WOMEN'S
POLITICAL
&SOCIAL
THOUGHT

WOMEN'S POLITICAL & SOCIAL THOUGHT

An Anthology

Edited by Hilda L. Smith and Berenice A. Carroll

With an Introduction by Berenice A. Carroll

INDIANA UNIVERSITY PRESS
BLOOMINGTON AND INDIANAPOLIS

This book is a publication of
Indiana University Press
601 North Morton Street
Bloomington, Indiana 47404-3797 USA

http://www.indiana.edu/~iupress

Telephone orders 800-842-6796

Fax orders 812-855-7931

Orders by email iuporder@indiana.edu

The paper used in this publication meets the
minimum requirements of American National
Standard for Information Sciences—Permanence of
Paper for Printed Library Materials, ANSI Z39.48-
1984.

Manufactured in the United States of America

Library of Congress Cataloging-in-Publication Data

Women's political and social thought : an anthology /
edited by Hilda L. Smith and Berenice A. Carroll.

    p.   cm.

Includes bibliographical references and index.
ISBN 0-253-33758-5 (cloth : alk. paper)—ISBN
0-253-21396-7 (pbk. : alk. paper)

    1. Women—Intellectual life—Sources. 2.
Political science—History—Sources. 3. Sociology—History—Sources. I. Smith, Hilda L.,
date II. Carroll, Berenice A.

HQ1111.W75 2000
301—dc21

                            99-088855

1   2   3   4   5   05   04   03   02   01   00

TO THE MEMORY OF OUR MOTHERS

Ava Lee Davolt & *Margaret Segall Jacobs*

AND FOR OUR CHILDREN AND GRANDCHILDREN

Gregory, Christopher, and Seamus

&

David, Victoria, Malcolm, Katherine, and Annette

CONTENTS

Contents

Preface

This anthology is intended as an initial contribution to fill the gap in availability of source texts by women political theorists. The collection is designed for classroom use in courses in intellectual history, political theory, and women's studies, but we hope it may also be of use to scholars in many disciplines and of interest to a broad range of readers.

The collection developed out of a National Endowment for the Humanities Institute for college and university faculty held at the University of Cincinnati in the summer of 1991, entitled "Re-reading Intellectual History: Integrating Women's Social and Political Thought into the Undergraduate Curriculum." The Institute originated from our experience that courses in intellectual history and social and political theory included few works by women, that feminist scholarship in those two areas was not devoted primarily to discussions of women's works, and that even women's studies courses often neglected women as intellectuals or thinkers across a broad range of viewpoints. Thus, we conducted an institute for faculty from across the United States and beyond, focusing on selected political writings by women and discussing how they fit into traditional intellectual history and political theory courses, as well as into women's studies classes. In our efforts to locate appropriate works (both in our teaching and for the Institute), we had the frustrating experience of finding the great majority of works of even the most prominent women thinkers out of print or not readily available for classroom use. Hence, we felt that an anthology of such writings was urgently needed.

The coeditors came to these interests from differ-ing but related intellectual backgrounds and interests. Berenice A. Carroll has taught courses in political thought including ancient, medieval, and modern western theory, as well as socialist, feminist, and pacifist theory. She began teaching courses and lecturing on women's political and social thought in 1974. Her interest in this area dates back to her early reassessment of the work of Mary Beard (1972) and of the political thought of Virginia Woolf (1978). Her study "The Politics of 'Originality': Women and the Class System of the Intellect" appeared in the *Journal of Women's History* in the fall of 1990. Hilda L. Smith came to the project from her work in women's intellectual history, especially the history of feminist ideas and women's writings, both feminist and more broadly, in seventeenth-century England. During the early 1970s when Smith was completing her study of seventeenth-century English feminists, *Reason's Disciples: Seventeenth-Century English Feminists*, social history dominated the interests of those focusing on the history of women. Thus the small attention often paid to women's writings while they were alive, as well as the resistance of both traditional intellectual historians and historians of women to exhibit interest after their death, has been an important motivation behind her interest in editing this collection.

In recent years, there has been a marked growth of interest in the history of women's contributions to science and philosophy, and a growing number of specialized studies relating to women in social and political theory. But the need for a collection presenting selected writings from a broad range of theorists across boundaries of time, geography, discipline, and ideology remains undiminished.

It may be well to emphasize that this is not an anthology of feminist theory. While many of the writers have been claimed as feminists or feminist precursors, and many of the writings included are explicitly feminist, many are not, and the varieties of "feminism" expressed have been open to vigorous challenge from contemporary feminist and womanist perspectives.

We have reached far back in time but have excluded (with one exception) selections from the second half of the twentieth century. We have chosen a varied selection of writings, diverse in form and content, by well-known and little-known writers. In general, we have omitted writings by the best-known contemporary political theorists, such as Hannah Arendt and Simone de Beauvoir, as well as by contemporary feminist theorists, mainly on the ground that their works are more readily available and more often studied today than those we have selected. For the same reasons, we have sometimes omitted the best-known writings of a given theorist, so as to bring to attention and make available other of her works. Thus, for example, we excluded here Mary Wollstonecraft's *Vindication of the Rights of Woman* (1792) in favor of her earlier and more neglected *Vindication of the Rights of Men* (1790), in which she had already signaled some of the central arguments of the later work. We have also chosen to provide relatively long selections. This offers a better sense of the work of the writer but limits us sharply in the number of authors we are able to include.

We are conscious that our selections are biased by our own training, knowledge, standpoints, and interests, as well as by the limitations of space, and that we omit hundreds, indeed thousands, of brilliant and influential theorists who deserve to be better known. Nevertheless, we have sought to convey in these selections some sense of the broad range of women's political and social thought across time, geographic area, class, race, culture, ideology, and genre. We offer this collection in hopes that the writings included will prove useful, illuminating, provocative, and delightful to others, as they have to us.

Acknowledgments

We owe thanks to many people for contributions to this work at various stages of its development, both in connection with the 1991 Institute supported by the National Endowment for the Humanities and in the development of the anthology itself. First, we thank the NEH for its confidence in the importance of the Institute and its generous support of the project. We especially appreciate the supportive assistance of our NEH program officer, Barbara Ashbrook, who provided highly valuable advice in the preparation of our grant proposal and offered support and wise counsel during a visit to the Institute and in many other communications. We also thank particularly those at the University of Cincinnati who cooperated in the administration and logistics of the Institute.

We are very grateful to all those who contributed to the Institute as faculty, participants, and guest lecturers. Hilda L. Smith served as director of the Institute and one of the three core faculty, together with Berenice Carroll and David Grimsted. The participants (the majority of whom were teaching women's studies, intellectual history, or political theory courses) made essential contributions of knowledge and critique throughout the discussions, in both formal and informal settings. Guest lecturers added insights in selected areas: Alice Deck (African American and African women writers), Kathryn Kish Sklar and David Noble (Progressive-era intellectual trends), J. G. A. Pocock (writings of women historians during the eighteenth century), Barbara Ramusack (women's standing within the professions and the women's movement of early twentieth-century India), Mikiso Hane (Chinese and Japanese women thinkers at the turn of the twentieth century), Joanne Meyerowitz (a reassessment of the image of women in popular culture during the 1950s), and Ann Michellini (an assessment of classics as a discipline which had left little room for women scholars within its ranks). We would also like to thank the then staff of the Center for Women's Studies at the University of Cincinnati—in particular Elizabeth Emrich, Michele Morgan, and Amy Myers—who worked tirelessly to organize and duplicate materials during the Institute and dealt cheerfully with difficult logistical arrangements and the needs of Institute participants who came from institutions throughout the United States and abroad.

We owe thanks to many assistants and friends who contributed to the preparation of the manuscript at various points in time, especially to Michele Morgan, who designed and copyedited a first draft of the collection, and to Beth Harley, Sheri Cole, Jane Ziki, Anna Suranyi, Kathleen Saunders, Priya Kurian, Ruchi Anand, River Karner, Phyllis Swanson, Susan Moynihan, Kerri Maple, Chun-hui Ho, Danielle Bolduc, and Christine Braunberger for their indispensable and painstaking help in entering, formatting, and editing text or assisting in library searches. Throughout the development and preparation of the work, Clinton F. Fink contributed generously of his time and knowledge to discussions, editing, indexing, proofreading, library searches, securing reprint permissions, and, last but not least, helping us to laugh now and then.

A number of libraries and archives have provided essential assistance to this work. We thank especially the Langsam Library at the University of Cincinnati; the Humanities, Social Sciences and Education Library at Purdue University; the University Library, the Women's Studies/WID Library, the Rare Book Room, and the Newspaper Library at the University of Illinois at Urbana-Champaign; the British Library; the Widener Library; and the Folger Library. We also thank the Women's Studies Center and History Department at the University of Cincinnati, the Political Science Department at the University of Illinois at Urbana-Champaign, and the Women's Studies Program and Political Science Department at Purdue University for their support of this endeavor.

Finally, we are grateful to the anonymous reviewers for Indiana University Press, who made constructive suggestions on the manuscript, and to the editors at the press, particularly to Terry L. Cagle for her meticulous copy-editing, and to Joan Catapano for her patience, assistance, and support.

Permissions Acknowledgments

We gratefully acknowledge those who have given permission to reprint items included in this anthology.

Enheduanna. "Nin-me-sar-ra," from *The Exaltation of Inanna*, translated and edited by William W. Hallo and J. J. A. van Dijk. Copyright © 1968 by Yale University Press. Reprinted by permission of Yale University Press.

Sappho. Poems and fragments. Reprinted by permission of the publisher from *Greek Lyric, Volume I*, edited and translated by David A. Campbell, Cambridge, Mass.: Harvard University Press, copyright © 1982 by the President and Fellows of Harvard College.

Sappho. "To Anaktoria." From *Sappho: Lyrics in the Original Greek with Translations* by Willis Barnstone. Copyright © 1965 by Willis Barnstone. Reprinted by permission of Willis Barnstone.

Sei Shōnagon. Excerpts from *The Pillowbook of Sei Shōnagon*, translated and edited by Ivan Morris. Copyright © [1967], 1971 by Columbia University Press. Reprinted with the permission of the publisher.

Catherine of Siena. Excerpts from *The Letters of St. Catherine of Siena, Volume I*, translated by Suzanne Noffke, O.P. Copyright © 1988 by the Center for Medieval and Early Renaissance Studies, State University of New York at Binghamton). Used by permission of the Center for Medieval and Renaissance Studies, Binghamton University.

Catherine of Siena. Excerpts from *Catherine of Siena: The Dialogue*, translation and introduction by Suzanne Noffke, O.P. Copyright © 1980 by The Missionary Society of St. Paul the Apostle in the State of New York. Used by permission of Paulist Press Inc.

Christine de Pizan. Excerpts from *The Book of the Body Politic*, edited and translated by Kate Langdon Forhan, copyright © 1994 by Cambridge University Press. Reprinted with the permission of Cambridge University Press.

Sor Juana Inés de la Cruz. Excerpts reprinted by permission of the publisher from *A Sor Juana Anthology*, translated by Alan S. Trueblood, Cambridge, Mass.: Harvard University Press, copyright © 1988 by the President and Fellows of Harvard College.

Olympe de Gouges. Excerpts from *Translating Slavery*, edited by Doris Y. Kadish and Françoise Massardier-Kenney. Copyright © 1994 by Kent State University Press. Used by permission of The Kent State University Press.

Olympe de Gouges. Excerpts reprinted from *Women, the Family, and Freedom: The Debate in Documents, Volume One: 1750–1880*, edited by Susan

Notes on the Text

The readings in this collection are presented in chronological order of author's birth date and date of writing, with some exceptions where several selections by one author overlap with those of another. When necessary to distinguish dates in ancient history, we use the secular designation B.C.E. (Before the Common Era), rather than "B.C." (Before Christ). The book is divided into four parts: Ancient and Medieval Writings, Seventeenth- and Eighteenth-Century Writings, Nineteenth-Century Writings, and Twentieth-Century Writings.

For each writer, we have included an introduction to the selections and a brief list of suggested readings and citations of the sources from which the selections are drawn. Citations within the introductions or the texts of readings are given in "social science" format (author, year: page), with the full reference listed in the "Sources and Suggested Readings" for the individual writer or in the bibliography at the end of the volume.

To maximize space for readings, we have omitted most discursive notes by the authors of the selections and have refrained from adding explanatory notes of our own. Where explanations or translations of unfamiliar terms seemed essential, we have included them in the introductions or in square brackets in the text.

Some brief footnotes and citations by the authors have been retained in the selections, including citations to the Judeo-Christian Bible, which are given in standard form (book, chapter number: verse).

In order to convey a better sense of the ideas and style of each writer, we have avoided very brief or abbreviated excerpts in favor of longer excerpts or full text of the selections. In general we have attempted to follow exactly the text as given in the source rather than to modernize spelling, punctuation, and usage. In some cases this has meant adoption of forms and spellings rather strange to many readers today, but which we hope give a truer flavor of the writer than would modern language. In a few cases, we have taken the liberty of breaking up very long paragraphs in order to give emphasis to points which might otherwise be obscured.

The development of this collection has been a collaborative work, but each of the coeditors has undertaken primary responsibility for individual selections and for the brief introductions to the readings. The initials at the end of each of these introductions, BAC for Berenice A. Carroll or HLS for Hilda L. Smith, indicate the responsible editor for each of the selections and introductions.

Introduction

BERENICE A. CARROLL

In the mid-nineteenth century, Sarah Grimké wrote:

> Thus far woman has struggled through life with bandaged eyes, accepting the dogma of her weakness and inability to take care of herself not only physically but intellectually. She has held out a trembling hand and received gratefully the proffered aid. She has foregone her right to study, to know the laws and purposes of government to which she is subject. But now there is awakened in her a consciousness that she is defrauded of her legitimate Rights and that she never can fulfil her mission until she is placed in that position to which she feels herself called by the divinity within. . . . There is now predominant in the minds of intelligent women to an extent never known before a struggling after freedom, an intense desire after a higher life. (Grimké, [1852] 1975: 254)

Nearly a century and a half later, these words still have an uncomfortably familiar ring. In the persistent stereotypes, science, reason, and intellect are still male. In the elite halls of academe, women are still a relatively small minority; in the recognized annals of intellectual history, a yet smaller minority.

But today there is growing recognition that the image of woman with bandaged eyes is as limited as the image of woman with trembling hand—that neither is true to the complex realities of women's participation in history. As Mary Daly put it: "[I]t is necessary to grasp the fundamental fact that women have had the power of *naming* stolen from us" (Daly, 1973: 8). "Stolen": that is, not that women never had the power, nor even that we are without it now, but that women have been denied the free and full exercise—and rewards—of this essential function of human intellect.

There is a compelling exploration of the power of naming in Ursula Le Guin's fantasy, *A Wizard of Earthsea*. The apprentice wizard sees there "that in this dusty and fathomless matter of learning the true name of every place, thing, and being, the power he wanted lay like a jewel at the bottom of a dry well. For magic consists in this, the true naming of a thing." Substitute "science" for "magic" (bearing in mind that this novel is an allegory on modern science) and we will understand better the meaning of this remark in contemporary terms. The power of naming is the power to define, comprehend, and seek to control reality.

Naming has appeared to be in the hands of men in the realm of social reality as much as in the realm of natural science, and a large proportion of feminist scholarship has focused on exposing the distortions and false consciousness arising from the oligopoly of what has been called "masculist" or "phallocratic" knowledge and the techniques by which it is maintained—discouraging, repressing, and ultimately suppressing namings by women and other unwelcome aspirants.

But if the power of naming has been stolen from women, some, unquestionably—like Sarah Grimké—have wrested it back, in every time and place, from

Enheduanna in the third millennium B.C.E. to the present. Some have always refused to forego the "right to study, to know the laws and purposes of government." Not all have been equally daring in questioning the dominant consciousness, but many have insisted on the right to formulate and put forward their own conceptions of political reality.

The readings in this anthology were selected to represent contributions of women specifically in the field of political and social theory, rather than the more general realm of women writers or intellectuals, though it is often difficult to draw the boundaries. Over the past three decades there has been explosive growth in the study of women in literature—women as poets, dramatists, and novelists. Women's education, "learned women," women in science, and women academics have also received attention. A project to restore the history of women philosophers has produced a four-volume collaborative history, and several other studies of women philosophers in particular periods have appeared in recent years. Substantial work has also been done on women as political activists, revolutionaries, and social reformers. The extensive intellectual tradition of feminist thought in particular has been explored in many works in recent decades. A selected list of studies of these kinds, such as the bibliography at the end of this volume, can only be suggestive of the impressive growth of knowledge in these areas.

Yet this rapidly growing scholarly literature has not produced a widespread awareness of women as creators of diverse theoretical contributions throughout the long history of social and political theory.

This has been almost as true of feminist scholarship as it is of "malestream" scholarship and education. The defensiveness of many feminists concerning the intellectual work of women is reflected, for example, in the title of Nancy J. Holland's book, *Is Women's Philosophy Possible?* (1990), or in Kate Fullbrook's remark that "It is no longer heretical to discuss [Simone de] Beauvoir as a philosopher" (quoted in *Chronicle of Higher Education*, September 4, 1998: A22). Holland acknowledges that "there is philosophy done by women" but passes over the history of their work in favor of seeking a new body of "women's philosophy" defined as "philosophical work (i.e., discussion of traditional philosophical issues) that arises from, explicitly refers to, and attempts to account for the experience of women" (p. 1). Of this, Holland finds that there is very little, and she directs her attention to the search for "what women's philosophy might be."

Gerda Lerner wrote in 1986: "Women have not only been educationally deprived throughout historical time in every known society, they have been excluded from theory-formation" (Lerner, 1986: 5). In-

deed there is no question that there have been processes of systematic exclusion of women from the institutions and recognized bodies of literature dominant in "the enterprise of creating symbol systems, philosophies, science, and law" (ibid.). But there exists nonetheless an extensive history of women's participation in the enterprise of theory-formation. It is not exclusively a history of feminist thought but ranges over the entire spectrum of political and social theory.

Ironically, this very diversity of perspectives has bolstered resistance to serious assessment of women as political theorists. The traditions of women's political thought do not fit neatly into contemporary ideological frames and therefore lack an assured base of recognition, acceptance, and adherents.

One problem is that women identified as "intellectuals" are generally of a small privileged class, and often "exceptional" even in that class; hence they are isolated from and unrepresentative of the overwhelming majority of women. The latter, even in middle and upper classes, have generally been denied the educational and occupational opportunities to produce recognized works of political and social theory, at least on the model of the male classics. Women of less privileged class, race, or ethnic groups experience even greater obstacles and isolation in asserting claims to formulate theory. Thus those who managed to produce written works of theory were often seen as "outsiders" in their own communities and lacked a following of admiring supporters. Those who did acquire such a following were generally perceived less as creators of social theory than as religious leaders (e.g., St. Catherine of Siena), popular reformers (e.g., Jane Addams, Ida B. Wells), or revolutionaries (e.g., Vera Figner, Rosa Luxemburg).

At the same time, women of all groups have been seen as marginal in the male-dominated arenas of intellectual and political activity, even where they succeeded in breaking barriers to enter those arenas. This "outsider" status often stamps their work with an innovative or dissimulating character that may seem deviant or dissenting even in the intellectual and political movements with which they are associated, making them appear on the periphery rather than at the center of the movement's intellectual tradition. For Virginia Woolf and others, this outsider status became a platform and badge of honor, but even for Woolf, it hid her message in the shadows of obscurity.

Women have adopted a remarkable diversity of responses to their status as intellectual outsiders, from appearing to ignore it to drawing on it as inspiration for their theoretical doctrines. Those who adopt the former model are often, particularly if successful and famous, heavily imbued with male attitudes, male doctrines, male "wisdom." They may have internalized and conformed to tradition, the "malestream" as Mary O'Brien named it (O'Brien, 1981: 21), more completely than other women, in order to gain a hearing in the male intellectual oligopoly, not to be locked out of the recognized realm of intellectual discourse. Thus some women who have written extensively on social and political questions have ignored or at times even demeaned women and have adopted the goals, values, and methods of the patriarchy. From the Neo-Pythagoreans of the ancient world to a Melanie Klein or Ayn Rand of the twentieth century, many women have adopted this stance in their works.

Feminist scholars today, not surprisingly, find these (and many other) women's writings troubling and have preferred to seek out those of our foremothers who anticipated or approximated what we now consider a correct "line," leaving the rest in an obscurity which admittedly saves us many discomforts. On the other hand, this practice leaves us in ignorance or near-ignorance of an enormous body of works constituting an integral part of the collective product of human consciousness. These works are important to restore to light and subject to analysis.

When we embark on this endeavor, seeking to find the women who contributed to the varied traditions of political thought and to explore and assess their works, we encounter many obstacles. The first, and still the most widespread and destructive obstacle, is their *omission* from standard courses, texts, and reference works in political theory and philosophy. Most older standard histories and anthologies of political theory, political and social philosophy, or intellectual history simply omit all women. This remains true of some today, but recent collections may include one woman theorist, such as Hannah Arendt, or a few, such as Arendt, Simone de Beauvoir, and Simone Weil. A striking advance is the introduction of a series of works by women among the Cambridge Texts in the History of Political Thought (now including works by Christine de Pizan, Mary Astell, and Mary Wollstonecraft).

The long-standing pattern of omission and neglect of women theorists has been addressed in the field of sociology and social theory by two outstanding works of the 1990s: *The Women Founders of the Social Sciences*, by Lynn McDonald (1994), and *The Women Founders: Sociology and Social Theory, 1830–1930—A Text/Reader*, edited by Patricia Madoo Lengermann and Jill Niebrugge-Brantley (1998). Lynn McDonald describes well the experience of discovering "the women founders" in the course of a study of the history of sociology, in which she set out to look for women's contributions and found far more than she anticipated:

The exercise of recovery was not easy, for there was so much to unlearn. It often took me a long time simply to believe what I was reading, to give full value to the original observations, insights, theories, propositions, and practical research examples provided by these women. I would frequently tell myself that what the woman had said reminded me of work by some other, prominent, male theorist, only to realize that her work predated his by years, even decades. (McDonald, 1994, 1996: x)

McDonald mentions and includes early political theorists among the women she discusses, but her emphasis is upon the founders and shapers of empirical social science in the period from the late sixteenth century to the beginning of the twentieth century. She defends empiricism against some contemporary feminist attacks and is chiefly concerned with recovering the important contributions of women to the methodology of sociology and empirical social research. Lengermann and Niebrugge-Brantley, like McDonald, address the contributions of women as sociologists and "the politics of erasure" but provide also selections from the writings of the "founders": Harriet Martineau, Jane Addams, Charlotte Perkins Gilman, Anna Julia Cooper, Ida B. Wells-Barnett, Marianne Weber, the Chicago women's school, and Beatrice Potter Webb. These are both very welcome and important contributions.

These works focus on a particular area of women's political and social thought. Methodology and social research are grounded in theory, but the range of women's political theory, as reflected in small part in the present volume, is much broader, more diverse, and often contrary to empiricist approaches. Moreover, as Lynn McDonald herself notes, there is reason to wonder about the security of such gains. Awareness of women's intellectual contributions is not entirely new today but rather a revival of knowledge that has been recovered and lost, recovered and lost again, repeatedly over time. This pattern of repeated loss and suppression may be discerned in the historical accounts given in such works as Joanna Russ, *How to Suppress Women's Writing* (1983); Dale Spender, *Women of Ideas and What Men Have Done to Them* (1982, 1988); Mary Ellen Waithe, ed., *A History of Women Philosophers* (4 vols., 1987–95), and others.

In this sense, it may be misleading to say, as stated above, that "most of the older standard histories" simply omit women altogether. While this may be true for general introductory texts, it is possible to find some older specialized works that give more attention to women than many recent texts. For example, Henry Osborn Taylor's *The Medieval Mind* (4th ed., 1930) devoted a chapter in volume 1 to five women (Elizabeth of Schönau, Hildegard of Bingen, Mary of Ognies, Liutgard of Tongern, and Mechtild of Magdeburg), and a chapter in volume 2 to Heloïse. Since Taylor concludes with the thirteenth century, he does not deal with such important figures as Catherine of Siena and Christine de Pizan. We might also find some grounds for regret or criticism concerning Taylor's presentation of these women's ideas. But two full chapters on medieval women writers goes beyond anything in even the most recent textbooks on intellectual history and philosophy, other than works in women's studies.

Taylor's work reflected a revival of knowledge concerning women's intellectual contributions that coincided with the development of the women's movement in the late nineteenth and early twentieth centuries, and we owe a great deal to that period. Henry Steele Commager's *The American Mind* (1949), now five decades old, marked a kind of turning point between that era and the regressive anti-feminism of the middle decades of the twentieth century, a reactionary era described for example by Kate Millett in *Sexual Politics* (1978) and Marilyn French in *Beyond Power* (1985). Commager, like Taylor, accorded some extended consideration to women writers, giving particular attention to a few novelists, above all Willa Cather and Ellen Glasgow. However, Commager's treatment of women as intellectuals was uneven. Mary Baker Eddy and Margaret Sanger appear, but no mention is made of Mercy Otis Warren, Emma Willard, Frances Wright, Angelina and Sarah Grimké, Catharine Beecher, Harriet Beecher Stowe, Margaret Fuller, Elizabeth Cady Stanton, Susan B. Anthony, Charlotte Perkins Gilman, Emma Goldman, or Eleanor Roosevelt. Mary Beard is not mentioned even when Commager discusses the *Rise of American Civilization*, which he treats as though it were solely the work of Charles Beard. No mention is made of Jane Addams except for the title of one of her books, included in passing. Even so, Commager gave more attention to women writers than many successors, and the decades of the 1950s and 1960s were singularly barren. Only since the 1970s has the cycle of recognition and recovery of women's intellectual work moved again into an upward path.

Insofar as the power of naming has been stolen from women, it has been mainly by this process of omission from general works of intellectual and social history, which makes inaccessible what women have named in the past, and implies its unimportance. Total omission is probably the most frequent approach and most effective in creating a void of silence from which the work of women is especially difficult to rescue. But where the presence of women has been noted, their contributions to political and social theory have often been obscured by *distortion, derision,* and *depreciation*—to which we return below—which rationalize the omission of their work in later collections and studies, and eventually the loss or deliberate destruction of the works themselves.

Outright *destruction* and physical loss of the body of works appears to have been the fate of the vast majority of women's writings from ancient times to the period of the Renaissance in Europe, and of many works since then. The entire writings of Sappho, as well as those of Hypatia and other women, have been lost to such destruction, with the exception of fragments and perhaps some works that survived under the names of male authors. Selective destruction to suit the predilections of male associates has also been practiced. Margaret Fuller's writings were heavily "edited" (or rather: censored) after her death by her friends (!) James Freeman Clarke, Ralph Waldo Emerson, and W. H. Channing, who went so far as to destroy the original manuscripts after editing to their taste (see Chevigny, 1976: 9).

A modified form of omission of women's work is *neglect* or *inattention* to their *intellectual* work as such, particularly in the case of women well known as political activists or social reformers, such as Jane Addams, Ida B. Wells, or Eleanor Roosevelt. The case of Jane Addams is particularly salient in view of Christopher Lasch's effort to rescue her intellectual contributions from obscurity in his anthology, *The Social Thought of Jane Addams*, where he describes Addams as "a thinker of originality and daring" (1965: xv). Unfortunately, in his treatment of her elsewhere, Lasch was not entirely without fault in the failure of this rescue mission. We are left, even in the late 1990s, without a comprehensive, full-length critical study of the political and social thought of Jane Addams.

The same must be said for the overwhelming majority of significant women theorists in the political and social realm. We have biographies, essays, anthologies, but still few full-length critical analyses. Some biographies contain incisive discussion of their subjects' ideas. But for purposes of intellectual history and the critique of political theory, a biography cannot substitute for a systematic critical study.

To the extent that women's intellectual work escapes from total invisibility or neglect, it is often subject to a pattern of *distorted representations* ranging from blatant depreciation and derision to wasteful defensiveness and uncritical apologetics. The analysis of women's political thought is often clouded also by judgments on their personal lives and motives. It is true that this is the case for men as well, and that on the positive side, a careful interweaving of biographical information with critical analysis may provide the richest comprehension of a writer's work. But too often the process degenerates into a focus on the personal characteristics and motivations of the writers rather than on their ideas as such.

In seeking to restore the body of works expressing the political and social theories of women, we must recognize that their ideas are more likely to be expressed in *vehicles other than formal treatises*. Women, excluded for centuries from the academies, the chambers of law, the divinity schools, and similar institutions, had fewer opportunities to learn, practice, and publish in the conventional style of the political treatise. This does not mean that they thought less, nor less rigorously and systematically, than men, but that the forms of expression open to them were more likely to be of other types: essays, letters, diaries, autobiographies, histories, speeches, pamphlets, textbooks for the school or the home, reviews, periodical articles, poetry, drama, and novels.

Poetry and drama have often been vehicles of political expression, particularly under repressive regimes. Works in these forms by male writers have often been recognized as "political theory," as in the case of Greek tragedy, the dialogues of Plato, and epic poetry by John Milton and Dante Alighieri. In such works, theory may be implicit rather than explicit, and the problems of interpretation and assessment are multiplied. But if we are not to accept an exclusionary double standard, we must search a wide range of materials for the political philosophy of women who were excluded from the recognized channels of theoretical discourse. We have therefore included in this collection examples of works by women in diverse genres, including poetry, drama, autobiography, letters, fiction, and others.

Similarly, in order to discern the political theory of ancient times we must turn to a variety of literary, historical, and religious sources in which the early ideas are embodied. Epic poetry and scriptures, temple hymns, fragments, and aphorisms quoted by later writers or rediscovered in cuneiform tablets, stone inscriptions or shreds of ancient papyri are among the sources from which we derive knowledge of the ideas and influence of the ancient theorists. Secular political philosophy emerges only in modern and contemporary times, and the mixing of political with religious or spiritual beliefs, especially the explanation and justification of political principles through religious doctrines, persists from ancient times throughout the history of political philosophy.

Finally, there is a need for balance in assessing the place of women's writings about women in their over-

all social philosophy. There has been a tendency to give attention to those writings which relate to women and gender, to the neglect of writings offering observations and theory on other questions. For example, Mary Wollstonecraft's *Vindication of the Rights of Woman* (1792) is well known today, but her *Vindication of the Rights of Men* (1790) is so little known and used that it is sometimes confused with the later work. For purposes of research and scholarship, what is crucial is not to dichotomize these areas of thought. Rather, we need to see them in the context of the writer and her time. Where the role of women in social action is seen by the writer as a central concern, as in the case of Angelina Grimké, we should consider it as such—that is, neither focus exclusively on her ideas on women's roles nor try to excise them from our examination of her ideas on other matters. On the other hand, where the roles and experiences of women are seldom directly addressed, as in the writings of Rosa Luxemburg, we must consider why that was so but give our attention mainly to understanding what she saw as essential to write about.

In seeking to achieve a better naming of political reality, feminist scholars have adopted two main approaches to the history of social thought: first, critical analysis of the traditional canon of political theory from a feminist perspective; and second, recovery and development of feminist theory both as an autonomous tradition in the history of political theory and in dialogue with other traditions both within and outside the accepted canon.

The *first* approach has produced a large body of scholarly literature. Some of the studies presenting critical analysis of the traditional literature also encompass exposition and critique of contemporary feminist theory. Almost all give at least brief attention to feminist writers, though the chapter titles or content may focus mainly on male theorists. Yet the emphasis is still upon the male theorists of the traditional canon. Indeed, attention often remains focused on the familiar names of the most authoritative "Fathers": Plato, Aristotle, Cicero, St. Augustine, St. Thomas Aquinas, Machiavelli, Luther, Hobbes, Locke, Rousseau, Kant, Mill, Hegel, Nietzsche, Marx, Freud, and Sartre. Some recent works in this genre address an updated male canon, including critique of currently more popular intellectual heroes: Heidegger, Merleau-Ponty, Barthes, Lacan, Foucault, Derrida (see, for example, Holland, 1990). The lists could be used for the syllabi in conventional courses in the history of political theory. In content such a course, taught from a variety of critical feminist perspectives, would be by no means conventional, but to the extent that dominance rests on a mystique of authority and control, the persistence of primary attention to the Fathers may have the unintended and undesired consequences of reinforcing this mystique.

The *second* approach escapes this difficulty by turning attention fully to the history and current development of feminist theory. While this body of theory does encompass the works of some male writers (such as John Stuart Mill or Friedrich Engels), the overwhelming majority of the literature of feminist theory has been written by women. This approach has produced a large, growing, and important body of literature dealing with the history and critical interpretation of feminist thought. However, this literature has been compartmentalized, so that feminist thought has been treated as though it were outside the body of political theory.

A *third* approach to the goal of transforming political theory and intellectual history is that of efforts to open up the traditional canon itself to works not usually represented in it, including works by people of subordinated races, cultures, or classes; works by advocates of marginalized philosophies such as utopianism, pacifism, and gay and lesbian identity; and works by women—of all races, cultures, classes, sexual orientations, and ideologies. These efforts are not yet far advanced, and as suggested above, the range and richness of women's political thought is little recognized.

This volume is offered as a contribution to the third approach to the goal of transforming political theory and intellectual history. It is divided into four sections, by historical era, designed to illustrate the presence and varied contributions of women in the political and social thought of their time. The editors hope that the volume will provoke discussion and provide material for exploration of questions hardly touched on to date concerning the continuities and discontinuities, consistencies and inconsistencies, of women's political thought over time and difference.

It is not possible to examine these substantive questions here, but one may venture the observation that, to varying degrees and in widely differing ways, women's political writings fall most often on the side of challenge to authority and the search for alternatives to relations of hierarchical dominance. These challenges may be embedded even in a conservative framing, as in the instances of seventeenth-century royalists Margaret Cavendish and Mary Astell. One may speculate that the outsider status of women theorists—even those most closely associated with ruling groups, such as Enheduanna—gives them an edge of indignation, a critical vision, provoking challenge to particular forms of dominant authority. As Hannah Arendt wrote: "It is only after one ceases to reduce public affairs to the business of dominion that the original data in the realm of human affairs will appear, or rather, reappear, in their authentic diversity" (Arendt, 1972: 142–43).

In this context, we may note the example of another theorist not included in this volume, Mary Parker Follett. Follett is little remembered today, and there is no full-length biography of her, though she is included in *Notable American Women*. She is not well known in feminist circles, for the good reasons that she apparently never dealt with the situation of women in her writings, and in the labor-management issues to which she addressed herself later in life, she spoke more to corporate management than to labor. Nevertheless, Follett's early writings provided an analysis of power that bears a striking resemblance to some contemporary feminist concepts, distinguishing "power-over" from "power-with." In *The New State* (1918) and *Creative Experience* (1924), Follett argued that genuine power is "coactive" rather than "coercive" and that both power and creativity are interactive functions of group processes: "Out of the intermingling, interacting activities of men and women surge up the forces of life: powers are born which we had not dreamed of, ideas take shape and grow, forces are generated which act and react on each other. . . ." (Follett, 1920: 149).

So it is, we may suggest, in our quest for the history of women's political and social thought. Taking a liberty with Follett's words, I would suggest that out of our recovery of works previously unknown or obscured to our understanding, out of the collective process of learning and naming, "forces are generated which act and react on each other, ideas take shape and grow, powers are born which we had not dreamed of."

References

Arendt, Hannah. "On Violence." In *Crises of the Republic*. New York: Harcourt, Brace, Jovanovich (Harvest), 1972.

Carroll, Berenice A. "The Politics of 'Originality': Women and the Class System of the Intellect." *Journal of Women's History* 2, 2 (Fall 1990): 136–163.

Chevigny, Bell Gale. *The Woman and the Myth: Margaret Fuller's Life and Writings*. Old Westbury, N.Y.: Feminist Press, 1976.

Commager, Henry Steele. *The American Mind*. New Haven: Yale University Press, 1949.

Daly, Mary. *Beyond God the Father: Toward a Philosophy of Women's Liberation*. Boston: Beacon Press, 1973.

Follett, Mary Parker. *Creative Experience*. New York: Longmans, Green, 1924.

———. *The New State: Group Organization, the Solution of Popular Government*. New York: Longmans, Green, 1920 (1918).

French, Marilyn. *Beyond Power: On Women, Men and Morals*. New York: Ballantine, 1985.

Fullbrook, Kate, and Edward Fullbrook. *Simone de Beauvoir and Jean-Paul Sartre: The Remaking of a Twentieth-Century Legend.* New York: Basic, 1998.

Grimké, Sarah. "Sisters of Charity," ca. 1852, edited with an introduction by Gerda Lerner. *Signs* 1, 1 (Autumn 1975): 254.

Holland, Nancy J. *Is Women's Philosophy Possible?* Savage, Md.: Rowman and Littlefield, 1990.

Lasch, Christopher. *The Social Thought of Jane Addams.* Indianapolis: Bobbs-Merrill, 1965.

Le Guin, Ursula. *A Wizard of Earthsea.* New York: Bantam, 1975.

Lengermann, Patricia Madoo, and Jill Niebrugge-Brantley, eds. *The Women Founders: Sociology and Social Theory, 1830–1930—A Text/Reader.* Boston: McGraw Hill, 1998.

Lerner, Gerda. *The Creation of Feminist Consciousness: From the Middle Ages to Eighteen-Seventy.* New York: Oxford University Press, 1993.

———. *The Creation of Patriarchy.* New York: Oxford University Press, 1986.

McDonald, Lynn. *The Women Founders of the Social Sciences.* Ottawa: Carleton University Press, 1994, 1996.

Millett, Kate. *Sexual Politics.* Garden City, N.Y.: Doubleday, 1970.

O'Brien, Mary. *The Politics of Reproduction.* London: Routledge and Kegan Paul, 1981.

Russ, Joanna. *How to Suppress Women's Writing.* Austin: University of Texas Press, 1983.

Simons, Margaret. *Beauvoir and "The Second Sex": Feminism, Race, and the Origins of Existentialism.* Savage, Md.: Rowman and Littlefield, 1999.

Spender, Dale. *Women of Ideas, and What Men Have Done to Them, From Aphra Behn to Adrienne Rich.* London: Routledge and Kegan Paul, 1982; Boston: Pandora, 1988.

Taylor, Henry Osborn. *The Medieval Mind.* 4th ed., in 2 vols. London: Macmillan, 1930.

Waithe, Mary Ellen, ed. *A History of Women Philosophers.* Volume 1, 600 B.C.–500 A.D., Dordrecht: Martinus Nijhoff, 1987; Volume 2, 500–1600, Dordrecht: Kluwer, 1989; Volume 3, 1600–1900, Dordrecht: Kluwer, 1991; Volume 4, 1900–today, Dordrecht: Kluwer, 1995.

PART ONE

Ancient and Medieval Writings

Enheduanna (ca. 2300 B.C.E.)

Enheduanna was the high priestess (en) of the moon god Nanna and his consort, Ningal, at the ancient Mesopotamian city-state of Ur, and later also of the god of heaven, An, at Uruk. Ur and Uruk were leading city-states of ancient Sumer, in what is now the modern state of Iraq. It is not possible to date exactly Enheduanna's birth and death, but it is likely that she lived and wrote around 2300 B.C.E. The surviving texts of her works date, however, from a period some five hundred years later. She was apparently the first of a long succession of royal high priestesses and priests of Ur whose names have been documented from contemporary inscriptions and seals. She is thought to have been appointed by her father, Sargon of Akkad, and to have held her office as high priestess for more than two decades, into the reign of Naram-Sin, her nephew. Sometime during this period she lived through a time of crisis, recounted in the selection below, in which she was driven into exile but later restored to her position.

Enheduanna's writings are the earliest significant body of literary-political works by a named author, male or female, that have survived to the present. Princess and priestess, her name was recorded as author-compiler of a major collection of Sumerian temple hymns and as author of poetic works including the "Myth of Inanna and Ebih" and "The Exaltation of Inanna." The latter, "Nin-me-sar-ra" (Lady of all the me's), is the selection presented below. The importance of this work is attested in part by the fact that it has survived over four millennia in nearly fifty tablets or fragments, an unusually large number for such ancient works. Enheduanna's works were models for scribes, poets, and priests for centuries after her death.

As noted in the Introduction to this volume, it is necessary to seek the political theory of ancient times in a variety of genres, such as epic poetry and temple hymns, in which religious or spiritual ideas are intermingled with political concepts. The selection below exemplifies this in the form of an epic poem, in which we find explicit and implicit rendering of concepts of political authority and legitimacy, justice, retribution, just war and rebellion, and right order in society.

Ancient religious texts, scriptures, and epics mention women as rulers and lawgivers, judges, seers, prophets, priestesses, poets, and philosophers. The images of women and men, human and divine, in these texts defy later stereotypes of dichotomous femininity and masculinity. In ancient Israel, the Old Testament tells us, Deborah was a judge, that is, a woman of wisdom, a law-giver, and a leader of the people ("and the people of Israel came up to her for judgment"—Judges 4: 4–5). The judges were also military leaders, and the story of Deborah (about twelfth century B.C.E.) makes clear that she directed Barak to raise an army to fight against the Canaanites of Hazor, laid out the strategy of the campaign, went herself with Barak to lead the battle, and like Enheduanna a thousand years earlier, wrote a hymn exulting in the victory (The Song of Deborah, Judges 5).

Enheduanna's works have been portrayed as promoting a royal political theology directed primarily to serve her father, Sargon, in establishing the hegemony of Akkad, through elevating the cult of the goddess Ishtar over those of the other city-states of ancient Sumer. Sargon is reputedly the first to have established a form of imperial primacy of one city-state over others. The "Exaltation of Inanna" does clearly reflect an intense political struggle, which some scholars identify with a rebellion against Sargon in the later years of his reign, or perhaps a still later rebellion against Naram-Sin. The poem concludes with an assertion of the supremacy of Inanna, hence of Ishtar, later identified with Inanna.

We may question, however, whether the struggle in which Enheduanna was engaged was for the primacy of her father's political rule or for her own dignity as a woman, for her prerogatives as high priestess, and for the authority of the great goddess as against male priests seeking to establish the preeminence of their male gods. Perhaps the struggles were intertwined, but the portrayal of Enheduanna's theology as merely an instrument of the designs of her male relatives is open to doubt on the evidence of the text.

We learn from the poem that Enheduanna was insulted and sexually importuned by Lugalanne, a king or priest of Uruk, whom she accuses of having altered the traditional rites which were properly her own function as high priestess. Enheduanna calls upon the moon god Nanna for help, but he "takes no heed" of her appeal and, in fact, "has driven me out of the sanctuary. . . . He made me walk in the bramble of the mountain. He stripped me of the crown appropriate for the high priesthood." Enheduanna thus turns to Inanna for aid.

Inanna is described as possessor and guardian of "the me's," a concept not easily translated. The term is used variously to refer to cosmic powers or divine attributes which regulate the universe as well as human life. They may be held by or transferred to a particular deity. In this poem, Inanna is said to be endowed with the me's by An, but elsewhere she is said to have received them from Enki, god of wisdom and the waters. An, god of heaven, is often referred to as the supreme deity of ancient Sumer. However, Inanna is described here and elsewhere as "Lady supreme over An" (line 59), or as his equal, and other gods, such as Enlil (An's son), are also referred to as "supreme." The pantheon of Sumerian gods and goddesses shows a pattern of shifting relationships between and among each other that may reflect both shifting patterns of relationships among the city-states and shifting patterns of gender relations, as well as an ancient form of egalitarianism that could accommodate competing claims of deities appearing under varying names and guises. Thus "Suen" and "Ashimbabbar" in this poem are other names or manifestations of Nanna.

The poem celebrates Inanna's defeat of Nanna, or the defeat of Lugalanne at the hands of Enheduanna and Sargon or Naram-Sin, and the elevation of Inanna over Nanna (significantly, her father!). The "magnificat" of the poem explicitly counterposes Inanna's magnificent and terrible powers ("be it known!") against the conscious assertion "That one has not recited (this) of Nanna," repeated both at the beginning and end of the liturgy (lines 122 and 133). Yet it should be remembered that the defeat of Nanna represented not extirpation of worship of the moon god or destruction of his temple but restoration of Enheduanna to her rightful place ("I am the brilliant high priestess of Nanna," lines 67 and 120) and of right order in society.

The version of "Nin-me-sar-ra" presented below is from The Exaltation of Inanna, translated and edited by William W. Hallo and J. J. A. Van Dijk (1968). Note that the section headings and parenthetical insertions within the text of the poem are attributions by the translators.

BAC

Sources and Suggested Readings

Hallo, William W., and J. J. A. Van Dijk. *The Exaltation of Inanna.* New Haven: Yale University Press, 1968.

Kramer, Samuel Noah. *From the Poetry of Sumer.* Berkeley: University of California Press, 1979.

Lerner, Gerda. *The Creation of Patriarchy.* New York: Oxford University Press, 1986.

Lewis, Brian. *The Sargon Legend.* Cambridge, Mass.: American Schools of Oriental Research, 1980.

Pritchard, James B., ed. *Ancient Near Eastern Texts Relating to the Old Testament.* 3rd ed. Princeton: Princeton University Press, 1969.

Sjöberg, Åke W., and E. Bergmann. *The Collection of the Sumerian Temple Hymns.* Texts from Cuneiform Sources, vol. 3. Locust Valley, N.Y.: J. J. Augustin, 1969.

Stone, Merlin. *When God Was a Woman.* New York: Harvest, 1978.

Wolkstein, Diane, and Samuel Noah Kramer. *Inanna.* New York: Harper and Row, 1983.

Nin-me-sar-ra [Lady of All the Me's]

A. Exordium

(i) Inanna and the me's

Lady of all the me's, resplendent light,   1
Righteous woman clothed in radiance, beloved of
    Heaven and Earth,

Hierodule of An (you) of all the great ornaments,
Enamored of the appropriate tiara, suitable for the
    high priesthood

Whose hand has attained (all) the "seven" me's,
Oh my lady, you are the guardian of all the great
    me's!

You have picked up the me's, you have hung the
    me's on your hand,
You have gathered up the me's, you have clasped the
    me's to your breast.

(ii) Inanna and An

Like a dragon you have deposited venom on the land
When you roar at the earth like Thunder, no
    vegetation can stand up to you.   10

A flood descending from its mountain,
Oh foremost one, you are the Inanna of heaven and
    earth!

Raining the fanned fire down upon the nation,
Endowed with me's by An, lady mounted on a beast,

Who makes decisions at the holy command of An.
(You) of all the great rites, who can fathom what is
    yours?

(iii) Inanna and Enlil

Devastatrix of the lands, you are lent wings by the
    storm.
Beloved of Enlil, you fly about in the nation.

You are at the service of the decrees of An.
Oh my lady, at the sound of you the lands bow
    down.   20

When mankind comes before you
In fear and trembling at (your) tempestuous
    radiance,
They receive from you their just deserts.

Proffering a song of lamentation, they weep before
    you,
They walk toward you along the path of the house of
    all the great sighs.

(iv) Inanna and Iskur
In the van of battle everything is struck down by you.
Oh my lady, (propelled) on your own wings, you
    peck away (at the land).

In the guise of a charging storm you charge.
With a roaring storm you roar.

With Thunder [Iskur] you continually thunder.   30
With all the evil winds you snort.

Your feet are filled with restlessness.
To (the accompaniment of) the harp of sighs you
    give vent to a dirge.

(v) Inanna and the Anunna
Oh my lady, the Anunna, the great gods,
Fluttering like bats fly off from before you to the
    clefts,

They who dare not walk(?) in your terrible glance,
Who dare not proceed before your terrible
    countenance.

Who can temper your raging heart?
Your malevolent heart is beyond tempering.

Lady (who) soothes the reins, lady (who) gladdens
    the heart,   40
Whose rage is not tempered, oh eldest daughter of
    Suen [Nanna]!
Lady supreme over the land, who has (ever) denied
    (you) homage?

(vi) Inanna and [Mt.] Ebih(?)
In the mountain where homage is withheld from
    you vegetation is accursed.
Its grand entrance you have reduced to ashes.

Blood rises in its rivers for you, its people have
    nought to drink.
It leads its army captive before you of its own accord.

It disbands its regiments before you of its own accord.

It makes its able-bodied young men parade before
    you of their own accord.

A tempest has filled the dancing of its city.
It drives its young adults before you as captives.   50

(vii) Inanna and Uruk
Over the city which has not declared "The land is
    yours,"
Which has not declared "It is your father's, your
    begettor's"

You have spoken your holy command, have verily
    turned it back from your path
Have verily removed your foot from out of its byre.

Its woman no longer speaks of love with her
    husband.
At night they no longer have intercourse.
She no longer reveals to him her inmost treasures.

Impetuous wild cow, great daughter of Suen,
Lady supreme over An who has (ever) denied (you)
    homage?

(viii) Invocation of Inanna
You of the appropriate me's, great queen of
    queens,   60
Issued from the holy womb, supreme over the
    mother who bore you,

Omniscient sage, lady of all the lands,
Sustenance of the multitudes, I have verily recited
    your sacred song!

True goddess, fit for the me's, it is exalting to
    acclaim you.
Merciful one, brilliantly righteous woman, I have
    verily recited your me's for you!

B. The Argument

(ix) The Banishment from Ur
Verily I had entered my holy *giparu* at your behest,
I, the high priestess, I, Enheduanna!

I carried the ritual basket, I intoned the acclaim.
(But now) I am placed in the lepers' ward I, even I,
    can no longer live with you!

They approach the light of day, the light is obscured
    about me,   70
The shadows approach the light of day, it is covered
    with a (sand)storm.

5

Enheduanna

My mellifluous mouth is cast into confusion.
My choicest features are turned to dust.

(x) The Appeal to Nanna-Suen
What is he to me, oh Suen, this Lugalanne!
Say thus to An: "May An release me!"

Say but to An "Now!" and An will release me.
This woman will carry off the manhood of
    Lugalanne.

Mountain (and?) flood lie at her feet.
That woman is as exalted (as he)—she will make the
    city divorce him.
Surely she will assuage her heartfelt rage for me. 80

Let me, Enheduanna, recite a prayer to her.
Let me give free vent to my tears like sweet drink for
    the holy Inanna!
Let me say "Hail!" to her!

(xi) The Indictment of Lugalanne(?)
I cannot appease Ashimbabbar.
(Lugalanne) has altered the lustrations of holy An
    and all his (other rites).

He has stripped An of (his temple) Eanna.
He has not stood in awe of An-lugal

That sanctuary whose attractions are irresistible,
    whose beauty is endless,
That sanctuary he has verily brought to destruction.

Having entered before you as a partner, he has even
    approached his sister-in-law.   90
Oh my divine impetuous wild cow, drive out this
    man, capture this man!

(xii) The Curse of Uruk
In the place of sustenance what am I, even I?
(Uruk) is a malevolent rebel against your Nanna—
    may An make it surrender!

This city—may it be sundered by An!
May it be cursed by Enlil!
May its plaintive child not be placated by his
    mother!

Oh lady, the (harp of) mourning is placed on the
    ground.
One had verily beached your ship of mourning on a
    hostile shore.
At (the sound of) my sacred song they are ready to
    die.

(xiii) The Indictment of Nanna
As for me, my Nanna takes no heed of me.   100
He has verily given me over to destruction in
    murderous straits.

Ashimbabbar has not pronounced my judgment.
Had he pronounced it: what is it to me? Had he not
    pronounced it: what is it to me?

(Me) who once sat triumphant he has driven out of
    the sanctuary.
Like a swallow he made me fly from the window, my
    life is consumed.

He made me walk in the bramble of the mountain.
He stripped me of the crown appropriate for the
    high priesthood.
He gave me dagger and sword—"it becomes you," he
    said to me.

(xiv) The Appeal to Inanna
Most precious lady, beloved of An,
Your holy heart is lofty, may it be assuaged on my
    behalf!   110

Beloved bride of Ushumgalanna,
You are the senior queen of the heavenly foundations and zenith.

The Anunna have submitted to you.
From birth on you were the "junior" queen.

How supreme you are over the great gods, the
    Anunna!
The Anunna kiss the ground with their lips (in
    obeisance) to you.

(But) my own sentence is not concluded, a hostile
    judgment appears before my eyes as my judgment.
(My) hands are no longer folded on the ritual couch,
I may no longer reveal the pronouncements of
    Ningal to man.

(Yet) I am the brilliant high priestess of Nanna, 120
Oh my queen beloved of An, may your heart take
    pity on me!

(xv) The Exaltation of Inanna
That one has not recited as a "Known! Be it known!"
    of Nanna, that one has recited as a "'Tis Thine!":

"That you are lofty as Heaven (An)—be it known!
That you are broad as the earth—be it known!

6

That you devastate the rebellious land—be it known!
That you roar at the land—be it known!   125a
That you smite the heads—be it known!
That you devour cadavers like a dog—be it known!
That your glance is terrible—be it known!
That you lift your terrible glance—be it known!
That your glance is flashing—be it known!   130
That you are ill-disposed toward the . . . —be it
    known!
That you attain victory—be it known!"

That one has not recited (this) of Nanna, that one
    has recited it as a "'Tis Thine"—
(That,) oh my lady, has made you great, you alone
    are exalted!

Oh my lady beloved of An, I have verily recounted
    your fury!

C. Peroration

(xvi) The Composition of the Hymn
One has heaped up the coals (in the censer)
    prepared the lustration
The nuptial chamber awaits you, let your heart be
    appeased!

With "It is enough for me, it is too much for me!" I
    have given birth, oh exalted lady, (to this song)
    for you.

That which I recited to you at (mid)night
May the singer repeat it to you at noon!   140

(Only) on account of your captive spouse, on
    account of your captive child,
Your rage is increased, your heart unassuaged.

(xvii) The Restoration of Enheduanna
The first lady, the reliance of the throne room,
Has accepted her offerings
Inanna's heart has been restored.

The day was favorable for her, she was clothed
    sumptuously, she was garbed in womanly beauty.
Like the light of the rising moon, how she was
    sumptuously attired!

When Nanna appeared in proper view,
They (all) blessed her (Inanna's) mother Ningal.

The (heavenly) doorsill called "Hail!"   150

(xviii) Doxology
For that her (Enheduanna's) speaking to the
    Hierodule was exalted,
Praise be (to) the devastatrix of the lands, endowed
    with me's from An,
(To) my lady wrapped in beauty, (to) Inanna!

Sappho (ca. 612–555 B.C.E.)

Of women intellectuals in the ancient world, Sappho (or Psappho, in her own Aeolian dialect) is certainly best known. Her poetry was famed in her own time, and for centuries after she was regarded as the equal of Homer, even as the Tenth Muse. In 1850 Philip Smith wrote in the Dictionary of Greek and Roman Biography and Mythology: "It is almost superfluous to refer to the numerous passages in which the ancient writers have expressed their unbounded admiration of the poetry of Sappho. . . . It may safely be affirmed that the loss of Sappho's poems is the greatest over which we have to mourn in the whole range of Greek literature." Rae Dalven, in her introduction to her collection of contemporary Greek women poets, offers tribute to Sappho's inspiration: "By means of her rhythmic lyricism, her faith in the poetic idea, and the free expression of her emotions, Sappho broke through the patriarchal structure of society and the moral authority of the male" (17). Her influence has been felt for more than two millennia and remains powerful today.

Little is known with certainty of the life of Sappho, whose birth and death dates have been set variously by scholars at about 612 (or 630) to 555 (or 570) B.C.E. To paraphrase Mary Barnard, the biographical tradition is full of contradictions: it is held that Sappho was born on the island of Lesbos in the city of Mytilene, or perhaps in Eresus; that she married a man named Kerkylas, or that this name is a crude pun and that she never married; that she had a daughter named Cleis, or that Cleis was not really her daughter; that she was a prostitute, or that she was not; that she committed suicide throwing herself off a cliff for love of Phaon, a ferryman, or that she did no such thing; that she taught a school for girls on Lesbos, or that she did not; that the women named in her poems, such as Atthis and Anaktoria, were her students, or that they were simply her friends, or that they were her lovers, or that they were not; that her flight from Lesbos to Sicily was a political banishment, or that it was not.

Sappho's poetry was collected in nine volumes in Hellenistic Alexandria, around the second century B.C.E. They appear to have been preserved in Europe through at least the early middle ages, despite public condemnations, burnings, and orders that they be destroyed wherever found—for example by St. Gregory, Bishop of Constantinople, about the year 380 and by Pope Gregory VII in 1073. The persistence of quotations from her poems in later works suggests that not all copies were destroyed, but today only one complete poem and numerous fragments are known to have survived, culled in part from the works of later grammarians and historians, in part from papyri found in Egypt, many in shreds used for wrapping the dead in tombs.

There are numerous editions of the surviving fragments, in Greek or in translation, often along with compilations of testimonia or biographical references and commentaries on Sappho in ancient Greek and Latin literature. Modern English versions are available either in literal translation or in verse. David A. Campbell's Greek Lyric, vol. 1 (1982), provides the most complete compilation of poems and fragments, in Greek and literal English translation, together with biographical references.

Most of the English verse translations, from Swinburne in the nineteenth century to the present, are elaborate reconstructions that often owe more to the poetic imagination and predilections of the translator than to the Sapphic remnants. Some are compelling poetry in their own right and many seek to be faithful to the spirit of Sappho's own words, but most present significant distortions, particularly by the introduction of ethnocentric substitutions (e.g., "God" for "Zeus") and patriarchal or misogynistic interpolations (e.g., the portrayal of Helen, in selection 1.C. below). Jane McIntosh Snyder, however, in Lesbian Desire in the Lyrics of Sappho (1997), provides an excellent collection of 192 poems and fragments in her own "relatively literal" verse translation, with both Greek text and transliteration in the Roman alphabet, to give a sense of the original lyric sound.

Sappho is generally thought of today as a lyric poet who wrote primarily about the private love between individuals, in particular between women. J. B. Bury in the Cambridge Ancient History in 1926 contrasted her work with that of her friend and colleague, Alcaeus: "Politics, war, his own exile, sea voyages were the leading themes of Alcaeus . . . , while Sappho confined her muse within a narrower circle of feminine interests" (1926: 4, 494–95). Yet Sappho's fame rested on her wisdom as well as on her eloquence. Plato in the Phaedrus reported that Socrates classed her with Anacreon among the "ancient sages, men and women."

The difficulties of translating the fragmentary remains of Sappho's poetry often leave us in doubt concerning their political context. A fragment cited by Hephaestion in the Handbook on Metres (second century) is translated by David A. Campbell as a somewhat petulant personal remark: " . . . having never yet found you more annoying, Irana" (Campbell, GL 91). But Mary Barnard, agreeing with J. M. Edmonds in interpreting the name to refer to Irene, goddess of peace, sets the fragment in the context of Sappho's experience of political exile: "As for the exiles: I think they had never found you, Peace, more difficult to endure!" (Barnard, # 90).

Sappho is thought to have been exiled twice from Lesbos for opposition to the populist tyrants Myrsilus and Pittacus of Mytilene, her home. Whether this makes her a partisan of liberty or merely an ally of Alcaeus in aristocratic conspiracies against democratic rule remains in dispute. There are few echoes of these events in the surviving fragments of Sappho's poetry—little more than a hostile reference to "ladies of the house of Penthilus," into which Pittacus had married. But the poems and fragments below give intimations of a wider-ranging political outlook that rejects military values, merges the sensual/erotic with the political, and asserts the freedom and primacy of love in human society.

Few modern treatments of Sappho have been without some commentary on her love relationships with women. Some deny their physical eroticism, claiming to maintain academic distance or defend (from a homophobic perspective) Sappho's "virtuous character." Others insist upon it as an issue of critical scholarship, historical accuracy, or contemporary lesbian politics. That the debate has persisted for more than a thousand years and retains its intensity today is sufficient testimony to the depth and importance of the political implications attached to Sappho's homoerotic poetry. The fragments available today remain open to conflicting interpretations, of which two of the most probing analyses are provided by Joan DeJean in Fictions of Sappho (1989) and Jane McIntosh Snyder, in Lesbian Desire in the Lyrics of Sappho (1997).

Sappho was sometimes described as small and dark, as in the Oxyrhynchus papyrus of the late second or early third century (Campbell, 3). Ovid's poem "Sappho to Phaon," which may have been partly based on poems of her own now lost, suggests she may have been black:

> Brown as I am, an Aethiopian dame
> Inspired young Perseus with a generous flame:
> Turtles and doves of different hue unite,
> And glossy jet is paired with shining white.

(trans. Alexander Pope, 1707: in Barnstone, 1965: 181)

This tradition, as well as the association of Sappho with same-sex desire between women, may have had reverberations in the works of twentieth-century African American writers, as in the case of Pauline E. Hopkins in the portrayal of Sappho Clark in Contending Forces (see Somerville, 1997).

The description of Sappho in the Oxyrhynchus papyrus as "quite ugly, being dark in complexion and of very small stature" has been linked with other hints that Sappho felt herself an outsider, visibly different from the people of the Aeolian and Ionian cultures in which she was situated. Jack Winkler, for example, has argued that Sappho's expressions of intense longing for the love of beautiful women reflected an underlying sense of alienation in her life.

In contrast with this view, Judy Grahn draws on the tradition of literature, history, and criticism that places Sappho in a matrilineal culture with a long matriarchal history, in which Lesbos figures as a protected island with a female-centered history. Grahn's vision of Sappho rejects the image of a privatized voice forced to conceal its meaning in hidden phrases, isolated in a hostile world, for that of a consciously public voice, addressed to a welcoming audience, and met with praise and even accolades in her own lifetime and for centuries after. For Grahn, the power of Sappho's public voice was so great that her memory and words were preserved for millennia, overcoming repeated efforts to eradicate them and surviving to be heard over the clamor of silencing misconstructions (The Highest Apple, 1985; see fragment GL 105, below).

The selections included in this volume are generally given in literal translation from the Greek. Two verse translations of the first selection (GL 16) are included to illustrate the diverse representations of Sappho's work in contemporary literature. The first, by Guy Davenport, provides a graphic image of the gaps in even the better preserved fragments; the second, by Willis Barnstone, is an example of significant interpolations by Sappho's translators.

In interpreting the selections provided here, it may be helpful to recall that in Sappho's time, Lydia was one of four major kingdoms in Asia Minor, particularly famed for its wealth and military glory; Sardis was its capital. The first two selections (GL 16, 132) are the most directly "political" in challenging the appeal of military and imperial values. The third (GL 1) reflects the centrality of the goddess Aphrodite in Sappho's poetry and the boldness of her summons to Aphrodite to be her "fellow-fighter," her ally, as Jane Snyder suggests, in winning a love founded in "reciprocity and exchange, not rejection or alienation" (Snyder, 14). Selections 4 through 10 exemplify Sappho's woman-centered love poems. Selections 11–17 reflect other significant values and concepts: the independence and greatness of another female model, Artemis; the importance of forthright speech in a good cause; the dependence of beauty on the good; the need to link wealth with virtue; the value of education in the search for immortality; the challenge of reaching "the highest apple"; and Sappho's confidence in continuity with the future.

The selections below are, except as noted, literal

translations by David A. Campbell in Greek Lyric, *vol. 1, 1982. The poems and fragments are identified by Campbell's numeration, for example, "GL 16."*

BAC

Sources and Suggested Readings

Barnard, Mary. *Sappho: A New Translation.* Berkeley: University of California Press, 1958 [reprinted Boston: Shambala Publications, 1994].

Barnstone, Willis. *Sappho: Lyrics in the Original Greek with translations.* New York: New York University Press, 1965.

Bury, J. B., S. A. Cook, and F. E. Adcock, eds. *Cambridge Ancient History,* vol. 4 (1926): 494–99.

Campbell, David A. *Greek Lyric,* vol. 1. Cambridge, Mass.: Harvard University Press, 1982.

Dalven, Rae, ed. and trans. *Daughters of Sappho: Contemporary Greek Women Poets.* Rutherford, N.J.: Fairleigh Dickinson University Press, 1994.

Davenport, Guy. *Sappho: Poems and Fragments.* Ann Arbor: University of Michigan Press, 1965.

DeJean, Joan. *Fictions of Sappho, 1546–1937.* Chicago: University of Chicago Press, 1989.

DuBois, Page. *Sappho Is Burning.* Chicago: University of Chicago Press, 1997.

Freedman, Nancy. *Sappho: The Tenth Muse.* New York: St. Martin's Press, 1998.

Grahn, Judy. *The Highest Apple: Sappho and the Lesbian Poetic Tradition.* San Francisco: Spinsters Ink, 1985.

Greene, Ellen, ed. *Reading Sappho: Contemporary Approaches.* Berkeley: University of California Press, 1996.

———. *Re-reading Sappho: Reception and Transmission.* Berkeley: University of California Press, 1997.

Gubar, Susan. "Sapphistries." *Signs: Journal of Women in Culture and Society* 10, 1 (1984): 43–62.

Skinner, Marilyn B. "Woman and Language in Archaic Greece, or, Why Is Sappho a Woman?" In *Feminist Theory and the Classics,* ed. Nancy Sorkin Rabinowitz and Amy Richlin. New York: Routledge, 1993.

Snyder, Jane McIntosh. *Lesbian Desire in the Lyrics of Sappho.* New York: Columbia University Press, 1997.

Somerville, Siobhan. "Passing through the Closet in Pauline E. Hopkins's *Contending Forces.*" *American Literature* 69, 1 (March 1997): 139–66.

Weigall, Arthur. *Sappho of Lesbos: Her Life and Times.* New York: Frederick A. Stokes Co., 1932.

Williamson, Margaret. *Sappho's Immortal Daughters.* Cambridge: Harvard University Press, 1995.

Winkler, Jack. "Gardens of Nymphs: Public and Private in Sappho's Lyrics." In *Reflections of Women in Antiquity,* ed. Helene P. Foley, 63–89. New York: Gordon and Breach, 1981.

Selected fragments and verse renditions

1.A. From a second-century papyrus

Some say a host of cavalry, others of infantry, and others of ships, is the most beautiful thing on the black earth, but I say it is whatsoever a person loves. It is perfectly easy to make this understood by everyone: for she who far surpassed mankind in beauty, Helen, left her most noble husband and went sailing off to Troy with no thought at all for her child or dear parents, but (love) led her astray . . . lightly . . . (and she?) has reminded me now of Anactoria who is not here; I would rather see her lovely walk and the bright sparkle of her face than the Lydians' chariots and armed infantry . . . impossible to happen . . . mankind . . . but to pray to share . . . unexpectedly.

GL 16, p. 67

1.B. [Verse translation of GL 16 by Guy Davenport, #25, I]

A company of horsemen or of infantry
Or a fleet of ships, some say,
Is the black earth's finest sight,
But to me it is what you love.

This can be understood in its round truth
By all, clearly, for she who in her beauty
Surpassed all mankind, Elena, left her husband,
The best of men,

And sailed to Troia, mindless of her daughter,
And of her parents whom she loved.
But[   ]
[   ]led her astray.

[   ]
[   ]lightness in her heart[   ]
That I remember Anaktoria now
So far away.

I would rather see the fetching way she walks
And the smiling brightness of her eyes
Than the chariots and charioteers of Lydia
In full armor charging.

[   ]cannot become
[   ]man[   ]approach with sacrifice
    and pray
[   ]
[   ].

1.C. [Verse translation of GL 16 by Willis Barnstone, p. 7]

To Anaktoria

Some say cavalry and others claim
infantry or a fleet of long oars
is the supreme sight on the black earth.
    I say it is

the one you love. And easily proved.
Did not Helen, who was queen of mortal
beauty, choose as first among mankind
    the very scourge

of Trojan honor? Haunted by Love
she forgot kinsmen, her own dear child,
and wandered off to a remote country.
    Weak and fitful

woman bending before any man!
So Anaktoria, although you are
far, do not forget your loving friends.
    And I for one

would rather listen to your soft step
and see your radiant face— than watch
all the dazzling chariots and armored
    hoplites of Lydia.

2. from Hephaestion, second century

I have a beautiful child who looks like golden flowers, my darling Cleis, for whom I would not (take) all Lydia or lovely . . .

GL 132, p. 149

3. from Dionysius of Halicarnassus, first century B.C.E.

Ornate-throned immortal Aphrodite, wile-weaving daughter of Zeus, I entreat you: do not overpower my heart, mistress, with ache and anguish, but come here, if ever in the past you heard my voice from afar and acquiesced and came, leaving your father's golden house, with chariot yoked: beautiful swift sparrows whirring fast-beating wings brought you above the dark earth down from heaven through the mid-air, and soon they arrived; and you, blessed one, with a smile on your immortal face asked what was the matter with me this time and why I was calling this time and what in my maddened heart I most wished to happen for myself: "Whom am I to persuade this time to lead you back to her love? Who wrongs you, Sappho? If she runs away,

soon she shall pursue; if she does not accept gifts, why, she shall give them instead; and if she does not love, soon she shall love even against her will." Come to me now again and deliver me from oppressive anxieties; fulfil all that my heart longs to fulfil, and you yourself be my fellow-fighter.

GL 1, pp. 53–55

4. from Hephaestion

I loved you, Atthis, once long ago.

GL 49, p. 95

5. from "Longinus," first century

He seems as fortunate as the gods to me, the man who sits opposite you and listens nearby to your sweet voice and lovely laughter. Truly that sets my heart trembling in my breast. For when I look at you for a moment, then it is no longer possible for me to speak; my tongue has snapped, at once a subtle fire has stolen beneath my flesh, I see nothing with my eyes, my ears hum, sweat pours from me, a trembling seizes me all over, I am greener than grass, and it seems to me that I am little short of dying. But all can be endured, since . . . even a poor man . . .

GL 31, pp. 79–81

6. from Hephaestion

Once again limb-loosening Love makes me tremble, the bitter-sweet, irresistible creature.

GL 130, p. 147

7. from Hephaestion

(But?), Atthis, the thought of me has grown hateful to you, and you fly off to Andromeda.

GL 131, p. 149

8. from Hephaestion

The moon has set and the Pleiades; it is midnight, and time goes by, and I lie alone.

GL 168B, pp. 171–73

9. sixth century parchment

. . . and honestly I wish I were dead. She was leaving me with many tears and said this: "Oh what bad luck has been ours, Sappho; truly I leave you against my will." I replied to her thus:

"Go and fare well and remember me, for you know how we cared for you. If not, why then I want to remind you . . . and the good times we had. You put on many wreaths of violets and roses and (crocuses?) together by

Sappho

my side, and round your tender neck you put many woven garlands made from flowers and . . . with much flowery perfume, fit for a queen, you anointed yourself . . . and on soft beds . . . you would satisfy your longing (for?) tender . . .

GL 94, pp. 117–19

10. from the same parchment

. . . Sardis . . . often turning her thoughts in this direction . . . (she honoured) you as being like a goddess for all to see and took most delight in your song. Now she stands out among Lydian women like the rosy-fingered moon after sunset, surpassing all the stars, and its light spreads alike over the salt sea and flowery fields; the dew is shed in beauty, and roses bloom and tender chervil and flowery melilot. Often as she goes to and from she remembers gentle Atthis and doubtless her tender heart is consumed because of your fate . . . to go there . . . this . . . mind . . . much . . . sings . . .

GL 96, p. 121

11. papyrus fragment written in second or third century

. . . (golden-haired Phoebus), whom the daughter of Coeus bore, having lain with Cronus' son, (god of high clouds), whose name is great; but Artemis swore the (gods') great oath; "By your head, I shall always be a virgin (unwed), (hunting) on the peaks of the (lonely) mountains; come, grant this for my sake." So she spoke, and the father of the blessed gods nodded his consent; and gods (and men) call her (the virgin, shooter of deer), huntress, a great title. Love, (loosener of limbs), never approaches her . . .

GL 44A, p. 91

12. from Aristotle, *Rhetoric,* fourth century B.C.E.

[Alcaeus said:] "I wish to say something to you, but shame prevents me."

[Sappho replied:] " . . . but if you had a desire for what is honourable or good, and your tongue were not stirring up something evil to say, shame would not cover your eyes, but you would state your claim."

GL 137, p. 153

13. from Galen, second century

for he that is beautiful is beautiful as far as appearances go, while he that is good will consequently also be beautiful.

GL 50, p. 97

14. from the Scholiast, fifth century?

Wealth without virtue is no harmless neighbour. [The blending of both brings the height] of happiness.

GL 148, p. 161

15. from Stobaeus, early fifth century

[Sappho to an uneducated woman]: But when you die you will lie there, and afterwards there will never be any recollection of you or any longing for you since you have no share in the roses of Pieria; unseen in the house of Hades also, flown from our midst, you will go to and fro among the shadowy corpses.

GL 55, p. 99

16. from Syrianus, second century

As the sweet-apple reddens on the bough-top, on the top of the topmost bough; the apple-gatherers have forgotten it—no they have not forgotten it entirely, but they could not reach it.

GL 105, p. 131

17. Dio Chrysostom, first century

Someone, I say, will remember us in the future . . .

GL 147, p. 159

Diotima (ca. 400 B.C.E.)

Diotima is known to us primarily through Plato's Symposium, *in which Socrates recounts in dialogue form how she instructed him in the philosophical understanding of Eros, exposing the fallacies of his own youthful misconceptions about love and those of other speakers at the banquet. Diotima is described there and in other sources as a priestess of Mantinea and as a Pythagorean philosopher of the fifth century* B.C.E., *who lived for a time in Athens and was Socrates' teacher.*

In the twentieth century the historical existence of Diotima has often been questioned, though earlier sources accepted that she was a historical person and no new evidence has been adduced. Classicist Robert G. Bury asserted flatly that "Diotima is a fictitious personage," but he offered no historical grounds for this conclusion. More recently, David M. Halperin has devoted a lengthy essay to the view that "Diotima's 'femininity' is illusory — a projection of male fantasy."

Mary Ellen Waithe (1987) and Susan Hawthorne (1994), however, argue persuasively on historical and internal textual grounds that there is good reason to accept the historical existence of Diotima as a real person, a philosopher whose ideas shaped those of Socrates and Plato. Andrea Nye (1994: 206–207) and Louis Ruprecht, Jr. (1992: 103–105) also call upon the history and cultural traditions of the Minoan past, and especially of Mantinea, to suggest the verisimilitude of Socrates having such a teacher and of Diotima having taught the ideas attributed to her by Plato.

The conception of Eros attributed to Diotima in the Symposium reappears in other dialogues of Plato, including the Republic, and has had profound and continuing influence on the history of political thought. At its core, it elevates love to a preeminent place in the soul and hence (as developed in the Republic) in the body politic. Viewed in this light, Diotima appears to carry forward the tradition of Sappho.

There is considerable debate today, however, as to the correct interpretation to be placed on Diotima's conception of love, or Eros. Some scholars maintain that Diotima rejects fleshly love in favor of the love of beauty and goodness, primarily the beauty and goodness of the creations of the mind. In this view, the argument which Plato portrays as the teaching of Diotima epitomizes a dualistic vision which separates the soul from the body, reason from emotion, and politics from compassion — subordinating the body, emotion, and compassion to the soul, reason, and state policy. With this conception of love, we may well understand Socrates' concluding comment, in the selection below: "And now and ever do I praise the energy and manliness of Eros with all the might I have" (emphasis added).

Other scholars, however, reject this view of Diotima's teaching. Christine Downing, for example, argues that Diotima's philosophy of love, set in the homoerotic ambience of Socrates and his male companions, emphasized relations of mutuality and offered a "'feminine' dimension to male love" in the form of analogies to birthing: the creation or procreation of beauty and goodness. Susan Hawthorne, in "Diotima Speaks through the Body," argues that Diotima's language and metaphors offer a distinctively "feminine" vision (with caveats on this term). Hawthorne emphasizes the metaphors of pregnancy, birth, and connectedness in Diotima's ideas, linking them to later women philosophers such as Simone Weil and Luce Irigaray, and concludes that Diotima may be "the earliest named woman philosopher to 'think through the body,' or to 'write the body.'"

Martha Nussbaum, who views Diotima as fictional, portrays the ideas attributed to Diotima as simply those of Plato himself, emphasizing passages that direct the concepts of love and beauty toward abstraction, unity, purity, even uniformity, in a life of contemplation of truth (1986: 177–83). But others, such as Susan Hawthorne, have argued that Diotima raised challenges to Socrates' "absolutist dualistic divisions," questioning dualist oppositions between beauty and ugliness, good and evil, wisdom and ignorance. Andrea Nye also denies that Diotima's concept of love would lead to political quietism. On the contrary, Nye finds in Diotima a vision of love as creating community, generating the goods that lead to human happiness, and "continually foment the kind of change which breaks up the old and creates new knowledge and virtues" (Nye, 1990: 150).

These contrary interpretations reflect underlying changes and contradictions in ideas of masculinity, femininity, procreation, love, and so forth, from Diotima's time to the present. But they may also stem from internal contradictions in the text of the Symposium itself. Diotima's words are reported by Plato at fifth hand, through various tellings by Socrates and others who attended or heard of his account. It is reasonable to accept Plato's representation that Socrates regarded Diotima's teachings as important, that they dealt generally with the subject of Eros, and that Socrates credited Diotima with certain key philosophical ideas of his own. It is also likely that Plato, writing in the lifetime of some who were present at the gathering, would have tried to render a version of Diotima's views approximating Socrates' telling. But internal inconsistencies in the dialogue suggest that Plato sought to put his own ideas on bodyless love into the mouth of Diotima, the wise woman and priestess, "honoured of Zeus," while retaining at least a core of her actual teachings. It is thus a challenge to discern that core, and the dialogue between Diotima and Socrates remains an intriguing puzzle, open to ongoing speculation and debate.

The selection presented here is from Lane Cooper's 1938 translation of Plato's Symposium.

BAC

Sources and Suggested Readings

Anonymous. *The Dialectics of Diotima*. With a foreword by Richard Church. Fontwell, Sussex: Centaur Press, 1969. [A modern dialogue on what Diotima might have thought about twentieth-century problems.]

Blair, Elena Duvergès. "Women: The Unrecognized Teachers of the Platonic Socrates." *Ancient Philosophy* 16 (1996): 333–50.

Bury, Robert G., ed. and trans. *The Symposium of Plato*. Cambridge: W. Heffer, 1932.

Cooper, Lane, ed. and trans. *Plato: Phaedrus, Ion, Gorgias, and Symposium*. London: Oxford University Press, 1938. 251–63.

Downing, Christine. "Diotima and Alcibiades: An Alternative Reading of the *Symposium*." *Soundings* 72, 4 (1989): 631–55.

Halperin, David M. "Why Is Diotima a Woman?" In *Before Sexuality: The Construction of Erotic Experience in the Ancient Greek World*, ed. D. Halperin, J. Winkler, and F. Zeitlin, 257–308. Princeton: Princeton University Press, 1990.

Hawthorne, Susan. "Diotima Speaks through the Body." In *Engendering Origins: Critical Feminist Readings in Plato and Aristotle*, ed. Bat Ami Bar On, 83–96. Albany: State University of New York Press, 1994.

Irigaray, Luce. "Sorcerer Love: A Reading of Plato's Symposium, Diotima's Speech." In *Feminist Interpretations of Plato*, ed. Nancy Tuana. University Park: Pennsylvania State University Press, 1994.

Lamb, W. R. M., ed. and trans. *Plato: With an English Translation*. Vol. 5. *Lysis, Symposium, Gorgias*. London: William Heinemann, rev. ed., 1946.

Nussbaum, Martha. *The Fragility of Goodness: Luck and Ethics in Greek Tragedy and Philosophy*. Cambridge: Cambridge University Press, 1986. Chaps. 6 and 7.

———. *Love's Knowledge: Essays on Philosophy and Literature*. Oxford: Clarendon Press, 1990.

Nye, Andrea. "Irigaray and Diotima at Plato's Symposium." In *Feminist Interpretations of Plato*, ed. Nancy Tuana. University Park: Pennsylvania State University Press, 1994.

———. "The Subject of Love: Diotima and Her Critics." *Journal of Value Inquiry* 24 (1990): 135–53.

Rosen, Stanley. *Plato's Symposium*. New Haven: Yale University Press, 1973.

Ruprecht, Louis A., Jr. "A Funny Thing Happens on the Way to Mantineia: Diotima and Martha Nussbaum on Love's Knowledge." *Soundings* 75, 1 (Spring 1992): 97–127.

Smith, William, ed. *Dictionary of Greek and Roman Biography and Mythology*. 3 vols. London: Taylor, Walton, and Maberly, 1850.

Tuana, Nancy, ed. *Feminist Interpretations of Plato*. University Park: Pennsylvania State University Press, 1994.

Waithe, Mary Ellen. "Diotima of Mantinea." In *A History of Women Philosophers*, vol. 1. Dordrecht: Martinus Nijhoff, 1987. 83–116.

The Discourse on Eros
(FROM PLATO, *THE SYMPOSIUM*)

[Socrates and Diotima.] . . . Now for the speech concerning Eros. It is one I heard from Diotima, a woman of Mantinea, who was wise on this and many another theme, and once, through sacrifice by the Athenians against the plague, she brought about a ten-years' respite from the sickness. And she it was who taught me on the theme of love. Accordingly, the speech that woman made to me I will attempt to give again to you, starting from the premises which Agathon and I agreed on; I will do it by myself, as well as I am able. The right procedure, Agathon, as you explained, is first to tell what Eros is, and what he is like, and then to tell of his works. I think the easiest way will be to follow through as she, the visitant, once did in answering me; for actually I said pretty much the same to her as Agathon just now said to me—that Eros was a mighty god, and was a thing of beauty; and she refuted me with just the arguments I used with him—that, by my reasoning, Eros was not beautiful, nor was he good. And I said: "How mean you, Diotima? You mean to say that Eros must be ugly and bad?" And she replied: "No blasphemy! Or do you hold that anything that is not beautiful must then perforce be ugly?" "Yes, certainly!" "And similarly that he who is not wise must of necessity be ignorant? Or are you not aware that there is something midway between ignorance and knowledge?" "What is that?" "Holding a correct opinion while yet unable to give a reason for it. Don't you know that this is neither understanding (for how could anything without a reason be called science?), nor is it ignorance (for when it tallies with reality, then how could it be nonsense?) Right opinion doubtless is some such thing as that, midway between intelligence and folly."

[Socrates.] That is true (said I).

[Diotima.] So you must not demand that that which is not beautiful must perforce be ugly, nor yet that that which is not good is evil. And so with Eros. When you personally admit that he is neither good nor beautiful, no more need you suppose that he is ugly and bad, but rather something intermediate (said she) between the two.

[Socrates and Diotima.] "And yet," said I, "it is agreed by all that he is a mighty god." "You mean, by all who do not know?" said she, "or by all who know as well?" "Absolutely all." At that she laughed, and said: "And how can that be, Socrates? How can it be admitted that he is a mighty god by those who hold that Eros is no god at all?" "And who are they?" said I. "You, for one," said she; "and I am one." And I rejoined: "What do you mean by that?" said I. "That is easy; tell me, now," said she, "do you not hold that all the gods are beautiful and happy? Or would you dare to say that any one of them is neither beautiful nor happy?" "By Heaven, not I!" said I. "But those whom you call happy, they are those who have the good and beautiful in their possession?" "Certainly." "But it is precisely Eros, you admitted, who, because he lacks the good and beautiful, desires these very things of which he stands in need." "I have admitted that." "How, then, could he be god, who is bereft of what is beautiful and good?" "In no way, it would seem." "So you see," said she, "that you yourself do not consider Eros god." "Well," said I, "and what is Eros, then? A mortal?" "Not at all." "But what, then?" "As in the previous cases, he is intermediate: between the mortal and immortal." "And so, what? Diotima!" "He is a mighty genius [*daimon*, spirit], Socrates, and hence, like all the race of spirits is midway between divine and mortal." "What function has it?" I inquired.

[Diotima.] It has for its office to interpret between gods and men, to fetch and carry to the gods from men, and to men from the gods—from the one side prayer and sacrifice, from the other their behests and recompense for worship; being central, it fills the gap between the two, and thus the universe is bound together in one whole. Through it proceeds all divination, together with the priestly art of such as are concerned with sacrifices, with initiations, with prophecy in general, and with magic. Divinity does not mingle with humanity; but through it is carried on the intercourse and converse of the gods with men, in waking hours as well as sleep. And he who is wise in matters of the sort is a spiritual man [*daimonios*]; but he who is wise in any other matter, about arts or handicrafts, is but an artisan. Now these spirits [*daimones*] are many and diverse; and one of them is Eros.

[Socrates.] What about his father and his mother? (I demanded). Who are they?

[Diotima.] The story is a rather long one (she replied), but I will tell you all the same. When Aphrodite was born, you see, that day the gods had a feast, and among the company was Plenty, son of Metis. When they had finished dinner, along came Poverty to beg, there being ample cheer, and hung about the door. Well, Plenty had got tipsy on the nectar (for wine did not yet exist), and went into the garden of Zeus, and sank down and went to sleep. So Poverty by reason of her want made a scheme to get herself with child by Plenty, and lay down beside him, and got Eros. And that is why Eros follows Aphrodite, and is her attendant: because he was begotten at her birthday festival, and is also by his nature a lover of the beautiful, and since Aphrodite is a lovely goddess.

Inasmuch, then, as he is the son of Plenty and Poverty, the state of Eros' fortune is like this. In the first place, he is for ever poor, and anything but delicate and beautiful, as the many think; no, he is rough, unkempt, unshod, and homeless, ever couching on the ground uncovered, sleeping beneath the open sky by doors and in the streets, because he has the nature of his mother, and is the constant mate of indigence. But again, in keeping with his father, he has designs upon the beautiful and good, for he is bold, headlong, and intense, a mighty hunter, always weaving some device or other, eager in invention and resourceful, searching after wisdom all through life, terrible as a magician, sorcerer, and sophist. Further, in his nature he is not immortal, nor yet mortal. No, on a given day, now he flourishes and lives, when things go well with him, and again he dies, but through the nature of his sire revives again. Yet his gain for ever slips away from him, so that Eros never is without resources, nor is ever rich.

As for ignorance and knowledge, here again he is midway between them. The case stands thus. No god seeks after wisdom, or wishes to grow wise (for he already is so), no more than anybody else seeks after wisdom if he has it. Nor, again, do ignorant folk seek after wisdom or long to grow wise; for here is just the trouble about ignorance, that what is neither beautiful and good, nor yet intelligent, to itself seems good enough. Accordingly, the man who does not think himself in need has no desire for what he does not think himself in need of.

[Socrates.] The seekers after knowledge, Diotima! If they are not the wise, nor yet the ignorant (said I), who are they, then?

[Diotima.] The point (said she) is obvious even to a child, that they are persons intermediate between these two, and that Eros is among them; for wisdom falls within the class of the most beautiful, while Eros is an *eros* for the beautiful. And hence it follows necessarily that Eros is a seeker after wisdom [a philosopher], and, being a philosopher, is midway between wise and ignorant. And the cause thereof in him lies in his birth, his father being wise and gifted, his mother lacking wisdom and ability. So there, dear Socrates, you have the nature of the spirit [*daimon*]. There is nothing strange about your taking Eros to be what you thought him. Judging by the evidence of what you say, I think that you took Eros for the object of desire, and not that which desires. That is why to you, I fancy, Eros appeared to be all beautiful. And indeed the lovable is that which in reality is beautiful, tender, perfect, and accounted blest; whereas desiring has another form, a nature such as I explained.

[Socrates and Diotima.] And I said: "So be it, stranger-friend, for you speak well. Yet if Eros is like that, what value has he for mankind?" "That is the next thing, Socrates," said she, "that I will try to show you. Eros is like that, and his origin was such; just so. And, as you say, he loves the beautiful. Now suppose that some one were to ask us: 'What actually is the love of beauty, Socrates and Diotima?' Or, to make it clearer, thus: 'He loves who is enamoured of the beautiful; what is it he desires?'" And I answered: "That the object may be his." "But the answer," said she, "demands a further question, namely: 'What happens to the man when the beauty becomes his?'" I replied that, for this question, I by no means had an answer ready. "But suppose," said she, "that one made a substitution, using 'good' instead of 'beautiful,' and inquired: 'Come, Socrates, he loves who is enamoured of the good; what is it he desires?'" "That the good," said I, "may be his." "'And what happens to the man when the good things become his?'" "On this," said I, "I am more ready with an answer: that he will be happy." "It is, in fact, by the possession of good things," said she, "that the happy man is happy, and there is no need of asking, further, about what he wishes to be happy when he wishes it. No, the question seems to have attained its final answer." "You are right," said I.

"Now this wish and *eros*, do you think that they are common to mankind, and that everybody wishes that the good shall be for ever theirs? Or would you put it otherwise?" "No, thus," said I—"that they are common to mankind." "Well then, why is it, Socrates," said she, "that we do not say that everybody is in love, if it be true that all are eager for the same things, and eternally? Why do we say, instead, that some love, and that some do not?" "I too," said I, "am wondering at that." "You need not wonder," said she; "for we begin by separating off a certain kind of love, to which, applying the inclusive term, we give the name of 'Eros,' while for the other species we use other names." "For instance, what?" said I. "For instance, this. You are aware

that *poiesis* [creation, poetry] is a term of wide extent. Thus, in every case, when anything whatever passes from not-being into being, the cause is *poiesis*. And hence the works produced by all the arts are acts of *poiesis*, and all the makers of them, poets." "You are right." "But nevertheless," said she, "you know that they are not called poets, but go by other names. But from poetry as a whole one section is marked off, the part concerned with music and with metre, and gets the designation of the whole; this part alone it is that is called 'poetry,' and only they who share this realm of poetry are known as 'poets.'" "You are right," said I. "Well then, it is just the same with Love. The universal concept is all the longing for the good, and to be happy:

The all-inclusive and the subtle Love in every heart.

Some, however, though in numerous other ways they are concerned therewith, whether in pecuniary thrift, or in pursuit of the gymnastic art, or in philosophy, are not spoken of as 'loving,' nor called 'lovers'; whereas others, following one special form of love, and eager in it, monopolize the general term, 'love,' 'loving,' 'lovers.'" "I dare say you are right," said I. "There is a theory, too," said she, "that it is they that seek their other half who love. My theory asserts that love is neither of the half nor of the whole, unless, my friend, the object happens somehow to be good; since men are willing actually to have their feet and hands cut off, if they think their own members offend them. It is not to his own, methinks, that each one cleaves, unless some one calls the good his proper nature and his own, and the evil alien to him; so true is it that there is nothing that men love except the good. Do you think otherwise of them?" "By Heaven! not I," said I. "Well then," said she, "may one thus simply say that men love what is good?" "Yes," I replied. "But what! Must one not add," said she, "that they desire besides to have possession of the good?" "That must be added." "And," said she, "not only the possession, but to possess the good for ever?" "This also must be added." "Accordingly," said she, "all put together, Eros is the longing that the good shall be one's own for ever." "Your statement is most eminently true," said I.

"Granted that love is always this," said she, "by what manner of pursuit and in what activity does the eagerness and straining for the object get the name of Eros? What may this action really be? Can you say?" "If I could do so, Diotima, I should not," said I, "be in amazement at your wisdom, or come to school to you for information on these very matters." "In that case, I," said she, "will teach you. This action is engendering in beauty, with relation both to body and to soul." "One needs," said I, "the power of divination in order to get your meaning, and I do not understand." "Come," she answered, "I will speak more plainly. All human beings, Socrates," she said, "are fecund, fecund both in body and in soul; and when they reach a certain age, our nature yearns to generate. But generate in ugliness it cannot; it must generate in beauty. The union of a man and a woman, is in fact, a generation; this is a thing divine; in a living creature that is mortal, it is an element of immortality, this fecundity and generation. But these things cannot occur in what is inharmonious; and the ugly is out of harmony with all that is divine, whereas beauty is harmonious with it. Therefore Beauty is the Moira and the Ilithyia [goddess of parturition] presiding over genesis. That is why the fecund, whenever it comes near a thing of beauty, becomes tranquil, expands with joy, and begets and generates. But when it draws near to the ugly, the fecund is depressed, in affliction shrouds itself, turns away, and shrivels up, and does not generate, but with pain endures the load of its fecundity. And hence there comes to the fecund, ripe and already swelling, the mighty transport over the beautiful, because possessing it frees the possessor from the cruel pain; for, Socrates," said she, "the aim of love is not the beautiful, as you suppose." "But, what, then, is it?" "It is generating and producing in the beautiful." "Let it be that," said I. "Yes, absolutely," she replied; "yet why precisely generation? Because, so far as may be to a mortal, generation is perpetual existence and eternal life. The bond between desiring immortality and the good arises necessarily from the premises, if it be true that *eros* means desire to have the good oneself for ever."

All this she taught me on the various occasions when she made discourse of love; and once she asked: "What do you imagine, Socrates, to be the cause of this desire and longing? Do you not mark how powerfully all the animals are affected when they desire to procreate, they that walk and they that fly, all frantic, and all amorously disposed, first for commerce, and then for the rearing of the progeny; and prepared to fight for these, the weakest even with the strongest, and to die for them, racking themselves with hunger, doing everything, in order that the offspring may be adequately nourished? With men," said she, "one might imagine that they acted thus from reason; but, in the beasts, what is the cause of this passionate behavior? Can you say?" And I said once more that I did not know. But she rejoined: "And so you think you will be competent some day upon the theme of love, when you are not aware of this?" "But, Diotima, there you have the very reason, as I just now said, why I come to you; it is because I know that I have need of masters. Do you, rather, tell me what the cause is of the things you mention, and of the other matters touching love."

"Well now," said she, "if you are convinced that the aim of love is by nature what we repeatedly have admitted it to be, you need not be astonished; for here the line of reasoning is the same as it was before: the mortal nature seeks, as far as it is able, to perpetuate itself and be immortal. But it can do so only by this means of generation, because thus it always leaves behind another individual, a new one, to replace the old. In proof of that, take what they call the lifetime of the individual creature and its identity; the fact, for instance, that one is said to be the same from childhood till old age comes on. This person is, in truth, still called the same, although he never has the same materials in him, but, on the contrary, is ever being formed anew, with certain losses, alike in hair, flesh, bones, and blood—in his body as a whole.

"And that is true not merely of the body, but also of the soul; true of our ways, our character, our notions, longings, pleasures, pains, and fears; not one of these remains the same in any individual, but some of them are being born while others are passing away. Yet a change that is odder by far than that takes place in our knowledge; for not only do some parts of it come to be while others are lost, so that we never remain the same with respect to the things we know, but even the single piece of knowledge has this very lot. Thus the act called 'recollection' implies that knowledge has departed; forgetting is, in fact, a departing of knowledge, and recollecting again is implanting a newborn memory in place of that which is leaving, thereby preserving knowledge, so that it seems to be the same. This is the fashion in which everything mortal is preserved, not in being always perfectly identical, as is divinity, but in that the disappearing and decaying object leaves behind it another new one such as it was. By this arrangement, Socrates," said she, "the mortal partakes of immortality, both in body and all else; the immortal does so in another way. So do not marvel if everything by nature prizes its own offspring; it is for the sake of immortality that every being has this urgency and love."

As for me, when I had listened to her words, I was amazed, and said: "Come, wisest Diotima, is that the way things really are?" said I. And she, replying like a finished Sophist:

[Diotima.] Socrates (said she), you may rest assured of it; and, for proof, only look, if you will, at men's ambition. You would marvel at their want of reason, if you did not keep in mind what I have said, when reflecting on the vehemence with which they are disposed by love to win a name,

And to lay up for endless time imperishable glory.

And for this they are prepared to encounter every peril, even more than for their children, to pour out all their money, to submit to any toils whatever, and to die for it. Because (said she), do you imagine that Alcestis would have died for Admetus, or that Achilles would have followed Patroclus in death, or that your Codrus would have perished in advance for the kingdom of his children, if they had not supposed that there would be the deathless memory of them, for their virtue, which we now possess? Far from it (said she). No, methinks they all do all they can for an eternity of virtue and for glorious renown like that, and the better men they are, the more they do it. The reason is that they love immortality.

Well then (said she), when men's fecundity is of the body, they turn rather to the women, and the fashion of their love is this: through begetting children to provide themselves with immortality, renown, and happiness, as they imagine—

Securing them for all time to come.

But when fecundity is of the soul—for indeed there are (said she) those persons who are fecund in their souls, even more than in their bodies, fecund in what it is the function of the soul to conceive and also to bring forth—what is this proper offspring? It is wisdom, along with every other spiritual value. Of these, the poets, all of them, are generators, and, among the artists, as many are called "original." By far the greatest and most beautiful form of wisdom (said she) is that which has to do with regulating states and households, and has the name, no doubt, of "temperance" and "justice." Now, when a person from his youth bears the germ of these within his soul, a godlike person, and with the coming of maturity desires to generate and procreate, he goes about, he too, in quest of the beauty in which he may beget, for never will he do it in deformity. And hence in his fecundity he is more drawn to bodies that are beautiful than to ugly ones; and if in one of them he meets a soul that is beautiful, high-minded, and well-born, he is powerfully attracted to this union of the two, and in the presence of this man he straightway becomes ready in discourse on virtue, and on the sort of things the good man ought to be concerned with, and be doing, and sets out to teach him. At the touch, methinks, of beauty, and in communion with it, he begets what he has long been fecund with, and brings it forth; present or absent, he has in mind the lovely being, and rears the progeny in common with that being; and thus such persons are united by a bond far closer than the tie through children, and continue in a firmer mutual affection, because their common offspring are more beautiful and deathless. Further, every one would rather have such children born to him than human offspring; and, when he considers Homer, Hesiod, and the other able poets, he is envious of such posterity as they have left behind

them, a posterity that confers on them immortal fame and memory, being itself immortal; such offspring, if you will (said she), as Lycurgus left behind in Lacedaemon, [the laws] which were the saviors of Lacedaemon, and, we may say, of Greece. With you [Athenians] Solon, too, has honor for the engendering of laws; as other men in many another place, alike among the Greeks and the barbarians, have brought many a noble work to light, engendering every kind of worth; for whom there have been, also, many shrines erected because of offspring of the sort, but never a shrine for any one because of human offspring.

The mysteries of love so far, I take it, Socrates, are such as even you may enter. To the complete initiation and final revelation which are the goal of these, if one follows the proper way, I do not know if you are fitted to attain. I will proceed (said she); I will do my utmost to instruct you. Do you try to follow as much as in you lies.

He who pursues the proper road to this result (said she) must in youth begin to visit beautiful forms, and first, if he be led aright by him who leads, must love one single object [physical form of beauty], and thereof must engender fair discourses. Then, however, he must come to see that the beauty in a given object is brother to the beauty of the next one, and, if he must hunt for beauty in the visible form, what folly if he failed to judge that the beauty in all objects is single and the same! But when he reflects on that, he will abate his violent love of one, disdaining this and deeming it a trifle, and will become a lover of all fair objects. Thereafter he must recognize that beauty in the soul is of a higher worth than beauty in the body [physical object], until, if perchance a person with a gentle soul should have but little comeliness of body, he is content to love that person, and to care for him, and to engender and discover such discourses as will improve the young. And thus, in turn, he will be forced to view the beauty in the pursuits of life, and in the law, and to see that it is all one self-consistent genus, till he takes the beauty of the body for a trifle. After occupations, he must needs be led to forms of knowledge, to behold, in turn, the beauty of the sciences, and, gazing at the realm, now vast, of beauty, no longer will he, like a menial, cleave to the individual form, to the beauty of a stripling or some man, or of some one pursuit, living in a wretched slavery and talking tattle; no, turned about towards the vast sea of beauty, and contemplating it, he will give birth to manifold and beautiful discourse of lofty import, and concepts born in boundless love of wisdom; till there, with powers implanted and augmented, he has the vision of one single science, the science of that beauty I go on to.

Try with all your might (continued she) to give

your mind to what I say. He who has been instructed thus far in the things of love, and who has come to see the beautiful in successive stages and in order due, when now he nears the goal of the initiation, will suddenly behold a beauty of wondrous nature, and, Socrates, this is that for which all the former labors were undertaken; a beauty, first of all, which is eternal, not growing up or perishing, increasing or decreasing; secondly, not beautiful in one point and ugly in another, not sometimes beautiful and sometimes not, nor beautiful in one relation and ugly in another, nor beautiful in this place and ugly in that, as if beautiful to some, to others ugly; again, this beauty will not be revealed to him in the semblance of a face, or hands, or any other element of the body, nor in any form of speech or knowledge, nor yet as if it appertained to any other being, a creature, for example, upon earth, or in the sky, or elsewhere; no, it will be seen as beauty in and for itself, consistent with itself in uniformity for ever, whereas all other beauties share it in such fashion that, while they are ever born and perish, that eternal beauty, never waxing, never waning, never is impaired. Now when a man, beginning with these transitory beauties, and through the rightful love of youths ascending, comes to have a sight of that eternal beauty, he is not far short of the goal. This is indeed the rightful way of going, or of being guided by another, to the things of love: starting from these transitory beauties, with that beauty yonder as a goal, ever to mount upwards, using these as rungs, from one going on to two, and from two to all fair bodies, and from beautiful bodies to beautiful pursuits, and from beautiful pursuits to beautiful domains of science, until, mounting from the sciences, he finally attains to yonder science which has no other object save eternal beauty in itself, and knows at last the beauty absolute.

There you have the life, dear Socrates (said the visitant from Mantinea), there if anywhere the life that is worth living by a man, in contemplation of the beauty absolute. If one day you behold it, it will not appear to you to be according to the measure of gold and raiment, or of lovely boys and striplings, at the sight of whom you now are entranced, and are ready, you along with many others, if you can gaze at your beloved and be for ever with them, to go (supposing it were somehow possible) without your food and drink, and only look at them and stay with them! What indeed (said she) do we think it would mean to a man to see the beauty absolute, authentic, pure, without alloy? Not beauty clogged with human flesh and hues and a vast deal of other mortal trumpery, but, instead, to be able to behold beauty divine in its own single nature? Do you believe (said she) that life can be ignoble for the man who looks up yonder, and with the rightful instrument beholds that beauty, and abides with it? Do you not conclude (said she) that then alone it will be his, when he sees the beautiful with that by which it can be seen, to bring to birth, not images of virtue, since what he holds to is no image, but real virtue, because he has laid hold on truth? And will it not be the lot of him who brings forth real virtue, and nourishes it, to be the friend of God, and to become, if it can come to any of mankind, immortal?

[Socrates.] There, Phaedrus and the rest of you, you have what Diotima said to me, and by it she convinced me. Once convinced, I labor to convince others also that, in order to attain this good, our human nature could not find a more efficient aid than Eros. And therefore it is my express opinion that every man should honor Eros; and, for myself, I prize the things of love, and train myself in them exceedingly, and urge the same on others. And now and ever do I praise the energy and manliness of Eros with all the might I have.

Accept then, Phaedrus, this discourse, if you are willing, as an encomium spoken upon Eros; at all events, whatever and however you are pleased to call it, call it so.

Sei Shōnagon (ca. 965–?)

The Pillow Book of Sei Shōnagon *is one of the classics of Japanese literature, and its author has been described as "one of the greatest writers of prose in the long history of Japanese literature." She was born about 965 and wrote the notes that comprise* The Pillow Book *during the time she was in service to Empress Sadako in the last decade of the tenth century, probably beginning about the year 994.*

We know little about the details of Sei Shōnagon's life outside of her experiences and observations at court around the turn of the tenth century. She was of the Kiyohara family, but the name by which we know her is simply the first character (Sei) of the family name and an honorary title (Shōnagon = "lesser counsellor"). Her writings give little information about her personal life, and we have no more than speculation about her possible marriage(s), children, private relationships, and later years.

The Pillow Book *has been paired with Murasaki Shikibu's* The Tale of Genji *as the two most outstanding works of Japanese prose literature of the mid-Heian period. In contrast with the situation in Europe around the year 1000, literature and scholarship held a prominent place in aristocratic circles in Japan, and women were leading figures in the literary life of the time. The poetic quality of* The Pillow Book *led Arthur Waley to describe Sei Shōnagon as "incomparably the best poet of her time" (Morris).* The Pillow Book, *a kind of diary, initiated a genre of Japanese writing known as zuihitsu ("to follow the brush"), a seemingly unstructured type of work allowing free rein to the writer's spirit and inclinations.* The Pillow Book *itself incorporated a variety of prose forms including tales, narratives, reflections, lists, word pictures, and commentaries.*

Shōnagon has been admired and imitated for the style, beauty, and originality of her writings, her wit and satire, her self-critical honesty, and the historical value of her accounts of court life. But she is reproached for her "scorn for the lower orders," her "adoration of the Imperial family," and her attitude toward men ("even those of a somewhat higher class than hers"), which has been described as "competitive . . . to the point of overt hostility" (Morris, xiv). In her own time, she was vilified by Murasaki Shikibu as "the very picture of conceit and arrogance" (Cranston), but Murasaki borrowed from Sei Shōnagon in writing The Tale of Genji *(Keene). Murasaki Shikibu served in the court of Akiko, literary and political rival to Empress Sadako, and there is* doubt whether to accept her attacks on Sei Shōnagon at face value.

The Pillow Book of Sei Shōnagon *poses for us many key questions about the history of women's writings on political and social issues. It reports and reflects features of the political and social institutions, assumptions, interactions, and ideas of her time, but its varied forms are not easily recognized today as "political theory." One must ask whether this doubt arises because* The Pillow Book *does not meet essential criteria for what constitutes political theory, or rather because our assumptions and notions (stated or unstated) of political theory's forms are too limited. Indeed there was little of what we would identify as formal political theory in Sei Shōnagon's time, yet there was certainly thought and writing on issues of governance, class and gender relations, right order in society, and other "political" questions.*

The selections included here were chosen to illustrate the stylistic variety of the Pillow Book *entries, Sei Shōnagon's observations of court life and politics, her social attitudes and values, the importance of learning and literary activities to women of her class, and her incisive comments on male-female relations and other matters. The latter are sometimes embodied in the brief lists scattered through the book, such as "Different Ways of Speaking" or "Words That Look Commonplace but That Become Impressive When Written in Chinese Characters."*

It is interesting to note that Sei Shōnagon, a thousand years ago, was aware of and interested in differences between the speech of men and women. But the differences did not deter her from conversing with men. As Donald Keene points out: "She not only associated with them as equals, but did not hesitate to assert her superiority when a man seemed an unworthy adversary" (1993: 426). She loved the court life of her time for those very opportunities to cross wits with both male and female associates—opportunities which became more limited for women in later centuries.

The following selections are from the translation of The Pillow Book *(vol. 1, 1967) by Ivan Morris.*

BAC

Sources and Suggested Readings

Cranston, Edwin A. "Sei Shōnagon." In *Kodansha Encyclopedia of Japan.* Vol. 7. New York: Kodansha, 1983. 52–54.

The Pillow Book of Sei Shōnagon (ca. 994)

Keene, Donald. *Seeds in the Heart: Japanese Literature from Earliest Times to the Late Sixteenth Century.* New York: Henry Holt, 1993. Chaps. 9 and 10.

Morris, Ivan, ed. and trans. *The Pillow Book of Sei Shōnagon.* 2 vols. New York: Columbia University Press, 1967.

Murasaki Shikibu. *The Tale of Genji.* New York: Knopf, 1976. Translated with an Introduction by Edward G. Seidensticker.

"Sei Shōnagon," with a seventeenth-century portrait. *Japan: An Illustrated Encyclopedia.* Vol. 2. New York: Kodansha, 1993. 1338.

Waley, Arthur, trans. *The Pillow-Book of Sei Shōnagon.* London: George Allen and Unwin, 1949. [Reprint of the 1928 translation of about one quarter of the *Pillow Book*, with an introductory chapter, "Japan in the Tenth Century."]

The Pillow Book of Sei Shōnagon (ca. 994)

In Spring It Is the Dawn

In spring it is the dawn that is most beautiful. As the light creeps over the hills, their outlines are dyed a faint red and wisps of purplish cloud trail over them.

In summer the nights. Not only when the moon shines, but on dark nights too, as the fireflies flit to and fro, and even when it rains, how beautiful it is!

In autumn the evenings, when the glittering sun sinks close to the edge of the hills and the crows fly back to their nests in threes and fours and twos; more charming still is a file of wild geese, like specks in the distant sky. When the sun has set, one's heart is moved by the sound of the wind and the hum of the insects.

In winter the early mornings. It is beautiful indeed when snow has fallen during the night, but splendid too when the ground is white with frost; or even when there is no snow or frost, but it is simply very cold and the attendants hurry from room to room stirring up the fires and bringing charcoal, how well this fits the season's mood! But as noon approaches and the cold wears off, no one bothers to keep the braziers alight, and soon nothing remains but piles of white ashes. . . .

Different Ways of Speaking

A priest's language.
The speech of men and of women.
The common people always tend to add extra syllables to their words. . . .

The Sliding Screen in the Back of the Hall

The sliding screen in the back of the hall in the north-east corner of Seiryō is decorated with paintings of the stormy sea and of the terrifying creatures with long arms and long legs that live there. When the doors of the Empress's room were open, we could always see this screen. One day we were sitting in the room, laughing at the paintings and remarking how unpleasant they were. By the balustrade of the veranda stood a large celadon vase, full of magnificent cherry branches; some of them were as much as five foot long, and their blossoms overflowed to the very foot of the railing. Towards noon the Major Counsellor, Fujiwara no Korechika, arrived. He was dressed in a cherry-coloured Court cloak, sufficiently worn to have lost its stiffness, a white under-robe, and loose trousers of dark purple; from beneath the cloak shone the pattern of another robe of dark red damask. Since His Majesty was present, Korechika knelt on the narrow wooden platform before the door and reported to him on official matters.

A group of ladies-in-waiting was seated behind the bamboo blinds. Their cherry-coloured Chinese jackets hung loosely over their shoulders with the collars pulled back; they wore robes of wistaria, golden yellow, and other colours, many of which showed beneath the blind covering the half-shutter. Presently the noise of the attendants' feet told us that dinner was about to be served in the Daytime Chamber, and we heard cries of "Make way. Make way."

The bright, serene day delighted me. When the Chamberlains had brought all the dishes into the Chamber, they came to announce that dinner was ready, and His Majesty left by the middle door. After accompanying the Emperor, Korechika returned to his previous place on the veranda beside the cherry blossoms. The Empress pushed aside her curtain of state and came forward as far as the threshold. We were overwhelmed by the whole delightful scene. It was then that Korechika slowly intoned the words of the old poem,

> The days and the months flow by,
> But Mount Mimoro lasts forever.

Deeply impressed, I wished that all this might indeed continue for a thousand years.

As soon as the ladies serving in the Daytime Chamber had called for the gentlemen-in-waiting to remove the trays, His Majesty returned to the Empress's room. Then he told me to rub some ink on the inkstone. Dazzled, I felt that I should never be able to take my eyes off his radiant countenance. Next he folded a piece of white paper. "I should like each of you," he said, "to copy down on this paper the first ancient poem that comes into your head."

"How am I going to manage this?" I asked Korechika, who was still out on the veranda.

"Write your poem quickly," he said, "and show it to His Majesty. We men must not interfere in this." Ordering an attendant to take the Emperor's inkstone to each of the women in the room, he told us to make haste. "Write down any poem you happen to remember," he said. "The Naniwazu or whatever else you can think of."

For some reason I was overcome with timidity; I flushed and had no idea what to do. Some of the other women managed to put down poems about the spring, the blossoms, and such suitable subjects; then they handed me the paper and said, "Now it's your turn." Picking up the brush, I wrote the poem that goes,

> The years have passed
> And age has come my way.
> Yet I need only look at this fair flower
> For all my cares to melt away.

I altered the third line, however, to read, "Yet I need only look upon my lord."

When he had finished reading, the Emperor said, "I asked you to write these poems because I wanted to find out how quick you really were.

"A few years ago," he continued, "Emperor Enyū ordered all his courtiers to write poems in a notebook. Some excused themselves on the grounds that their handwriting was poor; but the Emperor insisted, saying that he did not care in the slightest about their handwriting or even whether their poems were suitable for the season. So they all had to swallow their embarrassment and produce something for the occasion. Among them was His Excellency, our present Chancellor, who was then Middle Captain of the Third Rank. He wrote down the old poem,

> Like the sea that beats
> Upon the shores of Izumo
> As the tide sweeps in,
> Deeper it grows and deeper—
> The love I bear for you.

But he changed the last line to read, 'The love I bear my lord!' and the Emperor was full of praise."

When I heard His Majesty tell this story, I was so overcome that I felt myself perspiring. It occurred to me that no younger woman would have been able to use my poem and I felt very lucky. This sort of test can be a terrible ordeal: it often happens that people who usually write fluently are so overawed that they actually make mistakes in their characters.

Next the Empress placed a notebook of *Kokin Shū* poems before her and started reading out the first three lines of each one, asking us to supply the remainder. Among them were several famous poems that we had in our minds day and night; yet for some strange reason we were often unable to fill in the missing lines. Lady Saishō, for example, could manage only ten, which hardly qualified her as knowing her *Kokin Shū*. Some of the other women, even less successful, could remember only about half-a-dozen poems. They would have done better to tell the Empress quite simply that they had forgotten the lines; instead they came out with great lamentations like "Oh dear, how could we have done so badly in answering the questions that Your Majesty was pleased to put to us?"—all of which I found rather absurd.

When no one could complete a particular poem, the Empress continued reading to the end. This produced further wails from the women: "Oh, we all knew that one! How could we be so stupid?"

"Those of you," said the Empress, "who had taken the trouble to copy out the *Kokin Shū* several times would have been able to complete every single poem I have read. In the reign of Emperor Murakami there was a woman at Court known as the Imperial Lady of Senyō Palace. She was the daughter of the Minister of the Left who lived in the Smaller Palace of the First Ward, and of course you have all heard of her. When she was still a young girl, her father gave her this advice: 'First you must study penmanship. Next you must learn to play the seven-string zither better than anyone else. And also you must memorize all the poems in the twenty volumes of the *Kokin Shū*.'

"Emperor Murakami," continued Her Majesty, "had heard this story and remembered it years later when the girl had grown up and become an Imperial Concubine. Once, on a day of abstinence, he came into her room, hiding a notebook of *Kokin Shū* poems in the folds of his robe. He surprised her by seating himself behind a curtain of state; then, opening the book, he asked, 'Tell me the verse written by such-and-such a poet, in such-and-such a year and on such-and-such an occasion.' The lady understood what was afoot and that it was all in fun, yet the possibility of making a mistake or forgetting one of the poems must have worried her greatly. Before beginning the test, the Emperor had summoned a couple of ladies-in-waiting who were particularly adept in poetry and told them to mark each incorrect reply by a *go* stone. What a splendid scene it must have been! You know, I really envy anyone who attended that Emperor even as a lady-in-waiting.

"Well," Her Majesty went on, "he then began questioning her. She answered without any hesitation, just giving a few words or phrases to show that she knew each poem. And never once did she make a mistake. After a time the Emperor began to resent the lady's flawless memory and decided to stop as soon as he detected any error or vagueness in her replies. Yet, after he had gone through ten books of the *Kokin Shū*, he had still not caught her out. At this stage he declared that it would be useless to continue. Marking where he had left off, he went to bed. What a triumph for the lady!

"He slept for some time. On waking, he decided that he must have a final verdict and that if he waited until the following day to examine her on the other ten volumes, she might use the time to refresh her memory. So he would have to settle the matter that very night. Ordering his attendants to bring up the bedroom lamp, he resumed his questions. By the time he had finished all twenty volumes, the night was well advanced; and still the lady had not made a mistake.

"During all this time His Excellency, the lady's father, was in a state of great agitation. As soon as he was informed that the Emperor was testing his daughter, he sent his attendants to various temples to arrange for special recitations of the Scriptures. Then he turned in the direction of the Imperial Palace and spent a long time in prayer. Such enthusiasm for poetry is really rather moving."

The Emperor, who had been listening to the whole story, was much impressed. "How can he possibly have read so many poems?" he remarked when Her Majesty had finished. "I doubt whether I could get through three or four volumes. But of course things have changed. In the old days even people of humble station had a taste for the arts and were interested in elegant pastimes. Such a story would hardly be possible nowadays, would it?"

The ladies in attendance on Her Majesty and the Emperor's own ladies-in-waiting who had been admitted into Her Majesty's presence began chatting eagerly, and as I listened I felt that my cares had really "melted away."

When I Make Myself Imagine

When I make myself imagine what it is like to be one of those women who live at home, faithfully serving their husbands—women who have not a single exciting prospect in life yet who believe that they are perfectly happy—I am filled with scorn. Often they are of quite good birth, yet have had no opportunity to find out what the world is like. I wish they could live for a while in our society, even if it should mean taking service as Attendants, so that they might come to know the delights it has to offer.

I cannot bear men who believe that women serving in the Palace are bound to be frivolous and wicked. Yet I suppose their prejudice is understandable. After all, women at court do not spend their time hiding modestly behind fans and screens, but walk about, looking openly at people they chance to meet. Yes, they see everyone face to face, not only ladies-in-waiting like themselves, but even Their Imperial Majesties (whose august names I hardly dare mention), High Court Nobles, senior courtiers, and other gentlemen of high rank. In the presence of such exalted personages the women in the Palace are all equally brazen, whether they be the maids of ladies-in-waiting, or the relations of Court ladies who have come to visit them, or housekeepers, or latrine-cleaners, or women who are of no more value than a roof-tile or a pebble. Small wonder that the young men regard them as immodest! Yet are the gentlemen themselves any less so? They are not exactly bashful when it comes to looking at the great people in the Palace. No, everyone at Court is much the same in this respect.

Women who have served in the Palace, but who later get married and live at home, are called Madam and receive the most respectful treatment. To be sure, people often consider that these women, who have displayed their faces to all and sundry during their years at Court, are lacking in feminine grace. How proud they must be, nevertheless, when they are styled Assistant Attendants, or summoned to the Palace for occasional duty, or ordered to serve as Imperial envoys during the Kamo Festival! Even those who stay at home lose nothing by having served at Court. In fact they make very good wives. For example, if they are married to a provincial governor and their daughter is chosen to take part in the Gosechi dances, they do not have to disgrace themselves by acting like provincials and asking other people about procedure. They themselves are well versed in the formalities, which is just as it should be. . . .

Things That People Despise

The north side of a house.

Someone with an excessive reputation for goodness.

An old man who has lived to be *too* old.

A frivolous woman.

A mud wall that has started to crumble.

Hateful Things

One is in a hurry to leave, but one's visitor keeps chattering away. If it is someone of no importance, one can get rid of him by saying, "You must tell me all about it next time"; but, should it be the sort of visitor whose presence commands one's best behaviour, the situation is hateful indeed.

One finds that a hair has got caught in the stone on which one is rubbing one's inkstick, or again that gravel is lodged in the inkstick, making a nasty, grating sound.

Someone has suddenly fallen ill and one summons the exorcist. Since he is not at home, one has to send messengers to look for him. After one has had a long fretful wait, the exorcist finally arrives, and with a sigh of relief one asks him to start his incantations. But perhaps he has been exorcizing too many evil spirits recently; for hardly has he installed himself and begun praying when his voice becomes drowsy. Oh, how hateful!

A man who has nothing in particular to recommend him discusses all sorts of subjects at random as though he knew everything.

An elderly person warms the palms of his hands over a brazier and stretches out the wrinkles. No young man would dream of behaving in such a fashion; old people can really be quite shameless. I have seen some dreary old creatures actually resting their feet on the brazier and rubbing them against the edge while they speak. These are the kind of people who in visiting someone's house first use their fans to wipe away the dust from the mat and, when they finally sit on it, cannot stay still but are forever spreading out the front of their hunting costume or even tucking it up under their knees. One might suppose that such behaviour was restricted to people of humble station; but I have observed it in quite well-bred people, including a Senior Secretary of the Fifth Rank in the Ministry of Ceremonial and a former Governor of Suruga.

I hate the sight of men in their cups who shout, poke their fingers in their mouths, stroke their beards, and pass on the wine to their neighbors with great cries of "Have some more! Drink up!" They tremble, shake their heads, twist their faces, and gesticulate like children who are singing, "We're off to see the Governor." I have seen really well-bred people behave like this and I find it most distasteful.

To envy others and to complain about one's own lot; to speak badly about people; to be inquisitive about the most trivial matters and to resent and abuse people for not telling one, or, if one does manage to worm out

some facts, to inform everyone in the most detailed fashion as if one had known all from the beginning—oh, how hateful!

One is just about to be told some interesting piece of news when a baby starts crying.

A flight of crows circle about with loud caws.

An admirer has come on a clandestine visit, but a dog catches sight of him and starts barking. One feels like killing the beast.

One has been foolish enough to invite a man to spend the night in an unsuitable place—and then he starts snoring.

A gentleman has visited one secretly. Though he is wearing a tall, lacquered hat, he nevertheless wants no one to see him. He is so flurried, in fact, that upon leaving he bangs into something with his hat. Most hateful! It is annoying too when he lifts up the Iyo blind that hangs at the entrance of the room, then lets it fall with a great rattle. If it is a head-blind, things are still worse, for being more solid it makes a terrible noise when it is dropped. There is no excuse for such carelessness. Even a head-blind does not make any noise if one lifts it up gently on entering and leaving the room; the same applies to sliding-doors. If one's movements are rough, even a paper door will bend and resonate when opened; but, if one lifts the door a little while pushing it, there need be no sound.

One has gone to bed and is about to doze off when a mosquito appears, announcing himself in a reedy voice. One can actually feel the wind made by his wings and, slight though it is, one finds it hateful in the extreme.

A carriage passes with a nasty, creaking noise. Annoying to think that the passengers may not even be aware of this! If I am travelling in someone's carriage and I hear it creaking, I dislike not only the noise but also the owner of the carriage.

One is in the middle of a story when someone butts in and tries to show that he is the only clever person in the room. Such a person is hateful, and so, indeed, is anyone, child or adult, who tries to push himself forward.

One is telling a story about old times when someone breaks in with a little detail that he happens to know, implying that one's own version is inaccurate—disgusting behaviour!

Very hateful is a mouse that scurries all over the place.

Some children have called at one's house. One makes a great fuss of them and gives them toys to play with. The children become accustomed to this treatment and start to come regularly, forcing their way into one's inner rooms and scattering one's furnishings and possessions. Hateful!

A certain gentleman whom one does not want to

see visits one at home or in the Palace, and one pretends to be asleep. But a maid comes to tell one and shakes one awake, with a look on her face that says, "What a sleepyhead!" Very hateful.

A newcomer pushes ahead of the other members in a group; with a knowing look, this person starts laying down the law and forcing advice upon everyone—most hateful.

A man with whom one is having an affair keeps singing the praises of some woman he used to know. Even if it is a thing of the past, this can be very annoying. How much more so if he is still seeing the woman! (Yet sometimes I find that it is not as unpleasant as all that.)

A person who recites a spell himself after sneezing. In fact I detest anyone who sneezes, except the master of the house.

Fleas, too, are very hateful. When they dance about under someone's clothes, they really seem to be lifting them up.

The sound of dogs when they bark a long time in chorus is ominous and hateful.

I cannot stand people who leave without closing the panel behind them.

How I detest the husbands of nurse-maids! It is not so bad if the child in the maid's charge is a girl, because then the man will keep his distance. But, if it is a boy, he will behave as though he were the father. Never letting the boy out of his sight, he insists on managing everything. He regards the other attendants in the house as less than human, and, if anyone tries to scold the child, he slanders him to the master. Despite this disgraceful behaviour, no one dare accuse the husband; so he strides about the house with a proud, self-important look, giving all the orders.

I hate people whose letters show that they lack respect for worldly civilities, whether by discourtesy in the phrasing or by extreme politeness to someone who does not deserve it. This sort of thing is, of course, particularly odious should the letter be addressed to oneself.

As a matter of fact, most people are too casual, not only in their letters but in their direct conversation. Sometimes I am quite disgusted at noting how little decorum people observe when talking to each other. It is particularly unpleasant to hear some foolish man or woman omit the proper marks of respect when addressing a person of quality; and, when servants fail to use honorific forms of speech in referring to their masters, it is very bad indeed. No less odious, however, are those masters who, in addressing their servants, use such phrases as "When you were good enough to do such-and-such" or "As you so kindly remarked." No doubt there are some masters who, in describing their own actions to a servant, say, "I presumed to do so-and-so"!

Sometimes a person who is utterly devoid of charm will try to create a good impression by using very elegant language; yet he only succeeds in being ridiculous. No doubt he believes this refined language to be just what the occasion demands, but, when it goes so far that everyone bursts out laughing, surely something must be wrong.

It is most improper to address high-ranking courtiers, Imperial Advisers, and the like simply by using their names without any titles or marks of respect; but such mistakes are fortunately rare.

If one refers to the maid who is in attendance on some lady-in-waiting as "Madam" or "that lady," she will be surprised, delighted, and lavish in her praise.

When speaking to young noblemen and courtiers of high rank, one should always (unless Their Majesties are present) refer to them by their official posts. Incidentally, I have been very shocked to hear important people use the word "I" while conversing in Their Majesties' presence. Such a breach of etiquette is really distressing, and I fail to see why people cannot avoid it.

A man who has nothing in particular to recommend him but who speaks in an affected tone and poses as being elegant.

An inkstone with such a hard, smooth surface that the stick glides over it without leaving any deposit of ink.

Ladies-in-waiting who want to know everything that is going on.

Sometimes one greatly dislikes a person for no particular reason—and then that person goes and does something hateful.

A gentleman who travels alone in his carriage to see a procession or some other spectacle. What sort of a man is he? Even though he may be a person of the greatest quality, surely he should have taken along a few of the many young men who are anxious to see the sights. But no, there he sits by himself (one can see his silhouette through the blinds), with a proud look on his face, keeping all his impressions to himself. . . .

Rare Things

A son-in-law who is praised by his adoptive father; a young bride who is loved by her mother-in-law.

A silver tweezer that is good at plucking out the hair.

A servant who does not speak badly about his master.

A person who is in no way eccentric or imperfect, who is superior in both mind and body, and who remains flawless all his life.

People who live together and still manage to behave with reserve towards each other. However much these people may try to hide their weaknesses, they usually fail.

To avoid getting ink stains on the notebook into which one is copying stories, poems, or the like. If it is a very fine notebook, one takes the greatest care not to make a blot; yet somehow one never seems to succeed.

When people, whether they be men or women or priests, have promised each other eternal friendship, it is rare for them to stay on good terms until the end.

A servant who is pleasant to his master.

One has given some silk to the fuller and, when he sends it back, it is so beautiful that one cries out in admiration. . . .

Gloomy-Looking Things

A shabby carriage jogging along on a summer afternoon behind a wretched pair of oxen.

A carriage with the rain-mats spread out on a dry day; or a carriage without them when it is raining.

An old beggar on a very cold day or on a very hot one.

A woman of the lower classes, poorly dressed and with a child on her back.

A little, shingle-roofed cottage, dark, dirty and rain-spattered.

In a heavy downpour an outrider passes on a small horse; his head-dress has been squashed by the rain and his bedraggled robes are stuck together. What a gloomy sight! But in the summer I do not mind if it rains. . . .

Things without Merit

An ugly person with a bad character.

Rice starch that has become mixed with water. . . . I know that this is a very vulgar item and everyone will dislike my mentioning it. But that should not stop me. In fact I must feel free to include anything, even tongs used for the parting-fires. After all, these objects do exist in our world and people all know about them. I admit they do not belong to a list that others will see. But I never thought that these notes would be read by anyone else, and so I included everything that came into my head, however strange or unpleasant. . . .

When His Excellency, the Chancellor, Had Departed

When His Excellency, the Chancellor, had departed from among us, there was much stir and movement in the world. Her Majesty, who no longer came to the Imperial Palace, lived in the Smaller Palace of the Second Ward. Though I had done nothing to deserve it, things became very difficult for me and I spent

a long time at home. One day, when I was particularly concerned about Her Majesty and felt I could not allow our separation to continue, the Captain of the Left Guards Division came to see me. "I called on Her Majesty today," he said, "and found it very moving. Her ladies were dressed as elegantly as ever, with their robes, skirts, and Chinese jackets perfectly matching the season. The blind was open at the side and, when I looked in, I saw a group of about eight ladies, elegantly seated next to each other. They wore Chinese jackets of tawny yellow, light violet skirts, and robes of purple and dark red. Noticing that the grass in the garden outside the palace had been allowed to grow very high and thick, I told them they should have it cut. 'We've left it like this on purpose so that we might admire the dew when it settles on the blades.' The voice was Lady Saishō's and I found her reply delightful.

"Several of the ladies spoke about you and said it was a shame you were staying at home. 'Now that Her Majesty is living in a place like this,' they told me, 'she feels that Shōnagon should come back into waiting regardless of what business she may have at home. Why won't she return when Her Majesty wants her so much?' I definitely had the impression that they wanted me to pass this on to you. So please go. There's a charm about the place that will stir you deeply. The peonies in front of the terrace have a delightful Chinese air."

"No," I replied. "Since they dislike me so much, I've come to dislike them."

"You must try to be generous," he said with a smile.

Shortly afterwards I visited the Empress. I had no way of telling what she thought about it all; but I did hear some of her ladies-in-waiting whisper, "She is on close terms with people who are attached to the Minister of the Left." I was coming from my room when I saw them all standing there muttering to each other. Noticing me, they became silent and each of them went about her own business. I was not used to being treated like this and found it most galling. Thereafter Her Majesty summoned me on several occasions, but I paid no attention, and a long time passed without my visiting her. No doubt the ladies-in-waiting made out that I belonged to the enemy camp and told all sorts of lies about me.

One day, when there had been an unaccustomed silence from the Empress and I was sitting at home sunk in gloomy thoughts, a housekeeper brought me a letter. "Her Majesty ordered that this should be sent to you secretly by Lady Sakyō," she told me. Yet there could be no reason for such secrecy when I was living at home. Examining the letter, I gathered that it was a personal message from Her Majesty and my heart was pounding as I opened it. There was nothing written on the paper. It had been used to wrap up a single petal of mountain rose, on which I read the words, "He who does not speak his love." I was overjoyed; what a relief after the long, anxious days of silence! My eyes filled with "the things that one knows first of all." "The ladies-in-waiting are all wondering why you have stayed away so long," said the housekeeper, who had been watching me. "They consider it very strange, especially since you know how much Her Majesty is always thinking of you. Why don't you go?" Then she added, "I have a short errand near by. I'll be back for your answer presently."

But as I prepared to write my answer, I realized that I had completely forgotten the next line of the poem. "Amazing!" I muttered. "How can one possibly forget an old poem like that? I know it perfectly well and yet it just won't come." Hearing this a small page-boy who happened to be in the room said, "'Yet feels its waters seething underneath'—those are the words, Madam." Of course! How on earth could they have slipped my mind? To think that I should have to be taught by a mere child!

Shortly after sending my reply, I visited the Empress. Not knowing how she would receive me, I felt unusually nervous and remained half hidden behind a curtain of state. "Are you a newcomer?" asked Her Majesty with a laugh. "I am afraid it was not much of a poem," she went on, "but I felt it was the sort of thing I should write. When I do not see you, Shōnagon, I am wretched all the time."

Her Majesty had not changed. When I told her about the page-boy who had reminded me of the missing words, she was most amused. "That's just the sort of thing that can happen," she said, laughing, "especially with old poems that one considers too familiar to take seriously."

Then she told me the following story: "Some people were organizing a game of riddles when one of them, a clever man and a good player, said that he would like to set the first riddle presented by the team of the left, to which he belonged. His teammates cheerfully agreed, feeling confident that he would produce something good.

"When all the people in the team of the left had made up their riddles, they began to select the ones that would actually be used. 'Please tell us what yours is going to be?' they said to the man. 'No,' he replied. 'You must simply trust me. After speaking as I did, I am hardly likely to come out with something that will disappoint you.' His team-mates assumed that he must be right; but, when the day of the game drew near, they again asked him to let them know his riddle. 'What if you should have produced something very strange?'

they said. 'Well,' he said angrily, 'I don't know. If you are so uncertain about my riddle, you had better not depend on me at all.' When the day arrived, his partners were very worried about what he would do.

"The participants, men and women of quality including several senior courtiers, were divided into two teams and seated in rows. The time came to present the first set of riddles, and our man was chosen to lead off for the team of the left. He looked as if he had prepared his entry with great care, and all the players gazed at him anxiously, wondering what they would hear. 'Your riddle! Your riddle' they said impatiently.

"Finally he came out with 'A bow drawn in the sky,' which delighted the members of the opposing team. His partners were dumbfounded and disgusted with him. Surely, they thought, he must be working for the other side and trying to make his own team lose.

"Meanwhile his opponent on the team of the right was laughing at him. 'Dear me!' he said, beginning to pout. 'I haven't the slightest idea.' And, instead of answering the riddle, he began making jokes.

"'I've won!' cried the man who had posed the riddle. 'A point for our side!' A token was duly given to the team of the left.

"'Disgraceful!' said the members of the other team. 'Everyone knows the answer to that riddle. They certainly shouldn't get a point.'

"'But he said he did not know,' replied the man. 'How can you claim he hasn't lost?' In this and in each of the subsequent contests he argued so effectively that his side won.

"Later the player who had failed to answer the first riddle was being taken to task by his team-mates. 'We admit,' they said, 'that people can forget the answers to the most obvious questions and have to concede defeat. But what possible reason could you have to say you didn't know?' And they made him pay a forfeit."

When the Empress had finished her story, all the ladies burst out laughing. "The people on the team of the right had good reason to be annoyed with their man," said one of them. "I can see why they were disappointed. And how furious the other team must have been to hear their candidate lead off with such a silly riddle!"

"Indeed," I thought, "how could anyone possibly forget something so simple and commonplace?" . . .

Words That Look Commonplace but That Become Impressive When Written in Chinese Characters

Strawberries.
A dew-plant.
A prickly water-lily.

A walnut.

A Doctor of Literature.

A Provisional Senior Steward in the Office of the Empress's Household.

Red myrtle.

Knotweed is a particularly striking example, since it is written with the characters for "tiger's stick." From the look on a tiger's face one would imagine that he could do without a stick.

Words Written in Chinese Characters for Which There Must Be a Reason though One Cannot Really Understand It

Baked salt.

Short under-jackets.

Curtains.

Lacquered clogs.

Starch.

A bucket boat. . . .

When I First Went into Waiting

When I first went into waiting at Her Majesty's Court, so many different things embarrassed me that I could not even reckon them up and I was always on the verge of tears. As a result I tried to avoid appearing before the Empress except at night, and even then I stayed hidden behind a three-foot curtain of state.

On one occasion Her Majesty brought out some pictures and showed them to me, but I was so ill at ease that I could hardly stretch out my hand to take them. She pointed to one picture after another, explaining what each represented. Since the lamp had been put on a high stand, one could view the pictures even better than in the daytime, and every hair of the woman in one of them was clearly visible. I managed to control my embarrassment and had a proper look. It was a very cold time of the year and when Her Majesty gave me the paintings I could hardly see her hands; but, from what I made out, they were of a light pink hue that I found extraordinarily attractive. I gazed at the Empress with amazement. Simple as I was and unaccustomed to such wonderful sights, I did not understand how a being like this could possibly exist in our world.

At dawn I was about to hurry back to my room when Her Majesty said, "Even the God of Kazuraki would stay a little longer." So I sat down again, but I leant forward sideways in such a way that Her Majesty could not see me directly, and kept the lattice shut. One of the ladies who came into the room noticed this and said that it should be opened. A servant heard her and started towards it, but her Majesty said, "Wait. Leave the lattice as it is." The two women went out, laughing to each other.

Her Majesty then asked me various questions and finally said, "I am sure you want to return to your room. So off you go! But be sure to come again this evening—and early too."

As soon as I had crept out of Her Majesty's presence and was back in my room, I threw open all the lattices and looked out at the magnificent snow.

During the day I received several notes from Her Majesty telling me to come while it was still light. "The sky is clouded with snow," she wrote, "and no one will be able to see you clearly."

Noticing my hesitation, the lady in charge of my room urged me, saying, "I don't know how you can stay shut up like this all day long. Her Majesty has granted you the extraordinary good fortune of being admitted into her presence, and she must certainly have her reasons. To be unresponsive to another person's kindness is a most hateful way to behave." This was enough to make me hurry back to the Empress; but I was overcome with embarrassment, and it was not easy for me.

On my way I was delighted to see the snow beautifully piled on top of the fire huts. When I entered Her Majesty's room, I noticed that the usual square brazier was full to the brim with burning charcoal and that no one was sitting next to it. The Empress herself was seated in front of a round brazier made of Shen wood and decorated with pear-skin lacquer. She was surrounded by a group of high-ranking ladies who were in constant attendance upon her. In the next part of the room a tightly packed row of ladies-in-waiting sat in front of a long, rectangular brazier, with their Chinese jackets worn in such a way that they trailed on the floor. Observing how experienced they were in their duties and how easily they carried them out, I could not help feeling envious. There was not a trace of awkwardness in any of their movements as they got up to deliver notes to Her Majesty from the outside and sat down again by the brazier, talking and laughing to each other. When would I ever be able to manage like that, I wondered nervously. Still further in the back of the room sat a small group of ladies who were looking at pictures together.

After a while I heard the voices of outrunners loudly ordering people to make way. "His Excellency, the Chancellor, is coming," said one of the ladies, and they all cleared away their scattered belongings. I retired to the back of the room; but despite my modesty, I was curious to see the great man in person and I peeped through a crack at the bottom of the curtain of state where I was sitting. It turned out that it was not Michitaka, but his son, Korechika, the Major Counsellor. The purple of his Court cloak and trousers looked magnificent against the white snow. "I should not have come," he said, standing next to one of the pillars, "because both yesterday and today are days of abstinence. But it has been snowing so hard that I felt bound to call and find out whether all was well with you."

"How did you manage?" said Her Majesty. "I thought that all the paths were buried."

"Well," replied Korechika, "it occurred to me that I might move your heart."

Could anything surpass this conversation between the Empress and her brother? This was the sort of exchange that is so eloquently described in romances; and the Empress herself, arrayed in a white dress, a robe of white Chinese damask, and two more layers of scarlet damask over which her hair hung down loosely at the back, had a beauty that I had seen in paintings but never in real life: it was all like a dream.

Korechika joked with the ladies-in-waiting, and they replied without the slightest embarrassment, freely arguing with him and contradicting his remarks when they disagreed. I was absolutely dazzled by it all and found myself blushing without any particular reason. Korechika ate a few fruits and told one of the servants to offer some to the Empress. He must have asked who was behind the curtain of state and one of the ladies must have told him that it was I; for he stood up and walked to the back of the room. At first I thought he was leaving, but instead he came and sat very close to me; he began to talk about various things he had heard about me before I came into waiting and asked whether they were true. I had been embarrassed enough when I had been looking at him from a distance with the curtain of state between us; now that we were actually facing each other I felt extremely stupid and could hardly believe that this was really happening to me.

In the past, when I had gone to watch Imperial Processions and the like, Korechika had sometimes glanced in the direction of my carriage; but I had always pulled the inner blinds close together, and hidden my face behind a fan for fear that he might see my silhouette through the blinds. I wondered how I could ever have chosen to embark on a career for which I was so ill-suited by nature. What on earth should I say to him? I was bathed in sweat and altogether in a terrible state. To make matters worse, Korechika now seized the fan behind which I had prudently hidden myself, and I realized that my hair must be scattered all over my forehead in a terrible mess; no doubt everything about my appearance bespoke the embarrassment I felt at that moment.

I had hoped Korechika would leave quickly, but he showed no sign of doing so; instead he sat there, toying

with my fan and asking who had done the paintings on it. I kept my head lowered and pressed the sleeve of my Chinese jacket to my face—so tightly indeed, that bits of powder must have stuck to it, making my complexion all mottled.

The Empress, who no doubt realized how desperately I wanted Korechika to leave, turned to him and said, "Look at this notebook. Whose writing do you suppose it is?" I was relieved to think that now he would finally go; but instead he asked her to have the book brought to him so that he could examine it. "Really," she said. "You can perfectly well come here yourself and have a look." "No I can't," he replied. "Shōnagon has got hold of me and won't let go." It was a very fashionable sort of joke but hardly suited to my rank or age, and I felt terribly ill at ease. Her Majesty held up the book, in which something had been written in a cursive script, and looked at it. "Well indeed," said Korechika, "whose can it be? Let's show it to Shōnagon. I am sure she can recognize the handwriting of anyone in the world." The aim of all these absurd remarks, of course, was to draw me out.

As if a single gentleman were not enough to embarrass me, another one now arrived, preceded by outrunners who cleared the way for him. This gentleman too was wearing a Court cloak, and he looked even more splendid than Korechika. He sat down and started telling some amusing stories, which delighted the ladies-in-waiting. "Oh yes," they said, laughing, "we saw Lord So-and-so when he was ———." As I heard them mention the names of one senior courtier after another, I felt they must be talking about spirits or heavenly beings who had descended to earth. Yet, after some time had passed and I had grown accustomed to Court service, I realized that there had been nothing very impressive about their conversation. No doubt these same ladies, who talked so casually to Lord Korechika, had been just as embarrassed as I when they first came into waiting, but had little by little become used to Court society until their shyness had naturally disappeared.

The Empress spoke to me for a while and then asked, "Are you really fond of me?" "But Your Majesty," I replied, "how could I possibly not be fond of you?" Just then someone sneezed loudly in the Table Room. "Oh dear!" said the Empress. "So you're telling a lie. Well, so be it." And she retired into the back of the room.

To think that Her Majesty believed I was lying! If I had said that I was *fairly* fond of her, that would have been untrue. The real liar, I thought, was the sneezer's nose. Who could have done such a terrible thing? I dislike sneezes at the best of times, and whenever I feel like sneezing myself I deliberately smother it. All the more hateful was it that someone should have sneezed at this moment. But I was still far too inexperienced to say anything that might have repaired the damage; and, since the day was dawning, I retired to my room. As soon as I arrived, a servant brought me an elegant-looking letter, written on fine, smooth paper of light green. "This is what Her Majesty feels," I read.

How, if there were no God Tadasu in the sky,
And none to judge what is the truth and what a lie,
How should I know which words were falsely said?

My emotions were a jumble of delight and dismay, and once again I wished I could find out who had sneezed on the previous night. "Please give Her Majesty the following reply," I said, "and help me to make up for the harm that has been done.

'A simple sneeze might give the lie
To one whose love is small,
But sad indeed that she who truly loves,
Should suffer from so slight a thing!

The curse of God Shiki is of course very terrible.'"

Even after I had sent my reply I still felt most unhappy and wondered why someone should have had to sneeze at such an inopportune moment. . . .

Scriptures

I need hardly mention the Lotus Sutra. The Sutra of the Thousand Hands. The Ten Vows of Fugen. The Sutra of the Request. The Incantation of the Holy and Victorious. The Great Spell of Amida. The Incantation of the Thousand Hands.

Writings in Chinese

The collected works of Po Chü-i. The Anthology. Requests for promotion written by Doctors of Literature.

Buddhas

Grieved by what she perceives in people's hearts, the Bounteous One sits with her cheek resting on her hand. Seeing her, one is overcome with sorrow and with shame.

The Goddess of the Thousand Hands and all the other Six Kannons.

The Great Immovable One.

Yakushiji Buddha.

Gautama Buddha.

Miroku.

Fugen.

Jizō.

Monju.

Tales

Tales like *Sumiyoshi* and *The Hollow Tree*. *The Change of Palaces*. *The Lady who Awaited the Moon*. *The Captain of Katano*. *The Captain of Umetsubo*. *The Eyes of Men*. *The Yielding of the Land*. *The Buried Trees*. *The Pine Branch that Inspired Faith*.

In the *Tale of Komano* I enjoy the passage in which the hero leaves after presenting an old bat-fan. . . .

Things Worth Seeing

The Chancellor's pilgrimage to Kamo.

The Special Festival at Kamo. On one cold, overcast day the snow began to come down in scattered flakes, falling on the blue and white robes of the people in the procession and on the flowers that they wore in their head-dress. I found the sight immensely delightful. The sheaths of the dancers' swords shone magnificently, and the cords of their jackets, which hung over the sheaths, were so bright that they might have been polished. Beneath the printed material of their trouser-skirts I could see the brilliant, glossy silk of their under-robes, and for a moment I wondered whether they were made of ice. I was relishing the beauty of the procession when the envoys appeared. They were certainly a most undistinguished lot, having been chosen from among provincial governors and the like, common-looking men not worth one's attention. Yet so long as their faces were hidden by the sprays of wistaria in their head-dress, it was not too unpleasant to see them go by. While we were still watching the dancers, the musicians appeared, wearing willow-coloured robes and yellow roses in their head-dress. They were insignificant men of low rank, but it was delightful to hear them chanting,

The princess pines that grow outside
All-powerful Kamo Shrine.

and beating the measure loudly with their fans.

What can compare with an Imperial Progress? When the Emperor passes in his palanquin, he is as impressive as a God and I forget that my work in the Palace constantly brings me into his presence. Not only His Majesty himself, but even people like Ladies of the Escort who usually are of no importance, overawe me when I see them in an Imperial Progress. I particularly enjoy watching the Assistant Directors of the Bureau of Imperial Attendants as they walk past holding the cords of the Imperial palanquin, and also the Captains of the Inner Palace Guards, who serve as its escorts.

The Return Procession of the High Priestess from Kamo is a magnificent sight. I recall one year when everything was especially beautiful. On the day of the Festival itself we had stopped our carriage on that splendidly wide road, the First Avenue, and had sat there for a long time, hiding our faces behind our fans and waiting for the procession to arrive. A hot sun shone through the carriage blinds, dazzling us and making us perspire in a most unsightly fashion. On the following day we set out very early to see the High Priestess's procession. Though the sun had risen, the sky was overcast. As we reached the gates of Urin and Chisoku Temples, we noticed a number of carriages decorated with branches of faded hollyhock and maple. We could hear a loud chorus of *hototogisu*. This was the bird whose song so fascinated me that I would lie awake at night waiting for it. I was just thinking how delightful it was that I could now hear great numbers of these birds without making the slightest effort when an *uguisu* joined in with his rather croaky voice. He sounded as if he were trying to imitate the beautiful song of the *hototogisu*, and I found this unpleasant though at the same time rather amusing.

While we sat in our carriage waiting impatiently for the procession, we saw a group of men in red coming from the Upper Shrine. "What's happening? Is the procession on its way?" we asked them; but they replied that they had no idea and continued down the road, carrying the High Priestess's empty palanquins. It impressed me deeply that the High Priestess herself had travelled in one of these palanquins; but I was rather disturbed at the thought that low fellows like these could have come close to her sacred presence.

Though we had been told that there might be a long wait, the High Priestess and her retinue soon arrived from the Upper Shrine. First we could see the fans come into sight, then the yellow-green robes of the gentlemen from the Emperor's Private Office. It was a splendid sight. The men wore their under-robes in such a way that the white material stood out against the yellowish-green of their outer robes, and I was reminded so much of white *u no hana* blossoms in a green hedge that I almost expected to find a *hototogisu* lurking there.

On the previous day I had noticed several of these young noblemen crowded together in a carriage. They had taken down the blinds, and I could see that they were messily dressed in hunting costumes and violet cloaks; altogether they had made a very bizarre impression. Today these same young men were beautifully attired in full Court costume and ready to take part in the High Priestess's banquet, to which they had been invited as extra guests. They looked extremely demure as one by one they passed, each in his own carriage; and the young Palace pages who followed were also very attractive.

After the Procession had gone, things got out of hand. Everyone wanted to be the first to leave and there was a great crush of carriages, which I found rather frightening. I stuck my fan out of the window to summon my attendants. "Don't be in such a hurry," I scolded them. "Go slowly." Since they paid not the slightest attention and continued to push ahead, I became very flustered and ordered them to pull up the carriage in a place where the road was a little wider. The men were very impatient and it annoyed them to have to stop.

I enjoyed watching the carriages as they hurried along the road, each one trying to forge ahead of another. I allowed them all to get a good start before letting my men continue. It was a delightful road, rather like the paths that lead up to mountain villages. The thick hedges on both sides looked rough and shaggy; they were covered with *u no hana,* but the flowers had not yet come into bloom. I told my men to break off some of the branches and stuck them here and there in the carriage; they looked very pretty, all the more so since the decorations of maple and hollyhock had unfortunately begun to fade.

When I had glanced down the road from the distance, it had seemed impossible that all the carriages would get through, but now as we gradually advanced I was pleased to see it was not as crowded as I had thought. I noticed that the carriage of one man—I have no idea who he can have been—was following close behind mine, and I decided that this was much more pleasant than being alone on the road. When we came to a fork where our paths separated, he leaned out and recited the line, "That scatter on the peak," which I found delightful. . . .

Things That Should Be Large

Priests. Fruit. Houses. Provision bags. Inksticks for inkstones.

Men's eyes: when they are too narrow, they look feminine. On the other hand, if they were as large as metal bowls, I should find them rather frightening.

Round braziers. Winter cherries. Pine trees. The petals of yellow roses.

Horses as well as oxen should be large.

Things That Should Be Short

A piece of thread when one wants to sew something in a hurry.

A lamp stand.

The hair of a woman of the lower classes should be neat and short.

The speech of a young girl.

Things That Belong in a House

A kitchen.

A servants' hall.

A new broom.

Small tables.

Young maids and under-servants.

Sliding screens on stands.

Three-foot curtains of state.

A nicely decorated bag for carrying provisions.

Umbrellas.

A blackboard.

Small cupboards with shelves.

Vessels for warming and pouring wine.

Medium-sized tables.

Round straw cushions.

A corridor that turns at a right angle.

A brazier decorated with a painting. . . .

Letters Are Commonplace

Letters are commonplace enough, yet what splendid things they are! When someone is in a distant province and one is worried about him, and then a letter suddenly arrives, one feels as though one were seeing him face to face. Again, it is a great comfort to have expressed one's feelings in a letter even though one knows it cannot yet have arrived. If letters did not exist, what dark depressions would come over one! When one has been worrying about something and wants to tell a certain person about it, what a relief it is to put it all down in a letter! Still greater is one's joy when a reply arrives. At that moment a letter really seems like an elixir of life. . . .

Shrines

Furu, Ikuta, Tatsuta, Hanafuchi, and Mikuri. The sacred shrine of the cryptomeria. It is interesting that this tree should be a sign of virtue.

The deity of Koto no Mama deserves the trust that people put in him. I enjoy knowing that this is the shrine "where every prayer's been glibly answered by the God."

The deity of Aridōshi. It was past his shrine that Tsurayuki was riding when his horse was taken ill and he was told that this was due to the anger of the God; he then dedicated a poem to the God whereupon his horse was cured—a delightful incident.

I wonder whether the usual explanation for the name *Aridōshi* is correct. Long ago there was an Emperor who liked only young people and who ordered that everyone over forty should be put to death. The older people therefore went and hid in remote provinces, leaving the capital to their juniors. Now there was a Captain of the Guards whose parents were both almost seventy. They were absolutely terrified, realizing that, if even people of forty were proscribed, their own position was precarious indeed. The Captain, however, a most devoted son, who could not live without seeing his parents at least once a day, refused to let them go off to some distant hiding-place. Instead he spent night after night secretly digging a hole under his house and, when it was finished, he made it into a room where he installed his parents and went to visit them frequently, informing the Imperial authorities and everyone else that they had disappeared.

(Why should His Majesty have decided on this policy? After all, he had no need to concern himself with people who lived quietly at home and minded their own business.)

Since his son was a Captain, I imagine that the father was a High Court Noble or something of the sort. In any case he was a very clever, knowing old gentleman, and the Captain, despite his youth, was also able and intelligent, so that His Majesty regarded him as the outstanding young man of the day.

At this time the Emperor of China was planning to capture our country by tricking His Majesty, and for this purpose he was constantly sending puzzles to test His Majesty's ability. On one occasion he sent a round, glossy, beautifully planed log about two feet long and asked, "Which is the base and which is the top?" Since there was absolutely no way of telling, His Majesty was in great distress—so much so that the young Captain felt sorry for him and told his father what had happened. "All you need do," said the old man, "is to go to a rapid river, hold the log straight up, and throw it sideways into the water. It will then turn round by itself and the end that faces downstream will be the top. Mark the wood accordingly and return it to the Chinese Emperor." The Captain went to the Palace and, pretending to have thought of a plan by himself, told His Majesty that he would try to solve the puzzle. Accompanied by a group of people he proceeded to a river, threw in the log, and made a mark on the end that faced downstream. The log was then sent back and turned out to be correctly marked.

On another occasion the Chinese Emperor sent a pair of identical snakes, each about two feet in length, and the test was to tell which was male and which fe-male. Since no one had the faintest idea, the Captain again consulted his father, who told him to place the snakes next to each other and to hold a long, straight twig near their tails. "The one that moves its tail," he said, "will be the female." The son followed this advice and, as predicted, one of the snakes remained still while the other one moved; the Captain marked them accordingly and sent them back to China.

A long time afterwards the Chinese Emperor dis-patched to His Majesty a small jewel with seven curves and a passage that ran right through all the curves and was open at both ends. "Please pass a thread through the jewel," he wrote. "This is something that everyone in our country knows how to do." Outstanding crafts-men were summoned, but their skill was of no avail; everyone, from the High Court Nobles down, admit-ted defeat. Once more the Captain went to his father. "You must capture two large ants," said the old man. "Tie narrow threads round their middles and attach slightly thicker threads to the ends. Then smear some honey opposite one of the openings and place the ants at the opposite end." The Captain told this to His Majesty and two ants were duly put next to the open-ing. As soon as they smelt the honey, they started crawling through the passage and rapidly emerged at the other end. The threaded jewel was then returned to China, where it was decided that, after all, the in-habitants of Japan were clever people and there was no point in sending them any more puzzles.

Greatly impressed by the Captain's achievement, His Majesty asked what he could do for him and what rank he desired. "I want no rank or office at all," de-clared the young man. "Grant only that all the old people who have gone and hidden themselves be searched out and told that they may safely return to the capital." "That is a simple matter," said the Emperor. The old people were delighted when they heard the news and the Captain was appointed Great Minister. Evidently the Captain's father became a God; for it is said that the deity of Aridōshi appeared in a dream one night to someone who had come on a pilgrimage and that he recited the following poem:

Who is there who does not know
That the God of Aridōshi was so named
From the passage of the ants through a seven-
    curved jewel? . . .

If a Servant Girl

If a servant girl says about someone, "What a de-lightful gentleman he is!" one immediately looks down on him, whereas if she insulted the person in question

it would have the opposite effect. Praise from a ser-vant can also damage a woman's reputation. Besides, people of that class always manage to express them-selves badly when they are trying to say something nice. . . .

It Is Very Annoying

It is very annoying, when one has visited Hase Temple and has retired into one's enclosure, to be disturbed by a herd of common people who come and sit outside in a row, crowded so close together that the tails of their robes fall over each other in utter disarray. I remember that once I was overcome by a great desire to go on a pilgrimage. Having made my way up the log steps, deafened by the fearful roar of the river, I hurried into my enclosure, longing to gaze upon the sacred countenance of Buddha. To my dismay I found that a throng of commoners had settled themselves directly in front of me, where they were incessantly standing up, prostrating themselves, and squatting down again. They looked like so many basket-worms as they crowd-ed together in their hideous clothes, leaving hardly an inch of space between themselves and me. I really felt like pushing them all over sideways.

Important visitors always have attendants to clear such pests from their enclosures; but it is not so easy for ordinary people like me. If one summons one of the priests who is responsible for looking after the pil-grims, he simply says something like "You there, move back a little, won't you?" and, as soon as he has left, things are as bad as before.

Things That Are Hard to Say

I find it difficult to transmit a long message accu-rately from beginning to end; and the reply is no easier.

It is very hard to frame a reply to a message one has received from a person with whom one feels ill at ease.

A father hears that his grown-up son has done something that he would not have expected of him. How hard it is to reprimand him to his face! . . .

When the Middle Captain

When the Middle Captain of the Left Guards Di-vision was still Governor of Ise, he visited me one day at my home. There was a straw mat at the edge of the veranda, and I pulled it out for him. This notebook of mine happened to be lying on the mat, but I did not notice it in time. I snatched at the book and made a desperate effort to get it back; but the Captain instantly took it off with him and did not return it until much later. I suppose it was from this time that my book began to be passed about at Court.

It Is Getting So Dark

It is getting so dark that I can scarcely go on writing; and my brush is all worn out. Yet I should like to add a few things before I end.

I wrote these notes at home, when I had a good deal of time to myself and thought no one would notice what I was doing. Everything that I have seen and felt is included. Since much of it might appear malicious and even harmful to other people, I was careful to keep my book hidden. But now it has become public, which is the last thing I expected.

One day Lord Korechika, the Minister of the Centre, brought the Empress a bundle of notebooks. "What shall we do with them?" Her Majesty asked me. "The Emperor has already made arrangements for copying the 'Records of the Historian.'"

"Let me make them into a pillow," I said.

"Very well," said Her Majesty. "You may have them."

I now had a vast quantity of paper at my disposal, and I set about filling the notebooks with odd facts, stories from the past, and all sorts of other things, often including the most trivial material. On the whole I concentrated on things and people that I found charming and splendid; my notes are also full of poems and observations on trees and plants, birds, and insects. I was sure that when people saw my book they would say, "It's even worse than I expected. Now one can really tell what she is like." After all, it is written entirely for my own amusement and I put things down exactly as they came to me. How could my casual jottings possibly bear comparison with the many impressive books that exist in our time? Readers have declared, however, that I can be proud of my work. This has surprised me greatly; yet I suppose it is not so strange that people should like it, for, as will be gathered from these notes of mine, I am the sort of person who approves of what others abhor and detests the things they like.

Whatever people may think of my book, I still regret that it ever came to light.

St. Catherine of Siena (1347?–80)

Catherine Benincasa was canonized a saint of the Catholic Church in 1461 and named a Doctor of the Church in 1970—a rare distinction, placing her in the company of such men as Augustine and Aquinas. She was born about 1347, the twenty-fourth child of a family of the artisan class. Her father, a wool dyer, was a prosperous member of the popolo minore, or populist faction which for a time held political power in Siena. Catherine died in 1380, at thirty-three years of age.

From a very early age Catherine experienced visions of Christ and conceived a passionate commitment to devote her life to her understanding of truth and God. At age fifteen she cut off her hair to symbolize her determination not to marry, and at about eighteen she joined the Sisters of Penance of St. Dominic, a non-cloistered order of Mantellate (cloaked sisters), mainly older women and widows, devoted to service to the poor and the sick. After a period of seclusion, she emerged into her life of public service, at first through charities and spiritual healing, later through teaching, correspondence, missions of mediation and diplomacy, and providing counsel even to those at the highest levels of church and state.

The compelling qualities of Catherine's life and mind, personal asceticism, commitment to truth, and visionary exaltation, won her a large following across lines of class and politics. She offered advice, solace, correction, and exhortation to the poor and the rich alike. We have about 380 of Catherine's letters, directed to popes, cardinals, bishops, priests, queens, despots, and citizens—men and women—of the Italian city-states, prisoners and prostitutes, critics and suppliants, relatives and friends. Though she encountered substantial opposition and hostility to her public role, particularly on the ground that it was unacceptable for a woman, she drew strength, as Karen Scott has shown, from neighborhood friends and networks of lay religious women in Siena. She claimed the authorization of God to leave her cell and even her city, to "forget her sex" and mingle with men as well as women for the salvation of souls, and God's promise that "I will give you a mouth and a wisdom that no one will be able to resist" (Scott, 109).

From about 1372 until her death in 1380, Catherine engaged actively in the political struggles of her time. She was particularly concerned with the wars of the city-states against each other and against the papacy, with the "Babylonian Exile" of the Pope in Avignon and later the Great Schism, and with the urgent need for reform in the church and for justice and charity in the state. She urged peace and reconciliation among the Christian states, but this was not a fully pacifist stance, since she advocated that they turn their military exploits to the service of a Crusade against "the infidels." To Bernabo Visconti of Milan she wrote: "What a shame and disgrace it is for Christians to allow the base unbelievers to possess what is rightfully ours [the Holy Land]" (Letters, no. 17, p. 71). She helped to persuade Gregory XI to return from Avignon to Rome in hopes of reuniting Italy and the church, but she eventually found herself enmeshed in the struggles surrounding Urban VI, to whom she gave her full support in the Great Schism.

Catherine had no formal education, and it appears that she learned to read only during the years of her solitude after she joined the Dominican sisters. She did not learn to write until she was about thirty years old. Her voluminous correspondence and other writings were dictated to various companions and scribes, especially her close friend and confessor, Raymond of Capua. Her writings were in her Tuscan dialect, not the traditional Latin of the church, though they were later translated and published in Latin by her followers. The power and intensity of her writings reflect her own visionary ideas, but her reading of Scriptures and church writings is also evident. The fact that her works were largely dictated to others, and later subject to excisions and revisions in the various copies that have survived, has occasioned debate, but contemporary scholarly editions and translations accept their basic authenticity.

Catherine's writings include her letters, her prayers, and a theological work, The Dialogue, written in 1377–78. At present, only The Dialogue and selections from her letters and other writings are available in English. The Dialogue is a conversation with God, in which Catherine sets forth a series of questions and issues on which she seeks divine guidance. The temerity of both her questions and her claim to render the divine responses is striking. Though set, like her letters, in repeated assertions of her own humility, it is rather the image of her soul as "restless and aflame with tremendous desire" that she draws on to embolden her in this dialogue. Referring to herself in the third person, she declares (chap. 13): "more hungry than ever in her hope for the salvation of the whole world and the reform of holy Church, she stood up with confidence in the presence of the supreme Father." Both the letters and the Dialogue reflect what Edmund Gardner has called her "spiritualized political doctrine," the application to both Church and State of her philosophy of love, peace, justice, and charity.

The first two selections below are letters, written about the year 1376, in which Catherine urges the political leaders of Florence to make their peace with the Pope and urges the Pope to return to Rome. They are from volume 1 of the Letters, *translated by Suzanne Noffke (1988). These are followed by selections from* The Dialogue, *in the 1980 translation by Suzanne Noffke; the chapter numbers are as given in that edition.*

BAC

Sources and Suggested Readings

Catherine of Siena. *The Dialogue.* Trans. Suzanne Noffke. New York: Paulist Press, 1980.

——. *I, Catherine: Selected Writings of Catherine of Siena.* Trans. Kenelm Foster and Mary John Ronayne. London: Collins, 1980.

——. *The Letters of St. Catherine of Siena.* Vol. 1. Trans. Suzanne Noffke. Binghamton: State University of New York, Center for Medieval and Early Renaissance Studies, 1988.

——. *Selected Letters of Catherine Benincasa: Saint Catherine of Siena as Seen in Her Letters.* Trans. Vida Scudder. New York: Dutton, 1927.

Coogan, Robert. *Babylon on the Rhone: A Translation of Letters by Dante, Petrarch, and Catherine of Siena on the Avignon Papacy.* Potomac, Md.: Studia Humanitatis, 1983.

Curtayne, Alice. *Saint Catherine of Siena.* New York: Macmillan, 1930.

Gardner, Edmund G. *Saint Catherine of Siena: A Study in the Religion, History and Literature of the Fourteenth Century in Italy.* New York: Dutton, 1907.

O'Driscoll, Mary, O.P., ed. *Catherine of Siena—Passion for the Truth, Compassion for Humanity: Selected Spiritual Writings.* Hyde Park, N.Y.: New City Press, 1993.

Petroff, Elizabeth Alvilda. *Medieval Women's Visionary Literature.* New York: Oxford University Press, 1986. 238–41 and 263–75.

Scott, Karen. "Urban Spaces, Women's Networks, and the Lay Apostolate in the Siena of Catherine Benincasa." In *Creative Women in Medieval and Early Modern Italy: A Religious and Artistic Renaissance,* ed. E. Ann Matter and John Coakley, 105–19. Philadelphia: University of Pennsylvania Press, 1994.

Undset, Sigrid. *Catherine of Siena.* New York: Sheed and Ward, 1954.

Villegas, Diana L. "Discernment in Catherine of Siena." *Theological Studies* 58 (1997): 19–38.

Letter 68

To the Signori of Florence
[Probably directed to the leaders of the *Parte Guelfa* of Florence, seeking reconciliation between them and Pope Gregory XI, written about April 1376.]

In the name of Jesus Christ crucified and of gentle Mary, mother of God's Son.

Dearest, very loved brothers in Christ Jesus,

I Caterina, servant and slave of the servants of Jesus Christ, am writing to you in his precious blood. I am thinking of our Savior's words to his disciples, "With desire have I desired to celebrate the Pasch with you before I die." Now our Savior had been celebrating the Pasch with them for a long time, so what Pasch was he referring to? He was speaking of the very last Pasch which he was celebrating by communicating to them his very self. He shows clearly how in love he is with our salvation. He does not say, "I desire," but "with desire have I desired," as if to say, "For a long time I have desired to accomplish your redemption, to give myself to you as food, and to give myself up to death to restore life to you." This is the Pasch he was desiring, and so he is happy, rejoices, and celebrates within himself because he is seeing his desire fulfilled that he has so longed for. And as a sign that this makes him happy, he calls it a Pasch. Then he leaves them peace and unity and the command to love one another. He leaves this to them as a testament and as a sign by which people can recognize Christ's children and true disciples.

This true Father is leaving this to *us* as a testament. And we his children must not renounce our Father's testament, for whoever renounces the testament is not entitled to the inheritance. This is why I desire with tremendous desire to see you true children, not rebellious against your Father, not renouncing the testament of peace but realizing that peace by being bound and united in the bond, the love, of blazing charity. If you live in this love he will give himself to you as food, and you will receive the fruit of the blood of God's Son, through which we receive eternal life as our inheritance. For before his blood was shed eternal life was closed to us. None of us could journey to our goal, God—though this is why we were created. But death entered the picture because humankind would not live under the yoke of obedience but disobediently rebelled against God's commandment. Then God, moved by the fire of his divine charity, gave us the Word, his only-begotten Son. And he, in obedience to his Father, gave us his blood with such warm love that any proud foolish heart should be ashamed not to acknowledge such an enormous favor. His blood became a bath to wash away our weaknesses, and the nails became keys that unlocked the door to heaven. So, my sons and brothers, I don't want you to be ungrateful or unappreciative for all the boundless love

God is showing you—for you are well aware that ingratitude dries up the fountain of piety.

This is the Pasch my soul longs to celebrate with you: your becoming peaceable children, not rebellious against your head but submissive and obedient even to the point of death. You know well that Christ left us his vicar, and he left him as a help for our souls. There is nowhere we can have salvation except in the mystic body of holy Church, whose head is Christ and whose members we are. Whoever disobeys Christ on earth, who takes the place of Christ in heaven, will have no share in the fruit of the blood of God's Son. For God has decreed that through his hands this blood will be communicated and given to us, as well as all the sacraments of holy Church, which receive life from this blood. We cannot journey by any other road, nor can we enter through any other door, for First Truth said, "I am way and truth and life." Whoever keeps to this road is walking by way of truth, not falsehood. This is a way of hatred for the sin of selfish love of self, which is the cause of all evil. This way gives us love for the virtues, which give life to our souls and through which we are blessed with love and unity with our neighbors, so that we would rather die than sin against them. It becomes clear that if we sin against other creatures we sin against their Creator. So this is the way of truth. And it seems to me it is also the door through which we must enter once we have completed our journey, for he said, "No one can come to the Father except through me."

So you see, my dearest sons, that whoever like a gangrenous limb rebels against holy Church and against our father, Christ on earth, has fallen under the sentence of death, because whatever we do to him we are doing to Christ in heaven, whether it is reverence or dishonor. It is clear that by your disobedience and persecution (believe me, my brothers, I am saying this with heartfelt sorrow and tears), you have fallen into death and into hatred and contempt for God. And nothing worse could happen to you than to be deprived of his grace.

Human power would be of little use without divine power. Alas, those who guard the city are wearing themselves out for nothing unless God is guarding the city! If God has declared war on you because of the wrong you have done your father, his vicar, you are weak indeed, having lost his help. It's true that many do not believe they are offending God by this. It seems to them they are offering sacrifice to him. If they persecute the Church and its pastors they defend themselves by saying, "They are bad, and they are doing all kinds of evil." But I'm telling you that God wills, and has so commanded, that even if the pastors and

Christ on earth were devils incarnate (rather than good kind fathers), we must be submissive and obedient to them—not for what they are in themselves but out of obedience to God, because they take the place of Christ, who wants us to obey them. You know that a son never has a just case against his father, no matter how bad and unjust the latter may be, for the gift the son has received from his father, his very being, is so great that nothing can ever repay so great a debt. Now reflect that in the same way the being, the gift of grace, that we draw from the mystic body of holy Church is so great that no reverence or works we might offer could be sufficient to pay back this debt.

Ah, ah, my sons, I tell you weeping: I beg you, I urge you, in the name of Christ crucified, to be reconciled and make peace with him. Continue the war no longer. Don't wait for God's wrath to descend on you— for I tell you, he considers this wrong as done to him, and so it is. Make your decision to take shelter under the wings of love and fear of God, humbling yourselves and being willing to seek peace and unity with your father. Open, open the eye of your understanding, and don't walk so blindly! For we are not Jews or Saracens, but Christians baptized and ransomed in the blood of Christ. So we must not go against our head, no matter what injustice may have been done us. Nor must one Christian go against another. No, we should be going together against the unbelievers who are doing us an injustice because they are holding what is not theirs but ours.

Now, for love of God, no more sleeping in such unenlightened foolish obstinacy! Get up and run to your father's arms! If you do, he will receive you kindly, and you will have spiritual as well as material peace and tranquility, you and all of Tuscany. All this warring here will be turned against the unbelievers, by the raising of the standard of the most holy cross. But if you do not make any effort toward a wholesome peace, you and all of Tuscany will have a worse time than our ancestors ever had. Don't think that God is sleeping while his bride is being wronged. No, he is watching! It may not seem so to us, because we see things going well—but under the prosperity is hidden the discipline of God's powerful hand. Since God is ready to offer us his mercy, my brothers, don't be unyielding any more. Humble yourselves now, while you have time. For those who humble themselves will always be exalted (so said Christ), and those who exalt themselves will be humbled by God's discipline and whippings and beatings.

Walk in peace and unity: this is the Pasch I long to celebrate with you. And the only court in which we can celebrate this Pasch is the body of holy Church, because there we have the blood of God's Son as a bath to wash away the filth of our sins. There is the food that nourishes and satisfies our soul. And there is found the wedding garment we must have if we want to get into the wedding feast of eternal life, to which we are invited by the Lamb who was abandoned and slain on the cross for us. This is the garment of peace that calms our heart and covers the shame of our nakedness (I mean all our wretchedness and sin and divisiveness, which are the things that strip us of the garment of grace). Once God's gentle goodness gives us back this garment, don't be slow to put it on and go bravely and earnestly to your head, so that death won't find you naked. For we must die, but we don't know when. Don't wait for time, for time isn't waiting for you. It would be great folly to wait and rely on what I don't have and am not sure of having.

I'll say no more. Pardon my presumption, and blame it on my love for your well-being, physical as well as spiritual, and on my sorrow over the spiritual and temporal harm you are suffering. Keep in mind that I would rather say these things to you in person than by letter. If I can be of any use in advancing the honor of God and your reconciliation with holy Church, I am ready if necessary to give my life.

Keep living in God's holy and tender love.

Gentle Jesus! Jesus!

Letter 69

To Pope Gregory XI, at Avignon

[Urging Gregory to return to Rome without bringing troops, written about April 1376.]

In the name of Christ crucified and of gentle Mary.

Revered father in Christ gentle Jesus,

I Caterina, your unworthy daughter, servant and slave of the servants of Jesus Christ, am writing to you in his precious blood. I long to see you a courageous man, free of slavish fear, learning from the good gentle Jesus, whose vicar you are. Such was his boundless love for us that he ran to the shameful death of the cross heedless of torment, shame, insult, and outrage. He suffered them all, totally free of fear, such was his hungry desire for the Father's honor and our salvation. For love had made him completely let go of himself, humanly speaking. Now this is just what I want you to do, father. Let go of yourself wherever selfish love is concerned. Do not love yourself selfishly, nor others selfishly, but love yourself and your neighbors for God's sake and God for his own sake, since he is worthy of love, and since he is supreme eternal good. Take as

your example this slain Lamb, for the blood of this Lamb will give you courage for every battle. In the blood you will lose all fear, and you will become a good shepherd who will lay down your life for your little sheep.

Up then, father; don't sit still any longer! Fire yourself with tremendous desire, expecting divine help and providence. For it seems to me that divine Goodness is about to turn the great wolves into lambs. This is why I am coming there soon, to lay them in your lap, humbled. I am certain that you, as their father, will receive them in spite of their persecution and injustice against you. You will learn from gentle First Truth, who says that the good shepherd, once he has found the little lost sheep, will put it on his shoulders and take it back to the fold. So do that, father. Once your little lost sheep has been found, take it on love's shoulders and put it in the fold of holy Church. And right after that our gentle Savior wants and commands you to raise the standard of the most holy cross over the unbelievers, and let this whole war be picked up and directed against them. As for the soldiers you have hired to come here, hold them back and don't let them come, for they would ruin everything instead of setting things right.

My dear father, you ask me about your coming. I answer you in the name of Christ crucified: come as soon as you can. If you can, come before September, and if you cannot come earlier, don't delay beyond the end of September. Pay no attention to any opposition, but like a courageous and fearless man, come! And, as you value your life, see that you don't come with an army, but with the cross in your hand, as a meek lamb. If you do, you will fulfill God's will. But if you come in any other way you will be violating that will rather than fulfilling it. Be glad, father! Be jubilant! Come! Come!

I'll say no more. Keep living in God's holy and tender love.

Gentle Jesus! Jesus love!

Pardon me, father. I humbly ask your dear blessing.

The Dialogue (1378)

Prologue

In the Name of Christ Crucified and of Gentle Mary

1.

A soul rises up, restless with tremendous desire for God's honor and the salvation of souls. She has for some time exercised herself in virtue and has become accustomed to dwelling in the cell of self-knowledge in order to know better God's goodness toward her, since upon knowledge follows love. And loving, she seeks to pursue truth and clothe herself in it.

But there is no way she can so savor and be enlightened by this truth as in continual humble prayer, grounded in the knowledge of herself and of God. For by such prayer the soul is united with God, following in the footsteps of Christ crucified, and through desire and affection and the union of love he makes of her another himself. So Christ seems to have meant when he said, "If you will love me and keep my word, I will show myself to you, and you will be one thing with me and I with you." And we find similar words in other places from which we can see it is the truth that by love's affection the soul becomes another himself.

To make this clearer still, I remember having heard from a certain servant of God that, when she was at prayer, lifted high in spirit, God would not hide from her mind's eye his love for his servants. No, he would reveal it, saying among other things, "Open your mind's eye and look within me, and you will see the dignity and beauty of my reasoning creature. But beyond the beauty I have given the soul by creating her in my image and likeness, look at those who are clothed in the wedding garment of charity, adorned with many true virtues: They are united with me through love. So I say, if you should ask me who they are, I would answer," said the gentle loving Word, "that they are another me; for they have lost and drowned their own will and have clothed themselves and united themselves and conformed themselves with mine."

It is true, then, that the soul is united to God through love's affection.

Now this soul's will was to know and follow truth more courageously. So she addressed four petitions to the most high and eternal Father, holding up her desire for herself first of all—for she knew that she could be of no service to her neighbors in teaching or example or prayer without first doing herself the service of attaining and possessing virtue.

Her first petition, therefore, was for herself. The second was for the reform of holy Church. The third was for the whole world in general, and in particular for the peace of Christians who are rebelling against holy Church with great disrespect and persecution. In her fourth petition she asked divine providence to supply in general and in particular for a certain case which had arisen.

2.

This desire of hers was great and continuous. But it grew even more when First Truth showed her the world's need and how storm-tossed and offensive to God it is. And she had on her mind, besides, a letter she had received from her spiritual father, a letter in which he expressed pain and unbearable sadness over the offense against God, the damnation of souls, and persecutions against holy Church. All of this stirred up the flame of her holy desire with grief for the offense but with gladness in the hope by which she waited for God to provide against such great evils. . . .

From her deep knowledge of herself, a holy justice gave birth to hatred and displeasure against herself, ashamed as she was of her imperfection, which seemed to her to be the cause of all the evils in the world. In this knowledge and hatred and justice she washed away the stains of guilt, which it seemed to her were, and which indeed were, in her own soul, saying, "O eternal Father, I accuse myself before you, asking that you punish my sins in this life. And since I by my sins am the cause of the sufferings my neighbors must endure, I beg you in mercy to punish me for them."

The Way of Perfection

3.

Then eternal Truth seized her desire and drew it more strongly to himself. Just as in the Old Testament when sacrifice was offered to God a fire came and drew to himself the sacrifice that was acceptable to him, so gentle Truth did to that soul. He sent the fiery mercy of the Holy Spirit and seized the sacrifice of desire she had made of herself to him, saying:

Do you not know, my daughter, that all the sufferings the soul bears or can bear in this life are not enough to punish one smallest sin? For an offense against me, infinite Good, demands infinite satisfaction. So I want you to know that not all sufferings given in this life are given for punishment, but rather for correction, to chastise the child who offends. However, it is true that a soul's desire, that is, true contrition and sorrow for sin, can make satisfaction. True contrition satisfies for sin and its penalty not by virtue of any finite suffering you may bear, but by virtue of your infinite desire. For God, who is infinite, would have infinite love and infinite sorrow. . . .

So the glorious apostle Paul taught: "If I had an angelic tongue, knew the future, gave what is mine to the poor, and gave my body to be burned, but did not have charity, it would be worth nothing to me." Finite works are not enough either to punish or to atone unless they are seasoned with loving charity. . . .

5.

The willing desire to suffer every pain and hardship even to the point of death for the salvation of souls is very pleasing to me. The more you bear, the more you show your love for me. In loving me you come to know more of my truth, and the more you know, the more intolerable pain and sorrow you will feel when I am offended.

You asked for suffering, and you asked me to punish you for the sins of others. What you were not aware of was that you were, in effect, asking for love and light and knowledge of the truth. For I have already told you that suffering and sorrow increase in proportion to love: When love grows, so does sorrow. So I say to you: Ask and it shall be given to you; I will not say no to anyone who asks in truth. Consider that the soul's love in divine charity is so joined with perfect patience that the one cannot leave without the other. The soul, therefore, who chooses to love me must also choose to suffer for me anything at all that I give her. Patience is not proved except in suffering, and patience is one with charity, as has been said. Endure courageously, then. Otherwise you will not show yourselves to be—nor will you be—faithful spouses and children of my Truth, nor will you show that your delight is in my honor and in the salvation of souls.

6.

I would have you know that every virtue of yours and every vice is put into action by means of your neighbors. If you hate me, you harm your neighbors and yourself as well (for you are your chief neighbor), and the harm is both general and particular.

I say general because it is your duty to love your neighbors as your own self. In love you ought to help them spiritually with prayer and counsel, and assist them spiritually and materially in their need—at least with your good will if you have nothing else. If you do not love me you do not love your neighbors, nor will you help those you do not love. But it is yourself you harm most, because you deprive yourself of grace. And you harm your neighbors by depriving them of the prayer and loving desires you should be offering to me on their behalf. Every help you give them ought to come from the affection you bear them for love of me.

In the same way, every evil is done by means of your neighbors, for you cannot love them if you do not love me. This lack of charity for me and for your neighbors is the source of all evils, for if you are not doing good you are necessarily doing evil. And to whom is this evil shown and done? First of all to yourself and then to your neighbors—not to me, for you cannot harm me except insofar as I count whatever you do to them as done to me. You do yourself the harm of sin itself, depriving yourself of grace, and there is nothing worse you can do. You harm your neighbors by not giving them the pleasure of the love and charity

you owe them, the love with which you ought to be helping them by offering me your prayer and holy desire on their behalf. Such is the general help that you ought to give to every reasoning creature.

More particular are the services done to those nearest you, under your very eyes. Here you owe each other help in word and teaching and good example, indeed in every need of which you are aware, giving counsel as sincerely as you would to yourself, without selfishness. If you do not do this because you have no love for your neighbors, you do them special harm, and this as persistently as you refuse them the good you could do. How? In this Way:

Sin is both in the mind and in the act. You have already sinned in your mind when you have conceived a liking for sin and hatred for virtue. (This is the fruit of that sensual selfishness which has driven out the loving charity you ought to have for me and your neighbors.) And once you have conceived you give birth to one sin after another against your neighbors, however it pleases your perverse sensual will. Sometimes we see cruelty, general or particular, born. It is a general sort of cruelty to see yourself and others damned and in danger of death for having lost grace. What cruelty, to refuse to help either oneself or others by loving virtue and hating vice! But some actually extend their cruelty even further, not only refusing the good example of virtue but in their wickedness assuming the role of the devil by dragging others as much as they can from virtue and leading them to vice. This is spiritual cruelty: to make oneself the instrument for depriving others of life and dealing out death.

Bodily cruelty springs from greed, which not only refuses to share what is one's own but takes what belongs to others, robbing the poor, playing the overlord, cheating, defrauding, putting up one's neighbors' goods—and often their very persons—for ransom.

O wretched cruelty! You will find yourself deprived of my mercy unless you turn to compassion and kindness! At times you give birth to hurtful words, followed often enough by murder. At other times you give birth to indecency toward others, and the sinner becomes a stinking beast, poisoning not only one or two but anyone who might approach in love or fellowship.

And who is hurt by the offspring of pride? Only your neighbors. For you harm them when your exalted opinion of yourself leads you to consider yourself superior and therefore to despise them. And if pride is in a position of authority, it gives birth to injustice and cruelty, and becomes a dealer in human flesh.

O dearest daughter, grieve that I am so offended, and weep over these dead so that your prayer may destroy their death! For you see that everywhere, on every level of society, all are giving birth to sin on their neighbors' heads. For there is no sin that does not touch others, whether secretly by refusing them what is due them, or openly by giving birth to the vices of which I have told you.

It is indeed true, then, that every sin committed against me is done by means of your neighbors.

7.

I have told you how every sin is done by means of your neighbors, because it deprives them of your loving charity, and it is charity that gives life to all virtue. So that selfish love which deprives your neighbors of your charity and affection is the principle and foundation of all evil.

Every scandal, hatred, cruelty, and everything unbecoming springs from this root of selfish love. It has poisoned the whole world and sickened the mystic body of holy Church and the universal body of Christianity. For all virtues are built on charity for your neighbors. So I have told you, and such is the truth: Charity gives life to all the virtues, nor can any virtue exist without charity. In other words, virtue is attained only through love of me.

After the soul has come to know herself she finds humility and hatred for her selfish sensual passion, recognizing the perverse law that is bound up in her members and is always fighting against the spirit. So she rises up with hatred and contempt for that sensuality and crushes it firmly under the foot of reason. And through all the blessings she has received from me she discovers within her very self the breadth of my goodness. She humbly attributes to me her discovery of this self-knowledge, because she knows that my grace has drawn her from darkness and carried her into the light of true knowledge. Having come to know my goodness, the soul loves it both with and without intermediary. I mean she loves it without the intermediary of herself or her own advantage. But she does have as intermediary that virtue which is conceived through love of me, for she sees that she cannot be pleasing or acceptable to me except by conceiving hatred of sin and love of virtue.

Virtue, once conceived, must come to birth. Therefore, as soon as the soul has conceived through loving affection, she gives birth for her neighbors' sake. And just as she loves me in truth, so also she serves her neighbors in truth. Nor could she do otherwise, for love of me and love of neighbor are one and the same thing: Since love of neighbor has its source in me, the more the soul loves me, the more she loves her neighbors.

Such is the means I have given you to practice and prove your virtue. The service you cannot render me you must do for your neighbors. Thus it will be evident that you have me within your soul by grace, when with tender loving desire you are looking out for my honor and the salvation of your neighbors by bearing fruit for them in many holy prayers.

I showed you earlier how suffering alone, without desire, cannot atone for sin. Just so, the soul in love with my truth never ceases doing service for all the world, universally and in particular, in proportion to her own burning desire and to the disposition of those who receive. Her loving charity benefits herself first of all, as I have told you, when she conceives that virtue from which she draws the life of grace. Blessed with this unitive love she reaches out in loving charity to the whole world's need for salvation. But beyond a general love for all people she sets her eye on the specific needs of her neighbors and comes to the aid of those nearest her according to the graces I have given her for ministry: Some she teaches by word, giving sincere and impartial counsel; others she teaches by her example—as everyone ought to—edifying her neighbors by her good, holy, honorable life.

These are the virtues, with innumerable others, that are brought to birth in love of neighbor. But why have I established such differences? Why do I give this person one virtue and that person another, rather than giving them all to one person? It is true that all the virtues are bound together, and it is impossible to have one without having them all. But I give them in different ways so that one virtue might be, as it were, the source of all the others. So to one person I give charity as the primary virtue, to another justice, to another humility, to another a lively faith or prudence or temperance or patience, and to still another courage.

These and many other virtues I give differently to different souls, and the soul is most at ease with that virtue which has been made primary for her. But through her love of that virtue she attracts all the other virtues to herself, since they are all bound together in loving charity.

The same is true of many of my gifts and graces, virtue and other spiritual gifts, and those things necessary for the body and human life. I have distributed them all in such a way that no one has all of them. Thus have I given you reason—necessity, in fact—to practice mutual charity. For I could well have supplied each of you with all your needs, both spiritual and material. But I wanted to make you dependent on one another so that each of you would be my minister, dispensing the graces and gifts you have received from me. So whether you will it or not, you cannot escape the exercise of charity! Yet, unless you do it for love of me, it is worth nothing to you in the realm of grace.

So you see, I have made you my ministers, setting you in different positions and in different ranks to exercise the virtue of charity. For there are many rooms in my house. All I want is love. In loving me you will realize love for your neighbors, and if you love your neighbors you have kept the law. If you are bound by this love you will do everything you can to be of service wherever you are. . . .

10.

Do you know how these three virtues [charity, humility, discernment] exist?

Imagine a circle traced on the ground, and in its center a tree sprouting with a shoot grafted into its side. The tree finds its nourishment in the soil within the expanse of the circle, but uprooted from the soil it would die fruitless. So think of the soul as a tree made for love and living only by love. Indeed, without this divine love, which is true and perfect charity, death would be her fruit instead of life. The circle in which this tree's root, the soul's love, must grow is true knowledge of herself, knowledge that is joined to me, who like the circle have neither beginning nor end. You can go round and round within this circle, finding neither end nor beginning, yet never leaving the circle. This knowledge of yourself, and of me within yourself, is grounded in the soil of true humility, which is as great as the expanse of the circle (which is the knowledge of yourself united with me, as I have said). But if your knowledge of yourself were isolated from me there would be no full circle at all. Instead, there would be a beginning in self-knowledge, but apart from me it would end in confusion.

So the tree of charity is nurtured in humility and branches out in true discernment. The marrow of the tree (that is, loving charity within the soul) is patience, a sure sign that I am in her and that she is united with me.

This tree, so delightfully planted, bears many-fragranced blossoms of virtue. Its fruit is grace for the soul herself and blessing for her neighbors in proportion to the conscientiousness of those who would share my servants' fruits. To me this tree yields the fragrance of glory and praise to my name, and so it does what I created it for and comes at last to its goal, to me, everlasting Life, life that cannot be taken from you against your will.

And every fruit produced by this tree is seasoned with discernment, and this unites them all, as I have told you. . . .

Dialogue

13.

Then the soul was restless and aflame with tremendous desire because of the unspeakable love she had conceived in God's great goodness when she had come to see and know the expanse of his charity. How tenderly he had deigned to answer her petition and give her hope in her bitterness—bitterness over God's being offended and holy Church's being ravaged, and bitterness over her own wretchedness, which she saw through knowledge of herself! Her bitterness was softened and at the same time grew, for the supreme eternal Father, now that he had shown her the way of perfection, was showing her in a new light how he was being offended and souls were being harmed.

As the soul comes to know herself she also knows God better, for she sees how good he has been to her. In the gentle mirror of God she sees her own dignity: that through no merit of hers but by his creation she is the image of God. And in the mirror of God's goodness she sees as well her own unworthiness, the work of her own sin. For just as you can better see the blemish on your face when you look at yourself in a mirror, so the soul who in true self-knowledge rises up with desire to look at herself in the gentle mirror of God with the eye of understanding sees all the more clearly her own defects because of the purity she sees in him.

Now as light and knowledge grew more intense in this soul, a sweet bitterness was both heightened and mellowed. The hope that first Truth had given her mellowed it. But as a flame burns higher the more fuel is fed it, the fire in this soul grew so great that her body could not have contained it. She could not, in fact, have survived had she not been encircled by the strength of him who is strength itself.

Thus cleansed by the fire of divine charity, which she had found in coming to know herself and God, and more hungry than ever in her hope for the salvation of the whole world and the reform of holy Church, she stood up with confidence in the presence of the supreme Father. She showed him the leprosy of holy Church and the wretchedness of the world, speaking to him as with the words of Moses:

My Lord, turn the eye of your mercy on your people and on your mystic body, holy Church. How much greater would be your glory if you would pardon so many and give them the light of knowledge! For then they would surely all praise you, when they see that your infinite goodness has saved them from deadly sin and eternal damnation. How much greater this than to have praise only from my wretched self, who have sinned so much and am the cause and instrument of every evil! So I beg you, divine eternal Love, to take your revenge on me, and be merciful to your people. I will not leave your presence till I see that you have been merciful to them.

For what would it mean to me to have eternal life if death were the lot of your people, or if my faults especially and those of your other creatures should bring darkness upon your bride, who is light itself? It is my will, then, and I beg it as a favor, that you have mercy on your people with the same eternal love that led you to create us in your image and likeness. You said, "Let us make humankind in our image and likeness." And this you did, eternal Trinity, willing that we should share all that you are, high eternal Trinity! You, eternal Father, gave us memory to hold your gifts and share your power. You gave us understanding so that, seeing your goodness, we might share the wisdom of your only-begotten Son. And you gave us free will to love what our understanding sees and knows of your truth, and so share the mercy of your Holy Spirit.

Why did you so dignify us? With unimaginable love you looked upon your creatures within your very self, and you fell in love with us. So it was love that made you create us and give us being just so that we might taste your supreme eternal good.

Then I see how by our sin we lost the dignity you had given us. Rebels that we were, we declared war on your mercy and became your enemies. But stirred by the same fire that made you create us, you decided to give this warring human race a way to reconciliation, bringing great peace out of our war. So you gave us your only-begotten Son, your Word, to be mediator between us and you. He became our justice taking on himself the punishment for our injustices. He offered you the obedience you required of him in clothing him with our humanity, eternal Father, taking on our likeness and our human nature!

O depth of love! What heart could keep from breaking at the sight of your greatness descending to the lowliness of our humanity? We are your image, and now by making yourself one with us you have become our image, veiling your eternal divinity in the wretched cloud and dung heap of Adam. And why? For love! You, God, became human and we have been made divine! In the name of this unspeakable love, then, I beg you—I would force you even!—to have mercy on your creatures. . . .

16.

Then that soul stood before the divine majesty deeply joyful and strengthened in her new knowledge. What hope she had found in the divine mercy! What unspeakable love she had experienced! For she had seen how God, in his love and his desire to be merciful to humankind in spite of their enmity toward him, had given his servants a way to force his goodness and calm his wrath. So she was glad and fearless in the face of the world's persecution, knowing that God was on her side. And the fire of her holy longing grew so strong that she would not

rest there, but with holy confidence made her plea for the whole world.

In her second petition she had concerned herself with the good that both Christians and unbelievers would reap from the reform of holy Church. But as if that were not enough, she now stretched out her prayer, like one starved, to the whole world, and as if he himself were making her ask it, she cried out:

Have mercy, eternal God, on your little sheep, good shepherd that you are! Do not delay with your mercy for the world for already it almost seems they can no longer survive! Everyone seems bereft of any oneness in charity with you, eternal Truth, or even with each other: I mean, whatever love they have for each other has no grounding in you. . . .

25.

O immeasurably tender love! Who would not be set afire with such love? What heart could keep from breaking? You, deep well of charity, it seems you are so madly in love with your creatures that you could not live without us! Yet you are our God, and have no need of us. Your greatness is no greater for our well-being, nor are you harmed by any harm that comes to us, for you are supreme eternal Goodness. What could move you to such mercy? Neither duty nor any need you have of us (we are sinful and wicked debtors!)—but only love!

If I see clearly at all, supreme eternal Truth, it is I who am the thief, and you have been executed in my place. For I see the Word, your Son, nailed to a cross. And you have made him a bridge for me, as you have shown me, wretched servant that I am! My heart is breaking and yet cannot break for the hungry longing it has conceived for you!

I remember that you wanted to show me who are those who cross over the bridge and those who do not. So, if it would please your goodness to show me, I would gladly see and hear this from you.

The Bridge

26.

Then God eternal, to stir up even more that soul's love for the salvation of souls, responded to her:

Before I show you what I want to show you, and what you asked to see, I want to describe the bridge for you. I have told you that it stretches from heaven to earth by reason of my having joined myself with your humanity, which I formed from the earth's clay.

This bridge, my only-begotten Son, has three stairs. Two of them he built on the wood of the most holy cross, and the third even as he tasted the great bitterness of the gall and vinegar they gave him to drink. You will recognize in these three stairs three spiritual stages.

The first stair is the feet, which symbolize the affections. For just as the feet carry the body, the affections carry the soul. My Son's nailed feet are a stair by which you can climb to his side, where you will see revealed his inmost heart. For when the soul has climbed up on the feet of affection and looked with her mind's eye into my Son's opened heart, she begins to feel the love of her own heart in his consummate and unspeakable love. (I say consummate because it is not for his own good that he loves you; you cannot do him any good, since he is one with me.) Then the soul, seeing how tremendously she is loved, is herself filled to overflowing with love. So, having climbed the second stair, she reaches the third. This is his mouth, where she finds peace from the terrible war she has had to wage because of her sins.

At the first stair, lifting the feet of her affections from the earth, she stripped herself of sin. At the second she dressed herself in love for virtue. And at the third she tasted peace.

So the bridge has three stairs, and you can reach the last by climbing the first two. The last stair is so high that the flooding waters cannot strike it—for the venom of sin never touched my Son.

But though this bridge has been raised so high, it still is joined to the earth. Do you know when it was raised up? When my Son was lifted up on the wood of the most holy cross he did not cut off his divinity from the lowly earth of your humanity. So though he was raised so high he was not raised off the earth. In fact, his divinity is kneaded into the clay of your humanity like one bread. Nor could anyone walk on that bridge until my Son was raised up. This is why he said, "If I am lifted up high I will draw everything to myself."

When my goodness saw that you could be drawn in no other way, I sent him to be lifted onto the wood of the cross. I made of that cross an anvil where this child of humankind could be hammered into an instrument to release humankind from death and restore it to the life of grace. In this way he drew everything to himself: for he proved his unspeakable love, and the human heart is always drawn by love. He could not have shown you greater love than by giving his life for you. You can hardly resist being drawn by love, then, unless you foolishly refuse to be drawn.

I said that, having been raised up, he would draw everything to himself. This is true in two ways: First, the human heart is drawn by love, as I said, and with all its powers: memory, understanding, and will. If these three powers are harmoniously united in my name, everything else you do, in fact or in intention, will be drawn to union with me in peace through the move-

ment of love, because all will be lifted up in the pursuit of crucified love. So my Truth indeed spoke truly when he said, "If I am lifted up high, I will draw everything to myself." For everything you do will be drawn to him when he draws your heart and its powers.

What he said is true also in the sense that everything was created for your use, to serve your needs. But you who have the gift of reason were made not for yourselves but for me, to serve me with all your heart and all your love. So when you are drawn to me, everything is drawn with you, because everything was made for you.

It was necessary, then, that this bridge be raised high. And it had to have stairs so that you would be able to mount it more easily. . . .

31.

After thus expanding her heart a bit in singing the praises of God's mercy, the soul humbly waited for him to keep his promise. And in reply to her God said:

Dearest daughter, you have been carrying on about my mercy because I let you experience it when I said to you, "I beg you to pray to me on behalf of these people." But know that my mercy toward you is incomparably more than you can see, because your sight is imperfect and limited, and my mercy is perfect and without limit. So there can be no comparison except that of the finite to the infinite.

I wanted you to experience this mercy as well as your own dignity as I showed you before, so that you would better understand the cruelty and baseness of the wicked who travel beneath the bridge. Open your mind's eye and look at those who drown by their own choice, and see how low they have fallen by their sins.

First they became weak, and this is when they conceived deadly sin in their hearts. Then they gave birth to that sin and lost the life of grace. And now these who have drowned in the river of the world's disordered love are dead to grace, and like the senseless dead they cannot make a move except as they are picked up by others. Because they are dead they remember nothing of my mercy. Their minds neither see nor know my truth (for their sensitivity is dead, and they see nothing but themselves, and that with the dead love of selfish sensuality). And so their wills also are dead to my will, for they love nothing but what is dead.

Because these three powers (memory, understanding, and will) are dead, everything they do in intention or in fact is dead so far as grace is concerned. They can no longer defend themselves against their enemies. They are helpless unless I help them. But they do still have their freedom of choice as long as they are in the flesh, and any time these dead will ask for my help they can have it—but that is the limit of what they can do for themselves.

They become unbearable to themselves. They who wanted to rule the world find themselves ruled by nothingness, that is, by sin—for sin is the opposite of being, and they have become servants and slaves of sin.

I made them trees of love through the life of grace, which they received in holy baptism. But they have become trees of death, because they *are* dead.

Do you know where this tree of death is rooted? In the height of pride, which is nourished by their sensual selfishness. Its core is impatience and its offshoot is the lack of any discernment. These are the four chief vices, which together kill the souls of those I have called trees of death, since they have failed to feed on the life of grace.

Within these trees a worm of conscience nibbles. But as long as a person lives in deadly sin the worm is blinded and so is little felt.

The fruits of such trees are full of death, for their juice comes from the root of pride. So their wretched little souls are filled with thanklessness, the source of all evils. Had they been grateful for the blessings they received from me, they would know me. And in knowing me they would know themselves, and so live in my love. But instead they go on groping their way through the river as if they were blind, not seeing how completely undependable the water is.

32.

There are as many different death-dealing fruits on these trees of death as there are sins. Some are food for beasts: These are people who live indecently, using their bodies and minds like pigs rolling in the mud, for that is how they roll about in the mud of lust. O brutish souls! What have you done with your dignity? You who were created kin to the angels have made ugly beasts of yourselves! You have stooped so low that even the demons whose friends and servants you have become cannot stand the sight of such indecency—and much less I, who am purity itself.

No other sin is so hateful and so darkens the human mind as this. The philosophers knew this, not by the light of grace (since they did not have it) but by a natural light: that this sin beclouds the mind. So they were continent the better to be able to study. And they cast aside wealth so that the thought of material things would not clutter their hearts. But not so the foolish false Christians who have lost grace through their own fault.

33.

Others there are whose fruits are of clay. These are the greedy misers who act like the mole who feeds on nothing but dirt right up to the end. And when death comes where have they to turn? In their avarice they scorn my generosity, selling their time to their neighbors. They are usurers who become cruel robbers who blot my mercy from their memories. For if they did remember my mercy they would not be cruel either to themselves or their neighbors, but would rather be kind and merciful to themselves by living virtuously and to their neighbors by serving them with love.

How many evils come from this cursed sin of avarice! How many murders, thefts, and pillagings; how many unlawful profits and how much hard-heartedness and injustice toward others! It kills the spirit and makes people slaves to wealth who care nothing for God's commandments. Such people love no one except for their own profit.

This vice is born of pride and it feeds pride, because it is always so concerned about its own reputation that it necessarily links up with pride. And so, with wretched self-opinionated pride, it goes from bad to worse. It is a flame that always generates the smoke of vanity and arrogance, taking pride in what is not its own. It is a root with many branches, chief of which is a self-conceit that always wants to be greater than others. Another of its branches is the deceitful heart that is not sincere and generous but double, that says one thing but thinks another, that hides the truth and tells lies for its own profit. And avarice breeds envy, a worm that is always gnawing, letting the avaricious enjoy neither their own nor anyone else's good.

How can these wretched evil people share their possessions with the poor when they are already stealing from them? How can they rescue others from indecency when they are the ones who shoved them into it? For sometimes they are such animals that they have no respect for their own daughters and other relatives, but stoop to the meanest things with them. And yet my mercy holds them up, and I refrain from ordering the earth to swallow them up, giving them a chance to repent.

But if they will not share their possessions, how will they ever give their lives for the salvation of souls? How will they give affection if they are being eaten up by envy?

O miserable vices that tear down the heaven of the soul! I call the soul "heaven" because I make heaven wherever I dwell by grace. I made the soul my hiding place and by my love turned her into a mansion. But now she has left me like an adulteress because she loves herself and other created persons and things more than me. In fact, she has made a god of herself and strikes out at me with all sorts of sins. And she does all this because she gives no thought to the blood shed for her with such burning love.

34.

There are others who are so bloated with the power in their hands that the standard they carry is injustice. They inflict their injustice on God and their neighbors and even on themselves.

They are unjust to themselves by not being virtuous as they owe it to themselves to be. They do not give me the honor that is my due, nor praise my name as is their duty, but like thieves they steal what is mine and put it to the service of their own sensuality. So they are being unjust both to me and to themselves, for like blinded fools they do not recognize me in themselves.

And it is all because of selfishness, like those Jews and ministers of the Law who were so blinded by envy and selfishness that they did not recognize the Truth, my only-begotten Son. Therefore they did not, as they should have, recognize eternal Life when he was in their midst. My Truth told them, "The Kingdom of God is within you." But they failed to recognize it. Why? Because they had lost the light of reason and so they did not offer due honor and glory to me or to him who is one with me. And so they blindly committed the injustice of persecuting him shamefully even to death by crucifixion.

Such as these are unjust to themselves and to me and to their neighbors as well. They are unjust dealers in the flesh of their subjects and of anyone else who may fall into their hands. . . .

86.

Now I, eternal Truth, have let you see with your mind's eye and hear with your feeling's ear how you must behave if you would serve yourself and your neighbors in the teaching and knowledge of my truth. For I told you in the beginning that one comes to knowledge of the truth through self-knowledge. But self-knowledge alone is not enough: It must be seasoned by and joined with knowledge of me within you. This is how you found humility and contempt for yourself along with the fire of my charity, and so came to love and affection for your neighbors and gave them the service of your teaching and your holy and honorable living.

I showed you the bridge as well. And I showed you the three ordinary stairs that are set up in the soul's three powers, and how no one can have the life of grace without climbing all three stairs, without gathering all three powers in my name. Then I revealed to you how these stairs were in a special way a figure of the three spiritual stages, symbolized in the body of my only-begotten Son. I told you that he had made a stairway of his body, and showed it to you in his nailed

feet, in his open side, and in his mouth where the soul tastes peace and calm.

I showed you the imperfection of slavish fear and the imperfection of love that loves me for the delight it feels. And I showed you the perfection of the third stage, of those who have attained peace at his mouth. These have run with eager longing across the bridge of Christ crucified. They have climbed the three ordinary stairs, have gathered their souls' three powers and all their works in my name (as I explained for you more in detail before), and they have climbed the three special stairs and passed from imperfection to perfection. So you have seen how they run on in truth. I also gave you a taste of the soul's perfection as she is adorned with the virtues, as well as the delusions she is subject to before she reaches perfection if she does not use her time well in coming to know herself and me.

I told you about the wretchedness of those who let themselves be drowned in the river because they will not keep to the bridge of my Truth's teaching, the bridge I built for you so you would not drown. Like fools they have chosen to drown in the world's wretched filth.

I have told you all this to make you shake up the fire of your holy longing and your compassion and grief over the damnation of souls. I want your sorrow and love to drive you to pressure me with sweat and tears—tears of constant humble prayer offered to me in the flames of burning desire. And not just for yourself, but for so many others of my creatures and servants who will hear you and be compelled by my love (together with you and my other servants) to beg and pressure me to be merciful to the world and to the mystic body of holy Church, the Church for which you so earnestly plead with me.

You will recall that I already told you I would fulfill your desires by giving you refreshment in your labors, that I would satisfy your anguished longings by reforming holy Church through good and holy shepherds. I will do this, as I told you, not through war, not with the sword and violence, but through peace and calm, through my servants' tears and sweat. I have set you as workers in your own and your neighbors' souls and in the mystic body of holy Church. In yourselves you must work at virtue; in your neighbors and in the Church you must work by example and teaching. And you must offer me constant prayer for the Church and for every creature, giving birth to virtue through your neighbors. For I have already told you that every virtue and every sin is realized and intensified through your neighbors. Therefore, I want you to serve your neighbors and in this way share the fruits of your own vineyard.

Never cease offering me the incense of fragrant

prayers for the salvation of souls, for I want to be merciful to the world. With your prayers and sweat and tears I will wash the face of my bride, holy Church. I showed her to you earlier as a maiden whose face was all dirtied, as if she were a leper. The clergy and the whole of Christianity are to blame for this because of their sins, though they receive their nourishment at the breast of this bride! But I will tell you about those sins in another place. . . .

Tears . . .

97.

Then that soul was restless with a tremendous longing because Truth had so tenderly satisfied her by telling her about these stages of tears. And in love as she was, she said:

Thanks, thanks to you, high eternal Father, fulfiller of holy desires and lover of our salvation! Out of love you gave us love in the person of your only-begotten Son when we were still at war with you. This abyss of your flaming charity lets me ask you for grace and mercy so that I may come to you in sincerity in the light, and not run along darksomely after the teaching of your Truth. You have clearly shown me his truth to make me see two other real or possible delusions I fear. Before I go on, eternal Father, I wish you would explain these to me.

Here is the first: Sometimes people will come to me or to another of your servants asking for counsel in their desire to serve you and wanting me to instruct them. I know, gentle eternal God, that you have already told me, "I am one who takes delight in few words and many deeds." Still, if it would please your kindness to say a few more words on this, you would be doing me a great favor.

Also, sometimes when I am praying for your creatures and especially for your servants, it happens in the course of my prayer that I find this one spiritually well disposed, apparently rejoicing in you, and another seems to me to have a darksome spirit. Eternal Father, should I or can I judge the one to be in light and the other in darkness? Or if I should see one going the way of great penance and another not, should I judge that the one who does greater penance is more perfect than the other? I ask you, lest I be deluded by my own lack of insight, to be more specific about what you have told me in general terms.

Here is the second thing I want to ask you about: Be more clear to me about the sign you told me the soul receives to tell whether a spiritual visitation is from you, God eternal, or not.

If I remember well, you told me, eternal Truth, that [if the visitation is from you] it leaves the spirit glad and encouraged toward virtue. I would like to know whether this gladness can be disguised spiritual selfishness, for if that is the case I would hold only to the sign of virtue.

These are the things I am asking you so that I may be able to serve you and my neighbors in truth, and not fall into any false judgements about your creatures and your servants. For it seems to me that passing [rash] judgement alienates the soul from you, and I do not want to fall into that trap.

Truth

105.

. . . Now, dearest daughter, I have satisfied your desire by clarifying what you asked me to. I have told you how you should reprove your neighbors if you would not be deluded by the devil or your own meager insight, that is, that you should reprove in general terms, not specifically, unless you have had a clear revelation from me, and humbly reprove yourself along with them.

I also told you, and I will tell you again, that nothing in the world can make it right for you to sit in judgement on the intentions of my servants, either generally or in particular, whether you find them well or ill disposed.

And I told you the reason you cannot judge, and that if you do you will be deluded in your judgement. But compassion is what you must have, you and the others, and leave the judging to me.

I told you also the teaching and principal foundation you should give to those who come to you for counsel because they want to leave behind the darkness of deadly sin and follow the path of virtue. I told you to give them as principle and foundation an affectionate love for virtue through knowledge of themselves and of my goodness for them. And they should slay and annihilate their selfish will so that in nothing will they rebel against me. And give them penance as an instrument but not as their chief concern—not equally to everyone but according to their capacity for it and what their situation will allow, this one more and this one less, depending on their ability to manage these external instruments.

I told you that it is not right for you to reprove others except in general terms in the way I explained, and this is true. But I would not because of that have you believe that when you see something that is clearly sinful you may not correct it between that person and yourself, for you may. In fact, if that person is obstinate and refuses to change, you may reveal the matter to two or three others, and if this does not help, reveal it to the mystic body of holy Church. But I told you that it is not right for you to hand anyone over merely on the basis of what you see or feel within you or even what you see externally. Unless you have clearly seen the truth or have understood it through an explicit revelation from me, you are not to reprove anyone except in the manner I have already explained. Such is the more secure way for you because the devil will not be able to deceive you by using the cloak of neighborly charity.

Now, dearest daughter, I have finished telling you what is necessary if you would preserve and augment your soul's perfection. . . .

108.

Then that soul, truly like one drunk, seemed to be beside herself and separated from her bodily senses because of her loving union with her Creator. She lifted up her spirit and gazed into eternal Truth with her mind's eye. And as she had come to know the truth she was in love with truth, and she said:

O high eternal goodness of God! Who am I, wretched as I am, that you, high eternal Father, have revealed to me your truth and the hidden snares of the devil and the delusion of selfishness I and others can be subject to in this pilgrim life, so that we might not be deceived either by the devil or by ourselves? What moved you to this? Love. For you loved me without being loved by me. O fire of love! Thanks, thanks to you, eternal Father! . . .

And I would make yet another request, for those two pillars, the fathers you have appointed for me on earth to guide and teach me, who am so wretchedly weak, from the beginning of my conversion until now. Unite them and make of their two bodies a single soul. Let neither of them be concerned for anything but to fulfill in themselves, and in the ministries you have put in their care, the glory and praise of your name through the salvation of souls. And let me, unworthy wretched slave more than daughter, treat them with due reverence and holy fear for love of you, for your honor, for their peace and calm, and for the edification of our neighbors.

I am certain, eternal Truth, that you will not spurn my desire and the petitions I have addressed to you. For I know from having seen what you have been pleased to reveal to me, and even more from experience, that you are receptive to holy desires. I, your unworthy servant, will try as you give me grace to be faithful to your command and your teaching.

O eternal Father, I remember your telling me once, when you were speaking of the ministers of holy Church, that at another time you would talk more at length about the sins these ministers are committing this very day. Therefore, if it would please your goodness, say something about this, so that I may have reason to intensify my sorrow and compassion and restless longing for their salvation. For I recall that you have already said that through the suffering and tears and sorrow, the sweat and constant prayers of your servants, you would refresh us by reforming the Church with good and holy ministers. Therefore, I make my petition so that this may grow in me.

109.

Then God eternal looked on her with mercy. He did not spurn her desire but accepted her petition. Wishing to fulfill this last request that she had made because of his promise, he said:

O dearest daughter whom I so love! I will fulfill your desire in what you have asked of me only if you for your part will not be foolish or indifferent. For that would be much more serious for you and worthy of greater reproach now than before, because you have come to know more of my truth. Make it your concern, then, to offer prayers for all people and for the mystic body of holy Church and for those I have given you to love with a special love. Do not be guilty of indifference about offering prayers and the example of your living and the word of teaching. Reprove vice and commend virtue. Do all this to the greatest extent of your power.

Concerning the two pillars I have given you and of whom you have spoken to me (and you spoke truly), make yourself a channel for giving each of them what he needs, according to their disposition and what I, your Creator, give to you, for without me none of you can do anything. I for my part will fulfill your desires. But never fail—neither you nor they—to trust me, for my providence will not fail you. Let each of them receive humbly what he is ready to receive, and let each of them administer what I gave him to administer, each in his own way, as they have received and will continue to receive from my goodness.

The Mystic Body of Holy Church . . .

115.

This is how my gentle glorious ministers conduct themselves. I told you that I wanted you to see the excellence that is theirs beyond the dignity I have given them by making them my christs. When they exercise this dignity virtuously they are clothed in this gentle glorious Sun that I have entrusted to their ministry.

Consider those who have gone before them: the gentle Gregory, Sylvester, and the other successors of the chief pontiff Peter, to whom my Truth gave the keys of the heavenly kingdom when he said, "Peter, I am giving you the keys of the heavenly kingdom; whatever you loose on earth shall be loosed in heaven, and whatever you bind on earth shall be bound in heaven."

Listen well, dearest daughter. By showing you the magnificence of their virtues I shall show you more fully the dignity to which I have appointed these ministers of mine. This is the key to the blood of my only-begotten Son, that key which unlocked eternal life, closed for so long a time because of Adam's sin. But after I gave you my Truth, the Word, my only-begotten Son, he suffered and died, and by his death he destroyed your death by letting his blood be a cleansing bath for you. Thus his blood and his death, by the power of my divine nature joined with his human nature, unlocked eternal life.

And to whom did he leave the keys to this blood? To the glorious apostle Peter and to all the others who have come or will come from now until the final judgement day with the very same authority that Peter had. Nor is this authority lessened by any sinfulness on their part; nor can that sinfulness deprive the blood or any other sacrament of its perfection. I have already told you that no uncleanness can defile this Sun, nor is its light lost because of any darkness of deadly sin that may be in the minister or in those who receive it. Their sin cannot injure the sacraments of holy Church or lessen their power. But grace is lessened and sin increased in those who administer or receive them unworthily.

Christ on earth [the Pope], then, has the keys to the blood. If you remember, I showed you this in an image when I wanted to teach you the respect laypeople ought to have for these ministers of mine, regardless of how good or evil they may be, and how displeased I am with disrespect. You know that I set before you the mystic body of holy Church under the image of a wine cellar. In this wine cellar was the blood of my only-begotten Son, and from this blood all the sacraments derive their life-giving power.

Christ on earth stood at the door of this wine cellar. He had been commissioned to administer the blood, and it was his duty to delegate ministers to help him in the service of the entire universal body of Christianity. Only those accepted and anointed by him were to thus minister. He was the head of the whole clerical order, and he appointed each one to his proper office to administer this glorious blood.

Because he has sent them out as his helpers, it is his task to correct them for their faults, and it is my will that he do so. For by the dignity and authority I have bestowed on them I have freed them from slavery, that is, from submission to the authority of temporal rulers. Civil law has no power whatever to punish them; this right belongs solely to the one who has been appointed to rule and to serve according to divine law. These are my anointed ones, and therefore, it has been said through Scripture: "Dare not to touch my christs." Therefore, a person can do no worse violence than to assume the right to punish my ministers.

116.

And if you should ask me why I said that this sin of those who persecute holy Church is graver than any other sin, and why it is my will that the sins of the clergy should not lessen your reverence for them, this is how I would answer you: Because the reverence you pay to them is not actually paid to them but to me, in virtue of the blood I have entrusted to their ministry. If this were not so, you should pay them as much reverence as to anyone else, and no more. It is this ministry of theirs that dictates that you should reverence them and come to them, not for what they are in themselves but for the power I have entrusted to them, if you would receive the holy sacraments of the Church. For if you refuse these when it is in your power to have them, you would live and die condemned.

So the reverence belongs not to the ministers, but to me and to this glorious blood made one thing with me because of the union of divinity with humanity. And just as the reverence is done to me, so also is the irreverence, for I have already told you that you must not reverence them for themselves, but for the authority I have entrusted to them. Therefore you must not sin against them, because if you do, you are really sinning not against them but against me. This I have forbidden, and I have said that it is my will that no one should touch them.

For this reason no one has excuse to say, "I am doing no harm, nor am I rebelling against holy Church. I am simply acting against the sins of evil pastors." Such persons are deluded, blinded as they are by their own selfishness. They see well enough, but they pretend not to see so as to blunt the pricking of conscience. If they would look, they could see that they are persecuting not these ministers, but the blood. It is me they assault, just as it was me they reverenced. To me redounds every assault they make on my ministers: derision, slander, disgrace, abuse. Whatever is done to them I count as done to me. For I have said and I say it again: No one is to touch my christs. It is my right to punish them, and no one else's. . . .

119.

Now I would refresh your soul by softening your

grief over the darksomeness of those wretched ones with the holy lives of my ministers. I have told you that they have taken on the qualities of the Sun, so that the fragrance of their virtues mitigates the stench, and their lightsomeness the dark. By this very light I would have you know more deeply the sinful darksomeness of those other ministers of mine. So open your mind's eye and contemplate me, the Sun of justice, and you shall see these glorious ministers who by their stewardship of the Sun have taken on the qualities of the Sun. . . .

They have all, according to the positions I have chosen them for, given light to holy Church: Peter with his preaching and teaching and in the end with his blood; Gregory with his learning and [his knowledge of] Sacred Scripture and the mirror of his living; Sylvester by his struggles against unbelievers and above all in the disputations and argumentations for the holy faith that he made in deeds as well as in words with the power he received from me. And if you turn to Augustine, to the glorious Thomas, to Jerome and the others, you will see what great light they have shed on this bride, as lamps set on a lampstand, dispelling errors with their true and perfect humility. . . .

. . . They conducted themselves as good shepherds and followers of the good shepherd, my Truth, whom I sent to govern you, my little sheep, and to lay down his life for you.

These ministers of mine followed in his footsteps. Therefore they did not let my members grow rotten for want of correction. But they corrected lovingly, with the ointment of kindness along with the harshness of the fire that cauterizes the wound of sin through reproof and penance, now more, now less, according to the gravity of the sin. Nor did it concern them that such correcting and speaking the truth might bring them death.

They were true gardeners, and with care and holy fear they rooted out the brambles of deadly sin and put in their place the fragrant plants of virtue. Thus their subjects lived in truly holy fear and they grew up as fragrant flowers in the mystic body of holy Church because my ministers fearlessly gave them the correction they needed. Because there was in them no thorn of sin, they kept to the way of holy justice and administered reproof without any slavish fear. This was and is the shining pearl that sheds peace and light on people's spirits and establishes them in holy fear with hearts united. I want you, therefore, to know that nothing causes as much darkness and division in the world among both laypeople and religious, clergy and shepherds of holy Church, as does the lack of the light of justice and invasion of the darkness of injustice.

No rank, whether of civil or divine law, can be held in grace without holy justice. For those who are not corrected and those who do not correct are like members beginning to rot, and if the doctor were only to apply ointment without cauterizing the wound, the whole body would become fetid and corrupt.

So it is with prelates and with anyone else in authority. If they see the members who are their subjects rotting because of the filth of deadly sin and apply only the ointment of soft words without reproof, they will never get well. Rather, they will infect the other members with whom they form one body under their one shepherd. But if those in authority are truly good doctors to those souls, as were those glorious shepherds, they will not use ointment without the fire of reproof. And if the members are still obstinate in their evildoing, they will cut them off from the congregation so that they will not infect the whole body with the filth of deadly sin.

But [those who are in authority] today do not do this. In fact, they pretend not to see. And do you know why? Because the root of selfish love is alive in them, and this is the source of their perverse slavish fear. They do not correct people for fear of losing their rank and position and their material possessions. They act as if they were blind, so they do not know how to maintain their positions. For if they saw how it is by holy justice that their positions are to be maintained, they would maintain them. But because they are bereft of light they do not know this. They believe they can succeed through injustice, by not reproving the sins of their subjects. But they are deceived by their own sensual passion, by their hankering for civil or ecclesiastical rank.

Another reason they will not correct others is that they themselves are living in the same or greater sins. They sense that the same guilt envelops them, so they cast aside fervor and confidence and, chained by slavish fear, pretend they do not see. Even what they do see they do not correct, but let themselves be won over by flattery and bribes, using these very things as excuses for not punishing the offenders. In them is fulfilled what my Truth said in the holy Gospel: "They are blind and leaders of the blind. And if one blind person leads another, they both fall into the ditch."

Those who have been or would be my gentle ministers did not and would not act this way. I told you that these have taken on the qualities of the sun. Indeed, they are suns, for there is in them no darkness of sin or ignorance, because they follow the teaching of my Truth. Nor are they lukewarm, because they are set ablaze in the furnace of my charity. They have no use for the world's honors and ranks and pleasures. Therefore, they are not afraid to correct. Those who do not hanker after power or ecclesiastical rank have no fear of losing it. They reprove [sin] courageously, for those whose conscience does not accuse them of sin have nothing to fear. . . .

121.

. . . No matter where you turn, to secular or religious, clerics or prelates, lowly or great, young or old, you see nothing but sin. All of them pelt me with the filth of deadly sin. But their filth harms only themselves, not me. . . .

Do you know, dearest daughter—listen with grieving bitterness of heart—do you know where these have set their principle and foundation? In their own selfish self-centeredness. There is born the tree of pride with its offshoot of indiscretion. So, lacking in discernment as they are, they assume honor and glory for themselves by seeking higher office and adornments and delicacies for their bodies, repaying me with abuse and sin. They take to themselves what is not theirs and give me what is not mine. To me should be given glory and my name should be praised; to themselves is due contempt for their selfish sensuality. They ought to know themselves enough to consider themselves unworthy of the tremendous mystery they have received from me. But they do just the opposite, for, bloated with pride as they are, they never have their fill of gobbling up earthly riches and the pleasures of the world, while they are stingy, greedy, and avaricious toward the poor.

Because of this wretched pride and avarice born of their sensual selfishness, they have abandoned the care of souls and give themselves over completely to guarding and caring for their temporal possessions. They leave behind my little sheep, whom I had entrusted to them, like sheep without a shepherd. They neither pasture nor feed them either spiritually or materially. Spiritually they do administer the sacraments of holy Church (the power of which sacraments can neither be taken away nor lessened by any sin of theirs) but they do not feed them with sincere prayers, with hungry longing for their salvation, with holy and honorable living, nor do they feed their poor subjects with temporal assistance.

I told you they were to distribute their material goods in three portions: one for their own needs, one for the poor, and one for the use of the Church. But these do the opposite. Not only do they not give what they are in duty bound to give to the poor, but they rob them through simony and their hankering after money, selling the grace of the Holy Spirit. Some are so mean that they are unwilling to give to the needy the very things I have given them freely so that they might give them to you—unless their hands are filled [with money] or they are plentifully supplied with gifts [in return]. They love their subjects for what they can get from them, and no more. They spend all the goods of the Church on nothing but clothes for their bodies. They go about fancily dressed, not like clerics and religious, but like lords or court lackeys. They are concerned about having grand horses, many gold and silver vessels, and well-adorned homes. They have and keep what they ought not, all with huge vanity. Their heart babbles out its disordered vanity, and their whole desire is feasting, making a god of their bellies, eating and drinking inordinately. So they soon fall into impure and lustful living.

Woe, woe, to their wretched lives! For what the gentle Word, my only-begotten Son, won with such suffering on the wood of the most holy cross they spend on prostitutes. They devour the souls who were bought with Christ's blood, eating them up in so many wretched ways, and feeding their own children with what belongs to the poor. . . .

122.

I told you that the pearl of justice was luminous in those chosen ones. Now I tell you that the jewel these puny wretches wear over their heart is injustice. This injustice proceeds from and is mounted in their self-centeredness, for because of their selfishness they perpetrate injustice against their own souls and against me, along with their lack of discernment. . . .

Sometimes they administer correction as if to cloak themselves in this little bit of justice. But they will never correct persons of any importance, even though they may be guilty of greater sin than more lowly people, for fear that these might retaliate by standing in their way or deprive them of their rank and their way of living. They will, however, correct the little people, because they are sure these cannot harm them or deprive them of their rank. Such injustice comes from their wretched selfish love for themselves. . . .

123.

What is the source of such filth in their souls? Their own selfish sensuality. Their selfishness has made a lady of their sensuality, and their wretched little souls have become her slaves, whereas I made them to be free by the blood of my Son, when the whole human race was freed from slavery to the devil and his rule. Every person receives this grace, but these whom I have anointed I have freed from the world's service and appointed them to serve me alone, God eternal, by being stewards of the sacraments of holy Church.

I have made them so free, in fact, that it has never been my will, nor is it now, that any civil authority should presume to sit in judgement over them. . . .

My ministers should be standing at the table of the cross in holy desire, nourishing themselves there on the food of souls for my honor. . . .

But instead these have made the taverns their table, and there in public they swear and perjure themselves in sin upon miserable sin, as if they were blind and bereft of the light of reason. They have become beasts in their sinning, lustful in word and deed. They do not so much as know what the Divine Office is, and even if they say it from time to time they are saying it with their tongue while their heart is far from me. They are like criminal gamblers and swindlers: After they have gambled away their own souls into the devils' hands, they gamble away the goods of the Church as well, and they gamble and barter away whatever material goods they have been given in virtue of [my Son's] blood. So the poor go without what is due them, and the Church's needs are not provided for.

Because they have made themselves the devil's temple, they are no longer concerned about my temple. Rather, the things that should go for the adornment of the Church and her temples out of respect for the blood go instead to adorn the houses they live in. And worse: They act like husbands adorning their brides; these incarnate devils use the Church's property to adorn the she-devils with whom they live in sin and indecency. Shamelessly they let them come and stay and go. And while they, miserable devils, stand at the altar to celebrate, it does not even bother them to see their wretched she-devils coming up with their children by the hand, to make their offering with the other people!

O devils and worse than devils! At least let your iniquity be hid from the eyes of your subjects! Then at least, though you would still be offending me and harming yourselves, you would not be hurting your neighbors by actually setting your evil lives before their eyes. For by your example you give them reason not to leave their own sinful ways, but to fall into the same sins as yours and worse. Is this the kind of purity I demand of my ministers when they go to celebrate at the altar? This is the sort of purity they bring: They get up in the morning with their minds contaminated and their bodies corrupt. . . .

124.

. . . these wretches not only do not restrain their weakness; they make it worse by committing that cursed unnatural sin. As if they were blind and stupid, with the light of their understanding extinguished, they do not recognize what miserable filth they are wallowing in. The stench reaches even up to me, supreme Purity, and is so hateful to me that for this sin alone five cities were struck down by my divine judgement. For my divine justice could no longer tolerate it, so despicable to me is this abominable sin. . . .

You know, if you remember well, how before the great Death I showed you how despicable this sin is to me, and how the world is corrupted by it. At that time, when I lifted your spirit up above yourself in holy desire, I showed you the whole world, and in people of almost every walk of life you saw this miserable sin. You saw in that revelation how the devils fled. And you know that your spirit suffered so from the stench that you thought you would surely die. You could see nowhere that you and my other servants could go to escape being touched by this leprosy. It seemed you could not live among the lowly or the great, the old or the young, religious or clerics, superiors or subjects, masters or servants; for they were all contaminated in mind and body by this curse. . . .

So you see, dearest daughter, how abominable this sin is to me in any person. Now imagine how much more hateful it is in those I have called to live celibately. Among these celibates who have been lifted up above the world, some are religious and some are trees planted as my ministers in the mystic body of holy Church. You cannot imagine how much more I despise this sin in these celibates—even more than in ordinary people of the world. They are lamps set on a lampstand, to be stewards of me the true Sun, giving off the light of virtue and of holy and honorable living. But instead they minister in darksomeness. . . .

127.

. . . Do you see, dearest daughter, how much reason I have to grieve over such wretchedness? And how generous I have been with them and how miserly they have been with me? For just as I told you, some of them even lend for usury. Not that they set up shop as public usurers do, but have all sorts of subtle ways of selling time to their neighbors to satisfy their own greed. Now there is nothing in the world that can justify this. Even if it were the smallest of gifts, if their intention is to receive it as the price for the service they have done by lending their goods, this is usury as much as anything else that might be paid for the time [of the loan]. I appointed these wretches to forbid seculars [to practice usury], and here they are doing the same and more. For when someone comes to ask their advice about this matter, because they are guilty of the same sin and have lost the light of reason, the advice they give is darksome, tainted by the passion within their own souls.

This sin and many others are born of the tight, greedy, avaricious heart. One could use the words my Truth said when he entered the temple and found there the sellers and buyers. He chased them out with a whip of cords, saying, "Of my Father's house, which is a house of prayer, you have made a robbers' den."

You see well, sweetest daughter, how true it is that

they have made a robbers' den of my Church, which is a place of prayer. They sell and buy and have made the grace of the Holy Spirit a piece of merchandise. So you see, those who want the high offices and revenues of the Church buy them by bribing those in charge with money and provisions. And those wretches are not concerned about whether [the candidates] are good or bad, but only about pleasing them for love of the gifts they have received. So they make every effort to set these putrid plants in the garden of holy Church, and for this the wretches will give a good report of them to Christ on earth. Thus both use falsehood and deceit against Christ on earth, whereas they ought to behave sincerely and in all truth. But if my Son's vicar [the Pope] becomes aware of their sin he ought to punish them. He should relieve those of office who will not repent and change their evil way of living. As for those who do the bribing, they would do well to receive imprisonment for their bargaining, both to change their sinful ways and that others may see the example and be afraid to do the same thing any more. If Christ on earth does this, he is doing his duty. If he does not, his sin will not go unpunished when it is his turn to give me an account of his little sheep.

Believe me, my daughter. Today this is not done, and this is why such sins and abominations plague my Church. Those who make appointments to high offices do not investigate the lives of those they appoint, to see whether they are good or bad. Or if they do look into anything, they are questioning and asking information of those who are as evil as they are themselves, and these would not give anything but good testimony because they are guilty of the same sin. They are concerned about nothing but the grandeur of rank and nobility and wealth, about knowing polished rhetoric; and worse, they will recommend their candidate by saying he is good looking! Despicable, devilish things! Those who ought to be looking for the beautiful adornment of virtue are concerned about physical beauty! They ought to be searching out the humble poor folk who in their humility avoid high office, but instead they pick those who in their bloated pride go seeking promotions.

They look for learning. Now learning in itself is good and perfect when the scholar is at the same time good and honorable and humble. But if learning is combined with pride, indecency, and sinful living, it is venomous and understands nothing but the letter of Scripture. It understands in darkness, for it has lost the light of reason and its eye for understanding is clouded over. It was in this light, enlightened by faith, that Holy Scripture was proclaimed and understood by those of whom I have told you more at length elsewhere. So you see, knowledge is good in itself, but not in those who do not use it as it should be used, and it will be a punishing fire to those who do not amend their lives. . . .

. . . So many rebellions has my bride suffered that she should not have had! They ought to let the dead be buried by the dead. As for themselves, they should follow the teaching of my Truth and fulfill my will for them by doing what I appointed them to do. But they do exactly the opposite, for they set themselves to burying dead and passing things in their disordered care and affection, stealing their business from the hands of worldly folk. This displeases me and is harmful to holy Church. They ought to leave these things to the worldly, and let the one dead thing bury the other; that is, let those take care of worldly, temporal things who are appointed to do so.

I said, "Let the one dead thing bury the other," and I mean "dead" to be understood in two ways. The first is administering and governing bodily things in deadly sin because of one's disordered care and affection. The other stems from the fact that because these things are tangible it is the body's function [to care for them]; and the body is a dead thing because it has no life in itself except as it derives it from the soul, and it shares in life only so long as the soul remains in it.

Therefore, these anointed ones of mine, who ought to be living as angels, should leave dead things to the dead and concern themselves with governing souls. For souls are living things and do not ever die so far as their existence is concerned. So they should govern them and administer to them the sacraments and gifts and graces of the Holy Spirit, and pasture them on spiritual food through their own good and holy lives. In this way will my house be a house of prayer, abounding in grace and filled with their virtues. . . .

Christine de Pizan (1364–1430?)

Christine de Pizan has been called "France's first woman of letters," "the first feminist," and similar titles of precedence. Such titles are generally problematic because they erase the contributions of earlier women as writers and feminists, but there are some grounds for applying these titles to Christine. (She is properly called "Christine" alone, consistent with medieval nomenclature, like "Marsilius" of Padua.) Christine may well have been the first French woman (or man) to make her living as a writer, and the first woman to confront directly, through sustained works of literature and theory, the misogynist ideas and practices of the male intellectual establishment of her time. A woman of outstanding talent and courage, she was a pivotal figure in her time in the arena of gender struggle and in changes in the theory of the state, secularization of political thought, codification of military practice, development of international law, and the origins of peace theory.

Christine de Pizan was born in Venice in 1364. Her father, Thomas de Pizan, was court physician and astrologer to King Charles V of France, and in her youth she led a comfortable and happy life at court. Her father encouraged her in learning and writing, as did later her husband, Étienne du Castel, who was a secretary to Charles V. She bore three children, of whom two, a daughter named Marie and a son named Jean, survived. Her protected life was brought to an early end, however, by the successive deaths of Charles V (1380), Christine's father (1387), and her husband (1390). Charles V's death deprived her father and husband of their positions, and their untimely deaths in turn left Christine, her mother, her children, and a niece without a secure means of support and vulnerable to lawyers and creditors from whom it took years to secure much of her inheritance.

Christine may have supported herself at first as a manuscript copyist, thus learning many aspects of the process of book production. She began writing poetry as a personal consolation in the years after her husband's death, but as her own works won favor she turned to writing as a source of livelihood. She was able to secure the patronage of various members of the royal family and nobility of France, England, and Italy, who provided her with handsome gifts in return for her books, some of which were spontaneous offerings, while others, such as her biography of Charles V, were specifically commissioned. Christine was thus one of the first writers to earn her living primarily through her writings, not otherwise supported by a family estate, an established

profession, or a court or church sinecure. Her position as an independent intellectual and promoter of her own literary and political works was extraordinary for her time and a model for the development of professional writers in modern times.

Though Christine wrote from necessity and her works give evidence of the pressures imposed by her circumstances, her passionate involvement in many of the literary and political issues of her time determined the design and content of what she wrote. The era she lived in was one of the most tumultuous in the history of France, and as the ravages of internal and external conflicts intensified before her eyes, she withdrew eventually from secular life into the cloister. She spent the last decade of her life in a convent, where she died about the year 1430.

Christine wrote in her autobiographical Lavision-Christine, about the year 1406: "Nature willed that from my studies and experience there be born new works, and commanded: 'Take up your tools and hammer out on the anvil the material I shall give you, as lasting as iron and impervious to fire and everything else, and forge objects of delight. When your children were in your womb, you experienced great pain bringing them into the world. Now it is my wish that new works be born from your memory in joy and delight, which will carry your name forever all over the world, and to future generations of princes.'" This brief passage, like many others in Christine's writings, is rich in complex images and meanings, forging links between nature and learning, work and childbirth, body and mind, the pain of labor and the joy and delight of creation. Significantly, Christine attributes the source of her intellectual creations to "Nature" rather than "God" and portrays them as "objects of delight" rather than moral strictures.

Christine's hope that her works would survive as "objects of delight" in future generations has had an uneven fate. Her writings were well known in aristocratic circles in her own day and later enjoyed printings and translations bringing them to a wider literate audience in France, England, Italy, and other countries, particularly in the fifteenth and sixteenth centuries. But there were long periods in which they fell into total obscurity, interspersed with occasional revivals. Yet even centuries of obscurity did not spell the disappearance of her ideas and influence. Just as ideas are never created "de novo," out of nothing, and Christine drew hers from many written and unwritten sources that came her way, so her own words and thought became part of the intellectual subsoil of what today is called "modernity."

Christine and her significance were "rediscovered" by scholars in the nineteenth century, but she remained little known through most of the twentieth century. Over the past two decades, however, her work has achieved a level of recognition, attention, and critical scrutiny unusual for any woman writer of political theory, and certainly exceptional for any medieval woman writer. Particularly in recent years, many new editions and translations have appeared, many doctoral dissertations have been devoted to her works, and several new studies have been published addressing specifically her political ideas. She is the first woman theorist to be included in the Cambridge Texts in the History of Political Thought (The Book of the Body Politic, 1994).

Christine is best known today for her extraordinary Book of the City of Ladies (1405) and its sequel, the Book of Three Virtues (1405); and for her interventions in the debates surrounding Jean de Meun's Romance of the Rose (1401–1403). In the City of Ladies, Christine ponders the defamation of women and the hostility of the intellectual establishment to women's learning and calls up three allegorical figures—Reason, Rectitude, and Justice—to aid her in building a society in which the virtue, wisdom, and competence of women would be recognized, encouraged, and defended. Christine's "feminism" has been questioned by Sheila Delaney and other scholars who find her ideas on women's rights and participation in governance incompatible with contemporary feminist principles. But for Sarah Hanley and others, she was the heroic challenger of the male oligopoly of learning and power, who "instigated a long debate over political identity and the right to rule" and validated women's rule by historical example and legal and political argument (1998: 297-304).

Christine was also widely known in her own time and in later centuries for many other writings of political significance. Among these we may note her long poetic works, extended political allegories, such as The Letter of Othea to Hector (1401), The Book of the Long Road to Learning (1403), and The Book of the Mutation of Fortune (1404). Biography and autobiography too were vehicles for Christine's political commentary, particularly her biography of Charles V (1404) and Lavision-Christine (1405–1406). Christine also wrote directly and at length on topics conventionally recognized in the canon of political theory: the state and its institutions, the classes of society, war and just war, arms and chivalry, the nature and conditions of peace, the responsibilities of political authority, the horrors of civil war, and the causes of popular rebellion. Her works on these topics include among others: the Letter to Queen Isabel (1405), The Book of the Body Politic (ca. 1407), The Book of Feats of Arms and Chivalry (1410), the Lamentation on the Woes of France (1410), and The Book of Peace (1414).

There has been much debate about the "originality" of Christine's works. Many of the prose works were certainly composed in large part of materials taken from other sources, sometimes nearly word for word, sometimes rewritten to serve Christine's purposes. This was a common practice in her day, when "plagiarism" was not considered improper and the authority of ancient or learned sources was more prized than the inventiveness of contemporary writers. Christine herself explained her practice repeatedly using the metaphor of building an edifice, or a city, out of the timber or bricks and mortar of learning. As Charity Willard has noted, Christine argued in her biography of Charles V that, just as the worker in architecture or masonry uses stones and other materials which he has not made himself to build a house or a castle according to his design, so she uses whatever is appropriate to the end her imagination has devised.

These remarks suggest, however, that the medieval propensity to such borrowings was coming under challenge in Christine's time. That she was aware of an incipient demand for innovation or originality is evident from her comment on this subject in The Book of the City of Ladies: "For it is not such a great feat of mastery to study and learn some field of knowledge already discovered by someone else as it is to discover by oneself some new and unknown thing" (I.33.1). And while the overarching metaphor of The City of Ladies was that of building a city out of the materials and tools of learning, from which Christine still drew liberally, her own design of the whole, as well as revisions of the parts, made this a work of astonishing and daring originality. The book has been described as an early "utopia" (preceding by more than a century Thomas More's Utopia), offering a unique vision of a separatist women's society outside the confines of religious communities and upholding women's rights and abilities as rulers and intellectuals.

The selections included here, which exemplify Christine's ideas on the state, governance, class divisions, justice, and peace, are drawn from The Book of the Body Politic, translated by Kate Langdon Forhan (1994).

BAC

Sources and Suggested Readings

Brabant, Margaret, ed. Politics, Gender, and Genre: The Political Thought of Christine de Pizan. Boulder, Colo.: Westview Press, 1992.

Carroll, Berenice A. "Christine de Pizan and the Origins of Peace Theory." In Women Writers and the Early Modern British Political Tradition, ed. Hilda L.

Smith, 22–39. Cambridge: Cambridge University Press, 1998.

Christine de Pizan. *The Book of Deeds of Arms and Chivalry.* Trans. Sumner Willard, ed. Charity Cannon Willard. University Park, Pa.: Pennsylvania State University Press, 1999.

———. *The Book of the Body Politic* [1407]. Trans. Kate Langdon Forhan. New York: Cambridge University Press, 1994.

———. *The Book of the City of Ladies* [1405]. Trans. Earl Jeffrey Richards; with a foreword by Natalie Zeman Davis. New York: Persea Book, rev. ed., 1982.

———. *Lavision-Christine* [1405–1406]. Ed. Sister Mary Louis Towner. Washington, D.C.: Catholic University of America, 1932.

———. *Le Livre de la Paix* [1414]. Ed. Charity Cannon Willard. The Hague: Mouton, 1958.

———. *A Medieval Woman's Mirror of Honor: The Treasury of the City of Ladies* [*Le Livre de Trois Vertues*, 1405]. Trans. and ed. Charity Cannon Willard. New York: Persea, 1989.

———. *The Writings of Christine de Pizan.* Ed. Charity Cannon Willard. New York: Persea Books, 1994.

Green, Karen. "Christine de Pisan and Thomas Hobbes." *Philosophical Quarterly* 44, 177 (October 1994): 456–75.

Hanley, Sarah. "The Politics of Identity and Monarchic Government in France: The Debate over Female Exclusion." In *Women Writers and the Early Modern British Political Tradition*, ed. Hilda L. Smith, 289–304. Cambridge: Cambridge University Press, 1998.

Hicks, Eric, ed. *Le Débat sur le Roman de la Rose: Christine de Pisan, Jean Gerson, Jean de Montreuil, Gontier et Pierre Col.* Paris: H. Champion, 1977.

Kennedy, Angus J. *Christine de Pizan: A Bibliographical Guide.* 2nd ed. London: 1994.

Quilligan, Maureen. *The Allegory of Female Authority: Christine de Pizan's Cité des Dames.* Ithaca: Cornell University Press, 1991.

Willard, Charity C. *Christine de Pizan. Her Life and Works: A Biography.* New York: Persea Books, 1984.

Yenal, Edith. *Christine de Pisan: A Bibliography.* Metuchen, N.J.: Scarecrow Press, 1982.

Zimmerman, Margarete, and Dina De Rentiis, eds. *The City of Scholars: New Approaches to Christine de Pizan.* Berlin: Walter de Gruyter, 1994.

The Book of the Body Politic (1407)

Part One. On Princes

Here begins the Book of the Body Politic which speaks of virtue and manners and is divided into three parts. The first part is addressed to princes, the second to knights and nobles, and the third to the universal people.

Chapter 1. The first chapter gives the description of the Body Politic

If it is possible for vice to give birth to virtue, it pleases me in this part to be as passionate as a woman, since many men assume that the female sex does not know how to silence the abundance of their spirits. Come boldly, then and be shown the many inexhaustible springs and fountains of my courage, which cannot be stanched when it expresses the desire for virtue.

Oh, Virtue, noble and godly, how can I dare to flaunt myself by speaking of you, when I know that my understanding neither comprehends nor expresses you well?

But what comforts me and makes me bold is that I sense that you are so kind that it will not displease you if I speak of you, not about what is most subtle, but only in those areas which I can conceive or comprehend. So, I will speak about you as far as it concerns the teaching of good morals, by speaking first of the industry and rule of life for our superiors; that is, princes, whose majesties I humbly supplicate not to take wrongly nor disdain such a small intelligence as mine, that such a humble creature dares undertake to speak about the way of life for higher ranks. And may it please them to remember the teaching of the Philosopher, who said, "Do not disdain the wise words of the insignificant despite your own high position." Next by the grace of God, I hope to speak on the manner of life of knights and nobles. And then, thirdly, on the whole universal people.

These three types of estate ought to be one polity like a living body according to the words of Plutarch who in a letter which he sent to the Emperor Trajan compared the polity to a body having life. There the prince and princes hold the place of the head in as much as they are or should be sovereign and from them ought to come particular institutions just as from the mind of a person springs forth the external deeds that the limbs achieve. The knights and nobles take the place of the hands and arms. Just as a person's arms have to be strong in order to endure labor, so they have the burden of defending the law of the prince and the polity. They are also the hands because, just as the hands push aside harmful things, so they ought push all harmful and useless things aside. The other kinds of people are like the belly, the feet and the legs. Just as the belly receives all that the head and the limbs prepare for it, so, too, the activity of the prince and nobles ought to return to the public good, as will be better explained later. Just as the legs and feet sustain the human body, so, too, the laborers sustain all the other estates.

Chapter 2. Which describes how virtuous felicity is symbolized

First we have to discuss virtue, to the benefit of the rule of life for the three different estates. Virtue must regulate human life in all its works. Without it, no one can have honor. Whatever the degree of honor, Valerius says, honor is the plentiful food of virtue. And on this subject, Aristotle said, "Reverence is due to honor as a testimony of virtue," which means that honor must not be attributed but to a virtuous person, because he is not speaking about the powerful nor about the rich, but the virtuous. According to him, only the good are honored. Nothing is more desired by noble hearts than honor. As he says himself in the fourth book of the *Ethics*, neither power nor riches is without honor. Now it is true that kings and powerful princes are especially invested with honor, and as a consequence, virtue, so it is appropriate to distinguish the aspects of virtue. In chapter 20 of his book, *The City of God*, St. Augustine says that the philosophers say that virtue is the objective of all human good and evil. That is, human happiness comes from being virtuous.

Now it is fitting that there is great delight in happiness, otherwise it would not be happiness, and this joy and happiness ancient philosophers described and symbolized in this manner: Felicity is a very beautiful and refined queen seated on a royal throne, and the virtues are seated around her and look at her, waiting to hear her commands, to serve her, and to obey. She commands Prudence to inquire how she can stay healthy and in good condition so that she can reign a long time. And she commands Justice to do everything that she should and keep the laws so that there will be peace. And she commands Courage that if any pain should come to her body, to moderate it by resisting it with virtuous thought. She commands Temperance to take wine, food, and other delectable things in moderation so that anything she takes is for a reason and not to her detriment. This description allows one to understand that to be virtuous is nothing more than to have in one everything that attracts good and which pushes away evil and vice. Thus, in order to govern the body of the public polity well, it is necessary for the head to be healthy, that is, virtuous. Because if it is ill, the whole body will feel it. . . .

Chapter 8. Of the observance towards God and toward the law which the prince ought to practice

The good prince who loves God will know his commandments by memory, and how the worthy name of God must not be taken in vain. To this purpose he will proclaim an edict throughout his land, which will forbid on pain of severe punishment anyone swearing on or denying his Creator. Alas, there is great need in France at present for such an edict, because it is horrible that the whole of Christendom has the custom of such disrespect toward the Savior. One can scarcely hear any other language, whether it be in jest or another manner of speech, but everyone swears horribly at every word about the torments of the passion of our redeemer, and they forsake and deny him. I believe that the pagans of old would not have treated their gods and idols so!

All these things the good prince ought to forbid, because they are opposed to and disapproved by the Christian religion and could be the cause of the wrath of God and the subversion of kingdoms and countries where they take place, as some prophesies tell. And so, the good prince who loves God will carefully observe and keep the divine law and holy institutions in everything that is worthy and devout (which I will not discuss for reasons of brevity, and also because most people would prefer to hear of less boring things). But the good prince that keeps and observes these things ought to believe firmly that God will guard, defend, and increase him in virtue of soul and body. And why should he not have faith in God, the living, all powerful, and just, when the pagans trusted that their needs would be met generously, because of the worship that they gave to their gods and their idols? It appears, by what Valerius says, that the city of Rome desired to serve the gods conscientiously, and he said, "Our city has always set aside everything for the service of the gods," even those things that concerned the honor of the sovereign majesty, that is, the emperors, because they had, he says, firm belief that in doing thus they acquired the rule and the governance of the world, and also because of this "the emperors of our city have generally not abandoned the constant service of holy things."

This suffices for the first point of the first part, on the virtue of the prince, which should be founded on and should demonstrate the fact that he loves and serves God.

Chapter 9. How a good prince ought to resemble a good shepherd

Now we have discussed the first point on which the goodness of the prince ought principally to be founded, so next we shall speak of the second point, that is, that the good prince ought especially to love the public good and its augmentation more than his own good, according to the teaching of Aristotle's *Politics*, which says that tyranny is when the prince prefers his own good over the public good. This is against royal lordship as well, for he ought to care more for the benefit of his people than his own. Now he shall be advised on how to demonstrate this love.

The good prince who loves his country will guard it carefully, following the example of the good shepherd. As he guards his sheep from wolves and evil beasts, and keeps them clean and healthy so that they can increase and be fruitful and yield their fleece whole, sound, and well nourished by the land on which they are fed and kept, so that the shepherd will be well paid by their fleece, shorn in time and in season. But the rich good shepherd who gives them to others to keep because he cannot take care of all his flocks himself, provides himself with good and capable help. So he takes good, careful servants, wise and hard working in their craft, whom he understands and knows are loyal and prefer his interest. So he orders that those servants be equipped with good strong dogs with iron collars, well trained by being brought to the field to chase off wolves. So they let them loose at night in the fold so that thieves coming for the sheep are attacked by them. By day, they keep them tied to their belts while the sheep graze peacefully in the fields. But if these servants feel any fear of wolves or evil animals coming out of the woods or mountains, they then unleash the dogs, and let them run after them and nip at their heels. And to give the dogs greater boldness against the wolf or evil animal the servants run after them with good ironclad staffs. And if any sheep goes out of the flock, the good hounds go after it and, without doing it harm, they bring it back to the flock. In this manner, the wise servants defend and take care of them so well that they yield a good account to the head shepherd.

Just so, the good prince is mindful of the defense and care of his country and people, even though it is impossible in person. In every place he has responsibility, he will always provide himself with very good assistance, in deeds of knighthood and for other things; that is, the brave leaders whom he knows are good and loyal and who love him, such as constables, marshals, admirals and others, to whom he gives responsibility for furnishing other good soldiers, well-taught and experienced in war, whom he binds to him by an oath, not to leave without permission and are so ready to do his business that if needed they will go attack his enemies, so that the country is not despoiled, pillaged, nor the people killed.

This does not mean that the soldiers themselves should pillage and despoil the country like they do in France nowadays when in other countries they dare not do so. It is a great mischief and perversion of law when those who are intended for the defense of the people, pillage, rob, and so cruelly, that truly short of killing them or setting their houses on fire, their enemies could do no worse. This is not the right manner of warfare, which ought to be just and without extortion, and if not, the soldiers and the princes that send them to war are in great peril of the wrath of God falling on them and punishing them severely. Before God, there is no doubt that the justifiable curses of the people, when they have been oppressed too much, can cause evil fortune to fall, as, for example, one finds in many places in Holy Scripture; for everyone ought to know that God is just, and all this is the fault of an evil order.

For if soldiers were well paid, one could restrict the main pain of punishment to take nothing without paying for it, and by this means they could find provisions and everything that they needed economically and plentifully. It is too greatly astonishing how people can live under such a law without any compassion from the soldiers for the pity of their life. But the Holy Spirit, father of the poor, will visit them! Now, if a shepherd had a dog that ran after his sheep, he would hit him with his staff. It is not a thing a good prince who loves God and his people should bear, and just as one unleashed the dogs at night in the fold to keep them from thieves, so must the head keep watchmen and spies along the borders so that the country and the people are not surprised by thieves or by some trickery, and so that they can know the plans of their enemies.

The soldiers ought to have yet another duty. Just as the good dog brings back the strayed sheep, so they ought to bring back the common people or others who from fear or dread or evil want to rebel and take the wrong side. They ought to bring them back to the right path either by threats or by taking good care of them. Although it displeases some and surprises others, I compare the noble office of arms to the nature of the dog because, truly, the dog naturally has many characteristics which the good man-at-arms ought to have. The dog loves his master marvelously and is very loyal to him. And the man-at-arms should be also. He is tough and exposes himself to death for his master and when he is committed to guarding any place he is very alert and has excellent hearing in order to run after evil doers or thieves. He will not bite the friends of his master but naturally sniffs at them, nor does he bite the neighbors nor those of the household where he is fed, but he guards them instead. He is very tough and fights with great skill. He has a good understanding, knowledge, and is very amiable to those who do him kindness. And all these characteristics are those of the good soldier. . . .

Chapter 11. The love that the prince ought to have for his subjects

Now let us examine a little the rights of the prince according to the law; that is, whether the good prince can raise any new taxes or subsidies above his usual revenue over his demesne for any reason. It seems to me that the laws give enough freedom and permit him to do so for some cause. For example, to defend the land from his enemies if he is attacked by war, for which he ought to have paid soldiers for the defense of the country. Also for marrying his children, or paying ransom for them if they should be captured. And in this case especially, the good prince can raise a new tax over and above his natural demesne over his subjects without infringing on the law.

But this should be done compassionately and discretely [*sic*] so [as] to hinder the poor less, and without taking more than what is necessary for the particular cause, such as war or for whatever it was set. And the rich, in this case, ought to support the poor, and not exempt the rich, as is done nowadays, leaving the poor the more heavily burdened.

I dare say, no matter who is displeased, saving their reverence, it is a marvelous right that the rich and high officials of the king or princes who have their rank and power as a gift of the king and princes are able to carry the burden, are exempt from taxes, and the poor who have nothing from the king have to pay. Is it not reasonable if I have given a great gift to my servant, and give him a rich livelihood and his estate, and it happened that I had some need, that he comes to my aid more than the one who has had nothing from me? It is a strange custom that is used nowadays in this kingdom in the setting of taxes. But if it were changed, it must be uniform, not that some of the rich pay and others not, for this would bring envy, because some would despise those who paid as a form of servitude. If everyone paid, no one would be reproached. Nevertheless I do not mean that those who fought for the defense of the country should not be exempt. I say things for the poor. Compassion moves me because their tears and moans come bitterly forth. There are some who come to pay this money imposed on them and then they and their poor household starves afterwards, and sells their beds and other poor possessions cheaply and for nothing. . . .

. . . If I were allowed to say something more about this, how much more could I say; but the knowledge of these things does not please the evil ministers who have enriched themselves, and they will reprimand me. I could tell them without arrogance something

that Euripides, the great poet, said to the Athenian who asked him to quote a sentence from the tragedy that he had written. "Tragedy," said Valerius, "is a way of writing that represents misdeeds done on the orders of the polity; either by the community or by princes." He said that he did not write his sayings in order to reprimand nor to be reprimanded, but in order to teach us to live well. About the poet, Valerius said that he would not dishonor himself by obeying the words of the people and ignoring his own. . . .

Chapter 19. How the good prince ought to love justice

According to my judgment, we have sufficiently discussed the subject of the first two points and the branches that descend from them, on how the natural and non-tyrannical good prince ought to establish and build his government, as we promised before. First he ought to love and fear God above all else. Secondly, he loves and cares for the public good of his land and country more than his own good. Now it remains to speak of the third point, which is that he ought to keep and maintain justice. It is appropriate to speak first on what justice is. Afterwards, how to keep it is necessary, and how the ancients were well trained to keep it. We will use appropriate examples of things as we did previously.

"Justice," said Aristotle, "is a measure which renders to each his due," and much more could be said in describing this virtue. But on this subject I have spoken elsewhere, especially in the *Book of Human Wisdom*, so I will discuss this the more briefly at present so as to present some examples. The good prince ought to keep justice in such fashion that no favoritism will lead him to impede or to destroy it. Our ancestors loved justice so much that they did not spare even their own children. There was once an emperor who proclaimed an edict that anyone who broke a certain law would lose his two eyes. When it was broken by his own son, rather than blind his own heir so that he could not govern the republic, he found a remedy to satisfy the punishment without preventing the son from governing one day. But this remedy was too pitiful: his son had one of his eyes put out, and he put out his own, as the other. I say that justice was kept more rigorously than it is now. . . .

But to pass from examples of great rigor, let us discuss how the good prince keeps justice and what is necessary for him to do so. First, and principally, to do this he ought to be provided with wise and prudent men and good councillors, who love his soul and honor and the good of the country more than their own benefit. But I fear that presently there are not very many! If the prince has wise councillors he can maintain the rule of justice and other particular laws, and increase and multiply the virtue, strength, power and wealth of his country. Oh, who is the prince who can sufficiently deserve the wise, loyal, and good counsellor because of the great good that comes from following his advice if he wants to believe him? Is it not said in the *History of the Romans* that the wise Scipio Nasica (who was of the lineage of the other noble Scipios who were so valiant in warfare) despite the fact that he did not live by his weapons like the others, he was so wise and prudent in the council and governing of the republic that he did as much as the others did by their weapons?

Using his lively intelligence he fought against some of the powerful Romans who wanted to overpower the Senate and the good of the people. Valerius said about him that he deserved no less praise in his "coat of peace" than other warriors deserved in their "coat of arms" because he defended the city from many great problems and much good resulted because of him.

Chapter 20. What councillors the prince ought to have

Now it is appropriate to consider what people the prince should choose as his councillors. Should he choose from among the young? No, because they counselled Jeroboam badly in the past as they have many others. Therefore they should be chosen from the old, the most wise and experienced, because they are more capable and ready to advise than the young. It is necessary that the loyal councillor be well-informed on the things about which he counsels. He should not believe lightly in a thing that appears good before proving its truth, examining and inquiring. At first glance a thing may appear to be what it is not. In the *Rhetoric*, Aristotle said that the old and elderly did not have the habit of believing lightly, because they had been defrauded in their lives many times. They do not make decisions on doubtful things, but often interpret things for the worst, because many times they have seen the worst happen, thus they will not give advice hastily. They do not put great hopes on a little foundation and little evidence, because many times they have seen things come to pass differently from how one thought they would, and so they will not advise great undertakings without serious consideration. Most commonly these things are the opposite in the young, as other habits are naturally more weighty in the old.

But I do not say that all the old are wise! For Aristotle says that there are two kinds of age, one which fol-

lows after a well ordered and temperate youth, which Tully (Cicero) praises in his book *On Old Age*. The other is age which comes after a wasted and dissolute youth, and it is subject to many miseries and is not worth recommending. Thus I have said that the prince ought to choose councillors from the old and the wise. To speak more of them; although they do not have great bodily strength, like the young, all the same, they are greater in virtue and discreet in advice, which is more useful and more profitable than bodily strength, and is so much more to be praised. And the most noble virtues are understanding, discretion, and knowledge rather than strength of the body. Where the wisdom and counsel of the old and wise are followed, the royal majesties, cities, politics, and public affairs are well governed and sustained, which are often destroyed by the young, as Tully says, and which appears clear in many histories. Thus while age takes away bodily strength it abounds in strength of intelligence and understanding, which are more praiseworthy things. . . .

Chapter 21. How a good prince, despite being good natured and kind, ought to be feared

The nature of justice and what it serves and to what extent is well known and understood; it is appropriate for the good prince to punish (or have punished) evildoers. And so I will pass by this for a time and proceed to that which also befits the good prince: The virtue of justice, which renders to each that which is his due, according to his power. If he keeps this rule, which is just, he will not fail to do equity in everything, and thus, he will render to himself his due. For it is rational that he has the same right he gives to everyone, which means that he would be obeyed and feared by right and by reason, as is appropriate to the majesty of a prince.

For in whatever land or place where a prince is not feared, there is no true justice. How it is appropriate for the prince to be feared is shown by the worthy man Clearcus who was Duke of Lacedemonia (which is a large part of Greece where there once was a marvelously valiant people). This duke was so chivalrous and great a warrior that his people were more afraid of their prince than death and their enemies. Because of his words and also the punishment that he gave malefactors and cowards, they gave themselves without sparing, by which they achieved marvelous things. There is no doubt that the good prince ought to be feared despite being gentle and benign. His kindness ought to be considered a thing of grace which one ought to particularly heed rather than scorn. It is for this reason the ancients painted the goddess of lordship as a seated lady of very high rank on a royal throne, holding in one hand an olive branch and in the other a naked sword, showing that rule must include kindness and mercy as well as justice and power. . . .

Chapter 22. How the good prince ought to use the good counsel of the wise

We have said how the prince honors the wise. Now we will describe how he follows their advice. A knight, captain called Municius, as Valerius recounts, wanted to give thanks to Fabius, by whom he and his army were saved. "Fair Lords," he said to his knights, "I have often heard say that he is first in action who knows how to give good advice, and he is second who follows good advice, but the one who neither acknowledges advice nor follows it is useless. And because of this, fair lords," he said, "nature removes from us the first, that is, we are not wise enough to give advice, because we have not lively intelligence enough. Therefore let us do the second, that is, obey Fabius who is wise and gives good counsel." And so they did, and because of his wisdom, they were victorious in battle.

And on the subject of believing the wise and following their advice, [Aristotle's] great *Dialectic* says that one ought to believe each expert in his art. This means that the good prince ought to consult a variety of people according to the variety of things to do. For the governance of justice and the diverse important cases which he hears, he ought not to take advice from his soldiers nor his knights, but from jurists and clerks of this science. The same with warfare; not from clerks but from knights, and similarly in other matters. As Valerius said about Quintus Scaevola, despite his being a very wise jurist and interpreter of the law, every time someone came to him to ask advice on any custom of the offices of Rome, he sent those who asked to Furius or to Castellanus, who were experts on these customs, even if by chance he knew them just as well. But he wanted everyone to take care of the branch of knowledge to which one was devoted, no more. By which fact, said Valerius, he confirmed his authority, more because he did not claim for himself any office, than because of the superiority of his knowledge. This is unlike those who out of envy of others and arrogance want to meddle in everything.

The good prince should follow the advice of the wise in order to do justice and equity to himself and to others, ensure that those he has commissioned to office are not corrupted nor of evil life, and he should see to it that his judges do not favor one party more than another, as was discussed before, and ensure that the powerful are not spared more than the humble. Yet commonly the rich are favored over the poor, which is against God, against right, and against reason. Anacharsis, the philosopher compared law to spider webs, and said that the spider webs never caught fat flies nor

wasps, but catch little flies and frail butterflies, while letting strong birds go, which often destroy them when they fly through. So it is with the law, because the great and powerful often break it and pass through without fear, but the little flies are caught and trapped. This commonly happens to the poor and humble people because of the avarice of ministers of justice. And on this Pericles (who was a wise man and of great authority in the city of Athens, and the most virtuous as Tully tells us in his *On Duties*), said that whoever administers justice should have not only continent hands and tongue but also his eyes, which means that a judge ought to keep from receiving gifts which corrupt human judgment. Also he should keep himself both from talking too much and from incontinence of the flesh, for the common people take the life of the powerful as an example.

Chapter 23. How the good prince ought to observe the actions of his officers

. . . From this we have learned that in the well governed republic certain persons should be chosen from any rank, according to their proper position, as shown before. This means that soldiers and others who belong to that group are those who are capable for military offices; and clerks and students are appropriate for the speculative sciences, philosophy, and liberal arts, likewise for other offices, as Tully said. And the good prince ought to see them as a necessity, for the honor and glory of the kingdom, the land, and the country increases most through an abundance of clerks and wise scholars, because he is well advised by them, as I said before. On which Plato said (according to the first book of the *Consolation* by Boethius), the republic will be very happy if the wise govern it, or else if the governors of princes study wisdom. Through this, the whole community would obey the laws and rules of reason. And thus, as I have already often said, it would be appropriate to get rid of the presumption of many who desire honors without being worthy of them, so that the worthy are honored and receive them, and the unworthy reform themselves. And the worthy and unworthy are discerned by such practices, as is ordained by study of the sciences. . . .

Part Two. On Knights and Nobles

Here begins the second part of the book, which addresses chivalrous nobles.

Chapter 1. The first chapter describes how these nobles are the arms and hands of the body politic

Having concluded speaking to princes whom we

described according to Plutarch as the head of the living image of the body politic and exhorting them to virtuous life, it is appropriate in this second part of the present book to keep our promise and speak of the arms and hands of this image, which according to Plutarch, are the nobles, knights, and all those of their estate. In order to follow the style already begun, we ought to discuss their introduction to virtue and good manners, and particularly to deeds of chivalry, for they are responsible for guarding the public, according to the writing of the authors.

While the same virtue is just as appropriate and necessary for the ordinary person, the simple knight, or the noble, as for princes, nevertheless, the estates differ in their way of life, in their conversation, and kinds of activity; thus it is suitable for my treatment of the subject to differ as well. The thing that is appropriate for the prince to do is not appropriate for the simple knight or noble, and likewise the opposite. But there is no doubt that one can speak the same to nobles as to princes when it concerns the aforementioned virtues. This means that it is also their part to love God and fear Him above all else, to care for the public good for which they were established, to preserve and love justice according to their competences; just as it is for princes and other human beings. To be humane, liberal and merciful, to love the wise and good and to govern by their advice, and likewise they should have all the other virtues, which I do not think I will describe for them, as it suffices to have described them once. What I have said before concerning the virtues serves each estate in the polity, and each individual person, therefore I will not proceed much longer in this form. For it is sufficient to speak of the manner in which everyone ought to do his own part in the order that God has established, that is, nobles do as nobles should, the populace does as it is appropriate for them, and everyone should come together as one body of the same polity, to live justly and in peace as they ought. . . .

Chapter 5. How there are six good conditions that are necessary for nobles and knights, and the first of the six

It seems to me that according to the writings of the authors on the manners of noblemen, six conditions are especially necessary if they desire honor due for their merits. Otherwise their nobility is nothing but a mockery. The first is that they ought to love arms and the art of them perfectly, and they ought to practice that work. The second condition is that they ought to be very bold, and have such firmness and constancy in their courage that they never flee nor run from battles out of fear of death, nor spare their blood nor life, for the good of their prince and the safe keeping of their

country and the republic. Otherwise they will endure capital punishment through sentence of the law, and be dishonored forever.

Thirdly, they ought to give heart and steadiness to each other, counselling their companions to do well, and be firm and steadfast. The fourth is to be truthful and to uphold their fealty and oath. Fifthly, they ought to love and desire honor above all worldly things. Sixthly, they ought to be wise and crafty against their enemies and in all deeds of arms. To those who observe them and keep these conditions well there will be honor. But it is no doubt more difficult to do these things than it is to speak of them! Therefore, Aristotle said that the greatest honor is found where the greatest difficulty is.

On the first condition that the noble ought to have, which is to love and practice arms, and keep them right, we can give the examples of many noble knights. But since we have begun with the history of the Romans, let us continue with them, for it seems to me that they particularly loved warfare, and as a consequence were very noble (that is, the good ones who are mentioned in the writings of ancient authors where the deeds are told). And although they loved arms well, they also observed knightly discipline, that is they kept right in suitable things by rules, so that they failed in nothing. Those who broke the established rules were punished. Valerius said that the discipline of chivalry, that is keeping the rules and order appropriate to it, was the highest honor and firm foundation of the empire of Rome. Moreover, he said that they won their greatest victories, they secured the state, and the certain position of happy peace and tranquility because they kept their discipline well. . . .

Chapter 9. On the third good condition that knights and captains ought to have

It commonly happens that a person who has been instructed on or taught an art or custom, works hard and takes trouble to teach others, and incline them to the same thing; therefore, the sages say, "If you keep company with the good, you will come to resemble them, but if you often see the evil, you will become like them." And so if one desires to be master of an art or a science, it is necessary to associate with the masters and practitioners of whatever one desires to do. For as will be described in the last part of this book, one ought to believe every expert in his own art. On our subject, that is the third condition that the good knight or soldiers ought to have, as we have discussed in the beginning of this second part, any nobleman in arms ought to honor and emulate the good and noble both in the theory and practice of this science.

That I call it "science" could seem to be an error to

some, but it seems to me (to speak clearly without quibbling over subtleties), anything which has correct rules of order and measure that ought to be kept can be called science. And there is nothing in the world in which it is more necessary to keep measure and order than military activity, otherwise in battle everything is confusion, as we know from experience. Vegetius wrote his own book called *The Book of the Science and Art of Chivalry* where he speaks of the rules that ought to be kept. And to prove that it is true that there is no rational art where rules are more necessary, he quotes the very noble knight Scipio Africanus, saying, "The greatest shame in the activity of knighthood is to say I don't believe it." Something ought only to be done after such good advice and counsel and for such good reasons that it could not be a problem of believing or not; because there could be no room for doubt in battle. This saying is confirmed by the aforementioned Vegetius in the first book of *Chivalry*. In other things, if one errs one can correct the error or fault, but incorrect orders and misconduct in battle can not be rectified because the misdeed is immediately punished. If such a one dies dishonorably, or flees, or falls into slavery, it is fitting if he is captured and treated harshly because such things are more painful than death to the courageous.

And because we have entered into the chapter where we hope to discuss how good soldiers ought to encourage one another to be valiant, and good, and to have the manners and morals [moeurs] they ought (which words are particularly and principally appropriate for the instruction of leaders and captains of armies and battles), let us tell more about the valiant prince Scipio, mentioned above and what he said to his knights. He said that no one ought to fight his enemies, that is, attack them, without just cause. But if the cause is just, they ought to not wait until they are attacked, for in a just cause, right gives greater boldness. And in such a case a man ought to fight securely, but not unless he is forced to fight. But in the case where he is attacked, if he does not defend himself, it is shameful because it would be cowardice and show little confidence in good fortune, which would be bad. . . .

Part Three. On the Common People

Here begins the third part of this book, which is addressed to the universal people.

Chapter 1. The first chapter discusses how the estates must unite and come together

In the first part of this book concerning the instruction of princes, we depicted the aforementioned prince

or princes as the head of the body politic, as planned before. Thereafter followed the second part, on the education of nobles and knights, which are the arms and the hands. In this part, with God's help, let us continue with what we can pluck from the authorities on this subject of the life of the body of the aforementioned polity, which means the whole of the people in common, described as the belly, legs, and feet, so that the whole be formed and joined in one whole living body, perfect and healthy. For just as the human body is not whole, but defective and deformed when it lacks any of its members, so the body politic cannot be perfect, whole, nor healthy if all the estates of which we speak are not well joined and united together. Thus, they can help and aid each other, each exercising the office which it has to, which diverse offices ought to serve only for the conservation of the whole community, just as the members of a human body aid to guide and nourish the whole body. And in so far as one of them fails, the whole feels it and is deprived by it.

Thus it is appropriate to discuss the way the final parts of the body should be maintained in health and in well-being, for it seems to me that they are the support and have the burden of all the rest of the body, thus they need the strength and the power to carry the weight of the other parts. This is why, just as we said earlier, the good prince must love his subjects and his people, and we spoke of the office of nobles which is established to guard and defend the people.

It is suitable to speak of the love, reverence, and obedience that his people should have for the prince. So let us say to all universally: all the estates owe the prince the same love, reverence and obedience. But after I have said something about the increase of virtue in their life and manner of living, perhaps I will discuss the three ways the different classes ought to express the generalized principle. And because sometimes there are complaints among the three different estates— princes, knights and people—because it seems to each of them that the other two do not do their duty in their offices, which can cause discord among them, a most prejudicial situation, here is a moral tale told as a fable:

> Once upon a time there was great disagreement between the belly of a human body and its limbs. The belly complained loudly about the limbs and said that they thought badly of it and that they did not take care of it and feed it as well as they should. On the other hand, the limbs complained loudly about the belly and said they were all exhausted from work, and yet despite all their labor, coming and going and working, the belly wanted to have everything and was never satisfied. The limbs then decided that they would no longer suffer such pain and

labor, since nothing they did satisfied the belly. So they would stop their work and let the belly get along as best it might. The limbs stopped their work and the belly was no longer nourished. So it began to get thinner, and the limbs began to fail and weaken, and so, to spite one another, the whole body died.

Likewise, when a prince requires more than a people can bear, then the people complain against their prince and rebel by disobedience. In such discord, they all perish together. And thus I conclude that agreement preserves the whole body politic. And so attests Sallust, "in concord, little things increase, and by discord, great things decrease."

Chapter 2. On the differences between the several peoples

Although the writing of books and especially those on manners and instruction must be general and relate to the inhabitants of all countries (since books are carried to many places and regions), because we reside in France we will restrict our words and teaching to the French people, although these words and instruction would seem to generally serve as a good example in all other regions where good and correct understanding is desired.

Throughout the whole world, lands which are governed by humans are subject to different institutions according to the ancient customs or places. Some are governed by elected emperors, others by hereditary kings, and so on. And there are cities and countries which are self governed and are ruled by princes which they choose among themselves. Often these make their choice more by will than by reason. And sometimes, having chosen them by caprice, they seem to depose them the same way. Such government is not beneficial where it is the custom, as in Italy and many places.

Other cities are governed by certain families in the city that they call nobles, and they will allow no one not of their lineage to enter their counsels nor their discussions; this they do in Venice which has been governed thus since its foundation, which was very ancient. Others are governed by their elders who are called "aldermen." And in some places, the common people govern and every year a number of people are installed from each trade. I believe that such governance is not profitable at all for the republic and also it does not last very long once begun, nor is there peace in and around it, and for good reason. But I will not say more for reasons of brevity. Such was the government of Bologna. I would have too much to do to speak of each people separately, but when it comes to choosing the most suitable institution to govern the polity and

the community of people, Aristotle says in Book III of the *Politics*, that the polity of one is best, that is, governance and rule by one. Rule by a few is still good, he says, but rule by the many is too large to be good, because of the diversity of opinions and desires.

On our subject, I consider the people of France very happy. From its foundation by the descendants of the Trojans, it has been governed, not by foreign princes, but by its own from heir to heir, as the ancient chronicles and histories tell. This rule by noble French princes has become natural to the people. And for this reason and the grace of God, of all the countries and kingdoms of the world, the people of France has the most natural and the best love and obedience for their prince, which is a singular and very special virtue and praiseworthy of them and they deserve great merit.

Chapter 3. The obedience to the prince that a people ought to have

It pleases the good to have one's merits to be praised, although to be praised scarcely matters to those who are wise. As I have said before, no matter what anyone said to diminish their worth, it causes them to be pleased and delight more in goodness. For just as prudent persons who are curious about their health would like the advice of doctors, even though they have no symptoms of illness, but so they may live in health, it pleases them to have a regimen to preserve their health. Likewise, we will comfort the loyal people of France in order to preserve them in the good and faithful love that they are accustomed to and always have for their very noble, venerable, and above all, praiseworthy and redoubtable princes. And so that they understand and know that by doing so, they act as virtuous and good people, this will be demonstrated here by quotations on the subject from Holy Scripture and other examples.

The Holy Scriptures in many places advise subjects to render themselves humble subjects and to be readily obedient to their lords and rulers. So St. Paul says in the thirteenth chapter of the Epistle to the Romans: "All living creatures ought to be subject to powerful rulers, for those powers that princes have are commanded by God. And he who resists their power, he is recalcitrant or rebellious against the command of God."

And this same St. Paul, in chapter 3 of the Epistle to Titus, counsels the common people to hold themselves subject to princes and high powers. And this adage is given by St. Peter in his first epistle, chapter 2 where he says, "Be subject to your lords in fearful dread." But, so that no one can excuse oneself by saying that this only applies to princes that are good, St.

Peter declares plainly, "Suppose that the princes were bad," he says, "then subject yourself for the love of God, and especially to the king as the most excellent and to the leaders [ducz] sent by God for the punishment of evildoers and for the glory of the good and of their good deeds."

And for those who may complain about the tribute and taxes that it is suitable to pay to princes, they are to understand that it is a thing permitted and accepted by God. And so Holy Scripture gives an example to demonstrate how subjects ought not to refuse to pay that which is commanded. In chapter 22 of his gospel, Saint Matthew tells how the Pharisees asked Our Lord if they must pay taxes to Caesar the emperor, to which Our Lord answered, saying "Give to Caesar that which is Caesar's and to God that which is His," which means that taxes are due to the prince. In the seventeenth chapter of his gospel, Saint Matthew also tells how Our Lord sent St. Peter to the river and told him to look in the mouth of the first fish which he caught and he would find a coin. And He told him to take this coin to those who collected the taxes of the emperor in payment for the two of them. Thus, our Lord himself gave an example of being subject in deed and in word to revere and obey lords and princes. On this point of loyalty towards the prince, I believe that God has saved people of France from many perils, because of their goodness and merit. . . .

Chapter 4. Here we begin to discuss the third estate of the people, and first, clerics studying the branches of knowledge

In the community of people are found three estates, which means, especially in the city of Paris and other cities, the clergy, the burghers and merchants, and the common people, such as artisans and laborers. Now it is suitable to consider the things to say that are beneficial as examples of good living for each of the distinct estates since they are different. And because the clerical class is high, noble, and worthy of honor amongst others, I will address it first, that is, the students, whether at the University of Paris or elsewhere.

Oh well advised, oh happy people! I speak to you, the disciplines of the study of wisdom, who, by the grace and good fortune or nature apply yourselves to seek out the heights of the clear rejoicing star, that is, knowledge, do take diligently from this treasure, drink from this clear and healthy fountain. Fill yourself from this pleasant repast, which can so benefit and elevate you! For what is more worthy for a person than knowledge and the highest learning? Certainly, you who desire it and employ yourself with it, you have chosen the glorious life! For by it, you can understand the choice of virtue and the avoidance of vice as it counsels the one and forbids the other.

There is nothing more perfect than the truth and clarity of things which knowledge demonstrates how to know and understand. There is no treasure of the goods of fortune that he who has tasted of the highest knowledge would exchange for a drop of the dregs of wisdom. And truly, no matter what others say, I dare say there is no treasure the like of understanding. Who would not undertake any labor, you champions of wisdom, to acquire it? For if you have it and use it well, you are noble, you are rich, you are all perfect! And this is plain in the teachings of the philosophers, who teach and instruct the way to come through wisdom to the treasure of pure and perfect sufficiency. . . .

Chapter 6. On the second estate of people, that is the burghers and merchants

I said before that the second rank of people is composed of the burghers and merchants of the cities. Burghers are those who are from old city families and have a surname and an ancient coat of arms. They are the principal dwellers and inhabitants of cities, and they inherit the houses and manors on which they live. Books refer to them as "citizens." Such people ought to be honorable, wise and of good appearance, dressed in honest clothing without disguise or affectation. They must have true integrity and be people of worth and discretion, and it is the estate of good and beneficial citizens. In some places, they call the more ancient families noble, when they have been people of worthy estate and reputation for a long time. And so, in all places, one ought to praise good burghers and citizens of cities. It is a very good and honorable thing when there is a notable bourgeoisie in a city. It is a great honor to the country and a great treasure to the prince.

These people ought to be concerned with the situation and needs of the cities of which they are part. They are to ensure that everything concerning commerce and the situation of the population is well governed. For humble people do not commonly have great prudence in words or even in deeds that concern politics and so they should not meddle in the ordinances established by princes. Burghers and the wealthy must take care that the common people are not hurt, so that they have no reason to conspire against the prince or his council. The reason is that these conspiracies and plots by the common people always come back to hurt those that have something to lose. It always was and always will be that the end result is not at all beneficial to them, but evil and detrimental. And so, if there is a case sometime when the common people seem to be aggrieved by some burden, the merchants ought to assemble and from among them choose the wisest and most discreet in action and in speech, and go before the prince or the council and bring their claims for them in humility and state their case meekly for them, and not allow them to do anything, for that leads to the destruction of cities and of countries.

So, to the extent of their power, they should quiet the complaints of the people because of the evil that could come to all. They must restrain themselves this way, as well as others. And if sometimes the laws of princes and their council seem to them to appear, according to their judgment, to be wrong, they must not interpret this as in bad faith, and there may be danger in foolishly complaining, but they ought to assume that they have good intentions in what they do, although the cause might not be apparent. It is wisdom to learn when to hold one's tongue, said Valerius, citing Socrates, the most noble and praiseworthy philosopher. Once he was in a place where many complained of the laws of princes, and one of them asked him why he alone said nothing when the others spoke. "Because," said he, "I have sometimes repented of speaking but never of holding my tongue." . . .

Chapter 7. How the wise burghers ought to counsel the simple people in what they should do

As was said before, the wise should teach the simple and the ignorant to keep quiet about those things which are not their domain and from which great danger can come and no benefit. And as testimony to this, it is written in chapter 22 of the book of Exodus that the law forbids such complaints and says also "you will not complain about great rulers nor curse the princes of the people." And Solomon confirms this in the tenth chapter of Ecclesiastes, saying "Do not betray the king in your thought," which means that no subject ought to conspire against his lord.

It is also dangerous to complain about or disobey the laws of princes. . . .

These things could be given as an example in any country, but merciful God has not put cruel and bloody princes against their people in France. Because of all the nations of the world, I dare say without flattery, it is true that [there] are no more benign and humane princes than in France, and thus they ought all the more to be obeyed. And even if sometimes by chance it seems to the people that they are grieved and burdened, they should not believe that other places are less so, and even supposing that were true because of their chartered liberties that other peoples enjoy, yet they may have other services and usages that are more

detrimental, like great wrongs done to them, or murders amongst themselves, because there is no justice which guards them or treats them in another way. And in spite of those who contradict me, I hold that of all the countries in Christendom, in this one the people commonly live better both because of the benevolence of princes without cruelty, and because of the courtesy and amiability of the people of this nation. And I do not say this out of favoritism, because I was not born here. But, God be my witness at the end, I say what I think! And since I have enquired about the government of other countries and I know there is no paradise on earth, I know that everywhere has its own troubles. . . .

Chapter 8. On merchants

As we discussed before, the merchant class is very necessary, and without it neither the estate of kings and princes nor even the politics of cities and countries could exist. For by the industry of their labor, all kinds of people are provided for without their having to make everything themselves, because if they have money, merchants bring them afar all things necessary and proper for human beings to live. For it is a good thing that persons can occupy different offices in the world. For otherwise, one would be so busy with trying to make a living that no one could attend to other aspects of knowledge—thus God and reason have provided well.

And for the good that they do for everyone, this class of people—loyal merchants who in buying and selling, in exchanging things one for another by taking money or by other honest means—are to be loved and commended as necessary, and in many countries are held in high esteem. And there is no important citizen in any city who is not involved with trade, however, they are not considered thereby less noble. So Venice, Genoa, and other places have the most rich and powerful merchants who seek out good of all kinds, which they distribute all over the world. And thus is the world served all kinds of things, and without doubt, they act honestly. I hold that they have a meritorious office, accepted by God and permitted and approved by the laws.

These people ought to be well advised in their deeds, honest in their labor, truthful in their words, clever in what they do, because they have to know how to buy and resell things at such a price as not to lose money, and ought to be well informed about whether there are enough goods and where they are going short and when to buy and when to sell—otherwise their business will be gone.

They ought to be honest in their work, that is that

they ought not, under threat of damnation and awful punishment of the body, treat their goods with any tricks to make them seem better than they are in order to deceive people so that they might be more expensive or more quickly sold, because every trade is punished when there is fraud in one. And those that practice deception ought not to be called merchants but rather deceivers and evil doers. Above all, merchants should be truthful in words and in promises, accustomed to speaking and keeping the truth so that a simple promise by a merchant will be believed as certain as by a contract. And those that keep their promises and are always found honest should prefer to suffer damage rather than fail to keep an agreement, which is a very good and honest custom, and would please God, if others in France and elsewhere would do the same. Although there may be some that do wrong, I hold that by the mercy of God, there are those who are good, honest, and true. May God keep them rich, honorable and worthy of trust! For it is very good for a country and of great value to a prince and to the common polity when a city has trade and an abundance of merchants. This is why cities on the sea or major rivers are commonly rich and large, because of the goods that are brought by merchants from far away to be delivered there. So these people ought to be of fair and honest life without pomp or arrogance and ought to serve God in courage and reverence and to give alms generously from what God has given them, as one finds among those who give a tenth of their goods to the poor and who found many chapels, places of prayer, and hospitals for the poor. And so there are those of such goodness that if God pleases, they truly deserve merit in heaven and goodness and honor in the world.

Chapter 9. The third class of the people

Next comes the third rank of the people who are artisans and agricultural workers, which we call the last part of the body politic and who are like legs and feet, according to Plutarch, and who should be exceptionally well watched over and cared for so that they suffer no hurt, for that which hurts them can dangerously knock the whole body down. It is therefore more necessary to take good care and provide for them, since for the health of the body, they do not cease to go "on foot." The varied jobs that the artisans do are necessary for the human body and it cannot do without them, just as a human body cannot go without its feet. It would shamefully and uselessly drag itself in great pain on its hands and body without them, just as, he says, if the republic excluded laborers and artisans, it could not sustain itself. Thus although some think little of the office of the craftsman that the clerics call "arti-

sans," yet it is good, noble, and necessary, as said before. And among all other good things which exist, so this one should be even more praised because, of all the worldly estates, this one comes closest to science. Artisans put into practice what science teaches, as Aristotle says in his *Metaphysics*, because their works are the result of sciences, such as geometry, which is the science of measurement and proportion without which no craft could exist. To this a writer testifies, saying that the Athenians wanted to make a marvelous altar to Minerva, the goddess of wisdom, and because they wanted a notable and beautiful work above all, they sought advice from the best teachers. They went to the philosopher Plato as the most accomplished master of all sciences, but he sent them to Euclid instead as the master of the art of measurement, because he created geometry which is read everyday in general studies.

And from this can one see that artisans follow science. For masons, carpenters, and all other workers in whatever crafts work according to the teachings of the sciences. "To be praised is to master a craft," says Valerius, "so that art will follow nature." When a worker properly copies a thing which nature has made, as when a painter who is a great artist makes the portrait of a man so lifelike and so well, that everyone recognizes him, or when he makes a recognizable bird or other beast; so too the sculptor of images makes a likeness, and so on. And so some say that art is the "apess" or the "apes" of nature, because a monkey imitates many of the ways of man, just as art imitates many of the works of nature.

But nonetheless, they say, art can not imitate everything, so one ought to praise the skillful in art and believe those who have experience in it, for there is no doubt that no one speaks as appropriately of a thing as the one who knows it. And I believe the most skilled artisans of all crafts are more commonly in Paris than elsewhere, which is an important and beautiful thing. . . .

Chapter 10. On simple laborers

On the subject of simple laborers of the earth, what should I say of them when so many people despise and oppress them? Of all the estates, they are the most necessary, those who are cultivators of the earth which feed and nourish the human creature, without whom the world would end in little time. And really those who do them so many evils do not take heed of what they do, for anyone who considers himself a rational creature will hold himself obligated to them. It is a sin to be ungrateful for as many services as they give us! And really it is very much the feet which support the body politic, for they support the body of every person with their labor. They do nothing that is unpraiseworthy. God has made their office acceptable, first, because the two heads of the world, from whom all human life is descended, were laborers of the earth. The first head was Adam, the first father, of whom it is written in the second chapter of Genesis, "God took the first man and put him in a paradise of pleasures, to work, cultivate and take care of it." And from this scripture one can draw two arguments to prove the honesty of labor: The first is that God commanded it and made it first of all crafts. The second, that this craft was created during the state of innocence.

The second head of the world was Noah from whom, after the flood, all humans are descended. It is written in the ninth chapter that Noah was a laborer, and after the flood he put himself to work on the land and planted vineyards. And so our fathers, the ancient patriarchs were all cultivators of the earth and shepherds of beasts (whose stories I will not tell you for the sake of brevity), and in the olden days it was not an ignoble office nor unpraiseworthy. . . .

Because of these stories, we can understand that the estate of simple laborer or others of low rank should not be denigrated, as others would do. When those of the highest rank choose for their retirement a humble life of simplicity as the best for the soul and the body, then they are surely rich who voluntarily are poor. For they have no fear of being betrayed, poisoned, robbed, or envied, for their wealth is in sufficiency. For no one is rich without it, nor is there any other wealth. . . .

Anaxagoras agreed that happiness is to have sufficiency. In the prologue to the Almagest, Ptolemy says "he is happy who does not care in whose hands the world is." And that this saying is true is proven by all the sages, the poets, and especially, those perfect ones who have chosen a pure and poor life for the greatest surety.

For although one can be saved in any estate, nonetheless it is more difficult to pass by flames and not be burned. There is no doubt that the estate of the poor which everyone despises has many good and worthy persons in the purity of life.

Chapter 11. Christine concludes her book

I have come, God be praised, to the end I intended, that is I bring to an end the present book, which began, as Plutarch described, with the head of the body of the polity which is understood to be the princes. From them, I very humbly request first that the head of all, the King of France, and afterwards the princes and all those of their noble blood, that the diligent labor of writing by the humble creature Christine—this present work, as well as her others such as they might be—are agreeable to them. And since she is a woman of little knowledge, if by ignorance any faults are found, let her be pardoned and her good intention better known, for she intends only good to be the effect of her work. And I beg in payment from those living and their successors, the very noble kings and other French princes, in remembrance of my sayings in times to come when my soul is out of my body, that they would pray to God for me, requesting indulgence and remission of my sins.

And likewise, I ask of French knights, nobles, and generally of all, no matter from where they might be, that if they have any pleasure in the hours they saw or heard read from my little nothings, that they think of me and say an Our Father. And in the same way, I wish the universal people—the three estates and the whole together—that God by His holy mercy desire to maintain and increase them from better to better in all perfection of souls and bodies. Amen.

Here it ends.

PART TWO

Seventeenth- and
Eighteenth-Century Writings

Margaret Cavendish, Duchess of Newcastle (1623?–73)

Margaret Cavendish, Duchess of Newcastle, was a fascinating individual, a woman of strong character possessing varied and unpredictable intellectual interests. A creature of mid-seventeenth-century England—a period that has attracted the most historical and literary interest (especially for women) for its political and religious left—she was a complicated royalist but mainly uninterested in the major social and political debates of the day. Her political efforts were generally directed toward aiding her husband, William Cavendish, first Duke of Newcastle, who was a military leader under Charles I and a major target of parliamentary hostility following the king's death. Yet while the Duke was a classic conservative, the Duchess ranged from offering opinions similar to her husband's to ones diametrically opposed. With few clear religious convictions, she was interested in social and educational structures, the sciences, and especially women's status and abilities.

Margaret Cavendish was born a Lucas, which she later described as a respected and prosperous Essex gentry family. Born about 1623, she was the youngest daughter of a large family and, according to her autobiography, the subject of much love and adulation from her older sisters and brothers. She wrote lengthy stories and gained much praise and attention from her family because of her precocity. In her autobiography, appended to the more prominent biography of her husband, she noted that such attention made her shy outside the family circle. As a young woman, in 1644, she went into exile with the court of Queen Henrietta Maria. There she avoided court society but attracted the eye of the Marquis of Newcastle (about thirty years her senior), who expressed a not unusual affection for a younger woman endowed with a range of charms, not the least of which was an ample bosom. He wooed her with typically bad verse in the Cavalier mode, but he did work some surprising assurances into his claims as a suitor. One of the more interesting was his guarantee that an older man was less apt to dominate women than a young one. In reacting to the future duke's discussion of the twin motives of passion and respect in his desire to wed her, Margaret demonstrated a kind of common sense and skeptical vision that underlay her later feminist sentiments.

Newcastle lost much of his fortune in supporting Charles I and, in the opinion of himself and his wife, was not sufficiently recognized and recompensed for his sacrifices by the restored Charles II. But despite his relatively impoverished condition, he was determined to keep up his aristocratic and profligate lifestyle during their exile, forcing the Duchess to return to England to raise money and then to pawn one of her gowns for food rather than to give up his favorite pair of horses. He returned to England on the first possible ship, leaving his wife behind in Antwerp as collateral for their debts! On these and other grounds, there is reason to question whether the marriage was quite as idyllic as traditionally portrayed. However, the Duke's encouragement was surely the most important reason that Margaret Cavendish's works were published. In addition, as the Duke's wife she had an opportunity to meet individuals such as Thomas Hobbes and René Descartes and to learn from her husband and brother-in-law the principles of their thought, to be a part of an intellectual circle in Paris during the late 1640s when the recently married couple was in exile, and to continue to participate in intellectual discussions upon their return to England.

For those who seek early seeds of feminism, Cavendish is especially unsettling. She wrote the most radical critique of women's nature and women's status penned in the seventeenth century, yet she expressed some of the strongest doubts about women's intellectual and personal competence. In her one can find the unexpected viewpoint, the uncontrollable and unpredictable mind, an individual willing to take on any subject, even while apologizing at every turn for taking pen to paper. In her writings she created an imaginative world where she could be at the intellectual and political center, and in real life she offered opinions not spoken by others. In many of her writings she appears as an interesting, and perhaps even extreme, advocate for women's equal mental abilities and equal access to a serious education, but not systematically feminist. Others agreed with these sentiments, going back at least to Christine de Pizan, and including Bathsua Makin, Hannah Wooley, Anna van Schurman, Poullain de la Barre, and most prominently Mary Astell in her own day. But in her Female Orations and portions of her introductions, she went further than other feminists, perhaps rhetorically, but in a rhetoric that fits with her own life. She questioned the value of marriage altogether, the need for women to bear children and any gain to be had from them, and women's relationship or loyalty to the state.

Given the conflicting positions expressed in her writings, it is difficult to distinguish her genuine views from those that she stated purely for literary or argumentative effect. Still, she often spoke outside the range of acceptable royalist and Anglican positions. These positions are more significant and remarkable than when she repeated her husband's (and his circle's) positions. Thus her statements on behalf of social equality or freedom of conscience, while inconsistent, set her apart from those whose ideas she has been assumed to follow, and raised topics and ideas that others avoided.

Some of her more remarkable views are offered in an oration defending a man who had stolen to support his family, in which she appears to attack men such as Thomas Hobbes who is normally credited as having a significant influence on her. In contrast with her husband, who feared freedom of conscience above all things as encouraging political upheaval, the Duchess wrote an "Oration for Liberty of Conscience." Though this was followed by an oration arguing against liberty of conscience (on grounds of utility, not principle), she concluded with a compromise statement, siding more with the one favoring freedom of conscience: "if those Sects or Separatists . . . Disturb not the publick weal, why should you Disturb their Private Devotions?" Her lack of firm Christian loyalties is confirmed by her continual use of the term "gods" rather than God and her virtual ignoring of Christ altogether in her written works.

While those desiring intellectual or feminist consistency have never been comfortable with Margaret Cavendish, she was a thinker who tested the boundaries of acceptable views. She represented no movement or group and was an individual who spoke against or outside the values held by her class, her sex, and her age. About gender primarily, but also on issues of class, the pomp and circumstance of academics and academic life, and the social customs of the age, she was singularly original. Unlike women of the radical sects who often spoke more for the religious and political values of the group, normally articulated by male leaders, she did not represent a particular ideological position. She selected her causes and her positions in ways that seem idiosyncratic, remaining loyal only to husband (and indirectly to monarch), but never becoming a mouthpiece for others, either human or godly. No one has adequately explained the radical and often unseemly things she uttered. She wrote plays with obvious lesbian themes; she even included a defense of incest by a character in one of her plays. Her intellectual interests were as broad as her views were daring; her works encompassed the physical and biological sciences, drama, poetry, essays, moral philosophy, and model letters.

Her works were interspersed with judgments that the monarch should be supreme and not subject to question, that women were unworthy partners intellectually or socially to their male counterparts, that social and political stability were preferable to change and questioning. But unlike her husband and others around her, she criticized the abuse of animals, of the peasantry, and of women, and at points in virtually all of her writings, she broke from a social vision that saw some individuals more worthy than others.

Contemporaries and later scholars have resisted acknowledging the radical nature of her works. She was of the wrong social rank, on the wrong side of the English Civil War, tied (if only slightly) to the wrong religious establishment, to have reason to question gender or other relationships. Yet, even if offered in a rhetorical manner, grounded in an inconsistent vision of male-female relationships, and coming from a woman who was both admired and ridiculed as an eccentric, her writings posed a more broad-based, fundamental critique of women's legal, political, educational, and social status than did those of her contemporaries. Some scholars have emphasized the political and social imagery in her literary works as offering her most authentic voice, while others have turned to her essays and letters to view her attitudes toward the events and issues of her age. Wherever one turns, however, she was a unique individual. In many ways her life exemplified the desire expressed by a heroine in one of her plays, to be "a meteor singly alone" rather than a "star in a crowd."

The excerpts selected for this volume are from the original editions of Poems and Fancies (1653), Philosophical and Physical Opinions (1655), Orations of Divers Sorts (1662), and CCXI Sociable Letters (1664).

HLS

Sources and Suggested Readings

Battigelli, Anna. *Margaret Cavendish and the Exiles of the Mind.* Lexington: University Press of Kentucky, 1998.

Cavendish, Margaret, Duchess of Newcastle. *The Blazing World and Other Writings.* Ed. and with an introduction by Kate Lilley. London: Penguin Classic, 1994.

——. *Orations of Divers Sorts, Accommodated to Divers Places.* London, 1662.

——. *Philosophical and Physical Opinions.* London, 1655.

——. *Poems and Fancies.* London, 1653. 2nd ed., 1664; 3rd ed., 1668.

——. *CCXI Sociable Letters, Written by the Thrice Noble, Illustrious, and Excellent Princess, the Lady Marchioness of Newcastle.* London: Printed by William Wilson, 1664.

——. *Sociable Letters,* ed. James Fitzmaurice. New York: Garland Publishing, 1997.

Dash, Irene G. "Single-Sex Retreats in Two Early Modern Dramas: *Love's Labor's Lost* and *The Convent of Pleasure.*" *Shakespeare Quarterly* 47, 4 (1996): 387–95.

Ferguson, Moira, ed. *First Feminists: British Women Writers, 1578–1799.* Bloomington and New York: Indiana University Press and Feminist Press, 1985.

Gallagher, Catherine. "Embracing the Absolute: The Politics of the Female Subject in Seventeenth-Century England." *Genders* 1 (1988): 24–39.

Grant, Douglas. *Margaret the First: A Biography of Margaret Cavendish, Duchess of Newcastle, 1623–1673*. Toronto: University of Toronto Press, 1957.

Kahn, Victoria. "Margaret Cavendish and the Romance of Contract." *Renaissance Quarterly* 50 (1997): 526–66.

Mendelson, Sara H. *The Mental World of Stuart Women: Three Studies*. Amherst: University of Massachusetts Press, 1982.

Shaver, Anne, ed. *The Convent of Pleasure and Other Plays*. Baltimore: Johns Hopkins University Press, 1998.

Smith, Hilda L. "The Duty of Every Good Wife: Margaret Cavendish, Duchess of Newcastle." In *Women & History: Voices of Early Modern England*, ed. Valerie Frith, 119–44. Toronto: Coach House Press, 1995.

———. "'A General War amongst the Men [but] None amongst the Women': Political Differences between Margaret and William Cavendish." In *Politics and Political Culture in Late Stuart England*, ed. Howard Nenner. Rochester, N.Y.: Rochester University Press, 1997.

———. *Reason's Disciples: Seventeenth-Century English Feminists*. Urbana: University of Illinois Press, 1982.

Poems and Fancies (1653)

To All Noble, and Worthy Ladies

Noble, Worthy Ladies,

Condemne me not as a *dishonour* of your Sex, for setting forth this *Work*; for it is *harmlesse* and free from all *dishonesty*; I will not say from *vanity*: for that is so *natural* to our *Sex* that it were unnaturall, not to be so. Besides, *Poetry*, which is built upon *Fancy*, Women may claime, as a *worke* belonging most properly to themselves: for I have observ'd, that their Braines work usually in a *Fantasticall motion*; as in their *severall*, and *various dresses*, in their many and singular choices of *Cloaths*, and *Ribbons*, and the like; in their *curious shadowing*, and *mixing of Colours*, in their *Wrought works*, and divers sorts of *Stitches* they imploy their *Needle*, and many *Curious* things they make, as *Flowers*, *Boxes*, *Baskets* with *Beads*, *Shells*, *Silk*, *Straw*, or any thing else; besides all manner of Meats to eate: and thus their *Thoughts* are imployed perpetually with *Fancies*. For *Fancy* goeth not so much by *Rule*, & *Method*, as by *Choice*: and if I have chosen my silk with *fresh colours*, and matcht them in *good shadows*, although the stitches be not very true, yet it will please the *Eye*; so if my *Writing* please the *Readers*, though not the *Learned*, it will satisfie me; for I had rather be praised

in this, by the *most*, although not the *best*. For all I desire is *Fame*, and *Fame* is nothing but a *great noise*, and *noise* lives most in a *Multitude*; wherefore I wish my *Book* may set a worke every *Tongue*. But I imagine I shall be censur'd by my owne *Sex*; and *Men* will cast a *smile* of *scorne* upon my *Book*, because they think thereby, *Women* incroach too much upon their *Prerogatives*; for they hold *Books* as their *Crowne*, and the *Sword* as their *Scepter*, by which they rule, and governe. And very like they will say to me, as to the *Lady* that wrote the *Romancy*,

> *Work* Lady, *work, let writing* Books *alone,*
> *For surely* wiser Women *nere wrote one.*

But those that say so, shall give me leave to wish, that those of neerest Relation, as *Wives, Sisters and Daughters*, may imploy their time no worse then in *honest, Innocent*, and *harmlesse Fancies*; which if they do, *Men* shall have no cause to feare, that when they go abroad in their absence, they shall receive an *Iniury* by their *loose Carriages*. Neither will *Women* be desirous to *Gossip* abroad, when their *Thoughts* are well imployed at home. But if they do throw scorne, I shall intreat you, (as the *Woman* did in the *Play* of the *Wife*, for a *Month*, which caused many of the *Effeminate Sex*) to help her, to keep their *Right*, and *Priviledges*, making it their owne *Case*. Therefore pray strengthen my Side, in defending my *Book*; for I know *Womens Tongus* are as *sharp*, as two-edged *Swords*, and wound as much, when they are anger'd. And in this *Battel* may your *Wit* be *quick*, and your *Speech ready*, and your *Arguments* so *strong*, as to beat them out of the *Feild of Dispute*. So shall I get *Honour*, and *Reputation* by your *Favours*; otherwise I may chance to be cast into the *Fire*. But if I burn, I desire to die your *Martyr*; if I live, to be

> *Your humble Servant,*
> M.N.

An Epistle to Mistris Toppe:

Some may think an *Imperfection* of *wit* may be a *blemish* to the *Family* from whence I sprung: But *Solomon* says, A *wise man may get a Fool*. Yet there are as few *meer Fools*, as *wise men*: for *Understanding* runs in a *levell course*, that is, to know in *generall*, as of the *Effects*: but to know the *Cause* of any one thing of *Natures* works, *Nature* never gave us a *Capacity* thereto. Shee hath given us *Thoughts* which run wildly about, and if by *chance* they light on *Truth*, they do not know it for a *Truth*. But amongst many *Errours*, there are *huge Mountaines* of *Follies*; and though I add to the *Bulke* of one of them, yet I make not a *Mountaine* alone, and am the more *excusable*, because I have an *Opinion*, which troubles me like a *conscience*, that 'tis a part of *Honour* to aspire towards a *Fame*. . . .

Tis true, the *World* may wonder at my *Confidence*, how I dare put out a *Book*, especially in these *censorious times*; but which should I be ashamed, or affraid, where no *Evill* is, and not please my selfe in the *satisfaction* of *innocent desires*? For a *smile* of *neglect* cannot dishearten me, no more can a *Frowne* of *dislike* affright me; not but I should be well pleased, and delight to have my *Booke* commended. But the *Worlds dispraises* cannot make me a *mourning garment*: my mind's too big, and I had rather venture an *indiscretion*, then loose the *hopes* of a *Fame*. Neither am I ashamed of my *simplicity*, for Nature tempers not every *Braine* alike; but tis a *shame* to deny the *Principles* of their *Religion*, to break the *Lawes* of a *well-governed Kingdome*, to disturbe *Peace*, to be unnaturall, to break the *Union* and *Amity of honest Freinds*, for a *Man* to be a *Coward*, for a *Woman* to be a *Whore*; and by these *Actions*, they are not onely to be cast out of all *Civill society*, but to be blotted out of the *Roll of Mankinde*. And the reason why I summon up these *Vices*, is, to let my *Freinds* know, or rather to remember them, that my *Book* is none of them: yet in this Action of setting out of a *Booke*, I am not clear without fault, because I have not asked leave of any *Freind* thereto; for the *feare* of being denied, made me silent: and there is an *Old saying*; That it is easier to ask *Pardon*, then leave. . . . Besides, I print this *Book*, to give an *Account* to my *Freinds*, how I spend the *idle Time* of my *life*, and how I busie my Thoughts, when I thinke upon the *Objects* of the World. For the truth is, our *Sex* hath so much waste Time, having but little imployments, which makes our *Thoughts* run wildly about, having nothing to fix them upon, which *wilde thoughts* do not onely produce unprofitable, but indiscreet Actions; winding up the *Thread* of our *lives* in *snarles* on *unsound bottoms*. And since all times must be spent either *ill*, or *well*, or *indifferent*; I thought this was the *harmelessest Pastime*: for sure this *Worke* is better then to sit still, and censure my *Neighbours actions*, which nothing concernes me; or to condemne their *Humours*, because they do not *sympathize* with *mine*, or their *lawfull Recreations*, because they are not agreeable to my *delight*; or ridiculously to laugh at my *Neighbours Cloaths*, if they are not of the *Mode, Colour*, or *Cut*, or the *Ribbon* tyed with a *Mode Knot*, or to busie my selfe out of the *Sphear* of our *Sex*, as in *Politicks* of *State*, or to Preach *false Doctrine* in a Tub, or to entertaine my selfe in hearkning to *vaine Flatteries*, or to the *incitements* of evill *perswasions* where all these *Follies*, and many more, may be cut off by such innocent worke as

this. I write not this onely to satisfie you, which my *Love* makes me desire so to doe; but to defend my *Book* from spightefull Invaders, knowing *Truth* and *Innocence* are two good *Champions* against *Malice* and *Falshood*; and which is my *defence*, I am very confident is a great satisfaction to you. For being bred with me, your *Love* is twisted to my *Good*, which shall never be undone by any *unkinde Action* of Mine, but will alwayes remaine

Your loving Freind,
M. N.

Philosophical and Physical Opinions (1655)

Most Famously Learned,

I here present to you this philosophical work, not that I can hope wise school-men and industrious laborious students should value it for any worth, but to receive it without scorn, for the good encouragement of our sex, lest in time we should grow irrational as idiots, by the dejectedness of our spirits, through the careless neglects and despisements of the masculine sex to the female, thinking it impossible we should have either learning or understanding, wit or judgment, as if we had not rational souls as well as men, and we out of a custom of dejectedness think so too, which makes us quit all industry towards profitable knowledge, being imployed only in low and petty imployments which take away not only our abilities toward arts but higher capacities in speculations, so that we are become like worms, that only live in the dull earth of ignorance, winding ourselves sometimes out by the help of some refreshing rain of good education, which seldom is given us, for we are kept like birds in cages, to hop up and down in our houses. . . .; thus by an opinion, which I hope is but an erroneous one in men, we are shut out of all power and authority by reason we are never employed either in civil or martial affairs our counsels are despised and laughed at and the best of our actions are trodden down with scorn, by the overweening conceit men have of themselves and through a despisement of us.

Orations of Divers Sorts, Accommodated to Divers Places (1662)

Part III. *Orations*

An Oration for Liberty of Conscience

Fellow Citizens,

It is very probable, we shall fall into a Civil Warr, through the Divers Opinions in One and the same Religion, for what hath been the cause of this Hash in Religion, but the Suffering of Theological Disputations in Schools, Colleges, Churches, and Chambers, as also Books of Controversies? All which ought not to have been Suffered, but Prohibited, by making Laws of Restraint; but since that Freedome hath been given, the Inconveniency cannot be Avoided, unless the Magistrates will give, or at least not oppose a Free Liberty to all; for if the People of this Nation is so Follish, or Wilfull, or Factious, or Irreligious, as not to Agree in One Opinion, and to Unite in One Religion, but will be of Divers Opinions, if not of Divers Religions, the Governours must Yield, or they will Consume the Civil Government with the Fire of their Zeal; indeed they will Consume themselves at last in their own Confusion. Wherefore, the best remedy to prevent their Own ruine, with the ruine of the Commonwealth, is, to let them have Liberty of Conscience, Conditionally, that they do not meddle with Civil Government or Governours; and for Security that they Shall not, there must be a Law made and Inacted, that, whosoever doth Preach, Dispute, or Talk against the Government or Governours, not only in This, but of any other Nation, shall be Punished either with Death, Banishment, or Fine; also for the quiet and Peace of this Kingdome, there ought to be a strict Law, that no Governour or Magistrate shall any kind Infringe our Just Rights, our Civil or Common Laws, nor our Ancient Customs; for if the One Law should be made, and not the Other, the People would be Slaves, and the Governours their Tyrants.

An Oration against Liberty of Conscience

Fellow Citizens,

I am not of the former Orators opinion; for if you give Liberty in the Church, you must give Liberty in the State, and so let every one do what they will, which will be a Strange Government, or rather I may say, no Government; for if there be no Rules, their can be no Laws, and if there be no Laws, there can be no Justice,

and if no Justice, no Safety, and if no Safety, no Propriety, neither of Goods, Wives, Children, nor Lives, and if there be no Propriety, there will be no Husbandry, and the Lands will lye Unmanured; also there will be neither Trade nor Traffick, all which will cause Famine, Warr, and Ruine, and Such a Confusion, as the Kingdome will be like a Chaos, which the Gods keep us from.

An Oration proposing a Mean betwixt the two former Opinions

Fellow Citizens,

I am not of the two former Orators opinions, neither for an Absolute Liberty, nor a Forced Unity, but Between both, as neither to give them such Liberty, as for Several Opinions, to gather into Several Congregations, nor to force them to such Ceremonies, as Agree not with their Consciences; and if those Sects or Separatists Disturb not the Canon, Common, or Civil Laws, not to Disturb their Bodies, Minds, or Estates; for if they Disturb not the Publick Weal, why should you Disturb their Private Devotions? Wherefore, give them leave to follow their Several Opinions, in their Particular Families, otherwise if you Force them, you will make them Furious, and if you give them an Absolute Liberty, you will make them Factious.

Part IV. *Pleadings*

A *Cause Pleaded at the Barr before Judges, concerning Theft*

Plaintiff: Most Reverend, and Just Judges,

Here is a man, which is Accused for Stealing privately, and Robbing openly, against all Law and Right, the Goods of his Neighbours, for which we have brought him before your Honours, appealing to the Laws for satisfaction of the Injuries, Wrongs, and Losses, leaving him to your Justice and Judgement.

Defendant: Most Reverend Judges, I am come here to Plead for this poor man, my Client, who is Accused for Stealing, which is a silent obscure way of taking the Goods of other men, for his own use; also this Poor man, (for so I may say he is, having nothing of his own to Live on, but what he is Necessitated to take from other men) is accused of Robbery, which is to take away the Goods of other men in a Visible way and Forcible manner; All which he confesseth, as that the Accusation against him is true; for he did both Steal and Rob for his own Livelihood, and Maintenance of his Old Parents, which are Past Labouring, and for his Young Children, that are not Able to help themselves, and for his Weak, Sick Wife, that Labours in Child

Birth; For which he appeals to Nature, who made all things in Common, She made not some men to be Rich, and other men Poor, some to Surfeit with over-much Plenty, and others to be Starved for Want: for when she made the World and the Creatures in it, She did not divide the Earth, nor the rest of the Elements, but gave the use generally amongst them all. But when Governmental Laws were devised by some Usurping Men, who were the greatest Thieves and Robbers, (for they Robbed the rest of Mankind of their Natural Liberties and Inheritances, which is to be Equal Possessors of the World;) these Grand and Original Thieves and Robbers, which are call'd Moral Philosophers, or Common-wealth makers, were not only Thieves and Tyrants to the Generality of Mankind, but they were Rebels against Nature, Imprisoning Nature within the Jail of Restraint, Keeping her to the spare Diet of Temperance, Binding her with Laws, and Inslaving her with Propriety, whereas all is in Common with Nature. Wherefore, being against Nature's Laws for any man to Possess more of the World or the Goods of the World than an other man, those that have more Wealth or Power than other men, ought to be Punished as Usurpers and Robbers, and not those that are Poor and Powerless. Therefore, if you be Just Judges of Nature, and not of Art, Judges for Right, and not for Wrong, if you be Judges of the most Ancient Laws, and not Usurping Tyrants, you will not only quit this Poor man, and set him free from his Accusers, which are His and such Poor men's Abusers, but you will cause his Accusers, who are Rich, to Divide their Wealth Equally with Him and all his Family; for which Judgement you will gain Natures favor, which is the Empress of Mankind; Her Government is the Ancientest, Noblest, Generousest, Heroickest, and Royalest, and her Laws are not only the Ancientest, (for there are no Records before Nature's Laws, so that they are the Fundamental Laws of the Universe, and the most Common Laws extending to all Creatures,) but they are the Wisest Laws, and yet the Freest; also Nature is the most Justest Judge, both for Rewards and Punishments; for She Rewards her Creatures, that Observe her Laws as they ought to do, with Delight and Pleasure, but those that Break or abuse her Laws, as in destroying their fellow Creatures by untimely Deaths, or Unnatural Torments, or do Riot and oppress her with Excess, She Punishes them with Grief, Pains, and Sicknesses, and if you will avoid the Punishment of Remorse, Grief, and Repentance, Save this Poor necessitated man from Violence, and the Cruelty of these Inhuman, Unnatural, Destroying Laws.

Plaintiff: Most Reverend Judges, This man, who is Nature's Lawyer and Pleader, ought to be Banish'd from this Place, and his Profession of Pleading out of all Civilest Governments; for he Talks he knows not what of Nature's Laws, whereas there is no Law in Nature, for Nature is Lawless, and hath made all her Creatures so, as to be Wild and Ravenous, to be Unsatiable and Injurious, to be Unjust, Cruel, Destructive, and so Disorderous, that, if it were not for Civil Government, Ordained from an Higher Power, as from the Creator of Nature her self, all her Works would be in a Confusion, and so their own Destructions. But man is not all of Nature's Work, but only in his Outward Frame, having an Inward Celestial and Divine Composition, and a Supreme Power given him by the Gods to Rule and Govern Nature; So that if your Honours submit to the Plea of this Babler, you will make the Rulers and Governours of Nature, the Slaves of Nature; Wherefore, if you be Celestial and not Natural Judges, and will give Divine Judgement, and not Judge according to Brutal Senses, you will Condemn this Notorious Thief and Wild Robber to the Gallows, that his Life may be the Satisfaction for the Wrongs, and his Death an Example for a Warning to Prevent the like Crimes. . . .

Part VIII. *Orations*

A *Young New-Married Wif's Funeral Oration*

Beloved Brethren,

We are met together at this time, to see a New-Married Wife, which is here Dead, to be Buried. She hath made an unequal Change from a Lively Hot Husband, to a Deadly Cold Lover, yet will she be more Happy with her Dull, Dumb, Deaf, Blind, Numb Lover, than with her Lively, Talking, List'ning, Eyeing, Active Husband, were he the Best Husband that could be; for Death is far the Happier Condition than Marriage; and although Marriage at first is Pleasing, yet after a time it is Displeasing, like Meat which is Sweet in the Mouth, but proves Bitter in the Stomack; Indeed, the Stomack of Marriage is full of Evil Humours, as Choler, and Melancholy; and of very Evil Disgestion, for it cannot disgest Neglects, Disrespects, Absence, Dissembling, Adultery, Jealousy, Vain Expenses, Waste, Spoil, Idle Time, Laziness, Examinations, Cross Answers, Peevishness, Forwardness, Frowns, and many the like Meats, that Marriage Feeds on. As for Pains, Sickness, Cares, Fears, and other Troubles in Marriage, they are Accounted as wholesome Physic, which the Gods give them; for the Gods are the Best Physicians, and Death is a very Good Surgeon, Curing his Patients without Pain, for what Part soever he Touches, is Insensible. Death is only Cruel in Parting Friends from each other, for though they are Happy, whom he Takes away, yet those that are Left behind, are Unhappy, Living in Sorrow for their

Loss; so that this Young New-Married Wife, that is Dead, is Happy, but her Husband is a Sorrowfull Widdower; But leaving Her to her Happiness, and Him to be Comforted, let us put Her into the Grave, there to Remain until the day of Judgement, which Day will Imbody her Soul with Everlasting Glory.

A *Child-Bed Womans Funeral Oration*

Beloved Brethren,

We are met together to see a Young Dead Woman, who Died in Child-Bed, to be laid into the Bed of Earth, a Cold Bed, but yet she will not take any Harm there, nor we shall not fear she will Catch her Death, for Death has Catch'd her; the truth is, that although all Women are Tender Creatures, yet they Indure more than Men, and do oft'ner Venture and Indanger their Lives than Men, and their Lives are more Profitable than men's Lives are, for they Increase Life, when Men for the most part Destroy Life, as witness Warrs, wherein Thousands of Lives are Destroyed, Men Fighting and Killing each other, and yet Men think all Women meer cowards, although they do not only Venture and Indanger their Lives more than they do, but indure greater Pains with greater Patience than Men usually do: Nay, Women do not only indure the Extremity of Pain in Child-Birth, but in Breeding, the Child being for the most part Sick, and seldom at Ease. Indeed, Nature seems both Unjust and Cruel to her Femal Creatures, especially Women, making them to indure all the Pain and Sickness in Breeding and Bringing forth of their Young Children, and the Males to bear no part of their Pain or Danger; the truth is, Nature has made her Male Creatures, especially Mankind, only for Pleasure, and her Female Creatures for Misery; Men are made for Liberty, and Women for Slavery, and not only Slaves to Sickness, Pains, and Troubles, in Breeding, Bearing, and Bringing up their Children, but they are Slaves to Men's Humours, nay, to their vices and Wickedness, so that they are more Inslaved than any other Female Creatures, for other Female Creatures are not so Inslaved as they; Wherefore, those Women are most Happy that Never Marry, or Dye whilst they be Young, so that this Young Woman that Died in Child-Bed is Happy, in that she Lives not to Indure more Pain or Slavery, in which Happiness let us leave her, after we have laid her Corps to Rest in the Grave.

Part XI. *Femal Orations*

I.

Ladies, Gentlewomen, and other Inferiours, but not Less Worthy, I have been Industrious to Assemble you together, and wish I were so Fortunate, as to per-swade you to make a Frequentation, Association, and Combination amongst our Sex, that we may Unite in Prudent Counsels, to make our Selves as Free, Happy, and Famous as Men, whereas now we Live and Dye, as if we were Produced from Beast rather than from Men; for Men are Happy, and we Women are Miserable, they Possess all the Ease, Rest, Pleasure, Wealth, Power, and Fame, whereas Women are Restless with Labour, Easeless with Pain, Melancholy for want of Pleasures, Helpless for want of Power, and Dye in Oblivion for want of Fame. Nevertheless, Men are so Unconscionable and Cruel against us, as they Indeavour to Barr us of all Sorts or Kinds of Liberty, as not to Suffer us Freely to Associate amongst our own Sex, but would fain Bury us in their Houses or Beds, as in a Grave; the truth is, we live like Bats or Owls, Labour like Beasts, and Dye like Worms.

II.

Ladies, Gentlewomen, and other Inferiour Women, The Lady that Spoke to you, hath spoken Wisely and Eloquently in Expressing our Unhappiness, but she hath not Declared a Remedy, or Shew'd us a way to come Out of our Miseries; but if she could or would be our Guide, to lead us out of the Labyrinth Men have put us into, we should not only Praise and Admire her, but Adore and Worship her as our Goddess. But, Alas, Men, that are not only our Tyrants, but our Devils, keep us in the Hell of Subjection, from whence I cannot Perceive any Redemption or Getting out; we may Complain, and Bewail our Condition, yet that will not Free us; we may Murmur and Rail against Men, yet they Regard not what we say: In short, our Words to Men are as Empty Sounds, our Sighs as Puffs of Wind, and our Tears as Fruitless Showres, and our Power is so Inconsiderable, as Men Laugh at our Weakness.

III.

Ladies, Gentlewomen and other more Inferiours, The former *Orations* were Exclamations against Men, Repining at Their Condition, and Mourning for our Own; but we have no Reason to Speak against Men, who are our Admirers, and Lovers; they are our Protectors, Defenders, and Maintainers; they Admire our Beauties, and Love our Persons; they Protect us from Injuries, Defend us from Dangers, are Industrious for our Subsistence, and Provide for our Children; they Swim great Voyages by Sea, Travel long Journies by Land, to Get us Rarities and Curiosities; they Dig to the Centre of the Earth for Gold for us; they Dive to the Bottom of the Sea for Jewels for us; they Build to the Skies Houses for us; they Hunt, Fowl, Fish, Plant, and Reap for Food for us; all which we could not do our Selves, and yet we Complain of Men, as if they were our Enemies, when as we could not possibly Live without them: which shews, we are as Ungratefull, as Inconstant; But we have more Reason to Murmur against Nature than against Men, who hath made Men more Ingenious, Witty, and Wise than Women; more Strong, Industrious, and Laborious than Women, for Women are Witless, and Strengthless, and Unprofitable Creatures, did they not Bear Children. Wherefore, let us Love men, Praise men, and Pray for men, for without Men we should be the most Miserable Creatures that Nature Hath, or Could make.

IV.

Noble Ladies, Gentlewomen, and other Inferiour Women, The former Oratoress says, we are Witless, and Strengthless; if so, it is that we Neglect the One, and make no Use of the Other, for Strength is Increased by Exercise, and Wit is Lost for want of Conversation; but to shew Men we are not so Weak and Foolish, as the former Oratoress doth Express us to be, let us Hawk, Hunt, Race, and do the like Exercises as Men have, and let us Converse in Camps, Courts, and Cities, in Schools, Colleges, and Courts of Judicature, in Taverns, Brothels, and Gaming Houses, all which will make our Strength and Wit known, both to Men and to our own Selves, for we are as Ignorant of our Selves, as Men are of us. And how should we Know our Selves, when as we never made a Trial of our Selves? Or how should Men know us, when as they never Put us to the Proof? Wherefore, my Advice is, we should Imitate Men, so will our Bodies and Minds appear more Masculine, and our Power will Increase by our Actions.

V.

Noble, Honourable, and Vertuous Women, The former Oration was to Perswade us to Change the Custom of our Sex, which is a Strange and Unwise persuasion, since we cannot Change the Nature of our Sex, for we cannot make ourselves Men; and to have Femal Bodies, and yet to Act Masculine Parts, will be very Preposterous and Unnatural; In truth, we shall make our Selves like as the Defects of Nature, as to be Hermaphroditical, as neither to be Perfect Women nor Perfect Men, but Corrupt and Imperfect Creatures; Wherefore, let me Perswade you, since we cannot Alter the Nature of our Persons, not to Alter the Course of our Lives, but to Rule our Lives and Behaviours, as to be Acceptable and Pleasing to God and Men, which is to be Modest, Chaste, Temperate, Humble, Patient, and Pious; also to be Huswifely, Cleanly, and of few Words, all which will Gain us Praise from Men, and Blessing from Heaven, and Love in this World, and Glory in the Next.

VI.

Worthy Women, The former Oratoress's Oration indeavors to Perswade us, that it would not only be a Reproach and Disgrace, but Unnatural for Women in their Actions and Behaviour to Imitate Men; we may as well say, it will be a Reproach, Disgrace, and Unnatural to Imitate the Gods, which Imitation we are Commanded both by the Gods and their Ministers; and Shall we Neglect the Imitation of Men, which is more Easie and Natural than the Imitation of the Gods? For how can Terrestrial Creatures Imitate Celestial Deities? Yet one Terrestrial may Imitate an other, although in different sorts of Creatures; Wherefore, since all Terrestrial Imitations ought to Ascend to the Better, and not to Descend to the Worse, Women ought to Imitate Men, as being a Degree in Nature more Perfect, than they Themselves, and all Masculine Women ought to be as much Praised as Effeminate Men to be Dispraised, for the one Advances to Perfection, the other Sinks to Imperfection, that so by our Industry we may come at last to Equal Men both in Perfection and Power.

VII.

Noble ladies, Honourable Gentlewomen, and Worthy Femal Commoners, The former Oratress's Oration or Speech was to Perswade us Out of our Selves, as to be That, which Nature never Intended us to be, to wit Masculine; but why should we Desire to be Masculine, since our Own Sex and Condition is far the Better? for if Men have more Courage, they have more Danger; and if Men have more Strength, they have more Labour than Women have; if Men are more Eloquent in Speech, Women are more Harmonious in Voice; if Men be more Active, Women are more Gracefull; if Men have more Liberty, Women have more Safety; for we never Fight Duels, nor Battels, nor do we go Long Travels or Dangerous Voyages; we Labour not in Building, nor Digging in Mines, Quarries, or Pits, for Metal, Stone, or Coals; neither do we Waste or Shorten our Lives with University or Scholastic Studies, Questions, and Disputes; we Burn not our Faces with Smiths Forges, or Chymist Furnaces, and Hundreds of other Actions, which Men are Imployed in; for they would not only Fade the Fresh Beauty, Spoil the Lovely Features, and Decay the Youth of Women, causing them to appear Old, whilst they are Young, but would Break their Small Limbs, and Destroy their Tender Lives. Wherefore, Women have no Reason to Complain against Nature, or the God of Nature, for though the Gifts are not the Same they have given to Men, yet those Gifts they have given to Women, are much Better; for we Women are much more Favour'd by Nature than Men, in Giving us such Beauties, Features, Shapes, Gracefull Demeanour, and such Insinuating and Inticing Attractives, as Men are Forc'd to Admire us, Love us, and be Desirous of us, in so much as rather than not Have and Injoy us, they will Deliver to our Disposals, their Power, Persons, and Lives, Inslaving Themselves to our Will and Pleasures; also we are their Saints, whom they Adore and Worship, and what can we Desire more, than to be Men's Tyrants, Destinies, and Goddesses?

Part XIII. *Orations in the Field of Peace*

A *Peasants Oration to his Fellow Clowns*

Fellow Peasants,

For we are all Fellows in Labour, Profit, and Pleasure, though not Fellows in Arms, Spoils, and Danger, and though we Live in the Fields of Peace, and not in the Fields of Warr, yet our Fields of Peace resemble the Fields of Warr, for we are an Army of Clowns, though not of Souldiers, and our Commanders are our Landlords, who often Deceive us of the Increase of our Labours, as the Warring commanders Deceive their Common Souldiers of the Profit of their Spoils; also we have our Infantery, and our Cavallry; for all those that belong to the Keeping and Breeding of Beast, as Shepherds, Grasiers, Herdmen, Goat-herds, Swine-herds, and Carters, are of the Cavallry, but all they that belong to the Earth, as Sowers, Planters, Reapers, Threshers, Hedgers, Ditchers, Diggers, Delvers, are our Infantery; also we have Arms and Ammunition, for we are Arm'd with our Beast Skins, and our Arms of use are Pikes, Forks, Cutting Sickles, Mowing Sithes, Pruning Knives, Thrashing Flails, Plough-sherds, Shepherds Hooks, Herd-mens Staves, and the like, and our Match, Powder, and Bullets, are Puddings, Pease, and Porradge, and our Granadoes are Eggs of all Sorts and Sizes, our Carts are our Waggons, our Cottages our Tents, and our Victuals and Country Huswives our Bagg and Baggage, and the Lowing of our Herds, and Bleating of our sheep, are our Drums and Trumpets, not to Alarm us to Fight, but to Feed; also we have Enemies, which are Unseasonable Seasons, Rotting Moistures, Drowning Showres and Over-flows, Chilling Frost, Scorching Heat, and Devouring Worms, all which we Fight against, not with Force, but with Industry. And our Army of Clowns is more Skilfull to Destroy our Enemies, than an Army of Souldiers is to Destroy their Enemies, nay, our Army is an Army wherein is Peace and Plenty, whereas in their Army is Warr and Want: we become Rich with Safety, they become Poor with Danger, we be Gentle to Beast, they be Cruel to Men, they Thrive by Blood, we by Milk,

we get Health by our Labours, and Long Life by our Temperance, and they get Diseases in their Riots, and Death in their Warrs: Thus they Live Painfully, Die Violently, and only Leave their Bare Name to their Posterity and Beggarly Race, we Live Healthfully, Die Peaceably, and Leave our Goods to our Posterity, who by their Wealth come to be Gentlemen.

A *Peasants, or Clowns Oration spoken in the Field of Peace, concerning Husbandry*

Fellow Peasants,

I must tell you, we Live in a Happy Age, where Peace Sows, and Plenty Reaps, for whereas Warrs Destroy our Increase, now Peace Increases our Stores; also I would have you Know, that our Profession which is Husbandry, is one of the Noblest and Generousest Professions, which is, to Imploy our Selves like as the Gods and Nature; for though we cannot Create Creatures, as Nature doth, yet we by our Industry Increase Nature's Creatures, not only Vegetables, that we Produce in our Fields, and Store in our Barns, but Animals, which we Breed in our Farms, and Feed in our Fields; But as Nature Commits Errors and Defects in Producing her Creatures, so we for want of Knowledge have not the Good effect of our Labours; for though we are Bred up to Husbandry, yet we are not all so Knowing in Husbandry, as to Thrive and Grow Rich by our Labours; for as all Scholars are not Learned, that have Lived and Spent most of their time in Studies in Universities, but are meer Dunces; or as Artisans, are not all Excellent Workmen, although they have been Bound to their Trade, and have Wrought long in it, yet are but Bunglers: So for Husbandry, all Husbandmen are not so Knowing in their Profession as to Thrive . . . ; for as Learning without Practice is of No Effect, so Practice without Knowledge is of Small Profit; . . . but when Practice and Wit are joyned together, they beget Wisdom and Wealth, the One being Adorned with Gold, the Other Inthroned with Fame, for Emperours have Ascended from the Plough, and Kings from the Sheep-coats, Converting their Plough-sherds to Thrones, their Sickles to Crowns, and their Sheep-hooks to Scepters. Thus Clowns, Boors, or Peasants by Name, are become Princes in Power, and Princes in Power are become Beasts by Name and nature, witness *Nebuchadnezzar*.

A *Peasants Oration to his Fellow Peasants.*

Fellow Peasants,

Give me Leave to Tell you, we are the most Unhappy People in the World, for we Live to Labour, and Labour to Live; and we are not only the Unhappiest, but the Basest men in the World, for we are not only Bred with Beasts, and live with Beasts, and Dye like

Beasts, but we are the Bawds and Pimps too, to bring Beasts to Act Bestially together; also we are the Dungers of the Earth, to Carry and spread the several Excrements of several Creatures thereon, which makes us not only to have a Continual Stink in our Nostrils, but to be a meer Stink our Selves; Thus we are Beastly Within and Without, for all our Thoughts are Imployed on our Labours, which Labours are Brutish; neither have we such Fine and Pleasant Recreations as other Men, for our Recreation is only to Whistle, Pipe, and sometimes to Dance in a Crowd together, or rather Jump and Leap together, being ignorant of Dancing Measures; and the only Pleasure we have, is, to Rumble and Tumble our Country Lasses, who being more Foul than Fair, more Gross than Fine, more Noisome than Sweet, we soon Surfeit of them, and then they become a Trouble instead of a Delight, a Disease instead of a Pleasure, a Hate instead of a Love; and as they are to Us, so no Doubt but in the End we are to Them, a Loathing Surfeit; for we Meet Wildly, Associate Brutishly, and Depart Rudely; and as for our Profits, though we Labour, yet our Landlords have the Increase. In short, we are Slaves to Beasts, and Beasts in Comparison of other Men.

A *Peasants Oration to prove the Happiness of a Rural Life.*

Fellow Peasants,

The Peasant that formerly Spoke, hath rather shew'n his Ungratefulness to Nature, and his Unthankfulness to the Gods, by his Complaining Speech, than the Truth of our Condition and Life, for he sayes we are the Unhappiest, Miserablest, and Basest men in the World; all which is False; for can there be more Happiness than Peace and Plenty? can there be more Happiness than in the Repose of the Mind and Contemplations of Thoughts? can we Associate our Selves more Contentedly than with Innocent, Harmless, and sinless Creatures? are not Men more Stinking, Foul, and Wicked than Beasts? can there be more Odoriferous Perfumes, than the Sweet Vegetables on the Earth? or Finer Prospects than Stately Hills, Humble Vallies, Shady Groves, Clear Brooks, Green Hedges, Corn Fields, Feeding Cattel, and Flying Birds? can there be more Harmonious Musick than Warbling Nightingales and Singing Birds? can there be more Deligh[t]ful Sounds than Purling Brooks, Whispering Winds, Humming Bees, and Small-Voiced Grashoppers? can there be a more Delicious Sweet than Honey? more Wholesome Food than warm Milk, Fresh Butter, Prest Curds, New laid Eggs, Season'd Bacon, Savory Bread, Cooling Sallets, and Moist Fruits? or more Refreshing Drink than Whay, Whig, and Butter-milk? or more Strengthening Drink than Ale, Meath, Perry and Sider? and are not we at our Own Vintage? nay, should we Desire to Feed Highly, we may, for we are Masters of the Beasts of the Field, and the Poultry in the Grange, and know well how to catch the Fouls of the Air? can we have Warmer and Softer Garments than Cloth Spun from the Fleece of our Flocks; to keep out Freezing Cold? or can we be Cooler than under Shady Trees, whose Waving Leaves are Fans to Cool the Sultry Air? or can we Lye Softer than on the Downy Feathers of Cocks and Hens? and can we be Happier, than to be Free from Stately Ceremony, Court Envy, City Faction, Law Sutes, Corrupt Bribes, Malice, Treachery, and Quarrels? and as for our Recreation, although we do not Dance, Sing, and Play on Musick Artificially, yet we Pipe, Dance, and Sing Merrily; and if we do not Make Love Courtly, yet we Make Love Honestly; and for our Women, whom our Fellow Peasant doth Disgracefully, Scornfully, and Slanderously speak of, although they are but Plain Country Huswives, and not Fine Ladies, yet they be as Honest Women as They, for they Spend their time in Huswifry, and Waste not their time in Vanity; and as for their Beauty, their Faces are their Own, as Nature Gave them, not Borrowed of Art; and if they be not Fair, yet they are as Lovely, and as they use no Sweet Perfumes, for they use no Stinking Pomatum, and though their Hands be not Smooth, yet they are Clean, they use no Oyl'd Gloves to Grease them, but Rub their Hands, when Washed, with Coarse Cloth to Cleanse them; and as for their Garments, they are Plain, yet Commodious, Easie, and Decent, they are not Ribb'd up with Whale bones, nor Incumbred with Heavy Silver and Gold laces, nor Troubled with New Fashions; they Spend not half their time in Painting and Dressing, and though they Patch their Cloaths sometimes out of Good Huswifry, yet they Patch not their Faces out of Vanity, as Ladies do; neither do our Women Sweat to make their Faces Fair, but Sweat for their Children's Livelihood, and though they Breed not their Children Curiously, yet they Breed them up Carefully: But our Discontented and Ambitious Peasant, would Turn from a Clown to a Gallant, as to Waste Lavishly, to Spend Prodigally, to Live Idlely, to be Accoutred Fantastically, to Behave himself Proudly, to Boast Vaingloriously, to Speak Words Constraintly, to Make Love Amorously, to Flatter Falsely, to Quarrel Madly, and to Fight Foolishly, but not to Thrive Prudently, to Imploy Time Profitably, to Spend Wisely, to Live Temperately, to Speak Truly, to Behave himself Friendly, to Demean himself Civilly, to Make Love Chastly, to Live Peaceably, Innocently, and Safely, as we, that are of the Peasantry, do.

Sociable Letters (1664)

XVI.

Madam,

I Hope I have given the Lady *D.A.* no cause to believe I am not her Friend; for though she hath been of P[arliament']s. and I of K[ing']s. side, yet I know no reason why that should make a difference betwixt us, as to make us Enemies, no more than cases of Conscience in Religion, for one may be my very good Friend, and yet not of my opinion, every one's Conscience in Religion is betwixt God and themselves, and it belongs to none other. 'T is true, I should be glad my Friend were of my opinion, or if I thought my Friend's opinion were better than mine, I would be of the same; but it should be no breach of Friendship, if our opinions were different, since God is onely to be the Judg: And as for the matter of Governments, we Women understand them not, yet if we did, we are excluded from intermedling therewith, and almost from being subject thereto; we are not tied, nor bound to State or Crown; we are free, not Sworn to Allegiance, nor do we take the Oath of Supremacy; we are not made Citizens of the Commonwealth, we hold no Offices, nor bear we any Authority therein; we are accounted neither Useful in Peace, nor Serviceable in War; and if we be not Citizens in the Commonwealth, I know no reason we should be Subjects to the Commonwealth: And the truth is, we are no Subjects, unless it be to our Husbands, and not alwayes to them, for sometimes we usurp their Authority, or else by flattery we get their good wills to govern; but if Nature had not befriended us with Beauty, and other good Graces, to help us to insinuate our selves into men's Affections, we should have been more inslaved than any other of Natur's Creatures she hath made; but Nature be thank'd, she hath been so bountiful to us, as we oftener inslave men, than men inslave us; they seem to govern the world, but we really govern the world, in that we govern men: for what man is he, that is not govern'd by a woman more or less? None, unless some dull Stoick, or an old miserable Userer, or a cold, old, withered Batchelor, or a half-starved Hermit, and such like persons, which are but here and there one; And not only Wives and Mistresses have prevalent power with Men, but Mothers, Daughters, Sisters, Aunts, Cousins, nay, Maid-Servants have many times a perswasive power with their Masters, and a Land-lady with her Lodger, or a she-Hostess with her he-Guest; yet men will not believe this, and 'tis the better for us, for by that we govern as it were by an insensible power, so as men perceive not how their are Led, Guided, and Rul'd by the Feminine Sex. But howsoever, Madam, the disturbance in this Countrey hath made no breach of Friendship betwixt us, for though there hath been a Civil War in the Kingdom, and a general War amongst the Men, yet there hath been non amongst the Women, they have not fought pitch'd battels; and if they had, there hath been no particular quarrel betwixt her and me, for her Ladiship is the same in my affection, as if the Kingdom had been in a calm Peace; in which Friendship I shall alwayes remain hers, as also,

Your Ladiships

most Humble and Devoted S.

XCIII.

Madam,

You were pleased in your last Letter to express to me the Reason of the Lady *D. Ss.* and the Lady *E. Ks.* Melancholy, which was for Want of Children; I cannot Blame the Lady *D. S.* by reason her Husband is the Last of his Family unless he have Children, but the Lady *E. Ks.* Husband being a Widdower when he Married her, and having Sons to Inherit his Estate, and to Keep up his Family, I Know no Reason why she should be troubled for having no Children, for though it be the part of every Good Wife to desire Children to Keep alive the Memory of their Husbands Name and Family by Posterity, yet a Woman hath no such Reason to desire Children for her Own Sake, for first her Name is Lost as to her Particular in her Marrying, for she quits her Own, and is Named as her Husband; also her Family, for neither Name nor Estate goes to her Family according to the Laws and Customes of this Countrey; Also she Hazards her Life by Bringing them into the World, and hath the greatest share of Trouble in Bringing them up; neither can Women assure themselves of Comfort or Happiness by them, when they are grown to be Men, for their Name only lives in Sons, who Continue the Line of Succession, whereas Daughters are but Branches which by Marriage are Broken off from the Root from whence they Sprang, & Ingrafted into the Stock of another Family, so that Daughters are to be accounted but as Moveable Goods or Furnitures that wear out; and though sometimes, they carry the Lands with them, for want of Heirmales, yet the Name is not Kept nor the Line Continued with them, for these are buried in the Grave of the Males, for the Line, Name and Life of a Family ends with the Male issue; But many times Married Women desire Children, as Maids do Husbands, more for Honour than for Comfort or Happiness, thinking it a Disgrace to live Old Maids, and so likewise to be Barren, for in the Jews time it was some Disgrace to be Barren, so that for the most part Maids and Wives desire Husbands and Children upon any Condition, rather than to live Maids or Barren: But I am not of their minds, for I think a Bad Husband is far worse than No Husband, and to have Unnatural Children is more Unhappy than to have No Children, and where One Husband proves Good, as Loving and Prudent, a Thousand prove Bad, as Cross and Spendthrifts; and where One Child proves Good, as Dutiful and Wise, a Thousand prove Disobedient and Fools, as to do Actions both to the Dishonour and Ruine of their Familyes. Besides, I have observed, that Breeding Women, especially those that have been married some time, and have had No Children, are in their Behavior like New-married Wives, whose Actions of Behavior and Speech are so Formal and Constrain'd, and so Different from their Natural way, as it is Ridiculous; for New Married wives will so Bridle their Behaviour with Constraint, or Hang down their Heads so Simply, not so much out of True modesty, as a Forced Shamefulness; and to their Husbands they are so Coyly Amorous, or so Amorously Fond and so Troublesome Kind, as it would make the Spectators Sick, like Fulsome Meat to the Stomach; and if New-married Men were Wise men, it might make them Ill Husbands, at least to Dislike a Married Life, because they cannot Leave their Fond or Amorous Wives so Readily or Easily as a Mistress; but in Truth that Humour doth not last Long, for after a month or two they are like Surfeited Bodyes, that like any Meat Better than what they were so Fond of, so that in time they think their Husbands Worse Company than any other men. Also Women at the Breeding of their First Children make so many Sick Faces, although oftentimes the Sickness is only in their Faces, not but that some are Really Sick, but not every Breeding Women; Likewise they have such Feigned Coughs, and fetch their Breath Short, with such Feigning Laziness, and so many Unnecessary Complaints, as it would Weary the most Patient Husband to hear or see them: besides, they are so Expensive in their Longings and Perpetual Eating of several Costly Meats, as it would Undo a man that hath but an Indifferent Estate; but to add to their Charge, if they have not what they Please for Child-bed Linnen, Mantels, and a Lying-in bed, with Suitable Furniture for their Lying-Chamber, they will be so Fretfull and Discontented, as it will indanger their Miscarrying; Again to redouble the Charge, there must be Gossiping, not only with Costly Banquets at the Christening and Churching, but they have Gossiping all the time of their Lying-in, for then there is a more set or formal Gossiping than at other ordinary times. But I fear, that if this Letter come to the view of our Sex besides your self, they will throw more Spitefull or Angry Words out of their mouths against me, than the Unbeleeving Jews did hard Stones out of their hands at Saint *Stephan*; but the best is, they cannot Kill me with their Reproaches, I speak but the Truth of what I have observed amongst many of our Sex; Wherefore, Pray Madam, help to Defend me, as being my Friend, and I yours, for I shall Continue as long as I live,

Madam,

Your Ladyship's most Faithfull
and Humble Servant.

CLII.

Madam,

The messenger you sent is returning to you again, and with him I have sent some Babies, and other Toyes this City Affords, as a Token to your Daughter, I do not send them for Bribes, to Corrupt her from Edifying Learning, and Wise Instructions, for I would not have her Bred to Delight in Toyes, and Childish Pleasures, but I send them as Gifts, to Allure her to that which is most Profitable, and Happiest for her Life, for Children are sooner Perswaded by the Means of Tinsell-Toyes, and Flattering Words, to Listen to Wise Instruction, to Study Profitable Arts or Sciences, to Practice Good, Graceful Behaviours, and Civil Demeanours, than they can be Forced thereto, by Terrifying Threats, and Cruel Blows; 'tis true, they may be Forced to the Outward Forms, or Actions of Learning, but not to the Understanding, Profit, Grace, or Becoming, for Force Breaks the Understanding, Destroyes all Ingenuity, for the Fear of Punishment Confuses the Brain, and Disquiets the Mind so much, as it makes them Incapable of Right Impressions, whereas the Hope of Rewards Delights the Mind, and Regulates the Motions in the Brain, and makes them so Smooth, as the least Impression of Learning Prints Fairly therein, and so Plainly, as to be Remembered in their Elder Years; also it makes their Thoughts and Actions Industrious, to Merit those Rewards, and their Endeavours will be the more Active, through a Covetous Desire to Increase those Rewards; so that those Toyes which are given to Children in their Childish Years, may be a Means to Teach them, when Grown to Elder Years, to Know, and Acknowledge, that all Toyes are Vanities, and that nothing is to be Prized, or Esteemed, but what is Useful, and Best, either for their Present, or Future Life, as the Life of their Memory, or Renown. Thus, Madam, the Toyish Present is to a Good Design, and may prove to a Good End, which is the Wish of,

Madam,

Your faithful Friend
and Servant.

Sor Juana Inés de la Cruz (1648?–95)

Sor Juana Inés de la Cruz—who, like Sappho, was called "the tenth Muse"—was born in a village near Mexico City as Juana Asbaje y Ramírez. Her date of birth is generally given as 1651, but baptismal records indicate it was probably 1648. Her father was Basque, her mother was of a Spanish criollo family among whom Juana was raised. Juana's parents were not married, and though it appears that she was legally adopted by her father, he played little part in her life. She learned to read at about three years of age, developed very early a passionate interest in learning, devoured whatever books came to hand, and by the age of ten was already writing poetry and plays. She was sent to live with relatives in Mexico City, where she wished to study at the university, proposing to do so by dressing as a man. Though she was not permitted to do this, she did succeed in acquiring by her own efforts an extraordinary level of knowledge in the sciences, philosophy, and theology.

Presented at the court of the Marquis de Mancera, viceroy of Mexico, at about the age of fifteen, she became a protégée of the vicereine. Her literary accomplishments and renown grew rapidly. This was exceptional, but not wholly anomalous in an environment in which the ladies of the court were educated enough for Sor Juana to feel that talking with the vicereine, the "Laura" of her poems, was not time taken away from her studies, but a continuation of them. However, as a criolla without fortune in the precarious environment of the viceregal court, her future in a secular life as a lady-in-waiting was uncertain. In 1667, rejecting the prospect of marriage, Juana first entered a Carmelite convent. Her confessor, Bishop Antonio Núñez, was one of those who persuaded her to turn to the life of the convent, helping to pay her dowry and confession costs when she became a nun. She left the Carmelite order after only a few months, but in 1669 she entered a less restrictive convent, of the Order of St. Jerome, where she remained for the rest of her life.

For many years Sor Juana found it possible to pursue her literary, intellectual, musical, and scientific interests in the convent. Though not wealthy, neither was she poor. The convent "cells" were two-story apartments with many amenities, and the nuns often had several servants. Sor Juana entered the convent with a servant given to her by her mother, a mulatto slave woman named Juana de San José, about whom there is little information. Through gifts and purchases Sor Juana collected the best library in Mexico and many precious musical and scientific instruments. A new viceroy and his wife, the Count and Countess of Paredes, became her patrons in the period 1680 to 1688, and she received many visitors from court circles and invitations to write for public occasions. She was famous not only in Mexico but also—or perhaps more so—in Spain, for her prized lyric and philosophical poetry, comic drama, and scientific learning. The first collection of her works was published in Madrid in 1689. Her popularity and reputation were such that she was often requested to write works which she later described as pressed upon her by the desires, needs, or challenges of others.

At the same time, there were counterpressures upon her to desist from writing, perhaps even from studying, and to apply herself to strictly religious devotions. She recounted in later years the suffering and humiliation of being subjected to unrelenting criticism from those around her. In 1690 the Bishop of Puebla publicly chastised her for failing to write on religious subjects. He wrote under the female pseudonym Sor Philothea [Filotea]—a misogynist practice of seventeenth-century male anti-feminists (Kretsch, 375). This reproach appears, however, to have been occasioned rather by her temerity in entering the theological controversies surrounding the Jesuit Antonio Vieira's critique of the Church Fathers. Her former benefactor, Antonio Núñez, a Jesuit powerful in the Inquisition, broke off contact with her following the publication of her response to the Bishop of Puebla, her famous Reply to Sor Philothea in 1691. He returned to her support only when, in 1693, she renounced her studies and sold her books and instruments, giving the proceeds to the poor. She spent her last two years in charitable works and died tending the sick during the plague in 1695.

Sor Juana chose the life of the convent out of a combination of "total disinclination to marriage," the lack of honorable secular alternatives, and the hope of assuring her "ardently desired salvation," as she tells us explicitly in the Reply to Sor Philothea. But many of the "incidental" aspects of convent life were, as she says, "repellent to my nature," and it is clear that her life and her writings set her apart from other nuns. Many cloistered women of her time wrote in a variety of forms, such as biographies, histories, plays, poetry, letters, and confessional narratives. But as Asunción Lavrin has pointed out, these nuns' writings are characterized by penitential and mystical features—accounts of visions and mystical experiences, ecstasies, acts of penance and purification, discipline and mortification of the flesh, renunciation and humiliation. All these are generally absent from Sor Juana's writings, which more often deal with human love and its complexities, the festive aspects of religious celebrations, or the beauties, joys, and challenges of nature and knowledge.

Sor Juana's love poetry and portrayals of "manly" women in comic dramas have provided ground for speculation about her homoerotic relationships with women and for interpretation of her works in the context of lesbian literary criticism. Particularly in poems addressed to "Phyllis" or "Lysis" (María Luisa, Countess of Laredo), Sor Juana expressed a love more passionate and sensuous than that of ordinary loving friendship, and a consciousness of feelings out of the ordinary for a woman toward another woman. Octavio Paz has argued that this love was nonetheless a chaste and spiritual love, premised on a Platonic dualism separating body and soul, in which "the soul has no sex." Paz maintains: "For Sor Juana the pursuit of culture not only involved masculinization but carried with it the neutralization of sexuality" (85, 94, 214–15). Lisa Rabin, who leaves open the question of a sexual relationship, argues that Sor Juana's poetic portraits of beloved women — aristocratic patrons of her work — reflect a complex creole political consciousness (Rabin, 1997).

Two of Sor Juana's most important works are the philosophical poem, First Dream (El Sueño, or Primero Sueño), probably written about 1685 (Paz, 357), and the Reply to Sor Philothea (Respuesta a Sor Filotea), 1691, also known as the Response.

"We must underscore Sor Juana's absolute originality," writes Paz; "nowhere in all of Spanish literature of the sixteenth and seventeenth centuries [or earlier] is there anything like First Dream." It is possible, however, that Sor Juana was influenced in this poem, as well as in the feminist arguments of the Reply to Sor Philothea, by the writings of Christine de Pizan (Kretsch, 364). Sor Juana described First Dream as the only work she ever wrote to please herself. It is an allegorical poem variously interpreted as offering a theory of the limits of universal knowledge, a Thomistic argument against the sin of intellectual pride, or a feminist epic of women's pursuit and control of knowledge. Cast in allusions to classical mythology, it draws primarily on female figures and references, as well as analogies from nature for many aspects of politics and society. Some of the imagery reflects American Indian and black cultural influences. The poem has been seen as a narrative of the soul's pursuit of universal knowledge, drawing from both nature and history. It closes with the temporary, cyclical yielding of the heroine Night to the masculine realm of the day, mediated by the amazon of light, Aurora, the dawn. The inconclusive ending has been interpreted as a challenge to return to the struggle, again and again, in search of truth.

The Reply (Response) to Sor Philothea is Sor Juana's best-known work, embodying a spirited, eloquent,

learned, and carefully reasoned defense of women and intellectual freedom. It earned her mixed reactions of praise and blame in her own day and an enduring place in history as, some say, "the first feminist" of the Americas. The Response has been seen as a prose version of First Dream, but it goes beyond the philosophical poem in its explicit defense of the human pursuit of knowledge against dogmatic constraints and in its more direct challenge to hierarchical authority. In Montross's words: "The poem states that night will try again. So, too, does Sor Juana say that she pursued knowledge despite the persecution of others. Her intellect is free and must act."

The selections are excerpted from translations by Alan S. Trueblood in A Sor Juana Anthology (1988).

BAC

Sources and Suggested Readings

Chavez, Exequiel A. Sor Juana Inés de la Cruz. Mexico City: Editorial Porrúa, 1970.

Cruz, Juana Inés de la. Obras Completas. Ed. Alberta Salceda. Mexico: Fondo de Cultura Economica, 1957.

———. A Sor Juana Anthology. Trans. Alan S. Trueblood. Cambridge: Harvard University Press, 1988.

———. A Woman of Genius: The Intellectual Autobiography of Sor Juana Inés de la Cruz. Trans. Margaret Sayers Peden. Salisbury, Conn.: Lime Rock Press, 1982.

Hellner, Nancy Ann. "Marginal Laughter: Humor in Contemporary American Lesbian/Feminist Drama." Ph.D. diss., Arizona State University, 1992, chap. 2.

Kretsch, Donna R. "Sisters across the Atlantic: Aphra Behn and Sor Juana Inéz de la Cruz." Women's Studies 21 (1992): 361–79.

Lavrin, Asunción. "Unlike Sor Juana? The Model Nun in the Religious Literature of Colonial Mexico." In Stephanie Merrim, ed., Feminist Perspectives on Sor Juana Inés de la Cruz, 61–85. Detroit: Wayne State University Press, 1991.

Merrim, Stephanie. Early Modern Women's Writing and Sor Juana Inés de la Cruz. Nashville: Vanderbilt University Press, 1999.

Merrim, Stephanie, ed. Feminist Perspectives on Sor Juana Inés de la Cruz. Detroit: Wayne State University Press, 1991.

Montross, Constance M. Virtue or Vice? Sor Juana's Use of Thomistic Thought. Washington, D.C.: University Press of America, 1981.

Paz, Octavio. Sor Juana: or, the Traps of Faith. Cambridge: Harvard University Press, 1988.

Rabin, Lisa. "The Blasón of Sor Juana Inés de la Cruz: Politics and Petrarchism in Colonial Mexico." BHS (Bulletin of Hispanic Studies) 72, 1 (January 1995): 29–39.

———. "Speaking to Silent Ladies: Images of Beauty and Politics in Poetic Portraits of Women from Petrarch to Sor Juana Inés de la Cruz." MLN (Modern language notes) 112 (1997): 147–65.

Scott, Nina M. "Sor Juana Inés de la Cruz: 'Let Your

Women Keep Silence in the Churches . . .'" *Women's Studies International Forum* 8, 5 (1985): 511–19.

Warnke, Frank J., trans. *Three Women Poets, Renaissance and Baroque: Louise Labé, Gaspara Stampa, and Sor Juana Inés de la Cruz.* Lewisburg: Bucknell University Press, 1987.

First Dream (1685)

. . . In remote mountain hideaways,
misshapen hollow crags
whose ruggedness is less defense
than their darkness is protection,
abodes of utter blackness
where night is safe from daylight's glare,
to which sure foot of practiced hunter
has never yet ascended,
the legions of wild animals lay resting—
some shedding all ferocity,
others, their timorousness—
each to Nature's power
paying the tribute
imposed by her on all alike.
The king of beasts, though open-eyed
pretending to keep watch, lay fast asleep.
That once-illustrious monarch
cornered by his own dogs,
now a timid hart,
pricks up an ear
to catch the slightest motion
of the peaceful surrounding night,
the merest shift of atom,
and twitching each ear in turn,
perceives the faint and muffled sound
uneasily through his sleep.
In the quietude of the nest
built out of twigs and mud—
hammock hung where foliage is thickest—
the light-pinioned tribe
slumbers away and gives the wind
a respite from the slashes of its wings.

Jupiter's majestic bird,
the dutiful king of fowl, rejects
complete repose, holding it a vice,
too far indulged, and taking care
not to fall unwittingly asleep.
Entrusting all his weight to a single leg,
he keeps a pebble in the other foot—
an alarm for his light sleep—

so that, when slumber impends,
it may not be prolonged,
will rather be interrupted
by kingly pastoral concern.
Uneasy lies the head that wears a crown!
Not for one instant may he lay it down.
Mysterious explanation this may be
why crowns are circular,
the golden round betokening
the unending obligation of the king.

All was now bound in sleep,
all by silence occupied.
Even the thief was slumbering,
even the lover had closed his eyes.
The hour of silence is drawing to a close,
the dark time is half over
when, worn out by daily tasks—
oppressed not only
by the heavy burden
of bodily exertion, but fatigued
by pleasure as well (for any object
continually before the senses,
even if pleasurable, will cloy them:
hence Nature is always shifting weight
from one side of the balance to the other,
setting the unsettled needle to its task
of logging all activity—now leisurely,
now toilsome—as she directs
the universe's complicated clockwork);
the limbs, then, all were occupied
by deep and welcome sleep,
leaving the senses for a time
if not deprived, relieved
of their customary labor—
labor indeed but labor greatly loved,
if labor can be loved—
the senses, I say, had yielded
to the likeness of life's opponent,
who, slow to arm and cowardly in attack,
with sleepy weapons is a lazy victor
over lowly shepherd's crook and lofty scepter
and all that stands between,
purple and sackcloth being all one for him.
His level is all-powerful:
it never makes exceptions
for any man alive,
be he one who wears the sovereign tiara
made up of triple crowns, or one
who dwells in hut of straw,
a man whom the Danube gilds in mirrored glory
or a denizen of humble rushes:
with one unvarying measuring-rod
(Morpheus being, after all,

a powerful image of death)
he graduates brocade and sackcloth.

    The soul now being released
from outward governance, activity
which keeps her materially employed
for better or for worse the whole day through,
at some remove although not quite cut off,
pays out their wages
of vegetal heat only
to listless limbs and resting bones
oppressed by temporary death.
The body in unbroken calm,
a corpse with soul,
is dead to living, living to the dead,
the human clock attesting
by faintest signs of life
its vital wound-up state,
wounded not by hand but by arterial concert:
by throbbings which give tiny measured signs
of its well-regulated movement. . . .

    And that most marvelous and scientific
manufacturer of heat,
provident supplier of the limbs,
always at work and never stinting,
which neither favors the closest member
nor overlooks the farthest
but keeps exact account
on her natural dial
of the share she apportions to each one . . .
so this, if not forge of Vulcan,
moderate bonfire of human warmth,
was sending to the brain
vapors from the four well-tempered humors,
humid but so clear
it not only failed to cloud with them
the images which the estimative sense
furnished to the imaginative
and the latter, for safer keeping,
passed on in purer form
to diligent memory
to incise retentively and store with care,
but also offered the fantasy
a chance to put together
further images. . . .
so the fantasy was calmly copying
the images of everything,
and the invisible brush was shaping
in the mind's colors, without light
yet beautiful still, the likenesses
not just of all created things
here in this sublunary world, but those as well
that are the intellect's bright stars,

and as far as in her power lay
the conception of things invisible,
was picturing them ingeniously in herself
and displaying them to the soul.

    Meanwhile the latter, all intent
on her immaterial being,
was contemplating that most lovely spark,
that portion of highest being
in whose likeness in herself she took delight.
She thought herself almost loosed
from that bodily chain,
that always blocks her path,
obstructing crudely and grossly interfering
with the flight of intellect through which she plumbs
the vast immensity of the firmament
or ponders the well-regulated orbits
in which the celestial bodies
variously run their courses—
a heavy sin with punishment inherent,
the relentless shattering of inner peace,
when it lapses into vain astrology—
placed, so she thought, on the towering crest
of a mountain next to which that very Atlas,
which like a giant dominates all others,
becomes a mere obedient dwarf,
and Olympus, whose tranquil brow
has never admitted violation
by buffeting winds,
is unworthy of foothill status. . . .

    The two Pyramids—proud boast
of vainglorious Memphis, ultimate refinement
of architecture, pennants, if not fixed,
no fluttering ones surely—whose great mass,
crowned with barbaric trophies,
was tomb and ensign to the Ptolemies,
broadcasting to the wind and clouds
(if not to heaven as well)
Egyptian glories, deeds of Memphian prowess—
of that great city, Cairo now, I mean,
forever undefeated—
deeds never sung by Fame, too dumbstruck
by their very abundance,
glories still written in the wind and sky;
these Pyramids, in lifting higher and higher
in smooth and level stages, their vast bulk,
shrank so in girth and with such art
that the closer the lynxlike gaze
of the observing eye approached the heavens,
the more it lost its way amid the winds,
unable to discern the minute tip
that feigns a juncture with the lowest heaven, . . .
These, be they glories of Egypt

or high points of idolatry,
barbaric hieroglyphics
of purblind error, as that singer says,
that Greek, blind also, and a sweetest poet— . . .

In Homer's opinion, then,
the pyramids were mere material versions,
outward manifestations only
of inner dimensions instancing
the human spirit's attitude:
for just as the ambitious fiery flame
assumes pyramidal shape when mounting
heavenward, so the human mind
assumes this very shape
in ever aspiring to the one First Cause,
the center toward which the straight line tends,
if not indeed the circumference
containing every essence ad infinitum.

These two artificial mountains, then
(be they miracles or marvels),
and that lofty blasphemous Tower
whose unhappy remnants to this day—
languages diversely shaped, not stones,
lest voracious time devour them—
are the divers tongues which still obstruct
the easy intercourse of humankind
(causing those Nature formed as one
to seem entirely different
simply because their tongues are unfamiliar),
if those three were compared
to the elevated pyramid of mind
on which, not knowing how, the soul
found herself now placed, they would see themselves
so far below that anyone
would assume her perch was in another sphere,
since her ambitious urge,
making of her very flight a summit,
lifted her to the highest point
of her own mentality,
mounted so high above herself, she thought
she had emerged in some new region.

At this almost limitless elevation,
jubilant but perplexed,
perplexed yet full of pride,
and astonished although proud,
the sovereign queen of this sublunary world
let the probing gaze, by lenses unencumbered,
of her beautiful intellectual eyes
(unperturbed by distance
or worry lest some opaque obstacle
by intervening hide objects from her view)
range unrestricted over all creation.

Such an immense assemblage,
a mass so unencompassable,
though holding out to sight
some chance of being taken in,
held none to the understanding, which being dazed
by objects in such profusion, its powers
surpassed by their very magnitude,
turned coward and drew back. . . .

But, as one who has been deprived
by lengthy darkness of all color
in visible objects,
if suddenly assaulted by bright light
is made the blinder by its very brilliance— . . .
and appeals to that same shade which formerly
had been a shadowy obstacle to the sight,
against the light's offenses, . . .
natural procedure, this inborn wisdom,
which, with confirmation by experience,
a silent teacher perhaps,
but exemplary persuader,
has led physicians more than once
to mete out scrupulously
in proportions carefully determined
the secret harmful qualities
of deadly poisons,
now via an excess
of properties hot or cold,
now through the unknown sympathies
or antipathies whereby
natural causes carry out their action
(providing our astonished admiration
with a sure effect born of an unknown cause,
by taking endless pains and with observant
empirical attention tested first
in experiments performed on animals,
where the danger is not so great)
so that they might concoct in a healthful brew—
final goal of Apollonian science—
a marvelous counterpoison,
for thus at times from evil good arises;
not otherwise, then, did the soul,
astounded by the sight of such a mass
of objects, pull the attention back,
which, scattered over such diversity,
as yet had found recovery impossible
from the portentous shock
that had blocked her reasoning power,
allowing her scarcely more
than a rudimentary embryo
of muddled discourse, one so shapeless,
that from the confusion of species it embraced
it formed a picture of disordered chaos—
associating species in no order,

dissociating them in none,
so that the more they mix and intermingle,
the more they come apart in disarray
from sheer diversity—
forcibly cramming the vast overflow
of objects into a tiny vessel
unfit to hold even the humblest, most minute.

    In fine, the ship of the soul, sails furled,
whose inexperience she entrusted
to the treacherous sea, the fanning wind,
thoughtlessly presuming
the sea to be loyal, constant the wind,
against her will was forced
to run ashore on the beach
of the vast sea of knowing,
with rudder broken, yardarms snapped,
kissing each grain of sand
with every splinter.
Recovering there,
for calking she resorted
to prudent rumination,
the temperate wisdom born of thoughtful judgment,
which, reining in its operation,
considered as more appropriate
restriction to a single subject
or taking separate account
of each thing, one by one,
contained in every one
of those artfully constructed
categories, ten in number:
a metaphysical reduction teaching
(by encompassing generic entities
in the purely mental constructs
of abstract thought, eschewing
embodiment in matter)
the art of forming universals,
sagely compensating by such art
for a deficiency:
the inability to know by one sole act
of intuition every created thing,
the need instead to move up, step by step,
as on a ladder, from one concept
to the next, adopting of necessity
the relative order of understanding
required by the restricted power of Mind,
which must entrust its progress
to a graduated form of reasoning.

    The imparting of such doctrine fortifies
Mind's weaknesses with learned nourishment
and the lengthy, although smooth,
continuing course of discipline
endows it with lusty energies,
wherewith inspirited, its pride aspires

to the glorious banner that rewards
the most arduous undertaking;
to ascend the lofty stair,
by cultivation, first of one,
then of another form of knowledge
till honor's summit gradually comes in view,
the easeful goal of a most laborious climb
(from bitter seed a fruit delighting taste,
which even at such expense is inexpensive)
and treading valiantly, Mind implants
sure footsteps on the summit's lofty brow.

    Of this series now my mind
desired to pursue the method:
namely, from the basest level
of being—the inanimate
(the one least favored
by the second productive cause,
yet still not wholly destitute)—
to move on to the nobler hierarchy, . . .
a hierarchy furnished with some four
operations diverging in their action,
now attracting, now excluding carefully
whatever it judges unsuited to itself,
now expelling superfluities and making
the most useful of countless substances its own;

    then, this form once examined,
to scrutinize another form, more beautiful—
one that possesses feeling
(and, what is more, equipped with powers
of apprehending through imagination):
grounds for legitimate complaint—
if not indeed for claiming insult—
on the part of the brightest star
that sparkles, yet lacks all feeling,
however magnificent its brilliant light—
for the lowest, tiniest creature
surpasses even the loftiest of stars,
arousing envy;
and making of this bodily way of knowing
a foundation, however meager,
to move on to the wondrous
composite, triplicate
(set up on three concordant lines)
mysterious compendium
of all the lower forms:
the hinge that makes the link
between the purest nature,
that which occupies the highest throne,
and the least noble of the creatures,
the most abject,
equipped not only with the five
faculties of sense,
but ennobled also by the inner ones,

the three that rule the rest;
for not for nothing was he fitted out
by the powerful and knowing hand
to be supreme over all the others: . . .

    In short, I speak of man, the greatest wonder
the human mind can ponder,
complete compendium
resembling angel, plant, and beast alike:
whose haughty lowliness
partook of very nature. Why?
Perhaps that, being more fortunate
than any, he might be lifted high
by a grace of loving union.
Oh, grace repeated often,
yet never recognized sufficiently,
overlooked, so one might think,
so unappreciated is it,
so unacknowledged it remains. . . .

    Now if, from a single object—
my timid thought kept saying—
true knowledge shies away,
and reason ingloriously turns aside;
if on a species set apart
as independent of all others—
thought of as unrelated—
understanding turns her back;
if reason, overwhelmed, recoils
before so difficult a challenge,
refusing to take action resolutely,
doubting in her cowardice
that she can grasp even this single object,
how can she hope to function in the face
of so astounding and immense a system?
Its burden, terrible, unendurable—
were it not upheld at its very center—
would make the shoulders even of Atlas sag,
outdo the strength of Hercules,
and they, who proved sufficient counterweight
to the sphere of heaven,
would judge its fabric far less burdensome,
its framework less oppressive,
than the task of investigating Nature.

Bolder at other times,
my mind denounced as height of cowardice
yielding the laurels without one attempt
to meet the challenge of the lists.
Then it would seize upon the brave example
set by that famous youth, high-minded
charioteer of the chariot of flame;
then courage would be fired
by his grand and bold, if hapless, impulse,
in which the spirit finds

not, like timidity, a chastening lesson
but a pathway summoning it to dare;
once treading this, no punishment can deter
the spirit bent upon a fresh attempt
(I mean a thrust of new ambition).
Neither the nether pantheon—
cerulean tomb of his unhappy ashes—
nor the vengeful lightning bolt,
for all their warnings, ever will convince
the soaring spirit once resolved,
in lofty disregard of living,
to pluck from ruin an everlasting fame.
Rather, that youth is the very type, the model:
a most pernicious instance
(causing wings to sprout for further flights)
of that ambitious mettle,
which, finding in terror itself a spur
to prick up courage,
pieces together the name of glory
from letters spelling endless havoc.
Either the punishment should not be known
so that the crime would never become contagious,
a politic silence covering up instead,
with a statesman's circumspection,
all record of the proceedings;
or let a show of ignorance prevail,
or the insolent excess
meet its just deserts by secret sentence
without the noxious example
ever reaching public notice,
for broadcasting makes the wickedness
of the greatest crime all the greater
till it threatens a widespread epidemic,
while, left in unknown isolation,
repetition is far less likely
than if broadcast to all as a would-be lesson. . . .

    . . . The overtired limbs,
worn out by rest,
reacting to the lack of sustenance,
and neither wide-awake nor fast asleep,
were showing signs of wishing
to be stirring once again
by the languid, drawn-out stretching
the torpid sinews were engaging in.
Even without their owner's full assent,
the limbs were turning tired bones
from side to side;
the senses were beginning to resume
their functioning, despite mild interference
caused by the natural toxin,
half-opening the eyes;
and from the brain, now cleared,
phantasms had taken leave
and, being formed of lightest vapor,

converted easily to smoke or wind,
now let their shapes be dissipated.
Just so, the magic lantern
casts on white of wall
simulations of different painted figures,
made possible by shadow no less than light.
Maintaining amid shimmering reflections
the distances required
by the science of perspective
and confirmed in its true measurements
by a number of experiments,
the fleeting shadow
that faces into the brilliance of the light
simulates a body's form,
one possessing all dimensions, though it merits
no consideration even as surface.

    Meanwhile the father of flaming light
saw that the appointed hour was arriving
when he must climb the East.
He took his leave of our antipodes
with light departing down the West,
for through the flickers of his fading light
the same point serves to mark his going down
as ushers in the brightening of our East.
But not till Venus as the morning star,
beautiful and serene,
had pierced the first faint dawnlight,
and the fair wife of old Tithonus—
amazon arrayed in countless lights
(her armor against the night),
beautiful though bold,
valiant although tearful—
had let her lovely brow be seen
crowned with the lights of morning,
a tender prelude though a spirited one,
to the fiery planet,
who was busy marshaling his troops
of glimmering novices—
reserving glowing veterans, more robust,
to fill the rearguard—
against the tyrannical usurper
of the empire of daylight,
who wore a laurel girdle with countless shadows
and with her dreadful nighttime scepter
ruled over shadows
of whom she stood in awe herself.
But scarcely had the lovely harbinger
and standard-bearer of the Sun, unfurled
her luminous pennant in the East,
as all the bugles of the birds,
soft yet bellicose, sounded the call to arms
(resonate trumpeters and skilled,
though uninstructed)

when—cowardly as tyrants always are,
and beset by timorous misgivings—
although trying to put up a valiant front
with her forces, although flaunting
her funereal cloak as shield,
that took short wounds
from the stabbing brightness
(even though her uneasy bravery
was merely a crude cover for her fear
since she knew how weak was her resistance)—
as if relying more on flight
than belligerence for her salvation,
Night was blowing her raucous horn
to gather her swarthy squadrons in
and make an orderly retreat—
when a burst of bouncing light
assaulted her from closer by
as it bathed the topmost tip
of the loftiest of turrets in the world.

    The Sun appeared, the circle now complete
which he carves in gold against the sapphire blue.
From his luminous circumference there sprang
a thousand times a thousand golden specks,
a thousand streams of gold—
lines, I mean, of brilliant light
ruled on heaven's cerulean page,
drawn up for orderly attack
upon the dismal despot of his realm
who, in hasty headlong flight,
stumbling over her native terrors,
was treading on her very shadow
as she sought to reach the West
with the routed, broken ranks
of her shadow army, harassed by light
in close pursuit upon her heels.
At last her fleeing footsteps reached the point
where the West came into view
and, though rushing, regaining her composure,
plucking courage up from her very ruin,
she resolved, rebelling once again,
to see herself made sovereign
in that half of the globe
left unprotected by the sun
when the beauty of his golden locks
brought luster to our hemisphere.
Dealing judiciously with his light,
by orderly distribution he dispensed
to all things visible their colors,
restoring to every outer sense
full functioning,
flooding with light whatever had been opaque
throughout the world, and summoning me awake.

Sor Juana's Admonishment: The Letter of Sor Philothea [Filotea] de la Cruz [Bishop of Puebla] (1690)

Madam:

I have seen the letter in which you take issue with the Reverend Father Antonio de Vieira regarding the signs of Christ's love treated by him in his Maundy Thursday sermon. So subtle is his treatment that the most erudite persons have opined that, like a second Apocalyptic Eagle, his singular talent outsoared itself as it followed the scheme set forth earlier by the Most Illustrious Cesar Meneses, a Portuguese talent of the first rank. In my opinion, however, anyone following your exposition must admit that your quill was cut finer than either of theirs and that they might well have rejoiced at finding themselves confuted by a woman who does honor to her sex.

I at least have admired the keenness of your concepts, the skill of your proofs, and the vigorous clarity that lends conviction to the subject, a quality inseparably linked with wisdom. This is why the first word uttered by Divine Wisdom was *light*, for without illumination there can be no word of wisdom. Even Christ's words, cloaked in parables when He spoke of the deepest mysteries, were not held to be marvelous in the world. Only when He spoke out clearly did He win acclaim for knowing everything. This is one of the many special favors you owe to God, for clarity is not acquired by toil and diligence; it is a gift infused with the soul.

So that you may read yourself in clearer lettering in that document, I have had it printed; likewise, so that you may acknowledge the treasures God has placed in your soul and, being made thus more aware, may be more grateful, for gratitude and awareness are always born twins. . . .

I do not subscribe to the commonplace view of those who condemn the practice of letters in women, since so many have applied themselves to literary study, not failing to win praise from Saint Jerome. True, Saint Paul says women should not teach, but he does not order women not to study so as to grow wiser. He wished only to preclude any risk of presumptuousness in our sex, inclined as it is to vanity. . . .

Letters that breed arrogance God does not want in women. But the Apostle does not reject them so long as they do not remove women from a position of obedience. No one could say that study and learning have caused you to exceed your subordinate status. Indeed, they have served to perfect in you the finer forms of obedience. For if other nuns sacrifice their wills for the sake of obedience, you hold the mind captive, which is the most arduous and the most welcome sacrifice one can offer on the altars of Religion.

As this judgment shows, I do not mean you to modify your natural predisposition by giving up books; I do mean that you should improve it by sometimes reading the book of Jesus Christ. None of the Evangelists called the genealogy of Christ a book, except Saint Matthew [Matt. 1:1]. This was because at his conversion our Lord's wish was not so much to change his natural bent, as to improve upon it, so that if earlier as a publican his occupation was to keep books recording his transactions and interest, as an apostle he might better his nature, transforming the books of his ruin into the book of Jesus Christ. You have spent much time studying philosophers and poets. Surely it is only right for you now to better your occupation and upgrade your books.

Was there ever a nation more learned than Egypt? In it the world's first letters had their beginning and there were admirable hieroglyphics. In order to underscore Joseph's wisdom, Holy Scripture calls him a past master of Egyptian learning. Notwithstanding this, the Holy Ghost openly calls the people of Egypt barbarians, because all their learning served at most for probing into the courses of the stars and the heavens; it was not applied to curbing the unruliness of the passions. Their entire learning had as its goal perfecting men for political life, not lighting their way to the eternal. And learning which does not enlighten men for their salvation is deemed folly by God, who knows everything. . . .

I do not on this account ensure the reading of these authors, but I pass on to you some advice of Gerson's: Lend yourself to these studies; do not sell yourself to them, nor yet allow yourself to be carried away by them. The humanities are slaves and as such they have their usefulness for sacred studies. But they must be rejected when they dislodge Divine Wisdom from possession of the human mind and, though destined to be menials, take over as masters. They are to be recommended when the curiosity that has motivated them, which is a vice, gives way to studiousness, a virtue. . . .

Philothea de la Cruz [Bishop of Puebla]

The Reply to Sor Philothea (1691)

. . . Forgive, my Lady, the digression wrung from me by the force of truth; and, to tell the whole truth, as a way of eluding the difficulty of answering; indeed I had almost made up my mind to let silence be my answer. Yet, since silence is something negative, although it explains a great deal by its insistence on not explaining, some brief label is needed to enable one to understand what it is intended to mean. Otherwise, silence will say nothing. The vessel of election was transported to the third Heaven and, having seen the arcane secrets of God, he says: *Audivit arcana Dei, quae non licet homini loqui* ["He heard secret words, which it is not granted to man to utter" (2 Cor. 12:4)]. He does not tell what he saw; he says that he cannot tell it. Thus, of those things that cannot be spoken, it must at least be said that they cannot be, to make clear that keeping silent does not mean having nothing to say, but rather that words cannot encompass all there is to say. Saint John says [21:25] that were he to write down all the miracles worked by our Redeemer, there would be insufficient room in the whole world for the resultant books. About this passage Vieira says that the Evangelist spoke more in this one sentence than in everything else he wrote. And this is very well said (and does the Lusitanian Phoenix ever fail to say things well, even when it would be as well not to say them?), because with these words Saint John says all that he had left unsaid, and expresses whatever he had left unexpressed. . . .

Coming down to particulars, I confess to you, with the ingenuousness owed to you and the truth and clarity natural and habitual with me, that my not having written much on sacred subjects is not from disinclination or lack of application, but from an excess of the awe and reverence due those Sacred Letters, for the understanding of which I acknowledge myself so ill-equipped and which I am so unworthy to treat. . . . Then how should I dare to take this into my unworthy hands, when my sex, age, and especially my way of life all oppose it? And so I confess that many times this fear has taken the pen from my hand and caused the subject to sink back into the very mind from which it sought to emerge.

I encountered no such problem in secular subjects, since heresy against art is punished, not by the Holy Office, but by the laughter of the intelligent and the censure of the critical. The censure, *iusta vel iniusta, timenda non est* [whether deserved or not, is not to be feared], for it does not interfere with communion and attending mass, whence it concerns me little or not at all. For, in the opinion of the very people who slander me for writing, I am under no obligation to be learned nor do I possess the capacity never to err. Therefore my failure involves neither fault nor discredit: no fault since there is no chance of my not erring and *ad impossibilia nemo tenetur* [no one is obligated to attempt the impossible]. And in truth I have never written except when pressured and forced to and then only to please others and even then not only without enjoyment but with actual repugnance because I have never thought of myself as possessing the intelligence and educational background required of a writer. Hence my usual reply to those who urge me on, especially where sacred matters are involved: what aptitude have I, what preparation, what subjects, what familiarity do I possess for such a task, beyond a handful of superficial sophistries? Let such things be left to those who understand them: I want no trouble with the Holy Office. I am ignorant and shudder to think that I might utter some disreputable proposition or distort the proper understanding of some passage or other. My purpose in studying is not to write, much less to teach (this would be overbearing pride in my case), but simply to see whether studying makes me less ignorant. This is my reply and these are my feelings. . . .

. . . I became a nun because, although I knew that that way of life involved much that was repellent to my nature—I refer to its incidental, not its central aspects—nevertheless, given my total disinclination to marriage, it was the least unreasonable and most becoming choice I could make to assure my ardently desired salvation. To which first consideration, as most important, all the other small frivolities of my nature yielded and gave way, such as my wish to live alone, to have no fixed occupation which might curtail my freedom to study, nor the noise of a community to interfere with the tranquil stillness of my books. This made me hesitate a little before making up my mind, until, enlightened by learned persons that hesitation was temptation, I overcame it by the grace of God and entered upon the life I now pursue so unworthily. I thought I was escaping from myself, but, alas for me, I had brought myself along. In this propensity I brought my greatest enemy, given me by Heaven whether as a boon or a punishment I cannot decide, for far from dying out or being hindered by all the exercises religion entails, it exploded like gunpowder. *Privatio est causa appetitus* [Privation arouses the appetite] had its confirmation in me.

I went back (I misspeak: I had never stopped); I went on with the studious pursuit (in which I found relaxation during all the free time remaining from my obligations) of reading and more reading, study and more study, with no other teacher than books themselves. One can readily imagine how hard it is to study from those lifeless letters, lacking a teacher's live voice and explanations. Still I happily put up with all those drawbacks, for the sheer love of learning. Oh, if it had only been for the love of God, which would have been the sound way, what merit would have been mine! I *will* say that I tried to uplift my study as much as I could and direct it to serving Him, since the goal I aspired to was the study of theology, it seeming to me a mean sort of ineptitude for a Catholic not to know all that can be found out in this life through natural means concerning divine mysteries. I also felt that being a nun and not a lay person, I should, because of my ecclesiastical status, make a profession of letters—and furthermore that, as a daughter of Saint Jerome and Saint Paula, it would be a great disservice for the daughter of such learned parents to be a fool. This is what I took upon myself, and it seemed right to do so, unless of course—and this is probably the case—it was simply a way of flattering and applauding my own natural tendency, proposing its own pleasure to it as an obligation.

In this way I went on, continually directing the course of my study, as I have said, toward the eminence of sacred theology. To reach this goal, I considered it necessary to ascend the steps of arts and sciences, for how can one who has not mastered the style of ancillary branches of learning hope to understand that of the queen of them all? . . .

. . . How then, could I, remote as I was from virtue and learning, find the strength to write? Thus, for the acquisition of certain fundamentals, I would constantly study divers things, without inclining in particular to any given one, inclined rather to all generally. So it happened that my having concentrated on some more than others was not a matter of choice but came about through the chance of having found books dealing with the former subjects closer to hand, which gave them preference without any decision of mine. As I had no material goal in mind, nor any limitation of time constraining me to the study of any one thing to meet degree requirements, almost at once I was studying different things or dropping some to take up others, although this was not wholly unsystematic since some I called study and other diversion. The latter brought me relaxation from the former. It follows from this that I have studied many things, yet know nothing because each one always interfered with some other. True, I am referring to the operative aspect of those which have one, for, obviously, while the pen is in motion, the compass is at rest, and while the harp is being played, the organ is still, *et sic de caeteris.* For, because much bodily practice is required to develop a skill, one who

spreads herself out over a number of exercises will never acquire any one skill perfectly. In the formal and speculative realms, however, the opposite is true, and I should like to convince everyone by my own experience not only that different subjects do not interfere with one another, but that they actually support one another, since certain ones shed light on others, opening a way into them by means of variations and occult connections. It was to form this universal chain that the wisdom of their Author so put them in place that they appear correlated and bound together with marvelous concert and bonding. This is the chain that the ancients pretended emerged from Jupiter's mouth, on which all things were strung and linked together. So much is demonstrated by the Reverend Father Athanasius Kircher in his curious book *De magnete* [On the Magnet]. All things proceed from God, who is at once the center and the circumference from which all existing lines proceed and at which all end up. . . .

What I might point out in self-justification is how severe a hardship it is to work not only without a teacher but also without fellow students with whom to compare notes and try out what has been studied. Instead I have had nothing but a mute book as teacher, an unfeeling inkwell as fellow student, and, in place of explanation and exercises, many hindrances, arising not only from my religious duties (it goes without saying that these occupy one's time most profitably and beneficially) but also from things implicit in the life of a religious community—such as when I am reading, those in a neighboring cell take it upon themselves to play music and sing. Or when I am studying and two maids quarrel and come to me to settle their dispute. Or when I am writing and a friend comes to visit, doing me a great disservice with the best of intentions, whereupon I not only must put up with the bother but act grateful for the injury. This goes on all the time, because, since the times I devote to my studies are those remaining when the regular duties of the community are over, the others are also free then to come and bother me. Only those who have experienced communal religious life can know how true this is. Only the strength of my vocation allows my nature to take pleasure in this and the great bond of love between me and my beloved sisters, for since love is union, there are no poles too distant for it. . . .

. . . Well, the most arduous part of the difficulties still remains to be told, for those related up to now have been simply necessary or incidental annoyances which are such only indirectly. Still to come are the outright ones which have worked directly to hinder and to prohibit my pursuit of learning. Who could fail to believe, in view of such widespread plaudits, that I have sailed with a following wind on a glassy sea to the encomiums of general acclaim? Well, the Lord knows that it has hardly been so, for amidst the bouquets of that very acclaim, asps of such invidiousness and relentlessness as I could never describe have stirred and reared up. Those most harmful and painful to me are not the persons who have pursued me with open hatred and ill will, but those who, while loving me and wishing me well (and being possibly very meritorious in God's eyes for their good intentions), have mortified and tortured me much more than the others, with their: "This study is incompatible with the blessed ignorance to which you are bound. You will lose your way, at such heights your head will be turned by your very perspicacity and sharpness of mind." What have I not gone through to hold out against this? Strange sort of martyrdom, in which I was both the martyr and my own executioner!

Why, for the ability (doubly infelicitous in my case) to compose verse, even when it was sacred verse, what nastiness have I not been subjected to, what unpleasantness has not come my way! I must say, Madam, that sometimes I stop and reflect that anyone who stands out—or whom God singles out, for He alone can do so—is viewed as everyone's enemy, because it seems to some that he is usurping the applause due them or deflecting the admiration which they have coveted, for which reason they pursue him. . . .

. . . Oh singularity, set up as a target for envy and an object for contradiction! Any eminence, be it in dignity, nobility, wealth, beauty, learning, is subject to this penalty, but most implacably subject to it is eminence of mind. First of all, because it is the most defenseless, since wealth and power punish anyone daring to challenge them; but not mind, for the greater it is, the more modest and long-suffering, and the less prone to defend itself. Secondly, because, as Gracian so learnedly put it, superiority of mind goes with superiority of the whole being. The angel is superior to man for no other reason than superiority of mind; man surpasses animals in mind alone. Thus, as no one wished to be inferior to anyone else, no one will admit that another is superior in mind, since this proceeds from natural superiority. Anyone will allow and admit that another is nobler than he, richer, handsomer, and even more knowledgeable, but that someone else has a better mind scarcely anyone will grant. *Rarus est, qui velit cedere ingenio* [Rare is the man willing to acknowledge another's superiority of mind (Martial, *Epigrams* 8.8)]. That is why assaults on this gift are so successful. . . .

. . . I confess that I am far removed from wisdom's confines and that I have wished to pursue it, though *a longe*. But the sole result has been to draw me closer to the flames of persecution, the crucible of torture, and this has even gone so far as a formal request that study be forbidden me.

This was successful in one instance involving a very holy and very ingenuous prelate who thought studying was something for the Inquisition and ordered me to cease. I obeyed her (for the three months her right to so order me lasted) as regarded not taking a book in hand, but as to ceasing study altogether, it not being in my power, I could not carry it out. For, although I did not study from books, I did from everything God has created, all of it being my letters, and all this universal chain of being my book. I saw nothing without reflecting on it; I heard nothing without wondering at it—not even the tiniest, most material thing. For, as there is no created thing, no matter how lowly, in which one cannot recognize the *me fecit Deus* [God made me], there is none that does not confound the mind once it stops to consider it. Thus, I repeat, I looked and marveled at all of them, so much so that simply from the person with whom I spoke, and from what that person said to me, countless reflections arose in my mind. What could be the origin of so great a variety of characters and minds, when all belonged to one species? Which humors and hidden qualities could bring this about? If I saw a figure, I at once fell to working out the relationship of its lines, measuring it with my mind and recasting it along different ones. Sometimes I would walk back and forth across the front of a sleeping-room of ours—a very large one—and observe how, though the lines of its two sides were parallel and its ceiling horizontal, one's vision made it appear as if the lines inclined toward each other and the ceiling were lower at the far end, from which I inferred that visual lines run straight but not parallel, tending rather toward a pyramidal figure. . . .

This type of observation would occur to me about everything and still does, without my having any say in the matter; indeed, it continually irritates me because it tires my mind. I thought the same thing occurred in everyone's case, and with writing verse as well, until experience proved me wrong. This turn, or habit, of mind is so strong that I can look upon nothing without reflecting on it. Two little girls were playing with a top in my presence. The moment I saw its movement and form, I began, in my crazy way, to consider the easy motion of the spherical form, and how, the impulse once given, it continued independently of its cause, since at a distance from the girl's hand, which originated the motion, the top went on dancing. Nor was this enough for me. I had flour brought and sifted, so as to tell, when the top danced over it, whether the circles its motion described were perfect or not. I discovered that they were simply spirals which moved farther and farther from the circular in proportion as the impulse wore down. . . .

What could I not tell you, my Lady, of the secrets of Nature which I have discovered in cooking! That an egg hangs together and fries in fat or oil, and that, on the contrary, it disintegrates in syrup. That, to keep sugar liquid, it suffices to add the tiniest part of water in which a quince or some other tart fruit has been. That the yolk and white of the same egg are so different in nature, that when eggs are used with sugar, the yolks must be used separately from the white, never, together with them. I do not wish to tire you with such trivia, which I relate only to give you a full picture of my native turn of mind, which will, no doubt, make you laugh. But, Madam, what is there for us women to know, if not bits of kitchen philosophy? . . .

But to continue with the workings of my mind, let me say that this line of thought is so constant with me that I have no need of books. On one occasion, when, owing to some serious stomach trouble, the doctor forbade my studying, I obeyed for several days, but then I pointed out that allowing me books would be much less harmful, since my mental activity was so vigorous, so vehement, that it used up more spirits in a quarter of an hour than studying from books did in four days. So they agreed reluctantly to allow me to read. And not only that, my Lady: even my sleep was not free from this constant activity of my brain. In fact, it seems to go on during sleep with all the more freedom and lack of restraint, putting together the separate images it has carried over from waking hours with greater clarity and tranquility, debating with itself, composing verses, of which I could draw up a whole catalogue for you, including certain thoughts and subtleties I have arrived at more easily while asleep than while awake, which I won't go into, not wishing to bore you. . . .

I must admit, likewise, that although, as I have said, a truth such as this requires no exemplification; nevertheless the many precedents I have read about in both divine and humane letters have greatly assisted me. For I see a Debbora [Judges 4 and 5] setting up laws in both military and political spheres, and governing a nation that could boast so many learned men. I see a most wise Queen of Sheba [3 (1) Kings 10; 2 Paralipomenon (Chronicles) 9], so learned that she dared to challenge with enigmas the wisdom of the wisest of the wise, without suffering on that account any reproof. Rather, thanks to that, she becomes judge of the unbelieving. I see so many and such outstanding women, like Abigail [1 Kings (1 Sam.) 25], endowed with the gift of prophecy; others, like Esther, with that of persuasiveness; others, like Rahab [Josh. 2], with piety; others, like Anna, mother of Samuel [1 Kings (1 Sam.) 1 and 2], with perseverance; and an infinite number of others, all possessing other gifts and virtues.

If I look among the Gentiles, the first I come upon are the Sybils, chosen by God to prophesy the principal mysteries of our faith—and to do so in such learned and refined verse that it holds wonderment itself in suspense. I see worshiped as goddess of learning a woman like Minerva, daughter of the first Jupiter and giver of all the learning of Athens. I see a Polla Argentaria helping her husband, Lucan write the Pharsalian Battle. I see divine Tiresias' daughter, more learned than her father. I see a Zenobia, queen of the Palmyrans, as wise as she is brave. An Arete, daughter of Aristippus, learned in the extreme. A Nicostrata, inventor of Latin letters and extremely erudite in the Greek. An Aspasia of Miletus, teacher of philosophy and rhetoric and instructress of the philosopher Pericles. A Hypatia, who taught astrology and lectured for a long time in Alexandria. A Leoncia, the Greek woman who wrote in opposition to Theophrastus, the philosopher, and won him over. A Jucia [Julia], a Corinna, a Cornelia—in sum, the whole throng of those who earned a name for themselves—Grecians, muses, oracles, who all were simply women of learning, considered such, celebrated as such, and venerated as such by the ancients. Not to mention innumerable others, of whom the books are full, for I see that Egyptian Catherine, lecturing and winning over to her view all the wisdom of the sages of Egypt. I see a Gertrude reading, writing, and teaching. And, to stay with examples close to home, I see a most holy mother of mine, Paula, learned in the Hebrew, Greek, and Latin languages and most skilled at interpreting the Scriptures. And how could she fail to be, when the supreme Jerome, her chronicler, considered himself scarcely worthy of being such, for with that striking emphasis and power of expression, of which he has the secret, he says: If all the limbs in my body were tongues, they would still not suffice to publish abroad the wisdom and virtue of Paula. He was moved to similar praise of the widow Blesilla and the illustrious virgin Eustochium, daughters both of the same Saint, the latter so noteworthy that, by reason of her learning, she was called the Wonder of the World. Fabiola, the Roman woman, was also most versed in Holy Scripture. Proba Falconia, a Roman woman, wrote an elegant book in the mysteries of our Holy Faith, by putting together quotations from Virgil. Our Queen Isabella, the wife of Alfonso X, is known to have written on astrology. Not to mention others whom I shall pass over to avoid relaying what others have said (a vice I've always detested) and because in our day there flourishes the great Christina Alexandra, Queen of Sweden, as learned as she is courageous and great-hearted, and their Excellencies the Duchess of Aveiro and the Countess of Villaumbrosa.

The venerable Dr. Arce (in virtue and cultivation a worthy professor of Scripture) in his *Studioso Bibliorum*, raises this question: *An liceat foeminis sacrorum Bibliorum studio incumbere? eaque interpretari?* [Is it legitimate for women to apply themselves to study of the Holy Bible and to interpret it?] He brings in many opinions of saints in support of the opposing view, especially that of the Apostle: *Mulieres in Ecclesiis taceant, non enim permittitur eis loqui* etc. ["Let women keep silence in the churches, for it is not permitted them to speak" (1 Cor. 14:34)]. He then brings in other opinions and especially that of the same Apostle addressing Titus: *Anus similiter in habitu sancto, bene docentes* ["The aged women, in like manner, in holy attire . . . teaching well" (Tit. 2:3)], with interpretations of the Church Fathers. He finally decides, in his judicious way, that to lecture publicly in the classroom and to preach in the pulpit are not legitimate activities for women, but that studying, writing, and teaching privately are not only allowable but most edifying and useful. Of course this does not apply to all women—only to those whom God has endowed with particular virtue and discernment and who have become highly accomplished and erudite, and possess the talents and other qualities needed for such holy pursuits. So true is this that the interpretation of Holy Scripture should be forbidden not only to women, considered so very inept, but to men, who merely by virtue of being men consider themselves sages, unless they are very learned and virtuous, with receptive and properly trained minds. Failure to do so, in my view, has given rise precisely to all those sectarians and been the root cause of all the heresies. For there are many who study in order to become ignorant, especially those of an arrogant, restless, and overbearing turn of mind, who are partial to new interpretations of the Law (where precisely they are to be rejected). Hence, until they have uttered something heretical merely in order to say what no none else has, they will not rest. Of these the Holy Spirit says: *In Malevolam animam no intoibit sapientia* ["For wisdom will not enter into a malicious soul" (Wisdom 1:4)]. Learning does more harm to such than remaining ignorant would. A clever man once said that a person who does not know Latin is not a complete fool, but that one who does is well qualified to be one. And I add he is even better (if stupidity is a qualification) who has studied his bit of philosophy and theology and has a smattering of languages, for therewith he becomes a fool in many branches of learning and language, his mother tongue not offering room enough for a great fool. . . .

Oh, how much harm would be avoided in our country if older women were as learned as Laeta and knew how to teach in the way Saint Paul and my Father Saint Jerome direct! Instead of which, if fathers wish to educate their daughters beyond what is customary, for want of trained older women and on account of the extreme negligence which has become women's sad lot, since well-educated older women are unavailable, they are obliged to bring in men teachers to give instruction in reading, writing, and arithmetic, playing musical instruments, and other skills. No little harm is done by this, as we witness every day in the pitiful examples of ill-assorted unions; from the ease of contact and the close company kept over a period of time, there easily comes about something not thought possible. As a result of this, many fathers prefer leaving their daughters in a barbaric, uncultivated state to exposing them to an evident danger such as familiarity with men breeds. All of which would be eliminated if there were older women of learning, as Saint Paul desires, and instruction were passed down from one group to another, as is the case with needlework and other traditional activities. . . .

. . . This should be taken into account by those who, being wedded to that *Mulieres in Ecclesia taceant*, rail against women's being educated and becoming teachers, as if the Apostle himself had never said: *bene docentes*. Besides which, that injunction referred to a historical circumstance related by Eusebius, namely, that in the early Church women had begun to indoctrinate one another in places of worship and the noise interfered with the apostles' preaching, for which reason they were told to keep still—exactly as now it is the case that while the preacher is preaching one does not pray out loud.

The understanding of many passages doubtless requires much study of history, customs, ceremonies, proverbs, and even the ways of speaking of the times in which they were written, so as to learn to what certain locutions of Holy Writ are referring and alluding. . . . That reply of the virtuous matron to the irksome suitor: Hinges won't be greased nor will torches burn for me, a way of saying that she had no desire to marry, with an allusion to the ceremony of greasing doors with fat and lighting nuptial torches at marriages—as if we were now to say: there will be no outlay for dowry nor will the priest give his blessings on my account. And along these lines there are countless other observations of Virgil and Homer and all the poets and prose writers. Aside from these, how many difficulties cannot be found in Biblical passages, even in matters of grammar—the plural used for the singular, the second person giving way to the third, in those words of the *Canticle of Canticles: osculetur me osculo oris sui: quia meliora sunt ubera tua vino* ["Let him kiss me with the kiss of his mouth: for thy breasts are better than wine" (1:1)]? The adjective in the genitive instead of the accusative, as in *Calicem salutaris accipiam* ["I will take the chalice of salvation" (Ps. 115:13)]? The use of the feminine for the masculine and, on the contrary, calling any sin adultery?

All of this requires more study than is thought by some who, not having gone beyond the level of grammar or knowing at most a few terms of formal logic, undertake to interpret the Scriptures and fasten onto *Mulieres in Ecclesiis taceant*, with no idea of how it should be interpreted. And, from elsewhere in the Bible, onto: *Mulier in silentio discat* ["Let the woman learn in silence" (1 Tim. 2:11)], even though these words speak more in women's favor than against them, since they direct them to learn, and it is obvious that while women are learning they must keep silent. And it is also written: *Audi, Israel, et tace* ["Hear, Israel, and hold thy peace"], words which address the whole conglomeration of men and women telling them all to maintain silence, since anyone listening and learning must naturally be attentive and keep silent. . . . And nowadays we see the Church allowing women, both saints and not, to write, for the nun of Agreda and Maria de la Antigua are not canonized, yet their writings circulate, nor were Saint Teresa and the others when they wrote. Thus Saint Paul's prohibition referred only to speaking in public from pulpits; if the Apostle had prohibited writing, the Church would not allow it. So today I am not so bold as to teach—it would be the height of presumption in my case. Writing requires greater talent than I possess and a great deal of thought. So Saint Cyprian says: *Gravi condiseratione indigent, quae scribimus* [The things we write need to be very carefully considered]. My whole wish has been to study so as to be less ignorant, for, as Saint Augustine has it, some things are learned with a view to action, others only for the sake of knowing: *Discimus quedam, ut sciamus; quaedam, ut faciamus.* . . .

If I turn to the facility in writing verse which has been so censured in me, it is so innate that I am even doing violence to myself to keep this missive in prose and could cite that line *Quidquid conabar dicere, versus erat* [Anything I set out to say turned into verse (Ovid, *Tristia* 4.10.26, inexactly quoted)]. Seeing it so condemned and so impugned on all sides, I have expressly tried to determine what is so wrong about it and have not been able to. What I find instead is that verses are applauded on the lips of Sybils, sanctified in the pens of the Prophets, and especially of King David, of whom that great expounder and beloved father of mine, in explaining their metrical patterns, says: *In morem Flacci et Pindari nunc iambo currit, nunc al-*

caico personat, nunc sappico tumet, nunc semipede ingreditur [In the manner of Horace and Pindar, now it runs along in iambics, now it is resonant with alcaics, now it swells with sapphics, now it moves in half-feet]. Most of the sacred books are in meter—. . . .

Now if the wrong consists in the practice of verse by a woman, since so many have practiced it in a fashion so evidently praiseworthy, what can be so wrong about my being a poet? Though I readily confess that I am base and vile, I am not aware that anyone has seen an unseemly ditty by me. Furthermore, I have never written anything of my own volition, but always at the request, and to the specifications, of others. So much so that the only thing I can remember writing for my own pleasure is a trifle called *The Dream.* . . .

. . . If it should be your pleasure, my Lady, that I do the opposite of what I had proposed to your judgment and view, my decision will yield, as is right, to the least indication of your wishes. As I said, it had been to remain silent because, although Saint John Chrysostom says: *calumniatores convincere oportet, interrogatores docere* [slanderers should be won over, questioners enlightened], I see that Saint Gregory also says: *Victoria non minor est hostes tolerare, quam hostest vincere* [It is no less a victory to tolerate an enemy than to overcome him], and that patience conquers by tolerance and triumphs by sufferance. And it was the custom of the pagan Romans, at the highest peak of their captains' glory, when they returned home in triumph from the conquest of nations, dressed in purple and crowned with laurel; with, instead of animals, crowned heads of conquered kings pulling the chariot; with the rich spoils of the whole world in their train; with the victorious militia decorated with the insignia of their prowess; while they enjoyed the popular acclaim of such honorable and greatly reputed titles as Fathers of their Country, Mainstays of Empire, Bulwarks of Rome, Protectors of the Republic, and other titles to glory: it was, I say, the Romans' custom, in the full flush of human glory and felicity, to have a soldier go alongside the conqueror, saying to him in a loud voice, as if expressing his own sentiments and acting on the Senate's order: Don't forget you are mortal, that you have such and such a flaw, without sparing them the most shameful, as happened at Caesar's triumphs, when the lowliest soldiers shouted into his ears: *Cavete romani, adducimus vobis adulterum calvum* [Beware, Romans, we bring you one who is bald and adulterous!] This was done so that such great honors should not go to the conqueror's head, and so that the ballast of these affronts should counterbalance the sails of such acclaim, in order that the ship of judgment should not be endangered by the winds of so much cheering.

If this, I say, was done by pagans having solely the light of natural law, is it so much for us Catholics, who are required to love our enemies, to tolerate them? For my part, I can assure you that calumnies have sometimes mystified me but have never harmed me, since I consider very stupid the person who, having the opportunity to win merit, takes no less trouble to lose it, like those people who resist the thought of dying, yet die in the end, their resistance being of no avail in avoiding death and serving only to deprive them of the merit of acceptance and turning what could have been a fine death into a poor one. Thus, Madam, I consider these things more beneficial than harmful and hold the risk of applause the greater one for human weakness, which has a way of appropriating what does not belong to it. One must be very wary and keep those words of the Apostle written in one's heart: *Quid autem habes quod non accepisti? Si autem accepisti, quid gloriaris quasi no acceperis?* ["or what hast thou that thou hast not received? And if thou hast received, why doest thou glory, as if thou hadst not received it?" (1 Cor. 4:7)], that they may serve as a shield to resist the sharp spikes of praise, a lance which, when not attributed to God, to whom it belongs, takes our lives and turns us into robbers of God's honor and usurpers of the talents He has entrusted to us and the gifts he has lent us, of which we must give a most exact reckoning. I therefore fear praise more than censure, my Lady, for the latter, by only the simplest act of patience, may be turned to advantage, while the former, if it is not to do one harm, requires many reciprocal acts of humility and self-knowledge. . . .

If the style of this letter, my venerable Lady, should not have been such as is owed you, I ask you to pardon my homespun familiarity or inadequate respect, in treating you as a veiled nun, sister to me, and forgetting the distance that separates me from your most illustrious person. Had I seen you with no veil, this would not have happened. But with your good and benign judgment, you will fill in or emend the forms of address, and if you find incongruous my addressing you with no title, because I felt that considering the reverence I owe you, the title of Your Reverence would actually show very little reverence, replace my familiarity with any form of address you deem worthy of your merits, for I have not had the daring to exceed the limits of your style nor to infringe the margins of your modesty.

And keep me in your grace in order to obtain God's for me, and may He grant you great increase thereof and keep you, as I beg and need Him to do. From this convent of Our Father Saint Jerome of the City of Mexico, the first day of the month of March of the year sixteen hundred ninety-one. Your most favored servant kisses your hands,

Juana Inés de la Cruz

Mary Astell (1666–1731)

Mary Astell was an English feminist of the later seventeenth and early eighteenth century who wrote political works on a range of subjects from 1694 to 1713. She lived from 1666 to 1731 but did not continue active writing later in life. She is often termed a conservative feminist because she held uncompromising royalist principles and was a loyal follower of the Church of England during an age where some scholars have located feminist origins within the religious and political left. While Astell looked askance upon those who would undermine social and political order, this did not prevent her from questioning women's inferior status during the late 1600s. This conflictual perspective permeates her feminist, religious, and political writings, in which she often used conservative perspectives as a springboard for her feminist arguments. This complex mixture of loyalties and intellectual principles made her an intriguing figure among seventeenth-century political theorists and among early feminist theorists.

Her reputation grew from her first work, A Serious Proposal to the Ladies for the Advancement of Their True and Greatest Interest, written in 1694 when she was just twenty-eight years old. Interestingly, she signed it "by a Lover of Her Sex" and, like many seventeenth-century women, published it anonymously. It quickly became an open secret that the author was Mary Astell, a young woman from Newcastle upon Tyne, who came from a successful commercial family, her father being an innkeeper and her grandfather the mayor and a well-known royalist during the English Civil War of 1640–60. She did not come from aristocratic roots but from a respectable merchant family, and she later made friends among a circle of aristocratic women after she moved to London in 1690. She had no independent income to live on and had to work as a governess or teacher in a girls' school or accept financial help from her wealthier friends. Resentful of the teaching positions she was forced to accept, Astell became bitter in old age following the death of Queen Anne, when, to her mind, there was little support for an intellectual woman such as herself. She saw the failing as twofold: first, there was much ridicule of the educated woman and of ideas she had first offered thirty years ago in A Serious Proposal; second, although there were pensions for male intellectuals and institutions such as universities, the Inns of Court, and the Royal Society to perpetuate their work, there was nothing similar for women.

Although Astell wrote ten separate works, the Serious Proposal remained the one most closely associated with her name up to her death. In this work she combined advocacy of women's higher education with a proposed refuge for them to develop spiritual, moral, and intellectual qualities. As a strong Anglican, she grounded her arguments for women's learning in the promise from God that both men and women possessed rational minds and immortal souls capable and obligated to seek his truth and imitate his goodness. Reason was an effective tool to understand God's grandeur and his plan for humanity. Women's serious learning would always make them better Christians, and ones who realized the superiority of the Anglican church. But such learning would not merely produce within them sure Christian principles, it would make them serious beings, interested in issues of morality and social import. Above all, Astell resented her society's waste of women's potential, their languishing in lives focused on superficial beauty and social customs unworthy of a creature created in God's image. She disliked what many of her contemporaries believed was women's proper path to faith: reading scripture and memorizing the catechism while failing to grasp the reasoning behind God's teachings.

The first part of A Serious Proposal is written in often sarcastic, sharp language directed at women who would ignore their potential and, in her words, "be content to be in the World like Tulips in a Garden, to make a fine shew and be good for nothing; have all your Glories set in the Grave, or perhaps much sooner!" Yet her strongest rebuke was aimed at a society which cared so little about women that its members would leave them to wither among selections of lace, appropriate colors, and insignificant social customs. She railed at the fashions, neighborhood visits, and gossip that characterized the lives of upper-class women. Such a waste infuriated her, and she expressed this view especially through an unrelenting attack on chivalry which she saw as a hypocritical attempt by men to keep women ignorant, idle, and powerless while heaping praise upon them. The true meaning of chivalry was summed up in the following: "give me leave therefore to hope, that no Gentleman who has honourable designs, will henceforward decry Knowledge and Ingenuity in her he would pretend to Honour."

In the second part of the Serious Proposal, published separately in 1697, Astell outlined the systematic education she intended for women which included philosophy and theology, as well as history, along with traditional artistic and social lessons. She wanted women's minds to be tested because God would hold them accountable even if they could not live a life which allowed time for serious thought and spiritual contemplation.

Scholars have argued that Some Reflections upon Marriage, Occasion'd by the Duke and Duchess of Mazarine's Case (1700) holds her most radical feminist critique of seventeenth-century society because of its broad-based attack on the institution of marriage. Yet it, as well as the Serious Proposal, blunted the attack on male/female relationships and the family through a strong Christian overlay. Obviously Astell saw marriage as an institution that oppressed women, gave them few choices, and rendered them virtually powerless. Yet marriage was a Christian institution ordained by God for the propagation of humankind. Thus she did not openly attack it but argued that seventeenth-century men debased the institution, ignoring God's directive that they should seek a helpmeet. Rather, she contended, men were driven either by a desire for transitory beauty or by a grasping search for wealth, marrying a wife who had an estate to maintain them comfortably. This meant that few men sought intelligent, moral, and religious companions or gave a wife an opportunity to pursue such qualities following marriage. She argued that men often despised their wives because they held all women in contempt.

While stressing the goodness of Christian marriage, Astell contended that the seventeenth-century institution was one in which power dictated relationships. A woman had limited choice in establishing the union and virtually none following the marriage no matter how poor, cruel, or dishonest a companion she had married. Often her choice was made for her, and, following wedlock, the sexual double standard gave her little opportunity to find pleasure elsewhere whatever her husband's habits, and his legal control over her property left little economic flexibility. Marriage catered to men's needs, soothing their egos and supplying them with "an upper servant." Although she agreed that, according to scripture, men should have the upper hand, in reality she left little opportunity for them to use that superiority to control their wives. Some Reflections upon Marriage is an essay placed squarely in the feminist framework of an unequal power structure between the sexes.

Astell's explicit political tracts were royalist documents that lamented the execution of the Stuart monarch, Charles I, in 1649. Charles came quickly to be known as the royal martyr, and Astell was one of the most uncompromising royalists to vilify those who executed him and governed following his death. She argued that there was no justification whatsoever for opposition to Charles and that a group of evil men duped a naive public into believing that Charles was establishing a tyranny. She felt so strongly about this that she published a tract arguing against a sermon offered on January 30, 1704 (the anniversary of Charles's execution), by White Kennett, a leading Anglican divine. Such commemoration sermons were given well into the eighteenth century, and January 30 became a day of sacred memory for royalists. Kennett, while honoring the king's memory, admitted that people might have been misled about his arbitrary rule. Kennett's sermon seems reasonable and written in a compromising tone, trying to bring a wide spectrum of those loyal to the crown back into the royalist and Anglican fold. Yet Astell would allow no good words to be said about those "Miscreants, who set whole Nations on fire, only that their own despicable selves may be talk'd of." And, just as surely, she would allow no criticism of the royal martyr. For her, there was no honorable way to compromise with traitors. Her tract, An Impartial Enquiry into the Causes of Rebellion and Civil War in This Kingdom, took White Kennett to task in no uncertain terms and was the strongest expression of her antirevolutionary sentiments and her fear of social disorder.

Although all of her works are permeated with her attachment to the Church of England, she presented those views most fully in 1705 in The Christian Religion, as Profess'd by a Daughter of the Church of England. Her strong adherence to Anglicanism and the integration it offered between reason and faith convinced her that it was the best representative of the early church established by Christ. She had few doubts about its superiority, but this was not a proselytizing essay; rather, it reflects her genuine admiration and affection for the Anglican faith.

Although Mary Astell disliked the spreading heterodoxy of Protestant sectarians and any doctrine on the fundamental rights of the people to sovereignty or rebellion, she argued strongly for women to be able to resist, as she called it, "a private tyranny" within the home. Her feminism blended with her political views in that she saw that Puritans who supported revolution ignored women's rights and that the emotionalism of much radical Protestantism was dismissive of women's intelligence. Yet it is fair to say that she did not always honestly grapple with the contradictions within her thought. She was a conservative, and she was a feminist, but it seems clear that she was not a conservative feminist. For the 1690s, in many ways, she was a radical feminist, often more so than those who were more radical politically and religiously than she.

The selections are from A Serious Proposal to the Ladies (Part 1, 2nd ed., 1695; Part II, 1697); Some Reflections upon Marriage (4th ed., 1730); and An Impartial Enquiry into the Causes of Rebellion and Civil War in This Kingdom (1704).

HLS

Sources and Suggested Readings

Astell, Mary. *The Christian Religion, as Profess'd by a Daughter of the Church of England*. London, 1705.

——. *An Impartial Enquiry into the Causes of Rebellion and War in This Kingdom: In an Examination of Dr. Kennett's Sermon, Jan. 31. 1703/4. And Vindication of the Royal Martyr*. London: Printed by E. P. for R. Wilkin, 1704.

——. *Political Writings*. Ed. Patricia Springborg. New York: Cambridge University Press, 1996.

——. *A Serious Proposal to the Ladies for the Advancement of Their True and Greatest Interest*. Part I, 2nd ed., corrected. London: Printed by T. W. for R. Wilkin, 1695. Part II. London: Printed for Richard Wilkin, 1697.

——. *Some Reflections upon Marriage*. 4th ed. London: Printed for William Parker, 1730.

Hill, Bridget. "Mary Astell and the Feminist Critique of Possessive Individualism." *Eighteenth-Century Studies* 23, 4 (Summer 1990): 444–58.

Hill, Bridget, ed. *The First English Feminist: Reflections upon Marriage and Other Writings by Mary Astell*. New York: St. Martin's Press, 1986.

McDonald, Lynn. *The Women Founders of the Social Sciences*. Ottawa: Carleton University Press, 1994. 37–55.

Perry, Ruth. *The Celebrated Mary Astell: An Early English Feminist*. Chicago: University of Chicago Press, 1986.

Smith, Florence M. *Mary Astell*. New York: Columbia University Press, 1916.

Springborg, Patricia. "Mary Astell (1666–1731), Critic of Locke." *American Political Science Review* 89, 3 (1995): 621–33.

Sutherland, Christine Mason. "Outside the Rhetorical Tradition: Mary Astell's Advice to Women in Seventeenth-Century England." *Rhetorica* 9, 2 (1991): 147–63.

Thickstun, Margaret Olofson. "'This Was a Woman That Taught': Feminist Scriptural Exegesis in the Seventeenth Century." In *Studies in Eighteenth-Century Culture*, vol. 21. East Lansing, Mich.: American Society for Eighteenth-Century Studies (Colleagues Press), 1991.

A *Serious Proposal to the Ladies for the Advancement of Their True and Greatest Interest*

By a Lover of Her Sex

Part I (2nd ed., 1695)

Ladies,

Since the Profitable Adventures that have gone abroad in the World have met with so great Encouragement, . . . I therefore persuade my self, you will not be less kind to a Proposition that comes attended with more certain and substantial Gain; whose only design is to improve your Charms and heighten your Value, by suffering you no longer to be cheap and contemptible. Its aim is to fix that Beauty, to make it lasting and permanent, which Nature with all the helps of Art cannot secure, and to place it out of the reach of Sickness and Old Age, by transferring it from a corruptible Body to an immortal Mind. An obliging Design, which wou'd procure them *inward* Beauty, to whom Nature has unkindly denied the *outward*, and not permit those Ladies who have comely Bodies, to tarnish their Glory with deformed Souls. Wou'd have you all be wits, or what is better, Wise. Raise you above the Vulgar by something more truly illustrious, than a sounding Title or a great Estate. Wou'd excite in you a generous Emulation to excel in the best things, and not in such Trifles as every mean person who has but Money enough may purchase as well as you. Not suffer you to take up with the low thought of distinguishing your selves by any thing that is not truly valuable, and procure you such Ornaments as all the Treasures of the *Indies* are not able to purchase. Wou'd help you to surpass the Men as much in Vertue and Ingenuity, as you do in Beauty, that you may not only be as lovely, but as wise as Angels. Exalt and Establish your Fame, more than the best wrought *Poems* and loudest *Panegyricks*, by ennobling your Minds with such Graces as really deserve it. And instead of the Fustian Complements and Fulsome Flatteries of your Admirers, obtain for you the Plaudit of Good Men and Angels, and the approbation of Him who cannot err. In a word, render you the Glory and Blessing of the present Age, and the Admiration and Pattern of the next. . . .

Remember, I pray you, the famous Women of former Ages, the *Orinda's* of late [seventeenth-century poet Katherine Philips], and the more Modern Heroins, and blush to think how much is now, and will hereafter be said of them, when you your selves (as great a Figure as you make) must be buried in silence and forgetfulness! Shall your Emulation fail *there only* where 'tis commendable? Why are you so preposterously humble, as not to contend for one of the highest Mansions in the Court of Heav'n? Believe me, Ladies, this is the only *Place* worth contending for, you are neither better nor worse in your selves for going before, or coming after *now*, but you are really so much the better, by how much the higher your station is in an Orb of Glory. How can you be content to be in the World like Tulips in a Garden, to make a fine *shew* and be good for nothing; have all your Glories set in the Grave, or perhaps much sooner! What your own sentiments are I know not, but I can't without pity and resentment reflect, that those Glorious Temples on which your kind Creator has bestow'd such exquisite workmanship, shou'd enshrine no better than *Aegyptian* Deities; be like a garnish'd Sepulchre, which for all its glittering, has nothing within but emptiness or putrefaction! . . .

For shame let's abandon that *Old*, and therefore one wou'd think, unfashionable employment of pursuing Butterflies and Trifles! No longer drudge on in the dull beaten road of Vanity and Folly, which so many have gone before us, but dare to break the enchanted Circle that custom has plac'd us in, and scorn the vulgar way of imitating all the Impertinencies of our Neighbours. Let us learn to pride our selves in something more excellent than the invention of a Fashion, and not entertain such a degrading thought of our own *worth*, as to imagine that our Souls were given us only for the service of our Bodies, and that the best improvement we can make of these, is to attract the Eyes of Men. We value *them* too much, and our *selves* too little, if we place any part of our desert in their Opinion, and don't think our selves capable of Nobler Things than the pitiful Conquest of some worthless heart. She who has opportunities of making an interest in Heaven, of obtaining the love and admiration of GOD and Angels, is too prodigal of her Time, and injurious to her Charms, to throw them away on vain insignificant men. . . .

Pardon me the seeming rudeness of this Proposal, which goes upon a supposition that there's something amiss in you, which it is intended to amend. My design is not to expose, but to rectifie your Failures. To be exempt from mistake, is a priviledge few can pretend to, the greatest is to be past Conviction and too obstinate to reform. Even the *Men*, as exact as they wou'd seem, and as much as they divert themselves with our Miscarriages, are very often guilty of greater faults, and such, as considering the advantages they enjoy, are much more inexcusable. But I will not pretend to correct their Errors, who either are, or at least *think* themselves too wise to receive Instruction from a Womans Pen.

My earnest desire is, That you Ladies, would be as perfect and happy as 'tis possible to be in this imperfect state; for I love you too well to endure a spot upon your Beauties, if I can by any means remove and wipe it off. I would have you live up to the dignity of your Nature, and express your thankfulness to GOD for the benefits you enjoy by a due improvement of them: As I know very many of you do, who countenance that Piety which the men decry, and are the brightest Patterns of Religion that the Age affords, 'tis my grief that all the rest of our Sex do not imitate such Illustrious Ex-

amples, and therefore I would have them encreas'd and render'd more conspicuous, that Vice being put out of countenance, (because Vertue is the only thing in fashion) may sneak out of the World, and its darkness be dispell'd by the confluence of so many shining Graces.

The Men perhaps will cry out that I teach you false Doctrin, for because by their deductions some amongst us are become very mean and contemptible, they would fain persuade the rest to be as despicable and forlorn as they. We're indeed oblig'd to them for their management, in endeavouring to make us so, who use all the artifice they can to spoil, and deny us the means of improvement. So that instead of inquiring why all Women are not wise and good, we have reason to wonder that there are any so. Were the Men as much neglected, and as little care taken to cultivate and improve them, perhaps they wou'd be so far from surpassing those whom they now despise, that they themselves wou'd sink into the greatest stupidity and brutality. . . . Hither, Ladies, I desire you wou'd aspire, 'tis a noble and becoming Ambition, and to remove such Obstacles as lie in your way is the design of this Paper. We will therefore enquire what it is that stops your flight, that keeps you groveling here below, like *Domitian* catching Flies when you should be busied in obtaining Empires.

Altho' it has been said by Men of more Wit than Wisdom, and perhaps of more malice than either, that Women are naturally incapable of acting Prudently, or that they are necessarily determined to folly, I must by no meanes grant it; that Hypothesis would render my endeavours impertinent, for then it would be in vain to advise the one, or endeavour the Reformation of the other. Besides, there are Examples in all Ages, which sufficiently confute the Ignorance and Malice of this assertion.

The Incapacity, if there be any, is acquired not natural, and none of their Follies are so necessary, but that they might avoid them if they pleas'd themselves. Some disadvantages indeed they labour under, and what these are we shall see by and by and endeavour to surmount; but Women need not take up with mean things, since (if they are not wanting to themselves) they are capable of the best. Neither God nor Nature have excluded them from being Ornaments to their Families and useful in their Generation; there is therefore no reason they should be content to be Cyphers in the World, useless at the best, and in a little time a burden and nuisance to all about them. And 'tis very great pity that they who are so apt to overrate themselves in smaller Matters, shou'd, where it most concerns them to know and stand upon their Value, be so insensible of their own worth. The Cause therefore of the defects we labour under is, if not wholly, yet at least in the first place, to be ascribed to the mistakes of our Education, which like an Error in the first Concoction, spreads its ill Influence through all our Lives.

The Soil is rich and would if well cultivated produce a noble Harvest. . . . Women are from their very Infancy debar'd those Advantages, with the want of which they are afterwards reproached, and nursed up in those Vices which will hereafter be upbraided to them. So partial are Men as to expect Brick where they afford no Straw; and so abundantly civil as to take care we shou'd make good that obliging Epithet of *Ignorant*, which out of an excess of good Manners, they are pleas'd to bestow on us!

One would be apt to think indeed, that Parents shou'd take all possible care of their Childrens Education, not only for *their* sakes, but even for their *own*. And tho' the Son convey the Name to Posterity, yet certainly a great Part of the Honour of their Families depends on their Daughters. . . . To introduce poor Children into the World and neglect to fence them against the temptations of it, and so leave them expos'd to temporal and eternal Miseries, is a wickedness for which I want a Name; 'tis beneath Brutality; the Beasts are better natur'd for they take care of their offspring, till they are capable of caring for themselves. And if Mothers had a due regard to their Posterity, how *Great* soever they are, they wou'd not think themselves too *Good* to perform what Nature requires, nor through Pride and Delicacy remit the poor little one to the care of a Foster Parent. Or if necessity inforce them to depute another to perform *their* Duty, they wou'd be as choice at least, in the Manners and Inclinations, as they are in the complections of their Nurses, lest with their Milk they transfuse their Vices, and form in the Child such evil habits as will not easily be eradicated. . . .

. . . She who rightly understands wherein the perfection of her Nature consists, will lay out her Thoughts and Industry in the acquisition of such Perfections: But she who is kept ignorant of the matter, will take up with such Objects as first offer themselves, and bear any plausible resemblance to what she desires; a shew of advantage being sufficient to render them agreeable baits to her who wants Judgment and Skill to discern between reality and pretence. From whence it easily follows, that she who has nothing else to value her self upon, will be proud of her Beauty, or Money and what that can purchase, and think her self mightily oblig'd to him, who tells her she has those Perfections which she naturally longs for. Her inbred self-esteem and desire of good, which are degenerated

into Pride and mistaken Self-love, will easily open her Ears to whatever goes about to nourish and delight them; and when a cunning designing Enemy from without, has drawn over to his Party these Traitors within, he has the Poor unhappy Person, at his Mercy, who now very glibly swallows down his Poison, because 'tis presented in a Golden Cup, and credulously hearkens to the most disadvantageous Proposals, because they come attended with a seeming esteem. She whose Vanity makes her swallow praises by the wholesale, without examining whether she deserves them, or from what hand they come, will reckon it but gratitude to think well of him who values her so much, and think she must needs be merciful to the poor despairing Lover whom her Charms have reduc'd to die at her feet.

Love and Honour are what every one of us naturally esteem, they are excellent things in themselves and very worthy our regard, and by how much the readier we are to embrace what ever resembles them, by so much the more dangerous it is that these venerable Names should be wretchedly abus'd and affixt to their direct contraries, yet this is the Custom of the World: And how can she possibly detect the fallacy, who has no better Notion of either than what she derives from Plays and Romances? How can she be furnished with any solid Principles whose very Instructors are Froth and emptiness? Whereas Women were they rightly Educated, had they obtain'd a well inform'd and discerning Mind, they would be proof against all those Batteries, see through and scorn those little silly Artifices which are us'd to ensnare and deceive them. . . .

Whence is it but from ignorance, from a want of Understanding to compare and judge of things, to chuse a right End, to proportion the Means to the End, and to rate ev'ry thing according to its proper value, that we quit the Substance for the Shadow, Reality for Appearance, and embrace those very things which if we understood we shou'd hate and fly, but now are reconcil'd to, merely because they usurp the Name, tho' they have nothing of the Nature of those venerable Objects we desire and seek? Were it not for this delusion, is it probable a Lady who passionately desires to be admir'd, shou'd ever consent to such Actions as render her base and contemptible? . . . In sum, did not ignorance impose on us, we would never lavish out the greatest part of our Time and Care, on the decoration of a Tenement, in which our Lease is so very short, and which for all our industry, may loose it's Beauty e'er that Lease be out, and in the mean while neglect a more glorious and durable Mansion! We would never be so curious of the House and so careless of the

Inhabitant, whose beauty is capable of great improvement and will endure for ever without diminution or decay!

Thus Ignorance and a narrow Education lay the Foundation of Vice, and Imitation and Custom rear it up. Custom, that merciless torrent that carries all before it, and which indeed can be stem'd by none but such as have a great deal of Prudence and a rooted Vertue. For 'tis but Decorous that she who is not capable of giving better Rules, shou'd follow those she sees before her, least she only change the instance and retain the absurdity. 'Twou'd puzzle a considerate Person to account for all that Sin and Folly that is in the World (which certainly has nothing in it self to recommend it) did not Custom help to solve the difficulty. For Vertue without question has on all accounts the preeminence of Vice, 'tis abundantly more pleasant in the *Act*, as well as more advantageous in the *Consequences*, as any one who will but rightly use her reason, in a serious reflection on her self and the nature of things, may easily perceive. 'Tis Custom therefore, that Tyrant Custom, which is the grand motive to all those irrational choices which we daily see made in the World, so very contrary to our *present* interest and pleasure, as well as to our Future. We think it an unpardonable mistake not to do as our neighbours do, and part with our Peace and Pleasure as well as our Innocence and Vertue, meerly in complyance with an unreasonable Fashion. And having inur'd ourselves to Folly, we know not how to quit it; we go on in Vice, not because we find satisfaction in it, but because we are unacquainted with the Joys of Vertue. . . .

. . . She is it may be, taught the Principles and Duties of Religion, but not Acquainted with the Reasons and Grounds of them; being told 'tis enough for her to believe, to examine why, and wherefore, belongs not to her. And therefore, though her Piety may be tall and spreading, yet because it wants foundation and Root, the first rude Temptation overthrows and blasts it, or perhaps the short liv'd Gourd decays and withers of its own accord. But why should she be blamed for setting no great value on her Soul, whose noblest Faculty her Understanding is render'd useless to her? Or censur'd for relinquishing a course of Life, whose Prerogatives she was never acquainted with, and tho' highly reasonable in it self, was put upon the embracing it with as little reason as she now forsakes it? For if her Religion it self be taken up as the Mode of the Country, 'tis no strange thing that she lays it down again in conformity to the Fashion. Whereas she whose Reason is suffer'd to display it self, to inquire into the grounds and Motives of Religion, to make a disquisition of its Graces and search out its hidden Beauties;

who is a Christian out of Choice, not in conformity to those among whom she lives; and cleaves to Piety, because 'tis her Wisdom, her Interest, her Joy, not because she has been accustom'd to it; she who is not only eminently and unmoveably good, but able to give a Reason *why she is so*, is too firm and stable to be mov'd by the pitiful Allurements of sin, too wise and too well bottom'd to be undermin'd and supplanted by the strongest Efforts of Temptation. Doubtless a truly Christian Life requires a clear Understanding as well as regular Affections, that both together may move the Will to a direct choice of Good and a stedfast adherence to it. For tho' the heart may be honest, it is but by chance that the Will is right if the Understanding be ignorant and Cloudy. . . .

And now having discovered the Disease and its cause, 'tis proper to apply a Remedy; single Medicines are too weak to cure such complicated Distempers, they require a full Dispensatory; and what wou'd a good Woman refuse to do, could she hope by that to advantage the greatest part of the World, and to improve her Sex in Knowledge and true Religion? . . . I have therefore no more to do but to make the Proposal, to prove that it will answer these great and good Ends, and then 'twill be easy to obviate the Objections that Persons of more Wit than Vertue may happen to raise against it.

Now as to the Proposal, it is to erect a *Monastery*, or if you will (to avoid giving offence to the scrupulous and injudicious, by names which tho' innocent in themselves, have been abus'd by superstitious Practices,) we will call it a *Religious Retirement*, and such as shall have a double aspect, being not only a Retreat from the World for those who desire that advantage, but likewise, an Institution and previous discipline, to fit us to do the greatest good in it; such an Institution as this (if I do not mightily deceive my self,) would be the most probable method to amend the present, and improve the future Age. . . .

You are therefore Ladies, invited into a place, where you shall suffer no other confinement, but to be kept out of the road of sin: You shall not be depriv'd of your Grandeur but only exchange the vain Pomps and Pageantry of the world, empty Titles and Forms of State, for the true and solid Greatness of being able to despise them. You will only quit the Chat of insignificant people for an ingenious Conversation; the froth of flashy Wit for real Wisdom; idle tales for instructive discourses. . . . Happy Retreat! which will be the introducing you into such a *Paradise* as your Mother *Eve* forfeited, where you shall feast on Pleasures, that do not like those of the World, disappoint your expectations, pall your Appetites, and by the which when obtain'd are as empty as the former; but such as will make you *truly* happy now, and prepare you to be *perfectly* so hereafter. . . .

But because we were not made for our selves, nor can by any means so effectually glorify GOD, and do good to our own Souls, as by doing Offices of Charity and Beneficence to others; and to the intent that every Vertue, and the highest degrees of every Vertue may be exercis'd and promoted the most that may be; your Retreat shall be so manag'd as not to exclude the good works of an *Active*, from the pleasure and serenity of a *Contemplative* Life, but by a due mixture of both retain all the advantages and avoid the inconveniencies that attend either. It shall not so cut you off from the world as to hinder you from bettering and improving it, but rather qualify you to do it the greatest Good, and be a Seminary to stock the Kingdom with pious and prudent Ladies, whose good Example it is to be hop'd, will so influence the rest of their Sex, that Women may no longer pass for those little useless and impertinent Animals, which the ill conduct of too many has caus'd 'em to be mistaken for.

. . . Therefore, one great end of this Institution shall be, to expel that cloud of Ignorance which Custom has involv'd us in, to furnish our minds with a stock of solid and useful Knowledge, that the souls of Women may no longer be the only unadorn'd and neglected things. . . . Such a course of Study will neither be too troublesome nor out of the reach of a Female Virtuoso; for it is not intended that she shou'd spend her hours in learning *words* but *things*, and therefore no more Languages than are necessary to acquaint her with useful Authors. Nor need she trouble her self in turning over a great number of Books, but take care to understand and digest a few well chosen and good ones. Let her but obtain right Ideas, and be truly acquainted with the nature of those Objects that present themselves to her mind, and then no matter whether or no she be able to tell what fanciful people have said about them: And thoroughly to understand Christianity as profess'd by the *Church of England*, will be sufficient to confirm her in the truth, tho' she have not a Catalogue of those particular errors which oppose it. . . .

For since GOD has given Women and Men intelligent Souls, why should they be forbidden to improve them? Since he has not denied us the faculty of Thinking, why shou'd we not (at least in gratitude to him) employ our Thoughts on himself their noblest Object, and not unworthily bestow them on Trifles and Gaities and secular Affairs? Being the Soul was created for the contemplation of Truth as well as for the fruition of Good, is it not as cruel and unjust to exclude Women

from the knowledge of the one as from the enjoyment of the other? Especially since the Will is blind, and cannot chuse but by the direction of the Understanding; or to speak more properly, since the Soul always *Wills* according as she *Understands*, so that if she Understands amiss, she Wills amiss. . . .

Let such therefore as deny us the improvement of our Intellectuals, either take up *his* Paradox, who said that *Women have no Souls*, (which at this time a day, when they are allow'd to Brutes, wou'd be as unphilosophical as it is unmannerly,) or else let them permit us to cultivate and improve them. There is a sort of Learning indeed which is worse than the greatest Ignorance: A Woman may study Plays and Romances all her days, and be a great deal more knowing but never a jot wiser. Such a knowledge as this serves only to instruct and put her forward in the practice of the greatest Follies, yet how can they justly blame her who forbid, or at least won't afford opportunity of better? A rational mind *will* be employ'd, it will never be satisfy'd in doing nothing, and if you neglect to furnish it with good materials, 'tis like to take up with such as come to hand.

We pretend not that Women shou'd teach in the Church, or usurp Authority where it is not allow'd them; permit us only to understand our *own* duty, and not be forc'd to take it upon trust from others; to be at least so far learned, as to be able to form in our minds a true Idea of Christianity, it being so very necessary to fence us against the danger of these *last* and *perilous days*, in which Deceivers a part of whose Character is to *lead captive silly Women*, need not *creep into Houses* since they have Authority to proclaim their Errors on the *House top*. And let us also acquire a true Practical knowledge, such as will convince us of the absolute necessity of *Holy Living* as well as of *Right Believing*, and that no Heresy is more dangerous than that of an ungodly and wicked Life. And since the *French Tongue* is understood by most Ladies, methinks they may much better improve it by the study of Philosophy (as I hear the *French Ladies* do) *Des Cartes, Malebranche* and others, than by reading idle *Novels* and *Romances*. 'Tis strange that we shou'd be so forward to imitate their Fashions and Fopperies, and have no regard to what really deserves our Imitation. And why shall it not be thought as genteel to understand *French Philosophy*, as to be accoutred in a *French mode*? Let therefore the famous Madam *D'acier, Scudery*, &c, and our own incomparable *Orinda*, excite the Emulation of the English Ladies.

The Ladies, I'm sure, have no reason to dislike this Proposal, but I know not how the Men will resent it to have their enclosure broke down, and Women invited

[margin handwritten note: did she think that or conced that?]

[bottom handwritten note: compare to those who criminalize questioning tradition + changing it]

to taste of that Tree of knowledge they have so long unjustly *Monopoliz'd*. But they must excuse me, if I be as partial to my own Sex as they are to theirs, and think Women as capable of Learning as Men are, and that it becomes them as well. . . .

To enter into the detail of the particulars concerning the Government of the *Religious*, their Offices of Devotion, Employments, Work &c. is not now necessary. Suffice it at present to signify, that they will be more than ordinarily careful to redeem their Time. . . . For a stated portion of it being daily paid to GOD in Prayers and Praises, the rest shall be imploy'd in innocent, charitable, and useful Business; either in study in learning themselves or instructing others, for it is design'd that part of their Employment be the Education of those of their own Sex; or else in spiritual and corporal Works of Mercy, relieving the Poor, healing the Sick, mingling Charity to the Soul with that they express to the Body, instructing the Ignorant, counselling the Doubtful, comforting the Afflicted, and correcting those that err and do amiss. . . .

And as this institution will strictly enjoyn all pious and profitable Employments, so does it not only permit but recommend harmless and ingenious Diversions, Musick particularly, and such as may refresh the Body without enervating the Mind. They do a disservice to Religion who make it an enemy to innocent Nature, and injure the almighty when they represent him as imposing burdens that are not to be born. . . .

As to *Lodging*, *Habit*, and *Diet*, they may be quickly resolv'd on by the Ladies who shall subscribe; who I doubt not will make choice of what is most plain and decent, what Nature not Luxury requires. . . . She who considers to how much better account that Money will turn which is bestow'd on the Poor, than that which is laid out in unnecessary Expences on her self, needs no Admonitions against superfluities. . . .

In a word, this happy Society will be but one Body, whose Soul is love—animating and informing us; and perpetually breathing forth it self in flames of holy desires after GOD and acts of Benevolence to each other. . .

In the last place, by reason of this loss of time and the continual hurry we are in, we can find no opportunities for thoughtfulness and recollection; we are so busied with what passes abroad, that we have no leisure to look at home, nor to rectifie the disorders there. And such an unthinking mechanical way of living, when like Machines we are condemn'd every day to repeat the impertinencies of the day before, shortens our Views, contracts our Minds, exposes to a thousand practical Errors, and renders Improvement impossible, because it will not permit us to consider and recollect, which is the only means to attain it. So much

for the inconveniences of living in the World; if we enquire concerning Retirement, we shall find it does not only remove all these, but brings considerable advantages of its own.

For first, it helps us to mate Custom and delivers us from its Tyranny, which is the most considerable thing we have to do, it being nothing else but the habituating our selves to Folly that can reconcile us to it. . . .

And by that Learning which will be here afforded, and that leisure we have to enquire after it, and to know and reflect on our own minds, we shall rescue our selves out of that woeful incogitancy we have slept into, awaken our sleeping Powers and make use of that reason which GOD has given us. . . .

Farther yet, besides that holy emulation which a continual view of the brightest and most exemplary Lives will excite in us, we shall have opportunity of contracting the purest and noblest Friendship; a Blessing, the purchase of which were richly worth all the World besides! For she who possesses a worthy Person, has certainly obtain'd the richest Treasure. A Blessing that Monarchs may envy, and she who enjoys is happier than she who fills a Throne! A Blessing, which next to the love of GOD, is the choicest Jewel in our Celestial Diadem; which, were it duly practis'd wou'd both fit us for Heav'n and bring it down into our hearts whilst we tarry here. For Friendship is a Vertue which comprehends all the rest; none being fit for this, who is not adorn'd with every other Vertue. Probably one considerable cause of the degeneracy of the present Age, is the little true Friendship that is to be found in it; or perhaps you will rather say that this is the effect of our corruption. The cause and the effect are indeed reciprocal; for were the World better there wou'd be more Friendship, and were there more Friendship we shou'd have a better World. But because *Iniquity abounds*, therefore the *love of many* is not only *waxen cold*, but quite benumb'd and perish'd. But if we have such narrow hearts, be so full of mistaken Self-love, so unreasonably fond of our selves, that we cannot spare a hearty Goodwill to one or two choice Persons, how can it ever be thought, that we shou'd well acquit our selves of that Charity which is due to all Mankind? For Friendship is nothing else but Charity contracted; it is (in the words of an admired Author) a kind of revenging our selves on the narrowness of our Faculties, by exemplifying that extraordinary Charity on one or two, which we are willing, but not able to exercise towards all. . . .

. . . [I]t were well if we could look into the very Soul of the beloved Person, to discover what resemblance it bears to our own, and in this Society we shall have the best opportunities of doing so. There are no Interests here to serve, no contrivances for another to be a stale to; the Souls of all the *Religious* will be open and free, and those particular Friendships must be no prejudice to the general Amity. But yet, as in Heav'n that region of perfect Love, the happy Souls (as some are of opinion) now and then step aside from more general Conversations, to entertain themselves with a peculiar Friend; so, in this little emblem of that blessed place, what shou'd hinder, but that two Persons of a sympathizing disposition, the *make* and *frame* of whose Souls bears an exact conformity to each other, and therefore one wou'd think were purposely design'd by Heaven to unite and mix; what shou'd hinder them from entering into an holy combination to watch over each other for Good, to advise, encourage and direct, and to observe the minutest fault in order to its amendment. The truest effect of love being to endeavour the bettering the beloved Person. And therefore nothing is more likely to improve us in Vertue, and advance us to the very highest pitch of Goodness than unfeigned Friendship, which is the most beneficial, as well as the most pleasant thing in the world. . . .

If any object against a Learned Education, that it will make Women vain and assuming, and instead of correcting encrease their Pride: I grant that a smattering in Learning may, for it has this effect on the Men, none so Dogmatical and so forward to shew their Parts as your little *Pretenders* to Science. But I wou'd not have the Ladies content themselves with the *shew*, my desire is, that they shou'd not rest till they obtain the *Substance*. And then, she who is most knowing will be forward to own with the wise *Socrates* that she knows nothing: nothing that is matter of Pride and Ostentation; nothing but what is attended with so much ignorance and imperfection, that it cannot reasonably elate and puff her up. The more she knows, she will be the less subject to talkativeness and its sister Vices, because she discerns, that the most difficult piece of Learning is to know when to use and when to hold ones Tongue, and never to speak but to the purpose.

But the men if they rightly understand their own interest, have no reason to oppose the ingenious Education of the Women, since 'twou'd go a great way towards reclaiming the men. Great is the influence we have over them in their Childhood, in which time if a Mother be discreet and knowing as well as devout, she has many opportunities of giving such a *Form* and *Season* to the tender Mind of the Child, as will shew its good effects thro' all the stages of his Life. But tho' you should not allow her capable of doing *good*, 'tis certain she may do *hurt*; If she do not *make* the Child, she has the power to *marr* him, by suffering her fondness to get the better of discreet affection. But besides this, a good and prudent wife wou'd wonderfully work on an ill man; he must be a Brute indeed, who cou'd hold out against all those innocent Arts, those gentle persuasives

and obliging methods she wou'd use to reclaim him. Piety is often offensive when it is accompanied with indiscretion; but she who is as Wise as Good, possesses such Charms as can hardly fail of prevailing. Doubtless her Husband is a much happier Man and more likely to abandon all his ill Courses than he who has none to come home to, and an ignorant, froward and fantastick Creature. An ingenious Conversation will make his life comfortable, and he who can be so well entertain'd at home, needs not run into Temptations in search of diversions abroad. The only danger is that the Wife be more knowing than the Husband; but if she be 'tis his own fault, since he wants no opportunities of improvement; unless he be a natural *Blockhead*, and then such an one will need a wise Woman to govern him, whose prudence will conceal it from publick Observation, and at once both cover and supply his defects. Give me leave therefore to hope, that no Gentleman who has honourable designs, will henceforward decry Knowledge and Ingenuity in her he would pretend to Honour; If he does, it may serve for a Test to distinguish the feigned and unworthy from the real Lover.

Now who that has a spark of Piety will go about to oppose so Religious a design? What generous Spirit that has a due regard to the good of Mankind, will not be forward to advance and perfect it? Who will think 500 pounds too much to lay out for the purchase of so much Wisdom and Happiness? Certainly we shou'd not think them too dearly paid for by a much greater Sum did not our pitiful and sordid Spirits set a much higher value on Money than it deserves. But granting so much of that dear Idol were given away, a person thus bred, will easily make it up by her Frugality & other Vertues; if she bring less, she will not waste so much as others do in superflous and vain Expences. Nor can I think of any expedient so useful as this to Persons of Quality who are over-stock'd with Children, for thus they may honourably dispose of them without impairing their Estates. Five or six hundred pounds may be easily spar'd with a Daughter, when so many thousands would go deep; and yet as the world goes be a very inconsiderable Fortune for Ladies of their Birth, neither maintain them in that *Port* which Custom makes almost necessary, nor procure them an equal Match, those of their own Rank (contrary to the generous custom of the *Germans*) chusing rather to fill their Coffers than to preserve the purity of their Blood, and therefore think a weighty Bag the best Gentility, preferring a wealthy Upstart before the best Descended and best Qualified Lady; their own Extravagancies perhaps having made it necessary, that they may keep up an empty shadow of Greatness, which is all that remains to shew what their Ancestors have been. . . .

Part II (1697): *Wherein a Method is offer'd for the Improvement of their Minds*

Chap. III. *Concerning the Improvement of the Understanding. I. Of the Capacity of the Humane Mind in General. II. Of Particular Capacities. . . . IV. A Natural Logic. . . .*

The perfection of the Understanding consisting in the Clearness and Largeness of its view, it improves proportionably as its Ideas become Clearer and more Extensive. But this is not so to be understood as if all sorts of Notices contributed to our Improvement, there are some things which make us no wiser when we know 'em, others which 'tis best to be ignorant of. But that Understanding seems to me the most exalted, which has the Clearest and most Extensive view of such Truths as are suitable to its Capacity, and Necessary or Convenient to be Known in this Present State. For being that we are but Creatures, our Understanding in its greatest Perfection has only a limited excellency. It has indeed a vast extent, and it were not amiss if we tarried a little in the Contemplation of its Powers and Capacities, provided that the Prospect did not make us giddy, that we remember from whom we have receiv'd them, and ballance those lofty Thoughts which a view of our Intellectuals may occasion, with the depressing ones which the irregularity of our Morals will suggest, and that we learn from this inspection, how indecorous it is to busy this bright side of us in mean things, seeing it is capable of such noble ones.

Human Nature is indeed a wonderful Composure admirable in its outward structure, but much more excellent in the Beauties of its Inward, and she who considers in whose Image her Soul was Created, and whose Blood was shed to Redeem it, cannot prize it too much, nor forget to pay it her utmost regard. There's nothing in this Material World to be compar'd to't, all the gay things we dote on, and for which we many times expose our Souls to ruin, are of no consideration in respect of it. They are not the good of the Soul, it's happiness depends not on 'em, but they often deceive and withdraw it from its true Good. It was made for the Contemplation and Enjoyment of its GOD, and all Souls are capable of this tho in a different degree and by measures somewhat different, as we hope will appear from that which follows.

I. Truth in general is the Object of the Understanding, but all Truths are not equally Evident, because of the Limitation of the Humane Mind, which tho' it can gradually take in many Truths, yet cannot any more than our sight attend to many things at once: And likewise, because GOD has not thought fit to communicate such Ideas to us as are necessary to the disquisition of some particular Truths. For knowing nothing without us but by the Idea we have of it, and Judging only according to the Relation we find between two or more Ideas, when we cannot discover the Truth we search after by Intuition or the immediate comparison of two Ideas, 'tis necessary that we shou'd have a third by which to compare them. But if this middle Idea be wanting, though we have sufficient Evidence of those two which we wou'd compare, because we have a Clear and Distinct Conception of them, yet we are Ignorant of those Truths which wou'd arise from their Comparison, because we want a third by which to compare them. . . .

Tho the Human Intellect has a large extent, yet being limited as we have already said, this Limitation is the Cause of those different Modes of Thinking, which for distinction sake we call Faith, Science and Opinion. For in this present and imperfect State in which we know not any thing by Intuition, or immediate View, except a few first Principles which we call Self-evident, the most of our Knowledge is acquir'd by Reasoning and Deduction: And these three Modes of Understanding, Faith, Science and Opinion are no otherwise distinguish'd than by the different degrees of Clearness and Evidence in the Premises from whence the Conclusion is drawn. . . .

In this enumeration of the several ways of Knowing, I have not reckon'd the Senses, in regard that we're more properly said to be *Conscious* of than to *Know* such things as we perceive by Sensation. And also because that Light which we suppose to be let into our Ideas by our Senses is indeed very dim and fallacious, and not to be relied on till it has past the Test of Reason; neither do I think there's any Mode of Knowledge which mayn't be reduc'd to those already mentioned.

Now tho there's a great difference between Opinion and Science, true Science being immutable but Opinion variable and uncertain, yet there is not such a difference between Faith and Science as is usually suppos'd. The difference consists not in the Certainty but in the way of Proof; the Objects of Faith are as Rationally and as Firmly Prov'd as the Objects of Science, tho by another way. As Science Demonstrates things that are *Seen*, so Faith is the Evidence of such as are *Not Seen*. And he who rejects the Evidence of Faith in such things as belong to its Cognizance, is as unreasonable as he who denies Propositions in Geometry that are prov'd with Mathematical exactness.

There's nothing true which is not in it self demonstrable, or which we should not pronounce to be true had we a Clear and Intuitive View of it. But as was said above we see very few things by Intuition, neither are we furnish'd with Mediums to make the Process our selves in Demonstrating all Truths, and therefore there are some Truths which we must either be totally ignorant of, or else receive them on the Testimony of another Person, to whose Understanding they are clear and manifest tho not to ours. And if this Person be one who can neither be Deceiv'd nor Deceive, we're as sertain of those Conclusions which we prove by his Authority, as we're of those we demonstrate by our own Reason: nay more Certain, by how much his Reason is more Comprehensive and Infallible than our own.

Science is following the Process our Selves upon Clear and Evident principles; Faith is a Dependance on the Credit of another, in such matters as are out of our View. And when we have very good Reason to submit to the Testimony of the Person we Believe, Faith is as Firm, and those Truths it discovers to us as truly Intelligible, and as strongly Prov'd in their kind as Science.

In a word, as every Sense so every Capacity of the Understanding has its proper Object. The Objects of Science are things within our View, of which we may have Clear and Distinct Ideas, and nothing shou'd be determin'd here without Clearness and Evidence. To be able to repeat any Persons *Dogma* without forming a Distinct Idea of it our selves, is not to Know but to Remember; and to have a Confused Indeterminate Idea is to Conjecture not to Understand.

The Objects of Faith are as Certain and as truly, Intelligible in themselves as those of Science, as has been said already, only we become persuaded of the Truth of them by another Method, we do not *See* them so clearly and distinctly as to be unable to disbelieve them. Faith has a mixture of the Will that it may be rewardable, for who will thank us for giving our Assent where it was impossible to withold it? Faith then may be said to be a sort of Knowledge capable of Reward, and Men are Infidels not for want of Conviction, but thro an *Unwillingness* to Believe. . . .

II. It is therefore very fit that after we have consider'd the Capacity of the Understanding in general, we shou'd descend to the view of our own particular, observing the bent and turn of our own Minds, which way our Genius lies and to what it is most inclin'd. I see no reason why there may not be as great a variety in Minds as there is in Faces, that the Soul as well as the Body may not have something in it to distinguish it, not only from all other Intelligent Natures but even from those of its own kind. There are different proportions in Faces which recommend them to some Eyes sooner than to others, and tho *All* Truth is amiable to a Reasonable Mind, and proper to employ it, yet why may there not be some particular Truths, more agreeable to each individual Understanding than others are? Variety gives Beauty to the Material World and

why not to the Intellectual? We can discern the different Abilities which the Wise Author of all things has endow'd us with, the different Circumstances in which he has plac'd us in reference to this World and the Concerns of an Animal Life, that so we may be mutually useful, and that since each single Person is too limited and confin'd to attend to many, much less to all things, we may receive from each other a reciprocal advantage, and why may we not think he has done the like in respect of Truth? That since it is too much for one, our united Strength shou'd be employ'd in the search of her. Especially since the divine Being who contains in himself all Reality and Truth is Infinite in Perfection, and therefore shou'd be Infinitely Ador'd and Lov'd; and If Creatures are by their being so uncapable of rendering to their Incomprehensible Creator an Adoration and Love that's worthy of him, it is but decorous that they shou'd however do as much as they can. All that variety of sublime Truths of Beautiful and Wondrous Objects which surround us, are nothing else but a various display of his unbounded Excellencies, and why shou'd any of 'em pass unobserv'd? Why shou'd not every individual Understanding be in a more especial manner fitted for and employ'd in the disquisition of some particular Truth and Beauty? 'Tis true after all our researches we can no more sufficiently Know GOD than we can worthily Love him, and are as much unable to find out all his Works as we are his Nature, yet this shou'd only prompt us to exert *All* our Powers and to do our best, since even *that* were too little cou'd we possibly do more. We can never offer to him so much Praise as he deserves, and therefore it is but fit that he shou'd have *All* that Mankind can possibly render him. He is indeed immutable in his own Nature, but those discoveries we daily make of his Operations will always afford us somewhat New and Surprizing, for this All-glorious Sun the Author of Life and Light is as inexhaustible a Source of Truth as he is of Joy and Happiness. . . .

IV. As to the *Method* of Thinking, if it be proper for me to say any thing of that, after those better Pens which have treated of it already, it falls in with the Subject I'me now come to, which is, that *Natural Logic* I wou'd propose. I call it natural because I shall not send you further than your Own Minds to learn it, you may if you please take in the assistance of some well chosen Book, but a good Natural Reason after all, is the best Director, without this you will scarce Argue well, tho you had the Choicest Books and Tutors to Instruct you, but with it you may, tho' you happen to be destitute of the other. For as a very Judicious Writer on this Subject (to whose Ingenious Remarks and Rules I am much obliged) well observes, "These Operations (of the Mind) proceed meerly from Nature, and that sometimes more perfectly from those who are altogether ignorant of Logic, than from others who have learn'd it." (*Art of Thinking*)

That which we propose in all our Meditations and Reasonings is, either to deduce some Truth we are in search of, from such Principles as we're already acquainted with; or else, to dispose our Thoughts and Reasonings in such a manner, as to be able to Convince others of those Truths which we our selves are Convinc'd of. Other Designs indeed Men may have, such as the Maintenance of their Own Opinions, Actions and Parties without regard to the Truth and Justice of 'em, or the Seduction of their unwary Neighbours, but these are Mean and Base ones, beneath a Man, much more a Christian, who is or ought to be endow'd with greater Integrity and Ingenuity.

Now Reasoning being nothing else but a Comparison of Ideas, and a deducing of Conclusions from Clear and Evident Principles, it is in the first place requisite that our Ideas be Clear and Just, and our Principles True, else all our Discourse will be Nonsense and Absurdity, Falsehood and Error. And that our Idea may be Right, we have no more to do but to look attentively into our Minds, having as we said above, laid aside all Prejudices and whatever may give a false tincture to our Light, there we shall find a Clear and Lively Representation of what we seek for, unsophisticated with the Dross of false Definitions and unintelligible Expressions. But we must not imagine that a transient view will serve the turn, or that our Eye will be Enlightened if it be not fix'd. For tho' Truth be exceeding bright, yet since our Prejudices and Passions have darkned our Eye-sight, it requires no little Pains and Application of Mind to find her out, the neglect of which Application is the Reason that we have so little Truth, and that the little we have is almost lost in the Rubbish of Error which is mingled with it. And since Truth is so near at hand, since we are not oblig'd to tumble over many Authors, to hunt after every celebrated Genius, but may have it for enquiring after in our own Breasts, are we not inexcusable if we don't obtain it? Are we not unworthy of Compassion if we suffer our Understandings to be overrun with Error? Indeed it seems to me most Reasonable and most agreeable to the Wisdom and Equity of the Divine Operations, that every one shou'd have a Teacher in their own Bosoms, who will if they seriously apply themselves to him, immediately Enlighten them so far as that is necessary, and direct them to such Means as are sufficient for their Instruction both in Humane and Divine Truths; for as to the latter, Reason if it be Right and Solid, will not pretend to be our sole Instructor, but will send us to Divine Revelation when it may be had. . . .

The First and Principal thing therefore to be observed in all the Operations of the Mind is, That we determine nothing about those things of which we have not a Clear Idea, and as Distinct as the Nature of the Subject will permit, for we cannot properly be said to Know any thing which does not Clearly and Evidently appear to us. Whatever we see Distinctly we likewise see Clearly, Distinction always including Clearness, tho this does not necessarily include that, there being many Objects Clear to the view of the Mind, which yet can't be said to be Distinct.

That (to use the Words of a Celebrated Author) may be said to be "Clear which is Present and Manifest to an attentive Mind; so as we say we see Objects Clearly, when being present to our Eyes they sufficiently Act on 'em, and our Eyes are dispos'd to regard 'em. And that Distinct, which is so Clear, Particular, and Different from all other things, that it contains not any thing in it self which appears not manifestly to him who considers it as ought." (*Les Princip. De la Philos. De M. Des Cartes*, Part I, para 45.) Thus we may have a Clear, but not a Distinct and Perfect Idea of God and of our own Souls; their Existence and some of their Properties and Attributes may be Certainly and Indubitably Known, but we can't Know the Nature of our Souls Distinctly, for Reasons too long to be mentioned here, and less that of GOD, because he is Infinite. Now where our Knowledge is Distinct, we may boldly deny of a subject, all that which after a careful Examination we find not in it: But where our Knowledge is only Clear, and not Distinct, tho' we may safely Affirm what we see, yet we can't without a hardy Presumption Deny of it what we see not. And were it not very common to find People both Talking and Writing of things of which they have no Notion, no Clear Idea; nay and determining Dogmatically concerning the intire Nature of those of which they cannot possibly have an Adequate and distinct one, it might seem Impertinent to desire them to speak no farther than they Apprehend. They will tell you Peremptorily of Contradictions and Absurdities in such matters as they themselves must allow they cannot Comprehend, tho others as Sharp sighted as themselves can see no such thing as they complain of.

As Judgments are form'd by the Comparing of Ideas, so Reasoning or Discourse arises from the Comparison or Combination of several Judgments. Nature teaches us when we can't find out what Relation one Idea bears to another by a Simple view or bare Comparison, to seek for a Common Measure or third Idea, which Relating to the other two, we may by Comparing it with each of 'em, discern wherein they agree or differ. Our Invention discovers it self in proposing readily apt Ideas for this Middle Term, our Judgment in making Choice of such as are Clearest and most to our purpose, and the excellency of our Reasoning consists in our Skill and Dexterity in Applying them. . .

Some Reflections upon Marriage (4th ed., 1730)

Curiosity, which is sometimes an Occasion of Good, but more frequently of Mischief, by disturbing our own, or our Neighbour's Repose, having induc'd me to read the Account of an unhappy Marriage [of the Duke and Duchess of Mazarine], I thought an Afternoon would not be quite thrown away in pursuing such *Reflections* as it occasion'd. I am far from designing a Satire upon Marriage, as some pretend, either unkindly or ignorantly, through want of *Reflection* in that Sense wherein I use the Word. . . .

They only who have felt it, know the Misery of being forc'd to marry where they do not love; of being yok'd for Life to a disagreeable Person and imperious Temper, where Ignorance and Folly (the Ingredients of a Coxcomb, who is the most unsufferable Fool) tyrannizes over Wit and Sense: To be perpetually contradicted for Contradiction-sake, and bore down by Authority, not by Argument; to be denied one's most innocent Desires, for no other Reason but the absolute Will and Pleasure of a Lord and Master, whose Follies a Wife, with all her Prudence, cannot hide, and whose Commands she cannot but despise at the same Time that she obeys them. . . .

But shall a Wife retaliate? God forbid! no Provocation, though ever so great, can excuse the Sin, or lessen the Folly: It were indeed a revenging the Injury upon herself in the most terrible Manner. The *Italian* Proverb shews a much better Way, *If you would be revenged of your Enemies, live well.*

Devotion is the proper Remedy, and the only infallible belief in all Distresses; when this is neglected or turn'd into Ridicule, we run, as from one Wickedness, so from one Misfortune, to another. Unhappy is that Grandeur which is too great to be good, and that which sets us at a Distance from true Wisdom. Even Bigotry, as contemptible as it is, is preferable to profane Wit; for *that* requires our Pity, but *this* deserves our Abhorrence. . . .

An ill Husband may deprive a Wife of the Comfort and Quiet of her Life, give occasion of exercising her Vertue, try her Patience and Fortitude to the utmost, which is all he can do; it is herself only that can accomplish her Ruin. . . .

There are some Reasons, (for the Laws of God and Man allow Divorces in certain Cases) though not many, that authorize a Wife's leaving her Husband, but if any Thing short of absolute Necessity, from irreclaimable Vice and Cruelty, prevails with her to break these sacred and strongest Bonds, how is she expos'd to Temptations and Injuries, Contempt, and the just Censure of the World. A Woman of Sense, one shou'd think, could take but little pleasure in the Courtship and Flatteries of her Adorers, even when she is single: But for a married Woman to admit of Love Addresses, is worse than Folly; it is a Crime so ridiculous, that I will never believe a Woman of Sense can be guilty of it. For what does a Man pretend when he whines and dangles after a married Woman? Would he have her think he admires her, when he is treating her with the last Contempt? or that he loves her, when he is trying his Arts to gratify his brutal Passion, at the Price of all that is dear to her? His fine Speeches have either no Meaning, or a reproachful one; he affronts her Understanding as well as her Vertue, if he fancies she cannot discern, or wants Spirit to resent the Insults. She can look on him no otherwise than as the worst of Hypocrites, who flatters to betray, and fawns that he may ruin; who is laying Snares to entangle her in a Commerce founded on Injustice, and Breach of the most sacred Vows, carried on by Dissimulation, Treachery, Lyes, and Deceit, attended with Fear and Anxiety, Shame, Remorse, the bitter Stings of Guilt, whose fatal Consequences cannot be forseen, the least of which is the blasting of her Honour. And why all this Mischief? Why, because he professes to think her amiable, and with the blackest Treachery takes Advantage of her Weakness and the too good Opinion she has entertained of him, to render her odious! to render her contemptible to himself, as well as to the World.

These Destroyers avoided, and better Care taken than usual in Womens Education, Marriage might recover the Dignity and Felicity of its original Institution; and Men be very happy in a married State, if it be not their own Fault. The great Author of our Being, who does nothing in vain, ordained it as the only honourable Way of continuing our Race; as a Distinction between reasonable Creatures and meer Animals, into which we degrade our selves, by forsaking the Divine Institution. God ordained it for a Blessing, not a Curse: We are foolish as well as wicked, when that which was appointed for mutual Comfort and Assistance, has quite contrary Effect through our Folly and Perverseness. Marriage therefore, notwithstanding all the loose Talk of the Town, the Satires of antient, or modern Pretenders to Wit, will never lose its just Esteem from the Wise and Good.

Though much may be said against this, or that Match; though the ridiculousness of some, the Wickedness of others, and the Imprudence of too many, may provoke our Wonder, or Scorn, our Indignation or Pity; yet Marriage in general is too sacred to be treated with Disrespect, too venerable to be the Subject of Raillery and Buffoonery. None but the Impious will pretend to refine on a Divine Institution, or suppose there is a better Way for Society and Posterity. Whoever scoffs at this, and by odious Representation would possess the married Pair with a frightful Idea of each other, as if a Wife is nothing better than a Domestick Devil, an Evil he must tolerate for his own Conveniency; and an Husband must of necessity be a Tyrant or a Dupe; has ill Designs on both, and is himself a dangerous Enemy to the Publick, as well as to private Families. . . .

Is it the being tied to *One* that offends us? Why this ought rather to recommend it to us, and would really do so, were we guided by Reason, and not by Humour or brutish Passion. He who does not make Friendship the chief Inducement to his Choice, and prefer it before any other Consideration, does not deserve a good Wife, and therefore should not complain if he goes without one. Now we can never grow weary of our Friends; the longer we have had them the more they are endear'd to us; and if we have One well assur'd, we need seek no farther, but are sufficiently happy in her. The Love of Variety in this and other Cases, shews only the ill Temper of our own Mind; for instead of being content with a competent Share of Good, thankfully and chearfully enjoying what is afforded us, and patiently bearing with the Inconveniencies that attend it, we would set up our Rest here, and expect Felicity where it is not to be found.

The Christian Institution of Marriage provides the best that may be for Domestick Quiet and Content, and for the Education of Children; so that if we were not under the Tie of Religion, even the Good of Society and civil Duty, would oblige us to what Christianity requires: And since the very best of us are but poor frail Creatures, full of Ignorance and Infirmity, so that in Justice we ought to tolerate each other, and exercise that Patience towards our Companions to Day, which we shall give them occasion to shew towards us Tomorrow; the more we are accustom'd to any one's Conversation, the better shall we understand their Humour, be more able to comply with their Weakness, and less offended at it. . . .

But if Marriage be such a blessed State, how comes it, may you say, that there are so few happy Marriages? Now in answer to this, it is not to be wonder'd that so few succeed, we should rather be surpriz'd to find so many do, considering how imprudently Men engage, the Motives they act by, and the very strange Conduct they observe throughout.

For pray, what do Men propose to themselves in Marriage? What Qualifications do they look after in a Spouse? What will she bring? is the first Enquiry: How many Acres? Or how much ready Coin? Not that this is altogether an unnecessary Question, for Marriage without a Competency, that is, not only a bare Subsistence, but even a handsome and plentiful Provision, according to the Quality and Circumstances of the Parties, is no very comfortable Condition. They who marry for Love, as they call it, find Time enough to repent their rash Folly, and are not long in being convinc'd, that whatever fine Speeches might be made in the heat of Passion, there could be no *real Kindness* between those who can agree to make each other miserable. But tho' an Estate is to be consider'd, so it should not be the *Main*, much less the only Consideration, for Happiness does not depend on Wealth; That may be wanting, and too often is, where This abounds. He who Marries himself to a Fortune only, must expect no other Satisfaction than that can bring him; but let not him say that Marriage, but that his own covetous or prodigal Temper, has made him unhappy. What Joy has that Man in all his Plenty, who must either run from home to possess it, contrary to all the Rules of Justice, to the Laws of God and Man, nay, even in Opposition to good Nature, and good Breeding too . . . ; or else be forc'd to share it with a Woman whose Person or Temper is disagreeable . . . ?

Few Men have so much Goodness as to bring themselves to a Liking of what they loath'd, meerly because it is their duty to like; on the contrary, when they Marry with an Indifferency, to please their Friends or increase their Fortune, the Indifferency proceeds to an Aversion, and perhaps even the Kindness and Complaisance of the poor abus'd Wife, shall only serve to increase it. What follows then? There is no Content at home, so it is sought elsewhere, and the Fortune so unjustly got, is as carelessly squander'd; the Man takes a Loose, what should hinder him? He has all in his Hands, and Custom has almost taken off that small Restraint Reputation us'd to lay. The Wife finds too late what was the Idol the Man adored, which her Vanity, perhaps, or it may be the Commands and Importunities of Relations, would not let her see before; and now he has got That into his Possession, she must make court to him for a little sorry Alimony out of her own Estate. If Discretion and Piety prevail upon her Passions, she sits down quietly contented with her Lot, seeks no Consolation in the Multitude of Adorers, since he whom only she desir'd to please because it was her Duty to do so, will take no Delight in her Wit or Beauty: She follows no Diversion to allay her Grief, uses no Cordials to support her Spirit, that may sully her Vertue or bring a Cloud upon her Reputation; she makes no Appeals to the mis-judging Croud, hardly mentions her Misfortunes to her most intimate Acquaintance, nor lays a Load upon her Husband to ease her self; but would, if it were possible, conceal his Crimes, though her Prudence and Vertue give him a thousand Reproaches without her Intention or Knowledge; and retiring from the World, she seeks a more solid Comfort than it can give her, taking Care to do nothing that Censoriousness, or even Malice it self can misconstrue to her Prejudice. Now she puts on all her Reserves, and thinks even innocent Liberties scarce allowable in her disconsolate State; she has other Business to mind: Nor does she in her Retirements reflect so much upon the Hand that administers this bitter Cup, as consider what is the best Use she can make of it. And thus indeed, Marriage, however unfortunate in other respects, becomes a very great Blessing to her. . . .

But it must not be suppos'd that Womens Wit approaches those Heights which Men arrive at, or that they indulge those Liberties the other take. Decency lays greater Restraints on them, their Timorousness does them this one, and perhaps this only Piece of Service, it keeps them from breaking through these Restraints, and following their Masters and Guides in many of their daring and masculine Crimes. As the World goes, your Witty Men are usually distinguish'd by the Liberty they take with Religion, good Manners, or their Neighbour's Reputation: But, God be thank'd, it is not yet so bad, as that Women should form Cabals to propagate Atheism and Irreligion ([Author's note:] *This was wrote in the Beginning of the present Century.*) A Man then cannot hope to find a Woman whose Wit is of a Size with his, but when he doats on Wit, it is to be imagin'd he makes Choice of that which comes the nearest to his own.

In a word, when we have reckon'd up how many look no further than the making of their Fortune, as they call it; who don't so much propose to themselves any Satisfaction in the Woman to whom they Plight their Faith, seeking only to be Masters of her Estate, that so they may have Money enough to indulge all their irregular Appetites; who think they are as good as can be expected, if they are but, according to the fashionable Term, *Civil Husbands*; when we have taken the Number of your giddy Lovers, who are not more violent in their Passion than they are certain to repent of it; when to these you have added such as marry without any Thought at all, further than it is the Custom of the World, what others have done before them, that the Family must be kept up, the antient Race preserv'd, and therefore their kind Parents and Guard-

ians choose as they think convenient, without ever consulting the Young one's Inclinations, who must be satisfied or pretend so at least, upon Pain of their Displeasure, and that heavy Consequence of it, Forfeiture of their Estate: These set aside, I fear there will be but a small Remainder to Marry out of better Considerations; and even amongst the Few that do, not one in a Hundred takes Care to deserve his Choice.

But do the Women never choose amiss? Are the Men only in fault? That is not pretended; for he who will be just, must be forc'd to acknowledge, that neither Sex are always in the right. A Woman indeed can't properly be said to Choose; all that is allow'd her, is to Refuse or Accept what is offer'd. And when we have made such reasonable Allowances as are due to the Sex, perhaps they may not appear so much in Fault as one would at first imagine, and a generous Spirit will find more Occasion to Pity, than to Reprove . . . nor is there a Man of Honour amongst the whole Tribe, that would not venture his Life, nay, and his Salvation too, in their Defence, if any but himself attempts to injure them. But I must ask Pardon if I can't come up to these Heights, nor flatter them with the having no Faults, which is only a malicious Way of continuing and increasing their Mistakes.

Women, it's true, ought to be treated with Civility; for since a little Ceremony and out-side Respect is all their Guard, all the Privelege that's allow'd them, it were barbarous to deprive them of it; and because I would treat them civilly, I would not express my Civility at the usual rate. I would not, under Pretence of Honouring and paying a mighty Deference to the Ladies, call them Fools, or what's worse, to their Faces; For what are all the fine Speeches and Submissions that are made, but an abusing them in a well-bred Way? She must be a Fool with a Witness, who can believe a Man, Proud and Vain as he is, will lay his boasted Authority, the Dignity and Prerogative of his Sex, one Moment at her Feet, but in Prospect of taking it up again to more Advantage; he may call himself her Slave a few Days, but it is only in order to make her his all the rest of his Life. . . .

A Meer Obedience, such as is paid only to Authority, and not out of Love and a sense of the Justice and Reasonableness of the Command, will be of an uncertain Tenure. As it can't but be uneasy to the Person who pays it, so he who receives it will be sometimes disappointed when he expects to find it: for that Woman must be endow'd with a Wisdom and Goodness much above what we suppose the Sex capable of, I fear much greater than any Man can pretend to, who can so constantly conquer her Passions, and divest her self even of Innocent Self-love, as to give up the Cause when she is in the Right, and to submit her inlightned Reason, to the imperious Dictates of a blind Will, and wild Imagination, even when she clearly perceives the ill Consequences of it, the Imprudence, nay, Folly and Madness of such a Conduct.

And if a Woman runs such a Risque when she marries prudently, according to the Opinion of the World, that is, when she permits her self to be dispos'd of to a Man equal to her in Birth, Education and Fortune, and as good as the most of his Neighbours, (for if none were to marry, but Men of strict Vertue and Honour, I doubt the World would be but thinly Peopled) if at the very best her Lot is hard, what can she expect who is Sold, or any otherwise betray'd into mercenary Hands, to one who is in all, or most respects, unequal to her? A Lover who comes upon what is call'd equal Terms, makes no very advantageous Proposal to the Lady he Courts, and to whom he seems to be an humble Servant. For under many sounding Compliments, Words that have nothing in them, this is his true meaning; He wants one to manage his Family, an House-keeper, one whose Interest it will be not to wrong him, and in whom therefore he can put greater Confidence than in any he can hire for Money. One who may breed his Children, taking all the care and trouble of their Education, to preserve his Name and Family. One whose Beauty, Wit, or good Humour and agreeable Conversation, will entertain him at Home when he has been contradicted and disappointed Abroad; who will do him that Justice the ill-natur'd World denies him; that is, in any one's Language but his own, sooth his Pride and flatter his Vanity, by having always so much good Sense as to be on his Side, to conclude him in the Right, when others are so ignorant, or so rude, as to deny it. Who will not be Blind to his Merit nor contradict his Will and Pleasure, but make it her Business, her very Ambition to content him; whose Softness and gentle Compliance will calm his Passions, to whom he may safely disclose his troublesome Thoughts, and in her Breast discharge his Cares; whose Duty, Submission and Observance, will heal those Wounds other Peoples Opposition or Neglect have given him. In a word, one whom he can intirely Govern, and consequently may form her to his Will and Liking, who must be his for Life, and therefore cannot quit his Service, let him treat her how he will. . . .

And if this be what every Man expects, the Sum of his violent Love and Courtship, when it is put into Sense, and rendred Intelligible, to what a fine pass does she bring her self who purchases a Lord and Master, not only with her Money, but with what is of greater Value, at the Price of her Discretion! . . . She will not find him less a Governor because she was once

his Superior, on the contrary, the Scum of the People are most Tyrannical when they get the Power, and treat their Betters with the greatest Insolence. For, as the wise Man long since observ'd, A Servant when he Reigns, is one of those Things for which the Earth is disquieted, and which no body is able to bear. . . .

Let us see then what is their Part, what must they do to make the Matrimonial Yoke tolerable to themselves as well as pleasing to their Lords and Masters? That the World is an empty and deceitful Thing, that those Enjoyments which appear'd so desirable at a Distance, which rais'd our Hopes and Expectations to such a mighty Pitch, which we so passionately coveted, and so eagerly pursued, vanish at our first Approach, leaving nothing behind them but the Folly of Delusion, and the Pain of disappointed Hopes, is a common Outcry; and yet, as common as it is, though we complain of being deceiv'd this Instant, we do not fail of contributing to the Cheat the very next. Though in reality it is not the World that abuses us, 'tis we abuse ourselves; it is not the Emptiness of That, but our own false Judgments, our unreasonable Desires and Expectations that torment us; for he who exerts his whole Strength to lift a Straw, ought not to complain of the Burden, but of his own disproportionate Endeavour which gives him the Pain he feels. The World affords us all the Pleasure a sound Judgment can expect from it, and answers all those Ends and Purposes for which it was design'd; let us expect no more than is reasonable, and then we shall not fail of our Expectations.

It is even so in the Case before us; a Woman who has been taught to think Marriage her only Preferment, the Sum-Total of her Endeavours, the Completion of all her Hopes, that which must settle and make her Happy in this World, and very few, in their Youth especially, carry a Thought steadily to a greater Distance; She who has seen a Lover dying at her Feet, and can't therefore imagine that he who professes to receive all his Happiness from her, can have any other Design or Desire than to please her; whose Eyes have been dazled with all the Glitter and Pomp of a Wedding, and, who hears of nothing but Joy and Congratulation; who is transported with the Pleasure of being out of Pupillage, and Mistress not only of her self, but of a Family too: She who is either so simple or so vain, as to take her Lover at his Word either as to the Praises he gave her, or the Promises he made for himself; in sum, she whose Expectation has been rais'd by Courtship, by all the fine things that her Lover, her Governess and Domestic Flatterers say, will find a terrible Disappointment when the hurry is over, and when she comes calmly to consider her Condition, and views it no more under a false Appearance, but as it truly is. . . .

But how can a Woman scruple intire Subjection, how can she forbear to admire the Worth and Excellency of the superior Sex, if she at all considers it! Have not all the great Actions that have been perform'd in the World been done by Men? Have not they founded Empires and over-turn'd them? Do not they make Laws and continually repeal and amend them? Their vast Minds lay Kingdoms waste, no Bounds or Measures can be prescrib'd to their Desires. War and Peace depend upon them; they form Cabals and have the Wisdom and Courage to get over all the Rubs, the petty Restraints which Honour and Conscience may lay in the way of their desired Grandeur. What is it they cannot do? They make Worlds and ruin them, form Systems of universal Nature, and dispute eternally about them; their Pen gives Worth to the most trifling Controversy; nor can a fray be inconsiderable if they have drawn their Swords in't. . . . It is a Woman's Happiness to hear, admire and praise them, especially if a little Ill-nature keeps them at any time from bestowing due Applauses on each other! And if she aspires no further, she is thought to be in her proper Sphere of Action; she is as wise and as good as can be expected from her!

She then who Marries, ought to lay it down for an indisputable Maxim, that her Husband must govern absolutely and intirely, and that she has nothing else to do but to Please and Obey. She must not attempt to divide his Authority, or so much as dispute it; to struggle with her Yoke will only make it gall the more, but must believe him Wise and Good and in all respects the best, at least he must be so to her. She who can't do this is no way fit to be a Wife, she may set up for that peculiar Coronet the antient Fathers talk'd of, but is not qualified to receive that great Reward, which attends the eminent Exercise of Humility and Self-denial, Patience and Resignation, the Duties that a Wife is call'd to.

But some refractory Woman perhaps will say, how can this be? Is it possible for her to believe him Wise and Good who by a thousand Demonstrations convinces her, and all the World, of the contrary? Did the bare Name of Husband confer Sense on a Man, and the mere being in Authority infallibly qualify him for Government, much might be done. But since a wise Man and a Husband are not Terms convertible, and how loth soever one is to own it, Matter of Fact won't allow us to deny, that the Head many times stands in need of the Inferior's Brains to manage it, she must beg leave to be excus'd from such high Thoughts of her Sovereign, and if she submits to his Power, it is not so much Reason as Necessity that compels her. . . .

To wind up this Matter; If a Woman were duly principled, and taught to know the World, especially the true Sentiments that Men have of her, and the Traps they lay for her under so many gilded Compliments, and such a seemingly great Respect, that Disgrace would be prevented which is brought upon too many Families; Women would Marry more discreetly, and demean themselves better in a Married State, than some People say they do. The Foundation, indeed, ought to be laid deep and strong, she shou'd be made a good Christian, and understand why she is so, and then she will be everything else that is Good. . . .

Indeed nothing can assure Obedience, and render it what it ought to be, but the Conscience of Duty, the paying it for God's sake. Superiors don't rightly understand their own Interest when they attempt to put out their Subjects Eyes to keep them Obedient. A blind Obedience is what a Rational Creature should never Pay, nor would such an one receive it, did he rightly understand its Nature. For Human Actions are no otherwise valuable, than as they are conformable to Reason; but a blind Obedience is an Obeying *without Reason*, for ought we know, *against* it. God himself does not require our Obedience at this rate; he lays before us the Goodness and Reasonableness of his Laws, and were there any thing in them whose Equity we could not readily comprehend, yet we have this clear and sufficient Reason, on which, to found our Obedience, that nothing but what's just and fit, can be enjoin'd by a Just, a Wise and Gracious God; but this is a Reason will never hold in respect of Men's Commands, unless they can prove themselves Infallible, and consequently Impeccable too.

It is therefore very much a Man's Interest, that Women should be good Christians; in this as in every other Instance, he who does his Duty, finds his own Account in it. Duty and true Interest are one and the same Thing, and he who thinks otherwise is to be pitied for being so much in the Wrong; but what can be more the Duty of the Head, than to instruct and improve those who are under Government? She will freely leave him the quiet Dominion of this World, whose Thoughts and Expectations are plac'd on the next. A Prospect of Heaven, and that only, will cure that Ambition which all generous Minds are fill'd with, not by taking it away, but by placing it on a right Object. She will discern a Time when her Sex shall be no Bar to the best Employments, the highest Honour; a Time when that distinction, now so much us'd to her Prejudice, shall be no more; but, provided she is not wanting to her self, her Soul shall shine as bright as the greatest Heroe's. This is a true, and indeed, the only Consolation, this makes her a sufficient Compensation for all the Neglect and Contempt the ill-grounded Customs of the World throw on her; for all the Injuries brutal Power may do her, and is a sufficient Cordial to support her Spirits, be her Lot in this World what it may.

But some sage Persons may, perhaps object, that were Women allow'd to Improve themselves, and not, amongst other Discouragements, driven back by those wise Jests and Scoffs that are put upon a Woman of Sense or Learning, a Philosophical Lady as she is call'd by way of Ridicule; they would be too wise and too good for the Men; I grant it, for vicious and foolish Men. Nor is it to be wonder'd that He is afraid he should not be able to Govern them were their Understandings improv'd, who is resolv'd not to take too much Pains with his own. But these, 'tis to be hop'd, are no very considerable Number, the Foolish at least; and therefore this is so far from being an Argument against Womens Improvement, that it is a strong one for it, if we do but suppose the Men to be as capable of Improvement as the Women; but much more, if, according to Tradition, we believe they have greater Capacities. This, if any thing, would stir them up to be what they ought, and not permit them to waste their Time and abuse their Faculties, in the Service of their irregular Appetites and unreasonable Desires, and so let poor contemptible Women who have been their Slaves, excel them in all that is truly excellent. This would make them Blush at employing an immortal Mind no better than in making Provision for the Flesh to fulfil the Lusts thereof, since Women, by a wiser Conduct, have brought themselves to such a Reach of Thought, to such Exactness of Judgment, such Clearness and Strength of Reasoning, such Purity and Elevation of Mind, such Command of their Passions, such Regularity of Will and Affection, and in a Word, to such a Pitch of Perfection, as the Human Soul is capable of attaining in this Life by the Grace of God, such true Wisdom, such real Greatness, as though it does not qualify them to make a Noise in this World, to found or overturn Empires, yet it qualifies them for what is infinitely better, a Kingdom that cannot be mov'd, an incorruptible Crown of Glory. . . .

Again, it may be said, If a Wife's Case be as it is here represented, it is not good for a Woman to Marry, and so there's an End of Human Race. But this is no fair Consequence, for all that can justly be inferr'd from hence, is that a Woman has no mighty Obligations to the Man who makes Love to her; she has no Reason to be fond of being a Wife, or to reckon it a piece of Preferment when she is taken to be a Man's Upper-Servant; it is no Advantage to her in this World; if rightly manag'd it may prove one as to the next. For she who marries purely to do good, to educate Souls for Heaven, who can be so truly mortified as to lay aside her own Will and Desires, to pay such an intire

Submission for Life, to one whom she cannot be sure will always deserve it, does certainly perform a more Heroick Action than all the famous Masculine Heroes can boast of, she suffers a continual Martyrdom to bring Glory to God and Benefit to Mankind; which Consideration, indeed, may carry her through all Difficulties. . . .

To conclude. Perhaps I've said more than most Men will thank me for; I cannot help it, for how much soever I may be their Friend and humble Servant, I am more a Friend to Truth. . . . If they have usurp'd, I love Justice too much to wish Success and Continuance to Usurpations, which, though submitted to out of Prudence, and for Quietness sake, yet leave everybody free to regain their lawful Right whenever they have Power and Opportunity. I don't say that Tyranny *ought*, but we find in *Fact*, that it provokes the Oppress'd to throw off even a Lawful Yoke that sits too heavy: And if he who is freely Elected, after all his fair Promises and the fine Hopes he rais'd, proves a Tyrant, the Consideration that he was one's own Choice, will not render one more Submissive and Patient, but I fear, more Refractory. For though it is very unreasonable, yet we see 'tis the Course of the World, not only to return Injury for Injury, but Crime for Crime; both Parties indeed are Guilty, but the Aggressors have a double Guilt, they have not only their own, but their Neighbour's Ruin to answer for.

As to the Female Reader, I hope she will allow I've endeavoured to do her Justice; not betray'd her Cause as her Advocates usually do, under Pretence of defending it. A Practice too mean for any to be guilty of who have the least Sense of Honour, and who do any more than meerly pretend to it. I think I have held the Balance even, and not being conscious of Partiality, I ask no Pardon for it. To plead for the Oppress'd, and to defend the Weak, seem'd to me a generous Undertaking; for though it may be secure, 'tis not always Honourable, to run over to the strongest Party. And if she infers from what has been said, that marriage is a very Happy State for Men, if they think fit to make it so; that they govern the World, they have Prescription on their Side; Women are too weak to dispute it with them, therefore they, as all other Governors, are most, if not only, accountable, for what's amiss, for whether other Governments in their Original, were or were not confer'd according to the Merit of the Person, yet certainly in this Case, if Heaven has appointed the Man to Govern, it has Qualified him for it: So far I agree with her: But if she goes on to infer, that therefore, if a man has not these Qualifications, where is his Right? That if he misemploys, he abuses it? And if he abuses, according to modern Deduction, he forfeits it, I must leave her there. A peaceable Woman, indeed, will not carry it so far, she will neither question her Husband's Right nor his fitness to Govern, but how? Not as an absolute Lord and Master, with an arbitrary and tyrannical sway, but as Reason governs and conducts a Man, by proposing what is just and fit. And the Man who acts according to that Wisdom he assumes, who would have that Superiority he pretends to, acknowledg'd just, will receive no Injury by any thing that has been offer'd here. A Woman will value Him the more who is so wise and good, when she discerns how much he excels the rest of his noble Sex; the less he requires, the more will he merit that Esteem and Deference, which those who are so forward to exact, seem conscious they don't deserve. So then the Man's Prerogative is not at all infring'd, whilst the Woman's Privileges are secured; and if any Woman think her self injur'd, she has a Remedy in reserve, which few Men will envy, or endeavour to rob her of, the Exercise and Improvement of her Vertue Here, and the Reward of it Hereafter. . . .

An Impartial Enquiry into the Causes of Rebellion and Civil War in This Kingdom (1704)

In an Examination of Dr. Kennett's Sermon, Jan. 31. 1703/4 and Vindication of the Royal Martyr:

. . . [Charles I, executed January 30, 1649] was *an Orthodox and most Regular Prince, stedfast in the Faith and Communion of our Church,* to whose *Memory* we must in *Justice* own, no *Prince* had *his Heart more fix'd on the Improvement of the Church,* and *Support and Honour of the Clergy,* as the Dr. [Kennett] confesses; who besides that Impartiality and Sincerity of which he makes profession, gives us no reason, from the Beginning to the End of his Sermon, to think that he wou'd say any more in favour of the *Martyr* [Charles] than Truth extorted from him.

But sure we of this Age, who have this dismal Tragedy so fresh in our Memories, must be the greatest Fools in nature, if we suffer ourselves to be bubbled any more by Men of the same Principles, and by the same Artifices so often detected, and so justly abhorr'd. Have we not had Warnings enough to beware of those Miscreants, who set whole Nations on fire, only that their own despicable selves may be talk'd of, and that they may warm them at the Flame? Men who are equally ruinous to Prince and People, who effectually destroy the Liberties of the Subject under pretence of

defending them; who bring in Popery, for they act by some of the very worst Popish Principles, whilst they rail against it!

Far be it from us to think that the Body of the Nation ever concur'd in that Villany we deplore, or even the Majority, any further than by a Supine Neglect of opposing it vigorously and in time. Wicked Men are active and unwearied, they stick at no Methods, use the vilest Means to carry their Point. They become the Flatterers of Mens Follies, and the Panders of their Vices, to gain them to their Party. They Bribe, they Threaten, they Solicit, they Fawn, they Dissemble, they Lye, they break through all the Duties of Society, violate all the Laws of GOD and of Man, where they can do it with present Impunity. They fright the Timorous, and tire out the Impatient; if they meet with any of an invincible Spirit and Prudence to countermine them, all the hard Words, all the scandalous stories that may be are thrown upon these Men, they are Malignants, High-flyers, and what not: No Stratagems are omitted to make them weary of Well doing. No wonder then that by such ways as these they get what passes for a Majority, and draw in thoughtless Men, who are so far from approving their Villanies, that they do not so much as suspect them. For one of their Arts is to lay their own Designs of overturning the Government, at the Door of those very Men, who are it's most faithful Supporters.

But as it will ever become a wise Government to be watchful over every little Cloud of Faction, and to suppress it in its Rise, so there is no Artifice us'd by Factious Men that Governours ought to be more upon their Guard against, than those suspicious Fears and Jealousies, that are artfully instill'd into the Minds of the People, by Cunning Men and their Instruments. I do not only mean that Governours shou'd provide against this, by taking care that their *Good be not Evil-spoken of,* and by *cutting off occasion* as much as in them lies, *from those that desire* and seek *occasion;* for after all this caution, Factious men will still find something to misrepresent. A sad instance of which, we have in their Usage of our Royal Martyr; whose very best Actions, as well as those Mistakes and Infirmities that are incident to Humane Nature, they took occasion to Calumniate. But Governours must vigorously exert that lawful Authority GOD has given them, to *be a Terror to Evil-doers,* as well as a *Praise and Encouragement to those who do well.* They shou'd not suffer Men to infect the Peoples Minds with evil Principles and Representations, with Speeches that have double Meanings and equivocal Expressions, *Innuendo's,* and secret Hints and Insinuations.

An honest man dares always *speak out;* he who means well, needs no Softnings, no cautious Periphrases; no aimings at something he wou'd have you *think*, but which he does not care to *say*, laying in Provision to bring himself off, if you shou'd charge him with it. This, how well soever it may suit the Politicks of the Age, how much soever it may be the Practice of the *Wise Men, as the World calls them,* is not at all consistent with the *Simplicity of the Gospel,* or the Courage and Spirit of a Free-man, an *English-man.* Governours therefore may be very justly animadvert upon, and suppress it. For it is as much their Duty, and as necessary a Service to the Public, to restrain the Turbulent and Seditious, as it is to protect the Innocent, and to reward the Deserving. This, no doubt, the Doctor [Kennett] was very well aware of; and therefore takes care to inform us very particularly, how *Doubts* and *Fears* contributed to our deplorable Civil Wars. . . .

For till those Men have done pretending to Doubts and Fears, and I know not what Apprehensions, who have formerly destroy'd their innocent Neighbours, and overturn'd the Government by such Pretences, our Affairs can hardly be well manag'd Abroad, because we can never be united at Home. That supine Indifferency for excellent Establishments, which some are pleas'd to miscal *Charity*; that Faint Heart and Double Mind, that Want of Regular Zeal, which they would put upon us instead of *Meekness,* may hasten our Ruin, but can never *heal our Breaches.* For we have the sad Experience of our Civil Wars to inform us, that all the Concessions the King and his Loyal Subjects cou'd make to the Factious and Rebellious, cou'd not satisfie; no, not tho' they were at first, all that they had the confidence to desire, and their Confidence never fail'd them: They were ever stiff in their own way, still contending to bring over others to themselves, whilst they wou'd concede to nothing.

And, what was the thing they aim'd at, and at last unhappily effected? What but the Ruin of the Government in Church and State? The bringing *the Necks* of their Fellow Subjects, *Englishmen,* who *had the Spirit of a Free People!* under their own infamous *Yoke,* and *their Feet into* the most reproachful Chains; becoming themselves the Actors of those Arbitrary and Illegal Actions, which they had so loudly, and in great measure falsly imputed to their Lawful Superiors. And the *Freeborn* People of *England,* for all their *Spirit of Honour and Genius to Liberty,* even those great Fore-Fathers, whose *Off-spring we are,* had the *disdain of serving* in the most slavish manner, and of wearing the heavy and shameful *Yoke* of some of the vilest of their Fellow Subjects: Till GOD was pleas'd to restore our Monarch, and with him the Exercise of our Religion, and the Liberties of the *English* Nation. But this is a common Story, which every body knows, and there-

fore the Doctor wou'd not lose his time upon't; only in my mind, and whatever might be in his, methinks the whole course of his Sermon inculcates this necessary Lesson, Beware of every one who wou'd draw you into a *necessity of believing,* that your *Liberties and Estates are in some danger,* who wou'd give you such a *Prospect,* and work you into such a *Persuasion,* and so draw you in by the old Cant of *Self-Preservation,* tho' they seem to demonstrate ever so great a *necessity:* Much more ought you to abhor being *drawn in* by the bare *meaning* of it, at least if you have any regard to real Self Preservation, and think your Souls of greater moment than your Lives or Estates. Nay, even for the very Preservation of these Dear Lives of yours, since, if you dare believe our Lord himself, the surest way to save your Lives is to be ready to part with them; and the most likely way to lose them, is this unchristian Desire of saving them. For such Arts as those, the putting such *Thoughts* into the Heads of the *Good-natur'd English People,* was that which *seduc'd them into that Unnatural Rebellion,* which has had so many dismal Effects upon this Nation. . . .

But can we fancy, that the *Body of a Good-natur'd English People,* are of that Generation? Tho' *the least Attempts towards Slavery and Exorbitant Power,* has always *rais'd up the Appearance of a Yoke, that our Forefathers were not able to bear,* and Princes ought to remember *that we are their Off-spring:* Tho' the People of *England* are *Free,* and we are like to hear no such *fond* Answers from them, as the *Israelites* gave *Samuel,* when he told them the manner of the Kingdom, I *Sam.* 8. Yet surely, the *uncorrupted English Blood and Principles,* will never allow them to *use their Liberty for a Cloak of Maliciousness,* but to use it *as the Servants of* GOD; who has been pleas'd to declare his Will in this matter very particularly, and very frequently to enjoin us to render to *Caesar the things that are Caesar's, and unto GOD the things that are GODS;* to *Fear GOD, and to Honour the King;* to pay to all our Superiours what is any way their *due, not only to the Good and Gentle, but also to the Froward.* For to be *patient* when we suffer for our *Faults* is no great matter; but to do *well,* and patiently to *suffer* Evil for *doing so,* is an Heroic Action, it is the Christian's Business, that to which he is *call'd,* in imitation of his Great Master: See I S. *Pet.* 2.

It is not to be suppos'd therefore, that now we are Reform'd from Popery, one of whose worst Doctrines and Practices is Disobedience to the Civil Magistrate; it is not to be imagin'd, I say, that we shou'd have a *Thought,* or *Strength of Fear,* upon an *unjust Occasion,* especially we our selves being Judges! or that we shou'd be *drawn* into any necessary Revolutions; much less, any *Unnatural Rebellions,* but *for the meaning at least of Self-Preservation!* . . .

And, Oh! how happy had it been for the Peace of the Martyr's *Reign, if even Doubts and Suspicions had been wanting! If Hardships* (the softest Name we can call them by) *had not serv'd to exasperate the Minds of the People, and prepar'd them by degrees to be led out first in Riots and Tumults, and then in Troops and Armies, against their Lawful Sovereign!* Poor *good-natur'd People,* to be forc'd to this upon *Thoughts, Suspicions,* and *Hardships!* Doubtless, they never meant such *ill Effects,* any more than the King did those, which the Dr. tells us were *beyond his Intentions,* but which rais'd *such a Jealousy, and spread such a damp upon the English Subjects, that it was unhappily turn'd into one of the unjust Occasions of the Civil War.* But who cou'd help this Civil War? since the *People* THOUGHT *themselves too much under* French *Counsels and a* French *Ministry?* . . . But without this *Thought,* the good People, alas! *cou'd never have been drawn into this Great Rebellion!* How we come to call it a Rebellion, is another Question: which *Harrington* shall answer.

> *Treason does never prosper; what's the Reason?*
> *For if it prosper none dares call it Treason?*

The People were *not secure* in their *Legal Rights and Tenures,* at least they *thought so.* There was *Ship-mony, Loans,* and *Benevolences* exacted, which they, good Souls! had no Notion of. The King, 'tis true, had set this Right; but why shou'd you trust him who once has Injur'd you? or to whom you have been Injurious? There was *an unhappy Suspicion of an Arbitrary Executive Power,* and the *Spirit of a Free People* will always shake off the *Yoke. For Tyranny and Oppression were a Grievance Here in the remotest Times of Old. And for the Future* (hear, and take Warning O ye English Princes!) *it shall never be attempted,* or which is the same thing, *thought to be attempted, without bringing down Ruin and Confusion upon those who shall attempt it,* or whom Crafty Men, I shou'd say Good Patriots, shall tell the People, and make them *think* that they design to attempt it. . . .

I hope then *our Rights,* and the Rights of Englishmen, *tender Lovers of their Faith and Country, have been retrieved, and committed down to Posterity, beyond a Capacity of their being ever depriv'd of them;* for the Dr. has very wisely, and very industriously establish'd that Supreme Law, the Safety of the People: it being evident from him, that it is not enough that a Prince be *Orthodox, Regular,* free from *Ambition* and *Sinister Ends;* . . . if there be the *least Attempts towards Exorbitant Power,* . . . the *Appearance of a Yoke,* or so

much as *the Remoter Fears and Apprehensions of one;* . . . tho' *he himself* be ever so *innocent;* yet the *Good Prince,* we find by experience, must *answer* for all, and *pay down his Royalty and his Life!* . . .

. . . [A]nd tho' when a Prince does any irregular or disobliging Action this may be a good Pretence, yet a *Civil War* may be *indeed begun more out of Hatred to a Party,* who are, or who we fear may be uppermost, than out of *any Dissatisfaction* to the Prince: for these, and no doubt for other reasons, 'tis highly necessary, the *Truth* which we have taught of late, the *Justice* we have practis'd, and *Charity,* which always begins at home, taking care in the first place to make our own Fortunes, are all of them nearly concern'd to keep this Fundamental Right in the Peoples view, *viz.* "That Power is originally from the People, and that Princes are responsible to them for the exercise thereof." The People must ever and anon be reminded as plainly as we dare, and as Prudence, the Humour of the Times, and the Service of the Cause will permit; that this Right has often been exercis'd; that there are many Precedents, or that the Suspicion, the very *Thought and Dread of Popery, Oppression, and Illegal Power,* the very *Prospect* that *their Liberties and Estates were in some Danger,* have drawn in their great Forefathers to stand upon their Guard, *meaning Self-preservation;* and that Princes, how sacred soever they be, must not think to *attempt* upon the Liberties of a Free People, without *bringing down Ruin and Confusion upon themselves.*

For if a Busie Man, or Party of Men, have Policy and Courage enough, and some lucky Opportunities to persuade the People into Jealousies and Fears, and to Head them against their Sovereign, 'tis all a case whether the *Dangers* are Real or Imaginary; if they happen to succeed, they shall find Advocates enough to Justify them, Success will Crown the Work.

Is it not an Inconsistency to deplore the Fate of Char. I. and to justify that of other Princes? If we think their Fall to be Just, and his to be Unjust and Deplorable, we may in time come to abhor those Principles that brought him to the Block, and the Practices that flow from them, as being equally destructive of the Best, as well as of the worst Princes; and then what will become of the Peoples Right to shake off an Oppressor? Must we take that dull way which David took, and which the old-fashion'd Homilies talk of, Wait God's time, and let him go down to the Grave in Peace? Why at this rate we may tamely have our Throats cut; and sure it is better to be beforehand and with him! If you deny us the Lawfulness of the Self-defence, we have done twenty actions that we can't justifie. . . .

Is it not best therefore, when these 30th of *Januarys* come about, to persuade ourselves and the People, with as much respect to King *Charles's* Memory as the matter will bear, that this *Good Prince*, tho' he meant no hurt, was over-persuaded by a Popish Queen [Henrietta Maria], and high Church men, such as the *Laudean* Faction [of William Laud, Archbishop of Canterbury], and Arbitrary Ministers, to do things worthy of blame. That tho' matters were afterwards carry'd too far, farther than the Honest Presbyterians, and the *Tender* and *Loyal* moderate Men intended, yet the King may thank himself for it; for he gave the Occasion by the *French Alliance*, and the Consequences of it. . . .

Such an Indictment as this, drawn up against this unfortunate Prince, with *Plainness of Truth*, and *Sincerity of Heart*, even when it is said to *be dangerous*, and an *invidious Subject*, but yet entred upon with *Simplicity and godly Sincerity, for the sake of Truth, and Justice, and Charity*; may, it's like, open Peoples eyes, and convince them that a Friend to Popery, and an Invader of our Liberties, a Prince in whose Reign *the People*, the *good-natur'd* People, *thought themselves too much under* French *Counsels and a* French *Ministry*, ought not to stand as a Martyr in our *English* Calendars; the Example is dangerous, and the Consequences pernicious. . . .

What greater Service then can be done our Country, and those Noble Assertors of its Rights and Liberties, than to let Princes know, that they must, from the very beginning, avoid everything that may raise a *Suspicion*, a *Thought*, in the Peoples Minds, of their Inclinations to *France*, to Popery, or Arbitrary Power? Since it is not enough to retract past Mistakes, King *Charles* did this, but to no manner of purpose. Or rather, to prevent all Misunderstanding, 'tis best for them at first *To part with their Power, and Trust it to them*, as Mr. *Hambden* answered one of his Fellow Members, who ask'd him, What they cou'd desire more of the King, seeing he had granted them so much? . . .

Now they who are curious to know what Popery is, and who do not rail at it at a venture, know very well, that every Doctrine which is profess'd by the Church of *Rome*, is not Popish; GOD forbid it shou'd, for they receive the Holy Scriptures, and teach the Creeds. But that Superstructure of Hay and Stubble, those Doctrines of Men or Devils, which they have built upon this good Foundation, this is Popery; and it is upon account of our rejecting those Corruptions, that we stile our selves Reform'd. It is not necessary to enumerate those Errors here; the Learned Writers of the *Church of England* having sufficiently expos'd them in those excellent Tracts, whereby they most Gloriously defended the Truth with their Pens, in a Primitive manner, in the late Reign. I shall only take notice of one Error, which is proper to my present purpose, and that is the *Deposing Doctrine*, which is as rank Popery

as Transubstantiation, and has ever been so accounted by *Church of England* Writers. . . .

We see then, that this is the declar'd Doctrine of the *Roman* Doctors, of all Orders, and of all Nations; . . . And I shall only at present make a small Request to those good Protestants who profess it, (*viz.*) that if it is not Popish, but true Orthodox Protestant Doctrine, they wou'd be pleas'd to prove it to us from Authentick Protestant Authors; for I make no reckoning of a *Buchanan*, a *Milton*, or any of those Mercenary Scriblers whom all sober Men condemn, and who only write after the Fact, or in order to it, to make their own Fortunes, or to justifie their own wickedness. Or rather, and which is much better, let it be prov'd to us from Holy Scripture, and those best expositors, as well as Practisers of Holy Writ, the Primitive Church.

But if they will not, or cannot give us this Proof, then I wou'd beg them, for their own Credit sake, to talk no more against Popery, much less to affix this odious Name, either openly or indirectly, upon Men who are the greatest and truest Enemies to Popery, since they themselves espouse some of the vilest Popish Doctrines. . . . It is but setting up . . . Cunning and Popular Men, and good Speakers, . . . to obstruct the King's Business, and to weaken his Authority: And then, tho' the Royal and English Heart be continually labouring for the Good of the People, these evil Ministers may easily pervert and misrepresent the best Intentions and most noble Designs. For Princes, how good soever, are neither infallible in their Judgments, whether of Things or Persons, nor exempt from the Passions of Humane Nature. And if the Principles and Measures that brought the Royal Head to the Block be so tenderly handled, and so carefully pursu'd, woe unto us! for how much soever we make shew of detesting the Consequences, whilst the Premises please, we are in the high Road towards drawing the fatal Conclusion! We may harangue as much as we please against Popery and Arbitrary Power, so did our *Forefathers* whose *Off-spring we are*, and all the World knows to what End and Purpose; these being only the Baits that cover the Hook of home-bred Cabals and Rebellious Projects. Strange! that such Principles shou'd be suffered in a Christian Nation, a Nation that has smarted so severely by them! But stranger yet, that any Prince shou'd Employ and Trust Men of these Principles! 'Tis certain he can have no hold of them; for whenever they get Power, and *Think* that a Change will be for their Interest, they will never want Pretences to throw him out of the Saddle. Nor will they be long in persuading themselves that it will turn to their own Account, even tho' the Prince may have heap'd the utmost Favours on them. For in all Changes there's something to be got, by the Mercenary and Rebellious

Hands that effect them. Forbid it Heaven! that they shou'd ever any more be able to give us a Tryal of their Skill. . . .

Our Excellent Church . . . teaches us to acknowledge in our daily Prayers, That GOD is *the only Ruler of Princes;* that the Parliament is *assembled under our most Religious and Gracious Queen* [Queen Anne— 1700–1714]; and therefore can have no Coercive Power over their Princes. In the Communion Service we are taught to own in our very Prayers, That the *Queen* is *GOD's Chosen Servant, GOD's Minister,* but *our Queen and Governour;* that she has *GOD's Authority* that it is *GOD's Word and Ordinance* that we *should faithfully serve, honour, and humbly obey Her, in* GOD, and *for* GOD, that is, in the Apostle's words, *not only for Wrath, but for Conscience sake.* Where then is the Original and Supreme Authority of the People? Besides; this is the Law of the Land, as well as the Doctrine of the Church, for the Liturgy is Establish'd by Act of Parliament: which may be one Reason why some are so willing to have it Review'd. It is a lasting and daily Reproach to their Disloyalty, reminding them how far they have gone towards the breach of that excellent Constitution, about the Preservation of which they make so great and so Hypocritical a Clamour: For, allowing that the People have a Right to Design the Person of their Governour; it does by no means follow that they Give him his Authority, or that they may when they please resume it. None can give what they have not: The People have no Authority over their own Lives, consequently they can't invest such an Authority in their Governours. And tho' we shou'd grant that People, when they first enter into Society, may frame their Laws as they think fit; yet these Laws being once Establish'd, they can't legally and Honestly be chang'd, but by that Authority in which the Founders of the Society thought fit to place the Legislature. Otherwise we have been miserably impos'd upon by all those Arguments that were urg'd against a Dispensing Power.

And since our Constitution lodges the Legislative Power in the Prince and the Three Estates assembled in Parliament; as it is not in the Power of the Prince and one of the Houses, to Make or Abrogate any Law, without the Concurrence of the other House, so neither can it be Lawfully done by the Prince alone, or by the two Houses without the Prince. All such pretended Acts, and all the Consequences of them, being Illegal and Void in themselves, without the Formality of a Repeal, as is evident to every honest Man, if he will but attend to common Sense, plain *English,* and the unalterable Reason of things. I hope then we shall hear no more of the People's Supremacy till these Good Men have got *the Act of Uniformity* Repeal'd. But, alas, what

do Laws signifie to Rebels, who have Power to Break or Cunning to Evade them! For all sides must allow, that there are even yet many other Good Laws in force, which sufficiently condemn those Principles and Practices in which they glory. . . .

Popery was the Cry 'tis true, but the Establish'd Church was the thing aim'd at; . . .

The short is; The true and the principal Cause of that Great Rebellion, and that Horrid Fact which compleated it, and which we can never enough deplore, was this: Some Cunning and Self-ended Men, whose Wickedness was equal to their Craft, and their Craft sufficient to carry them thro' their Wickedness; these had *Thoughts* and *Meanings* to destroy the government in Church and State, and to set up a Model of their own Invention, agreeable to their own private Interests and Designs, under the specious Pretences of the Peoples Rights and Liberties. They did not indeed speak out, and declare this at first, for that wou'd have spoil'd the Intrigue, every body wou'd have abhorr'd them; but a little Discernment might have found what they drove at. For to lessen and incroach upon the Royal Authority, is the only way to null it by degrees, as an ingenious Person observes upon this Occasion. . . .

As little did we hear of *Illegal Acts* and *Arbitrary Power,* of *Oppression and Persecution,* in a Reign [of Oliver Cromwell] that tugg'd hard for a Standing Army in time of Peace; that had Interest to suspend the *Habeas Corpus* Act several times, tho' it be the great Security of the *English* Liberties; that outed 7 or 8 Reverend Prelates, the Ornament and Glory of the *English* Church, besides several of the inferiour Clergy, and Members of the Universities, and that only for *Conscience sake,* and because they cou'd not swallow such new Oaths, as they believ'd to be contrary to the old ones: And tho' 12 of them were thought so deserving, that there was a Provision made in their Favour, even by that Act that depriv'd them of their Freeholds and Subsistance, of their Rights as *English-men* and Ministers of GOD's Church, yet not one of them enjoy'd, in that Human, Charitable and Religious Reign! the Advantages which the *Body of Good-natur'd* English *People* designed them. Who cry'd out Persecution? or put in a word for a Sister Church, when Episcopacy was destroy'd Root and Branch in a Neighbouring Kingdom [Scotland], that us'd to interest itself mightily in our Affairs, and still believes it is under Covenant Engagements, to work the same Blessed Reformation here? And tho' all of the Clergy, who were but suspected to be favourers of Episcopacy, were treated in the most outragious and cruel manner; 'tho a whole Clan of defenceless Men were barbarously Massacred in cold Blood, after promises of Security; which Action, if not done by Authority, was done at least by connivance, the Actors being protected and kept from Punishment. When——etc. more might be said, but let this suffice; nor are these bare *Suspicions, Doubts, etc.* no, they are true and notorious Facts; which will be remembered, and call'd by their proper Names, whatever a Set of Men may endeavour to the contrary.

But no sooner was her Majesty happily plac'd in the Throne of her Fathers, thro' GOD's great and most seasonable Mercy to an unworthy People, but all the old Clamours are reviv'd, tho' she has done nothing to Provoke, but every thing to Oblige them! Tho' her only fault, if Duty and Respect will allow that Expression, consists in too much of the Royal Martyr's Clemency and Goodness; Her Majesty's Reign having left us nothing to wish, but that she had less of K. *Charles* and more of the Spirit of Q. *Elizabeth*, since a Factious People can no way be kept inbounds, but by a sprightly and vigorous Exertion of just Authority. . . .

To come then to account for the Causes of our deplorable Civil Wars, we may be allow'd to do it in this manner: Tho' Government is absolutely necessary for the Good of Mankind, yet no Government, no not that of GOD himself, can suit with their deprav'd and boundless Appetites. Few govern themselves by Reason, and they who transgress its Laws, will always find somewhat or other to be uneasy at, and consequently will ever desire, and as far as they can endeavour, to change their Circumstances. But since there are more Fools in the World than Wise Men, and even among those who pass for Wise, that is, who have Abilities to be truly so, too many abuse and warp their Understandings to petty and evil Designs, and to such Tricks and Artifices as appear the readiest way to attain them. Since Riches and Power are what Men covet, supposing these can procure them all they wish; Hopes to gain more, or at least to secure what one has, will always be a handle by which Humane nature may be

mov'd, and carry'd about as the cunning Manager pleases. And therefore of *Necessity* in all Civil Wars and Commotions, there must be some Knaves at the Head of a great many Fools, whom the other wheedle and cajole with many plausible Pretences, according to the Opportunity, and the Humour of those they manage. . . .

I will not pretend to justifie all the Actions of our Princes, but it is much more Difficult; nay, it is impossible to justifie, or honestly excuse the Behaviour of our People towards them. Tyranny and Oppression are no doubt a grievance; they are so to the Prince, as well as to the Subject. Nor shou'd I think a Prince wou'd fall into them, unless seduc'd by some of his Flattering Courtiers and Ambitious Ministers; and therefore our Law very Reasonably provides, that these, and these only, shou'd suffer for it. But are Sedition and Rebellion no Grievances? they are not less, perhaps more Grievous than Tyranny, even to the People; for they expose us to the Oppression of a multitude of Tyrants. And as *we here in this Nation* may have suffer'd by the former, so have we oftner and much more grievously by the latter. The accursed Roots of which are I fear still left among us, and there are but too many wicked ones who cultivate these Tares with the utmost Arts and Industry. May GOD inspire the Heart of his Viceregent with the Spirit of Courage and Understanding, to restrain and keep under *all such workers of Iniquity, as turn Religion into Rebellion, and Faith into Faction.* That so She may never leave it in their power to prevail either against her Royal Person or her Good and Faithful Subjects, *or to triumph in the Ruin of GOD's Church among us*; seeing they have not fail'd upon occasion to give us too evident Proof, that when they have the Power to hurt, they never want the Inclination.

FINIS

Phillis Wheatley (1753?–84)

Phillis Wheatley was one of the most renowned of poets in colonial America even though she was born in Africa and brought to the American colonies as a slave when she was a child. Although scholars are unsure of her birth place, the consensus is that she was born in Senegal and brought to Boston in 1761. She was then purchased by John and Susanna Wheatley. John Wheatley was a tailor who was also a successful merchant. The family was part of the evangelical reform movement in American Protestantism, prominent in Boston during the mid-eighteenth century. The Wheatleys quickly came to recognize the strong intellectual abilities of the young girl, and they decided to educate her along with their own children. She was even taught Latin, certainly something most white girls would not have studied in eighteenth-century Britain or New England.

While still quite young, she began writing poetry and in 1767 published her first poem in the Newport Mercury. Wheatley wrote in a formal style popular in her time, focusing often on religious topics but placing them in a universal context touching on questions of creation and teleology, issues of good and evil, and metaphysical questions more broadly. She has sometimes been criticized by current scholars seeking the roots of African American or feminist literature. She almost never spoke from her identity as a woman, but she did remind her readers that she came from another land, was not free, and could never share their free existence. In 1770 she published "Africa," a poem on her homeland. She later expressly contrasted the claims of freedom and independence from Britain put forward by colonialists against the condition of herself, and others like her, who were brought to American shores in chains. Her origins were laid out in "To S.M., a Young African Painter, On Seeing His Works" and "On Being Brought from Africa to America." Because of the fear of doubt concerning her authorship, the latter poem contained a foreword by eighteen prominent American men verifying that Phillis Wheatley was indeed its author.

In 1773 Wheatley traveled to Britain with a collection of her poems, entitled Poems on Various Subjects, Religious and Moral. With its publication in England, she became the first African American to publish a book, but the volume was not published in the colonies until 1777. In 1770 she had published a poem, "On the death of the Rev. Mr. George Whitefield" (Whitefield had been chaplain to the Countess of Huntingdon), and during her stay in England she was the guest of the countess, to whom she dedicated the book. Following a triumphal tour of Britain, where she especially capti-vated London literary society, she returned to Boston. The Wheatleys emancipated her, but she continued to live in their household.

In 1768 Wheatley had written "To the King's Most Excellent Majesty," praising George III for the repeal of the Stamp Act. But as the American Revolution approached, she wrote a number of poems siding with the colonists against his rule and that of the British parliament. She wrote verses praising individual leaders of the American Revolution, including one entitled "To His Excellency General Washington" in 1775, when he was appointed commander in chief of the continental army, and "On the Death of General Wooster," written in 1778.

Following the breakup of the Wheatley family with the death of John Wheatley, Phillis married a free black man, John Peters. The marriage between Peters and Wheatley was not a happy one, but she continued to write poetry and managed a boardinghouse as well. Not only did she have personal problems with her husband, but the family suffered great poverty and she had to devote much of her time to securing her family's economic survival. She published the poem "Liberty and Peace, A Poem" in 1784 and was planning a second volume of poetry when she died shortly after the birth of her third child in 1784.

While many prominent Americans praised her work, Thomas Jefferson denied that she could be considered seriously as a poet, in keeping with his arguments about the inherent inferiority of blacks. Wheatley was treated as an oddity by those who found it remarkable that a slave girl was educated and wrote poetry. Her abilities were cited by early abolitionists pointing out the evils of slavery. She was used as well by Jefferson and others upholding racist values as standing for what they saw as the ridiculous pretensions of black Americans who claimed to possess abilities similar to their white brothers and sisters. Later, she was criticized by some black scholars for not sufficiently identifying with her race; the religious, rational, and nonemotional quality of her verse was said to reveal her over-great identification with her white owners and their circle of friends.

Few have found it possible to treat her on her own terms, as a young African American poet who was deeply religious and who wrote in the literary form popular in her age. Her reliance on Alexander Pope as a model may have limited the range of topics to which her works were addressed, but it was a common practice among young poets of her generation. Nor can she be fairly judged either as an inferior imitator or as a writer without conscious identity of race or gender, conforming too greatly to the values of middle-class, Protestant Boston. Though she gained support especially from Susanna Wheatley and the circle of evangelical women to which she belonged, this did not define Phillis Wheatley's personal identity. One can find expressions of such identity not simply in her few poems about Africa and slavery but also in the fervent support for values of independence and liberty characterizing her poems supporting the American Revolution, and perhaps most poignantly in one of her earliest poems, "To the University of Cambridge, in New England," which reflected her frustrated intellectual goals as a black, a slave, and a female, in contrast to Harvard students of her age.

Washington and other leaders wrote her letters praising her writing, and the crowds of London flocked to see a sight as strange as a young American slave writing verse. Although the Wheatleys were kind to her and enabled her to pursue the career of a writer, after she left that family, she suffered the poverty facing free blacks living in eighteenth-century America. Not seeming to fit in any world, she ultimately died young, so distant from the fame she gained as the almost unbelievable blazing star, a young female slave poet. While those most interested in the works of Phillis Wheatley continue to be literary scholars, recent essays have concentrated on her biography, her place in eighteenth-century religious and intellectual production, and studies of her poetry as an expression of her perspective as a slave and African American, her "subtle war" against slave society (see especially Willard, 1995).

The following selections are from Poems on Various Subjects, Religious and Moral (1773) and from William H. Robinson's Phyllis Wheatley and Her Writings (1984).

HLS

Sources and Suggested Readings

Barker-Benfield, G. J. "Phillis Wheatley." Portraits of American Women: From Settlement to the Present. New York: St. Martin's Press, 1991.

Bennett, Paula Bernat, ed. Nineteenth-Century American Women Poets: An Anthology. Malden, Mass.: Blackwell, 1998.

Burke, Helen M. "The Rhetoric and Politics of Marginality: The Subject of Phillis Wheatley." Tulsa Studies in Women's Literature 10, 1 (1991): 31–45.

Felker, Christopher. "'The Tongues of the Learned Are Insufficient': Phillis Wheatley, Publishing Objectives, and Personal Liberty." In Texts and Textuality: Textual Instability, Theory, and Interpretation, ed. Philip Cohen, 81–119. New York: New York University Press, 1997.

Foster, Frances Smith. Written by Herself: Literary Production by African American Women, 1746–1892. Bloomington: Indiana University Press, 1993.

Gates, Henry Louis. Figures in Black: Words, Signs, and the "Racial" Self. New York: Oxford University Press, 1987.

Grimsted, David. "Anglo-American Racism and Phillis Wheatley's 'Sable Veil,' 'Length'ned Chain,' and 'Knitted Heart.'" Women in the Age of the American Revolution. Charlottesville: University Press of Virginia, 1989.

Jordan, June. "The Difficult Miracle of Black Poetry in America." Massachusetts Review 27 (Summer 1986): 252–62.

Levernier, James A. "Phillis Wheatley and the New England Clergy." Early American Literature 26, 1 (1991): 21–38.

Nott, Walt. "From 'Uncultivated Barbarian' to 'Poetical Genius': The Public Presence of Phillis Wheatley." MELUS: The Journal of the Society for the Study of Multi-Ethnic Literature of the United States 18, 3 (Fall 1993): 21–32.

O'Neale, Sondra. "A Slave's Subtle War: Phillis Wheatley's Use of Biblical Myth and Symbol." Early American Literature 21, 2 (1986): 144–65.

Richards, Phillip M. "Phillis Wheatley and Literary Americanization." American Quarterly 44, 2 (1992): 163–91.

Robinson, William H. Critical Essays on Phillis Wheatley. Boston: G. K. Hall, 1982.

———. Phyllis Wheatley: A Bio-Bibliography. Boston: G. K. Hall, 1981.

———. Phyllis Wheatley and Her Writings. New York: Garland, 1984.

Scheick, William J. "Subjection and Prophecy in Phillis Wheatley's Verse Paraphrases of Scripture." College Literature 22, 3 (1995): 122–30.

Scruggs, Charles. "Phillis Wheatley and the Poetical Legacy of Eighteenth-Century England." Studies in Eighteenth-Century Culture 10 (1981): 279–95.

Wheatley, Phillis [Peters]. Poems and Letters: First Collected Edition. Ed. Charles F. Heartman. With an Appreciation by Arthur A. Schomburg. Publisher and date unknown. Reprinted: Miami, Fla.: Mnemosyne, 1969.

———. The Poems of Phillis Wheatley. Ed. Julian D. Mason, Jr. Chapel Hill: University of North Carolina Press, 1989.

———. Poems on Various Subjects, Religious and Moral. London: Printed for A. Bell, Bookseller, Aldgate, 1773.

Willard, Carla. "Wheatley's Turns of Praise: Heroic Entrapment and the Paradox of Revolution." American Literature 67, 2 (June 1995): 233–56.

Poems on Various Subjects, Religious and Moral (1773)

To the University of Cambridge, in New-England. 1767.

While an intrinsic ardor prompts to write,
The muses promise to assist my pen;
'Twas not long since I left my native shore
The land of errors, and *Egyptian* gloom:
Father of mercy, 'twas thy gracious hand
Brought me in safety from those dark abodes.

    Students, to you 'tis giv'n to scan the heights
Above, to traverse the ethereal space,
And mark the systems of revolving worlds.
Still more, ye sons of science ye receive
The blissful news by messengers from heav'n,
How *Jesus*' blood for your redemption flows.
See him with hands out-stretcht upon the cross;
Immense compassion in his bosom glows;
He hears revilers, nor resents their scorn:
What matchless mercy in the Son of God!
When the whole human race by sin had fall'n,
He deign'd to die that they might rise again,
And share with him in the sublimest skies,
Life without death, and glory without end.

    Improve your privileges while they stay,
Ye pupils, and each hour redeem, that bears
Or good or bad report of you to heav'n.
Let sin, that baneful evil to the soul,
By you be shunn'd, nor once remit your guard;
Suppress the deadly serpent in its egg.
Ye blooming plants of human race divine,
An *Ethiop* tells you 'tis your greatest foe;
Its transient sweetness turns to endless pain,
And in immense perdition sinks the soul.

To the KING'S Most Excellent Majesty. 1768.

Your subjects hope, dread Sire—
The crown upon your brows may flourish long,
And that your arm may in your God be strong!
O may your sceptre num'rous nations sway,
And all with love and readiness obey!

    But how shall we the *British* king reward!
Rule thou in peace, our father, and our lord!
Midst the remembrance of thy favours past,
The meanest peasants most admire the last.*

May *George*, belov'd by all the nations round,
Live with heav'ns choicest constant blessings
    crown'd!
Great God, direct, and guard him from on high,
And from his head let ev'ry evil fly!
And may each clime with equal gladness see
A monarch's smile can set his subjects free!

*The Repeal of the Stamp Act.

On being brought from Africa to America.

'Twas mercy brought me from my *Pagan* land,
Taught my benighted soul to understand
That there's a God, that there's a *Saviour* too:
Once I redemption neither sought nor knew.
Some view our sable race with scornful eye,
"Their colour is a diabolic die."
Remember, *Christians*, *Negros*, black as *Cain*,
May be refin'd, and join th' angelic train.

On the Death of the Rev. Mr. GEORGE WHITEFIELD. 1770.

Hail, happy saint, on thine immortal throne,
Possest of glory, life, and bliss unknown;
We hear no more the music of thy tongue,
Thy wonted auditories cease to throng.
Thy sermons in unequall'd accents flow'd,
And ev'ry bosom with devotion glow'd;
Thou didst in strains of eloquence refin'd
Inflame the heart, and captivate the mind.
Unhappy we the setting sun deplore,
So glorious once, but ah! it shines no more.

    Behold the prophet in his tow'ring flight!
He leaves the earth for heav'n's unmeasur'd height,
And worlds unknown receive him from our sight.
There *Whitefield* wings with rapid course his way,
And sails to *Zion* through vast seas of day.
Thy pray'rs, great saint, and thine incessant cries
Have pierc'd the bosom of thy native skies.
Thou moon hast seen, and all the stars of light,
How he has wrestled with his God by night.
He pray'd that grace in ev'ry heart might dwell,
He long'd to see *America* excel;
He charg'd its youth that ev'ry grace divine
Should with full lustre in their conduct shine;
That Saviour, which his soul did first receive,
The greatest gift that ev'n a God can give;
He freely offer'd to the num'rous throng,
That on his lips with list'ning pleasure hung.

    "Take him, ye wretched, for your only good,
"Take him ye starving sinners, for your food;

"Ye thirsty, come to this life-giving stream,
"Ye preachers, take him for your joyful theme;
"Take him my dear *Americans,* he said,
"Be your complaints on his kind bosom laid:
"Take him, ye *Africans,* he longs for you,
"*Impartial Saviour* is his title due:
"Wash'd in the fountain of redeeming blood,
"You shall be sons, and kings, and priests to God."

Great *Countess,* * we *Americans* revere
Thy name, and mingle in thy grief sincere;
New England deeply feels, the *Orphans* mourn,
Their more than father will no more return.

But, though arrested by the hand of death,
Whitefield no more exerts his lab'ring breath,
Yet let us view him in th' eternal skies,
Let ev'ry heart to this bright vision rise;
While the tomb safe retains its sacred trust,
Till life divine re-animates his dust.

*The Countess of *Huntingdon,* to whom Mr.
Whitefield was Chaplain.

Thoughts on the Works of Providence.

Arise, my soul, on wings enraptur'd, rise
To praise the monarch of the earth and skies,
Whose goodness and beneficence appear
As round its centre moves the rolling year,
Or when the morning glows with rosy charms,
Or the sun slumbers in the ocean's arms:
Of light divine be a rich portion lent
To guide my soul, and favour my intent.
Celestial muse, my arduous flight sustain,
And raise my mind to a seraphic strain!

Ador'd for ever be the God unseen,
Which round the sun revolves this vast machine,
Though to his eye its mass a point appears:
Ador'd the God that whirls surrounding spheres,
Which first ordain'd that mighty *Sol* should reign
The peerless monarch of th' ethereal train:
Of miles twice forty millions is his height,
And yet his radiance dazzles mortal sight
So far beneath—from him th' extended earth
Vigour derives, and ev'ry flow'ry birth:
Vast through her orb she moves with easy grace
Around her *Phoebus* in unbounded space;
True to her course th' impetuous storm derides,
Triumphant o'er the winds, and surging tides.

Almighty, in these wond'rous works of thine,
What *Pow'r,* what *Wisdom,* and what *Goodness* shine?

And are thy wonders, Lord, by men explor'd,
And yet creating glory unador'd!

Creation smiles in various beauty gay,
While day to night, and night succeeds to day:
That *Wisdom,* which attends *Jehovah's* ways,
Shines most conspicuous in the solar rays:
Without them, destitute of heat and light,
This world would be the reign of endless night:
In their excess how would our race complain,
Abhorring life! how hate its length'ned chain!
From air adust what num'rous ills would rise?
What dire contagion taint the burning skies?
What pestilential vapours, fraught with death,
Would rise, and overspread the lands beneath?

Hail, smiling morn, that from the orient main
Ascending dost adorn the heav'nly plain!
So rich, so various are thy beauteous dies,
That spread through all the circuit of the skies,
That, full of thee, my soul in rapture soars,
And thy great God, the cause of all adores.

O'er beings infinite his love extends,
His *Wisdom* rules them, and his *Pow'r* defends.
When tasks diurnal tire the human frame,
The spirits faint, and dim the vital flame,
Then too that ever active bounty shines,
Which not infinity of space confines.
The sable veil, that *Night* in silence draws,
Conceals effects, but shews th'*Almighty Cause;*
Night seals in sleep the wide creation fair,
And all is peaceful but the brow of care.
Again, gay *Phoebus,* as the day before,
Wakes ev'ry eye, but what shall wake no more;
Again the face of nature is renew'd,
Which still appears harmonious, fair, and good.
May grateful strains salute the smiling morn,
Before its beams the eastern hills adorn!

Shall day to day and night to night conspire
To show the goodness of the Almighty Sire?
This mental voice shall man regardless hear,
And never, never raise the filial pray'r?
To-day, O hearken, nor your folly mourn
For time mispent, that never will return.

But see the sons of vegetation rise,
And spread their leafy banners to the skies.
All-wise Almighty Providence we trace
In trees, and plants, and all the flow'ry race;
As clear as in the nobler frame of man,
All lovely copies of the Maker's plan.

The pow'r the same that forms a ray of light,
That call'd creation from eternal night.
"Let there be light," he said: from his profound
Old *Chaos* heard, and trembled at the sound;
Swift as the word, inspir'd by pow'r divine,
Behold the light around its maker shine,
The first fair product of th' omnific God,
And now through all his works diffus'd abroad.

As reason's pow'rs by day our God disclose,
So we may trace him in the night's repose:
Say what is sleep? and dreams how passing strange!
When action ceases, and ideas range
Licentious and unbounded o'er the plains,
Where *Fancy's* queen in giddy triumph reigns.
Hear in soft strains the dreaming lover sigh
To a kind fair, or rave in jealousy;
On pleasure now, and now on vengeance bent,
The lab'ring passions struggle for a vent.
What pow'r, O man! thy *reason* then restores,
So long suspended in nocturnal hours?
What secret hand returns the mental train,
And gives improv'd thine active pow'rs again?
From thee, O man, what gratitude should rise!
And, when from balmy sleep thou op'st thine eyes,
Let thy first thoughts be praises to the skies.
How merciful our God who thus imparts
O'erflowing tides of joy to human hearts,
When wants and woes might be our righteous lot,
Our God forgetting, by our God forgot!

Among the mental pow'rs a question rose,
"What most the image of th' Eternal shows?"
When thus to *Reason* (so let *Fancy* rove)
Her great companion spoke immortal *Love*.

"Say, mighty pow'r, how long shall strife prevail,
"And with its murmurs load the whisp'ring gale?
"Refer the cause to *Recollection's* shrine,
"Who loud proclaims my origin divine,
"The cause whence heav'n and earth began to be,
"And is not man immortaliz'd by me?
"*Reason* let this most causeless strife subside."
Thus *Love* pronounc'd, and *Reason* thus reply'd.

"Thy birth, celestial queen! 'tis mine to own,
"In thee resplendent is the Godhead shown;
"Thy words persuade, my soul enraptur'd feels
"Resistless beauty which thy smile reveals."
Ardent she spoke, and, kindling at her charms,
She clasp'd the blooming goddess in her arms.

Infinite *Love* where'er we turn our eyes

Appears: this ev'ry creature's wants supplies;
This most is heard in *Nature's* constant voice,
This makes the morn, and this the eve rejoice;
This bids the fost'ring rains and dews descend
To nourish all, to serve one gen'ral end,
The good of man: yet man ungrateful pays
But little homage, and but little praise.
To him, whose works array'd with mercy shine,
What songs should rise, how constant, how divine!

Isaiah lxiii. I-8

Say, heav'nly muse, what king, or mighty God,
That moves sublime from *Idumea's* road?
In *Bozrah's* dies, with martial glories join'd,
His purple vesture waves upon the wind.
Why thus enrob'd delights he to appear
In the dread image of the *Pow'r* of war?

Compress'd in wrath the swelling wine-press
    groan'd,
It bled, and pour'd the gushing purple round.

"Mine was the act," th' Almighty Saviour said,
And shook the dazzling glories of his head,
"When all forsook I trod the press alone,
"And conquer'd by omnipotence my own;
"For man's release sustain'd the pond'rous load,
"For man the wrath of an immortal God:
"To execute th' Eternal's dread command
"My soul I sacrific'd with willing hand;
"Sinless I stood before the avenging frown,
"Atoning thus for vices not my own."
His eye the ample field of battle round
Survey'd, but no created succours found;
His own omnipotence sustain'd the fight,
His vengeance sunk the haughty foes in night;
Beneath his feet the prostrate troops were spread,
And round him lay the dying, and the dead.

Great God, what light'ning flashes from thine
    eyes?
What pow'r withstands if thou indignant rise?

Against thy *Zion* though her foes may rage,
And all their cunning, all their strength engage,
Yet she serenely on thy bosom lies,
Smiles at their arts, and all their force defies.

On Imagination.

Thy various works, imperial queen, we see,
How bright their forms! how deck'd with pomp by
    thee!

Thy wond'rous acts in beauteous order stand,
And all attest how potent is thine hand.

From *Helicon's* refulgent heights attend,
Ye sacred choir, and my attempts befriend:
To tell her glories with a faithful tongue,
Ye blooming graces, triumph in my song.

Now here, now there, the roving *Fancy* flies,
Till some lov'd object strikes her wand'ring eyes,
Whose silken fetters all the senses bind,
And soft captivity involves the mind.

Imagination! who can sing thy force?
Or who describe the swiftness of thy course?
Soaring through air to find the bright abode,
Th' empyreal palace of the thund'ring God,
We on thy pinions can surpass the wind,
And leave the rolling universe behind:
From star to star the mental optics rove,
Measure the skies, and range the realms above.
There in one view we grasp the mighty whole,
Or with new worlds amaze th' unbounded soul.

Though *Winter* frowns to *Fancy's* raptur'd eyes
The fields may flourish, and gay scenes arise;
The frozen deeps may break their iron bands,
And bid their waters murmur o'er the sands.
Fair *Flora* may resume her fragrant reign,
And with her flow'ry riches deck the plain;
Sylvanus may diffuse his honours round,
And all the forest may with leaves be crown'd:
Show'rs may descend, and dews their gems disclose,
And nectar sparkle on the blooming rose.

Such is thy pow'r, nor are thine orders vain,
O thou the leader of the mental train:
In full perfection all thy works are wrought,
And thine the sceptre o'er the realms of thought.
Before thy throne the subject-passions bow,
Of subject-passions sov'reign ruler Thou;
At thy command joy rushes on the heart,
And through the glowing veins the spirits dart.

Fancy might now her silken pinions try
To rise from earth, and sweep th' expanse on high;
From *Tithon's* bed now might *Aurora* rise,
Her cheeks all glowing with celestial dies,
While a pure stream of light o'erflows the skies.
The monarch of the day I might behold,
And all the mountains tipt with radiant gold,
But I reluctant leave the pleasing views,
Which *Fancy* dresses to delight the *Muse*;
Winter austere forbids me to aspire,

And northern tempests damp the rising fire;
They chill the tides of *Fancy's* flowing sea,
Cease then, my song, cease the unequal lay.

To the Right Honourable William, Earl of Dartmouth, His Majesty's Principal Secretary of State for North-America, &c. (1773)

Hail, happy day, when, smiling like the morn,
Fair *Freedom* rose *New-England* to adorn:
The northern clime beneath her genial ray,
Dartmouth, congratulates thy blissful sway:
Elate with hope her race no longer mourns,
Each soul expands, each grateful bosom burns,
While in thine hand with pleasure we behold
The silken reins, and *Freedom's* charms unfold.
Long lost to realms beneath the northern skies
She shines supreme, while hated *faction* dies:
Soon as appear'd the *Goddess* long desir'd,
Sick at the view, she languish'd and expir'd;
Thus from the splendors of the morning light
The owl in sadness seeks the caves of night.

No more, *America*, in mournful strain
Of wrongs, and grievance unredress'd complain,
No longer shall thou dread the iron chain,
Which wanton *Tyranny* with lawless hand
Had made, and with it meant t' enslave the land.

Should you, my lord, while you peruse my song,
Wonder from whence my love of *Freedom* sprung,
Whence flow these wishes for the common good,
By feeling hearts alone best understood,
I, young in life, by seeming cruel fate
Was snatch'd from *Afric's* fancy'd happy seat:
What pangs excruciating must molest,
What sorrows labour in my parent's breast?
Steel'd was that soul and by no misery mov'd
That from a father seiz'd his babe belov'd:
Such, such my case. And can I then but pray
Others may never feel tyrannic sway?

For favours past, great Sir, our thanks are due,
And thee we ask thy favours to renew,
Since in thy pow'r, as in thy will before,
To sooth the griefs, which thou did'st once deplore.
May heav'nly grace the sacred sanction give
To all thy works, and thou for ever live
Not only on the wings of fleeting *Fame*,
Though praise immortal crowns the patriot's name,
But to conduct to heav'ns refulgent fane,
May fiery coursers sweep th' ethereal plain,
And bear thee upwards to that blest abode,
Where, like the prophet, thou shalt find thy God.

Other writings

[*Virginia Gazette*, March 20, 1776]:

To His Excellency General Washington

Celestial choir! enthron'd in realms of light,
Columbia's scenes of glorious toils I write.
While freedom's cause her anxious breast alarms,
She flashes dreadful in refulgent arms.
See mother earth her offspring's fate bemoan,
And nations gaze at scenes before unknown!
See the bright beams of heaven's revolving light
Involv'd in sorrows and the veil of night!

The goddess comes, she moves divinely fair,
Olive and laurel bind her golden hair:
Wherever shines this native of the skies,
Unnumber'd charms and recent graces rise.

Muse! how propitious, while my pen relates
How pour her armies through a thousand gates;
As when Eolus heaven's fair face deforms,
Enwrap'd in tempest, and a night of storms;
Astonish'd ocean feels the wild uproar,
The refluent surges beat the sounding shore;
Or thick as leaves in autumn's golden reign,
Such, and so many, moves the warrior train.
In bright array they seek the work of war,
Where high unfurl'd the ensign waves in air.
Shall I to Washington their praise recite?
Enough thou know'st them in the fields of fight.
Thee, first in place and honours,—we demand
The grace and glory of thy martial band.
Fam'd for thy valour, for thy virtues more,
Hear every tongue thy guardian aid implore!

One century scarce perform'd its destin'd round,
When Gallic powers Columbia's fury found;
And so may you, whoever dares disgrace
The land of freedom's heaven-defended race!
Fix'd are the eyes of nations on the scales,
For in their hopes Columbia's arm prevails.
Anon Britannia droops the pensive head,
While round increase the rising hills of dead.
Ah! cruel blindness to Columbia's state!
Lament thy thirst of boundless power too late.

Proceed, great chief, with virtue on thy side,
Thy every action let the goddess guide.
A crown, a mansion, and a throne that shine,
With gold unfading, WASHINGTON! be thine.

On the Death of General Wooster (1778)

From this the Muse rich consolation draws
He nobly perish'd in his Country's cause
His Country's Cause that ever fir'd his mind
Where martial flames, and Christian virtues join'd.
How shall my pen his warlike deeds proclaim
Or paint them fairer on the list of Fame—
Enough, great Chief—now wrapt in Shades around
Thy grateful Country shall thy praise resound—
Tho' not with mortals' empty praise elate
That vainest vapour to th' immortal State
Inly serene the expiring hero lies
And thus (while heav'nward roll his swimming eyes)
Permit, great power while yet my fleeting breath
And Spirits wander to the verge of Death—
Permit me yet to paint fair freedom's charms
For her the Continent shines bright in arms
By thy high will, celestial prize she came—
For her we combat on the field of fame
Without her presence vice maintains full sway
And social love and virtue wing their way
O still propitious be thy guardian care
And lead *Columbia* thro' the toils of war.
With thine hand conduct them and defend
And bring the dreadful contest to an end—
For ever grateful let them live to thee
And keep them ever Virtuous, brave, and free—
But how, presumptuous shall we hope to find
Divine acceptance with th' Almighty mind—
While yet, O deed ungenerous! they disgrace
And hold in bondage Afric's blameless race?
Let virtue reign—And thou accord our prayers
Be victory our's, and generous freedom theirs.
The hero pray'd—the wond'ring Spirit fled
And sought the unknown regions of the dead—
Tis thine fair partner of his life, to find
The virtuous path and follow close behind—
A little moment steals him from thy sight
He waits thy coming to the realms of light
Freed from his labours in the ethereal Skies
Where in succession endless pleasures rise!

Liberty and Peace (1784)

Lo freedom comes. Th' prescient muse foretold,
All eyes th' accomplish'd prophecy behold:
Her port describ'd, "She moves divinely fair,
Olive and laurel bind her golden hair."
She, the bright progeny of Heaven, descends,
And every grace her sovereign step attends;
For now kind Heaven, indulgent to our prayer,
In smiling peace resolves the din of war.
Fix'd in Columbia her illustrious line,

And bids in thee her future council shine.
To every realm her portals open'd wide,
Receives from each the full commercial tide.
Each art and science now with rising charms,
Th' expanding heart with emulation warns.
E'en great Britannia sees with dread surprise,
And from the dazzling splendor turns her eyes.
Britain, whose navies swept th' Atlantic o'er,
And thunder sent to every distant shore;
E'en thou, in manners cruel as thou art,
The sword resign'd, resume the friendly part.
For Gallia's power espous'd Columbia's cause,
And new-born Rome shall give Britannia laws,
Nor unremember'd in the grateful strain,
Shall princely Louis' friendly deeds remain;
The generous prince th' impending vengeance eyes,
Sees the fierce wrong and to the rescue flies.
Perish that thirst of boundless power, that drew
On Albion's head the curse to tyrants due.
But thou appeas'd submit to Heaven's decree,
That bids this realm of freedom rival thee.
Now sheathe the sword that bade the brave atone
With guiltless blood for madness not their own.
Sent from th' enjoyment of their native shore,
Ill-fated—never to behold her more.
From every kingdom on Europe's coast
Throng'd various troops, their glory, strength, and boast.
With heart-felt pity fair Hibernia saw
Columbia menac'd by the Tyrant's law:
On hostile fields fraternal arms engage,
And mutual deaths, all dealt with mutual rage:
The muse's ear hears mother earth deplore
Her ample surface smoke with kindred gore:
The hostile field destroys the social ties,
And everlasting slumber seals their eyes.
Columbia mourns, the haughty foes deride,
Her treasures plunder'd and her towns destroy'd:
Witness how Charlestown's curling smokes arise,
In sable columns to the clouded skies.
The ample dome, high-wrought with curious toil,
In one sad hour the savage troops despoil.
Descending peace the power of war confounds;
From every tongue celestial peace resounds:
As from the east th' illustrious king of day,
With rising radiance drives the shades away,
So freedom comes array'd with charms divine,
And in her train commerce and plenty shine.
Britannia owns her independent reign,

Hibernia, Scotia and the realms of Spain;
And great Germania's ample coast admires
The generous spirit that Columbia fires.
Auspicious Heaven shall fill with fav'ring gales,
Where e'er Columbia spreads her swelling sails:
To every realm shall peace her charms display,
And heavenly freedom spread her golden ray.

[*Massachusetts Spy*, March 24, 1774]:

*The following is an extract of a letter from
Phillis, a Negro girl of Mr. Wheatley's of
this town to the Reverend Samson Occom,
which we are desired to insert as a specimen
of her ingenuity. It is dated the 11th of
February, 1774.*

Reverend and honoured Sir,
I have this Day received your obliging kind Epistle,
and am greatly satisfied with your Reasons respecting
the negroes, and think highly reasonable what you
offer in Vindication of their natural Rights: Those that
invade them cannot be insensible that the divine Light
is insensibly chasing away the thick Darkness which
broods over the Land of Africa; and the Chaos which
has reigned so long is converting into beautiful Order,
and reveals more and more clearly the glorious Dispensation of civil and religious Liberty, which are so
inseparably united, that there is little or no Enjoyment
of one without the other: Otherwise, perhaps the Israelites had been less solicitous for their Freedom from
Egyptian slavery; I do not say they would have been
contented without it, by no means, for in every human
Breast, God has implanted a Principle, which we call
Love of Freedom; it is impatient of oppression, and
pants for Deliverance—and by the Leave of our modern Egyptians I will assert that the same principle lives
in us. God grant Deliverance in his own Way and
Time, and get him honour upon all those whose
Avaraice impels them to countenance and help forward the Calamities of their fellow Creatures. This I
desire not for their Hurt, but to convince them of the
strange Absurdity of their Conduct whose Words and
Actions are so diametrically opposite. How well the
Cry for Liberty, and the reverse Disposition for the
exercise of oppressive power over others agree I humbly think it does not require the penetration of a Philosopher to determine.

Olympe de Gouges (1748?–93)

Olympe de Gouges is best known for her response to the National Assembly's adoption at the outset of the French Revolution of its famous set of principles, Declaration of the Rights of Man and Citizen, in August 1789. She replied in 1791 with the Declaration of the Rights of Woman and Citizen. This declaration both pointed to women's omission from the general goals of the French Revolution and laid out principles that postulated not simply women's equal political standing but their inclusion within a broader set of concepts about the nature of human beings and their inclusion within the values articulated in Rousseau's social contract.

The basic information about de Gouges's life is not easily discerned. It seems fairly certain that she was born in the town of Montauban in 1748; even so, she altered her date of birth to appear younger as she advanced in years. Her birth name was Marie Gouze and her legal father was listed as a butcher, but she claimed that she was actually the daughter of the Marquis de Pompignan. She was married in 1765 at age seventeen to Louis-Yves Aubry, a minor official in Montauban, and had one son, Pierre, later a state's attorney. We know very little about her relationship with her husband or their economic setting. It is also unclear whether she left him before his death, but she was widowed early and left Montauban in 1767, only two years after her marriage, when she followed her sister Jeanne to Paris. Jeanne had sometimes signed her name as "Gouges," perhaps an alternate spelling of the family patronymic, but the name "Olympe de Gouges" came neither from her father nor her husband. By adopting her own name and pursuing an independent life in Paris, de Gouges worked hard to guarantee herself an independent identity.

The principles of the Declaration written by Olympe de Gouges reflect both the anger of a woman who saw the actions of the National Assembly as arrogant and ignorant and her desire to draft a set of broad-based principles that would allow women to make the same elevated claims that Enlightenment thinkers claimed for men. The Declaration opens with an angry introduction in which she addresses the National Assembly directly (as representing men more broadly): "Who has given you the sovereign authority to oppress my sex?" She then moves to the body of the declaration and demands that women be constituted a "National Assembly" because "contempt for the rights of women" has led to "public misfortune and . . . government corruption." The document continues to build a case for equal rights of women citizens upon grounds of "nature and reason."

Other than common citizenship with their brothers, de Gouges demands that women be allowed to speak in public, to have equal access to public jobs and responsibilities, to help make the laws, to make decisions concerning taxation along with other citizens, and to have as inviolate a claim on their property as men. Following this set of demands, de Gouges turns her attention to other women and asks them to "wake up" to the forces of reason that are in the land. They have not given sufficient attention to understanding and protecting their own interests up to this point. If they do not alter their passive and self-destructive ways and their belief that they will thrive by dependence upon men, they will never gain the strength that comes from well-informed independence. While some women have gotten by on their beauty, they have always been subject to being "set . . . free, without compensation, at an age when the slave has lost all her charms." She makes clear the harm emerging from an integrated dependence that comes from women's nonpolitical standing, the legal ties of an unequal marriage, and the immorality and weakness that are attached to such realities. For the good of themselves, as well as for the good of society, women must fight to gain the standing and respect of equals in French society, or they will gain nothing from the Revolution. She concludes her Declaration with a contract for an equal relationship between a man and a woman. And thus for Olympe de Gouges the Revolution had a dual purpose: to guarantee rights to all French citizens and to forge equal relationships between individual men and women.

Scholars have seen Olympe de Gouges's emphasis on the need to include women in the revolutionary agenda, her writings on slavery and issues of race, and her uncompromising call for principles of unalloyed equality as one of the earliest integrated calls for a broad-based principle of respect for all human beings as individuals. That de Gouges submitted her Declaration in 1791 was no accident; although the 1789 Declaration put into place principles that omitted women, it was the constitution of September 1791 that promulgated the rules, as well as the principles, that defined only men as citizens of France. She realized this and thought it was essential to challenge the foundational principles of the Revolution before a constitution was adopted by the people's representatives.

De Gouges's most important contribution to debates about race and slavery at the outset of the French Revolution was her play, L'esclavage des noirs (Black Slavery, or The Happy Shipwreck), first produced at the

Comédie-Française *in December 1789. Despite a negative reception from critics and contemporary commentators, the play was performed at the most prestigious theater in Paris and was much discussed. Criticisms were typical of those directed against women's writings; it was lambasted as melodramatic, and as a slight, non-philosophical account of a serious political and moral subject. The play was closed after only four performances, but it has been argued by Marie-Pierre Le Hir that it had significant impact as* "a powerful drama committed to a double agenda of sociopolitical and dramatic reform" (Le Hir, 66).

De Gouges's attempt to tell the stories of actual slaves reflected her effort (and that of other cultural critics of French neoclassical drama and comedy) to replace the dramatic form of the seventeenth century with a more natural reality. Her emphasis on nature focuses on the inherent equality of all human beings, whether separated by race or gender, with nature standing as much for liberty as for a primitive setting for human relationships. In the preface to her play, de Gouges separates slavery from any misguided vision of racial inferiority: "It was force and prejudice that had condemned them to the horrible slavery, in which Nature plays no role." *She continues in her preface to call for the end, or at least the amelioration, of slavery and to judge French society by how it treats its weakest subjects, especially slaves in French West Indian colonies. Although the play reveals significant limits in de Gouges's understanding of racism and slavery, it presented challenges that, along with her feminist demands in the* Declaration, *combine to make her one of the most original and radical critics of those who led the French Revolution.*

Even so, Olympe de Gouges did not advocate the overthrow of the French monarchy, and she turned to Marie Antoinette as an individual who might protect the interests of the women of France. But as a political activist, playwright, and author, de Gouges lost her life because of her resistance to the Jacobin demands for a national government and the end of monarchy, and for her uncompromising feminist stance, as well as for her troublesome reminders regarding the lack of black citizenship in France and its colonies. She was arrested in July 1793 and was executed in November of that year. Immediately before her execution, the deputies of the National Assembly passed the following resolution with almost no debate on October 29: "The clubs and popular societies of women, under whatever denomination, are prohibited." *In the same month as her execution, a Parisian politician denounced a group of protesting women, stating that they should remember the* "shameless Olympe de Gouges, who was the first to set up women's clubs." *Thus while her execution has been ex-plained in terms of her opposition to the radical direction the Revolution was taking in 1793, there is little doubt that her public outspokenness and her feminist stance also played a significant role in her death.*

The following selections are taken from Doris Y. Kadish and Françoise Massardier-Kenney's Translating Slavery *(1994) and from* Women, the Family, and Freedom *(1983), edited by Susan Groag Bell and Karen M. Offen.*

HLS

Sources and Suggested Readings

Bell, Susan Groag, and Karen M. Offen. *Women, the Family, and Freedom: The Debate in Documents.* Vol. 1. 1750–1880. Stanford: Stanford University Press, 1983.

Blanc, Olivier. *Une femme de libertés: Olympe de Gouges.* Paris: Syros, 1989.

De Gouges, Olympe. *Black Slavery, or The Happy Shipwreck.* Trans. Maryann De Julio. With *Reflections on Negroes.* Trans. Sylvie Molta. In *Translating Slavery: Gender and Race in French Women's Writing, 1783–1823,* ed. Doris Y. Kadish and Françoise Massardier-Kenney. Kent, Ohio: Kent State University Press, 1994.

——. *Declaration of the Rights of Woman and Citizen* (1791). Trans. Nupur Chaudhuri. In Susan Groag Bell and Karen M. Offen, *Women, the Family and Freedom: The Debate in Documents.* Vol. 1. 1750–1880. Stanford: Stanford University Press, 1983. 104–109.

——. *Écrits Politiques, 1788–1793.* 2 vols. Paris: Côté-femmes éditions, 1993.

——. *Œuvres.* Ed. Benoîte Groult. Paris: Mercure de France, 1986.

Diamond, Marie Josephine. "Olympe de Gouges and the French Revolution: The Construction of Gender as Critique." *Dialectical Anthropology* 15, 2–3 (1990): 95–105.

——. "The Revolutionary Rhetoric of Olympe de Gouges." *Feminist Issues* 14, 1 (Spring 1994): 3–23.

Godineau, Dominique. *The Women of Paris and Their French Revolution.* Trans. Katherine Streip. Berkeley: University of California Press, 1998.

Harth, Erica. "Olympe de Gouges: 'Placed and Displaced. . . .'" In *Cartesian Women: Versions and Subversions of Rational Discourse in the Old Regime.* Ithaca: Cornell University Press, 1992. 213–34.

Hunt, Lynn, ed. *The French Revolution and Human Rights: A Brief Documentary History.* Boston: Bedford Books, 1996.

Kadish, Doris Y., and Françoise Massardier-Kenney, eds. *Translating Slavery: Gender and Race in French Women's Writing, 1783–1823.* Kent, Ohio: Kent State University Press, 1994.

Le Hir, Marie-Pierre. "Feminism, Theater, Race: *L'esclavage des noirs.*" In *Translating Slavery: Gender and Race in French Women's Writing, 1783–1823,* ed. Doris Y. Kadish and Françoise Massardier-Kenney, 65–83. Kent, Ohio: Kent State University Press, 1994.

Montfort, Catherine R., ed. *Literate Women and the French Revolution of 1789.* Birmingham, Ala.: Summa Publications, 1994.

Schröder, Hannelore. "The Declaration of Human and Civil Rights for Women (Paris, 1791) by Olympe de Gouges." *History of European Ideas* 11 (1989): 263–71.

Scott, Joan W. *Only Paradoxes to Offer: French Feminists and the Rights of Man.* Cambridge: Harvard University Press, 1996.

Trouille, Mary. "Eighteenth-Century Amazons of the Pen: Stéphanie de Genlis; Olympe de Gouges." In *Femmes savantes et femmes d'esprit: Women Intellectuals of the French Eighteenth Century,* ed. Roland Bonnel and Catherine Rubinger. New York: Peter Lang, 1994.

Reflections on Negroes (1788)

I have always been interested in the deplorable fate of the Negro race. I was just beginning to develop an understanding of the world, at that age when children hardly think about anything, when I saw a Negress for the first time. Seeing her made me wonder and ask questions about her color.

People I asked did not satisfy my curiosity and my reason. They called those people brutes, cursed by Heaven. As I grew up, I clearly realized that it was force and prejudice that had condemned them to that horrible slavery, in which Nature plays no role, and for which the unjust and powerful interests of Whites are alone responsible.

Convinced for a long time of this truth and troubled by their dreadful situation, I dealt with their story in the very first work I wrote. Several men had taken an interest in them and worked to lighten their burden; but none of them had thought of presenting them on stage in their costume and their color as I would have tried, if the Comédie-Française had not been against it.

Mirza had kept her native language, nothing was more touching; it added a lot to the interest of the play. All the experts agreed, except for the actors at the Comédie-Française. But let us not talk about the reception of my play. Now I hand it over to the Public.

Let us go back to the dreadful lot of the Negroes. When will we turn our attention to changing it, or at least to easing it? I know nothing about the Politics of Governments; but they are fair. Now the Law of Nature was never more apparent in them. People are equal everywhere. Fair kings do not want any slaves; they know that they possess obedient subjects, and France will not abandon the wretched in their suffer-

ing, ever since greed and ambition have inhabited the most remote islands. Europeans, thirsting for blood and for this metal that greed calls gold, have made Nature change in these happy lands. Fathers have repudiated their children, sons have sacrificed their fathers, brothers have fought, and the defeated have been sold like cattle at the market. What am I saying? It has become a trade in the four corners of the world.

Trading people! Heavens! And Nature does not quake! If they are animals, are we not also like them? How are the Whites different from this race? It is in the color. . . . Why do blonds not claim superiority over brunettes who bear a resemblance to Mulattos? Why is the Mulatto not superior to the Negro? Like all the different types of animals, plants, and minerals that Nature has produced, people's color also varies. Why does not the day argue with the night, the sun with the moon, and the stars with the sky? Everything is different, and herein lies the beauty of Nature. Why then destroy its Work?

Is mankind not its most beautiful masterpiece? Ottomans exploit Whites in the same way we exploit Blacks. We do not accuse them of being barbarian or inhuman, and we are equally cruel to people whose only means of resistance is their submissiveness.

But when submissiveness once starts to flag, what results from the barbaric despotism of the Islanders and West-Indians? Revolts of all kinds, carnage increased with the troops' force, poisonings, and any atrocities people can commit once they revolt. Is it not monstrous of Europeans, who have acquired vast plantations by exploiting others, to have Blacks flogged from morning to night? These miserable souls would cultivate their fields no less if they were allotted more freedom and kindness.

Is their fate not among the most cruel, and their labor the hardest, without having Whites inflict the most horrible punishments on them, and for the smallest fault? Some speak about changing their condition, finding ways to ease it, without fearing that this race of men misuse a kind of freedom that remains subordinate.

I understand nothing about Politics. Some predict that widespread freedom would make the Negro race as essential as the White race, and that after they have been allowed to be masters of their lives, they will be masters of their will, and able to raise their children at their side. They will be more exact and diligent in their work. Intolerance will not torment them anymore, and the right to rise up like others will make them wiser and more human. Deadly conspiracies will no longer have to be feared. They will cultivate freely their own land like the farmers in Europe and will not leave their fields to go to foreign Nations.

Their freedom will lead some Negroes to desert

their country, but much less than those who leave the French countryside. Young people hardly come of age with the requisite strength and courage, before they are on their way to Paris to take up the noble occupation of lackey or porter. There are a hundred servants for one position, whereas our fields lack farmers.

This freedom will produce a large number of idle, unhappy, and bad persons of any kind. May each nation set wise and salutary limits for its people; this is the art of Sovereigns and Republican States.

My instincts could help, but I will keep myself from presenting my opinion, for I should be more knowledgeable and enlightened about the Politics of Governments. As I have said, I do not know anything about Politics, and I freely give my observations either good or bad. I, more than anyone, must be interested in the fate of these unfortunate Negroes since it has been five years since I conceived a play based on their tragic History.

I have only one piece of advice to give to the actors of the Comédie-Française, and it is the only favor I will ask of them, that is to wear the color and costume of the Negro race. Never has the occasion been more opportune, and I hope that the Play will have an effect in favor of these victims of Whites' ambition.

The costume will contribute greatly to the interest of this Play, which will inspire the pens and the hearts of our best writers. My goal will thus be attained, my ambition satisfied, and the Comédie-Française will be honored rather than dishonored by the issue of color.

My happiness would be too immeasurable if I were to see my Play performed as I wish. This weak sketch would require a poignant group of scenes for it to serve posterity. Painters ambitious enough to paint the tableau would be considered Fathers of the wisest and most worthwhile Humanity, and I am convinced that they would favor the subject of this small Play over its dramatic expression.

So, Ladies and Gentlemen, act out my Play, it has waited long enough. As you have wanted, it is now published. I join every Nation in asking for its production, and I am convinced they will not disappoint me. This feeling that could be considered self-pride in others, results from the impact which the public outcry in favor of Negroes has had on me. Any reader who appreciates my work will be convinced of my sincerity.

Forgive me these last statements; they are painful to express, but therein lies my right to them. Farewell Ladies and Gentlemen, act my play as you see fit; I shall not attend the rehearsals. I turn over all rights to my son; may he make good use of them and protect himself from becoming a Writer for the Comédie-Française. If he believes me, he will never pick up a pen to write Literature.

Black Slavery, or The Happy Shipwreck (1789)

Preface

In the Dark Ages men made war; in the most Enlightened Age, they want to destroy themselves. Will there ever be a science, a regime, an epoch, or an age when men will live in peace? The Learned may dwell upon and lose themselves in these metaphysical observations. I, a woman, who have only studied the good principles of Nature, I no longer set forth man's nature; my rude learning has taught me to judge things only after my soul. My works, therefore, bear but the color of human nature.

Here, at last, is my Play, which avarice and ambition have proscribed, but which just men approve. What must my opinion be of these varying opinions? As an Author, I am permitted to approve this philanthropical work; but as an earwitness of the disastrous accounts of the troubles in America, I should abhor my Work, if an invisible hand had not performed this revolution in which I did not participate except to prophesy its occurrence. However, you blame me, you accuse me without even having seen *Black Slavery*, accepted in 1783 by the Comédie-Française, printed in 1786, and performed in December 1789. The Colonists, whose cruel ambition was effortlessly satisfied, won over the Comedians, and you can be sure . . . that the interception of my Play did not hurt their receipts; but it is neither the Comedians nor the Colonists whom I wish to put on trial, it is rather myself.

I denounce myself publicly; here I am under arrest: I am going to plead my own case before this august Tribunal, frivolous . . . but redoubtable. I deliver myself to a vote of conscience; I shall win or lose by a majority.

The author and friend of the truth who has no interest but to remind men of the charitable principles of Nature, who respects laws and social conventions no less, is still an estimable mortal, and if her writings do not produce all the good that she had hoped for, she is to be pitied more than blamed.

It is, therefore, important for me to convince the Public and the detractors of my Work, of the purity of my maxims. This work may lack talent but not morals. It is by means of these morals that public opinion must reconsider my case.

When the Public has read my Play, conceived in a time when it was to appear as a Novel drawn from an old Fairy tale play, it will recognize that it is the faithful tableau of the current situation in America. I give you, today, in the fourth year of the Republic, my Play such as it was approved under the despotism of the press. I offer my Play to the Public as an authentic document, which is necessary for my vindication. Is my work inflammatory? No. Is it insurgent? No. Does it have a moral? Yes, without doubt. What, then, do these Colonists want from me when they speak of me in such unsparing terms? But they are wretches; I pity them and shall respect their deplorable fate; I shall not even permit myself to remind them of their inhumanity: I shall permit myself only to mention all that I have written to preserve their properties and their most cherished interests: my Play is proof thereof.

I shall now address myself to you, slaves, men of color; perhaps I have an incontestable right to blame your ferocity: cruel, you justify tyrants when you imitate them. Most of your Masters were humane and charitable, and in your blind rage you do not distinguish between innocent victims and your persecutors. Men were not born in irons, and now you prove them necessary. If force majeure is on your side, why exercise all the fury of your fiery lands? Poison, irons, daggers, they say you invent the most barbarous and atrocious tortures with no effort. What cruelty! what inhumanity! Ah! How you make them moan, they who wanted to prepare you, by temperate means, a kinder fate, a fate more worthy of envy than all those illusory advantages whereby the authors of the calamities in France and America have misled you. Tyranny will follow you just as crime clings to depraved men. Nothing will reconcile you with yourselves. Fear my prediction, you know whether it be well-founded or not. My pronouncements are based on reason and divine justice. I retract nothing: I abhor your Tyrants, your cruelties horrify me.

Ah! If my counsel reaches you, if you recognize its worth, I dare believe that your untamed wits will be calmed and that my counsel will restore harmony, which is indispensable to the colonial commonweal and to your own interests. These interests consist only in social order, your rights within the wisdom of the Law; this Law recognizes that all men are brothers; this august Law that cupidity had plunged into chaos has been finally extricated from the dark. If the savage, a ferocious man, fails to recognize this Law, then he is made for irons, to be tamed like a brute.

Slaves, people of color, you who live closer to Nature than Europeans, than your Tyrants, recognize these gentle laws and show that an enlightened Nation was not mistaken to treat you like men and give you rights that you never had in America. To draw nearer to justice and humanity, remember, and never lose sight of this, your Fatherland condemns you to a frightful servitude and your own parents put you up for sale: men are hunted in your frightful climes like animals are hunted elsewhere. The true Philosophy of the enlightened man prompts him to snatch his fellow-man from the midst of a primitively horrible situation where men not only sold one another, but where they still ate each other. The true man has regards for all men. These are my principles, which differ greatly from those of these so-called defenders of Liberty, these firebrands, these incendiary spirits who preach equality and liberty with all the authority and ferocity of Despots. America, France, and perhaps the Universe, will owe their fall to a few energumen that France has produced, the decadence of Empires and the loss of the arts and sciences. This is perhaps a fatal truth. Men have grown old, they seem to want to be born again, and according to the principles of Brissot, animal life suits man perfectly; I love Nature more than he, she has placed the laws of humanity and wise equality in my soul; but when I consider this Nature, I often see her in contradiction with her principles, and everything then seems subordinate. Animals have their Empires, Kings, Chiefs, and their reign is peaceable; an invisible and charitable hand seems to conduct their administration. I am not entirely an enemy of M. Brissot's principles, but I believe them impracticable among men: I have treated this matter before him. I dared, after the august Author of *The Social Contract*, provide *Man's Original Happiness*, published in 1789. I wrote a Novel, and never will men be pure enough, great enough, to recover this original happiness, which I found only in a blissful fiction. Ah! If it were possible for them to achieve this, the wise and humane laws that I establish in this social contract would make all men brothers, the Sun would be the true God that they would invoke; but always fickle, the *Social Contract*, *Original Happiness* and the august Work of M. Brissot will always be chimerae and not a useful instruction. Imitations of Jean-Jacques are defaced in this new regime, what, then, would those of Madame de Gouges and M. Brissot be? It is easy, even for the most ignorant, to make revolutions in paper notebooks; but, alas! every People's experience, and now the French experience, teaches me that the most learned and the most wise do not establish their doctrines without producing all kinds of troubles.

I stray from the aim of my Preface, and time does not permit me to give free reign to philosophical reasons. It was a question of justifying *Black Slavery*, which the odious Colonists had proscribed and presented as an incendiary work. Let the public judge and pronounce, I await its decree for my justification.

DRAMATIS PERSONAE

Zamor, educated Indian
Mirza, young Indian, Zamor's lover
M. de Saint-Frémont, Governor of an island in the Indies
Mme de Saint-Frémont, his wife
Valère, French gentleman, Sophie's husband
Sophie, M. de Saint-Frémont's natural daughter
Betzi, Mme de Saint-Frémont's maid
Caroline, Slave
Indian, M. de Saint-Frémont's slave steward
Azor, M. de Saint-Frémont's valet
M. de Belfort, Major from the garrison
Judge
M. de Saint-Frémont's Man-Servant
Old Indian
Several Indian Planters of both sexes, and Slaves
Grenadiers and French Soldiers

THE SCENE IN THE FIRST ACT IS A DESERTED ISLAND; IN THE SECOND, A LARGE, NEIGHBORING CITY IN THE INDIES, AND IN THE THIRD, A NEARBY PLANTATION.

Act I

SHORE OF A DESERTED ISLAND, SURROUNDED BY STEEP CLIFFS, FROM WHICH THE HIGH SEA IS VISIBLE IN THE DISTANCE. ON ONE SIDE IN FRONT IS THE OPEN DOOR OF A HUT SURROUNDED BY FRUIT TREES FROM THE REGION: THE ENTRANCE TO A SEEMINGLY IMPENETRABLE FOREST FILLS THE OTHER SIDE. JUST AS THE CURTAIN RISES, A STORM AGITATES THE WAVES: A SHIP HAS JUST BROKEN TO PIECES ON THE ROCKS. THE WINDS DIE DOWN AND THE SEA BECOMES CALM.

Scene I

Zamor, Mirza

ZAMOR: Dispel your fears, my dear Mirza; this vessel is not sent by our persecutors: as far as I can judge, it is French. Alas! it has just broken to pieces on these rocks, none of the crew has escaped.

MIRZA: Zamor, I fear only for you; punishment does not frighten me; I shall bless my fate if we end our days together.

ZAMOR: O my Mirza! How you move me!

MIRZA: Alas! What have you done? my love has rendered you guilty. Without the unhappy Mirza you would never have run away from the best of all Masters, and you would not have killed his confidential agent.

ZAMOR: The barbarian! he loved you, and that made him your tyrant. Love rendered him fierce. The tiger dared charge me with the chastisement that he inflicted upon you for not wanting to respond to his unbridled passion. The education that our governor had given me added to the sensibility of my rude manners and rendered the frightful despotism that commanded me to punish you even more intolerable.

MIRZA: You should have let me die; you would be beside our Governor who cherishes you like his child. I have caused your troubles and his.

ZAMOR: Me, let you perish! Ah! Gods! Hey! Why remind me of the virtues and kindnesses of this respectable Master? I have performed my duty to him: I have paid for his kindnesses, rather with the tenderness of a son, than the devotion of a slave. He believes me guilty, and that is what renders my torment more frightful. He does not know what a monster he had honored with his confidence. I have saved my fellow-men from his tyranny; but, my dear Mirza, let us destroy a memory too dear and too fatal: we no longer have any protectors save Nature. Benevolent Mother! You know our innocence. No, you will not abandon us, and this deserted spot will hide us from all eyes.

MIRZA: The little that I know, I owe to you, Zamor; but tell me why Europeans and Planters have such advantage over us, poor slaves? They are, however, made like us: we are men like them: why, then, such a great difference between their kind and ours?

ZAMOR: That difference is very small; it exists only in color; but the advantages that they have over us are huge. Art has placed them above Nature: instruction has made Gods of them, and we are only men. They use us in these climes as they use animals in theirs. They came to these regions, seized the lands, the fortunes of the Native Islanders, and these proud ravishers of the properties of a gentle and peaceable people in its home, shed all the blood of its noble victims, sharing amongst themselves its bloody spoils and made us slaves as a reward for the riches that they ravished, and that we preserve for them. These are their own fields that they reap, sown with the corpses of the Planters, and these crops are now watered with our sweat and our tears. Most of these barbaric masters treat us with a cruelty that makes Nature shudder. Our wretched species has grown accustomed to these chastisements. They take care not to instruct us. If by chance our eyes were to open, we would be horrified by the state to which they have reduced us, and we would shake off a yoke as cruel as it is shameful; but is it in our power to change our fate? The man vilified by slavery has lost all his energy, and the most brutalized among us are the least unhappy. I have always shown the same zeal to my master, but I have taken care not to make my way of thinking known to my comrades. God! Divert the presage that still menaces these climes, soften the hearts of our Tyrants, and give man back the rights that he has lost in the very bosom of Nature.

MIRZA: How we are to be pitied!

ZAMOR: Perhaps our fate will change before long. A gentle and consoling morality has unveiled European error. Enlightened men gaze compassionately upon us: we shall owe them the return of this precious liberty, man's primary treasure, of which cruel ravishers have deprived us for so long.

MIRZA: I would be happy to be as well instructed as you; but I only know how to love you.

ZAMOR: Your artlessness charms me; it is the imprint of Nature. I leave you for a moment. Go and gather some fruit. I am going to take a walk down to the shore to collect the debris from this shipwreck. But, what do I see? A woman who is struggling against the waves! Ah! Mirza, I fly to her rescue. Must excessive misfortune excuse us from being humane? *(He descends toward the rock)*

Scene II

MIRZA: *(Alone)* Zamor is going to save this poor unfortunate soul! How can I not adore such a tender, compassionate heart? Now that I am unhappy, I am more conscious of how sweet it is to soothe the misfortunes of others. *(She exits toward the forest)*

Scene III

VALÈRE, ALONE, ENTERS FROM THE OPPOSITE SIDE

VALÈRE: Nothing in sight on the agitated waves. O my wife! You are lost forever! Hey! Could I survive you? No: I must be reunited with you. I gathered my strength to save your life, and I have only escaped the fury of the waves. I breathe but with horror: separated from you, each instant redoubles my sorrow. I search for you in vain, in vain do I call out your name: Your voice resounds in my heart, but it does not strike my ear. I fly from you. *(He descends with difficulty and falls at the back of the Theatre propped up against a boulder)* A thick cloud covers my eyes, my strength abandons me! Almighty God, grant me strength that I may drag myself as far as the sea! I can no longer hold myself up. *(He remains immobile from exhaustion)*

Scene IV

Valère, Mirza

MIRZA, RUSHING UP AND CATCHING SIGHT OF VALÈRE

MIRZA: Ah! God! Who is this man? Suppose he were coming to lay hands on Zamor and separate me from him! Alas! What would become of me? But, no, perhaps he does not have so evil a scheme; he is not one of our persecutors. I am suffering . . . Despite my fears, I cannot help myself from coming to his aid. I cannot see him in this state much longer. He looks like a French man. *(To Valère)* Monsieur, Frenchman . . . He does not respond. What to do! *(She calls out)* Zamor, Zamor. *(With reflection)* Let us climb upon the rock to see if he is coming. *(She runs up to it and immediately climbs down)* I do not see him. *(She returns to Valère)* Frenchman, Frenchman, answer me? He does not answer. What help can I give him? I have nothing; how unhappy I am! *(Taking Valère's arm and striking his hand)* Poor stranger, he is very ill, and Zamor is not here: he has more strength than I; but let us search in our hut for something that will revive him. *(She exits)*

Scene V

Valère, Zamor, Sophie

ZAMOR, ENTERING FROM THE SIDE BY THE ROCK, AND CARRYING SOPHIE WHO APPEARS TO HAVE FAINTED IN HIS ARMS, GARBED IN A WHITE DRESSING-GOWN, BELTED, AND WITH HER HAIR DISHEVELED

ZAMOR: Regain your strength, Madame; I am only an Indian slave, but I shall help you.

SOPHIE: *(In a dying voice)* Whoever you may be, leave me. Your pity is more cruel to me than the waves. I have lost what was most dear to me. Life is odious to me. O Valère! O my spouse! What has become of you?

VALÈRE: Whose voice is that I hear? Sophie!

SOPHIE: *(Noticing Valère)* What do I see . . . It is he!

VALÈRE: *(Getting up and falling at Sophie's feet)* Almighty God! You have returned my Sophie to me! O dear spouse! Object of my tears and my tenderness! I succumb to my suffering and to my Joy.

SOPHIE: Divine Providence! you have saved me! Complete your work, and return my father to me.

Scene VI

VALÈRE, ZAMOR, SOPHIE, MIRZA, BRINGING SOME FRUIT AND WATER; SHE ENTERS RUNNING, AND SURPRISED TO SEE A WOMAN, SHE STOPS

ZAMOR: Approach, Mirza, there is nothing to fear. These are two unfortunates like us; they have rights on our souls.

VALÈRE: Compassionate being to whom I owe my life and my spouse's life! You are not a Savage; you have neither the language nor the manners of one. Are you the master of this Island?

ZAMOR: No, but we have been living here alone for several days. You seem like a Frenchman to me. If the company of slaves does not seem contemptible to you, they will gladly share the possession of this Island with you, and if destiny wills it, we shall end our days together.

SOPHIE: *(To Valère)* How this language interests me! *(To the slaves)* Generous mortals, I would accept your offers, if I were not going farther to look for a father whom I shall perhaps never find again! We have been wandering the seas for two years, and we have found no trace of him.

VALÈRE: Well then! Let us remain in this spot: let us accept the hospitality of these Indians for awhile and be persuaded, my dear Sophie, that by dint of perseverance we shall find the author of your days on this Continent.

SOPHIE: Cruel destiny! We have lost everything; how can we continue our search?

VALÈRE: I share your sorrow. *(To the Indians)* Generous mortals, do not abandon us.

MIRZA: Us, abandon you! Never, no, never.

ZAMOR: Yes, my dear Mirza, let us console them in their misfortunes. *(To Valère and Sophie)* Rely upon me; I am going to examine the entire area by the cliff: if your lost goods are among the debris from the vessel, I promise to bring them to you. Enter our hut, unhappy Strangers; you need rest; I am going to try to calm your agitated spirits.

SOPHIE: Compassionate mortals, we must repay you for so much kindness! You have saved our lives, how shall I ever acquit myself toward you?

ZAMOR: You owe us nothing, in helping you I obey only the voice of my heart. *(He exits)*

Scene VII

Mirza, Sophie, Valère

MIRZA: *(To Sophie)* I like you, though you are not a slave. Come, I shall care for you. Give me your arm. Ah! what a pretty hand, so different from mine! Let us sit here. *(Gaily)* How happy I am to be with you! You are as fair as our Governor's wife.

SOPHIE: Yes? You have a Governor on this Island?

VALÈRE: It seems to me that you told us that you live here alone?

MIRZA: *(With frankness)* Oh! It is quite true, and Zamor has not deceived you. I spoke to you of the Governor of the Colony, who does not live with us. *(Aside)* I must be careful of what I am going to say; for if he knew that Zamor has killed a white man, he would not want to remain with us.

SOPHIE: *(To Valère)* Her ingenuousness delights me, her countenance is sweet, and prejudices in her favor.

VALÈRE: I have not seen a prettier Negress.

MIRZA: You mock me; I am not for all that the prettiest; but, tell me, are all French women as fair as you? They must be so; for Frenchmen are all good, and you are not slaves.

VALÈRE: No, Frenchmen have a horror of slavery. One day more free they will see about tempering your fate.

MIRZA: *(With surprise)* More free one day, how so, are you not free?

VALÈRE: We are free in semblance, but our irons are only the heavier. For several centuries the French have been groaning under the despotism of Ministers and Courtiers. The power of a single Master is in the hands of a thousand Tyrants who trample the People underfoot. This People will one day break its irons and, resuming all its rights under Natural Law, it will teach these Tyrants what the union of a people too long oppressed and enlightened by a sound philosophy can do.

MIRZA: Oh! Dear God! There are then evil men everywhere!

Scene VIII

Zamor, on the cliff, Sophie, Valère, Mirza

ZAMOR: The worst has happened, unhappy Strangers! You have no hope. A wave has just swallowed up the remains of the equipage along with all of your hopes.

SOPHIE: Alas! What shall become of us?

VALÈRE: A vessel can land on this Island.

ZAMOR: You do not know, unhappy Strangers, how dangerous this coast is. There are only unfortunates like Mirza and me, who have dared to approach it and overcome all perils to inhabit it. We are, however, only two leagues from one of the bigger towns in the Indies; a town that I shall never see again unless our tyrants come and tear us away from here to make us suffer the punishment to which we are condemned.

SOPHIE: Torture!

VALÈRE: What crime have you both committed? Ah! I see; you are too educated for a slave, and the person who gave you your instruction has paid a high price no doubt.

ZAMOR: Monsieur, do not hold your fellowmen's prejudices against me. I had a Master who was dear to me: I would have sacrificed my life to prolong his days, but his Steward was a monster whom I have purged from the land. He loved Mirza; but his love was scorned. He learned that she preferred me, and in his fury he had me suffer frightful treatment; but the most terrible was to demand that I become the instrument of his vengeance against my dear Mirza. I rejected such a commission with horror. Irritated by my disobedience, he came at me with his naked sword; I avoided the blow that he wanted to give me; I disarmed him and he fell dead at my feet. I had but the time to carry off Mirza and to flee with her in a longboat.

SOPHIE: How I pity him, this unhappy man! Though he has committed murder, this murder seems worthy of mercy to me.

VALÈRE: I am interested in their fate; they brought me back to life, they saved yours: I shall defend them at the cost of my days. I shall go myself to see his Governor: If he is a Frenchman, he must be humane and generous.

ZAMOR: Yes, Monsieur, he is a Frenchman and the best of men.

MIRZA: Ah! If all the Colonists were like him, we would be less unhappy.

ZAMOR: I have belonged to him since I was eight years old; he took pleasure in having me educated and loved me as if I had been his son; for he never had one, or perhaps he was deprived of one: he seems to regret something. Sometimes you hear him sighing; surely he strives to hide some great sorrow. I have often surprised him in tears: he adores his wife, and she him in kind. If it depended only upon him, I would be pardoned; but they need an example. There is no hope of a pardon for a slave who has raised a hand against his Commander.

SOPHIE: *(To Valère)* I do not know why this Governor interests me. The account of his sorrows lies heavy on my heart; he is generous, clement; he can pardon you. I shall go myself and throw myself at his feet. His name? If only we could leave this Island.

ZAMOR: His name is Monsieur de Saint-Frémont.

SOPHIE: Alas! This name is unknown to me; but no matter, he is a Frenchman: he will hear me, and I hope to move him to mercy. *(To Valère)* If with the longboat that saved them, we could guide ourselves into port, there is no peril that I would not brave to defend them.

VALÈRE: I admire you, my dear Sophie! I approve of your plan: we have only to make our way to their Governor. *(To the Slaves)* My friends, this step barely discharges us of our obligation to you. Happy if our entreaties and our tears move your generous Master! Let us leave, but what do I see? Here are some slaves who are examining us and who are hurrying toward us. They are carrying chains.

SOPHIE: Unhappy lovers, you are lost!

ZAMOR: *(Turns around and sees the Slaves)* Mirza, the worst has happened! They have found us.

Scene IX

The Same, an Indian, several slaves who are running down from the rock

INDIAN: *(To Zamor)* Scoundrel! At last, I find you; you will not escape punishment.

MIRZA: May they put me to death before him!

ZAMOR: O my dear Mirza!

INDIAN: Put them in chains.

VALÈRE: Monsieur, listen to our entreaties! What are you going to do with these Slaves?

INDIAN: A terrible example.

SOPHIE: You are taking them away to put them to death? You will take away our lives before tearing them from our arms.

VALÈRE: What are you doing? My dear Sophie! We can place all our hope in the Governor's indulgence.

INDIAN: Do not flatter yourself. The Governor must set an example for the Colony. You do not know this cursed race; they would slit our throats without pity if the voice of humanity spoke in their favor. That is what you must always expect, even from Slaves who have received some instruction. They are born to be savages and tamed like animals.

SOPHIE: What frightful prejudice! Nature did not make them Slaves; they are men like you.

INDIAN: What language do you speak, Madame?

SOPHIE: The same which I would speak before your

Governor. It is gratitude that interests me in these unfortunates, who know better than you the rights of pity; he whose position you uphold was no doubt a wicked man.

ZAMOR: Ah! Madame, cease your entreaties; his soul is hardened and does not know kindness. It is his daily task to make this rigor conspicuous. He believes that he would not be performing his duty if he did not push rigor to cruelty.

INDIAN: Wretch!

ZAMOR: I fear you no longer. I know my fate and shall submit to it.

SOPHIE: How their misfortune renders them interesting! What would I not do to save them!

VALÈRE: *(To the Indian)* Take us away with them, Monsieur. You will oblige us to withdraw from here. *(Aside)* I hope to move the Governor to mercy.

INDIAN: I consent with pleasure, especially as the danger leaving this Island is not the same as that risked to reach it.

VALÈRE: But Monsieur, how were you able to land here?

INDIAN: I risked everything for the good of the Colony. See if it is possible to pardon them. We are no longer the Masters of our Slaves. Our Governor's life is perhaps in danger, and order will be restored on the plantations once these two poor wretches are punished. *(To the Negroes)* Negroes, fire the cannon, and let the prearranged signal announce to the Fort that the criminals are taken.

ZAMOR: Let us go Mirza, we are going to die.

MIRZA: Ah! God! I am the cause of his death.

ZAMOR: Our good action in saving these Strangers will cast some charm on our last moments, and we shall taste at least the sweetness of dying together.

ZAMOR AND MIRZA ARE LED AWAY; THE OTHER CHARACTERS FOLLOW THEM, AND THEY ARE ALL ABOUT TO EMBARK. THE NEXT MOMENT THE SHIP CARRYING THEM GOES PAST.

End of Act One.

Act II

A COMPANY DRAWING-ROOM WITH INDIAN FURNISHINGS.

Scene I

Betzi, Azor

BETZI: Well, Azor, what do they say about Mirza and Zamor? They are searching for them everywhere.

AZOR: There is talk of putting them to death on the rock by the plantation; I even believe that preparations for their punishment are being readied. I tremble that they may find them.

BETZI: But the Governor can pardon them. He is their master.

AZOR: That must be impossible; for he loves Zamor, and he says that he never had any complaint with him. The whole Colony is asking for their death; he cannot refuse it without compromising himself.

BETZI: Our Governor was not made to be a Tyrant.

AZOR: How good he is to us! All Frenchmen are the same; but the Natives of this country are much more cruel.

BETZI: I have been assured that we were not originally slaves.

AZOR: Everything leads us to believe that. There are still climes where Negroes are free.

BETZI: How fortunate they are!

AZOR: Ah! We are really to be pitied.

BETZI: And no one undertakes our defense! We are even forbidden to pray for our fellow men.

AZOR: Alas! the father and mother of the unfortunate Mirza will witness their daughter's punishment.

BETZI: Such ferociousness!

AZOR: That is how they treat us.

BETZI: But, tell me, Azor, why did Zamor kill the Steward?

AZOR: I was assured that it was from jealousy. You know quite well that Zamor was Mirza's lover.

BETZI: Yes, it was you who informed me of it.

AZOR: The Commander loved her too.

BETZI: But he ought not to kill him for that.

AZOR: That is true.

BETZI: There were other reasons.

AZOR: That may well be, but I am unaware of them.

BETZI: If we could let them escape, I am sure that Monsieur and Madame de St-Frémont would not be angry.

AZOR: I think that too, but those who would serve them would put themselves at great risk.

BETZI: No doubt, but there would not be a death penalty.

AZOR: Perhaps, I still know that I would not risk it.

BETZI: We should at least talk to their friends; they could win over the other slaves. They all love Zamor and Mirza.

AZOR: There is talk of arming the entire regiment.

BETZI: It is hopeless.

AZOR: On the contrary, we must urge them to obey for the good of our comrades.

BETZI: You are right; do it if you can, for I would never have the strength for it.

Scene II

The Same, Coraline

CORALINE: *(Running)* O my dear comrades! What bad news I bring you! It is certain that cannon fire has been heard and that Zamor and Mirza are captured.

AZOR: Come, that is not possible, Coraline.

BETZI: Almighty God!

CORALINE: I was at the port when they announced this unfortunate news. Several Colonists were awaiting impatiently a ship that could be seen in the distance. It finally entered port, and all the planters surrounded it immediately. I ran away, trembling. Poor Mirza! unhappy Zamor! our tyrants will not pardon them.

AZOR: Oh! You may take my word for it; they will soon be dead.

BETZI: Without a hearing? Without a trial?

CORALINE: Trial! We are forbidden to be innocent and to justify ourselves.

AZOR: What generosity! And, in the bargain, they sell us like cattle at the market.

BETZI: A commerce of men! O Heaven! Humanity is repulsive.

AZOR: It is quite true, my father and I were bought on the Coast of Guinea.

CORALINE: There, there, my poor Azor, whatever our deplorable fate, I have a presentiment that we shall not always be in irons, and perhaps before long . . .

AZOR: Well then! What shall we see? Shall we be masters in our turn?

CORALINE: Perhaps; but no, we would be too wicked. Indeed, to be good, one must be neither master nor slave.

AZOR: Neither master, nor slave; Oh! Oh! And what do you want us to be? Do you know, Coraline, that you no longer know what you are saying, though our comrades assure us that you know more about this than we do?

CORALINE: There, there, my poor boy, if you knew what I know! I read in a certain Book that to be happy one need only be free and a good Farmer. We lack but liberty, let them give it to us, and you will see that there will no longer be masters or slaves.

AZOR: I do not understand you.

BETZI: Neither do I.

CORALINE: My God, how kind you both are! Tell me, was Zamor not free? And because of that, did he want to leave our kind Master?; we shall all do the same thing. Let the Masters give liberty; no

Slave will leave the workshop. Imperceptibly, the rudest among us will instruct themselves, recognize the laws of humanity and justice, and our superiors will find in our attachment, in our zeal, the reward for this kindness.

AZOR: You speak like a man! You sound like the Governor . . . Oh! One must have wit to retain everything that others say. But, here is Madame.

BETZI: Here is Madame, let us be silent!

CORALINE: We must not tell Madame that we fear that Zamor has been captured. That would grieve her too much.

AZOR: Oh! Yes.

Scene III

The Same, Mme de Saint-Frémont

MME DE SAINT-FRÉMONT: My children, I need to be alone. Leave me, and do not enter unless I call for you, or you have some news to announce. *(They exit)*

Scene IV

MME DE SAINT-FRÉMONT: *(Alone)* My spouse has gone out on account of this unfortunate matter: he went to one of the plantations where his attendance was requested. Since this catastrophe revolt reigns in the minds of our slaves. All maintain that Zamor is innocent, and that he only killed the Commander because he saw himself forced to; but the Colonists have gathered to ask for the death of Mirza and Zamor, and Mirza and Zamor are being sought everywhere. My husband really wanted to pardon Zamor, though he pronounced his judgment, as well as that of poor Mirza, who is to perish with her lover. Alas! Expectation of their punishment throws me into a profound sadness. I am thus not born to be happy! In vain am I adored by my spouse: my love cannot conquer the melancholy that consumes him. He has been suffering for more than ten years, and I cannot divine the cause of his sorrow. It is the only one of his secrets which he has not entrusted to me. When he returns I must redouble my efforts to wrench it from him. But I hear him.

Scene V

Mme de Saint-Frémont, M. de Saint-Frémont

MME DE SAINT-FRÉMONT: Well, then! My dear, did your presence dispel this unrest?

M. DE SAINT-FRÉMONT: All of my slaves have returned to their duties; but they ask me to pardon Zamor. This matter is quite delicate, *(Aside)* and as a crowning misfortune, I have just received heart-rending news from France.

MME DE SAINT-FRÉMONT: What are you saying, my dear, you seem to reproach yourself. Ah! If you are only guilty with regard to me, I forgive you so long as your heart is still mine. You look away; I see the tears in your eyes. Ah! My dear, I no longer have your trust; I am becoming tiresome to you; I am going to retire.

M. DE SAINT-FRÉMONT: You, become tiresome to me! Never, never. Ah! If I could have strayed from my duty, your sweetness alone would have brought me back to your feet, and your great virtues would render me still more in love with your charms.

MME DE SAINT-FRÉMONT: But you hide a secret worry from me. Confess it to me. Your stifled sighs make me suspect so. France was dear to you; she is your Country . . . Perhaps an inclination . . .

M. DE SAINT-FRÉMONT: Stop, stop, dear spouse, and do not reopen an old wound that had closed beside you. I fear distressing you.

MME DE SAINT-FRÉMONT: If I were dear to you, you must give me proof of it.

M. DE SAINT-FRÉMONT: What kind of proof do you demand?

MME DE SAINT-FRÉMONT: The kind that reveals the causes of your affliction to me.

M. DE SAINT-FRÉMONT: This is what you want?

MME DE SAINT-FRÉMONT: I demand it; be forgiven, by this complaisance, for this secret that you have kept from me for so long.

M. DE SAINT-FRÉMONT: I obey. I am from a Province where unjust and inhuman laws deprive younger children of the equal share that Nature gives to children born of the same father and mother. I was the youngest of seven; my parents sent me to the Court to ask for employment; but how could I have succeeded in a country where virtue is a chimera, and where nothing is obtained without intrigue and baseness. However, I made the acquaintance of a worthy Scottish Gentleman who had come in the same purpose. He was not rich, and had a daughter in a Convent: he took me there. This interview turned fatal for both of us. The father, after several months, left for the army: He enjoined me to go and see his daughter, and even said that she could be entrusted to me when she wanted to go out. This worthy friend, this good father, did not foresee the consequences occasioned by his imprudence. He was killed in battle. His daughter was all alone in the world, without family or friends. She saw only me, and appeared to desire only my presence.

Love rendered me guilty: Spare me the rest: I swore an oath to be her spouse; there is my crime.

MME DE SAINT-FRÉMONT: But, my dear, did you determine by yourself to abandon her?

M. DE SAINT-FRÉMONT: Who, me? to have abandoned such a fine woman? Ah! The longest absence would never have made me forget her. I could not marry her without the consent of my whole family. She became the mother of a daughter. Our liaison was discovered; I was banished. They procured me a commission as Captain in a regiment that was leaving for the Indies and made me embark in it. Not long after I received the false news that Clarisse was dead, and that only my daughter remained. I saw you every day; with time your presence weakened the impression that Clarisse's image still made on my heart. I requested your hand, you accepted my vows, and we were united; but by an over-refinement of barbarity, the cruel relation who had deceived me informed me that Clarisse was still living.

MME DE SAINT-FRÉMONT: Alas! At what fatal price have I the honor of being your spouse! My dear, you are more unhappy than guilty. Clarisse herself would forgive you, if she were witness to your remorse. We must conduct an intensive search, so that your property and mine may acquit us toward these unfortunates. I have no other relations but yours. I am making your daughter my heiress; but your heart is a treasure that it is not in my power to surrender to another.

M. DE SAINT-FRÉMONT: Ah! Worthy spouse, I admire your virtues. Alas! I see only Clarisse who was capable of imitating them. It is thus at opposite ends of the earth that I was destined to meet the fairest and the most virtuous of your sex!

MME DE SAINT-FRÉMONT: You deserve a companion worthy of yourself; but, my dear, consider that in marrying me you consented to take the name of my father, who, by giving you his name, had no other aim save yielding his position to you as to an adopted son. You must write your relations, especially your most faithful friends, that they renew the search, and give us prompt news of these unfortunates. I believe, my dear, that I shall have the strength to leave you in order to seek the daughter whom you fathered. I already feel a mother's compassion for her; but at the same time I shudder. O my dear, my dear! If I had to separate from you! If Clarisse tore you from my arms! . . . Her misfortunes, her virtues, her charms . . . Ah! Forgive, forgive my despair, forgive me, dear spouse, you are not capable of abandoning me and making two victims for one.

M. DE SAINT-FRÉMONT: Dear spouse! O half of myself! Cease breaking this heart which already grieves too much. No doubt Clarisse is no longer alive, as it has been two years now that all of the funds that I send to France for her and for my daughter are sent back to me. What has become of them is not even known. But someone is coming; we shall resume this conversation later.

Scene VI

M. and Mme de Saint-Frémont, a Judge

JUDGE: Monsieur, I have come to inform you that the criminals are captured.

MME DE SAINT-FRÉMONT: What! So soon! Time would have erased their crime.

M. DE SAINT-FRÉMONT: *(Grieved)* What a frightful example I am obliged to give!

JUDGE: Remember, Monsieur, your father-in-law's disgrace in this instance. He was constrained to give up his position for having exercised it with too much kindness.

M. DE SAINT-FRÉMONT: *(Aside)* Unhappy Zamor, you are going to perish! I have thus raised you from childhood only to see you dragged off to be tortured. *(Aloud)* That my good offices should become fatal for him! If I had left him in his rude manners, perhaps he would not have committed this crime. He had no vicious inclinations in his soul. Honesty and virtue distinguished him in the bosom of slavery. Raised in a simple and hard life, despite the instruction that he had received, he never forgot his roots. How sweet it would be for me to be able to justify him! As a simple planter, I would perhaps be able to temper his arrest; but as Governor I am forced to deliver him to the full rigor of the law.

JUDGE: They must be put to death at once, more especially as two Europeans have incited a general revolt among the Slaves. They depicted your Commander as a monster. The Slaves listened avidly to these seditious speeches, and all have promised not to execute the orders that they were given.

M. DE SAINT-FRÉMONT: Who are these foreigners?

JUDGE: They are French citizens who were found on the coast where these criminals had taken refuge. They claim that Zamor saved their lives.

M. DE SAINT-FRÉMONT: Alas! These unfortunate French citizens were no doubt shipwrecked, and gratitude alone has produced this indiscreet zeal.

JUDGE: You see, Governor, sir, that there is no time to lose, if you want to avoid the total ruin of our plantations. There is hopeless disorder.

M. DE SAINT-FRÉMONT: I do not have the good fortune of having been born in your climes; but what sway the unfortunate hold over sensitive souls! It is not your fault if the manners of your country familiarized you with these harsh treatments that you exercise without remorse on men who have no other defense save their timidity, and whose work, so ill recompensed, increases our fortunes by increasing our authority over them. They have a thousand tyrants for one. Sovereigns render their People happy: every Citizen is free under a good Master, and in this country of slavery one must be barbaric in spite of oneself. Hey! How can I help abandoning myself to these reflections, when the voice of humanity cries out from the bottom of my heart: "Be kind and sensitive to the cries of the wretched." I know that my opinion must displease you: Europe, however, takes care to justify it, and I dare hope that before long there will no longer be any slaves. O Louis! O adored Monarch! Would that I could this very moment put under your eyes the innocence of these condemned souls! In granting their pardon, you would render freedom to those too long unrecognized; but no matter: you want an example, it shall be done, though the Blacks assure us that Zamor is innocent.

JUDGE: Can you believe them in this?

M. DE SAINT-FRÉMONT: They cannot deceive me, and I know more than they the virtues of Zamor. You want him to die without a hearing? I consent with regret; but you will not be able to reproach me for having betrayed the interests of the Colony.

JUDGE: You must do it, Governor, sir, in this matter in which you see that we are threatened with a general revolt. You must give the orders to arm the troops.

M. DE SAINT-FRÉMONT: Follow me; we shall see what decision should be made.

MME DE SAINT-FRÉMONT: My dear, I see you go in sorrow.

M. DE SAINT-FRÉMONT: My presence is necessary to restore order and discipline.

Scene VII

MME DE SAINT-FRÉMONT: *(Alone)* How I pity these wretches! The worst has happened! They are going to die. What chagrin for my spouse; but a greater chagrin agitates me once more. All that bears the name of a French woman terrifies me! If it were Clarisse! Oh! Unhappy me, what would be my fate? I know the virtues of my spouse, but I am his wife. No, no! let us cease in our deception!

Clarisse, in misfortune, has greater rights on his soul! Let us hide the trouble that agitates me.

Scene VIII

Mme De Saint-Frémont, Betzi rushing up

MME DE SAINT-FRÉMONT: What news is there, Betzi?

BETZI: *(With exaltation)* The Governor is not here?

MME DE SAINT-FRÉMONT: No, he has just gone out, speak?

BETZI: Ah! Let me regain my senses . . . We were on the terrace; from time to time we glanced sadly at the plantation. We see Mirza's father arrive from afar with another Slave; amid them was a foreigner, her hair disheveled and sorrow coloring her face: her eyes stared at the ground, and though she walked quickly, she seemed very preoccupied. When she was near us, she asked for Mme de Saint-Frémont. She informed us that Zamor had saved her from the fury of the waves. She added: I shall die at the feet of the Governor if I do not obtain his pardon. She wants to implore your assistance. Here she is.

Scene IX

The Same, Sophie, followed by all the Slaves

SOPHIE: *(Throwing herself at the knees of Mme de Saint-Frémont)* Madame, I embrace your knees. Have pity on an unhappy stranger who owes everything to Zamor and has no other hope but in your kind actions.

MME DE SAINT-FRÉMONT: *(Aside)* Ah! I breathe again. *(Aloud, while lifting Sophie to her feet)* Rise, Madame, I promise to do all that is within my power. *(Aside)* Her youth, her sensibility, touch my heart beyond words. *(To Sophie)* Interesting Stranger, I shall use every means to make my spouse grant the pardon that you demand. Believe that I share your sorrows. I sense how dear these unfortunates must be to you.

SOPHIE: Without Zamor's help, as intrepid as it was humane, I would have perished in the waves. I owe him the good fortune of seeing you. What he did for me earns him my heartfelt assurance of his natural rights; but these rights do not render me unjust, Madame, and the testimony that they render to your rare qualities shows well enough that Zamor and Mirza cannot be reproached with a premeditated crime. What humanity! What zeal in succoring us! The fate that pursues them was to inspire them with fear rather than pity; but, far from shunning peril, Zamor has dared all. Judge,

Madame, if with these feelings of humanity, a mortal can be guilty; his crime was involuntary, and to acquit him as innocent is to treat him as he deserves.

MME DE SAINT-FRÉMONT: *(To the Slaves)* My children, we must unite with the Colonists and ask that Zamor and Mirza be pardoned. We have no time to lose: *(To Sophie)* and you, whom I am burning to know, you are a French woman, perhaps you could . . . but moments are dear to us. Go back beside these unfortunates; Slaves, accompany her.

SOPHIE: *(Transported)* Ah! Madame, so many kindnesses at once! Alas! I should like, as much as I desire it, to prove my gratitude to you. *(She kisses her hands)* Soon my spouse will come and acquit himself of his obligation to you. Dear Valère, what happy news I am going to tell you! *(She exits with the Slaves)*

Scene X

Mme de Saint-Frémont, Betzi, Coraline

MME DE SAINT-FRÉMONT: *(Aside)* I find a resemblance in the features of this Stranger . . . What a chimera! . . . *(Aloud)* And you, Coraline, summon M. de Saint-Frémont's Secretary.

CORALINE: Ah! Madame, you are unaware of what is happening: he has just commanded your doors closed by order of the Governor. Everything is ablaze . . . Listen, Madame . . . There is the call to arms . . . and the sound of bells . . . *(The alarm must be heard in the distance)*

MME DE SAINT-FRÉMONT: *(Going with fright to the back of the theatre)* Wretched! What is to become of me? What does my husband do?

BETZI: I tremble for my comrades.

MME DE SAINT-FRÉMONT: *(Having given way to the greatest sorrow)* God, my Spouse is perhaps in danger! I fly to his aid . . .

CORALINE: Set your mind at rest, Madame, there is nothing to fear for the Governor. He is at the head of the regiment. But even if he were in the midst of the tumult, all the Slaves would respect his life. He is too cherished for anyone to want to harm him. The Slaves bear ill will only against some planters: they reproach them with the punishment of Zamor and Mirza; they are certain that without these planters Zamor and Mirza would not have been condemned.

MME DE SAINT-FRÉMONT: *(Agitated)* What! They are going to put them to death.

CORALINE: Alas! Soon my poor comrades will be no longer.

MME DE SAINT-FRÉMONT: *(With alacrity)* No, my children, they shall not perish: my husband will be moved by my tears, by this Stranger's despair, who, perhaps better than I, will know how to move him. His heart does not need to be incited to do good; but he can take everything upon himself. *(Aside)* And if this French woman were to give him news of his daughter! Almighty God! he would owe everything to these victims who are being dragged off to torture. *(Aloud)* Let us go, Betzi, we must join my husband, tell him . . . But how to enter into an explanation just now? I must see him myself. Where is he now?

CORALINE: I do not know precisely with which regiment he is: the entire army is in rout. They say only that M. de Saint-Frémont restores calm and order wherever he passes. It would be very difficult to find him just now. We have but to return to the plantation, if we have not already been forestalled. But the roads are broken up or cut off. It is hardly conceivable that they could have done so much damage in so little time.

MME DE SAINT-FRÉMONT: No matter. I fear neither danger nor weariness when the lives of two unfortunates are at stake.

End of Act II

Act III

A WILD SPOT FROM WHICH TWO POINTED HILLS ARE VISIBLE, BORDERED BY CLUSTERS OF SHRUBBY TREES FOR AS FAR AS THE EYE CAN SEE. ON ONE SIDE IS A STEEP CLIFF WHOSE SUMMIT IS A PLATFORM AND WHOSE BASE IS PERPENDICULAR TO THE FORE-STAGE. ALL OF THE CHARACTERS COME ON STAGE FROM THE SIDE OF ONE OF THE HILLS SO THAT THE AUDIENCE CAN SEE THEM ENTER. A FEW NEGRO HUTS ARE SCATTERED HERE AND THERE.

Scene I

Valère, Zamor, Mirza

VALÈRE: Free! Both of you are free! I hasten to your chief. It will not be long before my wife reappears before our eyes. She will no doubt have obtained your pardon from M. de Saint-Frémont. I leave you for a moment but do not lose sight of you.

Scene II

Zamor, Mirza

ZAMOR: O my dear Mirza, our fate is deplorable! It is

becoming so frightful that I fear this Frenchman's zeal to save us will only harm him and his wife. What a devastating idea!

MIRZA: The same idea pursues me: but perhaps his worthy wife will have succeeded in moving our Governor to mercy; let us not grieve before her return.

ZAMOR: I bless my death since I die with you; but, how cruel it is to lose one's life a culprit! I have been judged such, our good master believes it; that is what makes me despair.

MIRZA: I want to see the Governor myself. This last wish must be granted me. I shall throw myself at his feet; I shall reveal everything to him.

ZAMOR: Alas! What could you say to him?

MIRZA: I shall make him know the cruelty of his Commander and of his ferocious love.

ZAMOR: Your tenderness for me blinds you: you want to accuse yourself to render me innocent! If you scorn life at this price, do you believe me miserly enough to want to preserve it at your expense? No, my dear Mirza, there is no happiness for me on earth if I do not share it with you.

MIRZA: It is the same for me; I could no longer live without seeing you.

ZAMOR: How sweet it would have been for us to prolong our days together! This spot reminds me of our first encounter. It is here that the tyrant received his death; it is here that they are going to end our lives. Nature seems to stand in contrast with herself in this spot. Formerly she smiled upon us: she has lost none of her attractions; but she shows us both the image of our past happiness and the horrible fate to which we shall be victim. Ah! Mirza, how cruel it is to die when one is in love.

MIRZA: How you move me! Do not distress me more. I feel that my courage abandons me; but this good Frenchman is returning to us; what shall we learn from him?

Scene III

Zamor, Mirza, Valère

VALÈRE: O my benefactors! You must run away. Avail yourselves of these precious moments that your comrades procure for you. They are blocking off the roads; respond to their zeal and their courage. They risk themselves for you; flee to another clime. It is quite possible that my wife will not obtain your pardon. Several troops of soldiers can be seen approaching: you have time to escape by this hill. Go and live in the forests: your fellow men will receive you in their bosom.

MIRZA: This Frenchman is right. Come, follow me. He loves us; let us profit from his advice. Run away with me, dear Zamor; do not fear returning to live in the heart of the forest. You scarcely remember our laws, but soon your dear Mirza will recall their gentle impression for you.

ZAMOR: Well! I yield. It is but for you that I cherish life. *(He embraces Valère)* Farewell, most generous of men!

MIRZA: Alas! I must leave you, then, without the pleasure of throwing myself at your wife's feet!

VALÈRE: She will share your regrets, you can be sure; but flee this fatal spot.

Scene IV

The Same, Sophie, Slaves

SOPHIE: *(Rushing into Valère's arms)* Ah!, my friend, thank Heaven: these victims shall not perish. Madame de Saint-Frémont promised me they would be pardoned.

VALÈRE: *(With joy)* Almighty God! What supreme happiness!

ZAMOR: Ah! I recognize her fair soul in these proceedings. *(To Valère)* Generous foreigners, may Heaven gratify your wishes! The Supreme Being will never abandon those who seek his likeness in good works.

VALÈRE: Ah! How happy you make our days!

MIRZA: How fortunate we are to have succored these French citizens! They owe us much; but we owe them even more.

SOPHIE: Madame de Saint-Frémont has assembled her best friends. I have instructed her of their innocence; she exerts all possible zeal in saving them. I had no trouble interesting her on their behalf; her soul is so fair, so sensitive to the troubles of the unfortunate.

ZAMOR: Her respectable husband equals her in merit and goodness.

SOPHIE: I did not have the good fortune of seeing him.

ZAMOR: *(Alarmed)* What do I see! A throng of soldiers arriving! Ah! All is over! You have been deceived, generous Frenchman; we are lost.

SOPHIE: Do not become alarmed; we must first find out . . .

VALÈRE: I shall risk my life to defend them. Alas! They were going to run away when you came to reassure them. I am going to ask the Officer in charge of this detachment what his mission is. *(A Company of Grenadiers and one of French Soldiers line up in the back of the Theatre, their bayonets extended. A troop of Slaves with bows and arrows stands in front of them; the troop is headed by the Major, the Judge, and M. de Saint-Frémont's Slave Steward.)*

Scene V

The Same, Major, Judge, Indian, Grenadiers and French Soldiers, several Slaves

VALÈRE: Monsieur, may I ask you what matter brings you here?

MAJOR: A cruel function. I come to execute the death sentence pronounced against these wretches.

SOPHIE: *(Upset)* You are going to have them put to death?

MAJOR: Yes, Madame.

VALÈRE: No, this frightful sacrifice will not be carried out.

SOPHIE: Madame de Saint-Frémont promised me they would be pardoned.

JUDGE: *(Harshly)* That is not within her power, the Governor himself could not grant them their pardon. Desist therefore in your stubborn wish to save them. You make their punishment more terrible. *(To the Major)* Major, sir, execute the order that you were given. *(To the Slaves)* And you, lead the criminals to the top of the rock.

INDIAN COMMANDER: Draw your bows!

VALÈRE: Stop! *(The Slaves listen only to Valère)*

JUDGE: Obey. *(The Major signals to the Soldiers; they run with their bayonets, which they point at the Slaves' chests; not one Slave budges)*

ZAMOR: *(Rushing up to meet them)* What are you doing? Only I deserve to die. What have my poor comrades done to you? Why slaughter them? Turn your arms against me. *(He opens his jacket)* Here is my breast! Cleanse their disobedience in my blood. The Colony asks only my death. Is it necessary that so many innocent victims who were not parties to my crime perish?

MIRZA: I am as guilty as Zamor; do not separate me from him: take my life out of pity; my days are bound to his destiny. I want to die first.

VALÈRE: *(To the Judge)* Monsieur, grant a stay of execution, I beg of you. I assure you they are to be pardoned.

MAJOR: *(To the Judge)* Monsieur, we can take this up ourselves; let us await the Governor.

JUDGE: *(Harshly)* I listen to nothing save my duty and the law.

VALÈRE: *(Furious)* Barbarian! Though your position makes the soul callous, your being even more cruel than the laws have prescribed, degrades what you do.

JUDGE: Major, sir, have this impudent man taken away to the Citadel.

MAJOR: He is a Frenchman: he will answer to the Governor for his conduct; I am not required to take orders from you in this matter.

JUDGE: Then execute those you were given.

SOPHIE: *(With heroism)* This excess of cruelty gives me courage. *(She runs and places herself between Zamor and Mirza, takes them both by the hand, and says to the Judge)* Barbarian! Dare to have me assassinated with them; I shall not leave them; nothing can wrench them from my arms.

VALÈRE: *(Transported)* Ah! My dear Sophie, this act of courage makes you even dearer to my heart.

JUDGE: *(To the Major)* Monsieur, have this impudent woman removed: you are not fulfilling your duty.

MAJOR: *(Indignant)* You demand it; but you will answer for the consequences. *(To the Soldiers)* Separate these foreigners from these slaves. *(Sophie screams while clasping Zamor and Mirza to her breast)*

VALÈRE: *(Furious, running after Sophie)* If there is the slightest violence against my wife, then I cannot be held responsible for my actions. *(To the Judge)* And You, Barbarian, tremble, you may be sacrificed to my righteous fury.

A SLAVE: Were they to put us all to death, we would defend them. *(The Slaves line up around them, forming a rampart, the Soldiers and Grenadiers approach with their bayonets)*

MAJOR: *(To the Soldiers)* Soldiers, stop. *(To the Judge)* I was not sent here to order carnage and bloodshed, but, rather to restore order. The Governor will not be long, and his prudence will best indicate what we must do. *(To the Foreigners and the Slaves)* Take heart; I will not use force; your efforts would be useless if I wanted to exercise it. *(To Sophie)* And you, Madame, you may stand aside with these wretches; I await the Governor. *(Sophie, Zamor and Mirza, exit with several Slaves)*

Scene VI

Valère, Major, Judge, Indian, Grenadiers and Soldiers, Slaves

VALÈRE: I cannot abandon my wife in this state. Do your utmost to sway M. de Saint-Frémont. I do not need to recommend clemency to you; it must reign in your soul. Warriors have always been generous.

MAJOR: Rely upon me; withdraw and appear when it is time.

(Valère exits)

Scene VII

The Same, Except Valère

MAJOR: *(To the Judge)* There, Monsieur, is the fruit of too much harshness.

JUDGE: We are losing the Colony today because of your moderation.

MAJOR: More exactly; moderation is what may save the Colony. You know only your cruel laws, but I know the art of war and human nature. These are not our enemies whom we are fighting; these are our Slaves, or rather our Farmers. You would have them put to the sword to drive them to defeat, but, in this instance, imprudence would take us further than you think.

Scene VIII

The Same, M. de Saint-Frémont, entering from one side of the stage and Valère from the other. Two Companies of Grenadiers and Soldiers escort several Slaves in irons.

VALÈRE: *(To M. de Saint-Frémont)* Ah! Monsieur, hear our prayers: you are a Frenchman, you will be just.

M. DE SAINT-FRÉMONT: I approve of your zeal; but in these climes zeal becomes indiscreet; it has even caused much trouble. I have just witnessed the most frightful attempt on a Magistrate. I had to use violence, contrary to my nature, to stop the slaves in their cruelty. I know all that you owe to these wretched creatures; but you do not have the right to defend them, nor to change the laws and manners of a country.

VALÈRE: I have at least the right that gratitude gives to all fair souls: whatever harshness you feign, my heart appeals to your heart.

M. DE SAINT-FRÉMONT: Cease your entreaties, it pains me too much to refuse you.

VALÈRE: Your worthy wife had made us hope against hope.

M. DE SAINT-FRÉMONT: She herself, Monsieur, is convinced of the absolute impossibility of what you ask.

VALÈRE: If it is a crime to have killed a monster who made nature shudder, this crime, at least, is excusable. Zamor was defending his own life, and that is his natural right.

JUDGE: You abuse the Governor's complaisance: you have already been told this. The laws condemn them as homicides; can you change the laws?

VALÈRE: No; but the laws could be tempered in favor of an involuntary crime.

JUDGE: Do you really think that? Temper the law in favor of a slave! We are not here in France; we need examples.

M. DE SAINT-FRÉMONT: The worst has happened; the general order must be executed.

VALÈRE: These words make my blood run cold and lie heavy on my heart . . . Dear wife, what will become of you? Ah! Monsieur, if you knew her sensibility, her misfortunes, you would be moved; she had placed all her hopes in your goodness; she even flattered herself that you would give her some particulars on the fate of a parent, her sole support, of whom she has been deprived since childhood, and who must be settled in some part of this Continent.

M. DE SAINT-FRÉMONT: Be assured that I shall do everything in my power to help you; but, as for the criminals, I can do nothing for them. Unhappy Stranger! Go and console her: she interests me without my knowing her. Deceive her even, if need be, so that she does not witness this frightful torture: tell her that they want to interrogate these wretches, that they must be left alone, and that their pardon depends perhaps upon this wise precaution.

VALÈRE: (Weeping) How we are to be pitied! I shall not survive their loss. (He exits)

Scene IX

The Same, Except Valère

M. DE SAINT-FRÉMONT: How this Frenchman grieves me! His regrets on behalf of these unfortunates increase mine. They must die, and in spite of my leaning towards clemency . . . (With reflection) Zamor saved this foreigner; she is a French woman, and if I believe her husband, she is searching for a parent who lives in these climes. Would he be afraid to explain himself? His sorrow, his searches, his misfortunes . . . Unfortunate, if it were she . . . where is nature going to mislead me! And why am I surprised? This Foreigner's adventure is so much like my daughter's . . . and my cankered heart would like to rediscover my daughter in her. It is the fate of the wretched to cherish hope and to find consolation in the slightest connections.

JUDGE: Major, sir, advance your Soldiers. (To the Indian) Commander, sir, escort the Slaves, and line them up as customary. (The Indian exits with the armed Slaves, while a troop of the others throw themselves at the feet of M. de Saint-Frémont)

Scene X

The Same, Except the Indian (Armed Slaves are replaced by unarmed Slaves)

A SLAVE: (Kneeling) Monseigneur, we have not been among the rebels' number. May we be permitted to ask for the pardon of our comrades! To redeem their lives we would suffer the most terrible chastisements. Increase our arduous toil; reduce our food rations; we would endure this punishment with courage. Monseigneur, you are moved to tears, I see the tears in your eyes.

M. DE SAINT-FRÉMONT: My children, my friends, what are you proposing? (To the Judge) How do you want me to respond to this act of heroism? Ah! Heavens! They show such greatness of soul, and we dare to regard them as the meanest of men! Civilized men! You believe yourselves superior to Slaves! From infamy and the vilest state, equity and courage raise them in one instant to the ranks of the most generous mortals. You see the example before your eyes.

JUDGE: They know your heart well; but you cannot yield to your inclination without compromising your dignity. I know them better than you; they promise everything in these moments; besides, these criminals are no longer in your power; they are delivered to the rigor of the law.

M. DE SAINT-FRÉMONT: Well, then, I abandon them to you. Alas! Here they are. Where can I hide? How cruel this duty is!

Scene XI

The Same, Indian, Zamor, Mirza

ZAMOR: There is no longer any hope; our benefactors are surrounded by soldiers. Embrace me for the last time, my dear Mirza!

MIRZA: I bless my fate, since the same torment reunites us. (To an old man and an old Slave woman) Adieu, dear authors of my days; do not cry for your dear Mirza; she is no longer to be pitied. (To the Slaves of her sex) Adieu, my companions.

ZAMOR: Slaves, Colonists, listen to me: I have killed a man; I deserve to die. Do not regret my punishment, it is necessary for the good of the Colony. Mirza is innocent; but she cherishes her death. (To the Slaves, in particular) And you, my dear friends, listen to me in my last hour. I leave this life, I die innocent but fear rendering yourself guilty by defending me: fear especially this factious spirit, and never deliver yourselves into excess to escape slavery; fear breaking your irons with too much violence; time and divine justice are on your side; stand by the Governor and his respectable spouse. Pay them by your zeal and your attachment for all that I owe them. Alas! I cannot fulfill my obligation to them. Cherish this good Master, this good father, with a filial tenderness as I have always done. I shall die happy if I can believe at least that he will miss me! *(He throws himself at his feet)* Ah! My dear Master, am I still permitted to name you thus?

M. DE SAINT-FRÉMONT: *(With intense sorrow)* These words wring my heart. Wretched man! What have you done? Go, I no longer hold it against you; I suffer enough from the fatal duty that I fulfill.

ZAMOR: *(Bows and kisses his feet)* Ah! My dear master, death holds nothing frightful for me. You still cherish me; I die happy. *(He takes his hands)* May I kiss these hands for the last time!

M. DE SAINT-FRÉMONT: *(Full of pity)* Leave me, leave me, you are breaking my heart.

ZAMOR: *(To the armed Slaves)* My friends, do your duty. *(He takes Mirza in his arms and climbs upon the rock with her, where they both kneel. The Slaves aim their arrows)*

Scene XII

The Same, Mme de Saint-Frémont, with her Slaves, Grenadiers and French Soldiers

MME DE SAINT-FRÉMONT: Stop, Slaves, and respect your governor's wife. *(To her husband)* Mercy, my friend, mercy!

Scene XIII and last

The Same, Valère, Sophie

SOPHIE: *(To Valère)* You restrain me in vain. I absolutely want to see them. Cruel one! You deceived me. *(To Mme de Saint-Frémont)* Ah! Madame, my strength abandons me. *(She falls into the arms of the Slaves)*

MME DE SAINT-FRÉMONT: *(To her husband)* My friend, you see this French woman's despair; would you not be moved?

SOPHIE: *(Recovering herself and throwing herself at the feet of M. de Saint Frémont)* Ah Monsieur! I shall die of sorrow at your feet if you do not grant their pardon. It is within your heart and depends upon your power. Ah! If I cannot obtain it life no longer matters to me! We have lost everything. Deprived of a mother and of my fortune, abandoned at the age of five by a father, my consolation was in saving two victims who are dear to you.

M. DE SAINT-FRÉMONT: *(Aside, in the keenest agitation)* My memory . . . these features . . . that time . . . her age . . . What confusion stirs my soul. *(To Sophie)* Ah Madame! Respond to my marked attention; may I ask you the names of those who gave you birth?

SOPHIE: *(Leaning on Valère)* Alas!

VALÈRE: Oh my dear Sophie!

M. DE SAINT-FRÉMONT: *(More warmly)* Sophie . . . *(Aside)* She was named Sophie. *(Aloud)* What name did you utter . . . Speak, answer me, for pity's sake, Madame, who was your mother?

SOPHIE: *(Aside)* What confusion agitates him, the more I examine him . . . *(Aloud)* The unfortunate Clarisse de Saint-Fort was my mother.

M. DE SAINT-FRÉMONT: Ah! My daughter, recognize me. Nature did not deceive me. Recognize the voice of a father too long absent from you and from your mother.

SOPHIE: Ah! My father! I am dying. *(She falls into the arms of the Soldiers)*

M. DE SAINT-FRÉMONT: O my daughter! O my blood!

SOPHIE: What did I hear? Yes, yes it is he . . . His features are still etched in my soul . . . What good fortune makes me find myself in your arms once more! I cannot express all the feelings that agitate me. But these wretched creatures, O my father, their fate is in your hands. Without their help your daughter would have perished. Grant to nature the first favor that she asks of you. Planters, Slaves, fall at the knees of the most generous of men; one finds clemency at the feet of virtue. *(All kneel, except the Judge and the Soldiers)*

SLAVES: Monseigneur!

PLANTERS: Governor, sir!

M. DE SAINT-FRÉMONT: What do you demand of me?

ALL: Their pardon.

M. DE SAINT-FRÉMONT: *(Moved)* My children, my wife, my friends, I grant it to you.

ALL: What happiness! *(The Grenadiers and soldiers genuflect)*

MAJOR: Brave warriors, do not blush at this show of sensibility; it purifies, not vilifies, courage.

MIRZA: Bless me! You change our unhappy fate; our happiness runneth over; manifestations of your justice never cease.

M. DE SAINT-FRÉMONT: My friends, I give you your liberty and shall look after your fortune.

ZAMOR: No, my master; keep watch over your kindnesses. The most precious kindness for our hearts would be to live in your midst along with all that you hold most dear.

M. DE SAINT-FRÉMONT: What! I have found my daughter again! I clasp her in my arms. A cruel fate thus ends its pursuit of me! O my dear Sophie! How I fear to learn of your mother's cruel fate.

SOPHIE: Alas! My poor mother is no longer! But, dear father, how sweet it is for me to see you. *(To Valère)* Dear Valère!

VALÈRE: I share your happiness.

MME DE SAINT-FRÉMONT: My daughter, see in me only a tender mother. Your father knows my intentions, and you will soon learn them yourself. Let us concern ourselves only with the marriage of Zamor and Mirza.

MIRZA: We are going to live to love each other. We shall live happily ever after.

ZAMOR: Yes, my dear Mirza; yes, we shall live happily ever after.

M. DE SAINT-FRÉMONT: My friends, I have just granted you your pardon. Would that I might also give liberty to all your fellow men, or at least temper their fate! Slaves, listen to me; if ever your destiny were to change, do not lose sight of the love of the public good, which until now has been unknown to you. Know that man, in his liberty, needs still to submit to wise and humane laws, and without disposing yourselves to reprehensible excesses, place all your hopes in a benevolent and enlightened Government. Let us go, my friends, my children, so that a general holiday may be the happy presage of this sweet liberty.

End

Declaration of the Rights of Woman and Citizen (1791)

Man, are you capable of being just? It is a woman who asks you this question; at least you will not deny her this right. Tell me! Who has given you the sovereign authority to oppress my sex? Your strength? Your talents? Observe the creator in his wisdom; regard nature in all her grandeur, with which you seem to want to compare yourself; and give me, if you dare, an example of this tyrannical empire. (From Paris to Peru, from Rome to Japan, the most stupid animal, in my opinion, is man.) Go back to the animals, consult the elements, study the plants, then glance over all the modifications of organized matter, and cede to the evidence when I offer you the means. Seek, search, and distinguish, if you can, the sexes in the administration of nature. Everywhere you will find them mingled, everywhere they cooperate in harmony with this immortal masterpiece. Only man has fashioned himself a principle out of this exception. Bizarre, blind, bloated by science and degenerate, in this century of enlightenment and wisdom, he, in grossest ignorance, wishes to exercise the command of a despot over a sex that has received every intellectual faculty; he claims to rejoice in the Revolution and claims his rights to equality, at the very least.

Declaration of the Rights of Woman and Citizen

To be decreed by the National Assembly in its last meetings or in those of the next legislature.

Preamble

The mothers, daughters, and sisters, representatives of the nation, demand to be constituted a national assembly. Considering that ignorance, disregard of or contempt for the rights of women are the only causes of public misfortune and of governmental corruption, they have resolved to set forth in a solemn declaration, the natural, inalienable and sacred rights of woman; to the end that this declaration, constantly held up to all members of society, may always remind them of their rights and duties; to the end that the acts based on women's power and those based on the power of men, being constantly measured against the goal of all political institutions, may be more respected; and so that the demands of female citizens, henceforth founded on simple and indisputable principles, may ever uphold the constitution and good morals, and may contribute to the happiness of all.

Consequently, the sex that is superior in beauty as well as in courage of maternal suffering, recognizes and declares, in the presence and under the auspices of the Supreme Being, the following rights of woman and citizen.

Article One. Woman is born free and remains equal in rights to man. Social distinctions can be founded only on general utility.

II. The goal of every political association is the preservation of the natural and irrevocable rights of Woman and Man. These rights are liberty, property, security, and especially resistance to oppression.

III. The principle of all sovereignty resides essentially in the Nation, which is none other than the union of Woman and Man; no group, no individual can exercise any authority that is not derived expressly from it.

IV. Liberty and Justice consist of rendering to persons those things that belong to them; thus, the exercise of woman's natural rights is limited only by the perpetual tyranny with which man opposes her; these limits must be changed according to the laws of nature and reason.

V. The laws of nature and of reason prohibit all acts harmful to society; whatever is not prohibited by these wise and divine laws cannot be prevented, and no one can be forced to do anything unspecified by the law.

VI. The law should be the expression of the general will: all female and male citizens must participate in its elaboration personally or through their representatives. It should be the same for all; all female and male citizens, being equal in the eyes of the law, should be equally admissible to all public offices, places, and employments, according to their capacities and with no distinctions other than those of their virtues and talents.

VII. No woman is immune; she can be accused, arrested, and detained in such cases as determined by law. Women, like men, must obey these rigorous laws.

VIII. Only punishments strictly and obviously necessary may be established by law. No one may be punished except under a law established and promulgated before the offense occurred, and which is legally applicable to women.

IX. If any woman is declared guilty, then the law must be enforced rigorously.

X. No one should be punished for their opinions. Woman has the right to mount the scaffold; she should likewise have the right to speak in public, provided that her demonstrations do not disrupt public order as established by law.

XI. Free communication of thoughts and opinions is one of the most precious rights of woman, since this liberty assures the legitimate paternity of fathers with regard to their children. Every female citizen can therefore freely say: "I am the mother of a child that belongs to you," without a barbaric prejudice forcing her to conceal the truth; she must also answer for the abuse of this liberty in cases determined by law.

XII. Guarantee of the rights of woman and female citizens requires the existence of public services. Such guarantee should be established for the advantage of everyone, not for the personal benefit of those to whom these services are entrusted.

XIII. For the maintenance of public forces and administrative expenses, the contributions of women and men shall be equal; the woman shares in all forced labor and all painful tasks, therefore she should have the same share in the distribution of positions, tasks, assignments, honors, and industry.

XIV. Female and male citizens have the right to determine the need for public taxes, either by themselves or through their representatives. Female citizens can agree to this only if they are admitted to an equal share not only in wealth but also in public administration, and by determining the proportion and extent of tax collection.

XV. The mass of women, allied for tax purposes to the mass of men, has the right to hold every public official accountable for his administration.

XVI. Any society in which the guarantee of rights is not assured, or the separation of powers determined, has no constitution. The constitution is invalid if the majority of individuals who compose the Nation have not cooperated in writing it.

XVII. The right of property is inviolable and sacred to both sexes, jointly or separately. No one can be deprived of it, since it is a true inheritance of nature except when public necessity, certified by law, clearly requires it, subject to just and prior compensation.

Postamble

Woman, wake up! The tocsin of reason is sounding throughout the Universe; know your rights. The powerful empire of nature is no longer surrounded by prejudices, fanaticism, superstition and lies. The torch of truth has dispelled all the clouds of stupidity and usurpation. Man enslaved has multiplied his forces; he has had recourse to yours in order to break his own chains. Having become free, he has become unjust toward his mate. Oh Women! Women! when will you cease to be blind? What advantages have you gained in the Revolution? A more marked scorn, a more signal disdain. During centuries of corruption, you reigned only over the weakness of men. Your empire is destroyed; what then remains for you? The proof of man's injustice. The claim of your patrimony founded on the wise decrees of nature—what have you to fear from such a splendid enterprise? The good word of the legislator at the marriage of Canaan? Do you not fear that our French legislators, who are correcting this morality, which was for such a long time appended to the realm of politics but is no longer fashionable, will again say to you, "Women, what do we have in common with you?" You must answer, "Everything!" If, in their weakness, they are obstinate in drawing this conclusion contrary to their principles, you must courageously invoke the force of reason against their vain pretensions of superiority. Unite yourselves under the banner of philosophy; deploy all the energy of your character, and soon you will see these prideful ones, your adoring servants, no longer grovelling at your feet but proud to share with you the treasures of the Supreme Being. Whatever the obstacles that are put in your way, it is in your power to overturn them; you have only to will it. Let us turn now to the frightful picture of what you have been in society; and since there is currently a question of national education, let us see if our wise legislators will think wisely about the education of women.

Women have done more evil than good. They have had their share in coercion and double-dealings. When forcibly abused, they have countered with stratagems; they have had recourse to all the resources of their charms, and the most blameless among them has not hesitated to use them. They have used poison and irons; they have commanded crime and virtue alike. For centuries, the government of France in particular has depended on the nocturnal administration of women; the cabinet had no secrets from their indiscretion: embassy, military command, ministry, presidency, pontificate, cardinalate—one might say everything profane and sacred subject to the foolishness of man has been subordinated to the greed and ambition of the female sex, which was formerly contemptible and respected but, since the revolution, is respectable and yet contemptible.

What could I not say about this paradox! I have only a moment for offering a few remarks, but this moment will attract the attention of the most remote posterity. Under the Old Regime, all were vicious, all were guilty; but could one not perceive the improvement of things, even in the substance of vice? A woman needed only to be beautiful or lovable; when she possessed these two advantages, she saw a hundred fortunes at her feet. If she did not profit from this situation, she had either a bizarre character or a rare philosophy that led her to despise wealth; in such a case she was relegated to the status of a brainless person; the most indecent woman could make herself respected with enough gold; the buying and selling of women was a kind of industry taken for granted in the first rank of society, which, henceforth, will have no credit. If it did, the revolution would be lost, and under the new order we would remain ever corrupt. Still, can reason hide the fact that all other routes to fortune are closed to woman, whom man buys like a slave on the African coast? The difference is great, as we know. The slave commands the master; but if the master sets her free, without compensation, at an age when the slave has lost all her charms, what becomes of this unfortunate creature? A contemptible toy; even the doors of charity are closed to her; she is poor and old, they say; why didn't she know how to make her fortune? Other more touching examples suggest themselves to reason. A young person without experience, seduced by a man she loves, will abandon her parents to follow him; the ungrateful fellow will leave her after a few years, and the older she has grown with him, the more inhuman will his inconstancy be. If she has children, he will abandon her all the same. If he is rich, he will think

himself exempt from sharing his fortune with his noble victims. If some commitment binds him to his duties, he will violate its power by using all legal loopholes. If he is married, other commitments lose their rights. What laws then remain to be made in order to destroy vice down to its very roots? One dealing with the sharing of fortunes between men and women, and another with public administration. It is clear that a woman born to a rich family gains a great deal from equal inheritance. But a woman born to a poor family of merit and virtue—what is her fate? Poverty and shame. If she does not excel in music or painting, she cannot be admitted to any public office, even though she might be quite capable. I wish only to give an overview of things. I will examine them more thoroughly in the new edition of my political works, with notes, which I propose to offer to the public in a few days.

I resume my text with regard to morals. Marriage is the tomb of confidence and love. A married woman can, with impunity, present bastards to her husband and the bastards with the fortune that does not belong to them. An unmarried woman has merely a slim right: ancient and inhuman laws have refused her the right to the name and property of the father of her children, and no new laws on this matter have been passed. If my attempt thus to give my sex an honorable and just stability is now considered a paradox on my part, an attempt at the impossible, I must leave to men yet to come the glory of discussing this matter; but meanwhile, one can pave the way through national education, the restoration of morals, and by conjugal contracts.

Model for a Social Contract between a Man and a Woman

We, N & N, of our own free will, unite ourselves for the remainder of our lives and for the duration of our mutual inclinations, according to the following conditions: We intend and desire to pool our fortunes as community property, while nevertheless preserving the right to divide them on behalf of our own children and those we might have with someone else, mutually recognizing that our fortune belongs directly to our children, from whatever bed they might spring, and that all of them have the right to carry the name of the fathers and mothers who have acknowledged them, and we obligate ourselves to subscribe to the law that punishes the renunciation of one's own flesh and blood. We obligate ourselves equally, in case of separation, to divide our fortune, and to set apart the portion belonging to our children as indicated by the law; and in the case of perfect union, the first to die would assign half the property to their children; and if one of us should die without children, the survivor would inherit everything, unless the dying party had disposed of his half of the common wealth in favor of someone else he might deem appropriate.

Here is the general formula for the conjugal agreement I am proposing. Upon reading this unorthodox piece, I envision all the hypocrites, prudes, clergy, and their gang of diabolic followers rising up against me. But would this plan not offer to the wise a moral means of achieving the perfectibility of a happy government? I shall prove it in a few words. A rich and childless epicurean fervently thinks fit to go to his poor neighbor's house to augment his family. Once a law is passed that will authorize the rich man to adopt the poor woman's children, the bonds of society will be strengthened and its morals purified. This law would perhaps save the wealth of the community and check the disorder that leads so many victims into the refuges of shame, servility, and degeneration of human principles, where nature has so long bemoaned its oppression. May the critics of rational philosophy therefore cease to protest against primitive morals or else go bury themselves in the sources they cite. (Abraham had some very legitimate children with Agar, the servant of his wife.)

I should like a law that protects widows and maidens deceived by the false promises of a man to whom they have become attached; I would like this law to force a fickle-minded man to stand by his agreements or else provide an indemnity proportional to his fortune. Moreover, I would like this law to be rigorous against women, at least against those impudent enough to appeal to a law which they themselves have violated by their own misconduct, if this can be proved. At the same time, I would like prostitutes to be placed in designated quarters, as I discussed in 1788 in *Le Bonheur primitif de l'homme*. It is not the prostitutes who contribute most to the depravation of morals; it is the women of Society. By reeducating the latter, one can modify the former. At first this chain of fraternal union will prove disorderly, but eventually it will result in perfect harmony. I am offering an invincible means of elevating the soul of women; it is for them to join in all the activities of men. If man insists on finding this means impracticable, let him share his fortune with woman, not according to his whim, but according to the wisdom of the law. Prejudice will tumble down; customs and manners will be purified; and nature will recapture all its rights. Add to this the marriage of priests, the reaffirmation of the King on his throne, and the French government will never perish.

Mary Wollstonecraft (1759–97)

Mary Wollstonecraft was born in London in 1759 and died from complications of childbirth in 1797 when she was thirty-eight years old. Wollstonecraft's writings fall within a number of intellectual traditions and genres including feminist theory, political theory, and educational theory. She wrote political and historical works, tracts, novels, and contributions to popular periodicals. Wollstonecraft was a participant in the radical, dissenting circles in London at the end of the eighteenth century, and she was important both for her place in those conversations and for her works which were well known at the time and have come to be widely read recently. Her present-day reputation rests mostly on the Vindication of the Rights of Woman, *published in 1792, but her* Vindication of the Rights of Men, *which appeared in 1790, was the earliest attack on the prominent, conservative assessment of the French Revolution by Edmund Burke entitled* Reflections on the Revolution in France. A Vindication of the Rights of Men *received a great deal of attention when it appeared and was more important among radical intellectuals than her writings on women, which were to gain her more lasting fame.*

Wollstonecraft was in many ways a surprising member of this radical group. She came from a once-successful merchant family. Her grandfather was a wealthy weaver, but her father, with little financial or entrepreneurial sense, failed in his hopes to parlay the family's wealth into respectability as a country gentleman. Her father's financial failures meant the family moved often, and Mary was able to gain only a haphazard education. Early on, she developed an unusually adult sense of responsibility for the family's economic status and, with a close adolescent friend, Fanny Blood, pledged to work to keep the family afloat financially. She resented the time and money that was bestowed upon her eldest brother's education and career, and her family situation influenced her feminism, which focused on women's inadequate education and lack of economic independence.

Mary Wollstonecraft's need for economic stability, and her sense that she was responsible for the lives of female friends and family, led her to take positions as a companion, governess, and teacher in a girls' school and regularly to interfere in the lives of those about her for what she considered to be their own good. Following some economic setbacks and the death of her friend Fanny, she determined to move to London and become a professional writer. There she wrote for a new publication, the Analytical Review, *and had earlier made some income from her* Thoughts on the Education of Daugh-ters *(1787) and a novel,* Mary, a Fiction *(1788). In the 1790s she became more closely associated with radical pamphleteers including Protestant dissenter Richard Price and political writers such as Thomas Paine and William Godwin. She was a prolific member of that circle, writing political tracts and literary criticism and focusing, as her colleagues did not, on the continual dismissal of women as serious, rational members of society who deserved the education and public responsibility appropriate to their equal abilities.*

She is sometimes reproached for having had singularly unsuccessful relationships with men, first falling in love with Henry Fuseli, a painter, who was a married man. He did not return her affection. Likely the most disastrous of her relationships was with Gilbert Imlay, an American businessman who was trying to make money from the economic and social dislocations of the French Revolution. They met in Paris after Wollstonecraft had traveled there in 1792 to assess the progress of the revolution. They lived together out of wedlock, and she had a daughter whom she called Fanny after her dead friend. As Imlay's interest in her waned she twice attempted suicide. By 1796 she returned to London to resume her writing career and put this unsuccessful relationship behind her.

After her return to London, she formed an unconventional relationship with William Godwin, the author of Political Justice *and one of the radical circle to which she had earlier belonged. She became pregnant and they married but even then maintained separate households. Her premarital pregnancy shocked much of respectable London, and Wollstonecraft's intellectual and personal reputation was disparaged following her death eleven days after the birth of her daughter, the novelist Mary Shelley. While Godwin was a better match for her than her earlier love interests, he is often criticized by feminist scholars for not maintaining all of Wollstonecraft's works and for emphasizing her unorthodox personal life over the intellectual and literary contributions of her writings.*

As noted earlier, the Vindication of the Rights of Woman *has gained Wollstonecraft a lasting reputation among feminist theorists. Her emphasis within that work on the superficial lives of most middle- and upper-class women and on the necessity to recognize women's rational natures laid the groundwork for many of the writings and efforts of those in nineteenth-century women's rights organizations. She argued strongly for the reformation of girls' education and the need for advanced training for women. Such views undergirded the efforts of women in the nineteenth century to establish women's colleges, to seek admission for women to various professions, to pass married women's property acts so that middle- and upper-class women could keep control of their property following marriage, and to allow women to support themselves independently.*

Her Vindication of the Rights of Men, *which has received much less attention either by feminist scholars or by political theorists, argued cogently and strongly against Burke's glorification of the British constitutional structure in which gradual change and political reform based on legislative bodies such as the British parliament was superior to radical or revolutionary change tied to events such as the French Revolution. She introduced arguments on property and class divisions, similar to some later offered by Karl Marx, to contend that only a limited number of citizens and interests were heard through British constitutionalism. As happened for numerous other women thinkers, Wollstonecraft's general political works have been subordinated to her writings and views about women, even though they were widely discussed during her lifetime. Thus it is valuable for us to reassess this work that appeared before her major feminist work, to understand the range of her contributions to radical debates and British reactions to the French Revolution in the late 1700s, and to understand the general social and political principles which underlay the* Vindication of the Rights of Woman.

The first printing of A Vindication of the Rights of Men *appeared anonymously in 1790; the excerpts below are from the second printing, in which the author's name was first acknowledged.*

HLS

Sources and Suggested Readings

Barker-Benfield, G. J. "Mary Wollstonecraft: Eighteenth-Century Commonwealthwoman." *Journal of the History of Ideas* 50, 1 (1989): 95–116.

Brown, Chandos Michael. "Mary Wollstonecraft, or, The Female Illuminati: The Campaign against Women and 'Modern Philosophy' in the Early Republic." *Journal of the Early Republic* 15, 3 (Fall 1995): 389–424.

Elfenbein, Andrew. "Lesbianism and Romantic Genius: The Poetry of Anne Bannerman." *ELH* 63, 4 (1996): 929–57, esp. pp. 930–35.

Falco, Maria J., ed. *Feminist Interpretations of Mary Wollstonecraft.* University Park: Pennsylvania State University Press, 1996.

Ferguson, Moira. *Colonialism and Gender Relations from Mary Wollstonecraft to Jamaica Kincaid: East Caribbean Connections.* New York: Columbia University Press, 1993.

Flexner, Eleanor. *Mary Wollstonecraft.* Baltimore: Penguin, 1973.

Frost, Cy. "Autocracy and the Matrix of Power: Issues of Propriety and Economics in the Work of Mary Wollstonecraft, Jane Austen, and Harriet Martineau." *Tulsa Studies in Women's Literature* 10, 2 (Fall 1991): 253–73.

Furniss, Tom. "Nasty Tricks and Tropes: Sexuality and Language in Mary Wollstonecraft's *Rights of Woman.*" *Studies in Romanticism* 32, 2 (Summer 1993): 177–209.

Huxman, Susan Schultz. "Mary Wollstonecraft, Margaret Fuller, and Angelina Grimke [*sic*]: Symbolic Convergence and a Nascent Rhetorical Vision." *Communication Quarterly* 44, 1 (Winter 1996): 16–28.

Jones, Vivien. "Femininity, Nationalism and Romanticism: The Politics of Gender in the Revolution Controversy." *History of European Ideas* [Great Britain] 16, 1–3 (1993): 299–305.

Kelly, Gary. *Revolutionary Feminism: The Mind and Career of Mary Wollstonecraft.* New York: St. Martin's, 1992.

McCrystal, J. "Revolting Women: The Use of Revolutionary Discourse in Mary Astell and Mary Wollstonecraft Compared." *History of Political Thought* 14, 2 (Summer 1993): 189–204.

Mulholland, Joan. "Constructing Woman's Authority: A Study of Wollstonecraft's Rhetoric in Her *Vindication,* 1792." *Prose Studies* 18, 2 (1995): 171–87.

Nicholson, Mervyn. "The Eleventh Commandment: Sex and Spirit in Wollstonecraft and Malthus." *Journal of the History of Ideas* 51, 3 (1990): 401–21.

Offen, Karen. "Was Mary Wollstonecraft a Feminist? A Contextual Re-Reading of *A Vindication of the Rights of Woman,* 1792–1992." In *Quilting a New Canon,* ed. Uma Parameswaran. Toronto: Sister Vision, Black Women and Women of Colour Press, 1996.

Ravetz, Alison. "The Trivialisation of Mary Wollstonecraft: A Personal and Professional Career Re-Vindicated." *Women's Studies International Forum* 6, 5 (1983): 491–99.

Sapiro, Virginia. *A Vindication of Political Virtue: The Political Theory of Mary Wollstonecraft.* Chicago: University of Chicago Press, 1992.

Spender, Dale. "Mary Wollstonecraft and Her Foremothers." In her *Women of Ideas and What Men Have Done to Them.* London: Routledge & Kegan Paul, 1982.

Taylor, Barbara. "Mary Wollstonecraft and the Wild Wish of Early Feminism." *History Workshop Journal* [Great Britain] 33 (1992): 197–219.

Weiss, Penny A. "Wollstonecraft and Rousseau: The Gendered Fate of Political Theorists." In *Feminist Interpretations of Mary Wollstonecraft,* ed. Maria J. Falco. University Park: Pennsylvania State University Press, 1996.

Wilson, Anna. "Mary Wollstonecraft and the Search for the Radical Woman." *Genders* 6 (1989): 88–101.

Wollstonecraft, Mary. *Political Writings.* Ed. Janet Todd. Toronto: University of Toronto Press, 1993.

———. *A Vindication of the Rights of Men, in a Letter to the Right Honourable Edmund Burke; occasioned by his Reflections on the Revolution in France.* 2nd ed. London: Printed for J. Johnson, 1790.

———. *A Vindication of the Rights of Men* and *A Vindication of the Rights of Woman*. Ed. Sylvana Tomaselli. Cambridge: Cambridge University Press (Cambridge Texts in the History of Political Thought), 1995.

———. *The Works of Mary Wollstonecraft*. Ed. Janet Todd and Marilyn Butler. New York: New York University Press, 1989.

A *Vindication of the Rights of Men* (1790)

In a Letter to the Right Honourable Edmund Burke; Occasioned by His Reflections on the Revolution in France

Advertisement.

Mr. Burke's Reflections on the French Revolution first engaged my attention as the transient topic of the day; and reading more for amusement than information, my indignation was roused by the sophistical arguments, that every moment crossed me, in the questionable shape of natural feelings and common sense.

Many pages of the following letter were the effusions of the moment; but, swelling imperceptibly to a considerable size, the idea was suggested of publishing a short vindication of *the Rights of Men*.

Not having leisure or patience to follow this desultory writer through all the devious tracks in which his fancy has started fresh game, I have confined my strictures, in a great measure, to the grand principles at which he has levelled many ingenious arguments in a very specious garb.

Sir,

It is not necessary, with courtly insincerity, to apologise to you for thus intruding on your precious time, not to profess that I think it an honour to discuss an important subject with a man whose literary abilities have raised him to notice in the state. I have not yet learned to twist my periods, nor, in the equivocal idiom of politeness, to disguise my sentiments, and imply what I should be afraid to utter: if, therefore, in the course of this epistle, I chance to express contempt, and even indignation, with some emphasis, I beseech you to believe that it is not a flight of fancy; for truth, in morals, has ever appeared to me the essence of the sublime; and, in taste, simplicity the only criterion of the beautiful. But I war not with an individual when I contend for the *rights of men* and the liberty of reason. You see I do not condescend to cull my words to avoid the invidious phrase, nor shall I be prevented from giving a manly definition of it, by the flimsy ridicule which a lively fancy has interwoven with the present acceptation of the term. Reverencing the rights of humanity, I shall dare to assert them; not intimidated by the horse laugh that you have raised, or waiting till time has wiped away the compassionate tears which you have elaborately laboured to excite.

From the many just sentiments interspersed through the letter before me, and from the whole tendency of it, I should believe you to be a good, though a vain man, if some circumstances in your conduct did not render the inflexibility of your integrity doubtful; and for this vanity a knowledge of human nature enables me to discover such extenuating circumstances, in the very texture of your mind, that I am ready to call it amiable, and separate the public from the private character.

I know that a lively imagination renders a man particularly calculated to shine in conversation and in those desultory productions where method is disregarded; and the instantaneous applause which his eloquence extorts is at once a reward and a spur. Once a wit and always a wit, is an aphorism that has received the sanction of experience; yet I am apt to conclude that the man who with scrupulous anxiety endeavours to support that shining character, can never nourish by reflection any profound, or, if you please, metaphysical passion. . . .

And though some dry reasoner might whisper that the arguments were superficial, and should even add, that the feelings which are thus ostentatiously displayed are often the cold declamation of the head, and not the effusions of the heart—what will these shrewd remarks avail, when the witty arguments and ornamental feelings are on a level with the comprehension of the fashionable world, and a book is found very amusing? Even the Ladies, Sir, may repeat your sprightly sallies, and retail in theatrical attitudes many of your sentimental exclamations. Sensibility is the *manie* of the day, and compassion the virtue which is to cover a multitude of vices, whilst justice is left to mourn in sullen silence, and balance truth in vain.

In life, an honest man with a confined understanding is frequently the slave of his habits and the dupe of his feelings, whilst the man with a clearer head and colder heart makes the passions of others bend to his interest; but truly sublime is the character that acts from principle, and governs the inferior springs of activity without slackening their vigour; whose feelings give vital heat to his resolves, but never hurry him into feverish eccentricities. . . .

Quitting now the flowers of rhetoric, let us, Sir, reason together; and, believe me, I should not have meddled with these troubled waters, in order to point out your inconsistencies, if your wit had not burnished up some rusty, baneful opinions, and swelled the shallow current of ridicule till it resembled the flow of reason, and presumed to be the test of truth.

I shall not attempt to follow you through 'horse-way and foot-path;' but, attacking the foundation of your opinions, I shall leave the superstructure to find a centre of gravity on which it may lean till some strong blast puffs it into air; or your teeming fancy, which the ripening judgment of sixty years has not tamed, produces another Chinese erection, to stare, at every turn, the plain country people in the face, who bluntly call such an airy edifice—a folly.

The birthright of man, to give you, Sir, a short definition of this disputed right, is such a degree of liberty, civil and religious, as is compatible with the liberty of every other individual with whom he is united in a social compact, and the continued existence of that compact.

Liberty, in this simple, unsophisticated sense, I acknowledge, is a fair idea that has never yet received a form in the various governments that have been established on our beauteous globe; the demon of property has ever been at hand to encroach on the sacred rights of men, and to fence round with awful pomp laws that war with justice. But that it results from the eternal foundation of right—from immutable truth—who will presume to deny, that pretends to rationality—if reason has led them to build their morality and religion on an everlasting foundation—the attributes of God?

I glow with indignation when I attempt, methodically, to unravel your slavish paradoxes, in which I can find no fixed first principle to refute; I shall not, therefore, condescend to shew where you affirm in one page what you deny in another; and how frequently you draw conclusions without any previous premises:—it would be something like cowardice to fight with a man who had never exercised the weapons with which his opponent chose to combat, and irksome to refute sentence after sentence in which the latent spirit of tyranny appeared.

I perceive, from the whole tenor of your Reflections, that you have a moral antipathy to reason; but, if there is any thing like argument, or first principles, in your wild declamation, behold the result:—that we are to reverence the rust of antiquity, and term the unnatural customs, which ignorance and mistaken self-interest have consolidated, the sage fruit of experience; nay, that, if we do discover some errors, our *feelings* should lead us to excuse, with blind love, or unprincipled filial affection, the venerable vestiges of ancient days. These are gothic notions of beauty—the ivy is beautiful, but, when it insidiously destroys the trunk from which it receives support, who would not grub it up?

Further, that we ought cautiously to remain for ever in frozen inactivity, because a thaw, whilst it nourishes the soil, spreads a temporary inundation; and the fear of risking any personal present convenience should prevent a struggle for the most estimable advantages. This is sound reasoning, I grant, in the mouth of the rich and short-sighted.

Yes, sir, the strong gained riches, the few have sacrificed the many to their vices; and, to be able to pamper their appetites, and supinely exist without exercising mind or body, they have ceased to be men.—Lost to the relish of true pleasure, such beings would, indeed, deserve compassion, if injustice was not softened by the tyrant's plea—necessity; if prescription was not raised as an immortal boundary against innovation. Their minds, in fact, instead of being cultivated, have been so warped by education, that it may require some ages to bring them back to nature, and enable them to see their true interest, with that degree of conviction which is necessary to influence their conduct.

The civilization which has taken place in Europe has been very partial, and, like every custom that an arbitrary point of honour has established, refines the manners at the expence of morals, by making sentiments and opinions current in conversation that have no root in the heart, or weight in the cooler resolves of the mind.—And what has stopped its progress?—hereditary property—hereditary honours. The man has been changed into an artificial monster by the station in which he was born, and the consequent homage that benumbed his faculties like the torpedo's touch;—or a being, with a capacity of reasoning, would not have failed to discover, as his faculties unfolded, that true happiness arose from the friendship and intimacy which can only be enjoyed by equals; and that charity is not a condescending distribution of alms, but an intercourse of good offices and mutual benefits, founded on respect for justice and humanity.

Governed by these principles, the poor wretch, whose *inelegant* distress extorted from a mixed feeling of disgust and animal sympathy present relief, would have been considered as a man, whose misery demanded a part of his birthright, supposing him to be industrious; but should his vices have reduced him to poverty, he could only have addressed his fellow-men as weak beings, subject to like passions, who ought to forgive, because they expect to be forgiven, for suffering the impulse of the moment to silence the suggestions of conscience, or reason, which you will; for, in my view of things, they are synonymous terms.

Will Mr. Burke be at the trouble to inform us, how far we are to go back to discover the rights of men, since the light of reason is such a fallacious guide that none but fools trust to its cold investigation?

In the infancy of society, confining our view to our own country, customs were established by the lawless power of an ambitious individual; or a weak prince was obliged to comply with every demand of the licentious barbarous insurgents, who disputed his authority with irrefragable arguments at the point of their swords; or the more specious requests of the Parliament, who only allowed him conditional supplies.

Are these the venerable pillars of our constitution? And is Magna Charta to rest for its chief support on a former grant, which reverts to another, till chaos becomes the base of the mighty structure—or we cannot tell what?—for coherence, without some pervading principle of order, is a solecism. . . .

The imperfection of all modern governments must, without waiting to repeat the trite remark, that all human institutions are unavoidably imperfect, in a great measure have arisen from this simple circumstance, that the constitution, if such an heterogeneous mass deserve that name, was settled in the dark days of ignorance, when the minds of men were shackled by the grossest prejudices and most immoral superstition. And do you, Sir, a sagacious philosopher, recommend night as the fittest time to analyze a ray of light?

Are we to seek for the rights of men in the ages when a few marks were the only penalty imposed for the life of a man, and death for death when the property of the rich was touched? when—I blush to discover the depravity of our nature—when a deer was killed! Are these the laws that it is natural to love, and sacrilegious to invade?—Were the rights of men understood when the law authorized or tolerated murder?—or is power and right the same in your creed?

But in fact all your declamation leads so directly to this conclusion, that I beseech you to ask your own heart, when you call yourself a friend of liberty whether it would not be more consistent to style yourself the champion of property, the adorer of the golden image which power has set up?—And, when you are examining your heart, if it would not be too much like mathematical drudgery, to which a fine imagination very reluctantly stoops, enquire further, how it is consistent with the vulgar notions of honesty, and the foundation of morality—truth; for a man to boast of his virtue and independence, when he cannot forget that he is at the moment enjoying the wages of falsehood (see Mr. Burke's Bills for œconomical reform); and that, in a skulking, unmanly way, he has secured himself a pension of fifteen hundred pounds per annum on the Irish establishment? Do honest men, Sir, for I am not rising to the refined principle of honour, ever receive the reward of their public services, or secret assistance, in the name of *another*?

But to return from a digression which you will more perfectly understand than any of my readers—on what principle you, Sir, can justify the reformation, which tore up by the roots an old establishment, I cannot guess—but, I beg your pardon, perhaps you do not wish to justify it—and have some mental reservation to excuse you, to yourself, for not openly avowing your reverence. Or, to go further back;—had you been a Jew—you would have joined in the cry—crucify him! The promulgator of a new doctrine, and the violator of old laws and customs, that not melting like ours, into darkness and ignorance, rested on Divine authority, must have been a dangerous innovator, in your eyes, particularly if you had not been informed that the Carpenter's Son was of the stock and lineage of David. But there is no end to the arguments which might be deduced to combat such palpable absurdities, by shewing the manifest inconsistencies which are necessarily involved in a direful train of false opinions.

It is necessary emphatically to repeat, that there are rights which men inherit at their birth, as rational creatures, who were raised above the brute creation by their improvable faculties; and that, in receiving these, not from their forefathers but, from God, prescription can never undermine natural rights.

A father may dissipate his property without his child having any right to complain;—but should he attempt to sell him for a slave, or fetter him with laws contrary to reason; nature, in enabling him to discern good from evil, teaches him to break the ignoble chain, and not to believe that bread becomes flesh, and wine blood, because his parents swallowed the Eucharist with this blind persuasion.

There is no end to this implicit submission to authority—some where it must stop, or we return to barbarism; and the capacity of improvement, which gives us a natural sceptre on earth, is a cheat, an *ignisfatuus*, that leads us from inviting meadows into bogs and dung-hills. And if it be allowed that many of the precautions, with which any alteration was made, in our government, were prudent, it rather proves its weakness than substantiates an opinion of the soundness of the stamina, or the excellence of the constitution.

But on what principle Mr. Burke could defend American independence, I cannot conceive; for the whole tenor of his plausible arguments settles slavery on an everlasting foundation. Allowing his servile reverence for antiquity, and prudent attention to self-interest to have the force which he insists on, the slave trade ought never to be abolished; and, because our ignorant forefathers, not understanding the native dignity of man, sanctioned a traffic that outrages every suggestion of reason and religion, we are to submit to the inhuman custom, and term an atrocious insult to humanity the love of our country, and a proper submission to the laws by which our property is secured.

—Security of property! Behold, in a few words, the definition of English liberty. And to this selfish principle every nobler one is sacrificed.—The Briton takes place of the man, and the image of God is lost in the citizen! But it is not that enthusiastic flame which in Greece and Rome consumed every sordid passion: no, self is the focus; and the disparting rays rise not above our foggy atmosphere. But softly—it is only the property of the rich that is secure; the man who lives by the sweat of his brow has no asylum from oppression; the strong man may enter—when was the castle of the poor sacred? and the base informer steal him from the family that depend on his industry for subsistence.

Fully sensible as you must be of the baneful consequences that inevitably follow this notorious infringement on the dearest rights of men, and that it is an infernal blot on the very face of our immaculate constitution, I cannot avoid expressing my surprise that when you recommended our form of government as a model, you did not caution the French against the arbitrary custom of pressing men in the sea service. You should have hinted to them, that property in England is much more secure than liberty, and not have concealed that the liberty of an honest mechanic—his all—is often sacrificed to secure the property of the rich. For it is a farce to pretend that a man fights *for his country, his hearth, or his altars,* when he has neither liberty nor property.—His property is in his nervous arms—and they are compelled to pull a strange rope at the surly command of a tyrannic boy, who probably obtained his rank on account of his family connections, or the prostituted vote of his father, whose interest in a borough, or voice as a senator, was acceptable to the minister.

Our penal laws punish with death the thief who steals a few pounds; but to take by violence, or trepan, a man, is no such heinous offence.—For who shall dare to complain of the venerable vestige of the law that rendered the life of a deer more sacred than that of a man? But it was the poor man with only his native dignity who was thus oppressed—and only metaphysical sophists and cold mathematicians can discern this insubstantial form; it is a work of abstraction—and a *gentleman* of lively imagination must borrow some drapery from fancy before he can love or pity a *man.*—Misery, to reach your heart, I perceive, must have its cap and bells; your tears are reserved, very *naturally*

considering your character, for the declamation of the theatre, or for the downfall of queens, whose rank alters the nature of folly, and throws a graceful veil over vices that degrade humanity; whilst the distress of many industrious mothers, whose *helpmates* have been torn from them, and the hungry cry of helpless babes, were vulgar sorrows that could not move your commiseration, though they might extort an alms. . . .

If I were not afraid to derange your nervous system by the bare mention of a metaphysical enquiry, I should observe, sir, that self-preservation is, literally speaking, the first law of nature; and that the care necessary to support and guard the body is the first step to unfold the mind, and inspire a manly spirit of independence. The mewing babe in swaddling-clothes, who is treated like a superior being, may perchance become a gentleman; but nature must have given him uncommon faculties if, when pleasure hangs on every bough, he has sufficient fortitude either to exercise his mind or body in order to acquire personal merit. The passions are necessary auxiliaries of reason: a present impulse pushes us forward, and when we discover that the game did not deserve the chace, we find that we have gone over much ground, and not only gained many new ideas, but a habit of thinking. The exercise of our faculties is the great end, though not the goal we had in view when we started with such eagerness.

It would be straying still further into metaphysics to add, that this is one of the strongest arguments for the natural immortality of the soul.—Every thing looks like a means, nothing like an end, or point of rest, when we can say, now let us sit down and enjoy the present moment; our faculties and wishes are proportioned to the present scene; we may return without repining to our sister clod. And, if no conscious dignity whisper that we are capable of relishing more refined pleasures, the thirst of truth appears to be allayed; and thought, the faint type of an immaterial energy, no longer bounding it knows not where, is confined to the tenement that affords it sufficient variety.—The rich man may then thank his God that he is not like other men—but when is retribution to be made to the miserable, who cry day and night for help, and there is no one at hand to help them? And not only misery but immorality proceeds from this stretch of arbitrary authority. The vulgar have not the power of emptying their mind of the only ideas they imbibed whilst their hands were employed; they cannot quickly turn from one kind of life to another. Pressing them entirely unhinges their minds; they acquire new habits, and cannot return to their old occupations with their former readiness; consequently they fall into idleness, drunkenness, and the whole train of vices which you stigmatise as gross.

A government that acts in this manner cannot be called a good parent, nor inspire natural (habitual is the proper word) affection, in the breasts of children who are thus disregarded.

The game laws are almost as oppressive to the peasantry as press-warrants to the mechanic. In this land of liberty what is to secure the property of the poor farmer when his noble landlord chooses to plant a decoy field near his little property? Game devour the fruit of his labour; but fines and imprisonment await him if he dare to kill any—or lift up his hand to interrupt the pleasure of his lord. How many families have been plunged, in the *sporting* countries, into misery and vice for some paltry transgression of these coercive laws, by the natural consequence of that anger which a man feels when he sees the reward of his industry laid waste by unfeeling luxury?—when his children's bread is given to dogs!

You have shewn, Sir, by your silence on these subjects, that your respect for rank has swallowed up the common feelings of humanity; you seem to consider the poor as only the live stock of an estate, the feather of hereditary nobility. When you had so little respect for the silent majority of misery, I am not surprised at your manner of treating an individual whose brow a mitre will never grace, and whose popularity may have wounded your vanity—for vanity is ever sore. Even in France, Sir, before the revolution, literary celebrity procured a man the treatment of a gentleman; but you are going back for your credentials of politeness to more distant times.—Gothic affability is the mode you think proper to adopt, the condescension of a Baron, not the civility of a liberal man. Politeness is, indeed, the only substitute for humanity; or what distinguishes the civilised man from the unlettered savage? And he who is not governed by reason should square his behaviour by an arbitrary standard; but by what rule your attack on Dr. Price was regulated we have yet to learn. . . .

Dr. Price, when he reasons on the necessity of men attending some place of public worship, concisely obviates an objection that has been made in the form of an apology, by advising those, who do not approve of our Liturgy, and cannot find any mode of worship out of the church, in which they can conscientiously join, to establish one for themselves. This plain advice you have tortured into a very different meaning, and represented the preacher as activated by a dissenting phrensy, recommending dissensions, 'not to diffuse truth, but to spread contradictions' (Page 15). A simple question will silence this impertinent declamation.—What is truth? A few fundamental truths meet the first enquiry of reason, and appear as clear to an unwarped mind, as that air and bread are necessary to enable the body to fulfil its vital functions; but the opinions which men discuss with so much heat must be simplified and brought back to first principles; or who can discriminate the vagaries of the imagination, or scrupulosity of weakness, from the verdict of reason? Let all these points be demonstrated, and not determined by arbitrary authority and dark traditions, lest a dangerous supineness should take place; for probably, in ceasing to enquire, our reason would remain dormant, and delivered up, without a curb, to every impulse of passion, we might soon lose sight of the clear light which the exercise of our understanding no longer kept alive. To argue from experience, it should seem as if the human mind, averse to thought, could only be opened by necessity; for, when it can take opinions on trust, it gladly lets the spirit lie quiet in its gross tenement. Perhaps the most improving exercise of the mind, confining the argument to the enlargement of the understanding, is the restless enquiries that hover on the boundary, or stretch over the dark abyss of uncertainty. These lively conjectures are the breezes that preserve the still lake from stagnating. We should be aware of confining all moral excellence to one channel, however capacious; or, if we are so narrow-minded, we should not forget how much we owe to chance that our inheritance was not Mahometism; and that the iron hand of destiny, in the shape of deeply rooted authority, has not suspended the sword of destruction over our heads. But to return to the misrepresentation.

Blackstone, to whom Mr. Burke pays great deference, seems to agree with Dr Price, that the succession of the King of Great Britain depends on the choice of the people, or that they have a power to cut it off; but this power, as you have fully proved, has been cautiously exerted, and might with more propriety be termed a *right* than a power. Be it so!—yet when you elaborately cited precedents to shew that our forefathers paid great respect to hereditary claims, you might have gone back to your favourite epoch, and shewn their respect for a church that fulminating laws have since loaded with opprobrium. The preponderance of inconsistencies, when weighed with precedents, should lessen the most bigotted veneration for antiquity, and force men of the eighteenth century to acknowledge, that our *canonized forefathers* were unable, or afraid, to revert to reason, without resting on the crutch of authority; and should not be brought as a proof that their children are never to be allowed to walk alone.

When we doubt the infallible wisdom of our ancestors, it is only advancing on the same ground to doubt the sincerity of the law, and the propriety of that servile appellation—our Sovereign Lord the King. Who were the dictators of this adulatory language of the law? Were they not courtly parasites and worldly priests? Besides, whoever at divine service, whose feelings were not deadened by habit, or their understanding quiescent, ever repeated without horror the same epithets applied to a man and his Creator? . . .

You further sarcastically animadvert on the consistency of the democratists, by wresting the obvious meaning of a common phrase, *the dregs of the people*; or your contempt for poverty may have led you into an error. Be that as it may, an unprejudiced man would have directly perceived the single sense of the word, and an old Member of Parliament could scarcely have missed it. He who had so often felt the pulse of the electors needed not have gone beyond his own experience to discover that the dregs alluded to were the vicious, and not the lower class of the community.

Again, Sir, I must doubt your sincerity or your discernment. — You have been behind the curtain; and, though it might be difficult to bring back your sophisticated heart to nature and make you feel like a man, yet the awestruck confusion in which you were plunged must have gone off when the vulgar emotion of wonder, excited by finding yourself a Senator, had subsided. Then you must have seen the clogged wheels of corruption continually oiled by the sweat of the laborious poor, squeezed out of them by unceasing taxation. You must have discovered that the majority in the House of Commons was often purchased by the crown, and that the people were oppressed by the influence of their own money, extorted by the venal voice of a packed representation.

You must have known that a man of merit cannot rise in the church, the army, or navy, unless he has some interest in a borough; and that even a paltry exciseman's place can only be secured by electioneering interest. I will go further, and assert that few Bishops, though there have been learned and good bishops, have gained the mitre without submitting to a servility of dependence that degrades the man. — All these circumstances you must have known, yet you talk of virtue and liberty, as the vulgar talk of the letter of the law; and the polite of propriety. It is true that these ceremonial observances produce decorum; the sepulchres are white-washed, and do not offend the squeamish eyes of high rank; but virtue is out of the question when you only worship a shadow, and worship it to secure your property.

Man has been termed, with strict propriety, a microcosm, a little world in himself. — He is so; — yet must, however, be reckoned an ephemera, or, to adopt your figure of rhetoric, a summer's fly. The perpetuation of property in our families is one of the privileges you most warmly contend for; yet it would not be very difficult to prove that the mind must have a very lim-

ited range that thus confines its benevolence to such a narrow circle, which, with great propriety, may be included in the sordid calculations of blind self-love.

A brutal attachment to children has appeared most conspicuous in parents who have treated them like slaves, and demanded due homage for all the property they transferred to them, during their lives. It has led them to force their children to break the most sacred ties; to do violence to a natural impulse, and run into legal prostitution [i.e., marriage — BAC] to increase wealth or shun poverty; and, still worse, the dread of parental malediction has made many weak characters violate truth in the face of Heaven; and, to avoid a father's angry curse, the most sacred promises have been broken. It appears to be a natural suggestion of reason, that a man should be freed from implicit obedience to parents and private punishments, when he is of an age to be subject to the jurisdiction of the laws of his country; and that the barbarous cruelty of allowing parents to imprison their children, to prevent their contaminating their noble blood by following the dictates of nature when they chose to marry, or for any misdemeanor that does not come under the cognizance of public justice, is one of the most arbitrary violations of liberty.

Who can recount all the unnatural crimes which the *laudable, interesting* desire of perpetuating a name has produced? The younger children have been sacrificed to the eldest son; sent into exile, or confined in convents, that they might not encroach on what was called, with shameful falsehood, the *family* estate. Will Mr. Burke call this parental affection reasonable or virtuous? — No; it is the spurious offspring of overweening, mistaken pride — and not that first source of civilization, natural parental affection, that makes no difference between child and child, but what reason justifies by pointing out superior merit.

Another pernicious consequence which unavoidably arises from this artificial affection is, the insuperable bar which it puts in the way of early marriages. It would be difficult to determine whether the minds or bodies of our youth are most injured by this impediment. Our young men become selfish coxcombs, and gallantry with modest women, and intrigues with those of another description, weaken both mind and body, before either has arrived at maturity. The character of a master of a family, a husband, and a father, forms the citizen imperceptibly, by producing a sober manliness of thought, and orderly behaviour; but, from the lax morals and depraved affections of the libertine, what results? — a sinical man of taste, who is only anxious to secure his own private gratifications, and to maintain his rank in society.

The same system has an equally pernicious effect

on female morals.—Girls are sacrificed to family convenience, or else marry to settle themselves in a superior rank, and coquet, without restraint, with the fine gentleman whom I have already described. And to such lengths has this vanity, this desire of shining, carried them, that it is not now necessary to guard girls against imprudent love matches; for if some widows did not now and then *fall* in love, Love and Hymen would seldom meet, unless at a village church.

I do not intend to be sarcastically paradoxical when I say, that women of fashion take husbands that they may have it in their power to coquet, the grand business of genteel life, with a number of admirers, and thus flutter the spring of life away, without laying up any store for the winter of age, or being of any use to society. Affection in the marriage state can only be founded on respect—and are these weak beings respectable? Children are neglected for lovers and we express surprise that adulteries are so common! A woman never forgets to adorn herself to make an impression on the senses of the other sex, and to extort the homage which it is gallant to pay, and yet we wonder that they have such confined understandings.

Have ye not heard that we cannot serve two masters? An immoderate desire to please contracts the faculties, and immerges, to borrow the idea of a great philosopher, the soul in matter, till it becomes unable to mount on the wing of contemplation.

It would be an arduous task to trace all the vice and misery that arise in society from the middle class of people apeing the manners of the great. All are aiming to procure respect on account of their property; and most places are considered as sinecures that enable men to start into notice. The grand concern of three parts out of four is to contrive to live above their equals, and to appear to be richer than they are. How much domestic comfort and private satisfaction is sacrificed to this irrational ambition! It is a destructive mildew that blights the fairest virtues; benevolence, friendship, generosity, and all those endearing charities which bind human hearts together, and the pursuits which raise the mind to higher contemplations, all that were not cankered in the bud by the false notions that 'grew with its growth and strengthened with its strength,' are crushed by the iron hand of property!

Property, I do not scruple to aver it, should be fluctuating, which would be the case, if it were more equally divided amongst all the children of a family; else it is an everlasting rampart, in consequence of a barbarous feudal institution, that enables the elder son to overpower talents and depress virtue. . . .

The only security of property that nature authorizes and reason sanctions is, the right a man has to enjoy the acquisitions which his talents and industry have acquired; and to bequeath them to whom he chooses. Happy would it be for the world if there were no other road to wealth or honour; if pride, in the shape of parental affection, did not absorb the man, and prevent friendship from having the same weight as relationship. Luxury and effeminacy would not then introduce so much idiotism into the noble families which form one of the pillars of our state: the ground would not lie fallow, nor would undirected activity of mind spread the contagion of restless idleness, and its concomitant, vice, through the whole mass of society.

Instead of gaming they might nourish a virtuous ambition, and love might take place of the gallantry which you, with knightly fealty, venerate. Women would probably then act like mothers, and the fine lady, become a rational woman, might think it necessary to superintend her family and suckle her children, in order to fulfil her part of the social compact. But vain is the hope, whilst great masses of property are hedged round by hereditary honours; for numberless vices, forced in the hot-bed of wealth, assume a sightly form to dazzle the senses and cloud the understanding. The respect paid to rank and fortune damps every generous purpose of the soul, and stifles the natural affections on which human contentment ought to be built. Who will venturously ascend the steeps of virtue, or explore the great deep for knowledge, when *the one thing needful*, attained by less arduous exertions, if not inherited, procures the attention man naturally pants after, and vice 'loses half its evil by losing all its grossness' (Page 113).—What a sentiment to come from a moral pen!

A surgeon would tell you that by skinning over a wound you spread disease through the whole frame; and, surely, they indirectly aim at destroying all purity of morals, who poison the very source of virtue, by smearing a sentimental varnish over vice, to hide its natural deformity. . . .

'On this scheme of things (p. 114) a king *is* but a man; a queen *is* but a woman; a woman *is* but an animal, and an animal not of the highest order.'—All true, Sir; if she is not more attentive to the duties of humanity than queens and fashionable ladies in general are. I will still further accede to the opinion you have so justly conceived of the spirit which begins to animate this age.—'All homage paid to the sex in general, as such, and without distinct views, is to be regarded as *romance* and folly.' Undoubtedly; because such homage vitiates them, prevents their endeavouring to obtain solid personal merit; and, in short, makes those beings vain inconsiderate dolls, who ought to be prudent mothers and useful members of society. 'Regicide and sacrilege are but fictions of superstition corrupting jurisprudence, by destroying its simplicity.

The murder of a king, or a queen, or a bishop, are only common homicide.'—Again I agree with you. . . .

It is an arduous task to follow the doublings of cunning, or the subterfuges of inconsistency; for in controversy, as in battle, the brave man wishes to face his enemy, and fight on the same ground. Knowing, however, the influence of a ruling passion, and how often it assumes the form of reason when there is much sensibility in the heart, I respect an opponent, though he tenaciously maintains opinions in which I cannot coincide; but, if I once discover that many of those opinions are empty rhetorical flourishes, my respect is soon changed into that pity which borders on contempt; and the mock dignity and haughty stalk, only reminds me of the ass in the lion's skin.

A sentiment of this kind glanced across my mind when I read the following exclamation. 'Whilst the royal captives, who followed in the train, were slowly moved along, amidst the horrid yells, and shrilling screams, and frantic dances, and infamous contumelies, and all the unutterable abominations of the furies of hell, in the abused shape of the vilest of women' (Page 106). Probably you mean women who gained a livelihood by selling vegetables or fish, who never had had any advantages of education; or their vices might have lost part of their abominable deformity, by losing part of their grossness. The queen of France—the great and small vulgar, claim our pity; they have almost insuperable obstacles to surmount in their progress towards true dignity of character; still I have such a plain downright understanding that I do not like to make a distinction without a difference. But it is not very extraordinary that *you* should, for throughout your letter you frequently advert to a sentimental jargon, which has long been current in conversation, and even in books of morals, though it never received the *regal* stamp of reason. A kind of mysterious instinct is *supposed* to reside in the soul, that instantaneously discerns truth, without the tedious labour of ratiocination. This instinct, for I know not what other name to give it, has been termed *common sense*, and more frequently *sensibility*; and, by a kind of *indefeasible* right, it has been *supposed*, for rights of this kind are not easily proved, to reign paramount over the other faculties of the mind, and to be an authority from which there is no appeal. . . .

Children are born ignorant, consequently innocent; the passions, are neither good nor evil dispositions, till they receive a direction, and either bound over the feeble barrier raised by a faint glimmering of unexercised reason, called conscience, or strengthen her wavering dictates till sound principles are deeply rooted, and able to cope with the headstrong passions that often assume her awful form. What moral purpose can be answered by extolling good dispositions, as they are called, when these good dispositions are described as instincts; for instinct moves in a direct line to its ultimate end, and asks not for guide or support. But if virtue is to be acquired by experience, or taught by example, reason, perfected by reflection, must be the director of the whole host of passions, which produce a fructifying heat, but no light, that you would exalt into her place. —She must hold the rudder, or, let the wind blow which way it list, the vessel will never advance smoothly to its destined port; for the time lost in tacking about would dreadfully impede its progress.

In the name of the people of England, you say, 'that we know *we* have made no discoveries; and we think that no discoveries are to be made in morality; nor many in the great principles of government, nor in the ideas of liberty, which were understood long before we were born, altogether as well as they will be after the grave has heaped its mould upon our presumption, and the silent tomb shall have imposed its law on our pert loquacity. In England we have not yet been completely emboweled of our natural entrails; we still feel within us, and we cherish and cultivate those inbred sentiments which are faithful guardians, the active monitors of our duty, the true supporters of all liberal and manly morals' (Page 128). —What do you mean by inbred sentiments? From whence do they come? How were they bred? Are they the brood of folly, which swarm like the insects on the banks of the Nile, when mud and putrefaction have enriched the languid soil? Were these *inbred* sentiments faithful guardians of our duty when the church was an asylum for murderers, and men worshipped bread as a God? when slavery was authorized by law to fasten her fangs on human flesh, and the iron eat into the very soul? If these sentiments are not acquired, if our passive dispositions do not expand into virtuous affections and passions, why are not the Tartars in the first rude horde endued with sentiments white and *elegant* as the driven snow? Why is passion or heroism the child of reflection, the consequence of dwelling with intent contemplation on one object? The appetites are the only perfect inbred powers that I can discern; and they like instincts have a certain aim, they can be satisfied—but improveable reason has not yet discovered the perfection it may arrive at—God forbid!

First, however, it is necessary to make what we know practical. Who can deny, that has marked the slow progress of civilization, that men may become more virtuous and happy without any new discovery in morals? Who will venture to assert that virtue would not be promoted by the more extensive cultivation of reason? If nothing more is to be done, let us eat and drink, for to-morrow we die—and die for ever! Who will pretend to say, that there is as much happiness diffused on this globe as it is capable of affording? as many social virtues as reason would foster, if she could gain the strength she is able to acquire even in this imperfect state; if the voice of nature was allowed to speak audibly from the bottom of the heart, and the *native* unalienable rights of men were recognized in their full force; if factitious merit did not take place of genuine acquired virtue, and enable men to build their enjoyment on the misery of their fellow creatures; if men were more under the dominion of reason than opinion, and did not cherish their prejudices 'because they were prejudices?' (Page 129). I am not, Sir, aware of your sneers, hailing a millennium, though a state of greater purity of morals may not be a mere poetic fiction; nor did my fancy ever create a heaven on earth, since reason threw off her swaddling clothes. I perceive, but too forcibly, that happiness, literally speaking, dwells not here; — and that we wander to and fro in a vale of darkness as well as tears. I perceive that my passions pursue objects that the imagination enlarges, till they become only a sublime idea that shrinks from the enquiry of sense, and mocks the experimental philosophers who would confine this spiritual phlogiston in their material crucibles. I know that the human understanding is deluded with vain shadows, and that when we eagerly pursue any study, we only reach the boundary set to human enquires. — Thus far shalt thou go, and no further, says some stern difficulty; and the cause we were pursuing melts into utter darkness. But these are only the trials of contemplative minds, the foundation of virtue remains firm. — The power of exercising our understanding raises us above the brutes; and this exercise produces that 'primary morality,' which you term 'untaught feelings.'

If virtue be an instinct, I renounce all hope of immortality; and with it all the sublime reveries and dignified sentiments that have smoothed the rugged path of life: it is all a cheat, a lying vision; I have disquieted myself in vain; for in my eye all feelings are false and spurious, that do not rest on justice as their foundation, and are not concentred by universal love.

I reverence the rights of men. — Sacred rights! For which I acquire a more profound respect, the more I look into my own mind; and, professing these heterodox opinions, I still preserve my bowels; my heart is human, beats quick with human sympathies — and I FEAR GOD!

I bend with awful reverence when I enquire on what my fear is built. — I fear that sublime power, whose motive for creating me must have been wise and good; and I submit to the moral laws which my reason deduces from this view of my dependence on him. — It is not his power that I fear — it is not to an arbitrary will, but to unerring *reason* that I submit. — Submit — yes; I disregard the charge of arrogance, to the law that regulates his just resolves. . . .

This fear of God makes me reverence myself. — Yes, Sir, the regard I have for honest fame, and the friendship of the virtuous, falls far short of the respect which I have for myself. And this, enlightened self-love, if an epithet the meaning of which has been grossly perverted will convey my idea, forces me to see; and, if I may venture to borrow a prostituted term, to *feel*, that happiness is reflected, and that, in communicating good, my soul receives its noble aliment. — I do not trouble myself, therefore, to enquire whether this is the fear the *people* of England feel: — and, if it be *natural* to include all the modifications which you have annexed — it is not (*Vide* Reflections, p. 128).

Besides, I cannot help suspecting that; if you had the enlightened respect for yourself, which you affect to despise, you would not have said that the constitution of our church and state, formed, like most other modern ones, by degrees, as Europe was emerging out of barbarism, was formed 'under the auspices, and was confirmed by the sanctions, of religion and piety.' You have turned over the historic page; have been hackneyed in the ways of men, and must know that private cabals and public feuds, private virtues and vices, religion and superstition, have all concurred to foment the mass and swell it to its present form; nay more, that it in part owes its sightly appearance to bold rebellion and insidious innovation. Factions, Sir, have been the leaven, and private interest has produced public good. . . .

Such a curious paragraph occurs in this part of your letter, that I am tempted to transcribe it, and must beg you to elucidate it, if I misconceive your meaning. ('When the people have emptied themselves of all the lust of selfish will, which without religion it is utterly impossible they ever should; when they are conscious that they exercise, and exercise perhaps in an higher link of the order of delegation, the power, which to be legitimate must be according to that eternal immutable law, in which will and reason are the same, they will be more careful how they place power in base and incapable hands. In their nomination to office, they will not appoint to the exercise of authority as to a pitiful job, but as to an holy function; not according to their sordid selfish interest, nor to their wanton caprice, nor to their arbitrary will; but they will confer that power (which any man may tremble to give or to receive) on those only, in whom they may discern that predominant proportion of active virtue and wisdom, taken together and fitted to the charge, such, as in the great and inevitable mixed mass of human imperfections and infirmities, is to be found.' P. 140.)

The only way in which the people interfere in government, religious or civil, is in electing representatives. And, Sir, let me ask you, with manly plainness—are these *holy* nominations? Where is the booth of religion? Does she mix her awful mandates, or lift her persuasive voice, in those scenes of drunken riot and beastly gluttony? Does she preside over those nocturnal abominations which so evidently tend to deprave the manners of the lower class of people? The pestilence stops not here—the rich and poor have one common nature, and many of the great families, which, on this side adoration, you venerate, date their misery, I speak of stubborn matters of fact, from the thoughtless extravagance of an electioneering frolic.— Yet, after the effervescence of spirits, raised by opposition, and all the little and tyrannic arts of canvassing are over—quiet souls! they only intend to march rank and file to say yes—or no.

Experience, I believe, will shew that sordid interest, or licentious thoughtlessness, is the spring of action at most elections.—Again, I beg you not to lose sight of my modification of general rules. So far are the people from being habitually convinced of the sanctity of the charge they are conferring, that the venality of their votes must admonish them that they have no right to expect disinterested conduct. But to return to the church, and the habitual conviction of the people of England.

So far are the people from being 'habitually convinced that no evil can be acceptable, either in the act or the permission, to him whose essence is good' (Page 140), that the sermons which they hear are to them almost as unintelligible as if they were preached in a foreign tongue. The language and sentiments rising above their capacities, very orthodox Christians are driven to fanatical meetings for amusement, if not for edification. The clergy, I speak of the body, not forgetting the respect and affection which I have for individuals, perform the duty of their profession as a kind of fee-simple, to entitle them to the emoluments accruing from it; and their ignorant flock think that merely going to church is meritorious.

So defective, in fact, are our laws, respecting religious establishments, that I have heard many rational pious clergymen complain, that they had no method of receiving their stipend that did not clog their endeavours to be useful; whilst the lives of many less conscientious rectors are passed in litigious disputes with the people they engaged to instruct; or in distant cities, in all the ease of luxurious idleness.

But you return to your old firm ground.—*Art thou there, True-penny?* Must we swear to secure property, and make assurance doubly sure, to give your perturbed spirit rest? Peace, peace to the manes of thy patriotic phrensy, which contributed to deprive some of thy fellow-citizens of their property in America: another spirit now walks abroad to secure the property of the church.—The tithes are safe!—We will not say forever—because the time may come, when the traveller may ask where proud London stood? When its *temples*, its laws, and its trade, may be buried in one common ruin, and only serve as a byword to point a moral, or furnish senators, who wage a wordy war, on the other side of the Atlantic, with tropes to swell their thundering bursts of eloquence. . . .

What, but the rapacity of the only men who exercised their reason, the priests, secured such vast property to the church, when a man gave his perishable substance to save himself from the dark torments of purgatory: and found it more convenient to indulge his depraved appetites, and pay an exorbitant price for absolution, than listen to the suggestions of reason, and work out his own salvation: in a word, was not the separation of religion from morality the work of the priests, and partly achieved in those *honourable* days which you so piously deplore?

That civilization, that the cultivation of the understanding, and refinement of the affections, naturally make a man religious, I am proud to acknowledge.— What else can fill the aching void in the heart, that human pleasures, human friendships can never fill? what else can render us resigned to live, though condemned to ignorance?—What but a profound reverence for the model of all perfection, and the mysterious tie which arises from a love of goodness? What can make us reverence ourselves, but a reverence for that Being, of whom we are a faint image? That mighty Spirit moves on the waters—confusion hears his voice, and the troubled heart ceases to beat with anguish, for trust in Him bade it be still. Conscious dignity may make us rise superior to calumny, and sternly brave the winds of adverse fortune,—raised in our own esteem by the very storms of which we are the sport—but when friends are unkind, and the heart has not the prop on which it fondly leaned, where can a tender suffering being fly but to the Searcher of hearts? and, when death has desolated the present scene, and torn from us the friend of our youth—when we walk along the accustomed path, and, almost fancying nature dead, ask, Where art thou who gave life to these well-known scenes? when memory heightens former pleasures to contrast our present prospects—there is but one source of comfort within our reach;—and in this sublime solitude the world appears to contain only the Creator and the creature, of whose happiness he is the source.—These are human feelings; but I know not of any common nature or common relation amongst men but what results from reason. The common affec-

Mary Wollstonecraft

tions and passions equally bind brutes together; and it is only the continuity of those relations that entitles us to the denomination of rational creatures; and this continuity arises from reflection—from the operations of that reason which you contemn with flippant disrespect.

If then it appears, arguing from analogy, that reflection must be the natural foundation of *rational* affections, and of that experience which enables one man to rise above another, a phenomenon that has never been seen in the brute creation, it may not be stretching the argument further than it will go to suppose, that those men who are obliged to exercise their reason have the most reason, and are the persons pointed out by Nature to direct the society of which they make a part, on any extraordinary emergency.

Time only will shew whether the general censure, which you afterwards qualify, if not contradict, and the unmerited contempt that you have ostentatiously displayed of the National Assembly, be founded on reason, the offspring of conviction, or the spawn of envy. Time may shew, that this obscure throng knew more of the human heart and of the legislation than the profligates of rank, emasculated by hereditary effeminacy.

It is not, perhaps, of very great consequence who were the founders of a state; savages, thieves, curates, or practitioners in the law. It is true, you might sarcastically remark, that the Romans had always a *smack* of the old leaven, and that the private robbers, supposing the tradition to be true, only became public depredators. You might have added, that their civilization must have been very partial, and had more influence on the manners than morals of the people; or the amusements of the amphitheatre would not have remained an everlasting blot not only on their humanity, but on their refinement, if a vicious elegance of behaviour and luxurious mode of life is not a prostitution of the term. However, the thundering censures which you have cast with a ponderous arm, and the more playful bushfiring of ridicule, are not arguments that will ever depreciate the National Assembly, for applying to their understanding rather than to their imagination, when they met to settle the newly acquired liberty of the state on a solid foundation. . . .

But, in settling a constitution that involved the happiness of millions, that stretch beyond the computation of science, it was, perhaps, necessary for the Assembly to have a higher model in view than the *imagined* virtues of their forefathers; and wise to deduce their respect for themselves from the only legitimate source, respect for justice. Why was it a duty to repair an ancient castle, built in barbarous ages, of Gothic materials? Why were the legislators obliged to rake amongst heterogeneous ruins; to rebuild old walls, whose foundations could scarcely be explored, when a simple structure might be raised on the foundation of experience, the only valuable inheritance our forefathers could bequeath? Yet of this bequest we can make little use till we have gained a stock of our own; and even then, their inherited experience would rather serve as lighthouses, to warn us against dangerous rocks or sand-banks, than as finger-posts that stand at every turning to point out the right road.

Nor was it absolutely necessary that they should be diffident of themselves when they were dissatisfied with, or could not discern the *almost obliterated* constitution of their ancestors (Page 53). They should first have been convinced that our constitution was not only the best modern, but the best possible one; and that our social compact was the surest foundation of all the *possible* liberty a mass of men could enjoy, that the human understanding could form. They should have been certain that our representation answered all the purposes of representation; and that an established inequality of rank and property secured the liberty of the whole community, instead of rendering it a sounding epithet of subjection, when applied to the nation at large. They should have had the same respect for our House of Commons that you, vauntingly, intrude on us, though your conduct throughout life has spoken a very different language; before they made a point of not deviating from the model which first engaged their attention.

That the British House of Commons is filled with every thing illustrious in rank, in descent, in hereditary, and acquired opulence, may be true,—but that it contains every thing respectable in talents, in military, civil, naval, and political distinction, is very problematical. Arguing from natural causes, the very contrary would appear to the speculatist to be the fact; and let experience say whether these speculations are built on sure ground.

It is true you lay great stress on the effects produced by the bare idea of a liberal descent (Page 49); but from the conduct of men of rank, men of discernment would rather be led to conclude, that this idea obliterated instead of inspiring native dignity, and substituted a factitious pride that disemboweled the man. The liberty of the rich has its ensigns armorial to puff the individual out with insubstantial honours; but where are blazoned the struggles of virtuous poverty? Who, indeed, would dare to blazon what would blur the pompous monumental inscription you boast of, and make us view with horror, as monsters in human shape, the superb gallery of portraits proudly set in battle array? . . .

Where is the dignity, the infallibility of sensibility, in the fair ladies, whom, if the voice of rumour is to be credited, the captive negroes curse in all the agony of bodily pain, for the unheard of tortures they invent? It is probable that some of them, after the sight of a flagellation, compose their ruffled spirits and exercise their tender feelings by the perusal of the last imported novel. — How true these tears are to nature, I leave you to determine. But these ladies may have read your Enquiry concerning the origin of our ideas of the Sublime and Beautiful, and, convinced by your arguments, may have laboured to be pretty, by counterfeiting weakness.

You may have convinced them that *littleness* and *weakness* are the very essence of beauty; and that the Supreme Being in giving women beauty in the most supereminent degree, seemed to command them, by the powerful voice of Nature, not to cultivate the moral virtues that might chance to excite respect, and interfere with the pleasing sensations they were created to inspire. Thus confining truth, fortitude, and humanity, within the rigid pale of manly morals, they might justly argue, that to be loved, women's high end and great distinction! they should 'learn to lisp, to totter in their walk, and nick-name God's creatures.' Never, they might repeat after you, was any man, much less a woman, rendered amiable by the force of those exalted qualities, fortitude, justice, wisdom, and truth; and thus forewarned of the sacrifice they must make to those austere, unnatural virtues, they would be authorized to turn all their attention to their persons, systematically neglecting morals to secure beauty. . . .

But should experience prove that there is a beauty in virtue, a charm in order, which necessarily implies exertion, a depraved sensual taste may give way to a more manly one — and *melting* feelings to rational satisfactions. Both may be equally natural to man; the test is their moral difference, and that point reason alone can decide.

Such a glorious change can only be produced by liberty. Inequality of rank must ever impede the growth of virtue, by vitiating the mind that submits or domineers; that is ever employed to procure nourishment for the body, or amusement for the mind. And if this grand example be set by an assembly of unlettered clowns, if they can produce a crisis that may involve the fate of Europe, and 'more than Europe' (Page 11), you must allow us to respect unsophisticated reason, and reverence the active exertions that were not relaxed by a fastidious respect for the beauty of rank, or a dread of the deformity produced by any *void* in the social structure.

After your contemptuous manner of speaking of the National Assembly, after descanting on the coarse vulgarity of their proceedings, which, according to your own definition of virtue, is a proof of its genuineness; was it not a little inconsistent, not to say absurd, to assert, that a dozen people of quality were not a sufficient counterpoise to the vulgar mob with whom they condescended to associate? Have we half a dozen leaders of eminence in our House of Commons, or even in the fashionable world? Yet the sheep obsequiously pursue their steps with all the undeviating sagacity of instinct.

In order that liberty should have a firm foundation, an acquaintance with the world would naturally lead cool men to conclude that it must be laid, knowing the weakness of the human heart, and the 'deceitfulness of riches,' either by *poor men*, or philosophers, if a sufficient number of men, disinterested from principle, or truly wise, could be found. Was it natural to expect that sensual prejudices should give way to reason, or present feelings to enlarged views? — No; I am afraid that human nature is still in such a weak state, that the abolition of titles, the corner-stone of despotism, could only have been the work of men who had no titles to sacrifice. The National Assembly, it is true, contains some honourable exceptions; but the majority had not such powerful feelings to struggle with, when reason led them to respect the naked dignity of virtue.

Weak minds are always timid. And what can equal the weakness of mind produced by servile flattery, and the vapid pleasures that neither hope nor fear seasoned? Had the constitution of France been new modelled, or more cautiously repaired, by the lovers of elegance and beauty, it is natural to suppose that the imagination would have erected a fragile temporary building; or the power of one tyrant, divided amongst a hundred, might have rendered the struggle for liberty only a choice of masters. And the glorious *chance* that is now given to human nature of attaining more virtue and happiness than has hitherto blessed our globe, might have been sacrificed to a meteor of the imagination, a bubble of passion. The ecclesiastics, indeed, would probably have remained in quiet possession of their sinecures; and your gall might not have been mixed with your ink on account of the daring sacrilege that brought them more on a level. The nobles would have had bowels for their younger sons, if not for the misery of their fellow-creatures. An august mass of property would have been transmitted to posterity to guard the temple of superstition, and prevent reason from entering with her officious light. And the pomp of religion would have continued to impress the senses, if she were unable to subjugate the passions. Is hereditary weakness necessary to render religion lovely? and will her form have lost the smooth delicacy that inspires love, when stripped of its Gothic drapery? Must every grand model be placed on the pedestal of property? and is there no beauteous proportion in virtue, when not clothed in a sensual garb?

Of these questions there would be no end, though they lead to the same conclusion;—that your politics and morals, when simplified, would undermine religion and virtue to set up a spurious, sensual beauty, that has long debauched your imagination, under the specious form of natural feelings.

And what is this mighty revolution in property [confiscation of the lands of the clergy, November 1789—BAC]? The present incumbents only are injured, or the hierarchy of the clergy, an ideal part of the constitution, which you have personified, to render your affection more tender. How has posterity been injured by a distribution of property snatched, perhaps, from innocent hands, but accumulated by the most abominable violation of every sentiment of justice and piety. Was the monument of former ignorance and iniquity to be held sacred, to enable the present possessors of enormous benefices to *dissolve* in indolent pleasures? Was not their convenience, for they have not been turned adrift on the world, to give place to a just partition of the land belonging to the state? And did not the respect due to the natural equality of man require this triumph over Monkish rapacity? Were those monsters to be reverenced on account of their antiquity, and their unjust claims perpetuated to their ideal children, the clergy, merely to preserve the sacred majesty of Property inviolate, and to enable the Church to retain her pristine splendor? Can posterity be injured by individuals losing the chance of obtaining great wealth, without meriting it, by its being diverted from a narrow channel, and disembogued into the sea that affords clouds to water all the land? Besides, the clergy not brought up with the expectation of great revenues will not feel the loss; and if bishops should happen to be chosen on account of their personal merit, religion may be benefited by the vulgar nomination.

The sophistry of asserting that Nature leads us to reverence our civil institutions from the same principle that we venerate aged individuals, is a palpable fallacy 'that is so like truth, it will serve the turn as well.' And when you add, 'that we have chosen our nature rather than our speculations, our breasts rather than our inventions' (Page 50), the pretty jargon seems equally unintelligible.

But it was the downfall of the visible power and dignity of the church that roused your ire; you could have excused a little squeezing of the individuals to supply present exigencies; the actual possessors of the property might have been oppressed with something like impunity, if the church had not been spoiled of its gaudy trappings. You love the church, your country, and its laws, you repeatedly tell us, because they deserve to be loved; but from you this is not a panegyric: weakness and indulgence are the only incitements to love and confidence that you can discern, and it cannot be denied that the tender mother you venerate deserves, on this score, all your affection.

It would be as vain a task to attempt to obviate all your passionate objections, as to unravel all your plausible arguments, often illustrated by known truths, and rendered forcible by pointed invectives. I only attack the foundation. On the natural principles of justice I build my plea for disseminating the property artfully said to be appropriated to religious purposes, but, in reality, to support idle tyrants, amongst the society whose ancestors were cheated or forced into illegal grants. Can there be an opinion more subversive of morality, than that time sanctifies crimes, and silences the blood that calls out for retribution, if not for vengeance? If the revenue annexed to the Gallic church was greater than the most bigoted protestant would now allow to be its reasonable share, would it not have been trampling on the rights of men to perpetuate such an arbitrary appropriation of the common flock, because time had rendered the fraudulent seizure venerable? Besides, if Reason had suggested, as surely she must, if the imagination had not been allowed to dwell on the fascinating pomp of ceremonial grandeur, that the clergy would be rendered both more virtuous and useful by being put more on a par with each other, and the mass of the people it was their duty to instruct;—where was there room for hesitation? The charge of presumption, thrown by you on the most reasonable innovations, may, without any violence to truth, be retorted on every reformation that has meliorated our condition, and even on the improvable faculty that gives us a claim to the pre-eminence of intelligent beings. . . .

A fallacy of this kind, I think, could not have escaped you when you were treating the subject that called forth your bitterest animadversions, the confiscation of the ecclesiastical revenue. Who of the vindicators of the rights of men ever ventured to assert, that the clergy of the present day should be punished on account of the intolerable pride and inhuman cruelty of many of their predecessors? (*Vide* Page 210). No; such a thought never entered the mind of those who warred with inveterate prejudices. A desperate disease required a powerful remedy. Injustice had no right to rest on prescription; nor has the character of the present clergy any weight on the argument.

You find it very difficult to separate policy from

justice: in the political world they have frequently been separated with shameful dexterity. To mention a recent instance. According to the limited views of timid, or interested politicians, an abolition of the infernal slave trade would not only be unsound policy, but a flagrant infringement of the laws (which are allowed to have been infamous) that induced the planters to purchase their estates. But is it not consonant with justice, with the common principles of humanity, not to mention Christianity, to abolish this abominable mischief? There is not one argument, one invective, levelled by you at the confiscators of the church revenue, which could not, with the strictest propriety, be applied by the planters and negro-drivers to our Parliament, if it gloriously dared to shew the world that British senators were men: if the natural feelings of humanity silenced the cold cautions of timidity, till this stigma on our nature was wiped off, and all men were allowed to enjoy their birth-right—liberty, till by their crimes they had authorized society to deprive them of the blessing they had abused.

The same arguments might be used in India, if any attempt were made to bring back things to nature, to prove that a man ought never to quit the cast that confined him to the profession of his lineal forefathers. The Bramins would doubtless find many ingenious reasons to justify this debasing, though venerable prejudice; and would not, it is to be supposed, forget to observe that time, by interweaving the oppressive law with many useful customs, had rendered it for the present very convenient, and consequently legal. Almost every vice that has degraded our nature might be justified by shewing that it had been productive of *some* benefit to society: for it would be as difficult to point out positive evil as unallayed good, in this imperfect state. What indeed would become of morals, if they had no other test than prescription? The manners of men may change without end; but, wherever reason receives the least cultivation—wherever men rise above brutes, morality must rest on the same base. And the more man discovers of the nature of his mind and body, the more clearly he is convinced, that to act according to the dictates of reason is to conform to the law of God.

The test of honour may be arbitrary and fallacious, and, retiring into subterfuge, elude close enquiry; but true morality shuns not the day, nor shrinks from the ordeal of investigation. Most of the happy revolutions that have taken place in the world have happened when weak princes held the reins they could not manage; but are they, on that account, to be canonized as saints or demi-gods, and pushed forward to notice on the throne of ignorance? Pleasure wants a zest, if experience cannot compare it with pain; but who courts

pain to heighten his pleasures? A transient view of society will further illustrate arguments which appear so obvious that I am almost ashamed to produce illustrations. How many children have been taught œconomy, and many other virtues, by the extravagant thoughtlessness of their parents; yet a good education is allowed to be an inestimable blessing. The tenderest mothers are often the most unhappy wives; but can the good that accrues from the private distress that produces a sober dignity of mind justify the inflictor?

Right or wrong may be estimated according to the point of sight, and other adventitious circumstances; but, to discover its real nature, the enquiry must go deeper than the surface, and beyond the local consequences that confound good and evil together. The rich and weak, a numerous train, will certainly applaud your system, and loudly celebrate your pious reverence for authority and establishments—they find it pleasanter to enjoy than to think; to justify oppression than correct abuses.—*The rights of men* are grating sounds that set their teeth on edge; the impertinent enquiry of philosophic meddling innovation. If the poor are in distress, they will make some *benevolent* exertions to assist them; they will confer obligations, but not do justice. Benevolence is a very amiable specious quality; yet the aversion which men feel to accept a right as a favour, should rather be extolled as a vestige of native dignity, than stigmatized as the odious offspring of ingratitude. The poor consider the rich as their lawful prey; but we ought not too severely to animadvert on their ingratitude. When they receive an alms they are commonly grateful at the moment; but old habits quickly return, and cunning has ever been a substitute for force.

That both physical and moral evil were not only foreseen, but entered into the scheme of Providence, when this world was contemplated in the Divine mind, who can doubt, without robbing Omnipotence of a most exalted attribute? But the business of the life of a good man should be, to separate light from darkness, to diffuse happiness, whilst he submits to unavoidable misery. And a conviction that there is much unavoidable wretchedness, appointed by the grand Disposer of all events, should not slacken his exertions: the extent of what is possible can only be discerned by God. The justice of God may be vindicated by a belief in a future state; but, only by believing that evil is educing good for the individual, and not for an imaginary whole. The happiness of the whole must arise from the happiness of the constituent parts, or the essence of justice is sacrificed to a supposed grand arrangement. And that may be good for the whole of a creature's existence, that disturbs the comfort of a small portion. The evil which an individual suffers for the good of the community is partial, it must be allowed, if the account is settled by death. — But the partial evil which it suffers, during one stage of existence, to render another stage more perfect, is strictly just. . . .

It may be confidently asserted that no man chooses evil, because it is evil; he only mistakes it for happiness, the good he seeks. And the desire of rectifying these mistakes, is the noble ambition of an enlightened understanding, the impulse of feelings that Philosophy invigorates. To endeavour to make unhappy men resigned to their fate, is the tender endeavour of short-sighted benevolence, of transient yearnings of humanity; but to labour to increase human happiness by extirpating error, is a masculine godlike affection. This remark may be carried still further. Men who possess uncommon sensibility, whose quick emotions shew how closely the eye and heart are connected, soon forget the most forcible sensations. Not tarrying long enough in the brain to be subject to reflection, the next sensations, of course, obliterate them. Memory, however, treasures up these proofs of native goodness; and the being who is not spurred on to any virtuous act, still thinks itself of consequence, and boasts of its feelings. Why? Because the sight of distress, or an affecting narrative, made its blood flow with more velocity, and the heart, literally speaking, beat with sympathetic emotion. We ought to beware of confounding mechanical instinctive sensations with emotions that reason deepens, and justly terms the feelings of *humanity*. This word discriminates the active exertions of virtue from the vague declamation of sensibility.

The declaration of the National Assembly, when they recognized the rights of men, was calculated to touch the humane heart—the downfall of the clergy, to agitate the pupil of impulse. On the watch to find fault, faults met your prying eye; a different prepossession might have produced a different conviction.

When we read a book that supports our favourite opinions, how eagerly do we suck in the doctrines, and suffer our minds placidly to reflect the images that illustrate the tenets we have previously embraced. We indolently acquiesce in the conclusion, and our spirit animates and corrects the various subjects. But when, on the contrary, we peruse a skilful writer, with whom we do not coincide in opinion, how attentive is the mind to detect fallacy. And this suspicious coolness often prevents our being carried away by a stream of natural eloquence, which the prejudiced mind terms declamation—a pomp of words! We never allow ourselves to be warmed; and, after contending with the writer, are more confirmed in our opinion; as much, perhaps, from a spirit of contradiction as from reason. A lively imagination is ever in danger of being betrayed into error by favourite opinions, which it almost personifies, the more effectually to intoxicate the understanding. Always tending to extremes, truth is left behind in the heat of the chace, and things are viewed as positively good, or bad, though they wear an equivocal face. . . .

But, among all your plausible arguments, and witty illustrations, your contempt for the poor always appears conspicuous, and rouses my indignation. The following paragraph in particular struck me, as breathing the most tyrannic spirit, and displaying the most factitious feelings. 'Good order is the foundation of all good things. To be enabled to acquire, the people, without being servile, must be tractable and obedient. The magistrate must have his reverence, the laws their authority. The body of the people must not find the principles of natural subordination by art rooted out of their minds. They *must* respect that property of which they *cannot* partake. *They must labour to obtain what by labour can be obtained; and when they find, as they commonly do, the success disproportioned to the endeavour, they must be taught their consolation in the final proportions of eternal justice.* Of this consolation, whoever deprives them, deadens their industry, and strikes at the root of all acquisition as of all conservation. He that does this, is the cruel oppressor, the merciless enemy, of the poor and wretched; at the same time that, by his wicked speculations, he exposes the fruits of successful industry, and the accumulations of fortune,' (ah! there's the rub) 'to plunder of the negligent, the disappointed, and the unprosperous' (Page 351).

This is contemptible hard-hearted sophistry, in the specious form of humility, and submission to the will of Heaven. — It is, sir, *possible* to render the poor happier in this world, without depriving them of the consolation which you gratuitously grant them in the next. They have a right to more comfort than they at present enjoy; and more comfort might be afforded them, without encroaching on the pleasures of the rich: not now waiting to enquire whether the rich have any right to exclusive pleasures. What do I say?—encroaching! No; if an intercourse were established between them, it would impart the only true pleasure that can be snatched in his land of shadows, this hard school of moral discipline.

I know, indeed, that there is often something disgusting in the distresses of poverty, at which the imagination revolts, and starts back to exercise itself in the more attractive Arcadia of fiction. The rich man builds a house, art and taste give it the highest finish. His gardens are planted, and the trees grow to recreate the fancy of the planter, though the temperature of the climate may rather force him to avoid the dangerous damps they exhale, than seek the umbrageous retreat. Every thing on the estate is cherished but man;—yet, to contribute to the happiness of man, is the most sublime of all enjoyments. But if, instead of sweeping pleasure-grounds, obelisks, temples, and elegant cottages, as *objects* for the eye, the heart was allowed to beat true to nature, decent farms would be scattered over the estate, and plenty smile around. Instead of the poor being subject to the griping hand of an avaricious steward, they would be watched over with fatherly solicitude, by the man whose duty and pleasure it was to guard their happiness, and shield from rapacity the beings who, by the sweat of their brow, exalted him above his fellows. . . .

What salutary dews might not be shed to refresh this thirsty land, if men were more *enlightened*! Smiles and premiums might encourage cleanliness, industry, and emulation.—A garden more inviting than Eden would then meet the eye, and springs of joy murmur on every side. The clergyman would superintend his own flock, the shepherd would then love the sheep he daily tended; the school might rear its decent head, and the buzzing tribe, let loose to play, impart a portion of their vivacious spirits to the heart that longed to open their minds, and lead them to taste the pleasures of man. Domestic comfort, the civilizing relations of husband, brother, and father, would soften labour, and render life contented.

Returning once from a despotic country to a part of England well cultivated, but not very picturesque—with what delight did I not observe the poor man's garden—The homely palings and twining woodbine, with all the rustic contrivances of simple, unlettered taste, was a sight which relieved the eye that had wandered indignant from the stately palace to the pestiferous hovel, and turned from the awful contrast into itself to mourn the fate of man, and curse the arts of civilization!

Why cannot large estates be divided into small farms? these dwellings would indeed grace our land. Why are huge forests still allowed to stretch out with idle pomp and all the indolence of Eastern grandeur? Why does the brown waste meet the traveller's view, when men want work? But commons cannot be enclosed without *acts of parliament* to increase the property of the rich! Why might not the industrious peasant be allowed to steal a farm from the heath? This sight I have seen;—the cow that supported the children grazed near the hut, and the cheerful poultry were fed by the chubby babes, who breathed a bracing air, far from the diseases and the vices of cities. Domination blasts all these prospects; virtue can only flourish amongst equals, and the man who submits to a fellow-creature, because it promotes his worldly interest, and he who relieves only because it is his duty to lay up a

treasure in heaven, are much on a par, for both are radically degraded by the habits of their life.

In this great city, that proudly rears its head, and boasts of its population and commerce, how much misery lurks in pestilential corners, whilst idle mendicants assail, on every side, the man who hates to encourage impostors, or repress, with angry frown, the plaints of the poor! How many mechanics, by a flux of trade or fashion, lose their employment; whom misfortunes, not to be warded off, lead to the idleness that vitiates their character and renders them afterwards averse to honest labour! Where is the eye that marks these evils, more gigantic than any of the infringements of property, which you piously deprecate? Are these remediless evils? And is the humane heart satisfied with turning the poor over to *another* world, to receive the blessings this could afford? If society was regulated on a more enlarged plan; if man was contented to be the friend of man, and did not seek to bury the sympathies of humanity in the servile appellation of master; if, turning his eyes from ideal regions of taste and elegance, he laboured to give the earth he inhabited all the beauty it is capable of receiving, and was ever on the watch to shed abroad all the happiness which human nature can enjoy;—he who, respecting the rights of men, wishes to convince or persuade society that this is true happiness and dignity, is not the cruel *oppressor* of the poor, nor a short-sighted philosopher—He fears God and loves his fellow-creatures.—Behold the whole duty of man!—the citizen who acts differently is a sophisticated being.

Surveying civilized life, and seeing, with undazzled eye, the polished vices of the rich, their insincerity, want of natural affections, with all the specious train that luxury introduces, I have turned impatiently to the poor, to look for man undebauched by riches or power—but alas! what did I see? a being scarcely above the brutes, over which he tyrannized; a broken spirit, worn-out body, and all those gross vices which the example of the rich, rudely copied, could produce. Envy built a wall of separation, that made the poor hate, whilst they bent to their superiors; who, on their part, stepped aside to avoid the loathsome sight of human misery.

What were the outrages of a day [October 6] to these continual miseries? Let those sorrows hide their diminished head before the tremendous mountain of woe that thus defaces our globe! Man preys on man; and you mourn for the idle tapestry that decorated a gothic pile, and the dronish bell that summoned the fat priest to prayer. You mourn for the empty pageant of a name, when slavery flaps her wing, and the sick heart retires to die in lonely wilds, far from the abodes of men. Did the pangs you felt for insulted nobility, the anguish that rent your heart when the gorgeous robes were torn off the idol human weakness had set up, deserve to be compared with the long-drawn sigh of melancholy reflection, when misery and vice are thus seen to haunt our steps, and swim on the top of every cheering prospect? Why is our fancy to be appalled by terrific perspectives of a hell beyond the grave?—Hell stalks abroad;—the lash resounds on the slave's naked sides; and the sick wretch, who can no longer earn the sour bread of unremitting labour, steals to a ditch to bid the world a long good night—or, neglected in some ostentatious hospital, breathes his last amidst the laugh of mercenary attendants.

Such misery demands more than tears—I pause to recollect myself; and smother the contempt I feel rising for your rhetorical flourishes and infantine sensibility. . . .

Is it absolute blasphemy to doubt of the omnipotence of the law, or to suppose that religion might be more pure if there were fewer baits for hypocrites in the church? . . .

Before I conclude my cursory remarks, it is but just to acknowledge that I coincide with you in your opinion respecting the *sincerity* of many modern philosophers. Your consistency in avowing a veneration for rank and riches deserves praise; but I must own that I have often indignantly observed that some of the *enlightened* philosophers, who talk most vehemently of the native rights of men, borrow many noble sentiments to adorn their conversation, which have no influence on their conduct. They bow down to rank, and are careful to secure property; for virtue, without this adventitious drapery, is seldom very respectable in their eyes—nor are they very quick-sighted to discern real dignity of character when no sounding name exalts the man above his fellows.—But neither open enmity nor hollow homage destroys the intrinsic value of those principles which rest on an eternal foundation, and revert for a standard to the immutable attributes of God.

The End

PART THREE

Nineteenth-Century Writings

Sarah M. Grimké (1792–1873) and Angelina E. Grimké (1805–79)

Sarah Moore Grimké and Angelina Emily Grimké have been remembered most lastingly as abolitionists and participants within the women's rights movement. They are less remembered for their writings which evolved from those commitments. Yet each wrote a range of polemical and analytical works attempting to break the bonds between Christian and respectable America and the ownership of slaves or subordination of women. They were thought to be scandalous individuals when they lived, and the details of their lives continue to dominate much of what is written about them by scholars today. Contemporaries marveled at these daughters of a family of prominent South Carolina slave owners, who fled the South, became abolitionists and members of the Society of Friends (Quakers), and spoke in public in favor of both abolition and women's rights. Not only were they vilified by the traditional Southerners from whom they had broken, they also parted company with abolitionists who did not support women's rights, and they developed breaches with the Society of Friends in Philadelphia when its members refused to grant full racial equality to black members of the Society. They had a strong, consistent, and enduring sense of justice, and such views emerge from their works as well as in their disputes with their enemies and allies.

Their growing perception of the evils of slavery emerged from their interaction with the slaves owned by their father. Sarah Grimké, as a Sunday school teacher, taught slaves to read, although such teaching was prohibited by South Carolina law. In 1819 at their father's death, the sisters freed their slaves. When Sarah Grimké was twenty-six years old she moved to the North and joined others (especially Quakers) who opposed the existence of slavery. By 1829 Angelina Grimké joined her sister in Philadelphia. The 1830s and 1840s were the most active period for them in their public organizing against slavery (and later against women's lack of rights), following Angelina Grimké's letter published in William Lloyd Garrison's The Liberator, in which she attacked the institution of slavery. As two prominent Southerners, the Grimkés were sought out by Northern abolitionists, but resistance arose to their speaking in public. Women were not expected to speak in public or before mixed (dual sex) audiences. Thus many who were excited about the prospect of these reformed slave owners making a case for abolition resisted their being able to do so because they were women. The sisters did speak for the American Anti-Slavery Society from 1836 on, but seldom without resistance from abolitionists and nonabolitionists alike.

The Grimké sisters, in their letters and writings, appealed to women, to Christians, and to Southerners to grasp the evil of slavery. While both sisters were devoted to abolition and women's rights, Angelina wrote more about, and was more active in, the cause of abolition, while Sarah devoted greater attention to women's causes. Angelina called upon women to act on the part of the slave, less in the interest of their sex, as in her first prominent work, An Appeal to the Christian Women of the South, published in 1836. The Appeal was excoriated in the South because it was directed to white Southern women who were asked to oppose slavery in part on grounds that it allowed white men (their husbands, brothers, and fathers) to pursue sexual ties with slave women and father children with them; yet this theme imbued it with risqué qualities in the North and enhanced its popularity there. During this period, Sarah Grimké was busy publishing works on both the evils of slavery and women's secondary position within U.S. society. From 1836 to 1838 she wrote Epistle to the Clergy of the Southern States, Appeal to the Women of the Nominally Free States, and her strongest feminist work, Letters on the Equality of the Sexes and the Condition of Woman.

In 1838 Angelina Grimké married Theodore Weld, a leading abolitionist, and their wedding in Philadelphia (which included African Americans) led to rioting that culminated in the burning of the Anti-Slavery Society offices and the Shelter for Colored Orphans. After 1839, the sisters engaged in fewer public appearances but still continued active support for both causes. They both devoted time to the Weld-Grimké household, with Sarah teaching her sister's children and aiding in the housekeeping following Angelina's difficult recovery from childbirth. In addition, following the Civil War, they adopted two slaves who they assumed were their nephews, since their brother was thought to be their father. While strong abolitionists, they parted company with a majority of male abolitionists by protesting the Fifteenth Amendment, which granted suffrage to male ex-slaves but failed to enfranchise women, either black or white. Following the war, much of their effort was through correspondence with suffrage leaders. Sarah did speak at women's rights conventions but never went on major speaking tours, and Angelina was even more restricted to her home in the last years before their deaths in the 1870s.

They wrote some of the most effective works using Christian doctrine to argue for the abolition of slavery and for fair and equal treatment of African Americans, and to argue against the treatment of and powerlessness of American women during the antebellum period. They held that God had a view for the equality of all of his creations, and they called upon believers to respect that equality and work earnestly and untiringly for justice on earth, not simply for salvation in heaven. Sarah Grimké's writings were some of the most impressive feminist writings of the mid nineteenth century, and the writings of both sisters are notable for the strength of their convictions and the effective use of both logic and social guilt to reach those who could be persuaded through arguments of Christian, and more broadly human, guilt and responsibility. While earlier scholars focused on the writings of the sisters, and on their roles within the abolitionist and women's rights movements, recently more attention has been placed on the language and symbols embedded in their public appearances during the 1830s.

The following selections include excerpts from Angelina Grimké's Appeal to the Christian Women of the South (1836) and from Sarah Grimké's Letters on the Equality of the Sexes and the Condition of Woman (1838).

HLS

Sources and Suggested Readings

Bartlett, Elizabeth Ann. *Liberty, Equality, Sorority: The Origins and Interpretation of American Feminist Thought: Frances Wright, Sarah Grimké, and Margaret Fuller.* Brooklyn, N.Y.: Carlson, 1994.

Browne, Stephen H. "Encountering Angelina Grimké: Violence, Identity, and the Creation of Radical Community." *Quarterly Journal of Speech* 82 (1996): 55–73.

Ceplair, Larry, ed. *The Public Years of Sarah and Angelina Grimké: Selected Writings, 1835–1839.* New York: Columbia University Press, 1989.

Grimké, A[ngelina] E. "Appeal to the Christian Women of the South." *Anti-Slavery Examiner* 1, 2 (September 1836): 16 pp.

[Grimké, Sarah]. *Letters on the Equality of the Sexes and the Condition of Woman. Addressed to Mary S. Parker, President of the Boston Female Anti-Slavery Society.* Boston: Isaac Knapp, 1838.

Grimké, Sarah. *"Letters on the Equality of the Sexes," and Other Essays.* Ed. Elizabeth Ann Bartlett. New Haven: Yale University Press, 1988.

Henry, Katherine. "Angelina Grimké's Rhetoric of Exposure." *American Quarterly* 42, 9 (June 1997): 328–55.

Huxman, Susan Schultz. "Mary Wollstonecraft, Margaret Fuller, and Angelina Grimke [sic]: Symbolic Convergence and a Nascent Rhetorical Vision." *Communication Quarterly* 44, 1 (Winter 1996): 16–28.

Isenberg, Nancy. *Sex and Citizenship in Antebellum America.* Chapel Hill: University of North Carolina Press, 1998.

Lerner, Gerda. *The Grimké Sisters from South Carolina: Pioneers for Woman's Rights and Abolition.* New York: Schocken, 1988 [1967].

Matthews, Jean. "Consciousness of Self and Consciousness of Sex in Antebellum Feminism." *Journal of Women's History* 5, 1 (Spring 1993): 61–78.

———. "Race, Sex, and the Dimensions of Liberty in Antebellum America." *Journal of the Early Republic* 6, 3 (1986): 275–91.

Weld, Theodore Dwight. *Letters of Theodore Dwight Weld, Angelina Grimké, and Sarah Grimké, 1822–1844.* Gloucester, Mass.: P. Smith, 1965 [1934].

ANGELINA EMILY GRIMKÉ

Appeal to the Christian Women of the South (1836)

Then Mordecai commanded to answer Esther. Think not within thyself that thou shalt escape in the king's house more than all the Jews. For if thou altogether holdest thy peace at this time, then shall there enlargement and deliverance arise to the Jews from another place: but thou and thy father's house shall be destroyed: and who knoweth whether thou art come to the kingdom for such a time as this. And Esther bade them return Mordecai this answer: —and so will I go unto the king, which is not according to law, and if I perish, I perish.

Esther IV. 13–16.

Respected Friends,

It is because I feel a deep and tender interest in your present and eternal welfare that I am willing thus publicly to address you. Some of you have loved me as a relative, and some have felt bound to me in Christian sympathy, and Gospel friendship; and even when compelled by a strong sense of duty, to break those outward bonds of union which bound us together as members of the same community, and members of the same religious denomination, you were generous enough to give me credit, for sincerity as a Christian, though you believed I had been most strangely deceived. I thanked you then for your kindness, and I ask you *now*, for the sake of former confidence, and friendship, to read the following pages in the spirit of calm investigation and fervent prayer. It is because you have known me, that I write thus unto you.

But there are other Christian women scattered over the Southern States, a very large number of whom have never seen me, and never heard my name, and who feel *no* interest whatever in *me*. But I feel an interest in *you*, as branches of the same vine from whose root I daily draw the principle of spiritual vitality—Yes! Sisters in Christ I feel an interest in *you*, and often has the secret prayer arisen on your behalf, Lord "open thou their eyes that they may see wondrous things out of thy Law"—It is then, because I *do feel* and *do pray* for you, that I thus address you upon a subject about which of all others, perhaps you would rather not hear any thing; but "would to God ye could bear with me a little in my folly, and indeed bear with me, for I am jealous over you with godly jealousy." Be not afraid then to read my appeal; it is *not* written in the heat of passion or prejudice, but in that solemn calmness which is the result of conviction and duty. It is true, I am going to tell you unwelcome truths, but I mean to speak those *truths in love*, and remember Solomon says, "faithful are the *wounds* of a friend." I do not believe the time has yet come when *Christian women* "will not endure sound doctrine," even on the subject of slavery, if it is spoken to them in tenderness and love, therefore I now address *you*.

To all of you then, known or unknown, relatives or strangers, (for you are all *one* in Christ,) I would speak. I have felt for you at this time, when unwelcome light is pouring in upon the world on the subject of slavery; light which even Christians would exclude, if they could, from our country, or at any rate from the southern portion of it, saying, as its rays strike the rock bound coasts of New England and scatter their warmth and radiance over her hills and valleys, and from thence travel onward over the Palisades of the Hudson, and down the soft flowing waters of the Delaware and gild the waves of the Potomac, "hitherto shalt thou come and no further"; I know that even professors of His name who has been emphatically called the "Light of the world" would, if they could, build a wall of adamant around the Southern States whose top might reach unto heaven, in order to shut out the light which is bounding from mountain to mountain and from the hills to the plains and valleys beneath, through the vast extent of our Northern States. But believe me, when I tell you, their attempts will be as utterly fruitless as were the efforts of the builders of Babel; and why? Because moral, like natural light, is so extremely subtle in its nature as to overleap all human barriers, and laugh at the puny efforts of man to control it. All the excuses and palliations of this system must inevitably be swept away, just as other "refuges of lies" have been, by the irresistible torrent of a rectified public opinion. "The *supporters* of the slave system," says Jonathan Dymond in his admirable work on the Principles of Morality, "will *hereafter* be regarded with the *same* public feeling, as he who was an advocate for the slave

trade *now* is." It will be, and that very soon, clearly perceived and fully acknowledged by all the virtuous and the candid, that in *principle* it is as sinful to hold a human being in bondage who has been born in Carolina, as one who has been born in Africa. All that sophistry of argument which has been employed to prove, that although it is sinful to send to Africa to procure men and women as slaves, who have never been in slavery, that still, it is not sinful to keep those in bondage who have come down by inheritance, will be utterly overthrown. We must come back to the good old doctrine of our forefathers who declared to the world, "this self evident truth that *all* men are created equal, and that they have certain *inalienable* rights among which are life, *liberty*, and the pursuit of happiness." It is even a greater absurdity to suppose a man can be legally born a slave under *our free Republican* Government, than under the petty despotisms of barbarian Africa. If then, we have no right to enslave an African, surely we can have none to enslave an American; if it is a self evident truth that *all* men, every where and of every color are born equal, and have an *inalienable right to liberty*, then it is equally true that *no* man can be born a slave, and no man can ever *rightfully* be reduced to *involuntary* bondage and held as a slave, however fair may be the claim of his master or mistress through will and title-deeds.

But after all, it may be said, our fathers were certainly mistaken, for the Bible sanctions Slavery, and that is the highest authority. Now the Bible is my ultimate appeal in all matters of faith and practice, and it is to *this test* I am anxious to bring the subject at issue between us. Let us then begin with Adam and examine the charter of privileges which was given to him. "Have dominion over the fish of the sea, and over the fowl of the air, and over every living thing that moveth upon the earth." In the eighth Psalm we have a still fuller description of this charter which through Adam was given to all mankind. "Thou madest him to have dominion over the works of thy hands; thou hast put all things under his feet. All sheep and oxen, yea, and the beasts of the field, the fowl of the air, the fish of the sea, and whatsoever passeth through the paths of the seas." And after the flood when this charter of human rights was renewed, we find *no additional* power vested in man. "And the fear of you and the dread of you shall be upon every beast of the earth, and every fowl of the air, and upon all that moveth upon the earth, and upon all the fishes of the sea, into your hand are they delivered." In this charter, although the different kinds of *irrational* beings are so particularly enumerated, and supreme dominion over *all of them* is granted, yet *man is never* vested with this dominion *over his fellow man*; he was never told that any of the human species were put *under his feet*; it was only *all things*, and man, who was created in the image of his Maker, *never* can properly be termed a *thing*, though the laws of Slave States do call him a "chattel personal"; *Man* then, I assert *never* was put *under the feet of man*, by that first charter of human rights which was given by God, to the Fathers of the Antediluvian and the Postdiluvian worlds, therefore this doctrine of equality is based on the Bible.

But it may be argued, that in the very chapter of Genesis from which I have last quoted, will be found the curse pronounced upon Canaan, by which his posterity was consigned to servitude under his brothers Shem and Japheth. I know this prophecy was uttered, and was most fearfully and wonderfully fulfilled, through the immediate descendants of Canaan, i.e. the Canaanites, and I do not know but it has been through all the children of Ham, but I do know that prophecy does *not* tell us what *ought to be*, but what actually does take place, ages after it has been delivered, and that if we justify America for enslaving the children of Africa, we must also justify Egypt for reducing the children of Israel to bondage, for the latter was foretold as explicitly as the former. I am well aware that prophecy has often been urged as an excuse for Slavery, but be not deceived, the fulfillment of prophecy *will not cover one sin* in the awful day of account. Hear what our Saviour says on this subject, "it must needs be that offences come, but *woe unto that man through whom they come*"—Witness some fulfillment of this declaration in the tremendous destruction of Jerusalem, occasioned by that most nefarious of all crimes the crucifixion of the Son of God. Did the fact of that event having been foretold, exculpate the Jews from sin in perpetrating it; No—for hear what the Apostle Peter says to them on this subject, "Him being delivered by the determinate counsel and foreknowledge of God, *ye* have taken, and by *wicked* hands have crucified and slain." Other striking instances might be adduced, but these will suffice.

But it has been urged that the patriarchs held slaves, and therefore, slavery is right. Do you really believe that patriarchal servitude was like American slavery? Can you believe it? If so, read the history of these primitive fathers of the church and be undeceived. . . .

But I shall be told, God sanctioned Slavery, yea commanded Slavery under the Jewish Dispensation. Let us examine this subject calmly and prayerfully. I admit that a species of *servitude* was permitted to the Jews, but in studying the subject I have been struck with wonder and admiration at perceiving how carefully the servant was guarded from violence, injustice and wrong. . . .

From these laws we learn that Hebrew men servants were bound to serve their masters *only* six years, unless their attachment to their employers, their wives and children, should induce them to wish to remain in servitude, in which case, in order to prevent the possibility of deception on the part of the master, the servant was first taken before the magistrate, where he openly declared his intention of continuing in his master's service, (probably a public register was kept of such) he was then conducted to the door of the house, (in warm climates doors are thrown open,) and *there* his ear was *publicly* bored, and by submitting to this operation he testified his willingness to serve him *forever*, i.e. during his life, for Jewish Rabbins who must have understood Jewish *slavery*, (as it is called,) "affirm that servants were set free at the death of their masters and did *not* descend to their heirs": or that he was to serve him until the year of Jubilee, when *all* servants were set at liberty. To protect servants from violence, it was ordained that if a master struck out the tooth or destroyed the eye of a servant, that servant immediately became *free*, for such an act of violence evidently showed he was unfit to possess the power of a master, and therefore that power was taken from him. All servants enjoyed the rest of the Sabbath and partook of the privileges and festivities of the three great Jewish Feasts; and if a servant died under the infliction of chastisement, his master was surely to be punished. . . .

There are however two other laws which I have not yet noticed. The one effectually prevented *all involuntary* servitude, and the other completely abolished Jewish servitude every fifty years. They were equally operative upon the Heathen and the Hebrew.

1. "Thou shalt *not* deliver unto his master the servant that is escaped from his master unto thee. He shall dwell with thee, even among you, in that place which he shall choose, in one of thy gates where it liketh him best: thou shalt *not* oppress him." Deut. xxiii, 15, 16.

2. "And ye shall hallow the fiftieth year, and proclaim *Liberty* throughout *all* the land, unto *all* the inhabitants thereof: it shall be a jubilee unto you." Lev. xxv, 10.

Here, then, we see that by this first law, the *door of Freedom was opened wide to every servant who* had any cause whatever for complaint; if he was unhappy with his master, all he had to do was to leave him, and *no man* had a right to deliver him back to him again, and not only so, but the absconded servant was to *choose* where he should live, and no Jew was permitted to oppress him. He left his master just as our Northern servants leave us; we have no power to compel them to remain with us, and no man has any right to oppress them; they go and dwell in that place where it chooseth them, and live just where they like. Is it so at the

South? Is the poor runaway slave protected *by law* from the violence of that master whose oppression and cruelty has driven him from his plantation or his house? No! no! Even the free states of the North are compelled to deliver unto his master the servant that is escaped from his master into them. By *human* law, under the *Christian Dispensation,* in the *nineteenth century we* are commanded to do, what *God* more than *three thousand* years ago, under the *Mosaic Dispensation, positively commanded* the Jews *not* to do. In the wide domain even of our free states, there is not *one* city of refuge for the poor runaway fugitive; not one spot upon which he can stand and say, I am a free man—I am protected in my rights as a *man,* by the strong arm of the law; no! *not one.* How long the North will thus shake hands with the South in sin, I know not. How long she will stand by like the persecutor Saul, *consenting* unto the death of Stephen, and keeping the raiment of them that slew him. I know not; but one thing I do know, *the guilt of the North* is increasing in a tremendous ratio as light is pouring in upon her on the subject and the sin of slavery. As the sun of righteousness climbs higher and higher in the moral heavens, she will stand still more and more abashed as the query is thundered down into her ear, "*Who* hath required *this* at thy hand?" It will be found *no* excuse then that the Constitution of our country required that *persons bound to service,* escaping from their masters should be delivered up; no more excuse than was the reason which Adam assigned for eating the forbidden fruit. *He was condemned and punished because* he hearkened to the voice of *his wife,* rather than to the command of his Maker; and *we* will assuredly be condemned and punished for obeying *Man* rather than *God,* if we do not speedily repent and bring forth fruits meet for repentance. Yea, are we not receiving chastisement even *now?*

But by the second of these laws a still more astonishing fact is disclosed. If the first effectually prevented *all involuntary servitude,* the last absolutely forbade even *voluntary servitude being perpetual.* On the great day of atonement every fiftieth year the Jubilee trumpet was sounded through the land of Judea, and *Liberty* was proclaimed to *all* the inhabitants thereof. I will not say that the servants' *chains* fell off and their *manacles* were burst, for there is no evidence that Jewish servants *ever* felt the weight of iron chains, and collars, and handcuffs; but I do say that even the man who had voluntarily sold himself and the *heathen* who had been sold to a Hebrew master, were set free, the one as well as the other. This law was evidently designed to prevent the oppression of the poor, and the possibility of such a thing as *perpetual servitude* existing among them.

Where, then, I would ask, is the warrant, the justification, or the palliation of American Slavery from Hebrew servitude? How many of the southern slaves would now be in bondage according to the laws of Moses? Not one. You may observe that I have carefully avoided using the term *slavery* when speaking of Jewish servitude; and simply for this reason, that *no such thing* existed among that people; the word translated servant does *not* mean *slave,* it is the same that is applied to Abraham, to Moses, to Elisha and the prophets generally. *Slavery* then *never* existed under the Jewish Dispensation at all, and I cannot but regard it as an aspersion on the character of Him who is "glorious in Holiness" for any one to assert that "*God sanctioned, yea commanded slavery* under the old dispensation." I would feign lift my feeble voice to vindicate Jehovah's character from so foul a slander. If slaveholders are determined to hold slaves as long as they can, let them not dare to say that the God of mercy and of truth *ever* sanctioned such a system of cruelty and wrong. It is blasphemy against Him.

We have seen that the code of laws framed by Moses with regard to servants was designed to *protect them as men and women,* to secure to them their *rights* as *human beings,* to guard them from oppression and defend them from violence of every kind. Let us now turn to the Slave laws of the South and West and examine them too. I will give you the substance only, because I fear I shall trespass too much on your time, were I to quote them at length.

1. *Slavery* is hereditary and perpetual, to the last moment of the slave's earthly existence, and to all his descendants to the latest posterity.

2. The labor of the slave is compulsory and uncompensated; while the kind of labor, the amount of toil, the time allowed for rest, are dictated solely by the master. No bargain is made, no wages given. A pure despotism governs the human brute; and even his covering and provender, both as to quantity and quality, depend entirely on the master's discretion.

3. The slave being considered a personal chattel may be sold or pledged, or leased at the will of his master. He may be exchanged for marketable commodities, or taken in execution for the debts or taxes either of a living or dead master. Sold at auction, either individually, or in lots to suit the purchaser, he may remain with his family, or be separated from them for ever.

4. Slaves can make no contracts and have no *legal* right to any property, real or personal. Their own honest earnings and the legacies of friends belong in point of law to their masters.

5. Neither a slave nor a free colored person can be a witness against any *white,* or free person, in a court of

justice, however atrocious may have been the crimes they have seen him commit, if such testimony would be for the benefit of a *slave*; but they may give testimony *against a fellow slave*, or free colored man, even in cases affecting life, if the *master* is to reap the advantage of it.

6. The slave may be punished at his master's discretion—without trial—without any means of legal redress; whether his offence be real or imaginary; and the master can transfer the same despotic power to any person or persons, he may choose to appoint.

7. The slave is not allowed to resist any free man under any circumstances, *his* only safety consists in the fact that his *owner* may bring suit and recover the price of his body, in case his life is taken, or his limbs rendered unfit for labor.

8. Slaves cannot redeem themselves, or obtain a change of masters, though cruel treatment may have rendered such a change necessary for their personal safety.

9. The slave is entirely unprotected in his domestic relations.

10. The laws greatly obstruct the manumission of slaves, even where the master is willing to enfranchise them.

11. The operation of the laws tends to deprive slaves of religious instruction and consolation.

12. The whole power of the laws is exerted to keep slaves in a state of the lowest ignorance.

13. There is in this country a monstrous inequality of law and right. What is a trifling fault in the *white* man, is considered highly criminal in the *slave*; the same offences which cost a white man a few dollars only, are punished in the negro with death.

14. The laws operate most oppressively upon free people of color. (See Mrs. [Lydia Maria] Child's *Appeal*, Chap. II.)

Shall I ask you now my friends, to draw the *parallel* between Jewish *servitude* and American *slavery*? No! For there is *no likeness* in the two systems; I ask you rather to mark the contrast. The laws of Moses *protected servants* in their *rights* as *men and women*, guarded them from oppression and defended them from wrong. The Code Noir of the South *robs the slave of all his rights* as a *man*, reduces him to a chattel personal, and defends the *master* in the exercise of the most unnatural and unwarrantable power over his slave. They each bear the impress of the hand which formed them. The attributers of justice and mercy are shadowed out in the Hebrew code; those of injustice and cruelty, in the Code Noir of America. Truly it was wise in the slaveholders of the South to declare their slaves to be "chattels personal"; for before they could be robbed of wages, wives, children, and friends, it was

absolutely necessary to deny they were human beings. It is wise in them, to keep them in abject ignorance, for the strong man armed must be bound before we can spoil his house—the powerful intellect of man must be bound down with the iron chains of nescience before we can rob him of his rights as a man; we must reduce him to a *thing* before we can claim the right to set our feet upon his neck, because it was only *all things* which were originally *put under the feet of man* by the Almighty and beneficent Father of all, who has declared himself to be *no respecter* of persons, whether red, white, or black. . . .

I have thus, I think, clearly proved to you seven propositions, viz.: First, that slavery is contrary to the declaration of our independence. Second, that it is contrary to the first charter of human rights given to Adam, and renewed to Noah. Third, that the fact of slavery having been the subject of prophecy, furnishes *no* excuse whatsoever to slavedealers. Fourth, that no such system existed under the patriarchal dispensation. Fifth, that *slavery never* existed under the Jewish dispensation; but so far otherwise, that every servant was placed under the *protection of law*, and care taken not only to prevent all *involuntary* servitude, but all *voluntary perpetual* bondage. Sixth, that slavery in America reduces a *man* to a *thing*, a "chattel personal," *robs him* of *all* his rights as a *human being*, fetters both his mind and body, and protects the *master* in the most unnatural and unreasonable power, whilst it *throws him out* of the protection of law. Seventh, that slavery is contrary to the example and precepts of our holy and merciful Redeemer, and of his apostles.

But perhaps you will be ready to query, why appeal to *women* on this subject? We do not make the laws which perpetuate slavery. *No* legislative power is vested in *us; we* can do nothing to overthrow the system, even if we wished to do so. To this I reply, I know you do not make the laws, but I also know that *you are the wives and mothers, the sisters and daughters of those who do*; and if you really suppose *you* can do nothing to overthrow slavery, you are greatly mistaken. You can do much in every way: four things I will name. First, you can read on this subject. Second, you can pray over this subject. Third, you can speak on this subject. Fourth, you can *act* on this subject. I have not placed reading before praying because I regard it more important, but because, in order to pray aright, we must understand what we are praying for; it is only then we can "pray with the understanding and the spirit also."

1. Read then on the subject of slavery. Search the Scriptures daily, whether the things I have told you are true. Other books and papers might be a great help to you in this investigation, but they are not necessary, and it is hardly probable that your Committees of

Vigilance will allow you to have any other. The *Bible* then is the book I want you to read in the spirit of inquiry, and the spirit of prayer. Even the enemies of Abolitionists, acknowledge that their doctrines are drawn from it. In the great mob in Boston last autumn, when the books and papers of the Anti-Slavery Society were thrown out of the windows of their office, an individual laid hold of the Bible and was about tossing it out to the ground, when another reminded him that it was the Bible he had in his hand. *"O! 'tis all one,"* he replied, and out went the sacred volume along with the rest. We thank him for the acknowledgment. Yes, *"it is all one,"* for our books and papers are mostly commentaries on the Bible, and the Declaration. Read the *Bible* then, it contains the words of Jesus, and they are spirit and life. Judge for yourselves whether *he sanctioned* such a system of oppression and crime.

2. Pray over this subject. When you have entered into your closets, and shut to the doors, then pray to your father, who seeth in secret, that he would open your eyes to see whether slavery is *sinful*, and if it is, that he would enable you to bear a faithful, open and unshrinking testimony against it, and to do whatsoever your hands find to do, leaving the consequences entirely to him, who still says to us whenever we try to reason away duty from the fear of consequences, *"What is that to thee, follow thou me."* Pray also for that poor slave, that he may be kept patient and submissive under his hard lot, until God is pleased to open the door of freedom to him without violence or bloodshed. Pray too for the master that his heart may be softened, and he made willing to acknowledge, as Joseph's brethren did, "Verily we are guilty concerning our brother," before he will be compelled to add in consequence of Divine judgment, "therefore is all this evil come upon us." Pray also for all your brethren and sisters who are laboring in the righteous cause of Emancipation in the Northern States, England and the world. There is great encouragement for prayer in these words of our Lord. "Whatsoever ye shall ask the Father *in my name*, he *will give* it to you"—Pray then without ceasing, in the closet and the social circle.

3. Speak on this subject. It is through the tongue, the pen, and the press, that truth is principally propagated. Speak then to your relatives, your friends, your acquaintances on the subject of slavery; be not afraid if you are conscientiously convinced it is *sinful*, to say so openly, but calmly, and to let your sentiments be known. If you are served by the slaves of others, try to ameliorate their condition as much as possible; never aggravate their faults, and thus add fuel to the fire of anger already kindled in a master and mistress's bosom; remember their extreme ignorance, and consider them as your Heavenly Father does the *less* culpable

on this account, even when they do wrong things. Discountenance *all* cruelty to them, all starvation, all corporal chastisement; these may brutalize and *break* their spirits, but will never bond them to willing, cheerful obedience. If possible, see that they are comfortably and *seasonably* fed, whether in the house or the field; it is unreasonable and cruel to expect slaves to wait for their breakfast until eleven o'clock, when they rise at five or six. Do all you can, to induce their owners to clothe them well, and to allow them many little indulgences which would contribute to their comfort. Above all, try to persuade your husband, father, brothers and sons, that *slavery is a crime against God and man*, and that it is a great sin to keep *human beings* in such abject ignorance; to deny them the privilege of learning to read and write. The Catholics are universally condemned, for denying the Bible to the common people, but, *slaveholders must not* blame them, for *they* are doing the *very same thing*, and for the very same reason, neither of these systems can bear the light which bursts from the pages of that Holy Book. And lastly, endeavour to inculcate submission on the part of the slaves, but whilst doing this be faithful in pleading the cause of the oppressed.

> Will *you* behold unheeding,
> Life's holiest feelings crushed,
> Where *woman's* heart is bleeding,
> Shall *woman's* heart be hushed?

4. Act on this subject. Some of you *own* slaves yourselves. If you believe slavery is *sinful*, set them at liberty, "undo the heavy burdens and let the oppressed go free." If they wish to remain with you, pay them wages, if not let them leave you. Should they remain teach them, and have them taught the common branches of an English education; they have minds and those minds, *ought to be improved.* So precious a talent as intellect, never was given to be wrapt in a napkin and buried in the earth. It is the *duty* of all, as far as they can, to improve their own mental faculties, because we are commanded to love God with *all our minds*, as well as with all our hearts, and we commit a great sin, if we *forbid or prevent* that cultivation of the mind in others, which would enable them to perform this duty. Teach your servants then to read &c, and encourage them to believe it is their *duty* to learn, if it were only that they might read the Bible.

But some of you will say, we can neither free our slaves nor teach them to read, for the laws of our state forbid it. Be not surprised when I say such wicked laws *ought to be no barrier* in the way of your duty, and I appeal to the Bible to prove this position. What was the conduct of Shiphrah and Puah, when the king of Egypt issued his cruel mandate, with regard to the

Hebrew children? "*They* feared *God*, and did *not* as the King of Egypt commanded them, but saved the men children alive." Did these *women* do right in disobeying that monarch? "*Therefore* (says the sacred text,) *God dealt well* with them, and made them houses." Ex. i. What was the conduct of Shadrach, Meshach, and Abednego, when Nebuchadnezzar set up a golden image in the plain of Dura, and commanded all people, nations, and languages to fall down and worship it? "Be it known, unto thee, (said these faithful *Jews*) O king, that *we will not* serve thy gods, nor worship the image which thou hast set up." Did these men *do right in disobeying the law* of their sovereign: Let their miraculous deliverance from the burning fiery furnace, answer; Dan. iii. What was the conduct of Daniel, when Darius made a firm decree that no one should ask a petition of any man or God for thirty days? Did the prophet cease to pray? No! "When Daniel *knew that the writing was signed*, he went into his house, and his windows being *open* towards Jerusalem, he kneeled upon his knees three times a day, and prayed and gave thanks before his God, as he did aforetime." Did Daniel do right thus to *break* the law of his king? Let his wonderful deliverance out of the mouths of the lions answer; Dan. vii. Look, too, at the Apostles Peter and John. When the rulers of the Jews, "*commanded them not* to speak at all, nor teach in the name of Jesus," what did they say? "Whether it be right in the sight of God, to hearken unto you more than unto God, judge ye." And what did they do? "They spake the word of God with boldness, and with great power gave the Apostles witness of the *resurrection* of the Lord Jesus"; although *this* was the very doctrine, for the preaching of which, they had just been cast into prison, and further threatened. Did these men do right? I leave *you* to answer, who now enjoy the benefits of their labors and sufferings, in that Gospel they dared to preach when positively commanded *not to teach any more* in the name of Jesus; Acts iv.

But some of you may say, if we do free our slaves, they will be taken up and sold, therefore there will be no use in doing it. Peter and John might just as well have said, we will not preach the gospel, for if we do, we shall be taken up and put in prison, therefore there will be no use in our preaching. *Consequences*, my friends, belong no more to *you*, than they did to these apostles. Duty is ours and events are God's. If you think slavery is sinful, all *you* have to do is to set your slaves at liberty, do all you can to protect them, and in humble faith and fervent prayer, commend them to your common Father. He can take care of them; but if for wise purposes he sees fit to allow them to be sold, this will afford you an opportunity of testifying openly, wherever you go, against the crime of *manstealing*.

Such an act will be *clear robbery*, and if exposed, might, under the Divine direction, do the cause of Emancipation more good, than any thing that could happen, for "He makes even the wrath of man to praise him, and the remainder of wrath he will restrain."

I know that this doctrine of obeying *God*, rather than man, will be considered as dangerous and heretical by many, but I am not afraid openly to avow it, because it is the doctrine of the Bible; but I would not be understood to advocate resistance to any law however oppressive, if, in obeying it, I was not obliged to commit *sin*. If for instance, there was a law, which imposed imprisonment or a fine upon me if I manumitted a slave, I would on no account resist that law, I would set the slave free, and then go to prison or pay the fine. If a law commands me to *sin I will break it*; if it calls me to *suffer*, I will let it take its course *unresistingly*. The doctrine of blind obedience and unqualified submission to *any human* power, whether civil or ecclesiastical, is the doctrine of despotism, and ought to have no place among Republicans and Christians.

But you will perhaps say, such a course of conduct would inevitably expose us to great suffering. Yes! my Christian friends, I believe it would, but this will *not* excuse you or any one else for the neglect of *duty*. If Prophets and Apostles, Martyrs, and Reformers had not been willing to suffer for the truth's sake, where would the world have been now? If they had said, we cannot speak the truth, we cannot do what we believe is right, because the *laws of our country or public opinion are against us*, where would our holy religion have been now? . . .

But you may say we are *women*, how can *our* hearts endure persecution? And why not? Have not *women* stood up in all the dignity and strength of moral courage to be the leaders of the people, and to bear a faithful testimony for the truth whenever the providence of God has called them to do so? Are there no *women* in that noble army of martyrs who are now singing the song of Moses and the Lamb? Who led out the women of Israel from the house of bondage, striking the timbrel, and singing the song of deliverance on the banks of that sea whose waters stood up like walls of crystal to open a passage for their escape? It was a *woman*; Miriam, the prophetess, the sister of Moses and Aaron. Who went up with Barak to Kadesh to fight against Jabin, King of Canaan, into whose hand Israel had been sold because of their iniquities? It was a *woman!* Deborah the wife of Lapidoth, the judge, as well as the prophetess of that backsliding people; Judges iv, 9. Into whose hands was Sisera, the captain of Jabin's host delivered? Into the hand of a *woman*. Jael the wife of Heber! Judges vi, 21. Who dared to *speak the truth* concerning those judgments which were coming upon Judea, when Josiah, alarmed at finding that his people "had not kept the word of the Lord to do after all that was written in the book of the Law," sent to enquire of the Lord concerning these things? It was a *woman*. Huldah the prophetess, the wife of Shallum; 2 Chron. xxxiv, 22. Who was chosen to deliver the whole Jewish nation from the murderous decree of Persia's King, which wicked Haman had obtained by calumny and fraud? It was a *woman*; Esther the Queen; yes, weak and trembling *woman* was the instrument appointed by God, to reverse the bloody mandate of the eastern monarch, and save the *whole visible church* from destruction. What human voice first proclaimed to Mary that she should be the mother of our Lord? It was a *woman!* Elizabeth, the wife of Zacharias; Luke i, 42, 43. Who united with the good old Simeon in giving thanks publicly in the temple, when the child, Jesus, was presented there by his parents, "and spake of him to all them that looked for redemption in Jerusalem"? It was a *woman!* Anna the prophetess. Who first proclaimed Christ as the true Messiah in the streets of Samaria, once the capital of the ten tribes? It was a *woman!* Who ministered to the Son of God whilst on earth a despised and persecuted Reformer, in the humble garb of a carpenter? They were *women!* Who followed the rejected King of Israel, as his fainting footsteps trod the road to Calvary? "A great company of people and of *women*": and it is remarkable that to *them alone*, he turned and addressed the pathetic language, "Daughters of Jerusalem, weep not for me, but weep for yourselves and your children." Ah! who went unto the Roman Governor when he was set down on the judgment seat, saying unto him, "Have thou nothing to do with that just man, for I have suffered many things this day in a dream because of him"? It was a *woman!* the wife of Pilate. Although "*he knew* that for envy the Jews had delivered Christ," yet *he* consented to surrender the Son of God into the hands of a brutal soldiery, after having himself scourged his naked body. Had the *wife* of Pilate sat upon that judgment seat, what would have been the result of the trial of this "just person"?

And who last hung around the cross of Jesus on the mountain of Golgotha? Who first visited the sepulchre early in the morning on the first day of the week, carrying sweet spices to embalm his precious body, not knowing that it was incorruptible and could not be holden by the bands of death? These were *women!* To whom did he *first* appear after his resurrection? It was to a *woman!* Mary Magdalene; Mark xvi, 9. Who gathered with the apostles to wait at Jerusalem, in prayer and supplication, for "the promise of the Father"; the spiritual blessing of the Great High Priest of his

Church, who had entered, *not* into the splendid temple of Solomon, there to offer the blood of bulls, and of goats, and the smoking censer upon the golden altar, but into Heaven itself, there to present his intercessions, after having "given himself for us, an offering and a sacrifice to God for a sweet smelling savor"? *Women* were among that holy company; Acts, i, 14. And did *women* wait in vain? Did those who had ministered to his necessities, followed in his train, and wept at his crucifixion, wait in vain? No! No! did the cloven tongues of fire descend upon the heads of *women* as well as men? Yes, my friends, "it sat upon *each of them*"; Acts ii, 3. *Women* as well as men were to be living stones in the temple of grace, and therefore *their* heads were consecrated by the descent of the Holy Ghost as well as those of men. Were *women* recognized as fellow laborers in the gospel field? They were! Paul says in his epistle to the Philippians, "help those *women* who labored with men, in the gospel"; Phil. iv, 3.

But this is not all. Roman *women* were burnt at the stake, *their* delicate limbs were torn joint from joint by the ferocious beasts of the Amphitheatre, and tossed by the wild bull in his fury, for the diversion of that idolatrous, warlike, and slaveholding people. Yes, *women* suffered under the ten persecutions of heathen Rome, with the most unshrinking constancy and fortitude; not all the entreaties of friends, nor the claims of new born infancy, nor the cruel threats of enemies could make *them* sprinkle one grain of incense upon the altars of Roman idols. Come now with me to the beautiful valleys of Piedmont. Whose blood stains the green sward, and decks the wild flowers with colors not their own, and smokes on the sword of persecuting France? Is it *woman's*, as well as man's? Yes, *women* were accounted as sheep for the slaughter, and were cut down as the tender saplings of the wood.

But time would fail me, to tell of all those hundreds and thousands of *women*, who perished in the Low countries of Holland, when Alva's sword of vengeance was unsheathed against the Protestants, when the Catholic Inquisitions of Europe became the merciless executioners of vindictive wrath, upon those who dared to worship God, instead of bowing down in unholy adoration before "my Lord God the *Pope*," and when England, too, burnt her Ann Ascoes at the stake of martyrdom. Suffice it to say, that the Church, after having been driven from Judea to Rome, and from Rome to Piedmont, and from Piedmont to England, and from England to Holland, at last stretched her fainting wings over the dark bosom of the Atlantic, and found on the shores of a great wilderness, a refuge from tyranny and oppression—as she thought, but *even here,* (the warm blush of shame mantles my cheeks as I write it,) *even there, woman* was beaten and banished, imprisoned, and hung upon the gallows, a trophy to the Cross.

And what, I would ask in conclusion, have *women* done for the great and glorious cause of Emancipation? Who wrote that pamphlet which moved the heart of Wilberforce to pray over the wrongs, and his tongue to plead the cause of the oppressed African? It was a *woman*, Elizabeth Heyrick. Who labored assiduously to keep the sufferings of the slave continually before the British public? They were *women*. And how did they do it? By their needles, paintbrushes and pens, by speaking the truth, and petitioning Parliament for the abolition of slavery. And what was the effect of their labors? Read it in the Emancipation bill of Great Britain. Read it, in the present state of her West India Colonies. Read it, in the impulse which has been given to the cause of freedom in the United States of America. Have English women then done so much for the Negro, and shall American women do nothing? Oh no! Already are there sixty female Anti-Slavery Societies in operation. These are doing just what the English women did, telling the story of the colored man's wrongs, praying for his deliverance, and presenting his kneeling image constantly before the public eye on bags and needlebooks, card-racks, pen-wipers, pin-cushions, &c. Even the children of the north are inscribing on their handiwork, "May the points of our needles prick the slaveholder's conscience." Some of the reports of these Societies exhibit not only considerable talent, but a deep sense of religious duty, and a determination to persevere through evil as well as good report, until every scourge, and every shackle, is buried under the feet of the manumitted slave.

The Ladies' Anti-Slavery Society of Boston was called last fall, to a severe trial of their faith and constancy. They were mobbed by "the gentlemen of property and standing," in that city at their anniversary meeting, and their lives were jeoparded by an infuriated crowd; but their conduct on that occasion did credit to our sex, and affords a full assurance that they will *never* abandon the cause of the slave. The pamphlet, "Right and Wrong in Boston," issued by them in which a particular account is given of that "mob of broad cloth in broad day," does equal credit to the head and the heart of her who wrote it. I wish my Southern sisters could read it; they would then understand that the women of the North have engaged in this work from a sense of *religious duty*, and that nothing will ever induce them to take their hands from it until it is fully accomplished. They feel no hostility to you, no bitterness or wrath; they rather sympathize in your trials and difficulties; but they well know that the first thing to be done to help you, is to pour in the light of truth on your minds, to urge you to reflect on, and pray

over the subject. This is all *they* can do for you, *you* must work out your own deliverance with fear and trembling, and with the direction and blessing of God, *you can do it*. Northern women may labor to produce a correct public opinion at the North, but if Southern women sit down in listless indifference and criminal idleness, public opinion cannot be rectified and purified at the South. It is manifest to every reflecting mind, that slavery must be abolished; the era in which we live, and the light which is overspreading the whole world on this subject, clearly show that the time cannot be distant when it will be done. Now there are only two ways in which it can be effected, by moral power or physical force, and it is for *you* to choose which of these you prefer. Slavery always has, and always will produce insurrections wherever it exists, because it is a violation of the natural order of things, and no human power can much longer perpetuate it. The opposers of abolitionists fully believe this; one of them remarked to me not long since, there is no doubt there will be a most terrible overturning at the South in a few years, such cruelty and wrong, must be visited with Divine vengeance soon. Abolitionists believe, too, that this must inevitably be the case if you do not repent, and they are not willing to leave you to perish without entreating you, to save yourselves from destruction; well may they say with the apostle, "am I then your enemy because I tell you the truth," and warn you to flee from impending judgments.

But why, my dear friends, have I thus been endeavoring to lead you through the history of more than three thousand years, and to point you to that great cloud of witnesses who have gone before, "from works to rewards"? Have I been seeking to magnify the sufferings, and exalt the character of woman, that she "might have praise of men"? No! no! my object has been to arouse *you*, as the wives and mothers, the daughters and sisters, of the South, to a sense of your duty as *women*, and as Christian women, on that great subject, which has already shaken our country, from the St. Lawrence and the lakes, to the Gulf of Mexico, and from the Mississippi to the shores of the Atlantic; *and will continue mightily to shake it*, until the polluted temple of slavery fall and crumble into ruin. I would say unto each one of you, "what meanest thou, O sleeper! arise and call upon thy God, if so be that God will think upon us that we perish not." Perceive you not that dark cloud of vengeance which hangs over our boasting Republic? Saw you not the lightnings of Heaven's wrath, in the flame which leaped from the Indian's torch to the roof of yonder dwelling, and lighted with its horrid glare the darkness of midnight? Heard you not the thunders of Divine anger, as the distant roar of the cannon came rolling onward, from the Texan country, where Protestant American Rebels are fighting with Mexican Republicans—for what? For the reestablishment of *slavery*; yes! of American slavery in the bosom of a Catholic Republic, where that system of robbery, violence, and wrong, had been legally abolished for twelve years. Yes! citizens of the United States, after plundering Mexico of her land, are now engaged in deadly conflict for the privilege of fastening chains, and collars, and manacles—upon whom? upon the subjects of some foreign prince? No! upon native born American Republican citizens, although the fathers of these very men declared to the whole world, while struggling to free themselves from the three penny taxes of an English king, that they believed it to be a *self-evident* truth that *all men* were created equal, and had an *inalienable right to liberty*.

Well may the poet exclaim in bitter sarcasm,

"The fustian flag that proudly waves
In solemn mockery o'er *a land of slaves.*"

Can you not, my friends, understand the signs of the time; do you not see the sword of retributive justice hanging over the South, or are you still slumbering at your posts?—Are there no Shiphrahs, no Puahs among you, who will dare in Christian firmness and Christian meekness, to refuse to obey the *wicked laws* which require *woman to enslave, to degrade and to brutalize woman*? Are there no Miriams, who would rejoice to lead out the captive daughters of the Southern States to liberty and light? Are there no Huldahs there who will dare to *speak the truth* concerning the sins of the people and those judgments, which it requires no prophet's eye to see must follow if repentance is not speedily sought? Is there no Esther among you who will plead for the poor devoted slave? Read the history of this Persian queen, it is full of instruction; she at first refused to plead for the Jews: but hear the words of Mordecai, "Think not within thyself, that *thou* shalt escape in the king's house more than all the Jews, for *if thou altogether holdest thy peace at this time,* then shall there enlargement and deliverance arise to the Jews from another place: but *thou and thy father's house shall be destroyed.*" Listen, too, to her magnanimous reply to this powerful appeal; "*I will* go in unto the king, which is *not* according to law, and if I perish, I perish." Yes! if there were but *one* Esther at the South, she *might* save her country from ruin; but let the Christian women there arise, as the Christian women of Great Britain did, in the majesty of moral power, and that salvation is certain. Let them embody themselves in societies, and send petitions up to their different legislatures, entreating their husbands, fathers, brothers, and sons, to abolish the institution of slavery; no

longer to subject *woman* to the scourge and the chain, to mental darkness and moral degradation; no longer to tear husbands from their wives, and children from their parents; no longer to make men, women, and children, work *without wages*; no longer to make their lives bitter in hard bondage; no longer to reduce *American citizens* to the abject condition of *slaves*, of "chattels personal"; no longer to barter the *image of God* in human shambles for corruptible things such as silver and gold.

The *women of the South can overthrow* this horrible system of oppression and cruelty, licentiousness and wrong. Such appeals to your legislatures would be irresistible, for there is something in the heart of man which *will bend under moral suasion*. There is a swift witness for truth in his bosom, which *will respond to truth* when it is uttered with calmness and dignity. If you could obtain but six signatures to such a petition in only one state, I would say, send up that petition, and be not in the least discouraged by the scoffs and jeers of the heartless, or the resolution of the house to lay it on the table. It will be a great thing if the subject can be introduced into your legislatures in any way, even by *women*, and *they* will be the most likely to introduce it there in the best possible manner, as a matter of *morals* and *religion*, not of expediency or politics. You may petition, too, the different ecclesiastical bodies of the slave states. Slavery must be attacked with the whole power of truth and the sword of the spirit. You must take it up on *Christian* ground, and fight against it with Christian weapons, whilst your feet are shod with the preparation of the gospel of peace. And *you are now* loudly called upon by the cries of the widow and the orphan, to arise and gird yourselves for this great moral conflict, with the whole armour of righteousness upon the right hand and on the left.

There is every encouragement for you to labor and pray, my friends, because the abolition of slavery as well as its existence, has been the theme of prophecy. "Ethiopia (says the Psalmist) shall stretch forth her hands unto God." And is he not doing so? Are not the Christian Negroes of the south lifting their hands in prayer for deliverance, just as the Israelites did when their redemption was drawing nigh? Are they not sighing and crying by reason of the hard bondage? And think you, that He, of whom it was said, "and God heard their groaning, and their cry came up unto him by reason of the hard bondage," think you that his ear is heavy that he cannot *now* hear the cries of his suffering children? Or that He who raised up a Moses, an Aaron, and a Miriam, to bring them up out of the land of Egypt from the house of bondage, cannot now, with a high hand and a stretched out arm rid the poor Negroes out of the hands of their masters? Surely you believe that his arm is not shortened that he cannot save. And would not such a work of mercy redound to his glory? But another string of the harp of prophecy vibrates to the song of deliverance: "But they shall sit every man under his vine, and under his fig-tree, and *none shall make them afraid*; for the mouth of the Lord of Hosts hath spoken it." The *slave* never can do this as long as he is a *slave*; whilst he is a "chattel personal" he can own *no* property; but the time *is to come* when *every* man is to sit under *his own* vine and *his own* fig-tree, and no domineering driver, or irresponsible master, or irascible mistress, shall make him afraid of the chain or the whip. Hear, too, the sweet tones of another string: "Many shall run to and fro, and *knowledge* shall be increased." Slavery is an insurmountable barrier to the increase of knowledge in every community where it exists; *slavery, then, must be abolished before* this prediction can be fulfilled. The last chord I shall touch, will be this, "They shall *not* hurt nor destroy in all my holy mountain."

Slavery, then, must be overthrown before the prophecies can be accomplished, but how are they to be fulfilled? Will the wheels of the millennial car be rolled onward by miraculous power? No! God designs to confer this holy privilege upon *man*; it is through *his* instrumentality that the great and glorious work of reforming the world is to be done. And see you not how the mighty engine of *moral power* is dragging in its rear the Bible and peace societies, anti-slavery and temperance, sabbath schools, moral reform, and missions? or to adopt another figure, do not these seven philanthropic associations compose the beautiful tints in that bow of promise which spans the arch of our moral heaven? Who does not believe, that if these societies were broken up, their constitutions burnt, and the vast machinery with which they are laboring to regenerate mankind was stopped, that the black clouds of vengeance would soon burst over our world, and every city would witness the fate of the devoted cities of the plain? Each one of these societies is walking abroad through the earth scattering the seeds of truth over the wide field of our world, not with the hundred hands of a Briareus, but with a hundred thousand.

Another encouragement for you to labor, my friends, is, that you will have the prayers and co-operation of English and Northern philanthropists. You will never bend your knees in supplication at the throne of grace for the overthrow of slavery, without meeting there the spirits of other Christians, who will mingle their voices with ours, as the morning or evening sacrifice ascends to God. . . .

But I will now say a few words on the subject of Abolitionism. Doubtless you have all heard Anti-Slavery Societies denounced as insurrectionary and mis-

chievous, fanatical and dangerous. It has been said they publish the most abominable untruths, and that they are endeavoring to excite rebellions at the South. Have you believed these reports, my friends? have *you* also been deceived by these false assertions? Listen to me, then, whilst I endeavor to wipe from the fair character of Abolitionism such unfounded accusations. You know that *I* am a Southerner; you know that my dearest relatives are now in a slave State. Can you for a moment believe I would prove so recreant to the feelings of a daughter and a sister, as to join a society which was seeking to overthrow slavery by falsehood, bloodshed, and murder? I appeal to you who have known and loved me in days that are passed, can *you* believe it? No! my friends. As a Carolinian I was peculiarly jealous of any movements on this subject; and before I would join an Anti-Slavery Society, I took the precaution of becoming acquainted with some of the leading Abolitionists, of reading their publications and attending their meetings, at which I heard addresses both from colored and white men; and it was not until I was fully convinced that their principles were *entirely pacific*, and their efforts *only moral*, that I gave my name as a member to the Female Anti-Slavery Society of Philadelphia. Since that time, I have regularly taken the *Liberator*, and read many Anti-Slavery pamphlets and papers and books, and can assure you I *never* have seen a single insurrectionary paragraph, and never read any account of cruelty which I could not believe. Southerners may deny the truth of these accounts, but why do they not *prove* them to be false. Their violent expressions of horror at such accounts being believed, *may* deceive some, but they cannot deceive *me*, for I lived too long in the midst of slavery, not to know what slavery is. When *I* speak of this system, "I speak that I do know," and I am not at all afraid to assert, that Anti-Slavery publications have *not* overdrawn the monstrous features of slavery at all. And many a Southerner *knows* this as well as I do. A lady in North Carolina remarked to a friend of mine, about eighteen months since, "Northerners know nothing at all about slavery; they think it is perpetual bondage only; but of the *depth of degradation* that word involves, they have no conception; if they had, *they would never cease* their efforts until so *horrible* a system was overthrown." She did not know how faithfully some Northern men and Northern women had studied this subject; how diligently they had searched out the cause of "him who had none to help him," and how fearlessly they had told the story of the Negro's wrongs. Yes, Northerners know *every* thing about slavery now. This monster of iniquity has been unveiled to the world, her frightful features unmasked, and soon, very soon will she be regarded with no more complacency by the American republic than is the idol of Juggernaut, rolling its bloody wheels over the crushed bodies of its prostrate victims.

But you will probably ask, if Anti-Slavery societies are not insurrectionary, why do Northerners tell us they are? Why, I would ask you in return, did Northern senators and Northern representatives give their votes, at the last sitting of congress, to the admission of Arkansas Territory as a state? Take those men, one by one, and ask them in their parlours, do you *approve of slavery?* ask them on *Northern* ground, where they will speak the truth, and I doubt not *every man* of them will tell you, *no!* Why then, I ask, did *they* give their votes to enlarge the mouth of that grave which has already destroyed its tens of thousands? All our enemies tell *us* they are as much anti-slavery as we are. Yes, my friends, thousands who are helping you to bind the fetters of slavery on the Negro despise you in their hearts for doing it; they rejoice that such an institution has not been entailed upon them. Why then, I would ask, do *they* lend you their help? I will tell you, "they love *the praise of men more* than the praise of God." The Abolition cause has not yet become so popular as to induce them to believe, that by advocating it in congress, they shall sit still more securely in their seats there and like the *chief rulers* in the days of our Saviour, though *many* believed on him, they did *not* confess him, lest they should *be put out of the synagogue;* John xii, 42, 43. Or perhaps like Pilate, thinking they could prevail nothing, and fearing a tumult, they determined to release Barabbas and surrender the just man, the poor innocent slave to be stripped of his rights and scourged. In vain will such men try to wash their hands, and say, with the Roman governor, "I am innocent of the blood of this just person." Northern American statesmen are no more innocent of the crime of slavery, than Pilate was of the murder of Jesus, or Saul of that of Stephen. These are high charges, but I appeal to *their hearts;* I appeal to public opinion ten years from now. Slavery then is a national sin.

But you will say, a great many other Northerners tell us so, who can have no political motives. The interests of the North, you must know, my friends, are very closely combined with those of the South. The Northern merchants and manufacturers are making *their* fortunes out of the *produce of slave labor;* the grocer is selling your rice and sugar; how then can these men bear a testimony against slavery without condemning themselves? But there is another reason, the North is most dreadfully afraid of Amalgamation. She is alarmed at the very idea of a thing so monstrous, as she thinks. And lest this consequence *might* flow from emancipation, she is determined to resist all efforts at emancipation without expatriation. It is not because *she approves of slavery*, or believes it to be "the cornerstone of our republic," for she is as much *anti-slavery* as we are; but amalgamation is too horrible to think of. Now I would ask *you*, is it right, is it generous, to refuse the colored people in this country the advantages of education and the privilege, or rather the *right*, to follow honest trades and callings merely because they are colored? The same prejudice exists here against our colored brethren that existed against the Gentiles in Judea. Great numbers cannot bear the idea of equality, and fearing lest, if they had the same advantages we enjoy, they would become as intelligent, as moral, as religious, and as respectable and wealthy, they are determined to keep them as low as they possibly can. Is this doing as they would be done by? Is this loving their neighbor as *themselves?* Oh! that *such* opposers of Abolitionism would put their souls in the stead of the free colored man's and obey the apostolic injunction, to "remember them that are in bonds *as bound with them.*" I will leave you to judge whether the fear of amalgamation ought to induce men to oppose anti-slavery efforts, when *they* believe *slavery* to be *sinful.* Prejudice against color, is the most powerful enemy we have to fight with at the North. . . .

Abolitionists understand the slaveholding spirit too well to be surprised at any thing that has yet happened at the South or the North; they know that the greater the sin is, which is exposed, the more violent will be the efforts to blacken the character and impugn the motives of those who are engaged in bringing to light the hidden things of darkness. They understand the work of Reform too well to be driven back by the furious waves of opposition, which are only foaming out of their own shame. They have stood "the world's dread laugh," when only twelve men formed the first Anti-Slavery Society in Boston in 1831. They have faced and refuted the calumnies of their enemies, and proved themselves to be emphatically *peace men* by *never resisting* the violence of mobs, even when driven by them from the temple of God, and dragged by an infuriated crowd through the streets of the emporium of New England, or subjected by *slaveholders* to the pain of corporal punishment. "None of these things move them"; and, by the grace of God, they are determined to persevere in this work of faith and labor of love: they mean to pray, and preach, and write, and print, until slavery is completely overthrown, until Babylon is taken up and cast into the sea, to "be found no more at all." They mean to petition Congress year after year, until the seat of our government is cleansed from the sinful traffic of "slaves and the souls of men." Although that august assembly may be like the unjust judge who "feared not God neither regarded man," yet it *must* yield just as he did, from the power of importunity. Like the unjust judge, Congress *must* redress the wrongs of the widow, lest by the continual coming up of petitions, it be wearied. This will be striking the dagger into the very heart of the monster, and once 'tis done, he must soon expire. . . .

Great fault has been found with the prints which have been employed to expose slavery at the North, but my friends, how could this be done so effectually in any other way? Until the pictures of the slave's sufferings were drawn and held up to public gaze, no Northerner had any idea of the cruelty of the system, it never entered their minds that such abominations could exist in Christian, Republican America; they never suspected that many of the *gentlemen* and *ladies* who came from the South to spend the summer months in travelling among them, were petty tyrants at home. And those who had lived at the South, and came to reside at the North, were too *ashamed of slavery* even to speak of it; the language of their hearts was, "tell it *not* in Gath, publish it *not* in the streets of Askelon"; they saw no use in uncovering the loathsome body to popular sight, and in hopeless despair, wept in secret places over the sins of oppression. To such hidden mourners the formation of Anti-Slavery Societies was as life from the dead, the first beams of hope which gleamed through the dark clouds of despondency and grief. Prints were made use of to effect the abolition of the Inquisition in Spain, and Clarkson employed them when he was laboring to break up the Slave trade, and English Abolitionists used them just as we are now doing. They are powerful appeals and have invariably done the work they were designed to do, and we cannot consent to abandon the use of these until the *realities* no longer exist. . . .

What can I say more, my friends, to induce *you* to set your hands, and heads, and hearts, to this great work of justice and mercy. Perhaps you have feared the consequences of immediate Emancipation, and been frightened by all those dreadful prophecies of rebellion, bloodshed and murder, which have been uttered. "Let no man deceive you"; they are the predictions of that same "lying spirit" which spoke through the four hundred prophets of old, to Ahab king of Israel, urging him on to destruction. *Slavery* may produce these horrible scenes if it is continued five years longer, but Emancipation *never will.*

I can prove the *safety* of immediate Emancipation by history. In St. Domingo in 1793 six hundred thousand slaves were set free in a white population of forty-two thousand. That Island "marched as by enchantment toward its ancient splendor, cultivation prospered, every day produced perceptible proofs of its progress and the negroes all continued quietly to work

on the different plantations, until in 1802, France determined to reduce these liberated slaves again to bondage. It was at *this time* that all those dreadful scenes of cruelty occurred, which we so often *unjustly* hear spoken of, as the effects of Abolition. They were occasioned *not* by Emancipation, but by the base attempt to fasten the chains of slavery on the limbs of liberated slaves.

In Guadaloupe eighty-five thousand slaves were freed in a white population of thirteen thousand. The same prosperous effects followed manumission here, that had attended it in Hayti, every thing was quiet until Buonaparte sent out a fleet to reduce these negroes again to slavery, and in 1802 this institution was re-established in that Island. In 1834, when Great Britain determined to liberate the slaves in her West India colonies, and proposed the apprenticeship system; the planters of Bermuda and Antigua, after having joined the other planters in their representations of the bloody consequences of Emancipation, in order if possible to hold back the hand which was offering the boon of freedom to the poor negro; as soon as they found such falsehoods were utterly disregarded, and Abolition must take place, came forward voluntarily, and asked for the compensation which was due to them, saying, *they preferred immediate emancipation,* and were not afraid of any insurrection. And how is it with these islands now? They are decidedly more prosperous than any of those in which the apprenticeship system was adopted, and England is now trying to abolish that system, so fully convinced is she that immediate Emancipation is the *safest* and the best plan.

And why not try it in the Southern States, if it *never* has occasioned rebellion; if *not a drop of blood* has ever been shed in consequence of it, though it has been so often tried, why should we suppose it would produce such disastrous consequences now? "Be not deceived then, God is not mocked," by such false excuses for not doing justly and loving mercy. There is nothing to fear from immediate Emancipation, but *every thing* from the continuance of slavery.

Sisters in Christ, I have done. As a Southerner, I have felt it was my duty to address you. I have endeavored to set before you the exceeding sinfulness of slavery, and to point you to the example of those noble women who have been raised up in the church to effect great revolutions, and to suffer for the truth's sake. I have appealed to your sympathies as women, to your sense of duty as *Christian women.* I have attempted to vindicate the Abolitionists, to prove the entire safety of immediate Emancipation, and to plead the cause of the poor and oppressed. I have done—I have sowed the seeds of truth, but I well know, that even if an Apollos were to follow in my steps to water them, "*God only* can give the increase." To Him then who is able to prosper the work of his servant's hand, I commend this Appeal in fervent prayer, that as he "hath *chosen the weak things of the world*, to confound the things which are mighty," so He may cause His blessing, to descend and carry conviction to the hearts of many Lydias through these speaking pages. Farewell—Count me not your "enemy because I have told you the truth," but believe me in unfeigned affection,

Your sympathizing Friend,
Angelina E. Grimké
Shrewsbury, N.J., 1836
Third Edition

Sarah M. Grimké

Letters on the Equality of the Sexes, and the Condition of Woman (1838)

Addressed to Mary S. Parker, President of the Boston Female Anti-Slavery Society.

Letter I.

The Original Equality of Woman

Amesbury, 7th Mo. 11th, 1837.

My Dear Friend,—In attempting to comply with thy request to give my views on the Province of Woman, I feel that I am venturing on nearly untrodden ground, and that I shall advance arguments in opposition to a corrupt public opinion, and to the perverted interpretation of Holy Writ, which has so universally obtained. But I am in search of truth; and no obstacle shall prevent my prosecuting that search, because I believe the welfare of the world will be materially advanced by every new discovery we make of the designs of Jehovah in the creation of woman. It is impossible that we can answer the purpose of our being, unless we understand that purpose. It is impossible that we should fulfil our duties, unless we comprehend them; or live up to our privileges, unless we know what they are.

In examining this important subject, I shall depend solely on the Bible to designate the sphere of woman, because I believe almost every thing that has

been written on this subject, has been the result of a misconception of the simple truths revealed in the Scriptures, in consequence of the false translation of many passages of Holy Writ. My mind is entirely delivered from the superstitious reverence which is attached to the English version of the Bible. King James's translators certainly were not inspired. I therefore claim the original as my standard, *believing that to have been inspired*, and I also claim to judge for myself what is the meaning of the inspired writers, because I believe it to be the solemn duty of every individual to search the Scriptures for themselves, with the aid of the Holy Spirit, and not be governed by the views of any man, or set of men.

We must first view woman at the period of her creation. 'And God said, Let us make man in our own image, after our likeness; and let them have dominion over the fish of the sea, and over the fowl of the air, and over the cattle, and over all the earth, and over every creeping thing that creepeth upon the earth. So God created man in his own image, in the image of God created he him, male and female created he them.' In all this sublime description of the creation of man, (which is a generic term including man and woman,) there is not one particle of difference intimated as existing between them. They were both made in the image of God; dominion was given to both over every other creature, but not over each other. Created in perfect equality, they were expected to exercise the viceregence intrusted to them by their Maker, in harmony and love. . . .

This blissful condition was not long enjoyed by our first parents. . . . Through the subtlety of the serpent, [Eve] was beguiled . . . [and ate of the fruit of the tree in the midst of the garden].

. . . Had Adam tenderly reproved his wife, and endeavored to lead her to repentance instead of sharing in her guilt, I should be much more ready to accord to man that superiority which he claims; but as the facts stand disclosed by the sacred historian, it appears to me that to say the least, there was as much weakness exhibited by Adam as by Eve. They both fell from innocence, and consequently from happiness, *but not from equality.*

Let us next examine the conduct of this fallen pair, when Jehovah interrogated them respecting their fault. They both frankly confessed their guilt. 'The man said, the woman whom thou gavest to be with me, she gave me of the tree and I did eat. And the woman said, the serpent beguiled me and I did eat.' And the Lord God said unto the woman, 'Thou wilt be subject unto thy husband, and he will rule over thee.' That this did not allude to the subjection of woman to man is manifest, because the same mode of expression is used in speaking to Cain of Abel. The truth is that the curse, as it is termed, which was pronounced by Jehovah upon the woman, is a simple prophecy. The Hebrew, like the French language, uses the same word to express shall and will. Our translators having been accustomed to exercise lordship over their wives, and seeing only through the medium of a perverted judgment, very naturally, though I think not very learnedly or very kindly, translated it *shall* instead of *will* and thus converted a prediction to Eve into a command to Adam; for observe, it is addressed to the woman and not to the man. The consequence of the fall was an immediate struggle for dominion, and Jehovah foretold which would gain the ascendancy; but as he created them in his image, as that image manifestly was not lost by the fall, because it is urged in Gen. 9:6, as an argument why the life of man should not be taken by his fellow man, there is no reason to suppose that sin produced any distinction between them as moral, intellectual, and responsible beings. . . .

Here then I plant myself: God created us equal;—he created us free agents;—he is our Lawgiver, our King and our Judge, and to him alone is woman bound to be in subjection, and to him alone is she accountable for the use of those talents with which her Heavenly Father has entrusted her. One is her Master even Christ.

Thine for the oppressed in the bonds of womanhood,

Sarah M. Grimké

Letter II.

Woman Subject Only to God.

Newburyport, *7th mo.* 17, 1837

My dear Sister,—In my last, I traced the creation and the fall of man and woman from that state of purity and happiness which their beneficent Creator designed them to enjoy. As they were one in transgression, their chastisement was the same. . . . We now behold them expelled from Paradise, fallen from their original loveliness, but still bearing on their foreheads the image and superscription of Jehovah; still invested with high moral responsibilities, intellectual powers, and immortal souls. They had incurred the penalty of sin, they were shorn of their innocence, but they stood on the same platform side by side, acknowledging *no superior* but their God. Notwithstanding what has been urged, woman I am aware stands charged to the present day with having brought sin into the world. I shall not repel the charge by any counter assertions, although, as was before hinted, Adam's ready acquiescence with his wife's proposal, does not savor much of that superiority *in strength of mind*, which is arrogated by man. Even admitting that Eve was the greater sinner, it seems to me man might be satisfied with the dominion he has claimed and exercised for nearly six thousand years, and that more true nobility would be manifested by endeavoring to raise the fallen and invigorate the weak, than by keeping woman in subjection. But I ask no favors for my sex. I surrender not our claim to equality. All I ask of our brethren is, that they will take their feet from off our necks, and permit us to stand upright on that ground which God designed us to occupy. . . .

The lust of dominion was probably the first effect of the fall; and as there was no other intelligent being over whom to exercise it, woman was the first victim of this unhallowed passion. We afterwards see it exhibited by Cain in the murder of his brother, by Nimrod in his becoming a mighty hunter of men, and setting up a kingdom over which to reign. Here we see the origin of that Upas of slavery, which sprang up immediately after the fall, and has spread its pestilential branches over the whole face of the known world. . . .

Woman has been placed by John Quincy Adams, side by side with the slave, whilst he was contending for the right side of petition. I thank him for ranking us with the oppressed; for I shall not find it difficult to show, that in all ages and countries, not even excepting enlightened republican America, woman has more or less been made a *means* to promote the welfare of man, without due regard to her own happiness, and the glory of God as the end of her creation. . . .

The cupidity of man soon led him to regard woman as property, and hence we find them sold to those, who wished to marry them, as far as appears, without any regard to those sacred rights which belong to a woman, as well as to man in the choice of a companion. That women were a profitable kind of property, we may gather from the description of a virtuous woman in the last chapter of Proverbs. . . . 'The spirit of that age was not favorable to intellectual improvement; but as there were wise men who formed exceptions to the general ignorance, and were destined to guide the world into more advanced states, so there was a corresponding proportion of wise women; and among the Jews, as well as other nations, we find a strong tendency to believe that women were in more immediate connection with heaven than men.'—L. M. Child's Con[dition] of Woman. If there be any truth in this tradition, I am at a loss to imagine in what the superiority of man consists.

Thine in the bonds of womanhood,

Sarah M. Grimké

Letter III.

The Pastoral Letter of the General Association of Congregational Ministers of Massachusetts.

Haverhill, 7th Mo. 1837.

Dear Friend,—When I last addressed thee, I had not seen the Pastoral Letter of the General Association. It has since fallen into my hands, and I must digress from my intention of exhibiting the condition of women in different parts of the world, in order to make some remarks on this extraordinary document. . . .

. . . How monstrous, how anti-christian, is the doctrine that woman is to be dependent on man! Where, in all the sacred Scriptures, is this taught? Alas! She has too well learned the lesson which MAN has labored to teach her. She has surrendered her dearest RIGHTS, and been satisfied with the privileges which man has assumed to grant her; she has been amused with the show of power, whilst man has absorbed all the reality into himself. . . . This doctrine of dependence upon man is utterly at variance with the doctrine of the Bible. In that book I find nothing like the softness of woman, nor the sternness of man: both are equally commanded to bring forth the fruits of the Spirit, love, meekness, gentleness, &c.

But we are told, 'the power of woman is in her dependence, flowing from a consciousness of that weakness which God has given her for her protection.' If physical weakness is alluded to, I cheerfully concede the superiority; if brute force is what my brethren are claiming, I am willing to let them have all the honor they desire; but if they mean to intimate, that mental or moral weakness belongs to woman, more than to man, I utterly disclaim the charge. Our powers of mind have been crushed, as far as man could do it, our sense of morality has been impaired by his interpretation of our duties; but no where does God say that he made any distinction between us, as moral and intelligent beings.

'We appreciate,' say the Association, 'the *unostentatious* prayers and efforts of woman in advancing the cause of religion at home and abroad, in leading religious inquirers TO THE PASTOR for instruction.' Several points here demand attention. If public prayers and public efforts are necessarily ostentatious, then 'Anna the prophetess, (or preacher,) who departed not from the temple, but served God with fastings and prayers night and day . . . and spake of Christ to all them that looked for redemption in Israel,' was ostentatious in her efforts. Then, the apostle Paul encourages women to be ostentatious in their efforts to spread the gospel, when he gives them directions how they should appear, when engaged in praying, or preaching in the public assemblies. Then, the whole association of Congregational ministers are ostentatious, in the efforts they are making in preaching and praying to convert souls.

But woman may be permitted to lead religious inquirers to the PASTORS for instruction. Now this is assuming that all pastors are better qualified to give instruction than woman. This I utterly deny. I have suffered too keenly from the teaching of man, to lead any one to him for instruction. The Lord Jesus says,— 'Come unto me and learn of me.' He points his followers to no man; and when woman is made the favored instrument of rousing a sinner to his lost and helpless condition, she has no right to substitute any teacher for Christ; all she has to do is, to turn the contrite inquirer to the 'Lamb of God which taketh away the sins of the world.' More souls have probably been lost by going down to Egypt for help, and by trusting in man in the early stages of religious experience, than by any other error. Instead of the petition being offered to God,— 'Lead me in thy truth, and TEACH me, for thou art the God of my salvation,'—instead of relying on the precious promises—'What man is he that feareth the Lord? him shall HE TEACH in the way that he shall choose . . . I will instruct thee and TEACH thee in the way which thou shalt go—I will guide thee with mine eye'—the young convert is directed to go to man, as if he were in the place of God, and his instructions essential to an advancement in the path of righteousness. That woman can have but a poor conception of the privilege of being taught of God, what he alone can teach, who would turn the 'religious inquirer aside' from the fountain of living waters, where he might slake his thirst for spiritual instruction, to those broken cisterns which can hold no water, and therefore cannot satisfy the panting spirit. The business of men and women, who are ORDAINED OF GOD to preach the unsearchable riches of Christ to a lost and perishing world, is to lead souls to Christ, and not to Pastors for instruction.

The General Association say, that 'when woman assumes the place and tone of man as a public reformer, our care and protection of her seem unnecessary; we put ourselves in self-defence against her, and her character becomes unnatural.' Here again the unscriptural notion is held up, that there is a distinction between the duties of men and women as moral beings; that what is virtue in man, is vice in woman; and women who dare to obey the command of Jehovah, 'Cry aloud, spare not, lift up thy voice like a trumpet, and show my people their transgressions,' are threatened with having the protection of the brethren withdrawn. If this is all they do, we shall not even know the time when our chastisement is inflicted; our trust is in the Lord Jehovah, and in him is everlasting strength. The motto of woman, when she is engaged in the great work of public reformation should be, — 'The Lord is my light and my salvation; whom shall I fear? The Lord is the strength of my life; of whom shall I be afraid?' She must feel, if she feels rightly, that she is fulfilling one of the important duties laid upon her as an accountable being, and that her character, instead of being 'unnatural,' is in exact accordance with the will of Him to whom, and to no other, she is responsible for the talents and the gifts confided to her. As to the pretty simile, introduced into the 'Pastoral Letter,' 'If the vine whose strength and beauty is to lean upon the trellis work, and half conceal its clusters, thinks to assume the independence and the overshadowing nature of the elm,' &c. I shall only remark that it might well suit the poet's fancy, who sings of sparkling eyes and coral lips, and knights in armor clad; but it seems to me utterly inconsistent with the dignity of a Christian body, to endeavor to draw such an anti-scriptural distinction between men and women. Ah! how many of my sex feel in the dominion, thus unrighteously exercised over them, under the gentle appellation of *protection*, that what they have leaned upon has proved a broken reed at best, and oft a spear.

Thine in the bonds of womanhood,

Sarah M. Grimké

Letter IV.

Social Intercourse of the Sexes

Andover, 7th Mo. 27th, 1837.

My Dear Friend, — Before I proceed with the account of that oppression which woman has suffered in every age and country from her *protector*, man, permit me to offer for your consideration, some views relative to the social intercourse of the sexes. Nearly the whole of this intercourse is, in my apprehension, derogatory to man and woman, as moral and intellectual beings. We approach each other, and mingle with each other, under the constant pressure of a feeling that we are of different sexes; and, instead of regarding each other only in the light of immortal creatures, the mind is fettered by the idea which is early and industriously infused into it, that we must never forget the distinction between male and female. Hence our intercourse, instead of being elevated and refined, is generally calculated to excite and keep alive the lowest propensities of our nature. Nothing, I believe, has tended more to destroy the true dignity of woman, than the

fact that she is approached by man in the character of a female. The idea that she is sought as an intelligent and heaven-born creature, whose society will cheer, refine and elevate her companion, and that she will receive the same blessings she confers, is rarely held up to her view. On the contrary, man almost always addresses himself to the weakness of woman. By flattery, by an appeal to her passions, he seeks access to her heart; and when he has gained her affections, he uses her as the instrument of his pleasure — the minister of his temporal comfort. He furnishes himself with a housekeeper, whose chief business is in the kitchen, or the nursery. And whilst he goes abroad and enjoys the means of improvement afforded by collision of intellect with cultivated minds, his wife is condemned to draw nearly all her instruction from books, if she has time to peruse them; and if not, from her meditations, whilst engaged in those domestic duties, which are necessary for the comfort of her lord and master.

Surely no one who contemplates, with the eye of a Christian philosopher, the design of God in the creation of woman, can believe that she is now fulfilling that design. The literal translation of the word 'help-meet' is a helper like unto himself; it is so rendered in the Septuagint, and manifestly signifies a companion. Now I believe it will be impossible for woman to fill the station assigned her by God, until her brethren mingle with her as an equal, as a moral being; and lose, in the dignity of her immortal nature, and in the fact of her bearing like himself the image and superscription of her God, the idea of her being a female. The apostle beautifully remarks, 'As many of you as have been baptized into Christ, have put on Christ. There is neither Jew nor Greek, there is neither bond nor free, there is neither *male* nor *female*; for ye are all one in Christ Jesus.' Until our intercourse is purified by the forgetfulness of sex, — until we rise above the present low and sordid views which entwine themselves around our social and domestic interchange of sentiment and feelings, we never can derive that benefit from each other's society which it is the design of our Creator that we should. Man has inflicted an unspeakable injury upon woman, by holding up to her view her animal nature, and placing in the background her moral and intellectual being. Woman has inflicted an injury upon herself by submitting to be thus regarded; and she is now called upon to rise from the station where *man*, not God, has placed her, and claim those sacred and inalienable rights, as a moral and responsible being, with which her Creator has invested her.

What but these views, so derogatory to the character of woman, could have called forth the remark contained in the Pastoral Letter? 'We especially deplore the intimate acquaintance and promiscuous conversation of *females* with regard to things 'which ought not to be named,' by which that modesty and delicacy, which is the charm of domestic life, and which constitutes the true influence of woman, is consumed.' How wonderful that the conceptions of man relative to woman are so low, that he cannot perceive that she may converse on any subject connected with the improvement of her species, without swerving in the least from that modesty which is one of her greatest virtues! Is it designed to insinuate that woman should possess a greater degree of modesty than man? This idea I utterly reprobate. Or is it supposed that woman cannot go into scenes of misery, the necessary result of those very things, which the Pastoral Letter says ought not to be named, for the purpose of moral reform, without becoming contaminated by those with whom she thus mingles?

This is a false position; and I presume has grown out of the never-forgotten distinction of male and female. The woman who goes forth, clad in the panoply of God, to stem the tide of iniquity and misery, which she beholds rolling through our land, goes not forth to her labor of love as a female. She goes as the dignified messenger of Jehovah, and all she does and says must be done and said irrespective of sex. She is in duty bound to communicate with all, who are able and willing to aid her in saving her fellow creatures, both men and women, from that destruction which awaits them.

So far from woman losing any thing of the purity of her mind, by visiting the wretched victims of vice in their miserable abodes, by talking with them, or of them, she becomes more and more elevated and refined in her feelings and views. While laboring to cleanse the minds of others from the malaria of moral pollution, her own heart becomes purified, and her soul rises to nearer communion with her God. Such a woman is infinitely better qualified to fulfil the duties of a wife and a mother, than the woman whose *false delicacy* leads her to shun her fallen sister and brother, and shrink from *naming those sins* which she knows exist, but which she is too fastidious to labor by deed and by word to exterminate. Such a woman feels, when she enters upon the marriage relation, that God designed that relation not to debase her to a level with the animal creation, but to increase the happiness and dignity of his creatures. Such a woman comes to the important task of training her children in the nurture and admonition of the Lord, with a soul filled with the greatness of the beings committed to her charge. She sees in her children, creatures bearing the image of God; and she approaches them with reverence, and treats them at all times as moral and accountable beings. Her own mind being purified and elevated, she

instills into her children that genuine religion which induces them to keep the commandments of God. Instead of ministering with ceaseless care to their sensual appetites, she teaches them to be temperate in all things. She can converse with her children on any subject relating to their duty to God, can point their attention to those vices which degrade and brutify human nature, without in the least defiling her own mind or theirs. She views herself, and teaches her children to regard themselves as moral beings; and in all their intercourse with their fellow men, to lose the animal nature of man and woman, in the recognition of that immortal mind wherewith Jehovah has blessed and enriched them.

Thine in the bonds of womanhood,
Sarah M. Grimké

Letter VIII.

On the Condition of Women in the United States

Brookline, 1837.

My Dear Sister,—I have now taken a brief survey of the condition of woman in various parts of the world. I regret that my time has been so much occupied by other things, that I have been unable to bestow that attention upon the subject which it merits, and that my constant change of place has prevented me from having access to books, which might probably have assisted me in this part of my work. I hope that the principles I have asserted will claim the attention of some of my sex, who may be able to bring into view, more thoroughly than I have done, the situation and degradation of woman. I shall now proceed to make a few remarks on the condition of women in my own country.

During the early part of my life, my lot was cast among the butterflies of the *fashionable* world; and of this class of women, I am constrained to say, both from experience and observation, that their education is miserably deficient; that they are taught to regard marriage as the one thing needful, the only avenue to distinction; hence to attract the notice and win the attentions of men, by their external charms, is the chief business of fashionable girls. They seldom think that men will be allured by intellectual acquirements, because they find, that where any mental superiority exists, a woman is generally shunned and regarded as stepping out of her 'appropriate sphere,' which, in their view, is to dress, to dance, to set out to the best possible advantage her person, to read the novels which inundate the press, and which do more to destroy her character as a rational creature, than any thing else. Fashionable women regard themselves, and are regarded by men, as pretty toys or as mere instruments of pleasure; and the vacuity of mind, the heartlessness, the frivolity which is the necessary result of this false and debasing estimate of women, can only be fully understood by those who have mingled in the folly and wickedness of fashionable life; and who have been called from such pursuits by the voice of the Lord Jesus, inviting their weary and heavy laden souls to come unto Him and learn of Him, that they may find something worthy of their immortal spirit, and their intellectual powers; that they may learn the high and holy purposes of their creation, and consecrate themselves unto the service of God; and not, as is now the case, to the pleasure of man.

There is another and much more numerous class in this country, who are withdrawn by education or circumstances from the circle of fashionable amusements, but who are brought up with the dangerous and absurd idea, that *marriage* is a kind of preferment; and that to be able to keep their husband's house, and render his situation comfortable, is the end of her being. Much that she does and says and thinks is done in reference to this situation; and to be married is too often held up to the view of girls as the sine qua non of human happiness and human existence. For this purpose more than for any other, I verily believe the majority of girls are trained. This is demonstrated by the imperfect education which is bestowed upon them, and the little pains taken to cultivate their minds, after they leave school, by the little time allowed them for reading, and by the idea being constantly inculcated, that although all household concerns should be attended to with scrupulous punctuality at particular seasons, the improvement of their intellectual capacities is only a secondary consideration, and may serve as an occupation to fill up the odds and ends of time. In most families, it is considered a matter of far more consequence to call a girl off from a pie, or a pudding, than to interrupt her whilst engaged in her studies. This mode of training necessarily exalts, in their view, the animal above the intellectual and spiritual nature, and teaches women to regard themselves as a kind of machinery, necessary to keep the domestic engine in order, but of little value as the *intelligent* companions of men.

Let no one think, from these remarks, that I regard a knowledge of housewifery as beneath the acquisition of women. Far from it: I believe that a complete knowledge of household affairs is an indispensable requisite in a woman's education,—that by the mistress of a family, whether married or single, doing her duty thoroughly and *understandingly*, the happiness of the family is increased to an incalculable degree, as well as a

vast amount of time and money saved. All I complain of is, that our education consists so almost exclusively in culinary and other manual operations. I do long to see the time, when it will no longer be necessary for women to expend so many precious hours in furnishing 'a well spread table,' but that their husbands will forego some of their accustomed indulgences in this way, and encourage their wives to devote some portion of their time to mental cultivation, even at the expense of having to dine sometimes on baked potatoes, or bread and butter.

I believe the sentiment expressed by the author of 'Live and let Live,' is true:

> 'Other things being equal, a woman of the highest mental endowments will always be the best housekeeper, for domestic economy, is a science that brings into action the qualities of the mind, as well as the graces of the heart. A quick perception, judgment, discrimination, decision and order are high attributes of mind, and are all in daily exercise in the well ordering of a family. If a sensible woman, an intellectual woman, a woman of genius, is not a good housewife, it is not because she is either, or all of those, but because there is some deficiency in her character or some omission of duty which should make her very humble, instead of her indulging in any secret self-complacency on account of a certain superiority, which only aggravates her fault.'

The influence of women over the minds and character of *children* of both sexes, is allowed to be far greater than that of men. This being the case by the very ordering of nature, women should be prepared by education for the performance of their sacred duties as mothers and sisters. A late American writer [Thomas S. Grimké], speaking on this subject, says in reference to an article in the Westminster Review:

> 'I agree entirely with the writer in the high estimate which he places on female education, and have long since been satisfied, that the subject not only merits, but *imperiously demands* a thorough reconsideration. The whole scheme must, in my opinion, be reconstructed. The great elements of usefulness and duty are too little attended to. Women ought, in my view of the subject, to approach to the best education now given to men, (I except mathematics and the classics,) far more I believe than has ever yet been attempted. Give me a host of educated, pious mothers and sisters, and I will do more to revolutionize a

country, in moral and religious taste, in manners and in social virtues and intellectual cultivation, than I can possibly do in double or treble the time, with a similar host of educated men. I cannot but think that the miserable condition of the great body of the people in all ancient communities, is to be ascribed in a very great degree to the degradation of women.'

There is another way in which the general opinion, that women are inferior to men, is manifested, that bears with tremendous effect on the laboring class, and indeed on almost all who are obliged to earn a subsistence, whether it be by mental or physical exertion—I allude to the disproportionate value set on the time and labor of men and of women. A man who is engaged in teaching, can always, I believe, command a higher price for tuition than a woman—even when he teaches the same branches, and is not in any respect superior to the woman. This I know is the case in boarding and other schools with which I have been acquainted, and it is so in every occupation in which the sexes engage indiscriminately. As for example, in tailoring, a man has twice, or three times as much for making a waistcoat or pantaloons as a woman, although the work done by each may be equally good. In those employments which are peculiar to women, their time is estimated at only half the value of that of men. A woman who goes out to wash, works as hard in proportion as a wood sawyer, or a coal heaver, but she is not generally able to make more than half as much by a day's work. The low remuneration which women receive for their work, has claimed the attention of a few philanthropists, and I hope it will continue to do so until some remedy is applied for this enormous evil. I have known a widow, left with four or five children, to provide for, unable to leave home because her helpless babes demand her attention, compelled to earn a scanty subsistence, by making coarse shirts at 12 1–2 cents a piece, or by taking washing, for which she was paid by some wealthy persons 12 1–2 cents per dozen. All these things evince the low estimation in which woman is held. There is yet another and more disastrous consequence arising from this unscriptural notion—women being educated, from earliest childhood, to regard themselves as inferior creatures, have not that self-respect which conscious equality would engender, and hence when their virtue is assailed, they yield to temptation with facility, under the idea that it rather exalts than debases, to be connected with a superior being.

There is another class of women in this country, to whom I cannot refer, without feelings of the deepest shame and sorrow. I allude to our female slaves. Our

southern cities are whelmed beneath a tide of pollution; the virtue of female slaves is wholly at the mercy of irresponsible tyrants, and women are bought and sold in our slave markets, to gratify the brutal lust of those who bear the name of Christians. In our slave States, if amid all her degradation and ignorance, a woman desires to preserve her virtue unsullied, she is either bribed or whipped into compliance, or if she dares resist her seducer, her life by the laws of some of the slave States may be, and has actually been sacrificed to the fury of disappointed passion. Where such laws do not exist, the power which is necessarily vested in the master over his property, leaves the defenseless slave entirely at his mercy, and the sufferings of some females on this account, both physical and mental are intense. Mr. Gholson, in the House of Delegates of Virginia, in 1832, said, 'He really had been under the impression that he owned his slaves. He had lately purchased four women and ten children, in whom he thought he had obtained a great bargain; for he supposed they were his own property, *as were his brood mares.*' But even if any laws existed in the United States, as in Athens formerly, for the protection of female slaves, they would be null and void, because the evidence of a colored person is not admitted against a white, in any of our Courts of Justice in the slave States. 'In Athens, if a female slave had cause to complain of any want of respect to the laws of modesty, she could seek the protection of the temple, and demand a change of owners; and such appeals were never discountenanced, or neglected by the magistrate.' In Christian America, the slave has no refuge from unbridled cruelty and lust.

S.A. Forrall, speaking to the state of morals at the South, says, 'Negresses when young and likely, are often employed by the planter, or his friends, to administer to their sensual desires. This frequently is a matter of speculation, for if the offspring, a mulatto, be a handsome female, 800 or 1000 dollars may be obtained for her in the New Orleans market. It is an occurrence of no uncommon nature to see a Christian father sell his own daughter, and the brother his own sister.' The following is copied by the N.Y. *Evening Star* from the *Picayune*, a paper published in New Orleans. 'A very beautiful girl, belonging to the estate of John French, a deceased gambler at New Orleans, was sold a few days since for the round sum of $7000. An ugly-looking bachelor named Gouch, a member of the Council of one of the Principalities, was the purchaser. The girl is a brunette; remarkable for her beauty and intelligence, and there was considerable contention, who should be the purchaser. She was, however, persuaded to accept Gouch, he having made her princely promises.' I will add but one more from the numerous testimonies respecting the degradation of female slaves, and the licentiousness of the South. It is from the *Circular* of the Kentucky Union, for the moral and religious improvement of the colored race. 'To the female character among our black population, we cannot allude but with feelings of the bitterest shame. A similar condition of moral pollution and utter disregard of a pure and virtuous reputation, is to be found *only without the pale of Christendom.* That such a state of society should exist in a Christian nation, claiming to be the most enlightened upon earth, without calling forth any *particular attention* to its existence, though ever before our eyes and *in our* families, is a moral phenomenon at once unaccountable and disgraceful.' Nor does the colored woman suffer alone: the moral purity of the white woman is deeply contaminated. In the daily habit of seeing the virtue of her enslaved sister sacrificed without hesitancy or remorse, she looks upon the crimes of seduction and illicit intercourse without horror, and although not personally involved in the guilt, she loses that value for innocence in her own, as well as the other sex, which is one of the strongest safeguards to virtue. She lives in habitual intercourse with men, whom she knows to be polluted by licentiousness, and often she is compelled to witness in her own domestic circle, those disgusting and heart-sickening jealousies and strifes which disgraced and distracted the family of Abraham. In addition to all this, the female slaves suffer every species of degradation and cruelty, which the most wanton barbarity can inflict; they are indecently divested of their clothing, sometimes tied up and severely whipped, sometimes prostrated on the earth, while their naked bodies are torn by the scorpion lash.

> 'The whip on WOMAN'S shrinking flesh!
> Our soil yet reddening with the stains
> Caught from her scourging warm and fresh.'

Can any American woman look at these scenes of shocking licentiousness and cruelty, and fold her hands in apathy, and say, 'I have nothing to do with slavery'? *She cannot and be guiltless.*

I cannot close this letter, without saying a few words on the benefits to be derived by men, as well as women, from the opinions I advocate relative to the equality of the sexes. Many women are now supported, in idleness and extravagance, by the industry of their husbands, fathers, or brothers, who are compelled to toil out their existence, at the counting house, or in the printing office, or some other laborious occupation, while the wife and daughters and sisters take no part in the support of the family, and appear to think that their sole business is to spend the hard bought earnings of their male friends. I deeply regret such a state of things, because I believe that if women felt their responsibility, for the support of themselves, or their families it would add strength and dignity to their characters, and teach them more true sympathy for their husbands, than is now generally manifested, — a sympathy which would be exhibited by actions as well as words. Our brethren may reject my doctrine, because it runs counter to common opinions, and because it wounds their pride; but I believe they would be 'partakers of the benefit' resulting from the Equality of the Sexes, and would find that woman, as their equal, was unspeakably more valuable than woman as their inferior, both as a moral and an intellectual being.

Thine in the bonds of womanhood,
Sarah M. Grimké

Letter XII.

Legal Disabilities of Women

Concord, 9th Mo., 6th, 1837.

My Dear Sister, — There are few things which present greater obstacles to the improvement and elevation of woman to her appropriate sphere of usefulness and duty, than the laws which have been enacted to destroy her independence, and crush her individuality; laws which, although they are framed for her government, she has had no voice in establishing, and which rob her of some of her *essential rights.* Woman has no political existence. With the single exception of presenting a petition to the legislative body, she is a cipher in the nation; or, if not actually so in representative governments, she is only counted, like the slaves of the South, to swell the number of law-makers who form decrees for her government, with little reference to her benefit, except so far as her good may promote their own. I am not sufficiently acquainted with the laws respecting women on the continent of Europe, to say anything about them. But Prof. Follen, in his essay on 'The Cause of Freedom in our Country,' says, 'Woman, though fully possessed of that rational and moral nature which is the foundation of all rights, enjoys amongst us fewer legal rights than under the civil law of continental Europe.' I shall confine myself to the laws of our country. These laws bear with peculiar rigor on married women. Blackstone, in the chapter entitled 'Of husband and wife,' says:—

> 'By marriage, the husband and wife are one person in law; that is, *the very being, or legal existence of the woman* is suspended during the marriage, or at least is incorporated and consolidated into that of the husband under

whose wing, protection and cover she performs everything. . . . For this reason, a man cannot grant anything to his wife, or enter into covenant with her; for the grant would be to suppose her separate existence, and to covenant with her would be to covenant with himself; and therefore it is also generally true, that all compacts made between husband and wife, when single, are voided by the intermarriage. A woman indeed may be attorney for her husband, but that implies no separation from, but is rather a representation of, her love.'

Here now, the very being of a woman, like that of a slave, is absorbed in her master. All contracts made with her, like those made with slaves by their owners, are a mere nullity. Our kind defenders have legislated away almost all our legal rights, and in the true spirit of such injustice and oppression, have kept us in ignorance of those very laws by which we are governed. They have persuaded us, that we have no right to investigate the laws, and that, if we did, we could not comprehend them; they alone are capable of understanding the mysteries of Blackstone, &c. But they are not backward to make us feel the practical operation of their power over our actions.

'The husband is bound to provide his wife with necessaries by law as much as himself; and if she contracts debts for them, he is obliged to pay for them; but for anything besides necessaries, he is not chargeable.'

Yet a man may spend the property he had acquired by marriage at the ale-house, the gambling table, or in any other way that he pleases. Many instances of this kind have come to my knowledge; and women, who have brought their husbands handsome fortunes, have been left, in consequence of the wasteful and dissolute habits of their husbands, in straitened circumstances, and compelled to toil for the support of their families.

'If the wife be indebted before marriage, the husband is bound afterwards to pay the debt; for he has adopted her and her circumstances together.'

The wife's property is, I believe, equally liable for her husband's debts contracted before marriage.

'If the wife be injured in her person or property, she can bring no action for redress without her husband's concurrence, and his name as well as her own: neither can she be sued, without making her husband a defendant.'

This law that 'a wife can bring no action,' &c., is similar to the law respecting slaves. 'A slave cannot bring a suit against his master, or any other person, for an injury—his master, must bring it.' So if any damages are recovered for an injury committed on a wife, the husband pockets it; in the case of the slave, the master does the same.

'In criminal prosecution, the wife may be indicted and punished separately, unless there be evidence of coercion from the fact that the offence was committed in the presence, or by the command of her husband. A wife is excused from punishment for theft committed in the presence, or by the command of her husband.'

It would be difficult to frame a law better calculated to destroy the responsibility of woman as a moral being, or a free agent. Her husband is supposed to possess unlimited control over her; and if she can offer the flimsy excuse that he bade her steal, she may break the eighth commandment with impunity, as far as human laws are concerned.

'Our law, in general, considers man and wife as one person; yet there are some instances in which she is separately considered, as inferior to him and acting by his compulsion. Therefore, all deeds executed, and acts done by her during her coverture (i.e., marriage) are void, except it be a fine, or like matter of record, in which case she must be solely and secretly examined, to learn if her act be voluntary.'

Such a law speaks volumes of the abuse of that power which men have vested in their own hands. Still the private examination of a wife, to know whether she accedes to the disposition of property made by her husband is, in most cases, a mere form; a wife dares not do what will be disagreeable to one who is, in his own estimation, her superior, and who makes her feel, in the privacy of domestic life, that she has thwarted him. With respect to the nullity of deeds or acts done by a wife, I will mention one circumstance. A respectable woman borrowed of a female friend a sum of money to relieve her son from some distressing pecuniary embarrassment. Her husband was from home, and she assured the lender, that as soon as he returned, he would gratefully discharge the debt. She gave her note, and the lender, entirely ignorant of the law that a man is not obliged to discharge such a debt, actually borrowed the money, and lent it to the distressed and weeping mother. The father returned home, refused to pay the debt, and the person who had loaned the money was obliged to pay both principal and interest to the friend who lent it to her. Women should certainly know the laws by which they are governed, and from which they frequently suffer; yet they are kept in ignorance, nearly as profound, of their legal rights, and of the legislative enactments which are to regulate their actions, as slaves.

> 'The husband, by the old law, might give his wife moderate correction, as he is to answer for her misbehavior. The law thought it reasonable to entrust him with this power of restraining her by domestic chastisement. The courts of law will still permit a husband to restrain a wife of her liberty, in case of any gross misbehavior.'

What a mortifying proof this law affords, of the estimation in which woman is held! She is placed completely in the hands of a being subject like herself to the outbursts of passion, and therefore unworthy to be trusted with power. Perhaps I may be told respecting this law, that it is a dead letter, as I am sometimes told about the slave laws; but this is not true in either case. The slaveholder does kill his slave by moderate correction, as the law allows; and many a husband, among the poor, exercises the right given him by the law, of degrading woman by personal chastisement. And among the higher ranks, if actual imprisonment is not resorted to, women are not unfrequently restrained of the liberty of going to places of worship by irreligious husbands, and of doing many other things about which, as moral and responsible beings, *they* should be the *sole* judges. Such laws remind me of the reply of some little girls at a children's meeting held recently at Ipswich. The lecturer told them that God had created four orders of beings with which he had made us acquainted through the Bible. The first was angels, the second was man, the third beasts; and now, children, what is the fourth? After a pause, several girls replied, 'WOMEN.'

> 'A woman's personal property by marriage becomes absolutely her husband's, which, at his death, he may leave entirely away from her.'

And farther, all the avails of her labor are absolutely in the power of her husband. All that she acquires by her industry is his; so that she cannot, with her own honest earnings, become the legal purchaser of any property. If she expends her money for articles of furniture, to contribute to the comfort of her family, they are liable to be seized for her husband's debts: and I know an instance of a woman, who by labor and economy had scraped together a little maintenance for herself and a do-little husband, who was left, at his death, by virtue of his last will and testament, to be supported by charity. I knew another woman, who by

great industry had acquired a little money which she deposited in a bank for safe keeping. She had saved this pittance whilst able to work, in hopes that when age or sickness disqualified her for exertion, she might have something to render life comfortable, without being a burden to her friends. Her husband, a worthless, idle man, discovered this hid treasure, drew her little stock from the bank and expended it all in extravagance and vicious indulgence. I know of another woman, who married without the least idea that she was surrendering her rights to all her personal property. Accordingly, she went to the bank as usual to draw her dividends, and the person who paid her the money, and to whom she was personally known as an owner of shares in that bank, remarking the change in her signature, withdrew the money, informing her that if she were married, she had no longer a right to draw her dividends without an order from her husband. It appeared that she intended having a little fund for private use, and had not even told her husband that she owned this stock, and she was not a little chagrined, when she found that it was not at her disposal. I think she was wrong to conceal the circumstance. The relation of husband and wife is too near and sacred to admit of secrecy about money matters, unless positive necessity demands it; and I can see no excuse for any woman entering a marriage engagement with a design to keep her husband ignorant that she was possessed of property. If she was unwilling to give up her property to his disposal, she had infinitely better have remained single.

The laws above cited are not very unlike the slave laws of Louisiana.

> 'All that a slave possesses belongs to his master; he possesses nothing of his own, except what his master chooses he should possess.'

> 'By the marriage, the husband is absolutely master of the profits of the wife's lands during the coverture, and if he has had a living child, and survives the wife, he retains the whole of those lands, if they are estates of inheritance, during his life; but the wife is entitled only to one third if she survives, out of the husband's estates of inheritance. But this she has, whether she has had a child or not . . . With regard to the property of women, there is taxation without representation; for they pay taxes without having the liberty of voting for representatives.'

And this taxation, without representation, be it remembered, was the cause of our Revolutionary war, a grievance so heavy, that it was thought necessary to purchase exemption from it at an immense expense of blood and treasure, yet the daughters of New England, as well as of all the other States of this free Republic, are suffering a similar injustice—but for one, I had rather we should suffer any injustice or oppression, than that my sex should have any voice in the political affairs of the nation.

The laws I have quoted, are, I believe, the laws of Massachusetts, and, with few exceptions, of all the States in this Union. 'In Louisiana and Missouri, and possibly, in some other southern States, a woman not only has half her husband's property by right at his death, but may always be considered as possessed of half his gains during his life; having at all times power to bequeath that amount.' That the laws which have generally been adopted in the United States, for the government of women, have been framed almost entirely for the exclusive benefit of men, and with a design to oppress women, by depriving them of all control over their property, is too manifest to be denied. Some liberal and enlightened men, I know, regret the existence of these laws; and I quote with pleasure an extract from Harriet Martineau's 'Society in America,' as a proof of the assertion. 'A liberal minded lawyer of Boston, told me that his advice to testators always is to leave the largest possible amount to the widow, subject to the condition of her leaving it to the children; but that it is with shame that he reflects that any woman should owe that to his professional advice, which the law should have secured to her as a right.' I have known a few instances where men have left their whole property to their wives, when they have died, leaving only minor children; but I have known more instances of 'the friend and helper of many years, being portioned off like a salaried domestic,' instead of having a comfortable independence secured to her, while the children were amply provided for.

As these abuses do exist, and women suffer intensely from them, our brethren are called upon in this enlightened age, by every sentiment of honor, religion and justice, to repeal these unjust and unequal laws, and restore to woman those rights which they have wrested from her. Such laws approximate too nearly to the laws enacted by slaveholders for the government of their slaves, and must tend to debase and depress the mind of that being, whom God created as a help meet for man, or 'helper like unto himself,' and designed to be his equal and his companion. Until such laws are annulled, woman never can occupy that exalted station for which she was intended by her Maker. And just in proportion as they are practically disregarded, which is the case to some extent, just so far is woman assuming that independence and nobility of character which she ought to exhibit.

The various laws which I have transcribed, leave women very little more liberty, or power, in some respects, than the slave. 'A slave,' says the civil code of Louisiana, 'is one who is in the power of a master, to whom he belongs. He can possess nothing, nor acquire anything, but what must belong to his master.' I do not wish by any means to intimate that the condition of free women can be compared to that of slaves in suffering, or in degradation; still, I believe the laws which deprive married women of their rights and privileges, have a tendency to lessen them in their own estimation as moral and responsible beings, and that their being made by civil law inferior to their husbands, has a debasing and mischievous effect upon them, teaching them practically the fatal lesson to look unto man for protection and indulgence.

Ecclesiastical bodies, I believe, without exception, follow the example of legislative assemblies, in excluding woman from any participation in forming the discipline by which she is governed. The men frame the laws, and, with few exceptions, claim to execute them on both sexes. In ecclesiastical, as well as civil courts, woman is tried and condemned, not by a jury of her peers, but by beings, who regard themselves as her superiors in scale of creation. Although looked upon as an inferior, when considered as an intellectual being, woman is punished with the same severity as man, when she is guilty of moral offences. Her condition resembles, in some measure, that of the slave, who, while he is denied the advantages of his more enlightened master, is treated with even greater rigor of the law. Hoping that in the various reformations of the day, women may be relieved from some of their legal disabilities, I remain,

Thine in the bonds of womanhood,
Sarah M. Grimké

Letter XIII.

Relation of Husband and Wife

Brookline, 9th Mo., 1837.

My Dear Sister,—Perhaps some persons may wonder that I should attempt to throw out my views on the important subject of marriage, and may conclude that I am altogether disqualified for the task, because I lack experience. However, I shall not undertake to settle the specific duties of husbands and wives, but only to exhibit opinions based on the word of God, and formed from a little knowledge of human nature, and close observation of the working of generally received notions respecting the dominion of man over woman.

When Jehovah ushered into existence man, created in his own image, he instituted marriage as a part of paradisaical happiness: it was a *divine ordination,* not a civil contract. God established it, and man, except by special permission, has no right to annul it. There can be no doubt that the creation of Eve perfected the happiness of Adam; hence, our all-wise and merciful Father made her as he made Adam in his own image after his likeness, crowned her with glory and honor, and placed in her hand, as well as in his, the sceptre of dominion over the whole lower creation. Where there was perfect equality, and the same ability to receive and comprehend divine truth, and to obey divine injunctions, there could be no superiority. If God had placed Eve under the guardianship of Adam, after having endowed her, as richly as him, with moral perceptions, intellectual faculties, and spiritual apprehensions, he would at once have interposed a fallible being between her and her Maker. He could not, in simple consistency with himself, have done this; for the Bible teems with instructions not to put any confidence in man.

The passage on which the generally received opinion, that husbands are invested by divine command with authority over their wives, as I have remarked in a previous letter, is a prediction; and I am confirmed in this belief, because the same language is used to Cain respecting Abel. The text is obscure; but on a comparison of it with subsequent events, it appears to me that it was a prophecy of the dominion which Cain would usurp over his brother, and which issued in the murder of Abel. I could not allude to any thing but physical dominion, because Cain had already exhibited those evil passions which subsequently led him to become an assassin.

I have already shown, that man has exercised the most unlimited and brutal power over woman, in the peculiar character of husband,—a word in most countries synonymous with tyrant. I shall not, therefore, adduce any further proofs of the fulfillment of that prophecy, 'He will rule over thee,' from the history of heathen nations, but just glance at the condition of woman in the relation of wife in Christian countries.

'Previous to the introduction of the religion of Jesus Christ, the state of society was wretchedly diseased. The relation of the sexes to each other had become so gross in its manifested forms, that it was difficult to perceive the pure conservative principle in its inward essence.' Christianity came in, at this juncture, with its hallowed influence, and has without doubt tended to lighten the yoke of bondage, to purify the manners, and give the spiritual in some degree an empire over the animal nature. Still, that state which was designed by God to increase the happiness of woman as well as man, often proves the means of lessening her comfort and degrading her into the mere machine of another's convenience and pleasure.

Woman, instead of being elevated by her union with man, which might be expected from an alliance with a superior being, is in reality lowered. She generally loses her individuality, her independent character, her moral being. She becomes absorbed into him, and henceforth is looked at, and acts through the medium of her husband.

In the wealthy classes of society, and those who are in comfortable circumstances, women are exempt from great corporeal exertion, and are protected by public opinion, and by the genial influence of Christianity, from much physical ill treatment. Still, there is a vast amount of secret suffering endured, from the forced submission of women to the opinions and whims of their husbands. Hence they are frequently driven to use deception, to compass their ends. They are early taught that to appear to yield, is the only way to govern. Miserable sophism! I deprecate such sentiments as being peculiarly hostile to the dignity of woman. If she submits, let her do it openly, honorably, not to gain her point, but as a matter of Christian duty. But let her beware how she permits her husband to be her conscience-keeper. On all moral and religious subjects, she is bound to think and to act for herself. Where confidence and love exist, a wife will naturally converse with her husband as with her dearest friend, on all that interests her heart, and there will be a perfectly free interchange of sentiment; but *she is no more bound to be governed by his judgment,* than he is by hers. They are standing on the same platform of human rights, are equally under the government of God, and accountable to him, and him alone.

I have sometimes been astonished and grieved at the servitude of women, and at the little idea many of them seem to have of their own moral existence and responsibilities. A woman who is asked to sign a petition for the abolition of slavery in the District of Columbia, or to join a society for the purpose of carrying forward the annihilation of American slavery, or any other great reformation, not unfrequently replies, 'My husband does not approve of it.' She merges her rights and her duties in her husband, and thus virtually chooses him for a savior and a king, and rejects Christ as her Ruler and Redeemer. I know some women are very glad of so convenient a pretext to shield themselves from the performance of duty; but there are others, who, under a mistaken view of their obligations as wives, submit conscientiously to this species of oppression, and go mourning on their way, for want of that holy fortitude, which would enable them to fulfil their duties as moral and responsible beings, without reference to poor fallen man. O that woman may arise in her dignity as an immortal creature, and speak, think and act as unto God, and not unto man!

There is, perhaps, less bondage of mind among the poorer classes, because their sphere of duty is more contracted, and they are deprived of the means of intellectual culture, and of the opportunity of exercising their judgment, on many moral subjects of deep interest and of vital importance. Authority is called into exercise by resistance, and hence there will be mental bondage only in proportion as the faculties of mind are evolved, and woman feels herself as a rational and intelligent being, on a footing with man. But women, among the lowest classes of society, so far as my observation has extended, suffer intensely from the brutality of their husbands. Duty as well as inclination has led me, for many years, into the abodes of poverty and sorrow, and I have been amazed at the treatment which women receive at the hands of those, who arrogate to themselves the epithet of *protectors*. Brute force, the law of violence, rules to a great extent in the poor man's domicile; and woman is little more than his drudge. They are less under the supervision of public opinion, less under the restraints of education, and unaided or unbiased by the refinements of polished society. Religion, wherever it exists, supplies the place of all these; but the real cause of woman's degradation and suffering in married life is to be found in the erroneous notion of her inferiority to man; and never will she be rightly regarded by herself, or others, until this opinion, so derogatory to the wisdom and mercy of God, is exploded, and woman arises in all the majesty of her womanhood, to claim those rights which are inseparable from her existence as an immortal, intelligent and responsible being.

Independent of the fact, that Jehovah could not, consistently with his character as the King, the Lawgiver, and the Judge of his people, give the reins of government over woman into the hands of man, I find that all his commands, all his moral laws, are addressed to women as well as to men. When he assembled Israel at the foot of Mount Sinai, to issue his commandments, we may reasonably suppose he gave all the precepts, which he considered necessary for the government of moral beings. Hence we find that God says, — 'Honor thy father and thy mother,' and he enforces this command by severe penalties upon those who transgress it: 'He that smiteth his father, or his mother, shall surely be put to death' — 'He that curseth his father, or his mother, shall surely be put to death' — Ex. 21: 15, 17. But in the decalogue, there is no direction given to women to obey their husbands: both are commanded to have no other God but Jehovah, and not to bow down, or serve any other. When the Lord Jesus delivered his sermon on the Mount, full of the practical precepts of religion, he did not issue any command to wives to obey their husbands. When he is

speaking on the subject of divorce, Mark 16: 11, 12, he places men and women on the same ground. And the Apostle, 1 Cor. 7: 12, 13, speaking of the duties of the Corinthian wives and husbands, who had embraced Christianity, to their unconverted partners, points out the same path to both, although our translators have made a distinction. 'Let him not put her away,' 12 — 'Let her not leave him,' 13 — is precisely the same in the original. If man is constituted the governor of woman, he must be her God; and the sentiment expressed to me lately, by a married man, is perfectly correct: 'In my opinion,' said he, 'the greatest excellence to which a married woman can attain, is to worship her husband.' He was a professor of religion — his wife a lovely and intelligent woman. He only spoke out what thousands think and act. Women are indebted to Milton for giving to this false notion, 'confirmation strong as proof of holy writ.' His Eve is embellished with every personal grace, to gratify the eye of her admiring husband; but he seems to have furnished the mother of mankind with just intelligence enough to comprehend her supposed inferiority to Adam, and to yield unresisting submission to her lord and master. Milton put into Eve's mouth the following address to Adam:

'My author and disposer, what thou bidst,
Unargued I obey; so God ordains —
God is thy law, thou mine: to know no more,
Is woman's happiest knowledge and her praise.'

This much admired sentimental nonsense is fraught with absurdity and wickedness. If it were true, the commandment of Jehovah should have run thus: Man shall have no other gods before Me, and woman shall have no other gods before MAN.

The principal support of the dogma of woman's inferiority, and consequent submission to her husband, is found in some passages of Paul's epistles. I shall proceed to examine those passages, premising 1st, that the antiquity of the opinions based on the false construction of those passages, has no weight with me: they are the opinions of interested judges, and I have no particular reverence for them, *merely* because they have been regarded with veneration from generation to generation. So far from this being the case, I examine any opinions of centuries standing, with as much freedom, and investigate them with as much care, as if they were of yesterday. I was educated to think for myself, and it is a privilege I shall always claim to exercise. 2d. Notwithstanding my full belief that the apostle Paul's testimony, respecting himself, is true, 'I was not a whit behind the chiefest of the apostles,' yet I believe his mind was under the influence of Jewish prejudices respecting women, just as Peter's and the apostles were about the uncleanness of the Gentiles. 'The Jews,' says Clarke, 'would not suffer a woman to read in the synagogue, although a servant, or even a child, had this permission.' When I see Paul shaving his head for a vow, and offering sacrifices, and circumcising Timothy, to accommodate himself to the prepossessions of his countrymen, I do not conceive that I derogate in the least from his character as an inspired apostle, to suppose that he may have been imbued with the prevalent prejudices against women.

In 1 Cor. 11: 3, after praising the Corinthian converts, because they kept the 'ordinances,' or 'traditions,' as the margin reads, the apostle says, 'I would have you know, that the head of every man is Christ, and the head of the woman is the man; and the head of Christ is God.' Eph. 5: 23, is a parallel passage. 'For the husband is the head of the wife, even as Christ is the head of the Church.' The apostle closes his remarks on this subject, by observing, 'This is a great mystery, but I speak concerning Christ and the Church.' I shall pass over this with simply remarking, that God and Christ are one. 'I and my Father are one,' and there can be no inferiority where there is no divisibility. The commentaries on this and similar texts, afford a striking illustration of the ideas which men entertain of their own superiority, I shall subjoin Henry's remarks on 1 Cor. 11: 5, as a specimen: 'To understand this text, it must be observed, that it was a signification either of shame, or subjection, for persons to be veiled, or covered in Eastern countries; contrary to the custom of ours, where the being bare-headed betokens subject, and being covered superiority and dominion; and this will help us the better to understand the reason on which he grounds his reprehension, 'Every man praying, &c. dishonoreth his head,' i.e. Christ, the head of every man, by appearing in a habit unsuitable to the rank in which God had placed him. The woman, on the other hand, that prays, &c. dishonoreth her head, i.e. the man. She appears in the dress of her *superior*, and throws off the token of her subjection; she might with equal decency cut her hair short, or cut it off, the common dress of the man in that age. Another reason against this conduct was, that the man is the image and glory of God, the representative of that glorious dominion and headship which God has over the world. It is the man who is set at the head of this lower creation, and therein bears the resemblance of God. The woman, on the other hand, is the glory of the man: she is his representative. Not but she has dominion over the inferior creatures, and she is a partaker of human nature, and so far is God's representative too, but it is at second hand. She is the image of God, inasmuch as she is the image of the man. The man was first made,

and made head of the creation here below, and therein the image of the divine dominion; and the woman was made out of the man, and shone with a *reflection of his glory*, being made superior to the other creatures here below, but in subjection to her husband, and deriving that *honor from him*, out of whom she was made. The woman was made for the man to be his help meet, and not the man for the woman. She was, naturally, therefore, made subject to him, because made for him, for HIS USE AND HELP AND COMFORT.'

We see in the above quotation, what degrading views even good men entertain of women. Pity the Psalmist had not thrown a little light on this subject, when he was paraphrasing the account of man's creation. 'Thou hast made him a little lower than the angels, and hast crowned him with glory and honor. Thou madest him to have dominion over the works of thy hands; thou hast put all things under his feet.' Surely if woman had been placed below man, and was to shine only by a lustre borrowed from him, we should have some clear evidence of it in the sacred volume. Henry puts her exactly on a level with the beasts; they were made for the use, help and comfort of man; and according to this commentator, this was the whole end and design of the creation of woman. The idea that man, as man is superior to woman, involves an absurdity so gross, that I really wonder how any man of reflection can receive it as of divine origin; and I can only account for it, by that passion for supremacy, which characterizes man as a corrupt and fallen creature. If it be true that he is more excellent than she, as man, independent of his moral and intellectual powers, then every man is superior by virtue of his manship, to every woman. The man who sinks his moral capacities and spiritual powers in his sensual appetites, is still, as a man, simply by the conformation of his body, a more dignified being, than the woman whose intellectual powers are highly cultivated, and whose approximation to the character of Jesus Christ is exhibited in a blameless life and conversation.

But it is strenuously urged by those, who are anxious to maintain their usurped authority, that wives are, in various passages of the new Testament, commanded to obey their husbands. Let us examine these texts.

> Eph. 5, 22. 'Wives, submit yourselves unto your own husbands as unto the Lord . . . As the church is subject unto Christ, so let the wives be to their own husbands in every thing.'
> Col. 3, 18. 'Wives, submit yourselves unto your own husbands, as it is fit in the Lord.'
> 1 Pet. 3, 2. 'Likewise ye wives, be in subjection

to your own husbands; that if any obey not the word, they may also without the word be won by the conversation of the wives.'

Accompanying all these directions to wives, are commands to husbands.

> Eph. 5, 25. 'Husbands, love your wives even as Christ loved the Church, and gave himself for it. . . . So ought men to love their wives as their own bodies. He that loveth his wife, loveth himself.'
> Col. 3, 19. 'Husbands, love your wives, and be not bitter against them.'
> 1 Pet. 3, 7. 'Likewise ye husbands, dwell with them according to knowledge, giving honor unto the wife as unto the weaker vessel, and as being heirs together of the grace of life.'

I may just remark, in relation to the expression 'weaker vessel,' that the word in the original has no reference to intellect: it refers to physical weakness merely.

The apostles were writing to Christian converts, and laying down rules for their conduct towards their unconverted consorts. It no doubt frequently happened, that a husband or a wife would embrace Christianity, while their companions clung to heathenism, and husbands might be tempted to dislike and despise those, who pertinaciously adhered to their pagan superstitions. And wives who, when they were pagans, submitted as a matter of course to their heathen husbands, might be tempted knowing that they were superior as moral and religious characters, to assert that superiority, by paying less deference to them than heretofore. Let us examine the context of these passages, and see what are the grounds of the directions here given to husbands and wives. The whole epistle to the Ephesians breathes a spirit of love. The apostle beseeches the converts to walk worthy of vocation wherewith they are called, with all lowliness and meekness, with long suffering, forbearing one another in love. The verse preceding 5, 22, is 'SUBMITTING YOURSELVES ONE TO ANOTHER IN THE FEAR OF GOD.' Colossians 3, from 11 to 17, contains similar injunctions. The 17th verse says, 'Whatsoever ye do in word, or in deed, do all in the name of the Lord Jesus.' Peter, after drawing a most touching picture of Christ's sufferings for us, and reminding the Christians, that he had left us an example that we should follow his steps, 'who did no sin, neither was guile found in his mouth,' exhorts wives to be in subjection, &c.

From an attentive consideration of these passages, and of those in which the same words 'submit,' 'subjec-

tion,' are used, I cannot but believe that the apostles designed to recommend to wives, as they did to subjects and to servants, to carry out the holy principle laid down by Jesus Christ, 'Resist not evil.' And this without in the least acknowledging the right of the governors, masters, or husbands, to exercise the authority they claimed. The recognition of the existence of evils does not involve approbation of them. God tells the Israelites, he gave them a king in his wrath, but nevertheless as they chose to have a king, he laid down directions for the conduct of that king, and had him anointed to reign over them. According to the generally received meaning of the passages I have quoted, they directly contravene the laws of God, as given in various parts of the Bible. Now I must understand the sacred Scriptures as harmonizing with themselves, or I cannot receive them as the word of God. The commentators on these passages exalt man to the station of a Deity in relation to woman. Clarke says, 'As the Lord Christ is the head, or governor of the church, and the head of the man, so is the man the head, or governor of the woman. This is God's ordinance, and should not be transgressed.' As unto the Lord. 'The word church seems necessarily to be understood here: that is, act under the authority of your husbands, as the church acts under the authority of Christ. As the church submits to the Lord, so let wives submit to their husbands.' Henry goes even further—'For the husband is the head of the wife. The metaphor is taken from the head in the natural body, which being the seat of reason, of wisdom and of knowledge, and the fountain of sense and motion, is more excellent than the rest of the body.' Now if God ordained man the governor of woman, he must be able to save her, and to answer in her stead for all those sins which she commits by his direction. Awful responsibility. Do husbands feel able and willing to bear it? And what becomes of the solemn affirmation of Jehovah? 'Hear this, all ye people, give ear all ye inhabitants of the world, both low and high, rich and poor. . . . None can by any means redeem his brother, or give to God a ransom for him, for the redemption of the soul is precious, and man cannot accomplish it.' —*French Bible.*

Thine in the bonds of womanhood,
Sarah M. Grimké

Letter XV.

Man Equally Guilty with Woman in the Fall.

Uxbridge, 10th Mo. 20th, 1837.

My Dear Sister,—It is said that 'modern Jewish women light a lamp every Friday evening, half an hour before sunset, which is the beginning of their Sabbath, in remembrance of their original mother, who first extinguished the lamp of righteousness,—to remind them of their obligation to rekindle it.' I am one of those who always admit, to its fullest extent, the popular charge, that woman brought sin into the world. I accept it as a powerful reason, why woman is bound to labor with double diligence, for the regeneration of that world she has been instrumental in ruining.

But although I do not repel the imputation, I shall notice some passages in the sacred Scriptures, where this transaction is mentioned, which prove, I think, the identity and equality of man and woman, and that there is no difference in their guilt in the view of that God who searcheth the heart and trieth the reins of the children of men. . . .

Conclusion

I have now, my dear sister, completed my series of letters. I am aware, they contain some new views; but I believe they are based on the immutable truths of the Bible. All I ask for them is, the candid and prayerful consideration of Christians. If they strike at some of our bosom sins, our deep-rooted prejudices, our long cherished opinions, let us not condemn them on that account, but investigate them fearlessly and prayerfully, and not shrink from the examination; because, if they are true, they place heavy responsibilities upon women. In throwing them before the public, I have been actuated solely by the belief, that if they are acted upon, they will exalt the character and enlarge the usefulness of my own sex, and contribute greatly to the happiness and virtue of the other. That there is a root of bitterness continually springing up in families and troubling the repose of both men and women, must be manifest to even a superficial observer; and I believe it is the mistaken notion of the inequality of the sexes. As there is an assumption of superiority on the one part, which is not sanctioned by Jehovah, there is an incessant struggle on the other to rise to that degree of dignity, which God designed women to possess in common with men, and to maintain those rights and exercise those privileges which every woman's common sense, apart from the prejudices of education, tells her are inalienable; they are a part of her moral nature, and can only cease when her immortal mind is extinguished. . . .

Thine in the bonds of womanhood,

Sarah M. Grimké

Flora Tristan (1803–44)

Flora Tristan was born in Paris on April 7, 1803, and died at Bordeaux on November 14, 1844. Her mother, a middle-class French woman named Thérèse Laisney (or Laine), had fled to Spain during the French Revolution and there met Don Mariano de Tristan de Moscoso, a Spanish Peruvian officer of aristocratic family claiming royal Indian ancestry. Against the wishes of Don Mariano's family and without the required military approval, they were married by a priest who failed to give them proper certification of the marriage. For the first years of Tristan's life, the family lived comfortably on an estate near Paris, where among the guests on occasion was a friend of Don Mariano, Simón Bolívar, later the hero of Latin American independence. But Don Mariano died suddenly in 1808 and his property was confiscated by France, then at war with Spain. Flora's mother was left without resources other than a small allowance from her brother, and she was unable to claim her inheritance because Don Mariano's family refused to recognize the legitimacy of the marriage. Thus Tristan grew up in relative poverty, first in a country village, later in a garret apartment on the Left Bank in Paris. She was almost entirely self-educated. In 1818 she learned for the first time of the technical illegitimacy of her birth, which abruptly terminated her youthful hopes of marriage and enforced upon her the sense that she was to be a pariah forever.

In 1820 Tristan went to work for a lithographer, André François Chazal, whom she soon married, under pressure from her mother and uncle, and to whom she bore three children. Aline, the third child, was closest to her mother in temperament and interests; through Aline, Flora was grandmother to the artist Paul Gauguin. But in 1825 she left a miserable marriage, beginning a prolonged battle for custody of her children and freedom from Chazal. She was then doubly a pariah, being born "illegitimate" and having abandoned her husband and left her children in the care of others in order to support herself, at first by going into domestic service (traveling to England and Italy as a chambermaid), later by writing. In 1837 Tristan published a petition, submitted to the Chamber of Deputies, for the reinstatement of divorce (which had been legalized during the Revolution in 1792 but abolished in 1816). In 1838 Chazal attempted to kill her by shooting her in broad daylight in the street. Tristan survived, and Chazal went to prison for eighteen years, but even under these conditions, divorce remained impossible.

Tristan voyaged to Peru in 1833, in a vain attempt to secure her inheritance from her uncle, Don Pío de Tristan de Moscoso, one of the most influential men in the new republic. On this journey she witnessed with horror sights of black slavery and the oppression of the Indian population, and she saw at close hand the civil war and chaotic political struggles of the early years of Peruvian independence. Tristan came away with only a small legacy from her grandmother, but with a wealth of new knowledge and experience and the extensive journals on which she drew for her later success as a writer, an activist, and a theorist.

In the politically volatile France, England, and South America of the 1820s and 1830s, Tristan encountered the ideas of late-eighteenth-century radicals such as Jean-Jacques Rousseau and Mary Wollstonecraft and early-nineteenth-century "utopian socialists" and workers' advocates, including Claude-Henri de Saint-Simon, Prosper Enfantin, Charles Fourier, Victor Considérant, Louis Blanc, P. J. Proudhon, Robert Owen, and William Lovett. Saint-Simon had died in 1825, but Tristan met the others at various times in Paris and London and plunged into the sometimes clandestine world of revolutionary debate and politics in cafés, journals, and salons. Her writings were greeted with acclaim and serialized in the socialist press.

Her first signed pamphlet in 1835 addressed the mortifications and difficulties faced by "women who are among strangers," including women traveling alone in a foreign country, unaccompanied women traveling in their own countries for education or business, women who choose or are forced to seek their own livelihood, and women cast off by society. Here Tristan put forward several ideas presaging her subsequent writings, including the need "to ameliorate the lot of women, of that part of humanity whose mission is to bring peace and love to mankind," and the need "for new institutions adapted to new needs, a demand for associations working by common consent to bring relief to the many who suffer and languish without being able to help themselves; for, divided, they are weak, unable even to struggle against the last efforts of a decrepit, dying civilization" (Flora Tristan: Utopian Feminist, 2). Doubting the prospects of creating "another brilliant utopia" without a clear means for its realization, she advocated "amelioration by degrees," to be undertaken by each person focusing on a particular aspect of the need for change. Her proposal at this time was an association of mutual aid and reciprocal hospitality to make it possible for women to travel freely for their own support, education, or other goals. The pamphlet was remarkable for its analysis of the different factors affecting women by class, and her internationalist hope for a day "when we shall all be mankind, *without distinctions as English, Germans, French, etc.*" (ibid., 7). As she wrote later in her London Journal (1840), "*I long ago renounced any notion of* nationality, *a mean and narrow concept which does nothing but harm*" (Cross and Gray, 49).

Tristan's first major work was the Peregrinations of a Pariah (serialized in 1836, published as a book in 1838). She described this as her autobiography, defending herself and other outcast women, such as doña Pencha Gamarra, the exiled Peruvian general and political leader who played a prominent role in the civil war during Tristan's stay in Peru. As Kathleen Hart has argued, Gamarra personified for Tristan "the reality of a woman who had sought to provide leadership for her country, but was finally calumnied and humiliated by its people," who, like the people of France in the Revolution of 1830, had "failed to recognize at once the leadership capabilities of women and the principle of association" (Hart, 62, 61). Addressed "To the Peruvians" as a contribution to their "present prosperity and future progress," the book presented an unflattering portrait of a country in which "the upper class is profoundly corrupted" and "the degradation of the people is extreme in all the races of which it is composed" (Utopian Socialist, 10). Don Pío had the book burned in Arequipa and cut off the small annuity he had been sending his niece, but the book was later translated into Spanish, and Tristan is now warmly remembered in Latin America and claimed as a Peruvian writer and early feminist socialist.

Several other important publications by Tristan appeared in 1838. Lettres de Bolívar, her edition of the letters between Bolívar and her parents, was serialized that July. A Petition for the Abolition of the Death Penalty to the Chamber of Deputies appeared in December. Tristan's only novel, Méphis, was also published that year. Though seen as of uneven literary merit, Méphis was an important expression of Tristan's ideas on class antagonisms and the image of the femme guide, the woman guide to humanity, sometimes identified with the "woman messiah" prefigured in Saint-Simonian socialism, yet significantly different from that concept (Cross and Gray, 38–43).

Tristan's commitment to the principle of association, particularly in the context of working-class struggles in the capitalist system of her time, was confirmed and sharpened by her return to England in 1839, where she walked through many streets and visited factories, foundries, gasworks, and the miserable living quarters of workers. She observed prisons, prostitution, and the ghettos of the Irish and the Jews. She met with Robert Owen, William Lovett, and others associated with the London Working Men's Association and the Chartist movement, and she returned to France to write Promenades dans Londres (1840, later translated as Flora Tristan's London Journal).

An immediate success, the book portrayed for the first time a broad view of the desperate conditions of life for the working classes and the poor at the center of the industrial revolution. It was an impressive contribution to the early history of sociology not only in its factual observations of social conditions but in its analysis of social structures and alienation. It preceded Friedrich Engels's Condition of the Working Class in England by five years and though shorter, it offered a more comprehensive—and materialist—critique of inequalities, prejudice, and oppressive conditions affecting various groups including women, prisoners, and despised minorities.

Engels, for example, asserted that poverty in Ireland "is owing to the character of the people" and described the Irish in England in vituperative language ("filth and drunkenness," "the lack of cleanliness . . . which is the Irishman's second nature," "his crudity, which places him but little above the savage"), lamenting that English workers' wages are driven down by competition with workers of this alien savage "race" who, having "grown up in filth, . . . have a strong, degrading influence on their English companions in toil. . . ." (Condition, 559, 366–67). But Tristan had already rejected such views—that the poor "themselves are the cause of their suffering"—as excuses by Malthus, Ricardo, "and the whole English school of economists" to dismiss and obscure the unbearable conditions of poverty. She insisted that one must go into the Irish quarter "to realize in all its horror the poverty which occurs in a rich and fertile country when it is governed by, and for, the aristocracy." Appalled by what she saw as she entered the quarter, she was about to turn back "when suddenly I remembered that these were human beings, my fellow men, all about me. . . . I overcame my distress . . . and I once again felt up to the task I had set myself, to examine these evils one by one" (London Journal, 134–36).

The enthusiastic reception of her London Journal inspired Tristan to move beyond her observations and critique of society and expound more fully her own proposals for social change and action. In introducing the third edition of the book, she wrote in the introduction: "the reader will find on every page the thought of unity that guides me in everything . . . envisaged from the point of view of European unity and of universal unity" (Schneider, 211). This was to be a central theme of her efforts in her few remaining years.

In 1842 Tristan completed her best-known work,

The Workers' Union, *which proposed the creation of an International Association of Working Men and Women to "constitute the working class" as a self-conscious force of solidarity among working people across national and gender boundaries. This proposal preceded by more than five years Marx and Engels's famed call, in the Com-*munist Manifesto, *that "Workers of the world, unite!" And it preceded by more than twenty years the actual founding in 1864 of the International Workingmen's Association, which largely ignored Tristan's concern for working women. Neither Marx nor Engels, nor any of their disciples, acknowledged her influence, but Marx and Engels made clear in* The Holy Family *that they were aware of her* Workers' Union *in 1845.*

The Workers' Union *was met at first with incomprehension and disbelief by publishers, and Tristan was obliged to publish it by subscription, which yielded sufficient contributions from a broad range of writers, socialist intellectuals, and workers to underwrite publication of the first edition. Next Tristan set out to carry the word to workers throughout France. By this time she had come to see herself in the role of the* femme guide *or the woman messiah. Whether Tristan's inspiration for this was fundamentally Christian, as some scholars argue, may be doubted in view of her critical stance toward religion and her intensely anticlerical positions on many points ranging from oppression of women to observations of "Christian" institutions of slavery in Peru. But she clearly had adopted the role of apostle of a new era of society, whose principles would be radical egalitarianism, feminism, cooperative organization, and working-class solidarity.*

A *powerful speaker driven by a sense of urgency and mission, Tristan succeeded in drawing audiences and gaining adherents to her cause in a whirlwind lecture tour, described in her posthumously published* Tour of France. *But her health, which had been poor for years, broke down completely under the strain, and at age forty-one she died in 1844 at Bordeaux, whence she had set out on her journey to Peru a little more than a decade before.*

In *testimony to the power and durability of her ideas and her influence, Tristan's works today are the subject of numerous debates, particularly as to whether to characterize her as primarily feminist, socialist, socialist-feminist, Christian socialist, or liberal individualist; whether to claim her as a romantic, a revolutionary, a Christian, a free thinker, a patriot, French or Peruvian, egomaniacal or selflessly dedicated. These debates will surely persist, but it may be well to recall, as Steven Hause notes, that "she spent her last days on a lecture tour exhorting workers and socialists to organize," and that "a carpenter and a tailor spoke at her grave." In*

1848, ten thousand workers gathered for the unveiling of a monument, paid for by subscription, inscribed: "To the memory of Madame Flora Tristan, author of The Workers' Union. *The grateful workers—Liberty-Equality-Fraternity-Solidarity." And following her dates of birth and death, the word "Solidarity" was inscribed again (Schneider, 249).*

The following selections are from the 1983 edition of The Workers' Union, *translated by Beverly Livingston.*
BAC

Sources and Suggested Readings

Cross, Máire, and Tim Gray. *The Feminism of Flora Tristan.* Oxford: Berg, 1992.

Desanti, Dominique. *Flora Tristan: Oeuvres et Vie Mêlées.* Paris: Union générale d'éditions, 1973.

Engels, Friedrich. *The Condition of the Working Class in England* [1845]. In *Karl Marx, Frederick Engels: Collected Works.* Vol. 4. New York: International Publishers, 1976.

Grogan, Susan K. *French Socialism and Sexual Difference: Women and the New Society, 1803–44.* Basingstoke: Macmillan, 1992.

Hart, Kathleen. "An I for an Eye: Flora Tristan and Female Visual Allegory." *Nineteenth-Century French Studies* 26, 1 & 2 (Fall–Winter 1997–98): 52–65.

Hause, Steven C. Review of M. Cross and T. Gray, *The Feminism of Flora Tristan. European History Quarterly* 24 (April 1994): 314–16.

Marx, Karl, and Friedrich Engels. *The Holy Family, or Critique of Critical Criticism.* In *Karl Marx, Frederick Engels: Collected Works.* Vol. 4. New York: International Publishers, 1976.

Moon, S. J. "Feminism and Socialism: The Utopian Synthesis of Flora Tristan." In *Socialist Women: European Socialist Feminism in the Nineteenth and Early Twentieth Centuries,* ed. Marilyn J. Boxer and Jean H. Quataert. New York: Elsevier, 1978.

Moses, Claire. *French Feminism in the Nineteenth Century.* Albany: New York State University Press, 1984.

Schneider, Joyce Anne. *Flora Tristan: Feminist, Socialist, and Free Spirit.* New York: William Morrow, 1980.

Struminger, Laura S. *The Odyssey of Flora Tristan.* New York: Peter Lang, 1988.

Tristan, Flora. *Flora Tristan: La Paria et son rêve. Correspondance.* Ed. Stéphane Michaud. Fontenay/St. Cloud: E. N. S. Editions, 1995.

———. *Flora Tristan, Utopian Feminist: Her Travel Diaries and Personal Crusade.* Trans. and ed. Doris and Paul Beik. Bloomington: Indiana University Press, 1993.

———. *Flora Tristan's London Journal: A Survey of London Life in the 1830s.* Trans. Dennis Palmer and Giselle Pincetl. London: George Prior, 1980.

———. *Peregrinations of a Pariah 1833–4* [1838]. Trans. Jean Hawkes. London: Virago, 1986.

———. *The Workers' Union.* Trans. Beverly Livingston. Urbana: University of Illinois Press, 1983.

The Workers' Union (1843)

To Working Men and Women

Listen to me. For twenty-five years the most intelligent and devoted men have given their lives to defending your sacred cause. In their writings, speeches, reports, memoirs, investigations, and statistics, they have pointed out, observed, and demonstrated to the government and the wealthy that the working class, in the current state of affairs, is morally and materially placed in an intolerable situation of poverty and grief. They have shown that, in this state of abandonment and suffering, most of the workers, inevitably embittered through misfortune and brutalized through ignorance, become dangerous to society. They have proven to the Government and the wealthy that not only justice and humanity call for the duty of aiding them through a law on labor organization, but that even the public interest and security imperiously demand such a measure. Well, for the last twenty-five years, so many eloquent voices have not been able to arouse the Government's concern regarding the risks to society with seven to eight million workers exasperated by suffering and despair, with many trapped between suicide and thievery!

Workers, what can be said now in defense of your cause? In the last twenty-five years, hasn't everything been said and repeated in every form? There is nothing more to be said, nothing more to be written, for your wretched position is well known by all. Only one thing remains to be done: *to act by virtue of the rights inscribed in the [1830 Constitutional] Charter.* Now the day has come when one must act, and it is up to you and *only you* to act in the interest of your own cause. At stake are your very lives . . . or death, that horrible, ever-menacing death: misery and starvation.

Workers, put an end to twenty-five years of waiting for someone to intervene on your behalf. Experience and facts inform you well enough that the Government cannot or will not be concerned with your lot when its improvement is at issue. It is up to you alone, if you truly want it, to leave this labyrinth of misery, suffering, and degradation in which you languish. Do you want to ensure good vocational education for your children and for yourselves, and certainty of rest in your old age? You can.

Your action is not to be armed revolt, public riots, arson, or plundering. No, because, instead of curing your ills, destruction would only make them worse. The Lyons and Paris riots have attested to that. You have but one legal and legitimate recourse permissible before God and man: THE UNIVERSAL UNION OF WORKING MEN AND WOMEN.

Workers, your condition in present society is miserable and painful: in good health, you do not have the right to work; sick, ailing, injured, old, you do not even have the right to care; poor, lacking everything, you are not entitled to benefits, and beggary is forbidden by law. This precarious situation relegates you to a primitive state in which man, living in nature, must consider every morning how he will get food for the day. Such an existence is true torture. The fate of the animal ruminating in a stable is a thousand times better than yours. He, at least, is certain of eating the next day; his master keeps hay and straw for him in winter. The bee in its tree hole is a thousand times better off than you. The ant who works in summer to live well in winter is a thousand times better off than you. Workers, you are miserable, yes, indubitably; but what is the main cause of your suffering? If a bee or an ant, instead of working with other bees and ants to stock the common dwelling for winter, decided to separate and work alone, it too would die of cold and hunger all alone in a corner. Then why do you remain isolated from each other? Individually, you are weak and fall from the weight of all kinds of miseries. So, leave your isolation: unite! *Unity gives strength.* You have numbers going for you, and numbers are significant.

I come to you to propose a general union among working men and women, regardless of trade, who reside in the same region—a union which would have as its goal the CONSOLIDATION OF THE WORKING CLASS and the construction of several establishments (Workers' Union palaces), distributed evenly throughout France. Children of both sexes six to eighteen would be raised there; and sick or disabled workers as well as the elderly would be admitted. Listen to the numbers and you will have an idea of what can be done with the union.

In France there are about five million working-class men and two million women—seven million workers united in thought and action. To realize a great, communal project for the benefit of all men and women, if each contributes two francs per year, at the end of one year, the Workers' Union will have the enormous sum of fourteen million francs. . . .

II. How to Consolidate the Working Class

It is very important for the workers to distinguish between the Workers' Union as I conceive of it and what exists today under the titles of guild associations, the Union, welfare societies, etc. The goal of all these various private groups is simply to give aid, mutually and individually, within each society. Thus they were set up to provide in case of sickness, accidents, and long periods of unemployment.

Given the working class's current state of isolation, desertion and misery, these kinds of societies serve a purpose. For their aim is to give a bit of aid to the most needy, thereby mitigating some personal suffering, which often surpasses the strength and stamina of those afflicted. So I highly approve of these societies and encourage the workers to increase them and get rid of the abuses they may have. But alleviating misery does not destroy it; mitigating the evil is not the same as *eradicating* it. If one really wants to attack the root of evil, obviously one needs something other than private societies, since their only goal is to relieve individual suffering.

Let us examine what happens in the private societies and see whether this mode of action can actually improve the lot of the working class. Each society uses its membership fees to give so much per diem (between 50 centimes and 2 francs) to the sick and in some cases to those who have been out of work for a certain length of time. If, by chance, something happens, such as a member's being sent to prison, aid is available up to the time of the verdict. In the guild associations mutual aid is even more effective: members obtain work for those coming from provincial towns and let the mother know what their expenses are, up to a certain limit, while waiting for work. That is what they do on the material side. To boost their morale, each member of the association makes it his duty to go and visit sick members in their homes or in the hospital, and prisoners, as well. I repeat, given the current state of affairs, these sorts of groups are at least very useful in showing great sympathy and in binding the workers, for they encourage good morals, civilize their customs, and alleviate their awful suffering. But is that sufficient? No! Indeed not, since, in the final analysis, these groups cannot (and do not claim to) change or improve in any way the material and moral condition of the working class.

A father belonging to one of these associations suffers miserably, and finds no solace in believing that his sons will be any better off than he. And in their turn, his sons as members of the same association will live miserably like their fathers, with no hope for their children. Mind you, each society acting in the name of the individual and trying to provide temporary relief invariably offers the same thing. Despite all its efforts, it will be able to create nothing great, good, or capable of notable results. Therefore, Workers, with your private societies as they have existed since the time of Solomon, the physical and psychological condition of the working class will not have changed in fifty centuries: its fate will always be poverty, ignorance, and slav-

ery, the only change being the types and names of slaves.

What is wrong? This kind of absurd, selfish, mean, bastard organization divides the working class into a multitude of small private groups, the way large empires, which we see today as so strong, rich, and powerful, were divided during the Middle Ages into small provinces, which in turn were further divided into small towns with their own rights and freedoms. Well, what rights! That is to say, the little towns and provinces, continually at war with each other (and today war is competition), were poor, weak, and had as their only right the ability to moan under the weight of their wretchedness, isolation, and the terrible calamities inevitably resulting from their divisive state.

So I am not afraid to repeat that the fundamental vice which must be attacked from every point is the system of separation, which decimates the workers and can only foster abuse.

I think this short analysis will suffice to enlighten the workers about the true cause of their ills—*division.*

Workers, you must leave behind this division and isolation as quickly as possible and march courageously and fraternally down the only appropriate path—*unity.* My union plan rests upon a broad base, and its spirit is capable of fully satisfying the moral and material needs of a great people.

What is the aim and what will result from the universal union of working men and women? Its goals are:

1. to establish the solid, indissoluble unity of the working class;

2. to provide the Workers' Union with great capital through the optional membership of every worker;

3. to acquire a real power backed by this capital;

4. by means of this power, to prevent poverty and eradicate abuse by giving working-class children a solid, rational education which will make them educated, reasonable, intelligent, and able men and women in their work;

5. to remunerate labor as it ought to be, generously and fairly. . . .

What is the social position of the French working class today, and what rights remain to be demanded? . . .

. . . From the Charter's standpoint, [the worker's] social position is as desirable as he could want! By virtue of the recognized principle, he enjoys absolute equality, complete freedom of thought, and the guarantee of security for his person and property. What more can he ask? But, let us hasten to say that to enjoy equality and freedom *in theory is* to live *in spirit.* And if he who brought the law of the spirit to the world spoke wisely, "Man can not live by bread alone," I believe it is also wise to say, "Man does not live in spirit alone."

Reading the 1830 Charter, one is struck by a serious omission. Our constitutional legislators forgot that preceding the rights of man and the citizen, there is an imperious, imprescriptible right engendering all the others, *the right to live*. Now, for the poor worker who possesses no land, shelter, capital, absolutely nothing except his hands, the rights of man and the citizen are of no value if his right to live is not recognized first of all (and in this case they are even bitterly derisory). For the worker, the right to live is the right to *work*, the only right that can give him the possibility of eating, and thus, of living. The first of the rights that every being enjoys by being born is precisely the one they *forgot* to inscribe in the Charter. This first right has yet to be proclaimed.

Today the working class must be concerned with this single claim, because it is based on the strictest equity. And anything short of granting this claim is an abrogation of fundamental rights. So, what is to be demanded? THE RIGHT TO WORK. The working class's own property and the only one it can ever possess is its hands. Yes, its hands. That is its patrimony, its sole wealth. Its hands are the only work tools it has. Therefore they constitute its property, and I do not think its legitimacy or utility can be denied. For if the earth produces, it is thanks to manual labor.

To deny that the worker's hands are his property is to refuse to understand the spirit of Article 8 of the Charter. Yet this property is uncontestable and, as soon as it comes under discussion, there will be a unanimous voice in support of it. To guarantee the working class's property (as Art. 8 indicates), this right and its free enjoyment must be recognized in principle (as well as in reality). Now, the exercise of this free enjoyment of property would consist in being able to use its hands when and how it pleases. And for that, it must have the right to work. So the guarantee of this property consists in a wise and equitable organization of labor. The working class thus has two important demands to make: *The right to work and the right to organize. . . .*

Workers, you see, if you want to save yourselves, you have but one means, you must unite. If I preach unity, it is because I know the strength and power you will find. Open your eyes, look around you, and you will see the advantages enjoyed by all those who have created unity in the goal of serving a common cause and common interests. . . .

In 1789 the bourgeoisie gained its independence. Its own charter dates from the capture of the Bastille. Workers, for more than two hundred years the bourgeois have fought courageously and ardently against the privileges of the nobility and for the victory of their rights. But when the day of victory came, and though

they recognized *de facto* equal rights for all, they seized all the gains and advantages of the conquest for themselves alone.

The bourgeois class has been established since 1789. Note what strength a body united in the same interest can have. As soon as this class is recognized, it becomes so powerful that it can exclusively take over all the country's powers. Finally in 1830 its power reaches its peak, and without being the least bit troubled by what might occur, it pronounces the fall of France's reigning king. It chooses its own king, proceeds to elect him without consulting the rest of the nation, and finally, being actually sovereign, it takes the lead in business and governs the country as it pleases. This bourgeois-owners class represents itself in the legislature and before the nation, not to defend its own interests, for no one threatens them, but to impose its conditions and commands upon 25 million proletarians. In a word, it is both counsel and judge, just like the feudal lords it triumphed over. Being capitalists, the bourgeois make laws with regard to the commodities they have to sell, and thereby regulate, as they will, the prices of wine, meat, and even the people's bread. You see, already more numerous and useful, the bourgeoisie has succeeded the nobility. The unification of the working class now remains to be accomplished. In turn, the workers, the vital part of the nation, must create a huge union to assert their unity! Then, the working class will be strong; then it will be able to make itself heard, to demand from the bourgeois gentlemen its right to work and to organize. . . .

III. Why I Mention Women . . .

In the life of the workers, woman is everything. She is their sole providence. If she is gone, they lack everything. So they say, "It is woman who makes or unmakes the home," and this is the clear truth: that is why it has become a proverb. However, what education, instruction, direction, moral or physical development does the working-class woman receive? None. As a child, she is left to the mercy of a mother and grandmother who also have received no education. One of them might have a brutal and wicked disposition and beat and mistreat her for no reason; the other might be weak and uncaring, and let her do anything. (As with everything I am suggesting, I am speaking in general terms; of course, there are numerous exceptions.) The poor child will be raised among the most shocking contradictions—hurt by unfair blows and treatment one day, then pampered and spoiled no less perniciously the next.

Instead of being sent to school, she is kept at home in deference to her brothers and so that she can share in the housework, rock the baby, run errands, or watch the soup, etc. At the age of twelve she is made an apprentice. There she continues to be exploited by her mistress and often continues to be as mistreated as she was at home.

Nothing embitters the character, hardens the heart, or makes the spirit so mean as the continuous suffering a child endures from unfair and brutal treatment. First, the injustice hurts, afflicts, and causes despair; then when it persists, it irritates and exasperates us and finally, dreaming only of revenge, we end up by becoming hardened, unjust, and wicked. Such will be the normal condition for a poor girl of twenty. Then she will marry, without love, simply because one must marry in order to get out from under parental tyranny. What will happen? I suppose she will have children, and she, in turn, will be unable to raise them suitably. She will be just as brutal to them as her mother and grandmother were to her. . . .

Poor working women! They have so many reasons to be irritated! First, their husbands. (It must be agreed that there are few working-class couples who are happily married.) Having received more instruction, being the head by law and also by the money he brings home, the husband thinks he is (and he is, in fact) very superior to his wife, who only brings home her small daily wage and is merely a very humble servant in her home.

Consequently, the husband treats his wife with nothing less than great disdain. Humiliated by his every word or glance, the poor woman either openly or silently revolts, depending upon her personality. This creates violent, painful scenes that end up producing an atmosphere of constant irritation between the master and the slave (one can indeed say *slave*, because the woman is, so to speak, her husband's property). This state becomes so painful that, instead of staying home to talk with his wife, the husband hurries out; and as if he had no other place to go, he goes to the tavern to drink blue wine in the hope of getting drunk, with the other husbands who are just as unhappy as he. . . .

And following the acute chagrins caused by the husband come the pregnancies, illnesses, unemployment, and poverty, planted by the door like Medusa's head. Add to all that the endless tension provoked by four or five loud, turbulent, and bothersome children clamoring about their mother, in a small worker's room too small to turn around in. My! One would have to be an angel from heaven not to be irritated, not to become brutal and mean in such a situation. However, in this domestic setting, what becomes of the children? They see their father only in the evening or on Sunday. Always either upset or drunk, their father speaks to them only angrily and gives them only insults

and blows. Hearing their mother continuously complain, they begin to feel hatred and scorn for her. They fear and obey her, but they do not love her, for a person is made that way—he cannot love someone who mistreats him. And isn't it a great misfortune for a child not to be able to love his mother! If he is unhappy, to whose breast will he go to cry? If he thoughtlessly makes a bad mistake or is led astray, in whom can he confide? Having no desire to stay close to his mother, the child will seek any pretext to leave the parental home. Bad associations are easy to make, for girls as for boys. Strolling becomes vagrancy, and vagrancy often becomes thievery. . . .

Are you beginning to understand, you men, who cry scandal before being willing to examine the issue, why I demand rights for women? Why I would like women placed in society on a footing of *absolute equality* with men to enjoy the legal birthright all beings have? I call for woman's rights because I am convinced that *all* the misfortunes in the world come from this neglect and scorn shown until now for the natural and inalienable rights of woman. I call for woman's rights because it is the only way to have her educated, and woman's education depends upon man's in general, and particularly the working-class man's. I call for woman's rights because it is the only way to obtain her rehabilitation before the church, the law, and society, and this rehabilitation is necessary before working men themselves can be rehabilitated. All working-class ills can be summed up in two words: poverty and ignorance. Now in order to get out of this maze, I see only one way: begin by educating women, because the women are in charge of instructing boys and girls. . . .

Workers, in 1791, your fathers proclaimed the immortal declaration of the rights of man, and it is to that solemn declaration that today you owe your being free and equal men before the law. May your fathers be honored for this great work! But, proletarians, there remains for you men of 1843 a no less great work to finish. In your turn, emancipate the last slaves still remaining in French society; proclaim the *rights of woman*, in the same terms your fathers proclaimed yours:

"We, French proletarians, after fifty-three years of experience, recognize that we are duly enlightened and convinced that the neglect and scorn perpetrated upon the natural rights of woman are the only cause of unhappiness in the world, and we have resolved to expose her sacred and inalienable rights in a solemn declaration inscribed in our charter. We wish women to be informed of our declaration, so that they will not let themselves be oppressed and degraded any more by man's injustice and tyranny, and so that men will respect the freedom and equality they enjoy in their wives and mothers.

1. The goal of society necessarily being the common happiness of men and women, the Workers' Union guarantees them the enjoyment of their rights as working men and women.

2. Their rights include equal admission to the Workers' Union palaces, whether they be children, or disabled or elderly.

3. Woman being man's equal, we understand that girls will receive as rational, solid, and extensive (though different) an education in moral and professional matters as the boys.

4. As for the disabled and the elderly, in every way, the treatment will be the same for women as for men.["]

Workers, rest assured, if you have enough equity and justice to inscribe in your Charter the few lines I have just traced, this declaration of the rights of woman will soon become custom, then law, and within twenty-five years you will see absolute equality of man and woman inscribed at the head of the book of law.

Then, my brothers, and only then, will human unity be established.

Sons of '89, that is the work your fathers bequeathed to you! . . .

IV. *Plan for the Universal Unionization of Working Men and Women*

71. The results the Workers' Union ought to have are immeasurable. This union is a bridge erected between a dying civilization and the harmonious social order foreseen by superior minds. First of all, it will bring about the rehabilitation of manual labor diminished by thousands of years of slavery. And this is a capital point. As soon as it is no longer dishonorable to work with one's hands, when work is even an honorable deed, the rich and the poor alike will work. For idleness is both a torture for mankind and the cause of its ills. All will work, and for this reason alone, prosperity will rule for everyone. Then, there will be no more poverty; and poverty ceasing, ignorance will too. Who causes the evil we suffer from today? Isn't it that thousand-headed monster, *selfishness*? But selfishness is not the primary cause; poverty and ignorance are what produce selfishness. . . .

73. Only when all men and women work with their hands and are dignified by it, will this great, desirable productivity take place. And this is the only way to eradicate the vices fostered by selfishness, and consequently to civilize men.

74. The second, but not lesser, result necessarily brought about by the Workers' Union will be to establish de facto real equality among all men. In fact, as soon as the day comes when working-class children are carefully raised and trained to develop their intellects, faculties, and physical strength—in a word, all that is good and beautiful in human nature—and as soon as there is no distinction between rich and poor children in their education, talent, and good manners, I ask: where could there be inequality? Nowhere, absolutely nowhere. Then only one inequality will be recognized, but that one must be experienced and accepted, for God is the One who established it. To one, he gives genius, love, intelligence, wit, strength, and beauty; to the other, he denies all these gifts and makes him stupid, dull-minded, weak-bodied, and ill-shapen. That is natural inequality before which man's pride must humble itself; that inequality indiscriminately touches the sons of kings as well as the sons of the poor.

75. I stop here, wanting to leave my readers the sweet joy of counting for themselves the important and magnificent results the Workers' Union will doubtless obtain. In this institution the country will find elements of order, prosperity, wealth, morality, and happiness, such as they can be desired. . . .

Summary of the ideas in this book, the goals of which are:

1. Consolidation of the working class by means of a tight, solid, and indissoluble Union.

2. Representation of the working class before the nation through a defender chosen and paid by the Workers' Union, so that the working class's need to exist and the other classes' need to accept it become evident.

3. Recognition of one's hands as legitimate property. (In France 25,000,000 proletarians have their hands as their only asset.)

4. Recognition of the legitimacy of the right to work for all men and women.

5. Recognition of the legitimacy of the right to moral, intellectual, and vocational education for all boys and girls.

6. Examination of the possibility of labor organizing in the current social state.

7. Construction of Workers' Union palaces in every department, in which working-class children would receive intellectual and vocational instruction, and to which the infirm and elderly as well as workers injured on the job would be admitted.

8. Recognition of the urgent necessity of giving moral, intellectual, and vocational education to the women of the masses so that they can become the moral agents for the men of the masses.

9. Recognition in principle of equal rights for men and women as the sole means of unifying humankind.

Josephine Elizabeth Grey Butler (1828–1906)

Josephine Butler was born in 1828 to an old and distinguished British reform family. Her father, John Grey, was an abolitionist and led one of the campaigns against the Corn Laws, the successful attempt during the 1840s to establish free trade policies in Parliament. Her uncle was prime minister when the Reform Bill of 1832 extended suffrage to middle-class men and urban areas which before were omitted from the franchise. Thus she had a strong tradition of association with progressive causes and a sense of standing and empowerment as regards political action. This self-confidence and sense of political heritage would stand her well in her most famous and controversial effort to overturn the Contagious Diseases Acts, which restricted the constitutional rights of women accused of prostitution in certain parts of England.

After marrying George Butler, a leader in the Anglican Church, she raised a family and lived a respected upper-middle-class life in Oxford and elsewhere but was never satisfied with the conditions of her own existence or those of other women. Her earliest interests concerning women involved the need for their higher education, and with Anne Jemima Clough, she founded the North of England Council for the Higher Education of Women and served as its president from 1867 to 1873. Yet there always seemed a need within her to pursue more fundamental and controversial causes. With the death of her daughter in 1864, she began her work with the poor and with prostitutes, during which time she visited Bridewell and established refuges for prostitutes who were often given the worst work within workhouses and prisons.

While beginning this activist effort, she also wrote works concerning the treatment of working- and middle-class women and published The Education and Employment of Women *in 1868 and* Woman's Work and Woman's Culture *in 1869. In these works, as in later ones, Butler drew upon earlier legal, political, social, and religious treatises to create a work which marshaled varied evidence and arguments to document her case. She was especially critical of dependent, middle-class women who had inadequate education and could not support themselves if their husbands died or became ill or their families were unable to take them in. In all of her works, she was more favorable to the insights and character of the English working classes, but her values and perspective still represented the privilege and moral values of her own class.*

Her greatest work began in 1869 when she assumed the leadership of the Ladies' National Association, an organization dedicated to ending state regulation of prostitution. Under her leadership, the association focused on shared identity of women across classes (especially sexual identity) and encouraged its mostly middle-class members to recognize the sexual double standard and to realize that they were also subject to arbitrary state control over their lives. It was a long campaign; the Contagious Diseases Acts were not repealed until 1886. It was a difficult effort in which respectable women often avoided Butler, and she was sometimes assaulted and pelted with rotten fruit and vegetables when she spoke for the cause, especially when she spoke to working-class audiences in the port cities and army garrisons where the acts were enforced, supposedly to protect soldiers and sailors from contracting venereal disease from local prostitutes. The main arguments she put forth throughout this campaign were that: (1) only women were given medical tests for venereal diseases or threatened with prison for resisting, although both sexes got the disease, and women at least as often from men as vice versa; (2) such testing and imprisoning without the women's consent constituted an illegal denial of habeas corpus to these poor women; and (3) the acts were enforced by military departments while all of the punishment was directed against female civilians, not male military personnel. She saw such efforts as a form of sexual slavery comparable to the slavery of people of color carried out by the British Empire before her father and others successfully gained an agreement of emancipation for slaves anywhere in the empire.

Not only did she lead one of the most important political crusades of the nineteenth century, she produced a number of works on the importance of maintaining the principles of the Magna Carta, the oppression of Ireland by the English, the degradation of women as citizens, and the lack of concern for African natives during the Boer War. In The Constitution Violated *(1871) and* Government by Police *(1879) she outlined the principles of her campaign and the imminent danger of the police state, along the lines of Big Brother as portrayed later by George Orwell in 1984. In* Our Christianity Tested by the Irish Question *(1887) she scathingly attacked the Christian smugness of most English Christians in their abuse of Irish Catholics, and, finally, in* Native Races and the War *(1900) she represented the superiority of the British constitution and of the Anglican Church over Boer institutions while claiming that the British had allowed race prejudice to dictate their policies with regard to African natives who, not the British or Dutch, were the most important people for the future of South Africa.*

Butler died in 1906 at the age of seventy-eight, after a long and distinguished career in which she had been vilified but in the long run greatly admired by a cross section of English society. In reviewing the writings of Josephine Butler, it is important to consider her as a Victorian who little questioned the superiority of British constitutionalism or of Christianity. However, in many ways she held the standards, beliefs, and structure of these institutions to account for the treatment of all people, not simply treatment of others such as herself. There is class and cultural superiority in Butler, but there is a kind of honesty and consistency in her writings often not found among her contemporaries. She should be read in a more complex fashion than is often the case by those who assess her only in regard to her work on the issue of prostitution and consider her there simply imposing bourgeois morality and unrealistic economics on her poorer sisters.

The excerpts below are from The Constitution Violated *(1871),* Government by Police *(1879), and* Native Races and the War *(1900).*

HLS

Sources and Suggested Readings

Barry, Kathleen. "Josephine Butler: The First Wave of Protest." In *The Prostitution of Sexuality.* New York: New York University Press, 1995.

Burton, Antoinette. "The White Woman's Burden: Josephine Butler and the Indian Campaign, 1886–1915." In *Burdens of History: British Feminists, Indian Women, and Imperial Culture, 1865–1915.* Chapel Hill: University of North Carolina Press, 1994.

[Butler, Josephine]. *The Constitution Violated. An Essay by the author of the "Memoir of John Grey of Dilston."* Edinburgh: Edmonston and Douglas, 1871.

Butler, Josephine E. *Government by Police.* London: Dyer Brothers, 1879.

——. *Josephine Butler Letter Collection.* Zug, Switzerland: Inter Documentation, 1982, 1984.

——. *Josephine E. Butler, An Autobiographical Memoir.* Bristol, London: J. W. Arrowsmith; Simpkin, Marshall, Hamilton, Bent & Co., Ltd., 1909.

——. *Native Races and the War.* London: Gay and Bird, 1900.

——. *Our Christianity Tested by the Irish Question.* London: Fisher Unwin, [1887].

——. *Personal Reminiscences of a Great Crusade.* London: Horace Marshall, 1910.

——, ed. *Woman's Work and Woman's Culture. A Series of Essays.* London: Macmillan, 1869.

Caine, Barbara. *Victorian Feminists.* New York: Oxford University Press, 1992.

Luddy, Maria. "Women and the Contagious Diseases Acts 1864–1886." *History Ireland* 1, 1 (1993): 32–34.

Spender, Dale. "Josephine Butler: Sexual Economics." In *Women of Ideas and What Men Have Done to Them.* London: Routledge and Kegan Paul, 1982. 334–46.

Uglow, Jenny. "Josephine Butler: From Sympathy to Theory." In *Feminist Theorists: Three Centuries of Key Women Thinkers,* ed. Dale Spender, 146–64. New York: Pantheon, 1983.

Walkowitz, Judith. "The Repeal Campaign" and "Class and Gender Conflict within the Repeal Movement." In *Prostitution in Victorian Society: Women, Class, and the State.* New York: Cambridge University Press, 1980. 90–112; 137–47.

The Constitution Violated (1871)

The object of the following Essay is to set forth the unconstitutional nature of certain recent Acts of the Legislature, and the danger arising therefrom, with the view of arousing the country to a sense of that danger.

The enactments called the Contagious Diseases Acts, passed respectively in 1866, 1868, and 1869, may be regarded from several points of view. With their medical aspect and the statistical consideration of their results on public health, it is not my intention to deal. It has been dwelt on by other people, and in other places, fully.

The moral side of the question is undoubtedly the most important, and has been dwelt upon by the religious portion of the community, almost to the exclusion of others, although it may be truly said that it of necessity includes all others.

There is, however, one aspect of the question which has not been sufficiently set forth, that is, the constitutional aspect, including the effect which such legislation must have on our social and moral life as a nation, from a political point of view.

In almost all the great meetings which have been held throughout the country on the subject of these Acts, resolutions have been passed embodying the word "unconstitutional" as characteristic of the Acts, proving that the mass of the people of England have a strong instinct, if it be nothing more, of what is constitutional and what is not. Few terms, it has been said, are more vaguely or loosely employed than this. It is affirmed with some truth that "Magna Charta is in everybody's lips but in nobody's hands." The careful study of the Acts in question leads me to the conclusion that the latter part of this saying must be eminently true of their framers. We, on the other hand, are charged by our opponents with ignorance of the words which we use. Yet what Sir Edward Creasy says is true, that "the English Constitution is susceptible of a full and accurate explanation"; and though the subject may require "more investigation than may suit hasty talkers and superficial thinkers, it is not more than every member of a great and free State ought gladly to bestow, in order that he may rightly comprehend and appreciate the polity and the laws in which and by which he lives, acts, and has his civic being" (*English Constitution*, Eighth edition, p. 2). He adds, . . . "These great primeval and enduring principles are the principles of the English Constitution; . . ." It is these enduring principles which are violated by the Contagious Diseases Acts. This I shall shortly show, but before doing so, I shall briefly set forth what these principles are.

I am convinced that the people of this country are as yet but very partially awakened to the tremendous issues involved in the controversy before us, considered as a matter of constitutional rights; therefore it is that I venture, though I am no lawyer, to bring before them its extreme importance under that aspect. For this time of agony for the patriot, who can in any degree foresee the future of that country which violates the eternal principles of just government, drives many of us, unlearned though we be, to search the annals of our country, to inquire into past crises of danger, and the motives and character of the champions who fought the battles of liberty, with that keenness and singleness of purpose with which, in the agony of spiritual danger, the well-nigh shipwrecked soul may search the Scriptures of God, believing that in them he has eternal life.

On the occasion of an infringement of a constitutional principle by Parliament itself, a century ago, Lord Chatham, when urging the House of Lords to retrace this fatal step, used the following words:—"If I had a doubt upon this matter, I should follow the example set us by the most reverend bench, with whom I believe it is a maxim, when any doubt in point of faith arises, or any question of controversy is started, to appeal at once to the greatest source and evidence of our religion—I mean the Holy Bible. The Constitution has its political Bible also, by which, if it be fairly consulted, every political question may and ought to be determined. Magna Charta, the Petition of Rights, and the Bill of Rights, form that code which I call the Bible of the English Constitution."

In following out this advice of Lord Chatham, it is to these authorities that I wish to appeal in determining the exact nature of those principles of the Constitution which I assert have been violated. I am aware that in doing so I may incur criticism on account of my ignorance of legal terms and definitions, and on account of unskillfulness in the arrangement of the matter before me. I shall be satisfied, however, if I succeed in commending my subject to those to whom I particularly address myself—I mean the working men and working women of England. Neither they nor I have had a legal training, but we may alike possess a measure of that plain English common sense which, to quote again Lord Chatham's words, is "the foundation of all our English jurisprudence,"—which common sense tells us that "no court of justice can have a power inconsistent with, or paramount to, the known laws of the land, and that the people, when they choose their representatives, never mean to convey to them a power of invading the rights or trampling upon the liberties of those whom they represent." (Lord Chatham's Speeches) Further on in this Essay I shall show that Parliament in making the Contagious Diseases Acts, has invaded and trampled on the liberties of the people. . . .

Among the clauses in Magna Charta, there is one upon which the importance of all the others hinges, and upon which the security afforded by the others practically depends. This clause, and the supplementary clause which follows it, have been those whose subject has formed, more than any other, matter and occasion for the great battles fought for English liberty and right since the Charter was signed by King John.

They are the 39th and 40th clauses of King John's Charter, and the 29th of that of King Henry III, and are as follows:—. . . .

> 39. No freeman shall be taken, or imprisoned, or disseised, or outlawed, or banished, or anyways destroyed, nor will we pass upon him, nor will we send upon him, unless by the lawful judgment of his peers, or by the law of the land.
> 40. We will sell to no man, we will not deny to any man either justice or right.

"These clauses are the crowning glories of the great charter" (*English Constitution*, p. 148). Mr. Hallam calls them its "essential clauses" (*Middle Ages*, chap. ii. p. 324), being those which "protect the personal liberty and property of all freemen, by giving security from arbitrary imprisonment and spoliation." The same high authority observes that these words of the Great Charter, "interpreted by any honest court of law, convey an ample security for the two main rights of civil society." The principles of this clause of the Great Charter, which, if we look backwards, are lost in antiquity, were subsequently confirmed and elucidated by statutes and charters of the reign of Henry III and Edward III entitled *"confirmationes cartarum."* "The famous writ of Habeas Corpus was framed in conformity with the spirit of this clause; that writ, rendered more actively remedial by the statute of Charles II, but founded upon the broad basis of Magna Charta, is the principal bulwark of English liberty, and if ever temporary circumstances, or the doubtful plea of necessity, shall lead men to look on its denial with apathy, the most distinguishing characteristic of our constitution will be effaced." . . .

I have now set forth the great principles of Magna Charta, and the foundations of these principles, and have endeavoured to show how much English liberty depends on the preservation of jury trial. I have now to show how the Contagious Diseases Acts destroy these bulwarks of English liberty.

. . . the Member . . . who . . . led the opposition in the House to Mr. Fowler's motion for the repeal of the Acts, based his arguments for the existence of these Acts on the State necessity of having a standing army! Such statements as these are calculated to lead the public to imagine that these Acts have at least some connection, more or less remote, with the army and navy, and in this way to allay those just alarms which must necessarily arise from the violation of the constitutional rights of civilians.

Now the fact is, that so far from these Acts applying particularly to the army and navy, they in no way whatsoever apply to the army and navy, but entirely and exclusively to the civil population. The one and only connection which they have with the army and navy is, that the districts to which they apply are those within at least ten miles of which soldiers or sailors are resident. But in these districts they apply not to soldiers or sailors, but to the civil population, and to the civil population only. The word soldier or sailor does not occur in the whole Act, nor is there anything whatsoever about the army or navy, or any hint, the most remote, of any connection with the army or navy, except this, that the whole powers of carrying out the Acts are intrusted to the Admiralty and War Office. In fact, the jurisdiction of these offices is by these Acts extended over a large portion of the civil population of England. Nay, so little has the Act to do with soldiers and sailors, that it does not even commence with the preamble which, unless it had distinctly acknowledged its necessary separation from the army and navy, we should have expected to find in some such words as these, "Considering the increase of contagious disease in her Majesty's army and navy," and so forth. Over and above the obvious fact, that women, to whom alone

the Act applies, are in no case members of these honourable services, the Acts do not even profess in any way whatsoever to apply particularly to those women who associate with soldiers and sailors, but distinctly leave us to infer the opposite; for in clause 4, Act 1869, directions are given for procedure against any woman whom the policeman believes to have been under certain circumstances, in the company of *men* resident within the limits to which the Act applies, the word "men" being used with no reference to soldiers or sailors at all. In fact, the idea that the Acts apply in any way to the army or navy is so absolutely unfounded, that a confutation of it seems almost absurd, and I would not have mentioned it but for the fallacious notion on this point promoted apparently by the supporters of the Acts . . . I would, however, point it out as a very grave objection to these Acts, that they extend the jurisdiction of the Admiralty and War Office over the civil population, and that they intrust to these offices such extensive and arbitrary powers as we shall shortly see that they do.

The Contagious Diseases Acts, as now in force, consist essentially of the following clauses:—

Act 1869, Clause 4.—"Where an information on oath is laid before a justice by a superintendent of police charging to the effect that the informant has good cause to believe that a woman, therein named, is a common prostitute, and either is resident within the limits of any place to which this Act applies, or, being resident within ten miles of these limits, or, having no settled place of abode, has within fourteen days before the laying of the information either been within those limits for the purpose of prostitution, or been outside of those limits for the purpose of prostitution in the company of men resident within those limits, the justice may, if he thinks fit, issue a notice thereof addressed to such woman, which notice the superintendent of police shall cause to be served on her."

Act 1866, Clause 16.—"In either of the following cases, namely,"—

"If the woman on whom such a notice is served appears herself, or by some person on her behalf, at the time and place appointed in the notice, or at some other time and place appointed by adjournment";—

"If she does not so appear, and it is shown (on oath) to the justice present that the notice was served on her a reasonable time before the time appointed for her appearance, or that reasonable notice of such adjournment was given to her (as the case may be)";—

"The justice present, on oath being made before him substantiating the matter of the information to his satisfaction, may, if he thinks fit, order that the woman be subject to a periodical medical examination by the visiting surgeon for any period not exceeding one year, for the purpose of ascertaining at the time of each such examination whether she is affected with a contagious disease; and thereupon she shall be subject to such a periodical medical examination, and the order shall be a sufficient warrant for the visiting surgeon to conduct such examination accordingly."

We who have combined to oppose this legislation maintain that this Act is unconstitutional, because it submits a case, in which the result is to the party concerned of the most enormous consequence, to trial without jury.

We are well aware, while making this statement, that there is a class of cases in England which at this present time are tried without a jury. But these cases are what are called "minor cases."

Now we maintain that a woman's honour is a point of very grave importance to her, and that no State can thrive in which it is not regarded as a very sacred question. And we maintain that a case which is to decide as to the question of a woman's honour is by no means, nor by any stretch of language or imagination, capable of being called a "minor case."

We therefore maintain that this law, which places the determination of the fact as to a woman's honour solely in the hands of a single justice of the peace, is as great an infringement of constitutional right, as if the determination of the fact as to whether a man were guilty of murder or not were placed in the hands of a single justice of the peace.

We maintain absolutely that to deprive of jury trial a woman whose honour is the subject in question, is a breach of the English Constitution, as fundamentally expressed in that clause of Magna Charta of which we have already pointed out the importance, "We will condemn no one except by the judgment of his peers."

The decision of the question as to her honour would itself, even if followed by no legal consequences, be a sufficiently grave one to warrant what I say. But let it be observed that when the case is decided against the woman, the deprivation of her honour is followed immediately, under these Acts, by those consequences which are especially indicated in Magna Charta as the consequences which shall ensue to no one except after trial by jury. She is not only subjected to that ordeal which we assert comes distinctly within the application of the words "or anyways destroyed"; but in order to the carrying out of that ordeal, she is, by the Act, both outlawed and imprisoned in the strict meaning of these terms as used in Magna Charta. She is in fact deprived of her liberties for the space of a year. She is outlawed practically during that period, inasmuch as she is handed over to the irresponsible action of surgeons, at whose simple fiat she may be detained and imprisoned without even any order before a justice, or

any oath or affidavit taken. Her whole liberty is curtailed, inasmuch as she is liable to be summoned for a repetition of this ordeal at whatever times and as frequently as the surgeon thinks fit; and the entire curtailment which this is of her liberty must be evident from the fact that she is bound to appear, subject to the penalty of imprisonment, with or without hard labour. I have already said that these Acts virtually introduce a species of villeinage or slavery. I use the word not sentimentally, but in the strictest legal sense. Slavery means that condition in which an individual is not master of his own person, and the condition of slavery is defined in Magna Charta by the omission of all slaves from the rights which that charter grants to every one else. There could be no more complete, galling, and oppressive deprivation of freedom than this which takes place under these Acts. . . . It is not however out of place to show here an additional consequence which follows directly on a woman's being registered as a "public woman," and which is by no means the least of the evils which accrue to her under this Act. Indeed, if we consider it rightly, it is virtually that which comprehends all the rest. According to Magna Charta it is not only a subject's person and liberty which shall be untouched, except after trial by jury, but also his property. Now the honour of a poor woman is often her only capital; it is in fact that part of her property the loss of which is ruin to her; the action of this law therefore, by registering a woman as infamous, deprives her of that character the possession of which is, in almost every case, her only hope of getting a living in an honest situation, and the loss of which, whether it be lost rightly or wrongly, is ruinous to her whole future life. . . .

In answer to our objections to these Acts, it is utter vanity and folly in any one to plead that they apply only to women who are prostitutes. Can it be supposed that there is any man in England so foolish as to think that the safeguards of English law exist for the sake of the guilty only? They exist for the sake of the innocent, who may be falsely accused, as well to protect them when accused, as to lessen the chances of unjust accusation. And can it be supposed that we are so blind as ever to be able to fancy that it is impossible that under this law an innocent woman may be accused? On the contrary, it is obvious that the question of a woman's honour is one in which mistaken accusations are peculiarly likely to occur. Hence it has been that in Christian countries the sin of unchastity in a woman has ceased to be treated as legally criminal, on account, first, of the extreme facility of false accusation; and, second, of the impossibility of rebutting such accusation; and in more enlightened communities the injustice has been apparent of treating penally this offence in one sex only. Yet here we see a law which, regardless of these considerations, not only takes in hand the determination as to the question of a woman's honour, but in the process of that determination deprives her of the only legal safeguard which it bestows in all other cases. We ought never to forget that the very fact of jury trial, which guards the person wrongfully accused, does itself also, more than any other thing, prevent such wrong accusations. Nor is there any accusation so likely to be multiplied by the absence of trial by jury as that against a woman's honour.

In presence of this enormity of these Acts, it is perhaps almost trivial to indicate a minor point in which they are unjust. It will be satisfactory to do so, however, in order to show the spirit of utter contempt for woman's honour which this law evinces. The Acts require no witness against the woman except the policeman, who, though he must substantiate on oath his own belief that the woman is a prostitute, is not bound to produce on oath what the grounds of that belief are. If the justice of [the] peace is satisfied with this substantiation, the woman is condemned under the Act.

The honour therefore of every woman is by this law intrusted to two men, the one the justice of the peace, and the other the policeman, who, let it be carefully observed, is expressly hired by Government for the one stated object of detecting unchaste women. . . .

For the rich and great there may be little danger in dispensing with jury trial in this particular instance. As there are classes in society whose position and wealth place them above any chance of being erroneously accused of theft, so there are classes whose position, wealth and surroundings place the women belonging to them equally above any chance of being erroneously accused of being prostitutes. To this fact we may probably trace the apathy and indifference of so many of the upper classes to the passing of the Contagious Diseases Acts, and the urbanity with which they assure us that our fears are ungrounded, and that the operation of these Acts can seldom err. Again we must quote the words of Junius, "Laws are intended not to trust to what men will do, but to guard against what they may do." But, at the same time, can we accept the assurance that the action of the officials who carry out these Acts will never be in error? We certainly cannot. Ladies who ride in their carriages through the streets at night are in little danger of being molested. But what of working women? What of the daughters, sisters, wives of working men, out, it may be on an errand of mercy, at night? And what, most of all, of that girl whose father, mother, friends are dead, or far away, who is struggling hard, in a hard world, to live uprightly and justly by the work of her own hands,—is she in no danger from this law? Lonely, and friendless, and poor,

is she in no danger of a false accusation from malice or from error? especially since one clause of the Act particularly marks out *homeless* girls as just subjects for its operation. And what has she, if accused, to rely on, under God, except that of which this law has deprived her, the appeal to be tried "by God and my country; by which she is understood to claim to be tried by a jury, and to have all the judicial means of defence to which the law entitles her" (De Lolme ["On the Constitution"], p. 171). . . .

In the expectation of having this proved to us in numerous pamphlets to the absolute satisfaction of the writers of the same, I cannot avoid this opportunity of investigating a little more closely the so-called moral arguments brought forward in favour of the Acts. In doing so I do not for a moment intend to return to that unprofitable dispute which they prolong regarding certain reclamations which they claim of a percentage of their patients in hospital. But I would call attention to the following fact, that our opponents always, and up to the present moment, in speaking of the "moral view," include in that expression only that wretchedly limited portion of the question which relates to the annual exodus from this degrading trade of a certain number of public women, an exodus which they who are acquainted with the circumstances of the lives of such women before the Acts ever came into existence, know to have been always going on to a very much greater extent than the upholders of these Acts take cognisance of. Whereas this has, without exception, been the limit of our opponents' view of the extent of the moral question involved, our view of that question has extended far beyond the moral influence of this legislation on the immediate victims of it, and has embraced its influence on the country at large, and that not only considered in its character as a direct encouragement to license, through the protection offered, but also in its character as a warping and blinding influence on the judgments and consciences of men of all classes who may themselves not be guilty of any personal impurity. It is a most inadequate and narrow view of the morality of which we speak as undermined by the Acts, which is exclusively confined to sexual morality. Injustice is immoral; oppression is immoral; the sacrifice of the interests of the weaker to the stronger is immoral; and all these immoralities embodied in these iniquitous Acts, and continually contemplated, as they must be, by all that portion of the nation who have no direct connection with the working of them, are a demoralizing influence of the most deadly character.

I cannot too much insist upon the weight which we who oppose these Acts attach to the statement which we have so frequently made, that they are calculated to transfer the essential element of guilt from the vice to the infringement of this law. Under the action of this law we maintain that gradually society at large comes to regard as evil and good, not vice and virtue absolutely, but, vice not regulated by this law, and vice regulated by this law. Men's talk, inferences, actions come to be all based upon a false distinction, the distinction between regulated and unregulated vice, and the true distinction between vice and virtue is lost sight of. . . .

The Contagious Diseases Acts would never have been possible in this country, if Englishmen had not become gradually accustomed, through the educational influences of the gross state of the laws of which I have just spoken, to despise the claims of women as such, and to cease, both in theory and in practice, to grant them that equality of citizenship which the Constitution originally bestowed upon them. . . .

I have said that we live under a system of just laws, and I have praised our representative government. But we owe the existence of the Acts of Parliament which we condemn, in a great measure to a grave fault in these laws, and a grave inadequacy in that representative government. I have already spoken of that fault in our laws. It cannot be expected that due attention will ever be paid to the interests of any class which is not duly represented in the government of the country. If women had possessed the franchise, the Contagious Diseases Acts could not have been passed. I have preferred in this Essay to treat these Acts as a matter affecting the whole community rather than as one which concerns women particularly, inasmuch as the claims which women and men have to jury trial and to all constitutional rights are equal, and rest on the same foundation, which cannot be destroyed for one sex only. I can never view this question as fundamentally any more a woman's question than it is a man's. These Acts secure the enslavement of women and the increased immorality of men; and history and experience alike teach us that these two results are never separated. Slavery and immorality lead to degradation, political ruin, and intellectual decay, and therefore it is that these Acts are a question for the whole nation at large. Yet we cannot shut our eyes to the fact that these Acts of Parliament in the first instance affect women only; it is by their necessary consequences, not by their immediate action, that men are also affected.

It is the beneficent arrangement of God that the interests of men and of women are identical; to this we owe it that women have not been more the sufferers from the partial representative system of this country than they have yet been. But let us not forget that the same great ordinance of God holds equally of the interests of all mankind, in all lands, and of all ranks; the interests of all are identical; yet there are oppressions manifold among mankind. It is to the recognition which necessarily follows sooner or later of that great law of God, that we may, under Providence, attribute the fact that the world is not worse than it is. For when men act in neglect of this great law, evils ensue more or less immediately; if they continue so to act, their neglect of this law brings eventually disturbance or decay, and an overturning of the fabric of society.

The object of a complete representation of the people is to establish a government which, by its own natural action, shall follow out and not violate this great principle. Hence it is that a just representative government—that is, one in which there is no class unrepresented—is the only form of government which bears in itself the elements and means of its own continuance or revival. All other governments bear in them the necessary seeds of revolution; they must all be corrected from without; it alone is able to correct itself from within. The possession of the franchise by women is not only the pledge of security for women—the only satisfactory pledge that the interests of women shall be duly respected,—but it is also the pledge of security for the nation that it shall not be in danger of violating the great principle, that the interests of all are identical, and shall not therefore incur the evil consequences of such a violation.

The object of representative government is to make the recognition of the principle that the interests of all are identical, preventive rather than remedial. . . . [and] a continual and natural process; and until women have votes, that which stands between this nation and the evil consequences of violating this principle is only the precarious barrier of "agitation." Until women possess the franchise the system of our government will be unstable and not self-corrective. And this is much more evident, in the present day than in former times, and is daily becoming more evident. There are great social questions pressing for consideration and for settlement; and so long as one sex undertakes to consider these questions alone, we shall be hurried into errors similar to the Contagious Diseases Acts, and into legislation based upon the neglect of the interests of women—a neglect which in all instances will prove, as in this it most emphatically proves, fatal to those imagined interests on behalf of which these are neglected. Legislation can never in these days, and at the stage of civilisation which we have reached, be just and pure until women are represented. Do not let the reader here for a moment suppose that I am attributing to men any intentional injustice, or that I am supposing that they will be actuated in general by anything but benevolent intentions towards women. But the safety and stability of all that is done in the nation depends, not upon the benevolent intentions of the enfranchised towards the unenfranchised, but upon the just representation of all. . . .

Government by Police (1879)

The substance of this Essay was published nine years ago, in the endeavour to rouse the attention of the public to the dangers (in a special connection) of a centralised police system under the direct control of the Executive Government. The warnings then uttered are signally justified by the position of our country to-day, which calls loudly for a renewal of the same battle of principles, extending over a wider field. . . .

This group should consist of men both in and out of Parliament, and it should include women. It is in the ranks of the Liberals that we look for these men of tomorrow, who would prove to be not only the party of progress, but of true conservatism, watchers for and guardians of the preservation of precious principles which are constantly threatened with destruction by the classes who cling to privilege, to the disadvantage of their brother men. It is not enough to be men of today; there is an urgent necessity for some to look on in advance. We need Seers as well as workers. How much we need them, and how much human suffering has been needlessly inflicted and prolonged by the want of such Seers and men of tomorrow among us, we have learned from the long, sad drama of Ireland's wrongs and struggles. It is impossible not to be struck by the almost universal confession on the part of our best Liberals, from their great leader himself down to the rank and file, of past ignorance in regard to Ireland. "We did not know, we did not perceive; and only now we have learned, and only now we begin to see." There is a deep sadness in this confession, though well it is that it is honestly made; for what does it mean but wrong done and persevered in generation after generation, which can never be undone for those who have suffered under it, who have gone to their last resting-place in the gloom of misery, poverty, homelessness, or with hearts embittered by the sense of wrong and thoughts of vengeance engendered, which have passed on as a heritage to their children. What does it mean but that still greater evils have been wrought in the character of the succeeding generations of those who, consciously or unconsciously, inflicted the wrong? It is

well to ask ourselves honestly and truthfully before God the question: How far has our ignorance the character of moral guilt? and it is well that we should realise that that moral guilt needs nonetheless to be repented of and purged away because it is shared by many, and because it even may chiefly be chargeable to generations gone by.

There is a lesson to be learned from the great question of Ireland which is now being fought out—a lesson deeper than seems yet to have been expressed, though it may be taking root in some few minds who have given themselves leisure to hold communion with their own hearts concerning the great events, past and present, which are so pregnant with teaching, and with the just God, the Judge of all. That lesson is one of warning for the future. It points to our past folly in having been contented to wait till great problems vitally affecting the interests of our fellow men were "at our door," knocking loudly for immediate solution. A wise foresight and a humbler and more disinterested direction of our thoughts to what is vital for tomorrow, though it certainly does not so immediately "pay" in political life, would have found us ready instead of unready when the confused rush and the pent-up torrent of the inevitable strife begins to sound in our ears.

The lesson we have to take to heart is simply that we must in future look ahead. To do so is a solemn responsibility on the part of the educated, and those who have present opportunities and historical teaching. It is their duty towards the masses of the toilers and the poor who are, and ever will be the chief sufferers from protracted wrong and postponed reforms.

This urgent necessity for Seers who will stand upon their watchtower as the men of tomorrow does not apply only to what are called Imperial questions, unhappy rumours and prospects of war, extended territorial possessions in other parts of the globe, but also, and with far greater force, to the awful problems at home: the poverty of our people and its remedies, the unrighteous inequality in the distribution of the good things of this world, the land question, self-government, a pure representative system, and many other things. . . .

The Police Question

A question in regard to which a few voices have been raised but scarcely seriously hearkened to, may now be said to be "at the door." It has been found in certain European States, and we shall soon prove it to be in our own day and land, one of the most difficult of problems, namely, that of discovering the best means of effectually counteracting or holding in check the strongly bureaucratic tendencies which we see to be stealing over almost every civilised nation. On the one hand we see imperially governed countries; and on the other democratic republics, with traditions and aspirations wholly different, but alike only in this? that police rule in each has so established itself as to become a standing menace to liberty, and an embarrassment and even a rival to the governments which aim at its reform or at the restriction of its functions.

The object of the present paper is to indicate the position of England in respect to this subject, to suggest certain lessons to be derived from the present struggle in France for decentralisation and the curbing of the power of the police, and to point out briefly the danger of the threatening tyranny—a tyranny which may establish itself under the shelter of a liberal or democratic government, no less than under an autocracy or empire. It is not difficult to recognise the present abuses and dangers which have been allowed to establish themselves in this department of the Executive. But to see the path which leads out of the actual complication is not so easy. To denounce the police, to pronounce what it ought not to be and do, is a simple enough task, so palpable are the inconveniences and wrongs to which the public in various lands are daily subjected by the growing influence of the ubiquitous and overshadowing Bureau; but to decide the question of what the police ought to be in a free nation, is a problem which will require for its solution the exercise of the wisest heads and the firmest hands among those alike who govern, and those who influence that public opinion whose support is required for the maintenance of any Government.

The principles which our forefathers held in regard to free government, however sound we may recognise them to be, have become less easy of application in these modern days of overgrown cities, crowded populations, perpetual locomotion, and complex social life. "Self-government," said Grattan, "is life." It is indeed life; life for the individual, for the family, for all organised communities, for municipalities, and for nations. The opposite is gradual death for each of these. Protests enough have been uttered against the evil influence of an absolute monarchy on the life of a people; but it is doubtful whether we have yet sufficiently considered, or whether our Liberal leaders are at all adequately awake to the fact, that precisely the same evils are accumulating under a bureaucracy (created it may be by the most Liberal Parliament), which forces to act, and does not encourage and fructify the principle of self-action. De Tocqueville, alluding to a tyranny represented, not by one man, but by many (in the case of a fully enfranchised people), says: "For myself, when I feel the hand of power lie heavy upon me, I care little to know who oppresses me, and I am

not the more disposed to pass under the yoke because it is held out to me by the arms of a million of men." Modern Police Government in its worst forms combines the evil of extreme centralisation with the activity, in every corner of the nation, of a vast and numerous agency of surveillance, whose very presence tends by slow degrees to enfeeble the sense of responsibility in the citizens in regard to the order and well-being of society. "It is necessary," says Lieber, in his "Political Ethics," "to have seen nations who have been forced for centuries to submit to constant and minute police interference, in order to have any conception of the degree to which manly action, self-dependence, and inventiveness of proper means, can be eradicated from a whole community." Personal security against bodily violence or harm (the benefit above all others supposed to be guaranteed to the citizen by the ever-present police) is itself purchased at too great a cost, if it be obtained at the price of personal liberty. An extensive preventive police might, by fettering all free individual action, prevent many offences; but mere physical security is not the highest object of pursuit for society, although it is desirable, in order that it may obtain its highest objects. There is something bordering on the ludicrous, in the unconscious condemnation of the system which they represent, contained in the often repeated and somewhat sentimental lamentations of our metropolitan superintendents of police, over the growing dependence and carelessness of the population of London. A certain superintendent having reported the numbers of doors and windows found unguarded or open at night, asks despondingly, "When will the people of England ever learn to take care of themselves?" The answer is at hand, "Never, so long as they are educated by the constant presence of persons delegated by Government to take care of them, even in the minutest particulars." Here is the fulfilment of Lieber's words—inventiveness, self-protection, and manly self-dependence are gradually driven out of a people by the delegation of the simplest and most primitive duties of citizens to the agents of the Government. . . .

Chartist Meetings and Police

The reports of debates in Parliament at this time [early 1800s], and other public documents, prove how strongly the instinct of the people (whether reasonable or not) rose up against the proposed change [to a centralized and military police force]. Sir Robert Peel obtained in 1828 the appointment of a committee of the House of Commons, to inquire into the expediency of establishing a uniform system of police in the metropolis. The Committee reported favourably of the scheme. . . . and in [1829] the Act of 10th George

IV. Cap. 44, passed both Houses and became law. A great conflict of opinion concerning the introduction of a principle of police rule foreign to English habits continued to prevail; in fact, it came to be more than a conflict of opinion when in 1833 an actual collision took place between the new police force and a meeting of Chartists in Coldbath Fields. Directions had been given to the police to disperse the meeting; in attempting to do so three police officers were stabbed, and one of them fell dead on the spot. A contemporary writer, favourable to the new system of police, remarked: "It might have been thought that such a resistance of a constituted authority ending in murder would have excited the indignation of the more respectable class of citizens; but precisely the contrary was the fact." A coroner's jury returned a verdict of justifiable homicide, a very significant sign of the feeling towards the new force of the class of citizens from which the jury was selected. Such an agitation was stirred up that a commission was called for to inquire into the conduct of the police, in order to satisfy the public. The same special pleader for the new system, above quoted, says, "Thus we see that this essential change in this branch of criminal justice was not made without creating a deep sensation. That stalking-horse, the liberty of the subject, which in truth meant the liberty to rob and plunder, was immediately paraded before the public; and indeed for Englishmen, jealous of their personal liberty, the establishment of this new force might at first have created some well-founded alarm. It was no longer a question of a few constables under municipal or local direction, but of a standing army of nearly 6000 men drilled like soldiers, taught to act in masses, *entirely independent of the control of the ratepayers, and solely under that of a minister of State."* . . .

Illegal and Cruel Treatment of Prisoners

In close connection with the arbitrary powers granted to a State police is the subject of the treatment of prisoners both before and after trial. We may well ask, What has become of the first principles of English law in these days? Many even of the best of our public men do not seem fully impressed with the fact of the constant violation of the law in some of its highest principles by the Executive and their officers. The utterances of our greatest lawyers are very impressive on the subject of the sacredness of the persons of citizens at all times, and not least when condemned and in a condemned cell, awaiting, it may be, the extreme punishment awarded by law. Not Blackstone alone, but all great defenders of justice and law, have set forth this

principle in the clearest and strongest manner. And well they might do so: for the brutality and secret tyranny, even to murder, which would be exercised on defenceless persons confined within the four walls of a narrow cell can be imagined, were not the persons of prisoners considered by the law as inviolable in the matter of private assault, as those of any citizen walking in the street or any magistrate sitting on the Bench.

The Pall Mall Gazette of December 1, 1887, under the head, "The Black Hole of Scotland-yard," recorded some horrible facts of the brutality of the police to men in their power, whom they had just arrested. Surely, if "assault and battery" are punishable by law at any time, they are punishable in such a case; and every one of those policemen guilty of assault ought to be punished. Why is it that there is, apparently, so little said about it except among the poor people themselves? The want of general interest in the matter is a deadly sign. Even while repressing the natural feeling of compassion for the poor people thus maltreated, this apathy is in itself enough to stir the soul to its depths. It is to be hoped that these events may teach us again to defend the law with that zeal for it which once characterised the English people. No doubt there is a difficulty in bringing these police offenders to justice when the assault has been made in a narrow cell, with locked doors, and there is no witness on the side of the sufferer. Something might be done, however, by an observation being taken of the condition of the poor man's head and face and general appearance before entering the cell, and of the same when he leaves it. If he enters sound, and comes out again with black eyes and bandaged and bleeding head, &c., surely there is sufficient proof of assault within the cell, although no doubt the cowards who wounded him would be ready to swear, one and all, that he had wounded himself and blackened his own eyes. Persons cognisant of the matter assert that these cases of battery and assault by the police upon prisoners in cells, upon persons not tried or condemned, are now so common that they excite but little surprise.

Several typical cases in the past century or two have turned upon this question of the inviolability of the person of the citizen, no matter how obnoxious that citizen may have been to the existing Government. There is upon the Statute Book of England an Act to this day entitled the Coventry Act. The occasion of its enactment was as follows, and it is an illustration of the jealous spirit in which the slightest bodily injury inflicted by the public authority outside the law has been resented by the people of England. It is the case of Sir John Coventry. This gentleman had animadverted upon the immoralities of the king, Charles II. The king declared that "if this kind of talk was not summarily punished, it would become a fashion to talk so," and he sent some of his police—his personal bodyguard—to watch about the streets where Sir John lived, and to "leave some mark upon his person which should teach him not to talk at that rate for the future." Bishop Burnet, in his "History of his Own Times," says:— "The king's men, Sands and O'Brian, went there, and finding Coventry going home they drew round him. He stood up to the wall, and snatching the flambeau from his servant's hand, with that in one hand and his sword in the other, he fought so well that he got much credit by it. He wounded some of the men, but they inflicted a severe cut on his nose, to teach him to remember the respect he owed to his king, and so they left him. . . . This put the House of Commons in a *furious uproar.* They passed a Bill of punishment against the assailants, and put a clause in it that it should never be in the king's power to pardon them."

Observe the parallel. Certain London citizens had animadverted on the action of the Government in the matter of William O'Brien and Coercion in Ireland. The Government believed, apparently, that if it did not punish this sort of thing "it would grow into a fashion to talk so," and therefore sent its Sir Charles Warren and his men to watch in the streets where these citizens were likely to be found, and "to leave some mark upon their persons which should teach them not to talk at that rate in the future." But there the parallel ends. Other citizens have in some cases defended themselves as bravely as Sir John Coventry did, though only with sticks and umbrellas. They have got more than a wound upon their noses—a great deal more. But the representatives of London, being largely pledged to centralised and coercive policy, were *not* put into a furious uproar, unless it was against the people themselves, who claimed the right of free speech. It is, however, to be hoped that some day an Act of Parliament may be passed to punish future official assaulters of the citizens. . . .

The Police as Disturbers of the Peace

The late Chief Commissioner of the Metropolitan Police, Sir Edmund Henderson, being a man of high principle and acknowledged prudence in the control of the immense machine over which he presided, we had for some years comparatively few of those outrages which a Government police is so constantly liable to commit, owing to the extensive and unconstitutional powers placed in their hands. But under a less prudent chief the scene has changed. In Paris and every bureaucratically governed capital we have the fullest proofs that not only is a State police apt to fail in its duty of protecting the persons of the citizens, but that its agents become themselves the violators of personal liberties, the assailants of the modesty and chastity of women, and the cause frequently of public disorders. . . .

The danger of this growing tyranny on the part of the police is so much the greater now for us in England, because of the existence of that very element which has so rapidly and so deeply corrupted the *personnel* of the police in many other capitals, i.e., the encouragement of a portion of the metropolitan force as an organised body of women-hunters, with the most frightfully arbitrary and irresponsible powers to pursue, to accuse, and to condemn any woman who may be an immoral person, or not, or to whom they may have a personal enmity. To devote a certain number of the police force, acting under Government, to such an education as this, and for the exercise of such powers and functions, is a sure method of introducing into the whole force an arbitrary spirit, and immoral traditions and modes of action, which must exercise a deteriorating influence on the principles and personal character of the whole of the official staff under Government rule.

The people of England will endure for a long time, and with tolerable patience, tyranny and abuses of this nature; they endure them, until some great scandal occurs which agitates the public mind and brings about, not the abolition of the system, but the mere transfer of the unconstitutional power into the hands of a more trusted chief. Such a transfer will not essentially mend matters, and the same abuses will again spring up and flourish. The transfer must be made into the hands of the people themselves; and even then there will be danger enough, unless, taught by adversity and sore conflict, our people of all classes rise to a higher tone and to a greater respect for justice and for the liberties of all. The half of the human race, namely women, must not in future be left out of consideration, nor excluded from their right of equality before the law, as has, till now, been the case through all political struggles. They must be admitted to and rise to full citizenship. They already possess the municipal franchise, by which, happily for themselves, the women of London, under a future London Municipal Government, will be able in some measure to make their voice heard in many matters, including police hunting of women, a form of persecution which now goes on unchecked in all its abuses, under the cover of Vagrancy Acts and of sundry vague and unequal by-laws or police customs.

Summing-up of Proposed Reforms

To sum up in regard to the reforms which we propose, what measures shall we adopt in order to counteract the despotic tendencies which have been indicated? The following suggestions are offered:—

First—The placing of all police under municipal control.

Secondly—Its decentralisation, not only by removing it from the direct control of the central Government, but by relegating certain duties now combined under one great organisation to other persons and offices; and by inviting and encouraging as much as possible the action of the citizens themselves, in the guardianship of their own persons and property, and in the maintenance of order.

Thirdly—The severe restriction of the functions of a future municipal police to what is essentially legal and constitutional, and the guarding against that needless and mischievous multiplication of laws enacted year by year, whereby the police service and staff are necessarily greatly increased, and its functions enormously enlarged beyond what is good or safe for the public. . . .

A Revolution Needed in the Consciences of Men

A hope at last seems to be dawning that the necessity of such a revolution in the consciences of men as will lead to large self-sacrifices is acknowledged even by the most privileged classes to some extent.

If this hope decays, we are left to the contemplation of the inevitable alternative of violent retribution. But surely we may hope that the privileged classes, possessors of wealth and of the soil, are awaking to the consciousness of the great responsibility weighing upon them; the consciousness may come darkly, vaguely, uneasily, as a nightmare to a sleeping man, driven away again and again, but still returning. The supposed awful sacredness of the "rights of property" is beginning to be estimated at its real and comparative worth; and the right of the hungry to eat forces itself to the front as a right at least as sacred. London poverty should be teaching to the most stupid the lesson that wherever there is a monopoly of advantages on the one hand, there is loss, misery, and a disinherited mass of humanity on the other. But will the privileged classes awake in time to avert calamity, bitter suffering, and crime? Will they acknowledge in time the insufficiency of the tax on their resources, for ordinary charity, and the dire necessity of sacrifice to the extent of self-spoliation, in order to restore the balance, and avert confusion and destruction?

There is no truer kindness than to remind those who, themselves just, perhaps, and generous, have been born to an inheritance of monopolised privileges, of the duties which such an inheritance entails. A man born to the possession of a great neglected estate, on which he finds his labourers degraded, cottages in ruins, and fields, which ought to be storehouses of sustenance for city populations, going to waste, undrained and untilled, will scarcely think he has done his duty to society if, having any available means of improving it, he dies, leaving his estate as he found it, content to charge the ruin and neglect upon his forefathers or upon a series of accidents. It would not be thought that an unjust accusation had been brought against such a landowner, if a friend were to take him by the hand and lead him through the dwellings of his tenants and labourers, and bid him mark the moral as well as the material harvest of misery which each year of continued neglect was preparing for a number of human beings: even if such a friend were to reason with him of "righteousness, temperance, and judgment to come," until he trembled in the waking sense of deep responsibility, it would not be thought to be a harsh or needless counsel. Similarly it will be believed, that it is with an equal regard for the happiness of all human beings alike, men and women, the highly favoured and responsible as well as the spoiled and neglected, that upper-class men of the present generation are reminded that there is an entail even more grievous than that which spreads its blight over so many estates in our fair England—an entail which is injurious to those who are supposed to be benefiting by it, no less than to the human fields which it desolates. There is a moral deterioration which is the invariable attendant upon the habit of the careless and irresponsible enjoyment of possession at the expense of the happiness and good of others. No portion of the human family can continue from age to age in the enjoyment of advantages which are not justly shared with others, nor in an attitude of indifference to the disabilities of another and a dependent portion of the community—even though a monopoly of such advantages may have been an heritage to which they were born—without suffering deterioration, gradual but sure, in the deepest part of their nature. For persons in such a case, whether they or their forefathers be chargeable with the blame of it, there is no moral health possible save in the awakened perception of existing wrong, and the conscious will to restore the balance to society, as far as it lies in their power to do so, by bringing a share of monopolised blessings into the lot of those classes who have suffered deprivation. . . .

Native Races and the War (1900)

I.

Apology for "yet another book" on the South African Question. Future Peace must be based on Justice,—to coloured as well as white men. Difference between Legalized Slavery and the subjection of Natives by Individuals. . . .

In the midst of the manifold utterances and discussions on the burning question of to-day,—the War in South Africa,—there is one side of the subject which, it seems to me, has not as yet been considered with the seriousness which it deserves,—and that is the question of Slavery, and of the treatment of the native races of South Africa. Though this question has not yet in England or on the Continent been cited as one of the direct causes of the war, I am convinced,—as are many others,—that it lies very near to the heart of the present trouble.

The object of this paper is simply to bring witnesses together who will testify to the past and present condition of the native races under British, Dutch, and Transvaal rule. These witnesses shall not be all of one nation; they shall come from different countries, and among them there shall be representatives of the native peoples themselves. I shall add little of my own to the testimony of these witnesses. But I will say, in advance, that what I desire to make plain for some sincere persons who are perplexed, is this,—that where a Government has established by Law the principle of the complete and final abolition of Slavery, and made its practice illegal for all time,—as our British Government has done,—there is hope for the native races;—there is always hope that, by an appeal to the law and to British authority, any and every wrong done to the natives, which approaches to or threatens the reintroduction of slavery, shall be redressed. The Abolition of Slavery, enacted by our Government in 1834, was the proclamation of a great principle, strong and clear, a straight line by which every enactment dealing with the question, and every act of individuals, or groups of individuals, bearing on the liberty of the natives can be measured, and any deviation from that straight line of principle can be exactly estimated and judged.

When we speak of injustice done to the natives by the South African Republics, we are apt to be met with the reproach that the English have also been guilty of cruelty to native races. This is unhappily true, and

shall not be disguised in the following pages;—but mark this,—that it is true of certain individuals bearing the English name, true of groups of individuals, of certain adventurers and speculators. But this fact does not touch the far more important and enduring fact that *wherever British rule is established, slavery is abolished, and illegal.*

This fact is the ground of the hope for the future of the Missionaries of our own country, and of other European countries, as well as of the poor natives themselves, so far as they have come to understand the matter; and in several instances they have shown that they do understand it, and appreciate it keenly.

Those English persons, or groups of persons, who have denied to the native labourers their hire (which is the essence of slavery), have acted on their own responsibility, and *illegally*. This should be made to be clearly understood in future conditions of peace, and rendered impossible henceforward.

That future peace which we all desire, on the cessation of the present grievous war, must be a peace founded on justice, for there is no other peace worthy of the name; and it must be not only justice as between white men, but as between white men and men of every shade of complexion.

A speaker at a public meeting lately expressed a sentiment which is more or less carelessly repeated by many. I quote it, as helping me to define the principle to which I have referred, which marks the difference between an offence or crime committed by an individual *against* the law, and an offence or crime sanctioned, permitted, or enacted by a State or Government itself, or by public authority in any way.

This speaker, after confessing, apparently with reluctance, that "the South African Republic had not been stainless in its relations towards the blacks," added, "but for these deeds—every one of them—we could find a parallel among our own people." I think a careful study of the history of the South African races would convince this speaker that he has exaggerated the case as against "our own people" in the matter of deliberate cruelty and violence towards the natives. However that may be, it does not alter the fact of the wide difference between the evil deeds of men acting on their own responsibility and the evil deeds of Governments, and of Communities in which the Governmental Authorities do not forbid, but sanction, such actions.

As an old Abolitionist, who has been engaged for thirty years in a war against slavery in another form, may I be allowed to cite a parallel? That Anti-Slavery War was undertaken against a Law introduced into England, which endorsed, permitted, and in fact, legalized, a moral and social slavery already existing—a slavery to the vice of prostitution. The pioneers of the opposition to this law saw the tremendous import, and the necessary consequences of such a law. They had previously laboured to lessen the social evil by moral and spiritual means, but now they turned their whole attention to obtaining the abolition of the disastrous enactment which took that evil under its protection. They felt that the action of Government in passing that law brought the whole nation (which is responsible for its Government) under a sentence of guilt—a sentence of moral death. It lifted off from the shoulders of individuals, in a measure, the moral responsibility which God had laid upon them, and took that responsibility on its own shoulders, as representing the whole nation; it foreshadowed a national blight. My readers know that we destroyed that legislation after a struggle of eighteen years. In the course of that long struggle, we were constantly met by an assertion similar in spirit to that made by the speaker to whom I have referred; and to this day we are met by it in certain European countries. They say to us, "But for every scandal proceeding from this social vice, which you cite as committed under the system of Governmental Regulation and sanction, we can find a parallel in the streets of London, where no Governmental sanction exists." We are constantly taunted with this, and possibly we may have to admit its truth in a measure. But our accusers do not see the immense difference between Governmental and individual responsibility in this vital matter, neither do they see how additionally hard, how hopeless, becomes the position of the slave who, under the Government sanction, has no appeal to the law of the land; an appeal to the Government which is itself an upholder of slavery, is impossible. The speaker above cited concluded by saying: "The best precaution against the abuse of power on the part of whites living amidst a coloured population is to make the punishment of misdeeds come home to the persons who are guilty of those misdeeds; and if he could but get his countrymen to act up to that view he believed we should really have a better prospect for the future of South Africa than we had had in the past."

With this sentiment I am entirely in accord. It is our hope that the present national awakening on the whole subject of our position and responsibilities in South Africa will—in case of the re-establishment of peace under the principles of British rule—result in a change in the condition of the native races, both in the Transvaal, and at the hands of our countrymen and others who may be acting in their own interests, or in the interests of Commercial Societies.

I do not intend to sketch anything approaching to a history of South African affairs during the last seventy or eighty years; that has been ably done by others, writing from both the British and the Boer side. I shall only attempt to trace the condition of certain native tribes in connection with some of the most salient events in South Africa of the century which is past.

In 1877, as my readers know, the Transvaal was annexed by Sir Theophilus Shepstone. There are very various opinions as to the justice of that annexation. I will only here remark that it was at the earnest solicitation of the Transvaal leaders of that date that an interference on the part of the British Commissioner was undertaken. . . . The results, however, for the Republic were for the time, financial relief and prosperity, and better treatment of the natives. The financial condition of the country, as I have said, at the time of the annexation, was one of utter bankruptcy. "After three years of British rule, however, the total revenue receipts for the first quarter of 1879 and 1880 amounted to £22,773 and £47,982 respectively. That is to say, that, during the last year of British rule, the revenue of the country more than doubled itself . . ." (quoted from Parliamentary Blue Book).

In 1881, the Transvaal (under Prime Minister Gladstone's administration) was liberated from British control. It was given back to its own leaders, under certain conditions, agreed to and solemnly signed by the President. These are the much-discussed conditions of the Convention of 1881, one of these conditions being that Slavery should be abolished. This condition was indeed, insisted on in every agreement or convention made between the British Government and the Boers; the first being that of 1852, called the Sand River Convention; the second, a convention entered into two years later called the Bloemfontein Convention (which created the Orange Free State); a third agreement as to the cessation of Slavery was entered into at the period of the Annexation, 1877; a fourth was the Convention of 1881; a fifth the Convention of 1884. I do not here speak of the other terms of these Conventions, I only remark that in each a just treatment of the native races was demanded and agreed to.

The retrocession of the Transvaal in 1881 has been much lauded as an act of magnanimity and justice. There is no doubt that the motive which prompted it was a noble and generous one; yet neither is there any doubt, that in certain respects, the results of that act were unhappy, and were no doubt unanticipated. It was on the natives, whose interests appeared to have had no place in the generous impulses of Mr. Gladstone, that the action of the British Government fell most heavily, most mournfully. In this matter, it must be confessed that the English Government broke faith with the unhappy natives, to whom it had promised protection, and who so much needed it. In this, as in many other matters, our country, under successive Governments, has greatly erred; at times neglecting responsibilities to her loyal Colonial subjects, and at other times interfering unwisely.

In one matter, England has, however, been consistent, namely, in the repeated proclamations that Slavery should never be permitted under her rule and authority.

The formal document of agreement between Her Majesty's Government and the Boer leaders, known as the Convention of 1881, was signed by both parties at Pretoria on the afternoon of the 3rd August, in the same room in which, nearly four years before, the Annexation Proclamation was signed by Sir T. Shepstone.

This formality was followed by a more unpleasant duty for the Commissioners appointed to settle this business, namely, the necessity of conveying their message to the natives, and informing them that they had been handed back by Great Britain, "poor Canaanites," to the tender mercies of their masters, the "Chosen people," in spite of the despairing appeals which many of them had made to her.

Some three hundred of the principal native chiefs were called together in the Square at Pretoria, and there the English Commissioner read to them the proclamation of Queen Victoria. Sir Hercules Robinson, the Chief Commissioner, having "introduced the native chiefs to Messrs. Kruger, Pretorius, and Joubert," having given them good advice as to indulging in manual labour when asked to do so by the Boers, and having reminded them that it would be necessary to retain the law relating to Passes, which is, in the hands of a people like the Boers, almost as unjust a regulation as a dominant race can invent for the oppression of a subject people, concluded by assuring them that their "interests would never be forgotten or neglected by Her Majesty's Government." Having read this document, the Commission hastily withdrew, and after their withdrawal the Chiefs were "allowed" to state their opinions to the Secretary for Native Affairs.

In availing themselves of this permission, it is noticeable that no allusion was made by the Chiefs to the advantages they were to reap under the Convention. All their attention was given to the great fact that the country had been ceded to the Boers, and that they were no longer the Queen's subjects. I beg attention to the following appeals from the hearts of these oppressed people. They got very excited, and asked whether it was thought that they had no feelings or hearts, that they were thus treated as a stick or piece of tobacco, which could be passed from hand to hand without question.

Umgombarie, a Zoutpansberg Chief, said: "I am Umgombarie. I have fought with the Boers, and have many wounds, and they know that what I say is true. I will never consent to place myself under their rule. I belong to the English Government. I am not a man who eats with both sides of his jaw at once; I only use one side. I am English. I have said."

Silamba said: "I belong to the English. I will never return under the Boers. You see me, a man of my rank and position; is it right that such as I should be seized and laid on the ground and flogged, as has been done to me and other Chiefs?"

Sinkanhla said: "We hear and yet do not hear, we cannot understand. We are troubling you, Chief, by talking in this way; we hear the Chiefs say that the Queen took the country because the people of the country wished it, and again, that the majority of the owners of the country did not wish her rule, and that therefore the country was given back. We should like to have the man pointed out from among us black people who objects to the rule of the Queen. We are the real owners of the country; we were here when the Boers came, and without asking leave, settled down and treated us in every way badly. The English Government then came and took the country; we have now had four years of rest, and peaceful and just rule. We have been called here to-day, and are told that the country, our country, has been given to the Boers by the Queen. This is a thing which surprises us. Did the country, then, belong to the Boers? Did it not belong to our fathers and forefathers before us, long before the Boers came here? We have heard that the Boers' country is at the Cape. If the Queen wishes to give them their land, why does she not give them back the Cape?"

Umyethile said: "We have no heart for talking. I have returned to the country from Sechelis, where I had to fly from Boer oppression. Our hearts are black and heavy with grief to-day at the news told us. We are in agony; our intestines are twisting and writhing inside of us, just as you see a snake do when it is struck on the head. We do not know what has become of us, but we feel dead. It may be that the Lord may change the nature of the Boers, and that we will not be treated like dogs and beasts of burden as formerly; but we have no hope of such a change, and we leave you with heavy hearts and great apprehension as to the future." In his Report (made on the spot), Mr. Shepstone (Secretary for Native Affairs) says, "One chief, Jan Sibilo, who had been personally threatened with death by the Boers after the English should leave, could not restrain his feelings, but cried like a child." . . .

Many more of such extracts might be quoted, but it is not my motive to multiply horrors. These are given exactly as they stand in the original, which may all be found in Blue Books presented to Parliament.

It has frequently been denied on behalf of the Transvaal, and is denied at this day, in the face of innumerable witnesses to the contrary, that slavery exists in the Transvaal. Now, this may be considered to be verbally true. Slavery, they say, did not exist; but apprenticeship did, and does exist. It is only another name. It is not denied that some Boers have been kind to their slaves, as humane slave-owners frequently were in the Southern States of America. But kindness, even the most indulgent, to slaves, has never been held by abolitionists to excuse the existence of slavery. . . .

There is unhappily a tendency among persons living for any length of time among heathen people, to think and speak with a certain contempt for those people, at whose moral elevation they may even be sincerely aiming. They see all that is bad in these "inferior races," and little that is good. This was not so in the case of the greatest and most successful Missionaries. They never lost faith in human nature, even at its lowest estate, and hence they were able to raise the standard of the least promising of the outcast races of the world. This faith in the possibility of the elevation of these races has been firmly held, however, by some who know them best, and have lived among them the longest.

Mr. Rider Haggard writes thus on this subject:— "So far as my own experience of natives has gone, I have found that in all the essential qualities of mind and body they very much resemble white men. Of them might be aptly quoted the speech Shakespeare puts into Shylock's mouth: 'Hath not a Jew eyes? hath not a Jew hands, organs, dimensions, senses, affections, passions?' In the same way, I ask, has a native no feelings or affections? does he not suffer when his parents are shot, or his children stolen, or when he is driven a wanderer from his home? Does he not know fear, feel pain, affection, hate, and gratitude? Most certainly he does; and this being so, I cannot believe that the Almighty, who made both white and black, gave to the one race the right or mission of exterminating or of robbing or maltreating the other, and calling the process the advance of civilization. It seems to me, that on only one condition, if at all, have we the right to take the black men's land; and that is, that we provide them with an equal and a just Government, and allow no maltreatment of them, either as individuals or tribes, but, on the contrary, do our best to elevate them, and wean them from savage customs. Otherwise, the practice is surely undefensible.

"I am aware, however, that with the exception of a small class, these are sentiments which are not shared by the great majority of the public, either at home or abroad." . . . .

VII.

Transvaal Policy since 1884. . . . Transvaal law. The Grondwet or Constitution. The High Courts of Justice Subservient to the Volksraad or Parliament. Article 9 of the Grondwet referring to Natives. Native Marriage Laws. The Pass System. . . .

. . . I cannot find it in my heart to criticize the character of the Boers at a time when they have held on so bravely in a desperate war, and have suffered so much. There are Boers and Boers,—good and bad among them,—as among all nations. We have heard of kind and generous actions towards the British wounded and prisoners, and we know that there are among them men who, in times of peace, have been good and merciful to their native servants. But it is not magnanimity nor brutality on the part of individuals which are in dispute. Our controversy is concerning the presence or absence of Justice among the Boers, concerning the purity of their Government and the justice of their Laws, or the reverse.

I turn to their Laws, and in judging these, it is hardly possible to be too severe. Law is a great teacher, a trainer, to a great extent, of the character of the people. The Boers would have been an exceptional people under the sun had they escaped the deterioration which such Laws and such Government as they have had the misfortune to live under inevitably produce.

A pamphlet has lately been published containing a defence of the Boer treatment of Missionaries and Natives, and setting forth the efforts which have been made in recent years to Christianize and civilize the native populations in their midst. This paper is signed by nine clergymen of the Dutch Reformed Church, and includes the name of the Rev. Andrew Murray, a name respected and beloved by many in our own country. It is welcome news that such good work has been undertaken, that the President has himself encouraged it, and that a number of Zulus or Kaffirs have recently been baptized in the Dutch Reformed Church of the Transvaal. But the fact strikes one painfully that in this pleading, (which has a pathetic note in it,) these clergymen appear to have obliterated from their mind and memory the whole past history of their nation, and to have forgotten that the harvest from seed sown through many generations may spring up and bear its bitter fruit in their own day. . . .

Their Grondwet, or Constitution, must be removed out of its place for ever; their unequal laws, and the administrative corruption which unequal laws inevitably foster, must be swept away, and be replaced by a very different Constitution and very different Laws. If this had been done during the two last decades of Transvaal history, while untrammeled (as was desired) by British interference, the sincerity of this recent utterance would have deserved full credit, and would have been recognized as the beginning of a radical reformation.

The following is from the last Report of the Aborigines Protection Society (Jan., 1900). Its present secretary leans towards a favourable judgment of the recent improvements in the policy of the Transvaal, and condemns severely every act on the part of the English which does not accord with the principles of our Constitutional Law, and therefore this statement will not be regarded as the statement of a partisan: — "It is laid down as a fundamental principle in the Transvaal Grondwet that there is no equality of rights between white men and blacks. In theory, if not in practice, the Boers regard the natives, all of whom they contemptuously call Kaffirs, whatever their tribal differences, pretty much as the ancient Jews regarded the Philistines and others whom they expelled from Palestine, or used as hewers of wood and drawers of water, but with added prejudice due to the difference of colour. So it was in the case of the early Dutch settlers, and so it is to-day, with a few exceptions, due mainly to the influence of the missionaries, whose work among the natives has from the first been objected to and hindered. It is only by social sufferance, and not by law, that the marriage of natives with Christian rites is recognised, and it carries with it none of the conditions as regards inheritance and the like, which are prescribed by the Dutch Roman code in force with white men. As a matter of fact, natives have no legal rights whatever. If they are in the service of humane masters, mindful of their own interests and moral obligations, they may be properly lodged and fed, not overworked, and fairly recompensed; but from the cruelties of a brutal master, perpetrated in cold blood or a drunken fit, the native practically has no redress." . . .

I am especially concerned with what affects the natives.

Article 1 of this section says: — A native must not own fixed property.

(2) He must not marry by civil or ecclesiastical process.

(3) He must not be allowed access to Civil Courts in any action against a white man.

Article 9 of the Grondwet is not only adhered to, but is exaggerated in its application as follows: — "The people shall not permit any equality of coloured persons with white inhabitants, neither in the Church, nor in the State."

. . . . As to the access by the natives to the Courts of Law.

"If you ask a native he will tell you that access to the lawcourts is much too easy, but they are the Criminal Courts of the Field Cornets and Landdrosts. He suffers so much from these, that he cannot entertain the idea that the Higher Courts are any better than the ordinary Field Cornets' or Landdrosts'. However, there are times when with fear and trepidation he does appeal to a Higher Court. With what result? If the decision is in favour of the native, the burghers are up in arms, crying out against the injustice of a judgment given in favour of a black against a white man; burghers sigh and say that a great disaster is about to befall the State when a native can have judgment against a white man. . . .

No. 2. — The Native Marriage Laws. "Think," says Mr. Bovill, "what it would mean to our social life in England if we were a conquered nation, and the conquerors should say: 'All your laws and customs are abrogated; your marriage laws are of no consequence to us; you may follow or leave them as you please, but we do not undertake to support them, and you may live like cattle if you wish; we cannot recognise your marriage laws as binding, nor yet will we legalise any form of marriage among you.' Such is in effect, the present position of the natives in the Transvaal. . . .

"The injustice of such a law must be apparent; it places a premium on vice. It gives an excuse to any 'person of colour' to commit the most heinous offences against the laws of morality and social order, and protects such a one from the legal consequences which would necessarily follow in any other civilised State."

It is stated on the authority of *The Sentinel* (London, June, 1900), that Mr. Kruger was asked some years ago to permit the introduction in the Johannesburg mining district of the State regulation of vice, and that Mr. Kruger stoutly refused to entertain such an idea. Very much to his credit! Yet it seems to me that the refusal to legalize native marriages comes rather near, in immorality of principle and tendency, to the legalizing of promiscuous intercourse.

Mr. Bovill has an instructive chapter on the "Compound system," and the condition of native compounds. This is a matter which it is to be hoped will be taken seriously to heart by the Chartered Company, and any other company or group of employers throughout African mining districts. "The Compound system of huddling hundreds of natives together in tin shanties is the very opposite to the free life to which they are accustomed. If South African mining is to become a settled industry, we must have the conditions of the labour market settled, and also the conditions of living. We cannot expect natives to give up their free open-air style of living, and their home life. They love their homes, and suffer from homesickness as much as, or probably more than most white people. The reason so many leave their work after six months is that they are constantly longing to see their wives and children. . . ."

Mr. Bovill goes into much detail on the subject of the "Pass Laws." I should much desire to reproduce his chapter on that subject, if it were not too long. That system must be wholly abolished, he says: "it is at present worse than any conditions under which slavery exists. It is a criminal-making law. Brand a slave, and you have put him to a certain amount of physical pain for once, but penalties under the Pass Law system mean lashes innumerable at the direction of any Boer Field Cornet or Landdrost. It is a most barbarous system, as brutal as it is criminal-making, alone worthy of a Boer with an exaggerated fear of and cowardly brutality towards a race he has been taught to despise."

Treating of the prohibition imposed on the Natives as to the possession in any way or by any means of a piece of land, he writes: "Many natives are now earning and saving large sums of money, year by year, at the various labour centres. They return home with every intention of following a peaceful life; why should they not be encouraged to put their money into land, and follow their 'peaceful pursuits' as well as any Boer farmer? They are capable of doing it. Besides, if they held fixed property in the State, it would be to their advantage to maintain law and order, when they had everything they possessed at stake. With no interest in the land, the tendency must always be to a nomadic life. They are as thoroughly well capable of becoming true, peaceful, and loyal citizens of the State as are any other race of people. Their instincts and training are all towards law and order. Their lives have been disciplined under native rule, and now that the white man is breaking up that rule, what is he going to give as a substitute? Anarchy and lawlessness, or good government which tends to peace and prosperity?

VIII.

. . . . *Exploitation of Natives by Capitalists. British colonizing. — its causes and nature. . . . The moral teachings of the war. Our responsibilities. Hasty judgments. Denunciations of England by Englishmen. The open book. My last word is for the Native Races.*

This elimination of the Imperial Factor is precisely that which is the least desired by those who see our Imperialism to mean the continuance of obedience to the just traditions of British Law and Government. The granting of a Charter to a Company lends the au-

thority (or the appearance of it) of the Queen's name to acts of the responsible heads of that company, which may be opposed to the principles of justice established by British Law; and such acts may have disastrous results. It is to be hoped that the present awakening on the subject of past failures of our government to enforce respect for its own principles may be a warning to all concerned against any transgression of those principles.

Continental friends with whom I have conversed on the subject of the British Colonies have sometimes appeared to me to leave out of account some considerations special to the subject. They regard British Colonization as having been accomplished by a series of acts of aggression, solely inspired by the love of conquest and desire for increased territory. This is an error.

I would ask such friends to take a Map of Europe, or of the World, and steadily to regard it in connection with the following facts. Our people are among the most prolific, — if not the most prolific, — of all nations. Energy and enterprise are in their nature, together with a certain love of free-breathing, adventure and discovery. Now look at the map, and observe how small is the circumference of the British Isles. "Our Empire has no geographical continuity like the Russian Empire; it is that larger Venice with no narrow streets, but with the sea itself for a high-road. It is bound together by a moral continuity alone." What are our Sons to do? Must our immense population be debarred from passing through these ocean tracts to lands where there are great uninhabited wastes capable of cultivation? What shall we do with our sons and our daughters innumerable, as the ways become overcrowded in the mother land, and energies have not the outlets needful to develop them. Shall we place legal restrictions on marriage, or on the birth of children, or prescribe that no family shall exceed a certain number? You are shocked, naturally. It follows then that some members of our large British families must cross the seas and seek work and bread elsewhere.

The highest and lowest, representing all ranks, engage in this kind of initial colonization. Our present Prime Minister, a "younger son," went out in his youth, — as others of his class have done, — with his pickaxe, to Australia, to rank for a time among "diggers," until called home by the death of the elder son, the heir to the title and estate. This necessity and this taste for wandering and exploring has helped in some degree to form the independence of character of our men, and also to strengthen rather than to weaken the ties of affection and kinship with the Motherland. Many men, "nobly born and gently nurtured," have thus learned self-dependence, to endure hardships, and to share manual labour with the humblest; and such an experience does not work for evil. Then when communities have been formed, some sort of government has been necessitated. An appeal is made to the Mother Country, and her offspring have grown up more or less under her regard and care, until self-government has developed itself.

The great blot on this necessary and natural expansion is the record (from time to time) of the displacement of native tribes by force and violence, when their rights seemed to interfere with the interests of the white man. Of such action we have had to repent in the past, and we repent more deeply than ever now when our responsibilities towards native races have been brought with startling clearness before those among us who have been led to look back and to search deeply into the meanings of the present great "history-making war." . . .

It can hardly be supposed that I underrate the horrors of war. I have imagination enough and sympathy enough to follow almost as if I beheld it with my eyes, the great tragedy which has been unfolded in South Africa. The spirit of Jingoism is an epidemic of which I await the passing away more earnestly than we do that of any other plague. I deprecate, as I have always done, and as strongly as anyone can do, rowdyism in the form of violent opposition to free speech and freedom of meeting. It is as wholly unjustifiable, as it is unwise. Nothing tends more to the elucidation of truth than evidence and freedom of speech from all sides. Good works on many hands are languishing for lack of the funds and zeal needful to carry them on. The Public Press, and especially the Pictorial Press, fosters a morbid sentiment in the public mind by needlessly vivid representations of mere slaughter; to all this may be added (that which some mourn over most of all) the drain upon our pockets, — upon the country's wealth. All these things are a part of the great tribulation which is upon us. They are inevitable ingredients of the chastisement by war.

I see frequent allusions to the "deplorable state of the public mind," which is so fixed on this engrossing subject, the war, that its attention cannot be gained for any other. I hear our soldiers called "legalized murderers," and the war spoken of as a "hellish panorama," which is a blight even to look upon.

But, — I am impelled to say it at the risk of sacrificing the respect of certain friends, — there is to me another view of the matter. It is this. In this present woe, as in all other earthly events, God has something to say to us, — something which we cannot receive if we wilfully turn away the eye from seeing and the ear from hearing. . . .

It is good and necessary to protest against War; but at the same time, reason and experience teach that we must, with equal zeal, protest against other great evils, the accumulation of which makes for war and not for peace. War in another sense — moral and spiritual war — must be doubled, trebled, quadrupled, in the future, in order that material war may come to an end. We all wish for peace; every reasonable person desires it, every anxious and bereaved family longs for it, every Christian prays for it. But *what* Peace? [Is it] the Peace of God which we pray for? the Peace on Earth, which He alone can bring about? His hand alone, which corrects, can also heal. We do not and cannot desire the peace which some of those are calling for who dare not face the open book of present day judgment, or who do not wish to read its lessons! Such a peace would be a mere plastering over of an unhealed wound, which would break out again before many years were over. . . .

My last word must be on behalf of the Natives. When, thirty years ago, a few among us were impelled to take up the cause of the victims of the modern white slavery in Europe, we were told that in our pleadings for principles of justice and for personal rights, we ought not to have selected a subject in which are concerned persons who may deserve pity, but who, in fact, are not so important a part of the human family as to merit such active and passionate sympathy as that which moved our group. To this our reply was: "We did not *choose* this question, we did not ourselves deliberately elect to plead for these persons. The question was *imposed upon us*, and once so imposed, we could not escape from the claims of the oppressed class whose cause we had been called to take up. And generally, (we replied,) the work of human progress has not consisted in protecting and supporting any outward forms of government, or the noble or privileged classes, but in undertaking the defence of the weak, the humble, of beings devoted to degradation and contempt, or brought under any oppression or servitude."

It is the same now. My father was one of the energetic promoters of the Abolition of Slavery in the years before 1834, a friend of Clarkson and Wilberforce. The horror of slavery in every form, and under whatever name, which I have probably partly inherited, has been intensified as life went on. It is my deep conviction that Great Britain will in future be judged, condemned or justified, according to her treatment of those innumerable coloured races, heathen or partly Christianized, over whom her rule extends, or who, beyond the sphere of her rule, claim her sympathy and help as a Christian and civilizing power to whom a great trust has been committed.

It grieves me to observe that (so far as I am able to judge) our politicians, public men, and editors, (with the exception of the editors of the "religious press,") appear to a great extent unaware of the immense importance of this subject, even for the future peace and stability of our Empire, apart from higher interests. It *will* be "imposed upon them," I do not doubt, sooner or later, as it has been imposed upon certain missionaries and others who regard the Divine command as practical and sensible men should do: "Go ye and teach *all* nations." All cannot *go* to the ends of the earth; but all might cease to hinder by the dead weight of their indifference, and their contempt of all men of colour. Dr. Livingstone rebuked the Boers for contemptuously calling all coloured men Kaffirs, to whatever race they belonged. Englishmen deserve still more such a rebuke for their habit of including all the inhabitants of India, East and West, and of Africa, who have not European complexions, under the contemptuous title of "niggers." Race prejudice is a poison which will have to be cast out if the world is ever to be Christianized, and if Great Britain is to maintain the high and responsible place among the nations which has been given to her.

"It may be that the Kaffir is sometimes cruel," says one who has seen and known him, — "he certainly requires supervision. But he was bred in cruelty and reared in oppression—the child of injustice and hate. As the springbok is to the lion, as the locust is to the hen, so is the Kaffir to the Boer; a subject of plunder and leaven of greed. But the Kaffir is capable of courage and also of the most enduring affection. He has been known to risk his life for the welfare of his master's family. He has worked without hope of reward. He has laboured in the expectation of pain. He has toiled in the snare of the fowler. Yet shy a brickbat at him!—for he is only a Kaffir!" However much the Native may excel in certain qualities of the heart, still, until purged of the poison of racial contempt, that will be the expression of the practical conclusion of the white man regarding him; "Shy a brickbat at him. He is only a nigger."

A merely theoretical acknowledgment of the vital nature of this question,—of the future of the Native races and of Missionary work will not suffice. The Father of the great human family demands more than this.

"Is not this the fast that I have chosen?
To loose the bands of wickedness,
To undo the heavy burdens,
To let the oppressed go free,
And that ye break every yoke?"
(Isaiah lviii.6.)

Vera Figner (1852–1942)

Vera Nikolaevna Figner, born on June 24, 1852, was one of those revolutionary women who were leaders of the Narodnaya Volya (People's Will), the terrorist branch of the populist movement in Russia in the closing decades of the nineteenth century. It was her close associate, Sofia Perovskaia, who directed and carried out the assassination of Tzar Alexander II on March 1, 1881, for which Perovskaia and others were executed on April 3 of that year. Vera Figner, who had participated in the assassination plot and helped to prepare the bombs, escaped arrest for nearly two years. As the sole surviving member of the Executive Committee of the Narodnaya Volya, she became the party's leader and succeeded in rallying and reorganizing its forces until betrayed to Alexander III's police by one of her most trusted associates, Sergei Degayev. She was arrested on February 10, 1883, in a sweep which led to the destruction of the party through the imprisonment, exile, and executions of many of its remaining leaders and members.

At the Trial of the Fourteen in September 1884, Vera Figner was condemned to death, but the sentence was reduced to life imprisonment. In October 1884 she was sent to the Schlusselberg fortress, the most oppressive and hated of the Tzarist prisons, where many died of the physical and mental abuse and deprivations to which they were subjected. There was only one other woman, Ludmilla Wolkenstein, in the prison. Figner was kept for nearly twenty years in solitary confinement at Schlusselberg but was released in 1904 to live in exile, at first in Siberia, later in Europe. From 1906 until 1914 she lived in Switzerland, France, and England, but she returned to Russia at the outbreak of World War I. She was detained again in Nijni-Novgorod but was permitted to go to St. Petersburg in 1916, and she lived to see the Russian Revolution, its aftermath, and the fateful events leading to World War II. She died in Moscow on June 16, 1942, at ninety years of age.

During her imprisonment in the Peter Paul fortress in St. Petersburg while awaiting trial in 1883–84, Figner wrote pre-trial testimony preserved in police files, and at the trial, though weakened by the conditions of her imprisonment and fearful that her voice would fail because of the months of enforced silence she had endured, she was able to offer a sustained and powerful defense of the beliefs, motives, and resort to violence of the Narodnaya Volya. Her trial statement was kept from publication in Russia until after the Revolution of 1905; it was first published in 1906, while she was still living in Siberian exile. Her voice and her pen were silenced during the twenty years she spent at Schlusselberg, where she was not allowed books or paper for thirteen years, and by the time she was released she found herself wholly disoriented by the changes that had taken place. But in later years she became dedicated to writing her autobiography (beginning with Zapechatlennyi Trud [The Unforgettable Effort], published in 1921–22) and to preserving the memoirs of other populist revolutionaries of the Tzarist era, through the Society of Former Political Prisoners and Exiles and the Granat Encyclopedia, for which she edited a collection of forty-four memoirs in 1926.

Figner grew up in an isolated country environment with little to direct her toward the political course she adopted as a young woman. Her mother was the source of her early education and her aspirations for higher education for herself and other women. Her first introduction to liberal social views came from an uncle, a liberal democrat, and later influences on her thought were the radical press and the women's movement. But like thousands of young men and women of the middle and upper classes in late-nineteenth-century Russia, she was swept up, in revulsion against the brutality of Russian czarism, into the movement "to the people," the mission of bringing education, medical care, and reform to the masses of Russian peasantry and factory workers. Her first steps in this direction were modest but plunged her rapidly into the maelstrom. To extricate herself from her limited opportunities at home, she married in 1870 an accommodating liberal lawyer, Alexei Filipov, and with him and one of her younger sisters, Lydia, went to study medicine at the University of Zurich in 1872, conscious that she and other women who pursued this opportunity in that period were, as she later expressed it, "pioneers in the struggle for women's higher education."

In Zurich, Figner encountered the clandestine study circles—at first of women only, later of men and women—in which she was introduced to a wide range of radical and socialist thought and debate. She came to Zurich with vague ideals of service to the poor and admiration for democratic governments but soon came into contact with more radical concepts and ideas such as class, capital, proletariat, and the social parasitism of the privileged classes. As she later recorded, it was in conversations with Sofia Bardina, a student she met in a mineralogy class, that she was shaken to the core by recognition of her own heretofore unwitting role, by virtue of her class position, as oppressor and exploiter of the poor. Filipov, alienated by the political direction Vera was pursuing, returned to Russia and they were soon divorced. But it was her sister Lydia who first became deeply engaged in revolutionary activities and drew Vera into a solemn pact to commit her life to the movement. After Lydia returned to Russia and was arrested in 1875, convicted in one of the famous mass political trials of the period—the Trial of the 50—and sent into exile, Vera gave up her hopes of a medical degree and returned to Russia to engage herself fully in the revolutionary struggle.

Initially, Figner and her sister Eugénie worked with a new organization, Land and Liberty, founded in 1876. They undertook to work in country districts, teaching, providing health care, and seeking to raise political consciousness. But like many other young people with the same ideals, they were met with suspicion and hostility from the upper classes and discomfort from many of the poor, and as their efforts to work for change through such pacific means stumbled or were met by brutal police repression, they turned to the policy of selective violence that was adopted formally at the founding of the Narodnaya Volya in 1879.

In this they were inspired and followed the example—though not the program—of Vera Zasulich, who initiated the campaign of revolutionary terrorism by shooting Governor-General Trepov of St. Petersburg on January 25, 1878, in the reception room of the governor's offices in front of more than twenty witnesses. Although Zasulich had been briefly acquainted with the nihilist Sergei Nechaiev, she was not a nihilist and did not advocate terrorist violence as a policy. She shot Trepov in reaction to an especially sadistic and unjustified public whipping of a prisoner. She did not particularly try to kill him (and did not), and she testified at her trial that she shot him in order to make a public statement "that no one can be allowed to carry his contempt for human dignity to such lengths" (Maxwell, 11). Public sentiment was so hostile to Trepov and sympathy for Zasulich so great that she was acquitted, and though the police attempted to rearrest her, she managed to escape abroad. In later years she became, with George Plekhanov and P. B. Axelrod, a founder of the Russian Marxist group, Emancipation of Labor. Though Zasulich differed from Plekhanov in her theoretical approach to Marxism, she shared his opposition to the policy of revolutionary terrorism adopted by the Narodnaya Volya. Nevertheless the image of her decisive action and spectacular escape and the public enthusiasm her actions aroused went far to persuade Vera Figner and others struggling inside Russia to gain ground for the revolution that the best option open to them was that of selective terrorism.

As the public response to Zasulich's action made clear, sentiment in favor of democratic political reform was widespread throughout the different classes of soci-

ety, despite the success of the czarist police in driving the opposition underground. One significant aspect of this was the spread of democratic and socialist ideas even into the military forces and the officer corps. Vera Figner was remarkably successful in winning support and protection among the officers at Kronstadt, St. Petersburg, Odessa, and other locations, even after the assassination of the Tzar in 1881. Indeed, though the uprising that Narodnaya Volya had hoped would follow the assassination never materialized, the possibility was debated seriously amongst the revolutionary sympathizers in the military, and they welcomed Figner, the sole surviving member of the Executive Committee that had planned and executed the assassination, to stir their imaginations and challenge their ideas. This she did, exhorting them to question the nature of their obligations and see that duty, honor, and patriotism all called them to join the revolution. "You can stand with the liberators of our people or you can be their hangmen. And let him who wavers remember the foul path he must tread if he chooses to serve tyranny. He must deaden his conscience, spit on human dignity, blind himself to the shootings and beatings by the mercenary police, and be ready to order his troops to shoot innocent people. . . . Say 'No!' to this. . . . In the open war with tyranny which is at hand, the true officers will carry the flag of the people" (Maxwell, 90–91).

And many were won over or strengthened by her. As one admirer wrote: "Figner appeared to be a super-revolutionary. A lot was said about her beauty, elegance, education, intelligence and ability to conduct herself properly in all social circles, aristocratic included. For us she was an ideal revolutionary, a woman with an iron will. After the fall of Perovskaia and Zheliabov, she was the only one everyone recognized as having unlimited revolutionary authority" (Engel and Rosenthal, 3). Perhaps this recognition was a reflection of the integrity of her commitment to the cause, and her conviction that there could be no separation between theory and action. "I made no distinctions between word and deed. . . . I believed in the power of words and the might of the human will," she wrote (Engel and Rosenthal, xiii).

The following selections are from the 1991 reprint of Figner's Memoirs of a Revolutionist (1927), the abridged English translation of Zapechatlennyi Trud. Her trial statement (1884) was reproduced by her in the Memoirs and is included among the excerpts given here, as are several statements by the Executive Committee of the Narodnaya Volya, which also reflect her views.

BAC

Sources and Suggested Readings

Engel, Barbara Alpern. *Mothers and Daughters: Women of the Intelligentsia in Nineteenth-Century Russia.* Cambridge: Cambridge University Press, 1983.

Engel, Barbara Alpern, and Clifford N. Rosenthal, eds. *Five Sisters: Women against the Tsar.* New York: Knopf: 1975.

Figner, Vera. *Memoirs of a Revolutionist* [1927]. Dekalb, Ill.: Northern Illinois University Press, 1991.

Goldsmith, Margaret. *Seven Women against the World.* London: Methuen, 1935.

Hoogenboom, Hilde. "Vera Figner and Revolutionary Autobiographies: The Influence of Gender on Genre." In *Women in Russia and Ukraine*, ed. Rosalind March. Cambridge: Cambridge University Press, 1996.

Maxwell, Margaret. *Narodniki Women: Russian Women Who Sacrificed Themselves for the Dream of Freedom.* New York: Pergamon Press (Athene Series), 1990.

Memoirs of a Revolutionist (1927) [1921–22]

Author's foreword to the American edition

More than one hundred years ago the advanced portion of Russian society became imbued with the idea of the necessity of overthrowing the Autocracy, and replacing it by a representative government. But from the military conspiracy of the Decembrists (1825) to the seventies, only individual persons or small isolated groups figured as the opponents of absolutism, and they were swiftly crushed by the repressive measures of the government. Only with the liberation of the serfs (1861) and the inauguration of reforms during the early years of the reign of Alexander II (1818–1881) was Russian life rejuvenated, and social forces received a chance for a broader activity. However, the land and court reforms, and the introduction of county (zemstvo) and city self-government, could not satisfy the progressive men of Russia, as long as the obsolete political order remained. Despite the abolition of serfdom the economic condition of the people was quite unsatisfactory; the long-expected "freedom" failed to fulfil the hopes of the peasantry. On the other hand, the educated class, now increased in numbers, demanded a wider field of activity, and this was impossible in the absence of civil liberties.

These were the two causes of the incessant turmoil which reigned in the internal life of Russia and generated a revolutionary movement with the permanent slogan of *Land and Freedom.* At first the social-revolutionary movement was directed toward the organisation of the peasant masses for an uprising, with the aim of overthrowing the existing economic order. It was expected that this would inevitably result in the fall of the political order and its replacement by a new one. Such a formulation of the revolutionary programme implied no direct struggle against the government. But toward the end of the seventies, a new tendency ripened, owing to the lack of response on the part of the peasants, and to the persecutions and intolerable oppression of the unlimited Autocracy: the overthrow of absolutism was formulated as a definite task. In 1879 was formed the revolutionary socialist party, The Will of the People, headed by its Executive Committee. Planning the organisation of a military conspiracy backed by factory workers and by all the discontented, this party resolved to throw its own forces without delay into a ruthless battle with the Autocracy, directing its blows against the head of the state, who personally assumed the responsibility for the rule of the millions and millions of his people. This battle by means of violence against violence was waged for three years with unexampled energy and obstinacy. It culminated on March 1 (14), 1881, when Emperor Alexander II fell on the streets of St. Petersburg from the bombs hurled by two members of the party.

The first part of my book comprises the brief period of 1876–1884, describing the consecutive activity of the secret society, Land and Freedom, and later, of the party, The Will of the People. I took part in working out the programme of Land and Freedom, and was the last member of the Executive Committee of The Will of the People when arrested, in 1883. I describe the events as an eye-witness and participant.

The Executive Committee perished to the last person, the party was smashed, but its significance in the history of the revolutionary movement was extraordinary. After The Will of the People, political struggle became an essential part of the programmes of all the subsequent revolutionary generations. Seventy-two members of the party appeared before court within five years. Those who were not executed or exiled to Siberia, were incarcerated in the Fortress of Sts. Peter and Paul, and from 1884, in the Schlüsselburg Fortress. In the latter, I, too, was confined. The majority of us died, and I was freed in 1904, after twenty years of confinement, and sent into exile. Life in Schlüsselburg, mine and that of my comrades—this epilogue of our struggle against Autocracy—is described in the second part of my book.

Vera Figner.

Moscow, Spring, 1927.

P.S. For those who may be dismayed by the cruel methods employed by The Will of the People in its struggle against Autocracy, I should like to recall the declaration of the Executive Committee of our party, on the occasion of the assassination of President James A. Garfield in 1881:

"Expressing its profound sympathy for the American people, on the occasion of the death of President James Abram Garfield, the Executive Committee regards it as its duty to declare in the name of the Russian revolutionists its protest against such acts of violence as that of Guiteau. In a land where personal freedom gives an opportunity for an honest conflict of ideas, where the free will of the people determines not only the law but also the personality of the ruler, in such a land political murder as a means of struggle presents a manifestation of that despotic spirit which we aim to destroy in Russia. Personal despotism is as condemnable as group despotism, and violence may be justified only when it is directed against violence."

(Signed) The Executive Committee.
September 10 (23), 1881.
V. F.

THE EXECUTIVE COMMITTEE OF THE WILL OF THE PEOPLE

In conformity with the demands of intensive warfare against our mighty antagonist, the plan of organisation of The Will of the People was designed along lines of strict centralisation, and on an all-Russian scale. A net of secret societies, groups of party members, some of whom might busy themselves with tasks of a general revolutionary nature in a limited region, while others might pursue special aims, having chosen for themselves one branch or another of revolutionary work, was to have one common centre, the Executive Committee, through which a general solidarity and bond was established. The local groups were obliged to obey this centre, to surrender to it their members and resources upon demand. All general party functions and business of an all-Russian nature, came under the direction of this centre. At a time of uprising, it was to direct all the available forces of the party, and might call upon them for revolutionary purposes. But until such a time, its main attention was to be directed towards the planning of a conspiracy, that work of organisation which alone provided for the possibility of a revolution, through which the authority was to be transferred to the hands of the people. The forces of the party were generally applied in this direction. All the stranger was the title of terrorist organisation which it later acquired. The public gave it that name because of the external aspect of its activity, the

one characteristic which caught their attention. Terror for its own sake was never the aim of the party. It was a weapon of protection, of self-defence, regarded as a powerful instrument for agitation, and employed only for the purpose of attaining the ends for which the organisation was working. The assassination of the Tsar came under this head as one detail. In the fall of 1879, it was a necessity, a question of the day, which caused some to accept this assassination and terroristic activity in general as the most essential point of our entire programme. The desire to check the further development of reaction which hampered our organising activity, and the wish to assume our work as soon as possible, were the only reasons which induced the Executive Committee immediately upon its formation as the centre of The Will of the People, to plan for an attempt on the life of Alexander II to be made simultaneously in four different places. And yet the members of the Committee at the same time carried on active propaganda both among the intelligentsia and the workingmen. Zhelyabov directed it in Kharkov, Rolodkevich and I in Odessa, Alexander Mikhaylov in Moscow, and Kvyatkovsky, Rorba and others in St. Petersburg. The work of propaganda and organisation always went hand in hand with that of destruction; it was less evident, but was nevertheless destined to bear its fruits.

Uniting the dissatisfied elements into a general conspiracy against the government, the new party fully understood the meaning of the support which a peasant uprising would give them at the moment of the government's overthrow. Accordingly it assigned a requisite place for activity among the people, and always regarded the ones who wished to devote themselves to it, as its natural allies.

The by-laws of the Executive Committee, by which we bound ourselves, were also written by those who had called the congress at Lipetsk. These requirements of the constitution consisted: first, in the promise to devote all one's mental and spiritual strength to the revolutionary work, to forget for its sake all ties of kinship, and all personal sympathies, love and friendships; second, to give one's life also, if necessary, taking no thought of anything else, and sparing no one and nothing; third, to have no personal property, nothing of one's own, which was not shared in common by the organisation of which one was a member; fourth, to devote oneself entirely to the secret society, to renounce one's individual desires, subordinating them to the will of the majority as expressed in the ordinances of that society; fifth, to preserve complete secrecy with respect to all the affairs, personnel, plans and proposals of the organisation; sixth, never in dealings of private or social nature, or in official acts and declarations, to call ourselves members of the Executive Committee, but only its agents; and seventh, in case of withdrawal from the society, to preserve an unbroken silence as to the nature of its activity, and the business transacted before the eyes and with the participation of the one withdrawing.

These demands were great, but they were easily fulfilled by one fired with the revolutionary spirit, with that intense emotion which knows neither obstacles nor impediments, but goes forward, looking neither backward nor to the right nor the left. If these demands had been less exigent, if they had not stirred one's spirit so profoundly, they would not have satisfied us; but now, by their severe and lofty nature they exalted us and freed us from every petty or personal consideration. One felt more vividly that in him there lived, there must live, an ideal. . . .

THE FIRST OF MARCH

By the order of the Committee I was to remain at home until two o'clock on that first day of March, to receive the Kobozevs, for Bogdanovich was to leave the shop an hour before the Tsar's party should pass that way, and Yakimova was to leave directly after the signal that the Tsar had made his appearance on the Nevsky. A third person (Frolenko) was to switch on the electric current, and then leave the shop as a casual customer, in case he should escape perishing in the ruins from the explosion wrought by his own hand.

At ten o'clock Frolenko came to see me. With astonishment I saw him take from a package that he had brought with him, a bottle of red wine and a sausage, which he put on the table, preparing to have a little lunch. In my state of intense excitement, after our decision and the sleepless night spent in preparations, it seemed to me that to eat and drink was impossible.

"What are you doing?" I asked, almost with horror, as I beheld this matter-of-fact procedure on the part of a man who was destined to an almost certain death under the ruin caused by the explosion.

"I must be in full possession of my strength," calmly replied my comrade, and he imperturbably began to eat.

I could only bow in silent admiration before this disregard of the thought of possible death, this all-absorbing realisation that, in order to fulfil the mission which he had taken upon himself, he must be in full possession of his strength.

Neither Bogdanovich nor Yakimova came to the apartment. Isayev returned, and with him a few members of the party, with the news that the Tsar had not passed the shop, but had gone home from the Manège. Forgetting entirely that they had not followed the re-

turn route of the Tsar, and also had not been informed of the last decision of the Committee, to act, whatever might occur, though it be only with bombs, I left the house thinking that for some unforeseen reasons the attempt had not taken place.

And indeed, the Tsar did not pass through the Sadovaya; but it was at this point that Sofia Perovskaya displayed all her self-possession. Quickly concluding that the Tsar would return by way of the quay along the Ekaterininskaya Canal, she changed the entire plan of action, deciding to employ only the bombs. She made the rounds of the bomb-throwers and instructed them to take new positions, after they had agreed that she was to give the signal by waving her handkerchief.

Shortly after two o'clock, two detonations that sounded like shots from a cannon, thundered out, one after another. Rysakov's bomb wrecked the Tsar's carriage, while Grinyevitsky's struck the Tsar. Both the Tsar and Grinyevitsky were mortally wounded, and died within a few hours.

When I left the house after Isayev's return, everything was quiet, but half an hour after I had made my appearance at Glyeb Uspensky's, Ivanchin-Pisarev came to him with the news that there had been some explosions and that a rumour was circulating to the effect that the Tsar had been killed, and that in the churches the people were already swearing allegiance to the heir.

I rushed home. The streets hummed with talk, and there was evident excitement. People were speaking of the Tsar, of his wounds, of blood and death. When I entered my own dwelling and saw my friends who as yet suspected nothing, I was so agitated that I could hardly utter the words announcing the death of the Tsar. I wept, and many of us wept; that heavy nightmare, which for ten years had strangled young Russia before our very eyes, had been brought to an end; the horrors of prison and exile, the violence, executions, and atrocities inflicted on hundreds and thousands of our adherents, the blood of our martyrs, all were atoned for by this blood of the Tsar, shed by our hands. A heavy burden was lifted from our shoulders; reaction must come to an end and give place to a new Russia. In this solemn moment, all our thoughts centred in the hope for a better future for our country.

Shortly afterwards Sukhanov joined us, joyful and excited, and embraced and congratulated us all in the name of that future. The letter to Alexander III [see *Appendix*], drawn up a few days later, is characteristic of the general state of mind of the members of the party in St. Petersburg, during the period that followed the first of March. The letter was composed with a moderation and tact that won the sympathetic approval of all Russian society. Upon its publication in the West, it produced a sensation throughout all the European press. The most moderate and conservative periodicals expressed their approval of the demands of the Russian Nihilists, finding them reasonable, just, and such as had in large measure been long ago realised in the daily life of Western Europe. . . .

I must here say a few more words about the demoralisation brought about in society by the methods of the struggle between the government and the revolutionary party. This struggle was accompanied by violence, as is the case with any conflict waged by means of force rather than ideas. And violence, whether committed against a thought, an action, or a human life, never contributed to the refinement of morals. It arouses ferocity, develops brutal instincts, awakens evil impulses, and prompts acts of disloyalty. Humanity and magnanimity are incompatible with it. And from this point of view, the government and the revolutionary party, when they entered into what may be termed a hand-to-hand battle, vied with one another in corrupting everything and every one around them. On the one hand, the party declared that all methods were fair in the war with its antagonist, that here the end justified the means. At the same time, it created a cult of dynamite and the revolver, and crowned the terrorist with a halo; murder and the scaffold acquired a magnetic charm and attraction for the youth of the land, and the weaker their nervous system, and the more oppressive the life around them, the greater was their exaltation at the thought of revolutionary terror. Since the effects of ideas are hardly perceptible to a revolutionist during the brief span of his lifetime, he desires to see some concrete, palpable manifestation of his own will, his own strength, and at that time only a terroristic act with all its violence could be such a manifestation. Society saw no escape from the existing condition; one group sympathised with the violence practised by the party, while others regarded it only as a necessary evil—but even they applauded the valour and skill of the champion. And the repetition of such events made them a normal element of society's life.

But the gloomy side of revolutionary activity was brightened by the concord and brotherhood which existed among the revolutionists themselves; moreover, the party committed its deeds of violence under the banner of the people's welfare, in defence of the oppressed and insulted. Outsiders became reconciled to terrorism because of the disinterestedness of its motives; it redeemed itself through renunciation of material benefits, through the fact that the revolutionist was not satisfied with personal well-being, the possibility of which he rejected, once he had set out on his dangerous path; it redeemed itself by prison, exile, penal

servitude and death. Thus, though society became somewhat callous by accustoming itself to the violence practised by the revolutionary party, yet it nevertheless beheld, if not in the party as a whole, at least in individual representatives of it, examples of self-sacrifice and heroism, persons of rare civic virtues.

Parallel with the violence practised by the revolutionary party, but on a larger scale, was the violence practised by the government. It enchained thought, forbade free speech, and despoiled the people of life and freedom. Administrative exile was an ordinary occurrence, the prisons were filled to overflowing, executions were numbered by the dozen. In addition to this, prisoners were violently abused in the Siberian mines, and humiliating treatment was common in the central prisons. Throughout all the prisons harshness and violence were the daily order; in the House of Preliminary Detention, Bogolyubov was flogged and the modesty of women was insulted.

The officials who carried out the orders became callous, the sufferers and their relatives, friends and acquaintances became more and more incensed. Society became accustomed to this degradation of human dignity. The spectacle of public executions aroused mob bloodthirst; retaliation, an eye for an eye and a tooth for a tooth, became the watchword of all. Secret police were necessary in order to avert the government from impending danger; official gold created an army of spies. These were recruited from all ranks of society; among them were generals and baronesses, officers and advocates, journalists and doctors, college men and women; alas, there were even high-school students, little girls fourteen years old, while in Simferopol the department of the gendarmerie induced an eleven year-old high-school boy to become a paid spy. We know well that there is no stronger passion, or one leading to baser crimes than the passion for gold. Persian gold forced the Greek chieftains to sell their native land; thirty pieces of silver seduced Judas Iscariot. Our government took every advantage of the greed and covetousness of the human race, and utilised in every possible way the power of gold. Young women used the charms of their beauty and youth to seduce and betray; spies played the parts of initiators, organisers, and moving spirits in revolutionary work; secret accusations, treachery of the most perfidious kind, a clever trick at an examination, as a means of extorting a confession, or the inauguration of a great trial, under the most artificial pretences, and at the price of the well-being of dozens of people—such were the exploits that won the prize of gold, or advancement in office. In addition to all this, the government enticed the weak members of the party to become renegades. Remission of penalties, an agreement to forget the past, freedom and money—all served as a means for seduction. This was the greatest moral blow dealt to us revolutionists, a blow which shook our faith in mankind. It was not so hard to lose one's freedom, as to see a former comrade for whose sake you had been ready to risk your life, whom you had trusted and protected, and for whom you had performed every possible brotherly service—to see him helping the gendarmes to arrest you, and to hear his cynical words, "So you didn't expect it, did you?" Of course, all this was done in the name of "legal" justice, for the sake of saving the fatherland, or rather that state of society in which they wished to preserve the fatherland. But who, who will deny the base degradation of human character made manifest by these facts? . . .

There came at last the most memorable day of my life, the most profoundly moving moment in any trial, when the president turning to the accused, says in a peculiarly solemn voice, "Defendant, the last word is yours!"

The last word! How great, and how deep a significance is in that brief phrase! The accused is given an opportunity, unique in its tragic setting, and perhaps the last, the very last opportunity in his life, to express his spiritual individuality, to explain the moral justification of his acts and conduct, and to speak aloud, for all to hear, those things which he wishes to say, which he must say, and may say. A few minutes more, and this opportunity, this last possibility, drops into the past, retreats irrevocably and forever. If this moment is allowed to escape, the man whom they are trying, and whom they are ready to condemn, will never more lift his voice in speech: they will not listen to him, and his voice will either grow dumb in prison, or die with him on the scaffold.

How many torturing fears did I experience, in awaiting that day and hour in the loneliness of my cell!

Under the circumstances created by the investigation, I was the central figure of the trial, the person of most importance in the case under consideration. The previous trials (dating from 1879 to 1884), of Alexander Soloviev, Alexander Kvyatkovsky, of the conspirators of the first of March, and the trials of the twenty, and of the seventeen members of The Will of the People, during which my name had been frequently mentioned, had created for me, the last of them all to be arrested, an exceptional position. This position demanded that, as the last member of the Executive Committee, and as a representative of The Will of the People, I should speak at the trial.

But I was in no mood for making speeches. I was crushed by the general situation in our native land. There was no doubt that the conflict and the protest were ended; a long, dark period of reaction had come

upon us, all the more difficult to endure morally, because we had not expected it, but had hoped for an entirely new form of social life and government. The warfare had been waged by methods of unheard-of cruelty, but we had paid for such methods with our lives, and had believed and hoped. But the common people had remained silent, and had not understood. The advanced elements had remained silent, though they had understood. The wheel of history had been against us; we had anticipated by twenty-five years the course of events, the general political development of the city people and the peasantry—and we were left alone. The carefully selected and organised forces, small in number, but audacious in spirit, had been swept from life's arena, suppressed and annihilated. My comrades on the Executive Committee had been arrested and condemned before me. Some of them had died on the scaffold, others had died slowly from exhaustion and ill-treatment behind the walls of the Alexey Ravelin. The entire organisation of The Will of the People party, insofar as it had not been destroyed, had been reduced to fragments, over the ruins of which played the demoralising activity of Sergey Degayev, who, after the founders of The Will of the People had met their fate, began his career of betrayal in prison, and, emerging therefrom by means of a pretended escape, continued his career of treachery and espionage outside.

So it came about that at the time of the trial in 1884, in which, betrayed by Degayev, I was the central figure, the secret society which had striven to destroy autocracy, and which through its activities had not only shaken to the foundations our native land, but had aroused the whole civilised world, now lay prostrate. It lay prostrate, with no hope of soon arising from its ruin.

And at the very time when my body was shaken and weakened by the conditions of my preliminary imprisonment in the Fortress, when my spirit was broken and devastated by all that I had lived through, the moment arrived in which I was inexorably bound to fulfil my duty to my dead comrades and to our shattered party, to confess my faith, to declare before the court the spiritual impulses which had governed our activities, and to point out the social and political ideal to which we had aspired.

The presiding judge had spoken; my name was called. There was an unnatural silence, and the eyes of those present, strangers and comrades alike, turned to me, and they were all listening, though as yet I had not uttered a word.

I was nervous and timid: what if in the midst of my carefully thought-out speech that mental darkness should suddenly descend upon me, which in those decisive days frequently overwhelmed me, without causing me to lose consciousness?

And in the midst of the stillness, vibrant with the general attention, I spoke my last words in a voice wherein sounded my repressed emotion.

"The court has been examining my revolutionary activities since the year 1879. The public prosecutor has expressed astonishment in his speech of indictment, both with respect to the character and to the extent of those activities. But these crimes, like all others, have their own history. They are logically and closely bound up with my whole previous life. During the period of my preliminary imprisonment, I have often debated whether my life could have followed a different course, or could have ended in any other spot than this Criminal Court. And every time I have replied to myself, No!

"I began my life under very happy surroundings. I had no lack of guides in the formation of my character; it was not necessary to keep me in leading strings. My family was intelligent and affectionate, so that I never experienced the disharmony which often exists between the older and younger generations. I had no knowledge of material want, and no anxiety concerning daily necessities or self-support. When, at the age of seventeen, I left the Institute, the thought was borne in upon me for the first time that not every one lived under such happy conditions as I. The vague idea that I belonged to the cultured minority, aroused in me the thought of the obligations which my position imposed upon me with respect to the remaining uneducated masses, who lived from day to day, submerged in manual toil, and deprived of all those things which are usually called the blessings of civilisation. This visualisation of the contrast between my position and the position of those who surrounded me, aroused in me the first thought of the necessity of creating for myself a purpose in life which should tend to benefit those others.

"Russian journalism of that period, and the feminist movement which was in full swing at the beginning of the seventies, gave a ready answer to the questions which arose in my mind, and indicated the medical profession as being a form of activity which would satisfy my philanthropic aspirations.

"The Women's Academy in St. Petersburg had already been opened, but from its very beginning it was characterised by the weakness for which it has been distinguished up to the present time, in its constant struggle between life and death; and since I had firmly made up my mind, and did not wish to be forced to abandon the course which I had undertaken, I decided to go abroad.

"And so, having considerably recast my life, I departed for Zurich, and entered the University. Life abroad presented a sharp contrast to Russian life. I saw there things which were entirely new to me. I had not been prepared for them by what I had previously seen and known; I had not been prepared to make a correct evaluation of everything which came into my life. I accepted the idea of socialism at first almost instinctively. It seemed to me that it was nothing more than a broader conception of that altruistic thought which had earlier awakened in my mind. The teaching which promised equality, fraternity, and universal happiness, could not help but dazzle me. My horizon became broader; in place of my native village and its inhabitants, there appeared before me a picture of the common people, of humanity. Moreover, I had gone abroad at the time when the events which had taken place in Paris, and the revolution which was progressing in Spain, were evoking a mighty echo from the entire labouring world of the west. At the same time I became acquainted with the doctrines and the organisation of the International. Not till later did I begin to realise that much of what I saw there was only the brighter side of the picture. Moreover, I did not regard the working-class movement with which I had become acquainted, as a product of western-European life, but I thought that the same doctrine applied to all times, and to every locality.

"Attracted by socialist ideas while abroad, I joined the first revolutionary circle in the work of which my sister Lydia was engaged. Its plan of organisation was very weak; each member might take up revolutionary work in any form he chose, and at any time suited to his convenience. This work consisted of spreading the ideas of socialism, in the optimistic hope that the common people of Russia, already socialists because of their poverty and their social position, could be converted to socialism by a mere word. What we termed at that time the social revolution was rather in the nature of a peaceful social reorganisation; that is, we thought that the minority who opposed socialism, on seeing the impossibility of carrying on the strife, would be forced to yield to the majority who had become conscious of their own interests; and so there was no mention of bloodshed.

"I remained abroad for almost four years. I had always been more or less conservative, in the sense that I did not make speedy decisions, but having once made them, I withdrew from them only with great difficulty. Even when in the spring of 1874, almost the entire circle left for Russia, I remained abroad to continue my medical studies.

"My sister and the other members of the circle ended their careers most miserably. Two or three months' work as labourers in factories, secured for them two-and three-year terms of preliminary detention, after which a trial condemned some of them to penal servitude, others, to lifelong exile in Siberia. While they were in prison, the summons came to me: they asked me to return to Russia to support the cause of the circle. Inasmuch as I had already received a sufficiently thorough medical education, so that the conferring of the title of doctor of medicine and surgery upon me would satisfy only my vanity, I cut short my course and returned to Russia.

"There, from the very first, I found a critical and difficult situation. The movement 'To the People' had already suffered defeat. Nevertheless, I found a fairly large group of persons who seemed congenial, whom I trusted, and with whom I became intimate. Together with them I participated in the working out of that programme which is known as the Programme of the Populists [*Narodniki*].

"I went to live in the country. The programme of the Populists, as the court knows, had aims which the law could not sanction, for its problem was to effect the transfer of all the land into the hands of the peasant communes. But before this could be accomplished, the rôle which the revolutionists living among the people must play, consisted in what is called in all countries, cultural activity. So it was that I too went to live in the country with designs of a purely revolutionary nature, and yet I do not think that my manner towards the peasants, or my actions in general, would have aroused persecution in any other country save Russia; elsewhere I might even have been considered a useful member of society.

"I became an assistant surgeon in the Zemstvo.

"A whole league was formed against me in a very short time, at the head of which stood the marshal of the nobility, and the district police captain, while in the rear were the village constable, the county clerk and others. Rumours of every kind were spread about me: that I had no passport, while I really had one, and was living under my own name; that my diploma was forged, and so forth. When the peasants did not wish to enter into an unprofitable agreement with the proprietor, it was said that I was to blame; when the county assembly reduced the clerk's salary, it was said that I was again to blame.

"Public and secret inquiries were made: the police captain came; several of the peasants were arrested; my name figured in the cross-questioning; two complaints were made to the governor, and it was only through the efforts made by the president of the executive board of the County Zemstvo that I was left in peace. Police espionage rose up around me; people began to be afraid of me. The peasants came to my house by stealthy and circuitous routes.

"These obstacles naturally led me to the question: what could I accomplish under such conditions?

"I shall speak frankly. When I settled in the village,

I was at an age when I could no longer make gross mistakes through any lack of tact, at an age when people become more tolerant, more attentive to the opinions of others. I wanted to study the ground, to learn what the peasant himself thought, what he wished. I saw that there were no acts of mine which could incriminate me, that I was being persecuted only for my spirit, for my private views. They did not think that it was possible for a person of some culture to settle in the village without some horrible purpose.

"And so I was deprived of the possibility of even physical contact with the people, and was unable not only to accomplish anything, but even to hold the most simple, everyday relations with them.

"Then I began to ponder: had I not made some mistake from which I could escape by moving to another locality and repeating my attempt? It was hard for me to give up my plans. I had studied medicine for four years and had grown accustomed to the thought that I was going to work among the peasants.

"On considering this question, and hearing the stories that others had to tell, I became convinced that it was not a question of my own personality, or the conditions of a given locality, but of conditions in general, namely, the absence of political freedom in Russia.

"I had already received more than one invitation from the organisation Land and Freedom, to become one of its members, and to work among the intelligentsia. But as I always clung fast to a decision once made, I did not accept these invitations, and stayed in the village as long as there was any possibility of my doing so. Thus, not vacillation but bitter necessity forced me to give up my original views and to set out on another course.

"At that time individual opinions had begun to arise to the effect that the political element was to play an important role in the problems of the revolutionary party. Two opposing divisions grew up in the society Land and Freedom, and pulled in opposite directions. When I had come to the end of my attempts in the country, I notified the organisation that I now considered myself free.

"At that time two courses were open to me: I could either take a step backwards, go abroad and become a physician—no longer for the peasants, to be sure, but for wealthy people—which I did not wish to do, or I could choose the other course, which I preferred: employ my energy and strength in breaking down that obstacle which had thwarted my desires. After entering Land and Freedom, I was invited to attend the conference at Voronezh, where there took place no immediate split in the party, but where the position of each member was more or less clearly defined. Some said that we must carry on our work on the old basis, that is, live in the village and organise a popular insurrection in some definite locality; others believed that it was necessary to live in the city and direct our efforts against the imperial authority.

"From Voronezh I went to St. Petersburg, where shortly afterwards Land and Freedom broke up, and I received and accepted an invitation to become a member of the Executive Committee of The Will of the People. My previous experience had led me to the conviction that the only course by which the existing order of things might be changed was a course of violence. Peaceful methods had been forbidden me; we had of course no free press, so that it was impossible to think of propagating ideas by means of the printed word. If any organ of society had pointed out to me another course than violence, I might have chosen it, at least, I would have tried it. But I had seen no protest either from the Zemstvo, or from the courts, or from any institutions whatsoever; neither had literature exerted any influence to change the life which we were leading, and so I concluded that the only escape from the position in which we found ourselves, lay in militant resistance.

"Having once taken this position, I maintained my course to the end. I had always required logical and harmonious agreement of word and action from others, and so, of course, from myself; and it seemed to me that if I admitted theoretically that only through violence could we accomplish anything I was in duty bound to take active part in whatever programme of violence might be undertaken by the organisation which I had joined. Many things forced me to take this attitude. I could not with a quiet conscience urge others to take part in acts of violence if I myself did not do so; only personal participation could give me the right to approach other people with various proposals. The organisation really preferred to use me for other purposes, for propaganda among the intelligentsia, but I desired and demanded a different role. I knew that the court would always take cognisanse of whether or not I had an immediate part in our work, and that the only public opinion which is permitted to express itself freely, always descends with especial rancour upon those who take immediate part in acts of violence. And so I considered it nothing short of baseness to thrust others into a course which I myself did not enter.

"This is the explanation of that 'bloodthirst,' which must seem so terrible and incomprehensible, and which is expressed in those acts, the very enumeration of which would seem cynical to the court, had they not proceeded from motives which at all events do not seem to be dishonourable.

"The most essential part of the programme in accordance with which I worked, and which had the greatest significance for me, was the annihilation of the autocratic form of government. I really ascribe no practical importance to the question whether our programme advocates a republic or a constitutional monarchy. We may dream of a republic, but only that form of government will be realised for which society proves itself ready—and so this question has no special meaning for me. I consider it most important, most essential, that such conditions should be established as will allow the individual to develop his abilities to the fullest extent, and to devote them wholeheartedly to the good of society. And it seems to me that under our present order, such conditions do not exist."

When I had finished, the president asked gently, "Have you said all that you wish to say?"

"Yes," I replied.

And no earthly power could have urged me to speak further, so great was my agitation and weariness.

The sympathetic glances, handshakes and congratulations of my comrades and defenders at the end of my speech, and in the following intermission, convinced me that my address had produced an impression. . . .

Appendices

I. The Letter of the Executive Committee of the Will of the People to Tsar Alexander III

Your Majesty:—

Fully comprehending the sorrow which you are experiencing during these present moments, the Executive Committee does not, however, feel it right to yield to the impulse of natural delicacy, which demands, perhaps, a certain interval of waiting before the following explanation should be made. There is something higher than the most legitimate emotions of a human being: that is one's duty to his native land, a duty for which every citizen is obliged to sacrifice himself and his own feelings, and even the feelings of others. In obedience to this primal duty, we have determined to address you at once, without any delay, since that historical process does not wait, which threatens us in the future with rivers of blood and the most violent convulsions.

The bloody tragedy which was played on the shores of the Ekaterininsky Canal, was not accidental, and surprised no one. After all that has passed in the course of the last decade, it was absolutely inevitable, and in this lies its profound meaning—a meaning which must be understood by the man whom fate has placed at the head of the state power. To interpret such facts as being the evil plots of separate individuals, or even of a band of criminals, would be possible only to a man who is quite incapable of analysing the life of nations. In the course of ten years we have seen how, notwithstanding the most severe persecutions, notwithstanding the fact that the government of the late Emperor sacrificed everything, freedom, the interests of all classes, the interests of industry and even its own dignity, everything, unconditionally, in its attempt to suppress the revolutionary movement, that movement has nevertheless tenaciously grown and spread, attracting to itself the best elements of the nation, the most energetic and self-denying people of Russia, and for three years now has engaged in desperate, partisan warfare with the government. You know well, your Majesty, that it is impossible to accuse the government of the late Emperor of lack of energy. They have hanged our followers, both guilty and innocent; they have filled the prisons and distant provinces with exiles. Whole dozens of our leaders have been seized and hanged. They have died with the courage and calmness of martyrs, but the movement has not been suppressed, it has grown and gained strength. Yes, your Majesty, the revolutionary movement is not such as to depend on individual personalities. It is a function of the national organism, and the gallows, erected to hang the most energetic exponents of that function, is as powerless to save this outworn order of life, as was the death of the Saviour on the cross, to save the corrupt, ancient world from the triumph of reforming Christianity.

Of course, the government may continue to arrest and hang a great multitude of separate individuals. It may destroy many revolutionary groups. Let us grant that it will destroy even the most important of the existing revolutionary organisations. This will not change the state of affairs in the least. The conditions under which we are living, the general dissatisfaction of the people, Russia's aspiration towards a new order of life, all these create revolutionists. You cannot exterminate the whole Russian people, you cannot therefore destroy its discontent by means of reprisals; on the contrary, discontent grows thereby. This is the reason that fresh individuals, still more incensed, still more energetic, are constantly arising from the ranks of the people in great numbers to take the place of those who are being destroyed. These individuals, in the interests of the conflict, will of course organise themselves, having at hand the ready experience of their predecessors, and therefore the revolutionary movement in the course of time must grow stronger, both in quality and quantity. This we have actually seen in the last ten years. What did the death of the adherents of Dolgushin, Tchaikovsky, the agitators of the year 1784, avail the government? The far more determined populists arose to take their place. The terrible reprisals of the government called forth upon the stage the terrorists of '78 and '79. In vain did the government exterminate such men as

the adherents Kovalsky, Dubrovin, Osinsky, and Lizogub; in vain did it destroy dozens of revolutionary circles. From those imperfect organisations, by the course of natural selection there developed still hardier forms. There appeared at last the Executive Committee, with which the government has not yet been able to cope.

Casting a dispassionate glance over the depressing decade through which we have lived, we can accurately foretell the future progress of the movement if the political tactics of the government do not change. The movement must go on growing, gaining strength; terroristic acts will be repeated in ever more alarming and intensified forms. A more perfect, stronger revolutionary organisation will take the place of the groups that are wiped out. In the meantime, the number of malcontents in the land will increase, popular faith in the government will lapse, and the idea of revolution, of its possibility and inevitability, will take root and grow more and more rapidly in Russia. A terrible outburst, a bloody subversion, a violent revolutionary convulsion throughout all Russia, will complete the process of the overthrow of the old order.

What evokes this terrible perspective, what is responsible for it? Yes, your Majesty, a terrible and sad perspective. Do not take this for a mere phrase. We understand better than any one else, how sad is the perishing of so much talent, such energy, in a labour of destruction, in bloody conflicts, when, under different conditions, these forces might be directly applied to creative work, to the progress of the people, the development of their minds, and the well-being of their national life. Whence comes this sad necessity for bloody strife?

From the fact, your Majesty, that there exists among us now no actual government, in the true meaning of the word. A government, according to its fundamental principle, should express only the aspirations of the people, should accomplish only the Will of the People. While in Russia, pardon us for the expression, the government has degenerated into a veritable camarilla, and deserves to be called a band of usurpers far more than does the Executive Committee.

Whatever may have been the intentions of the Sovereign, the acts of the government have had nothing in common with the popular welfare and desires. The Imperial Government has subjugated the people to the state of bondage, it has delivered the masses into the power of the nobility; and now it is openly creating a pernicious class of speculators and profiteers. All its reforms lead to but one result, that the people have sunk into ever greater slavery, into a state of more complete exploitation. It has brought Russia to such a point that at the present time the popular masses find themselves in a state of utter beggary and ruin, not free even at their own domestic firesides from the most insulting surveillance, powerless even in their own communal village affairs. Only the spoiler, the exploiter, is favoured by the protection of the law and the government. The most revolting depredations remain unpunished. But what a terrible fate awaits the man who sincerely thinks and plans for the public welfare! You know well, your Majesty, that it is not only the socialists who are exiled and persecuted. What kind of a government is this, then, which protects such an "order"? Is it not rather a band of rascals, an absolute usurpation?

This is the reason why the Russian government has no moral influence, no support in the people; this is why Russia gives birth to so many revolutionists; this is why even such a fact as regicide awakens joy and sympathetic approval in an enormous part of the population. Yes, your Majesty, do not deceive yourself with the declarations of fawners and flatterers. Regicide is very popular in Russia.

There are two possible escapes from this situation: either a revolution, quite inevitable, which cannot be averted by any number of executions, or a voluntary turning to the people on the part of the Supreme Authority. In the interests of our native land, in the desire to avoid those terrible calamities which always accompany a revolution, the Executive Committee turns to your Majesty with the advice to choose the second course. Believe us that as soon as the Supreme Authority ceases to be arbitrary, as soon as it firmly determines to accomplish only the demands of the nation's consciousness and conscience, you may boldly drive out the spies who defile your government, send your convoys into their barracks, and burn the gallows which are depraving your people. The Executive Committee itself will cease its present activity, and the forces organised around it will disperse and consecrate themselves to cultural work for the benefit of their own people. A peaceful conflict of ideas will take the place of the violence which is more repugnant to us than to your servants, and which we practise only from sad necessity.

We turn to you, casting aside all prejudices, stifling that distrust, which the age-long activity of the government has created. We forget that you are the representative of that power which has so deceived the people, and done them so much harm. We address you as a citizen and an honourable man. We hope that the feeling of personal bitterness will not suppress in you the recognition of your duties, and the desire to know the truth. We too might be embittered. You have lost your father. We have lost not only our fathers, but also our brothers, our wives, our children, our best friends.

But we are ready to suppress our personal feelings if the good of Russia demands it. And we expect the same from you also. We do not lay conditions upon you. Do not be shocked by our proposition. The conditions which are indispensable in order that the revolutionary movement shall be transformed into peaceful activity, have been created, not by us, but by history. We do not impose them, we only recall them to your mind.

In our opinion there are two such conditions:

1. A general amnesty for all political crimes committed in the past, inasmuch as these were not crimes, but the fulfilment of a civic duty.

2. The convocation of an assembly of representatives of all the Russian people, for the purpose of examining the existing forms of our state and society, and revising them in accord with the desires of the people.

We consider it necessary to mention, however, that in order that the legality of the Supreme Authority may be confirmed by popular representation, the process of selecting delegates must be absolutely unrestricted. Therefore the elections must be held under the following conditions:

1. The deputies must be sent from all ranks and classes alike, and in numbers proportionate to the population.

2. There must be no restrictions imposed upon either the electors or the deputies.

3. Electioneering, and the elections themselves, must be carried out in complete freedom, and therefore the government must grant as a temporary measure, prior to the decision of the popular assembly:

    a. Complete freedom of the press,

    b. Complete freedom of speech,

    c. Complete freedom of assembly,

    d. Complete freedom of electoral programmes.

This is the only way in which Russia can be restored to a course of normal and peaceful development. We solemnly declare before our native land and all the world, that our party will submit unconditionally to the decision of a Popular Assembly which shall have been chosen in accord with the above-mentioned conditions; and in the future we shall offer no armed resistance whatever to a government that has been sanctioned by the Popular Assembly.

And so, your Majesty, decide. Before you are two courses. On you depends the choice; we can only ask Fate that your reason and conscience dictate to you a decision which will conform only to the good of Russia, to your own dignity, and to your duty to your native land.

(Signed) The Executive Committee.
March 10 (23), 1881.

Tekahionwake [E. Pauline Johnson] (1861–1913)

Tekahionwake, or Emily Pauline Johnson, was born on March 10, 1861, at Chiefswood, her childhood home, on the Six Nations Reservation in the Grand River valley, Ontario, Canada. She died in Vancouver, British Columbia, on March 7, 1913. From the 1890s until her death she was acclaimed as a leading poet, writer, and performer in Canada, England, and the United States. To honor her contributions, a Canadian commemorative postage stamp was issued in 1961, upon the centennial of her birth.

Her mother, Emily Susanna Howells, was from an English Quaker family that migrated to Ohio after the death of Emily's mother and remarriage of her father. Henry Charles Howells was a stern and strange schoolmaster who became deeply involved in the movement to abolish slavery and hid numerous slaves in his home as a station on the Underground Railway. In her story "My Mother" (1909), Pauline Johnson described her maternal grandfather as "a man of vast peculiarities, prejudices and extreme ideas—a man of contradictions so glaring that even his own children never understood him," who despite his Quaker beliefs beat and terrorized his numerous children. Through his brother, Pauline was cousin to William Dean Howells, the influential literary critic and prolific novelist of radical ideas. Emily left her father's home in 1845 to join her younger sister Eliza and Eliza's husband, the Reverend Adam Elliot, in the Tuscarora parsonage on the Six Nations Reservation in Ontario. There she met George Henry Martin Johnson, a Mohawk of distinguished ancestry, whose grandmother was a white woman adopted by the Mohawks. Emily and George Johnson married, over the objections of both families, in 1853. Emily Pauline, who went by the name Pauline, was the youngest of their four children. Pauline had only a few years of formal schooling and was educated primarily by Emily, who read her children Keats and Byron instead of nursery rhymes and introduced them to works by many distinguished poets and writers of English and American literary history.

George Johnson's parents were reconciled to his marriage with Emily after the birth of their first child, and Pauline grew up in the warm and stimulating family environment of the eminent Mohawks of Brantford (the town named for the Mohawk chief Joseph Brant). George was educated in both Mohawk and English language and traditions, knew all six languages of the confederation, and was the official interpreter for the English church missions on the reservation. He was a powerful orator and a respected leader, one of nine Mohawk chiefs on the Grand Council of the Six Na-

tions. The Six Nations had supported the British and Canadians in the Revolutionary War and the War of 1812, for which the British had provided them a large tract of land in the Grand River valley in compensation for lands they lost in those wars, and the Brantford Mohawks were particularly renowned for their loyalty and heroism. Pauline was deeply influenced by the stories of Mohawk history and traditions that she learned from her father and her paternal grandparents, Helen and John "Smoke" Johnson, whose Indian family name was Tekahionwake ("Double Wampum"). For his marriage, George Johnson had built the ample family estate overlooking the Grand River, Chiefswood (now restored as a museum), where the Johnsons extended gracious hospitality to both Indian and white visitors of varied station and interests. These were happy years, in which Pauline began to write verse and perform in private theatricals. But George Johnson's life was shortened by a series of severe beatings he sustained at the hands of whites because of his efforts to defend Indian rights and stop the illegal traffic in liquor and timber on the reservation. After his death in 1884, the family moved to modest lodgings in Brantford, and Pauline turned to writing to earn her living.

Among her early publications, beginning in 1885, were some of her most famous poems, particularly "A Cry from an Indian Wife" and "The Song My Paddle Sings," representing on the one hand the politics and on the other hand the lyrical qualities that were both central to her later work. In 1892 she gave the first of the public readings of her own work that electrified audiences for whom she later performed with conviction and passion as "The Mohawk Princess." In 1894 she performed to acclaim in London and was able to secure publication of her first volume of collected poems, The White Wampum, at the Bodley Head, then the foremost publisher of new poetry in England.

From then until 1910, Tekahionwake maintained a heavy schedule of writing and performances, touring Canada repeatedly from coast to coast, returning to London to perform at the Steinway Hall and other theaters in 1906 and 1907, and appearing also in the United States. Her second volume of poetry, Canadian Born, appeared in 1903, and her short stories and articles were in demand for the popular press, including Harper's Weekly, Saturday Night, the Toronto Globe, the Canadian Magazine, Mother's Magazine, and Boy's World. Beginning in 1897 she often toured with Walter McRaye as her performing partner and manager. She was engaged in January 1898 to Charles Drayton of

Toronto, but the engagement was broken off by the end of the year, in the face of his family's opposition to the mixed marriage and her continuing career as a stage performer. She never married, nor did her older sister Evelyn and brother Henry. Despite various rumors, little is known about her intimate relations, in part because many of Pauline's personal papers were destroyed or heavily edited after her death by Walter McRaye and Evelyn Johnson.

In London in 1906 Tekahionwake met Chief Joe of the Capilano Squamish Indians, on his mission to protest to King Edward VII infringements of Indian rights by the Columbia Games Act. When she settled in Vancouver in 1909, she learned from him the legends of the Pacific Coast Indians that she shaped into the book published in 1912 as Legends of Vancouver. He emphasized that she was the first English-speaking person to whom he had told these tales, and her preservation of them is seen as one of her lasting contributions. Already severely ill with cancer, she was helped by friends and supporters to publish a collected edition of her poetry under the title Flint and Feather, and a collection of short stories, published shortly after her death in 1913, under the title The Moccasin Maker. Another collection entitled The Shagganappi, stories for boys, was also published posthumously in 1913.

Johnson's work is filled with the tensions of race and gender conflict, the anguish and joys of love and nature, and the contradictions of pride and patriotism, identity and unity. Her poetry, prose, and performances reflected her multiple roots but also shaped the complex ideas, emotions, and social relations of her peoples. Her poetry and prose reached wide audiences, from highly educated white elites who purchased her books and attended elegant stage performances in the East to the mixed audiences of her tours of western Canada and the six hundred thousand readers of the Mother's Magazine. To most of her white readers and audiences she brought knowledge and insights of Indian life and culture they had never previously encountered. To many western audiences she brought experiences of literary and performance arts that were rare in their communities. To Indian peoples she brought her voice and her pen to speak and write their history, their anger, their values, refracted through her insider/outsider vision.

Among the Indian traditions that Pauline Johnson admired were the power and status of women in the governance of the Six Nations. In "My Mother," she wrote of her Mohawk grandmother: "She was 'Chief Matron' of her entire blood relations, and commanded the enviable position of being the one and only person, man or woman, who could appoint a chief to fill the vacancy of one of the great Mohawk law-makers." In an article for the London Daily Express in 1906 she wrote:

"I have heard that the daughters of this vast city cry out for a voice in the Parliament of this land. There is no need for an Iroquois woman to clamour for recognition in our councils; she has had it for upwards of four centuries. The highest title known to us is that of the 'chief matron,'" who names the successor to a chief's seat on the council. "The old and powerful chiefs-in-council never attempt to question her decision; her appointment is final and . . . the chief matron may, if she so desires, enter the council-house and publicly make an address to the chiefs, braves, and warriors assembled, and she is listened to not only with attention, but respect. There are fifty matrons possessing this right in the Iroquois Confederacy. I have not heard of fifty white women even among those of noble birth who may speak and be listened to in the lodge of the law-makers here" (Moccasin Maker, 232).

Many of Johnson's writings express her anger at white racism and experiences of oppression, injustice, and violence of whites toward Indians and "mixed bloods," as in "The Cattle Thief," "Wolverine," and "A Red Girl's Reasoning" (below). But she also portrays the pain and violence suffered by Indians, whites, and "mixed bloods" at the hands of Indians, as in "A Cry from an Indian Wife" and "Dawendine" (below), as well as in some passages of her autobiographical story, "My Mother." Yet throughout, she offered powerful models of resistance and survival.

These models were not always pacific, even for women. In the poem "Ojistoh" a captive woman deceives and kills her captor. In "As It Was in the Beginning" (one of the "woman-warrior" stories selected by Paula Gunn Allen for Spiderwoman's Granddaughters), "Esther" takes control of her fate, as an Indian and as a woman, by poisoning her white lover Laurence with snake venom when he cravenly abandons her before the racist insults of his uncle, the mission parson. The latter, who has raised her since childhood as a Christian (forbidding her use of her Cree language and contact with her people) now declares that being of mixed blood, "a bad, bad mixture," she is untrustworthy as "a caged animal that has once been wild . . . a strange snake." Though he claims to have devoted his whole life to bringing Indians into the church, "it is a different thing to marry with one of them" (Moccasin Maker, 152). Esther returns to her people, and although she is suspected of Laurence's murder, there is no proof. Brooding on what she has done, she thinks: "They account for it by the fact that I am a Redskin. They seem to have forgotten I am a woman." In the poem "A Cry from an Indian Wife," an Indian woman curses the fate that sends young warriors to kill and be killed and laments the pain of the pale-faced women praying for their own, yet she sends her warrior into battle: "Go forth, nor bend to greed of white men's hands / By right, by birth we Indians own these lands. . . ."

Despite such metaphoric calls to battle against whites to reclaim Indian heritage, Johnson also wrote patriotic poems celebrating Canadian unity, the Northwest Mounted Police, and the British Empire. She claimed and promoted a Canadian identity encompassing both the European and the Indian peoples. As she wrote in the "Inscription" for Canadian Born: "Let him who is Canadian born regard these poems as written to himself—whether he be my paleface compatriot who has given to me his right hand of good fellowship, in the years I have appealed to him by pen and platform, or whether he be that dear Red brother of whatsoever tribe or Province, it matters not—White Race and Red are one if they are but Canadian born." Many of her admirers saw this as one of her greatest contributions. In her tours of remote communities across Canada, "she brought word of a great new country stretching from the Atlantic to the Pacific. . . . And in her own person she was tangible proof that Canada had a past that extended back beyond the arrival of the white man—a past, moreover, in which she proclaimed that all Canadians should take unqualified pride" (Van Steen, 26).

But as a "mixed blood" herself, Johnson was acutely conscious of the current problems, responsibilities, and opportunities of this group. In the title story of The Shagganappi, she addressed the terminology applied to mixed-race children, arguing in favor of "half-blood" in place of "half-breed" (for "breed" was "a term for cattle" and should not be applied to human beings) and questioning why "white people of mixed nations are never called half-breeds." Yet in the end, the mixed-race boy heroes of her story embrace "half-breed" with defiant pride. This remarkable story, serialized in Boy's World in 1908, confronts issues of prejudice, discrimination, "passing," and resistance at a boys' school with astonishing frankness, if with more hope than realism in its happy ending. Unfortunately, the persistence of stereotypes she had struggled to overcome remained evident even in the eulogy written in 1913 by Theodore Watts-Dunton for the revised edition of Flint and Feather. "Of all Canadian poets," he wrote, "she was the most distinctly a daughter of the soil, inasmuch as she inherited the blood of the great primeval race now so rapidly vanishing, and of the greater race that has supplanted it" (Flint and Feather, 1914, xvi).

Johnson herself would not have accepted the image of her Indian people as a "primeval race now so rapidly vanishing" nor that whites were "the greater race." Indeed, she identified herself primarily as Indian. In his memorial note for Shagganappi, Ernest Thompson Seton wrote that she rejected being called a white woman and that she spoke of the name she was known by as

forced upon her by whites: "Was not my Indian name good enough? Do you think you help us by bidding us forget our blood? by teaching us to cast off all memory of our high ideals and our glorious past? I am an Indian. My pen and my life I devote to the memory of my own people. Forget that I was Pauline Johnson, but remember always that I was Tekahionwake, the Mohawk that humbly aspired to be the saga singer of her people. . . ." Beth Brant has written that she "began a movement that has proved unstoppable in its momentum—the movement of First Nations women to write down our stories of history, of revolution, of sorrow, of love."

The following selections include four poems from The White Wampum (1895) and the short story "A Red Girl's Reasoning" (1893).

BAC

Sources and Suggested Readings

Allen, Paula Gunn, ed. Spider Woman's Granddaughters: Traditional Tales and Contemporary Writing by Native American Women. New York: Fawcett Columbine, 1989.

Brant, Beth. "The Good Red Road: Journeys of Homecoming in Native Women's Writing." American Indian Culture and Research Journal 21, 1 (1997): 193–206.

Foster, Annie (Mrs. W. Garland). The Mohawk Princess, Being Some Account of the Life of Teka-hion-wake (E. Pauline Johnson). Vancouver: Lion's Gate, 1931.

Johnson, E. Pauline (Tekahionwake). Canadian Born. Toronto: Morang, 1903.

———. Flint and Feather. Collected Verse. Introduction by Theodore Watts-Dunton. 3rd ed. Toronto: Musson Book Company, 1914.

———. The Moccasin Maker. Vancouver: Briggs, 1913.

———. The Moccasin Maker. Introduction, Annotation, and Bibliography by A. LaVonne Brown Ruoff. Tucson: University of Arizona Press, 1987.

———. "A Red Girl's Reasoning." Dominion Magazine 2, 1 (February 1893): 19–28.

———. The Shagganappi. Toronto: Ryerson Press, 1913. "Dedicated to the Boy Scouts." Introduction by Ernest Thompson Seton.

———. The White Wampum. London: John Lane, The Bodley Head, 1895.

Keller, Betty. Pauline: A Biography of Pauline Johnson. Vancouver: Douglas & McIntyre, 1981.

Ruoff, A. LaVonne Brown. "Justice for Indians and Women: The Protest Fiction of Alice Callahan and Pauline Johnson." World Literature Today 66, 2 (Spring 1992): 249–55.

Simard, Rodney. "American Indian Literatures, Authenticity, and the Canon." World Literature Today 66, 2 (Spring 1992): 243–48.

Van Steen, Marcus. Pauline Johnson: Her Life and Work. Toronto: Hodder and Stoughton, 1965.

The White Wampum (1895)

The Cattle Thief

They were coming across the prairie, they were
    galloping hard and fast;
For the eyes of those desperate riders had
    sighted their man at last—
Sighted him off to Eastward, where the Cree
    encampment lay,
Where the cotton woods fringed the river, miles
    and miles away.
Mistake him? Never! Mistake him? the famous
    Eagle Chief!
That terror to all the settlers, that desperate
    Cattle Thief—
That monstrous, fearless Indian, who lorded it
    over the plain,
Who thieved and raided, and scouted, who rode
    like a hurricane!
But they've tracked him across the prairie;
    they've followed him hard and fast;
For those desperate English settlers have sighted
    their man at last.

Up they wheeled to the tepees, all their British
    blood aflame,
Bent on bullets and bloodshed, bent on
    bringing down their game;
But they searched in vain for the Cattle Thief:
    that lion had left his lair,
And they cursed like a troop of demons—for the
    women alone were there.
"The sneaking Indian coward," they hissed; "he
    hides while yet he can;
He'll come in the night for cattle, but he's
    scared to face a *man*."
"Never!" and up from the cotton woods rang
    the voice of Eagle Chief;
And right out into the open stepped, unarmed,
    the Cattle Thief.
Was that the game they had coveted? Scarce
    fifty years had rolled
Over that fleshless, hungry frame, starved to the
    bone and old;
Over that wrinkled, tawny skin, unfed by the
    warmth of blood.
Over those hungry, hollow eyes that glared for
    the sight of food.

He turned, like a hunted lion: "I know not
    fear," said he;
And the words outleapt from his shrunken lips
    in the language of the Cree.
"I'll fight you, white-skins, one by one, till I kill
    you *all*," he said;
But the threat was scarcely uttered, ere a dozen
    balls of lead
Whizzed through the air about him like a
    shower of metal rain,
And the gaunt old Indian Cattle Thief dropped
    dead on the open plain.
And that band of cursing settlers gave one
    triumphant yell,
And rushed like a pack of demons on the body
    that writhed and fell.
"Cut the fiend up into inches, throw his carcass
    on the plain;
Let the wolves eat the cursed Indian, he'd have
    treated us the same."
A dozen hands responded, a dozen knives
    gleamed high,
But the first stroke was arrested by a woman's
    strange, wild cry.
And out into the open, with a courage past
    belief,
She dashed, and spread her blanket o'er the
    corpse of the Cattle Thief;
And the words outleapt from her shrunken lips
    in the language of the Cree,
"If you mean to touch that body, you must cut
    your way through *me*."
And that band of cursing settlers dropped
    backward one by one,
For they knew that an Indian woman roused,
    was a woman to let alone.
And then she raved in a frenzy that they
    scarcely understood,
Raved of the wrongs she had suffered since her
    earliest babyhood:
"Stand back, stand back, you white-skins, touch
    that dead man to your shame;
You have stolen my father's spirit, but his body I
    only claim.
You have killed him, but you shall not dare to
    touch him now he's dead.
You have cursed, and called him a Cattle Thief,
    though you robbed him first of bread—
Robbed him and robbed my people—look
    there, at that shrunken face,
Starved with a hollow hunger, we owe to you
    and your race.
What have you left to us of land, what have you
    left of game,

What have you brought but evil, and curses
    since you came?
How have you paid us for our game? how paid
    us for our land?
By a *book*, to save our souls from the sins *you*
    brought in your other hand.
Go back with your new religion, we never have
    understood
Your robbing an Indian's *body*, and mocking his
    soul with food.
Go back with your new religion, and find—if
    find you can—
The *honest* man you have ever made from out a
    starving man.
You say your cattle are not ours, your meat is
    not our meat;
When *you* pay for the land you live in, *we'll* pay
    for the meat we eat.
Give back our land and our country, give back
    our herds of game;
Give back the furs and the forests that were ours
    before you came;
Give back the peace and the plenty. Then
    come with your new belief,
And blame, if you dare, the hunger that *drove*
    him to be a thief."

A Cry from an Indian Wife

My Forest Brave, my Red-skin love, farewell;
We may not meet to-morrow; who can tell
What mighty ills befall our little band,
Or what you'll suffer from the white man's hand?
Here is your knife! I thought 'twas sheathed for
    aye.
No roaming bison calls for it to-day;
No hide of prairie cattle will it maim;
The plains are bare, it seeks a nobler game:
'Twill drink the life-blood of a soldier host.
Go; rise and strike, no matter what the cost.
Yet stay. Revolt not at the Union Jack,
Nor raise Thy hand against this stripling pack
Of white-faced warriors, marching West to quell
Our fallen tribe that rises to rebel.
They all are young and beautiful and good;
Curse to the war that drinks their harmless
    blood.
Curse to the fate that brought them from the
    East
To be our chiefs—to make our nation least
That breathes the air of this vast continent.
Still their new rule and council is well meant.
They but forget we Indians owned the land

From ocean unto ocean; that they stand
Upon a soil that centuries agone
Was our sole kingdom and our right alone.
They never think how they would feel to-day,
If some great nation came from far away,
Wresting their country from their hapless
    braves,
Giving what they gave us—but wars and graves.
Then go and strike for liberty and life,
And bring back honour to your Indian wife.
Your wife? Ah, what of that, who cares for me?
Who pities my poor love and agony?
What white-robed priest prays for your safety
    here,
As prayer is said for every volunteer
That swells the ranks that Canada sends out?
Who prays for vict'ry for the Indian scout?
Who prays for our poor nation lying low?
None—therefore take your tomahawk and go.
My heart may break and burn into its core,
But I am strong to bid you go to war.
Yet stay, my heart is not the only one
That grieves the loss of husband and of son;
Think of the mothers o'er the inland seas;
Think of the pale-faced maiden on her knees;
One pleads her God to guard some sweet-faced
    child
That marches on toward the North-West wild.
The other prays to shield her love from harm,
To strengthen his young, proud uplifted arm.
Ah, how her white face quivers thus to think,
Your tomahawk his life's best blood will drink.
She never thinks of my wild aching breast,
Nor prays for your dark face and eagle crest
Endangered by a thousand rifle balls,
My heart the target if my warrior falls.
O! coward self I hesitate no more;
Go forth, and win the glories of the war.
Go forth, nor bend to greed of white men's
    hands,
By right, by birth we Indians own these lands,
Though starved, crushed, plundered, lies our
    nation low . . .
Perhaps the white man's God has willed it so.

Dawendine

There's a spirit on the river, there's a ghost upon
    the shore,
They are chanting, they are singing through the
    starlight evermore,
As they steal amid the silence,
        And the shadows of the shore.

You can hear them when the Northern candles
    light the Northern sky,
Those pale, uncertain candle flames, that
    shiver, dart and die,
Those dead men's icy finger tips,
        Athwart the Northern sky.

You can hear the ringing war-cry of a long-
    forgotten brave
Echo through the midnight forest, echo o'er the
    midnight wave,
And the Northern lanterns tremble
        At the war-cry of that brave.

And you hear a voice responding, but in soft
    and tender song;
It is Dawendine's spirit singing, singing all night
    long;
And the whisper of the night wind
        Bears afar her Spirit song.

And the wailing pine trees murmur with their
    voice attuned to hers,
Murmur when they 'rouse from slumber as the
    night wind through them stirs;
And you listen to their legend,
        And their voices blend with hers.

There was feud and there was bloodshed near
    the river by the hill;
And Dawendine listened, while her very heart
    stood still:
Would her kinsman or her lover
        Be the victim by the hill?

Who would be the great unconquered? who
    come boasting how he dealt
Death? and show his rival's scalplock fresh and
    bleeding at his belt.
Who would say, "O Dawendine!
        Look upon the death I dealt?"

And she listens, listens, listens—till a war-cry
    rends the night,
Cry of her victorious lover, monarch he of all
    the height;
And his triumph wakes the horrors,
        Kills the silence of the night.

Heart of her! it throbs so madly, then lies
    freezing in her breast,
For the icy hand of death has chilled the
    brother she loved best;

And her lover dealt the death-blow;
        And her heart dies in her breast.

And she hears her mother saying, "Take thy belt
    of wampum white;
Go unto yon evil savage while he glories on the
    height;
Sing and sue for peace between us:
        At his feet lay wampum white.

"Lest thy kinsmen all may perish, all thy
    brothers and thy sire
Fall before his mighty hatred as the forest falls
    to fire;
Take thy wampum pale and peaceful,
        Save thy brothers, save thy sire."

And the girl rises softly, softly slips toward the
    shore;
Loves she well the murdered brother, loves his
    hated foeman more,
Loves, and longs to give the wampum;
        And she meets him on the shore.

"Peace," she sings, "O mighty victor, Peace! I
    bring thee wampum white.
Sheathe thy knife whose blade has tasted my
    young kinsman's blood to-night
Ere it drink to slake its thirsting,
        I have brought thee wampum white."

Answers he, "O Dawendine! I will let thy
    kinsman be,
I accept thy belt of wampum; but my hate
    demands for me
That they give their fairest treasure,
        Ere I let thy kinsman be.

"Dawendine, for thy singing, for thy suing, war
    shall cease;
For thy name, which speaks of dawning, *Thou*
    shalt be the dawn of peace;
For thine eyes whose purple shadows tell of dawn,
        My hate shall cease.

"Dawendine, Child of Dawning, hateful are thy
    kin to me;
Red my fingers with their heart blood, but my
    heart is red for thee:
Dawendine, Child of Dawning,
        Wilt thou fail or follow me?"

And her kinsmen still are waiting her returning
    from the night,

Waiting, waiting for her coming with her belt of
    wampum white;
But forgetting all, she follows,
      Where he leads through day or night.

There's a spirit on the river, there's a ghost upon
    the shore,
And they sing of love and loving through the
    starlight evermore,
As they steal amid the silence,
      And the shadows of the shore.

Wolverine

"Yes, sir, it's quite a story, though you won't
    believe it's true,
But such things happened often when I lived
    beyond the Soo."
And the trapper tilted back his chair and filled
    his pipe anew.

"I ain't thought of it neither fer this many 'n
    many a day,
Although it used to haunt me in the years that's
    slid away;
The years I spent a-trappin' for the good old
    Hudson's Bay.

"Wild? You bet, 'twas wild then, an' few an' far
    between
The squatters' shacks, for whites was scarce as
    furs when things is green,
An' only reds an' 'Hudson's' men was all the
    folk I seen.

"No. Them old Indyans ain't so bad, not if you
    treat 'em square.
Why, I lived in amongst 'em all the winters I
    was there,
An' I never lost a copper, an' I never lost a hair.

"But I'd have lost my life the time that you've
    heard tell about;
I don't think I'd be settin' here, but dead
    beyond a doubt,
If that there Indyan 'Wolverine' jest hadn't
    helped me out.

"'Twas freshet time, 'way back, as long as sixty-
    six or eight,
An' I was comin' to the Post that year a kind of
    late,

For beaver had been plentiful, and trappin' had
    been great.

"One day I had been settin' traps along a bit of
    wood,
An' night was catchin' up to me jest faster 'an it
    should,
When all at once I heard a sound that curdled
    up my blood.

"It was the howl of famished wolves—I didn't
    stop to think
But jest lit out across for home as quick as you
    could wink,
But when I reached the river's edge I brought
    up at the brink.

"That mornin' I had crossed the stream straight
    on a sheet of ice
An' now, God help me! There it was, churned
    up an' cracked to dice,
The flood went boiling past—I stood like one
    shut in a vice,

"No way ahead, no path aback, trapped like a
    rat ashore,
With naught but death to follow, and with
    naught but death afore;
The howl of hungry wolves aback—ahead, the
    torrent's roar.

"An' then—a voice, an Indyan voice, that called
    out clear and clean,
'Take Indyan's horse, I run like deer, wolf can't
    catch Wolverine.'
I says, 'Thank Heaven.' There stood the chief
    I'd nicknamed Wolverine.

"I leapt on that there horse, an' then jest like a
    coward fled,
An' left that Indyan standin' there alone, as
    good as dead,
With the wolves a-howlin' at his back, the
    swollen stream ahead.

"I don't know how them Indyans dodge from
    death the way they do,
You won't believe it, sir, but what I'm tellin' you
    is true,
But that there chap was 'round next day as
    sound as me or you.

"He came to get his horse, but not a cent he'd
    take from me.

251

Yes, sir, you're right, the Indyans now ain't like
    they used to be;
We've got 'em sharpened up a bit an' *now*
    they'll take a fee.

"No, sir, you're wrong, they ain't no 'dogs.' I'm
    not through tellin' yet;
You'll take that name right back again, or else
    jest out you get!
You'll take that name right back when you hear
    all this yarn, I bet.

"It happened that same autumn, when some
    Whites was comin' in,
I heard the old Red River carts a-kickin' up a
    din,
So I went over to their camp to see an English
    skin.

"They said, 'They'd had an awful scare from
    Injuns,' an' they swore
That savages had come around the very night
    before
A-brandishing their tomahawks and painted up
    for war.

"But when their plucky Englishmen had put a
    bit of lead
Right through the heart of one of them, an'
    rolled him over, dead,
The other cowards said that they had come on
    peace instead.

"'That they (the Whites) had lost some stores,
    from off their little pack,
An' that the Red they peppered dead had
    followed up their track,
Because he'd found the packages an' came *to
    give them back.*'

"'Oh!' they said, 'they were quite sorry, but it
    wasn't like as if
They had killed a decent Whiteman by mistake
    or in a tiff,
It was only some old Injun dog that lay there
    stark an' stiff.'

"I said, 'You are the meanest dogs that ever yet I
    seen,'
Then I rolled the body over as it lay out on the
    green;
I peered into the face—My God! 'twas poor old
    Wolverine."

A Red Girl's Reasoning (1893)

"Be pretty good to her, Charlie, my boy, or she'll balk sure as shooting."

That was what old Jimmy Robinson said to his brand new son-in-law, while they waited for the bride to reappear.

"Oh! you bet, there's no danger of much else. I'll be good to her, help me Heaven," replied Charlie McDonald, brightly.

"Yes, of course you will," answered the old man, "but don't you forget, there's a good big bit of her mother in her, and," closing his left eye significantly, "you don't understand these Indians as I do."

"But I'm just as fond of them, Mr. Robinson," Charlie said assertively, "and I get on with them too, now, don't I?"

"Yes, pretty well for a town boy; but when you have lived forty years among these people, as I have done; when you have had your wife as long as I have had mine—for there's no getting over it, Christine's disposition is as native as her mother's, every bit—and perhaps when you've owned for eighteen years a daughter as dutiful, as loving, as fearless, and, alas! as obstinate as that little piece you are stealing away from me today—I tell you, youngster, you'll know more than you know now. It is kindness for kindness, bullet for bullet, blood for blood. Remember, what you are, she will be," and the old Hudson Bay trader scrutinized Charlie McDonald's face like a detective.

It was a happy, fair face, good to look at, with a certain ripple of dimples somewhere about the mouth, and eyes that laughed out the very sunniness of their owner's soul. There was not a severe nor yet a weak line anywhere. He was a well-meaning young fellow, happily dispositioned, and a great favorite with the tribe at Robinson's Post, whither he had gone in the service of the Department of Agriculture, to assist the local agent through the tedium of a long census-taking.

As a boy he had had the Indian relic-hunting craze, as a youth he had studied Indian archaeology and folklore, as a man he consummated his predilections for Indianology by loving, winning and marrying the quiet little daughter of the English trader, who himself had married a native woman some twenty years ago. The country was all backwoods, and the Post miles and miles from even the semblance of civilization, and the lonely young Englishman's heart had gone out to the girl who, apart from speaking a very few words of English, was utterly uncivilized and uncultured, but had withal that marvellously innate refinement so universally possessed by the higher tribes of North American Indians.

Like all her race, observant, intuitive, having a horror of ridicule, consequently quick at acquirement and teachable in mental and social habits, she had developed from absolute pagan indifference into a sweet, elderly Christian woman, whose broken English, quiet manner, and still handsome copper-colored face, were the joy of old Robinson's declining years.

He had given their daughter Christine all the advantages of his own learning—which, if truthfully told, was not universal; but the girl had a fair common education, and the native adaptability to progress.

She belonged to neither and still to both types of the cultured Indian. The solemn, silent, almost heavy manner of the one so commingled with the gesticulating Frenchiness and vivacity of the other, that one familiar with native Canadian life would find it difficult to determine her nationality.

She looked very pretty to Charles McDonald's loving eyes, as she reappeared in the doorway, holding her mother's hand and saying some happy words of farewell. Personally she looked much the same as her sisters, all Canada through, who are the offspring of red and white parentage—olive-complexioned, grey-eyed, black-haired, with figure slight and delicate, and the wistful, unfathomable expression in her whole face that turns one so heart-sick as they glance at the young Indians of to-day—it is the forerunner too frequently of "the white man's disease," consumption—but McDonald was pathetically in love, and thought her the most beautiful woman he had ever seen in his life.

There had not been much of a wedding ceremony. The priest had cantered through the service in Latin, pronounced the benediction in English, and congratulated the "happy couple" in Indian, as a compliment to the assembled tribe in the little amateur sanctuary that did service at the post as a sanctuary.

But the knot was tied as firmly and indissolubly as if all Charlie McDonald's swell city friends had crushed themselves up against the chancel to congratulate him, and in his heart he was deeply thankful to escape the flower-pelting, white gloves, rice-throwing, and ponderous stupidity of a breakfast, and indeed all the regulation gimcracks of the usual marriage celebrations, and it was with a hand trembling with absolute happiness that he assisted his little Indian wife into the old muddy buckboard that, hitched to an underbred-looking pony, was to convey them over the first stages of their journey. Then came more adieus, some hand-clasping, old Jimmy Robinson looking very serious just at the last, Mrs. Jimmy, stout, stolid, betraying nothing of visible emotion, and then the pony, roughshod and shaggy, trudged on, while mutual hand-waves were kept up until the old Hudson's Bay Post dropped out of sight, and the buckboard with its lightsome load of hearts, deliriously happy, jogged on over the uneven trail.

She was "all the rage" that winter at the provincial capital. The men called her a "deuced fine little woman." The ladies said she was "just the sweetest wildflower." Whereas she was really but an ordinary, pale, dark girl who spoke slowly and with a strong accent, who danced fairly well, sang acceptably, and never stirred outside the door without her husband.

Charlie was proud of her; he was proud that she had "taken" so well among his friends, proud that she bore herself so complacently in the drawing rooms of the wives of pompous Government officials, but doubly proud of her almost abject devotion to him. If ever human being was worshipped that being was Charlie McDonald; it could scarcely have been otherwise, for the almost godlike strength of his passion for that little wife of his would have mastered and melted a far more invincible citadel than an already affectionate woman's heart.

Favorites socially, McDonald and his wife went everywhere. In fashionable circles she was "new"—a potent charm to acquire popularity, and the little velvet-clad figure was always the centre of interest among all the women in the room. She always dressed in velvet. No woman in Canada, has she but the faintest dash of native blood in her veins, but loves velvets and silks. As beef to the Englishman, wine to the Frenchman, fads to the Yankee, so are velvet and silk to the Indian girl, be she wild as prairie grass, be she on the borders of civilization, or, having stepped within its boundary, mounted the steps of culture even under its superficial heights.

"Such a dolling little appil blossom," said the wife of a local M.P., who brushed up her etiquette and English once a year at Ottawa. "Does she always laugh so sweetly, and gobble you up with those great big grey eyes of hers, when you are togetheah at home, Mr. McDonald? If so, I should think youah pooah brothah would feel himself terribly *de trop*."

He laughed lightly. "Yes, Mrs. Stuart, there are not two of Christie; she is the same at home and abroad, and as for Joe, he doesn't mind us a bit; he's no end fond of her."

"I'm very glad he is. I always fancied he did not care for her, d'you know."

If ever a blunt woman existed it was Mrs. Stuart.

She really meant nothing, but her remark bothered Charlie. He was fond of his brother, and jealous for Christie's popularity. So that night when he and Joe were having a pipe he said:

"I've never asked you yet what you thought of her, Joe." A brief pause, then Joe spoke. "I'm glad she loves you."

"Why?"

"Because that girl has but two possibilities regarding humanity—love or hate."

"Humph! Does she love you or hate *you*?"

"Ask her."

"You talk bosh. If she hated you, you'd get out. If she loved you I'd *make* you get out."

Joe McDonald whistled a little, then laughed.

"Now that we are on the subject, I might as well ask—honestly, old man, wouldn't you and Christie prefer keeping house alone to having me always around?"

"Nonsense, sheer nonsense. Why, thunder, man, Christie's no end fond of you, and as for me—you surely don't want assurances from me?"

"No, but I often think a young couple—"

"Young couple be blowed! After a while when they want you and your old surveying chains, and spindle-legged tripod telescope kickshaws, farther west, I venture to say the little woman will cry her eyes out—won't you, Christie?" This last in a higher tone, as through clouds of tobacco smoke he caught sight of his wife passing the doorway.

She entered. "Oh, no, I would not cry; I never do cry, but I would be heart-sore to lose you, Joe, and apart from that"—a little wickedly—"you may come in handy for an exchange some day, as Charlie does always say when he hoards up duplicate relics."

"Are Charlie and I duplicates?"

"Well—not exactly"—her head a little to one side, and eyeing them both merrily, while she slipped softly on to the arm of her husband's chair—"but, in the event of Charlie's failing me"—everyone laughed then. The "some day" that she spoke of was nearer than they thought. It came about in this wise.

There was a dance at the Lieutenant-Governor's, and the world and his wife were there. The nobs were in great feather that night, particularly the women, who flaunted about in new gowns and much splendor. Christie McDonald had a new gown also, but wore it with the utmost unconcern, and if she heard any of the flattering remarks made about her she at least appeared to disregard them.

"I never dreamed you could wear blue so splendidly," said Captain Logan, as they sat out a dance together.

"Indeed she can, though," interposed Mrs. Stuart, halting in one of her gracious sweeps down the room with her husband's private secretary.

"Don't shout so, captain. I can hear every sentence you uttah—of course Mrs. McDonald can wear blue—she has a morning gown of cadet blue that she is a picture in."

"You are both very kind," said Christie. "I like blue; it is the color of all of the Hudson's Bay posts, and the factor's residence is always decorated in blue."

"Is it really? How interesting—do tell us some more of your old home, Mrs. McDonald; you so seldom speak of you life at the post, and we fellows so often wish to hear of it all," said Logan eagerly.

"Why do you not ask me of it, then?"

"Well—er, I'm sure I don't know; I'm fully interested in the Ind—in your people—your mother's people, I mean, but it always seems so personal, I suppose; and a—a—"

"Perhaps you are, like all other white people, afraid to mention my nationality to me."

The captain winced, and Mrs. Stuart laughed uneasily. Joe McDonald was not far off, and he was listening, and chuckling, and saying to himself, "That's you, Christie, lay 'em out; it won't hurt 'em to know how they appear once in a while."

"Well, Captain Logan" she was saying, "what is it you would like to hear—of my people, or my parents, or myself?"

"All, all, my dear" cried Mrs. Stuart clamorously. "I'll speak for him—tell us of yourself and your mother—your father is delightful. I am sure—but then he is only an ordinary Englishman, not half as interesting as a foreigner, or—or, perhaps I should say, a native."

Christie laughed. "Yes," she said, "my father often teases my mother now about how *very* native she was when he married her; then, how could she have been otherwise? She did not know a word of English, and there was not another English-speaking person besides my father and his two companions within sixty miles."

"Two companions, eh? One a Catholic priest and the other a wine merchant, I suppose, and with your father in the Hudson's Bay, they were good representatives of the pioneers in the New World," remarked Logan, waggishly.

"Oh, no, they were all Hudson's Bay men. There were no rumsellers and no missionaries in that part of the country then."

Mrs. Stuart looked puzzled. "*No missionaries?*" she repeated with an odd intonation.

Christie's insight was quick. There was a peculiar expression of interrogation in the eyes of her listeners, and the girl's blood leapt angrily up into her temples as she said hurriedly, "I know what you mean; I know

254

what you are thinking. You are wondering how my parents were married—"

"Well—er, my dear, it seems peculiar—if there was no priest, and no magistrate, why—a—" Mrs. Stuart paused awkwardly.

"The marriage was performed by Indian rites," said Christie.

"Oh, do tell me about it; is the ceremony very interesting and quaint—are your chieftains anything like Buddhist priests?" It was Logan who spoke.

"Why, no," said the girl in amazement at that gentleman's ignorance. "There is no ceremony at all, save a feast. The two people just agree to live only with and for each other, and the man takes his wife to his home, just as you do. There is no ritual to bind them; they need none; an Indian's word was his law in those days, you know."

Mrs. Stuart stepped backwards. "Ah!" was all she said. Logan removed his eye-glass and stared blankly at Christie. "and did McDonald marry you in this singular fashion?" he questioned.

"Oh, no, we were married by Father O'Leary. Why do you ask?"

"Because if he had, I'd have blown his brains out to-morrow."

Mrs. Stuart's partner, who had hitherto been silent, coughed and began to twirl his cuff stud nervously, but nobody took any notice of him. Christie has risen, slowly, ominously—risen, with the dignity and pride of an empress.

"Captain Logan," she said, "what do you dare to say to me? What do you dare to mean? Do you presume to think it would not have been lawful for Charlie to marry me according to my people's rites? Do you for one instant dare to question that my parents were not as legally—"

"Don't, dear, don't," interrupted Mrs. Stuart hurriedly; "it is bad enough now, goodness knows; don't make—" Then she broke off blindly. Christie's eyes glared at the mumbling woman, at her uneasy partner, at the horrified captain. Then they rested on the McDonald brothers, who stood within earshot, Joe's face scarlet, her husband's white as ashes, with something in his eyes she had never seen before. It was Joe who saved the situation. Stepping quickly across towards his sister-in-law, he offered her his arm, saying, "The next dance is ours, I think, Christie."

Then Logan pulled himself together, and attempted to carry Mrs. Stuart off for the waltz, but for once in her life that lady had lost her head. "It is shocking!" she said, "outrageously shocking! I wonder if they told Mr. McDonald before he married her!" Then looking hurriedly round, she too saw the young husband's face and knew that they had not.

"Humph! deuced nice kettle of fish—poor old Charlie has always thought so much of honorable birth."

Logan thought he spoke in an undertone, but "poor old Charlie" heard him. He followed his wife and brother across the room. "Joe," he said, "will you see that a trap is called?" Then to Christie, "Joe will see that you get home all right." He wheeled on his heel then and left the ball-room.

Joe *did* see.

He tucked a poor, shivering, pallid little woman into a cab, and wound her bare throat up in the scarlet velvet cloak that was hanging uselessly over her arm. She crouched down beside him, saying, "I am so cold, Joe; I am so cold," but she did not seem to know enough to wrap herself up. Joe felt all through this long drive that nothing this side of Heaven would be so good as to die, and he was glad when the poor little voice at his elbow said, "What is he so angry at, Joe?"

"I don't know exactly, dear," he said gently, "But I think it was what you said about this Indian marriage."

"But why should I not have said it? Is there anything wrong about it?" she asked pitifully.

"Nothing, that I can see—there was no other way; but Charlie is very angry, and you must be brave and forgiving with him, Christie, dear."

"But I did never see him like that before, did you?"

"Once."

"When?"

"Oh, at college, one day, a boy tore his prayerbook in half, and threw it into the grate, just to be mean, you know. Our mother had given it to him at his confirmation."

"And did he look so?"

"About, but it all blew over in a day—Charlie's tempers are short and brisk. Just don't take any notice of him; run off to bed, and he'll have forgotten it by the morning."

They reached home at last. Christie said goodnight quietly, going directly to her room. Joe went to his room also, filled a pipe and smoked for an hour. Across the passage he could hear her slippered feet pacing up and down, up and down the length of her apartment. There was something panther-like in those restless footfalls, a meaning velvetyness that made him shiver, and again he wished he were dead—or elsewhere.

After a time the hall door opened, and someone came upstairs, along the passage, and to the little woman's room. As he entered, she turned and faced him.

"Christie," he said harshly, "do you know what you have done?"

"Yes," taking a step nearer him, her whole soul springing up to her eyes, "I have angered you, Charlie, and—"

"Angered me? You have disgraced me; and more-over, you have disgraced yourself and both your parents."

"*Disgraced?*"

"Yes, *disgraced;* you have literally declared to the whole city that your father and mother were never married, and that you are the child of—what shall we call it—love? Certainly not legality."

Across the hallway sat Joe McDonald, his blood freezing; but it leapt into every vein like fire at the awful anguish in the little voice that cried simply, "Oh! Charlie!"

"How could you do it, how could you do it, Christie, without shame either for yourself or for me, let alone your parents?"

The voice was like an angry demon's—not a trace was there in it of the yellow-haired, blue-eyed, laugh-ing-lipped boy who had driven away so gaily to the dance five hours before.

"Shame? Why should I be ashamed of the rites of my people any more than you should be ashamed of the customs of yours—of a marriage more sacred and holy than half of your white man's mockeries?"

It was the voice of another nature in the girl—the love and the pleading were dead in it.

"Do you mean to tell me, Charlie—you who have studied my race and their laws for years—do you mean to tell me that, because there was no priest and no magistrate, my mother was not married? Do you mean to say that all my forefathers, for hundreds of years back, have been illegally born? If so, you blacken my ancestry beyond—beyond—beyond all reason."

"No, Christie, I would not be so brutal as that; but your father and mother live in more civilized times. Father O'Leary has been at the post for nearly twenty years. Why was not your father straight enough to have the ceremony performed when he did get the chance?"

The girl turned upon him with the face of a fury. "Do you suppose," she almost hissed, "that my mother would be married according to your *white* rites after she had been five years a wife, and I had been born in the meantime? *No,* a thousand times I say *no.* When the priest came with his notions of Christianizing, and talked to them of re-marriage by the Church, my moth-er arose and said, 'Never—never—I have never had but this one husband; he has had none but me for wife, and to have you re-marry us would be to say as much to the whole world as that we had never been married before. You go away; *I* do not ask that *your* people be re-married; talk not so to me. I *am* married, and you or the Church cannot do or undo it.'"

"Your father was a fool not to insist upon the law, and so was the priest."

"Law? *My* people have *no* priest, and my nation cringes not to law. Our priest is purity, and our law is honor. Priest? Was there a *priest* at the most holy marriage known to humanity—that stainless marriage whose offspring is the God you white men told my pagan mother of?"

"Christie—you are *worse* than blasphemous; such a profane remark shows how little you understand the sanctity of the Christian faith—"

"I know what I *do* understand; it is that you are hating me because I told some of the beautiful cus-toms of my people to Mrs. Stuart and those men."

"Pooh! Who cares for them? It is not them; the trouble is they won't keep their mouths shut. Logan's a cad and will toss the whole tale about at the club before to-morrow night; and as for the Stuart woman, I'd like to know how I'm going to take you to Ottawa for presentation and the opening, while she is blabbing the whole miserable scandal in every drawing-room, and I'll be pointed out as a romantic fool, and you—as worse; I *can't* understand why your father didn't tell me before we were married; I at least might have warned you to never mention it." Something of recklessness rang up through his voice, just as the panther-likeness crept up from her footsteps and couched itself in hers. She spoke in tones quiet, soft, deadly.

"Before we were married! Oh! Charlie, would it have—made—any—difference?"

"God knows," he said, throwing himself into a chair, his blonde hair rumpled and wet. It was the only boyish thing about him now.

She walked towards him, then halted in the centre of the room. "Charlie McDonald," she said, and it was as if a stone had spoken, "look up." He raised his head, startled by her tone. There was a threat in her eyes that, had his rage been less courageous, his pride less bit-terly wounded, would have cowed him.

"There was no such time as that before our mar-riage, for we *are not married now.* Stop," she said, outstretching her palms against him as he sprang to his feet, "I tell you we are not married. Why should I recognize the rites of your nation when you do not acknowledge the rites of mine? According to your own words, my parents should have gone through your church ceremony as well as through an Indian con-tract; according to *my* words, *we* should go through an Indian contract as well as through a church marriage. If their union is illegal, so is ours. If you think my father is living in dishonor with my mother, my people will think I am living in dishonor with you. How do I know when another nation will come and conquer you as you white men conquered us? And they will have another marriage rite to perform, and they will tell us another truth, that you are not my husband, that you are but disgracing and dishonoring me, that you are keeping me here, not as your wife, but as your—your *squaw.*"

The terrible word had never passed her lips before, and the blood stained her face to her very temples. She snatched off her wedding ring and tossed it across the room, saying scornfully, "That thing is as empty as the Indian rites to you."

He caught her by the wrists; his small white teeth were locked tightly, his blue eyes blazed into hers.

"Christine, do you dare to doubt my honor towards you? *you,* whom I should have died for; do you *dare* to think I have kept you here, not as my wife, but—"

"Oh, God! You are hurting me; you are breaking my arm," she gasped.

The door was flung open, and Joe McDonald's sinewy hands clinched like vices on his brother's shoulders.

"Charlie, you're mad, mad as the devil. Let go of her this minute."

The girl staggered backwards as the iron fingers loosed her wrists. "Oh, Joe," she cried, "I am not his wife, and he says I am born—nameless."

"Here," said Joe, shoving his brother towards the door. "Go downstairs till you can collect your senses. If ever a being acted like an infernal fool, you're the man."

The young husband looked from one to the other, dazed by his wife's insult, abandoned to a fit of ridiculously childish temper. Blind as he was with passion, he remembered long afterwards seeing them standing there, his brother's face darkened with a scowl of anger—his wife, clad in the mockery of her ball dress, her scarlet velvet cloak half covering her bare brown neck and arms, her eyes like flames of fire, her face like a piece of sculptured greystone.

Without a word he flung himself furiously from the room, and immediately afterwards they heard the heavy hall door bang behind him.

"Can I do anything for you, Christie?" asked her brother-in-law calmly.

"No, thank you—unless—I think I would like a drink of water, please."

He brought her up a goblet filled with wine; her hand did not even tremble as she took it. As for Joe, a demon arose in his soul as he noticed she kept her wrists covered.

"Do you think he will come back?" she said.

"Oh, yes, of course; he'll be all right in the morning. Now go to bed like a good little girl, and—and, I say, Christie, you can call me if you want anything; I'll be right here, you know."

"Thank you, Joe; you are kind—and good."

He returned then to his apartment. His pipe was out, but he picked up a newspaper instead, threw himself into an armchair, and in a half-hour was in the land of dreams.

When Charlie came home in the morning, after a six-mile walk into the country and back again, his foolish anger was dead and buried. Logan's "Poor old Charlie" did not ring so distinctly in his ears. Mrs. Stuart's horrified expression had faded considerably from his recollection. He thought only of that surprisingly tall, dark girl, whose eyes looked like coals, whose voice pierced him like a flint-tipped arrow. Ah, well, they would never quarrel again like that, he told himself. She loved him so, and would forgive him after he had talked quietly to her, and told her what an ass he was. She was simple-minded and awfully ignorant to pitch those old Indian laws at him in her fury, but he could not blame her; oh, no, he could not for one moment blame her. He had been terribly severe and unreasonable, and the horrid McDonald temper had got the better of him; and he loved her so. Oh! He loved her so! She would surely feel that, and forgive him, and—He went straight to his wife's room. The blue velvet evening dress lay on the chair into which he had thrown himself when he doomed his life's happiness by those two words, "God knows." A bunch of dead daffodils and her slippers were on the floor, everything—but Christie.

He went to his brother's bedroom door.

"Joe," he called, rapping nervously thereon; "Joe, wake up; where's Christie, d'you know?"

"Good Lord, no," gasped that youth, springing out of his armchair and opening the door. As he did so a note fell from off the handle. Charlie's face blanched to his very hair while Joe read aloud, his voice weakening at every word:

DEAR OLD JOE—I went into your room at daylight to get that picture of the Post on your bookshelves. I hope you do not mind, but I kissed your hair while you slept; it was so curly and yellow, and soft, just like his. Good-bye, Joe.

"CHRISTIE"

And when Joe looked into his brother's face and saw the anguish settle in those laughing blue eyes, the despair that drove the dimples away from that almost girlish mouth; when he realized that this boy was but four-and-twenty years old, and that all his future was perhaps darkened and shadowed for ever, a great, deep sorrow arose in his heart, and he forgot all things, all but the agony that rang up through the voice of the fair, handsome lad as he staggered forward, crying, "Oh, Joe—what shall I do—what shall I do?"

It was months and months before he found her, but during all that time he had never known a hopeless moment; discouraged he often was, but despondent, never. The sunniness of his ever-boyish heart radiated with a warmth that would have flooded a much deeper gloom than that which settled within his eager young life. Suffer? ah! Yes, he suffered, not with locked teeth and stony stoicism, not with the masterful self-command, the reserve, the conquered bitterness of the still-water sort of nature, that is supposed to run to such depths. He tried to be bright, and his sweet old boyish self. He would laugh sometimes in a pitiful, pathetic fashion. He took to petting dogs, looking into their large, solemn eyes with his wistful, questioning blue ones; he would kiss them, as women sometimes do, and call them "dear old fellow," in tones that had tears; and once in the course of his travels, while at a little way-station, he discovered a huge St. Bernard imprisoned by some mischance in an empty freight car; the animal was nearly dead from starvation, and it seemed to salve his own sick heart to rescue back the dog's life. Nobody claimed the big starving creature, the train hands knew nothing of its owner, and gladly handed it over to its deliverer. "Hudson," he called it, and afterwards when Joe McDonald would relate the story of his brother's life he invariably terminated it with, "And I really believe that big lumbering brute saved him." From what, he was never known to say.

But all things end, and he heard of her at last. She had never returned to the Post, as he at first thought she would, but had gone to the little town of B—, in Ontario, where she was making her living at embroidery and plain sewing.

The September sun had set redly when at last he reached the outskirts of the town, opened up the wicket gate, and walked up the weedy, unkept path leading to the cottage where she lodged.

Even through the twilight, he could see her there, leaning on the rail of the verandah—oddly enough she had about her shoulders the scarlet velvet cloak she wore when he had flung himself so madly from the room that night.

The moment the lad saw her his heart swelled with a sudden heat, burning moisture leapt into his eyes, and clogged his long, boyish lashes. He bounded up the steps—"Christie," he said, and the word scorched his lips like audible flame.

She turned to him, and for a second stood magnetized by his passionately wistful face; her peculiar grey-ish eyes seemed to drink the very life of his unquenchable love, though the tears that suddenly sprang into his seemed to absorb every pulse in his body through those hungry, pleading eyes of his that had, oh! so

often, been blinded by her kisses when once her whole world lay in their blue depths.

"You will come back to me, Christie, my wife? My wife, you will let me love you again?"

She gave a singular little gasp, and shook her head. "Don't, oh! Don't," he cried piteously. "You will come to me, dear? It is all such a bitter mistake—I did not understand. Oh! Christie, I did not understand, and you'll forgive me, and love me again, won't you—won't you?"

"No," said the girl with quick, indrawn breath.

He dashed the back of his hand across his wet eyelids. His lips were growing numb, and he bungled over the monosyllable "Why?"

"I do not like you," she answered quietly.

"God! Oh, God, what is there left?"

She did not appear to hear the heart-break in his voice; she stood like one wrapped in sombre thought; no blaze, no tear, nothing in her eyes; no hardness, no tenderness about her mouth. The wind was blowing her cloak aside, and the only visible human life in her whole body was once when he spoke the muscles of her brown arm seemed to contract.

"But, darling, you are mine—*mine*—we are husband and wife! Oh, heaven, you *must* love me, you *must* come to me again."

"You cannot *make* me come," said the icy voice, "neither church, nor law, nor even"—and the voice softened—"nor even love can make a slave of a red girl."

"Heaven forbid it," he faltered. "No, Christie, I will never claim you without your love. What reunion would that be? But, oh, Christie, you are lying to me, you are lying to yourself, you are lying to heaven."

She did not move. If only he could touch her he felt as sure of her yielding as he felt sure there was a hereafter. The memory of times when he had but to lay his hand on her hair to call a most passionate response from her filled his heart with a torture that choked all words before they reached his lips; at the thought of those days he forgot she was unapproachable; forgot how forbidding were her eyes, how stony her lips. Flinging himself forward, his knees on the chair at her side, his face pressed hardly in the folds of the cloak on her shoulder, he clasped his arms about her with a boyish petulance, saying, "Christie, Christie, my little girl wife, I love you, I love you, and you are killing me."

She quivered from head to foot as his fair, wavy hair brushed her neck, his despairing face sank lower until his cheek, hot as fire, rested on the cool, olive flesh of her arm. A warm moisture oozed up through her skin, and as he felt its glow he looked up. Her teeth, white and cold, were locked over her under lip, and her eyes as grey stones.

Not murderers alone know the agony of a death sentence.

"Is it all useless? All useless, dear?" he said, with lips starving for hers.

"All useless," she repeated. "I have no love for you now. You forfeited me and my heart months ago, when you said those two words."

His arms fell away from her wearily, he arose mechanically, he placed his little grey checked cap on the back of his yellow curls, the old-time laughter was dead in the blue eyes that now looked scared and haunted, the boyishness and the dimples crept away for ever from the lips that quivered like a child's; he turned from her, but she had looked once into his face as the Law Giver must have looked at the land of Canaan outspread at his feet. She watched him go down the long path and through the picket gate, she watched the big yellowish dog that had waited for him lumber up to its feet—stretch—then follow him. She was conscious of but two things, the vengeful lie in her soul, and a little space on her arm that his wet lashes had brushed.

It was hours afterwards when he reached his room. He had said nothing, done nothing—what use were words or deeds? Old Jimmy Robinson was right; she had "balked" sure enough.

What a bare, hotelish room it was! He tossed off his coat and sat for ten minutes looking blankly at the sputtering gas jet. Then his whole life, desolate as a desert, loomed up before him with appalling distinctness. Throwing himself on the floor beside his bed, with clasped hands and arms outstretched on the white counterpane, he sobbed. "Oh! God, dear God, I thought you loved me; I thought you'd let me have her again, but you must be tired of me, tired of loving me, too. I've nothing left now, nothing! It doesn't seem that I even have you to-night."

He lifted his face then, for his dog, big and clumsy and yellow, was licking at his sleeve.

Ida B. Wells-Barnett (1862–1931)

Ida B. Wells-Barnett, the most prominent opponent of the widespread lynching of African Americans occurring from 1890–1910 and again in the 1920s, was born in 1862 in Mississippi to slave parents. Her parents died when she was still a teenager. She thus assumed the responsibility of supporting five younger siblings while attending a school established for ex-slaves, Rust College, in her hometown of Holly Springs, Mississippi. Later a journalist of national stature, she trained early to be a teacher and in 1884 moved to Memphis where she both studied and taught at Fisk University. By 1887 she began her career in journalism, publishing articles and becoming active in the Colored Press Association, in which she was an elected officer. From the outset she was an activist in a range of civil rights causes: under the pen name "Iola" she criticized Fisk University for its lack of financial support for black students, and she sued a railroad for segregated seating. Such actions led the Memphis school board to refuse to renew her contract in 1891.

She bought a one-third interest in the Memphis paper, Free Speech and Highlight, increasing its circulation by 40 percent during the first year. Her editorial focus was the disenfranchisement of freedmen during Reconstruction, and she denounced Reconstruction officials for depriving black men of the vote. However, her greatest campaign was against lynching in the South, and she used her paper's forum to generate blistering attacks on the evils of lynching and its threat to any freedom African Americans might have gained from the Civil War amendments which freed them, protected their civil rights, and gave black men the vote. White journalists accused her of inciting violence through her denunciation of lynching.

Her campaign against lynching involved newspaper publishing, authorship of books on the subject—such as Southern Horrors in 1892—and political action, including urging boycotts of Memphis streetcars and militant resistance when necessary. Her work focused on the mythology of African American men's raping white women, and she inverted the sexual stereotypes by pointing out that it was white men who regularly raped black women. She denounced the stereotypes of the sexual promiscuity of black women, the purity and innocence of white women, the sexual prowess of black men, and the hero and savior status of white men who claimed their violent acts were simply to protect the purity of white Southern womanhood.

After fleeing Memphis in 1893 to escape threats and attacks against her life and newspaper, she wrote for papers in Chicago and New York and lived most of her remaining years in Chicago. She maintained lifelong involvement as a writer and activist in the causes for justice for African Americans and others. She gained national prominence in her writings concerning the exclusion of African Americans from the Columbian Exposition (or World's Fair) in Chicago in 1893. She organized a black women's club in Chicago called the Ida B. Wells Club, which she continued to head until her death. Through a lecture tour of Britain, she attracted large numbers to the anti-lynching campaign, winning their agreement to boycott American cotton in protest. In 1895 she published A Red Record, her most famous statement on the widespread evils of Southern lynching. She married Ferdinand L. Barnett, and they had four children. Barnett was a lawyer who had been the publisher of the Chicago Conservator, the city's first black weekly, which she purchased. She published this paper but also contributed to other newspapers throughout the nation, writing most often on the topic of lynching.

Wells supported women's suffrage but emphasized black women's role within the movement and formed the Alpha Suffrage Club which marched in suffrage parades with whites, despite opposition from some white suffrage leaders. In addition, she was appointed the first black female probation officer in the City of Chicago. She often worked with white women leaders such as Jane Addams, but she prodded them on issues of justice for African Americans while they focused on the sexual abuse of white women, as in the white slavery campaign against forced prostitution led by Addams and other white leaders. Along with Addams, she was a founding member of the National Association for the Advancement of Colored People but opposed its often gradualist efforts. In the disputes over immediate and radical action versus slower and more compromising efforts that occurred among black leaders during the period—with W. E. B. Du Bois being the most prominent spokesman for more radical action and Booker T. Washington for greater accommodation—Wells-Barnett sided with the radicals. However, as a woman, she was not accepted as an equal in the radical camp and openly quarreled with them. In 1928 she began her autobiography, Crusade for Justice, and, as the Great Depression worsened, in 1930 she ran as an independent for the Illinois Senate to address the appalling economic condition of blacks in Chicago slums but was defeated. She died in 1931. Her autobiography did not appear until 1970, when it was edited and published by her daughter.

As an African American woman activist and author, she was often given less respect and attention than male leaders of her race or her white counterparts within the women's movement. Scholars continue to concentrate on Wells-Barnett's recognition and reputation within the movement to enhance the status of blacks and of women at the turn of the twentieth century, but it is a struggle that continues to be needed in both arenas. She was the earliest and most effective critic of lynching in the South and the widespread loss of political rights for African Americans in the late nineteenth and early twentieth centuries, but she is seldom given the prominence she deserves in either American women's history or the history of African Americans.

The following selections are from Southern Horrors (1892) and A Red Record (1895).

HLS

Sources and Suggested Readings

Andrews, William L. "Crusader for Justice: Ida B. Wells." In *African American Autobiography: A Collection of Critical Essays.* Englewood Cliffs, N.J.: Prentice Hall, 1993.

Bederman, Gail. "'The White Man's Civilization on Trial': Ida B. Wells, Representations of Lynching, and Northern Middle-Class Manhood." In *Manliness and Civilization: A Cultural History of Gender and Race in the United States, 1880–1917.* Chicago: University of Chicago Press, 1995.

Boyd, Melba Joyce. "Review Essay: Canon Configuration for Ida B. Wells-Barnett." *Black Scholar* 24, 1 (1994): 8–13.

Carby, Hazel V. "'On the Threshold of Woman's Era': Lynching, Empire, and Sexuality in Black Feminist Theory." *Critical Inquiry* 12 (Autumn 1985) 262–77.

Davis, Simone W. "The 'Weak Race' and the Winchester: Political Voices in the Pamphlets of Ida B. Wells-Barnett." *Legacy* 12, 2 (1995): 77–97.

"Ida B. Wells: A Founder Who Never Knew Her Place." *The Crisis* 101, 1 (January 1994).

James, Joy. "The Anti-Violence Legacy of an 'Ancestor Mother.'" *Community Times* (West Lafayette, Ind.) 2, 2 (February 1995): 1, 8.

———. *Transcending the Talented Tenth: Black Leaders and American Intellectuals.* New York: Routledge, 1997.

Lengermann, Patricia Madoo, and Jill Niebrugge-Brantley. "Anna Julia Cooper (1858–1964) and Ida B. Wells-Barnett (1862–1931): The Foundations of Black Feminist Sociology." In *The Women Founders: Sociology and Social Theory 1830–1930.* Boston: McGraw Hill, 1998.

Marriott, Lucretia. *Guide to the Ida B. Wells Papers.* [Chicago]: Joseph Regenstein Library, 1978.

Wells-Barnett, Ida B. *Crusade for Justice: The Autobiography of Ida B. Wells.* Ed. Alfreda M. Duster. Chicago: University of Chicago Press, 1972.

———. *The Memphis Diary of Ida B. Wells.* Ed. Miriam DeCosta-Willis. Boston: Beacon Press, 1995.

———. *On Lynchings: Southern Horrors, A Red Record, Mob Rule in New Orleans.* New York: Arno Press and New York Times, 1969.

———. *Selected Works of Ida B. Wells-Barnett.* Comp. Trudier Harris. New York: Oxford University Press, 1991.

———. *Southern Horrors and Other Writings: The Anti-Lynching Campaign of Ida B. Wells, 1892–1900.* Ed. Jacqueline Jones Royster. Boston: St. Martin's Press (Bedford Books), 1997.

Southern Horrors: Lynch Law in All Its Phases (1892)

To the Afro-American women of New York and Brooklyn, whose race love, earnest zeal and unselfish effort at Lyric Hall, in the City of New York, on the night of October 5, 1892,—made possible its publication, this pamphlet is gratefully dedicated by the author.

Hon. Fred. Douglass's Letter.

Dear Miss Wells:

Let me give you thanks for your faithful paper on the lynch abomination generally practiced against colored people in the South. There has been no word equal to it in convincing power. I have spoken, but my word is feeble in comparison. You give us what you know and testify from actual knowledge. You have dealt with the facts with cool, painstaking fidelity and left those naked and uncontradicted facts to speak for themselves.

Brave woman! you have done your people and mine a service which can neither be weighed nor measured. If American conscience were only half alive, if the American church and clergy were only half christianized, if American moral sensibility were not hardened by persistent infliction of outrage and crime against colored people, a scream of horror, shame and indignation would rise to Heaven wherever your pamphlet shall be read.

But alas! even crime has power to reproduce itself and create conditions favorable to its own existence. It sometimes seems we are deserted by earth and Heaven —yet we must still think, speak and work, and trust in the power of a merciful God for final deliverance.

Very truly and gratefully yours,
Frederick Douglass.
Cedar Hill, Anacostia, D.C., Oct. 25, 1892.

Chapter I. The Offense

Wednesday evening May 24th, 1892, the city of Memphis was filled with excitement. Editorials in the daily papers of that date caused a meeting to be held in the Cotton Exchange Building; a committee was sent for the editors of the "Free Speech" an Afro-American journal published in that city, and the only reason the open threats of lynching that were made were not carried out was because they could not be found. The cause of all this commotion was the following editorial published in the "Free Speech" May 21st, 1892, the Saturday previous.

EIGHT NEGROES LYNCHED SINCE LAST ISSUE OF THE "FREE SPEECH" ONE AT LITTLE ROCK, ARK., LAST SATURDAY MORNING WHERE THE CITIZENS BROKE (?) INTO THE PENITENTIARY AND GOT THEIR MAN; THREE NEAR ANNISTON, ALA., ONE NEAR NEW ORLEANS; AND THREE AT CLARKSVILLE, GA., THE LAST THREE FOR KILLING A WHITE MAN, AND FIVE ON THE SAME OLD RACKET — THE NEW ALARM ABOUT RAPING WHITE WOMEN. THE SAME PROGRAMME OF HANGING, THEN SHOOTING BULLETS INTO THE LIFELESS BODIES WAS CARRIED OUT TO THE LETTER.

NOBODY IN THIS SECTION OF THE COUNTRY BELIEVES THE OLD THREADBARE LIE THAT NEGRO MEN RAPE WHITE WOMEN. IF SOUTHERN WHITE MEN ARE NOT CAREFUL, THEY WILL OVERREACH THEMSELVES AND PUBLIC SENTIMENT WILL HAVE A REACTION; A CONCLUSION WILL THEN BE REACHED WHICH WILL BE VERY DAMAGING TO THE MORAL REPUTATION OF THEIR WOMEN.

"The Daily Commercial" of Wednesday following, May 25th, contained the following leader:

THOSE NEGROES WHO ARE ATTEMPTING TO MAKE THE LYNCHING OF INDIVIDUALS OF THEIR RACE A MEANS FOR AROUSING THE WORST PASSIONS OF THEIR KIND ARE PLAYING WITH A DANGEROUS SENTIMENT. THE NEGROES MAY AS WELL UNDERSTAND THAT THERE IS NO MERCY FOR THE NEGRO RAPIST AND LITTLE PATIENCE WITH HIS DEFENDERS. A NEGRO ORGAN PRINTED IN THIS CITY, IN A RECENT ISSUE PUBLISHES THE FOLLOWING ATROCIOUS PARAGRAPH: 'NOBODY IN THIS SECTION OF THE COUNTRY BELIEVES THE OLD THREADBARE LIE THAT NEGRO MEN RAPE WHITE WOMEN. IF SOUTHERN WHITE MEN ARE NOT CAREFUL THEY WILL OVER-REACH THEMSELVES, AND PUBLIC SENTIMENT WILL HAVE A REACTION; AND A CONCLUSION WILL BE REACHED WHICH WILL BE VERY DAMAGING TO THE MORAL REPUTATION OF THEIR WOMEN.'

THE FACT THAT A BLACK SCOUNDREL IS ALLOWED TO LIVE AND UTTER SUCH LOATHSOME AND REPULSIVE CALUMNIES IS A VOLUME OF EVIDENCE AS TO THE WONDERFUL PATIENCE OF SOUTHERN WHITES. BUT WE HAVE HAD ENOUGH OF IT.

THERE ARE SOME THINGS THAT THE SOUTHERN WHITE MAN WILL NOT TOLERATE, AND THE OBSCENE INTIMATIONS OF THE FOREGOING HAVE BROUGHT THE WRITER TO THE VERY OUTERMOST LIMIT OF PUBLIC PATIENCE. WE HOPE WE HAVE SAID ENOUGH.

The "Evening Scimitar" of same date, copied the "Commercial's" editorial with these words of comment: "Patience under such circumstances is not a virtue. If the negroes themselves do not apply the rem-edy without delay it will be the duty of those whom he has attacked to tie the wretch who utters these calumnies to a stake at the intersection of Main and Madison Sts., brand him in the forehead with a hot iron and perform upon him a surgical operation with a pair of tailor's shears."

Acting upon this advice, the leading citizens met in the Cotton Exchange Building the same evening, and threats of lynching were freely indulged, not by the lawless element upon which the deviltry of the South is usually saddled — but by the leading business men, in their leading business centre. Mr. Fleming, the business manager and owning a half interest [in] the Free Speech, had to leave town to escape the mob, and was afterwards ordered not to return; letters and telegrams sent me in New York where I was spending my vacation advised me that bodily harm awaited my return. Creditors took possession of the office and sold the outfit, and the "Free Speech" was as if it had never been.

The editorial in question was prompted by the many inhuman and fiendish lynchings of Afro-Americans which have recently taken place and was meant as a warning. Eight lynched in one week and five of them charged with rape! The thinking public will not easily believe freedom and education more brutalizing than slavery, and the world knows that the crime of rape was unknown during four years of civil war, when the white women of the South were at the mercy of the race which is all at once charged with being a bestial one.

Since my business has been destroyed and I am an exile from home because of that editorial, the issue has been forced, and as the writer of it I feel that the race and the public generally should have a statement of the facts as they exist. They will serve at the same time as a defense for the Afro-American Sampsons who suffer themselves to be betrayed by white Delilahs.

The whites of Montgomery, Ala., knew J.C. Duke sounded the keynote of the situation — which they would gladly hide from the world, when he said in his paper, "The Herald," five years ago: "Why is it that white women attract negro men now more than in former days? There was a time when such a thing was unheard of. There is a secret to this thing, and we greatly suspect it is the growing appreciation of white Juliets for colored Romeos." Mr. Duke, like the "Free Speech" proprietors, was forced to leave the city for reflecting on the "honah" of white women and his paper suppressed; but the truth remains that Afro-American men do not always rape (?) white women without their consent.

Mr. Duke, before leaving Montgomery, signed a card disclaiming any intention of slandering Southern white women. The editor of the "Free Speech" has no disclaimer to enter, but asserts instead that there are many white women in the South who would marry colored men if such an act would not place them at once beyond the pale of society and within the clutches of the law. The miscegenation laws of the South only operate against the legitimate union of the races; they leave the white man free to seduce all the colored girls he can, but it is death to the colored man who yields to the force and advances of a similar attraction in white women. White men lynch the offending Afro-American, not because he is a despoiler of virtue, but because he succumbs to the smiles of white women.

Chapter II. The Black and White of It

The "Cleveland Gazette" of January 16, 1892, publishes a case in point. Mrs. J. S. Underwood, the wife of a minister of Elyria, Ohio, accused an Afro-American of rape. She told her husband that during his absence in 1888, stumping the State for the Prohibition Party, the man came to the kitchen door, forced his way in the house and insulted her. She tried to drive him out with a heavy poker, but he overpowered and chloroformed her, and when she revived her clothing was torn and she was in a horrible condition. She did not know the man but could identify him. She pointed out William Offett, a married man, who was arrested and, being in Ohio, was granted a trial.

The prisoner vehemently denied the charge of rape, but confessed he went to Mrs. Underwood's residence at her invitation and was criminally intimate with her at her request. This availed him nothing against the sworn testimony of a minister's wife, a lady of the highest respectability. He was found guilty, and entered the penitentiary, December 14, 1888, for fifteen years. Some time afterwards the woman's remorse led her to confess to her husband that the man was innocent.

These are her words: "I met Offett at the Post Office. It was raining. He was polite to me, and as I had several bundles in my arms he offered to carry them home for me, which he did. He had a strange fascination for me, and I invited him to call on me. He called, bringing chestnuts and candy for the children. By this means we got them to leave us alone in the room. Then I sat on his lap. He made a proposal to me and I readily consented. Why I did so, I do not know, but that I did is true. He visited me several times after that and each time I was indiscreet. I did not care after the first time. In fact I could not have resisted, and had no desire to resist."

When asked by her husband why she told him she had been outraged, she said: "I had several reasons for telling you. One was the neighbors saw the fellow here, another was, I was afraid I had contracted a loathsome disease, and still another was that I feared I might give birth to a Negro baby. I hoped to save my reputation by telling you a deliberate lie." Her husband, horrified by the confession, had Offett, who had already served four years, released and secured a divorce.

There are thousands of such cases throughout the South, with the difference that the Southern white men in insatiate fury wreak their vengeance without intervention of law upon the Afro-Americans who consort with their women. A few instances to substantiate the assertion that some white women love the company of the Afro-American will not be out of place. Most of these cases were reported by the daily papers of the South.

In the winter of 1885–6 the wife of a practicing physician in Memphis, in good social standing whose name has escaped me, left home, husband and children, and ran away with her black coachman. She was with him a month before her husband found and brought her home. The coachman could not be found. The doctor moved his family away from Memphis, and is living in another city under an assumed name.

In the same city last year a white girl in the dusk of evening screamed at the approach of some parties that a Negro had assaulted her on the street. He was captured, tried by a white judge and jury, that acquitted him of the charge. It is needless to add if there had been a scrap of evidence on which to convict him of so grave a charge he would have been convicted.

Sarah Clark of Memphis loved a black man and lived openly with him. When she was indicted last spring for miscegenation, she swore in court that she was *not* a white woman. This she did to escape the penitentiary and continued her illicit relation undisturbed. That she is of the lower class of whites, does not disturb the fact that she is a white woman. "The leading citizens" of Memphis are defending the "honor" of *all* white women, *demi-monde* included.

Since the manager of the "Free Speech" has been run away from Memphis by the guardians of the honor of Southern white women, a young girl living on Poplar St., who was discovered in intimate relations with a handsome mulatto young colored man, Will Morgan by name, stole her father's money to send the young fellow away from that father's wrath. She has since joined him in Chicago.

The Memphis *Ledger* for June 8th has the following: "If Lillie Bailey, a rather pretty white girl seventeen years of age, who is now at the City Hospital, would be somewhat less reserved about her disgrace there would be some very nauseating details in the story of her life. She is the mother of a little coon. The truth might reveal fearful depravity or it might reveal the evidence of a rank outrage. She will not divulge the name of the man who has left such black evidence of her disgrace, and, in fact, says it is a matter in which there can be no interest to the outside world. She came to Memphis nearly three months ago and was taken in at the Woman's Refuge in the southern part of the city. She remained there until a few weeks ago, when the child was born. The ladies in charge of the Refuge were horrified. The girl was at once sent to the City Hospital, where she has been since May 30th. She is a country girl. She came to Memphis from her father's farm, a short distance from Hernando, Miss. Just when she left there she would not say. In fact she says she came to Memphis from Arkansas, and says her home is in that State. She is rather good looking, has blue eyes, a low forehead and dark red hair. The ladies at the Woman's Refuge do not know anything about the girl further than what they learned when she was an inmate of the institution; and she would not tell much. When the child was born an attempt was made to get the girl to reveal the name of the Negro who had disgraced her, she obstinately refused and it was impossible to elicit any information from her on the subject."

Note the wording. "The truth might reveal fearful depravity or rank outrage." If it had been a white child or Lillie Bailey had told a pitiful story of Negro outrage, it would have been a case of woman's weakness or assault and she could have remained at the Woman's Refuge. But a Negro child and to withhold its father's name and thus prevent the killing of another Negro "rapist." A case of "fearful depravity."

The very week the "leading citizens" of Memphis were making a spectacle of themselves in defense of all white women of every kind, an Afro-American, M. Stricklin, was found in a white woman's room in that city. Although she made no outcry of rape, he was jailed and would have been lynched, but the woman stated she bought curtains of him (he was a furniture dealer) and his business in her room that night was to put them up. A white woman's word was taken as absolutely in this case as when the cry of rape is made, and he was freed.

What is true of Memphis is true of the entire South. The daily papers last year reported a farmer's wife in Alabama had given birth to a Negro child. When the Negro farmhand who was plowing in the field heard it he took the mule from the plow and fled. The dispatches also told of a woman in South Carolina who gave birth to a Negro child and charged three men with being its father, *every one of whom has since disappeared.* In Tuscumbia, Ala., the colored boy who was lynched there last year for assaulting a white girl

told her before his accusers that he had met her there in the woods often before.

Frank Weems of Chattanooga who was not lynched in May only because the prominent citizens became his body guard until the doors of the penitentiary closed on him, had letters in his pocket from the white woman in the case, making the appointment with him. Edward Coy who was burned alive in Texarkana, January 1, 1892, died protesting his innocence. Investigation since as given by the "Bystander" in the "Chicago Inter-Ocean," October 1, proves:

"1. The woman who was paraded as a victim of violence was of bad character; her husband was a drunkard and a gambler.

"2. She was publicly reported and generally known to have been criminally intimate with Coy for more than a year previous.

"3. She was compelled by threats, if not by violence, to make the charge against the victim.

"4. When she came to apply the match Coy asked her if she would burn him after they had 'been sweethearting' so long.

"5. A large majority of the 'superior' white men prominent in the affair are the reputed fathers of mulatto children.

"These are not pleasant facts, but they are illustrative of the vital phase of the so-called 'race question,' which should properly be designated an earnest inquiry as to the best methods by which religion, science, law and political power may be employed to excuse injustice, barbarity and crime done to a people because of race and color. There can be no possible belief that these people were inspired by any consuming zeal to vindicate God's law against miscegenationists of the most practical sort. The woman was a willing partner in the victim's guilt, and being of the 'superior' race must naturally have been more guilty."

In Natchez, Miss., Mrs. Marshall, one of the *creme de la creme* of the city, created a tremendous sensation several years ago. She has a black coachman who was married, and had been in her employ several years. During this time she gave birth to a child whose color was remarked, but traced to some brunette ancestor, and one of the fashionable dames of the city was its godmother. Mr. Marshall's social position was unquestioned, and wealth showered every dainty on this child which was idolized with its brothers and sisters by its white papa. In course of time another child appeared on the scene, but it was unmistakably dark. All were alarmed, and "rush of blood, strangulation" were the conjectures, but the doctor, when asked the cause, grimly told them it was a Negro child. There was a family conclave, the coachman heard of it and leaving his own family went West, and has never returned. As soon as Mrs. Marshall was able to travel she was sent away in deep disgrace. Her husband died within the year of a broken heart.

Ebenzer Fowler, the wealthiest colored man in Issaquena County, Miss., was shot down on the street in Mayersville, January 30, 1885, just before dark by an armed body of white men who filled his body with bullets. They charged him with writing a note to a white woman of the place, which they intercepted and which proved there was an intimacy existing between them.

Hundreds of such cases might be cited, but enough have been given to prove the assertion that there are white women in the South who love the Afro-American's company even as there are white men notorious for their preference for Afro-American women.

There is hardly a town in the South which has not an instance of the kind which is well-known, and hence the assertion is reiterated that "nobody in the South believes the old threadbare lie that negro men rape white women." Hence there is a growing demand among Afro-Americans that the guilt or innocence of parties accused of rape be fully established. They know the men of the section of the country who refuse this are not so desirous of punishing rapists as they pretend. The utterances of the leading white men show that with them it is not the crime but the *class*. Bishop Fitzgerald has become apologist for lynchers of the rapists of *white* women only. Governor Tillman, of South Carolina, in the month of June, standing under the tree in Barnwell, S.C., on which eight Afro-Americans were hung last year, declared that he would lead a mob to lynch a ["]negro who raped a *white* woman." So say the pulpits, officials and newspapers of the South. But when the victim is a colored woman it is different.

Last winter in Baltimore, Md., three white ruffians assaulted a Miss Camphor, a young Afro-American girl, while out walking with a young man of her own race. They held her escort and outraged the girl. It was a deed dastardly enough to arouse Southern blood, which gives its horror of rape as excuse for lawlessness, but she was an Afro-American. The case went to the courts, and an Afro-American lawyer defended the men and they were acquitted.

In Nashville, Tenn., there is a white man, Pat Hanifan, who outraged a little Afro-American girl, and, from the physical injuries received, she has been ruined for life. He was jailed for six months, discharged, and is now a detective in that city. In the same city, last May, a white man outraged an Afro-American girl in a drug store. He was arrested, and released on bail at the trial. It was rumored that five hundred Afro-Americans had organized to lynch him. Two hundred and fifty white citizens armed themselves with Winchesters and

guarded him. A cannon was placed in front of his home, and the Buchanan Rifles (State Militia) ordered to the scene for his protection. The Afro-American mob did not materialize. Only two weeks before Eph. Grizzard, who had only been *charged* with rape upon a white woman, had been taken from the jail, with Governor Buchanan and the police and militia standing by, dragged through the streets in broad daylight, knives plunged into him at every step, and with every fiendish cruelty a frenzied mob could devise, he was at last swung out on the bridge with hands cut to pieces as he tried to climb up the stanchions. A naked, bloody example of the blood-thirstiness of the nineteenth century civilization of the Athens of the South! No cannon or military was called out in his defense. He dared to visit a white woman.

At the very moment these civilized whites were announcing their determination "to protect their wives and daughters," by murdering Grizzard, a white man was in the same jail for raping eight-year-old Maggie Reese, an Afro-American girl. He was not harmed. The "honor" of grown women who were glad enough to be supported by the Grizzard boys and Ed Coy, as long as the liaison was not known, needed protection; they were white. The outrage upon helpless childhood needed no avenging in this case; she was black.

A white man in Guthrie, Oklahoma Territory, two months ago inflicted such injuries upon another Afro-American child that she died. He was not punished, but an attempt was made in the same town in the month of June to lynch an Afro-American who visited a white woman.

In Memphis, Tenn., in the month of June, Ellerton L. Dorr, who is the husband of Russell Hancock's widow, was arrested for attempted rape on Mattie Cole, a neighbor's cook; he was only prevented from accomplishing his purpose, by the appearance of Mattie's employer. Dorr's friends say he was drunk and not responsible for his actions. The grand jury refused to indict him and he was discharged.

Chapter III. The New Cry

The appeal of Southern whites to Northern sympathy and sanction, the adroit, insidious plea made by Bishop Fitzgerald for suspension of judgment because those "who condemn lynching express no sympathy for the *white* woman in the case," falls to the ground in the light of the foregoing.

From this exposition of the race issue in lynch law, the whole matter is explained by the well-known opposition growing out of slavery to the progress of the race. This is crystallized in the oft-repeated slogan: "This is a white man's country and the white man must rule."

The South resented giving the Afro-American his freedom, the ballot box and the Civil Rights Law. The raids of the Ku-Klux and White Liners to subvert reconstruction government, the Hamburg and Ellerton, S.C., the Copiah County Miss., and the Layfayette Parish, La., massacres were excused as the natural resentment of intelligence against government by ignorance.

Honest white men practically conceded the necessity of intelligence murdering ignorance to correct the mistake of the general government, and the race was left to the tender mercies of the solid South. Thoughtful Afro-Americans with the strong arm of the government withdrawn and with the hope to stop such wholesale massacres urged the race to sacrifice its political rights for sake of peace. They honestly believed the race should fit itself for government, and when that should be done, the objection to race participation in politics would be removed.

But the sacrifice did not remove the trouble, nor move the South to Justice. One by one the Southern States have legally (?) disfranchised the Afro-American, and since the repeal of the Civil Rights Bill nearly every Southern State has passed separate car laws with a penalty against their infringement. The race regardless of advancement is penned into filthy, stifling partitions cut off from smoking cars. All this while, although the political cause has been removed, the butcheries of black men at Barnwell, S.C., Carrolton, Miss., Waycross, Ga., and Memphis, Tenn., have gone on; also the flaying alive of a man in Kentucky, the burning of one in Arkansas, the hanging of a fifteen-year-old girl in Louisiana, a woman in Jackson, Tenn., and one in Hollendale, Miss., until the dark and bloody record of the South shows 728 Afro-Americans lynched during the past 8 years. Not 50 of these were for political causes; the rest were for all manner of accusations from that of rape of white women, to the case of the boy Will Lewis who was hanged at Tullahoma, Tenn., last year for being drunk and "sassy" to white folks.

These statistics compiled by the Chicago "Tribune" were given the first of the year (1892). Since then, not less than one hundred and fifty have been known to have met violent death at the hands of cruel bloodthirsty mobs during the past nine months.

To palliate this record (which grows worse as the Afro-American becomes intelligent) and excuse some of the most heinous crimes that ever stained the history of a country, the South is shielding itself behind the plausible screen of defending the honor of its women. This, too, in the face of the fact that only *one-third* of the 728 victims to mobs have been *charged* with rape, to say nothing of those of that one-third who were innocent of the charge. A white correspondent of the Baltimore Sun declares that the Afro-American who was lynched in Chestertown, Md., in May for assault on a white girl was innocent; that the deed was done by a white man who had since disappeared. The girl herself maintained that her assailant was a white man. When that poor Afro-American was murdered, the whites excused their refusal of a trial on the ground that they wished to spare the white girl the mortification of having to testify in court.

This cry has had its effect. It has closed the heart, stifled the conscience, warped the judgment and hushed the voice of press and pulpit on the subject of lynch law throughout this "land of liberty." Men who stand high in the esteem of the public for christian character, for moral and physical courage, for devotion to the principles of equal and exact justice to all, and for great sagacity, stand as cowards who fear to open their mouths before this great outrage. They do not see that by their tacit encouragement, their silent acquiescence, the black shadow of lawlessness in the form of lynch law is spreading its wings over the whole country.

Men who, like Governor Tillman, start the ball of lynch law rolling for a certain crime, are powerless to stop it when drunken or criminal white toughs feel like hanging an Afro-American on any pretext.

Even to the better class of Afro-Americans the crime of rape is so revolting they have too often taken the white man's word and given lynch law neither the investigation nor condemnation it deserved.

They forget that a concession of the right to lynch a man for a certain crime, not only concedes the right to lynch any person for any crime, but (so frequently is the cry of rape now raised) it is in a fair way to stamp us a race of rapists and desperadoes. They have gone on hoping and believing that general education and financial strength would solve the difficulty, and are devoting their energies to the accumulation of both.

The mob spirit has grown with the increasing intelligence of the Afro-American. It has left the out-of-the-way places where ignorance prevails, has thrown off the mask and with this new cry stalks in broad daylight in large cities, the centres of civilization, and is encouraged by the "leading citizens" and the press.

Chapter IV. The Malicious and Untruthful White Press

The "Daily Commercial" and "Evening Scimitar" of Memphis, Tenn., are owned by leading businessmen of that city, and yet, in spite of the fact that there had been no white woman in Memphis outraged by an Afro-American, and that Memphis possessed a thrifty law-abiding, property owning class of Afro-Americans the "Commercial" of May 17th, under the head of "More Rapes, More Lynchings" gave utterance to the following:

THE LYNCHING OF THREE NEGRO SCOUNDRELS REPORTED IN OUR DISPATCHES FROM ANNISTON, ALA., FOR A BRUTAL OUTRAGE COMMITTED UPON A WHITE WOMAN WILL BE A TEXT FOR MUCH COMMENT ON 'SOUTHERN BARBARISM' BY NORTHERN NEWSPAPERS; BUT WE FANCY IT WILL HARDLY PROVE EFFECTIVE FOR CAMPAIGN PURPOSES AMONG INTELLIGENT PEOPLE. THE FREQUENCY OF THESE LYNCHINGS CALLS ATTENTION TO THE FREQUENCY OF THE CRIMES WHICH CAUSES LYNCHING. THE 'SOUTHERN BARBARISM' WHICH DESERVES THE SERIOUS ATTENTION OF ALL PEOPLE NORTH AND SOUTH, IS THE BARBARISM WHICH PREYS UPON WEAK AND DEFENSELESS WOMEN. NOTHING BUT THE MOST PROMPT, SPEEDY AND EXTREME PUNISHMENT CAN HOLD IN CHECK THE HORRIBLE AND BESTIAL PROPENSITIES OF THE NEGRO RACE. THERE IS A STRANGE SIMILARITY ABOUT A NUMBER OF CASES OF THIS CHARACTER WHICH HAVE LATELY OCCURRED.

IN EACH CASE THE CRIME WAS DELIBERATELY PLANNED AND PERPETRATED BY SEVERAL NEGROES. THEY WATCHED FOR AN OPPORTUNITY WHEN THE WOMEN WERE LEFT WITHOUT A PROTECTOR. IT WAS NOT A SUDDEN YIELDING TO A FIT OF PASSION, BUT THE CONSUMMATION OF A DEVILISH PURPOSE WHICH HAS BEEN SEEKING AND WAITING FOR THE OPPORTUNITY. THIS FEATURE OF THE CRIME NOT ONLY MAKES IT THE MOST FIENDISHLY BRUTAL, BUT IT ADDS TO THE TERROR OF THE SITUATION IN THE THINLY SETTLED COUNTRY COMMUNITIES. NO MAN CAN LEAVE HIS FAMILY AT NIGHT WITHOUT THE DREAD THAT SOME ROVING NEGRO RUFFIAN IS WATCHING AND WAITING FOR THIS OPPORTUNITY. THE SWIFT PUNISHMENT WHICH INVARIABLY FOLLOWS THESE HORRIBLE CRIMES DOUBTLESS ACTS AS A DETERRING EFFECT UPON THE NEGROES IN THAT IMMEDIATE NEIGHBORHOOD FOR A SHORT TIME. BUT THE LESSON IS NOT WIDELY LEARNED NOR LONG REMEMBERED. THEN SUCH CRIMES, EQUALLY ATROCIOUS, HAVE HAPPENED IN QUICK SUCCESSION, ONE IN TENNESSEE, ONE IN ARKANSAS, AND ONE IN ALABAMA. THE FACTS OF THE CRIME APPEAR TO APPEAL MORE TO THE NEGRO'S LUSTFUL IMAGINATION THAN THE FACTS OF THE PUNISHMENT DO TO HIS FEARS. HE SETS ASIDE ALL FEAR OF DEATH IN ANY FORM WHEN OPPORTUNITY IS FOUND FOR THE GRATIFICATION OF HIS BESTIAL DESIRES.

THERE IS SMALL REASON TO HOPE FOR ANY CHANGE FOR THE BETTER. THE COMMISSION OF THIS CRIME GROWS MORE FREQUENT EVERY YEAR. THE GENERATION OF NEGROES WHICH HAVE GROWN UP SINCE THE WAR HAVE LOST IN LARGE MEASURE THE TRADITIONAL AND WHOLESOME AWE OF THE WHITE RACE WHICH KEPT THE NEGROES IN SUBJECTION, EVEN WHEN THEIR MASTERS WERE IN THE ARMY, AND THEIR FAMILIES LEFT UNPROTECTED EXCEPT BY THE SLAVES THEMSELVES. THERE IS NO LONGER A RESTRAINT UPON THE BRUTE PASSION OF THE NEGRO.

WHAT IS TO BE DONE? THE CRIME OF RAPE IS ALWAYS HORRIBLE, BUT THE SOUTHERN MAN THERE IS NOTHING WHICH SO FILLS THE SOUL WITH HORROR, LOATHING AND FURY AS THE OUTRAGING OF A WHITE WOMAN BY A NEGRO. IT IS THE RACE QUESTION IN THE UGLIEST, VILEST, MOST DANGEROUS ASPECT. THE NEGRO AS A POLITICAL FACTOR CAN BE CONTROLLED. BUT NEITHER LAWS NOR LYNCHINGS CAN SUBDUE HIS LUSTS. SOONER OR LATER IT WILL FORCE A CRISIS. WE DO NOT KNOW IN WHAT FORM IT WILL COME.

In its issue of June 4th, the Memphis "Evening Scimitar" gives the following excuse for lynch law:

ASIDE FROM THE VIOLATION OF WHITE WOMEN BY NEGROES, WHICH IS THE OUTCROPPING OF A BESTIAL PERVERSION OF INSTINCT, THE CHIEF CAUSE OF TROUBLE BETWEEN THE RACES IN THE SOUTH IS THE NEGRO'S LACK OF MANNERS. IN THE STATE OF SLAVERY HE LEARNED POLITENESS FROM ASSOCIATION WITH WHITE PEOPLE, WHO TOOK PAINS TO TEACH HIM. SINCE THE EMANCIPATION CAME AND THE TIE OF MUTUAL INTEREST AND REGARD BETWEEN MASTER AND SERVANT WAS BROKEN, THE NEGRO HAS DRIFTED AWAY INTO A STATE WHICH IS NEITHER FREEDOM NOR BONDAGE. LACKING THE PROPER INSPIRATION OF THE ONE AND THE RESTRAINING FORCE OF THE OTHER HE HAS TAKEN UP THE IDEA THAT BOORISH INSOLENCE IS INDEPENDENCE, AND THE EXERCISE OF A DECENT DEGREE OF BREEDING TOWARD WHITE PEOPLE IS IDENTICAL WITH SERVILE SUBMISSION. IN CONSEQUENCE OF THE PREVALENCE OF THIS NOTION THERE ARE MANY NEGROES WHO USE EVERY OPPORTUNITY TO MAKE THEMSELVES OFFENSIVE, PARTICULARLY WHEN THEY THINK IT CAN BE DONE WITH IMPUNITY.

WE HAVE HAD TOO MANY INSTANCES RIGHT HERE IN MEMPHIS TO DOUBT THIS, AND OUR EXPERIENCE IS NOT EXCEPTIONAL. *THE WHITE PEOPLE WON'T STAND THIS SORT OF THING, AND WHETHER THEY BE INSULTED AS INDIVIDUALS OR AS A RACE, THE RESPONSE WILL BE PROMPT AND EFFECTUAL.* THE BLOODY RIOT OF 1866, IN WHICH SO MANY NEGROES PERISHED, WAS BROUGHT ON PRINCIPALLY BY THE OUTRAGEOUS CONDUCT OF THE BLACKS TOWARD THE WHITES ON THE STREETS. IT IS ALSO A REMARKABLE AND DISCOURAGING FACT THAT THE MAJORITY OF SUCH SCOUNDRELS ARE NEGROES WHO HAVE RECEIVED EDUCATIONAL ADVANTAGES AT THE HANDS OF THE WHITE TAXPAYERS. THEY HAVE GOT JUST ENOUGH OF LEARNING TO MAKE THEM REALIZE HOW HOPELESSLY THEIR RACE IS BEHIND THE OTHER IN EVERYTHING THAT MAKES A GREAT PEOPLE, AND THEY ATTEMPT TO 'GET EVEN' BY INSOLENCE, WHICH IS EVER THE RESENTMENT OF INFERIORS. THERE ARE WELL-BRED NEGROES AMONG US, AND IT IS TRULY UNFORTUNATE THAT THEY SHOULD HAVE TO PAY, EVEN IN PART, THE PENALTY OF THE OFFENSES COMMITTED BY THE BASER SORT, BUT THIS IS THE WAY OF THE WORLD. THE INNOCENT MUST SUFFER FOR THE GUILTY. IF THE NEGROES AS A PEOPLE POSSESSED A HUNDREDTH PART OF THE SELF-RESPECT WHICH IS EVIDENCED BY THE COURTEOUS BEARING OF SOME THAT THE "SCIMITAR" COULD NAME, THE FRICTION BETWEEN THE RACES WOULD BE REDUCED TO A MINIMUM. IT WILL NOT DO TO BEG THE QUESTION BY PLEADING THAT MANY WHITE MEN ARE ALSO STIRRING UP STRIFE. THE CAUCASIAN BLACKGUARD SIMPLY OBEYS THE PROMPTINGS OF A DEPRAVED DISPOSITION, AND HE IS SELDOM DELIBERATELY ROUGH OR OFFENSIVE TOWARD STRANGERS OR UNPROTECTED WOMEN.

THE NEGRO TOUGH, ON THE CONTRARY, IS GIVEN TO JUST THAT KIND OF OFFENDING, AND HE ALMOST INVARIABLY SINGLES OUT WHITE PEOPLE AS HIS VICTIMS.

On March 9th, 1892, there were lynched in this same city three of the best specimens of young since-the-war Afro-American manhood. They were peaceful, law-abiding citizens and energetic businessmen.

They believed the problem was to be solved by eschewing politics and putting money in the purse. They owned a flourishing grocery business in a thickly populated suburb of Memphis, and a white man named Barrett had one on the opposite corner. After a personal difficulty which Barrett sought by going into the "People's Grocery" drawing a pistol and was thrashed by Calvin McDowell, he (Barrett) threatened to "clean them out." These men were a mile beyond the city limits and police protection; hearing that Barrett's crowd was coming to attack them Saturday night, they mustered forces and prepared to defend themselves against the attack.

When Barrett came he led a *posse* of officers, twelve in number, who afterward claimed to be hunting a man for whom they had a warrant. That twelve men in citizen's clothes should think it necessary to go in the night to hunt one man who had never before been arrested, or made any record as a criminal has never been explained. When they entered the back door the young men thought the threatened attack was on, and fired into them. Three of the officers were wounded, and when the *defending* party found it was the officers of the law upon whom they had fired, they ceased and got away.

Thirty-one men were arrested and thrown in jail as "conspirators," although they all declared more than once they did not know they were firing on officers. Excitement was at fever heat until the morning papers, two days after, announced that the wounded deputy sheriffs were out of danger. This hindered rather than helped the plans of the whites. There was no law on the statute books which would execute an Afro-American for wounding a white man, but the "unwritten law" did. Three of these men, the president, the manager and clerk of the grocery—"the leaders of the conspiracy"—were secretly taken from jail and lynched in a shockingly brutal manner. "The Negroes are getting too independent," they say, "we must teach them a lesson."

What lesson? The lesson of subordination. "Kill the leaders and it will cow the Negro who dares to shoot a white man, even in self-defense."

Although the race was wild over the outrage, the mockery of law and justice which disarmed men and locked them up in jails where they could be easily and safely reached by the mob—the Afro-American ministers, newspapers and leaders counselled obedience to the law which did not protect them.

Their counsel was heeded and not a hand was uplifted to resent the outrage; following the advice of the "Free Speech," people left the city in great numbers.

The dailies and associated press reports heralded these men to the country as "toughs," and "Negro desperadoes who kept a low dive." This same press service printed that the Negro who was lynched at Indianola, Miss., in May, had outraged the sheriff's eight-year-old daughter. The girl was more than eighteen years old, and was found by her father in this man's room, who was a servant on the place.

Not content with misrepresenting the race, the mob-spirit was not to be satisfied until the paper which was doing all it could to counteract this impression was silenced. The colored people were resenting their bad treatment in a way to make itself felt, yet gave the mob no excuse for further murder, until the appearance of the editorial which is construed as a reflection on the "honor" of the Southern white women. It is not half so libelous as that of the "Commercial" which appeared four days before, and which has been given in these pages. They would have lynched the manager of the "Free Speech" for exercising the right of free speech if they had found him as quickly as they would have hung a rapist, and glad of the excuse to do so. The owners were ordered not to return, "The Free Speech" was suspended with as little compunction as the business of the "People's Grocery" broken up and the proprietors murdered.

Chapter V. The South's Position

Henry W. Grady in his well-remembered speeches in New England and New York pictured the Afro-American as incapable of self-government. Through him and other leading men the cry of the South to the country has been "Hands off! Leave us to solve our problem." To the Afro-American the South says, "the white man must and will rule." There is little difference between the Ante-bellum South and the New South.

Her white citizens are wedded to any method however revolting, any measure however extreme, for the subjugation of the young manhood of the race. They have cheated him out of his ballot, deprived him of civil rights or redress therefore in the civil courts, robbed him of the fruits of his labor, and are still murdering, burning and lynching him.

The result is a growing disregard of human life. Lynch law has spread its insidious influence till men in New York State, Pennsylvania and on the free Western plains feel they can take the law in their own hands with impunity, especially where an Afro-American is concerned. The South is brutalized to a degree not realized by its own inhabitants, and the very foundation of government, law and order, are imperilled.

Public sentiment has had a slight "reaction" though not sufficient to stop the crusade of lawlessness and lynching. The spirit of christianity of the great M. E. Church was aroused to the frequent and revolting crimes against a weak people, enough to pass strong condemnatory resolutions at its General Conference in Omaha last May. The spirit of justice of the grand old party asserted itself sufficiently to secure a denunciation of the wrongs, and a feeble declaration of the belief in human rights in the Republican platform at Minneapolis, June 7th. Some of the great dailies and weeklies have swung into line declaring that lynch law must go. The President of the United States issued a proclamation that it be not tolerated in the territories over which he has jurisdiction. Governor Northern and Chief Justice Bleckley of Georgia have proclaimed against it. The citizens of Chattanooga, Tenn., have set a worthy example in that they not only condemn lynch law, but her public men demanded a trial for Weems, the accused rapist, and guarded him while the trial was in progress. The trial only lasted ten minutes, and Weems chose to plead guilty and accept twenty-one years sentence, than invite the certain death which awaited him outside that cordon of police if he had told the truth and shown the letters he had from the white woman in the case.

Col. A.S. Colyar, of Nashville, Tenn., is so overcome with the horrible state of affairs that he addressed the following earnest letter to the Nashville "American." "Nothing since I have been a reading man has so impressed me with the decay of manhood among the people of Tennessee as the dastardly submission to the mob reign. We have reached the unprecedented low level; the awful criminal depravity of substituting the mob for the court and jury, of giving up the jail keys to the mob whenever they are demanded. We do it in the largest cities and in the country towns; we do it in midday; we do it after full, not to say formal, notice, and so thoroughly and generally is it acquiesced in that the murderers have discarded the formula of masks. They go into the town where everybody knows them, sometimes under the gaze of the governor, in the presence of the courts, in the presence of the sheriff and his deputies, in the presence of the entire police force, take out the prisoner, take his life, often with fiendish glee, and often with acts of cruelty and barbarism which impress the reader with a degeneracy rapidly approaching savage life. That the State is disgraced but faintly expresses the humiliation which has settled upon the once proud people of Tennessee. The State, in its majesty, through its organized life, for which the people pay liberally, makes but one record, but one note, and that a criminal falsehood, 'was hung by persons to the jury unknown.' The murder at Shelbyville is only a verification of what every intelligent man knew would come, because with a mob a rumor is as good as a proof."

These efforts brought forth apologies and a short halt, but the lynching mania was raged again through the past three months with unabated fury.

The strong arm of the law must be brought to bear upon lynchers in severe punishment, but this cannot and will not be done unless a healthy public sentiment demands and sustains such action.

The men and women in the South who disapprove of lynching and remain silent on the perpetration of such outrages, are particeps criminis, accomplices, accessories before and after the fact, equally guilty with the actual law-breakers who would not persist if they did not know that neither the law nor militia would be employed against them.

Chapter VI. Self Help

In the creation of this healthier public sentiment, the Afro-American can do for himself what no one else can do for him. The world looks on with wonder that we have conceded so much and remain law-abiding under such great outrage and provocation.

To Northern capital and Afro-American labor the South owes its rehabilitation. If labor is withdrawn capital will not remain. The Afro-American is thus the backbone of the South. A thorough knowledge and judicious exercise of this power in lynching localities could many times effect a bloodless revolution. The white man's dollar is his god and to stop this will be to stop outrages in many localities.

The Afro-Americans of Memphis denounced the lynching of three of their best citizens, and urged and waited for the authorities to act in the matter and bring the lynchers to justice. No attempt was made to do so, and the black men left the city by thousands, bringing about great stagnation in every branch of business. Those who remained so injured the business of the street car company by staying off the cars, that the superintendent, manager and treasurer called personally on the editor of the "Free Speech," asked them to urge our people to give them their patronage again. Other business men became alarmed over the situation and the "Free Speech" was run away that the colored people might be more easily controlled. A meeting of white citizens in June, three months after the lynching, passed resolutions for the first time, condemning it. *But they did not punish the lynchers.* Every one of them was known by name, because they had been selected to do the dirty work, by some of the very citizens who passed these resolutions. Memphis is fast losing her black population, who proclaim as they go that there is not protection for the life and property of any Afro-American citizen in Memphis who is not a slave.

The Afro-American citizens of Kentucky, whose intellectual and financial improvement has been phenomenal, have never had a separate car law until now.

Delegations and petitions poured into the Legislation against it, yet the bill passed and the Jim Crow Car of Kentucky is a legalized institution. Will the great mass of Negroes continue to patronize the railroad? A special from Covington, Ky., says:

COVINGTON, JUNE 13TH. — THE RAILROADS OF THE STATE ARE BEGINNING TO FEEL VERY MARKEDLY, THE EFFECTS OF THE SEPARATE COACH BILL RECENTLY PASSED BY THE LEGISLATURE. NO CLASS OF PEOPLE IN THE STATE HAVE SO MANY AND SO LARGELY ATTENDED EXCURSIONS AS THE BLACKS. ALL THESE HAVE BEEN ABANDONED, AND REGULAR TRAVEL IS REDUCED TO A MINIMUM. A COMPETENT AUTHORITY SAYS THE LOSS TO THE VARIOUS ROADS WILL REACH $1,000,000 THIS YEAR.

A call to a State Conference in Lexington, Ky., last June had delegates from every county in the State. Those delegates, the ministers, teachers, heads of secret and others orders, and the head of every family should pass the word around for every member of the race in Kentucky to stay off railroads unless obliged to ride. If they did so, and their advice was followed persistently the convention would not need to petition the Legislature to repeal the law or raise money to file a suit. The railroad corporations would be so affected they would in self-defense lobby to have the separate car law repealed. On the other hand, as long as the railroads can get Afro-American excursions they will always have plenty of money to fight all the suits brought against them. They will be aided in so doing by the same partisan public sentiment which passed the law. White men passed the law, and white judges and juries would pass upon the suits against the law, and render judgment in line with their prejudices and in deference to the greater financial power.

The appeal to the white man's pocket has ever been more effectual than all the appeals ever made to his conscience. Nothing, absolutely nothing, is to be gained by a further sacrifice of manhood and self-respect. By the right exercise of his power as the industrial factor of the South, the Afro-American can demand and secure his rights, the punishment of lynchers, and a fair trial for accused rapists.

Of the many inhuman outrages of this present year, the only case where the proposed lynching did *not* occur, was where the men armed themselves in Jacksonville, Fla., and Paducah, Ky., and prevented it. The only times an Afro-American who was assaulted got away has been when he had a gun and used it in self-defense.

The lesson this teaches and which every Afro-American should ponder well, is that a Winchester rifle should have a place of honor in every black home, and it should be used for that protection which the law

refuses to give. When the white man who is always the aggressor knows he runs as great risk of biting the dust every time his Afro-American victim does, he will have greater respect for Afro-American life. The more the Afro-American yields and cringes and begs, the more he has to do so, the more he is insulted, outraged and lynched.

The assertion has been substantiated throughout these pages that the press contains unreliable and doctored reports of lynchings, and one of the most necessary things for the race to do is to get these facts before the public. The people must know before they can act, and there is no educator to compare with the press.

The Afro-American papers are the only ones which will print the truth, and they lack means to employ agents and detectives to get at the facts. The race must rally a mighty host to the support of their journals, and thus enable them to do much in the way of investigation.

A lynching occurred at Port Jarvis, N.Y., the first week in June. A white and colored man were implicated in the assault upon a white girl. It was charged that the white man paid the colored boy to make the assault, which he did on the public highway in broad day time, and was lynched. This, too was done by "parties unknown." The white man in the case still lives. He was imprisoned and promises to fight the case on trial. At the preliminary examination, it developed that he had been a suitor of the girl's. She had repulsed and refused him, yet had given him money, and he had sent threatening letters demanding more.

The day before this examination she was so wrought up, she left home and wandered miles away. When found she said she did so because she was afraid of the man's testimony. Why should she be afraid of the prisoner? Why should she yield to his demands for money if not to prevent him exposing something he knew? It seems explainable only on the hypothesis that a *liaison* existed between the colored boy and the girl, and the white man knew of it. The press is singularly silent. Has it a motive? We owe it to ourselves to find out.

The story comes from Larned, Kansas, Oct. 1st, that a young white lady held at bay until daylight, without alarming any one in the house, "a burly Negro" who entered her room and bed. The "burly Negro" was promptly lynched without investigation or examination of inconsistent stories.

A house was found burned down near Montgomery, Ala., in Monroe County, Oct. 13th, a few weeks ago; also the burned bodies of the owners and melted piles of gold and silver.

These discoveries led to the conclusion that the

awful crime was not prompted by motives of robbery. The suggestion of the whites was that "brutal lust was the incentive, and as there are nearly 200 Negroes living within a radius of five miles of the place the conclusion was inevitable that some of them were the perpetrators."

Upon this "suggestion" probably made by the real criminal, the mob acted upon the "conclusion" and arrested ten Afro-Americans, four of whom, they tell the world, confessed to the deed of murdering Richard L. Johnson and outraging his daughter, Jeanette. These four men, Berrell Jones, Moses Johnson, Jim and John Packer, none of them 25 years of age, upon this conclusion, were taken from jail, hanged, shot, and burned while yet alive the night of Oct. 12th. The same report says Mr. Johnson was on the best terms with his Negro tenants.

The race thus outraged must find out the facts of this awful hurling of men into eternity on supposition, and give them to the indifferent and apathetic country. We feel this to be a garbled report, but how can we prove it?

Near Vicksburg, Miss., a murder was committed by a gang of burglars. Of course it must have been done by Negroes, and Negroes were arrested for it. It is believed that 2 men, Smith Tooley and John Adams belonged to a gang controlled by white men and, fearing exposure, on the night of July 4th, they were hanged in the Courthouse yard by those interested in silencing them. Robberies since committed in the same vicinity have been known to be by white men who had their faces blackened. We strongly believe in the innocence of these murdered men, but we have no proof. No other news goes out to the world save that which stamps us as a race of cutthroats, robbers and lustful wild beasts. So great is Southern hate and prejudice, they legally (?) hung poor little thirteen-year-old Mildrey Brown at Columbia, S.C., Oct. 7th, on the circumstantial evidence that she poisoned a white infant. If her guilt had been proven unmistakably, had she been white, Mildrey Brown would never have been hung.

The country would have been aroused and South Carolina disgraced forever for such a crime. The Afro-American himself did not know as he should have known as his journals should be in a position to have him know and act.

Nothing is more definitely settled than he must act for himself. I have shown how he may employ the boycott, emigration and the press, and I feel that by a combination of all these agencies can be effectually stamped out lynch law, that last relic of barbarism and slavery. "The gods help those who help themselves."

A Red Record (1895)

Chapter I. The Case Stated

The student of American sociology will find the year 1894 marked by a pronounced awakening of the public conscience to a system of anarchy and outlawry which had grown during a series of ten years to be so common, that scenes of unusual brutality failed to have any visible effect upon the humane sentiments of the people of our land.

Beginning with the emancipation of the Negro, the inevitable result of unbridled power exercised for two and a half centuries, by the white man over the Negro, began to show itself in acts of conscienceless outlawry. During the slave regime, the Southern white man owned the Negro body and soul. It was to his interest to dwarf the soul and preserve the body. Vested with unlimited power over his slave, to subject him to any and all kinds of physical punishment, the white man was still restrained from such punishment as tended to injure the slave by abating his physical powers and thereby reducing his financial worth. While slaves were scourged mercilessly, and in countless cases inhumanly treated in other respects, still the white owner rarely permitted his anger to go so far as to take a life, which would entail upon him a loss of several hundred dollars. The slave was rarely killed, he was too valuable; it was easier and quite as effective, for discipline or revenge, to sell him "Down South."

But Emancipation came and the vested interests of the white man in the Negro's body were lost. The white man had no right to scourge the emancipated Negro, still less has he a right to kill him. But the Southern white people had been educated so long in that school of practice, in which might makes right, that they disdained to draw strict lines of action in dealing with the Negro. In slave times the Negro was kept subservient and submissive by the frequency and severity of the scourging, but, with freedom, a new system of intimidation came into vogue; the Negro was not only whipped and scourged; he was killed.

Not all nor nearly all of the murders done by white men during the past thirty years in the South, have come to light, but the statistics as gathered and preserved by white men, and which have not been questioned, show that during these years more than ten thousand Negroes have been killed in cold blood, without the formality of judicial trial and legal execution. And yet, as evidence of the absolute impunity with which the white man dares to kill a Negro, the same record shows that during all these years, and for all these murders only three white men have been tried, convicted, and executed. As no white man has been lynched for the murder of colored people, these three executions are the only instances of the death penalty being visited upon white men for murdering Negroes.

Naturally enough the commission of these crimes began to tell upon the public conscience, and the Southern white man, as a tribute to the nineteenth century civilization, was in a manner compelled to give excuses for his barbarism. His excuses have adapted themselves to the emergency, and are aptly outlined by that greatest of all Negroes, Frederick Douglass, in an article of recent date, in which he shows that there have been three distinct eras of Southern barbarism, to account for which three distinct excuses have been made.

The first excuse given to the civilized world for the murder of unoffending Negroes was the necessity of the white man to repress and stamp out alleged "race riots." For years immediately succeeding the war there was an appalling slaughter of colored people, and the wires usually conveyed to northern people and the world the intelligence, first, that an insurrection was being planned by Negroes, which, a few hours later, would prove to have been vigorously resisted by white men, and controlled with a resulting loss of several killed and wounded. It was always a remarkable feature in these insurrections and riots that only Negroes were killed during the rioting, and that all the white men escaped unharmed.

From 1865 to 1872, hundreds of colored men and women were mercilessly murdered and the almost invariable reason assigned was that they met their death by being alleged participants in an insurrection or riot. But this story at last wore itself out. No insurrection ever materialized; no Negro rioter was ever apprehended and proven guilty, and no dynamite ever recorded the black man's protest against oppression and wrong. It was too much to ask thoughtful people to believe this transparent story, and the southern white people at last made up their minds that some other excuse must be had.

Then came the second excuse, which had its birth during the turbulent times of reconstruction. By an amendment to the Constitution the Negro was given the right of franchise, and, theoretically at least, his ballot became his invaluable emblem of citizenship. In a government "of the people, for the people, and by the people," the Negro's vote became an important factor in all matters of state and national politics. But this did not last long. The southern white man would not consider that the Negro had any right which a white man was bound to respect, and the idea of a republican form of government in the southern states grew into general contempt. It was maintained that "This is a white man's government," and regardless of numbers the white man should rule. "No Negro domination" became the new legend on the sanguinary banner of the sunny South, and under it rode the Ku Klux Klan, the Regulators, and the lawless mobs, which for any cause chose to murder one man or a dozen as suited their purpose best. It was a long, gory campaign; the blood chills and the heart almost loses faith in Christianity when one thinks of Yazoo, Hamburg, Edgefield, Copiah, and the countless massacres of defenseless Negroes, whose only crime was the attempt to exercise their right to vote.

But it was a bootless strife for colored people. The government which had made the Negro a citizen found itself unable to protect him. It gave him the right to vote, but denied him the protection which should have maintained that right. Scourged from his home; hunted through the swamps; hung by midnight raiders, and openly murdered in the light of day, the Negro clung to his right of franchise with a heroism which would have wrung admiration from the hearts of savages. He believed that in that small white ballot there was a subtle something which stood for manhood as well as citizenship, and thousands of brave black men went to their graves, exemplifying the one by dying for the other.

The white man's victory soon became complete by fraud, violence, intimidation and murder. The franchise vouchsafed to the Negro grew to be a "barren ideality," and regardless of numbers, the colored people found themselves voiceless in the councils of those whose duty it was to rule. With no longer the fear of "Negro Domination" before their eyes, the white man's second excuse became valueless. With the Southern governments all subverted and the Negro actually eliminated from all participation in state and national elections, there could be no longer an excuse for killing Negroes to prevent "Negro Domination."

Brutality still continued; Negroes were whipped, scourged, exiled, shot and hung whenever and wherever it pleased the white man so to treat them, and as the civilized world with increasing persistency held the white people of the South to account for its outlawry, the murderers invented the third excuse—that Negroes had to be killed to avenge their assaults upon women. There could be framed no possible excuse more harmful to the Negro and more unanswerable if true in its sufficiency for the white man.

Humanity abhors the assailant of womanhood, and this charge upon the Negro at once placed him beyond the pale of human sympathy. With such unanimity, earnestness and apparent candor was this charge made and reiterated that the world has accepted the story that the Negro is a monster which the Southern white man has painted him. And today, the Christian world feels, that while lynching is a crime, and lawlessness and anarchy the certain precursors of a nation's fall, it can not by word or deed, extend sympathy or help to a race of outlaws, who might mistake their plea for justice and deem it an excuse for their continued wrongs.

The Negro has suffered much and is willing to suffer more. He recognizes that the wrongs of two centuries can not be righted in a day, and he tries to bear his burden with patience for to-day and be hopeful for to-morrow. But there comes a time when the veriest worm will turn, and the Negro feels to-day that after all the work he has done, all the sacrifices he has made, and all the suffering he has endured, if he did not, now, defend his name and manhood from this vile accusation, he would be unworthy even of the contempt of mankind. It is to this charge he now feels he must make answer.

If the Southern people in defense of their lawlessness, would tell the truth and admit that colored men and women are lynched for almost any offense, from murder to a misdemeanor, there would not now be the necessity for this defense. But when they intentionally, maliciously and constantly belie the record and bolster up these falsehoods by the words of legislators, preachers, governors and bishops, then the Negro must give to the world his side of the awful story.

A word as to the charge itself. In considering the third reason assigned by the Southern white people for the butchery of blacks, the question must be asked, what the white man means when he charges the black man with rape. Does he mean the crime which the statutes of the civilized states describe as such? Not by any means. With the Southern white man, any mesalliance existing between a white woman and a colored man is a sufficient foundation for the charge of rape. The Southern white man says that it is impossible for a voluntary alliance to exist between a white woman and a colored man, and therefore, the fact of an alliance is a proof of force. In numerous instances where colored men have been lynched on the charge of rape, it was positively known at the time of lynching and indisputably proven after the victim's death, that the relationship sustained between the man and woman was voluntary and clandestine, and that in no court of law could even the charge of assault have been successfully maintained.

It was for the assertion of this fact, in the defense of her own race, that the writer hereof became an exile; her property destroyed and her return to her home forbidden under penalty of death, for writing the following editorial which was printed in her paper, the "Free Speech," in Memphis, Tenn., May 21, 1892:

EIGHT NEGROES LYNCHED SINCE LAST ISSUE OF THE "FREE SPEECH" ONE AT LITTLE ROCK, ARK., LAST SATURDAY MORNING WHERE THE CITIZENS BROKE (?) INTO THE PENITENTIARY AND GOT THEIR MAN; THREE NEAR ANNISTON, ALA., ONE NEAR NEW ORLEANS; AND THREE AT CLARKSVILLE, GA., THE LAST THREE FOR KILLING A WHITE MAN, AND FIVE ON THE SAME OLD RACKET—THE NEW ALARM ABOUT RAPING WHITE WOMEN. THE SAME PROGRAMME OF HANGING, THEN SHOOTING BULLETS INTO THE LIFELESS BODIES WAS CARRIED OUT TO THE LETTER. NOBODY IN THIS SECTION OF THE COUNTRY BELIEVES THE OLD THREADBARE LIE THAT NEGRO MEN RAPE WHITE WOMEN. IF SOUTHERN WHITE MEN ARE NOT CAREFUL, THEY WILL OVERREACH THEMSELVES AND PUBLIC SENTIMENT WILL HAVE A REACTION; A CONCLUSION WILL THEN BE REACHED WHICH WILL BE VERY DAMAGING TO THE MORAL REPUTATION OF THEIR WOMEN.

But threats cannot suppress the truth, and while the Negro suffers the soul deformity, resultant from two and a half centuries of slavery, he is no more guilty of this vilest of all vile charges than the white man who would blacken his name.

During all the years of slavery, no such charge was ever made, not even during the dark days of the rebellion, when the white man, following the fortunes of war went to do battle for the maintenance of slavery. While the master was away fighting to forge the fetters upon the slave, he left his wife and children with no protectors save the Negroes themselves. And yet during those years of trust and peril, no Negro proved recreant to his trust and no white man returned to a home that had been dispoiled.

Likewise during the period of alleged "insurrection," and alarming "race riots," it never occurred to the white man, that his wife and children were in danger of assault. Nor in the Reconstruction era, when the hue and cry was against "Negro Domination," was there ever a thought that the domination would ever contaminate a fireside or strike to death the virtue of womanhood. It must appear strange indeed, to every thoughtful and candid man, that more than a quarter of a century elapsed before the Negro began to show signs of such infamous degeneration.

In his remarkable apology for lynching, Bishop Haygood [Atticus Haygood, former president of Emory University], of Georgia, says: "No race, not the most savage, tolerates the rape of woman, but it may be said without reflection upon any other people that the Southern people are now and always have been most sensitive concerning the honor of their women—their mothers, wives, sisters and daughters." It is not the purpose of this defense to say one word against the white women of the South. Such need not be said, but it is their misfortune that the chivalrous white men of that section, in order to escape the deserved execration of the civilized world, should shield themselves by their cowardly and infamously false excuse, and call into question that very honor about which their distinguished priestly apologist claims they are most sensitive. To justify their own barbarism they assume a chivalry which they do not possess. True chivalry respects all womanhood, and no one who reads the record, as it is written in the faces of the million mulattoes in the South, will for a minute conceive that the southern white man had a very chivalrous regard for the honor due the women of his own race or respect for the womanhood which circumstances placed in his power. That chivalry which is "most sensitive concerning the honor of women" can hope for but little respect from the civilized world, when it confines itself entirely to the women who happen to be white. Virtue knows no color line, and the chivalry which depends upon complexion of skin and texture of hair can command no honest respect.

When emancipation came to the Negroes, there arose in the northern part of the United States an almost divine sentiment among the noblest, purest and best white women of the North, who felt called to a mission to educate and Christianize the millions of southern ex-slaves. From every nook and corner of the North, brave young white women answered that call and left their cultured homes, their happy associations and their lives of ease, and with heroic determination went to the South to carry light and truth to the benighted blacks. It was a heroism no less than that which calls for volunteers for India, Africa and the Isles of the sea. To educate their unfortunate charges; to teach them the Christian virtues and to inspire in them the moral sentiments manifest in their own lives, these young women braved dangers whose record reads more like fiction than fact. They became social outlaws in the South. The peculiar sensitiveness of the southern white men and women, never shed its protecting influence about them. No friendly word from their own race cheered them in their work; no hospitable doors gave them the companionship like that from which they had come. No chivalrous white man doffed his hat in honor or respect. They were "Nigger teachers"—unpardonable offenders in the social ethics of the South, and were insulted, persecuted and ostracized, not by Negroes, but by the white manhood which boasts of its chivalry toward women.

And yet these northern women worked on, year after year, unselfishly, with a heroism which amounted almost to martyrdom. Threading their way through dense forests, working in schoolhouse, in the cabin and in the church, thrown at all times and in all places among the unfortunate and lowly Negroes, whom they

had come to find and to serve, these northern women, thousands and thousands of them, have spent more than a quarter of a century in giving to the colored people their splendid lessons for home and heart and soul. Without protection, save that which innocence gives to every good woman, they went about their work, fearing no assault and suffering none. Their chivalrous protectors were hundreds of miles away in their northern homes, and yet they never feared any "great dark faced mobs," they dared night or day to "go beyond their own roof trees." They never complained of assaults, and no mob was ever called into existence to avenge crimes against them. Before the world adjudges the Negro a moral monster, a vicious assailant of womanhood and a menace to the sacred precincts of home, the colored people ask the consideration of the silent record of gratitude, respect, protection and devotion of the millions of the race in the South, to the thousands of northern white women who have served as teachers and missionaries since the war.

The Negro may not have known what chivalry was, but he knew enough to preserve inviolate the womanhood of the South which was entrusted to his hands during the war. The finer sensibilities of his soul may have been crushed out by years of slavery, but his heart was full of gratitude to the white women of the North, who blessed his home and inspired his soul in all these years of freedom. Faithful to his trust in both of these instances, he should now have the impartial ear of the civilized world, when he dares to speak for himself as against the infamy wherewith he stands charged.

It is his regret, that, in his own defense, he must disclose to the world that degree of dehumanizing brutality which fixes upon America the blot of a national crime. Whatever faults and failings other nations may have in their dealings with their own subjects or with other people, no other civilized nation stands condemned before the world with a series of crimes so peculiarly national. It becomes a painful duty of the Negro to reproduce a record which shows that a large portion of the American people avow anarchy, condone murder and defy the contempt of civilization.

These pages are written in no spirit of vindictiveness, for all who give the subject consideration must concede that far too serious is the condition of that civilized government in which the spirit of unrestrained outlawry constantly increases in violence, and casts its blight over a continually growing area of territory. We plead not for the colored people alone, but for all victims of the terrible injustice which puts men and women to death without form of law. During the year 1894, there were 132 persons executed in the United States by due form of law, while in the same year, 197 persons were put to death by mobs who gave the victims no opportunity to make a lawful defense. No comment need be made upon a condition of public sentiment responsible for such alarming results.

The purpose of the pages which follow shall be to give the record which has been made, not by colored men, but that which is the result of compilations made by white men, of reports sent over the civilized world by white men in the South. Out of their own mouths shall the murderers be condemned. For a number of years the Chicago Tribune, admittedly one of the leading journals of America, has made a specialty of the compilation of statistics touching upon lynching. The data compiled by that journal and published to the world January 1st, 1894, up to the present time has not been disputed. In order to be safe from the charge of exaggeration, the incidents hereinafter reported have been confined to those vouched for by the Tribune.

Chapter VI. History of Some Cases of Rape

It has been claimed that the Southern white women have been slandered because, in defending the Negro race from the charge that all colored men, who are lynched, only pay penalty for assaulting women. It is certain that lynching mobs have not only refused to give the Negro a chance to defend himself, but have killed their victim with a full knowledge that the relationship of the alleged assailant with the woman who accused him, was voluntary and clandestine. As a matter of fact, one of the prime causes of the Lynch Law agitation has been a necessity for defending the Negro from this awful charge against him. This defense has been necessary because the apologists for outlawry insist that in no case has the accusing woman been a willing consort of her paramour, who is lynched because overtaken in wrong. It is well known, however, that such is the case. In July of this year, 1894, John Paul Bocock, a Southern white man living in New York, and assistant editor of the New York Tribune, took occasion to defy the publication of any instance where the lynched Negro was the victim of a white woman's falsehood. Such cases are not rare, but the press and people conversant with the facts, almost invariably suppress them.

The New York Sun of July 30th, 1894, contained a synopsis of interviews with leading congressmen and editors of the South. Speaker Crisp, of the House of Representatives, who was recently a Judge of the Supreme Court of Georgia, led in declaring that lynching seldom or never took place, save for vile crime against women and children. Dr. Hoss, editor of the leading organ of the Methodist Church South, published in its columns that it was his belief that more

than three hundred women had been assaulted by Negro men within three months. When asked to prove his charges, or give a single case upon which his "belief" was founded, he said that he could do so, but the details were unfit for publication. No other evidence but his "belief" could be adduced to substantiate this grave charge, yet Bishop Haygood, in the Forum of October, 1893, quotes this "belief" in apology for lynching, and voluntarily adds: "It is my opinion that this is an underestimate." The "opinion" of this man, based upon a "belief," had greater weight coming from a man who has posed as a friend to "Our Brother in Black," and was accepted as authority. An interview of Miss Frances E. Willard, the great apostle of temperance, the daughter of abolitionists and a personal friend and helper of many individual colored people, has been quoted in support of the utterance of this calumny against a weak and defenseless race. In the New York Voice of October 23, 1890, after a tour in the South, where she was told all these things by the "best white people," she said: "The grogshop is the Negro's center of power. Better whisky and more of it is the rallying cry of great, dark-faced mobs. The colored race multiplies like the locusts of Egypt. The grogshop is its center of power. The safety of woman, of childhood, the home, is menaced in a thousand localities at this moment, so that men dare not go beyond the sight of their own roof-tree."

These charges so often reiterated, have had the effect of fastening the odium upon the race of a peculiar propensity for this foul crime. The Negro is thus forced to a defense of his good name. . . . He is not the aggressor in this fight, but the situation demands that the facts be given, and they will speak for themselves. Of the 1,115 Negro men, women and children hanged, shot and roasted alive from January 1st, 1882, to January 1st, 1894, inclusive, only 348 of that number were charged with rape. Nearly 700 of these persons were lynched for any other reason which could be manufactured by a mob wishing to indulge in a lynching bee. . . .

Chapter VIII. Miss Willard's Attitude

No class of American citizens stands in greater need of the humane and thoughtful consideration of all sections of our country than do the colored people, nor does any class exceed us in the measure of grateful regard for acts of kindly interest in our behalf. It is, therefore, to us, a matter of keen regret that a Christian organization so large and influential as the Woman's Christian Temperance Union, should refuse to give its sympathy and support to our oppressed people who ask no further favor than the promotion of public sentiment which shall guarantee to every person accused of crime the safeguard of a fair and impartial trial, and protection from butchery by brutal mobs. Accustomed as we are to the indifference and apathy of Christian people, we would bear this instance of ill fortune in silence, had not Miss Willard gone out of her way to antagonize the cause so dear to our hearts by including in her Annual Address to the W.C.T.U. Convention at Cleveland, November 5, 1894, a studied, unjust and wholly unwarranted attack upon our work.

In her address Miss Willard said:

THE ZEAL FOR HER RACE OF MISS IDA B. WELLS, A BRIGHT YOUNG COLORED WOMAN, HAS, IT SEEMS TO ME, CLOUDED HER PERCEPTION AS TO WHO WERE HER FRIENDS AND WELL-WISHERS IN ALL HIGH-MINDED AND LEGITIMATE EFFORTS TO BANISH THE ABOMINATION OF LYNCHING AND TORTURE FROM THE LAND OF THE FREE AND THE HOME OF THE BRAVE. IT IS MY FIRM BELIEF THAT IN THE STATEMENTS MADE BY MISS WELLS CONCERNING WHITE WOMEN HAVING TAKEN THE INITIATIVE IN NAMELESS ACTS BETWEEN THE RACES SHE HAS PUT AN IMPUTATION UPON HALF THE WHITE RACE IN THIS COUNTRY THAT IS UNJUST, AND, SAVE IN THE RAREST EXCEPTIONAL INSTANCES, WHOLLY WITHOUT FOUNDATION. THIS IS THE UNANIMOUS OPINION OF THE MOST DISINTERESTED AND OBSERVANT LEADERS OF OPINION WHOM I HAVE CONSULTED ON THE SUBJECT, AND I DO NOT FEAR TO SAY THAT THE LAUDABLE EFFORTS SHE IS MAKING ARE GREATLY HANDICAPPED BY STATEMENTS OF THIS KIND, NOR TO URGE HER AS A FRIEND AND WELL-WISHER TO BANISH FROM HER VOCABULARY ALL SUCH ALLUSIONS AS A SOURCE OF WEAKNESS TO THE CAUSE SHE HAS AT HEART.

This paragraph, brief as it is, contains two statements which have not the slightest foundation in fact. At no time, nor in any place, have I made statements "concerning white women having taken the initiative in nameless acts between the races." Further, at no time, or place nor under any circumstance, have I directly or inferentially "put an imputation upon half the white race in this country" and I challenge this "friend and well-wisher" to give proof of the truth of her charge. Miss Willard protests against lynching in one paragraph and then, in the next, deliberately misrepresents my position in order that she may criticise a movement, whose only purpose is to protect our oppressed race from vindictive slander and Lynch Law.

What I have said and what I now repeat—in answer to her first charge—is, that colored men have been lynched for assault upon women, when the facts were plain that the relationship between the victim lynched and the alleged victim of his assault was voluntary, clandestine and illicit. For that very reason we maintain, that, in every section of our land, the accused should have a fair, impartial trial, so that a man who is colored shall not be hanged for an offense, which, if he were white, would not be adjudged a crime. Facts cited in another chapter—"History of Some Cases of Rape" —amply maintain this position. The publication of these facts in defense of the good

name of the race casts no "imputation upon half the white race in this country" and no such imputation can be inferred except by persons deliberately determined to be unjust.

But this is not the only injury which this cause has suffered at the hands of our "friend and well-wisher." It has been said that the Women's Christian Temperance Union, the most powerful organization of women in America, was misrepresented by me while I was in England. Miss Willard was in England at the time and knowing that no such misrepresentation came to her notice, she has permitted that impression to become fixed and widespread, when a word from her would have made the facts plain.

I never at any time or place or in any way misrepresented that organization. When asked what concerted action had been taken by churches and great moral agencies in America to put down Lynch Law, I was compelled in truth to say that no such action had occurred, that pulpit, press and moral agencies in the main were silent and for reasons known to themselves, ignored the awful conditions which to the English people appeared so abhorrent. Then the question was asked what the great moral reformers like Miss Frances Willard and Mr. Moody had done to suppress Lynch Law and again I answered—nothing. That Mr. Moody had never said a word against lynching in any of his trips to the South, or in the North either, so far as was known, and that Miss Willard's only public utterance on the situation had condoned lynching and other unjust practices of the South against the Negro. When proof of these statements was demanded, I sent a letter containing a copy of the New York Voice, Oct, 23, 1890, in which appeared Miss Willard's own words of wholesale slander against the colored race and condonation of Southern white people's outrages against us. My letter in part reads as follows:

But Miss Willard, the great temperance leader, went even further in putting the seal of her approval upon the southerners' method of dealing with the Negro. In October, 1890, the Women's Christian Temperance Union held its national meeting at Atlanta, Georgia. It was the first time in the history of the organization that it had gone south for a national meeting, and met the southerners in their own homes. They were welcomed with open arms. The governor of the state and the legislature gave special audiences in the halls of state legislation to the temperance workers. They set out to capture the northerners to their way of seeing things, and without troubling to hear the Negro side of the question, these temperance people accepted the white man's story of the problem with which he had to deal. State organizers were appointed that year, who had gone through the southern states since then, but in obedience to southern prejudices have confined their work to white persons only. It is only after Negroes are in prison for crimes that efforts of these temperance women are exerted without regard to "race, color, or previous condition." No "ounce of prevention" is used in their case; they are black, and if these women went among the Negroes for this work, the whites would not receive them. Except here and there, are found no temperance workers of the Negro race; "the great dark-faced mobs" are left the easy prey of the saloonkeepers.

There was pending in the National Congress at this time a Federal Election Bill, the object being to give the National Government control of the national elections in the several states. Had this bill become a law, the Negro, whose vote has been systematically suppressed since 1875 in the southern states, would have had the protection of the National Government, and his vote counted. The South would have been no longer "solid"; the Southerners saw that the balance of power which they unlawfully held in the House of Representatives and the Electoral College, based on the Negro population, would be wrested from them. So they nick-named the pending elections law the "Force Bill"—probably because it would force them to disgorge their ill-gotten political gains—and defeated it. While it was being discussed, the question was submitted to Miss Willard: "What do you think of the race problem and the Force Bill?"

Said Miss Willard: "Now, as to the 'race problem' in its minified, current meaning, I am a true lover of the southern people—have spoken and worked in, perhaps, 200 of their towns and cities; have been taken into their love and confidence at scores of hospitable firesides; have heard them pour out their hearts in the splendid frankness of their impetuous natures. And I have said to them at such times: 'When I go North there will be wafted to you no word from pen or voice that is not loyal to what we are saying here and now.' Going South, a woman, a temperance woman, and a Northern temperance woman—three great barriers to their good will yonder—I was received by them with a confidence that was one of the most delightful surprises of my life. I think we have wronged the South, though we did not mean to do so. The reason was, in part, that we had irreparably wronged ourselves by putting no safeguards on the ballot box at the North that would sift out alien illiterates. They rule our cities today; the saloon is their palace, and the toddy stick their sceptre. It is not fair that they should vote, nor is it fair that a plantation Negro, who can neither read nor write, whose ideas are bounded by the fence of his own field and the price of his own mule, should be

entrusted with the ballot. We ought to have put an educational test upon that ballot from the first. The Anglo-Saxon race will never submit to be dominated by the Negro so long as his altitude reaches no higher than the personal liberty of the saloon, and the power of appreciating the amount of liquor that a dollar will buy. New England would no more submit to this than South Carolina. 'Better whisky and more of it' has been the rallying cry of great dark-faced mobs in the Southern localities where local option was snowed under by the colored vote. Temperance has no enemy like that, for it is unreasoning and unreasonable. To-night it promises in a great congregation to vote for temperance at the polls tomorrow; but tomorrow twenty-five cents changes that vote in favor of the liquor-seller.

"I pity the southerners, and I believe the great mass of them are as conscientious and kindly-intentioned toward the colored man as an equal number of white church-members of the North. Would-be demagogues lead the colored people to destruction. Half-drunken white roughs murder them at the polls, or intimidate them so that they do not vote. But the better class of people must not be blamed for this, and a more thoroughly American population than the Christian people of the South does not exist. They have the traditions, the kindness, the probity, the courage of our forefathers. The problem on their hands is immeasurable. The colored race multiplies like the locusts of Egypt. The grogshop is its center of power. 'The safety of woman, of childhood, of the home, is menaced in a thousand localities at this moment, so that the men dare not go beyond the sight of their own roof-tree.' How little we know of all this, seated in comfort and affluence here at the North, descanting upon the rights of every man to cast one vote and have it fairly counted; that well-worn shibboleth invoked once more to dodge a living issue.

"The fact is that illiterate colored men will not vote at the South until the white population chooses to have them do so; and under similar conditions they would not at the North." Here we have Miss Willard's words in full, condoning fraud, violence, murder, at the ballot box; rapine, shooting, hanging and burning; for all these things are done and being done now by the Southern white people. She does not stop there, but goes a step further to aid them in blackening the good name of an entire race, as shown by the sentences quoted in the paragraph above. These utterances, for which the colored people have never forgiven Miss Willard, and which Frederick Douglass has denounced as false, are to be found in full in the Voice of October 23, 1890, a temperance organ published at New York City.

This letter appeared in the May number of Fraternity, the organ of the first Anti-Lynching society of Great Britain. When Lady Henry Somerset learned through Miss Florence Balgarnie that this letter had been published she informed me that if the interview was published she would take steps to let the public know that my statements must be received with caution. As I had no money to pay the printer to suppress the edition which was already published and these ladies did not care to do so, the May number of Fraternity was sent to its subscribers as usual. Three days later there appeared in the daily Westminster Gazette an "interview" with Miss Willard, written by Lady Henry Somerset, which was so subtly unjust in its wording that I was forced to reply in my own defense. In that reply I made only statements which, like those concerning Miss Willard's Voice interview, have not been and cannot be denied. It was as follows:

LADY HENRY SOMERSET'S INTERVIEW WITH MISS WILLARD

To the Editor of the *Westminster Gazette:* Sir— The interview published in your columns today hardly merits a reply, because of the indifference to suffering manifested. Two ladies are represented sitting under a tree at Reigate, and, after some preliminary remarks on the terrible subject of lynching, Miss Willard laughingly replies by cracking a joke. And the concluding sentence of the interview shows the object is not to determine how best they may help the Negro who is being hanged, shot and burned, but "to guard Miss Willard's reputation."

With me it is not myself nor my reputation, but the life of my people, which is at stake and I affirm that this is the first time to my knowledge that Miss Willard has said a single word in denunciation of lynching or demand for law. The year 1890, the one in which the interview appears, had a larger lynching record than any previous year, and the number and territory have increased, to say nothing of the human beings burnt alive.

If so earnest as she would have the English public believe her to be, why was she silent when five minutes were given me to speak last June at Princes' Hall, and in Holborn Town Hall this May? I should say it was as President of the Women's Christian Temperance Union of America she is timid, because all these unions in the South emphasize the hatred of the Negro by excluding him. There is not a single colored woman admitted to the Southern W.C.T.U., but still Miss Willard blames the Negro for the defeat of Prohibition in the South. Miss Willard quotes from Fraternity, but forgets to add my immediate recognition of her presence on the platform at Holborn Town Hall, when, amidst many other resolutions on temperance and other subjects in which she is interested, time was granted to carry an anti-lynching resolution. I was so thankful for this crumb of her speechless presence that I hurried off to the editor of Fraternity and added a postscript to my article blazoning forth that fact.

Any statements I have made concerning Miss Willard are confirmed by the Hon. Frederick Douglass (late United States minister to Hayti) in a speech delivered by him in Washington in January of this year, which has since been published in a pamphlet. The fact is, Miss Willard is no better or worse than the great bulk of white Americans on the Negro questions. They are all afraid to speak out, and it is only British public opinion which will move them, as I am thankful to see it has already begun to move Miss Willard. I am, etc., May 21. Ida B. Wells.

Unable to deny the truth of these assertions, the charge has been made that I have attacked Miss Willard and misrepresented the W.C.T.U. If to state facts is misrepresentation, then I plead guilty to the charge.

I said then and repeat now, that in all the ten terrible years of shooting, hanging and burning of men, women and children in America, the Women's Christian Temperance Union never suggested one plan or made one move to prevent those awful crimes. If this statement is untrue the records of that organization would disprove it before the ink is dry. It is clearly an issue of fact and in all fairness this charge of misrepresentation should either be substantiated or withdrawn.

It is not necessary, however, to make any representation concerning the W.C.T.U. and the lynching question. The record of that organization speaks for itself. During all the years prior to the agitation begun against Lynch Law, in which years men, women and children were scourged, hanged, shot and burned, the W.C.T.U. had no word, either of pity or protest; its great heart, which concerns itself about humanity the world over, was, toward our cause, pulseless as a stone. Let those who deny this speak by the record. Not until after the first British campaign, in 1893, was even a resolution passed by the body which is the self-constituted guardian for "God, home and native land."

Nor need we go back to other years. The annual session of that organization held in Cleveland in November, 1894, made a record which confirms and emphasizes the silence charged against it. At that session, earnest efforts were made to secure the adoption of a resolution of protest against lynching. At that very time two men were being tried for the murder of six colored men who were arrested on charge of barn burning, chained together, and on pretense of being taken to jail, were driven into the woods where they were ambushed and all six shot to death. The six widows of the butchered men had just finished the most pathetic recital ever heard in any court room, and the mute appeal of twenty-seven orphans for justice touched the stoutest hearts. Only two weeks prior to the session, Gov. Jones of Alabama, in his last message to the retiring state legislature, cited the fact that in the two years just past, nine colored men had been taken from the legal authorities by lynching mobs and butchered in cold blood—and not one of these victims was even charged with an assault upon womanhood.

It was thought that this great organization, in face of these facts, would not hesitate to place itself on record in a resolution of protest against this awful brutality towards colored people. Miss Willard gave assurance that such a resolution would be adopted, and that assurance was relied on. The record of the session shows in what good faith that assurance was kept. After recommending an expression against Lynch Law, the President attacked the anti-lynching movement, deliberately misrepresenting my position, and in her annual address, charging me with a statement I never made.

Further than that, when the committee on resolutions reported their work, not a word was said against lynching. In the interest of the cause I smothered the resentment I felt because of the unwarranted and unjust attack of the President, and labored with members to secure an expression of some kind, tending to abate the awful slaughter of my race. A resolution against lynching was introduced by Mrs. Fessenden and read, and then that great Christian body, which in its resolutions had expressed itself in opposition to the social amusement of card playing, athletic sports and promiscuous dancing; had protested against the licensing of saloons, inveighed against tobacco, pledged its allegiance to the Prohibition party, and thanked the Populist party in Kansas, the Republican party in California and the Democratic party in the South, wholly ignored the seven millions of colored people of this country whose plea was for a word of sympathy and support for the movement in their behalf. The resolution was not adopted, and the convention adjourned.

In the Union Signal Dec. 6, 1894, among the resolutions is found this one:

RESOLVED, THAT THE NATIONAL W.C.T.U., WHICH HAS FOR YEARS COUNTED AMONG ITS DEPARTMENTS THAT OF PEACE AND ARBITRATION, IS UTTERLY OPPOSED TO ALL LAWLESS ACTS IN ANY AND ALL PARTS OF OUR COMMON LANDS AND IT URGES THESE PRINCIPLES UPON THE PUBLIC, PRAYING THAT THE TIME MAY SPEEDILY COME WHEN NO HUMAN BEING SHALL BE CONDEMNED WITHOUT DUE PROCESS OF LAW; AND WHEN THE UNSPEAKABLE OUTRAGES WHICH HAVE SO OFTEN PROVOKED SUCH LAWLESSNESS SHALL BE BANISHED FROM THE WORLD, AND CHILDHOOD, MAIDENHOOD AND WOMANHOOD SHALL NO MORE BE THE VICTIMS OF ATROCITIES WORSE THAN DEATH.

This is not the resolution offered by Mrs. Fessenden. She offered the one passed last year by the W.C.T.U. which was a strong unequivocal denunciation of lynching. But she was told by the chairman of the committee on resolutions, Mrs. Rounds, that there was already a lynching resolution in the hands of the committee. Mrs. Fessenden yielded the floor on that assurance, and no resolution of any kind against lynching was submitted and none was voted upon, not even the one above, taken from the columns of the Union Signal, the organ of the national W.C.T.U.!

Even the wording of this resolution which was printed by the W.C.T.U., reiterates the false and unjust charge which has been so often made as an excuse for lynchers. Statistics show that less than one-third of the lynching victims are hanged, shot and burned alive for "unspeakable outrages against womanhood, maidenhood and childhood"; and that nearly a thousand, including women and children, have been lynched upon any pretext whatsoever; and that all have met death upon the unsupported word of white men and women. Despite these facts this resolution which was printed, cloaks an apology for lawlessness, in the same paragraph which affects to condemn it, where it speaks of "the unspeakable outrages which have so often provoked such lawlessness."

Miss Willard told me the day before the resolutions were offered that the Southern women present had held a caucus that day. This was after I, as fraternal delegate from the Woman's Mite Missionary Society of the A.M.E. Church at Cleveland, O., had been introduced to tender its greetings. In so doing I expressed the hope of the colored women that the W.C.T.U. would place itself on record as opposed to lynching which robbed them of husbands, fathers, brothers and sons and in many cases of women as well. No note was made either in the daily papers or the Union Signal of that introduction and greeting, although every other incident of that morning was published. The failure to submit a lynching resolution and the wording of the one above appears to have been the result of that Southern caucus.

On the same day I had a private talk with Miss Willard and told her she had been unjust to me and the cause in her annual address, and asked that she correct the statement that I had misrepresented the W.C.T.U., or that I had "put an imputation on one-half the white race in this country." She said that somebody in England told her it was a pity that I attacked the white women of America. "Oh," said I, "then you went out of your way to prejudice me and my cause in your annual address, not upon what you had heard me say, but what somebody had told you I said?" Her reply was that I must not blame her for her rhetorical expressions—that I had my way of expressing things and she had hers. I told her I most assuredly did blame her when those expressions were calculated to do such harm. I waited for an honest, an unequivocal retraction of her statements based on "hearsay." Not a word of retraction or explanation was said in the convention and I remained misrepresented before that body through her connivance and consent.

The editorial notes in the Union Signal, Dec. 6, 1894, however, contains the following:

IN HER REPUDIATION OF THE CHARGES BROUGHT BY MISS IDA WELLS AGAINST WHITE WOMEN AS HAVING TAKEN THE INITIATIVE IN NAMELESS CRIMES BETWEEN THE RACES, MISS WILLARD SAID IN HER ANNUAL ADDRESS THAT 'THIS STATEMENT PUT AN UNJUST IMPUTATION UPON HALF THE WHITE RACE.' BUT AS THIS EXPRESSION HAS BEEN MISUNDERSTOOD SHE DESIRES TO DECLARE THAT SHE DID NOT INTEND A LITERAL INTERPRETATION TO BE GIVEN TO THE LANGUAGE USED, BUT EMPLOYED IT TO EXPRESS A TENDENCY THAT MIGHT ENSUE IN PUBLIC THOUGHT AS A RESULT OF UTTERANCES SO SWEEPING AS SOME THAT HAVE BEEN MADE BY MISS WELLS.

Because this explanation is as unjust as the original offense, I am forced in self-defense to submit this account of differences. I desire no quarrel with the W.C.T.U., but my love for the truth is greater than my regard for an alleged friend who, through ignorance or design misrepresents in the most harmful way the cause of a long suffering race, and then unable to maintain the truth of her attack excuses herself as it were by the wave of the hand, declaring that "she did not intend a literal interpretation to be given to the language used." When the lives of men, women and children are at stake, when the inhuman butchers of innocents attempt to justify their barbarism by fastening upon a whole race the obloque of the most infamous of crimes, it is little less than criminal to apologize for the butchers today and tomorrow to repudiate the apology by declaring it a figure of speech.

Chapter X. The Remedy

It is a well established principle of law that every wrong has a remedy. Herein rests our respect for law. The Negro does not claim that all of the one thousand black men, women and children, who have been hanged, shot and burned alive during the past ten years, were innocent of the charges made against them. We have associated too long with the white man not to have copied his vices as well as his virtues. But we do insist that the punishment is not the same for both classes of criminals. In lynching, opportunity is not given the Negro to defend himself against the unsupported accusations of white men and women. The word of the accuser is held to be true and the excited blood-thirsty mob demands that the rule of law be reversed and instead of proving the accused to be guilty, the victim of their hate and revenge must prove himself innocent. No evidence he can offer will satisfy the mob; he is bound hand and foot and swung into eternity. Then to excuse its infamy, the mob almost invariably reports the monstrous falsehood that its victim made a full confession before he was hanged.

With all military, legal and political power in their hands, only two of the lynching States have attempted a check by exercising the power which is theirs. Mayor Trout, of Roanoke, Virginia, called out the militia in 1893, to protect a Negro prisoner, and in so doing nine men were killed and a number wounded. Then the mayor and militia withdrew, left the Negro to his fate and he was promptly lynched. The business men realized the blow to the town's financial interests, called the mayor home, the grand jury indicted and prosecuted the ringleaders of the mob. They were given light sentences, the highest being one of twelve months in State prison. The day he arrived at the penitentiary, he was pardoned by the governor of the State.

The only other real attempt made by the authorities to protect a prisoner of the law, and which was more successful, was that of Gov. McKinley, of Ohio, who sent the militia to Washington Courthouse, O., in October, 1894, and five men were killed and twenty wounded in maintaining the principle that the law must be upheld.

In South Carolina, in April, 1893, Gov. Tillman aided the mob by yielding up to be killed, a prisoner of the law, who had voluntarily placed himself under the Governor's protection. Public sentiment by its representatives has encouraged Lynch Law, and upon the revolution of this sentiment we must depend for its abolition.

Therefore, we demand a fair trial by law for those accused of crime, and punishment by law after honest conviction. No maudlin sympathy for criminals is solicited, but we do ask that the law shall punish all alike. We earnestly desire those that control the forces which make public sentiment to join with us in the demand. Surely the humanitarian spirit of this country which reaches out to denounce the treatment of the Russian Jews, the Armenian Christians, the laboring poor of Europe, the Siberian exiles and the native women of India—will not longer refuse to lift its voice on this subject. If it were known that the cannibals or the savage Indians had burned three human beings alive in the past two years, the whole of Christendom would be roused, to devise ways and means to put a stop to it. Can you remain silent and inactive when such things are done in our own community and country? Is your duty to humanity in the United States less binding?

What can you do, reader, to prevent lynching, to thwart anarchy and promote law and order throughout our land?

1st. You can help disseminate the facts contained in this book by bringing them to the knowledge of every one with whom you come in contact, to the end that public sentiment may be revolutionized. Let the facts speak for themselves, with you as a medium.

2d. You can be instrumental in having churches,

missionary societies, Y. M. C. A.'s, W.C.T.U's and all Christian and moral forces in connection with your religious and social life, pass resolutions of condemnation and protest every time a lynching takes place; and see that they are sent to the place where these outrages occur.

3d. Bring to the intelligent consideration of Southern people the refusal of capital to invest where lawlessness and mob violence hold sway. Many labor organizations have declared by resolution that they would avoid lynch infested localities as they would the pestilence when seeking new homes. If the South wishes to build up its waste places quickly, there is no better way than to uphold the majesty of the law by enforcing obedience to the same, and meting out the same punishment to all classes of criminals, white as well as black. "Equality before the law," must become a fact as well as a theory before America is truly the "land of the free and the home of the brave."

4th. Think and act on independent lines in this behalf, remembering that after all, it is the white man's civilization and the white man's government which are on trial. This crusade will determine whether that civilization can maintain itself by itself, or whether anarchy shall prevail; whether this Nation shall write itself down a success at self government, or in deepest humiliation admit its failure complete; whether the precepts and theories of Christianity are professed and practiced by American white people as Golden Rules of thought and action, or adopted as a system of morals to be preached to heathen until they attain to the intelligence which needs the system of Lynch Law.

5th. Congressman Blair offered a resolution in the House of Representatives, August, 1894. The organized life of the country can speedily make this a law by sending resolutions to Congress indorsing Mr. Blair's bill and asking Congress to create the commission. In no better way can the question be settled, and the Negro does not fear the issues. The following is the resolution:

"Resolved, By the House of Representatives and Senate in congress assembled, That the committee on labor be instructed to investigate and report the number, location and date of all alleged assaults by males upon females throughout the country during the ten years last preceding the passing of this joint resolution, for or on account of which organized but unlawful violence has been inflicted or attempted to be inflicted. Also to ascertain and report all facts of organized but unlawful violence to the person, with the attendant facts and circumstances, which have been inflicted upon accused persons alleged to have been guilty of crimes punishable by due process of law which have taken place in any part of the country within the ten years last preceding the passage of this resolution. Such investigation shall be made by the usual methods and agencies of the Department of Labor, and report made to Congress as soon as the work can be satisfactorily done, and the sum of $25,000, or so much thereof as may be necessary, is hereby appropriated to pay the expenses out of any money in the treasury not otherwise appropriated."

The belief has been constantly expressed in England that in the United States, which has produced Wm. Lloyd Garrison, Henry Ward Beecher, James Russell Lowell, John G. Whittier and Abraham Lincoln there must be those of their descendants who would take hold of the work of inaugurating an era of law and order. The colored people of this country who have been loyal to the flag believe the same, and strong in that belief have begun this crusade. . . .

PART FOUR

Twentieth-Century Writings

Jane Addams (1860–1935)

Jane Addams was likely the most prominent of American women who devoted their lives to social inquiry and social reform. A leading Progressive, she is most associated with the settlement house movement and with the founding of Hull House on Chicago's near west side, certainly the most well-known social settlement in the United States around the turn of the twentieth century. The settlement movement was based on the principle that one had to share the living experiences of the urban poor in order to assist them effectively. Thus Jane Addams and other middle- and upper-class women and men lived at Hull House and set up institutions to aid their poorer neighbors. Social reform and assistance were not sufficient alone, however; they believed one must have solid social analysis and statistical evidence to convince governmental and business leaders to establish social policies beneficial to poor urban neighborhoods. Thus residents at Hull House began publishing a series entitled Hull House Maps and Papers, which outlined the population density and economic realities of surrounding immigrant neighborhoods.

While Jane Addams, with the exception of a few First Ladies, may be the best-known American woman of the past, she is known primarily as an activist. She is often pictured in textbooks in her later years as a kindly grandmother figure surrounded by children at Hull House who came to the nation's first organized kindergarten and to a range of girls' and boys' clubs. Her standing as one of the most influential social analysts in the early twentieth century has been less recognized. Yet she strongly influenced the emergence of the fields of social work and sociology, especially its most important early manifestation known as the Chicago School, identified with the Sociology Department of the University of Chicago founded in 1893. Important intellectuals ranging from John Dewey to George Santayana have written of her essential contribution to their thought and writings. Her basic contention was that modern industrial and urban society demanded that individuals discard an individual morality for a social one, recognizing that they were as responsible for their neighbors' well-being as for their own. These views, which Addams published in a range of articles, were brought together as a collection and printed in 1902 as Democracy and Social Ethics.

Jane Addams was also an individual of broad-ranging concerns. As a young woman living in Baltimore, she had worked for the interests of African Americans, and she later became one of the founders and the vice president of the National Association for the Advancement of Colored People. She was important in Progressive politics and nominated Theodore Roosevelt for president on the Progressive ticket in 1912. She held a lifelong interest in the needs of women and was an officer in the National American Women's Suffrage Association as well as working to rid the nation of forced prostitution and unfair and unsafe working conditions for her sisters. She and others at Hull House were especially concerned with the needs of children, and they became the driving force in establishing in Illinois the nation's first juvenile court system and in being the single most influential group working for the abolition of child labor in this country. She supported the position of workers generally, and a Hull House resident became the first factory inspector in the nation.

Other than these broad-based domestic concerns, Jane Addams devoted herself most significantly and passionately to issues of peace. In 1906 Addams published Newer Ideals of Peace, setting forth "the claims of the newer, more aggressive ideals of peace, as over against the older dovelike ideal." In World War I, unlike many pacifists who yielded to the propaganda of "the war to end all wars," Addams persisted in her opposition to the war. One of the most important leaders of the Women's International League for Peace and Freedom, she and other women met in the Hague in 1915 to secure a peaceful end to World War I. In 1922, in Peace and Bread in Time of War, she recounted the history of the women's struggle and her own analysis of the experience of the war. Her pacifism led to the strongest criticisms of her as an individual, and many accused her of being a traitor for attempting to negotiate with representatives of the Central Powers. Because of this, along with the demise of Progressive values, her reputation was tarnished in the period following the end of World War I, but she ultimately shared the Nobel Prize for Peace in 1933, two years before her death.

It is difficult to think of a single woman since 1950 who has gained the range of accomplishments of Jane Addams from 1890 to 1930. Hull House became the model for today's community center. It offered an effective model for socially conscious citizens to influence a local, and often hostile, government; and it provided the springboard for the National Consumers' League and for the first women to head federal agencies, the Children's Bureau and the Women's Bureau of the United States Department of Labor. Moreover, the settlement movement led Frances Perkins to be the first woman cabinet member as Secretary of Labor under Franklin Delano Roosevelt. Values from the social settlement movement, as well as the efforts of individuals associated with the movement, are credited with the passage of the Social Security Act in 1935 and Aid to Families with Dependent Children, the basis of our current welfare system, in order to meet the financial and nutritional needs of poor families.

All of these accomplishments are truly impressive, but it is Jane Addams's ideas about social justice and the integrated interests of rural and urban, rich and poor, young and old that may prove to be her most important legacy. The first essay we include here, "Charitable Effort," provides more insightful views on the issue of welfare reform than much of the social science and political perspectives heard today on the subject. The selection which follows, from Newer Ideals of Peace, also introduces ideas (such as conceptualizations of negative and positive peace) usually attributed to much later (male) theorists. These writings exemplify the contributions of Jane Addams not as a leading social reformer but as an intellectual who provided many leading figures in social reform with their ideas and blueprints for social change.

The following selections are from Democracy and Social Ethics (1907 printing) and Newer Ideals of Peace (1906).

HLS

Sources and Suggested Readings

Addams, Jane. *Democracy and Social Ethics.* New York: Macmillan, 1907 [1902].

———. *The Jane Addams Papers.* Ed. Mary Lynn McCree Bryan. Ann Arbor: University Microfilms, 1985.

———. *The Long Road of Woman's Memory.* New York: Macmillan, 1916.

———. *A New Conscience and an Ancient Evil.* New York: Macmillan, 1912.

———. *Newer Ideals of Peace.* New York: Macmillan, 1906.

———. *Peace and Bread in Time of War.* New York: Macmillan, 1922.

———. *The Spirit of Youth and the City Streets.* New York: Macmillan, 1909.

———. *Twenty Years at Hull-House, with Autobiographical Notes.* New York: Penguin, 1981 [1938].

———, ed. *Hull House Maps and Papers* [1895]. New York: Arno Press, 1970.

Davis, Allen Freeman. *American Heroine: The Life and Legend of Jane Addams.* New York: Oxford University Press, 1973.

Deegan, Mary Jo. *Jane Addams and the Men of the Chicago School, 1892–1918.* New Brunswick, N.J.: Transaction, 1988.

Fish, Virginia Kemp. "Hull House: Pioneer in Urban Research during Its Creative Years." *History of Sociology* 6, 1 (1985): 33–54.

Franklin, Donna L. "Mary Richmond and Jane Addams: From Moral Certainty to Rational Inquiry in Social Work Practice." *Social Service Review* 60, 4 (1986): 504–25.

Harkavy, Ira, and John L. Puckett. "Lessons from Hull House for the Contemporary Urban University." *Social Services Review* 37 (1994): 299–321.

Herman, Sondra R. *Eleven against War: Studies in American Internationalist Thought, 1898–1921.* Stanford, Calif.: Hoover Institution Press, 1969.

Horowitz, Helen Lefkowitz. "Hull-House as Women's Space." *Chicago History* 12, 4 (1983–1984): 40–55.

Kopping, Linda J. "John Dewey: A Study of His Role in the Academic Advancement of Women." *Vitae Scholasticae* 6, 2 (1987): 11–36.

Leffers, M. Regine. "Pragmatists Jane Addams and John Dewey Inform the Ethic of Care." *Hypatia* 8, 2 (1993): 64–77.

Lengermann, Patricia Madoo, and Jill Niebrugge-Brantley. "Jane Addams: Ethics and Society." In *The Women Founders: Sociology and Social Theory 1830–1930.* Boston: McGraw Hill, 1998.

McCarthy, Michael P. "Urban Optimism and Reform Thought in the Progressive Era." *Historian* 51, 2 (1989): 239–62.

Mahowald, Mary B. "What Classic American Philosophers Missed: Jane Addams, Critical Pragmatism, and Cultural Feminism." *Journal of Value Inquiry* 31 (1997): 39–54.

Schott, Linda. "Jane Addams and William James on Alternatives to War." *Journal of the History of Ideas* 54, 2 (1993): 241–53.

Seigfried, Charlene Haddock. *Pragmatism and Feminism: Reweaving the Social Fabric.* Chicago: University of Chicago Press, 1996.

Sklar, Kathryn Kish. "Jane Addams' Peace Activism, 1914–1922: A Model for Women Today?" *Women's Studies Quarterly* 3 (1995): 32–47.

Townsend, Lucy Forsyth. "The Education of Jane Addams: Myth and Reality." *Vitae Scholasticae* 5, 1–2 (1986): 225–46.

Zeiger, Susan. "She Didn't Raise Her Boy to Be a Slacker: Motherhood, Conscription, and the Culture of the First World War." *Feminist Studies* 22, 1 (1996): 7–39.

Democracy and Social Ethics (1902)

Chapter II. Charitable Effort

All those hints and glimpses of a larger and more satisfying democracy, which literature and our own hopes supply, have a tendency to slip away from us and to leave us sadly unguided and perplexed when we attempt to act upon them.

Our conceptions of morality, as all our other ideas, pass through a course of development; the difficulty comes in adjusting our conduct, which has become hardened into customs and habits, to these changing moral conceptions. When this adjustment is not made, we suffer from the strain and indecision of believing one hypothesis and acting upon another.

Probably there is no relation in life which our democracy is changing more rapidly than the charitable relation—that relation which obtains between benefactor and beneficiary; at the same time there is no point of contact in our modern experience which reveals so clearly the lack of that equality which democracy implies. We have reached the moment when democracy has made such inroads upon this relationship, that the complacency of the old-fashioned charitable man is gone forever; while, at the same time, the very need and existence of charity, denies us the consolation and freedom which democracy will at last give.

It is quite obvious that the ethics of none of us are clearly defined, and we are continually obliged to act in circles of habit, based upon convictions which we no longer hold. Thus our estimate of the effect of environment and social conditions has doubtless shifted faster than our methods of administrating charity have changed. Formerly when it was believed that poverty was synonymous with vice and laziness, and that the prosperous man was the righteous man charity was administered harshly with a good conscience; for the charitable agent really blamed the individual for his poverty, and the very fact of his own superior prosperity gave him a certain consciousness of superior morality. We have learned since that time to measure by other standards, and have ceased to accord to the money-earning capacity exclusive respect; while it is still rewarded out of all proportion to any other, its possession is by no means assumed to imply the possession of the highest moral qualities. We have learned to judge men by their social virtues as well as by their business capacity, by their devotion to intellectual and disinterested aims, and by their public spirit, and we naturally resent being obliged to judge poor people so solely upon the industrial side. Our democratic instinct instantly takes alarm. It is largely in this modern tendency to judge all men by one democratic standard, while the old charitable attitude commonly allowed the use of two standards, that much of the difficulty adheres. We know that unceasing bodily toil becomes wearing and brutalizing, and our position is totally untenable if we judge large numbers of our fellows solely upon their success in maintaining it.

The daintily clad charitable visitor who steps into the little house made untidy by the vigorous efforts of her hostess, the washerwoman, is no longer sure of her superiority to the latter; she recognizes that her hostess after all represents social value and industrial use, as over against her own parasitic cleanliness and a social standing attained only through status.

The only families who apply for aid to the charitable agencies are those who have come to grief on the industrial side; it may be through sickness, through loss of work, or for other guiltless and inevitable reasons; but the fact remains that they are industrially ailing, and must be bolstered and helped into industrial health. The charity visitor, let us assume, is a young college woman, well-bred and open-minded; when she visits the family assigned to her, she is often embarrassed to find herself obliged to lay all the stress of her teaching and advice upon the industrial virtues, and to treat the members of the family almost exclusively as factors in the industrial system. She insists that they must work and be self-supporting, that the most dangerous of all situations is idleness, that seeking one's own pleasure, while ignoring claims and responsibilities, is the most ignoble of actions. The members of her assigned family may have other charms and virtues—they may possibly be kind and considerate of each other, generous to their friends, but it is her business to stick to the industrial side. As she daily holds up these standards, it often occurs to the mind of the sensitive visitor, whose conscience has been made tender by much talk of brotherhood and equality, that she has no right to say these things; that her untrained hands are no more fitted to cope with actual conditions than those of her broken-down family. . . .

Added to this is a consciousness, in the mind of the visitor, of a genuine misunderstanding of her motives by the recipients of her charity, and by their neighbors. Let us take a neighborhood of poor people, and test their ethical standards by those of the charity visitor, who comes with the best desire in the world to help them out of their distress. A most striking incongruity, at once apparent, is the difference between the emotional kindness with which relief is given by one poor neighbor to another poor neighbor, and the guarded care with which relief is given by a charity visitor to a charity recipient. The neighborhood mind is at once confronted not only by the difference of method, but by an absolute clashing of two ethical standards.

A very little familiarity with the poor districts of any city is sufficient to show how primitive and genuine are the neighborly relations. There is the greatest willingness to lend or borrow anything, and all the residents of the given tenement know the most intimate family affairs of all the others. The fact that the economic condition of all alike is on a most precarious level makes the ready outflow of sympathy and material assistance the most natural thing in the world. There are numberless instances of self-sacrifice quite un-known in the circles where greater economic advantages make that kind of intimate knowledge of one's neighbors impossible. An Irish family in which the man has lost his place, and the woman is struggling to eke out the scanty savings by day's work, will take in the widow and her five children who have been turned into the street, without a moment's reflection upon the physical discomforts involved. The most maligned landlady who lives in the house with her tenants is usually ready to lend a scuttle full of coal to one of them who may be out of work, or to share her supper. A woman for whom the writer had long tried in vain to find work failed to appear at the appointed time when employment was secured at last. Upon investigation it transpired that a neighbor further down the street was taken ill, that the children ran for the family friend, who went of course, saying simply when reasons for her non-appearance were demanded, "It broke me heart to leave the place, but what could I do?" A woman whose husband was sent up to the city prison for the maximum term, just three months, before the birth of her child found herself penniless at the end of that time, having gradually sold her supply of house-hold furniture. She took refuge with a friend whom she supposed to be living in three rooms in another part of town. When she arrived, however, she discov-ered that her friend's husband had been out of work so long that they had been reduced to living in one room. The friend, however, took her in, and the friend's hus-band was obliged to sleep upon a bench in the park every night for a week, which he did uncomplaining-ly if not cheerfully. Fortunately it was summer, "and it only rained one night." The writer could not discover from the young mother that she had any special claim upon the "friend" beyond the fact that they had for-merly worked together in the same factory. The hus-band she had never seen until the night of her arrival, when he at once went forth in search of a midwife who would consent to come upon his promise of future payment.

The evolutionists tell us that the instinct to pity, the impulse to aid his fellows, served man at a very early period, as a rude rule of right and wrong. There is no doubt that this rude rule still holds among many people with whom charitable agencies are brought into contact, and that their ideas of right and wrong are quite honestly outraged by the methods of these agen-cies. When they see the delay and caution with which relief is given, it does not appear to them a conscien-tious scruple, but as the cold and calculating action of a selfish man. It is not the aid that they are accustomed to receive from their neighbors, and they do not under-stand why the impulse which drives people to "be

good to the poor" should be so severely supervised. They feel, remotely, that the charity visitor is moved by motives that are alien and unreal. They may be supe-rior motives, but they are different, and they are "agin nature." They cannot comprehend why a person whose intellectual perceptions are stronger than his natural impulses, should go into charity work at all. The only man they are accustomed to see whose intellectual perceptions are stronger than his tenderness of heart, is the selfish and avaricious man who is frankly "on the make." If the charity visitor is such a person, why does she pretend to like the poor? Why does she not go into business at once?

We may say, of course, that it is a primitive view of life, which thus confuses intellectuality and business ability; but it is a view quite honestly held by many poor people who are obliged to receive charity from time to time. In moments of indignation the poor have been known to say: "What do you want, anyway? If you have nothing to give us, why not let us alone and stop your questionings and investigations?" "They investi-gated me for three weeks, and in the end gave me nothing but a black character," a little woman has been heard to assert. This indignation, which is for the most part taciturn, and a certain kindly contempt for her abilities, often puzzles the charity visitor. The lat-ter may be explained by the standard of worldly suc-cess which the visited families hold. Success does not ordinarily go, in the minds of the poor, with charity and kindheartedness, but rather with the opposite qual-ities. The rich landlord is he who collects with stern-ness, who accepts no excuse, and will have his own. There are moments of irritation and of real bitterness against him, but there is still admiration, because he is rich and successful. The good-natured landlord, he who pities and spares his poverty-pressed tenants, is seldom rich. He often lives in the back of his house, which he has owned for a long time, perhaps has inherited; but he has been able to accumulate little. He commands the genuine love and devotion of many a poor soul, but he is treated with a certain lack of respect. In one sense he is a failure. The charity visitor, just because she is a person who concerns herself with the poor, receives a certain amount of this good-na-tured and kindly contempt, sometimes real affection, but little genuine respect. The poor are accustomed to help each other and to respond according to their kindliness; but when it comes to worldly judgment, they use industrial success as the sole standard. In the case of the charity visitor who has neither natural kind-ness nor dazzling riches, they are deprived of both standards, and they find it of course utterly impossible to judge of the motive of organized charity.

Even those of us who feel most sorely the need of

more order in altruistic effort and see the end to be desired, find something distasteful in the juxtaposition of the words "organized" and "charity." We say in defence that we are striving to turn this emotion into a motive, that pity is capricious, and not to be depended on; that we mean to give it the dignity of conscious duty. But at bottom we distrust a little a scheme which substitutes a theory of social conduct for the natural promptings of the heart, even although we appreciate the complexity of the situation. The poor man who has fallen into distress, when he first asks aid, instinctively expects tenderness, consideration, and forgiveness. If it is the first time, it has taken him long to make up his mind to take the step. He comes somewhat bruised and battered, and instead of being met with warmth of heart and sympathy, he is at once chilled by an investigation and an intimation that he ought to work. He does not recognize the disciplinary aspect of the situation.

The only really popular charity is that of the visiting nurses, who by virtue of their professional training render services which may easily be interpreted into sympathy and kindness, ministering as they do to obvious needs which do not require investigation.

The state of mind which an investigation arouses on both sides is most unfortunate; but the perplexity and clashing of different standards, with the consequent misunderstandings, are not so bad as the moral deterioration which is almost sure to follow.

When the agent or visitor appears among the poor, and they discover that under certain conditions food and rent and medical aid are dispensed from some unknown source, every man, woman, and child is quick to learn what the conditions may be, and to follow them. Though in their eyes a glass of beer is quite right and proper when taken as any self-respecting man should take it; though they know that cleanliness is an expensive virtue which can be required of few; though they realize that saving is well-nigh impossible when but a few cents can be laid by at a time; though their feeling for the church may be something quite elusive of definition and quite apart from daily living: to the visitor they gravely laud temperance and cleanliness and thrift and religious observance. The deception in the first instances arises from a wondering inability to understand the ethical ideals which can require such impossible virtues, and from an innocent desire to please. It is easy to trace the development of the mental suggestions thus received. When A discovers that B, who is very little worse off than he, receives good things from an inexhaustible supply intended for the poor at large, he feels that he too has a claim for his share, and step by step there is developed the competitive spirit which so horrifies charity visitors

when it shows itself in a tendency to "work" the relief-giving agencies. . . .

If a poor woman knows that her neighbor next door has no shoes, she is quite willing to lend her own, that her neighbor may go decently to mass, or to work; for she knows the smallest item about the scanty wardrobe, and cheerfully helps out. When the charity visitor comes in, all the neighbors are baffled as to what her circumstances may be. They know she does not need a new pair of shoes, and rather suspect that she has a dozen pairs at home; which, indeed, she sometimes has. They imagine untold stores which they may call upon, and her most generous gift is considered niggardly, compared with what she might do. She ought to get new shoes for the family all round, "she sees well enough that they need them." It is no more than the neighbor herself would do, has practically done, when she lent her own shoes. The charity visitor has broken through the natural rule of giving, which, in a primitive society, is bounded only by the need of the recipient and the resources of the giver; and she gets herself into untold trouble when she is judged by the ethics of that primitive society.

The neighborhood understands the selfish rich people who stay in their own part of town, where all their associates have shoes and other things. Such people don't bother themselves about the poor; they are like the rich landlords of the neighborhood experience. But this lady visitor, who pretends to be good to the poor, and certainly does talk as though she were kind-hearted, what does she come for, if she does not intend to give them things which are so plainly needed?

The visitor says, sometimes, that in holding her poor family so hard to a standard of thrift she is really breaking down a rule of higher living which they formerly possessed; that saving, which seems quite commendable in a comfortable part of town, appears almost criminal in a poorer quarter where the next-door neighbor needs food, even if the children of the family do not.

She feels the sordidness of constantly being obliged to urge the industrial view of life. The benevolent individual of fifty years ago honestly believed that industry and self-denial in youth would result in comfortable possessions for old age. It was, indeed, the method he had practised in his own youth, and by which he had probably obtained whatever fortune he possessed. He therefore reproved the poor family for indulging their children, urged them to work long hours, and was utterly untouched by many scruples which afflict the contemporary charity visitor. She says sometimes, "Why must I talk always of getting work and saving money, the things I know nothing about? If it were anything else I had to urge, I could do it; anything like Latin prose, which I had worried through myself, it would not be so hard." But she finds it difficult to connect the experiences of her youth with the experiences of the visited family. . . .

The charity visitor may blame the women for lack of gentleness toward their children, for being hasty and rude to them, until she learns that the standard of breeding is not that of gentleness toward the children so much as the observance of certain conventions, such as the punctilious wearing of mourning garments after the death of a child. The standard of gentleness each mother has to work out largely by herself, assisted only by the occasional shame-faced remark of a neighbor, "That they do better when you are not too hard on them"; but the wearing of mourning garments is sustained by the definitely expressed sentiment of every woman in the street. The mother would have to bear social blame, a certain social ostracism, if she failed to comply with that requirement. It is not comfortable to outrage the conventions of those among whom we live, and, if our social life be a narrow one, it is still more difficult. The visitor may choke a little when she sees the lessened supply of food and the scanty clothing provided for the remaining children in order that one may be conventionally mourned, but she doesn't talk so strongly against it as she would have done during her first month of experience with the family since bereaved.

The subject of clothes indeed perplexes the visitor constantly, and the result of her reflections may be summed up somewhat in this wise: The girl who has a definite social standing, who has been to a fashionable school or to a college, whose family live in a house seen and known by all her friends and associates, may afford to be very simple, or even shabby as to her clothes, if she likes. But the working girl, whose family lives in a tenement, or moves from one small apartment to another, who has little social standing and has to make her own place, knows full well how much habit and style of dress has to do with her position. Her income goes into her clothing, out of all proportion to the amount which she spends upon other things. But, if social advancement is her aim, it is the most sensible thing she can do. She is judged largely by her clothes. Her house furnishing, with its pitiful little decorations, her scanty supply of books, are never seen by the people whose social opinions she most values. Her clothes are her background, and from them she is largely judged. It is due to this fact that girls' clubs succeed best in the business part of town, where "working girls" and "young ladies" meet upon an equal footing, and where the clothes superficially look very much alike. Bright and ambitious girls will come to these down-town clubs to eat lunch and rest at noon, to study all sorts of subjects and listen to lectures, when they might hesitate a long time before joining a club identified with their own neighborhood, where they would be judged not solely on their own merits and the unconscious social standing afforded by good clothes, but by other surroundings which are not nearly up to these. For the same reason, girls' clubs are infinitely more difficult to organize in little towns and villages, where every one knows every one else, just how the front parlor is furnished, and the amount of mortgage there is upon the house. These facts get in the way of a clear and unbiassed [sic] judgment; they impede the democratic relationship and add to the self-consciousness of all concerned. Every one who has had to do with down-town girls' clubs has had the experience of going into the home of some bright, well-dressed girl, to discover it uncomfortable and perhaps wretched, and to find the girl afterward carefully avoiding her, although the working girl may not have been at home when the call was made, and the visitor may have carried herself with the utmost courtesy throughout. In some very successful down-town clubs the home address is not given at all, and only the "business address" is required. Have we worked out our democracy further in regard to clothes than anything else? . . .

The charity visitor finds herself still more perplexed when she comes to consider such problems as those of early marriage and child labor; for she cannot deal with them according to economic theories, or according to the conventions which have regulated her own life. She finds both of these fairly upset by her intimate knowledge of the situation, and her sympathy for those into whose lives she has gained a curious insight. She discovers how incorrigibly bourgeois her standards have been, and it takes but a little time to reach the conclusion that she cannot insist so strenuously upon the conventions of her own class, which fail to fit the bigger, more emotional, and freer lives of working people. The charity visitor holds well-grounded views upon the imprudence of early marriages, quite naturally because she comes from a family and circle of professional and business people. A professional man is scarcely equipped and started in his profession before he is thirty. A business man, if he is on the road to success, is much nearer prosperity at thirty-five than twenty-five, and it is therefore wise for these men not to marry in the twenties; but this does not apply to the workingman. In many trades he is laid upon the shelf at thirty-five, and in nearly all trades he receives the largest wages in his life between twenty and thirty. If the young workingman has all his wages to himself, he will probably establish habits of personal comfort, which he cannot keep up when he has to divide with a family—habits which he can, perhaps, never overcome.

The sense of prudence, the necessity for saving, can never come to a primitive, emotional man with the force of a conviction; but the necessity of providing for his children is a powerful incentive. He naturally regards his children as his savings-bank; he expects them to care for him when he gets old, and in some trades old age comes very early. A Jewish tailor was quite lately sent to the Cook County poorhouse, paralyzed beyond recovery at the age of thirty-five. Had his little boy of nine been but a few years older, he might have been spared this sorrow of public charity. He was, in fact, better able to well support a family when he was twenty than when he was thirty-five, for his wages had steadily grown less as the years went on. Another tailor whom I know, who is also a Socialist, always speaks of saving as a bourgeois virtue, one quite impossible to the genuine working-man. He supports a family consisting of himself, a wife and three children, and his two parents on eight dollars a week. He insists it would be criminal not to expend every penny of this amount upon food and shelter, and he expects his children later to care for him.

This economic pressure also accounts for the tendency to put children to work over-young and thus cripple their chances for individual development and usefulness, and with the avaricious parent also leads to exploitation. "I have fed her for fourteen years, now she can help me pay my mortgage" is not an unusual reply when a hard-working father is expostulated with because he would take his bright daughter out of school and put her into a factory. . . .

The child who is prematurely put to work is constantly oppressed by this never ending question of the means of subsistence, and even little children are sometimes almost crushed with the cares of life through their affectionate sympathy. The writer knows a little Italian lad of six to whom the problems of food, clothing, and shelter have become so immediate and pressing that, although an imaginative child, he is unable to see life from any other standpoint. The goblin or bugaboo, feared by the more fortunate child, in his mind, has come to be the need of coal which caused his father hysterical and demonstrative grief when it carried off his mother's inherited linen, the mosaic of St. Joseph, and, worst of all, his own rubber boots. He once came to a party at Hull-House, and was interested in nothing save a gas stove which he saw in the kitchen. He became excited over the discovery that fire could be produced without fuel. "I will tell my father of this stove. You buy no coal, you need only a match. Anybody will give you a match." He was taken to visit at a country-house and at once inquired how much rent was paid for it. On being told carelessly by his hostess that they paid no rent for that house, he came back quite wild with interest that the problem was solved. "Me and my father will go to the country. You get a big house, all warm, without rent." Nothing else in the country interested him but the subject of rent, and he talked of that with an exclusiveness worthy of a single taxer.

The struggle for existence, which is so much harsher among people near the edge of pauperism, sometimes leaves ugly marks on character, and the charity visitor finds these indirect results most mystifying. Parents who work hard and anticipate an old age when they can no longer earn, take care that their children shall expect to divide their wages with them from the very first. Such a parent, when successful, impresses the immature nervous system of the child thus tyrannically establishing habits of obedience, so that the nerves and will may not depart from this control when the child is older. The charity visitor, whose family relation is lifted quite out of this, does not in the least understand the industrial foundation for this family tyranny.

The head of a kindergarten training-class once addressed a club of working women, and spoke of the despotism which is often established over little children. She said that the so-called determination to break a child's will many times arose from a lust of dominion, and she urged the ideal relationship founded upon love and confidence. But many of the women were puzzled. One of them remarked to the writer as she came out of the club room, "If you did not keep control over them from the time they were little, you would never get their wages when they are grown up." Another one said, "Ah, of course she (meaning the speaker) doesn't have to depend upon her children's wages. She can afford to be lax with them, because even if they don't give money to her, she can get along without it."

There are an impressive number of children who uncomplainingly and constantly hand over their weekly wages to their parents, sometimes receiving back ten cents or a quarter for spending-money, but quite as often nothing at all; and the writer knows one girl of twenty-five who for six years has received two cents a week from the constantly falling wages which she earns in a large factory. Is it habit or virtue which holds her steady in this course? If love and tenderness had been substituted for parental despotism, would the mother have had enough affection, enough power of expression to hold her daughter's sense of money obligation through all these years? This girl who spends her paltry two cents on chewing-gum and goes plainly clad in clothes of her mother's choosing, while many of her friends spend their entire wages on those clothes which factory girls love so well, must be held by some powerful force.

The charity visitor finds these subtle and elusive problems most harrowing. The head of a family she is visiting is a man who has become black-listed in a strike. He is not a very good workman, and this, added to his agitator's reputation, keeps him out of work for a long time. The fatal result of being long out of work follows: he becomes less and less eager for it, and gets a "job" less and less frequently. In order to keep up his self-respect, and still more to keep his wife's respect for him, he yields to the little self-deception that this prolonged idleness follows because he was once black-listed, and he gradually becomes a martyr. Deep down in his heart perhaps—but who knows what may be deep down in his heart? Whatever may be in his wife's, she does not show for an instant that she thinks he has grown lazy, and accustomed to see her earn, by sewing and cleaning, most of the scanty income for the family. The charity visitor, however, does see this, and she also sees that the other men who were in the strike have gone back to work. She further knows by inquiry and a little experience that the man is not skilful. She cannot, however, call him lazy and good-for-nothing, and denounce him as worthless as her grandmother might have done, because of certain intellectual conceptions at which she has arrived. She sees other workmen come to him for shrewd advice; she knows that he spends many more hours in the public library reading good books than the average workman has time to do. He has formed no bad habits and has yielded only to those subtle temptations toward a life of leisure which come to the intellectual man. He lacks the qualifications which would induce his union to engage him as a secretary or organizer, but he is a constant speaker at workingmen's meetings, and takes a high moral attitude on the questions discussed there. He contributes a certain intellectuality to his friends, and he has undoubted social value. The neighboring women confide to the charity visitor their sympathy with his wife, because she has to work so hard, and because her husband does not "provide." Their remarks are sharpened by a certain resentment toward the superiority of the husband's education and gentle manners. The charity visitor is ashamed to take this point of view, for she knows that it is not altogether fair. She is reminded of a college friend of hers, who told her that she was not going to allow her literary husband to write unworthy potboilers for the sake of earning a living. "I insist that we shall live within my own income; that he shall not publish until he is ready, and can give his genuine message." The charity visitor recalls what she has heard of another acquaintance, who urged her husband to decline a lucrative position as a railroad attorney, because she wished him to be free to take municipal positions, and handle public questions without the inevitable suspicion which unaccountably attaches itself in a corrupt city to a corporation attorney. The action of these two women seemed noble to her, but in their cases they merely lived on a lesser income. In the case of the working-man's wife, she faced living on no income at all, or on the precarious one which she might be able to get together.

She sees that this third woman has made the greatest sacrifice, and she is utterly unwilling to condemn her while praising the friends of her own social position. She realizes, of course, that the situation is changed by the fact that the third family needs charity, while the other two do not; but after all, they have not asked for it, and their plight was only discovered through an accident to one of the children. The charity visitor has been taught that her mission is to preserve the finest traits to be found in her visited family, and she shrinks from the thought of convincing the wife that her husband is worthless and she suspects that she might turn all this beautiful devotion into complaining drudgery. To be sure, she could give up visiting the family altogether, but she has become much interested in the progress of the crippled child who eagerly anticipates her visits, and she also suspects that she will never know many finer women than the mother. She is unwilling, therefore, to give up the friendship, and goes on bearing her perplexities as best she may. . . .

In the first year of their settlement the Hull-House residents took fifty kindergarten children to Lincoln Park, only to be grieved by their apathetic interest in trees and flowers. As they came back with an omnibus full of tired and sleepy children, they were surprised to find them galvanized into sudden life because a patrol wagon rattled by. Their eager little heads popped out of the windows full of questioning: "Was it a man or a woman?" "How many policemen inside?" and eager little tongues began to tell experiences of arrests which baby eyes had witnessed.

The excitement of a chase, the chances of competition, and the love of a fight are all centered in the outward display of crime. The parent who receives charitable aid and yet provides pleasure for his child, and is willing to indulge him in his play, is blindly doing one of the wisest things possible; and no one is more eager for playgrounds and vacation schools than the conscientious charity visitor.

This very imaginative impulse and attempt to live in a pictured world of their own, which seems the simplest prerogative of childhood, often leads the boys into difficulty. Three boys aged seven, nine, and ten were once brought into a neighboring police station under the charge of pilfering and destroying property. They had dug a cave under a railroad viaduct in which they had spent many days and nights of summer vacation. They had "swiped" potatoes and other vegetables from hucksters' carts, which they had cooked and eaten in true brigand fashion; they had decorated the interior of the excavation with stolen junk, representing swords and firearms, to their romantic imaginations. The father of the ringleader was a janitor living in a building five miles away in a prosperous portion of the city. The landlord did not want an active boy in the building, and his mother was dead; the janitor paid for the boy's board and lodging to a needy woman living near the viaduct. She conscientiously gave him his breakfast and supper, and left something in the house for his dinner every morning when she went to work in a neighboring factory; but was too tired by night to challenge his statement that he "would rather sleep outdoors in the summer," or to investigate what he did during the day. In the meantime the three boys lived in a world of their own, made up from the reading of adventurous stories and their vivid imaginations, steadily pilfering more and more as the days went by, and actually imperilling the safety of the traffic passing over the street on the top of the viaduct. In spite of vigorous exertions on their behalf, one of the boys was sent to the Reform School, comforting himself with the conclusive remark, "Well, we had fun anyway, and maybe they will let us dig a cave at the School; it is in the country, where we can't hurt anything."

In addition to books of adventure, or even reading of any sort, the scenes and ideals of the theatre largely form the manners and morals of the young people. "Going to the theatre" is indeed the most common and satisfactory form of recreation. Many boys who conscientiously give all their wages to their mothers have returned each week ten cents to pay for a seat in the gallery of a theatre on Sunday afternoon. It is their one satisfactory glimpse of life—the moment when they "issue forth from themselves" and are stirred and thoroughly interested. They quite simply adopt as their own, and imitate as best they can, all that they see there. In moments of genuine grief and excitement the words and the gestures they employ are those copied from the stage, and the tawdry expression often conflicts hideously with the fine and genuine emotion of which it is the inadequate and vulgar vehicle. . . .

Such a situation brings out the impossibility of substituting a higher ethical standard for a lower one without similarity of experience, but it is not as painful as that illustrated by the following example, in which the highest ethical standard yet attained by the charity

recipient is broken down, and the substituted one not in the least understood: —

A certain charity visitor is peculiarly appealed to by the weakness and pathos of forlorn old age. She is responsible for the well-being of perhaps a dozen old women to whom she sustains a sincerely affectionate and almost filial relation. Some of them learn to take her benefactions quite as if they came from their own relatives, grumbling at all she does, and scolding her with a family freedom. One of these poor old women was injured in a fire years ago. She has but the fragment of a hand left, and is grievously crippled in her feet. Through years of pain she had become addicted to opium, and when she first came under the visitor's care, was only held from the poorhouse by the awful thought that she would there perish without her drug. Five years of tender care have done wonders for her. She lives in two neat little rooms, where with her thumb and two fingers she makes innumerable quilts, which she sells and gives away with the greatest delight. Her opium is regulated to a set amount taken each day, and she has been drawn away from much drinking. She is a voracious reader, and has her head full of strange tales made up from books and her own imagination. At one time it seemed impossible to do anything for her in Chicago, and she was kept for two years in a suburb, where the family of the charity visitor lived, and where she was nursed through several hazardous illnesses. She now lives a better life than she did, but she is still far from being a model old woman. The neighbors are constantly shocked by the fact that she is supported and comforted by a "charity lady," while at the same time she occasionally "rushes the growler," scolding at the boys lest they jar her in her tottering walk. The care of her has broken through even that second standard, which the neighborhood had learned to recognize as the standard of charitable societies, that only the "worthy poor" are to be helped; that temperance and thrift are the virtues which receive the plums of benevolence. The old lady herself is conscious of this criticism. Indeed, irate neighbors tell her to her face that she doesn't in the least deserve what she gets. In order to disarm them, and at the same time to explain what would otherwise seem loving-kindness so colossal as to be abnormal, she tells them that during her sojourn in the suburb she discovered an awful family secret, —a horrible scandal connected with the long-suffering charity visitor; that it is in order to prevent the divulgence of this that she constantly receives her ministrations. Some of her perplexed neighbors accept this explanation as simple and offering a solution of this vexed problem. Doubtless many of them have a glimpse of the real state of affairs, of the love and patience which ministers to need irrespective of worth.

But the standard is too high for most of them, and it sometimes seems unfortunate to break down the second standard, which holds that people who "rush the growler" are not worthy of charity, and that there is a certain justice attained when they go to the poorhouse. It is certainly dangerous to break down the lower, unless the higher is made clear.

Just when our affection becomes large enough to care for the unworthy among the poor as we would care for the unworthy among our own kin, is certainly a perplexing question. To say that it should never be so, is a comment upon our democratic relations to them which few of us would be willing to make.

Of what use is all this striving and perplexity? Has the experience any value? It is certainly genuine, for it induces an occasional charity visitor to live in a tenement house as simply as the other tenants do. It drives others to give up visiting the poor altogether, because, they claim, it is quite impossible unless the individual becomes a member of a sisterhood, which requires, as some of the Roman Catholic sisterhoods do, that the member first take the vows of obedience and poverty, so that she can have nothing to give save as it is first given to her, and thus she is not harassed by a constant attempt at adjustment.

Both the tenement-house resident and the sister assume to have put themselves upon the industrial level of their neighbors, although they have left out the most awful element of poverty, that of imminent fear of starvation and a neglected old age.

The young charity visitor who goes from a family living upon a most precarious industrial level to her own home in a prosperous part of the city, if she is sensitive at all, is never free from perplexities which our growing democracy forces upon her.

We sometimes say that our charity is too scientific, but we would doubtless be much more correct in our estimate if we said that it is not scientific enough. We dislike the entire arrangement of cards alphabetically classified according to streets and names of families, with the unrelated and meaningless details attached to them. Our feeling of revolt is probably not unlike that which afflicted the students of botany and geology in the middle of the last century, when flowers were tabulated in alphabetical order, when geology was taught by colored charts and thin books. No doubt the students, wearied to death, many times said that it was all too scientific, and were much perplexed and worried when they found traces of structure and physiology which their so-called scientific principles were totally unable to account for. But all this happened before science had become evolutionary and scientific at all, before it had a principle of life from within. The very

indications and discoveries which formerly perplexed, later illumined and made the study absorbing and vital.

We are singularly slow to apply this evolutionary principle to human affairs in general, although it is fast being applied to the education of children. We are at last learning to follow the development of the child; to expect certain traits under certain conditions; to adapt methods and matter to his growing mind. No "advanced educator" can allow himself to be so absorbed in the question of what a child ought to be as to exclude the discovery of what he is. But in our charitable efforts we think much more of what a man ought to be than of what he is or of what he may become; and we ruthlessly force our conventions and standards upon him, with a sternness which we would consider stupid indeed did an educator use it in forcing his mature intellectual convictions upon an undeveloped mind. . . .

On the other hand, the young woman who has succeeded in expressing her social compunction through charitable effort finds that the wider social activity, and the contact with the larger experience, not only increases her sense of social obligation but at the same time recasts her social ideals. She is chagrined to discover that in the actual task of reducing her social scruples to action, her humble beneficiaries are far in advance of her, not in charity or singleness of purpose, but in self-sacrificing action. She reaches the old-time virtue of humility by a social process, not in the old way, as the man who sits by the side of the road and puts dust upon his head, calling himself a contrite sinner, but she gets the dust upon her head because she has stumbled and fallen in the road through her efforts to push forward the mass, to march with her fellows. She has socialized her virtues not only through a social aim but by a social process.

The Hebrew prophet made three requirements from those who would join the great forward-moving procession led by Jehovah. "To love mercy" and at the same time "to do justly" is the difficult task; to fulfil the first requirement alone is to fall into the error of indiscriminate giving with all its disastrous results; to fulfil the second solely is to obtain the stern policy of withholding, and it results in such a dreary lack of sympathy and understanding that the establishment of justice is impossible. It may be that the combination of the two can never be attained save as we fulfil still the third requirement—"to walk humbly with God," which may mean to walk for many dreary miles beside the lowliest of His creatures, not even in that peace of mind which the company of the humble is popularly supposed to afford, but rather with the pangs and

throes to which the poor human understanding is subjected whenever it attempts to comprehend the meaning of life.

Newer Ideals of Peace (1906)

Chapter I. Introduction

The following pages present the claims of the newer, more aggressive ideals of peace, as over against the
older dovelike ideal. These newer ideals are active and
dynamic, and it is believed that if their forces were
made really operative upon society, they would, in the
end, quite as a natural process, do away with war. The
older ideals have required fostering and recruiting,
and have been held and promulgated on the basis of
a creed. Their propaganda has been carried forward
during the last century in nearly all civilized countries
by a small body of men who have never ceased to cry
out against war and its iniquities and who have
preached the doctrines of peace along two great lines.
The first has been the appeal to the higher imaginative pity, as it is found in the modern, moralized man.
This line has been most effectively followed by two
Russians, Count Tolstoy in his earlier writings and
Verestchagin in his paintings. With his relentless power of reducing all life to personal experience Count
Tolstoy drags us through the campaign of the common
soldier in its sordidness and meanness and constant
sense of perplexity. We see nothing of the glories we
have associated with warfare, but learn of it as it appears to the untutored peasant who goes forth at the
mandate of his superior to suffer hunger, cold, and
death for issues which he does not understand, which,
indeed, can have no moral significance to him. Verestchagin covers his canvas with thousands of wretched
wounded and neglected dead, with the waste, cruelty,
and squalor of war, until he forces us to question
whether a moral issue can ever be subserved by such
brutal methods.

High and searching as is the preaching of these two
great Russians who hold their art of no account save as
it serves moral ends, it is still the appeal of dogma, and
may be reduced to a command to cease from evil. And
when this same line of appeal is presented by less gifted
men, it often results in mere sentimentality, totally
unenforced by a call to righteousness.

The second line followed by the advocates of peace
in all countries has been the appeal to the sense of
prudence, and this again has found its ablest exponent
in a Russian subject, the economist and banker, Jean
de Bloch. He sets forth the cost of warfare with pitiless
accuracy, and demonstrates that even the present
armed peace is so costly that the burdens of it threaten
social revolution in almost every country in Europe.
Long before the reader comes to the end of de Bloch's
elaborate computation he is ready to cry out on the
inanity of the proposition that the only way to secure
eternal peace is to waste so much valuable energy and
treasure in preparing for war that war becomes impossible. Certainly no theory could be devised which is
more cumbersome, more roundabout, more extravagant, than the *reductio ad absurdum* of the peace-
secured-by the preparation-for-war theory. This appeal
to prudence was constantly emphasized at the first
Hague Conference and was shortly afterward demonstrated by Great Britain when she went to war in
South Africa, where she was fined one hundred million pounds and lost ten thousand lives. The fact that
Russia also, and the very Czar who invited the Conference, disregarded the conclusions of the Hague Tribunal makes this line of appeal at least for the moment
seem impotent to influence empires which command
enormous resources and which lodge the power of
expenditure in officials who have nothing to do with
accumulating the treasure they vote to expend.

It would, however, be the height of folly for responsible statesmen to ignore the sane methods of
international discussion and concession which have
been evolved largely as a result of these appeals. The
Interparliamentary Union for International Arbitration and the Institute of International Law represent
the untiring efforts of the advocates of peace through
many years. Nevertheless universal peace, viewed from
the point of the World's Sovereignty or the Counsel of
Nations, is discouraging even when stated by the most
ardent promoters of the peace society. Here it is quite
possible that the mistake is being repeated which the
old annalists of history made when they never failed to
chronicle the wars and calamities which harassed their
contemporaries, although, while the few indulged in
fighting, the mass of them peacefully prosecuted their
daily toil and followed their own conceptions of kindliness and equity. . . .

Assuming that the two lines of appeal—the one to
sensibility and the other to prudence—will persist,
and that the international lawyers, in spite of the fact
that they have no court before which to plead and no
executive to enforce their findings, will continue to
formulate into codes the growing moral sense of the
nations, the following pages hope not only to make
clear the contention that these forces within society
are so dynamic and vigorous that the impulses to war

seem by comparison cumbersome and mechanical, but also to point out the development of those newer social forces which it is believed will at last prove a "sovereign intervention" by extinguishing the possibility of battle at its very source.

It is difficult to formulate the newer dynamic peace, embodying the later humanism, as over against the old dogmatic peace. The word "non-resistance" is misleading, because it is much too feeble and inadequate. It suggests passivity, the goody-goody attitude of ineffectiveness. The words "overcoming," "substituting," "re-creating," "readjusting moral values," "forming new centres of spiritual energy" carry much more of the meaning implied. For it is not merely the desire for a conscience at rest, for a sense of justice no longer outraged, that would pull us into new paths where there would be no more war nor preparations for war. There are still more strenuous forces at work reaching down to impulses and experiences as primitive and profound as are those of struggle itself. That "ancient kindliness which sat beside the cradle of the race," and which is ever ready to assert itself against ambition and greed and the desire for achievement, is manifesting itself now with unusual force, and for the first time presents international prospects. . . .

In the midst of the modern city which, at moments, seems to stand only for the triumph of the strongest, the successful exploitation of the weak, the ruthlessness and hidden crime which follow in the wake of the struggle for existence on its lowest terms, there come daily—at least to American cities—accretions of simple people, who carry in their hearts a desire for mere goodness. They regularly deplete their scanty livelihood in response to a primitive pity, and, independent of the religions they have professed, or the wrongs they have suffered, and of the fixed morality they have been taught, have an unquenchable desire that charity and simple justice shall regulate men's relations. . . .

. . . If we would adduce evidence that we are emerging from a period of industrialism into a period of humanitarianism, it is to such quarters that we must betake ourselves. These are the places in which it is easiest to study the newer manifestations of government, in which personal welfare is considered a legitimate object; for a new history of government begins with an attempt to make life possible and human in large cities, in those crowded quarters which exhibit such an undoubted tendency to barbarism and degeneracy when the better human qualities are not nourished. Public baths and gymnasiums, parks and libraries, are provided first for those who are without the security for bare subsistence, and it does not seem strange to them that it should be so. Such a community

is made up of men who will continue to dream of Utopian Governments until the democratic government about them expresses kindliness with protection. . . . As their hopes and dreams are a prophecy of the future development in city government, in charity, in education, so their daily lives are a forecast of coming international relations. Our attention has lately been drawn to the fact that it is logical that the most vigorous efforts in governmental reform, as well as the most generous experiments in ministering to social needs, have come from the larger cities and that it is inevitable that they should be to-day "the centers of radicalism," as they have been traditionally the "cradles of liberty."

If we once admit the human dynamic character of progress, then it is easy to understand why the crowded city quarters become focal points of that progress.

A deeper and more thorough-going unity is required in a community made up of highly differentiated peoples than in a more settled and stratified one, and it may be logical that we should find in this commingling of many peoples a certain balance and concord of opposing and contending forces; a gravitation toward the universal. Because of their difference in all external matters, in all of the non-essentials of life, the people in a cosmopolitan city are forced to found their community of interests upon the basic and essential likenesses of their common human nature; for, after all, the things that make men alike are stronger and more primitive than the things that separate them. It is natural that this synthesis of the varying nations should be made first at the points of the greatest congestion, quite as we find that selfishness is first curbed and social feeling created at the points where the conflict of individual interests is sharpest. One dares not grow too certain as to the wells of moral healing which lie under the surface of the sullen work-driven life which the industrial quarters of the modern city present. They fascinate us by their mere size and diversity, as does the city itself; but certain it is, that these quarters continually confound us by their manifestations of altruism. . . .

It is possible that we shall be saved from warfare by the "fighting rabble" itself, by the "quarrelsome mob" turned into kindly citizens of the world through the pressure of a cosmopolitan neighborhood. It is not that they are shouting for peace—on the contrary, if they shout at all, they will continue to shout for war—but that they are really attaining cosmopolitan relations through daily experience. . . . They are developing the only sort of patriotism consistent with the intermingling of the nations; for the citizens of a cosmopolitan quarter find an insuperable difficulty when they attempt to hem in their conception of patriotism either to the "old country" or to their adopted one. There arises the hope that when this newer patriotism becomes large enough, it will overcome arbitrary boundaries and soak up the notion of nationalism. We may then give up war, because we shall find it as difficult to make war upon a nation at the other side of the globe as upon our next-door neighbor. . . .

. . . An American philosopher [William James, Professor of Philosophy at Harvard University] has lately reminded us of the need to "discover in the social realm the moral equivalent for war—something heroic that will speak to men as universally as war has done, and yet will be as compatible with their spiritual natures as war has proved itself to be incompatible." It may be true that we are even now discovering these moral substitutes, although we find it so difficult to formulate them. Perhaps our very hope that these substitutes may be discovered has become the custodian of a secret change that is going on all about us. We care less each day for the heroism connected with warfare and destruction, and constantly admire more that which pertains to labor and the nourishing of human life. The new heroism manifests itself at the present moment in a universal determination to abolish poverty and disease, a manifestation so widespread that it may justly be called international. . . .

We are much too timid and apologetic in regard to this newer humanitarianism, and do not yet realize what it may do for us in the way of courage and endurance. We continue to defend war on the ground that it stirs the nobler blood and the higher imagination of the nation, and thus frees it from moral stagnation and the bonds of commercialism. We do not see that this is to borrow our virtues from a former age and to fail to utilize our own. We find ourselves in this plight because our modern morality has lacked fibre, because our humanitarianism has been much too soft and literary, and has given itself over to unreal and high-sounding phrases. It appears that our only hope for a genuine adjustment of our morality and courage to our present social and industrial developments, lies in a patient effort to work it out by daily experience. We must be willing to surrender ourselves to those ideals of the humble, which all religious teachers unite in declaring to be the foundations of a sincere moral life.

The following pages attempt to uncover these newer ideals as we may daily experience them in the modern city. It may be found that certain survivals of militarism in municipal government are responsible for much of the failure in the working of democratic institutions. We may discover that the survivals of warfare in the labor movement and all the other dangers of class morality rest largely upon an appeal to loyalties which are essentially a survival of the virtues of a war-

like period. The more aggressive aspects of the newer humanitarianism may be traced in the movement for social amelioration and in the protective legislation which regards the weakest citizen as a valuable asset. The same spirit which protests against the social waste of child labor also demands that the traditional activity of woman shall be utilized in civic life. . . .

It is no easy task to detect and to follow the tiny paths of progress which the unencumbered proletarian with nothing but his life and capacity for labor, is pointing out for us. These paths lead to a type of government founded upon peace and fellowship as contrasted with restraint and defence. They can never be discovered with the eyes of the doctrinaire. From the nature of the case he who would walk these paths must walk with the poor and oppressed, and can only approach them through affection and understanding. The ideals of militarism would forever shut him out from this new fellowship.

Chapter II. Survivals of Militarism in Civil Government

We are accustomed to say that the machinery of government incorporated in the charters of the early American cities, as in the Federal and State constitutions, was worked out by men who were strongly under the influence of the historians and doctrinaires of the eighteenth century. The most significant representative of these men is Thomas Jefferson, and their most telling phrase, the familiar opening that "all men are created free and equal."

We are only now beginning to suspect that the present admitted failure in municipal administration, the so-called "shame of American cities," may be largely due to the inadequacy of those eighteenth-century ideals, with the breakdown of the machinery which they provided. We recognize the weakness inherent in the historic and doctrinaire method when it attempts to deal with growing and human institutions. While these men were strongly under the influence of peace ideals which were earnestly advocated, both in France and in America, even in the midst of their revolutionary periods, and while they read the burning poets and philosophers of their remarkable century, their idealism, after all, was largely founded upon theories concerning "the natural man," a creature of their sympathetic imaginations.

Because their idealism was of the type that is afraid of experience, these founders refused to look at the difficulties and blunders which a self-governing people were sure to encounter, and insisted that, if only the people had freedom, they would walk continuously in the paths of justice and righteousness. It was inevitable, therefore, that they should have remained quite untouched by that worldly wisdom which counsels us to know life as it is, and by that very modern belief that if the world is ever to go right at all, it must go right in its own way.

A man of this generation easily discerns the crudeness of "that eighteenth-century conception of essentially unprogressive human nature in all the empty dignity of its 'inborn rights'" [from Josiah Royce *The Spirit of Modern Philosophy*]. Because he has grown familiar with a more passionate human creed, with the modern evolutionary conception of the slowly advancing race whose rights are not "inalienable," but hard-won in the tragic processes of experience, he realizes that these painfully acquired rights must be carefully cherished or they may at any moment slip out of our hands. We know better in America than anywhere else that civilization is not a broad road, with mile-stones indicating how far each nation has proceeded upon it, but a complex struggle forward, each race and nation contributing its quota; that the variety and continuity of this commingled life afford its charm and value. We would not, if we could, conform them to one standard. But this modern attitude, which may even now easily subside into negative tolerance, did not exist among the founders of the Republic, who, with all their fine talk of the "natural man" and what he would accomplish when he obtained freedom and equality, did not really trust the people after all.

They timidly took the English law as their prototype, "whose very root is in the relation between sovereign and subject, between lawmaker and those whom the law restrains," which has traditionally concerned itself more with the guarding of prerogative and with the rights of property than with the spontaneous life of the people. They serenely incorporated laws and survivals which registered the successful struggle of the barons against the aggressions of the sovereign, although the new country lacked both nobles and kings. Misled by the name of government, they founded their new government by an involuntary reference to a lower social state than that which they actually saw about them. They depended upon penalties, coercion, compulsion, remnants of military codes, to hold the community together; and it may be possible to trace much of the maladministration of our cities to these survivals, to the fact that our early democracy was a moral romanticism, rather than a well-grounded belief in social capacity and in the efficiency of the popular will.

It has further happened that as the machinery, groaning under the pressure of new social demands put upon it, has broken down that from time to time,

we have mended it by giving more power to administrative officers, because we still distrusted the will of the people. We are willing to cut off the dislocated part or to tighten the gearing, but are afraid to substitute a machine of newer invention and greater capacity. In the hour of danger we revert to the military and legal type although they become less and less appropriate to city life in proportion as the city grows more complex, more varied in resource and more highly organized, and is, therefore, in greater need of a more diffused local autonomy.

A little examination will easily show that in spite of the fine phrases of the founders, the Government became an entity by itself away from the daily life of the people. There was no intention to ignore them nor to oppress them. But simply because its machinery was so largely copied from the traditional European Governments which did distrust the people, the founders failed to provide the vehicle for a vital and genuinely organized expression of the popular will. The founders carefully defined what was germane to government and what was quite outside its realm, whereas the very crux of local self-government, as has been well said, is involved in the "right to locally determine the scope of the local government," in response to the needs as they arise.

They were anxious to keep the reins of government in the hands of the good and professedly public-spirited, because, having staked so much upon the people whom they really knew so little, they became eager that they should appear well, and should not be given enough power to enable them really to betray their weaknesses. This was done in the same spirit in which a kind lady permits herself to give a tramp five cents, believing that, although he may spend it for drink, he cannot get very drunk upon so small a sum. In spite of a vague desire to trust the people, the founders meant to fall back in every crisis upon the old restraints which government has traditionally enlisted in its behalf, and were, perhaps, inevitably influenced by the experiences of the Revolutionary War. Having looked to the sword for independence from oppressive governmental control, they came to regard the sword as an essential part of the government they had succeeded in establishing.

Regarded from the traditional standpoint, government has always needed this force of arms. The king, attempting to control the growing power of the barons as they wrested one privilege after another from him, was obliged to use it constantly; the barons later successfully established themselves in power only to be encroached upon by the growing strength and capital of the merchant class. These are now, in turn, calling upon the troops and militia for aid, as they are shorn of a pittance here and there by the rising power of the proletariat. The imperial, the feudal, the capitalistic forms of society each created by revolt against oppression from above, preserved their own forms of government only by carefully guarding their hardly won charters and constitutions. But in the very countries where these successive social forms have developed, full of survivals of the past, some beneficent and some detrimental, governments are becoming modified more rapidly than in this democracy where we ostensibly threw off traditional governmental oppression only to encase ourselves in a theory of virtuous revolt against oppressive government, which in many instances has proved more binding than the actual oppression itself.

Did the founders cling too hard to that which they had won through persecution, hardship, and finally through a war of revolution? Did these doctrines seem so precious to them that they were determined to tie men up to them as long as possible, and allow them no chance to go on to new devices of government, lest they slight these that had been so hardly won? Did they estimate, not too highly, but by too exclusive a valuation, that which they had secured through the shedding of blood?

Man has ever overestimated the spoils of war, and tended to lose his sense of proportion in regard to their value. He has ever surrounded them with a glamour beyond their deserts. This is quite harmless when the booty is an enemy's sword hung over a household fire, or a battered flag decorating a city hall, but when the spoil of war is an idea which is bound on the forehead of the victor until it cramps his growth, a theory which he cherishes in his bosom until it grows so large and near that it afflicts its possessor with a sort of disease of responsibility for its preservation, it may easily overshadow the very people for whose cause the warrior issued forth.

Was this overestimation of the founders the cause of our subsequent failures? or rather did not the fault lie with their successors, and does it not now rest with us, that we have wrapped our inheritance in a napkin and refused to add thereto? The founders fearlessly took the noblest word of their century and incorporated it into a public document. They ventured their fortunes and the future of their children upon its truth. We, with the belief of a progressive, developing human life, apparently accomplish less than they with their insistence upon rights and liberties which they so vigorously opposed to mediaeval restrictions and obligations. We are in that first period of conversion when we hold a creed which forecasts newer and larger possibilities for governmental development, without in the least understanding its spiritual implications. Although we have scrupulously extended the franchise to the varied immigrants among us, we have not yet admitted them into real political fellowship. . . .

The philosophers and statesmen of the eighteenth century believed that the universal franchise would cure all ills; that liberty and equality rested only upon constitutional rights and privileges; that to obtain these two and to throw off all governmental oppression constituted the full duty of the progressive patriot. We still keep to this formalization because the philosophers of this generation give us nothing newer. We ignore the fact that world-wide problems can no longer be solved by a political constitution assuring us against opposition, but that we must frankly face the proposition that the whole situation is more industrial than political. Did we apprehend this, we might then realize that the officers of the Government who are dealing with naturalization papers and testing the knowledge of the immigrants concerning the Constitution of the United States, are only playing with counters representing the beliefs of a century ago, while the real issues are being settled by the great industrial and commercial interests which are at once the products and the masters of our contemporary life. . . .

At the present moment, as we know, the actual importing of immigrants is left largely to the energy of steamship companies and to those agents for contract labor who are keen enough to avoid the restrictive laws. The business man is here again in the saddle, as he so largely is in American affairs. From the time that the immigrants first make the acquaintance of the steamship agent in their own villages, at least until a grandchild is born on the new soil, they are subjected to various processes of exploitation from purely commercial and self-seeking interests. It begins with the representatives of the transatlantic lines and their allies, who convert the peasant holdings into money, and provide the prospective emigrants with needless supplies, such as cartridge belts and bowie knives. The brokers, in manufactured passports, send their clients by successive stages for a thousand miles to a port suiting their purposes. On the way the emigrants' eyes are treated that they may pass the physical test; they are taught to read sufficiently well to meet the literacy test; they are lent enough money to escape the pauper test, and by the time they have reached America, they are so hopelessly in debt that it requires months of work to repay all they have received. During this time they are completely under the control of the last broker in the line, who has his dingy office in an American city. The exploitation continues under the employment agency whose operations verge into those of the politician, through the naturalization henchman, the petty lawyers who foment their quarrels and grievances by the statement that in a free country everybody "goes to law," by the liquor dealers who stimulate a lively trade among them, and, finally, by the lodging-house keepers and the landlords who are not obliged to give them the housing which the American tenant demands. It is a long dreary road, and the immigrant is successfully exploited at each turn. . . .

The sinister aspect of this exploitation lies in the fact that it is carried on by agents whose stock in trade are the counters and terms of citizenship. It is said that at the present moment there are more of these agents in Palermo than perhaps in any other European port, and that those politicians who have found it impossible to stay even in that corrupt city are engaged in the brokerage of naturalization papers in the United States. Certainly one effect of the stringent contract labor laws has been to make the padrones more powerful because "smuggled alien labor" has become more valuable to American corporations, and also to make simpler the delivery of immigrant votes according to the dictates of commercial interests. . . .

Pending a recent election, a Chicago reformer begged his hearers to throw away all selfish thoughts of themselves when they went to the polls and to vote in behalf of the poor and ignorant foreigners of the city. It would be difficult to suggest anything which would result in a more serious confusion than to have each man, without personal knowledge and experiences, consider the interests of the newly arrived immigrant. The voter would have to give himself over to a veritable debauch of altruism in order to persuade himself that his vote would be of the least value to those men of whom he knew so little, and whom he considered so remote and alien to himself. In truth the attitude of the advising reformer was in reality so contemptuous that he had never considered the immigrants really partakers and molders of the political life of his country. . . .

. . . But the social results of the contemptuous attitude are even more serious and nowhere so grave as in the modern city.

Men are there brought together by multitudes in response to the concentration of industry and commerce without bringing with them the natural social and family ties or the guild relationships which distinguished the mediaeval cities and held even so late as the eighteenth century, when the country people came to town in response to the normal and slowly formed ties of domestic service, family affection, and apprenticeship. Men who come to a modern city by immigration break all these older ties and the national bond in addition. There is all the more necessity to develop that cosmopolitan bond which forms their substitute.

The immigrants will be ready to adapt themselves to a new and vigorous civic life founded upon the recognition of their needs if the Government which is at present administered in our cities, will only admit that these needs are germane to its functions. The framers of the carefully prepared charters, upon which the cities are founded, did not foresee that after the universal franchise had once been granted, social needs and ideals were bound to enter in as legitimate objects of political action. . . .

The traditional governments which the founders had copied, in proceeding by fixed standards to separate the vicious from the good, and then to legislate against the vicious, had enforced these restrictive measures by trained officials, usually with a military background. . . .

In order to meet this situation, there is almost inevitably developed a politician of the corrupt type so familiar in American cities, the politician who has become successful because he has made friends with the vicious. . . .

As the policeman who makes terms with vice, and almost inevitably slides into making gain from vice, merely represents the type of politician who is living off the weakness of his fellows, so the over-zealous reformer who exaggerates vice until the public is scared and awestruck, represents the type of politician who is living off the timidity of his fellows. With the lack of civic machinery for simple democratic expression, for a direct dealing with human nature as it is, we seem doomed to one type or the other—corruptionists or anti-crime committees.

And one sort or the other we will continue to have so long as we distrust the very energy of existence, the craving for enjoyment, the pushing of vital forces, the very right of every citizen to be what he is without pretense or assumption of virtue. Too often he does not really admire these virtues, but he imagines them somewhere as a standard adopted by the virtuous whom he does not know. That old Frankenstein, the ideal man of the eighteenth century, is still haunting us, although he never existed save in the brain of the doctrinaire.

This dramatic and feverish triumph of the self seeker, see-sawing with that of the interested reformer, does more than anything else, perhaps, to keep the American citizen away from the ideals of genuine evolutionary democracy. Whereas repressive government, from the nature of the case, has to do with the wicked who are happily always in a minority in the community, a normal democratic government would naturally have to do with the great majority of the population in their normal relations to each other.

After all, the so-called "slum politician" ventures

his success upon an appeal to human sentiment and generosity. This venture often results in an alliance between the popular politician and the humblest citizens, quite as naturally as the reformer who stands for honest business administration usually becomes allied with the type of business man whose chief concern it is to guard his treasure and to prevent a rise in taxation. The community is again insensibly divided into two camps, the repressed, who is dimly conscious that he has no adequate outlet for his normal life and the repressive, represented by the cautious, careful citizen holding fast to his own,—once more the conqueror and his humble people. . . .

Chapter VIII. Passing of the War Virtues

Of all the winged words which Tolstoy wrote during the war between Russia and Japan, perhaps none are more significant than these: "The great strife of our time is not that now taking place between the Japanese and the Russians, nor that which may blaze up between the white and the yellow races, nor that strife which is carried on by mines, bombs, and bullets, but that spiritual strife which, without ceasing, has gone on and is going on between the enlightened consciousness of mankind now awaiting for manifestation and that darkness and that burden which surrounds and oppresses mankind." In the curious period of accommodation in which we live, it is possible for old habits and new compunctions to be equally powerful, and it is almost a matter of pride with us that we neither break with the old nor yield to the new. We call this attitude tolerance, whereas it is often mere confusion of mind. . . .

We quote the convictions and achievements of the past as an excuse for ourselves when we lack the energy either to throw off old moral codes which have become burdens or to attain a morality proportionate to our present sphere of activity.

At the present moment the war spirit attempts to justify its noisy demonstrations by quoting its greatest achievements in the past and by drawing attention to the courageous life which it has evoked and fostered. It is, however, perhaps significant that the adherents of war are more and more justifying it by its past record and reminding us of its ancient origin. They tell us that it is interwoven with every fibre of human growth and is at the root of all that is noble and courageous in human life, that struggle is the basis of all progress, that it is now extended from individuals and tribes to nations and races. . . .

This confusion between the contemporaneous stage of development and the historic rôle of certain qualities, is intensified by our custom of referring to social evolution as if it were a force and not a process. We assume that social ends may be obtained without the application of social energies, although we know in our hearts that the best results of civilization have come about only through human will and effort. To point to the achievement of the past as a guarantee for continuing what has since become shocking to us is stupid business; it is to forget that progress itself depends upon adaptation, upon a nice balance between continuity and change. . . .

. . . The task that is really before us is first to see to it, that the old virtues bequeathed by war are not retained after they have become a social deterrent and that social progress is not checked by certain contempt for human nature which is but the inherited result of conquest. Second, we must act upon the assumption that spontaneous and fraternal action as virile and widespread as war itself is the only method by which substitutes for the war virtues may be discovered. . . .

It has been the time-honored custom to attribute unjust wars to the selfish ambition of rulers who remorselessly sacrifice their subjects to satisfy their greed. But, as Lecky has recently pointed out, it remains to be seen whether or not democratic rule will diminish war. Immoderate and uncontrolled desires are at the root of most national as well as of most individual crimes, and a large number of persons may be moved by unworthy ambitions quite as easily as a few. If the electorate of a democracy accustom themselves to take the commercial view of life, to consider the extension of trade as the test of a national prosperity, it becomes comparatively easy for mere extension of commercial opportunity to assume a moral aspect and to receive the moral sanction. Unrestricted commercialism is an excellent preparation for governmental aggression. The nation which is accustomed to condone the questionable business methods of a rich man because of his success, will find no difficulty in obscuring the moral issues involved in any undertaking that is successful. It becomes easy to deny the moral basis of self-government and to substitute militarism. The soldier formerly looked down upon the merchant whom he now obeys, as he still looks down upon the laborer as a man who is engaged in a business inferior to his own, as someone who is dull and passive and ineffective. When our public education succeeds in freeing the creative energy and developing the skill which the advance of industry demands, this attitude must disappear. . . .

. . . Tolstoy would make non-resistance aggressive. He would carry over into the reservoirs of moral influence all the strength which is now spent in coercion and resistance. It is an experiment which in its fullness has never been tried in human history, and it is worthy of a genius. . . . It does not matter that he has entered these new moral fields through the narrow gateway of personal experience; that he sets forth his convictions with the limitations of the Russian governmental environment; that he is regarded at this moment by the Russian revolutionists as a quietist and reactionary. He has nevertheless reached down into the moral life of the humble people and formulated for them as for us the secret of their long patience and unremitting labor. Therefore, in the teachings of Tolstoy, as in the life of the peasants, coextensive with the doctrine of non-resistance, stress is laid upon productive labor. The peasant Bandereff, from whom Tolstoy claims to have learned much, has not only proclaimed himself as against war, but has written a marvelous book entitled "Bread Labor," expressing once more the striking antithesis, the eternal contrast between war and labor, and between those who abhor the one and ever advocate the other.

War on the one hand—plain destruction, Von Moltke called it—represents the life of the garrison and the tax-gatherer, the Roman emperor and his degenerate people, living upon the fruits of their conquest. Labor, on the other hand, represents productive effort, holding carefully what has been garnered by the output of brain and muscle, guarding the harvest jealously because it is the precious bread men live by. . . .

That this world peace movement should be arising from the humblest without the sanction and in some cases with the explicit indifference, of the church founded by the Prince of Peace, is simply another example of the strange paths of moral evolution.

To some of us it seems clear that marked manifestations of this movement are found in the immigrant quarters of American cities. The previous survey of the immigrant situation would indicate that all the peoples of the world have become part of the American tribunal, and that their sense of pity, their clamor for personal kindness, their insistence upon the right to join in our progress, can no longer be disregarded. The

burdens and sorrows of men have unexpectedly become intelligent and urgent to this nation, and it is only by accepting them with some magnanimity that we can develop the larger sense of justice which is become world-wide and is lying in ambush, as it were, to manifest itself in governmental relations. Men of all nations are determining upon the abolition of degrading poverty, disease, and intellectual weakness, with their resulting industrial inefficiency, and are making a determined effort to conserve even the feeblest citizen to the State. To join in this determined effort is to break through national bonds and to unlock the latent fellowship between man and man. . . .

The International Peace Conference held in Boston in 1904 was opened by a huge meeting in which men of influence and modern thought from four continents, gave reasons for their belief in the passing of war. But none was so modern, so fundamental and trenchant, as the address which was read from the prophet Isaiah. He founded the cause of peace upon the cause of righteousness, not only as expressed in political relations, but also in industrial relations. He contended that peace could be secured only as men abstained from the gains of oppression and responded to the cause of the poor; that swords would finally be beaten into plowshares and pruning-hooks, not because men resolved to be peaceful, but because all the metal of the earth would be turned to its proper use when the poor and their children should be abundantly fed. It was as if the ancient prophet foresaw that under an enlightened industrialism peace would no longer be an absence of war, but the unfolding of world-wide processes making for the nurture of human life. He predicted the moment which has come to us now that peace is no longer an abstract dogma but has become a rising tide of moral enthusiasm slowly engulfing all pride of conquest and making war impossible.

Rokeya Sakhawat Hossain (ca. 1880–1932)

Rokeya Sakhawat Hossain was born about 1880 in Rangpur, Bengal (now Bangladesh), into a well-to-do orthodox Muslim family. Her upbringing and her ideas both reflected the tensions between traditional practices, the demands of cultural and political modernization, and the emergence of nationalist and feminist movements around the world. Roushan Jahan calls her "the first and foremost feminist" of Bengali Muslim society. She was equally dedicated to the national and humanist aspirations of the Bengali literary renaissance of her time.

Strict observance of purdah, as Roushan Jahan has pointed out, was to some degree an upper-class phenomenon, a status symbol for those who could afford the separate quarters, servants, and other expenses necessary to support it. Rokeya's family maintained purdah so rigidly that as a young girl she was required to hide herself from being seen even by women visitors. Her mother, Rohatunnessa Sabera Chowdhurani, first of four wives of Mohammad Abu Ali Saber, was strictly observant, and Rokeya later dedicated to her The Secluded Ones, her biting exposé of the restrictions imposed by purdah. Yet Saber had his sons educated in several languages and sent them to St. Xavier's College in Calcutta. And when he discovered that Rokeya's older sister, Karimunessa, had been learning secretly from her brothers, he was at first willing to go on teaching her himself. When the mullahs vigorously opposed this, he sent Karimunessa away to be married at the age of fourteen, but he married her into a more liberal family where she was able to pursue her interests in learning. For similar reasons, Rokeya, on the urging of her eldest brother, Ibrahim Saber, was married in 1896, at about age sixteen, to Syed Sakhawat Hossain. Sakhawat, though a widower much older than Rokeya, was a highly educated and progressive man who actively encouraged her not only to expand her education but also to write and publish her work despite its outspokenly feminist politics.

Rokeya Sakhawat Hossain was a prolific writer, educator, organizer, and political essayist from 1903 until her sudden death from heart failure in 1932. Her husband had fallen ill in 1907 and died in 1909, leaving her a bequest specifically dedicated to founding a school for Muslim women. Rokeya attempted this at first in Bhagalpur but was forced by family disapproval to move to Calcutta with her mother and a widowed younger sister. There in 1911 she founded the Sakhawat Memorial Girl's School, which survives today, in testimony to her ability to overcome stubborn opposition and rally enduring support for her vision of education for women. In 1916 she founded the Bengal branch of the Anjuman-i-Khawatin Islam (All-India Muslim Women's Association), the first such organization for Muslim women in Bengal, and hosted a national conference of the association in Calcutta in 1919.

Rokeya Hossain's native language was Bangla, but Muslim girls of her class were taught to read only some Urdu, the preferred language of the Bengali elite, primarily so that they might read didactic works on women's proper roles and conduct. English and Bangla were frowned upon as unnecessary and potentially dangerous for women. With the help and encouragement of Karimunessa and Ibrahim, however, Rokeya had early learned to read both Bangla and English, and in later years she expanded her linguistic skills and published translations into Bangla of works she regarded as important to reach her audience, such as Fatima Begum's report of the progressive policies of Amanullah Khan in Afghanistan and writings by Annie Besant, the English-born socialist, theosophist, and Indian nationalist.

The educational and political philosophy of Rokeya was both feminist and nationalist, traditional and modernist. She was deeply dedicated to the liberation of women from dependency and subordination to men and found herself in conflict even with the national leadership of the Anjuman-i-Khawatin Islam over issues of seclusion and the purposes of women's education. But she was equally dedicated to the preservation of Muslim religion and culture and the national independence of India from British rule and Western domination. The accusation that "to her everything Indian is bad and everything Euro-American is good" was unfounded. She was interested in Western feminist ideas and aspirations but skeptical and critical of the limitations and obstacles to women's true equality in the West. She advocated state-supported compulsory education for all children but not co-education. Thus her model for Muslim girls' education was sex-segregated and Islamic while providing a wide-ranging curriculum to prepare women for active and productive lives and participation in the public political arena.

Rokeya Sakhawat Hossain's early essays were collected in two volumes, Motichur, Parts 1 and 2, published in Calcutta in 1908 and 1921. The second volume was dedicated to Karimunessa. Two early novels, Niriho Bangali and Gyanphol, reflect her opposition to the partition of 1905 and to British colonial rule. "Sultana's Dream," originally published in the Indian Ladies' Magazine in Madras in 1905, first appeared as a book in Calcutta in 1908. Rokeya's novel Padmaraga (Ruby) was published in Calcutta in 1924, dedicated to her brother Ibrahim. Like other female characters in Rokeya's fiction, Siddiqua, the central character of Padmaraga, offers readers the model of a woman who rejects marriage for an independent, productive life of teaching and service to other women. The Secluded Ones (Avarodhbasini), a series of vignettes of life under strict seclusion (including reports of Hindu forms of purdah), was published as a book in Calcutta in 1928 and serialized in the Monthly Mohammadi in 1928–29; the first English translation, by Roushan Jahan, did not appear until 1981. The collected works, Rokeya Racanavali, edited by Abdul Quadir, were published by the Bangla Academy in Dhaka in 1973.

"Sultana's Dream" is probably the best known of Rokeya's works, now reprinted in many anthologies. It is one of the earliest examples of feminist utopian fiction, preceding by ten years Charlotte Perkins Gilman's Herland. Unlike Christine de Pizan's City of Ladies and Gilman's Herland, Rokeya did not resort to banishing men entirely but presented a reversal of roles, with men confined in seclusion instead of women. Her husband called it "a terrible revenge," but it was he who urged her to publish it. Rokeya wrote the tale in English as a demonstration of her ability to write in this, her fifth language, but she preferred to write in Bengali, and few of her other works have been translated into English. As Frances Bonner has pointed out, "Sultana's Dream" offered a science-based utopia in which women supplant men's destructive and militaristic uses of science with uses directed to an ecology of beauty and happiness.

The version of "Sultana's Dream" presented here is from the Feminist Press edition (1988), edited by Roushan Jahan.

BAC

Sources and Suggested Readings

Amin, Sonia Nishat. "Rokeya Sakhawat Hossain and the Legacy of the 'Bengal Renaissance.'" Journal of the Asiatic Society of Bangladesh 34, 2 (1989): 185–92.

Bonner, Frances. Introduction to "Sultana's Dream." In Inventing Women: Science, Technology and Gender, ed. Gill Kirkup and Laurie Smith Keller, 294–95. London: Polity Press, 1992.

Hossain, Rokeya Sakhawat. Inside Seclusion: The Avarodh-basini of Rokeya Sakhawat Hossain. Ed. and trans. Roushan Jahan. Dacca: Women for Women, 1981.

———. Sultana's Dream and Selections from The Secluded Ones. Ed. and trans. Roushan Jahan. Afterword by Hanna Papanek. New York: Feminist Press at the City University of New York, 1988.

Hossain, Yasmin. "The Begum's Dream: Rokeya Sakhawat Hossain and the Broadening of Muslim Women's Aspirations in Bengal." South Asia Research 12, 1 (May 1992): 1–19.

Jahan, Roushan. "'Sultana's Dream': Purdah Reversed"; "The Secluded Ones: Purdah Observed"; and "Rokeya: An Introduction to Her Life." In Sultana's Dream and Selections from The Secluded Ones, ed. and trans. Roushan Jaha . New York: Feminist Press at the City University of New York, 1988.

Tharu, Susie, and K. Lalita, eds. "Rokeya Sakhawat Hossain (1880–1932)." Introduction to "Sultana's Dream." In Women Writing in India, 600 B.C. to the Present. Vol. 1. 340–42. New York: Feminist Press at the City University of New York, 1991.

Sultana's Dream (1905)

One evening I was lounging in an easy chair in my bedroom and thinking lazily of the condition of Indian womanhood. I am not sure whether I dozed off or not. But, as far as I remember, I was wide awake. I saw the moonlit sky sparkling with thousands of diamondlike stars, very distinctly.

All on a sudden a lady stood before me; how she came in, I do not know. I took her for my friend, Sister Sara.

"Good morning," said Sister Sara. I smiled inwardly as I knew it was not morning, but starry night. However, I replied to her, saying, "How do you do?"

"I am all right, thank you. Will you please come out and have a look at our garden?"

I looked again at the moon through the open window, and thought there was no harm in going out at that time. The menservants outside were fast asleep just then, and I could have a pleasant walk with Sister Sara.

I used to have my walks with Sister Sara, when we were at Darjeeling. Many a time did we walk hand in hand and talk lightheartedly in the botanical gardens there. I fancied Sister Sara had probably come to take me to some such garden, and I readily accepted her offer and went out with her.

When walking I found to my surprise that it was a fine morning. The town was fully awake and the streets alive with bustling crowds. I was feeling very shy, thinking I was walking in the street in broad daylight, but there was not a single man visible.

Some of the passersby made jokes at me. Though I could not understand their language, yet I felt sure they were joking. I asked my friend, "What do they say?"

"The women say you look very mannish."

"Mannish?" said I. "What do they mean by that?"

"They mean that you are shy and timid like men."

"Shy and timid like men?" It was really a joke. I

became very nervous when I found that my companion was not Sister Sara, but a stranger. Oh, what a fool had I been to mistake this lady for my dear old friend Sister Sara.

She felt my fingers tremble in her hand, as we were walking hand in hand.

"What is the matter, dear, dear?" she said affectionately.

"I feel somewhat awkward," I said, in a rather apologizing tone, "as being a purdahnishin woman I am not accustomed to walking about unveiled."

"You need not be afraid of coming across a man here. This is Ladyland, free from sin and harm. Virtue herself reigns here."

By and by I was enjoying the scenery. Really it was very grand. I mistook a patch of green grass for a velvet cushion. Feeling as if I were walking on a soft carpet, I looked down and found the path covered with moss and flowers.

"How nice it is," said I.

"Do you like it?" asked Sister Sara. (I continued calling her "Sister Sara," and she kept calling me by my name.)

"Yes, very much; but I do not like to tread on the tender and sweet flowers."

"Never mind, dear Sultana. Your treading will not harm them; they are street flowers."

"The whole place looks like a garden," said I admiringly. "You have arranged every plant so skillfully."

"Your Calcutta could become a nicer garden than this, if only your countrymen wanted to make it so."

"They would think it useless to give so much attention to horticulture, while they have so many other things to do."

"They could not find a better excuse," said she with [a] smile.

I became very curious to know where the men were. I met more than a hundred women while walking there, but not a single man.

"Where are the men?" I asked her.

"In their proper places, where they ought to be."

"Pray let me know what you mean by 'their proper places.'"

"Oh, I see my mistake, you cannot know our customs, as you were never here before. We shut our men indoors."

"Just as we are kept in zenana?"

"Exactly so."

"How funny." I burst into a laugh. Sister Sara laughed too.

"But, dear Sultana, how unfair it is to shut in the harmless women and let loose the men."

"Why? It is not safe for us to come out of the zenana, as we are naturally weak."

"Yes, it is not safe so long as there are men about the streets, nor is it so when a wild animal enters a marketplace."

"Of course not."

"Suppose some lunatics escape from the asylum and begin to do all sorts of mischief to men, horses, and other creatures: in that case what will your countrymen do?"

"They will try to capture them and put them back into their asylum."

"Thank you! And you do not think it wise to keep sane people inside an asylum and let loose the insane?"

"Of course not" said I, laughing lightly.

"As a matter of fact, in your country this very thing is done! Men, who do or at least are capable of doing no end of mischief, are let loose and the innocent women shut up in the zenana! How can you trust those untrained men out of doors?"

"We have no hand or voice in the management of our social affairs. In India man is lord and master. He has taken to himself all powers and privileges and shut up the women in the zenana."

"Why do you allow yourselves to be shut up?"

"Because it cannot be helped as they are stronger than women."

"A lion is stronger than a man, but it does not enable him to dominate the human race. You have neglected the duty you owe to yourselves, and you have lost your natural rights by shutting your eyes to your own interests."

"But my dear Sister Sara, if we do everything by ourselves, what will the men do then?"

"They should not do anything, excuse me; they are fit for nothing. Only catch them and put them into the zenana."

"But would it be very easy to catch and put them inside the four walls?" said I. "And even if this were done, would all their business—political and commercial—also go with them into the zenana?"

Sister Sara made no reply. She only smiled sweetly. Perhaps she thought it was useless to argue with one who was not better than a frog in a well.

By this time we reached Sister Sara's house. It was situated in a beautiful heart-shaped garden. It was a bungalow with a corrugated iron roof. It was cooler and nicer than any of our rich buildings. I cannot describe how neat and nicely furnished and how tastefully decorated it was.

We sat side by side. She brought out of the parlor a piece of embroidery work and began putting on a fresh design.

"Do you know knitting and needlework?"

"Yes: we have nothing else to do in our zenana."

"But we do not trust our zenana members with embroidery!" she said laughing, "as a man has not patience enough to pass thread through a needlehole even!"

"Have you done all this work yourself?" I asked her, pointing to the various pieces of embroidered teapoy cloths.

"Yes."

"How can you find time to do all these? You have to do the office work as well? Have you not?"

"Yes. I do not stick to the laboratory all day long. I finish my work in two hours."

"In two hours! How do you manage? In our land the officers, magistrates, for instance, work seven hours daily."

"I have seen some of them doing their work. Do you think they work all the seven hours?"

"Certainly they do!"

"No, dear Sultana, they do not. They dawdle away their time in smoking. Some smoke two or three choroots during the office time. They talk much about their work, but do little. Suppose one choroot takes half an hour to burn off, and a man smokes twelve choroots daily; then, you see, he wastes six hours every day in sheer smoking."

We talked on various subjects; and I learned that they were not subject to any kind of epidemic disease, nor did they suffer from mosquito bites as we do. I was very much astonished to hear that in Ladyland no one died in youth except by rare accident.

"Will you care to see our kitchen?" she asked me.

"With pleasure," said I, and we went to see it. Of course the men had been asked to clear off when I was going there. The kitchen was situated in a beautiful vegetable garden. Every creeper, every tomato plant, was itself an ornament. I found no smoke, nor any chimney either in the kitchen—it was clean and bright; the windows were decorated with flower garlands. There was no sign of coal or fire.

"How do you cook?" I asked.

"With solar heat," she said, at the same time showing me the pipe, through which passed the concentrated sunlight and heat. And she cooked something then and there to show me the process.

"How did you manage to gather and store up the sun heat?" I asked her in amazement.

"Let me tell you a little of our past history, then. Thirty years ago, when our present Queen was thirteen years old, she inherited the throne. She was Queen in name only, the Prime Minister really ruling the country.

"Our good Queen liked science very much. She circulated an order that all the women in her country should be educated. Accordingly a number of girls' schools were founded and supported by the Government. Education was spread far and wide among wom-

en. And early marriage also was stopped. No woman was to be allowed to marry before she was twenty-one. I must tell you that, before this change, we had been kept in strict purdah."

"How the tables are turned," I interposed with a laugh.

"But the seclusion is the same," she said. "In a few years we had separate universities, where no men were admitted.

"In the capital, where our Queen lives, there are two universities. One of these invented a wonderful balloon, to which they attached a number of pipes. By means of this captive balloon, which they managed to keep afloat above the cloudland, they could draw as much water from the atmosphere as they pleased. As the water was incessantly being drawn by the university people, no cloud gathered and the ingenious Lady Principal stopped rain and storms thereby."

"Really! Now I understand why there is no mud here!" said I. But I could not understand how it was possible to accumulate water in the pipes. She explained to me how it was done; but I was unable to understand her, as my scientific knowledge was very limited. However, she went on:

"When the other university came to know of this, they became exceedingly jealous and tried to do something more extraordinary still. They invented an instrument by which they could collect as much sun heat as they wanted. And they kept the heat stored up to be distributed among others as required.

"While the women were engaged in scientific researches, the men of this country were busy increasing their military power. When they came to know that the female universities were able to draw water from the atmosphere and collect heat from the sun, they only laughed at the members of the universities and called the whole thing 'a sentimental nightmare'!"

"Your achievements are very wonderful indeed! But tell me how you managed to put the men of your country into the zenana. Did you entrap them first?"

"No."

"It is not likely that they would surrender their free and open air life of their own accord and confine themselves within the four walls of the zenana! They must have been overpowered."

"Yes, they have been!"

"By whom?—by some lady warriors, I suppose?"

"No, not by arms."

"Yes, it cannot be so. Men's arms are stronger than women's. Then?"

"By brain."

"Even their brains are bigger and heavier than women's. Are they not?"

"Yes, but what of that? An elephant also has got a bigger and heavier brain than a man has. Yet man can enchain elephants and employ them, according to his own wishes."

"Well said, but tell me, please, how it all actually happened. I am dying to know it!"

"Women's brains are somewhat quicker than men's. Ten years ago, when the military officers called our scientific discoveries 'a sentimental nightmare,' some of the young ladies wanted to say something in reply to those remarks. But both the Lad\) Principals restrained them and said they should reply not by word but by deed, if ever they got the opportunity. And they had not long to wait for that opportunity."

"How marvelous!" I heartily clapped my hands.

"And now the proud gentlemen are dreaming sentimental dreams themselves.

"Soon afterward certain persons came from a neighboring country and took shelter in ours. They were in trouble, having committed some political offense. The king, who cared more for power than for good government, asked our kindhearted Queen to hand them over to his officers. She refused, as it was against her principle to turn out refugees. For this refusal the king declared war against our country.

"Our military officers sprang to their feet at once and marched out to meet the enemy.

"The enemy, however, was too strong for them. Our soldiers fought bravely, no doubt. But in spite of all their bravery the foreign army advanced step by step to invade our country.

"Nearly all the men had gone out to fight; even a boy of sixteen was not left home. Most of our warriors were killed, the rest driven back, and the enemy came within twenty-five miles of the capital.

"A meeting of a number of wise ladies was held at the Queen's palace to advise [as] to what should be done to save the land.

"Some proposed to fight like soldiers; others objected and said that women were not trained to fight with swords and guns, nor were they accustomed to fighting with any weapons. A third party regretfully remarked that they were hopelessly weak of body.

"If you cannot save your country for lack of physical strength, said the Queen, try to do so by brain power.

"There was a dead silence for a few minutes. Her Royal Highness said again, 'I must commit suicide if the land and my honor are lost.'

"Then the Lady Principal of the second university (who had collected sun heat), who had been silently thinking during the consultation, remarked that they were all but lost; and there was little hope left for them. There was, however, one plan [that] she would like to try, and this would be her first and last effort; if she

failed in this, there would be nothing left but to commit suicide. All present solemnly vowed that they would never allow themselves to be enslaved, no matter what happened.

"The Queen thanked them heartily, and asked the Lady Principal to try her plan.

"The Lady Principal rose again and said, 'Before we go out the men must enter the zenanas. I make this prayer for the sake of purdah.' 'Yes, of course,' replied Her Royal Highness.

"On the following day the Queen called upon all men to retire into zenanas for the sake of honor and liberty.

"Wounded and tired as they were, they took that order rather for a boon! They bowed low and entered the zenanas without uttering a single word of protest. They were sure that there was no hope for this country at all.

"Then the Lady Principal with her two thousand students marched to the battlefield, and arriving there directed all the rays of the concentrated sun light and heat toward the enemy.

"The heat and light were too much for them to bear. They all ran away panic-stricken, not knowing in their bewilderment how to counteract that scorching heat. When they fled away leaving their guns and other ammunitions of war, they were burned down by means of the same sun heat.

"Since then no one has tried to invade our country any more."

"And since then your countrymen never tried to come out of the zenana?"

"Yes, they wanted to be free. Some of the Police Commissioners and District Magistrates sent word to the Queen to the effect that the Military Officers certainly deserved to be imprisoned for their failure; but they [had] never neglected their duty and therefore they should not be punished, and they prayed to be restored to their respective offices.

"Her Royal Highness sent them a circular letter, intimating to them that if their services should ever be needed they would be sent for, and that in the meanwhile they should remain where they were.

"Now that they are accustomed to the purdah system and have ceased to grumble at their seclusion, we call the system *mardana* instead of zenana."

"But how do you manage," I asked Sister Sara, "to do without the police or magistrates in case of theft or murder?"

"Since the mardana system has been established, there has been no more crime or sin; therefore we do not require a policeman to find out a culprit, nor do we want a magistrate to try a criminal case."

"That is very good, indeed. I suppose if there were

any dishonest person, you could very easily chastise her. As you gained a decisive victory without shedding a single drop of blood, you could drive off crime and criminals too without much difficulty!"

"Now, dear Sultana, will you sit here or come to my parlor?" she asked me.

"Your kitchen is not inferior to a queen's boudoir!" I replied with a pleasant smile, "but we must leave it now; for the gentlemen may be cursing me for keeping them away from their duties in the kitchen so long." We both laughed heartily.

"How my friends at home will be amused and amazed, when I go back and tell them that in the far-off Ladyland, ladies rule over the country and control all social matters, while gentlemen are kept in the mardanas to mind babies, to cook, and to do all sorts of domestic work; and that cooking is so easy a thing that it is simply a pleasure to cook!"

"Yes, tell them about all that you see here."

"Please let me know how you carry on land cultivation and how you plow the land and do other hard manual work."

"Our fields are tilled by means of electricity, which supplies motive power for other hard work as well, and we employ it for our aerial conveyances too. We have no railroad nor any paved streets here."

"Therefore neither street nor railway accidents occur here," said I. "Do not you ever suffer from want of rainwater?" I asked.

"Never since the 'water balloon' had been set up. You see the big balloon and pipes attached thereto. By their aid we can draw as much rainwater as we require. Nor do we ever suffer from flood or thunderstorms. We are all very busy making nature yield as much as she can. We do not find time to quarrel with one another as we never sit idle. Our noble Queen is exceedingly fond of botany; it is her ambition to convert the whole country into one grand garden."

"The idea is excellent. What is your chief food?"

"Fruits."

"How do you keep your country cool in hot weather? We regard the rainfall in summer as a blessing from heaven."

"When the heat becomes unbearable, we sprinkle the ground with plentiful showers drawn from the artificial fountains. And in cold weather we keep our rooms warm with sun heat."

She showed me her bathroom, the roof of which was removable. She could enjoy a shower [or] bath whenever she liked, by simply removing the roof (which was like the lid of a box) and turning on the tap of the shower pipe.

"You are a lucky people!" ejaculated I. "You know no want. What is your religion, may I ask?"

"Our religion is based on Love and Truth. It is our religious duty to love one another and to be absolutely truthful. If any person lies, she or he is . . ."

"Punished with death?"

"No, not with death. We do not take pleasure in killing a creature of God—especially a human being. The liar is asked to leave this land for good and never to come to it again."

"Is an offender never forgiven?"

"Yes, if that person repents sincerely."

"Are you not allowed to see any man, except your own relations?"

"No one except sacred relations."

"Our circle of sacred relations is very limited, even first cousins are not sacred."

"But ours is very large; a distant cousin is as sacred as a brother."

"That is very good. I see Purity itself reigns over your land. I should like to see the good Queen, who is so sagacious and farsighted and who has made all these rules."

"All right," said Sister Sara.

Then she screwed a couple of seats on to a square piece of plank. To this plank she attached two smooth and well-polished balls. When I asked her what the balls were for, she said they were hydrogen balls and they were used to overcome the force of gravity. The balls were of different capacities, to be used according to the different weights desired to be overcome. She then fastened to the air-car two winglike blades, which, she said, were worked by electricity. After we were comfortably seated she touched a knob and the blades began to whirl, moving faster and faster every moment. At first we were raised to the height of about six or seven feet and then off we flew. And before I could realize that we had commenced moving, we reached the garden of the Queen.

My friend lowered the air-car by reversing the action of the machine, and when the car touched the ground the machine was stopped and we got out.

I had seen from the air-car the Queen walking on a garden with her little daughter (who was four years old) and her maids of honor.

"Halloo! you here!" cried the Queen, addressing Sister Sara. I was introduced to Her Royal Highness and was received by her cordially without any ceremony.

I was very much delighted to make her acquaintance. In [the] course of the conversation I had with her, the Queen told me that she had no objection to permitting her subjects to trade with other countries. "But," she continued, "no trade was possible with countries where the women were kept in the zenanas and so unable to come and trade with us. Men, we find, are rather of lower morals and so we do not like dealing with them. We do not covet other people's land, we do not fight for a piece of diamond though it may be a thousandfold brighter than the Koh-i-Noor ["mountain of light" diamond], nor do we grudge a ruler his Peacock Throne. We dive deep into the ocean of knowledge and try to find out the precious gems [that] Nature has kept in store for us. We enjoy Nature's gifts as much as we can."

After taking leave of the Queen, I visited the famous universities, and was shown over some of their factories, laboratories, and observatories.

After visiting the above places of interest, we got again into the air-car, but as soon as it began moving I somehow slipped down and the fall startled me out of my dream. And on opening my eyes, I found myself in my own bedroom still lounging in the easy chair!

Rosa Luxemburg (1871–1919)

Rosa Luxemburg was born on March 5, 1871, in the town of Zamosc in Russian Poland, to assimilated Jewish parents with strong affinities to German culture. She grew up in Warsaw, where the family moved when she was three and where she became involved in revolutionary politics while still in her teens. She died on January 15, 1919, murdered at age forty-seven in Berlin by paramilitary troops operating under the authority of the Defense Minister of the Weimar Republic, during an abortive insurrection by the Spartakus Party, which she and Karl Liebknecht had founded after World War I.

Luxemburg held an unparalleled position of intellectual and political leadership as a woman in the predominantly male circles of the European left in the late nineteenth and early twentieth centuries. The Hungarian Marxist Georg Lukács wrote in 1922: "Alone among Marx's disciples, Rosa Luxemburg made a real advance on his life's work in both the content and method of his economic doctrines" (1922/1971: xli). In the introduction to the published volume of Luxemburg's letters to the Kautskys, Luise Kautsky chose the image of Athena to describe Luxemburg's appearance on the German Social Democratic scene in the 1890s: "In short, a new Pallas Athene, sprung from the head of Zeus, she stood before us, resplendent in her armor" (1925: 18).

Luxemburg, emulating perhaps the male-identified Athena, directed her energies primarily to what was sometimes called "Big Politics" rather than engagement in "women's issues" or organizing women, and she was a fierce critic of "bourgeois feminism." But Luxemburg explicitly endorsed women's suffrage, was conscious of issues of gender equality in left politics, and supported the efforts of her close friends Luise Kautsky and Clara Zetkin to organize women and promote women's rights and political leadership.

Rosa was ten years old when Tsar Alexander II was assassinated in 1881. The assassination was carried out by a small group of terrorists of the Narodnaya Volya (the People's Will), under the direction of Sofia Perovskaia. Russian women had achieved an exceptional degree of equality with men in this most radical revolutionary movement of Europe in the nineteenth century, and they were often the central figures in the terrorist groups of the 1870s and 1880s. Besides Sofia Perovskaia, the leading revolutionary women included among others Ekaterina Breshkovskaya, Vera Figner, Sofia Bardina, and Vera Zasulich.

Thus Luxemburg, in entering the revolutionary circles of Poland and Russia in her mid-teens, entered a

political culture in which women's equality in revolutionary action was firmly established and visibly played out, at least in terms of the roles played by certain well-known figures or martyrs of the revolution. Though Luxemburg and her associates rejected the politics of the Narodnaya Volya in favor of Marxism, or Social Democracy, the revolutionary tradition offered her both the role models and the acceptance among men that were the foundation of her early leadership in the Polish Social Democracy, in turn the base from which she moved into prominence in the German Social Democratic Party.

In 1889, in danger of arrest for her political activities, she was smuggled out of Poland and went to Zurich, Switzerland, where she took her Ph.D. from the University of Zurich in 1897. In Zurich she became deeply involved with the Marxist political exiles of the Second Socialist International and in 1894 founded, with Leo Jogiches, and other antinationalist emigrés, the Social Democratic Party of the Kingdom of Poland and Lithuania. In 1898 she moved to Germany to be closer to the heart of organized socialism, making her living as a journalist. To obtain German citizenship, she married for form a German, Gustav Lübeck, and divorced him five years later. They never actually lived as man and wife. Leo Jogiches was her closest intimate until 1906, when she broke with him personally on learning that he had been unfaithful to her; however, they remained close as political associates.

In December 1905, Luxemburg went back to Poland to observe the revolution of 1905–1906. In 1906 she was imprisoned there, then released. She went to Finland, along with Lenin, Zinoviev, and other political exiles, and then returned to Germany. In the years prior to World War I, she was increasingly engaged in antimilitarist, anti-imperialist activities, and in August 1914 she was sentenced to prison again in Germany for antimilitarist speeches. She was released for a short time early in 1916, but arrested again in July 1916 and held without trial in different prisons for the rest of the war, until the overthrow of the kaiser's government in November 1918.

The prominence of Luxemburg's role as a theorist in German Social Democracy and European socialist politics at large was extraordinary at the time—indeed, would still be extraordinary today. She was engaged at the highest levels of party and international revolutionary politics in free-wheeling open debate with the leading male intellectuals of her time, and she engaged them on the same terms that they dealt with each other. Or perhaps, rather, she engaged them on a higher level of abstraction and theoretical complexity than her male comrades and adversaries generally ventured themselves, while at the same time it can be argued that she succeeded in maintaining a more consistent linkage between theory and practice.

Rosa Luxemburg's most important theoretical ideas fall in two main areas: the theory of imperialism and militarism, and the theory of social change and revolution.

Luxemburg's theory of social change and revolution developed over about two decades between 1899 and 1919 and was embodied in a series of important polemical works including Reform or Revolution? (1899), Organizational Questions of Social Democracy (1904), The Mass Strike, the Political Party, and the Trade Unions (1906), her "Address to the Judges" at her trial for antimilitary propaganda (1914), the Junius Pamphlet: The Crisis in German Social Democracy and Theses on the Tasks of International Social Democracy (both smuggled out of prison in 1915), and The Russian Revolution (1918). The doctrine most associated with her name in this context is that of "spontaneity" and the mass strike. In Reform or Revolution? she posed a daring and vigorous challenge to the revisionist socialism of Eduard Bernstein. Organizational Questions of Social Democracy was an acerbic, brilliant response to Vladimir Lenin's arguments for absolute control and centralization of the Social Democratic Party by an intellectual elite. In The Mass Strike, the Political Party, and the Trade Unions, she presented the fullest exposition of her theory of social change and revolution, drawing on her observations of the revolutions of 1905 in Poland and Russia. Throughout these and other works, Luxemburg argued that revolutionary change must emerge from the historical conditions, class consciousness, and free political action of the masses, and that it cannot be "called at will" or fruitfully directed from above by a central party leadership.

Luxemburg's analysis of imperialism and militarism was set forth primarily in The Accumulation of Capital, published in 1913. This was Luxemburg's longest and most theoretically ambitious work. In a letter to Konstantin Zetkin in November 1911 she wrote: "I want to find the cause of imperialism. . . . it will be a strictly scientific explanation of imperialism and its contradictions." In this she went beyond Marx and other Marxist theorists, including the later work of Lenin (Imperialism: The Highest Stage of Capitalism, 1917), which described economic aspects of imperialism and assumed or declared its links to capitalism but failed to explain fully the necessary relationship between capitalism and imperialism.

In brief summary, her argument was that Marx's explanation of the economic dynamics of capitalism, in particular of what is called "expanded reproduction" of capital, was inadequate. She maintained that capitalism requires continuing sources of "accumulation of capital," for which it must look outside the capitalist economy itself, namely, to any remaining pre-capitalist strata within the boundaries of developed capitalism and to non-capitalist societies outside those boundaries. Thus the necessity for capitalism to exploit non-capitalist strata and societies drives capitalism itself, and states serving the interests of the capitalist bourgeoisie, to imperialist policies. With prophetic foresight and eloquence she portrayed the increasing militarization of imperialist countries to compete successfully amongst themselves for these external resources as well as to destroy the natural or peasant economies of non-capitalist regions and forcibly subjugate their peoples to the needs of capitalism.

Luxemburg's position on issues of peace and the use of violence was ambivalent. She distanced herself from "bourgeois pacifism" and anarchism and supported armed revolution in Russia and (reluctantly) the armed insurrection of the Spartacists in Germany in 1919. But she devoted herself to the struggle against militarism in the decade before World War I and spent most of the war years in debilitating imprisonment for her "antimilitarist propaganda." Moreover, her theoretical work made important contributions to understanding the modern war system and to the theory of nonviolent direct action. Her "Address to the Judges" at her trial in 1914 and her Theses on the Tasks of International Social Democracy in 1915 encapsulated her theoretical and political principles under the test of war. The Theses constituted a ringing indictment of the failure of the Social Democratic leadership to stand against war and imperialism and declared: "The final goal of socialism will be realized by the international proletariat only if it opposes imperialism all along the line, and if it makes the issue 'war against war' the guiding line of its practical policy."

The critical and interpretive literature on Luxemburg is extensive but suffused and weighed down by an almost impenetrable web of sectarian polemics. Peter Nettl, in his biography of Luxemburg, describes at length many of the competing claims and repudiations to which her life and works have been subjected by a wide range of would-be heirs or rectifiers. The intensity and persistence of the ideological struggles to possess or annihilate Luxemburg are so extraordinary that Nettl could remark: "These opposed yet continued claims of both Communists and anti-Communists to represent the true heritage of Rosa Luxemburg's ideas are shared only by Marx himself" (1969: ix).

The selections below are from the 1970 Pathfinder Press edition of Luxemburg's writings, edited by Mary

Alice Waters, and the 1968 edition of The Accumulation of Capital.

BAC

Sources and Suggested Readings

Arendt, Hannah. "Rosa Luxemburg: 1971–1919." In *Men in Dark Times*. New York: Harcourt, Brace & World (Harvest), 1968. 33–56.

Dunayevskaya, Raya. *Rosa Luxemburg, Women's Liberation, and Marx's Philosophy of Revolution*. 2nd ed. Urbana: University of Illinois Press, 1991.

Engel, Barbara Alpern. "From Separatism to Socialism: Women in the Russian Revolutionary Movement of the 1870s." In *Socialist Women*, ed. Marilyn J. Boxer and Jean H. Quataert. New York: Elsevier, 1978.

Foner, Philip S., ed. *Clara Zetkin: Selected Writings*. New York: International Publishers, 1984.

Geras, Norman. *The Legacy of Rosa Luxemburg*. London: NLB, 1976.

Goldsmith, Margaret. *Seven Women against the World*. London: Methuen, 1935. Hyperion reprint, 1976.

Kautsky, Luise, ed. *Rosa Luxemburg: Letters to Karl and Luise Kautsky from 1896 to 1918*. New York: Robert M. McBride, 1925.

Lim, Jie-Hyun. "Rosa Luxemburg and the Dialectics of Proletarian Internationalism and Social Patriotism." *Science and Society* 59, 4 (Winter 1995–96): 498–530.

Lukács, Georg. *History and Class Consciousness*. Cambridge: MIT Press, 1971 [1922].

Luxemburg, Rosa. *The Accumulation of Capital*. New York: Monthly Review Press, 1968 [1913].

——. *Comrade and Lover: Rosa Luxemburg's Letters to Leo Jogiches*. Ed. and trans. Elbieta Ettinger. Cambridge: MIT Press, 1979.

——. *The Letters of Rosa Luxemburg*. Ed. Stephen Eric Bronner. Boulder, Colo.: Westview Press, 1978.

——. *Rosa Luxemburg Speaks*. Ed. Mary Alice Waters. New York: Pathfinder Press, 1970.

——. *Selected Political Writings of Rosa Luxemburg*. Ed. Dick Howard. New York: Monthly Review Press, 1971.

Nettl, Peter. *Rosa Luxemburg*. London: Oxford University Press, 1966. 2 vols. Abridged, 1969, 1 vol.

Nye, Andrea. *Philosophia: The Thought of Rosa Luxemburg, Simone Weil, and Hannah Arendt*. New York: Routledge, 1994.

Stites, Richard. *The Women's Liberation Movement in Russia*. Princeton: Princeton University Press, 1978.

Vollrath, Ernst. "Rosa Luxemburg's Theory of Revolution." *Social Research* 40, 1 (Spring 1973): 83–109.

Weitz, Eric D. "'Rosa Luxemburg Belongs to Us!': German Communism and the Luxemburg Legacy." *Central European History* 27, 1 (1994): 27–64.

The Mass Strike, the Political Party, and the Trade Unions (1906)

I. The Russian Revolution, Anarchism and the General Strike

Almost all works and pronouncements of international socialism on the subject of the mass strike date from the time before the Russian Revolution [of 1905], the first historical experiment on a very large scale with this means of struggle. It is therefore evident that they are, for the most part, out-of-date. Their standpoint is essentially that of Engels who in 1873 wrote as follows in his criticism of the revolutionary blundering of the Bakuninist in Spain:

"The general strike, in the Bakuninists' program, is the lever which will be used for introducing the social revolution. One fine morning all the workers in every industry in a country, or perhaps in every country, will cease work, and thereby compel the ruling classes either to submit in about four weeks, or to launch an attack on the workers so that the latter will have the right to defend themselves, and may use the opportunity to overthrow the old society. The proposal is by no means new: French and Belgian socialists have paraded it continually since 1848, but for all that it is of English origin. During the rapid and powerful development of Chartism among the English workers that followed the crisis of 1837, the 'holy month'—a suspension of work on a national scale—was preached as early as 1839, and was received with such favor that in July 1842 the factory workers of the north of England attempted to carry it out. And at the Congress of the Alliancists at Geneva on September 1, 1873, the general strike played a great part, but it was admitted on all sides that to carry it out it was necessary to have a perfect organization of the working class and a full war chest. And that is the crux of the question. On the one hand, the governments, especially if they are encouraged by the workers' abstention from political action, will never allow the funds of the workers to become large enough, and on the other hand, political events and the encroachments of the ruling classes will bring about the liberation of the workers long before the proletariat gets the length of forming this ideal organization and this colossal reserve fund. But if they had these, they would not need to make use of the roundabout way of the general strike in order to attain their object."

Here we have the reasoning that was characteristic of the attitude of international social democracy towards the mass strike in the following decades. It is based on the anarchist theory of the general strike—that is, the theory of the general strike as a means of inaugurating the social revolution, in contradistinction to the daily political struggle of the working class—and exhausts itself in the following simple dilemma: either the proletariat as a whole are not yet in possession of the powerful organization and financial resources required, in which case they cannot carry through the general strike; or they are already sufficiently well organized, in which case they do not need the general strike. This reasoning is so simple and at first glance so irrefutable that, for a quarter of a century, it has rendered excellent service to the modern labor movement as a logical weapon against the anarchist phantom and as a means of carrying the idea of political struggle to the widest circles of the workers. The enormous strides taken by the labor movement in all capitalist countries during the last twenty-five years are the most convincing evidence of the value of the tactics of political struggle, which were insisted upon by Marx and Engels in opposition to Bakuninism; and German social democracy, in its position of vanguard of the entire international labor movement is not in the least the direct product of the consistent and energetic application of these tactics.

The Russian Revolution has now effected a radical revision of the above piece of reasoning. For the first time in the history of the class struggle it has achieved a grandiose realization of the idea of the mass strike and—as we shall discuss later—has even matured the general strike and thereby opened a new epoch in the development of the labor movement. It does not, of course, follow from this that the tactics of political struggle recommended by Marx and Engels were false or that the criticism applied by them to anarchism was incorrect. . . . A tendency patterned entirely upon the "first blow" and "direct action," a tendency "revolutionary" in the most naked pitchfork sense, can only temporarily languish in the calm of the parliamentarian day and, on a return of the period of direct open struggle, can come to life again and unfold its inherent strength.

Russia, in particular, appeared to have become the experimental field for the heroic deeds of anarchism. A country in which the proletariat had absolutely no political rights and extremely weak organizations, a many-colored complex of various sections of the population, a chaos of conflicting interests, a low standard of education amongst the masses of the people, extreme brutality in the use of violence on the part of the prevailing regime—all this seemed as if created to raise anarchism to a sudden if perhaps short-lived power. And finally, Russia was the historical birthplace of anarchism. But the fatherland of Bakunin was to become the burial-place of its teachings. Not only did and do the anarchists in Russia not stand at the head of the mass strike movement; not only does the whole political leadership of revolutionary action and also of the mass strike lie in the hands of the social democratic organizations, which are bitterly opposed as "bourgeois parties" by the Russian anarchists, or partly in the hands of such socialist organizations as are more or less influenced by the social democracy and more or less approximate to it—such as the terrorist party, the "socialist revolutionaries"—but the anarchists simply do not exist as a serious political tendency in the Russian Revolution. Only in a small Lithuanian town with particularly difficult conditions—a confused medley of different nationalities among the workers, an extremely scattered condition of small-scale industry, a very severely oppressed proletariat—in Bialystok, there is, amongst the seven or eight different revolutionary groups a handful of half-grown "anarchists" who promote confusion and bewilderment amongst the workers to the best of their ability; and lastly in Moscow, and perhaps in two or three other towns, a handful of people of this kidney make themselves noticeable.

But apart from these few "revolutionary" groups, what is the actual role of anarchism in the Russian Revolution? It has become the sign of the common thief and plunderer; a large proportion of the innumerable thefts and acts of plunder of private persons are carried out under the name of "anarchist-communism"—acts which rise up like a troubled wave against the revolution in every period of expression and in every period of temporary defensive [action]. . . .

On the other hand, the mass strike in Russia has been realized not as means of evading the political struggle of the working class, and especially of parliamentarism, not as a means of jumping suddenly into the social revolution by means of a theatrical coup, but as a means, firstly, of creating for the proletariat the conditions of the daily political struggle and especially of parliamentarism. The revolutionary struggle in Russia, in which mass strikes are the most important weapon, is, by the working people, and above all by the proletariat, conducted for those political rights and conditions whose necessity and importance in the struggle for the emancipation of the working class Marx and Engels first pointed out, and in opposition to anarchism fought for with all their might in the International. Thus has historical dialectics, the rock on which the whole teaching of Marxian socialism rests, brought it about that today anarchism, with which the idea of the mass strike is indissolubly associated, has itself come to be opposed to the mass strike in practice; while on the contrary, the mass strike which, as the opposite of the political activity of the proletariat, was combatted appears today as the most powerful weapon of the struggle for political rights. . . .

II. The Mass Strike, A Historical and Not an Artificial Product

The first revision of the question of the mass strike which results from the experience of Russia relates to the general conception of the problem. . . .

For the anarchist there exist only two things as material suppositions of his "revolutionary" speculations—first imagination, and second goodwill and courage to rescue humanity from the existing capitalist vale of tears. This fanciful mode of reasoning sixty years ago gave the result that the mass strike was the shortest, surest and easiest means of springing into the better social future. The same mode of reasoning recently gave the result that the trade-union struggle was the only real "direct action of the masses" and also the only real revolutionary struggle—which, as is well known, is the latest notion of the French and Italian "syndicalists." The fatal thing for anarchism has always been that the methods of struggle improvised in the air were not only a reckoning without their host, that is, they were purely utopian, but that they, while not reckoning in the least with the despised evil reality, unexpectedly became in this evil reality, practical helps to the reaction, where previously they had only been for the most part, revolutionary speculations.

On the same ground of abstract, unhistorical methods of observation stand those today who would, in the manner of a board of directors, put the mass strike in Germany on the calendar on an appointed day, and those who, like the participants in the trade-union congress at Cologne, would by a prohibition of "propaganda" eliminate the problem of the mass strike from the face of the earth. Both tendencies proceed on the common purely anarchistic assumption that the mass strike is a purely technical means of struggle which can be "decided" at pleasure and strictly according to conscience, or "forbidden"—a kind of pocketknife which can be kept in the pocket clasped "ready for any emergency," and according to decision, can be unclasped and used. . . .

If it depended on the inflammatory "propaganda" of revolutionary romanticists or on confidential or public decisions of the party direction, then we should not even yet have had in Russia a single serious mass strike. In no country in the world—as I pointed out in March 1905 in the *Sachsische Arbeiterzeitung*—was the mass strike so little "propagated" or even "discussed" as in Russia. And the isolated examples of decisions and agreements of the Russian party executive which really

sought to proclaim the mass strike of their own accord—as, for example, the last attempt in August of this year after the dissolution of the Duma—are almost valueless.

If, therefore, the Russian Revolution teaches us anything, it teaches above all that the mass strike is not artificially "made," not "decided" at random, not "propagated," but that it is a historical phenomenon which, at a given moment, results from social conditions with historical inevitability. It is not therefore by abstract speculations on the possibility or impossibility, the utility or the injuriousness of the mass strike, but only by an examination of those factors and social conditions out of which the mass strike grows in the present phase of the class struggle—in other words, it is not by *subjective criticism* of the mass strike from the standpoint of what is desirable, but only by *objective investigation* of the sources of the mass strike from the standpoint of what is historically inevitable, that the problem can be grasped or even discussed. . . .

If anyone were to undertake to make the mass strike generally, as a form of proletarian action, the object of methodical agitation, and to go house-to-house canvassing with this "idea" in order to gradually win the working class to it, it would be as idle and profitless and absurd an occupation as it would be to seek to make the idea of the revolution or of the fight at the barricades the object of a special agitation. The mass strike has now become the center of the lively interest of the German and the international working class because it is a new form of struggle, and as such is the sure symptom of a thoroughgoing internal revolution in the relations of the classes and in the conditions of the class struggle. It is a testimony to the sound revolutionary instinct and to the quick intelligence of the mass of the German proletariat that, in spite of the obstinate resistance of their trade-union leaders, they are applying themselves to this new problem with such keen interest.

But it does not meet the case, in the presence of this interest and of this fine, intellectual thirst and desire for revolutionary deeds on the part of the workers, to treat them to abstract mental gymnastics on the possibility or impossibility of the mass strike; they should be enlightened on the development of the Russian Revolution, the international significance of that revolution, the sharpening of class antagonisms in Western Europe, the wider political perspectives of the class struggle in Germany, and the role and the tasks of the masses in the coming struggles. Only in this form will the discussion on the mass strike lead to the widening of the intellectual horizon of the proletariat, to the sharpening of their way of thinking, and to the steeling of their energy. . . .

IV. The Interaction of the Political and the Economic Struggle

We have attempted in the foregoing to sketch the history of the mass strike in Russia in a few strokes. Even a fleeting glance at this history shows us a picture which in no way resembles that usually formed by the discussions in Germany on the mass strike. Instead of the rigid and hollow scheme of an arid political action carried out by the decision of the highest committees and furnished with a plan and panorama, we see a bit of pulsating life of flesh and blood, which cannot be cut out of the large frame of the revolution but is connected with all parts of the revolution by a thousand veins.

The mass strike, as the Russian Revolution shows it to us, is such a changeable phenomenon that it reflects all phases of the political and economic struggle, all stages and factors of the revolution. Its adaptability, its efficiency, the factors of its origin are constantly changing. It suddenly opens new and wide perspectives of the revolution when it appears to have already arrived in a narrow pass and where it is impossible for anyone to reckon upon it with any degree of certainty. It flows now like a broad billow over the whole kingdom, and now divides into a gigantic network of narrow streams; now it bubbles forth from under the ground like a fresh spring and now is completely lost under the earth. Political and economic strikes, mass strikes and partial strikes, demonstrative strikes and fighting strikes, general strikes of individual branches of industry and general strikes in individual towns, peaceful wage struggles and street massacres, barricade fighting—all these run through one another, run side by side, cross one another, flow in and over one another—it is a ceaselessly moving, changing sea of phenomena. And the law of motion of these phenomena is clear: it does not lie in the mass strike itself nor in its technical details, but in the political and social proportions of the forces of the revolution.

The mass strike is merely the form of the revolutionary struggle and every disarrangement of the relations of the contending powers, in party development and in class division, in the position of the counterrevolution—all this immediately influences the action of the strike in a thousand invisible and scarcely controllable ways. But strike action itself does not cease for a single moment. It merely alters its forms, its dimensions, its effect. It is the living pulsebeat of the revolution and at the same time its most powerful driving wheel. In a word, the mass strike, as shown to us in the Russian Revolution, is not a crafty method discovered by subtle reasoning for the purpose of making the proletarian struggle more effective, *but the method of motion of the proletarian mass,* the phenomenal form of the proletarian struggle in the revolution.

Some general aspects may now be examined which may assist us in forming a correct estimate of the problem of the mass strike.

1. It is absurd to think of the mass strike as one act, one isolated action. The mass strike is rather the indication, the rallying idea, of a whole period of the class struggle lasting for years, perhaps for decades. Of the innumerable and highly varied mass strikes which have taken place in Russia during the last four years, the scheme of the mass strike was a purely political movement, begun and ended after a cut and dried plan, a short single act of one variety only and that a subordinate variety—pure demonstration strike. In the whole course of the five-year period we see in Russia only a few demonstration strikes, which be it noted, were generally confined to single towns. Thus the annual May Day general strike in Warsaw and Lodz in Russia proper on the first of May has not yet been celebrated to any appreciable extent by abstention from work; the mass strike in Warsaw on September 11, 1905, as a memorial service in honor of the executed Martin Kasprzak; that of November 1905 in Petersburg in protest demonstration against the declaration of a state of siege in Poland and Livonia; that of January 22, 1906 in Warsaw, Lodz, Czentochon and in the Dombrowa coal basin, as well as, in part those in a few Russian towns as anniversary celebrations of the Petersburg bloodbath; in addition, in July 1906 a general strike in Tiflis as demonstration of sympathy with soldiers sentenced by court-martial on account of the military revolt; and finally from the same cause, in September 1906, during the deliberations of the court-martial in Reval. All the above great and partial mass strikes and general strikes were not demonstration strikes but fighting strikes, and as such they originated for the most part spontaneously, in every case from specific local accidental causes, without plan and undesignedly, and grew with elemental power into great movements, and then they did not begin an "orderly retreat," but turned now into economic struggles, now into street fighting, and now collapsed of themselves.

In this general picture the purely political demonstration strike plays quite a subordinate role—isolated small points in the midst of a mighty expanse. Thereby, temporarily considered, the following characteristic discloses itself: the demonstration strikes which, in contradistinction to the fighting strikes, exhibit the greatest mass of party discipline, conscious direction and political thought, and therefore must appear as the highest and most mature form of the mass strike, play in reality the greatest part in the *beginnings* of the movement. Thus for example, the absolute cessation of work on May 1, 1905, in Warsaw, as the first instance of a decision of the social democrats carried throughout in such an astonishing fashion, was an experience of great importance for the proletarian movement in Poland. In the same way the sympathetic strike of the same year in Petersburg made a great impression as the first experiment of conscious systematic mass action in Russia. Similarly the "trial mass strike" of the Hamburg comrades on January 17, 1906, will play a prominent part in the history of the future German mass strike as the first vigorous attempt with the much disputed weapon, and also a very successful and convincingly striking test of the fighting temper and the lust for battle of the Hamburg working class. And just as surely will the period of the mass strike in Germany, when it has once begun in real earnest, lead of itself to a real, general cessation of work on May first. The May Day festival may naturally be raised to a position of honor as the first great demonstration under the aegis of the mass struggle. In this sense the "lame horse," as the May Day festival was termed at the trade-union congress at Cologne, has still a great future before it and an important part to play, in the proletarian class struggle in Germany.

But with the development of the earnest revolutionary struggle the importance of such demonstrations diminishes rapidly. It is precisely those factors which objectively facilitate the realization of the demonstration strike after a preconceived plan and at the party's word of command — namely, the growth of political consciousness and the training of the proletariat — make this kind of mass strike impossible; today the proletariat in Russia, the most capable vanguard of the masses, does not want to know about mass strikes; the workers are no longer in a mood for jesting and will now think only of a serious struggle with all its consequences. And when, in the first great mass strike in January 1905, the demonstrative element, not indeed in an intentional, but more in an instinctive spontaneous form, still played a great part, on the other hand, the attempt of the Central Committee of the Russian social democrats to call a mass strike in August as a demonstration for the dissolved Duma was shattered by, among other things, the positive disinclination of the educated proletariat to engage in weak half-actions and mere demonstrations.

2. When, however, we have in view the less important strike of the demonstrative kind, instead of the fighting strike as it represents in Russia today the actual vehicle of proletarian action, we see still more clearly that it is impossible to separate the economic factors from one another. Here also the reality deviates from the theoretical scheme, and the pedantic representation in which the pure political mass strike is logically derived from the trade-union general strike as the ripest and highest stage, but at the same time is kept distinct from it, is shown to be absolutely false. This is expressed not merely in the fact that the mass strikes, from that first great wage struggle of the Petersburg textile workers in 1896–97 to the last great mass strike in December 1905, passed imperceptibly from the economic field to the political, so that it is almost impossible to draw a dividing line between them.

Again, every one of the great mass strikes repeats, so to speak, on a small scale, the entire history of the Russian mass strike, and begins with a pure economic, or at all events, a partial trade-union conflict, and runs through all the stages to the political demonstration. The great thunderstorm of mass strikes in South Russia in 1902 and 1903 originated, as we have seen, in Baku from a conflict arising from the disciplinary punishment of the unemployed, in Rostov from disputes about wages in the railway workshops, in Tiflis from a struggle of the commercial employees for reduction of working hours, in Odessa from a wage dispute in one single small factory. The January mass strike of 1905 developed from an internal conflict in the Putilov works, the October strike from the struggle of the railway workers for a pension fund, and finally the December strike from the struggle of the postal and telegraph employees for the right of combination. The progress of the movement on the whole is not expressed in the circumstances that the economic initial stage is omitted, but much more in the rapidity with which all the stages to the political demonstration are run through and in the extremity of the point to which the strike moves forward.

But the movement on the whole does not proceed from the economic to the political struggle, nor even the reverse. Every great political mass action, after it has attained its political highest point, breaks up into a mass of economic strikes. And that applies not only to each of the great mass strikes, but also to the revolution as a whole. With the spreading, clarifying and involution of the political struggle, the economic struggle not only does not recede, but extends, organizes and becomes involved in equal measure. Between the two there is the most complete reciprocal action.

Every new onset and every fresh victory of the political struggle is transformed into a powerful impetus for the economic struggle, extending at the same time its external possibilities and intensifying the inner urge of the workers to better their position, and their desire to struggle. After every foaming wave of political action a fructifying deposit remains behind from which a thousand stalks of economic struggle shoot forth. And conversely. The workers' condition of ceaseless economic struggle with the capitalists keeps their fighting energy alive in every political interval; it forms, so to speak, the permanent fresh reservoir of the strength of the proletarian classes, from which the political fight ever renews its strength, and at the same time leads the indefatigable economic sappers of the proletariat at all times, now here and now there, to isolated sharp conflicts, out of which political conflicts on a large scale unexpectedly explode.

In a word: the economic struggle is the transmitter from one political center to another; the political struggle is the periodic fertilization of the soil for the economic struggle. Cause and effect here continually change places; and thus the economic and the political factor in the period of the mass strike, now widely removed, completely separated or even mutually exclusive, as the theoretical plan would have them, merely form the two interlacing sides of the proletarian class struggle in Russia. And their unity is precisely the mass strike. If the sophisticated theory proposes to make a clever logical dissection of the mass strike for the purpose of getting at the "purely political mass strike," it will by this dissection, as with any other, not perceive the phenomenon in its living essence, but will kill it altogether.

3. Finally, the events in Russia show us that the mass strike is inseparable from the revolution. The history of the Russian mass strikes is the history of the Russian Revolution. When, to be sure, the representatives of our German opportunism hear of "revolution," they immediately think of bloodshed, street fighting or powder and shot, and the logical conclusion thereof is: the mass strike leads inevitably to the revolution, therefore we dare not have it. In actual fact we see in Russia that almost every mass strike in the long run leads to an encounter with the armed guardians of czarist order, and therein the so-called political strikes exactly resemble the larger economic struggle. The revolution, however, is something other and something more than bloodshed. In contradiction to the police interpretation, which views the revolution exclusively from the standpoint of street disturbances and rioting, that is, from the standpoint of "disorder," the interpretation of scientific socialism sees in the revolution above all a thoroughgoing internal reversal of social class relations. And from this standpoint an altogether different connection exists between revolution and mass strike in Russia from that contained in the commonplace conception that the mass strike generally ends in bloodshed.

We have seen above the inner mechanism of the Russian mass strike which depends upon the ceaseless reciprocal action of the political and economic struggles. But this reciprocal action is conditioned during the revolutionary period. Only in the sultry air of the period of revolution can any partial little conflict between labor and capital grow into a general explosion. In Germany the most violent, most brutal collisions between the workers and employers take place every year and every day without the struggle overleaping the bounds of the individual departments or individual towns concerned, or even those of the individual factories. Punishment of organized workers in Petersburg and unemployment as in Baku, wage struggles as in Odessa, struggles for the right of combination as in Moscow are the order of the day in Germany. No single one of these cases however changes suddenly into a common class action. And when they grow into isolated mass strikes, which have without question a political coloring, they do not bring about a general storm. The general strike of the Dutch railwaymen, which died away in spite of the warmest sympathy, in the midst of the complete impassivity of the proletariat of the country, affords a striking proof of this.

And conversely, only in the period of the revolution, when the social foundations and the walls of the class society are shaken and subjected to a constant process of disarrangement, any political class action of the proletariat can arouse from their passive condition in a few hours whole sections of the working class who have hitherto remained unaffected, and this is immediately and naturally expressed in a stormy economic struggle. The worker, suddenly aroused to activity by the electric shock of political action, immediately seizes the weapon lying nearest his hand for the fight against his condition of economic slavery: the stormy gesture of the political struggle causes him to feel with unexpected intensity the weight and the pressure of his economic chains. And while, for example, the most violent political struggle in Germany—the electoral struggle or the parliamentary struggle on the customs tariff—exercised a scarcely perceptible direct influence upon the course and the intensity of the wage struggles being conducted at the same time in Germany, every political action of the proletariat in Russia immediately expresses itself in the extension of the area and the deepening of the intensity of the economic struggle.

The revolution thus first creates the social conditions in which this sudden change of the economic struggle into the political and of the political struggle into the economic is possible, a change which finds its expression in the mass strike. And if the vulgar scheme sees the connection between mass strike and revolution only in bloody street encounters with which the mass strikes conclude, a somewhat deeper look into the Russian events shows an exactly opposite connection: in reality the mass strike does not produce the revolution, but the revolution produces the mass strike.

4. It is sufficient in order to comprehend the foregoing to obtain an explanation of the question of the conscious direction and initiative in the mass strike. If the mass strike is not an isolated act but a whole period of the class struggle, and if this period is identical with a period of revolution, it is clear that the mass strike cannot be called at will, even when the decision to do so may come from the highest committee of the strongest social democratic party. As long as the social democracy has not the power to stage and countermand revolutions according to its fancy, even the greatest enthusiasm and impatience of the social democratic troops will not suffice to call into being a real period of mass strike as a living, powerful movement of the people. On the basis of a decision of the party leadership and of party discipline, a single short demonstration may well be arranged similar to the Swedish mass strike, or to the latest Austrian strike, or even to the Hamburg mass strike of January 17. These demonstrations, however, differ from an actual period of revolutionary mass strikes in exactly the same way that the well-known demonstrations in foreign ports during a period of strained diplomatic relations differ from a naval war. A mass strike born of pure discipline and enthusiasm will, at best, merely play the role of an episode, of a symptom of the fighting mood of the working class upon which, however, the conditions of a peaceful period are reflected.

Of course, even during the revolution, mass strikes do not exactly fall from heaven. They must be brought about in some way or another by the workers. The resolution and determination of the workers also play a part and indeed the initiative and the wider direction naturally fall to the share of the organized and most enlightened kernel of the proletariat. But the scope of this initiative and this direction, for the most part, is confined to application to individual acts, to individual strikes, when the revolutionary period is already begun, and indeed, in most cases, is confined within the boundaries of a single town. Thus, for example, as we have seen, the social democrats have already, on several occasions, successfully issued a direct summons for a mass strike in Baku, in Warsaw, in Lodz and in Petersburg. But this succeeds much less frequently when applied to general movements of the whole proletariat.

Further, there are quite definite limits set to initiative and conscious direction. During the revolution it is extremely difficult for any directing organ of the proletarian movement to foresee and to calculate which occasions and factors can lead to explosions and which cannot. Here also initiative and direction do not consist in issuing commands according to one's inclinations, but in the most adroit adaptability to the given situation, and the closest possible contact with the mood of the masses. The element of spontaneity, as we have seen, plays a great part in all Russian mass strikes without exception, be it as a driving force or as a restraining influence. This does not occur in Russia, however, because social democracy is still young or weak, but because in every individual act of the struggle so very many important economic, political and social, general and local, material and psychical, factors react upon one another in such a way that no single act can be arranged and resolved as if it were a mathematical problem. The revolution, even when the proletariat, with the social democrats at their head, appear in the leading role, is not a maneuver of the proletariat in the open field, but a fight in the midst of the incessant crashing, displacing and crumbling of the social foundation. In short, in the mass strikes in Russia the element of spontaneity plays such a predominant part, not because the Russian proletariat are "uneducated," but because revolutions do not allow anyone to play the schoolmaster with them.

On the other hand, we see in Russia that the same revolution which rendered the social democrats' command of the mass strike so difficult, and which struck the conductor's baton from, or pressed it into, their hand at all times in such a comical fashion—we see that it resolved of itself all those difficulties of the mass strike which, in the theoretical scheme of German discussion, are regarded as the chief concern of the "directing body": the question of "provisioning," "discovery of cost," and "sacrifice." It goes without saying that it does not resolve them in the way that they would be resolved in a quiet confidential discussion between the higher directing committees of the labor movement, the members sitting pencil in hand. The "regulation" of all these questions consists in the circumstance that the revolution brings such an enormous mass of people upon the stage that any computation or regulation of the cost of the movement such as can be effected in a civil process, appears to be an altogether hopeless undertaking.

The leading organizations in Russia certainly attempt to support the direct victims to the best of their ability. Thus, for example, the brave victims of the gigantic lockout in St. Petersburg, which followed upon the eight-hour day campaign, were supported for weeks. But all these measures are, in the enormous balance of the revolution, but as a drop in the ocean.

At the moment that a real, earnest period of mass strikes begins, all these "calculations" of "cost" become merely projects for exhausting the ocean with a tumbler. And it is a veritable ocean of frightful privations and sufferings which is brought by every revolution to the proletarian masses. And the solution which a revolutionary period makes of this apparently invincible difficulty consists in the circumstances that such an immense volume of mass idealism is simultaneously released that the masses are insensible to the bitterest sufferings. With the psychology of a trade unionist who will not stay off his work on May Day unless he is assured in advance of a definite amount of support in the event of his being victimized, neither revolution nor mass strike can be made. But in the storm of the revolutionary period even the proletarian is transformed from a provident pater familias demanding support, into a "revolutionary romanticist," for whom even the highest good, life itself, to say nothing of material well-being, possesses but little in comparison with the ideal of the struggle.

If, however, the direction of the mass strike in the sense of command over its origin, and in the sense of the calculating and reckoning of the cost, is a matter of the revolutionary period itself, the directing of the mass strike becomes, in an altogether different sense, the duty of social democracy and its leading organs. Instead of puzzling their heads with the technical side, with the mechanism, of the mass strike, the social democrats are called upon to assume *political* leadership in the midst of the revolutionary period.

To give the cue for, and the direction to, the fight; to so regulate the tactics of the political struggle in its every phase and at its every moment that the entire sum of the available power of the proletariat which is already released and active, will find expression in the battle array of the party; to see that the tactics of the social democrats are decided according to their resoluteness and acuteness and that they never fall below the level demanded by the actual relations of forces, but rather rise above it—that is the most important task of the directing body in a period of mass strikes. And this direction changes of itself, to a certain extent, into technical direction. A consistent, resolute, progressive tactic on the part of the social democrats produces in the masses a feeling of security, self-confidence and desire for struggle; a vacillating weak tactic, based on an underestimation of the proletariat, has a crippling and confusing effect upon the masses. In the first case mass strikes break out "of themselves" and "opportunely"; in the second case they remain ineffective amidst direct summonses of the directing body to mass strikes. And of both the Russian Revolution affords striking examples. . . .

VI. Cooperation of Organized and Unorganized Workers Necessary for Victory

In connection with this, the question of organization in relation to the problem of the mass strike in Germany assumes an essentially different aspect.

The attitude of many trade-union leaders to this question is generally summed up in the assertion: "We are not yet strong enough to risk such a hazardous trial of strength as a mass strike." Now this position is so far untenable that it is an insoluble problem to determine the time, in a peaceful fashion by counting heads, when the proletariat are "strong enough" for any struggle. Thirty years ago the German trade unions had 50,000 members. That was obviously a number with which a mass strike on the above scale was not to be thought of. Fifteen years later the trade unions were four times as strong, and counted 237,000 members. If, however, the present trade-union leaders had been asked at the time if the organization of the proletariat was then sufficiently ripe for a mass strike, they would assuredly have replied that it was still far from it and that the number of those organized in trade unions would first have to be counted by millions.

Today the number of trade unionists already runs into the second million, but the views of the leaders are still exactly the same, and may very well be the same to the end. The tacit assumption is that the entire working class of Germany, down to the last man and the last woman, must be included in the organization before it "is strong enough" to risk a mass action, which then, according to the old formula, would probably be represented as "superfluous." This theory is nevertheless absolutely utopian, for the simple reason that it suffers from an internal contradiction, that it goes in a vicious circle. Before the workers can engage in any direct class struggle they must all be organized. The circumstances, the conditions, of capitalist development and of the bourgeois state make it impossible that, in the normal course of things, without stormy class struggles, certain sections—and these the greatest, the most important, the lowest and the most oppressed by capital, and by the state—can be organized at all. We see even in Britain, which has had a whole century of indefatigable trade-union effort without any "disturbances"—except at the beginning in the period of the chartist movement—without any "romantic revolutionary" errors or temptations, it has not been possible to do more than organize a minority of the better-paid sections of the proletariat.

On the other hand the trade unions, like all fighting organizations of the proletariat, cannot permanently maintain themselves in any other way than by struggle, and that not struggles of the same kind as the war between the frogs and the mice in the stagnant waters of the bourgeois parliamentary period, but struggle in the troubled revolutionary periods of the mass strike. The rigid, mechanical-bureaucratic conception cannot conceive of the struggle save as the product of organization at a certain stage of its strength. On the contrary the living, dialectical explanation makes the organization arise as a product of the struggle. We have already seen a grandiose example of this phenomenon in Russia, where a proletariat almost wholly unorganized created a comprehensive network of organizational appendages in a year and a half of stormy revolutionary struggle.

Another example of this kind is furnished by the history of the German unions. In the year 1878 the number of trade-union members amounted to 50,000. According to the theory of the present-day trade-union leaders this organization, as stated above, was not nearly "strong enough" to enter upon a violent political struggle. The German trade unions however, weak as they were at the time, did take up the struggle—namely the struggle against the antisocialist law—and showed that they were "strong enough," not only to emerge victorious from the struggle, but to increase their strength fivefold: in 1891, after the repeal of the antisocialist laws, their membership was 277,659. It is true that the methods by which the trade unions conquered in the struggle against the antisocialist laws do not correspond to the ideal of a peaceful, beelike, uninterrupted process: they first went into the fight absolutely in ruins, to rise again on the next wave and to be born anew. But this is precisely the specific method of growth corresponding to the proletarian class organizations: to be tested in the struggle and to go forth from the struggle with increased strength.

On a closer examination of German conditions and of the condition of the different sections of the working class, it is clear that the coming period of stormy political mass struggles will not bring the dreaded, threatening downfall of the German trade unions, but on the contrary, will open up hitherto unsuspected prospects of the extension of their sphere of power—an extension that will proceed rapidly by leaps and bounds. But the question has still another aspect. The plan of undertaking mass strikes as a serious political class action with organized workers only is absolutely hopeless. If the mass strike, or rather, mass strikes, and the mass struggle are to be successful they must become a real people's movement, that is, the widest sections of the proletariat must be drawn into the fight. Already in the parliamentary form the might of the proletarian class struggle rests not on the small organized group, but on the surrounding periphery of the revolutionary-minded proletariat. If the social democrats were to enter the electoral battle with their few hundred thousand organized members alone, they would condemn themselves to futility. And although it is the tendency of social democracy wherever possible to draw the whole great army of its voters into the party organization, its mass of voters after thirty years experience of social democracy is not increased through the growth of the party organization, but on the contrary, the new sections of the proletariat, won for the time being through the electoral struggle, are the fertile soil for the subsequent seed of organization. Here the organization does not supply the troops for the struggle, but the struggle, in an ever growing degree, supplies recruits for the organization.

In a much greater degree does this obviously apply to direct political mass action than to the parliamentary struggle. If the social democrats, as the organized nucleus of the working class, are the most important vanguard of the entire body of the workers and if the political clarity, the strength, and the unity of the labor movement flow from this organization, then it is not permissible to visualize the class movement of the proletariat as a movement of the organized minority. Every real, great class struggle must rest upon the support and cooperation of the widest masses, and a strategy of class struggle which does not reckon with this cooperation, which is based upon the idea of the finely stage-managed marchout of the small, well-trained part of the proletariat is foredoomed to be a miserable fiasco.

Mass strikes and political mass struggles cannot, therefore, possibly be carried through in Germany by the organized workers alone, nor can they be appraised by regular "direction" from the central committee of a party. In this case, again—exactly as in Russia—they depend not so much upon "discipline" and "training" and upon the most careful possible regulation beforehand of the questions of support and cost, as upon a real revolutionary, determined class action, which will be able to win and draw into the struggle the widest circles of the unorganized workers, according to their mood and their conditions.

The overestimate and the false estimate of the role of organizations in the class struggle of the proletariat is generally reinforced by the underestimate of the unorganized proletarian mass and of their political maturity. In a revolutionary period, in the storm of great unsettling class struggles, the whole educational effect of the rapid capitalist development and of social democratic influences first shows itself upon the widest sections of the people, of which, in peaceful times the tables of the organized, and even election statistics, give only a faint idea.

We have seen that in Russia, in about two years a

great general action of the proletariat can forthwith arise from the smallest partial conflict of the workers with the employers, from the most insignificant act of brutality of the government organs. Everyone, of course, sees and believes that, because in Russia "the revolution" is there. But what does that mean? It means that class feeling, the class instinct, is alive and very active in the Russian proletariat, so that immediately they regard every partial question of any small group of workers as a general question, as a class affair, and quick as lightning they react to its influence as a unity. While in Germany, France, Italy and Holland the most violent trade-union conflicts call forth hardly any general action of the working class—and when they do, only the organized part of the workers moves—in Russia the smallest dispute raises a storm. That means nothing else however, than that at present—paradoxical as it may sound—the class instinct of the youngest, least trained, badly educated and still worse organized Russian proletariat is immeasurably stronger than that of the organized, trained and enlightened working class of Germany or of any other west European country. And that is not to be reckoned a special virtue of the "young, unexhausted East" as compared with the "sluggish West," but is simply a result of direct revolutionary mass action. . . .

VIII. Need for United Action of Trade Unions and Social Democracy

The most important desideratum which is to be hoped for from the German working class in the period of great struggles which will come sooner or later is, after complete resoluteness and consistency of tactics, the utmost capacity for action, and therefore the utmost possible unity of the leading social democratic part of the proletarian masses. Meanwhile the first weak attempts at the preparation of great mass actions have discovered a serious drawback in this connection: the total separation and independence of the two organizations of the labor movement, the social democracy and the trade unions. . . .

As a matter of fact the separation of the political and the economic struggle and the independence of each is nothing but an artificial product of the parliamentarian period, even if historically determined. . . . There are not two different class struggles of the working class, an economic and a political one, but only *one* class struggle, which aims at one and the same time at the limitation of capitalist exploitation within bourgeois society, and at the abolition of exploitation together with bourgeois society itself. . . .

The most important conclusion to be drawn from the facts above cited is that the *complete unity* of the

trade-union and the social democratic movements, which is absolutely necessary for the coming mass struggles in Germany, *is actually here*, and that it is incorporated in the wide mass which forms the basis at once of social democracy and trade unionism, and in whose consciousness both parts of the movement are mingled in a mental unity. The alleged antagonism between social democracy and trade unions shrinks to an antagonism between social democracy and a certain part of the trade-union officials, which is, however, at the same time an antagonism within the trade unions between this part of the trade-union leaders and the proletarian mass organized in trade unions. . . .

. . . Not above amongst the heads of the leading directing organizations and in their federative alliance, but below amongst the organized proletarian masses, lies the guarantee of the real unity of the labor movement. . . .

. . . Such a revolution will inevitably call forth a vigorous opposition from a part of the trade-union leadership. But it is high time for the working masses of social democracy to learn how to express their capacity for decision and action, and therewith to demonstrate their ripeness for that time of great struggles and great tasks in which they, the masses, will be the actual chorus and the directing bodies will merely act the "speaking parts," that is, will only be the interpreters of the will of the masses. . . .

The Accumulation of Capital (1913)

Chapter I. The Object of Our Investigation

. . . In a society producing by capitalist methods, reproduction assumes a peculiar form, as a mere glance at certain striking phenomena will show us. In every other society known to history, reproduction recurs in a regular sequence as far as its preconditions, the existing means of production and labour power, make this possible. As a rule, only external influences such as a devastating war or a great pestilence, depopulating vast areas of former cultural life, and consequently destroying masses of labour power and of accumulated means of production, can result in a complete interruption of reproduction or in its contraction to any considerable extent for longer or shorter periods. . . .

Societies which produce according to capitalist methods present a different picture. We observe that in certain periods all the ingredients of reproduction may be available, both labour and means of production, and yet some vital needs of society for consumer goods may be left unfulfilled. We find that in spite of these resources reproduction may in part be completely suspended and in part curtailed. Here it is no despotic interference with the economic plan that is responsible for the difficulties in the process of production. Quite apart from all technical conditions, reproduction here depends on purely social considerations: only those goods are produced which can with certainty be expected to sell, and not merely to sell, but to sell at the customary profit. Thus profit becomes an end in itself, the decisive factor which determines not only production but also reproduction. Not only does it decide in each case what work is to be undertaken, how it is to be carried out, and how the products are to be distributed; what is more, profit decides, also, at the end of every working period, whether the labour process is to be resumed, and, if so, to what extent and in what direction it should be made to operate. . . .

. . . A producer who produces not only commodities but capital must above all create surplus value [profit]. The capitalist producer's final goal, his main incentive, is the production of surplus value. The proceeds from the commodities he has manufactured must not only recompense him for all his outlay, but in addition they must yield him a value which does not correspond with any expense on his part, and is pure gain. If we consider the process of production from the point of view of the creation of surplus value, we see that the capital advanced by the capitalist is divided into two parts: the first part represents his expenses on means of production such as premises, raw material, partly finished goods and machinery. The second part is spent on wages. This holds good, even if the capitalist producer does not know it himself, and in spite of the pious stuff about fixed and circulating capital with which he may delude himself and the world. Marx called this first part constant capital. Its value is not changed by its utilisation in the labour process — it is transferred *in toto* to the finished product. The second part Marx calls the variable capital. This gives rise to an additional value, which materialises when the results of unpaid labour are appropriated [surplus value]. The various components which make up the value of every commodity produced by capitalist methods may be expressed by the formula: $c + v + s$. In this formula c stands for the value of the constant capital laid out in inanimate means of production and transferred to the commodity, v stands for the value of the variable capital advanced in form of wages, and s stands for the surplus value of the unpaid part of wage labour. Every type of goods shows these three components of value, whether we consider an individual commodity or the aggregate of commodities as a whole, whether we consider cotton textiles or ballet performances, cast-iron tubes or liberal newspapers. Thus for the capitalist producer the manufacture of commodities is not an end in itself, it is only a means to the appropriation of surplus value. . . .

. . . In every other economic system known to history, reproduction is determined by the unceasing need of society for consumer goods, whether they are the needs of all the workers determined in a democratic manner as in an agrarian and communist market community, or the despotically determined needs of an antagonistic class society, as in an economy of slave labour or *corvée* and the like. But in a capitalist system of production, it is not consideration of social needs which actuates the individual private producer who alone matters in this connection. His production is determined entirely by the effective demand, and even this is to him a mere means for the realisation of surplus value which for him is indispensable. Appropriation of surplus value is his real incentive, and production of consumer goods for the satisfaction of the effective demand is only a detour when we look to the real motive, that of appropriation of surplus value, although for the individual capitalist it is also a rule of necessity. This motive, to appropriate surplus value, also urges him to re-engage in reproduction over and over again. It is the production of surplus value which turns reproduction of social necessities into a *perpetuum mobile*. . . .

Now we come to a second important point. Under a system of private economy, it is the individual producer who determines the volume of reproduction at his discretion. His main incentive is appropriation of surplus value, indeed an appropriation increasing as rapidly as possible. An accelerated appropriation of surplus value, however, necessitates an increased production of capital to generate this surplus value. Here a large-scale enterprise enjoys advantages over a small one in every respect. In fine, the capitalist method of production furnishes not only a permanent incentive to reproduction in general, but also a motive for its expansion, for reproduction on an ever larger scale. . . .

As a rule, an increased production of surplus value results from an increase of capital brought about by addition of part of the appropriated surplus value to the original capital, no matter whether this capitalist surplus value is used for the expansion of an old enterprise or for founding a new one, an independent offshoot. Capitalist expanding reproduction thus acquires the specific characteristics of an increase in capital by means of a progressive capitalisation of surplus value, or, as Marx has put it, by the accumulation of capital. . . .

Chapter XXVI. The Reproduction of Capital and Its Social Setting

Marx's diagram of enlarged reproduction cannot explain the actual and historical process of accumulation. And why? Because of the very premises of the diagram. The diagram sets out to describe the accumulative process on the assumption that the capitalists and workers are the sole agents of capitalist consumption. We have seen that Marx consistently and deliberately assumes the universal and exclusive domination of the capitalist mode of production as a theoretical premise of his analysis in all three volumes of *Capital*. Under these conditions, there can admittedly be no other classes of society than capitalists and workers; as the diagram has it, all 'third persons' of capitalist society—civil servants, the liberal professions, the clergy, etc.,—must, as consumers, be counted in with these two classes, and preferably with the capitalist class. This axiom, however, is a theoretical contrivance— real life has never known a self-sufficient capitalist society under the exclusive domination of the capitalist mode of production. . . .

In real life the actual conditions for the accumulation of the aggregate capital are quite different from those prevailing for individual capitals and for simple reproduction. . . . The workers and capitalists themselves cannot possibly realise that part of the surplus value [profit] which is to be capitalised. Therefore, the realisation of the surplus value for the purposes of accumulation is an impossible task for a society which consists solely of workers and capitalists. Strangely enough, all theorists who analysed the problem of accumulation, from Ricardo and Sismondi to Marx, started with the very assumption which makes their problem insoluble. . . .

. . . Nevertheless, a solution of the problem of accumulation, in harmony both with other parts of Marx's doctrine and with the historical experience and daily practice of capitalism, is implied in Marx's complete analysis of simple reproduction and his characterisation of the capitalist process as a whole which shows up its immanent contradictions and their development (in *Capital*, vol. iii). In the light of this, the deficiencies of the diagram can be corrected. All the relations being, as it were, incomplete, a closer study of the diagram of enlarged reproduction will reveal that it points to some sort of organisation more advanced than purely capitalist production and accumulation.

Up to now we have only considered one aspect of enlarged reproduction, the problem of realising the surplus value, whose difficulties hitherto had claimed the sceptics' whole attention. Realisation of the surplus value is doubtless a vital question of capitalist accumulation. It requires as its prime condition—ignoring, for simplicity's sake, the capitalists' fund of consumption altogether—that there should be strata of buyers outside capitalist society. Buyers, it should be noted, not consumers, since the material form of the surplus value is quite irrelevant to its realisation. The decisive fact is that the surplus value cannot be realised by sale either to workers or to capitalists, but only if it is sold to such social organisations or strata whose own mode of production is not capitalistic. Here we can conceive of two different cases:

1. Capitalist production supplies consumer goods over and above its own requirements, the demand of its workers and capitalists, which are bought by non-capitalist strata and countries. The English cotton industry, for instance, during the first two-thirds of the nineteenth century, and to some extent even now, has been supplying cotton textiles to the peasants and petty-bourgeois townspeople of the European continent, and to the peasants of India, America, Africa and so on. The enormous expansion of the English cotton industry was thus founded on consumption by non-capitalist strata and countries. . . .

2. Conversely, capitalist production supplies means of production in excess of its own demand and finds buyers in non-capitalist countries. English industry, for instance, in the first half of the nineteenth century supplied materials for the construction of railroads in the American and Australian states. (The building of railways cannot in itself be taken as evidence for the domination of capitalist production in a country. As a matter of fact, the railways in this case provided only one of the first conditions for the inauguration of capitalist production.) Another example would be the German chemical industry which supplies means of production such as dyes in great quantities to Asiatic, African and other countries whose own production is not capitalistic. . . .

In addition, there is no obvious reason why means of production and consumer goods should be produced by capitalist methods alone. This assumption, for all Marx used it as the corner-stone of his thesis, is in conformity neither with the daily practice, and the history, of capital, nor with the specific character of this mode of production. In the first half of the nineteenth century, a great part of the surplus value in England was produced in form of cotton fabrics. Yet the material elements for the capitalism of this surplus value, although they certainly represented a surplus product, still were by no means all capitalist surplus value, to mention only raw cotton from the slave states of the American Union, or grain (a means of subsistence for the English workers) from the fields of serf-owning Russia. How much capitalist accumulation depends upon means of production which are not produced by capitalist methods is shown for example by the cotton crisis in England during the American War of Secession, when the cultivation of the plantations came to a standstill, or by the crises of European linen-weaving during the war in the East, when flax could not be imported from serf-owning Russia. We need only recall that imports of corn raised by peasants—i.e. not produced by capitalist methods—played a vital part in the feeding of industrial labour, as an element, that is to say, of variable capital, for a further illustration of the close ties between non-capitalist strata and the material elements necessary to the accumulation of capital.

Moreover, capitalist production, by its very nature, cannot be restricted to such means of production as are produced by capitalist methods. Cheap elements of constant capital are essential to the individual capitalist who strives to increase his rate of profit. In addition, the very condition of continuous improvements in labour productivity as the most important method of increasing the rate of surplus value, is unrestricted utilisation of all substances and facilities afforded by nature and soil. To tolerate any restriction in this respect would be contrary to the very essence of capital, its whole mode of existence. After many centuries of development, the capitalist mode of production still constitutes only a fragment of total world production. Even in the small Continent of Europe, where it now chiefly prevails, it has not yet succeeded in dominating entire branches of production, such as peasant agriculture and the independent handicrafts; the same holds true, further, for large parts of North America and for a number of regions in the other continents. In general, capitalist production has hitherto been confined mainly to the countries in the temperate zone, whilst it made comparatively little progress in the East, for instance, and the South. Thus, if it were dependent exclusively on elements of production obtainable within such narrow limits, its present level and indeed its development in general would have been impossible. From the very beginning, the forms and laws of capitalist production aim to comprise the entire globe as a store of productive forces. Capital, impelled to appropriate productive forces for purposes of exploitation, ransacks the whole world, it procures its means of production from all corners of the earth, seizing them, if necessary by force, from all levels of civilisation and from all forms of society. The problem of the material elements of capitalist accumulation, far from being solved by the material form of the surplus value that has been produced, takes on quite a different aspect. It becomes necessary for capital progressively to dispose ever more fully of the whole globe,

to acquire an unlimited choice of means of production, with regard to both quality and quantity, so as to find productive employment for the surplus value it has realised. . . .

Hitherto we have considered accumulation solely with regard to surplus value and constant capital. The third element of accumulation is variable capital which increases with progressive accumulation. In Marx's diagram, the social product contains ever more means of subsistence for the workers as the material form proper to this variable capital. The variable capital, however, is not really the means of subsistence for the workers but is in fact living labour for whose reproduction these means of subsistence are necessary. One of the fundamental conditions of accumulation is therefore a supply of living labour which can be mobilised by capital to meet its demands. This supply can be increased under favourable conditions—but only up to a certain point—by longer hours and more intensive work. Both these methods of increasing the supply, however, do not enlarge the variable capital, or do so only to a small extent (e.g. payment for overtime). Moreover, they are confined to definite and rather narrow limits which they cannot exceed owing to both natural and social causes. The increasing growth of variable capital which accompanies accumulation must therefore become manifest in ever greater numbers of employed labour. Where can this additional labour be found? . . .

. . . Marx himself has most brilliantly shown that natural propagation cannot keep up with the sudden expansive needs of capital. If natural propagation were the only foundation for the development of capital, accumulation, in its periodical swings from overstrain to exhaustion, could not continue, nor could the productive sphere expand by leaps and bounds, and accumulation itself would become impossible. The latter requires an unlimited freedom of movement in respect of the growth of variable capital equal to that which it enjoys with regard to the elements of constant capital—that is to say it must needs dispose over the supply of labour power without restriction. Marx considers that this can be achieved by an 'industrial reserve army of workers.' His diagram of simple reproduction admittedly does not recognise such an army, nor could it have room for it, since the natural propagation of the capitalist wage proletariat cannot provide an industrial reserve army. Labour for this army is recruited from social reservoirs outside the dominion of capital—it is drawn into the wage proletariat only if need arises. Only the existence of non-capitalist groups and countries can guarantee such a supply of additional labour power for capitalist production. . . .

Since capitalist production can develop fully only

with complete access to all territories and climes, it can no more confine itself to the natural resources and productive forces of the temperate zone than it can manage with white labour alone. Capital needs other races to exploit territories where the white man cannot work. It must be able to mobilise world labour power without restriction in order to utilise all productive forces of the globe—up to the limits imposed by a system of producing surplus value. This labour power, however, is in most cases rigidly bound by the traditional pre-capitalist organisation of production. It must first be 'set free' in order to be enrolled in the active army of capital. The emancipation of labour power from primitive social conditions and its absorption by the capitalist wage system is one of the indispensable historical bases of capitalism. For the first genuinely capitalist branch of production, the English cotton industry, not only the cotton of the Southern states of the American Union was essential, but also the millions of African Negroes who were shipped to America to provide the labour power for the plantations, and who later, as a free proletariat, were incorporated in the class of wage labourers in a capitalist system. Obtaining the necessary labour power from non-capitalist societies, the so-called 'labour problem,' is ever more important for capital in the colonies. All possible methods of 'gentle compulsion' are applied to solving this problem, to transfer labour from former social systems to the command of capital. . . .

Admittedly, Marx dealt in detail with the process of appropriating non-capitalist means of production as well as with the transformation of the peasants into a capitalist proletariat. Chapter xxiv of *Capital*, vol. i, is devoted to describing the origin of the English proletariat, of the capitalistic agricultural tenant class and of industrial capital, with particular emphasis on the looting of colonial countries by European capital. Yet we must bear in mind that all this is treated solely with a view to so-called primitive accumulation. For Marx, these processes are incidental, illustrating merely the genesis of capital, its first appearance in the world; they are, as it were, travails by which the capitalist mode of production emerges from a feudal society. As soon as he comes to analyse the capitalist process of production and circulation, he reaffirms the universal and exclusive domination of capitalist production.

Yet, as we have seen, capitalism in its full maturity also depends in all respects on non-capitalist strata and social organisations existing side by side with it. . . . Capital needs the means of production and the labour power of the whole globe for untrammelled accumulation; it cannot manage without the natural resources and the labour power of all territories. Seeing that the overwhelming majority of resources and labour power

is in fact still in the orbit of pre-capitalist production—this being the historical *milieu* of accumulation—capital must go all out to obtain ascendancy over these territories and social organisations. There is no *a priori* reason why rubber plantations, say, run on capitalist lines, such as have been laid out in India, might not serve the ends of capitalist production just as well. Yet if the countries of those branches of production are predominantly non-capitalist, capital will endeavour to establish domination over these countries and societies. And in fact, primitive conditions allow of a greater drive and of far more ruthless measures than could be tolerated under purely capitalist social conditions. . . .

Whatever the theoretical aspects, the accumulation of capital, as an historical process, depends in every respect upon non-capitalist social strata and forms of social organisation.

Chapter XXVII. The Struggle against Natural Economy

Capitalism arises and develops historically amidst a non-capitalist society. In Western Europe it is found at first in a feudal environment from which it in fact sprang—the system of bondage in rural areas and the guild system in the towns—and later, after having swallowed up the feudal system, it exists mainly in an environment of peasants and artisans, that is to say in a system of simple commodity production both in agriculture and trade. European capitalism is further surrounded by vast territories of non-European civilisation ranging over all levels of development, from the primitive communist hordes of nomad herdsmen, hunters and gatherers to commodity production by peasants and artisans. This is the setting for the accumulation of capital.

We must distinguish three phases: the struggle of capital against natural economy, the struggle against commodity economy, and the competitive struggle of capital on the international stage for the remaining conditions of accumulation.

The existence and development of capitalism requires an environment of non-capitalist forms of production, but not every one of these forms will serve its ends. Capitalism needs non-capitalist social strata as a market for its surplus value, as a source of supply for its means of production and as a reservoir of labour power for its wage system. For all these purposes, forms of production based upon a natural economy are of no use to capital. In all social organisations where natural economy prevails, where there are primitive peasant communities with common ownership of the land, a feudal system of bondage or anything of this nature, economic organisation is essentially in response to the internal demand; and therefore there is no demand, or very little, for foreign goods, and also, as a rule, no surplus production, or at least no urgent need to dispose of surplus products. What is most important, however, is that, in any natural economy, production only goes on because both means of production and labour power are bound in one form or another. The communist peasant community no less than the feudal *corvée* farm and similar institutions maintain their economic organisation by subjecting the labour power, and the most important means of production, the land, to the rule of law and custom. A natural economy thus confronts the requirements of capitalism at every turn with rigid barriers. Capitalism must therefore always and everywhere fight a battle of annihilation against every historical form of natural economy that it encounters, whether this is slave economy, feudalism, primitive communism, or patriarchal peasant economy. The principal methods in this struggle are political force (revolution, war), oppressive taxation by the state, and cheap goods; they are partly applied simultaneously, and partly they succeed and complement one another. In Europe, force assumed revolutionary forms in the fight against feudalism (this is the ultimate explanation of the bourgeois revolutions in the seventeenth, eighteenth and nineteenth centuries); in the non-European countries, where it fights more primitive social organisations, it assumes the forms of colonial policy. These methods, together with the systems of taxation applied in such cases, and commercial relations also, particularly with primitive communities, form an alliance in which political power and economic factors go hand in hand.

In detail, capital in its struggle against societies with a natural economy pursues the following ends:

1. To gain immediate possession of important sources of productive forces such as land, game in primeval forests, minerals, precious stones and ores, products of exotic flora such as rubber, etc.

2. To 'liberate' labour power and to coerce it into service.

3. To introduce a commodity economy.

4. To separate trade and agriculture.

At the time of primitive accumulation, i.e., at the end of the Middle Ages, when the history of capitalism in Europe began, and right into the nineteenth century, dispossessing the peasants in England and on the Continent was the most striking weapon in the large-scale transformation of means of production and labour power into capital. Yet capital in power performs the same task even to-day, and on an even more important scale—by modern colonial policy. It is an illusion to hope that capitalism will ever be content with the means of production which it can acquire by

way of commodity exchange. In this respect already, capital is faced with difficulties because vast tracts of the globe's surface are in the possession of social organisations that have no desire for commodity exchange or cannot, because of the entire social structure and the forms of ownership, offer for sale the productive forces in which capital is primarily interested. The most important of these productive forces is of course the land, its hidden mineral treasure, and its meadows, woods and water, and further the flocks of the primitive shepherd tribes. If capital were here to rely on the process of slow internal disintegration, it might take centuries. To wait patiently until the most important means of production could be alienated by trading in consequence of this process were tantamount to renouncing the productive forces of those territories altogether. Hence derives the vital necessity for capitalism in its relations with colonial countries to appropriate the most important means of production. Since the primitive associations of the natives are the strongest protection for their social organisations and for their material bases of existence, capital must begin by planning for the systematic destruction and annihilation of all the non-capitalist social units which obstruct its development. With that we have passed beyond the stage of primitive accumulation; this process is still going on. Each new colonial expansion is accompanied, as a matter of course, by a relentless battle of capital against the social and economic ties of the natives, who are also forcibly robbed of their means of production and labour power. Any hope to restrict the accumulation of capital exclusively to 'peaceful competition,' i.e. to regular commodity exchange such as takes place between capitalist producer-countries, rests on the pious belief that capital can accumulate without mediation of the productive forces and without the demand of more primitive organisations, and that it can rely upon the slow internal process of a disintegrating natural economy. Accumulation, with its spasmodic expansion, can no more wait for, and be content with, a natural internal disintegration of non-capitalist formations and their transition to commodity economy, than it can wait for, and be content with, the natural increase of the working population. Force is the only solution open to capital; the accumulation of capital, seen as an historical process, employs force as a permanent weapon, not only at its genesis, but further on down to the present day. From the point of view of the primitive societies involved, it is a matter of life or death; for them there can be no other attitude than opposition and fight to the finish—complete exhaustion and extinction. Hence permanent occupation of the colonies by the military, native risings and punitive expeditions are the order of the day for any colonial regime. The method of violence, then, is the immediate consequence of the clash between capitalism and the organisations of a natural economy which would restrict accumulation. Their means of production and their labour power no less than their demand for surplus products is necessary to capitalism. Yet the latter is fully determined to undermine their independence as social units, in order to gain possession of their means of production and labour power and to convert them into commodity buyers. This method is the most profitable and gets the quickest results, and so it is also the most expedient for capital. In fact, it is invariably accompanied by a growing militarism whose importance for accumulation will be demonstrated below in another connection. British policy in India and French policy in Algeria are the classical examples of the application of these methods by capitalism. . . .

Chapter XXXII. Militarism as a Province of Accumulation

Militarism fulfils a quite definite function in the history of capital, accompanying as it does every historical phase of accumulation. It plays a decisive part in the first stages of European capitalism, in the period of the so-called 'primitive accumulation,' as a means of conquering the New World and the spice-producing countries of India. Later, it is employed to subject the modern colonies, to destroy the social organisations of primitive societies so that their means of production may be appropriated, forcibly to introduce commodity trade in countries where the social structure had been unfavourable to it, and to turn the natives into a proletariat by compelling them to work for wages in the colonies. It is responsible for the creation and expansion of spheres of interest for European capital in non-European regions, for extorting railway concessions in backward countries, and for enforcing the claims of European capital as international leader. Finally, militarism is a weapon in the competitive struggle between capitalist countries for areas of non-capitalist civilisation.

In addition, militarism has yet another important function. From the purely economic point of view, it is a pre-eminent means for the realisation of surplus value; it is in itself a province of accumulation. In examining the question who should count as a buyer for the mass of products containing the capitalised surplus value, we have again and again refused to consider the state and its organs as consumers. Since their income is derivative, they were all taken to belong to the special category of those who live on the surplus value (or partly on the wage of labour), together with the liberal professions and the various parasites of present-day society ('king, professor, prostitute, mercenary'). But this interpretation will only do on two assumptions: first, if we take it, in accordance with Marx's diagram, that the state has no other sources of taxation than capitalist surplus value and wages, and secondly, if we regard the state and its organs as consumers pure and simple. If the issue turns on the personal consumption of the state organs (as also of the 'mercenary') the point is that consumption is partly transferred from the working class to the hangers-on of the capitalist class, in so far as the workers foot the bill. . . .

With indirect taxation and high protective tariffs, the bill of militarism is footed mainly by the working class and the peasants. The two kinds of taxation must be considered separately. From an economic point of view, it amounts to the following, as far as the working class is concerned: provided that wages are not raised to make up for the higher price of foodstuffs—which is at present the fate of the greatest part of the working class, including even the minority that is organised in trade unions, owing to the pressure of cartels and employers' organisations—indirect taxation means that part of the purchasing power of the working class is transferred to the state. Now as before the variable capital, as a fixed amount of money, will put in motion an appropriate quantity of living labour, that is to say it serves to employ the appropriate quantity of constant capital in production and to produce the corresponding amount of surplus value. As soon as capital has completed this cycle, it is divided between the working class and the state: the workers surrender the state part of the money they received as wages. Capital has wholly appropriated the former variable capital in its material form, as labour power, but the working class retains only a part of the variable capital in the form of money, the state claiming the rest. . . .

What would normally have been hoarded by the peasants and the lower middle classes until it has grown big enough to invest in savings banks and other banks is now set free to constitute an effective demand and an opportunity for investment. Further the multitude of individual and insignificant demands for a whole range of commodities, which will become effective at different times and which might often be met just as well by simple commodity production, is now replaced by a comprehensive and homogeneous demand of the state. And the satisfaction of this demand presupposes a big industry of the highest order. It requires the most favourable conditions for the production of surplus value and for accumulation. In the form of government contracts for army supplies the scattered purchasing power of the consumers is concentrated in large quantities and, free of the vagaries and subjective fluctuations of personal consumption, it achieves an almost automatic regularity and rhythmic growth. Capital itself ultimately controls this automatic and rhythmic movement of militarist production through the legislature and a press whose function is to mould so-called 'public opinion.' That is why this particular province of capitalist accumulation at first seems capable of infinite expansion. All other attempts to expand markets and set up operational bases for capital largely depend on historical, social and political factors beyond the control of capital, whereas production for militarism represents a province whose regular and progressive expansion seems primarily determined by capital itself.

In this way capital turns historical necessity into a virtue: the ever fiercer competition in the capitalist world itself provides a field for accumulation of the first magnitude. Capital increasingly employs militarism for implementing a foreign and colonial policy to get hold of the means of production and labour power of non-capitalist countries and societies. This same militarism works in a like manner in the capitalist countries to divert purchasing power away from the non-capitalist strata. The representatives of simple commodity production and the working class are affected alike in this way. At their expense, the accumulation of capital is raised to the highest power, by robbing the one of their productive forces and by depressing the other's standard of living. Needless to say, after a certain stage the conditions for the accumulation of capital both at home and abroad turn into their very opposite—they become conditions for the decline of capitalism.

The more ruthlessly capital sets about the destruction of non-capitalist strata at home and in the outside world, the more it lowers the standard of living for the workers as a whole, the greater also is the change in the day-to-day history of capital. It becomes a string of political and social disasters and convulsions, and under these conditions, punctuated by periodical economic catastrophes or crises, accumulation can go on no longer.

But even before this natural economic impasse of capital's own creating is properly reached it becomes a necessity for the international working class to revolt against the rule of capital.

Capitalism is the first mode of economy with the weapon of propaganda, a mode which tends to engulf the entire globe and to stamp out all other economies, tolerating no rival at its side. Yet at the same time it is also the first mode of economy which is unable to exist by itself, which needs other economic systems as a medium and soil. Although it strives to become universal, and, indeed, on account of this its tendency, it must break down—because it is immanently incapable

of becoming a universal form of production. In its living history it is a contradiction in itself, and its movement of accumulation provides a solution to the conflict and aggravates it at the same time. At a certain stage of development there will be no other way out than the application of socialist principles. The aim of socialism is not accumulation but the satisfaction of toiling humanity's wants by developing the productive forces of the entire globe. And so we find that socialism is by its very nature an harmonious and universal system of economy.

Theses on the Tasks of International Social Democracy (1915)

A large number of comrades from different parts of Germany have adopted the following theses, which constitute an application of the Erfurt program to the contemporary problems of international socialism.

1. The world war has annihilated the work of forty years of European socialism: by destroying the revolutionary proletariat as a political force; by destroying the moral prestige of socialism; by scattering the workers' International; by setting its sections one against the other in fratricidal massacre; and by tying the aspirations and hopes of the masses of the people of the main countries in which capitalism has developed to the destinies of imperialism.

2. By their vote for war credits and by their proclamation of national unity, the official leaderships of the socialist parties in Germany, France and England (with the exception of the Independent Labor Party) have reinforced imperialism, induced the masses of the people to suffer patiently the misery and horrors of the war, contributed to the unleashing, without restraint, of imperialist frenzy, to the prolongation of the massacre and the increase in the number of its victims, and assumed their share in the responsibility for the war itself and for its consequences.

3. This tactic of the official leaderships of the parties in the belligerent countries, and in the first place in Germany, until recently at the head of the International, constitutes a betrayal of the elementary principles of international socialism, of the vital interests of the working class, and of all the democratic interests of the peoples. By this alone socialist policy is condemned to impotence even in those countries where

the leaders have remained faithful to their principles: Russia, Serbia, Italy and—with hardly an exception—Bulgaria.

4. By this alone official social democracy in the principal countries has repudiated the class struggle in wartime and adjourned it until after the war; it has guaranteed to the ruling classes of all countries a delay in which to strengthen, at the proletariat's expense, and in a monstrous fashion, their economic, political and moral positions.

5. The world war serves neither the national defense nor the economic or political interests of the masses of the people whatever they may be. It is but the product of the imperialist rivalries between the capitalist classes of the different countries for world hegemony and for the monopoly in the exploitation and oppression of areas still not under the heel of capital. In the era of the unleashing of this imperialism, national wars are no longer possible. National interests serve only as the pretext for putting the laboring masses of the people under the domination of their mortal enemy, imperialism.

6. The policy of the imperialist states and the imperialist war cannot give to a single oppressed nation its liberty and its independence. The small nations, the ruling classes of which are the accomplices of their partners in the big states, constitute only the pawns on the imperialist chessboard of the great powers, and are used by them, just like their own working masses, in wartime, as instruments, to be sacrificed to capitalist interests after the war.

7. The present world war signifies, under these conditions, either in the case of "defeat" or "victory," a defeat for socialism and democracy. It increases, whatever the outcome—excepting the revolutionary intervention of the international proletariat—and strengthens militarism, national antagonisms, and economic rivalries in the world market. It accentuates capitalist exploitation and reaction in the domain of internal policy, renders the influence of public opinion precarious and derisory, and reduces parliaments to tools more and more obedient to imperialism. The present world war carries within itself the seeds of new conflicts.

8. World peace cannot be assured by projects utopian or, at bottom, reactionary, such as tribunals of arbitration by capitalist diplomats, diplomatic, "disarmament" conventions, "the freedom of the seas," abolition of the right of maritime arrest, "the United States of Europe," a "customs union for central Europe," buffer states, and other illusions. Imperialism, militarism and war can never be abolished nor attenuated so long as the capitalist class exercises, uncontested, its class hegemony. The sole means of successful resistance, and the only guarantee of the peace of the world, is the capacity for action and the revolutionary will of the international proletariat to hurl its full weight into the balance.

9. Imperialism, as the last phase in the life, and the highest point in the expansion of the world hegemony of capital, is the mortal enemy of the proletariat of all countries. . . . In peace time as in war, the struggle of the proletariat as a class has to be concentrated first of all against imperialism. For the international proletariat, the struggle against imperialism is at the same time the struggle for power, the decisive settling of accounts between socialism and capitalism. The final goal of socialism will be realized by the international proletariat only if it opposes imperialism all along the line, and if it makes the issue "war against war" the guiding line of its practical policy; and on condition that it deploys all its forces and shows itself ready, by its courage to the point of extreme sacrifice, to do this.

10. In this framework, socialism's principal mission today is to regroup the proletariat of all countries into a living revolutionary force; to make it, through a powerful international organization which has only one conception of its tasks and interests, and only one universal tactic appropriate to political action in peace and war alike, the decisive factor in political life: so that it may fulfill its historic mission.

11. The war has smashed the Second International. Its inadequacy has been demonstrated by its incapacity to place an effective obstacle in the way of the segmentation of its forces behind national boundaries in time of war, and to carry through a common tactic and action by the proletariat in all countries.

12. In view of the betrayal, by the official representatives of the socialist parties in the principal countries, of the aims and interests of the working class; in view of their passage from the camp of the working-class International to the political camp of the imperialist bourgeoisie; it is vitally necessary for socialism to build a new workers' International, which will take into its own hands the leadership and coordination of the revolutionary class struggle against world imperialism. . . .

Virginia Woolf (1882–1941)

Virginia Woolf was one of the foremost feminist political theorists of the twentieth century. She was born into a modestly well-to-do literary family in London, England, on January 25, 1882. Her father, Leslie Stephen, was a figure of some renown in his time, editor of the monumental Dictionary of National Biography *and an influential literary critic and historian. Her mother, Julia Jackson, was a stern but generous and beautiful woman, in many ways the very ideal of Victorian womanhood—best described by Virginia Woolf in* To the Lighthouse, *in the image of Mrs. Ramsay.*

Virginia Stephen was raised in a highly intellectual environment, in touch with many of the best-known writers of late-nineteenth-century England, and she read and wrote extensively even in her childhood. But as her nephew and biographer, Quentin Bell, put it: "It was taken for granted that the boys would go to public schools and then to Cambridge University. As for the girls, they would, in a decorous way, become accomplished and then marry" (Bell, vol. 1, 21). By the phrase "become accomplished" was meant, at the time, to acquire a proper kind and amount of learning from their mother or father and from governesses, and develop harmless and appropriate talents such as writing letters, playing the piano, and painting. Virginia's elder sister, Vanessa, in fact became a successful painter. The contrast between the formal education accorded to her brothers and the informal education accorded to her and her sister was apparent to Virginia from an early date.

Julia Jackson Stephen died when Virginia was about thirteen years old. The Stephen household was taken over first by Stella Duckworth, Julia's daughter by a previous marriage, and later by Vanessa, until her marriage to Clive Bell. For most of Virginia's early life she had literally no "room of her own," the Stephen household being relatively crowded with members of the family and servants. Virginia had memories of being sexually molested by her elder step-brothers. After the death of Julia, the household was made miserable by Leslie Stephen's repeated outbursts of self-pity and rage, which he took out on his step-daughter Stella and then on his daughter Vanessa, who were expected not only to run his household, entertain his guests, and manage his accounts, but also to minister to his irascible temper, all in patient and submissive silence. This is the portrait painted of Mr. Ramsay in To the Lighthouse *(1927), epitomizing the emotional relationship between the sexes as Virginia Woolf perceived it first in the relations between her mother and father: Mr. Ramsay is por-*

*trayed as "selfish, vain, egotistical; he is spoilt; he is a tyrant; he wears Mrs. Ramsay to death." His boundless need is a consuming and stifling force in women's lives, their strength "flaring up to be drunk and quenched by the beak of brass, the arid scimitar of the male, which smote mercilessly, again and again, demanding sympathy" (*To the Lighthouse, *40, 59).*

After her father's death in 1904, Virginia Stephen moved with her sister and brothers into a rather unconventional ménage in Bloomsbury. Their home became the center of the Bloomsbury literary circle, which included Lytton Strachey, Clive Bell, Leonard Woolf, John Maynard Keynes, E. M. Forster, and Roger Fry (of whom Virginia later wrote a biography). When her brother Thoby died unmarried in 1906, she inherited one third of his estate, and she inherited some additional small sums from female relatives; the total appears to have given her an income of her own of about £400 per year. In 1929 she wrote in A Room of One's Own *that "£500 a year will keep one alive in the sunshine." To make up the difference, she began writing for the* Times Literary Supplement *and other reviews. Virginia married Leonard Woolf in 1912. Leonard was a Jew, a liberal socialist, an outsider who had made it into her circle by being educated with her brothers at Cambridge. Leonard began a career in the British colonial service as an administrator in Ceylon but gave it up in order to marry Virginia, who would not have any part of the British Empire. Thereafter, Leonard held various lower government or political posts.*

Both Leonard and Virginia earned money by writing books. In 1917 they also founded a publishing house of their own, the Hogarth Press, which was in part a form of recreation (they were intrigued by hand-printing) and therapy for Virginia—but became an outlet for avant-garde works, including the first English-language edition of Freud's complete works. Between them they had enough income to live fairly comfortably, to have a servant or two, and eventually to buy a car and their printing press, but never to live lavishly. They usually had to scrimp on clothes and sometimes even on food. Representations of the relationship between them vary widely, from idyllic images of love and devotion to skeptical assessments noting Leonard's affairs with other women, Virginia's relationship with Vita Sackville-West, and other strains in their marriage.

The Woolfs never had children. Virginia was in fact forbidden to have children by Leonard, on the advice of a psychiatrist who thought the strain would be too much for her delicate mental balance. Virginia had had a nervous breakdown after the death of her mother and had several during her married years. She was confined by Leonard to a severe regimen of bed-rest at a private clinic after the first of her breakdowns during their marriage. Later the treatment was again bed-rest, though at home. What Virginia thought about this may be deduced from her portrayal of the psychiatrist Sir William Bradshaw in Mrs. Dalloway (1925): "Worshipping proportion, Sir William not only prospered himself but made England prosper, secluded her lunatics, forbade childbirth, penalised despair, made it impossible for the unfit to propagate their views" (p. 150).

There were undoubtedly deep positive bonds between Virginia Woolf and the men of her family, as well as a number of close male friends. When she committed suicide in 1941, she left Leonard a note in which she wrote: "I owe all the happiness of my life to you. You have been entirely patient and incredibly good. . . . I don't think two people could have been happier than we have been." Her suicide, she wrote, was to spare Leonard Woolf the agony of another bout with her madness. One must respect her dying words, but perhaps it is no disrespect to doubt they tell the whole story. In fact, despite her real affection and even gratitude toward her father, her brothers, and Leonard, Woolf was at the same time intensely angry with them for their treatment of women in general, and herself in particular, in many points central to her intellectual and emotional life.

For the most part, she deliberately concealed her anger, which has invited highly conflicting interpretations of her novels. Yet we know, from her letters and her prose works, that concealment of anger against men was a deliberate policy. She wrote in A Room of One's Own in 1929: "Lies will flow from my lips, but there may perhaps be some truth mixed up with them; it is for you to seek out the truth and to decide whether any part of it is worth keeping" (p. 4). For herself, she nearly abandoned concealment in Three Guineas in 1938 yet declared it as a political policy for women: "Secrecy is essential. We [women] must still hide what we are doing and thinking. . . . When salaries are low, . . . and jobs are hard to get and keep, . . . it is, 'to say the least, rather tactless,' as the newspaper puts it, to criticize your master" (p. 120).

Woolf early developed a strong interest in women. She read widely in history, including biographies and other historical works on women, and in fact one of her earliest sustained writings was A History of Women, the manuscript of which appears to be lost. She was not very active in feminist organizations but as a young woman did volunteer office work in the suffrage movement. Over the years, she wrote many reviews and essays on women's work. She taught history for a time to working women at Morley College, and she gave occasional lectures on

women. Her most active engagement in later years was with the Women's Cooperative Guild, and she wrote the introduction to Life as We Have Known It, a collection of memoirs of the lives of working women, published by the Hogarth Press in 1931. It may be argued that the main focus of her nine published novels from The Voyage Out in 1915 to Between the Acts in 1941 was on the lives, experiences, roles, and relationships of women. At the same time, her analysis of the lives of women brought her to a broad-ranging critique of patriarchal society as a whole.

Woolf's work, whether in the form of fiction or prose, was intensely political at the core. This fact has been obscured partly by her own deliberate efforts to conceal her political message from her own male intimates and the male intellectual oligopoly at large, and partly by the predilections of that oligopoly in its control of later literary criticism and political theory. There is thus an enormous literature today on strictly literary and aesthetic aspects of Woolf's work. However, the political character of much of her work has come to be recognized by a growing number of critics, especially in the field of feminist criticism, though they are not all in agreement as to the substance and implications of her ideas. More recently, too, there has been increased attention to Woolf's broader analysis of society and in particular her ideas on gender, war, and empire. Three Guineas embodied the most explicit statement of her theoretical analysis, but her novels gave vivid, passionate expression to her conviction "that the public and the private worlds are inseparably connected; that the tyrannies and servilities of the one are the tyrannies and servilities of the other."

The following selection is from the 1966 edition of Three Guineas.

BAC

Sources and Suggested Readings

Bell, Quentin. Virginia Woolf: A Biography. New edition. 2 vols. London: Hogarth, 1990.

Carroll, Berenice A. "'To Crush Him in Our Own Country': The Political Thought of Virginia Woolf." Feminist Studies 4, 1 (February 1978): 99–131.

Davies, Margaret L., ed. Life as We Have Known It, by Cooperative Working Women. New York: Norton, 1975 [1931].

DeSalvo, Louise A. Virginia Woolf: The Impact of Childhood Sexual Abuse on Her Life and Work. Boston: Beacon Press, 1989.

Dusinberre, Juliet. "Virginia Woolf and Montaigne." Textual Practice 5, 2 (Summer 1991): 219–41.

Hussey, Mark, ed. Virginia Woolf and War: Fiction, Reality, and Myth. Syracuse, N.Y.: Syracuse University Press, 1991.

Jones, Ellen Carol, ed. Special issue on Virginia Woolf, *Modern Fiction Studies* 38, 1 (Spring 1992).

Kirkpatrick, B. J. *A Bibliography of Virginia Woolf*. New York: Oxford University Press, 1980. 3rd ed.

Marcus, Jane. *Art and Anger: Reading Like a Woman*. Columbus: Ohio State University Press, 1988.

———. *Virginia Woolf and the Languages of Patriarchy*. Bloomington: Indiana University Press, 1987.

Marcus, Jane, ed. *New Feminist Essays on Virginia Woolf*. Lincoln: University of Nebraska Press, 1981.

———. *Virginia Woolf: A Feminist Slant*. Lincoln: University of Nebraska Press, 1983.

Marder, Herbert. *Feminism and Art: A Study of Virginia Woolf*. Chicago: University of Chicago Press, 1968.

Phillips, Kathy J. *Virginia Woolf against Empire*. Knoxville: University of Tennessee Press, 1994.

Raitt, Susanne. *Vita and Virginia: The Work and Friendship of V. Sackville-West and Virginia Woolf*. New York: Oxford University Press, 1993.

Sandbach-Dahlstrom, Catherine. "Virginia Woolf's *Three Guineas*: A Theory of Liberation for the Modern World?" *Women's Studies International Forum* 17, 2/3 (1994): 229–34.

Silver, Brenda R. "The Authority of Anger: *Three Guineas* as a Case Study." *Signs* 16, 2 (1991): 340–70.

Woolf, Virginia. *Moments of Being*. Ed. Jeanne Schulkind. 2nd ed. New York: Harcourt, 1985.

———. *Mrs. Dalloway*. New York: Harcourt, Brace and World, 1953 [1925].

———. *A Room of One's Own*. New York: Harcourt, Brace and World, 1957 [1929].

———. *Three Guineas*. New York: Harcourt, Brace and World, 1966 [1938].

———. *To the Lighthouse*. New York: Harcourt, Brace and World, 1955 [1927].

Zwerdling, Alex. *Virginia Woolf and the Real World*. Berkeley: University of California Press, 1986.

Three Guineas (1938)

1

Three years is a long time to leave a letter unanswered, and your letter has been lying without an answer even longer than that. I had hoped that it would answer itself, or that other people would answer it for me. But there it is with its question—How in your opinion are we to prevent war?—still unanswered.

It is true that many answers have suggested themselves, but none that would not need explanation, and explanations take time. In this case, too, there are reasons why it is particularly difficult to avoid misunderstanding. A whole page could be filled with excuses

and apologies; declarations of unfitness, incompetence, lack of knowledge, and experience: and they would be true. But even when they were said there would still remain some difficulties so fundamental that it may well prove impossible for you to understand or for us to explain. But one does not like to leave so remarkable a letter as yours—a letter perhaps unique in the history of human correspondence, since when before has an educated man asked a woman how in her opinion war can be prevented?—unanswered. Therefore let us make the attempt; even if it is doomed to failure. . . .

It is now that the first difficulty of communication between us appears. Let us rapidly indicate the reason. We both come of what, in this hybrid age when, though birth is mixed, classes still remain fixed, it is convenient to call the educated class. When we meet in the flesh we speak with the same accent; use knives and forks in the same way; expect maids to cook dinner and wash up after dinner; and can talk during dinner without much difficulty about politics and people; war and peace; barbarism and civilization—all the questions indeed suggested by your letter. Moreover, we both earn our livings. But . . . those three dots mark a precipice, a gulf so deeply cut between us that for three years and more I have been sitting on my side of it wondering whether it is any use to try to speak across it. Let us then ask someone else—it is Mary Kingsley—to speak for us. "I don't know if I ever revealed to you the fact that being allowed to learn German was *all* the paid-for education I ever had. Two thousand pounds was spent on my brother's, I still hope not in vain" (Stephen Gwynne, *The Life of Mary Kingsley*, p. 15). Mary Kingsley is not speaking for herself alone; she is speaking, still, for many of the daughters of educated men. And she is not merely speaking for them; she is also pointing to a very important fact about them, a fact that must profoundly influence all that follows: the fact of Arthur's Education Fund. You, who have read *Pendennis*, will remember how the mysterious letters A.E.F. figured in the household ledgers. Ever since the thirteenth century English families have been paying money into that account. From the Pastons to the Pendennises, all educated families from the thirteenth century to the present moment have paid money into that account. It is a voracious receptacle. Where there were many sons to educate it required a great effort on the part of the family to keep it full. For your education was not merely in book-learning; games educated your body; friends taught you more than books or games. Talk with them broadened your outlook and enriched your mind. In the holidays you travelled; acquired a taste for art; a knowledge of foreign politics; and then, before you could earn your own living, your father made you an allowance upon which it was possible for you to live while you learnt the profession which now entitles you to add the letters K.C. to your name. All this came out of Arthur's Education Fund. And to this your sisters, as Mary Kingsley indicates, made their contribution. Not only did their own education, save for such small sums as paid the German teacher, go into it; but many of those luxuries and trimmings which are, after all, an essential part of education—travel, society, solitude, a lodging apart from the family house—they were paid into it too. It was a voracious receptacle, a solid fact—Arthur's Education Fund—a fact so solid indeed that it cast a shadow over the entire landscape. And the result is that though we look at the same things, we see them differently. What is that congregation of buildings there, with a semi-monastic look, with chapels and halls and green playing-fields? To you it is your old school, Eton or Harrow; your old university, Oxford or Cambridge; the source of memories and of traditions innumerable. But to us, who see it through the shadow of Arthur's Education Fund, it is a schoolroom table; an omnibus going to a class; a little woman with a red nose who is not well educated herself but has an invalid mother to support; an allowance of £50 a year with which to buy clothes, give presents and take journeys on coming to maturity. Such is the effect that Arthur's Education Fund has had upon us. So magically does it change the landscape that the noble courts and quadrangles of Oxford and Cambridge often appear to educated men's daughters like petticoats with holes in them, cold legs of mutton, and the boat train starting for abroad while the guard slams the door in their faces. (Our ideology is still so inveterately anthropocentric that it has been necessary to coin this clumsy term—educated man's daughter—to describe the class whose fathers have been educated at public schools and universities. Obviously, if the term "bourgeois" fits her brother, it is grossly incorrect to use it of one who differs so profoundly in the two prime characteristics of the bourgeoisie—capital and environment.)

The fact that Arthur's Education Fund changes the landscape—the halls, the playing grounds, the sacred edifices—is an important one; but that aspect must be left for future discussion. Here we are only concerned with the obvious fact, when it comes to considering this important question—how we are to help you prevent war—that education makes a difference. Some knowledge of politics, of international relations, of economics, is obviously necessary in order to understand the causes which lead to war. Philosophy, theology even, might come in usefully. Now you the uneducated, you with an untrained mind, could not possibly deal with such questions satisfactorily. War, as the result of impersonal forces, is you will agree beyond the grasp of the untrained mind. But war

as the result of human nature is another thing. Had you not believed that human nature, the reasons, the emotions of the ordinary man and woman, lead to war, you would not have written asking for our help. You must have argued, men and women, here and now, are able to exert their wills; they are not pawns and puppets dancing on a string held by invisible hands. They can act, and think for themselves. Perhaps even they can influence other people's thoughts and actions. Some such reasoning must have led you to apply to us; and with justification. For happily there is one branch of education which comes under the heading "unpaid-for education"—that understanding of human beings and their motives which, if the word is rid of its scientific associations, might be called psychology. Marriage, the one great profession open to our class since the dawn of time until the year 1919; marriage, the art of choosing the human being with whom to live life successfully, should have taught us some skill in that. But here again another difficulty confronts us. For though many instincts are held more or less in common by both sexes, to fight has always been the man's habit, not the woman's. Law and practice have developed that difference, whether innate or accidental. Scarcely a human being in the course of history has fallen to a woman's rifle; the vast majority of birds and beasts have been killed by you, not by us; it is difficult to judge what we do not share.

How then are we to understand your problem, and if we cannot, how can we answer your question, how to prevent war? The answer based upon our experience and our psychology—Why fight?—is not an answer of any value. Obviously there is for you some glory, some necessity, some satisfaction in fighting which we have never felt or enjoyed. . . .

. . . [H]owever many dissentients there are, the great majority of your sex are today in favour of war. The Scarborough Conference of educated men, the Bournemouth Conference of working men are both agreed that to spend £300,000,000 annually upon arms is a necessity. They are of opinion that Wilfred Owen was wrong; that it is better to kill than to be killed. Yet since biography shows that differences of opinion are many, it is plain that there must be one reason which prevails in order to bring about this overpowering unanimity. Shall we call it, for the sake of brevity, "patriotism"? . . .

. . . But the educated man's sister—what does "patriotism" mean to her? Has she the same reasons for being proud of England, for loving England, for defending England? Has she been "greatly blessed" in England? History and biography when questioned would seem to show that her position in the home of freedom has been different from her brother's; and psychology would seem to hint that history is not without its effect upon mind and body. Therefore her interpretation of the word "patriotism" may well differ from his. And that difference may make it extremely difficult for her to understand his definition of patriotism and the duties it imposes. If then our answer to your question, "How in your opinion are we to prevent war?" depends upon understanding the reasons, the emotions, the loyalties which lead men to go to war, this letter had better be torn across and thrown into the waste-paper basket. For it seems plain that we cannot understand each other because of these differences. . . . Let us then refer the question of the rightness or wrongness of war to those who make morality their profession—the clergy. Surely if we ask the clergy the simple question: "Is war right or is war wrong?" they will give us a plain answer which we cannot deny. But no—the Church of England, which might be supposed able to abstract the question from its worldly confusions, is of two minds also. The bishops themselves are at loggerheads. The Bishop of London maintained that "the real danger to the peace of the world today were the pacifists. Bad as war was dishonour was far worse" (*The Daily Telegraph*, February 5th, 1937). On the other hand, the Bishop of Birmingham described himself as an "extreme pacifist. . . . I cannot see myself that war can be regarded as consonant with the spirit of Christ" (ibid.). So the Church itself gives us divided counsel—in some circumstances it is right to fight; in no circumstances is it right to fight. It is distressing, baffling, confusing, but the fact must be faced; there is no certainty in heaven above or on earth below. Indeed the more lives we read, the more speeches we listen to, the more opinions we consult, the greater the confusion becomes and the less possible it seems, since we cannot understand the impulses, the motives, or the morality which lead you to go to war, to make any suggestion that will help you to prevent war.

But besides these pictures of other people's lives and minds—these biographies and histories—there are also other pictures—pictures of actual facts; photographs. Photographs, of course, are not arguments addressed to the reason; they are simply statements of fact addressed to the eye. But in that very simplicity there may be some help. Let us see then whether when we look at the same photographs we feel the same things. Here then on the table before us are photographs. The Spanish Government sends them with patient pertinacity about twice a week. (Written in the winter of 1936–37.) They are not pleasant photographs to look upon. They are photographs of dead bodies for the most part. This morning's collection contains the photograph of what might be a man's body, or a woman's; it is so mutilated that it might, on the other hand, be the body of a pig. But those certainly are dead children, and that undoubtedly is the section of a house. A bomb has torn open the side; there is still a bird-cage hanging in what was presumably the sitting-room, but the rest of the house looks like nothing so much as a bunch of spilikins suspended in mid-air.

Those photographs are not an argument; they are simply a crude statement of fact addressed to the eye. But the eye is connected with the brain; the brain with the nervous system. That system sends its messages in a flash through every past memory and present feeling. When we look at those photographs some fusion takes place within us; however different the education, the traditions behind us, our sensations are the same; and they are violent. You, Sir, call them "horror and disgust." We also call them horror and disgust. And the same words rise to our lips. War, you say, is an abomination; a barbarity; war must be stopped at whatever cost. And we echo your words. War is an abomination; a barbarity; war must be stopped. For now at last we are looking at the same picture; we are seeing with you the same dead bodies, the same ruined houses.

Let us then give up, for the moment, the effort to answer your question, how we can help you to prevent war, by discussing the political, the patriotic or the psychological reasons which lead you to go to war. The emotion is too positive to suffer patient analysis. Let us concentrate upon the practical suggestions which you bring forward for our consideration. There are three of them. The first is to sign a letter to the newspapers; the second is to join a certain society; the third is to subscribe to its funds. Nothing on the face of it could sound simpler. To scribble a name on a sheet of paper is easy; to attend a meeting where pacific opinions are more or less rhetorically reiterated to people who already believe in them is also easy; and to write a cheque in support of those vaguely acceptable opinions, though not so easy, is a cheap way of quieting what may conveniently be called one's conscience. Yet there are reasons which make us hesitate; reasons into which we must enter, less superficially, later on. Here it is enough to say that though the three measures you suggest seem plausible, yet it also seems that, if we did what you ask, the emotion caused by the photographs would still remain unappeased. That emotion, that very positive emotion, demands something more positive than a name written on a sheet of paper; an hour spent listening to speeches; a cheque written for whatever sum we can afford—say one guinea. Some more energetic, some more active method of expressing our belief that war is barbarous, that war is inhuman, that war, as Wilfred Owen put it, is insupportable, horrible and beastly seems to be required. But, rhetoric apart, what active method is open to us? . . . all the weapons with which an educated man can enforce his opinions are either beyond our grasp or so nearly beyond it that even if we used them we could scarcely inflict one scratch. If the men in your profession were to unite in any demand and were to say: "If it is not granted we will stop work," the laws of England would cease to be administered. If the women in your profession said the same thing it would make no difference to the laws of England whatever. Not only are we incomparably weaker than the men of our own class; we are weaker than the women of the working class. If the working women of the country were to say: "If you go to war, we will refuse to make munitions or to help in the production of goods," the difficulty of war-making would be seriously increased. But if all the daughters of educated men were to down tools tomorrow, nothing essential either to the life or to the war-making of the community would be embarrassed. Our class is the weakest of all the classes in the state. We have no weapon with which to enforce our will.

The answer to that is so familiar that we can easily anticipate it. The daughters of educated men have no direct influence, it is true; but they possess the greatest power of all; that is, the influence that they can exert upon educated men. If this is true, if, that is, influence is still the strongest of our weapons and the only one that can be effective in helping you to prevent war, let us, before we sign your manifesto or join your society, consider what that influence amounts to. . . .

[T]here was of course one political cause which the daughters of educated men had much at heart during the past 150 years: the franchise. But when we consider how long it took them to win that cause, and what labour, we can only conclude that influence has to be combined with wealth in order to be effective as a political weapon, and that influence of the kind that can be exerted by the daughters of educated men is very low in power, very slow in action, and very painful in use. Certainly the one great political achievement of the educated man's daughter cost her over a century of the most exhausting and menial labour; kept her trudging in processions, working in offices, speaking at street corners; finally, because she used force, sent her to prison, and would very likely still keep her there, had it not been, paradoxically enough, that the help she gave her brothers when they used force at last gave her the right to call herself, if not a full daughter, still a step-daughter of England. . . .

But what light does our difference here throw upon the problem before us? What connection is there between the sartorial splendours of the educated man and the photograph of ruined houses and dead bodies? Obviously the connection between dress and war is not far to seek; your finest clothes are those that you wear as soldiers. Since the red and the gold, the brass and the feathers are discarded upon active service, it is plain that their expensive and not, one might suppose, hygienic splendour is invented partly in order to impress the beholder with the majesty of the military office, partly in order through their vanity to induce young men to become soldiers. Here, then, our influence and our difference might have some effect; we, who are forbidden to wear such clothes ourselves, can express the opinion that the wearer is not to us a pleasing or an impressive spectacle. He is on the contrary a ridiculous, a barbarous, a displeasing spectacle. But as the daughters of educated men we can use our influence more effectively in another direction, upon our own class—the class of educated men. For there, in courts and universities, we find the same love of dress. There, too, are velvet and silk, fur and ermine. We can say that for educated men to emphasize their superiority over other people, either in birth or intellect, by dressing differently, or by adding titles before, or letters after their names are acts that rouse competition and jealousy—emotions which, as we need scarcely draw upon biography to prove, nor ask psychology to show, have their share in encouraging a disposition towards war. If then we express the opinion that such distinctions make those who possess them ridiculous and learning contemptible, we should do something, indirectly, to discourage the feelings that lead to war. Happily we can now do more than express an opinion; we can refuse all such distinctions and all such uniforms for ourselves. This would be a slight but definite contribution to the problem before us—how to prevent war; and one that a different training and a different tradition put more easily within our reach than within yours . . .

Here, fortunately, the year, the sacred year 1919, comes to our help. Since that year put it into the power of educated men's daughters to earn their livings they have at last some real influence upon education. They have money. They have money to subscribe to causes. Honorary treasurers invoke their help. To prove it, here, opportunely, cheek by jowl with your letter, is a letter from one such treasurer asking for money with which to rebuild a women's college. And when honorary treasurers invoke help, it stands to reason that they can be bargained with. We have the right to say to her, "You shall only have our guinea with which to help you to rebuild your college if you will help this gentleman whose letter also lies before us to prevent war." We can say to her, "You must educate the young to hate war. You must teach them to feel the inhumanity, the beastliness, the insupportability of war." But what kind of education shall we bargain for? What sort of education will teach the young to hate war? . . .

History at once informs us that there are now, and have been since about 1870, colleges for the sisters of educated men both at Oxford and at Cambridge. But history also informs us of facts of such a nature about those colleges that all attempt to influence the young against war through the education they receive there must be abandoned. . . .

. . . For do they [the facts of history] not prove that education, the finest education in the world, does not teach people to hate force, but to use it? Do they not prove that education, far from teaching the educated generosity and magnanimity, makes them on the contrary so anxious to keep their possessions, that "grandeur and power" of which the poet speaks, in their own hands, that they will use not force but much subtler methods than force when they are asked to share them? And are not force and possessiveness very closely connected with war? Of what use then is a university education in influencing people to prevent war? But history goes on of course; year succeeds to year. The years change things; slightly but imperceptibly they change them. And history tells us that at last, after spending time and strength whose value is immeasurable in repeatedly soliciting the authorities with the humility expected of our sex and proper to suppliants the right to impress head mistresses by putting the letters B.A. after the name was granted. But that right, history tells us, was only a titular right. At Cambridge, in the year 1937, the women's colleges—you will scarcely believe it, Sir, but once more it is the voice of fact that is speaking, not of fiction—the women's colleges are not allowed to be members of the university; and the number of educated men's daughters who are allowed to receive a university education is still strictly limited; though both sexes contribute to the university funds. As for poverty, *The Times* newspaper supplies us with figures; any ironmonger will provide us with a foot-rule; if we measure the money available for scholarships at the men's colleges with the money available for their sisters at the women's colleges, we shall save ourselves the trouble of adding up; and come to the conclusion that the colleges for the sisters of educated men are, compared with their brothers' colleges, unbelievably and shamefully poor.

Proof of that last fact comes pat to hand in the honorary treasurer's letter, asking for money with which to rebuild her college. . . . What answer ought we to make her when she asks us to help her to rebuild her college? History, biography, and the daily paper between them make it difficult either to answer her letter or to dictate terms. . . . But we have sworn that we will do all we can to help you to prevent war by using our influence—our earned money influence. And education is the obvious way. Since she is poor, since she is

asking for money, and since the giver of money is entitled to dictate terms, let us risk it and draft a letter to her, laying down the terms upon which she shall have our money to help rebuild her college. Here, then is an attempt:

"Your letter, Madam, has been waiting some time without an answer. But certain doubts and questions have arisen. . . .

". . . Shall I send it or shan't I? If I send it, what shall I ask them to do with it? Shall I ask them to rebuild the college on the old lines? Or shall I ask them to rebuild it, but differently? Or shall I ask them to buy rags and petrol and Bryant & May's matches and burn the college to the ground?

"These are the questions, Madam, that have kept your letter so long unanswered. They are questions of great difficulty and perhaps they are useless questions. But can we leave them unasked in view of this gentleman's questions? He is asking us how we can help him to prevent war. He is asking us how we can help him to defend liberty; to defend culture. Also consider these photographs: they are pictures of dead bodies and ruined houses. Surely in view of these questions and pictures you must consider very carefully before you begin to rebuild your college what is the aim of education, what kind of society, what kind of human being it should seek to produce. At any rate, I will only send you a guinea with which to rebuild your college if you can satisfy me that you will use it to produce the kind of society, the kind of people that will help to prevent war.

"Let us then discuss as quickly as we can the sort of education that is needed. Now since history and biography—the only evidence available to an outsider—seem to prove that the old education of the old colleges breeds neither a particular respect for liberty nor a particular hatred of war it is clear that you must rebuild your college differently. It is young and poor; let it therefore take advantage of those qualities and be founded on poverty and youth. Obviously, then, it must be an experimental college, an adventurous college. Let it be built on lines of its own. It must be built not of carved stone and stained glass, but of some cheap, easily combustible material which does not hoard dust and perpetrate traditions. Do not have chapels. Do not have museums and libraries with chained books and first editions under glass cases. Let the pictures and the books be new and always changing. Let it be decorated afresh by each generation with their own hands cheaply. The work of the living is cheap; often they will give it for the sake of being allowed to do it. Next, what should be taught in the new college, the poor college? Not the arts of dominating other people; not the arts of ruling, of killing, of acquiring land and capital. They require too many overhead expenses; salaries and uniforms and ceremonies. The poor college must teach only the arts that can be taught cheaply and practised by poor people; such as medicine, mathematics, music, painting and literature. It should teach the arts of human intercourse; the art of understanding other people's lives and minds, and the little arts of talk, of dress, of cookery that are allied with them. The aim of the new college, the cheap college, should be not to segregate and specialize, but to combine. It should explore the ways in which mind and body can be made to co-operate; discover what new combinations make good wholes in human life. The teachers should be drawn from the good livers as well as from the good thinkers. There should be no difficulty in attracting them. For there would be none of the barriers of wealth and ceremony, of advertisement and competition which now make the old and rich universities such uneasy dwelling-places—cities of strife, cities where this is locked up and that is chained down; where nobody can walk freely or talk freely for fear of transgressing some chalk mark, of displeasing some dignitary. But if the college were poor it would have nothing to offer; competition would be abolished. Life would be open and easy. People who love learning for itself would gladly come there. Musicians, painters, writers, would teach there, because they would learn. What could be of greater help to a writer than to discuss the art of writing with people who were thinking not of examinations or degrees or of what honour or profit they could make literature give them but of the art itself?

"And so with the other arts and artists. They would come to the poor college and practise their arts there because it would be a place where society was free; not parcelled out into the miserable distinctions of rich and poor, of clever and stupid; but where all the different degrees and kinds of mind, body and soul merit co-operated. Let us then found this new college; this poor college; in which learning is sought for itself; where advertisement is abolished; and there are no degrees; and lectures are not given, and sermons are not preached, and the old poisoned vanities and parades which breed competition and jealousy . . ."

The letter broke off there. It was not from lack of things to say; the peroration indeed was only just beginning. It was because the face on the other side of the page—the face that a letter-writer always sees—appeared to be fixed with a certain melancholy, upon a passage in the book from which quotation has already been made. "Head mistresses of schools therefore prefer a belettered staff, so that students of Newnham and Girton, since they could not put B.A. after their name, were at a disadvantage in obtaining appointments."

The honorary treasurer of the Rebuilding Fund had her eyes fixed on that. "What is the use of thinking how a college can be different," she seemed to say, "when it must be a place where students are taught to obtain appointments?" "Dream your dreams," she seemed to add, turning, rather wearily, to the table which she was arranging for some festival, "fire off your rhetoric, but we have to face realities."

That then was the "reality" on which her eyes were fixed; students must be taught to earn their livings. And since that reality meant that she must rebuild her college on the same lines as the others, it followed that the college for the daughters of educated men must also make Research produce practical results which will induce bequests and donations from rich men; it must encourage competition; it must accept degrees and coloured hoods; it must accumulate great wealth; it must exclude other people from a share of its wealth; and, therefore, in 500 years or so, that college, too, must ask the same question that you, Sir, are asking now: "How in your opinion are we to prevent war?"

An undesirable result that seemed; why then subscribe a guinea to procure it? That question at any rate was answered. No guinea of earned money should go to rebuilding the college on the old plan; just as certainly none could be spent upon building a college upon a new plan; therefore the guinea should be earmarked "Rags. Petrol. Matches." And this note should be attached to it. "Take this guinea and with it burn the college to the ground. Set fire to the old hypocrisies. Let the light of the burning building scare the nightingales and incarnadine the willows. And let the daughters of educated men dance round the fire and heap armful upon armful of dead leaves upon the flames. And let their mothers lean from the upper windows and cry, 'Let it blaze! Let it blaze! For we have done with this "education"!'"

That passage, Sir, is not empty rhetoric, for it is based upon the respectable opinion of the late head master of Eton, the present Dean of Durham. Nevertheless, there is something hollow about it, as is shown by a moment's conflict with fact. We have said that the only influence which the daughters of educated men can at present exert against war is the disinterested influence that they possess through earning their livings. If there were no means of training them to earn their livings, there would be an end of that influence. They could not obtain appointments. If they could not obtain appointments they would again be dependent upon their fathers and brothers; and if they were again dependent upon their fathers and brothers they would again be consciously and unconsciously in favour of war. History would seem to put that beyond doubt. Therefore we must send a guinea to the honorary treasurer of the college rebuilding fund, and let her do what she can with it. It is useless as things are to attach conditions as to the way in which that guinea is to be spent.

Such then is the rather lame and depressing answer to our question whether we can ask the authorities of the colleges for the daughters of educated men to use their influence through education to prevent war. It appears that we can ask them to do nothing; they must follow the old road to the old end; our influence as outsiders can only be of the most indirect sort. If we are asked to teach, we can examine very carefully into the aim of such teaching, and refuse to teach any art or science that encourages war. Further, we can pour mild scorn upon chapels, upon degrees, and upon the value of examinations. We can intimate that a prize poem can still have merit in spite of the fact that it has won a prize; and maintain that a book may still be worth reading in spite of the fact that its author took a first class with honours in the English tripos. If we are asked to lecture we can refuse to bolster up the vain and vicious system of lecturing by refusing to lecture. And, of course, if we are offered honours and degrees for ourselves we can refuse them—how, indeed, in view of the facts, could we possibly do otherwise? But there is no blinking the fact that in the present state of things the most effective way in which we can help you through education to prevent war is to subscribe as generously as possible to the colleges for the daughters of educated men. For, to repeat, if those daughters are not going to be educated they are not going to earn their livings; if they are not going to earn their livings, they are going once more to be restricted to the education of the private house; and if they are going to be restricted to the education of the private house they are going, once more, to exert all their influence both consciously and unconsciously in favour of war.

. . . We are asking why did such an education make the person so educated consciously and unconsciously in favour of war? Because consciously, it is obvious, she was forced to use whatever influence she possessed to bolster up the system which provided her with maids; with carriages; with fine clothes; with fine parties—it was by these means that she achieved marriage. Consciously she must use whatever charm or beauty she possessed to flatter and cajole the busy men, the soldiers, the lawyers, the ambassadors, the cabinet ministers who wanted recreation after their day's work. Consciously she must accept their views, and fall in with their decrees because it was only so that she could wheedle them into giving her the means to marry or marriage itself. In short, all her conscious effort must be in favour of what Lady Lovelace called "our splen-

did Empire" . . . "the price of which," she added, "is mainly paid by women." And who can doubt her, or that the price was heavy?

But her unconscious influence was even more strongly perhaps in favour of war. How else can we explain that amazing outburst in August 1914, when the daughters of educated men who had been educated thus rushed into hospitals, some still attended by their maids, drove lorries, worked in fields and munition factories, and used all their immense stores of charm, of sympathy, to persuade young men that to fight was heroic, and that the wounded in battle deserved all her care and all her praise? The reason lies in that same education. So profound was her unconscious loathing for the education of the private house with its cruelty, its poverty, its hypocrisy, its immorality, its inanity that she would undertake any task however menial, exercise any fascination however fatal that enabled her to escape. Thus consciously she desired "our splendid Empire"; unconsciously she desired our splendid war.

So, Sir, if you want us to help you to prevent war the conclusion seems to be inevitable; we must help to rebuild the college which, imperfect as it may be, is the only alternative to the education of the private house. We must hope that in time that education may be altered. That guinea must be given before we give you the guinea that you ask for your own society. But it is contributing to the same cause—the prevention of war. Guineas are rare; guineas are valuable, but let us send one without any condition attached to the honorary treasurer of the building fund, because by so doing we are making a positive contribution to the prevention of war.

2

Now that we have given one guinea towards rebuilding a college we must consider whether there is not more that we can do to help you to prevent war. And it is at once obvious, if what we have said about influence is true, that we must turn to the professions, because if we could persuade those who can earn their livings, and thus actually hold in their hands this new weapon, our only weapon, the weapon of independent opinion based upon independent income, to use that weapon against war, we should do more to help you than by appealing to those who must teach the young to earn their livings; or by lingering, however long, round the forbidden places and sacred gates of the universities where they are thus taught. This, therefore, is a more important question than the other.

Let us then lay your letter asking for help to prevent war, before the independent, the mature, those who are earning their livings in the professions. There is no need of rhetoric; hardly, one would suppose, of argument. . . . Nevertheless, doubts and hesitations there are; and the way to understand them is to place before you another letter, a letter as genuine as your own, a letter that happens to lie beside it on the table (Extract from a letter from the London and National Society for Women's Service. [1938]).

It is a letter from another honorary treasurer, and it is again asking for money. "Will you," she writes, "send a subscription to" [a society to help the daughters of educated men to obtain employment in the professions] "in order to help us to earn our livings? Failing money," she goes on, "any gift will be acceptable — books, fruit or cast-off clothing that can be sold in a bazaar." Now that letter has so much bearing upon the doubts and hesitations referred to above, and upon the help we can give you, that it seems impossible either to send her a guinea or to send you a guinea until we have considered the questions which it raises.

The first question is obviously, Why is she asking for money? Why is she so poor, this representative of professional women, that she must beg for cast-off clothing for a bazaar? . . . Let us then question her about her financial position and certain other facts before we give her a guinea, or lay down the terms upon which she is to have it. Here is the draft of such a letter:

"Accept a thousand apologies, Madam, for keeping you waiting so long for an answer to your letter. The fact is, certain questions have arisen, to which we must ask you to reply before we send you a subscription. In the first place you are asking for money — money with which to pay your rent. But how can it be, how can it possibly be, my dear Madam, that you are so terribly poor? The professions have been open to the daughters of educated men for almost 20 years. Therefore, how can it be, that you, whom we take to be their representative, are standing, like your sister at Cambridge, hat in hand, pleading for money, or failing money, for fruit, books, or cast-off clothing to sell at a bazaar? How can it be, we repeat? Surely there must be some very grave defect, of common humanity, of common justice, or of common sense. Or can it simply be that you are pulling a long face and telling a tall story like the beggar at the street corner who has a stocking full of guineas safely hoarded under her bed at home? In any case, this perpetual asking for money and pleading of poverty is laying you open to very grave rebukes, not only from indolent outsiders who dislike thinking about practical affairs almost as much as they dislike signing cheques, but from educated men. You are drawing upon yourselves the censure and contempt of men of established reputation as philosophers and novelists — of men like Mr. Joad and Mr. Wells. Not only do they deny your poverty, but they accuse you of apathy and indifference. Let me draw your attention to the charges that they bring against you. Listen, in the first place, to what Mr. C. E. M. Joad has to say of you (*The Testament of Joad*). He says: 'I doubt whether at any time during the last fifty years young women have been more politically apathetic, more socially indifferent than at the present time. . . . Before the war money poured into the coffers of the W.S.P.U. in order that women might win the vote which, it was hoped, would enable them to make war a thing of the past. The vote is won,' Mr. Joad continues, 'but war is very far from being a thing of the past. . . . Is it unreasonable,' he goes on, 'to ask that contemporary women should be prepared to give as much energy and money, to suffer as much obloquy and insult in the cause of peace, as their mothers gave and suffered in the cause of equality?' . . . Your lethargy is such that you will not fight even to protect the freedom which your mothers won for you. That charge is made against you by the most famous of living English novelists — Mr. H. G. Wells. . . . [who] says, 'There has been no perceptible woman's movement to resist the practical obliteration of their freedom by Fascists or Nazis' (*Experiment in Autobiography*, p. 486). Rich, idle, greedy and lethargic as you are, how have you the effrontery to ask me to subscribe to a society which helps the daughters of educated men to make their livings in the professions? For as these gentlemen prove in spite of the vote and the wealth which that vote must have brought with it, you have not ended war; in spite of the vote and the power which that vote must have brought with it, you have not resisted the practical obliteration of your freedom by Fascists and Nazis. What other conclusion then can one come to but that the whole of what was called 'the woman's movement' has proved itself a failure. . . ."

There, Sir, the letter stopped; for on the face at the other side of the letter — the face that a letter-writer always sees — was an expression, of boredom was it, or was it of fatigue? The honorary treasurer's glance seemed to rest upon two dull little facts which, since they have some bearing upon the question we are discussing, how the daughters of educated men who are earning their livings in the professions can help you to prevent war, may be copied here. The first fact was that the income of the W.S.P.U. upon which Mr. Joad has based his estimate of their wealth was (in the year 1912 at the height of their activity) £42,000. The second fact was that: "To earn £250 a year is quite an achievement even for a highly qualified woman with years of experience." The date of that statement is 1934. . . .

. . . We have nevertheless to explain the curious

fact that though a certain number of daughters enter for the examination and pass the examination those to whose names the word "Miss" is attached do not seem to enter the four-figure zone. The sex distinction seems . . . possessed of a curious leaden quality, liable to keep any name to which it is fastened circling in the lower spheres. . . .

. . . Thus it is quite possible that the name "Miss" transmits through the board [of examiners] or division some vibration which is not registered in the examination room. "Miss" transmits sex; and sex may carry with it an aroma. "Miss" may carry with it the swish of petticoats, the savour of a scent or other odour perceptible to the nose on the further side of the partition and obnoxious to it. What charms and consoles in the private house may distract and exacerbate in the public office. . . . Let us turn to the public press and see if we can discover from the opinions aired there any hint that will guide us in our attempt to decide the delicate and difficult question as to the aroma, the atmosphere that surrounds the word "Miss" in Whitehall. We will consult the newspapers.

First:

"I think your correspondent . . . correctly sums up this discussion in the observation that woman has too much liberty. It is probable that this so-called liberty came with the war, when women assumed responsibilities so far unknown to them. They did splendid service during those days. Unfortunately, they were praised and petted out of all proportion to the value of their performances" (*Daily Telegraph*, January 20th, 1936).

That does very well for a beginning. But let us proceed:

"I am of the opinion that a considerable amount of the distress which is prevalent in this section of the community [the clerical] could be relieved by the policy of employing men instead of women, wherever possible. There are today in Government offices, post offices, insurance companies, banks and other offices, thousands of women doing work which men could do. At the same time there are thousands of qualified men, young and middle-aged, who cannot get a job of any sort. There is a large demand for woman labour in the domestic arts, and in the process of re-grading a large number of women who have drifted into clerical service would become available for domestic service" (*Daily Telegraph*, 1936).

The odour thickens, you will agree.
Then once more:

"I am certain I voice the opinion of thousands of young men when I say that if men were doing the work that thousands of young women are now doing the men would be able to keep those same women in decent homes. Homes are the real places of the women who are now compelling men to be idle. It is time the Government insisted upon employers giving work to more men, thus enabling them to marry the women they cannot now approach" (*Daily Telegraph*, January 22nd, 1936).

There! There can be no doubt of the odour now. The cat is out of the bag; and it is a Tom.

After considering the evidence contained in those three quotations, you will agree that there is good reason to think that the word "Miss," however delicious its scent in the private house, has a certain odour attached to it in Whitehall which is disagreeable to the noses on the other side of the partition; and that it is likely that a name to which "Miss" is attached will, because of this odour, circle in the lower spheres where the salaries are small rather than mount to the higher spheres where the salaries are substantial. As for "Mrs.," it is a contaminated word; an obscene word. The less said about that word the better. Such is the smell of it, so rank does it stink in the nostrils of Whitehall, that Whitehall excludes it entirely. In Whitehall, as in heaven, there is neither marrying nor giving in marriage.

Odour then — or shall we call it "atmosphere"? — is a very important element in professional life; in spite of the fact that like other important elements it is impalpable. It can escape the noses of examiners in examination rooms, yet penetrate boards and divisions and affect the senses of those within. . . . It is true that women civil servants deserve to be paid as much as men; but it is also true that they are not paid as much as men. The discrepancy is due to atmosphere.

Atmosphere plainly is a very mighty power. Atmosphere not only changes the sizes and shapes of things; it affects solid bodies, like salaries, which might have been thought impervious to atmosphere. An epic poem might be written about atmosphere, or a novel in ten or fifteen volumes. But since this is only a letter, and you are pressed for time, let us confine ourselves to the plain statement that atmosphere is one of the most powerful, partly because it is one of the most impalpable, of the enemies with which the daughters of educated men have to fight. If you think that statement exaggerated, look once more at the samples of atmosphere contained in those three quotations. We shall find there not only the reason why the pay of the professional woman is still so small, but something more dangerous, something which, if it spreads, may poison both sexes equally. There, in those quotations, is the egg of the very same worm that we know under other names in other countries. There we have in embryo the creature, dictator as we call him when he is Italian or German, who believes that he has the right, whether given by God, Nature, sex or race is immaterial, to dictate to other human beings how they shall live; what they shall do. Let us quote again: "Homes are the real places of the women who are now compelling men to be idle. It is time the Government insisted upon employers giving work to more men, thus enabling them to marry the women they cannot now approach." Place beside it another quotation: "There are two worlds in the life of the nation, the world of men and the world of women. Nature has done well to entrust the man with the care of his family and the nation. The woman's world is her family, her husband, her children, and her home." One is written in English, the other in German. But where is the difference? Are they not both saying the same thing? Are they not both the voices of Dictators, whether they speak English or German, and are we not all agreed that the dictator when we meet him abroad is a very dangerous as well as a very ugly animal? And he is here among us, raising his ugly head, spitting his poison, small still, curled up like a caterpillar on a leaf, but in the heart of England. Is it not from this egg, to quote Mr. Wells again, that "the practical obliteration of [our] freedom by Fascists or Nazis" will spring? And is not the woman who has to breathe that poison and to fight that insect, secretly and without arms, in her office, fighting the Fascist or the Nazi as surely as those who fight him with arms in the limelight of publicity? And must not that fight wear down her strength and exhaust her spirit? Should we not help her to crush him in our own country before we ask her to help us to crush him abroad? And what right have we, Sir, to trumpet our ideal of freedom and justice to other countries when we can shake out from our most respectable newspapers any day of the week eggs like these? . . .

. . . [T]he influence which the daughters of educated men have at present from their money-earning power cannot be rated very highly. Yet since it has become more than ever obvious that it is to them that we must look for help, for they alone can help us, it is to them that we must appeal. This conclusion then brings us back to the letter from which we quoted above—the honorary treasurer's letter, the letter asking for a subscription to the society for helping the daughters of educated men to obtain employment in the professions. You will agree, Sir, that we have strong selfish motives for helping her—there can be no doubt about that. For to help women to earn their livings in

the professions is to help them to possess that weapon of independent opinion which is still their most powerful weapon. It is to help them to have a mind of their own and a will of their own with which to help you to prevent war. But . . . —here again, in those dots, doubts and hesitations assert themselves. Can we, considering the facts given above, send her our guinea without laying down very stringent terms as to how that guinea shall be spent?

For the facts which we have discovered in checking her statement as to her financial position have raised questions which make us wonder whether we are wise to encourage people to enter the professions if we wish to prevent war. You will remember that we are using our psychological insight (for that is our only qualification) to decide what kind of qualities in human nature are likely to lead to war. And the facts disclosed above are of a kind to make us ask, before we write our cheque, whether if we encourage the daughters of educated men to enter the professions we shall not be encouraging the very qualities that we wish to prevent? Shall we not be doing our guinea's worth to ensure that in two or three centuries not only the educated men in the professions but the educated women in the professions will be asking—oh, of whom? as the poet says—the very question that you are asking us now: How can we prevent war? If we encourage the daughters to enter the professions without making any conditions as to the way in which the professions are to be practised shall we not be doing our best to stereotype the old tune which human nature, like a gramophone whose needle has stuck, is now grinding out with such disastrous unanimity? "Here we go round the mulberry tree, the mulberry tree, the mulberry tree. Give it all to me, give it all to me, all to me. Three hundred millions spent upon war." With that song, or something like it, ringing in our ears we cannot send our guinea to the honorary treasurer without warning her that she shall only have it on condition that she shall swear that the professions in future shall be practised so that they lead to a different song and a different conclusion. She shall only have it if she can satisfy us that our guinea shall be spent in the cause of peace. It is difficult to formulate such conditions; in our present psychological ignorance perhaps impossible. But the matter is so serious, war is so insupportable, so horrible, so inhuman, that an attempt must be made. Here then is another letter to the same lady.

"Your letter, Madam, has waited a long time for an answer, but we have been examining into certain charges made against you and making certain enquiries. We have acquitted you, Madam, you will be relieved to learn, of telling lies. It would seem to be true that you are poor. We have acquitted you further, of idleness, apathy and greed. The number of causes that you are championing, however secretly and ineffectively, is in your favour. . . . But though we are willing to deplore your poverty and to commend your industry we are not going to send you a guinea to help you to help women to enter the professions unless you can assure us that they will practise those professions in such a way as to prevent war. . . .

. . . Now we are here to consider facts; now we must fix our eyes upon the procession—the procession of the sons of educated men.

"There they go, our brothers who have been educated at public schools and universities, mounting those steps, passing in and out of those doors, ascending those pulpits, preaching, teaching, administering justice, practising medicine, transacting business, making money. It is a solemn sight always—a procession . . . The questions that we have to ask and to answer about that procession during this moment of transition are so important that they may well change the lives of all men and women for ever. For we have to ask ourselves, here and now, do we wish to join that procession, or don't we? On what terms shall we join that procession? Above all, where is it leading us, the procession of educated men? . . . Think we must. Let us think in offices; in omnibuses; while we are standing in the crowd watching Coronations and Lord Mayor's Shows; let us think as we pass the Cenotaph; and in Whitehall; in the gallery of the House of Commons; in the Law Courts; let us think at baptisms and marriages and funerals. Let us never cease from thinking—what is this 'civilization' in which we find ourselves? What are these professions and why should we make money out of them? Where in short is it leading us, the procession of the sons of educated men?

" . . . They were great fighters, it seems, the professional men in the age of Queen Victoria. There was the battle of Westminster. There was the battle of the universities. There was the battle of Whitehall. There was the battle of Harley Street. There was the battle of the Royal Academy. Some of these battles, as you can testify, are still in progress. . . . Now the books in your library record so many of these battles that it is impossible to go into them all; but . . . they all seem to have been fought on much the same plan, and by the same combatants, that is by professional men v. their sisters and daughters. . . .

" . . . The whole proceeding is so familiar that the battle of Harley Street in the year 1869 might well be the battle of Cambridge at the present moment. On both occasions there is the same waste of strength, waste of temper, waste of time, and waste of money.

Almost the same daughters ask almost the same brothers for almost the same privileges. Almost the same gentlemen intone almost the same refusals for almost the same reasons. It seems as if there were no progress in the human race, but only repetition. We can almost hear them, if we listen, singing the same old song, 'Here we go round the mulberry tree, the mulberry tree, the mulberry tree,' and if we add, 'of property, of property, of property,' we shall fill in the rhyme without doing violence to the facts.

"But we are not here to sing old songs or to fill in missing rhymes. We are here to consider facts. And the facts which we have just extracted from biography seem to prove that the professions have a certain undeniable effect upon the professors. They make the people who practise them possessive, jealous of any infringement of their rights, and highly combative if anyone dares dispute them. Are we not right then in thinking that if we enter the same professions we shall acquire the same qualities? And do not such qualities lead to war? In another century or so if we practise the professions in the same way, shall we not be just as possessive, just as jealous, just as pugnacious, just as positive as to the verdict of God, Nature, Law and Property as these gentlemen are now? Therefore this guinea, which is to help you to help women to enter the professions, has this condition as a first condition attached to it. You shall swear that you will do all in your power to insist that any woman who enters any profession shall in no way hinder any other human being, whether man or woman, white or black, provided that he or she is qualified to enter that profession, from entering it; but shall do all in her power to help them.

"You are ready to put your hand to that, here and now, you say, and at the same time stretch out that hand for the guinea. But wait. Other conditions are attached to it before it is yours. For consider once more the procession of the sons of educated men; ask yourself once more, where is it leading us? One answer suggests itself instantly. To incomes, it is obvious, that seem, to us at least, extremely handsome. . . . All this wealth may in the course of time come our way if we follow the professions. In short, we may change our position from being the victims of the patriarchal system, paid on the truck system, with £30 or £40 a year in cash and board and lodging thrown in, to being the champions of the capitalist system, with a yearly income in our own possession of many thousands which, by judicious investment, may leave us when we die possessed of a capital sum of more millions than we can count.

"It is a thought not without its glamour. Consider

what it would mean if among us there were now a woman motor-car manufacturer who, with a stroke of her pen, could endow the women's colleges with two or three hundred thousand pounds apiece. The honorary treasurer of the rebuilding fund, your sister at Cambridge, would have her labours considerably lightened then. There would be no need of appeals and committees, of bazaars and strawberries and cream. And suppose that there were not merely one rich woman, but that rich women were as common as rich men. What could you not do? You could shut up your office at once. You could finance a woman's party in the House of Commons. You could run a daily newspaper committed to a conspiracy, not of silence, but of speech. You could get pensions for spinsters; those victims of the patriarchal system, whose allowance is insufficient and whose board and lodging are no longer thrown in. You could get equal pay for equal work. You could provide every mother with chloroform when her child is born; you could bring down the maternal death-rate from four in every thousand to none at all, perhaps. In one session you could pass Bills that will now take you perhaps a hundred years of hard and continuous labour to get through the House of Commons. There seems at first sight nothing that you could not do, if you had the same capital at your disposal that your brothers have at theirs. Why not, then, you exclaim, help us to take the first step towards possessing it? The professions are the only way in which we can earn money. Money is the only means by which we can achieve objects that are immensely desirable. Yet here you are, you seem to protest, haggling and bargaining over conditions. But consider this letter from a professional man asking us to help him to prevent war. Look also at the photographs of dead bodies and ruined houses that the Spanish Government sends almost weekly. That is why it is necessary to haggle and to bargain over conditions.

"For the evidence of the letter and of the photographs when combined with the facts with which history and biography provide us about the professions seem together to throw a certain light, a red light, shall we say, upon those same professions. You make money in them; that is true; but how far is money in view of those facts in itself a desirable possession? A great authority upon human life, you will remember, held over two thousand years ago that great possessions were undesirable. . . . If extreme wealth is undesirable and extreme poverty is undesirable, it is arguable that there is some mean between the two which is desirable. What then is that mean—how much money is needed to live upon in England today? And how should that money be spent? What is the kind of life, the kind of

human being, you propose to aim at if you succeed in extracting this guinea? Those, Madam, are the questions that I am asking you to consider and you cannot deny that those are questions of the utmost importance. . . .

"There it is then, before our eyes, the procession of the sons of educated men, ascending those pulpits, mounting those steps, passing in and out of those doors, preaching, teaching, administering justice, practising medicine, making money. And it is obvious that if you are going to make the same incomes from the same professions that those men make you will have to accept the same conditions that they accept. Even from an upper window and from books we know or can guess what those conditions are. You will have to leave the house at nine and come back to it at six. That leaves very little time for fathers to know their children. You will have to do this daily from the age of twenty-one or so to the age of about sixty-five. That leaves very little time for friendship, travel or art. You will have to perform some duties that are very arduous, others that are very barbarous. You will have to wear certain uniforms and profess certain loyalties. If you succeed in those professions the words 'For God and the Empire' will very likely be written, like the address on a dog-collar, round your neck. And if words have meaning, as words perhaps should have meaning, you will have to accept that meaning and do what you can to enforce it. In short, you will have to lead the same lives and profess the same loyalties that professional men have professed for many centuries. There can be no doubt of that. . . .

" . . . [W]e, daughters of educated men, are between the devil and the deep sea. Behind us lies the patriarchal system; the private house, with its nullity, its immorality, its hypocrisy, its servility. Before us lies the public world, the professional system, with its possessiveness, its jealousy, its pugnacity, its greed. The one shuts us up like slaves in a harem; the other forces us to circle, like caterpillars head to tail, round and round the mulberry tree, the sacred tree, of property. It is a choice of evils. Each is bad. Had we not better plunge off the bridge into the river; give up the game; declare that the whole of human life is a mistake and so end it?

"But before you take that step, Madam, . . . let us see if another answer is not possible.

"Another answer may be staring us in the face on the shelves of your own library, once more in the biographies. Is it not possible that by considering the experiments that the dead have made with their lives in the past we may find some help in answering the very difficult question that is now forced upon us? . . .

" . . . For when Mary Kingsley says '. . . being allowed to learn German was *all* the paid-for education I ever had,' she suggests that she had an unpaid-for education. The other lives that we have been examining corroborate that suggestion. What then was the nature of that 'unpaid-for education' which, whether for good or for evil, has been ours for so many centuries? If we mass the lives of the obscure behind four lives that were not obscure, but were so successful and distinguished that they were actually written, the lives of Florence Nightingale, Miss Clough, Mary Kingsley and Gertrude Bell, it seems undeniable that they were all educated by the same teachers. And those teachers, biography indicates, obliquely, and indirectly, but emphatically and indisputable none the less, were poverty, chastity, derision, and—what word however covers 'lack of rights and privileges'? Shall we press the old word 'freedom' once more into service? 'Freedom from unreal loyalties,' then, was the fourth of their teachers; that freedom from loyalty to old schools, old colleges, old churches, old ceremonies, old countries which all those women enjoyed, and which, to a great extent, we still enjoy by the law and custom of England. We have no time to coin new words, greatly though the language is in need of them. Let 'freedom from unreal loyalties' then stand as the fourth great teacher of the daughters of educated men.

"Biography thus provides us with the fact that the daughters of educated men received an unpaid-for education at the hands of poverty, chastity, derision and freedom from unreal loyalties. It was this unpaid-for education, biography informs us, that fitted them, aptly enough, for the unpaid-for professions. And biography also informs us that those unpaid-for professions had their laws, traditions, and labours no less certainly than the paid-for professions. Further, the student of biography cannot possibly doubt from the evidence of biography that this education and these professions were in many ways bad in the extreme, both for the unpaid themselves and for their descendants. The intensive childbirth of the unpaid wife, the intensive money-making of the paid husband in the Victorian age had terrible results, we cannot doubt, upon the mind and body of the present age. To prove it we need not quote once more the famous passage in which Florence Nightingale denounced that education and its result; nor stress the natural delight with which she greeted the Crimean war; nor illustrate from other sources—they are, alas, innumerable—the inanity, the pettiness, the spite, the tyranny, the hypocrisy, the immorality which it engendered as the lives of both sexes so abundantly testify. Final proof of its harshness upon one sex at any rate can be found in the annals of our 'great war,' when hospitals, harvest fields and munition works were largely staffed by refugees flying from its horrors to their comparative amenity.

"But biography is many-sided; biography never returns a single and simple answer to any question that is asked of it. Thus the biographies of those who had biographies—say Florence Nightingale, Anne Clough, Emily Bronte, Christina Rossetti, Mary Kingsley—prove beyond a doubt that this same education, the unpaid for, must have had great virtues as well as great defects, for we cannot deny that these, if not educated, still were civilized women. We cannot, when we consider the lives of our uneducated mothers and grandmothers, judge education simply by its power to 'obtain appointments,' to win honour, to make money. We must, if we are honest, admit that some who had no paid-for education, no salaries and no appointments were civilized human beings—whether or not they can rightly be called 'English' women is matter for dispute; and thus admit that we should be extremely foolish if we threw away the results of that education or gave up the knowledge that we have obtained from it for any bribe or decoration whatsoever. Thus biography, when asked the question we have put to it—how can we enter the professions and yet remain civilized human beings, human beings who discourage war, would seem to reply: If you refuse to be separated from the four great teachers of the daughters of educated men—poverty, chastity, derision and freedom from unreal loyalties—but combine them with some wealth, some knowledge, and some service to real loyalties then you can enter the professions and escape the risks that make them undesirable.

" . . . such are the conditions attached to this guinea. You shall have it, to recapitulate, on condition that you help all properly qualified people, of whatever sex, class or colour, to enter your profession; and further on condition that in the practise of your profession you refuse to be separated from poverty, chastity, derision and freedom from unreal loyalties. Is the statement now more positive, have the conditions been made more clear and do you agree to the terms? You hesitate. Some of the conditions, you seem to suggest, need further discussion. Let us take them, then, in order. By poverty is meant enough money to live upon. That is, you must earn enough to be independent of any other human being and to buy that modicum of health, leisure, knowledge and so on that is needed for the full development of body and mind. But no more. Not a penny more.

"By chastity is meant that when you have made enough to live on by your profession you must refuse to sell your brain for the sake of money. That is you must cease to practise your profession, or practise it for the sake of research and experiment; or, if you are an artist, for the sake of the art; or give the knowledge acquired professionally to those who need it for nothing. But directly the mulberry tree begins to make you circle, break off. Pelt the tree with laughter.

"By derision—a bad word, but once again the English language is much in need of new words—is meant that you must refuse all methods of advertising merit, and hold that ridicule, obscurity and censure are preferable, for psychological reasons, to fame and praise. Directly badges, order, or degrees are offered you, fling them back in the giver's face.

"By freedom from unreal loyalties is meant that you must rid yourself of pride of nationality in the first place; also of religious pride, college pride, school pride, family pride, sex pride and those unreal loyalties that spring from them. Directly the seducers come with their seductions to bribe you into captivity, tear up the parchments; refuse to fill up the forms.

" . . . We have seen in the quotations given above how great a part chastity, bodily chastity, has played in the unpaid education of our sex. It should not be difficult to transmute the old ideal of bodily chastity into the new ideal of mental chastity—to hold that if it was wrong to sell the body for money it is much more wrong to sell the mind for money, since the mind, people say, is nobler than the body. Then again, are we not greatly fortified in resisting the seductions of the most powerful of all seducers—money—by those same traditions? For how many centuries have we not enjoyed the right of working all day and every day for £40 a year with board and lodging thrown in? And does not Whitaker prove that half the work of educated men's daughters is still unpaid-for work? Finally, honour, fame, consequence—is it not easy for us to resist that seduction, we who have worked for centuries without other honour than that which is reflected from the coronets and badges on our father's or husband's brows and breasts?

"Thus, with law on our side, and property on our side, and ancestral memory to guide us, there is no need of further argument; you will agree that the conditions upon which this guinea is yours are, with the exception of the first, comparatively easy to fulfil. They merely require that you should develop, modify and direct by the findings of the two psychometers the traditions and the education of the private house which have been in existence these 2,000 years. And if you will agree to do that, there can be an end of bargaining between us. Then the guinea with which to pay the rent of your house is yours—would that it were a thousand! For if you agree to these terms then you can join the professions and yet remain uncontaminated by them; you can rid them of their possessiveness, their jealousy, their pugnacity, their greed. You can use

them to have a mind of your own and a will of your own. And you can use that mind and will to abolish the inhumanity, the beastliness, the horror, the folly of war. Take this guinea then and use it, not to burn the house down, but to make its windows blaze. And let the daughters of uneducated women dance round the new house, the poor house, the house that stands in a narrow street where omnibuses pass and the street hawkers cry their wares, and let them sing, 'We have done with war! We have done with tyranny!' And their mothers will laugh from their graves, 'It was for this that we suffered obloquy and contempt! Light up the windows of the new house, daughters! Let them blaze!' . . ."

Such then, Sir, was the letter finally sent to the honorary treasurer of the society for helping the daughters of educated men to enter the professions. In it such influence as a guinea can exert has been framed so far as our psychological competence allows to ensure that she shall do all that is in her power to help you to prevent war. Whether the terms have been rightly defined it is impossible to say. But as you will see, it was necessary to answer her letter and the letter from the honorary treasurer of the college rebuilding fund, and to send them both guineas before answering your letter, because unless they are helped, first to educate the daughters of educated men, and then to earn their livings in the professions, those daughters cannot possess an independent and disinterested influence with which to help you to prevent war. The causes it seems are connected. But having shown this to the best of our ability, let us return to your own letter and to your request for a subscription to your own society.

3

Here then is your own letter. In that, as we have seen, after asking for an opinion as to how to prevent war, you go on to suggest certain practical measures by which we can help you to prevent it. These are it appears that we should sign a manifesto, pledging ourselves "to protect culture and intellectual liberty"; that we should join a certain society, devoted to certain measures whose aim is to preserve peace; and, finally, that we should subscribe to that society which like the others is in need of funds.

First, then, let us consider how we can help you to prevent war by protecting culture and intellectual liberty, since you assure us that there is a connection between those rather abstract words and these very positive photographs—the photographs of dead bodies and ruined houses. . . .

. . . We can only help you to defend culture and intellectual liberty by defending our own culture and our own intellectual liberty. That is to say, we can hint, if the treasurer of one of the women's colleges asks us for a subscription, that some change might be made in that satellite body when it ceases to be satellite; or again, if the treasurer of some society for obtaining professional employment for women asks us for a subscription, suggest that some change might be desirable, in the interests of culture and intellectual liberty, in the practice of the professions. But as paid-for education is still raw and young, and as the number of those allowed to enjoy it at Oxford and Cambridge is still strictly limited, culture for the great majority of educated men's daughters must still be that which is acquired outside the sacred gates, in public libraries or in private libraries, whose doors by some unaccountable oversight have been left unlocked. It must still, in the year 1938, largely consist in reading and writing our own tongue. The question thus becomes more manageable. Shorn of its glory it is easier to deal with. What we have to do now, then, Sir is to lay your request before the daughters of educated men and to ask them to help you to prevent war, not by advising their brothers how they shall protect culture and intellectual liberty, but simply by reading and writing their own tongue in such a way as to protect those rather abstract goddesses themselves.

. . . Is it not possible that if we knew the truth about war, the glory of war would be scotched and crushed where it lies curled up in the rotten cabbage leaves of our prostituted fact-purveyors; and if we knew the truth about art instead of shuffling and shambling through the smeared and dejected pages of those who must live by prostituting culture, the enjoyment and practice of art would become so desirable that by comparison the pursuit of war would be a tedious game for elderly dilettantes in search of a mildly sanitary amusement— the tossing of bombs instead of balls over frontiers instead of nets? In short, if newspapers were written by people whose sole object in writing was to tell the truth about politics and the truth about art we should not believe in war, and we should believe in art.

Hence there is a very clear connection between culture and intellectual liberty and those photographs of dead bodies and ruined houses. And to ask the daughters of educated men who have enough to live upon not to commit adultery of the brain is to ask them to help in the most positive way now open to them—to prevent war.

Thus, Sir, we might address this lady, crudely, briefly it is true; but time presses and we cannot define further. And to this appeal she might well reply, if indeed she exists: "What you say is obvious; so obvious that every educated man's daughter already knows it for herself, or if she does not, has only to read the newspapers to be sure of it. But suppose she were well

enough off not merely to sign this manifesto in favour of disinterested culture and intellectual liberty but to put her opinion into practice, how could she set about it? And do not," she may reasonably add, "dream dreams about ideal worlds behind the stars; consider actual facts in the actual world." Indeed, the actual world is much more difficult to deal with than the dream world. Still, Madam, the private printing press is an actual fact, and not beyond the reach of a moderate income. Typewriters and duplicators are actual facts and even cheaper. By using these cheap and so far unforbidden instruments you can at once rid yourself of the pressure of boards, policies and editors. They will speak your own mind, in your own words, at your own time, at your own length, at your own bidding. And that, we are agreed, is our definition of "intellectual liberty." "But," she may say, "'the public'? How can that be reached without putting my own mind through the mincing machine and turning it into sausage?" "'The public,' Madam," we may assure her, "is very like ourselves; it lives in rooms; it walks in streets, and is said moreover to be tired of sausage. Fling leaflets down basements; expose them on stalls; trundle them along streets on barrows to be sold for a penny or given away. Find out new ways of approaching 'the public'; single it into separate people instead of massing it into one monster, gross in body, feeble in mind. And then reflect—since you have enough to live on, you have a room, not necessarily 'cosy' or 'handsome' but still silent, private; a room where safe from publicity and its poison you could, even asking a reasonable fee for the service, speak the truth to artists, about pictures, music, books without fear of affecting their sales, which are exiguous, or wounding their vanity, which is prodigious. Such at least was the criticism that Ben Jonson gave Shakespeare at the Mermaid and there is no reason to suppose, with *Hamlet* as evidence, that literature suffered in consequence. Are not the best critics private people, and is not the only criticism worth having spoken criticism? Those then are some of the active ways in which you, as a writer of your own tongue, can put your opinion into practice. But if you are passive, a reader, not a writer, then you must adopt not active but passive methods of protecting culture and intellectual liberty." "And what may they be?" she will ask. "To abstain, obviously. Not to subscribe to papers that encourage intellectual slavery; not to attend lectures that prostitute culture; for we are agreed that to write at the command of another what you do not want to write is to be enslaved, and to mix culture with personal charm or advertisement is to prostitute culture. By these active and passive measures you would do all in your power to break the ring, the vicious circle, the dance round and round the mulberry tree, the poison tree of intellectual harlotry. The ring once broken, the captives would be freed. For who can doubt that once writers had the chance of writing what they enjoy writing they would find it so much more pleasurable that they would refuse to write on any other terms; or that readers once they had the chance of reading what writers enjoy writing, would find it so much more nourishing than what is written for money that they would refuse to be palmed off with the stale substitute any longer? Thus the slaves who are now kept hard at work piling words into books, piling words into articles, as the old slaves piled stones into pyramids, would shake the manacles from their wrists and give up their loathsome labour. And 'culture,' that amorphous bundle, swaddled up as she now is in insincerity, emitting half truths from her timid lips sweetening and diluting her message with whatever sugar or water serves to swell the writer's fame or his master's purse, would regain her shape and become, as Milton, Keats and other great writers assure us that she is in reality, muscular, adventurous, free. Whereas now, Madam, at the very mention of culture the head aches, the eyes close, the doors shut, the air thickens; we are in a lecture room, rank with the fumes of stale print, listening to a gentleman who is forced to lecture or to write every Wednesday, every Sunday, about Milton or about Keats, while the lilac shakes its branches in the garden free, and the gulls, swirling and swooping, suggest with wild laughter that such stale fish might with advantage be tossed to them. That is our plea to you, Madam; those are our reasons for urging it. Do not merely sign this manifesto in favour of culture and intellectual liberty; attempt at least to put your promise into practice."

. . . To protect culture and intellectual liberty in practice would mean, as we have said, ridicule and chastity, loss of publicity and poverty. But those, as we have seen, are [women's] familiar teachers. Further, Whitaker with his facts is at hand to help them; for since he proves that all the fruits of professional culture—such as directorships of art galleries and museums, professorships and lectureships and editorships are still beyond their reach, they should be able to take a more purely disinterested view of culture than their brothers, without for a moment claiming, as Macaulay asserts, that they are by nature more disinterested. Thus helped by tradition and by facts as they are, we have not only some right to ask them to help us to break the circle, the vicious circle of prostituted culture, but some hope that if such people exist they will help us. To return then to your manifesto: we will sign it if we can keep these terms; if we cannot keep them, we will not sign it.

Now that we have tried to see how we can help you to prevent war by attempting to define what is meant by protecting culture and intellectual liberty let us consider your next and inevitable request: that we should subscribe to the funds of your society. For you, too, are an honorary treasurer, and like the other honorary treasurers in need of money. Since you, too, are asking for money it might be possible to ask you, also, to define your aims, and to bargain and to impose terms as with the other honorary treasurers. What then are the aims of your society? To prevent war, of course. And by what means? Broadly speaking, by protecting the rights of the individual; by opposing dictatorship; by ensuring the democratic ideals of equal opportunity for all. Those are the chief means by which as you say, "the lasting peace of the world can be assured." Then, Sir, there is no need to bargain or to haggle. If those are your aims, and if, as it is impossible to doubt, you mean to do all in your power to achieve them, the guinea is yours—would that it were a million! The guinea is yours; and the guinea is a free gift, given freely.

But the word "free" is used so often, and has come, like used words, to mean so little, that it may be well to explain exactly, even pedantically, what the word "free" means in this context. It means here that no right or privilege is asked in return. The giver is not asking you to admit her to the priesthood of the Church of England; or to the Stock Exchange; or to the Diplomatic Service. The giver has no wish to be "English" on the same terms that you yourself are "English." The giver does not claim in return for the gift admission to any profession; any honour, title, or medal; any professorship or lectureship; any seat upon any society, committee or board. The gift is free from all such conditions because the one right of paramount importance to all human beings is already won. You cannot take away her right to earn a living. Now then for the first time in English history an educated man's daughter can give her brother one guinea of her own making at his request for the purpose specified above without asking for anything in return. It is a free gift, given without fear, without flattery, and without conditions. That, Sir, is so momentous an occasion in the history of civilization that some celebration seems called for. . . . Let us invent a new ceremony for this new occasion. What more fitting than to destroy an old word, a vicious and corrupt word that has done much harm in its day and is now obsolete? The word "feminist" is the word indicated. That word, according to the dictionary, means "one who champions the rights of women." Since the only right, the right to earn a living, has been won, the word no longer has a meaning. And a word without a meaning is a dead word, a corrupt word. Let us therefore celebrate this occasion by cremating the corpse. Let us write that word in large black

Virginia Woolf

letters on a sheet of foolscap; then solemnly apply a match to the paper. Look, how it burns! What a light dances over the world! Now let us bray the ashes in a mortar with a goose-feather pen, and declare in unison singing together that anyone who uses that word in future is a ring-the-bell-and-run-away-man, a mischief maker, a groper among old bones, the proof of whose defilement is written in a smudge of dirty water upon his face. The smoke has died down; the word is destroyed. Observe, Sir, what has happened as the result of our celebration. The word "feminist" is destroyed; the air is cleared; and in that clearer air what do we see? Men and women working together for the same cause. The cloud has lifted from the past too. What were they working for in the nineteenth century—those queer dead women in their poke bonnets and shawls? The very same cause for which we are working now. "Our claim was no claim of women's rights only;"—it is Josephine Butler who speaks—"it was larger and deeper; it was a claim for the rights of all—all men and women—to the respect in their persons of the great principles of Justice and Equality and Liberty." The words are the same as yours; the claim is the same as yours. The daughters of educated men who were called, to their resentment, "feminists" were in fact the advance guard of your own movement. They were fighting the same enemy that you are fighting and for the same reasons. They were fighting the tyranny of the patriarchal state as you are fighting the tyranny of the Fascist state. Thus we are merely carrying on the same fight that our mothers and grandmothers fought; their words prove it; your words prove it. But now with your letter before us we have your assurance that you are fighting with us, not against us. That fact is so inspiring that another celebration seems called for. What could be more fitting than to write more dead words, more corrupt words, upon more sheets of paper and burn them—the words, Tyrant, Dictator, for example? But, alas, those words are not yet obsolete. We can still shake out eggs from newspapers; still smell a peculiar and unmistakable odour in the region of Whitehall and Westminster. And abroad the monster has come more openly to the surface. There is no mistaking him there. He has widened his scope. He is interfering now with your liberty; he is dictating how you shall live; he is making distinctions not merely between the sexes, but between the races. You are feeling in your own persons what your mothers felt when they were shut out, when they were shut up, because they were women. Now you are being shut out, you are being shut up, because you are Jews, because you are democrats, because of race, because of religion. It is not a photograph that you look upon any longer; there you go, trapesing along in the proces-

sion yourselves. And that makes a difference. The whole iniquity of dictatorship, whether in Oxford or Cambridge, in Whitehall or Downing Street, against Jews or against women, in England, or in Germany, in Italy or in Spain is now apparent to you. But now we are fighting together. The daughters and sons of educated men are fighting side by side. That fact is so inspiring, even if no celebration is yet possible, that if this one guinea could be multiplied a million times all those guineas should be at your service without any other conditions than those that you have imposed upon yourself. Take this one guinea then and use it to assert "the rights of all—all men and women—to the respect in their persons of the great principles of Justice and Equality and Liberty." Put this penny candle in the window of your new society, and may we live to see the day when in the blaze of our common freedom the words tyrant and dictator shall be burnt to ashes, because the words tyrant and dictator shall be obsolete.

That request then for a guinea answered, and the cheque signed, only one further request of yours remains to be considered—it is that we should fill up a form and become members of your society. . . . What reason or what emotion can make us hesitate to become members of a society whose aims we approve, to whose funds we have contributed? It may be neither reason nor emotion, but something more profound and fundamental than either. It may be difference. Different we are, as facts have proved, both in sex and in education. And it is from that difference, as we have already said, that our help can come, if help we can, to protect liberty, to prevent war. But if we sign this form which implies a promise to become active members of your society, it would seem that we must lose that difference and therefore sacrifice that help. . . .

. . . The very word "society" sets tolling in memory the dismal bells of a harsh music: shall not, shall not, shall not. You shall not learn; you shall not earn; you shall not own; you shall not—such was the society relationship of brother to sister for many centuries. And though it is possible, and to the optimistic credible, that in time a new society may ring a carillon of splendid harmony, and your letter heralds it, that day is far distant. Inevitably we ask ourselves, is there not something in the conglomeration of people into societies that releases what is most selfish and violent, least rational and humane in the individuals themselves? Inevitably we look upon society, so kind to you, so harsh to us, as an ill-fitting form that distorts the truth; deforms the mind; fetters the will. Inevitably we look upon societies as conspiracies that sink the private brother, whom many of us have reason to respect, and inflate in his stead a monstrous male, loud of voice, hard of fist, childishly intent upon scoring the floor

348

of the earth with chalk marks, within whose mystic boundaries human beings are penned, rigidly, separately, artificially; where, daubed red and gold, decorated like a savage with feathers he goes through mystic rites and enjoys the dubious pleasures of power and dominion while we, "his" women, are locked in the private house without share in the many societies of which his society is composed. For such reasons compact as they are of many memories and emotions—for who shall analyse the complexity of a mind that holds so deep a reservoir of time past within it?—it seems both wrong for us rationally and impossible for us emotionally to fill up your form and join your society. For by so doing we should merge our identity in yours; follow and repeat and score still deeper the old worn ruts in which society, like a gramophone whose needle has stuck, is grinding out with intolerable unanimity "Three hundred millions spent upon arms." We should not give effect to a view which our own experience of "society" should have helped us to envisage. Thus, Sir, while we respect you as a private person and prove it by giving you a guinea to spend as you choose, we believe that we can help you most effectively by refusing to join your society; by working for our common ends—justice and equality and liberty for all men and women—outside your society, not within.

. . . In the first place, this new society, you will be relieved to learn, would have no honorary treasurer, for it would need no funds. It would have no office, no committee, no secretary; it would call no meetings; it would hold no conferences. If name it must have, it could be called the Outsiders' Society. That is not a resonant name, but it has the advantage that it squares with facts—the facts of history, of law, of biography; even, it may be, with the still hidden facts of our still unknown psychology. It would consist of educated men's daughters working in their own class—how indeed can they work in any other?—and by their own methods for liberty, equality and peace. Their first duty, to which they would bind themselves not by oath, for oaths and ceremonies have no part in a society which must be anonymous and elastic before everything, would be not to fight with arms. This is easy for them to observe, for in fact, as the papers inform us, "the Army Council have no intention of opening recruiting for any women's corps" (*The Times*, October 22nd, 1937). The country ensures it. Next they would refuse in the event of war to make munitions or nurse the wounded. Since in the last war both these activities were mainly discharged by the daughters of working men, the pressure upon them here too would be slight, though probably disagreeable. On the other hand the next duty to which they would pledge themselves is one of considerable difficulty, and calls not only for

courage and initiative, but for the special knowledge of the educated man's daughter. It is, briefly, not to incite their brothers to fight, or to dissuade them, but to maintain an attitude of complete indifference. But the attitude expressed by the word "indifference" is so complex and of such importance that it needs even here further definition. Indifference in the first place must be given a firm footing upon fact. As it is a fact that she cannot understand what instinct compels him, what glory, what interest, what manly satisfaction fighting provides for him—"without war there would be no outlet for the manly qualities which fighting develops"—as fighting thus is a sex characteristic which she cannot share, the counterpart some claim of the maternal instinct which he cannot share, so is it an instinct which she cannot judge. The outsider therefore must leave him free to deal with this instinct by himself, because liberty of opinion must be respected, especially when it is based upon an instinct which is as foreign to her as centuries of tradition and education can make it. This is a fundamental and instinctive distinction upon which indifference may be based. But the outsider will make it her duty not merely to base her indifference upon instinct, but upon reason. When he says, as history proves that he has said, and may say again, "I am fighting to protect our country" and thus seeks to rouse her patriotic emotion, she will ask herself, "What does 'our country' mean to me an outsider?" To decide this she will analyse the meaning of patriotism in her own case. She will inform herself of the position of her sex and her class in the past. She will inform herself of the amount of land, wealth and property in the possession of her own sex and class in the present—how much of "England" in fact belongs to her. From the same sources she will inform herself of the legal protection which the law has given her in the past and now gives her. And if he adds that he is fighting to protect her body, she will reflect upon the degree of physical protection that she now enjoys when the words "Air Raid Precaution" are written on blank walls. And if he says that he is fighting to protect England from foreign rule, she will reflect that for her there are no "foreigners," since by law she becomes a foreigner if she marries a foreigner. And she will do her best to make this a fact, not by forced fraternity, but by human sympathy. All these acts will convince her reason (to put it in a nutshell) that her sex and class has very little to thank England for in the past; not much to thank England for in the present; while the security of her person in the future is highly dubious. But probably she will have imbibed, even from the governess, some romantic notion that Englishmen, those fathers and grandfathers whom she sees marching in the picture of history, are "superior" to the men of other countries. This she will consider it her duty to check by comparing French historians with English; German with French; the testimony of the ruled—the Indians or the Irish, say—with the claims made by their rulers. Still some "patriotic" emotion, some ingrained belief in the intellectual superiority of her own country over other countries may remain. Then she will compare English painting with French painting; English music with German music; English literature with Greek literature, for translations abound. When all these comparisons have been faithfully made by the use of reason, the outsider will find herself in possession of very good reasons for her indifference. She will find that she has no good reason to ask her brother to fight on her behalf to protect "our" country. "'Our' country,'" she will say, "throughout the greater part of its history has treated me as a slave; it has denied me education or any share in its possessions. 'Our' country still ceases to be mine if I marry a foreigner. 'Our' country denies me the means of protecting myself, forces me to pay others a very large sum annually to protect me, and is so little able, even so, to protect me that Air Raid precautions are written on the wall. Therefore if you insist upon fighting to protect me, or 'our' country, let it be understood, soberly and rationally between us, that you are fighting to gratify a sex instinct which I cannot share; to procure benefits which I have not shared and probably will not share; but not to gratify my instincts, or to protect myself or my country. For," the outsider will say, "in fact, as a woman, I have no country. As a woman I want no country. As a woman my country is the whole world." And if, when reason has said its say, still some obstinate emotion remains, some love of England dropped into a child's ears by the cawing of rooks in an elm tree, by the splash of waves on a beach, or by English voices murmuring nursery rhymes, this drop of pure, if irrational, emotion she will make serve her to give to England first what she desires of peace and freedom for the whole world.

Such then will be the nature of her "indifference" and from this indifference certain actions must follow. She will bind herself to take no share in patriotic demonstrations; to assent to no form of national self-praise; to make no part of any claque or audience that encourages war; to absent herself from military displays, tournaments, tattoos, prize-givings and all such ceremonies as encourage the desire to impose "our" civilization or "our" dominion upon other people. The psychology of private life, moreover, warrants the belief that this use of indifference by the daughters of educated men would help materially to prevent war. For psychology would seem to show that it is far harder for human beings to take action when other people are

indifferent and allow them complete freedom of action, than when their actions are made the centre of excited emotion. The small boy struts and trumpets outside the window: implore him to stop; he goes on; say nothing; he stops. That the daughters of educated men then should give their brothers neither the white feather of cowardice nor the red feather of courage, but no feather at all; that they should shut the bright eyes that rain influence, or let those eyes look elsewhere when war is discussed—that is the duty to which outsiders will train themselves in peace before the threat of death inevitably makes reason powerless.

Such then are some of the methods by which the society, the anonymous and secret Society of Outsiders would help you, Sir, to prevent war and to ensure freedom. Whatever value you may attach to them you will agree that they are duties which your own sex would find it more difficult to carry out than ours; and duties moreover which are specially appropriate to the daughters of educated men. For they would need some acquaintance with the psychology of educated men, and the minds of educated men are more highly trained and their words subtler than those of working men. There are other duties, of course—many have already been outlined in the letters to the honorary treasurers. But at the risk of some repetition let us roughly and rapidly repeat them, so that they may form a basis for a society of outsiders to take its stand upon. First, they would bind themselves to earn their own livings. The importance of this as a method of ending war is obvious; sufficient stress has already been laid upon the superior cogency of an opinion based upon economic independence over an opinion based upon no income at all or upon a spiritual right to an income to make further proof unnecessary. It follows that an outsider must make it her business to press for a living wage in all the professions now open to her sex; further that she must create new professions in which she can earn the right to an independent opinion. Therefore she must bind herself to press for a money wage for the unpaid worker in her own class—the daughters and sisters of educated men who, as biographies have shown us, are now paid on the truck system, with food, lodging and a pittance of £40 a year. But above all she must press for a wage to be paid by the State legally to the mothers of educated men. The importance of this to our common fight is immeasurable; for it is the most effective way in which we can ensure that the large and very honourable class of married women shall have a mind and a will of their own, with which, if his mind and will are good in her eyes, to support her husband, if bad to resist him, in any case to cease to be "his woman" and to be her self. You will agree, Sir, without any aspersion upon the lady who bears your name, that to depend upon her for your income would effect a most subtle and undesirable change in your psychology. Apart from that, this measure is of such importance directly to yourselves, in your own fight for liberty and equality and peace, that if any condition were to be attached to the guinea it would be this: that you should provide a wage to be paid by the State to those whose profession is marriage and motherhood. . . .

The outsiders then would bind themselves not only to earn their own livings, but to earn them so expertly that their refusal to earn them would be a matter of concern to the work master. They would bind themselves to obtain full knowledge of professional practices, and to reveal any instance of tyranny or abuse in their profession. And they would bind themselves not to continue to make money in any profession, but to cease all competition and to practise their profession experimentally, in the interests of research and for love of the work itself, when they had earned enough to live upon. Also they would bind themselves to remain outside any profession hostile to freedom, such as the making or the improvement of the weapons of war. And they would bind themselves to refuse to take office or honour from any society which, while professing to respect liberty, restricts it, like the universities of Oxford and Cambridge. And they would consider it their duty to investigate the claims of all public societies to which, like the Church and the universities, they are forced to contribute as taxpayers as carefully and fearlessly as they would investigate the claims of private societies to which they contribute voluntarily. They would make it their business to scrutinize the endowments of the schools and universities and the objects upon which that money is spent. As with the educational, so with the religious profession. By reading the New Testament in the first place and next those divines and historians whose works are all easily accessible to the daughters of educated men, they would make it their business to have some knowledge of the Christian religion and its history. Further they would inform themselves of the practice of that religion by attending Church services, by analysing the spiritual and intellectual value of sermons; by criticizing the opinions of men whose profession is religion as freely as they would criticize the opinions of any other body of men. Thus they would be creative in their activities, not merely critical. By criticizing education they would help to create a civilized society which protects culture and intellectual liberty. By criticizing religion they would attempt to free the religious spirit from its present servitude and would help, if need be, to create a new religion based, it might well be, upon the New Testament, but, it might well be, very different from the religion now

erected upon that basis. And in all this, and in much more than we have time to particularize, they would be helped, you will agree, by their position as outsiders, that freedom from unreal loyalties, that freedom from interested motives which are at present assured them by the State.

It would be easy to define in greater number and more exactly the duties of those who belong to the Society of Outsiders, but not profitable. Elasticity is essential; and some degree of secrecy, as will be shown later, is at present even more essential. But the description thus loosely and imperfectly given is enough to show you, Sir, that the Society of Outsiders has the same ends as your society—freedom, equality, peace; but that it seeks to achieve them by the means that a different sex, a different tradition, a different education, and the different values which result from those differences have placed within our reach. Broadly speaking, the main distinction between us who are outside society and you who are inside society must be that whereas you will make use of the means provided by your position—leagues, conferences, campaigns, great names, and all such public measures as your wealth and political influence place within your reach—we, remaining outside, will experiment not with public means in public but with private means in private. Those experiments will not be merely critical but creative. To take two obvious instances:—the outsiders will dispense with pageantry not from any puritanical dislike of beauty. On the contrary, it will be one of their aims to increase private beauty; the beauty of spring, summer, autumn; the beauty of flowers, silks, clothes; the beauty which brims not only every field and wood but every barrow in Oxford Street; the scattered beauty which needs only to be combined by artists in order to become visible to all. But they will dispense with the dictated, regimented, official pageantry, in which only one sex takes an active part—those ceremonies, for example, which depend upon the deaths of kings, or their coronations to inspire them. Again, they will dispense with personal distinctions—medals, ribbons, badges, hoods, gowns—not from any dislike of personal adornment, but because of the obvious effect of such distinctions to constrict, to stereotype and to destroy. Here, as so often, the example of the Fascist States is at hand to instruct us—for if we have no example of what we wish to be, we have, what is perhaps equally valuable, a daily and illuminating example of what we do not wish to be. With the example then, that they give us of the power of medals, symbols, orders and even, it would seem, of decorated ink-pots to hypnotize the human mind it must be our aim not to submit ourselves to such hypnotism. We must extinguish the coarse glare of advertisement and publicity, not merely because the limelight is apt to be held in incompetent hands, but because of the psychological effect of such illumination upon those who receive it. Consider next time you drive along a country road the attitude of a rabbit caught in the glare of a head-lamp—its glazed eyes, its rigid paws. Is there not good reason to think without going outside our own country, that the "attitudes," the false and unreal positions taken by the human form in England as well as in Germany, are due to the limelight which paralyses the free action of the human faculties and inhibits the human power to change and create new wholes much as a strong head-lamp paralyses the little creatures who run out of the darkness into its beams? It is a guess; guessing is dangerous; yet we have some reason to guide us in the guess that ease and freedom, the power to change and the power to grow, can only be preserved by obscurity; and that if we wish to help the human mind to create, and to prevent it from scoring the same rut repeatedly, we must do what we can to shroud it in darkness.

But enough of guessing. To return to facts—what chance is there, you may ask, that such a Society of Outsiders without office, meetings, leaders or any hierarchy, without so much as a form to be filled up, or a secretary to be paid, can be brought into existence, let alone work to any purpose? Indeed it would have been waste of time to write even so rough a definition of the Outsiders' Society were it merely a bubble of words, a covert form of sex or class glorification, serving, as so many such expressions do, to relieve the writer's emotion, lay the blame elsewhere, and then burst. Happily there is a model in being, a model from which the above sketch has been taken, furtively it is true, for the model, far from sitting still to be painted, dodges and disappears. That model then, the evidence that such a body, whether named or unnamed, exists and works is provided not yet by history or biography, for the outsiders have only had a positive existence for twenty years—that is since the professions were opened to the daughters of educated men. But evidence of their existence is provided by history and biography in the raw—by the newspapers that is—sometimes openly in the lines, sometimes covertly between them. There, anyone who wishes to verify the existence of such a body, can find innumerable proofs. Many, it is obvious, are of dubious value. For example, the fact that an immense amount of work is done by the daughters of educated men without pay or for very little pay need not be taken as a proof that they are experimenting of their own free will in the psychological value of poverty. Nor need the fact that many daughters of educated men do not "eat properly" serve as a proof that they are experimenting in the physical value of undernourishment. Nor need the fact that a very small proportion of women compared with men accept honours be held to prove that they are experimenting in the virtues of obscurity. Many such experiments are forced experiments and therefore of no positive value. But others of a much more positive kind are coming daily to the surface of the Press. . . .

"Speaking at a bazaar last week at the Plumstead Common Baptist Church the Mayoress (of Woolwich) said:

   . . . I myself would not even do as much as darn a sock to help in a war.

These remarks are resented by the majority of the Woolwich public, who hold that the Mayoress was, to say the least, rather tactless. Some 12,000 Woolwich electors are employed in Woolwich Arsenal on armament making" (*Evening Standard*, December 20th, 1937).

There is no need to comment upon the tactlessness of such a statement made publicly, in such circumstances; but the courage can scarcely fail to command our admiration, and the value of the experiment, from a practical point of view, should other mayoresses in other towns and other countries where the electors are employed in armament making follow suit, may well be immeasurable. At any rate, we shall agree that the Mayoress of Woolwich, Mrs. Kathleen Rance, has made a courageous and effective experiment in the prevention of war by not knitting socks. . . .

. . . Keen observers . . . could, if they liked, discover many more proofs that experiments are being made. . . . Mr. Wells even might be led to believe if he put his ear to the ground that a movement is going forward, not altogether imperceptibly, among educated men's daughters against the Nazi and the Fascist. But it is essential that the movement should escape the notice even of keen observers and of famous novelists.

Secrecy is essential. We must still hide what we are doing and thinking even though what we are doing and thinking is for our common cause. The necessity for this, in certain circumstances, is not hard to discover. When salaries are low, as Whitaker proves that they are, and jobs are hard to get and keep, as everybody knows them to be, it is, "to say the least, rather tactless," as the newspaper puts it, to criticize your master. Still, in country districts, as you yourself may be aware, farm labourers will not vote Labour. Economically, the educated man's daughter is much on a level with the farm labourer. But it is scarcely necessary for us to waste time in searching out what reason it is that inspires both his and her secrecy. Fear is a powerful reason; those who are economically dependent have strong reasons for fear. We need explore no further. But here you may remind us of a certain guinea, and draw our attention to the proud boast that our gift, small though it was, had made it possible not merely to burn a certain corrupt word, but to speak freely without fear or flattery. The boast it seems had an element of brag in it. Some fear, some ancestral memory prophesying war, still remains, it seems. There are still subjects that educated people, when they are of different sexes, even though financially independent, veil or hint at in guarded terms and then pass on. You may have observed it in real life; you may have detected it in biography. Even when they meet privately and talk, as we have boasted, about "politics and people, war and peace, barbarism and civilization," yet they evade and conceal. But it is so important to accustom ourselves to the duties of free speech, for without private there can be no public freedom, that we must try to uncover this fear and to face it. What then can be the nature of the fear that still makes concealment necessary between educated people and reduces our boasted freedom to a farce? . . . Again there are three dots; again they represent a gulf—of silence this time, of silence inspired by fear. And since we lack both the courage to explain it and the skill, let us lower the veil of St. Paul between us—in other words take shelter behind an interpreter. Happily we have one at hand whose credentials are above suspicion. It is none other than the pamphlet from which quotation has already been made, the Report of the Archbishops' Commission on the Ministry of Women. . . .

The Commissioners, you will agree, have performed the delicate and difficult task that we asked them to undertake. They have acted as interpreters between us. They have given us an admirable example of a profession in its purest state; and shown us how a profession bases itself upon mind and tradition. They have further explained why it is that educated people when they are of different sexes do not speak openly upon certain subjects. They have shown why the outsiders, even when there is no question of financial dependence, may still be afraid to speak freely or to experiment openly. And, finally, in words of scientific precision, they have revealed to us the nature of that fear. For as Professor Grensted gave his evidence, we, the daughters of educated men, seemed to be watching a surgeon at work—an impartial and scientific operator, who, as he dissected the human mind by human means laid bare for all to see what cause, what root lies at the bottom of our fear. It is an egg. Its scientific name is "infantile fixation." We, being unscientific, have named it wrongly. An egg we called it; a germ. We smelt it in the atmosphere; we detected its presence in Whitehall, in the universities, in the

Church. Now undoubtedly the Professor has defined it and described it so accurately that no daughter of an educated man, however uneducated she may be, can miscall it or misinterpret it in future. Listen to the description. "Strong feeling is aroused by any suggestion that women be admitted"—it matters not to which priesthood; the priesthood of medicine or the priesthood of science or the priesthood of the Church. Strong feeling, she can corroborate the Professor, is undoubtedly shown should she ask to be admitted. "This strength of feeling is clear evidence of the presence of powerful and subconscious motive." . . . But whatever the powerful and subconscious motives may be that lie behind the exclusion of women from the priesthoods, and plainly we cannot count them, let alone dig to the roots of them here, the educated man's daughter can testify from her own experience that they "commonly, and even usually, survive in the adult and betray their presence, below the level of conscious thought, by the strength of the emotions to which they give rise." And you will agree that to oppose strong emotion needs courage; and that when courage fails, silence and evasion are likely to manifest themselves.

But now that the interpreters have performed their task, it is time for us to raise the veil of St. Paul and to attempt, face to face, a rough and clumsy analysis of that fear and of the anger which causes that fear; for they may have some bearing upon the question you put us, how we can help you to prevent war. Let us suppose, then, that in the course of that bi-sexual private conversation about politics and people, war and peace, barbarism and civilization, some question has cropped up, about admitting, shall we say, the daughters of educated men to the Church or the Stock Exchange or the diplomatic service. The question is adumbrated merely; but we on our side of the table become aware at once of some "strong emotion" on your side "arising from some motive below the level of conscious thought" by the ringing of an alarm bell within us; a confused but tumultuous clamour: You shall not, shall not, shall not. . . . The physical symptoms are unmistakable. Nerves erect themselves; fingers automatically tighten upon spoon or cigarette; a glance at the private psychometer shows that the emotional temperature has risen from ten to twenty degrees above normal. Intellectually, there is a strong desire either to be silent; or to change the conversation; to drag in, for example, some old family servant, called Crosby, perhaps, whose dog Rover has died . . . and so evade the issue and lower the temperature.

But what analysis can we attempt of the emotions on the other side of the table—your side? Often, to be candid, while we are talking about Crosby, we are asking questions—hence a certain flatness in the dialogue—about you. What are the powerful and subconscious motives that are raising the hackles on your side of the table? . . .

The infantile fixation in the fathers then was, it is clear, a strong force, and all the stronger because it was a concealed force. But the fathers were met, as the nineteenth century drew on, by a force which had become so strong in its turn that it is much to be hoped that the psychologists will find some name for it. The old names as we have seen are futile and false. "Feminism," we have had to destroy. "The emancipation of women" is equally inexpressive and corrupt. To say that the daughters were inspired prematurely by the principles of anti-Fascism is merely to repeat the fashionable and hideous jargon of the moment. To call them champions of intellectual liberty and culture is to cloud the air with the dust of lecture halls and the damp dowdiness of public meetings. Moreover, none of these tags and labels express the real emotions that inspired the daughters' opposition to the infantile fixation of the fathers, because, as biography shows, that force had behind it many different emotions, and many that were contradictory. Tears were behind it, of course—tears, bitter tears: the tears of those whose desire for knowledge was frustrated. . . . Others wanted to travel; to explore Africa; to dig in Greece and Palestine. Some wanted to learn music, not to tinkle domestic airs, but to compose—operas, symphonies, quartets. Others wanted to paint, not ivy-clad cottages, but naked bodies. They all wanted—but what one word can sum up the variety of the things that they wanted, and had wanted, consciously or subconsciously, for so long? Josephine Butler's label—Justice, Equality, Liberty—is a fine one; but it is only a label, and in our age of innumerable labels, of multicoloured labels, we have become suspicious of labels; they kill and constrict. Nor does the old word "freedom" serve, for it was not freedom in the sense of license that they wanted; they wanted, like Antigone, not to break the laws, but to find the law. Ignorant as we are of human motives and ill supplied with words, let us then admit that no one word expresses the force which in the nineteenth century opposed itself to the force of the fathers. All we can safely say about that force was that it was a force of tremendous power. It forced open the doors of the private house. It opened Bond Street and Piccadilly; it opened cricket grounds and football grounds; it shrivelled flounces and stays; it made the oldest profession in the world (but Whitaker supplies no figures) unprofitable. In fifty years, in short, that force made the life lived by Lady Lovelace and Gertrude Gell unlivable, and almost incredible. The fathers, who had triumphed over the strongest emotions of strong men, had to yield.

If that full stop were the end of the story, the final slam of the door, we could turn at once to your letter, Sir, and to the form which you have asked us to fill up. But it was not the end; it was the beginning. Indeed though we have used the past, we shall soon find ourselves using the present tense. The fathers in private, it is true, yielded; but the fathers in public, massed together in societies, in professions, were even more subject to the fatal disease than the fathers in private. The disease had acquired a motive, had connected itself with a right, or a conception, which made it still more virulent outside the house than within. The desire to support wife and children—what motive could be more powerful, or deeply rooted? For it was connected with manhood itself—a man who could not support his family failed in his own conception of manliness. And was not that conception as deep in him as the conception of womanhood in his daughter? It was those motives, those rights and conceptions that were now challenged. To protect them, and from women, gave, and gives, rise it can scarcely be doubted to an emotion perhaps below the level of conscious thought but certainly of the utmost violence. The infantile fixation develops, directly the priest's right to practise his profession is challenged, to an aggravated and exacerbated emotion to which the name sex taboo is scientifically applied. . . . But since the emotion itself had increased in strength it became necessary to invoke the help of stronger allies to excuse and conceal it. Nature was called in; Nature it was claimed who is not only omniscient but unchanging, had made the brain of woman of the wrong shape or size. "Anyone," writes Bertrand Russell, "who desires amusement may be advised to look up the tergiversations of eminent craniologists in their attempts to prove from brain measurements that women are stupider than men" (*The Scientific Outlook*, p. 17). Science, it would seem, is not sexless; she is a man, a father, and infected too. Science, thus infected, produced measurements to order: the brain was too small to be examined. Many years were spent waiting before the sacred gates of the universities and hospitals for permission to have the brains that the professors said that Nature had made incapable of passing examinations examined. When at last permission was granted the examinations were passed. . . .

And if, Sir, pausing in England now, we turn on the wireless of the daily press we shall hear what answer the fathers who are infected with infantile fixation now are making to those questions now. "Homes are the real places of women. . . . Let them go back to their homes. . . . The Government should give work to men. . . . A strong protest is to be made by the Ministry of Labour. . . . Women must not rule over men. . . . There

are two worlds, one for women, the other for men. . . .
Let them learn to cook our dinners. . . . Women have
failed. . . . They have failed. . . . They have failed. . . ."

Even here, even now, the clamour, the uproar that
infantile fixation is making is such that we can hardly
hear ourselves speak; it takes the words out of our
mouths; it makes us say what we have not said. As we
listen to the voices we seem to hear an infant crying in
the night, the black night that now covers Europe, and
with no language but a cry, Ay, ay, ay, ay. . . . But it is
not a new cry, it is a very old cry. Let us shut off the
wireless and listen to the past. We are in Greece now;
Christ has not been born yet, nor St. Paul either. But
listen:

"Whomsoever the city may appoint, that man must
be obeyed, in little things and great, in just things and
unjust . . . disobedience is the worst of evils. . . . We
must support the cause of order, and in no wise suffer
a woman to worst us. . . . They must be women, and not
range at large. Servants, take them within." That is the
voice of Creon, the dictator. To whom Antigone, who
was to have been his daughter, answered, "Not such
are the laws set among men by the justice who dwells
with the gods below." But she had neither capital nor
force behind her. And Creon said: "I will take her
where the path is loneliest, and hide her, living, in a
rocky vault." And he shut her not in Holloway or in a
concentration camp, but in a tomb. And Creon we
read brought ruin on his house, and scattered the land
with the bodies of the dead. It seems, Sir, as we listen
to the voices of the past, as if we were looking at the
photograph again, at the picture of dead bodies and
ruined houses that the Spanish Government sends us
almost weekly. Things repeat themselves it seems. Pictures and voices are the same today as they were 2,000
years ago.

Such then is the conclusion to which our enquiry
into the nature of fear has brought us—the fear which
forbids freedom in the private house. That fear, small,
insignificant and private as it is, is connected with the
other fear, the public fear, which is neither small nor
insignificant, the fear which has led you to ask us to
help you to prevent war. Otherwise we should not be
looking at the picture again. But it is not the same
picture that caused us at the beginning of this letter to
feel the same emotions—you called them "horror and
disgust"; we called them horror and disgust. For as this
letter has gone on, adding fact to fact, another picture
has imposed itself upon the foreground. It is the figure
of a man; some say, others deny, that he is Man himself, the quintessence of virility, the perfect type of
which all the others are imperfect adumbrations. He is
a man certainly. His eyes are glazed; his eyes glare. His
body, which is braced in an unnatural position, is

tightly cased in uniform. Upon the breast of that uniform are sewn several medals and other mystic symbols. His hand is upon a sword. He is called in German
and Italian Führer or Duce; in our own language
Tyrant or Dictator. And behind him lie ruined houses
and dead bodies—men, women, and children. But we
have not laid that picture before you in order to excite
once more the sterile emotion of hate. On the contrary
it is in order to release other emotions such as the
human figure, even thus crudely in a coloured photograph, arouses in us who are human beings. For it
suggests a connection and for us a very important
connection. It suggests that the public and the private
worlds are inseparably connected; that the tyrannies
and servilities of the one are the tyrannies and servilities of the other. But the human figure even in a
photograph suggests other and more complex emotions. It suggests that we cannot dissociate ourselves
from that figure but are ourselves that figure. It suggests that we are not passive spectators doomed to
unresisting obedience but by our thoughts and actions
can ourselves change that figure. A common interest
unites us; it is one world, one life. How essential it is
that we should realise that unity the dead bodies, the
ruined houses prove. For such will be our ruin if you in
the immensity of your public abstractions forget the
private figure, or if we in the intensity of our private
emotions forget the public world. Both houses will be
ruined, the public and the private, the material and
the spiritual, for they are inseparably connected. But
with your letter before us we have reason to hope. For
by asking our help you recognise that connection; and
by reading your words we are reminded of other connections that lie far deeper than the facts on the surface. Even here, even now your letter tempts us to shut
our ears to these little facts, these trivial details, to
listen not to the bark of the guns and the bray of the
gramophones but to the voices of the poets, answering
each other, assuring us of a unity that rubs out divisions
as if they were chalk marks only; to discuss with you the
capacity of the human spirit to overflow boundaries
and make unity out of multiplicity. But that would be
to dream—to dream the recurring dream that has
haunted the human mind since the beginning of time;
the dream of peace, the dream of freedom. But, with
the sound of the guns in your ears you have not asked
us to dream. You have not asked us what peace is; you
have asked us how to prevent war. Let us then leave it
to the poets to tell us what the dream is; and fix our eyes
upon the photograph again: the fact.

Whatever the verdict of others may be upon the
man in uniform—and opinions differ—there is your
letter to prove that to you the picture is the picture of
evil. And though we look upon that picture from differ-

ent angles our conclusion is the same as yours—it is evil. We are both determined to do what we can to destroy the evil which that picture represents, you by your methods, we by ours. And since we are different, our help must be different. What ours can be we have tried to show—how imperfectly, how superficially there is no need to say. But as a result the answer to your question must be that we can best help you to prevent war not by repeating your words and following your methods but by finding new words and creating new methods. We can best help you to prevent war not by joining your society but by remaining outside your society but in co-operation with its aim. That aim is the same for us both. It is to assert "the rights of all—all men and women—to the respect in their persons of the great principles of Justice and Equality and Lib-

erty." To elaborate further is unnecessary, for we have every confidence that you interpret those words as we do. And excuses are unnecessary, for we can trust you to make allowances for those deficiencies which we foretold and which this letter has abundantly displayed.

To return then to the form that you have sent and ask us to fill up: for the reasons given we will leave it unsigned. But in order to prove as substantially as possible that our aims are the same as yours, here is the guinea, a free gift, given freely, without any other conditions than you choose to impose upon yourself. It is the third of three guineas; but the three guineas, you will observe, though given to three different treasurers are all given to the same cause, for the causes are the same and inseparable. . . .

Ding Ling (1904–85)

In a review of I Myself Am a Woman: Selected Writings of Ding Ling, edited by Tani E. Barlow, David Der-wei Wang has epitomized the heroic and perplexing images of Ding Ling as follows:

> Writer, editor, feminist, revolutionary, and ideologue, Ding Ling is one of the most controversial figures of modern Chinese literary and cultural history. Her writings, be they decadent or didactic, erotic or political, appear crude to contemporary readers, while her romantic liaisons, ideological conversions, revolutionary adventures, purges and sufferings, and her resurgence in the late seventies after having been "missing" for more than two decades, make her a larger-than-life figure.

In this focus on the "larger-than-life" dimensions of Ding Ling's political and personal engagements, the substance of her theoretical ideas has been somewhat obscured. For those who do not read Chinese, especially readers reliant mainly on English, the problem is exacerbated by the limited availability of Ding Ling's writings in English translation. Moreover, her fiction and other works defy ready categorization by style or ideology.

Ding Ling was born into a declining family of the gentry in 1904 as Jiang Bingzhi, adopting the pseudonym Ding Ling in later years. Her father died when she was three years old, and her mother, Yu Manzhen (memorialized in Ding Ling's 1933 novel Mother), exemplified the struggles of a class of Chinese women liberating themselves from bound feet and dependency, herself becoming an innovative educator and political activist. In 1919 Ding Ling entered the world of radical politics and culture inaugurated by the May Fourth movement, moving first to Changsha and later Shanghai. There she met the poet Hu Yepin, a member of the League of Left-Wing Writers, with whom she lived until his arrest and summary execution by the Nationalist government in early 1931, only a few months after the birth of their child. Ding Ling herself was arrested in 1933 and held until 1936, when she escaped to join the Communist forces in Yan'an, where she came to hold a number of high posts in political training, culture, and the arts.

The short story "Miss Sophie's Diary" (1927) first drew attention to Ding Ling as a writer and later figured in repeated attacks upon her for alleged sexual immorality. "Yecao" (1929), a story from the same period, reflects her developing sense of the tensions between (in her words) the "level-headed and rational woman" and "unduly passionate emotions," between love and work, between "the social environment that caused women to overemphasize emotions" and the absorbing experience of creative work for a woman writer (1989: 105). "When I Was in Xia Village" (1941) reflects a more multifaceted and mature treatment of the complexities of women's experience—especially the experience of rape—in the political context of a village in the Yan'an period. Indirectly, the story expressed Ding Ling's belief that literature should embody criticism as well as propaganda for the social and cultural transformations promoted by the Yan'an government.

As editor and writer for the literary page of the party newspaper, Liberation Daily, Ding Ling published in 1942 her "Thoughts on March 8," International Women's Day. Her critique of ongoing inequality of women even under the new regime opened the way for others to raise criticisms of the official party line and policies. In response, Mao Zedong issued his "Talks at the Yan'an Forum on Arts and Literature," in which he laid down a set of restrictive principles asserting the primacy of revolutionary needs over the freedom of art and literature, and leading to the rectification campaign imposed in the later years of World War II. Ding Ling was removed from her positions but after a period of study in the party school and reform work in the countryside, she was recalled to favor and in the subsequent years, particularly after the establishment of the People's Republic of China, she became increasingly prominent in the party hierarchy and literary circles. In 1948 she published The Sun Shines over the Sanggan River, a novel about the process of land reform and class struggle in the countryside, which won widespread international acclaim and brought her the Stalin prize in 1951.

In 1957, however, she was denounced for rightist activity, her works were banned, she was expelled from the Communist Party and exiled to a state labor farm in the northeast wilderness, together with Chen Ming, a younger writer whom she had married in 1942. Her fate was unknown for many years. After a difficult period of adjustment she was assigned to teach adult literacy and was able to resume writing, but during the Cultural Revolution in 1966 she was subjected to more intense attacks and abuse and her manuscripts were destroyed. From 1970 to 1975 she was held in a Beijing prison in solitary confinement for five years. Released in 1975, she was officially rehabilitated in 1979, allowed to resume her literary career, and even permitted to travel to the United States in 1981. She continued to write until her death from breast cancer in 1985.

In "When I Was in Xia Village," the characters speak of "Jap devils," a usage then current in China under war conditions. The story portrays the physical, social, and psychological destruction wrought by the Japanese occupation. Focusing on Zhenzhen, a young village woman secretly sent on intelligence missions to Japanese military units, it raises issues of sexual abuse and disease in wartime, and explores their complex consequences. These issues have contemporary resonance in international movements to gain reparations for so-called "comfort women" and secure recognition of rape and sexual slavery as violations of human rights.

There has been extensive debate about Ding Ling's feminism, her political loyalties, and her refusal to use her persecution "as a stick to beat the party" (Feuerwerker, 1984). However, the overall theoretical significance and impact of her works remain to be fully explored. What is clear is that for Ding Ling, literature and politics were inseparable to the end.

The selections below are from I Myself Am a Woman: Selected Writings of Ding Ling, edited by Tani E. Barlow with Gary J. Bjorge.

BAC

Sources and Suggested Readings

Barlow, Tani E. "Gender and Identity in Ding Ling's Mother. In Modern Chinese Women Writers: Critical Appraisals, ed. Michael S. Duke. Armonk, N.Y.: M. E. Sharpe, 1989.

Chow, Rey. Woman and Chinese Modernity: The Politics of Reading between West and East. Minneapolis: University of Minnesota Press, 1991.

Ding Ling. I Myself Am a Woman: Selected Writings of Ding Ling. Ed. Tani E. Barlow with Gary J. Bjorge. Boston: Beacon Press, 1989.

———. The Sun Shines over the Sanggan River. Trans. Yang Hsien-yi and Gladys Yang. Peking: Foreign Languages Press, 1954.

Feuerwerker, Yi-tsi Mei. Ding Ling's Fiction: Ideology and Narrative in Modern Chinese Literature. Cambridge: Harvard University Press, 1982.

———. "In Quest of the Writer Ding Ling." Feminist Studies 10, 1 (Spring 1984): 65–83.

Liu, Lydia H. "The Female Tradition in Modern Chinese Literature: Negotiating Feminisms across East/West Boundaries." Genders 12 (Winter 1991): 22–44.

Nienling, Liu. "The Vanguards of the Women's Liberation Movement—Lu Yin, Bingxin, and Ding Ling." Chinese Studies in History (Winter 1989–90): 22–45.

Titov, A. "From the Cohort of the Unbending (In Memory of Ding Ling)." Far Eastern Affairs 1 (1988): 98–103.

Wang, David Der-Wei. Review of I Myself Am a Woman,

ed. Tani E. Barlow with Gary J. Bjorge. Journal of the American Oriental Society 111, 3 (1991): 617–18.

Wei, William. "From Miss Sophia to Comrade Wanxiang." American Book Review 12, 4 (September 1990).

When I Was in Xia Village (1941)

Because of the turmoil in the Political Department, Comrade Mo Yü decided to send me to stay temporarily in a neighboring village. Actually, I was already completely well, but the opportunity to rest for a while in a quiet environment and arrange my notes from the past three months did have its attractions. So I agreed to spend two weeks in Xia Village, a place about ten miles from the Political Department.

A female comrade from the Propaganda Department, who was apparently on a work assignment, went with me. Since she wasn't a person who enjoyed conversation, however, the journey was rather lonely. Also, because her feet had once been bound and my own spirits were low, we traveled slowly. We set out in the morning, but it was nearly sunset by the time we reached our destination.

The village looked much like any other from a distance, but I knew it contained a very beautiful Catholic church that had escaped destruction and a small grove of pine trees. The place where I would be staying was in the midst of these trees, which clung to the hillside. From that spot it would be possible to look straight across to the church. By now I could see orderly rows of cave dwellings and the green trees above them. I felt content with the village.

My traveling companion had given me the impression that the village was very busy, but when we entered it, not even a single child or dog was to be seen. The only movement was dry leaves twirling about lightly in the wind. They would fly a short distance, then drop to earth again.

"This used to be an elementary school, but last year the Jap devils destroyed it. Look at those steps over there. That used to be a big classroom," my companion, Agui, told me. She was somewhat excited now, not so reserved as she had been during the day. Pointing to a large empty courtyard, she continued: "A year and a half ago, this area was full of life. Every evening after supper, the comrades gathered here to play soccer or basketball." Becoming more agitated, she asked, "Why isn't anyone here? Should we go to the assembly hall or head up the hill? We don't know where they've taken our luggage either. We have to straighten that out first."

On the wall next to the gate of the village assembly hall, many white paper slips had been pasted. They read "Office of the [Communist] Association," "Xia Village Branch of the [Communist] Association," and so on. But when we went inside, we couldn't find a soul. It was completely quiet, with only a few tables set about. We were both standing there dumbly when suddenly a man rushed in. He looked at us for a moment, seemed about to ask us something, but swallowed his words and prepared to dash away. We called to him to stop, however, and made him answer our questions.

"The people of the village? They've all gone to the west door. Baggage? Hmm. Yes, there was baggage. It was carried up the hill some time ago to Liu Erma's home." As he talked, he sized us up.

Learning that he was a member of the Peasant's Salvation Association, we asked him to accompany us up the hill and also asked him to deliver a note to one of the local comrades. He agreed to take the note, but he wouldn't go with us. He seemed impatient and ran off by himself.

The street too was very quiet. The doors of several shops were closed. Others were still open, exposing pitch-black interiors. We still couldn't find anyone. Fortunately, Agui was familiar with the village and led me up the hill. It was already dark. The winter sun sets very quickly.

The hill was not high, and a large number of stone cave dwellings were scattered here and there from the bottom to the top. In a few places, people were standing out in front peering into the distance. Agui knew very well that we had not yet reached our destination, but whenever we met someone she asked, "Is this the way to Liu Erma's house?" "How far is it to Liu Erma's house?" "Could you please tell me the way to Liu Erma's house?" Or, she would ask, "Did you notice any baggage being sent to Liu Erma's house? Is Liu Erma home?"

The answers we received always satisfied us, and this continued right up to the most distant and highest house, which was the Liu family's. Two small dogs were the first to greet us. Then a woman came out and asked who we were. As soon as they heard it was me, two more women came out. Holding a lantern, they escorted us into the courtyard and then into a cave on the side toward the east. The cave was virtually empty. On the *kang* under the window were piled my bedroll, my small leather carrying case, and Agui's quilt.

Some of the people there knew Agui. They took her hand and asked her many questions, and after a

while they led her out, leaving me alone in the room. I arranged my bed and was about to lie down when suddenly they all crowded back in again. One of Liu Erma's daughters-in-law was carrying a bowl of noodles. Agui, Liu Erma, and a young girl were holding bowls, chopsticks, and a dish of onions and pepper. The young girl also brought in a brazier of burning coal.

Attentively, they urged me to eat some noodles and touched my hands and arms. Liu Erma and her daughter-in-law also sat down on the *kang*. There was an air of mystery about them as they continued the conversation interrupted by their entry into the room.

At first I thought I had caused their amazement, but gradually I realized that this wasn't the case. They were interested in only one thing—the topic of their conversation. Since all I heard were a few fragmentary sentences, I couldn't understand what they were talking about. This was especially true of what Liu Erma said because she frequently lowered her voice, as if afraid that someone might overhear her. Agui had changed completely. She now appeared quite capable and was very talkative. She listened closely to what the others were saying and seemed able to grasp the essence of their words. The daughter-in-law and the young girl said little. At times they added a word or two, but for the most part they just listened intently to what Agui and Liu Erma were saying. They seemed afraid to miss a single word.

Suddenly the courtyard was filled with noise. A large number of people had rushed in, and they all seemed to be talking at once. Liu Erma and the others climbed nervously off the *kang* and hurried outside. Without thinking, I followed along behind them to see what was happening.

By this time the courtyard was in complete darkness. Two red paper lanterns bobbed and weaved above the crowd. I worked my way into the throng and looked around. I couldn't see anything. The others also were squeezing in for no apparent reason. They seemed to want to say more, but they did not. I heard only simple exchanges that confused me even more.

"Yüwa, are you here too?"

"Have you seen her yet?"

"Yes, I've seen her. I was a little afraid."

"What is there to be afraid of? She's just a human being, and prettier than ever too."

At first I was sure that they were talking about a new bride, but people said that wasn't so. Then I thought there was a prisoner present, but that was wrong too. I followed the crowd to the doorway of the central cave, but all there was to see was more people packed tightly together. Thick smoke obscured my vision, so I had no choice but to back away. Others were also leaving by now, and the courtyard was much less crowded.

Since I couldn't sleep, I set about rearranging my carrying case by the lantern light. I paged through several notebooks, looked at photographs, and sharpened some pencils. I was obviously tired, but I also felt the kind of excitement that comes just before a new life begins. I prepared a time schedule for myself and was determined to adhere to it, beginning the very next day.

At that moment there was a man's voice at the door. "Are you asleep, comrade?" Before I could reply, the fellow entered the room. He was about twenty years old, a rather refined-looking country youth. "I received Director Mo's letter some time ago," he said. "This area is relatively quiet. Don't worry about a thing. That's my job. If you need something, don't hesitate to ask Liu Erma. Director Mo said you wanted to stay here for two weeks. Fine. If you enjoy your visit, we'd be happy to have you stay longer. I live in a neighboring cave, just below these. If you need me, just send someone to find me."

He declined to come up on the kang, and since there was no bench on the floor to sit on, I jumped down and said, "Ah! You must be Comrade Ma. Did you receive the note I sent you? Please sit down and talk for a while."

I knew that he held a position of some responsibility in the village. As a student he had not yet finished junior high school.

"They tell me you've written a lot of books," he responded. "It's too bad we haven't seen a single one." As he spoke he looked at my open carrying case that was lying on the kang. Our conversation turned to the subject of the local level of study. Then he said, "After you've rested for a few days, we'll definitely invite you to give a talk. It can be to a mass meeting or to a training class. In any case, you'll certainly be able to help us. Our most difficult task here is 'cultural recreation.'"

I had seen many young men like him at the Front. When I first met them, I was always amazed. I felt that these youth, who were somewhat remote from me, were really changing fast. Changing the subject, I asked him, "What was going on just now?"

"Zhenzhen, the daughter of Liu Dama, has returned," he answered. "I never thought she could be so great." I immediately sensed a joyful, radiant twinkle in his eyes. As I was about to ask another question, he added, "She's come back from the Japanese area. She's been working there for over a year."

"Oh my!" I gasped.

He was about to tell me more when someone outside called for him. All he could say was that he'd be sure to have Zhenzhen call on me the next day. As if to provoke my interest further, he added that Zhenzhen must certainly have a lot of material for stories.

It was very late when Agui came back. She lay down on the kang but could not sleep. She tossed and turned and sighed continuously. I was very tired, but I still wished that she would tell me something about the events of the evening.

"No, comrade," she said. "I can't talk about it now. I'm too upset. I'll tell you tomorrow. Ahh . . . How miserable it is to be a woman." After this she covered her head with her quilt and lay completely still, no longer sighing. I didn't know when she finally fell asleep.

Early the next morning I stepped outside for a stroll, and before I knew it I had walked down to the village. I went into a general store to rest and buy red dates for Liu Erma to put in the rice porridge. As soon as the owner learned that I was living with Liu Erma, his small eyes narrowed and he asked me in a low, excited voice, "Did you get a look at her niece? I hear her disease has even taken her nose. That's because she was abused by the Jap devils." Turning his head, he called to his wife, who was standing in the inner doorway, "She has nerve, coming home! It's revenge against her father, Liu Fusheng."

"That girl was always frivolous. You saw the way she used to roam around the streets. Wasn't she Xia Dabao's old flame? If he hadn't been poor, wouldn't she have married him a long time ago?" As she finished speaking, the old woman lifted her skirts and came into the store.

The owner turned his face back toward me and said, "There are so many rumors." His eyes stopped blinking and his expression became very serious. "It's said that she has slept with at least a hundred men. Humph! I've heard that she even became the wife of a Japanese officer. Such a shameful woman should not be allowed to return."

Not wanting to argue with him, I held back my anger and left. I didn't look back, but felt that he had again narrowed his small eyes and was feeling smug as he watched me walk away. As I neared the corner by the Catholic church, I overheard a conversation by two women who were drawing water at the well. One said, "She sought out Father Lu and told him she definitely wanted to be a nun. When Father Lu asked her for a reason, she didn't say a word, just cried. Who knows what she did there? Now she's worse than a prostitute . . ."

"Yesterday they told me she walks with a limp. Achh! How can she face people?"

"Someone said she's even wearing a gold ring that a Jap devil gave her!"

"I understand she's been as far away as Datong and has seen many things. She can even speak Japanese."

My walk was making me unhappy, so I returned home. Since Agui had already gone out, I sat alone in my room and read a small pamphlet. After a while, I raised my eyes and noticed two large baskets for storing grain sitting near the wall. They must have had a long history, because they were as black as the wall itself. Opening the movable portion of the paper window, I peered out at the gray sky. The weather had changed completely from what it had been when I arrived the day before. The hard ground of the courtyard had been swept clean, and at the far edge a tree with a few withered branches stood out starkly against the leaden sky. There wasn't a single person to be seen.

I opened my carrying case, took out pen and paper, and wrote two letters. I wondered why Agui had not yet returned. I had forgotten that she had work to do. I was somehow thinking that she had come to be my companion. The days of winter are very short, but right then I was feeling that they were even longer than summer days.

Some time later, the young girl who had been in my room the night before came out into the courtyard. I immediately jumped down off the *kang*, stepped out the door, and called to her, but she just looked at me and smiled before rushing into another cave. I walked around the courtyard twice and then stopped to watch a hawk fly into the grove of trees by the church. The courtyard there had many large trees. I started walking again and, on the right side of the courtyard, picked up the sound of a woman crying. She was trying to stop, frequently blowing her nose.

I tried hard to control myself. I thought about why I was here and about all my plans. I had to rest and live according to the time schedule I had made. I returned to my room, but I couldn't sleep and had no interest in writing in my notebook.

Fortunately, a short while later Liu Erma came to see me. The young girl was with her, and her daughter-in-law arrived soon after. The three of them climbed up on the *kang* and took seats around the small brazier. The young girl looked closely at my things, which were laid out on the little square *kang* table.

"At that time no one could take care of anyone else," Liu Erma said, talking about the Japanese attack on Xia Village a year and a half before. "Those of us who lived on the hilltop were luckier. We could run away quickly. Many who lived in the village could not escape. Apparently it was all fate. Just then, on that day, our family's Zhenzhen had run over to the Catholic church. Only later did we learn that her unhappiness about what was happening had caused her to go to talk to the foreign priest about becoming a nun. Her father was in the midst of negotiating a marriage for her with the young proprietor of a rice store in Xiliu Village. He was almost thirty, a widower, and his family was well respected. We all said he would be a good match, but Zhenzhen said no and broke into tears before her father. In other matters, her father had always deferred to her wishes, but in this case the old man was adamant. He had no son and had always wanted to betroth his daughter to a good man. Who would have thought that Zhenzhen would turn around in anger and run off to the Catholic church. It was at that moment that the Japs caught her. How could her mother and father help grieving?"

"Was that her mother crying?"

"Yes."

"And your niece?"

"Well, she's really just a child. When she came back yesterday, she cried for a long time, but today she went to the assembly in high spirits. She's only eighteen."

"I heard she was the wife of a Japanese. Is that true?"

"It's hard to say. We haven't been able to find out for sure. There are many rumors, of course. She's contracted a disease, but how could anyone keep clean in such a place? The possibility of her marrying the merchant seems to be over. Who would want a woman who was abused by the Jap devils? She definitely has the disease. Last night she said so herself. This time she's changed a lot. When she talks about those devils, she shows no more emotion than if she were talking about an ordinary meal at home. She's only eighteen, but she has no sense of embarrassment at all."

"Xia Dabao came again today," the daughter-in-law said quietly, her questioning eyes fixed on Erma.

"Who is Xia Dabao?" I asked.

"He's a young man who works in the village flour mill," replied Liu Erma. "When he was young, he and Zhenzhen were classmates for a year. They like each other very much, but his family was poor, even poorer than ours. He didn't dare do anything, but our Zhenzhen was head over heels in love with him and kept clinging to him. Then she was upset when he didn't respond. Isn't it because of him that she wanted to be a nun? After Zhenzhen fell into the hands of the Jap devils, he often came to see her parents. At first just the sight of him made Zhenzhen's father angry. At times he cursed him, but Xia Dabao would say nothing. After a scolding he would leave and then come back another day. Dabao is really a good boy. Now he's even a squad leader in the self-defense corps. Today he came once again, apparently to talk with Zhenzhen's mother about marrying Zhenzhen. All I could hear was her crying. Later he left in tears himself."

"Does he know about your niece's situation?"

"How could he help knowing? There is no one in this village who doesn't know everything. They all know more than we do ourselves."

"Mother, everyone says the Xia Dabao is foolish," the young girl interjected.

"Humph! The boy has a good conscience. I approve of this match. Since the Jap devils came, who has any money? Judging from the words of Zhenzhen's parents, I think they approve too. If not him, who? Even without mentioning her disease, her reputation is enough to deter anyone."

"He was the one wearing the dark blue jacket and the copper-colored felt hat with the turned-up brim," the young girl said. Her eyes were sparkling with curiosity, and she seemed to understand this matter very well.

His figure began to take shape in my memory. When I went out for my walk earlier that morning, I had seen an alert, honest-looking young man who fit this description. He had been standing outside my courtyard, but had not shown any intention of coming in. On my way home, I had seen him again, this time emerging from the pine woods beyond the cave dwellings. I had thought he was someone from my courtyard or from a neighboring one and hadn't paid much attention to him. As I recalled him now, I felt that he was a rather capable man, not a bad young man at all.

I now feared that my plan for rest and recuperation could not be realized. Why were my thoughts so confused? I wasn't particularly anxious to meet anybody, and yet my mind still couldn't rest. Agui had come in during the conversation, and now seemed to sense my feelings. As she went out with the others, she gave me a knowing smile. I understood her meaning and busied myself with arranging the *kang*. My bedroll, the lamp, and the fire all seemed much brighter. I had just placed the tea kettle on the fire when Agui returned. Behind her I heard another person.

"We have a guest, comrade!" Agui called. Even before she finished speaking, I heard someone giggling.

Standing in the doorway, I grasped the hands of this person whom I had not seen before. They were burning hot, and I couldn't help being a bit startled. She followed Agui up onto the *kang* and sat down. A single long braid hung down her back.

In the eyes of the new arrival, the cave that depressed me seemed to be something new and fresh. She looked around at everything with an excited glint in her eyes. She sat opposite me, her body tilted back slightly and her two hands spread apart on the bedroll for support. She didn't seem to want to say anything. Her eyes finally came to rest on my face.

The shadows lengthened her eyes and made her chin quite pointed. But even though her eyes were in deep shadow, her pupils shone brightly in the light of the lamp and the fire. They were like two open windows in a summer home in the country, clear and clean.

I didn't know how to begin a conversation without touching an open wound and hurting her self-respect. So my first move was to pour her a cup of hot tea.

It was Zhenzhen who spoke first: "Are you a Southerner? I think so. You aren't like the people from this province."

"Have you seen many Southerners?" I asked, thinking it best to talk about what she wanted to talk about.

"No," she said, shaking her head. Her eyes still fixed on me, she added, "I've only seen a few. They always seem a little different. I like you people from the South. Southern women, unlike us, can all read many, many books. I want to study with you. Will you teach me?"

I expressed my willingness to do so, and she quickly continued, "Japanese women also can read a lot of books. All those devil soldiers carried a few well-written letters, some from wives, some from girlfriends. Some were written by girls they didn't even know. They would include a photograph and use syrupy language. I don't know if those girls were sincere or not, but they always made the devils hold their letters to their hearts like precious treasures."

"I understand that you can speak Japanese," I said. "Is that true?"

Her face flushed slightly before she replied, in a very open manner, "I was there for such a long time. I went around and around for over a year. I can speak a fair amount. Being able to understand their language had many advantages."

"Did you go to a lot of different places with them?"

"I wasn't always with the same unit. People think that because I was the wife of a Jap officer I enjoyed luxury. Actually, I came back here twice before. Altogether, this is my third time. I was ordered to go on this last mission. There was no choice. I was familiar with the area, the work was important, and it was impossible to find anyone else in a short time. I won't be sent back anymore. They're going to treat my disease. That's fine with me because I've missed my dad and mom, and I'm glad to be able to come back to see them. My mother, though, is really hopeless. When I'm not home, she cries. When I'm here, she still cries."

"You must have known many hardships."

"She has endured unthinkable suffering," Agui interrupted, her face twisted in a pained expression. In a voice breaking with emotion, she added, "It's a real tragedy to be a woman, isn't it, Zhenzhen?" She slid over to be next to her.

"Suffering?" Zhenzhen asked, her thoughts apparently far, far away. "Right now I can't say for certain. Some things were hard to endure at the time, but when I recall them now they don't seem like much. Other things were no problem to do when I did them, but when I think about them now I'm very sad. More than a year . . . It's all past. Since I came back this time, a great many people have looked at me strangely. As far as the people of this village are concerned, I'm an outsider. Some are very friendly to me. Others avoid me. The members of my family are just the same. They all like to steal looks at me. Nobody treats me the way they used to. Have I changed? I've thought about this a great deal, and I don't think I've changed at all. If I have changed, maybe it's that my heart has become somewhat harder. But could anyone spend time in such a place and not become hardhearted? People have no choice. They're forced to be like that!"

There was no outward sign of her disease. Her complexion was ruddy. Her voice was clear. She showed no signs of inhibition or rudeness. She did not exaggerate. She gave the impression that she had never had any complaints or sad thoughts. Finally, I could restrain myself no longer and asked her about her disease.

"People are always like that, even if they find themselves in worse situations. They brace themselves and see it through. Can you just give up and die? Later, after I made contact with our own people, I became less afraid. As I watched the Jap devils suffer defeat in battle and the guerrillas take action on all sides as a result of the tricks I was playing, I felt better by the day. I felt that even though my life was hard, I could still manage. Somehow I had to find a way to survive, and if at all possible, to live a life that was meaningful. That's why I'm pleased that they intend to treat my disease. It will be better to be cured. Actually, these past few days I haven't felt too bad. On the way home, I stayed in Zhangjiayi for two days and was given two shots and some medicine to take orally. The worst time was in the fall. I was told that my insides were rotting away, and then, because of some important information and the fact that no one could be found to take my place, I had to go back. That night I walked alone in the dark for ten miles. Every single step was painful. My mind was filled with the desire to sit down and rest. If the work hadn't been so important, I definitely wouldn't have gone back. But I had to. Ahh! I was afraid I might be recognized by the Jap devils, and I was also worried about missing my rendezvous. After it was over, I slept for a full week before I could pull myself together. It really isn't all that easy to die, is it?"

Without waiting for me to respond, she continued on with her story. At times she stopped talking and looked at us. Perhaps she was searching for reactions on our faces. Or maybe she was only thinking of something else. I could see that Agui was more troubled than Zhenzhen. For the most part she sat in silence, and when she did speak, it was only for a sentence or two. Her words gave voice to a limitless sympathy for Zhenzhen, but her expression when silent revealed even more clearly how moved she was by what Zhenzhen was saying. Her soul was being crushed. She herself was feeling the suffering that Zhenzhen had known before.

It was my impression that Zhenzhen had no intention whatever of trying to elicit sympathy from others. Even as others took upon themselves part of the misfortune that she had suffered, she seemed unaware of it. But that very fact made others feel even more sympathetic. It would have been better if, instead of listening to her recount the events of this period with a calmness that almost made you think she was talking about someone else, you could have heard her cry. Probably you would have cried with her, but you would have felt better.

After a while Agui began to cry, and Zhenzhen turned to comfort her. There were many things that I had wanted to discuss with Zhenzhen, but I couldn't bring myself to say anything. I wished to remain silent. After Zhenzhen left, I forced myself to read by the lamp for an hour. Not once did I look at Agui or ask her a question, even though she was lying very close to me, even though she tossed and turned and sighed all the time, unable to fall asleep.

After this Zhenzhen came to talk with me every day. She did not talk about herself alone. She very often showed great curiosity about many aspects of my life that were beyond her own experiences. At times, when my words were far removed from her life, it was obvious that she was struggling to understand, but nevertheless she listened intently. The two of us also took walks together down to the village. The youth were very good to her. Naturally, they were all activists. People like the owner of the general store, however, always gave us cold, steely stares. They disliked and despised Zhenzhen. They even treated me as someone not of their kind. This was especially true of the women, who, all because of Zhenzhen, became extremely self-righteous, perceiving themselves as saintly and pure. They were proud about never having been raped.

After Agui left the village, I grew even closer to

Zhenzhen. It seemed that neither of us could be without the other. As soon as we were apart, we thought of each other. I like people who are enthusiastic and lively, who can be really happy or sad, and at the same time are straightforward and candid. Zhenzhen was just such a person. Our conversations took up a great deal of time, but I always felt that they were beneficial to my studies and to my personal growth. As the days went by, however, I discovered that Zhenzhen was not being completely open about something. I did not resent this. Moreover, I was determined not to touch upon this secret of hers. All people have things buried deeply in their hearts that they don't want to tell others. This secret was a matter of private emotions. It had nothing to do with other people or with Zhenzhen's own morality.

A few days before my departure, Zhenzhen suddenly began to appear very agitated. Nothing special seemed to have happened, and she showed no desire to talk to me about anything new. Yet she frequently came to my room looking disturbed and restless, and after sitting for a few minutes, she would get up and leave. I knew she had not eaten well for several days and was often passing up meals. I had asked her about her disease and knew that the cause of her uneasiness was not simply physical. Sometimes, after coming to my room, she would make a few disjointed remarks. At other times, she put on an attentive expression, as if asking me to talk. But I could see that her thoughts were elsewhere, on things that she didn't want others to know. She was trying to conceal her emotions by acting as if nothing was wrong.

Twice I saw that capable young man come out of Zhenzhen's home. I had already compared my impression of him with Zhenzhen, and I sympathized with him deeply. Zhenzhen had been abused by many men, and had contracted a stigmatized, hard-to-cure disease, but he still patiently came to see her and still sought the approval of her parents to marry her. He didn't look down on her. He did not fear the derision or the rebukes of others. He must have felt she needed him more than ever. He understood what kind of attitude a man should have toward the woman of his choice at such a time and what his responsibilities were.

But what of Zhenzhen? Although naturally there were many aspects of her emotions and her sorrows that I had not learned during this short period, she had never expressed any hope that a man would marry her or, if you will, comfort her. I thought she had become so hard because she had been hurt so badly. She seemed not to want anything from anyone. It would be good if love, some extraordinarily sympathetic commiseration, could warm her soul. I wanted her to find a place where she could cry this out. I was hoping for a chance

to attend a wedding in this family. At the very least, I wanted to hear of an agreement to marry before I left.

"What is Zhenzhen thinking of?" I asked myself. "This can't be delayed indefinitely, and it shouldn't be turned into a big problem."

One day Liu Erma, her daughter-in-law, and her young daughter all came to see me. I was sure they intended to give me a report on something, but when they started to speak, I didn't allow them the opportunity to tell me anything. If my friend wouldn't confide in me, and I wouldn't ask her about it directly, then I felt it would be harmful to her, to myself, and to our friendship to ask others about it.

That same evening at dusk, the courtyard was again filled with people milling about. All the neighbors were there, whispering to one another. Some looked sad, but here were also those who appeared to find it all exciting. The weather was frigid, but curiosity warmed their hearts. In the severe cold, they drew in their shoulders, hunched their backs, thrust their hands into their sleeves, puffed out their breath, and looked at each other as if they were investigating something very interesting.

At first all I heard was the sound of quarreling coming from Liu Dama's dwelling. Then I heard Liu Dama crying. This was followed by the sound of a man crying. As far as I can tell, it was Zhenzhen's father. Next came a crash of dishes breaking. Unable to bear it any longer, I pushed my way through the curious onlookers and rushed inside.

"You've come at just the right time," Liu Erma said as she pulled me inside. "You talk to our Zhenzhen."

Zhenzhen's face was hidden by her long disheveled hair, but two wild eyes could still be seen peering out at the people gathered there. I walked over to her and stood beside her, but she seemed completely oblivious to my presence. Perhaps she took me as one of the enemy and not worth a moment's concern. Her appearance had changed so completely that I could hardly remember the liveliness, the bright pleasantness I had found in her before. She was like a cornered animal. She was like an evening goddess. Whom did she hate? Why was her expression so fierce?

"You're so heartless. You don't think about your mother and father at all. You don't care how much I've suffered because of you in the last year." Liu Dama pounded on the *kang* as she scolded her daughter, tears like raindrops dropping to the *kang* or the floor and flowing down the contours of her face. Several women had surrounded her and were preventing her from coming down off the *kang*. It was frightening to see a person lose her self-respect and allow all her feelings to come out in a blind rage. I thought of telling her that such crying was useless, but at the same time,

I realized that nothing I could say now would make any difference.

Zhenzhen's father looked very weak and old. His hands hung down limply. He was sighing deeply. Xia Dabao was seated beside him. There was a helpless look in his eyes as he stared at the old couple.

"You must say something. Don't you feel sorry for your mother?"

"When the end of a road is reached, one must turn. After water has flowed as far as it can, it must change direction. Aren't you going to change at all? Why make yourself suffer?" The women were trying to persuade Zhenzhen with such words.

I could see that this affair could not turn out the way that everyone was hoping. Zhenzhen had shown me much earlier that she didn't want anyone's sympathy. She, in turn, had no sympathy for anyone else. She had made her decision long ago and would not change. If people wanted to call her stubborn, then so be it. With teeth tightly clenched, she looked ready to stand up to all of them.

At last the others agreed to listen to me, and I asked Zhenzhen to come to my room and rest. I told them that everything could be discussed later that night. But when I led Zhenzhen out of the house, she did not follow me to my room. Instead, she ran off up the hillside.

"That girl has big ideas."

"Humph! She looks down on us country folk."

"She's such a cheap little hussy and yet she puts on such airs. Xia Dabao deserves it . . ."

These were some of the comments being made by the crowd in the courtyard. Then, when they realized that there was no longer anything of interest to see, the crowd drifted away.

I hesitated for a while in the courtyard before deciding to go up the hillside myself. On the top of the hill were numerous graves set among the pine trees. Broken stone tablets stood before them. No one was there. Not even the sound of a falling leaf broke the stillness. I ran back and forth calling Zhenzhen's name. What sounded like a response temporarily comforted my loneliness, but in an instant the vast silence of the hills became even deeper. The colors of sunset had completely faded. All around me a thin, smokelike mist rose silently and spread out to the middle slopes of the hills, both nearby and in the distance. I was worried and sat down weakly on a tombstone. Over and over I asked myself, "Should I go on up the hill or wait for her here?" I was hoping that I could relieve Zhenzhen of some of her distress.

At that moment I saw a shadow moving toward me from below. I quickly saw that it was Xia Dabao. I remained silent, hoping that he wouldn't see me and would continue on up the hill, but he came straight at me. At last I felt that I had to greet him and called, "Have you found her? I still haven't seen her."

He walked over to me and sat down on the dry grass. He said nothing, only stared into the distance. I felt a little uneasy. He really was very young. His eyebrows were long and thin. His eyes were quite large, but now they looked dull and lifeless. His small mouth was tightly drawn. Perhaps before it had been appealing, but now it was full of anguish, as if trying to hold in his pain. He had an honest-looking nose, but of what use was it to him now?

"Don't be sad," I said. "Maybe tomorrow everything will be all right. I'll talk to her this evening."

"Tomorrow, tomorrow—she'll always hate me. I know that she hates me." He spoke in a sad low voice that was slightly hoarse.

"No," I replied, searching my memory. "She has never shown me that she hates anyone." This was not a lie.

"She wouldn't tell you. She wouldn't tell anyone. She won't forgive me as long as she lives."

"Why should she hate you?"

"Of course—" he began. Suddenly he turned his face toward me and looked at me intently. "Tell me," he said, "at that time I had nothing. Should I have encouraged her to run away with me? Is all of this my fault? Is it?"

He didn't wait for my answer. As if speaking to himself, he went on, "It is my fault. Could anyone say that I did the right thing? Didn't I bring this harm to her? If I had been as brave as she, she never would have—I know her character. She'll always hate me. Tell me, what should I do? What would she want me to do? How can I make her happy? My life is worthless. Am I of even the slightest use to her? Can you tell me? I simply don't know what I should do. Ahhh! How miserable things are! This is worse than being captured by the Jap devils." Without a break, he continued to mumble on and on.

When I asked him to go back home with me, he stood up and we took several steps together. Then he stopped and said that he had heard a sound coming from the very top of the hill. There was nothing to do but encourage him to go on up, and I watched until he had disappeared into the thick pines. Then I started back. By now it was almost completely dark. It was very late when I went to bed that night, but I still hadn't received any news. I didn't know what had happened to them.

Even before I ate breakfast the next morning, I finished packing my suitcase. Comrade Ma had promised that he would be coming this day to help me move, and I was all prepared to return to the Political

Department and then go on to [my next assignment]. The enemy was about to start another "mopping-up campaign," and my health would not permit me to remain in this area. Director Mo had said that the ill definitely had to be moved out first, but I felt uneasy. Should I try to stay? If I did, I could be a burden to others. What about leaving? If I went, would I ever be able to return? As I was sitting on my bedroll pondering these questions, I sensed someone slipping quietly into my room.

With a single thrust of her body, Zhenzhen jumped up onto the kang and took a seat opposite me. I could see that her face was slightly swollen, and when I grasped her hands as she spread them over the fire, the heat that had made such an impression on me before once again distressed me. Then and there I realized how serious her disease was.

"Zhenzhen," I said, "I'm about to leave. I don't know when we'll meet again. I hope you'll listen to your mother—"

"I have come to tell you," she interrupted, "that I'll be leaving tomorrow too. I want to leave home as soon as possible."

"Really?" I asked.

"Yes," she said, her face again revealing that special vibrancy. "They've told me to go in for medical treatment."

"Ah," I sighed, thinking that perhaps we could travel together. "Does your mother know?"

"No, she doesn't know yet. But if I say that I'm going for medical treatment and that after my disease is cured I'll come back, she'll be sure to let me go. Just staying at home doesn't have anything to offer, does it?"

At this moment I felt that she had a rare serenity about her. I recalled the words that Xia Dabao had spoken to me the previous evening and asked her directly, "Has the problem of your marriage been resolved?"

"Resolved? Oh, well, it's all the same."

"Did you heed your mother's advice?" I still didn't dare express my hopes for her. I didn't want to think of the image left in my mind by that young man. I was hoping that someday he would be happy.

"Why should I listen to what they say? Did they ever listen to me?"

"Well, are you really angry with them?"

There was no response.

"Well, then, do you really hate Xia Dabao?"

For a long time she did not reply. Then, in a very calm voice, she said, "I can't say that I hate him. I just feel now that I'm someone who's diseased. It's a fact that I was abused by a large number of Jap devils. I don't remember the exact number. In any case, I'm unclean, and with such a black mark I don't expect any

good fortune to come my way. I feel that living among strangers and keeping busy would be better than living at home where people know me. Now that they've approved sending me to [Yan'an] for treatment, I've been thinking about staying there and doing some studying. I hear it's a big place with lots of schools and that anyone can attend. It's better for each of us to go our own separate ways than it is to have everyone stay together in one place. I'm doing this for myself, but I'm also doing it for the others. I don't feel that I owe anyone an apology. Neither do I feel especially happy. What I do feel is that after I go to [Yan'an], I'll be in a new situation. I will be able to start life fresh. A person's life is not just for one's father and mother, or even for oneself. Some have called me young, inexperienced, and bad-tempered. I don't dispute it. There are some things that I just have to keep to myself."

I was amazed. Something new was coming out of her. I felt that what she had said was really worth examining. There was nothing for me to do but express approval of her plan.

When I took my departure, Zhenzhen's family was there to see me off. She, however, had gone to the village office. I didn't see Xia Dabao before I left either.

I wasn't sad as I went away. I seemed to see the bright future that Zhenzhen had before her. The next day I would be seeing her again. That had been decided. And we would still be together for some time. As soon as Comrade Ma and I walked out the door of Zhenzhen's home, he told me of her decision and confirmed that what she had told me that morning would quickly come to pass.

(Translated by Gary J. Bjorge)

Thoughts on March 8 (1942)

When will it no longer be necessary to attach special weight to the word "woman" and raise it specially?

Each year this day comes round. Every year on this day, meetings are held all over the world where women muster their forces. Even though things have not been as lively these last two years in Yan'an as they were in previous years, it appears that at least a few people are busy at work here. And there will certainly be a congress, speeches, circular telegrams, and articles.

Women in Yan'an are happier than women elsewhere in China. So much so that many people ask enviously: "How come the women comrades get so rosy and fat on millet?" It doesn't seem to surprise anyone that women make up a big proportion of the staff in the hospitals, sanatoria, and clinics, but they are inevitably the subject of conversation, as a fascinating problem, on every conceivable occasion.

Moreover, all kinds of women comrades are often the target of deserved criticism. In my view these reproaches are serious and justifiable.

People are always interested when women comrades get married, but that is not enough for them. It is virtually impossible for women comrades to get onto friendly terms with a man comrade, and even less likely for them to become friendly with more than one. Cartoonists ridicule them: "A departmental head getting married too?" The poets say, "All the leaders in Yan'an are horsemen, and none of them are artists. In Yan'an it's impossible for an artist to find a pretty sweetheart." But in other situations, they are lectured: "Damn it, you look down on us old cadres and say we're country bumpkins. But if it weren't for us country bumpkins, you wouldn't be coming to Yan'an to eat millet!" But women invariably want to get married. (It's even more of a sin not to be married, and single women are even more of a target for rumors and slanderous gossip.) So they can't afford to be choosy, anyone will do: whether he rides horses or wears straw sandals, whether he's an artist or a supervisor. They inevitably have children. The fate of such children is various. Some are wrapped in soft baby wool and patterned felt and looked after by governesses. Others are wrapped in soiled cloth and left crying in their parents' beds, while their parents consume much of the child allowance. But for this allowance (twenty-five yuan a month, or just over three pounds of pork), many of them would probably never get a taste of meat. Whoever they marry, the fact is that those women who are compelled to bear children will probably be publicly derided as "Noras who have returned home." Those women comrades in a position to employ governesses can go out once a week to a prim get-together and dance. Behind their backs there will also be the most incredible gossip and whispering campaigns, but as soon as they go somewhere, they cause a great stir and all eyes are glued to them. This has nothing to do with our theories, our doctrines, and the speeches we make at meetings. We all know this to be a fact, a fact that is right before our eyes, but it is never mentioned.

It is the same with divorce. In general there are three conditions to pay attention to when getting married: (1) political purity; (2) both parties should be more or less the same age and comparable in looks; (3) mutual help. Even though everyone is said to fulfill these conditions—as for point 1, there are no open traitors in Yan'an; as for point 3, you can call anything "mutual help," including darning socks, patching shoes, and even feminine comfort—everyone nev-

ertheless makes a great show of giving thoughtful attention to them. And yet the pretext for divorce is invariably the wife's political backwardness. I am the first to admit that it is a shame when a man's wife is not progressive and retards his progress. But let us consider to what degree they are backward. Before marrying, they were inspired by the desire to soar in the heavenly heights and lead a life of bitter struggle. They got married partly because of physiological necessity and partly as a response to sweet talk about "mutual help." Thereupon they are forced to toil away and become "Noras returned home." Afraid of being thought "backward," those who are a bit more daring rush around begging nurseries to take their children. They ask for abortions and risk punishment and even death by secretly swallowing potions to produce abortions. But the answer comes back: "Isn't giving birth to children also work? You're just after an easy life; you want to be in the limelight. After all, what indispensable political work have you performed? Since you are so frightened of having children and are not willing to take responsibility once you have had them, why did you get married in the first place? No one forced you to." Under these conditions, it is impossible for women to escape this destiny of "backwardness." When women capable of working sacrifice their careers for the joys of motherhood, people always sing their praises. But after ten years or so, they have no way of escaping the tragedy of "backwardness." Even from my point of view, as a woman, there is nothing attractive about such "backward" elements. Their skin is beginning to wrinkle, their hair is growing thin, and fatigue is robbing them of their last traces of attractiveness. It should be self-evident that they are in a tragic situation. But whereas in the old society they would probably have been pitied and considered unfortunate, nowadays their tragedy is seen as something self-inflicted, as their just deserts. Is it not so that there is a discussion going on in legal circles as to whether divorces should be granted simply on the petition of one party or on the basis of mutual agreement? In the great majority of cases, it is the husband who petitions for divorce. For the wife to do so, she must be leading an immoral life, and then of course she deserves to be cursed.

I myself am a woman, and I therefore understand the failings of women better than others. But I also have a deeper understanding of what they suffer. Women are incapable of transcending the age they live in, of being perfect, or of being hard as steel. They are incapable of resisting all the temptations of society or all the silent oppression they suffer here in Yan'an. They each have their own past written in blood and tears; they have experienced great emotions—in elation as in depression, whether engaged in the lone battle of life or drawn into the humdrum stream of life. This is even truer of the women comrades who come to Yan'an, and I therefore have much sympathy for those fallen and classified as criminals. What is more, I hope that men, especially those in top positions, as well as women themselves, will consider the mistakes women commit in their social context. It would be better if there were less empty theorizing and more talk about real problems, so that theory and practice would not be divorced, and better if all Communist Party members were more responsible for their own moral conduct. But we must also hope for a little more from our women comrades, especially those in Yan'an. We must urge ourselves on and develop our comradely feeling.

People without ability have never been in a position to seize everything. Therefore, if women want equality, they must first strengthen themselves. There is no need to stress this point, since we all understand it. Today there are certain to be people who make fine speeches bragging about the need to acquire political power first. I would simply mention a few things that any frontliner, whether a proletarian, a fighter in the war of resistance, or a woman, should pay attention to in his or her everyday life:

1. Don't allow yourself to fall ill. A wild life can at times appear romantic, poetic, and attractive, but in today's conditions it is inappropriate. You are the best keeper of your life. There is nothing more unfortunate nowadays than to lose your health. It is closest to your heart. The only thing to do is keep a close watch on it, pay careful attention to it, and cherish it.

2. Make sure you are happy. Only when you are happy can you be youthful, active, fulfilled in your life, and steadfast in the face of all difficulties; only then will you see a future ahead of you and know how to enjoy yourself. This sort of happiness is not a life of contentment, but a life of struggle and of advance. Therefore we should all do some meaningful work each day and some reading, so that each of us is in a position to give something to others. Loafing about simply encourages the feeling that life is hollow, feeble, and in decay.

3. Use your brain, and make a habit of doing so. Correct any tendency not to think and ponder, or to swim with the current. Before you say or do anything, think whether what you are saying is right, whether that is the most suitable way of dealing with the problem, whether it goes against your own principles, whether you feel you can take responsibility for it. Then you will have no cause to regret your actions later. This is what is known as acting rationally. It is the best way of avoiding the pitfalls of sweet words and honeyed phrases, of being sidetracked by petty gains, of wasting our emotions and wasting our lives.

4. Resolution in hardship, perseverance to the end. Aware, modern women should identify and cast off all their rosy illusions. Happiness is to take up the struggle in the midst of the raging storm and not to pluck the lute in the moonlight or recite poetry among the blossoms. In the absence of the greatest resolution, it is very easy to falter in midpath. Not to suffer is to become degenerate. The strength to carry on should be nurtured through the quality of "perseverance." People without great aims and ambitions rarely have the firmness of purpose that does not covet petty advantages or seek a comfortable existence. But only those who have aims and ambitions for the benefit, not of the individual, but of humankind as a whole can persevere to the end.

August 3, dawn

Postscript. On rereading this article, it seems to me that there is much room for improvement in the passage on what we should expect from women, but because I have to meet a deadline with the manuscript, I have no time to revise it. But I also feel that there are some things that, if said by a leader before a big audience, would probably evoke satisfaction. But when they are written by a woman, they are more than likely to be demolished. But since I have written it, I offer it as I always intended, for the perusal of those people who have similar views.

(Translated by Gregor Benton)

Simone Weil (1909–43)

Simone Weil was born in 1909 in Paris and died in London in 1943, at the age of thirty-four. In a period of less than two decades before her death, Weil was engaged in an extraordinary range of political, intellectual, and spiritual commitments that have won her the most intense hostility and devotion, ridicule and respect, isolation and acclaim, of any theorist of her time. In the same period, she produced a body of political and philosophical writings of exceptional brilliance and importance. Albert Camus wrote of her Oppression and Liberty that "Western political and social thought has not produced anything more penetrating and more prophetic since Marx" (McLellan, 91).

Weil studied with the philosopher Alain (Émile Chartier) at the Henri IV preparatory school and later went to the Sorbonne. There she met Simone de Beauvoir, on whom she made a strong but not congenial impression, consistent with Alain's comment that Weil "was nothing like us and she judged us all in a sovereign manner" (Fiori, 27). As Weil later made clear, she took a harsh view of the left intellectuals who "never think at all of undermining the privileges of the intellectual caste—far from it; instead, they elaborate a complicated and mysterious doctrine which serves to maintain the bureaucratic oppression at the heart of the working class movement" (Oppression and Liberty).

Weil became engaged quite early in pacifist and left-wing activism but was never satisfied to join any party. She repudiated not only the Communist Party but also others including the anarcho-syndicalists with whom she felt more in common. She was drawn to Leon Trotsky's ideas and in 1933 arranged to host him while in Paris at an apartment of her parents, allowing him to hold there what Trotsky, on departing, called the founding meeting of the Fourth International. But this did not prevent her, at twenty-four years of age, from engaging in a heated argument with her eminent guest. Weil rejected Trotsky's view that the Soviet Union was still a workers' state (even if "deformed") and reproached him for his role in suppressing opposition to the early Soviet regime (Nevin, 94).

In the early 1930s, Weil taught philosophy to young women at the lycée Le Puy, where she was an unconventional yet inspirational teacher. At the same time, she became increasingly involved in labor action and politics. Indignant at the treatment of the local unemployed, who were required to break stones for a pittance, she joined them in presenting their demands, which subsequently led to a strike. She was attacked in the right-wing press as the "red virgin [a reference to Louise Michel, anarchist heroine of the Paris Commune] of the tribe of Levi, bearer of the Muscovite gospels." Alain's comment was: "Who else but she could start a strike among the unemployed!" (McLellan, 42). She became convinced that it was necessary to learn by personal experience the conditions of workers' lives, and after several short-term jobs, she took a year's leave from teaching in 1934 to work in factories, recording her observations and experiences in a journal, published later as "Factory Work." This was also the period in which she wrote her "Reflections concerning the Causes of Liberty and Social Oppression" (1934, first published in 1955; see below).

Weil's pacifist convictions were tested by the Spanish Civil War, when she went to join the anarchist-syndicalist forces in the area of Barcelona in 1936. She was injured in an accident and returned to France confirmed in her revulsion against the excesses of violence in war. She wrote to Georges Bernanos of the pressure to encourage killing, of how "Right in the middle of a meal replete with comradeship, I have heard them recount with a good fraternal smile how many priests and how many 'Fascists' . . . they had killed. . . . Any possible revulsion is smothered, for fear of 'lacking manhood' . . ." (Fiori, 148; Panichas, 76–77). In the period from 1936 to 1939, Weil continued to oppose war, but with Hitler's occupation of Czechoslovakia and the spread of Nazi and fascist domination throughout Europe, she concluded "despite my pacifist inclinations, that my first responsibility was to pursue the destruction of Hitler" (Fiori, 253). Written in 1939 at this crucial turning point in her life and thought, her powerful essay "The Iliad: Poem of Force" may be read as a compelling pacifist argument on the ultimate futility of force, even in the face of its overwhelming presence.

Like Rosa Luxemburg and Hannah Arendt, with whom Weil is sometimes compared, she was born into an assimilated Jewish family. In Weil's case, the assimilation was so complete that she and her brother, famed mathematician André Weil, were not aware they were Jews until they entered school. In 1939, however, the Weils escaped to Vichy France, and in the period of hardship and reflection enforced upon her by her assigned status as a Jew, she developed a deep spiritual attachment to Catholicism, which had interested her for many years. Yet Weil never accepted baptism. In one of her last letters before her death, she wrote that while she believed in God, the Trinity, and other doctrines of

Catholic faith, "I do not grant the Church any right to limit the operations of the mind or the illuminations of love in the realm of thought. . . . I do not grant her the right to impose her comments on the mysteries of faith as being the truth. Even less do I grant her the right to use threats and force . . . to impose that truth" (Fiori, 317).

Among the most controversial and painful of her ideas were her ill-informed and contemptuous attacks on Judaism (bearing a bitter edge of shame in her forced identification as a Jew) and her proposals for the eradication of Jewish religion in France by a process of accelerated assimilation in which "Jewish racism" would be overcome by "the germ that cures," Christianity. After two or three generations following her prescriptions, she argued, "the only ones to remain conscious of being Jews would be fanatical racists," who should be deprived of French nationality (Nevin, 245). In his brilliant and balanced intellectual biography, Simone Weil: Portrait of a Self-Exiled Jew, Thomas Nevin argues that these aspects of Weil's thought must be taken seriously, not sealed off or excused. Despite her explicit rejection of her own Jewishness, Nevin claims, Weil was profoundly Jewish in her ideas and her being, even in "her passionate wrestling, often bitter and violent, with God," in her adoption of her role as "tzeddik, the just person," and her own description of her destiny: "that it had been prescribed to me to find myself alone, a stranger and in exile in relation to any human milieu whatsoever" (Nevin, 390, 389, 239). But he concludes: "That a mind of abundant energy, a mind that has cast brilliant lights on some of the abiding problems of this century, could do itself harm and give hurt to the Jewish people must be reckoned one of the intellectual and moral catastrophes of a dark age" (Nevin, 256).

In 1942 Weil and her family left France for New York, but Weil was unhappy there, having conceived a passionate desire to engage herself directly in some form of action against the forces of Nazism in Europe. She made her way to London later that year, hoping to gain permission to carry out some services to the Free French, but her proposals (including one to organize women for front-line nursing service) were rejected as fantastic. She fell seriously ill with tuberculosis and digestive problems and died in August 1943. Before her death she wrote The Need for Roots, in later years her most widely renowned work, to set forth her ideas and proposals for the postwar reconstruction of politics and society in France.

Like Rosa Luxemburg, whom she greatly admired, Simone Weil left an extensive body of writings, most published after her death and some not yet translated into English. Though less enmeshed in party politics ¿ nd polemics than Luxemburg, Weil too has been the subject of many claims and counterclaims between those who see her as a potential Catholic saint, as a political conservative and intellectual anti-Semite, or as a "fanatical ascetic," and those who see her as a powerful spiritual philosopher or a radical theorist of liberation. Perhaps in consequence of these contested interpretations of her work, or simply in testimony to the wide-ranging impact her ideas have had, an extensive critical literature has developed around Weil's religious, philosophical, and political thought.

Among the major contributions identified by her critics and admirers are Weil's analyses of freedom and power, bureaucratic centralism, work, workers' control, and the necessity of liberated work as central to a free society. These are themes she put forward in her 1934 essay "Reflections concerning the Causes of Liberty and Social Oppression." The following selection is drawn from the 1973 publication of this essay in the volume Oppression and Liberty.

BAC

Sources and Suggested Readings

Bell, Richard H., ed. Simone Weil's Philosophy and Culture: Readings toward a Divine Humanity. New York: Cambridge University Press, 1993.

Blum, Lawrence A., and Victor J. Seidler. A Truer Liberty: Simone Weil and Marxism. New York: Routledge, 1990.

De Beauvoir, Simone. The Prime of Life. Cleveland: World, 1962.

Dietz, Mary G. Between the Human and the Divine: The Political Thought of Simone Weil. Totowa, N.J.: Rowman and Littlefield, 1988.

Fiori, Gabriella. Simone Weil: An Intellectual Biography. Athens: University of Georgia Press, 1989.

Hellman, John. Simone Weil: An Introduction to Her Thought. Waterloo, Ontario: Wilfrid Laurier University Press, 1982.

McFarland, Dorothy Tuck. Simone Weil. New York: Ungar, 1983.

McLane-Iles, Betty. Uprooting and Integration in the Writings of Simone Weil. New York: Peter Lang, 1987.

McLellan, David. Utopian Pessimist: The Life and Thought of Simone Weil. New York: Poseidon Press, 1990.

Nevin, Thomas. Simone Weil: Portrait of a Self-Exiled Jew. Chapel Hill: University of North Carolina Press, 1991.

O'Brien, Conor Cruise. "The Anti-Politics of Simone Weil." New York Review of Books 24, 8 (May 12, 1977): 23–28.

Pétrement, Simone. Simone Weil: A Life. New York: Pantheon, 1976.

———. La Vie de Simone Weil. 2 vols. Paris: Fayard, 1973.

Strickland, Stephanie. The Red Virgin: A Poem of Simone Weil. Madison: University of Wisconsin Press, 1993.

Terry, Megan. Approaching Simone: A Play. Introduction by Phyllis Jane Wagner. Old Westbury, N.Y.: Feminist Press, 1973.

Veto, Miklos. The Religious Metaphysics of Simone Weil. Albany: State University of New York Press. 1994.

Weil, Simone. *Formative Writings, 1929–1941.* Ed.
Dorothy Tuck McFarland and Wilhelmina Van Ness.
Amherst: University of Massachusetts Press, 1988.

——. *Lectures on Philosophy.* Introduction by Peter
Winch. New York: Cambridge University Press, 1978
[1959].

——. *The Need for Roots.* Preface by T. S. Eliot. Boston:
Beacon, 1955.

——. *Oppression and Liberty.* Introduction by F. C.
Ellert. Amherst: University of Massachusetts Press,
1973.

——. *Selected Essays, 1934–1945.* Ed. Richard Rees.
London: Oxford, 1962.

——. *The Simone Weil Reader.* Ed. George A. Panichas.
New York: David McKay, 1977.

——. *Waiting for God.* Introduction by Leslie A. Fiedler.
New York: Harper & Row, 1973 [1951].

White, George Abbott. *Simone Weil: Interpretations of a
Life.* Amherst: University of Massachusetts Press, 1981.

Winch, Peter. *Simone Weil: "The Just Balance."* New York:
Cambridge University Press 1989.

Reflections concerning the Causes of Liberty and Social Oppression (1934)

The present period is one of those when everything that seems normally to constitute a reason for living dwindles away, when one must, on pain of sinking into confusion or apathy, call everything in question again. That the triumph of authoritarian and nationalist movements should blast almost everywhere the hopes that well-meaning people had placed in democracy and in pacifism is only a part of the evil from which we are suffering; it is far deeper and far more widespread. One may well ask oneself if there exists a single sphere of public or private life where the very spring-heads of activity and of hope have not been poisoned by the conditions under which we live. Work is no longer done with the proud consciousness that one is being useful, but with the humiliating and agonizing feeling of enjoying a privilege bestowed by a temporary stroke of fortune, a privilege from which one excludes several human beings by the mere fact that one enjoys, in short, a job. The leaders of industry themselves have lost that naive belief in unlimited economic progress which made them imagine that they had a mission. Technical progress seems to have gone bankrupt, since instead of happiness it has only brought the masses that physical and moral wretchedness in which we see them floundering; moreover, technical innovations are now banned everywhere, or very nearly so, except in industries connected with war. As for scientific progress, it is difficult to see what can be the use of piling up still more knowledge on to a heap already much too vast to be able to be embraced by the minds even of specialists; and experience has shown that our forefathers were mistaken in believing in the spread of enlightenment, since all that can be revealed to the masses is a miserable caricature of modern scientific culture, a caricature which, far from forming their judgment, accustoms them to be credulous. Art itself suffers the backlash of the general confusion, which partly deprives it of its public, and by that very fact impairs inspiration. Finally, family life has become nothing but anxiety, now that society is closed to the young. The very generation for whom a feverish expectation of the future is the whole of life, vegetates, all over the world, with the feeling that it has no future, that there is no room for it in our world. But if this evil is felt more sharply by youth, it remains common to the whole of humanity today. We are living through a period bereft of a future. Waiting for that which is to come is no longer a matter of hope, but of anguish.

However, ever since 1789, there has been one magic word which contains within itself all imaginable futures, and is never so full of hope as in desperate situations—that word is revolution. That is why, for some time now, we have often been hearing it uttered. We ought, so it seems, to be in a period of full revolution; but in fact everything goes on as if the revolutionary movement were falling into decay with the very system it aspires to destroy. For more than a century, each new generation of revolutionaries has, in turn, placed its hopes in an impending revolution; today, these hopes have lost everything which was able to serve them as buttresses. Neither in the régime that emerged from the October Revolution, nor in the two Internationals, nor in the independent socialist or communist parties, nor in the trade unions, nor in the anarchist organizations, nor in the small youth groups that have sprung up in such profusion in recent times, can one find anything vigorous, healthy or pure; for a long time now the working class has shown no sign of that spontaneity on which Rosa Luxemburg counted, and which, moreover, has never manifested itself without being promptly drowned in blood; the middle classes are only attracted by revolution when it is conjured up for demagogic purposes by apprentice dictators. It is often said that the situation is objectively revolutionary, and that all that is lacking is the "subjective factor"; as if the complete absence of that very force which alone could transform the system were not an objective characteristic of the present situation, whose origins must be sought in the structure of our society! That is why the first duty the present period imposes on us is to have enough intellectual courage to ask ourselves if the term "revolution" is anything else but a name, if it has any precise content, if it is not simply one of the numerous lies produced by the capitalist system in its rise to power which the present crisis is doing us the service of dissipating. . . .

Critique of Marxism

Up to now all those who have experienced the need to buttress their revolutionary feelings with precise concepts have found or thought they found these concepts in Marx. It is accepted once and for all that Marx, thanks to his general theory of history and to his analysis of bourgeois society, demonstrated the ineluctable necessity of an early upheaval, in which the oppression we suffer under capitalism would be abolished; and indeed, by dint of being persuaded of the fact, we generally dispense with examining the demonstration more closely. "Scientific socialism" has attained the status of a dogma, exactly in the same way as have all the results obtained by modern science, results in which each one thinks it is his duty to believe, without ever dreaming of enquiring into the method employed. As far as Marx is concerned, if one tries really to grasp his demonstration intellectually, one at once perceives that it contains very many more difficulties than the advocates of "scientific socialism" lead one to suppose.

Actually, Marx gives a first-rate account of the mechanism of capitalist oppression; but so good is it that one finds it hard to visualize how this mechanism could cease to function. As a rule, it is only the economic aspect of this oppression that holds our attention, that is to say the extortion of surplus value; and, if we confine ourselves to this point of view, it is certainly easy to explain to the masses that this extortion is bound up with competition, which latter is in turn bound up with private property, and that the day when property becomes collective all will be well. Nevertheless, even within the limits of this apparently simple reasoning, a thousand difficulties present themselves on careful examination. For Marx showed clearly that the true reason for the exploitation of the workers is not any desire on the part of the capitalists to enjoy and consume, but the need to expand the undertaking as rapidly as possible so as to make it more powerful than its rivals. Now not only a business undertaking, but any sort of working collectivity, no matter what it may be, has to exercise the maximum restraint on the consumption of its members so as to devote as much time

as possible to forging weapons for use against rival collectivities; so that as long as there is, on the surface of the globe, a struggle for power, and as long as the decisive factor in victory is industrial production, the workers will be exploited. As a matter of fact, what Marx assumed, without, however, proving it, was that every kind of struggle for power will disappear on the day socialism is established in all industrial countries; the only trouble is that, as Marx himself recognized, revolution cannot take place everywhere at once; and when it does take place in one country, it does not for that country do away with the need for exploiting and oppressing the mass of workers, but on the contrary accentuates the need, lest it be found weaker than the other nations. The history of the Russian Revolution furnishes a painful illustration of this.

If we consider other aspects of capitalist oppression, other still more formidable difficulties appear, or rather the same difficulty under a more glaring light. The power which the bourgeoisie has to exploit and oppress the workers lies at the very foundations of our social life, and cannot be destroyed by any political and juridical transformation. This power consists in the first place and essentially in the modern system of production itself, that is to say big industry. Pungent dicta abound in Marx's writings on this subject of living labour being enslaved to dead labour, "the reversal of the relationship between subject and object," "the subordination of the worker to the material conditions of work." "In the factory," he writes in *Capital*, "there exists a mechanism independent of the workers, which incorporates them as living cogs. . . . The separation of the spiritual forces that play a part in production from manual labour, and the transformation of the former into power exercised by capital over labour, attain their fulfilment in big industry founded on mechanization. The detail of the individual destiny of the machineworker fades into insignificance before the science, the tremendous natural forces and the collective labour which are incorporated in the machines as a whole and constitute with them the employer's power." Thus the worker's complete subordination to the undertaking and to those who run it is founded on the factory organization and not on the system of property. Similarly, "the separation of the spiritual forces that play a part in production from manual labour," or, according to another formula, "the degrading division of labour into manual and intellectual labour," is the very foundation of our culture, which is a culture of specialists. Science is a monopoly, not because public education is badly organized, but by its very nature; non-scientists have access only to the results, not to the methods, that is to say they can only believe, not assimilate. "Scientific socialism" has itself remained the monopoly of a select few, and the "intellectuals" possess, unfortunately, the same privileges in the working-class movement as they do in bourgeois society. And the same applies, furthermore, on the political plane.

Marx had clearly perceived that State oppression is founded on the existence of organs of government that are permanent and distinct from the population, namely, the bureaucratic, military and police machines; but these permanent organs are the inevitable result of the radical distinction existing, in fact, between the managerial and executive functions. In this respect again, the working-class movement reproduces in full the vices of bourgeois society. At all levels we are brought up against the same obstacle. The whole of our civilization is founded on specialization, which implies the enslavement of those who execute to those who co-ordinate; and on such a basis one can only organize and perfect oppression, not lighten it. Far from capitalist society having developed within itself the material conditions for a regime of liberty and equality, the establishment of such a regime presupposes a preliminary transformation in the realm of production and that of culture.

We can only understand how Marx and his disciples could still believe in the possibility of a real democracy based on our present civilization if we take into account their theory of the development of productive forces. It is well known that, in Marx's eyes, this development constitutes, in the last analysis, the true motive power of history, and that it is practically unlimited. Every social system, every dominant class has the "task," the "historic mission," of carrying the productive forces to an ever higher level, until the day when all further progress is arrested by the social cadres; at that moment the productive forces rebel, break up these cadres, and a new class takes over power. The recognition of the fact that the capitalist system grinds down millions of men only enables one to condemn it morally; what constitutes the historic condemnation of the system is the fact that, after having made productive progress possible, it is now an obstacle in its way. The essential task of revolutions consists in the emancipation not of men but of productive forces. As a matter of fact, it is clear that, as soon as these have reached a level of development high enough for production to be carried out at the cost of little effort, the two tasks coincide; and Marx assumed that such was the case in our time. It was this assumption that enabled him to establish a harmony, indispensable to his moral tranquility, between his idealistic aspirations and his materialistic conception of history. In his view, modern technique, once freed from capitalist forms of economy, can give men, here and now, sufficient leisure to enable them to develop their faculties harmoni-

ously, and consequently bring about the disappearance, to a certain extent, of the degrading specialization created by capitalism; and above all the further development of technique must lighten more and more, day by day, the burden of material necessity, and as an immediate consequence that of social constraint, until humanity reaches at last a truly paradisal state in which the most abundant production would be at the cost of a trifling expenditure of effort and the ancient curse of work would be lifted; in short, in which the happiness of Adam and Eve before the fall would be regained.

One can understand very well, starting from this conception, the attitude of the Bolsheviks, and why all of them, including Trotsky, treat democratic ideas with supreme disdain. They have found themselves powerless to bring about the workers' democracy foreshadowed by Marx; but such a minor detail does not worry them, convinced as they are, on the one hand, that all attempts at social action which do not consist of developing productive forces are doomed to failure, on the other hand, that all progress in productive forces causes humanity to advance along the road leading to emancipation, even if it is at the cost of a temporary oppression. It is not surprising that, backed up by such moral certainty as this, they have astonished the world by their strength.

It is seldom, however, that comforting beliefs are at the same time rational. Before even examining the Marxist conception of productive forces, one is struck by the mythological character it presents in all socialist literature, where it is assumed as a postulate. Marx never explains why productive forces should tend to increase; by accepting without proof this mysterious tendency, he allies himself not with Darwin, as he liked to think, but with Lamarck, who in similar fashion founded his biological system on an inexplicable tendency of living creatures to adapt themselves. In the same way, why is it that, when social institutions are in opposition to the development of productive forces, victory should necessarily belong beforehand to the latter rather than the former? Marx evidently does not assume that men consciously transform their social conditions in order to improve their economic conditions; he knows perfectly well that up to the present social transformations have never been accompanied by any clear realization of their real long-term consequences; he therefore implicitly assumes that productive forces possess a secret virtue enabling them to overcome obstacles. Finally, why does he assert without demonstration, and as a self-evident truth, that the productive forces are capable of unlimited development?

The whole of this doctrine, on which the Marxist conception of revolution entirely rests, is absolutely devoid of any scientific basis. In order to understand it, we must remember the Hegelian origins of Marxist thought. Hegel believed in a hidden mind at work in the universe, and that the history of the world is simply the history of this world mind, which, as in the case of everything spiritual, tends indefinitely towards perfection. Marx claimed to "put back on its feet" the Hegelian dialectic, which he accused of being "upside down," by substituting matter for mind as the motive power of history; but by an extraordinary paradox, he conceived history, starting from this rectification, as though he attributed to matter what is the very essence of mind—an unceasing aspiration towards the best. In this he was profoundly in keeping, moreover, with the general current of capitalist thought; to transfer the principle of progress from mind to things is to give a philosophical expression to that "reversal of the relationship between subject and object" in which Marx discerned the very essence of capitalism. The rise of big industry made of productive forces the divinity of a kind of religion whose influence Marx came under, despite himself, when formulating his conception of history. The term religion may seem surprising in connection with Marx; but to believe that our will coincides with a mysterious will which is at work in the universe and helps us to conquer is to think religiously, to believe in Providence. Besides, Marx's vocabulary itself testifies to this since it contains quasi-mystical expressions such as "the historic mission of the proletariat."

This religion of productive forces, in whose name generations of industrial employers have ground down the labouring masses without the slightest qualm, also constitutes a factor making for oppression within the socialist movement. All religions make man into a mere instrument of Providence, and socialism, too, puts men at the service of historical progress, that is to say of productive progress. That is why, whatever may be the insult inflicted on Marx's memory by the cult which the Russian oppressors of our time entertain for him, it is not altogether undeserved. Marx, it is true, never had any other motive except a generous yearning after liberty and equality; but this yearning, once separated from the materialistic religion with which it was merged in his mind, no longer belongs to anything except what Marx contemptuously called utopian socialism. If Marx's writings contained nothing more valuable than this, they might without loss be forgotten, at any rate except for his economic analyses.

But such is not the case; we find in Marx a different conception from that Hegelian doctrine turned inside out, namely, a materialism which no longer has anything religious about it and forms not a doctrine but a method of understanding and of action. It is no un-

common thing to find thus in quite great minds two distinct and even incompatible conceptions mingling together under cover of the inevitable looseness of language; absorbed as they are in formulating new ideas, such minds have not the time to make a critical examination of what they have discovered. Marx's truly great idea is that in human society as well as in nature nothing takes place otherwise than through material transformations. "Men make their own history, but within certain fixed conditions." To desire is nothing; we have got to know the material conditions which determine our possibilities of action; and in the social sphere these conditions are defined by the way in which man obeys material necessities in supplying his own needs, in other words, by the method of production. A methodical improvement in social organization presupposes a detailed study of the method of production, in order to try to find out on the one hand what we may expect from it, in the immediate or distant future, from the point of view of output, and on the other hand what forms of social and cultural organization are compatible with it, and, finally, how it may itself be transformed. Only irresponsible human beings can neglect such a study and yet claim the right to domineer over society; and, unfortunately, such is the case everywhere, as much in revolutionary circles as among the ruling classes. The materialistic method—that instrument which Marx bequeathed us—is an untried instrument; no Marxist has ever really used it, beginning with Marx himself. The only really valuable idea to be found in Marx's writings is also the only one that has been completely neglected. It is not surprising that the social movements springing from Marx have failed.

The first question to consider is that concerning output. Are there any reasons for supposing that modern technique, at its present level, is capable—always supposing a fair distribution—of guaranteeing to everyone sufficient welfare and leisure so that the development of the individual may cease to be hampered by modern working conditions? It seems that on this subject there are many illusions, purposely kept alive by demagogic interests. It is not profits which have to be calculated; those of them that are reinvested in production would for the most part be taken away from the workers under any system. We should have to be able to calculate the total amount of labour that could be dispensed with at the cost of a transformation of the property system. Even that would not solve the problem; we must bear in mind the labour involved in the complete reorganization of the productive machine, a reorganization necessary for production to be adapted to its new end, namely, the welfare of the masses; we must not forget that the manufacture of armaments would not be abandoned before the capitalist system had been everywhere destroyed; above all, we must provide for the fact that the abolition of individual profit, while causing certain forms of waste to disappear, would at the same time necessarily create others. It is impossible, of course, to make exact calculations; but they are not indispensable for discerning that the abolition of private property would be far from sufficient in itself to prevent work in the mines and in the factories from continuing to weigh as a servitude on those who are subjected to it.

But if the present state of technique is insufficient to liberate the workers, is there at any rate a reasonable hope that an unlimited development lies before it, which would imply an unlimited increase in productivity? This is what everybody assumes, both among capitalists and socialists, without the smallest preliminary study of the question; it is enough that the productivity of human effort should have increased in an unheard-of manner for the last three centuries for it to be expected that this increase will continue at the same rate. Our so-called scientific culture has given us this fatal habit of generalizing, of arbitrarily extrapolating, instead of studying the conditions of a given phenomenon and the limits implied by them; and Marx, whose dialectical method should have saved him from such an error, fell into it on this point just like other people.

The problem is fundamental, and of a kind to determine all our future prospects; it must be formulated with the utmost precision. To this end, the first thing is to know in what technical progress consists, what factors play a part in it, and to examine each factor separately; for we mix up under the name of technical progress entirely different procedures that offer different possibilities of development.

The first procedure that offers itself to man for producing more with less effort is the utilization of natural sources of energy; and it is true, in a sense, that it is impossible to assign a precise limit to the benefits of this procedure, because we do not know what new sources of energy we shall one day be able to use; but this does not mean to say that there can be prospects of unlimited progress in this direction, nor that progress in it is, generally speaking, assured. For nature does not give us this energy, whatever may be the form in which it offers itself—animal power, coal or petroleum; we have to wrest it from her and transform it through our labour so as to adapt it to our own ends. Now, this labour does not necessarily become less as time goes on; at present the very opposite is happening to us, since the extraction of coal and petroleum becomes continually and automatically less profitable and more costly. What is more, the deposits at present known are destined to become exhausted at the end of a relatively short time. Perhaps new deposits will be found; but prospecting, the development of new workings, some of which will doubtless fail to pay—all that will be costly; furthermore, we do not know how many unknown deposits there are in general, and in any case their number will not be unlimited. We may also—and no doubt some day we are bound to—discover new sources of energy; but there is nothing to guarantee that their utilization will call for less labour than the utilization of coal or heavy oils; the opposite is just as possible. It may even happen, at the worst, that the utilization of a natural source of energy involves more labour than the human expenditure of energy one is seeking to replace. In this field it is chance which decides; for the discovery of a new and easily accessible source of energy or of an economic transformation process for a known source of energy is not one of those things one is sure of reaching on a basis of thinking methodically and spending the necessary time thereon. . . .

Apart from this, there exists only one other resource making it possible to diminish the total sum of human effort, namely, what we may call, to use a modern expression, the rationalization of labour. Two aspects of it may be distinguished; one which concerns the relationship between simultaneous efforts, the other that between successive efforts; in both cases progress resides in increasing the productivity of the efforts by the way in which these are combined. It is clear that in this field one can, strictly speaking, leave chance out of account, and that here the notion of progress has meaning; the question is to know whether this progress is unlimited, and, if not, whether we are still a long way from the limit. . . .

A serious study of the question ought, strictly speaking, to take many other elements into consideration. The various factors that go to increase productivity do not develop separately, although they have to be separated in analysis; they combine together, and these combinations produce results difficult to foresee. Besides, technical progress does not only serve to obtain at low cost what one used to obtain before with considerable effort; it also makes it possible to undertake what without it would have been almost unimaginable. It would be as well to examine the value of these new possibilities, while bearing in mind the fact that they are not only possibilities of construction, but also of destruction. But such a study would be forced to take into account the economic and social relations which necessarily go hand in hand with a given form of technical achievement. For the moment it is enough to have understood that the possibility of future progress so far as concerns productivity is not beyond question; that, to all appearances, we have at present as many reasons for expecting to see it diminish as increase; and, what is most important of all, that a continuous and unlimited increase in productivity is, strictly speaking, inconceivable. It is solely the frenzy produced by the speed of technical progress that has brought about the mad idea that work might one day become unnecessary. On the plane of pure science, this idea has found expression in the search for the "perpetual motion machine," that is to say a machine which would go on producing work indefinitely without ever consuming any; and the scientists made short work of it by propounding the law of the conservation of energy. In the social sphere, divagations are better received. The "higher stage of communism," regarded by Marx as the final term of social evolution, is, in effect, a utopia absolutely analogous to that of perpetual motion.

It is in the name of this utopia that revolutionaries have shed their blood. Or rather, they have shed their blood in the name either of this utopia or of the equally utopian belief that the present system of production could be placed by a mere decree at the service of a society of free and equal men. Is it surprising, then, if all this blood has been shed in vain? The history of the working-class movement is thus lit up with a cruel, but singularly vivid, light. The whole of it can be summarized by remarking that the working class has never manifested strength save in so far as it has served something other than the workers' revolution. The working-class movement was able to give the illusion of power as long as it was still a question for it of helping to liquidate the vestiges of feudalism or to prepare the way for capitalist domination, whether under the form of private capitalism or that of State capitalism, as happened in Russia; now that its role in that field is over and the industrial crisis confronts it with the problem of the effective seizure of power by the working masses, it is crumbling away and dissolving with a rapidity that breaks the hearts of those who had placed their faith in it. On its ruins interminable arguments are held which can only be smoothed over by the most ambiguous formulas; for among all those who still persist in talking about revolution, there are perhaps not two who attach the same content to the term. And that is not in the least surprising. The word "revolution" is a word for which you kill, for which you die, for which you send the labouring masses to their death, but which does not possess any content.

Yet perhaps one can give a meaning to the revolutionary ideal, if not as a possible prospect in view, at any rate as a theoretical limit of feasible social transformations. What we should ask of the revolution is the abolition of social oppression; but for this notion to

have at least a chance of possessing some meaning, we must be careful to distinguish between oppression and subordination of personal whims to a social order. So long as such a thing as a society exists, it will circumscribe the life of individuals within quite narrow limits and impose its rules on them; but this inevitable constraint does not merit the name of oppression except in so far as, owing to the fact that it brings about a division between those who exercise it and those who are subject to it, places the latter at the disposal of the former and thus causes those who command to exert a crushing physical and moral pressure over those who execute. Even when this distinction has been made, nothing entitles us to assume *a priori* that the abolition of oppression is either possible or even simply conceivable by way of limit. Marx demonstrated forcibly, in the course of analyses of whose far-reaching scope he was himself unaware, that the present system of production, namely, big industry, reduces the worker to the position of a wheel in the factory and a mere instrument in the hands of his employers; and it is useless to hope that technical progress will, through a progressive and continuous reduction in productive effort, alleviate, to the point of almost causing it to disappear, the double burden imposed on man by nature and society.

The problem is, therefore, quite clear; it is a question of knowing whether it is possible to conceive of an organization of production which, though powerless to remove the necessities imposed by nature and the social constraint arising therefrom, would enable these at any rate to be exercised without grinding down souls and bodies under oppression. At a time like ours, to have grasped this problem clearly is perhaps a condition for being able to live at peace with oneself. If we can manage to conceive in concrete terms the conditions of this liberating organization, then it only remains for us to exercise, in order to move towards it, all the powers of action, small or great, at our disposal; and if, on the other hand, we realize clearly that the possibility of such a system of production is not even conceivable, we at least gain the advantage of being able legitimately to resign ourselves to oppression and of ceasing to regard ourselves as accomplices in it because we fail to do anything effective to prevent it.

Analysis of Oppression

The problem is, in short, to know what it is that links oppression in general and each form of oppression in particular to the system of production; in other words, to succeed in grasping the mechanism of oppression, in understanding by what means it arises, subsists, transforms itself, by what means, perhaps, it might theoretically disappear. This is, to all intents and purposes, a novel question. For centuries past, noble minds have regarded the power of oppressors as constituting a usurpation pure and simple, which one had to try to oppose either by simply expressing a radical disapproval of it, or else by armed force placed at the service of justice. In either case, failure has always been complete; and never was it more strikingly so than when it took on momentarily the appearance of victory, as happened with the French Revolution, when, after having effectively succeeded in bringing about the disappearance of a certain form of oppression, people stood by, helpless, watching a new oppression immediately being set up in its place.

In his ponderings over this resounding failure, which had come to crown all previous ones, Marx finally came to understand that you cannot abolish oppression so long as the causes which make it inevitable remain, and that these causes reside in the objective—that is to say material—conditions of the social system. He consequently elaborated a completely new conception of oppression, no longer considered as the usurpation of a privilege, but as the organ of a social function. This function is that very one which consists in developing the productive forces, in so far as this development calls for severe efforts and serious hardships; and Marx and Engels perceived a reciprocal relationship between this development and social oppression.

In the first place, according to them, oppression becomes established only when improvements in production have brought about a division of labour sufficiently advanced for exchange, military command and government to constitute distinct functions; on the other hand, oppression, once established, stimulates the further development of the productive forces, and changes in form as and when this development so demands, until the day when, having become a hindrance to it instead of a help, it disappears purely and simply.

However brilliant the concrete analyses may be by which Marxists have illustrated this thesis, and although it constitutes an improvement on the naive expressions of indignation which it replaced, one cannot say that it throws light on the mechanism of oppression. It only partially describes its origins; for why should the division of labour necessarily turn into oppression? It by no means entitles us to a reasonable expectation of its ending; for if Marx believed himself to have shown how the capitalist system finally hinders production, he did not even attempt to prove that, in our day, any other oppressive system would hinder it in like manner. Furthermore, one fails to understand why oppression should not manage to continue, even

after it has become a factor of economic regression. Above all, Marx omits to explain why oppression is invincible as long as it is useful, why the oppressed in revolt have never succeeded in founding a non-oppressive society, whether on the basis of the productive forces of their time, or even at the cost of an economic regression which could hardly increase their misery; and, lastly, he leaves completely in the dark the general principles of the mechanism by which a given form of oppression is replaced by another.

What is more, not only have Marxists not solved a single one of these problems, but they have not even thought it their duty to formulate them. It has seemed to them that they had sufficiently accounted for social oppression by assuming that it corresponds to a function in the struggle against nature. Even then, they have only really brought out this correspondence in the case of the capitalist system; but, in any case, to suppose that such a correspondence constitutes an explanation of the phenomenon is to apply unconsciously to social organisms Lamarck's famous principle, as unintelligible as it is convenient, "the function creates the organ." Biology only started to be a science on the day when Darwin replaced this principle by the notion of conditions of existence. . . .

It is clear that this luminous method is not only valid in biology, but wherever one is confronted by organized structures which have not been organized by anybody. In order to be able to appeal to science in social matters, we ought to have effected with respect to Marxism an improvement similar to that which Darwin effected with respect to Lamarck. The causes of social evolution must no longer be sought elsewhere than in the daily efforts of men considered as individuals. These efforts are certainly not directed haphazardly; they depend, in each individual case, on temperament, education, routine, customs, prejudices, natural or acquired needs, environment, and above all, broadly speaking, human nature, a term which, although difficult to define, is probably not devoid of meaning. But given the almost infinite diversity of individuals, and especially the fact that human nature includes among other things the ability to innovate, to create, to rise above oneself, this warp and woof of incoherent efforts would produce anything whatever in the way of social organization, were it not that chance found itself restricted in this field by the conditions of existence to which every society has to conform on pain of being either subdued or destroyed. The men who submit to these conditions of existence are more often than not unaware of them, for they act not by imposing a definite direction on the efforts of each one, but by rendering ineffective all efforts made in directions disallowed by them.

These conditions of existence are determined in the first place, as in the case of living beings, on the one hand by the natural environment and on the other hand by the existence, activity and especially competition of other organisms of the same species, that is to say here of other social groups. But still a third factor enters into play, namely, the organization of the natural environment, capital equipment, armaments, methods of work and of warfare; and this factor occupies a special position owing to the fact that, though it acts upon the form of social organization, it in turn undergoes the latter's reaction upon it. Furthermore, this factor is the only one over which the members of a society can perhaps exercise some control.

This outline is too abstract to serve as a guide; but if on the basis of this summary view we could arrive at some concrete analyses, it would at last become possible to formulate the social problem. The enlightened goodwill of men acting in an individual capacity is the only possible principle of social progress; if social necessities, once clearly perceived, were found to lie outside the range of this goodwill in the same way as those which govern the stars, each man would have nothing more to do but to watch history unfolding as one watches the seasons go by, while doing his best to spare himself and his loved ones the misfortune of being either an instrument or a victim of social oppression. If this is not so, it would be necessary first of all to define by way of an ideal limit the objective conditions that would permit of a social organization absolutely free from oppression; then seek out by what means and to what extent the conditions actually given can be transformed so as to bring them nearer to this ideal; find out what is the least oppressive form of social organization for a body of specific objective conditions; and lastly, define in this field the power of action and responsibilities of individuals as such. Only on this condition could political action become something analogous to a form of work, instead of being, as has been the case hitherto, either a game or a branch of magic.

Unfortunately, in order to reach this stage, what is required is not only searching, rigorous thinking, subjected, so as to avoid all possibility of error, to the most exacting checking, but also historical, technical and scientific investigations of an unparalleled range and precision, and conducted from an entirely new point of view. However, events do not wait; time will not stop in order to afford us leisure; the present forces itself urgently on our attention and threatens us with calamities which would bring in their train, amongst many other harrowing misfortunes, the material impossibility of studying or writing otherwise than in the service of the oppressors. What are we to do? There would be no point in letting oneself be swept along in

the *mêlée* by an ill-considered enthusiasm. No one has the faintest idea of either the objectives or the means of what is still from force of habit called revolutionary action. As for reformism, the principle of the lesser evil on which it is based is certainly eminently reasonable, however discredited it may be through the fault of those who have hitherto made use of it; though remember, if it has so far served only as a pretext for capitulation, this is due not to the cowardice of a few leaders, but to an ignorance unfortunately common to all; for as long as the worst and the best have not been defined in terms of a clearly and concretely conceived ideal, and then the precise margin of possibilities determined, we do not know which is the lesser evil, and consequently we are compelled to accept under this name anything effectively imposed by those who dispose of force, since any existing evil whatever r is always less than the possible evils which uncalculating action invariably runs the risk of bringing about. Broadly speaking, blind men such as we are in these days have only the choice between surrender and adventure. And yet we cannot avoid the duty of determining here and now the attitude to adopt with regard to the present situation. That is why, until we have—if, indeed, such a thing is possible—taken to pieces the social mechanism, it is permissible perhaps to try to outline its principles; provided it be clearly understood that such a rough sketch rules out any kind of categorical assertion, and aims solely at submitting a few ideas, by way of hypotheses, to the critical examination of honest people. Besides, we are far from being without a guide on the subject. If Marx's system, in its broad outlines, is of little assistance, it is a different matter when it comes to the analyses he was led to make by the concrete study of capitalism, and in which, while believing that he was limiting himself to describing a system, he probably more than once seized upon the hidden nature of oppression itself.

Among all the forms of social organization which history has to show, there are very few which appear to be really free from oppression; and these few are not very well known. All of them correspond to an extremely low level of production, so low that the division of labour is pretty well unknown, except between the sexes, and each family produces little more than its own requirements. It is sufficiently obvious, moreover, that such material conditions necessarily rule out oppression, since each man, compelled to sustain himself personally, is continually at grips with outside nature; war itself, at this stage, is war of pillage and extermination, not of conquest, because the means of consolidating a conquest and especially of turning it to account are lacking. What is surprising is not that oppression should make its appearance only after higher forms of economy have been reached, but that it should always accompany them. This means, therefore, that as between a completely primitive economy and more highly developed forms of economy there is a difference not only of degree, but also of kind. And, in fact, although from the point of view of consumption there is but a change-over to slightly better conditions, production, which is the decisive factor, is itself transformed in its very essence. This transformation consists at first sight in a progressive emancipation with respect to nature. In completely primitive forms of production—hunting, fishing, gathering—human effort appears as a simple reaction to the inexorable pressure continually exercised on man by nature, and that in two ways. To start with, it takes place, to all intents and purposes, under immediate compulsion, under the ever-present spur of natural needs; and, by an indirect consequence, the action seems to receive its form from nature herself, owing to the important part played therein by an intuition comparable to animal instinct and a patient observation of the most frequent natural phenomena, also owing to the indefinite repetition of methods that have often succeeded without men's knowing why, and which are doubtless regarded as being welcomed by nature with special favour. At this stage, each man is necessarily free with respect to other men, because he is in direct contact with the conditions of his own existence, and because nothing human interposes itself between them and him; but, on the other hand, and to the same extent, he is narrowly subjected to nature's dominion, and he shows this clearly enough by deifying her. At higher stages of production, nature's compulsion continues certainly to be exercised, and still pitilessly, but in an apparently less immediate fashion; it seems to become more and more liberalized and to leave an increasing margin to man's freedom of choice, to his faculty of initiative and decision. Action is no longer tied moment by moment to nature's exigencies; men learn how to store up reserves on a long-term basis for meeting needs not yet actually felt; efforts which can be only of indirect usefulness become more and more numerous; at the same time a systematic co-ordination in time and in space becomes possible and necessary, and its importance increases continually. In short, man seems to pass by stages, with respect to nature, from servitude to dominion. At the same time nature gradually loses her divine character, and divinity more and more takes on human shape. Unfortunately, this emancipation is only a flattering semblance. In reality, at these higher stages, human action continues, as a whole, to be nothing but pure obedience to the brutal spur of an immediate necessity; only, instead of being harried by nature, man is henceforth harried by man.

However, it is still the same pressure exerted by nature that continues to make itself felt, although indirectly; for oppression is exercised by force, and in the long run all force originates in nature.

The notion of force is far from simple, and yet it is the first that has to be elucidated in order to formulate the problems of society. Force and oppression—that makes two; but what needs to be understood above all is that it is not the manner in which use is made of some particular force, but its very nature, which determines whether it is oppressive or not. Marx clearly perceived this in connection with the State; he understood that this machine for grinding men down, cannot stop grinding as long as it goes on functioning, no matter in whose hands it may be. But this insight has a far more general application. Oppression proceeds exclusively from objective conditions. The first of these is the existence of privileges; and it is not men's laws or decrees which determine privileges, nor yet titles to property; it is the very nature of things. Certain circumstances, which correspond to stages, no doubt inevitable, in human development, give rise to forces which come between the ordinary man and his own conditions of existence, between the effort and the fruit of the effort, and which are, inherently, the monopoly of a few, owing to the fact that they cannot be shared among all; thenceforward these privileged beings, although they depend, in order to live, on the work of others, hold in their hands the fate of the very people on whom they depend, and equality is destroyed. This is what happens to begin with when the religious rites by which man thinks to win nature over to his side, having become too numerous and complicated to be known by all, finally become the secret and consequently the monopoly of a few priests; the priest then disposes, albeit only through a fiction, of all of nature's powers, and it is in their name that he exercises authority. Nothing essential is changed when this monopoly is no longer made up of rites but of scientific processes, and when those in possession of it are called scientists and technicians instead of priests.

Arms, too, give rise to a privilege from the day when, on the one hand, they are sufficiently powerful to render any defence by unarmed against armed men impossible, and, on the other, the handling of them has become sufficiently advanced, and consequently difficult, to require a long apprenticeship and continuous practice. For henceforth the workers are powerless to defend themselves, whereas the warriors, albeit incapable of production, can always take forcible possession of the fruits of other people's labour; the workers are thus at the mercy of the warriors, and not the other way about. The same thing applies to gold, and more generally to money, as soon as the division of labour is so far developed that no worker can live off his own products without having exchanged at any rate some of them for those of others; the organization of exchange then becomes necessarily the monopoly of a few specialists who, having money under their control, can both obtain for themselves, in order to live, the products of others' labour, and at the same time deprive the producers of the indispensably necessary.

In short, wherever, in the struggle against men or against nature, efforts need to be multiplied and co-ordinated to be effective, co-ordination becomes the monopoly of a few leaders as soon as it reaches a certain degree of complexity, and execution's primary law is then obedience; this is true both of the management of public affairs and for that of private undertakings. There may be other sources of privilege, but these are the chief ones; furthermore, except in the case of money, which appears at a given moment of history, all these factors enter into play under all the systems of oppression; what changes is the way in which they are distributed and combined, the degree of concentration of power, and also the more or less closed and consequently more or less mysterious character of each monopoly. Nevertheless, privileges, of themselves, are not sufficient to cause oppression. Inequality could be easily mitigated by the resistance of the weak and the feeling for justice of the strong; it would not lead to a still harsher form of necessity than that of natural needs themselves, were it not for the intervention of a further factor, namely, the struggle for power.

As Marx clearly understood in the case of capitalism, and as a few moralists have perceived in a more general way, power contains a sort of fatality which weighs as pitilessly on those who command as on those who obey; nay more, it is in so far as it enslaves the former that, through their agency, it presses down upon the latter. The struggle against nature entails certain inescapable necessities which nothing can turn aside, but these necessities contain within themselves their own limits; nature resists, but she does not defend herself, and where she alone is involved, each situation presents certain well-defined obstacles which arouse the best in human effort. It is altogether different as soon as relations between man and man take the place of direct contact between man and nature. The preservation of power is a vital necessity for the powerful, since it is their power which provides their sustenance; but they have to preserve it both against their rivals and against their inferiors, and these latter cannot do otherwise than try to rid themselves of dangerous masters; for, through a vicious circle, the master produces fear in the slave by the very fact that he is afraid of him, and vice versa; and the same is true as between rival powers.

What is more, the struggles that every man of power has to wage—first against those over whom he rules, secondly against his rivals—are inextricably bound up together and each is all the time rekindling the other. A power, whatever it may be, must always tend towards strengthening itself at home by means of successes gained abroad, for such successes provide it with more powerful means of coercion; besides, the struggle against its rivals rallies behind it its own slaves, who are under the illusion they have a personal interest in the result of the battle. But, in order to obtain from the slaves the obedience and sacrifices indispensable to victory, that power has to make itself more oppressive; to be in a position to exercise this oppression, it is still more imperatively compelled to turn outwards; and so on. We can follow out the same chain of events by starting from another link; show how a given social group, in order to be in a position to defend itself against the outside powers threatening to lay hands on it, must itself submit to an oppressive form of authority; how the power thus set up, in order to maintain its position, must stir up conflicts with rival powers; and so on, once again. Thus it is that the most fatal of vicious circles drags the whole society in the wake of its masters in a mad merry-go-round.

There are only two ways of breaking the circle, either by abolishing inequality, or else by setting up a stable power, a power such that there exists a balance between those who command and those who obey. It is this second solution that has been sought by all whom we call upholders of order, or at any rate all those among them who have been moved neither by servility nor by ambition; it was doubtless so with the Latin writers who praised "the immense majesty of the Roman peace," with Dante, with the reactionary school at the beginning of the nineteenth century, with Balzac, and is so today with sincere and thoughtful men of the Right. But this stability of power—objective of those who call themselves realists—shows itself to be a chimera, if one examines it closely, on the same grounds as the anarchists' utopia.

Between man and matter, each action, whether successful or not, establishes a balance that can only be upset from outside; for matter is inert. A displaced stone accepts its new position; the wind consents to guide to her destination the same ship which it would have sent off her course if sails and rudder had not been properly adjusted. But men are essentially active beings and have a faculty of self-determination which they can never renounce, even should they so desire, except on the day when, through death, they drop back into the state of inert matter; so that every victory won over men contains within itself the germ of a possible defeat, unless it goes as far as extermination. But extermination abolishes power by abolishing its object. Thus there is, in the very essence of power, a fundamental contradiction that prevents it from ever existing in the true sense of the word; those who are called the masters, ceaselessly compelled to reinforce their power for fear of seeing it snatched away from them, are for ever seeking a dominion essentially impossible to attain; beautiful illustrations of this search are offered by the infernal torments in Greek mythology. It would be otherwise if one man could possess in himself a force superior to that of many other men put together; but such is never the case; the instruments of power—arms, gold, machines, magical or technical secrets—always exist independently of him who disposes of them, and can be taken up by others. Consequently all power is unstable.

Generally speaking, among human beings, since the relationships between rulers and ruled are never fully acceptable, they always constitute an irremediable disequilibrium which is continually aggravating itself; the same is true even in the sphere of private life, where love, for example, destroys all balance in the soul as soon as it seeks to dominate or to be dominated by its object. But here at any rate there is nothing external to prevent reason from returning and putting everything to rights by establishing liberty and equality; whereas social relationships, in so far as the very methods of labour and of warfare rule to equality, seem to cause madness to weigh down on mankind in the manner of an external fatality. For, owing to the fact that there is never power, but only a race for power, and that there is no term, no limit, no proportion set to this race, neither is there any limit or proportion set to the efforts that it exacts; those who give themselves up to it, compelled to do always better than their rivals, who in their turn strive to do better than they, must sacrifice not only the existence of the slaves, but their own also and that of their nearest and dearest; so it is that Agamemnon sacrificing his daughter lives again in the capitalists who, to maintain their privileges, acquiesce lightheartedly in wars that may rob them of their sons.

Thus the race for power enslaves everybody, strong and weak alike. Marx saw this clearly with reference to the capitalist system. Rosa Luxemburg used to inveigh against the aspect of "aimless merry-go-round" presented by the Marxist picture of capitalist accumulation, that picture in which consumption appears as a "necessary evil" to be reduced to the minimum, a mere means for keeping alive those who devote themselves, whether as leaders or as workers, to the supreme object, which is none other than the manufacture of capital equipment, that is to say of the means of production. And yet it is the profound absurdity of this

picture which gives it its profound truth; a truth which extends singularly beyond the framework of the capitalist system. The only characteristic peculiar to this system is that the instruments of industrial production are at the same time the chief weapons in the race for power; but always the methods pursued in the race for power, whatever they may be, bring men under their subjection through the same frenzy and impose themselves on them as absolute ends. It is the reflection of this frenzy that lends an epic grandeur to works such as the *Comédie Humaine*, Shakespeare's *Histories*, the *chansons de geste*, or the *Iliad*. The real subject of the *Iliad* is the sway exercised by war over the warriors, and, through them, over humanity in general; none of them knows why each sacrifices himself and all his family to a bloody and aimless war, and that is why, all through the poem, it is the gods who are credited with the mysterious influence which nullifies peace negotiations, continually revives hostilities, and brings together again the contending forces urged by a flash of good sense to abandon the struggle.

Thus in this ancient and wonderful poem there already appears the essential evil besetting humanity, the substitution of means for ends. At times war occupies the forefront, at other times the search for wealth, at other times production; but the evil remains the same. The common run of moralists complain that man is moved by his private interest: would to heaven it were so! Private interest is a self-centered principle of action, but at the same time restricted, reasonable and incapable of giving rise to unlimited evils. Whereas, on the other hand, the law of all activities governing social life, except in the case of primitive communities, is that here each one sacrifices human life—in himself and in others—to things which are only means to a better way of living. This sacrifice takes on various forms, but it all comes back to the question of power. Power, by definition, is only a means; or to put it better, to possess a power is simply to possess means of action which exceed the very limited force that a single individual has at his disposal. But power-seeking, owing to its essential incapacity to seize hold of its object, rules out all consideration of an end, and finally comes, through an inevitable reversal, to take the place of all ends. It is this reversal of the relationship between means and end, it is this fundamental folly that accounts for all that is senseless and bloody right through history. Human history is simply the history of the servitude which makes men—oppressors and oppressed alike—the plaything of the instruments of domination they themselves have manufactured, and thus reduces living humanity to being the chattel of inanimate chattels.

Thus it is things, not men, that prescribe the limits

and laws governing this giddy race for power. Men's desires are powerless to control it. The masters may well dream of moderation, but they are prohibited from practising this virtue, on pain of defeat, except to a very slight extent; so that, apart from a few almost miraculous exceptions, such as Marcus Aurelius, they quickly become incapable even of conceiving it. As for the oppressed, their permanent revolt, which is always simmering, though it only breaks out now and then, can operate in such a way as to aggravate the evil as well as to restrict it; and on the whole it rather constitutes an aggravating factor in that it forces the masters to make their power weigh ever more heavily for fear of losing it.

From time to time the oppressed manage to drive out one team of oppressors and to replace it by another, and sometimes even to change the form of oppression; but as for abolishing oppression itself, that would first mean abolishing the sources of it, abolishing all the monopolies, the magical and technical secrets that give a hold over nature, armaments, money, co-ordination of labour. Even if the oppressed were sufficiently conscious to make up their minds to do so, they could not succeed. It would be condemning themselves to immediate enslavement by the social groupings that had not carried out the same change; and even were this danger to be miraculously averted, it would be condemning themselves to death, for, once men have forgotten the methods of primitive production and have transformed the natural environment into which these fitted, they cannot recover immediate contact with nature.

It follows that, in spite of so many vague desires to put an end to madness and oppression, the concentration of power and the aggravation of its tyrannical character would know no bounds were these not by good fortune found in the nature of things. It behooves us to determine roughly what these bounds can be; and for this purpose we must keep in mind the fact that, if oppression is a necessity of social life, this necessity has nothing providential about it. It is not because it becomes detrimental to production that oppression can come to an end; the "revolt of the productive forces," so naively invoked by Trotsky as a factor in history, is a pure fiction. We should be mistaken likewise in assuming that oppression ceases to be ineluctable as soon as the productive forces have been sufficiently developed to ensure welfare and leisure for all. Aristotle admitted that there would no longer be anything to stand in the way of the abolition of slavery if it were possible to have the indispensable jobs done by "mechanical slaves," and when Marx attempted to forecast the future of the human species, all he did was

to take up this idea and develop it. It would be true if men were guided by considerations of welfare; but from the days of the *Iliad* to our own times, the senseless demands made by the struggle for power have taken away even the leisure for thinking about welfare. The raising of the output of human effort will remain powerless to lighten the load of this effort as long as the social structure implies the reversal of the relationship between means and ends, in other words, as long as the methods of labour and of warfare give to a few men a discretionary power over the masses; for the fatigues and privations that have become unnecessary in the struggle against nature will be absorbed by the war carried on between men for the defence or acquisition of privileges. Once society is divided up into men who command and men who execute, the whole of social life is governed by the struggle for power, and the struggle for subsistence only enters in as one factor, indispensable to be sure, of the former.

The Marxist view, according to which social existence is determined by the relations between man and nature established by production, certainly remains the only sound basis for any historical investigation; only these relations must be considered first of all in terms of the problem of power, the means of subsistence forming simply one of the data of this problem. This order seems absurd, but it merely reflects the essential absurdity lying at the very heart of social life. A scientific study of history would thus be a study of the actions and reactions which are perpetually arising between the organization of power and the methods of production; for although power depends on the material conditions of life, it never ceases to transform these conditions themselves. Such a study goes very far beyond our possibilities at the moment; but before grappling with the infinite complexity of the facts, it is useful to make an abstract diagram of this interplay of actions and reactions, rather in the same way as astronomers have had to invent an imaginary celestial sphere so as to find their way about among the movements and positions of the stars.

We must try first of all to draw up a list of the inevitable necessities which limit all species of power. In the first place, any sort of power relies upon instruments which have in each situation a given scope. Thus you do not command in the same way, by means of soldiers armed with bows and arrows, spears and swords as you do by means of aeroplanes and incendiary bombs; the power of gold depends on the role played by exchanges in economic life; that of technical secrets is measured by the difference between what you can accomplish with their aid and what you can accomplish without them; and so on. As a matter of fact, one must always include in this balance-sheet the subterfuges by which the powerful obtain through persuasion what they are totally unable to obtain by force, either by placing the oppressed in a situation such that they have or think they have an immediate interest in doing what is asked of them, or by inspiring them with a fanaticism calculated to make them accept any and every sacrifice. Secondly, since the power that a human being really exercises extends only to what is effectively under his control, power is always running up against the actual limits of the controlling faculty, and these are extremely narrow. For no single mind can encompass a whole mass of ideas at once; no man can be in several places at once; and for master and slave alike there are never more than twenty-four hours in a day. Collaboration apparently constitutes a remedy for this drawback; but as it is never absolutely free from rivalry, it gives rise to infinite complications. The faculties of examining, comparing, weighing, deciding, combining are essentially individual, and consequently the same thing applies also to power, whose exercise is inseparable from these faculties; collective power is a fiction, at any rate in final analysis. As for the number of interests that can come under the control of one single man, that depends to a very large extent on individual factors such as breadth and quickness of intelligence, capacity for work, firmness of character; but it also depends on the objective conditions of the control exercised, more or less rapid methods of transport and communication, simplicity or otherwise of the machinery of power. Lastly, the exercise of any form of power is subject to the existence of a surplus in the production of commodities, and a sufficiently large surplus so that all those engaged, whether as masters or as slaves, in the struggle for power, may be able to live. Obviously, the extent of such surplus depends on the methods of production, and consequently also on the social organization. Here, therefore, are three factors that enable one to conceive political and social power as constituting at each moment something analogous to a measurable force. However in order to complete the picture, one must bear in mind that the men who find themselves in relationship, whether as masters or as slaves, with the phenomenon of power are unconscious of this analogy. The powerful, be they priests, military leaders, kings or capitalists, always believe that they command by divine right; and those who are under them feel themselves crushed by a power which seems to them either divine or diabolical, but in any case supernatural. Every oppressive society is cemented by this religion of power, which falsifies all social relations by enabling the powerful to command over and above what they are able to impose; it is only

otherwise in times of popular agitation, times when, on the contrary, all—rebellious slaves and threatened masters alike—forget how heavy and how solid the chains of oppression are. . . .

. . . In general, one can only regard the world in which we live as subject to laws if one admits that every phenomenon in it is limited; and it is the same for the phenomenon of power, as Plato had understood. If we want to consider power as a conceivable phenomenon, we must think that it can extend the foundations on which it rests up to a certain point only, after which it comes up, as it were, against an impassable wall. But even so it is not in a position to stop; the spur of competition forces it to go ever farther and farther, that is to say to go beyond the limits within which it can be effectively exercised. It extends beyond what it is able to control; it commands over and above what it can impose; it spends in excess of its own resources. Such is the internal contradiction which every oppressive system carries within itself like a seed of death; it is made up of the opposition between the necessarily limited character of the material bases of power and the necessarily unlimited character of the race for power considered as relationship between men. . . .

Generally speaking, the sudden reversal of the relationship between forces which is what we usually understand by the term "revolution" is not only a phenomenon unknown in history, but furthermore, if we examine it closely, something literally inconceivable, for it would be a victory of weakness over force, the equivalent of a balance whose lighter scale were to go down. What history offers us is slow transformations of régimes, in which the bloody events to which we give the name "revolutions" play a very secondary role, and from which they may even be absent. . . .

We must pose once again the fundamental problem, namely, what constitutes the bond which seems hitherto to have united social oppressions in the relations between man and nature? If one considers human development as a whole up to our own time, if above all, one contrasts primitive tribes, organized practically without inequality, with our present-day civilization, it seems as if man cannot manage to lighten the yoke imposed by natural necessities without an equal increase in the weight of that imposed by social oppression, as though by the play of a mysterious equilibrium. And even, what is stranger still, it would seem that if, in fact, the human collectivity has to a large extent freed itself from the crushing burden which the gigantic forces of nature place on frail humanity, it has, on the other hand, taken in some sort nature's place to the point of crushing the individual in a similar manner. . . .

... Thus it is that man escapes to a certain extent from the caprices of blind nature only by handing himself over to the no less blind caprices of the struggle for power. This is never truer than when man reaches—as in our case—a technical development sufficiently advanced to give him the mastery over the forces of nature; for, in order that this may be so, co-operation has to take place on such a vast scale that the leaders find they have to deal with a mass of affairs which lie utterly beyond their capacity to control. As a result, humanity finds itself as much the plaything of the forces of nature, in the new form that technical progress has given them, as it ever was in primitive times; we have had, are having, and will continue to have bitter experience of this. As for attempts to preserve technique while shaking off oppression, they at once provoke such laziness and such confusion that those who have engaged in them are more often than not obliged to place themselves again almost immediately under the yoke; the experiment was tried out on a small scale in the producers' co-operatives, on a vast scale at the time of the Russian Revolution. It would seem that man is born a slave, and that servitude is his natural condition.

Theoretical Picture of a Free Society

And yet nothing on earth can stop man from feeling himself born for liberty. Never, whatever may happen, can he accept servitude; for he is a thinking creature. He has never ceased to dream of a boundless liberty, whether as a past state of happiness of which a punishment has deprived him, or as a future state of happiness that is due to him by reason of a sort of pact with some mysterious providence. The communism imagined by Marx is the most recent form this dream has taken. This dream has always remained vain, as is the case with all dreams, or, if it has been able to bring consolation, this has only been in the form of an opium; the time has come to give up dreaming of liberty, and to make up one's mind to conceive it.

Perfect liberty is what we must try to represent clearly to ourselves, not in the hope of attaining it, but in the hope of attaining a less imperfect liberty than is our present condition; for the better can be conceived only by reference to the perfect. One can only steer towards an ideal. The ideal is just as unattainable as the dream, but differs from the dream in that it concerns reality; it enables one, as a mathematical limit, to grade situations, whether real or realizable, in an order of value from least to greatest. Perfect liberty cannot be conceived as consisting merely in the disappearance of that necessity whose pressure weighs continually upon us; as long as man goes on existing, that is to say as long

as he continues to constitute an infinitesimal fraction of this pitiless universe, the pressure exerted by necessity will never be relaxed for one single moment. ... If one were to understand by liberty the mere absence of all necessity, the word would be emptied of all concrete meaning; but it would not then represent for us that which, when we are deprived of it, takes away the value from life.

One can understand by liberty something other than the possibility of obtaining without effort what is pleasurable. There exists a very different conception of liberty, an heroic conception which is that of common wisdom. True liberty is not defined by a relationship between desire and its satisfaction, but by a relationship between thought and action; the absolutely free man would be he whose every action proceeded from a preliminary judgment concerning the end which he set himself and the sequence of means suitable for attaining this end. It matters little whether the actions in themselves are easy or painful, or even whether they are crowned with success; pain and failure can make a man unhappy, but cannot humiliate him as long as it is he himself who disposes of his own capacity for action. And ordering one's own actions does not signify in any way acting arbitrarily; arbitrary actions do not proceed from any exercise of judgment, and cannot properly speaking be called free. Every judgment bears upon an objective set of circumstances, and consequently upon a warp and woof of necessities. Living man can on no account cease to be hemmed in on all sides by an absolutely inflexible necessity; but since he is a thinking creature, he can choose between either blindly submitting to the spur with which necessity pricks him on from outside, or else adapting himself to the inner representation of it that he forms in his own mind; and it is in this that the contrast between servitude and liberty lies. ...

Man would then have his fate constantly in his own hands; at each moment he would forge the conditions of his own existence by an act of mind. Mere desire, it is true, would lead him nowhere; he would receive nothing gratuitously; and even the possibilities of effective effort would for him be strictly limited. But the very fact of not being able to obtain anything without having brought into action, in order to acquire it, all the powers of mind and body would enable man to tear himself away for good from the blind grip of the passions. A clear view of what is possible and what impossible, what is easy and what difficult, of the labours that separate the project from its accomplishment—this alone does away with insatiable desires and vain fears; from this and not from anything else proceed moderation and courage, virtues without which life is nothing but a disgraceful frenzy. Besides, the source of any kind of virtue lies in the shock produced by the human intelligence being brought up against a matter devoid of lenience and of falsity. It is not possible to conceive of a nobler destiny for man than that which brings him directly to grips with naked necessity, without his being able to expect anything except through his own exertions, and such that his life is a continual creation of himself by himself. Man is a limited being to whom it is not given to be, as in the case of the God of the theologians, the direct author of his own existence; but he would possess the human equivalent of that divine power if the material conditions that enable him to exist were exclusively the work of his mind directing the effort of his muscles. This would be true liberty.

Such liberty is only an ideal, and cannot be found in reality any more than a perfectly straight line can be drawn with a pencil. But it will be useful to conceive this ideal if we can discern at the same time what it is that separates us from it, and what are the circumstances that can cause us to move away from it or approach nearer to it. The first obstacle which appears is formed by the complexity and size of this world with which we have to deal: these infinitely outstrip our mental range. The difficulties of real life do not constitute problems made to our scale; they are like problems possessing an innumerable quantity of data, for matter is doubly indefinite, from the point of view of extent and from that of divisibility. That is why it is impossible for a human mind to take into account all the factors on which the success of what seems to be the simplest action depends; any given situation whatever leaves the door open to innumerable chance possibilities, and things escape our mind as water does between the fingers of our cupped hands. Hence it would seem that the mind is only able to exercise itself upon unreal combinations of signs, and that action must be reduced to the blindest form of groping. But, in fact, this is not so. It is true that we can never act with absolute certainty; but that does not matter so much as one might suppose. We can easily accept the fact that the results of our actions are dependent on accidents outside our control; what we must at all costs preserve from chance are our actions themselves, and that in such a way as to place them under the control of the mind. . . . The world is too full of situations whose complexity is beyond us for instinct, routine, trial and error, improvising ever to be able to cease playing a role in our labours; all man can do is to restrict this role more and more, thanks to scientific and technical progress. What matters is that this role should be subordinate and should not prevent method from constituting the very soul of work. It is also necessary that it should appear as provisional, and that routine and trial

and error should always be regarded not as principles of action, but as make-shifts for the purpose of filling up the gaps in methodical conception; in this scientific hypotheses are a powerful aid by making us conceive half-understood phenomena as governed by laws comparable to those which determine the most clearly understood phenomena. And even in cases where we know nothing at all, we can still assume that similar laws are applicable; this is sufficient to eliminate, in default of ignorance, the feeling of mystery, and to make us understand that we live in a world in which man has only himself to look to for miracles.

There is, however, one source of mystery that we cannot eliminate, and which is none other than our own body. The extreme complexity of vital phenomena can perhaps be progressively unravelled, at any rate to a certain extent; but the immediate relationship linking our thoughts to our movements will always remain wrapped in impenetrable obscurity. . . . We can thus understand how primitive men, in spite of their very great dexterity in accomplishing all they have to do in order to continue to exist, visualize the relationship between man and the world under the aspect not of work but of magic. . . . These beliefs survive in the form of superstitions, and, contrary to what we like to think, no man is completely free from them; but their spell loses its potency in proportion as, in the struggle against nature, the living body assumes a secondary importance and passive instruments a primary importance. Such is the case when instruments, ceasing to be fashioned according to the structure of the human organism, force the latter, on the contrary, to adapt its movements to their own shape. Thenceforward there is no longer any correspondence between the motions to be carried out and the passions; the mind has to get away from desire and fear and apply itself solely to establishing an exact relationship between the movements imparted to the instruments and the objective aimed at. The docility of the body in such a case is a kind of miracle, but a miracle which the mind may ignore; the body, rendered as it were fluid through habit, to use Hegel's beautiful expression, simply causes the movements conceived in the mind to pass into the instruments. The attention is directed exclusively to the combinations formed by the movements of inert matter, and the idea of necessity appears in its purity, without any admixture of magic. For example, on dry land and borne along by the desires and fears that move his legs for him, man often finds that he has passed from one place to another without being aware of it; on the sea, on the other hand, as desires and fears have no hold over the boat, one has continually to use craft and strategy, set sails and rudder, transmute the thrust of the wind by means of a series of devices which can only be the work of a clear intelligence. You cannot entirely reduce the human body to this docile intermediary role between mind and instrument, but you can reduce it more and more to that role; this is what every technical advance helps to bring about.

But, unfortunately, even if you did manage strictly and in full detail to subject all forms of work without exception to methodical thought, a new obstacle to liberty would immediately arise on account of the profound difference in kind which separates theoretical speculation from action. In reality, there is nothing in common between the solution of a problem and the carrying out of an even perfectly methodical piece of work, between the sequence of ideas and the sequence of movements. The man who tackles a difficulty of a theoretical order proceeds by moving from what is simple to what is complex, from what is clear to what is obscure; the movements of the manual worker, on the other hand, are not some of them clearer and simpler than others, it is merely that those which come before are the condition of those which come after. . . . Hence one is brought face to face with a paradoxical situation; namely, that there is method in the motions of work, but none in the mind of the worker. It would seem as though the method had transferred its abode from the mind into the matter. Automatic machines present the most striking image of this. From the moment when the mind which has worked out a method of action has no need to take part in the job of execution, this can be handed over to pieces of metal just as well as and better than to living members; and one is thus presented with the strange spectacle of machines in which the method has become so perfectly crystallized in metal that it seems as though it is they which do the thinking, and it is the men who serve them who are reduced to the condition of automata. . . .

But there is still another factor making for servitude; it is, in the case of each man, the existence of other men. And indeed, when we look into it more closely, it is strictly speaking, the only factor; man alone can enslave man. Even primitive men would not be the slaves of nature if they did not people her with imaginary beings comparable to man, whose wills are, furthermore, interpreted by men. In this case, as in all the others, it is the outside world that is the source of power; but if behind the infinite forces of nature there did not lie, whether as a result of fiction or in reality, divine or human wills, nature could break man, but she could not humiliate him. Matter can give the lie to expectations and ruin efforts, it remains none the less inert, made to be understood and handled from the outside; but the human mind can never be understood or handled from the outside. To the extent to which a man's fate is dependent on other men, his own life

escapes not only out of his hands, but also out of the control of his intelligence; judgment and resolution no longer have anything to which to apply themselves; instead of contriving and acting, one has to stoop to pleading or threatening; and the soul is plunged into bottomless abysses of desire and fear, for there are no bounds to the satisfactions and sufferings that a man can receive at the hands of other men. This degrading dependence is not the characteristic of the oppressed only; it is for the same reason, though in different ways, that of both the oppressed and the powerful. As the man of power lives only by his slaves, the existence of an inexorable world escapes him almost entirely; his orders seem to him to contain within themselves some mysterious efficacy; he is never capable, strictly speaking, of willing, but is a prey to desires to which the clear perception of necessity never comes to assign any limit. Since he cannot conceive of any other mode of action than that of commanding, when he happens, as he inevitably does, to issue commands in vain, he passes all of a sudden from the feeling of absolute power to that of utter impotence, as often happens in dreams; and his fears are then all the more overwhelming in that he feels himself continually threatened by his rivals. As for the slaves, they are continually striving with material elements; only their lot does not depend on these material elements which they handle, but on masters whose whims are unaccountable and insatiable.

But it would still be a small matter to be dependent on other beings who, although strangers, are at any rate real and whom one can, if not penetrate, at least see, hear, divine by analogy with oneself. Actually, in all oppressive societies, any man, whatever his rank may be, is dependent not only on those above or below him, but above all on the very play of collective life—a blind play which alone determines the social hierarchies; and it does not matter much in this respect whether power allows its essentially collective origin to appear or else seems to reside in certain specific individuals after the manner of the dormitive virtue in opium. Now, if there is one thing in the world which is completely abstract, wholly mysterious, inaccessible to the senses and to the mind, it is the collectivity; the individual who is a member of it cannot, it would seem, reach up to or lay hold of it by any artifice, bring his weight to bear on it by the use of any lever; with respect to it he feels himself to be something infinitely small. If an individual's caprices seem arbitrary to everybody else, the shocks produced by collective life seem to be so to the second power. Thus between man and this universe which is assigned to him by destiny as the sole matter of his thoughts and actions, the relation oppression-servitude permanently sets the impenetrable screen of human arbitrariness. Why be surprised, then, if instead of ideas one encounters little but opinions, instead of action a blind agitation? One could only visualize the possibility of any progress in the true sense of the word, that is to say progress in the order of human values, if one could conceive as an ideal limit a society which armed man against the world without separating him from it.

Man is not made to be the plaything of the blind collectivities that he forms with his fellows, any more than he is made to be the plaything of a blind nature; but in order to cease being delivered over to society as passively as a drop of water is to the sea, he would have to be able both to understand and to act upon it. In all spheres, it is true, collective strength infinitely surpasses individual strength; thus you can no more easily conceive of an individual managing even a portion of the collective life than you can of a line extending itself by the addition of a point. Such, at any rate, is the appearance; but in reality there is one exception and one only, namely, the sphere of the mind. In the case of the mind, the relation is reversed; here the individual surpasses the collectivity to the same extent as something surpasses nothing, for thought only takes shape in a mind that is alone face to face with itself; collectivities do not think. It is true that mind by no means constitutes a force by itself. Archimedes was killed, so it is said, by a drunken soldier; and if he had been made to turn a millstone under the lash of a slave-overseer, he would have turned it in exactly the same manner as the most dull-witted man. To the extent to which the mind soars above the social *mêlée*, it can judge, but it cannot transform. All forms of force are material; the expression "spiritual force" is essentially contradictory; mind can only be a force to the extent to which it is materially indispensable. To express the same idea under another aspect, man has nothing essentially individual about him, nothing which is absolutely his own, apart from the faculty of thinking; and this society on which he is in close dependence every minute of his existence depends in its turn a little on him from the moment his thinking is necessary to it. For all the rest can be imposed from outside by force, including bodily movements, but nothing in the world can compel a man to exercise his powers of thought, nor take away from him the control over his own mind. If you require a slave to think, the lash had better be put away; otherwise you will run very little chance of obtaining high-quality results. Thus, if we wish to form in a purely theoretical way, the conception of a society in which collective life would be subject to men as individuals instead of subjecting them to itself, we must visualize a form of material existence wherein only efforts exclusively directed by a clear intelligence would take place, which would im-

ply that each worker himself had to control, without referring to any external rule, not only the adaptation of his efforts to the piece of work to be produced, but also their co-ordination with the efforts of all the other members of the collectivity. The technique would have to be such as to make continual use of methodical thought; the analogy between the techniques employed in the various tasks would have to be sufficiently close, and technical education sufficiently widespread, to enable each worker to form a clear idea of all the specialized procedures; co-ordination would have to be arranged in sufficiently simple a manner to enable each one continually to have a precise knowledge of it, as concerns both co-operation between workers and exchange of products; collectivities would never be sufficiently vast to pass outside the range of a human mind; community of interests would be sufficiently patent to abolish competitive attitudes; and as each individual would be in a position to exercise control over the collective life as a whole, the latter would always be in accordance with the general will. Privileges founded upon the exchange of products, secrets of production or co-ordination of labour would automatically be done away with. The function of co-ordinating would no longer imply power, since a continual check exercised by each individual would render any arbitrary decision impossible. Generally speaking, men's dependence with regard to one another would no longer imply that their fate rested in the hands of arbitrary factors, and would cease to introduce into human life any mysterious element whatever, since each would be in a position to verify the activities of all the rest by using his own reason. There is but one single and identical reason for all men; they only become estranged from and impenetrable to each other when they depart from it; thus a society in which the whole of material existence had as its necessary and sufficient condition that each individual should exercise his reason could be absolutely clearly understood by each individual mind. As for the stimulus necessary to overcome fatigue, sufferings and dangers, each would find it in the desire to win the esteem of his fellows, but even more so in himself; in the case of creative work by the mind, outward constraint, having become useless and harmful, is replaced by a sort of inward constraint; the sight of the unfinished task attracts the free man as powerfully as the overseer's whip stimulates the slave. Such a society alone would be a society of men free, equal and brothers. Men would, it is true, be bound by collective ties, but exclusively in their capacity as men; they would never be treated by each other as things. Each would see in every workfellow another self occupying another post, and would love him in the way that the Gospel maxim enjoins.

Thus we should possess, over and above liberty, a still more precious good; for if nothing is more odious than the humiliation and degradation of man by man, nothing is so beautiful or so sweet as friendship.

The above picture, considered by itself, is, if possible, still farther removed from the actual conditions of human existence than is the fiction of a Golden Age. But, unlike that fiction, it is able to serve, by way of an ideal, as a standard for the analysis and evaluation of actual social patterns. The picture of a completely oppressive social life where every individual is subject to the operation of a blind mechanism was also purely theoretical; an analysis which situated a society with respect to these two pictures would already come much closer to reality, while still remaining very abstract. There thus emerges a new method of social analysis which is not that of Marx, although it starts, as Marx wanted, from the relationships of production; but whereas Marx, whose conception is in any case not very precise on this point, seems to have wanted to classify the modes of production in terms of output, these would be analysed in terms of the relationships between thought and action. It goes without saying that such a point of view in no way implies that humanity has evolved, in the course of history, from the least conscious to the most conscious forms of production; the idea of progress is indispensable for whoever seeks to design the future in advance, but it can only lead the mind astray when it is the past that is being studied. We must then replace it by the idea of a scale of values conceived outside time; but it is not possible, either, to arrange the various social patterns in serial order according to such a scale. What one can do is to refer to this scale such and such an aspect of social life, taken at a given period.

It is clear enough that one kind of work differs substantially from another by reason of something which has nothing to do with welfare, or leisure, or security, and yet which claims each man's devotion; a fisherman battling against wind and waves in his little boat, although he suffers from cold, fatigue, lack of leisure and even of sleep, danger and a primitive level of existence, has a more enviable lot than the manual worker on a production-line, who is nevertheless better off as regards nearly all these matters. That is because his work resembles far more the work of a free man, despite the fact that routine and blind improvisation sometimes play a fairly large part in it. The craftsman of the Middle Ages also occupies, from this point of view, a fairly honourable position, although the "tricks of the trade" which play so large a part in all work carried out by hand are to a great extent something blind; as for the fully skilled worker, trained in modern technical methods, he perhaps resembles most closely the perfect workman.

Similar differences are found in collective action; a team of workers on a production-line under the eye of a foreman is a sorry spectacle, whereas it is a fine sight to see a handful of workmen in the building trade, checked by some difficulty, ponder the problem each for himself, make various suggestions for dealing with it, and then apply unanimously the method conceived by one of them, who may or may not have any official authority over the remainder. At such moments the image of a free community appears almost in its purity. As for the relationship between the nature of the work and the condition of the worker, that, too, is clearly apparent, as soon as one takes a look at history or at our present-day society; even the slaves of antiquity were treated with consideration when they were employed as physicians or as pedagogues. However, all these remarks are still concerned only with details. A method enabling one to reach general views concerning the various modes of social organization in terms of the ideas of servitude and of liberty would be more valuable.

It would first of all be necessary to draw up something like a map of social life, a map indicating the spots where it is indispensable that thought should be exercised, and consequently, if one may so express it, the individual's zones of influence over society. It is possible to distinguish three ways in which thought can play a part in social life; it can formulate purely theoretical speculations, the results of which will afterwards be applied by technicians; it can be exercised in execution; it can be exercised in command and management. In all these cases, it is only a question of a partial and, as it were, maimed exercise of thought, since the mind is never able fully to embrace its object; but it is enough to ensure that those who are obliged to think when they are discharging their social function preserve the human aspect better than others. This is true not only for the oppressed, but also for all degrees of the social scale. In a society founded on oppression, it is not only the weak but also the most powerful who are bondslaves to the blind demands of collective life, and in each case heart and mind suffer a diminution, though in different ways. If we compare two oppressive social strata such as, for example, the citizens of Athens and the Soviet bureaucracy, we find a distance between them at least as great as that between one of our skilled workmen and a Greek slave. As for the conditions under which thought plays a greater or lesser part in the exercise of power, it would be easy to tabulate them according to the degree of complexity and range of business, the general nature of the difficulties to be solved and the allocation of functions. Thus the members of an oppressive society are not only distinguished according to the higher or lower position in the social mechanism to which they cling, but also by the more conscious or more passive character of their relationship with it, and this second distinction—the more important of the two—has no direct connection with the first. As for the influence that men charged with social functions subject to the control of their own intelligence can exercise on the society of which they form a part, that depends, of course, on the nature and importance of these functions; it would be very interesting, but also very difficult, to carry out a detailed analysis with regard to this point.

Another very important factor in the relations between social oppression and individuals arises from the more or less extensive powers of control that can be exercised over the various functions essentially concerned in co-ordinating by men who are not themselves invested with such powers; it is obvious that the more these functions cannot be controlled, the more crushing collective life becomes for the general body of individuals. Finally, one must bear in mind the nature of the ties which keep the individual in material dependence upon the society surrounding him; at times these ties are looser, at other times tighter, and considerable differences may be found at this point, according to whether a man is more or less forced, at every moment of his existence, to address himself to others in order to have the wherewithal to live, the wherewithal to produce, and to protect himself from outside danger. For example, a workman who has a large enough garden to supply himself with vegetables is more independent than those of his comrades who have to get all their food from the shopkeepers; an artisan who has his own tools is more independent than a factory worker whose hands become useless as soon as it pleases the boss to stop him from working his machine. As for protection against danger, the individual's position in this respect depends on the method of warfare practised by the society in which he finds himself; where fighting is the monopoly of those belonging to a certain social stratum, the security of everybody else depends on these privileged persons; where the destructive power of armaments and the collective nature of warfare give the central government the monopoly of military force, that government disposes of the security of the citizens as it likes. To sum up, the least evil society is that in which the general run of men are most often obliged to think while acting, have the most opportunities for exercising control over collective life as a whole, and enjoy the greatest amount of independence. Furthermore, the necessary conditions for diminishing the oppressive weight of the social mechanism run counter to each other as soon as certain limits are overstepped; thus the thing to do is not to proceed forward as far as possible in a specific direction, but, what is much more difficult, to discover a certain optimum balance.

The purely negative idea of a lessening of social oppression cannot by itself provide an objective for people of good will. It is indispensable to form at any rate a vague mental picture of the sort of civilization one wishes humanity to reach; and it matters little if this mental picture is derived more from mere reverie than from real thought. If the foregoing analyses are correct, the most fully human civilization would be that which had manual labour constituted the supreme value. It is not a question of anything comparable to the religion of production which reigned in America during the period of prosperity, and has reigned in Russia since the Five Year Plan; for the true object of that religion is the product of work and not the worker, material objects and not man. It is not in relation to what it produces that manual labour must become the highest value, but in relation to the man who performs it; it must not be made the object of honours and rewards, but must constitute for each human being what he is most essentially in need of if his life is to take on of itself a meaning and a value in his own eyes. . . .

. . . Those who have so far maintained that applications are the goal of science meant to say that truth is not worth seeking and that success alone counts; but it could be understood differently; one can conceive of a science whose ultimate aim would be the perfecting of technique not by rendering it more powerful, but simply more conscious and more methodical. Besides, output might well increase in proportion with clear thinking; "seek ye first the kingdom of God . . . and all these things shall be added unto you." Such a science would be, in effect, a method for mastering nature, or a catalogue of concepts indispensable for attaining to such mastery, arranged according to an order that would make them palpably clear to the mind. Presumably Descartes conceived science after this fashion. As for the art of such a civilization, it would crystallize in its works the expression of that happy balance between mind and body, between man and the universe, which can exist in action only in the noblest forms of physical labour; moreover, even in the past, the purest works of art have always expressed the sentiment, or to speak perhaps with greater precision, the presentiment of such a balance. The essential aim of sport would be to give the human body that suppleness and, as Hegel says, that fluidity which renders it pervious to thought and enables the latter to enter directly into contact with material objects. Social relations would be directly modelled upon the organizations of labour; men would group themselves in small working collectivities, where co-operation would be the sovereign law, and where each would be able to understand clearly and to verify the connection between the rules to which his life was subjected and the public interest. Moreover, every moment of existence would afford each the opportunity to understand and to feel how profoundly all men are one, since they all have to bring one same reason to bear on similar obstacles; and all human relations, from the most superficial to the very tenderest, would have about them something of that manly and brotherly feeling which forms the bond between workmates.

No doubt all this is purely utopian. But to give even a summary description of a state of things which would be better than what actually exists is always to build a utopia; yet nothing is more necessary to our life than such descriptions, provided it is always reason that is responsible for them. The whole of modern thought since the Renaissance is, moreover, impregnated with more or less vague aspirations towards such a utopian civilization; for some time it was even thought that this civilization was beginning to take shape, and that men were entering upon a period when Greek geometry would descend upon earth. Descartes certainly believed this, as also did some of his contemporaries. Furthermore, the idea of labour considered as a human value is doubtless the one and only spiritual conquest achieved by the human mind since the miracle of Greece; this was perhaps the only gap in the ideal of human life elaborated by Greece and left behind by her as an undying heritage. Bacon was the first to put forward this idea. For the ancient and heart-breaking curse contained in Genesis, which made the world appear as a convict prison and labour as the sign of men's servitude and abasement, he substituted in a flash of genius the veritable charter expressing the relations between man and the world: "We cannot command Nature except by obeying her." This simple pronouncement ought to form by itself the Bible of our times. It suffices to define true labour, the kind which forms free men, and that to the very extent to which it is an act of conscious submission to necessity. After Descartes, scientists progressively slipped into considering pure science as an end in itself; but the ideal of a life devoted to some free form of physical labour began, on the other hand, to be perceived by writers; and it even dominates the masterpiece of the poet usually regarded as the most aristocratic of all, namely, Goethe. Faust, a symbol of the human soul in its untiring pursuit of the good, abandons with disgust the abstract search for truth, which has become in his eyes an empty and barren occupation; love merely leads him to destroy the loved one; political and military power reveals itself as nothing but a game of appearances; the meeting with beauty fulfils his dreams, but only for the space of a second; his position as industrial leader gives him a power which he believes to be substantial, but which nevertheless delivers him up to the tyranny of the passions. Finally, he longs to be stripped of his magic power, which can be regarded as the symbol of all forms of power, and he exclaims: "If I could stand before thee, Nature, simply as a man, then it would be worth while being a human creature"; and he ends by having, at the moment of death, a foretaste of the most complete happiness, by representing to himself a life spent freely among a free people and entirely taken up by hard and dangerous physical labour, which would, however, be carried out in the midst of brotherly co-operation. It would be easy to cite yet other famous names, amongst them Rousseau, Shelley and, above all, Tolstoy, who developed this theme throughout the whole of his work in matchless accents. As for the working-class movement, every time it has managed to escape from demagogy, it is on the dignity of labour that it has based the workers' demands. Proudhon dared to write: "The genius of the humblest artisan is as much superior to the materials with which he works as is the mind of a Newton to the lifeless spheres whose distances, masses and revolutions he calculates." Marx, whose work contains a good many contradictions, set down as man's essential characteristic, as opposed to the animals, the fact that he produces the conditions of his own existence and thus himself indirectly produces himself. The revolutionary syndicalists, who place at the core of the social problem the dignity of the producer as such, are linked up with the same current of ideas. On the whole, we may feel proud to belong to a civilization which has brought with it the presage of a new ideal.

Emma Mashinini (1929–)

Emma Mashinini was born in 1929 in Johannes-burg, South Africa. She was conscious of being, as she later wrote, "the one with the least education in a family of six" (Russell, 180). Though her parents were able to send their eldest daughter to a boarding school, Emma was needed at home to help her mother care for younger sisters and was unable to go to school beyond the tenth grade. The family was subjected to a series of traumatic removals that forced them eventually to live in Soweto. For a time they lived in Sophiatown, where Emma went to Bantu High School. She was proud to note that it was "the same school that our Archbishop Desmond Tutu went to" (ibid.). In Soweto she married at age eighteen but left her first husband in 1959. She had six daugh-ters, the first at age twenty, of whom only two survived. Three died of yellow jaundice, victims of inadequate health care, and one died in an accident. Her second husband, Tom Mashinini, worked with and supported her in her union organizing efforts and later, in response to her imprisonment, became very active in the anti-apartheid struggle.

In 1956, at age twenty-seven, Mashinini started working in the garment industry. She worked for more than nineteen years in the same factory, where she was promoted eventually to factory supervisor. From the start she had joined the Garment Workers Union Number 3, a black workers' union that was represented by the white garment workers' union in negotiations with manage-ment. She became shop steward and then a member of the national executive of the union. Blacks were ex-cluded from white unions and black workers' unions were not legally recognized, but they were sometimes recognized by management. Strikes were illegal. Never-theless, in the early 1970s there was a great increase in strikes and black union organizing, and in 1975 Ma-shinini left her factory job to start a union among the previously unorganized black shop workers. Police ar-rested and harassed her but she succeeded nonetheless, in part with the help of white union leaders, in organiz-ing many workers into a union which was able to secure management recognition and negotiations. She became the General Secretary of the union—later the Commer-cial Catering and Allied Workers' Union—and held that position for eleven years. In 1989 she was proud to observe that the union she had co-founded had grown very powerful, with more than seventy thousand mem-bers. She was also proud of the union's record of protec-tion of women workers.

In November 1981 Mashinini was arrested and held incommunicado for six months in Pretoria Central Pris-on, at first without charge, and never brought to trial. She was subjected most of that time to solitary con-finement and severe deprivation, which affected her mental and physical health. During the same period, one of the white union leaders she had worked with, Neil Aggett, died in detention. The international outcry against Aggett's death focused attention on the deten-tions of others, and Mashinini was released along with another woman trade unionist, Rita Ndzanga, whose disorientation was so great that she had to be helped to find her home. Mashinini tried to resume her work with the union, but her health problems forced her to with-draw in 1985. Before her retirement from union work she played a role in the formation of COSATU, the Con-gress of South African Trade Unions, a nonracial fed-eration of worker-controlled unions that constituted an important force in the struggle against apartheid. Ma-shinini later became director of the Department of Jus-tice and Reconciliation for the Anglican Church in the Province of Southern Africa, working with Archbishop Tutu.

The selections included in this volume are from Emma Mashinini's autobiography, Strikes Have Fol-lowed Me All My Life. It is a powerful example of this genre of writing as a vehicle for the expression of politi-cal thought. Though the book has been welcomed as a document of the oppressions suffered by a black woman under apartheid, and the active resistance of black wom-en in South Africa, little attention has been accorded to her ideas as such. But as Dorothy Driver has shown, Mashinini's autobiography is in a tradition of recon-struction of the "self" in colonized cultures, "the indi-vidual life as exemplary of a social truth about those intended to be mute and invisible as subjects" (Driver, 338). Threading through the simplicity of language and narrative is a complex and subtle process of self-interro-gation and interrogation of human values and behavior, resisting both the structures and the dichotomized po-larities of class, gender, and race in apartheid South Africa.

BAC

Sources and Suggested Readings

Driver, Dorothy. "Imagined Selves, (Un)Imagined Marginalities." *Journal of Southern African Studies* 17, 2 (1991): 337–54.

Hoskins, Linus A. "Life in South Africa: Personal Views." *Current Bibliography on African Affairs* 24, 1 (1992–93): 53–58.

Mashinini, Emma. "Life as a Trade-Union Leader." In *Lives*

Emma Mashinini

of *Courage: Women for a New South Africa*, by Diana E. H. Russell. New York: Basic Books, 1989. 178–89.

————. *Strikes Have Followed Me All My Life: A South African Autobiography.* New York: Routledge, 1991 [London: The Women's Press, 1989].

Rose, Phyllis, ed. *The Norton Book of Women's Lives.* Introduction to selection by Emma Mashinini, p. 530. New York: Norton, 1993.

Russell, Diana E. H. Introduction, Conclusion, and Epilogue. *Lives of Courage: Women for a New South Africa.* New York: Basic Books, 1989.

Strikes Have Followed Me All My Life (1989)

1. Early Years . . .

I was married in 1947, and then I stayed at home. I was a housewife. My first child was born in 1949, and thereafter I had another baby in 1951, and another in 1952, and another in 1954, so it was just babies, babies, babies, all the time. My last baby was born in 1956. I bore six in all, but three died within days of their birth. I didn't know at the time what had caused their deaths, although I can see now it must have been yellow jaundice. Then, in my ignorance, I didn't see that anything was wrong with them. At that time black people wanted their skin to be lighter. Those children seemed to me beautiful, with their lovely light yellow complexions. And the jaundice was never diagnosed.

It might surprise some people that I could lose three babies, each time soon after birth, and not know the cause. But it is typical of white doctors working in our black hospitals to treat patients, and cram them with pills and mixtures, without ever telling them the cause of their illness. Even when you are brave enough to ask, the doctor gets irritable and asks you not to waste his time. I don't know whether it's because our hospitals are overcrowded and therefore the doctors cannot cope with the workload; or whether they think they are doing us a favour because black doctors are few, and so we should be grateful and shut up. To me, on the contrary, it seems that we are doing them a favour, because all our hospitals are training hospitals attached to their medical schools, and with all the peculiar diseases we suffer from, we make excellent guinea-pigs. Sadly, though, some of our own black nurses have fallen victim to this bad habit of not discussing the patient's illness and are spiteful when you

ask what is wrong with you. They have even coined a word for a patient who wants information: they call her '*i Graju*,' meaning you are a graduate, too educated for your own good.

I remember when the first of my children died. The nurse came from the clinic to wash the baby and so forth. I think it was the third day or so that she'd visited, and she said we must go to the clinic. I asked why, and then thought it must be something to do with the baby's extra finger, which they'd tied off, to cut off the circulation.

When we got to the clinic we were taken by ambulance to Baragwanath. I was holding this lovely baby of mine—she was very plump, and everybody was taking her hand saying, 'Look at this lovely baby.' I wasn't the only one who thought she was beautiful. Then the doctors took her and examined her, and said they had to rush her to the ward. And when I got to the ward, that lovely yellow baby of mine had turned almost blue, and no one told me why. There was a drip, and I was upset, and I remember my husband had come looking for me—and the next thing the baby was dead. That beautiful yellow baby.

This thinking that anything that is light-skinned is beautiful has caused so much harm. I don't think anyone escaped it. I myself used skin lighteners when I was working, but I'm one of the lucky people who didn't get cancer from them. Most of the people have damaged skins, just because we thought that if we were light we'd have the same privileges as the whites. When you're working side by side with someone with a lighter skin in a factory and you find they're given preference, it's hard not to believe a lighter skin is better for you. Now black consciousness has saved us from hating the colour of our skin. We used to wear wigs, too, to help give the appearance of being fair, and we used to have terrible struggles with our own hair, to make it straighter. And when we had our photographs taken the negatives would be lightened for us, to make us look as much like white people as possible. I have a photograph of myself wearing my wig, and it saddens me. Even then, looking at my face, I don't think that wig made me too happy.

The only thing we still have a quarrel with, even today, is our weight, and that we continue to fight against, because to be overweight is bad for our health. We know it is the food we eat that is to blame, and that the cheapest food is the most fattening food, and the least nutritious. So we can fight this problem with pride, because we want to be healthy and to look good as people—not as white people. Many young black people are very slim, including my own children. They take exercise, where we just worked and didn't have enough money for food, let alone sport.

When I met my first husband, Roger, I thought he

was very nice because he was handsome and he used to dress well. And when he chose me to be his wife I was proud, because he had chosen me from all the women he could have had.

It was the tradition then that a newly married woman should spend much of her time staying with her in-laws, on her own. It was a point of pride to be able to say, 'I am well accepted. My in-laws love me.' If your husband sent money to you, he didn't have to send it to you as his wife, but would send it to his mother, who would tell you, or not tell you. I was lucky with my mother-in-law, who lived in a rural area in what was once known as Mafeking. She would pass everything he sent on to me, and although she wasn't working, she was ploughing and had some stock cattle and so on, so we lived from all that she could get as produce. I went to live with her when I had Molly, and I lived quite well there.

Then I went back to my husband and brought up our children in our one-roomed house in Kliptown. We lived behind the landlord's cottage, in one of the rooms at the back of the yard. There were three houses like ours facing the front, and three facing almost the back, and ours was a corner room facing the back. A fence divided one house from the other. I had a bed and a wardrobe, and I'd put empty apple boxes one on top of another. In the bottom one I'd store my pots, and in the top one the plates and cups, and on top of these boxes I'd put the two water buckets, and a pot and kettle, which were all aluminium. We had a small black stove in the corner, and two benches and a table.

I would spend the whole day at that table. There were the nappies to be changed, and the children and myself to feed, and then I'd clean those buckets and the pot and kettle with Brasso or whatever until they glittered like mirrors. And I'd polish the black stove, and scrub the benches and the tables. Cleanliness, you see, was another matter of pride among us. We polished in order to keep some self-respect, because the conditions we lived in were so terrible.

I was fortunate that in the yard where I was living there was a well. The others had to come to this same well, and some people had to travel a long way for water. Then came a time when we were told we shouldn't drink the water, as it was polluted, but should use it only for household and laundry work. So I would put my glittering bucket on my head and travel a long way to another well to draw water, but we could never be sure that well was clean, and whether the person doing the inspection was reliable. Looking back, I realise how often my children were ill, and wonder about that water. And of course the toilets were also in the yard, and they weren't drained properly but were really just another well. They smelled very bad.

To my disappointment, within five years I had to admit that my marriage was no longer what it had been. There were just too many quarrels. Always it would be one problem that would lead to the quarrels, and that was money. He was working in the clothing industry, in the cutting room, and so was earning slightly more than some of his colleagues, but still we could not manage on his pay. It would be used up before pay day and there would be no money to pay for food for the babies. . . .

In 1955 we moved into our own four-roomed house in Orlando West, which is in Soweto. The arrangement was that you would pay rent, and if you could afford to pay for thirty years then you would be granted the lease of the house, but never the freehold, because the law forbids black people to own freeholds. That is the privilege of whites only.

Well, it was our pride to have such a big house. Such luxury! We even had our own yard, for a garden or vegetable plot. But the financial problems came with us. These new homes were not electrified, and this added to our difficulties, because just to have light in the evening cost us money we did not have, and the rent was always increasing.

I kept on thinking, 'It will improve.' When we had our fights I would try hard to get money together so that I could take my kids and travel to Mafeking, which was just twelve hours by train, to go to my mother-in-law, who always welcomed me.

In our tradition, when a girl married she was married, body and soul, into the family of her husband. And after the wedding, before she went to live with her husband, all the elderly women—grannies, aunties, mothers—would convene a meeting where she was told what to do when she got to her new home. All the taboos were spelt out—how to behave to her husband, her parents-in-law. And especially she was told never to expose the dirty linen in public. This is why it was always to my mother-in-law that I would go when things got really bad between Roger and me, because wife-battering was regarded as dirty linen, and a woman would suffer that in silence and never admit to a doctor what was the real cause of her injuries. Only nowadays, and this I am pleased to be able to say, this practice has been exposed to such an extent that we have refugee centres in our townships, something that was unheard of a few years ago. But then I would say to the doctors, 'I fell,' or 'I tripped myself.' And his mother would be furious, and even when he'd calmed down and wanted me to come back she'd say, 'No,' but she didn't mention divorce. That wasn't the language we spoke. For her, the way to get away from him was to stay with her.

But one day we started arguing and I said to my husband, 'I'm going to leave you. I'm going home.'

And this man knew I cared about my family, my family unit, and he thought I'd never leave him. So he just said, 'If you want to go, why don't you?'

I took my bag—no clothes or suitcases—and I left. I walked to the bus stop and took a bus all the way to my father's place, and that's the last time I walked away from my husband.

My children came afterwards. My people had to go and fetch them. It was not possible to do it any other way.

2. "Push Your Arse!"

. . . The church was my one pleasure, until we working women got together and had what we called *stokvels*. A *stokvel* is a neighbourhood group that is very supportive, socially and financially. Many black women earn meagre wages and cannot afford to buy the necessary comforts of a home, so we set up these *stokvels*, where we could pool our resources. You have to be a member to enjoy the benefits of a *stokvel*, and they are properly run. The members decide what is the greatest need. It could be a ceiling, a refrigerator, or pots, or anything that you could not pay for yourself. The members collect money in proportion to their wages, and put it into a pool for one person in the group to purchase what has been decided. After that they pass on to the next person, and the group identifies another pressing need, and so it goes until you find that each person in the group has managed to buy some household gadgets without getting into a hire-purchase contract, which has been disastrous to many a housewife.

Another important aspect of *stokvels* is social. Women in the townships are very lonely because their husbands tend to leave them at home when they go to soccer matches, or to the movies, or to taverns to have a drink with the boys. The *stokvel* meetings change from one member's house to another, and you are obliged to serve tea or drinks. After the money has been collected the women start conversing about current affairs, sharing their problems, which leads them to politics. And that is why African women are often much more politically aware than their Coloured and Indian counterparts, who do not have the opportunity of meeting in such a way.

That was the way my neighbourhood was. My house was the second from the corner, and there were no fences dividing the houses from each other. The woman in the first house from the corner worked in a white kindergarten, and she would be able to bring leftovers of sandwiches from rich children, and as she had no young children of her own she would pass those leftovers to me. And so we sustained each other, woman to woman—a woman-to-woman sustaining. . . .

I struggled from the first day I got into the factory. After I had learned the machine better I thought that perhaps the most important thing was to do whatever I had to do perfectly, but because I wanted to do this I couldn't produce the number of garments I was supposed to. It was not possible to chase perfection along with production. They made the choice for you, and they wanted production.

As a result of my attempt to work in this way I was screamed at more than anyone else, but still I couldn't get myself to work as fast as all those other people. Every morning when I walked into that factory I really thought, 'Today it will be my turn to be dismissed.' But then I was elected a shop steward, and soon after, to my surprise (though looking back it does not seem so unexpected), I was promoted. It was after about three or four years, and I was promoted first to be a set leader and then a supervisor, which was unheard of—a black supervisor in that factory. Instead of dismissing me, they were trying to make me one of them.

We were members of the Garment Workers' Union Number 3. There were three garment workers' trade unions at that time. The Garment Workers' Union Number 1 was for whites, headed by Johanna Cornelius, and Number 2 was for Coloureds and Indians. Number 3 was for blacks, headed by Lucy Mvubelo, who had sent me to Henochsberg's in the first place. The union for Africans wasn't registered, of course, but the employers accepted it was there. Our subscriptions at that time were deducted from our pay and went to the Number 1 and 2 unions, who would negotiate for working conditions and wages for garment workers. We had an agreement which served for all three branches—whites, Indians and Coloureds, and Africans—and we would benefit from their negotiations in that whatever minimum wage was set we would be paid that amount. The other workers would get over and above that wage, but they would be sure to set a minimum wage for the African workers. In my factory we black women workers made up about 70 per cent of the work force, all earning that basic flat wage. There was no machinery to challenge that wage. It was for the employer to decide to pay over the minimum wage. It was purely voluntary, and that is in fact what it was called, a 'voluntary increase.' So our union just had to sit and wait for what came out of the negotiations with the Industrial Council. Any action we took over their decision was illegal. For us to strike was illegal.

None the less, on occasion we did strike, or go on a 'go slow.' I think the strikes that meant the most to me were in the early 1970s, when we fought to earn an extra cent, and also to narrow our hours. When I first started work the day would be from seven-thirty to four-thirty, and we fought, all of us, for the narrowing down of the time, and succeeded in bringing it down to five minutes past four for leaving the factory. We were fighting for a forty-hour week, and in the course of the fight we did go out on strike. . . .

On the occasion when we fought for our extra cent, I remember what a struggle we had, and how hostile the employers were. We went on a go slow strike, and they were so angry, being used to dismissing us for the least mistake, for being late or whatever. It took months for us to win—but when we did, we felt joy, great joy. . . .

It was not easy to act for the workers at that time. A lot of awareness has been created over the last years, but then they were often frightened to say aloud that they were not happy with their salaries. Also, they didn't always tell their plans to me, as shop steward. They would always be surprising me. They would say to each other, without my knowledge, 'Tomorrow we are not going to start work until a certain demand is met.' I would always be early at work, because I would arrange things before the workers came in, and when I got there I would see people were not coming to start work, and I would stand there like a fool. I, a black person and a worker, would be inside with all these whites standing around with me and saying, 'Why aren't they coming in to work?' And when the whites would address the workers and say, 'What is your problem?' perhaps somebody would answer, 'We do have a problem.' So they would say, 'Who are your spokespeople? Let your spokespeople come in and talk to us.' And they would say their spokesperson was Emma, meaning me. So the whites would think I had instigated the stoppage, that I was playing a double role, making the workers stand outside and pretending I didn't know.

They could have sacked me if they had wanted. I was a shop steward, but if they wanted to sack you they could still sack you. Instead, they would try and use me to stop the trouble. They would use me like a fire extinguisher, always there to stop trouble. I would have to go to meet with the workers and ask, 'Now what is actually going on?' And they would tell me they wanted money, or they wanted that person who had been shouting and yelling at us to behave him or herself. I would listen to all that, and then I would convey it to the employers. They would be adamant, and so the workers would stay outside and not come in. Often the police would arrive with dogs and surround the workers. Many times with the help of the union we would

eventually receive assistance, and perhaps the people would achieve a part of what they wanted and go back to work. But during those days, in the factory I worked in, there was one strike after another. And this has followed me all my life. Wherever I am it seems there must always be trouble.

3. Speaking Back

I don't know exactly when I became politicised. In 1955, for example, I was in Kliptown when the Freedom Charter was drawn up there, and the square that became known as Freedom Charter Square was like a stone's throw from where I was living. But . . . it was only when my friends approached me that I really took notice of it. . . .

The ANC had a uniform then, and these women were wearing black skirts and green blouses. The gold colour was not anywhere in them then, just green and black. So my friends were all in their colours, and I didn't have that, but every other thing which affected them and made that occasion so wonderful for them affected me as well. I was not a card-carrying member, but at that meeting I was a member in body, spirit and soul.

It was so good to be there, just to hear them speaking. Every race was there, everybody, intermingling. I would sit under the shade of a tree and listen to everything, and it was as though everything I heard was going to happen, in the next few days. I feel the same when I listen to the Freedom Charter now—just for those few moments I take heart that it will all come true, that there will be houses for everyone, schooling, prosperity, everything we need.

There were speeches against the pass laws, and cheering, and clapping, and we sang '*Mayibuye Afrika!*' —'Africa come back!'—and '*Nkosi Sikelei' i Afrika*'— 'God Bless Africa.' It was a moving meeting, yet with all this—the shouting, the strong talk, the mixing of races—it was a peaceful meeting. It has been a long time since we've had those kinds of meetings, with no interference or people having to run. I don't know if they'd invented tear-smoke, nobody running away from anything. I can't even remember seeing any police present, and the police station wasn't far from where the meeting was held. Maybe the police were there, enjoying the meeting as well, because Kliptown was the right place for this meeting to be held. It was a non-racial area. There were very many Indian people, and it was almost like a coloured area, but we were there as well. And there must have been some whites and so forth. So everyone was there. It wasn't like in Soweto, where you find only Africans, or Lenz (Len-

Emma Mashinini

asia), where you find Indians, or in other areas with so-called Coloureds only. It was total racial harmony.

So I think that congress was really an eye-opener for me. That, maybe, is when I started to be politicised. Although there is another thing, which I have always felt, which is that I have always resented being dominated. I resent being dominated by a man, and I resent being dominated by white people, be they man or woman. I don't know if that is being politicised. It is just trying to say, 'I am human. I exist. I am a complete person.'

The 1960s were a bad time for unions. Many were forced to go underground by the government, which was arresting people and banning meetings. The ANC and the Pan African Congress were banned in 1960, after the Sharpeville massacre, and because of the close ties of SACTU [South African Congress of Trade Unions] with the ANC very many union leaders had to go underground or to leave the country.

In 1962 the Garment Workers' Union, which was an all-women union, combined with the Men's Clothing Union and became the National Union of Clothing Workers, and I was elected to sit on the national executive of that union, where I stayed for twelve years. We would meet with the workers and look at their demands, and then pass these demands on to the non-African unions to negotiate for us.

Soon after this, it happened that we went on strike in our factory over our wages, which were still so terribly low, and during one of our meetings somebody came from the Labour Department to drive away the representative who was addressing us at the time, one of my colleagues on the national executive. He said we had no right to go out on strike at that time, because there was an Industrial Council contract in existence, and we were therefore breaking the law. We knew nothing of this, and to us it wasn't important which law we were breaking. The important thing was that we were starving.

These meetings were an opportunity for us to speak out, and say some of the things that had been boiling up inside us, so this man—I remember he was an Afrikaner, and he had only one arm—found himself faced with perhaps more than he expected. His attitude was so rude. He didn't even introduce himself properly. The first thing he did, instead of explaining who he was and that he was supposed to be representing us, was to send our union people away, and to tell us that unions weren't recognised—meaning black unions weren't recognised—and that he was the only one who could speak for us.

Well, we challenged him, and all the workers booed

him, and I, because I am not so good at booing, spoke back instead. It was very satisfying to be able to speak out and say we didn't even know who he was—that since we were seeing him for the first time we didn't see how he could be our representative, and that he was driving away the only people who had come into our factory to help us and organise us. I also asked him which law it was that we were breaking, and in what circumstances that law would not be operating, making it possible for us to go out on strike, because the Industrial Council made sure an agreement was always in operation, and that before one expired they would always have negotiated another agreement, leaving no gap in between. This was a law we had always known about. It existed already and had done since I had become a union member. But because of the suppression of the unions in those years it was not being strictly enforced. And this man, instead of giving us due warning that this was the case, chose to come to our meeting and try to bully us, and drive our representatives away.

At that meeting was Tom Mashinini. He was there as an organiser, and he also was driven away by this man. We were to come across each other soon after this, when Tom was standing to be a full-time union organiser. In fact I voted for the other candidate, but I must have grown to appreciate Tom more over the next few years, since we eventually married, in 1967. He has always respected my independence, and this, I am sorry to say, is unusual in South Africa. . . .

. . . I think it was on that day that the employers really took heed of me, because soon after I was called in to Mr. Herman, the top man in the factory, who told me he had information that a strike was going to take place within a week, and that I was the one who had instigated it.

I thought he was lying, because I had no idea there was going to be any strike, and he said he'd got the information from the people in the Labour Department. They worked very closely with the police, he said, and the police had informed the Labour Department that they had been investigating the Henochsberg workers at this factory for a long time, and that I was the one who was inciting them to strike illegally. I said, 'You'll be proved wrong, because nothing of that nature is going to happen.' But unfortunately, and to my great disappointment, the workers did go out on strike that week, and Mr. Herman called me in and said, 'There it is now, you see, there it is.'

Strangely, though, they still didn't dismiss me from work.

Always, when I addressed those whites, I would have to

stand. We wore uniform for our work, and so I would stand there, dressed in my blue overalls, with my hands behind my back. In all the nineteen and a half years I worked at Henochsberg's I was never once asked to sit down. You just accepted that was the order of the day when you spoke to the white boss—standing, in uniform, hands behind your back, completely deferential. . . .

. . . around 1970 . . . I was earning around 15 rand a week, and that was after fifteen years. I used to take five rand home with me, and the other 10 rand was kept by the factory, so that I would get it all at once at the end of the year in January and be able to meet all my school fees for my children and so forth. It was very hard to live on five rand a week, but I didn't want my children ending up in the factory like I had. I didn't have much knowledge of these things. I didn't know that if I had taken the money to the bank myself there would have been some interest, which I did not get from the factory. . . .

One thing that was worrying me at this time was that I could not understand why we black workers were expected to take tablets against TB, which were handed out to us as a group in our workplaces. I had heard of many bad experiences of 'medical attention,' and because I felt suspicious of these tablets I protested at one of our shop steward meetings. Little did I know that the whites also were getting the same tablet, but that they received theirs person to person, and not publicly, in a group. It will always be difficult to convince us to believe that anything supposedly done for us is really to help us when it is not done for all the people as one. Among my people there are those who have learnt to be suspicious even of family planning methods, and we will always blame the side-effects that have been suffered by some of us on the fact that our treatment is of lesser importance than of the whites.

However, after that meeting a man called Loet Douwes Dekker, a trade unionist working for the Urban Training Project (UTP), approached me and said, 'Emma, I think you would be the right person to go and start a union for the textile workers.' Now all this was a foreign language to me then, and I thought he must be joking. I said no, it wasn't for me, I was okay where I was. But that wasn't the end of it. Next I was approached about a glassworkers' union, and again I didn't accept. But then I was approached by the senior people of the National Union of Distributive Workers (NUDW), the union for white shopworkers, and this time I accepted. I still don't know why, but I did. I discussed it with Lucy Mvubelo and handed in my notice. . . .

4. Birth of a Union

Morris Kagan and Ray Altman were my first real experience of friendship between whites and blacks. I had met them before, along with other white trade unionists, at TUCSA [Trade Union Council of South Africa] meetings, since the NUDW, was an affiliate, and I had admired the brilliant speakers there. One woman especially, Bobby Robarts, who was working for the NUDW, was a fine speaker, and she was one reason why I accepted the job—because of the challenge. But it was those two, Morris and Ray, who supported and helped me in a new way, especially Morris.

They acted as officials for both NUDW and the National Union of Commercial and Allied Workers (NUCAW), which was formed in order to represent Coloured and Indian shopworkers. I was starting the union for black shopworkers from scratch, most of the leaders for the original union having been detained or having left the country. My starting salary was 200 rand a month, which was a big jump, and to cover our first few months Kagan's union gave our union a 1000 rand loan, interest free. We were to be called CCAWUSA: the Commercial, Catering and Allied Workers' Union of South Africa.

The union offices were in Princess House, in the centre of Johannesburg. My office was on the second floor. Because of the Group Areas Act we could not, as blacks, rent offices in town, so Morris Kagan rented my office in the name of NUDW. I had an office, a desk and a chair.

My first day was a terrible experience. I had come out of a factory of over a thousand workers, with the machines roaring for the whole day, everybody busy, people shouting and so forth, and here I found myself all alone. The silence was deafening. It was spring, and I was very cold in that office. I was afraid. There were no formalities to be gone through, I just had to get myself ready to go out and find some members. I didn't know where to start or what to do. When I went home that afternoon I thought I'd made the worst mistake of my life.

I had never been a shopworker and I knew nothing of the ordinances and regulations. I was an ordinary factory worker. I would listen to Morris Kagan speaking and quoting and quoting, and I just thought, 'My God, will I ever catch up?'

In a way, this was my university education, at last, my chance to study. And I was lucky to have a man like Morris Kagan to talk to me and say, 'Here are the books. Read.'

Morris came from Latvia, and arrived in South Africa around 1929, when he was about twenty. He started working as a bus driver and bus conductor, and ended up working in a shop, and from there he became very active as a union member, eventually becoming a full-time union official. He was a junior to Ray Altman, who was a very educated man. Altman was in Cape Town, and Kagan and I were in Johannesburg.

All my admiration goes to Morris Kagan, who struggled with me. He used to say that I reminded him of his late wife, Katie Kagan, who was as short as myself and was a trade unionist ahead of him. He would say, 'Until you are as efficient in your work as the capitalists, you will never beat them.' Even the last time I saw him, the day before he died, in 1983, he scolded me because the name of CCAWUSA was not correctly spelt in the telephone directory. After that he said 'I'm tired and I want to sleep. You will all have to go.' (I was there with Alan Fine and Morris's son-in-law.) 'First, Emma, put me properly on my pillow and cover me with my sheet. Okay. All of you—go.' And by the time I got home there was a call from his daughter to say he had died.

I invited many black unionists to his funeral. There were more blacks than whites there, and we sang 'Nkosi Sikelele.' I thought it was important that Morris Kagan should have a funeral that would show what kind of life he had lived. I remember one elderly white union colleague asked me, 'Emma, could I have the same as Morris Kagan at my funeral?' But Morris had deserved it. . . .

There were other black trade unions that were being set up at that time. Every union was busy getting on its feet, and although their focus wasn't on the particular industry we were representing, at least it was on other problems that we shared, like legislation or recognition. That was very helpful and good—to work as black unions together, not just with Morris's union which was registered and recognised. Even when we worked with unions belonging to FOSATU [Federation of South African Trade Unions], for example, we weren't tempted to federate with them because the FOSATU leadership was dominated by white intellectuals, and although we valued the support of its unions we did not want to be swallowed up by their way of thinking. . . .

The obstacles management put in our way! They were so determined not to let us near the workers. Not only did I have no access to the stores, but even distributing leaflets out in the different shopping centres brought me to my first brush with the police.

The best way of getting the leaflets distributed, to get information across to the workers about the fact that there was a union called CCAWUSA, and where

the headquarters were, and what it could do for them, was to go to their workplace and wait for them to come in to work. They had their meals in the canteen, and it was difficult to catch them going home because most of the stores had several different doors, and you wouldn't know where to wait. So I would try to catch them in the morning, as they came streaming in to work.

Management was very upset by this. They used to blame me for making the workers late, even though all I did was hand them the leaflets as they went in. Then they challenged me with trespassing on private property, which was quite interesting, since if I wasn't trespassing as a shopper then I wasn't trespassing by being there with my leaflets. But then the management would phone the police, and the police would come with their dogs, often very many of them, and bundle me into their van, leaflets and all. Oh, it was disheartening to see all those leaflets disappear into their hands, with all the printing that had gone into them. And they would mishandle me, but there was nothing they could charge me with, and that was more important to me than any fear of being injured. I remember the first time they came roaring up to me with their vans and packed me off to the police station, I was horrified, thinking I was now a criminal. I had broken no law, but that was my main fear.

I was married to Tom by this time, and he would help me out, either standing with me to hand out leaflets or driving me around to the various points before dropping me at work and then going on to his own work. He would sometimes be taken to the police station along with me, but we kept on popping up the next day, at a different place, and a different set of police would come and take us away again.

What the police were not aware of was that by intimidating me in full view of the workers they were in a way assisting me, because the workers became interested in this woman who was being arrested, as it seemed, and wished to know who I was and what was going on. So I didn't give up, and when I managed to save up and buy a very old second-hand Fiat car and to learn to drive it properly I could visit many more people. It wasn't easy learning to drive at the age of forty-six, but I was glad I did! . . .

One thing I insisted upon, when asking NUDW to convey a message from us to management or when management, in trouble with their workers, called upon me to help them out, was that CCAWUSA was for black workers only, and when I spoke for shopworkers, I was speaking for black shopworkers. This was not simply keeping clear the distinction imposed by the South African government, between blacks, who could in theory not be union members, and other workers. Our insistence on CCAWUSA's black identity was important for other reasons too.

Our problems were very different from the problems of those white and Coloured workers, and this was vital to us as a group, to keep together in order to tackle injustice. We felt this in 1979, when the chance came to join with NUDW and NUCAW. They could not have included us before and stayed registered, but when the law changed they began to tell us they wanted to form a single union.

Decisions in trade unions are never made by the officials but by the people who are making up the union itself. Decisions come from the workers, and in this case the workers voted against forming one union. It was hard for us to forget that in the 1960s, when blacks were ousted from trade unions, the white trade unions acted very quickly in that process, and did not demonstrate for us. . . .

. . . we remained a blacks only union until 1984, when the CCAWUSA constitution was amended to admit Coloureds and Indians, and in 1985, a few months before COSATU was formed, we removed all reference to race from our constitution.

It is hard for black workers in South Africa to identify with other workers' problems. Other workers are seen as human beings, and the black workers are seen as underdogs. And it was not exactly a common thing to see a white person speak out against their own promotion for the sake of a black fellow worker. It is all the menial jobs, all the lowest jobs in the workplaces, that are the jobs of the black workers. And as a black worker, if I speak about a transport problem I am speaking about a different transport problem from anything the white worker will have to suffer. We have these very long distances to travel, and we have the poorest possible transport facilities, and our problems concern the pass laws and schooling and hospitals, exhaustion, and poor diet. And while white mothers have problems of their own, such as having to see one of their boys leave to fight on the border, we can understand them, because we also must lose our children—to the security forces, or to fight against apartheid. But white mothers in this country do not have to suffer anxiety over what we call breadline problems. There is no other word for them. Breadline problems are questions of who will care for the children when their mother goes to work? Who will pay the bills when the grandmother or friend cannot come one day and the mother must stay at home, even though she is not paid enough to be able to afford to lose that one day's money? Who will pay when she has to spend a day at the hospital waiting for an appointment?

No. Our problems are not the same. We had to fight for our identity as a black union. And we had to fight the dependency we had on the white workers and their unions. It was vital that we should be recognised for who we were, and that we should fight for our identity and respect as human beings. That was the battle we had to fight then. And human dignity is the battle we still must fight. . . .

6. The Arrest of a Commie . . .

They said to me, 'Emma Mashinini, we are detaining you under Section 22,' and that I still take exception to, because they should have made that statement in the presence of my family and not to me alone.

They searched the house, the dustbin, outside in the yard. They took complete charge of everything while I stayed in my nightie. With the shock and everything I wanted to go to the toilet, and whenever I went there was one policewoman who came with me, accompanied me literally into the toilet—as though something would come out of that place to attack them and she had to be there all the time. And they went on searching. They searched through the piles of letters from my children, and from the friends I had made all over the world, and from the shopworkers' unions in different countries.

The letters were very interesting to them, and the books, especially all the books that had something to do with trade union work. They took piles of them, piles and piles of things, and put them on the table, and just at the time when they were about to leave the house my family was called in and they said to my husband that he should attach his signature to a form saying they were taking these books and materials that had been found in the house.

Tom refused to sign. 'I am not going to attach my signature to this when I don't know whether you brought these things along with you or what.' They were very rude to him and said he was not making life easier for me, but he said he would not do it. . . .

They took me out to their cars. Now I was in the street, and my neighbours were standing on the corners to see what was happening. It was as though they had come to arrest a murderer, a criminal. It was only about six-thirty in the morning, and I was busy working over in my mind why it was they had come to arrest me, what offence I had committed. And after some time it came to me—oh no, maybe it is like the other trade unionists who were arrested in September. And then I thought, Section 22 is fourteen days. I was counting—oh my God, fourteen days, two weeks' time, in two weeks' time it'll be . . . I'll be back, I'll be out, just before Christmas, I'll be back home . . . But why, why?

They drove me to town, to Khotso House, where we now had our offices. They didn't even ask me where our union offices were. They went straight to that place to search it. . . .

When eventually we did go in, they searched our offices, through all the files—and there was a lot of paper then, not like when I first started the union, when I didn't have one letter. Again they were interested in all of it, and again they took piles of the files and books. . . .

Finally we went out to the car again, and when the lift stopped at the ground floor we met a group of inmates of Khotso House who were coming from the chapel, because in Khotso House every morning they have prayer meetings held at eight-thirty before people start work. It had been announced that I had been seen accompanied by police and that my offices were being ransacked. Several young men came to say, 'What are you doing to Emma?' And even though the police said, 'Get away, get away,' they still came, just to show that they were with me. . . .

I was strengthened by these people, and all the goodbyes, the waving at me, and the good things they were saying, that there will come a day when all this will be over, one day. Right in front of the car they were standing, and they sang the national anthem and chanted, 'Amandla Ngawethu'—'The power is ours'— and I was raising my clenched fist back.

We went to John Vorster Square, where I was put into a room, and there I was interrogated and harassed and given a number. And after some time I was called in by other policemen, who were looking through all the books and things which had been collected from my home.

'You're fat, Kaffir meid,' one said to me. 'You're a nuisance and a troublemaker.' And afterwards he said to me, in Afrikaans, 'Are you a commie?'

Well, my understanding of that was, 'Are you a communicant?' because I saw some Bibles and I thought he meant was I communicant of the Church. So I said yes.

And he said, 'Well, I'm not going to give you the damned Bible, because you are a Communist and you admit it.'

I was shocked, and all by myself, and it seemed everyone had an insult for me, that everyone who walked past had a word of insult to say to me. I was just in the centre of a mess. Who was I to argue over anything and say I misunderstood and that the last thing I was was a commie? That is how they work. They put you in a room, and confine you there so that you must just think you are the only person who is arrested and detained. They don't want you to be exposed to the knowledge that there are other people who are detained as well.

As fate would have it, with all the shock, I kept needing to go to the toilet, and time and time again I had to say to this lady, 'Now I want to go to the toilet.'

But this time when I went, just before we turned into the toilet, we passed the lift, and it stopped, and someone walked out and said, 'Hello, Emma.' It was Neil Aggett. I wanted to respond, to say hello back to him, but the relief of finding I was not the only one who was arrested took it away from me, and I could not bring out even that one word. I always regretted that, that I did not say hello to Neil, because I was not to see him again. But he was being pushed one way, and I that way, and he did manage to say, 'Hello, Emma.'

From the toilet I went back to the office where they were writing down my details. They took photographs and fingerprinted me, and later on I was taken downstairs to the car, with just the little bit of clothing I had brought with me. They told me, in Afrikaans, that they were going to drive me to the Wilds, which is a place where all the muggers and criminals hang out. One understands Afrikaans, but only as much as one has to. There is not the willingness to learn to communicate very well. . . .

I don't know where we went. They took me many different ways, just to cause me more confusion, and they were insulting me all the time.

But then we stopped, and I saw we were in Pretoria.

I think it was then I realised I was really in trouble. I was taken to the offices and put into a cell. And I thought then, now I am arrested. Now I am detained.

Because, to me, Pretoria Central Prison was a place for people who have been sentenced to death. . . .

8. Jeppe Police Station

In January I was moved from Pretoria to Johannesburg. Once again I wasn't told anything. It was, 'Pack your things, pack your things and you go.' And I thought perhaps I was going home. . . .

The first day I just said, 'Yes, yes,' but as the days went by I complained to say, 'Can I have an extra blanket or an extra mat?' meaning just something to make this floor softer. She gave me that. And when I asked her about the food she said everybody ate this kind of food. She said it was the same food, cooked from the same pot as for every other arrested person, black and white. Because I was saying, 'Is it food just for detainees?' And she told me detainees and white persons eat the same food. So I got encouraged and started eating again.

But I was so glad—oh my God, I was so glad to see

a black person, even a black police person. I was so sick of seeing those white people. To see always white people, white people pushing your food at you through the door, white people pushing you and telling you 'Come' or 'Go' and what to do—it was making me ill. Because when you are black you have a need for persons of your own colour. And with my envy of white people, now to be surrounded by them made me realise again how stupid that was, to envy their skin or hair. It was no privilege to be among them. It was a misery and a deprivation.

To the doctor I complained time and time again about sleeping on the ground and not having a chair. It meant that all the time I was squatting on the floor. For my age and size, all I had to do was squat. And the doctor said, 'Okay, I will tell them.' I would go for weekly check-ups and each time he would say, 'All right, I'm going to report that you've got to have a chair.' A chair, not a bed.

It was for me an outing, to visit the doctor, or the dentist, even if the reason was pain with my back, or my teeth falling out. And this was how I felt about my interrogation when it began. An outing to get out of my cell.

I was fetched one day in February to go to John Vorster Square from Jeppe, by car. I was manacled again. I soon got used to that. It meant nothing.

And there came now this questioning time.

There could be about four people, at times six people. At times I would stand, at times I would sit, and these people would take turns. This could go on for the whole day. Questioning you about this, questioning you about that. Sometimes they would ask me if I wanted coffee, but I would always ask for water instead. I didn't want to be seen sitting drinking coffee with these people. They would be at one end of the room with a table. I would be at the far end of the room. They worked in shifts. One shift would go to lunch and leave me with another shift. Once they gave me some lunch, bread and tea, but I wasn't ever hungry there, and anyway when I went back to my cell my plate of food would be there. Maybe that's why they didn't bother to give me any. They knew my food would be waiting for me at the end of the day, and what did I know about lunch-times? I was nothing but a Kaffir. Then, at the end of the questioning, they would just leave me. They wouldn't say goodbye or anything. They would just go, and the next thing would be another policeman coming to say, 'Follow me.' Not to say where to. Just, 'Follow me.'

Even in the car they would play tricks on you and confuse you about where you were going. They would conceal from you any cars coming in or out with other detainees. There would always be a driver, and one policeman next to him with a gun, and two escorts sitting either side of me—all just to take me from prison to prison. The waste of manpower in this! Sometimes it would depress me very much, the waste of these working people, with more education just handed to them than we blacks could get with all our struggles—for what? To sit there in a room learning nothing, doing nothing, always questioning and never understanding what they were being told. It is frightening. Very frightening.

There were times when I would believe them, that with all that manpower I must be a very dangerous person. And then again I would not believe them, but would see that I was helpless, like a child, and that even to go to the toilet was beyond my powers in that room, because I must ask, and wait for permission to be allowed, and then someone must escort me. At first this was very embarrassing for me, but after a time I managed to make myself see that it was the white women warders who should feel humiliated, to have to watch me wipe my bottom.

I was thoroughly questioned about my trade union work. They weren't interested in the GWU, just in CCAWUSA. And they seemed very interested in the Allied Publishing strike of newspaper workers, which I suppose was really a turning point for us, and showed how strong we had grown. They were also very interested in my relationship with the other leaders who had been arrested before me. At times they would tell me directly that I had been very obstinate and very difficult to the employers. They would remind me of instances, saying, 'Do you remember that this is what you were saying to a certain employer?' One interrogator told me that he was among those people who were talking to me, saying that the workers had to go back to work and that I was being difficult. And sometimes they would leave me and I would hear in another room a tape being played, and I guessed they had recordings of some of the meetings I had been involved with. So it seems that in our industrial relations in South Africa you not only deal with the employers when you negotiate but you deal with the police as well.

Most of them were not intelligent. They were even very stupid. I know I never had the opportunity to complete my education, but they were very stupid, I must say. There was one who had read a lot about trade unions, I think, and one particular man would question me about my friends. What was I doing with Alan Fine, and what was I doing with Neil Aggett, and what was I doing with Barbara Hogan? I knew all these people had been arrested and were in prison. And they were questioning me about our meetings and our trade union centre and where this idea had come from, that somebody must have put this or that idea into my head. They wanted to know if I had ever read certain books—I can't remember the names, because in fact I hadn't read them, but they were Marxist books, because Marxists were the sort of people who have that type of thought, of bringing people together. I was interested in a trade union centre for worker education. Not necessarily with any ulterior motives behind it. But I was interrogated for hours to come up with the truth about the idea and where I got it from.

Always they wanted the truth, when I had no more truth to tell. I don't think they ever really understood that in fact there was nothing to give away. But they always tried to find it, this nothing. They'd make me sit down and write, and perhaps in my writing they wanted me to say things, but there was nothing I could write that would give anybody away, because I'd write about my trade union matters. I would sit and write, and write, and this was better for me. Maybe it was a way of being able to think what to say without for once anyone pushing me and going on—'Come on, come on, now. Speak.' And being rough about it.

I was never physically abused by them. Just pushed around, but not battered or assaulted. It was an emotional battery, I suppose. There was a woman who would say, 'If you tell the truth and nothing else you will be able to go back to your children in good time.' And then there was a policeman who was very angry and bullying, called Whitehead, who would tell me I was fat, but that I was not to worry because by the time I left this place I would be the size of a marble, I would have lost so much weight. And that I would lose my position with the union, which had made me so hot-headed. And that when I came out my husband would no longer be there. . . .

I was at times going again to John Vorster Square to meet my husband, but we could not speak of all he was doing outside for me. It was still not allowed. But now I knew that there were still problems continuing about that, and that my husband was still standing firm.

Worst of all was one particular day when I was being driven to John Vorster Square and we were going down Commissioner Street. Out of anxiety I would always look round to see if I could see people I knew. I would see them, but I couldn't wave to them because I was with two policemen, sitting next to me. That day I saw on the posters, 'DETAINEE DIES IN CELL.'

'Detainee dies in cell, detainee dies in cell. . . .' And I can't ask these people what has happened or what is going on.

When I got to John Vorster Square my father, my husband, my brother and my sister-in-law were there, and I was excited to see them, but at the back of my mind my concern was for those posters. 'Detainee dies in cell.' . . .

When I went back to Jeppe I wanted to know from the policeman, 'I understand there is a detainee who has died in the cell. Who is this detainee?' And one policeman said, 'Okay, I will call you somebody senior who will come in and talk to you.' I think it was a Section 6 inspector who came. And he said, 'I believe you have got a question.' I said, 'Yes, I want to know who is this detainee who has died in the cells.' He said, 'Who told you that? Who told you that?' I said, 'Nobody told me.' He said, 'Where did you get it from?' He was becoming aggressive. I told him I had read the posters at the corner of the street. And he said, 'Can you guess who it is?'

Guessing. How could I guess who it was? He was amused then, smiling and amused.

I started calling names of people who I knew could never have been arrested. I wasn't so stupid as to call the names of persons I knew were in prison. There would be more demands for the 'truth' then, more 'How did you know? Who told you? Tell us the truth.' So I mentioned all the other names and he was very amused. I was like a fool.

He never told me who that person was. And this was a torture and a hell to me. But a few weeks thereafter I went to John Vorster Square again and there was my husband. He was now bringing me fruit juice in five-litre boxes. One time it was peach, orange, apple and so forth. I had these boxes in my cell. When they were empty I kept them. The colour meant much to me—the green, the orange—it was my closeness to nature. It kept me going. It was fun. But then my husband also brought me a transistor radio, which was a gift from my friend David Webster, a founding member of the DPSC who was later assassinated, shot dead by a passenger in a speeding car as he entered his home on 1 May 1989.

He showed me how to put the batteries in, and I was so nervous. I didn't know if this was going to be allowed and he said, 'Look, you must have it.'

I took it back with me. Now I had company. There was music. But also I could listen to the news. And one day when I was listening to the news I just heard the radio say that Australian trade unions refused to offload goods from South Africa because of Neil Aggett's death in detention.

9. Dudu

'. . . Australian trade unions are refusing to offload . . . because of the death in detention of . . .' They said the name and then they linked to say he was a trade unionist. I waited for a few hours and then the news came again and they said it again. I still did not believe what I had heard. I got such a shock. Here was I, all by myself, and I couldn't tell anyone about the death of my friend.

It was stale, old news. It was weeks since I'd seen those posters, very many weeks. When I questioned the white police who brought the food, saying, 'Is it true that Neil Aggett has died?' they said, 'I don't know.' And then I spoke to the black policeman and said, 'Is it true?' and he said, 'Yes. It is true.' I questioned the black policewoman and the black policeman, and they said, 'Okay, we'll try and see if we can get the newspapers.'

The first cuttings they brought me were from an Afrikaans newspaper. There was a picture of Neil and the name, but I could not pretend to understand what had happened. So I asked if I could see the *Rand Daily Mail* and they said, 'Okay, we'll try.'

So now they were bringing me the *Rand Daily Mail* concealed in their clothing. They'd walk into my cell, and speak to me, and then they would just pass on the newspaper to me. It was great joy to read it. I'd read every bit, but I had to be careful. In Pretoria I'd never have been able to do it, but this window was so high nobody could see me through it. They had to actually come in, through the door, and I could hear them, with the keys jangling. I'd read the newspaper and then hide it under the mat. And when I'd read the newspaper I'd tear it into little pieces, then flush it.

In the newspapers I read about the people who were admitted to hospital. I read that somebody from the South African and Allied Workers' Union (SAAWU) was taken in for psychiatric treatment, and that Liz Floyd, Neil Aggett's girlfriend, had been admitted to the general hospital. And I started realising that there were many of us inside here. It made me feel braver. I all of a sudden just gained strength. . . .

But under all this was Neil Aggett. His death affected me very deeply. We were very close friends with this man.

I would remember when Alan Fine was detained and Neil Aggett came to take his place in my life. He used to visit my office every day to enquire, 'Is there anything I can do?' I was very concerned about Alan Fine, because I like him dearly, and I knew Neil Aggett did too. I couldn't visit him. All I could do was call his mother to find out how he was and she would always tell me, 'He's okay.'

Neil was the first white person to die in detention. He had his profession as a doctor, which he could have concentrated on safely, without ever getting himself involved in trade union work. He was supposed to have

killed himself, but everybody who dies in detention is supposed to have killed himself. I don't know what they find to kill themselves with in those cells. There was no chair for me, not even to burn myself to death.

The police hated that white people should work for justice for black people. When they interrogated me they didn't know I had found out that Neil Aggett was dead. They would time and time again tell me, 'We're going to question him about this.' I remember Whitehead would use very vulgar words when he spoke about Neil. I could see he was furious and mad about him, that there was no more price that Neil could pay, because he had died on them. And in fact it was this man who was questioned about Neil's death, and as a result was demoted from the security forces and made a policeman, working in the robbery squad. He was mad about Liz and Liz, too: Liz Thompson and Liz Floyd.

Strangely, I was not made more frightened when I went in for my interrogation. Instead I was furious about the whole thing. I was sort of arguing back. I started kicking out to say, 'I'm not going to be questioned about things I don't know.' I'm a very well travelled person, and when I was questioned about my travels I would say whatever I wanted to say because my travels were genuine. It wasn't to plan for people to come and take over the workers, or whatever it was they thought.

I was still getting the newspapers, and one thing really gave me a lot of pride when I saw it. There was a cutting with a photograph of my husband standing as a lone demonstrator in front of the Supreme Court, demanding my release. Tom standing there, alone, with a placard, demanding. And I read about him even coming to Cape Town and demanding my release, and demanding the release of all the other detainees.

The main important thing they were saying was, 'Why are they not being charged?' They insisted we had to be charged, rather than be kept in prison all this time. And he was arguing that he knew of no offence that I'd committed, and that it seemed I'd been arrested for my trade union work. And these people kept saying I wasn't arrested for my trade union work, but for being a political activist. And the big thing was that Tom seemed to be negotiating as an equal, and did not feel any intimidation. His first act the day they detained me had been to refuse to sign for the books that they were removing from my house, and this was sufficient to prove that Tom was a very strong and conscientious person. But he was not one to speak out. My being detained, him demonstrating in front of the Supreme Court, the police station, demanding my release and going to Cape Town to demand my release there—this Tom was a person who spoke out, which he hadn't been before. So sometimes when the police think they're doing you down, they're building you up. They built me up by harassing me in front of the shopworkers, and helped make the union what it is. And they made my husband speak out, so that today if the police knocked on the door I would look around to say, 'Who are they after?'—unlike before, when I would always think it was me. . . .

10. A Kind of Freedom

One morning in May a chair was brought to my cell, so the doctor's orders were at last complied with. I had a chair. But I had not sat on that chair for too long when there was a knock on the door to say, 'Pack your things. Come with us.'

This wasn't anything new for me, to bring my things for interrogation. But I had not had any interrogation for so long, I just thought it was a change from one prison to another again. Leaving that chair behind, that chair which I'd waited so long for, I thought, 'O, my God, I'm going to start life all over again without a chair.' The cruelty of people. The cruelty of that chair. I ached. My back ached. I needed that chair.

I was taken to John Vorster Square with all my things, into that office, and in that office I was made to sign papers to say that I would appear in court on a certain day. I don't know what the charges were, and I never did appear in court. It was just a further threat to leave hanging over me. But I did attach my signature, and I was given my things back. My rings, my watch, everything. Only my gold necklace which my daughters bought for me for my fiftieth birthday was not there. I said I wanted my necklace amongst my things, and that it was not there. They said they were going to find that necklace, but they never did. Then an officer made me sign very many more papers. And still I thought I was being transferred to another prison, and stripped again of all my things. It was only after signing all those papers and after being made to make oaths about not talking about being in prison that I realised, 'Oh, I'm being released.'

Then they said, 'How are you going home?'

I asked if I could please phone my husband, to tell him that I was being released. They knew the number. Of course. They knew everything about my husband, and myself. During the interrogation they used to tell me about my husband and myself. They rang him and told him that I was released from prison.

We went down into the basement and out with all my things, and I was left alone at the gate. . . .

It was not long before my husband came. He came accompanied by a friend, Athol Margolis, who was in the National Union of Garment Workers with him. And Athol Margolis jumped in the air because he was so excited. . . .

So now it was time for me to go home. It was so exciting. My child Nomsa was there, and my neighbours. My neighbours came in very great numbers, and there was one visit especially which was very important to me. Morris Kagan, who until that time had never been to Soweto, came to my house. He said—it was before the permits were abolished—'Permit or no permit, I'm going to Soweto. I'm going to see Emma.' All this was very wonderful, but also too much, because in the evening, when I went to bed, I was very exhausted from being alone for so long then all of a sudden having so many people coming.

At night the cars driving back and forth seemed to me now to be interrogators. Every time there was a car I was terrified, and thought that they were coming back to collect me. These people know what they do when they lock you up. You torture yourself.

So the excitement was short-lived. I now had a period when I was very concerned and worried and wanted to run away from my home. My home was no longer suitable for accommodating me safely, because they knew where it was and I thought they were coming back to get me.

We called the doctor, and he gave me something to put me to rest, to sleep. But still that feeling went on, for days and days. And all the time people were coming to see me. They were coming in their tens, in their hundreds. We actually had to have arrangements to say which people were going to visit on a certain day. People from trade unions, people from the Church, from prayer meetings. It was just traffic, one after another. And international friends. I was one of those lucky people who had a telephone in the home, and all the time there were telephone calls from all angles.

I'm sure the people could tell from my speech that I wasn't normal. And in the end my *FIET* colleagues in Geneva said, 'We want you to come to Geneva, and we are prepared for you to travel with your husband. We are not going to take the risk of you travelling alone.'

In May I was out of prison, and now in June I was to travel to Geneva. And from Geneva I was whisked away to go to Denmark, to a clinic for detainees and people who had been tortured.

In Denmark I was given the most royal treatment one could expect. I had wonderful doctors who paid the most important attention to me, I had a ward which was like a suite, I had everything I wanted.

But to me it was yet another detention. Tom had to

leave me there, and he went to Germany to spend a few days with the children and then went back to South Africa. And mostly I just felt I'd been away from my family for too long, and now again I was away from my family. So in spite of all the good work that was done by this clinic—the good work which I appreciated very much—the fact remains that I wanted to be with my family again. I think this was bad timing, for me to go to that clinic then. I think, for all their good treatment, it was another disorientation.

I was with other people who were torture victims, coming from other countries. We could not speak because we knew different languages. Only the doctors and nurses could come and speak to me. And when you look at these people who are themselves tortured and derailed, it does not give much courage. It just put me off.

There were mostly men, from Chile, South American men. Some of them had brought their families with them. You could see their wives and children, and there was a lot of unpleasantness. These husbands had been away from home in prison, where they were derailed, and they were different people now—they were not who they had been. There must be unpleasantness in such a circumstance. So these families did not come excited. There was misery all around.

The doctors there were very nice. I remember they tried to keep my presence a secret, so that it would not be known in South Africa that I was having this treatment. They didn't want to use my real name. They wanted to give me a name to cover up who I was. This I refused. It was important to me that I had come and that my name was Emma Mashinini. I wanted to go down on record. This was very important. I wasn't going to accept another name.

The doctor who started the clinic was Inge Genefke, a woman about ten or twelve years younger than myself, and a very brave, intelligent person. She said the idea had come to her with the aid and help of another woman, who was in Paris. When I was there the clinic was still in a hospital, in a separate wing. But they were building a separate hospital for torture victims.

Inge Genefke used to want me to speak out, to tell her what happened during the whole time of my imprisonment and what the torture was. I had to dig it out. I forgot some of the things, but she was so patient. She wanted me to dig and dig and speak about everything.

But for me I was speaking to a white doctor, and I had spent so much time with white police, surrounded by white people. It was a white woman who had refused me chewing gum, and a white woman who had put those bracelets on me. And it was hard, very hard,

to trust her, this new white woman. As well as that, I had been told when I was released never, never to speak about my detention. So whenever I spoke I was leaving something out. I was fearful, terribly fearful, that this would leak out and get to them, and I would be rearrested and charged for having spoken about things.

Then the newspapers found out I was in that hospital, and again I had that fear of being betrayed and that the people who said they were helping me would hand me over and return me to prison. The journalist who most hounded me was black. His name was Z. B. Molefe, and he printed an article on 18 July 1982 in the Golden City Press in Johannesburg under the headline: 'MYSTERY OF SICK EMMA': . . .

11. Just a Tiny Giant . . .

So by the end of that year we had won these four big battles, and with these recognitions we really had in our hands the power to change things. In reaction to this, from their fear of us, the management did all they could to discredit CCAWUSA. In 1983 a magazine called Hard Labour, edited by Gavin Brown, a legal adviser to OK Bazaars, produced a pamphlet discrediting CCAWUSA that had been widely distributed in shopping centres, parking lots and ware-houses. In it were questions like: Who is controlling CCAWUSA? Where does the subscription money go? And so on. It was 'signed' by the Edgars shop stewards, but at a meeting of the Edgars shop stewards shortly after they all said the pamphlet was not their work. I am glad to say that our members were not so easily fooled! . . .

Those six months brought about a great change in me. I tried to get it all out at the time, all the bad feelings and memories, but I could not, and even now there are things that come up, and I remember. These are long-term effects. I have had long-term physical effects, and long-term mental effects.

The first time I had caught sight of myself in a mirror after all that time I had been shocked. I was a different person altogether. I am a very big person by stature, a fat person, though not tall. But now I was so thin and small, and my complexion had gone so fair from being in the shade for all that time, that I couldn't believe my eyes that this was me. It shook me a lot. I thought it was my sister in that bathroom with me, my sister who is very fair.

After the loss of my teeth, caused by the terrible food I was given in Pretoria, I had to be fitted for dentures when I was in Denmark. And I have to put something on my nails to patch them, because they are always splitting and they hurt. And I have a problem

405

with my bladder, from sitting flat on concrete floors for all that time. I'd never had these problems before, not like most women. I've always been a person who was troubled with tonsils, but never with gyn problems. But now I was advised to have a hysterectomy, much earlier than I should have had it because I was suffering with fibroids.

I was admitted to the Johannesburg General Hospital, which was originally a hospital only for whites. But the white community built a very modern, up-to-date hospital for their community and turned over their rundown hospital to black patients. The white-only hospital which dominates the horizon of Johannesburg stands as a symbol of the attitude of whites to their own health-care and welfare: for their comparatively small community they have built an enormous hospital; our infinitely larger community has inherited their rejects.

On my day of admission a young male white doctor came to my bedside and a tray with instruments was brought. He was joined by another white doctor, an elderly man. They stood on either side of my bed and the young doctor started examining my vagina and was taking notes. While the young doctor was inserting something into me they were talking. Then the elderly doctor left and the young doctor was joined by another white male doctor. The young doctor was now relating what he had previously done to me in the first examination and I realized that he was being examined by a professor. I was inwardly fuming, and when they had finished and were about to move away I said to them that I regretted that their bedside manner was so horrible. I asked why they never informed me that I was going to be used as a guinea pig for their exams. I added that I had been humanely examined by a gynaecologist the previous year in Denmark, where I was treated as a human being. I said that they had also failed to prepare me for what they were going to do—that the speculum would feel cold and that it would hurt as they inserted it. They answered defensively, saying they did not know that I could speak English, but neither was at all apologetic. . . .

Two other bad things were the exhaustion and the loss of memory. When I went back to work that first time, in August, I was almost like a cabbage. I, who had always been a very productive person, now had to struggle to keep going. For a long time I felt like this. I felt that although I was free, I was still a condemned person. . . .

Perhaps the effects of my detention would not be so unpleasant if I was not constantly bothered by the security forces. But since I have been out of prison, practically every eve of every black commemoration day—like 16 June (Soweto Massacre), 26 June (Freedom Charter), 21 March (Sharpeville Day)—I have been reminded of these dates by the shining torches and loud knocks at my door which mean I am once again being visited by the security branch. They search my home as though I am harbouring people who are their targets. . . .

12. Violent Times

When I started CCAWUSA I can remember I told myself I would give it ten years and then it would be time to move. Well, after ten years, in May 1985, I announced I would leave the following year, and I did. I felt it was time to go, and not once since have I looked back with regret that I left at that time. To have gone before, when I came out of detention, would have been to tell the government that they had won. And to have stayed for longer would have been to wear out my strength and my energy. I felt I had seen CCAWUSA through its opening, from being a union with no members to being a union with over 80,000, with power and influence and with great achievements behind it. . . .

No country that lives by a system of apartheid can claim a sense of justice for itself, not in the area of black and white relations, and not in the area of relations between men and women either, whether white or black. The segregation, the setting of one off against another—this breeds a corruption from which none of us, whatever our colour, can be free. This was brought home to me when I left CCAWUSA, and I wanted so very much for my position to be filled by a woman. It would have made me so happy to see a woman ready there, wanting to do that job, and prepared to jostle the men around her for it. I had had a bitter experience in the time when COSATU came to be formed, when I had taken such a lot of interest, and worked so hard, and had seen how all the men were very happy to consult with me because of the size and importance of my union. It didn't matter then that I was a woman. But then came the day when the names were put forward of those who would go on the National Executive. And each and every one of those names were men's names. Even CCAWUSA was represented in the end not by me, who was its General Secretary, but by Makhulu Ledwaba, who was the President, even though he was to be the youngest of all the people on the executive, and most ironic of all, when they were having an important person to come and meet them, from abroad or whatever, then they would say, 'Oh, Emma, please, you must meet them.' And I would say, 'Am I again just to be used as a valve, just to patch up what you have done wrong?'

There was in fact worse to come, because the next step was to choose a logo for COSATU. And all the logos that came about, every single one, had the image of a man. There was not a single image of a woman. So it means that our presence — our efforts, our work, our support — was not even recognised. And CCAWUSA, which is regarded as a very strong woman-oriented group fighting for women's rights, with a majority, 60 per cent, of women as members, had to speak up for the very rights we had fought for from the different employers.

All this must be the concern of the union movement. The trade union movement is a very powerful organisation, and it is not there just to look at the bread and butter problems of workers. The trade union movement is concerned with the liberation of the people in South Africa. Because if the trade union organisation cannot take on the issue of the liberation of the country, who will? Much as they have abolished the pass laws, who wants to be a member of the Nationalist Party? Who wants to be a member of the PFP? No black wants to be a member of these organisations. There have been two organisations for my people and they have been banned. These are the Pan-African Congress, the ANC, and now the UDF. So the government has got to unban these organisations, and allow the people the choice of saying which political organisation they want to belong to. But until then, in the absence of these organisations, the trade unions are the people who must fight their battles. The whole life of a worker needs trade union involvement. And together with that goes the whole question of equality between men and women. . . .

Sadly, as black determination to be free increases, so does the virulent right wing grow in number. Their fear and greed increases their hatred. The numerous right-wing organisations in South Africa may differ on certain issues of policy, strategy and tactics, but one idea is common to them all: they identify blacks as the enemy. The grotesque slaughter in Pretoria in 1988 epitomises the right wing. Mr Strydom, a member of the Afrikaner Weerstand Beweging (AWB), simply woke up one morning and with his sawn-off shotgun went on a hunting expedition. He killed seven innocent black people and wounded many others. He is a man in his twenties. He has been declared sane and will stand trial. He smiles and waves to his family and friends in the courtroom and looks distinctly proud of his achievement on behalf if the Boere Volk (Boer Nation). One lives in a constant state of fear of these people. They cannot be underestimated, and as their numbers grow they remain a very real and dangerous threat to black people, and even to those white people

who stand up to be counted with us in the struggle and are labelled by their right-wing white brethren as Communists and Kaffir-boeties (black brothers).

This is the kind of violence which surrounds the apartheid regime. This is the kind of society we live in — a society where children disappear, where mothers go from prison to prison to try and find their children, where some of those picked up by the troops or the police are as young as eleven years old. And in this kind of society it is not difficult to fan hatred, mistrust and revenge. The authorities have skillfully manipulated black people, creating ethnic divisions by encouraging malicious rumours, and turning black against black rather than against their real enemy, which is apartheid. The horror of South Africa is that the life of a black person is very cheap. Under this brutal regime, the saddest turn of all is that some of our own people have become brutalised and a prey to violent feelings. . . .

13. Justice and Reconciliation?

Among the delegates present at the meeting of the Eminent Persons Group in 1986 which I attended was Sheena Duncan, who was at that time President of the Black Sash. At the end of the meeting she approached me to say that she had read in the newspaper that I was now retiring from the union, and she wanted to know what my qualifications were. I told her with pride that I am a self-made person with very little and low qualifications, as I had left school at the age of fourteen years, without completing my Junior Certificate, after my parents divorced and our home was broken. Sheena told me then that the Anglican Church requires the minimum of a Matric pass of its employees, but that in spite of my low educational level she urged me to apply for a vacancy in the Department of Justice and Reconciliation.

Although one of my major fights on behalf of CCAWUSA workers was for pension rights, especially for women, I failed to negotiate any pension for myself. I needed to find another job, and this should have seemed a great opportunity, but because of my non-qualifications I did not do anything about it until Sheena phoned me and insisted that I should. I will always be grateful to Sheena for her faith in me.

I was awarded the post, to my great surprise, . . . My work as Director of the Department of Justice and Reconciliation is to guide and co-ordinate all resource persons in the eighteen dioceses of the Province, consisting of South Africa, Namibia, Swaziland, Lesotho, Mozambique and St. Helena, in the Indian Ocean.

One of the very important challenges in my new

job is working with detainees. I am part of a task force which draws up a register of detainees and political prisoners, and I suppose it is because I have served many months in detention that I am so acutely aware of the plight of detainees since the State of Emergency. Many people, especially our young people, have been detained, without a crime necessarily having been committed, and they are often subjected to violence and abuse. In the absence of detailed official figures, the DPSC keeps the most comprehensive records available to the public. In 1986 the DPSC knew about the detention of 2840 people under security laws. The police later revealed that 4132 had been detained under security laws that year.

One of the shocking revelations made by the DPSC was the detention of school pupils, some of whom were as young as eleven years old. The children's consciousness of the discriminatory laws, and of the harsh security measures used by the government to suppress their requests for change, has led to an inevitable clash between the victims and the enforcers of the laws. A very popular campaign, Free the Children Alliance, was very active in highlighting the plight of children in detention. It is a crying shame to see children who are ten years old relating their nasty experiences while in detention. I grieve when I think of them as fathers and mothers of tomorrow; what are they going to tell and teach their children? The two predominating effects of detention, say social workers who have observed the results in children who have been released, are depression and anxiety, resulting in loss of interest in life, a loss of esteem, terror, sleeplessness, nightmares, lack of trust and serious medical problems. Some of these effects could last a lifetime.

I notice that their methods with detainees have changed, and I can, even despite all the terrible feelings I suffer because of my detention, count myself lucky to have been able to pick up my life and try to go on with it. The dying in detention seems not to be growing rapidly, as it was, but the people who come out from there are literally vegetables. The methods of torturing people are different.

They are also developing another way of damaging us more. You can see the trend—first it is trade unionists, then it is one-time students. Now—after the restriction on other organisations speaking against apartheid, which society used as their windows for ventilating their oppression and suppression—it is the Church which has emerged to speak on behalf of the people. They never used to detain so many people who work for the Church.

Another ingredient of South African society is the very high numbers of people killed with capital punishment, a means of retribution I can nowhere find it

in my heart to condone, however bad the crime committed, or said to have been committed. On 26 February 1988 the *South African Barometer* published the figures for executions in South Africa since 1977. They are as follows:

1977	93	1983	93
1978	132	1984	131
1979	138	1985	161
1980	132	1986	128
1981	100	1987	164
1982	107		

In 1988 (up to 5 January 1989) 213 death sentences were pronounced, 117 people executed, 48 reprieved and 27 appeals against the death sentence were successful. The South African figures for capital punishment are among the worst in the world.

They kill them seven at a time. And the sorest part of it is that the black families do not believe that their people have been executed, because they cannot see the bodies. It is an absolute African tradition to see the bodies of the dead. We pay our last respects by seeing the body. If you don't see the body inside the coffin, then how do you know what is in that coffin? People could just be removed. Who knows what could have happened to them?

It is very bad for the mothers, not to see the body. The grief at never knowing what is in that coffin, of not being able to see for the last time a child of yours, is just horrible. Terrible grief. I remember I was in Pretoria when Solomon Mahlangu was executed. Immediately after that execution we women from Soweto went and wanted to be with his mother, and when we got there they didn't even give her that sealed coffin or her child to be buried. This body was chased all over, from one cemetery to another, but never was there access to it. And all we could do to sustain her was to share her anger. To identify the solidarity and to share her anger. And at every memorial service of an executed person all the mothers of those who have been executed come to that service and give support to the one whose child has been executed. All the mothers know one another, and have met, and can link together, so your problem is never your problem alone, you are never an island in your problem, and the divisions the government has been trying to create, they are all gone. We unite, and especially we unite in our crisis times. . . .

I have heard white liberals say, 'The black children are throwing their lives away thinking that liberation is just round the corner. And it's not round the corner. The South African government could hold on for five, ten, fifteen years.' And this is so. But this is still only a delay of what will happen. It's just delaying tactics, so that more of us will die. And our black children, they are not afraid to die. None of them. They are prepared to die now. I have heard young girls speaking and saying, 'I definitely am not afraid to die. Because many children have been killed in South Africa. And many are in detention because of fighting for the struggle. So why should we question which child should die and which child should be arrested when all of us are fighting for the same cause?' And I have heard of a boy who said, 'I'm not afraid to die now, but when Mandela's released, *then* I'll be afraid to die.'

The youth are prepared to die now, but they are not prepared to die when liberation comes. And I have been afraid to die, but when liberation is achieved, then, I must say, I am prepared. I've lived a hard life, in many ways a horrible life, but I have always wanted to see the day of liberation. And when we get there, as a coward, perhaps, I am prepared to die, to say: I've lived and struggled for all these years. Now that we've achieved justice—now that we've attained that—now may I not rest in peace?

End

Selected Bibliography

This bibliography provides a selection of works pertinent to the general history of women's political and social thought. No general history of the subject exists, but there are studies of particular periods or categories of women's political thought, or on individual writers. Some general works on the history of women, such as those by Mary Beard and Elise Boulding, also provide valuable information on the contributions of women intellectuals.

Note that the sources and suggested readings for the individual writers and works featured in this collection are listed in the introductions to the selections throughout the volume and are *not* included below, except for some items of substantial breadth or general applicability.

The bibliography is divided into four sections:

1. Women writers and theorists: selected histories, criticism, and anthologies;

2. Mainstream and "malestream" political theory: texts, anthologies, and interpretation;

3. Feminist critique of mainstream and "malestream" political theory;

4. Feminist political theory: history, anthologies, and analysis.

The works included in the bibliography are intended to provide a broad perspective on the scope of women's contributions to political and social thought and to suggest opportunities for further study. Section 1 lists mainly general works, but studies of a few individual theorists not presented in this volume are included.

The titles listed in Section 2 include a substantial number of what we might call "object lessons"—works that illustrate the exclusion or distorted treatment of women's contributions—as well as some that illustrate growing recognition of women's political thought in some quarters of the mainstream. Works listed in Section 3 exemplify the critical approach of many feminist studies, exposing the phallocratic biases of mainstream/"malestream" political theory. Section 4 offers a small sampling of the burgeoning field of feminist political theory and its many branches, with special attention to works that may throw light on the history of women's political and social thought.

BAC

1. Women Writers and Theorists: Selected Histories, Criticism, and Anthologies

Agosin, Marjorie, ed. *Landscapes of a New Land: Fiction by Latin American Women.* Buffalo, N.Y.: White Pine Press, 1989.

——. *These Are Not Sweet Girls: Latin American Women Poets.* Fredonia, N.Y.: White Pine Press, 1994.

Allen, Paula Gunn. *Grandmothers of the Light: A Medicine Woman's Sourcebook.* Boston: Beacon Press, 1991.

——. *The Sacred Hoop: Recovering the Feminine in American Indian Traditions.* Boston: Beacon Press, 1986.

Allen, Paula Gunn, ed. *Spider Woman's Granddaughters: Traditional Tales and Contemporary Writing by Native American Women.* New York: Fawcett Columbine, 1989.

Arens, Katherine. "Between Hypatia and Beauvoir:

Philosophy as Discourse." *Hypatia* 10, 4 (Fall 1995): 46–75.

Atherton, Margaret, ed. *Women Philosophers of the Early Modern Period.* Indianapolis: Hackett, 1994.

Barth, Else M. *Women Philosophers: A Bibliography of Books through 1990.* Bowling Green, Ohio: Philosophy Documentation Center, 1992.

Beard, Mary Ritter. *On Understanding Women.* New York: Grosset and Dunlap, 1931.

———. *Woman as Force in History: A Study in Traditions and Realities.* London: Macmillan (Collier), [1946] 1962; New York: Persea, 1987.

Bell, Susan G. *Women: From the Greeks to the French Revolution.* Belmont, Calif.: Wadsworth, 1973.

Bell, Susan G., and Karen M. Offen. *Women, the Family, and Freedom: The Debate in Documents.* Vol. 1: *1750–1880;* Vol. 2: *1880–1950.* Stanford: Stanford University Press, 1983.

Bonnel, Roland, and Catherine Rubinger, eds. *Femmes savantes et femmes d'esprit: Women Intellectuals of the French Eighteenth Century.* New York: P. Lang, 1994.

Boulding, Elise. *The Underside of History: A View of Women through Time.* Rev. ed. 2 vols. Newbury Park, Calif.: Sage, 1992.

Brill, Alida, ed. *A Rising Public Voice: Women in Politics Worldwide.* New York: Feminist Press, City University of New York, 1995.

Brink, J. R. *Female Scholars: A Tradition of Learned Women before 1800.* Montreal: Eden Press Women's Publications, 1980.

Cambridge Women's Peace Collective. *My Country Is the Whole World: An Anthology of Women's Work on Peace and War.* London: Pandora, 1984.

Carroll, Berenice A. "The Politics of 'Originality': Women and the Class System of the Intellect." *Journal of Women's History* 2,2 (Fall 1990): 136–163.

Conrad, Susan. *Perish the Thought: Intellectual Women in Romantic America, 1830–1860.* New York: Oxford University Press, 1978; Secaucus, N.J.: Citadel Press, 1976.

Cooke, Miriam, and Roshni Rustomji-Kerns. *Blood into Ink: South Asian and Middle Eastern Women Write War.* Boulder, Colo.: Westview Press, 1994.

David, Deirdre. *Intellectual Women and Victorian Patriarchy: Harriet Martineau, Elizabeth Barrett Browning, George Eliot.* Ithaca: Cornell University Press, 1987.

Delamotte, Eugenia, Natania Meeker, and Jean O'Barr, eds. *Women Imagine Change: A Global Anthology of Women's Resistance, from 600 BCE to Present.* New York: Routledge, 1997.

Douglas, Ann. *The Feminization of American Culture.* New York: Knopf, 1977; New York: Avon, 1978.

Dykeman, Therese Boos. *American Women Philosophers, 1650–1930: Six Exemplary Thinkers.* Lewiston: Edwin Mellen Press, 1993.

Elkins, Sharon K. *Holy Women of Twelfth-Century England.* Chapel Hill: University of North Carolina Press, 1988.

Faderman, Lillian. *Surpassing the Love of Men: Romantic Friendship and Love between Women from the Renaissance to the Present.* New York: William Morrow, 1981.

Felder, Deborah G. *The 100 Most Influential Women of All Time: A Ranking Past and Present.* Secaucus, N.J.: Carol Pub. Group/Citadel Press, 1996.

Foner, Philip. *The Factory Girls.* Urbana: University of Illinois Press, 1977.

Foster, Frances Smith. *Written by Herself: Literary Production by African American Women, 1746–1892.* Bloomington: Indiana University Press, 1993.

Frith, Valerie. *Women and History: Voices of Early Modern England.* Toronto: Coach House Press, 1995.

Gambrell, Alice. *Women Intellectuals, Modernism, and Difference: Transatlantic Culture, 1919–1945.* Cambridge: Cambridge University Press, 1997.

Garfield, Evelyn Picon. *Women's Voices from Latin America.* Detroit: Wayne State University Press, 1985.

Giddings, Paula. *When and Where I Enter: The Impact of Black Women on Race and Sex in America.* New York: Morrow, 1984; New York: Bantam, 1985.

Gilbert, Sandra M., and Susan Gubar. *The Norton Anthology of Literature by Women: The Tradition in English.* 2nd ed. New York: Norton, 1996.

Greer, Germaine, et al. *Kissing the Rod: An Anthology of Seventeenth-Century Women's Verse.* New York: Noonday Press, 1988.

Hane, Mikiso. *Reflections on the Way to the Gallows: Voices of Japanese Rebel Women.* New York: Random House (Pantheon), 1988.

Harvey, Elizabeth D. and Kathleen Okruhlik, eds. *Women and Reason.* Ann Arbor: University of Michigan Press, 1992.

Hewitt, Nancy A. *Women's Activism and Social Change: Rochester, New York, 1822–1872.* Ithaca: Cornell University Press, 1984.

Hinds, Hilary. *God's Englishwomen: Seventeenth-Century Radical Sectarian Writing and Feminist Criticism.* Manchester: Manchester University Press, 1996.

Holland, Nancy J. *Is Women's Philosophy Possible?* Savage, Md.: Rowman and Littlefield, 1990.

Honig, Bonnie, ed. *Feminist Interpretations of Hannah Arendt.* University Park: Pennsylvania State University Press, 1995.

Hull, Gloria, Patricia Bell Scott, and Barbara Smith, eds. *But Some of Us Are Brave: Black Women's Studies.* Old Westbury, N.Y.: Feminist Press, 1982.

James, Joy. *Transcending the Talented Tenth: Black Leaders and American Intellectuals.* New York: Routledge, 1997.

Johnson, Pauline. *Feminism as Radical Humanism.* Boulder, Colo.: Westview Press, 1994.

Katz, Jonathan. *Gay American History: Lesbians and Gay Men in the U.S.A.: A Documentary.* New York: Avon, 1976.

Kersey, Ethel M. *Women Philosophers: A Bio-Critical Source Book.* New York: Greenwood Press, 1989.

King, Margaret L., and Albert Rabil, Jr. *Her Immaculate Hand: Selected Works by and about the Women Humanists of Quattrocento Italy.* Binghamton, N.Y.: Medieval and Renaissance Texts and Studies, 1983.

Labalme, Patricia H., ed. *Beyond Their Sex: Learned Women of the European Past*. New York: New York University Press, 1984.

Lengerman, Patricia Madoo, and Jill Niebrugge-Brantley, eds. *The Women Founders: Sociology and Social Theory, 1830–1930*. San Francisco: McGraw-Hill, 1998.

Lerner, Gerda. *The Creation of Feminist Consciousness: From the Middle Ages to Eighteen-Seventy*. New York: Oxford University Press, 1993.

Levenson, E. R., and E. S. Levi Elwell. *Jewish Women's Studies*. Fresh Meadows, N.Y.: Biblio Press, 1982.

Lyeser, Henrietta. *Medieval Women: A Social History of Women in England, 450–1500*. Part 4. "Culture and Spirituality." New York: St. Martin's Press, 1995.

McAlister, Linda Lopez, ed. *Hypatia's Daughters: Fifteen Hundred Years of Women Philosophers*. Bloomington: Indiana University Press, 1996.

———. "Special Issue: The History of Women in Philosophy." *Hypatia*, 4, 1 (Spring 1989).

McDonald, Lynn. *The Early Origins of the Social Sciences*. Montreal: McGill-Queens University Press, 1994.

———. *The Women Founders of the Social Sciences*. Ottawa: Carleton University Press, 1994.

Ménage, Gilles. *The History of Women Philosophers* [1692]. Trans. Beatrice H. Zedler. Lanham, Md.: University Press of America, 1984.

Mirandé, Alfredo, and Evangelina Enríquez. *La Chicana: The Mexican-American Woman*. Chicago: University of Chicago Press, 1979.

Morris, Celia. *Fanny Wright: Rebel in America*. Urbana: University of Illinois Press, 1992.

Oden, Amy, ed. *In Her Words: Women's Writings in the History of Christian Thought*. Nashville: Abingdon Press, 1994.

Petroff, Elizabeth Alvilda, ed. *Medieval Women's Visionary Literature*. New York: Oxford University Press, 1986.

Pomeroy, Sarah B. *Goddesses, Whores, Wives, and Slaves: Women in Classical Antiquity*. New York: Schocken, 1975.

———. *Women in Hellenistic Egypt*. New York: Schocken, 1984.

Resources for Feminist Research (Canada) 16, 3 (1987): 53–63. [Resources and sketches of women in the history of philosophy.]

Ruether, Rosemary, and Eleanor McLaughlin, eds. *Women of Spirit: Female Leadership in the Jewish and Christian Traditions*. New York: Simon and Schuster, 1979.

Russ, Joanna. *How to Suppress Women's Writing*. Austin: University of Texas Press, 1983.

The Schomburg Library of Nineteenth-Century Black Women Writers. General editor, Henry Louis Gates, Jr. New York: Oxford University Press. 30 vols. 1988–92.

Smith, Hilda L., ed. *Women Writers and the Early Modern British Political Tradition*. Cambridge: Cambridge University Press, 1998.

Solomon, Barbara Miller. *In the Company of Educated Women: A History of Women and Higher Education in America*. New Haven: Yale University Press, 1985.

Spender, Dale. *The Writing or the Sex? or Why You Don't Have to Read Women's Writing to Know It's No Good*. New York: Pergamon Press (Athene), 1989.

Stewart, Maria W. *America's First Black Woman Political Writer: Essays and Speeches*. Ed. Marilyn Richardson. Bloomington: Indiana University Press, 1987.

Stites, Richard. *The Women's Liberation Movement in Russia: Feminism, Nihilism, and Bolshevism*. Princeton: Princeton University Press, 1978.

Stone, Merlin. *When God Was a Woman*. New York: Harcourt Brace Jovanovich, 1976.

Taylor, Henry Osborn. *The Medieval Mind*. 4th ed. 2 vols. London: Macmillan, 1930. [Vol. 1, chap. 20: "Mystic Visions of Ascetic Women"; vol. 2, chap. 26: "The Heart of Heloise."]

Tharu, Susie, and K. Lalita, eds. *Women Writing in India: 600 B.C. to the Present*. 2 vols. New York: Feminist Press at the City University of New York, 1993.

Thiébaux, Marcelle, trans. *The Writings of Medieval Women*. New York: Garland, 1987.

Tuesday Magazine. *Black Heroes in World History*. [Queen of Sheba, Phillis Wheatley.] New York: Bantam, 1969.

Van Sertima, Ivan, ed. *Black Women in Antiquity*. New Brunswick, N.J.: Transaction, 1988.

Waithe, Mary Ellen, ed. *A History of Women Philosophers*. Vol. 1, 600 B.C.–500 A.D., Dordrecht: Martinus Nijhoff, 1987; Vol. 2, 500–1600, Dordrecht: Kluwer, 1989; Vol. 3, 1600–1900, Dordrecht: Kluwer, 1991; Vol. 4, 1900–today, Dordrecht: Kluwer, 1995.

Warnock, Mary. *Women Philosophers*. London: Dent, 1996.

Wilson, Katharina M., ed. *Medieval Women Writers*. Athens: University of Georgia Press, 1984.

———. *Women Writers of the Renaissance and Reformation*. Athens: University of Georgia Press, 1987.

Wilson, Katharina M., and Frank J. Warnke. *Women Writers of the Seventeenth Century*. Athens: University of Georgia Press, 1989.

Wolf, Margery, and Roxane Witke, eds. *Women in Chinese Society*. Stanford: Stanford University Press, 1975.

Yalom, Marilyn. *Blood Sisters: The French Revolution in Women's Memory*. New York: Basic, 1993.

2. Mainstream and "Malestream" Political Theory: Texts, Anthologies, and Interpretation

Allen, J. W. *A History of Political Thought in the Sixteenth Century*. London: Methuen (University Paperbacks), [1928] 1961.

Appleby, Joyce, et al., eds. *Knowledge and Postmodernism: in Historical Perspective*. New York: Routledge, 1996.

Arnhart, Larry. *Political Questions: Political Philosophy from Plato to Rawls*. 2nd ed. Prospect Heights, Ill.: Waveland Press, 1993.

Arthur, John, ed. *Democracy: Theory and Practice*. Belmont, Calif.: Wadsworth, 1992.

Ball, Terence. *Reappraising Political Theory: Revisionist Studies in the History of Political Thought*. New York: Oxford University Press, 1995.

Baumer, Franklin L., ed. *Main Currents in Western*

Thought. 4th ed. New Haven: Yale University Press, 1978.

Berlin, Isaiah. "Does Political Theory Still Exist?" In *Philosophy, Politics and Society,* ed. Peter Laslett and W. G. Runciman. Oxford: Basil Blackwell, 1962.

Bluhm, William T. *Theories of the Political System: Classics of Political Thought and Modern Political Analysis.* Englewood Cliffs, N.J.: Prentice-Hall, 1971.

Broyles, David D. "Political Philosophy and Liberal Education." Special issue of *Teaching Political Science* 12, 2 (Winter 1984–85).

Commager, Henry Steele. *The American Mind.* New Haven: Yale University Press, 1949.

Contemporary Civilization Staff of Columbia College. *Introduction to Contemporary Civilization in the West: A Source Book.* 2 vols. New York: Columbia University Press, 3rd ed. 1960.

Farr, James, and Raymond Seidelman, eds. *Discipline and History: Political Science in the United States.* Ann Arbor: University of Michigan Press, 1993.

Foucault, Michel. *Power/Knowledge.* New York: Pantheon, 1980.

Fowler, Robert Booth. 1983. "Does Political Theory Have a Future?" In *What Should Political Theory Be Now?,* ed. Nelson, 549–80. Albany: State University of New York Press, 1983.

Garner, Richard T., and Andrew Oldenquist, eds. *Society and the Individual: Readings in Political and Social Philosophy.* Belmont, Calif.: Wadsworth, 1990.

John G. Gunnell. *Political Theory: Tradition and Interpretation.* Lanham, Md.: University Press of America, 1987.

Kymlicka, Will. *Contemporary Political Philosophy: An Introduction.* Oxford: Clarendon Press, 1990.

Laslett, Peter, and W. G. Runciman, eds. *Philosophy, Politics and Society.* Second Series. Oxford: Basil Blackwell, 1962.

Lerner, Ralph, and Muhsin Mahdi. *Medieval Political Philosophy.* Ithaca: Cornell University Press, 1963.

Nelson, Cary. *Theory in the Classroom.* Urbana: University of Illinois Press, 1986.

Nelson, John S. "Political Theory as Political Rhetoric." In *What Should Political Theory Be Now,* ed. Nelson, 169–240. Albany: State University of New York Press, 1983.

———. *Tradition, Interpretation, and Science: Political Theory in the American Academy.* Albany: State University of New York Press, 1986.

Nelson, John S., ed. *What Should Political Theory Be Now?* Albany: State University of New York Press, 1983.

Porter, Jene M., ed. *Classics in Political Philosophy.* 2nd ed. Scarborough, Ont.: Prentice Hall Canada, 1997.

Rabb, Theodore K. *Origins of the Modern West: Essays and Sources in Renaissance and Early Modern European History.* Sources edited and introduced by Sherrin Marshall. New York: McGraw-Hill, 1993.

Sabine, George H. *A History of Political Theory.* 3rd ed. New York: Holt, Rinehart, Winston, 1961.

Sibley, Mulford Q. *Nature and Civilization: Some Implications for Politics.* Itasca, Ill.: F. E. Peacock, 1977.

Spragens, Thomas A., Jr. *Understanding Political Theory.* New York: St. Martin's Press, 1976.

Stewart, Robert M. *Readings in Social and Political Philosophy.* New York: Oxford University Press, 1986.

Strauss, Leo, and Joseph Cropsey, eds. *History of Political Philosophy.* 2nd ed. Chicago: Rand McNally, 1972.

Stumpf, Samuel E. *Philosophical Problems: Selected Readings in Ethics, Religion, Political Philosophy, Epistemology, and Metaphysics.* 3rd ed. New York: McGraw-Hill, 1989.

Taylor, Henry Osborn. *The Medieval Mind.* 4th ed. 2 vols. London: Macmillan, 1930.

Thompson, Karl F. *Classics of Western Thought.* 3 vols. New York: Harcourt, Brace and World, 1964.

Ullman, Walter. *A History of Political Thought: The Middle Ages.* Harmondsworth, Middlesex: Penguin (Pelican), 1965.

University of Chicago Readings in Western Civilization. 1986–1988. General editors, Julius Kirshner and Karl F. Morrison. Chicago: University of Chicago Press.

Weber, Eugen, comp. *The Western Tradition.* 5th ed. Lexington, Mass.: D.C. Heath, 1995.

Weinstein, Michael. *Philosophy, Theory, and Method in Contemporary Political Thought.* Glenview, Ill.: Scott Foresman, 1971.

Wintz, Cary D. *African American Political Thought, 1890–1930.* Armonk, N.Y.: M. E. Sharpe, 1996.

3. Feminist Critique of Mainstream and "Malestream" Political Theory

Benhabib, Seyla, and Drucilla Cornell, eds. *Feminism as Critique.* Minneapolis: University of Minnesota Press, 1987.

Brodribb, Somer. *Nothing Mat(t)ers: A Feminist Critique of Postmodernism.* Toronto: James Lorimer, 1993.

Brown, Wendy. *Manhood and Politics: A Feminist Reading in Political Theory.* Totowa, N.J.: Rowman and Littlefield, 1988.

Clark, Lorenne, and Lynda Lange, eds. *The Sexism of Social and Political Theory: Women and Reproduction from Plato to Nietzsche.* Toronto: University of Toronto Press, 1979.

Coole, Diana H. *Women in Political Theory: From Ancient Misogyny to Contemporary Feminism.* Boulder, Colo.: Lynne Rienner, 1988.

Cruikshank, Margaret, ed. *Lesbian Studies: Present and Future.* Old Westbury, N.Y.: Feminist Press, 1982.

Davies, Miranda, comp. *Third World/Second Sex.* London: Zed, 1983.

Di Stefano, Christine. *Configurations of Masculinity: A Feminist Perspective on Modern Political Theory.* Ithaca: Cornell University Press, 1991.

Elshtain, Jean Bethke. *Meditations on Modern Political Thought: Masculine/Feminine Themes from Luther to Arendt.* New York: Praeger, 1986.

———. *Public Man, Private Woman: Women in Social and Political Thought.* Princeton: Princeton University Press, 1981.

Evans, Judith, et al. *Feminism and Political Theory.* London: Sage, 1986.

Figes, Eva. *Patriarchal Attitudes.* Greenwich, Conn.: Fawcett, 1971.

French, Marilyn. *Beyond Power: On Women, Men and Morals.* New York: Ballantine, 1986 (1985).

Gould, Carol C., and Marx W. Wartofsky. *Women and Philosophy: Toward a Theory of Liberation.* New York: G. P. Putnam's, 1976.

Grimshaw, Jean. *Philosophy and Feminist Thinking.* Minneapolis: University of Minnesota Press, 1986.

Kennedy, Ellen, and Susan Mendus. *Women in Western Political Philosophy: Kant to Nietzsche.* New York: St. Martin's Press, 1987.

Meehan, Johanna. *Feminists Read Habermas: Gendering the Subject of Discourse.* New York: Routledge, 1995.

Millett, Kate. *Sexual Politics.* New York: Simon and Schuster, 1990; Garden City, N.Y.: Doubleday, 1970.

O'Brien, Mary. *The Politics of Reproduction.* London: Routledge and Kegan Paul, 1981.

——. *Reproducing the World: Essays in Feminist Theory.* Boulder, Colo.: Westview Press, 1989.

O'Faolain, Julia, and Lauro Martines. *Not in God's Image.* New York: Harper and Row, 1973.

Okin, Susan Moller. *Women in Western Political Thought.* Princeton: Princeton University Press, 1979.

Pateman, Carole. *The Disorder of Women: Democracy, Feminism and Political Theory.* Stanford: Stanford University Press, 1989.

——. *The Sexual Contract.* Stanford: Stanford University Press, 1988.

Pellikaan-Engel, Maja, ed. *Against Patriarchal Thinking.* Proceedings of the VIth Symposium of the International Association of Women Philosophers. Amsterdam: VU University Press, 1992.

Saxonhouse, Arlene W. *Fear of Diversity: The Birth of Political Science in Ancient Greek Thought.* Chicago: University of Chicago Press, 1992.

——. *Women in the History of Political Thought: Ancient Greece to Machiavelli.* New York: Praeger, 1985.

Spender, Dale. *Man Made Language.* London: Routledge and Kegan Paul, 1980.

Thompson, Janna L., ed. *Women and Philosophy.* *Australasian Journal of Philosophy.* Supplement, vol. 64 (June), 1986.

Ward, Julie K. *Feminism and Ancient Philosophy.* New York: Routledge, 1996.

Weiss, Penny A. *Gendered Community: Rousseau, Sex, and Politics.* New York: New York University Press, 1993.

4. Feminist Political Theory: History, Anthologies, and Analysis

Agarwal, Bina, ed. *Structures of Patriarchy: The State, the Community and the Household.* New Delhi: Kali for Women, 1988; London: Zed, 1988.

Akkerman, Tjitske, and Siep Stuurman, eds. *Perspectives on Feminist Political Thought in European History: From the Middle Ages to the Present.* London: Routledge, 1998.

Alcoff, Linda, and Elizabeth Potter, eds. *Feminist Epistemologies.* New York: Routledge, 1993.

Al-Hibri, Azizah Y., and Margaret A. Simons, eds. *Hypatia Reborn: Essays in Feminist Philosophy.* Bloomington: Indiana University Press, 1990.

Badran, Margot, and Miriam Cooke. *Opening the Gates: A Century of Arab Feminist Writing.* Bloomington: Indiana University Press, 1990.

Beck, Evelyn Torton. *Nice Jewish Girls: A Lesbian Anthology.* Watertown, Mass.: Persephone Press, 1982.

Bell, Diane, and Renate Klein, eds. *Radically Speaking: Feminism Reclaimed.* London: Zed Books in association with Spinifex Press, 1996.

Bell, Susan Groag, and Karen M. Offen. *Women, the Family, and Freedom: The Debate in Documents.* 2 vols. 1750–1880, 1880–1950. Stanford: Stanford University Press, 1983.

Benhabib, Seyla, et al. *Feminist Contentions: A Philosophical Exchange.* New York: Routledge, 1995.

Boxer, Marilyn J., and Jean H. Quataert, eds. *Socialist Women: European Socialist Feminists in the Nineteenth and Early Twentieth Centuries.* New York: Elsevier, 1978.

Bowles, Gloria, and Renate Duelli Klein, eds. *Theories of Women's Studies.* London: Routledge and Kegan Paul, 1983.

Brock-Utne, Birgit. *Feminist Perspectives on Peace and Peace Education.* New York: Pergamon Press (now Teachers College Press, Athene Series), 1989.

Butler, Judith, and Joan W. Scott, eds. *Feminists Theorize the Political.* New York: Routledge, 1992.

Cade, Toni, ed. *The Black Woman.* New York: Signet, 1970.

Carroll, Berenice A., ed. *Liberating Women's History: Theoretical and Critical Essays.* Urbana: University of Illinois Press, 1976.

Collins, Patricia Hill. *Black Feminist Thought: Knowledge, Consciousness, and the Politics of Empowerment.* Boston: Unwin Hyman, 1990.

Cott, Nancy F. *The Grounding of Modern Feminism.* New Haven: Yale University Press, 1987.

Daley, Caroline, and Melanie Nolan, eds. *Suffrage and Beyond: International Feminist Perspectives.* Annandale: Pluto Press Australia, 1994; New York: New York University Press, 1994.

Daly, Mary. *Beyond God the Father: Toward a Philosophy of Women's Liberation.* Boston: Beacon Press, 1985, c. 1973.

——. *Gyn/ecology: The Metaethics of Radical Feminism.* Boston: Beacon Press, 1990.

Donahue, Francis. "Feminists in Latin America." *Arizona Quarterly* 41, 1 (1985): 38–50.

Donovan, Josephine. *Feminist Theory: The Intellectual Traditions of American Feminism.* New York: Ungar, 1986.

DuBois, Ellen. *Feminism and Suffrage: The Emergence of an Independent Women's Movement in America, 1848–1869.* Ithaca: Cornell University Press, 1978.

Eisenstein, Hester. *Contemporary Feminist Theory.* Boston: G. K. Hall, 1983.

Eisenstein, Zillah. *The Radical Future of Liberal Feminism.*

New York: Longman, 1986; Boston: Northeastern University Press, 1981.

Elshtain, Jean Bethke. *Power Trips and Other Journeys: Essays in Feminism as Civic Discourse.* Madison: University of Wisconsin Press, 1990.

Enloe, Cynthia. *Bananas, Beaches and Bases: Making Feminist Sense of International Politics.* Berkeley: University of California Press, 1989.

Faderman, Lillian, and Brigette Eriksson, eds. *Lesbian-Feminism in Turn-of-the-Century Germany.* Tallahassee, Fla.: Naiad Press, 1980.

Falco, Maria, ed. *Feminist Interpretations of Mary Wollstonecraft.* University Park: Pennsylvania State University Press, 1996.

Ferguson, Moira, ed. *First Feminists: British Women Writers, 1578–1799.* Bloomington, Ind., and Old Westbury, N.Y.: Indiana University Press and Feminist Press, 1985.

Flexner, Eleanor. *Century of Struggle: The Women's Rights Movement in the United States.* New York: Atheneum, 1970.

Fraser, Elizabeth. *The Politics of Community: A Feminist Critique of the Liberal-Communitarian Debate.* Toronto: University of Toronto Press, 1993.

Fraser, Nancy. *Unruly Practices: Power, Discourse, and Gender in Contemporary Social Theory.* Minneapolis: University of Minnesota Press, 1989.

Frye, Marilyn. *The Politics of Reality: Essays in Feminist Theory.* Trumansburg, N.Y.: Crossing Press, 1983.

Fullbrook, Kate, and Edward Fullbrook. *Simone de Beauvoir and Jean-Paul Sartre: The Remaking of a Twentieth-Century Legend.* New York: Basic, 1994.

Garcia, Alma M., and Mario T. Garcia, eds. *Chicana Feminist Thought: The Basic Historical Writings.* New York: Routledge, 1997.

Gates, Henry Louis, Jr., ed. *Reading Black, Reading Feminist: A Critical Anthology.* New York: Penguin (Meridian), 1990.

Grimshaw, Jean. *Philosophy and Feminist Thinking.* Minneapolis: University of Minnesota Press, 1986.

Haraway, Donna. *Primate Visions: Gender, Race, and Nature in the World of Modern Science.* New York: Routledge, 1989.

———. *Simians, Cyborgs, and Women: The Reinvention of Nature.* New York: Routledge, 1991.

Harding, Sandra. *The Science Question in Feminism.* Ithaca: Cornell University Press, 1986.

———. *Whose Science? Whose Knowledge?* Ithaca: Cornell University Press, 1991.

Harding, Sandra, ed. *The "Racial" Economy of Science: Toward a Democratic Future.* Bloomington: Indiana University Press, 1993.

Hartsock, Nancy. *Money, Sex and Power: Toward a Feminist Historical Materialism.* New York: Longman, 1983.

Hirschmann, Nancy J., and Christine Di Stefano, eds. *Revisioning the Political: Feminist Reconstructions of Traditional Concepts in Western Political Theory.* Boulder, Colo.: Westview Press, 1996.

hooks, bell. *Feminist Theory: From Margin to Center.* Boston: South End Press, 1984.

Jayawardena, Kumari. *Feminism and Nationalism in the Third World.* London: Zed, 1986.

Kadish, Doris Y., and Françoise Massardier-Kenney, eds. *Translating Slavery: Gender and Race in French Women's Writing, 1783–1823.* Kent, Ohio: Kent State University Press, 1994.

Kauffman, Linda S. *American Feminist Thought at Century's End: A Reader.* Cambridge, Mass.: Blackwell, 1993.

Kaur, Manmohan. *Women in India's Freedom Struggle.* New Delhi: Sterling, 1985.

Kelly, Joan. *Women, History, and Theory: The Essays of Joan Kelly.* Chicago: University of Chicago Press, 1984.

Kenney, Sally J., and Helen Kinsella, eds. *Politics and Feminist Standpoint Theories.* Binghamton, N.Y.: Haworth Press, 1997.

Kerber, Linda. *No Constitutional Right to Be Ladies: Women and the Obligations of Citizenship.* New York: Hill and Wang, 1998.

Klosko, George, and Margaret G. Klosko. *The Struggle for Women's Rights: Theoretical and Historical Sources.* Upper Saddle River, N.J.: Prentice Hall, 1999.

Kourany, Janet A., ed. *Philosophy in a Feminist Voice: Critiques and Reconstructions.* Princeton: Princeton University Press, 1998.

Kraditor, Aileen. *The Ideas of the Woman Suffrage Movement, 1890–1920.* New York: Columbia University Press, 1965.

Lerner, Gerda. *The Creation of Feminist Consciousness: From the Middle Ages to Eighteen-Seventy.* New York: Oxford University Press, 1993.

Lorde, Audre. *Sister Outsider: Essays and Speeches.* Trumansburg, N.Y.: Crossing Press, 1984.

Marchand, Marianne H., and Jane L. Parpart, eds. *Feminism/Postmodernism/Development.* London: Routledge, 1995.

Meyers, Diana Tietjens, ed. *Feminist Social Thought: A Reader.* New York: Routledge, 1997.

Mies, Maria. *Patriarchy and Accumulation on a World Scale: Women in the International Division of Labor.* London: Zed, 1986.

Mill, Harriet Taylor. *The Complete Works of Harriet Taylor Mill.* Ed. Jo Ellen Jacobs, with Paula Harms Payne. Bloomington: Indiana University Press, 1998.

Moraga, Cherríe, and Gloria Anzaldúa, eds. *This Bridge Called My Back: Writings by Radical Women of Color.* Watertown, Mass.: Persephone Press, 1981; New York: Kitchen Table, Women of Color Press, 1983.

Nicholson, Linda, ed. *Feminism/Postmodernism.* New York: Routledge, 1990.

Okin, Susan Moller. "Feminism and Political Theory." In *Philosophy in a Feminist Voice: Critiques and Reconstructions,* ed. Janet A. Kourany, 16–144. Princeton: Princeton University Press, 1998.

Olson, Gary A., and Elizabeth Hirsh, eds. *Women Writing Culture.* Albany: State University of New York Press, 1995.

Pateman, Carole, and Elizabeth Gross. *Feminist Challenges: Social and Political Theory.* Boston: Northeastern University Press, 1987.

Peterson, V. Spike, ed. *Gendered States: Feminist (Re)Visions of International Relations Theory.* Boulder: Lynne Rienner, 1992.

Pettman, Jan Jindy. *Worlding Women: A Feminist International Politics.* London: Routledge, 1996.

Pierson, Ruth R., ed. *Women and Peace: Theoretical, Historical, and Practical Perspectives.* London: Croom Helm, 1987.

Quataert, Jean H. *Reluctant Feminists in German Social Democracy, 1885–1917.* Princeton: Princeton University Press, 1979.

Rabinowitz, Nancy Sorkin, and Amy Richlin, eds. *Feminist Theory and the Classics.* New York: Routledge, 1993.

Radtke, H. Lorraine, and Henderikus J. Stam, eds. *Power/Gender: Social Relations in Theory and Practice.* Thousand Oaks, Calif.: Sage, 1994.

Robinson, Pat, Patricia Haden, and Donna Middleton. "A Historical and Critical Essay for Black Women in the Cities, June 1969." In *The Black Woman*, ed. Toni Cade. New York: Signet, 1970; *Voices from Women's Liberation*, ed. Leslie Tanner. New York: New American Library, 1970.

Rossi, Alice, ed. *The Feminist Papers: From Adams to de Beauvoir.* New York: Bantam, 1974.

Ruddick, Sara. *Maternal Thinking: Toward a Politics of Peace.* Boston: Beacon Press, 1989.

Saadawi, Nawal el. *The Hidden Face of Eve.* London: Zed, 1980. Boston: Beacon Press, 1982.

——. *The Nawal el Saadawi Reader.* London: Zed, 1997.

Salleh, Ariel. *Ecofeminism as Politics: Nature, Marx, and the Postmodern.* London: Zed, 1997.

Schneir, Miriam. *Essential Works of Feminism.* New York: Random House/Vintage, 1972.

Scott, Joan Wallach. *Only Paradoxes to Offer: French Feminists and the Rights of Man.* Cambridge: Harvard University Press, 1996.

Shanley, Mary Lyndon, and Carole Pateman, eds. *Feminist Interpretations and Political Theory.* University Park: Pennsylvania State University Press, 1991.

Simons, Margaret. *Beauvoir and "The Second Sex": Feminism, Race, and the Origins of Existentialism.* Lanham, Md.: Rowman and Littlefield, 1999.

Simons, Margaret, ed. *Feminist Interpretations of Simone de Beauvoir.* University Park: Pennsylvania State University Press, 1995.

Smith, Barbara, ed. *Home Girls: A Black Feminist Anthology.* New York: Kitchen Table, Women of Color Press, 1983.

Smith, Hilda L. "Intellectual Bases for Feminist Analyses: The Seventeenth and Eighteenth Centuries" In *Women and Reason*, ed. Elizabeth D. Harvey and Kathleen Okruhlik. Ann Arbor: University of Michigan Press, 1992.

——. *Reason's Disciples: Seventeenth-Century English Feminists.* Urbana: University of Illinois Press, 1982.

Spender, Dale. *Women of Ideas, and What Men Have Done to Them, from Aphra Behn to Adrienne Rich.* London: Routledge and Kegan Paul, 1982.

Spender, Dale, ed. *Feminist Theorists: Three Centuries of Key Women Thinkers.* New York: Pantheon, 1983.

——. *There's Always Been a Women's Movement This Century.* London: Routledge and Kegan Paul (Pandora), 1983.

Stanton, Domna C., and Abigail J. Stewart, eds. *Feminisms in the Academy.* Ann Arbor: University of Michigan Press, 1995.

Sylvester, Christine. *Feminist Theory and International Relations in a Postmodern Era.* Cambridge: Cambridge University Press, 1994.

Tanner, Leslie, ed. *Voices from Women's Liberation.* New York: New American Library, 1970.

Taylor, Barbara. *Eve and the New Jerusalem: Socialism and Feminism in the Nineteenth Century.* New York: Pantheon, 1983.

Tong, Rosemarie Putnam. *Feminist Thought: A More Comprehensive Introduction.* 2nd ed. Boulder, Colo.: Westview Press, 1998.

Treichler, Paula. "Teaching Feminist Theory." In *Theory in the Classroom*, ed. Cary Nelson. Urbana: University of Illinois Press, 1986.

Trinh T. Minh-ha. *Woman, Native, Other: Writing Postcoloniality and Feminism.* Bloomington: Indiana University Press, 1989.

Tuana, Nancy, and Rosemarie Tong, eds. *Feminism and Philosophy: Essential Readings in Theory, Reinterpretation, and Application.* Boulder, Colo.: Westview Press, 1995.

Weiss, Penny A. *Conversations with Feminism: Political Theory and Practice.* Lanham, Md.: Rowman and Littlefield, 1998.

Weiss, Penny A., and Marilyn Friedman, eds. *Feminism and Community.* Philadelphia: Temple University Press, 1995.

West, Lois A., ed. *Feminist Nationalism.* New York: Routledge, 1997.

Zalewski, Marysia, and Jane Parpart, eds. *The Man Question in International Relations.* Boulder: Westview Press, 1996.

Subject Index

abolition of slavery (abolitionism, -ists), 169, 175, 180–189, 200, 225, 226, 230, 231, 243, 245, 274, 382; anti-slavery societies, 184, 186–189; effects of (in Antigua, Bermuda, and Haiti), 188; English, 188, 213, 225, 231; expatriation, 187; nonviolent (pacific), 186, 187; *The Liberator*, 175, 186; Underground Railway, 245. *See also* emancipation (manumission); slave(s); slavery

action(s) (activism), 115, 300; against lynching, 260–262, 268–273, 278–281; agreement of word and, 242; biblical and historical examples of women's, 181–183, 185; boycotts, 269–270; collective, 388; conscious systematic mass, 316; consequences (risks) of, 181, 182; decisive, 234; deeds, not words, 47; "direct action," 311, 313, 314; disobedience to unjust laws, 182; effectiveness of women's, 176, 184; by needlework, pictures, and prints, 181, 184, 188; from principle, 156; deeds of anarchism, 313; house-to-house canvassing, 314; indifference as, 349; mass, 314–316; methodical agitation, 314; militant resistance, 242; active and contemplative life, 105;

under the control of mind, 385; nonviolent direct, 311; not armed revolt, 208; of Outsiders, 350–352; petitions, 184, 185, 187, 188, 205; political, 314, 317, 378; prayer as, 176, 180–183, 187; preaching, 187; proletarian, 314, 316; public speaking and writing, 151, 175, 176, 180–188; reading as, 180–181; reciprocal, of economic and political struggle, 316–317; reform (reformism), 186, 378; relationship to theory (ideas, thought), 234, 386, 388; resistance, 150, 182, 247, 301, 391; revolutionary, 314, 378; "spontaneity," 311; to consolidate the working class, 208; to educate and emancipate slaves, 181, 188; to form societies, 185; without certainty, 385; women to fight for equality, 131, 151–153. *See also* disobedience; rebellion (revolt, insurrection); revolution(s) (revolutionary-[ies]); strike(s); struggle; women's legal/political status and activism

Adam, 43, 49, 68, 177, 179; and Eve, 189–190, 200–201, 373. *See also* Eve

Addams, Jane, xvi, xvii, xviii, 260, 285–286; Nobel Peace Prize (1933), 285

Africa and Africans, 123–126, 128, 130, 177–179, 184, 213–214, 225–232, 274, 323, 325, 391–409; Ethiop(ian), 125; Pan-African Congress, 396, 407. *See also* South Africa

African [Afro-]Americans, 123, 124, 175, 260–281, 285; action against lynching, 269–271; allegedly incapable of self-government, 268; crimes against, 261; disenfranchised in southern U.S., 266; freedmen, 260; law-abiding, 269; lynched and murdered by whites in the South (statistics), 266, 271; women, 261, 265; writers, 9. *See also* black(s); slave(s); slavery

age, 24; and male-female relations, 71; older women, in non-cloistered lay order, 35; of councillors, 60; of women teachers, 96; rights and care of the elderly, 208, 212; youth, 285, 360, 363, 371, 408

allegorical figures: Aurora, 128; Chaos, 127, 130; Columbia, 129, 130; Eolus, 129; Hibernia, 130; Reason, Rectitude, and Justice, 55

America(s), 123–125, 128, 135, 158, 165, 274, 276, 278; "first feminist of the," 84; Latin American independence, 205–206; North, 324; South, 205. *See*

Name and Place Index

BERENICE A. CARROLL is Professor of Political Science and Women's Studies at Purdue University and Professor Emerita at the University of Illinois at Urbana-Champaign. Her books and articles include *Design for Total War: Arms and Economics in the Third Reich*; *Liberating Women's History: Theoretical and Critical Essays*; "The Politics of 'Originality': Women and the Class System of the Intellect"; and "Christine de Pizan and the Origins of Peace Theory."

HILDA L. SMITH is Professor of History at the University of Cincinnati. She is author of *Reason's Disciples: Seventeenth-Century English Feminists*, co-compiler with Susan Cardinale of *Women and the Literature of the Seventeenth Century: An Annotated Bibliography Based on Wing's Short Title Catalogue*, and editor of *Women Writers and the Early Modern British Political Tradition*.